Lecture Notes in Computer Science   9191

Commenced Publication in 1973
Founding and Former Series Editors:
Gerhard Goos, Juris Hartmanis, and Jan van Leeuwen

More information about this series at http://www.springer.com/series/7409

Fiona Fui-Hoon Nah · Chuan-Hoo Tan (Eds.)

HCI in Business

Second International Conference, HCIB 2015
Held as Part of HCI International 2015
Los Angeles, CA, USA, August 2–7, 2015
Proceedings

Springer

Editors
Fiona Fui-Hoon Nah
Department of Business
   and Information Technology
Missouri University of Science
   and Technology
Rolla, MO
USA

Chuan-Hoo Tan
Department of Information Systems
City University of Hong Kong
Kowloon Tong
Hong Kong SAR

ISSN 0302-9743   ISSN 1611-3349 (electronic)
Lecture Notes in Computer Science
ISBN 978-3-319-20894-7   ISBN 978-3-319-20895-4 (eBook)
DOI 10.1007/978-3-319-20895-4

Library of Congress Control Number: 2015942243

LNCS Sublibrary: SL3 – Information Systems and Applications, incl. Internet/Web, and HCI

Printed on acid-free paper

Springer International Publishing AG Switzerland is part of Springer Science+Business Media
(www.springer.com)

Foreword

The 17th International Conference on Human-Computer Interaction, HCI International 2015, was held in Los Angeles, CA, USA, during 2–7 August 2015. The event incorporated the 15 conferences/thematic areas listed on the following page.

A total of 4843 individuals from academia, research institutes, industry, and governmental agencies from 73 countries submitted contributions, and 1462 papers and 246 posters have been included in the proceedings. These papers address the latest research and development efforts and highlight the human aspects of design and use of computing systems. The papers thoroughly cover the entire field of Human-Computer Interaction, addressing major advances in knowledge and effective use of computers in a variety of application areas. The volumes constituting the full 28-volume set of the conference proceedings are listed on pages VII and VIII.

I would like to thank the Program Board Chairs and the members of the Program Boards of all thematic areas and affiliated conferences for their contribution to the highest scientific quality and the overall success of the HCI International 2015 conference.

This conference could not have been possible without the continuous and unwavering support and advice of the founder, Conference General Chair Emeritus and Conference Scientific Advisor, Prof. Gavriel Salvendy. For their outstanding efforts, I would like to express my appreciation to the Communications Chair and Editor of HCI International News, Dr. Abbas Moallem, and the Student Volunteer Chair, Prof. Kim-Phuong L. Vu. Finally, for their dedicated contribution towards the smooth organization of HCI International 2015, I would like to express my gratitude to Maria Pitsoulaki and George Paparoulis, General Chair Assistants.

May 2015

Constantine Stephanidis
General Chair, HCI International 2015

HCI International 2015 Thematic Areas and Affiliated Conferences

Thematic areas:

- Human-Computer Interaction (HCI 2015)
- Human Interface and the Management of Information (HIMI 2015)

Affiliated conferences:

- 12th International Conference on Engineering Psychology and Cognitive Ergonomics (EPCE 2015)
- 9th International Conference on Universal Access in Human-Computer Interaction (UAHCI 2015)
- 7th International Conference on Virtual, Augmented and Mixed Reality (VAMR 2015)
- 7th International Conference on Cross-Cultural Design (CCD 2015)
- 7th International Conference on Social Computing and Social Media (SCSM 2015)
- 9th International Conference on Augmented Cognition (AC 2015)
- 6th International Conference on Digital Human Modeling and Applications in Health, Safety, Ergonomics and Risk Management (DHM 2015)
- 4th International Conference on Design, User Experience and Usability (DUXU 2015)
- 3rd International Conference on Distributed, Ambient and Pervasive Interactions (DAPI 2015)
- 3rd International Conference on Human Aspects of Information Security, Privacy and Trust (HAS 2015)
- 2nd International Conference on HCI in Business (HCIB 2015)
- 2nd International Conference on Learning and Collaboration Technologies (LCT 2015)
- 1st International Conference on Human Aspects of IT for the Aged Population (ITAP 2015)

Conference Proceedings Volumes Full List

HCI in Business

Program Board Chairs: Fiona Fui-Hoon Nah, USA and Chuan-Hoo Tan, Hong Kong

- Andreas Auinger, Austria
- Michel Avital, Denmark
- Hock Chuan Chan, Singapore
- Patrick Chau, Hong Kong
- Constantinos K. Coursaris, USA
- Soussan Djamasbi, USA
- Brenda Eschenbrenner, USA
- Ann L. Fruhling, USA
- Nobuyuki Fukawa, USA
- Jie Mein Goh, Canada
- Richard Hall, USA
- Khaled Hassanein, Canada
- Milena Head, Canada
- Susanna (Shuk Ying) Ho, Australia
- Jack Zhenhui Jiang, Singapore
- Yi-Cheng Ku, Taiwan
- Roderick L. Lee, USA
- Honglei Li, UK
- Yan Li, France
- Eleanor T. Loiacono, USA
- Mei Lu, USA
- Robbie Nakatsu, USA
- David Chee Wei Phang, P.R. China
- Robin Suzanne Poston, USA
- Lingyun Qiu, P.R. China
- Rene Riedl, Austria
- April Savoy, USA
- Norman Shaw, Canada
- Choong Ling Sia, Hong Kong
- Juliana Sutanto, Switzerland
- Chee-Wee Tan, Denmark
- Horst Treiblmaier, Austria
- Virpi Kristiina Tuunainen, Finland
- Dezhi Wu, USA
- I-Chin Wu, Taiwan
- Cheng Yi, P.R. China
- Dezhi Yin, USA

The full list with the Program Board Chairs and the members of the Program Boards of all thematic areas and affiliated conferences is available online at:

http://www.hci.international/2015/

HCI International 2016

The 18th International Conference on Human-Computer Interaction, HCI International 2016, will be held jointly with the affiliated conferences in Toronto, Canada, at the Westin Harbour Castle Hotel, 17–22 July 2016. It will cover a broad spectrum of themes related to Human-Computer Interaction, including theoretical issues, methods, tools, processes, and case studies in HCI design, as well as novel interaction techniques, interfaces, and applications. The proceedings will be published by Springer. More information will be available on the conference website: http://2016.hci.international/.

General Chair
Prof. Constantine Stephanidis
University of Crete and ICS-FORTH
Heraklion, Crete, Greece
Email: general_chair@hcii2016.org

http://2016.hci.international/

Contents

Electronic, Mobile and Ubiquitous Commerce

Enterprise Systems, Business and Gamification

Industry, Academia, Innovation and Market

Social Media for Business

Ruhi (2014), Social Media Analytics metrics should clarify the relationship between corporate objectives, supporting business unit metrics and social media activities. The majority of these Social Media Analytics metrics are based on web metrics (Brauer et al. 2014). Currently there exist a great variety of Social Media Analytics metrics to analyse the different social media. In this regard, e.g. Facebook Insights offers the administrator of the Facebook page more than 200 different Facebook metrics, e.g. the number of likes, the number of posts, negative posts etc. to analyse a Facebook page.[1]

At present only a few research studies have investigated the importance and usage of Social Media Analytics metrics within the organization. For example a research study of the Association of National Advertisers conducted by Ipsos OTX (2014) has revealed that number of likes, click-through rate, retweets, daily or monthly user, conversation volume, reach, influence, advocacy, sales, ROI are the most important metrics for US marketers. Due to different time and personal constraints, it is difficult for the majority of organizations to select the appropriate Social Media Analytics metrics in order to analyse the different social media activities within the organizations. Therefore some companies have outsourced the analysis of social media activities to a media agency or to other companies (Alfaro et al. 2013).

2.2 Social Media Analytics Software

At present a variety of Social Media Analytics software exists (Chen et al. 2012; Stieglitz and Linh 2013), but only relatively few research studies about Social Media Analytics software are available in the literature. Currently few companies use Social Media Analytics software to analyse and monitor the different social media activities within the organisation (Ruhi 2014). In this regard, Frauenhofer (2011, pp. 11–15) have revealed that companies use Social Media Analytics software to analyse, for example, the corporate reputation, crises (shitstorms), competitors, corporate brand, marketing campaigns, market/trends, price and innovation.

Since 2011 Facebook offers free of charge Facebook Insights to monitor the organization´s Facebook page. Regarding to Facebook "Page admins are interested in understanding if people are engaging with the content they publish. To help them with this, Facebook provides Page admins aggregated anonymous insights about people's activity on their Page." (Facebook 2014). Facebook Insights is only available for Facebook pages (not for Facebook profiles) and requires at least 30 fans. Based on anonymized data, Facebook analyses different user activities on the Facebook page, e.g. visits, click-through rate etc. and enables the analysis of deeper information about the Facebook fans and their user behaviour. The different Facebook metrics which are offered via Facebook Insights can be grouped into several categories: total interactions, over time interactions, interactions per posts, fan over time, page views and impressions per post and ads (Borthakur et al. 2011; Killekar et al. 2013).

---

[1] https://developers.facebook.com/docs/graph-api/reference/v2.0/insights.

3 Research Design

As Zeng et al. (2010) and Stieglitz and Linh (2013) have already stated, Social Media Analytics is multidisciplinary and offers the application of various research methods from different research disciplines, e.g. statistics, computational linguistics, corporate management, marketing, sociology. The delphi study is recommended for complex research questions and if a lack of historical statistical data exists. Furthermore, the delphi study was also employed in previous IS research to develop different models and frameworks (Nevo and Chan 2007). The delphi method is a method for " [...] achieving convergence of opinion concerning real world knowledge solicited from experts within certain topic areas. The idea of the delphi study is to achieve a group consensus" (Hsu and Sandford 2007, p. 1) by mitigating halo or bandwagon effects (Keller and von der Gracht 2014, p. 6). The group consensus is attained by a series of questionnaires that offers the participants the possibility to reflect their answers according to the group results from previous delphi study rounds. Therefore we conducted an international 2-round delphi study between May 2014 and August 2014 based on an online questionnaire.

Due to the required experience and the profound background knowledge in the field of Social Media Analytics, professional staff was selected for this delphi study. There is no general rule about the sample size of a delphi study (Walker and Selfe 1996). During the investigation period, 315 higher education institutions in German-speaking countries out of 530 (60 %) had a Facebook page. We selected HEIs based on the number of Facebook fans and the country. Therefore HEIs were excluded which did not provide continuously content on their Facebook page. Based on four month investigation period of the delphi study and to ensure the execution of international delphi study we selected HEIs from Germany, Switzerland and Austria. We contacted 30 possible participants via telephone in Germany, Austria and Switzerland. 14 HEIs participated on the delphi study; nine universities were from Germany, three universities from Austria and two universities from Switzerland. The average time that participating HEIs have used Facebook amounts to 1.149 days. The Engagement Rate varies between 0.50 % and 3.59 %. All HEIs took part on all delphi study rounds, thus we had no panel mortality.

Based on Walker and Selfe (1996) at least two delphi rounds are required. The determination of the necessary rounds can be made ex post or ex ante. We used Kendall's Coefficient of Concordance (W) to determine the level of agreement on the final evaluations. An analysis of the final evaluations resulted in a W of 0.435 and 0.349, which is significant at $p < 0.001$. In the run-up of the first delphi round, a comprehensive list with the Facebook metrics was provided to all participants to ensure the same understanding between the participants.

The objective of the first delphi round was to determine the current usage of Social Media Analytics and the different Facebook metrics in HEIs in German-speaking countries. The online survey was divided into two parts and comprised 68 questions. The first part included questions concerning the Facebook strategy, the organizational integration of Social Media Analytics and the applied Social Media Analytics software. The second part included questions concerning the usage of the different Facebook metrics. The first round of the delphi study was conducted from 11–24 June 2014. We reminded participants either via mail or phone from 19–24 June to take part. We then analysed the results of the first delphi round via SPSS and implemented the online questionnaire for the second delphi round. The objective of the second delphi round was to reach a group consensus concerning the importance of the different Facebook metrics. The survey of the second delphi round comprised 20 questions and was conducted from 2–20 July 2014. The mean and standard deviation were selected to present the group opinion of experts. Also in the second delphi round a reminder mail was sent between starting on 10 July 2014. The analysis of results of the second delphi round was carried out from 20 July to 13 August 2014.

4 Research Results

4.1 Usage of Social Media Analytics Exemplified by Facebook in HEIs

9 out of 14 experts stated that they have a written social media strategy for their social media activities. 8 out of 9 experts mentioned that they have specific objectives for their Facebook page and their Facebook strategy. In the first delphi round the participating universities in German-speaking countries consider Facebook Analytics as very important. More than 50 % of the participants (8) assess Facebook Analytics as very important (4), 4 as import and 2 as slightly less important. In the second delphi round the participants evaluated the importance of Facebook Analytics higher (m = 3.89). The organizational integration of Social Media Analytics in HEIs is closely linked with the organizational integration of social media marketing. Social media marketing is carried out in almost all participating universities in German-speaking countries (10) by the PR department. Only two universities have established a social media department and two universities consider social media marketing as a part of the marketing department. Concerning the organizational integration of Social Media Analytics, the majority of the universities have integrated Social Media Analytics into the same department that is responsible for social media activities. Only one HEI has outsourced Social Media Analytics to an external provider. Between 1.5 and 2 employees are responsible for the support of the Facebook page and between 0.5 and 1 employee is responsible for the analysis of the Facebook page within HEIs in German-speaking countries. All investigated HEIs analyse their Facebook page via Facebook Insights. Furthermore, 11 out of 14 universities have stated that they use additional Social Media Analytics software to analyse the development of their Facebook page, e.g. Fanpage Karma, Hootsuite, Buzz or Meltwater.

4.2 Current Usage of Facebook Metrics in HEIs

The analysis of the used Facebook metrics by HEIs allows deeper insights into the usage of Social Media Analytics in HEIs and their Social Media Analytics strategy. Previous research has revealed that the number of total likes is the most analysed Facebook metric, which is also confirmed by our analysis. Our findings show that 13 out of 14 HEIs in German-speaking countries analyse the number of total likes (see Fig. 1). However, a more differentiated analyses of the number of total likes by considering demographic information, gender, age, organic, viral and paid is done by fewer HEIs. While eight out of 14 HEIs analyse the number of total likes [age] and six participating HEIs analyse the number of total likes [region] and [gender], only three HEIs measure the number of total likes [organic] and only one HEI analyses the

Facebook metric	N	M	Mode of Time interval	After post (6)	Daily (5)	Weekly (4)	Monthly (3)	Quarterly(2)	Yearly (1)
Total Likes	13	0.93	3.00				●		
Post Reach	13	0.93	2.00					●	
Post Interactions	14	0.86	4.00			●			
Post Likes	14	0.86	4.00			●			
Post Comments	14	0.86	4.00			●			
Post Shares	14	0.86	4.00			●			
Post Engagement	14	0.79	4.00			●			
Growth Rate Likes	10	0.71	2.00					●	
Total Reach	10	0.71	2.00					●	
Talking About	8	0.57	3.00				●		
Likes [Age]	8	0.57	3.00				●		
Unlikes	7	0.50	2.00					●	
Response Rate	6	0.43	2.00					●	
Likes [Gender]	6	0.43	3.00				●		
Likes [Region]	6	0.43	3.00				●		
Negative Posts	5	0.36	1.00						●
Positive Posts	5	0.36	2.00					●	
Trending Topics	5	0.36	2.00					●	
Reach [Age]	5	0.36	3.00				●		
Reach [Organic]	5	0.29	3.00				●		
Reach [Viral]	5	0.29	3.00				●		
Reach [Region]	4	0.29	3.00				●		
Net Likes	3	0.21	3.00				●		
Response Time	3	0.21	3.00				●		
Influencers	3	0.21	3.00				●		
Likes [Organic]	3	0.21	3.00				●		
Reach [Paid]	5	0.21	3.00				●		
Reach [Gender]	3	0.21	3.00				●		
Referrals to Website	2	0.14	2.00					●	
Referrals from Website	2	0.14	3.00				●		
Likes [Viral]	2	0.14	3.00				●		
Likes [Paid]	2	0.14	2.67				●		

Fig. 1. Usage and time periods of Facebook metrics ordered by application of Facebook metrics

number of total likes [viral] and the number of total likes [paid]. Equally important as the metric number of total likes is the post reach for HEIs. The second most common group of analysed Facebook metrics are metrics concerning post interactions. The number of post likes, the number of post comments, the number of post shares and the post engagement are analysed by 11–12 HEIs. The third mostly analysed group of Facebook metrics comprises the growth rate likes, the total reach and the number of post clicks. These Facebook metrics are analysed by 10 out of 14 HEIs in German-speaking countries. The number of talking about, the unlikes and the response rate are only analysed by half or less than the half the participating universities. The next group of Facebook metrics refers again on Facebook posts, respectively the content of the posts. Nearly half of universities analyse the positive posts, the negative posts and the trending topics. Furthermore, the high standard deviation demonstrates that there is a limited group consensus concerning the current usage of these Facebook metrics among HEIs in German-speaking countries. The next group of applied Facebook metrics focuses on the reach of the Facebook page. The total reach [age], the total reach [region], the total reach [organic] and the total reach [viral] are only analysed by 4–5 HEIs. The following group includes six different Facebook metrics. The net likes, the top influencer, the response time, the total likes [organic], the total reach [gender], the total reach [paid] are only analysed by 3 out of 14 HEIs in German-speaking countries. The last group comprises referrals from the website, the referrals to the website, total likes [organic] and total likes [paid]. Only 2 out of 14 HEIs analyse these Facebook metrics. The low usage of referrals from/to website demonstrates a lack of an integrated social media strategy among German-speaking HEIs.

4.3   Time Periods of Analysed Facebook Metrics in HEIs

In order to get a deeper insight into the analysis of the Facebook page in HEIs, the participants were asked to name the time periods the different Facebook metrics are analysed. As Fig. 1 illustrates, only the metric negative posts is analysed yearly by HEIs in German-speaking countries. The Facebook metrics post reach, growth rate likes, total reach, the number of unlikes, the response rate, positive posts, trending topics and the referrals to website are measured quarterly by HEIs. The majority of Facebook metrics are analysed on a monthly basis. Post interactions, post likes, post comments and post shares are analysed on a weekly basis. Therefore, it can be concluded that the Facebook page is mainly analysed on a monthly basis in HEIs in German-speaking countries.

5   Conclusion and Limitations

The present research results allow for deeper insights into the usage of Social Media Analytics in HEIs in German-speaking countries with the example of Facebook. Our research results have revealed that not all participating HEIs have a social media strategy, but all participating HEIs are analysing their Facebook page with one or more Social Media Analytics software applications. All of them use Facebook Insights to analyse the development of their Facebook pages. Closely linked with organizational integration of social media activities is the organizational integration of Social Media Analytics. Currently this integration is not clearly dedicated in most HEIs. Currently, Social Media Analytics is mainly assigned to the PR department. In this regard, further research on the organizational integration of Social Media Analytics seems warranted, maybe comparing industries and branches. At present, HEIs analyse a variety of Facebook metrics to develop their Facebook page. Total Likes, Post Reach, Post Interactions, Total Reach and Talking About are the most important Facebook metrics for HEIs. In this context, the importance of the different Facebook metrics from the perspective of HEIs has to be discussed. For example, the Facebook metric Total Likes has a limited significance regarding to the long-term developments of Facebook page; the growth rate of total likes would be more meaningful in this context. In this regard, the number of analysed Facebook metrics and which metrics are analysed indicate that only few HEIs pursue an integrated social media strategy despite the majority reporting an explicit Facebook strategy with objectives. Only two universities analyse the referrals from/to their website, which is important to understand an integrated social media strategy including the website. It seems that the majority of HEIs in German-speaking countries do not exploit the range of Facebook metrics linked with an overall social media strategy. Our research also revealed that many HEIs analyse their Facebook page on a monthly basis. The monthly analysis period has to be discussed against the background of the real-time analysis capability offered by Social Media Analytics software. Furthermore, we recognize that there is a lack of integrated and cross-network Social Media Analytics frameworks (cf. Alt and Wittwer 2014). Therefore, Social Media Analytics measurement frameworks which classify the variety of the different Social Media Analytics metrics are missing.

One limitation of the present research study is the focus of HEIs in German-speaking countries. Further research studies about the usage of Social Media Analytics in other countries are required. Due to high penetration of social networks in the USA and Asian countries further research in these regions is recommend and would be interesting to in comparison with the present research results. Another limitation of our research study results from low number of participating HEIs in German-speaking countries. As mentioned before, Social Media Analytics is a very young and multi-disciplinary research field; therefore only a small number of experts took part in the international delphi study. Nonetheless the present research results provide first exploratory insights into Social Media Analytics in HEIs exemplified by Facebook. Further research studies are required to validate and extend our initial results. Finally one limitation results from the focus on Facebook. Due to a great variety of online social networks it is difficult to analyse all social online networks. In particular it would be a very challenging and rewarding future research effort to develop a performance metric framework for all online social networks.

References

Ajmera, J., Ahn, H.I., Nagarajan, M., Verma, A., Contractor, D., Dill, S., Denesuk, M.: A crm system for social media: challenges and experiences. In: Proceedings of the 22nd international conference on World Wide Web, pp. 49–58. International World Wide Web Conferences Steering Committee (2013)

Alfaro, I., Bhattacharyya, S., Watson-Manheim, M.B.: Organizational adoption of social media in the USA: a mixed method approach. In: Proceedings of the European Conference on Information Systems (2013). http://aisel.aisnet.org

Alt, R., Wittwer, M.: Towards An Ontology-Based Approach For Social Media Analysis. In: Proceedings of 22 European Conference on Information Systems (ECIS 2014) (2014)

van Barnefeld, A., Arnold, K.E., Campbell, J.P.: Analytics in higher education: establishing a common language. EDUCAUSE Learn. Initiative 1, 1–11 (2012)

Borthakur, D., Gray, J., Sarma, J.S., Muthukkaruppan, K., Spiegelberg, N., Kuang, H., Aiyer, A.: Apache hadoop goes realtime at Facebook. In: Proceedings of the 2011 ACM SIGMOD International Conference on Management of data, pp. 1071–1080 (2011)

Brauer, C., Reischer, D., Mödritscher, F.: What web analysts can do for human-computer interaction? In: Fui-Hoon Nah, F. (ed.) HCIB 2014. LNCS, vol. 8527, pp. 471–481. Springer, Switzerland (2014)

Chen, H., Chiang, R.H., Storey, V.C.: Business intelligence and analytics: from big data to big impact. MIS Q. 36(4), 1165–1188 (2012)

Etlinger, S., Li, C.: A framework for social analytics. Altimeter Group, USA. Accessed Oct 2011

Facebook (2014). www.facebook.com

Fan, W., Gordon, M.: The power of social media analytics. Commun. ACM 57(6), 74–81 (2013)

Ferguson, R.: Learning analytics: drivers, developments and challenges. Int. J. Technol. Enhanced Learn. 4(5), 304–317 (2012)

Frauenhofer (2011). https://shop.iao.fraunhofer.de/details.php-?id=474&source=2&actio-n=schnellsuche&suche_autor=&suche_jahr=&-suche_titel=&suche-=&suche1=social+media+monitoring&SID=e1330-d471de08ed02e675173db071d1b

Hsu, C.C., Sandford, B.A.: The delphi technique: making sense of consensus. Pract. Assess. Res. Eval. 12(10), 1–8 (2007)

Ipsos OTX (2014). Association for national advertisers (ANA) 2014 Social Media Content Development Survey

Keller, J., von der Gracht, H.: The influence of information and communication technology on future foresight processes—results from a delphi study. Technol. Forecast. Soc. Chang. 85, 81–92 (2014). doi:10.1016/j.techfore.2013.07.010

Kurniawati, K., Shanks, G., Bekmamedova, N.: The business impact of social media analytics (2013)

Kilner, D.: 3 big reasons universities need a social media monitoring tool (2014). http://digimind.com/blog/social-media/3-reasons-schools-need-smm-tool/

Killekar, O., Shah, H., Kolge, A.: Social media metrics, tools & analytics. PRIMA Pract. Res. Mark. 3(2), 35–47 (2013)

Leskovec, J.: Social media analytics: tracking, modeling and predicting the flow of information through networks. In: Proceedings of the 20th International Conference Companion on World Wide Web, pp. 277–278 (2011)

Nevo, D., Chan, Y.: A delphi study of knowledge management systems: scope and requirements. Inf. Manage. 44(6), 583–597 (2007)

Permatasari, H. P., Harlena, S., Erlangga, D., & Chandra, R. (2014). Effect of social media on website popularity: differences between public and private Universities in Indonesia. arXiv: 1403.1956

Peters, K., Chen, Y., Kaplan, A.M., Ognibeni, B., Pauwels, K.: Social media metrics—a framework and guidelines for managing social media. J. Interact. Mark. 27(4), 281–298 (2013)

Romero, C., Ventura, S.: Educational data mining: a survey from 1995 to 2005. Expert Syst. Appl. 33(1), 135–146 (2007)

Ruhi, U.: Social Media Analytics as a business intelligence practice: current landscape & future prospects. J. Internet Soc. Netw. Virtual Communities 2014(2014), 1–12 (2014)

Stieglitz, S., Linh, D.-X.: Social media and political communication: a social media analytics framework. Soc. Netw. Anal. Min. 3(4), 1277–1291 (2013)

Walker, A.M., Selfe, J.: The delphi method: a useful tool for the allied health researcher. Br. J. Ther. Rehabil. 3(12), 677–681 (1996)

Zeng, D., Chen, H., Lusch, R., Li, S.-H.: Social media analytics and intelligence. IEEE Intell. Syst. 25(6), 13–16 (2010)

Engaging Online Review Writing Experience: Effect of Motivational Affordance on Review Quality

Xiaofang Cai[✉] and Patrick Y.K. Chau

Faculty of Business and Economics, The University of Hong Kong,
Pok Fu Lam, Hong Kong
Cai2013@connect.hku.hk

Abstract. Online review has become an important repository for consumers to make online buying decisions. However, writing online reviews is a voluntary behavior lacking guidelines and it is hard to guarantee the review quality generated. How to improve online review quality has become a challenge to online retailers and review aggregators. In this study, we explore the design of review writing interface in order to provide engaging writing experience for online reviewers. Using the motivational affordance theory as the theory basis, we define the motivational factors and corresponding design elements, which support reviewers to fulfill their motivation to write their online reviews. We explore how the engaging experience supported by cognitive and social affordances will affect reviewers' writing performance.

Keywords: Motivational affordance theory · Online review quality · Engagement · Social presence · Review writing · Interface design

1 Introduction

Online review is an important information source for consumers to reduce product uncertainty in making buying decisions. But with the increasing volume of online reviews, consumers are struggling with large volume of information in pre-purchase decision phases, and simplicity and good quality information has become more important to consumer stickiness, leading to higher recommendation to friends and repurchase intention.

In order to relief consumer from online review overload, researchers, online retailers and review aggregators attempt to develop personalization techniques and online review filtering strategy to selectively display online review [1, 2]. Yelp.com rejects more than one quarter of online reviews because they are fake or of poor quality [3]. Such techniques may fail when faced the issues such as cold startup and product review spam, and can be effective only if there are reviews of high quality.

Writing online review is a voluntary post-consumption behavior of consumers motivated by extreme experiences, and the desire to share such experiences. Previous literature on online product communication has found different drivers of online review writing behavior, and researchers have proposed suggestions on how to improve online

© Springer International Publishing Switzerland 2015
F.F.-H. Nah and C.-H. Tan (Eds.): HCIB 2015, LNCS 9191, pp. 13–21, 2015.
DOI: 10.1007/978-3-319-20895-4_2

review performance by leveraging their findings [4]. Besides, studies on online review helpfulness also suggested guidelines for writing helpful online reviews, which imply the need and the potential of guiding online reviewers to improve their review writing [5, 6]. In this study, we study online review writing as a computer mediated communication behavior, in which online review writing interface serves as a supportive technology to engage online reviewers to achieve their goal. Taken a motivational affordance perspective, this study proposes motivational supportive design of online review writing improves online review quality by providing reviewers engaging experience.

This paper is organized as follows. First, we discuss the extant findings of online review motivation and online review quality. Second, we introduce motivational affordance theory, and propose the research model of this study. Based on this theory, two key motivational affordances are proposed and analyzed: cognitive motivational affordance and social motivational affordance. These two types of affordances generate positive experiences, measured by engagement and perceived social presence, which then encourage online reviewers to write online reviews of better quality. Experiment in movie review setting is designed to test the effectiveness of such design. Finally, potential contributions of this research are discussed.

2   Literature Review

2.1   Online Review Motivation

After consuming a product or a service, consumers may be motivated by various reasons to share their experiences or feelings via different channels. Online review writing is a social voluntary behavior motivated by the need for reputation, reciprocity and sense of belongingness to the online community [7].

Writing online is motivated by the affiliation to existing online product or review community. The need to belongingness is one of the fundamental drive of human being, and such need motivate people to interact and maintain social bond in order to be satisfied [8]. Online review writing is an act of joining the existing online product communication and fulfilling the sense of belongingness [7]. Social benefit is the most influential determinant motive to online review platform visit frequency and comment writing behavior [9]. According to [4], consumers tend to write reviews on a popular product which has a lot of reviews because the number of previous reviews indicate the popularity of the topics and the presence of potential audience. Such information will attract reviewers to join the conversation as part of the community. When people perceive themselves as the community member, they are intrinsically to share and act for the benefit of other group members [10]. The affiliation to virtual community is one distinct characteristic of online review compared with traditional word of mouth. Reputation is another important motives of online information sharing behavior [11]. Online reviewers perceive the online review platform as the opportunity to establish their reputation by writing online reviews [7]. People are writing reviews to share their experience or opinion to influence or persuade potential audience. The audience of the online review includes the product retailers, the existing product communication community and potential consumers who are interested in the focal product.

To further the present work on online review motivation, our study explores how such motivation can be further exploit to the design online review writing interface. When reviewers are expressing their opinion, their audiences are invisible. Online review editing interface has different social design elements that serve to visualize certain social presence to reviewers.

2.2 Online Review Quality

Although online review provides additional information for consumers to make the purchase decision, it may cause information overload among consumers [12, 13]. The quality, rather than the volume of online review becomes the focus of research in order to improve online buying experience. Previous studies have identified the characteristics, antecedents and consequences of online review quality or helpfulness [5, 13, 14]. However, how to improve online review quality remains a question.

One of the common practice is to use consumers or participants to evaluate the online review quality (or helpfulness), especially using the number of the helpfulness votes. It refers to the helpful votes cast from the consumers who have read the review [15]. In experiment setting, the helpfulness of online review can be measured with the subjective scores given by trained coders [16]. Helpfulness votes of online review is a design feature provided in many e-commerce websites, such as Amazon.com. Consumers can vote for the piece of review they found helpful by clicking the helpfulness button. Besides subjective votes of online review, the linguistic characteristics of online review such as readability [15], online review depth [14], as well as source features such as the status of online reviewers are powerful predictors of online review quality [14, 17, 18].

With the predictors of online review helpfulness, designers can develop personalization strategy in display the sequence of online review [19]. However, such attempts cannot solve the low-quality review problem. Although studies [6, 21] have suggest guidelines to help online reviewers, there lacks empirical research on the implementation of such findings to influence online review behavior, which is susceptible to the manipulation of writing context [20].

2.3 Motivational Affordance

Motivation can affect human behavior in two aspects: the direction and the strength of the behavior. Motivational affordance in information technology design is proposed [22] following the recent work in positive psychology. Affordance is a concept from eco-psychology, referring the properties of an object or environment and how such properties control or affect human behavior [23]. In interaction design, affordance refers to design features and what such design features offer to the product users, i.e. how things can be designed in a way that the user can easily infer what they afford [24]. Motivational affordance includes two components: the interaction or interface design elements and the process of how such design elements support users to fulfill their motivational need [22].

According to motivational affordance theory, information system or application should be designed to support the major motivational needs of users, which vary according to the contexts and task types [25]. Therefore, designers should first understand what motivates users to adopt and use certain type of information technology. There are three major types of motivational needs: emotional, cognitive and social needs [22]. For example, in the context of group idea generation, people are motivated to achieve self-efficacy and demotivated by social evaluation apprehension [26]. Therefore, goal-setting and timely feedback are identified to provide cognitive support to gain sense of achievement and finally towards better performance [27]. Empirical studies on gamification have examined the design of motivational affordance and its positive effects on psychological and behavior outcomes [28]. Enhancing the motivational affordance design in information system can lead to positive user experience such as engagement and enjoyment, and such positive user experience is associated with the desired behavioral outcomes according to the contexts.

3 Hypothesis Development

In this study, we aims to design online review writing interface to enhance individual performance of online review writing. We propose that online review writing needs two types of motivational support: one is social motivation affordance, and the other is cognitive motivational affordance. In the following part, we will provide the rationale of our hypothesis of design guidelines for the effect of engaging online review experience (Fig. 1).

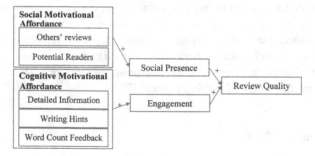

Fig. 1. Research model

3.1 Social Motivational Affordance

Two design features are proposed here to improve the social presence of online product community and the potential audience of online review. Others' reviews of a product refer to the individual comments written by the previous reviewers. Potential readers refer to the consumers, who are interested in the product, i.e. online consumers who have marked down the products for future buying.

Different types of communication cues can change perceived social presence in computer mediated communication context, and such changes in social presence level will influence group communication behavior [26, 29]. Low social presence level leads to lower commitment behavior to social group, such as greater group polarization [26]. The media of high social richness could evoke the quality of social interaction during a mediated social interaction [30]. In online review writing, presenting previous online reviews and the potential readers of the online product review can be visualized as the communication cues to demonstrate the presence of community to belong and audience to reach. Supported by such communication clues, online reviewers can enhance the perceived social presence level of online community and audience. Social presence of the website in turn, enable the sense of connection between the website and its visitors [31]. More specifically, empirical evidence has shown that the provision of online reviews increased the level of social presence, which strengthened the social bonds between the readers and the website [32].

Hypothesis 1. Social motivational affordance (others' reviews, potential readers) is positively associated with perceived social presence.

People are motivated to write online as a way to establish social connection with online product community. Enhancing the social motivational affordance in online review writing contexts can improve the quality of online review performance for several reasons. First, visual cues of previous reviews makes the presence of online product community or online word of mouth community more salience. Second, salient online product community motivates reviewers to feel stronger social presence of other reviewers and exemplify the need to communicate and establish social bond. Third, to some extends, writing online review serves as a way for online reviewers to share their personal feelings on the same item with community members. Therefore, with the presence of visual cues of online product community, online reviewers will be more motivated to write online reviews. People tend to share their personal feeling and experience with the audience of closer social distance. Emotion information also influences how consumer perceives the helpfulness of online review [21].

Hypothesis 2. Perceived social presence is positively associated with online review quality.

3.2 Cognitive Motivational Affordance

Competence is a psychological need that everyone strives to fulfill. Competence as psychological need provides a source of motivation for exerting efforts necessary to overcome optimal challenges [33]. Optimal challenge is represented a level of difficulty and complexity that fit the focal individual's current knowledge and skill. With the provision of cognitive support in the writing interface, online reviewers form an engaging writing experience because the level of task difficulty is lessen with the design of cognitive affordance. Three cognitive motivational affordances are proposed in the context of online review writing: detailed product information, writing hints and word count feedback.

Detailed product information can assist reviewers in recalling product related information. According to cue-summation theory, the number of available cues or stimuli increases effectiveness of learning [34]. Rich product presentation enhances consumers product knowledge, which leads to higher perceived usefulness of the website [35]. Supported with more information cues in the writing phase, online reviewers can relate their consumption experience with the information and write more informative reviews. The presence of an external memory can serve to reduce the burden on the consumer's internal memory. That is, both internal memory and external memory can be viewed functionally as sources of information [36]. Besides, people are more cognitively absorbed in the task when perceiving task-related cues [37]. Therefore, we propose that providing product-related information can increase user engagement in writing online reviews. Writing hint module is often adopted in blog writing assistant system, and study has shown that such function can improve users' writing performance with higher system satisfaction [38].

Timely feedback combined with optimal challenge supports people to evaluate their performance. Word count feedback refers to the number of words that user has written. Length of online review is an important indicator of online review depth [14]. Online reviewers can use review length as a timely feedback to evaluate their contribution compared with their past performance or norms of online review community. With such meaningful evaluation supported by the feedback, reviewers are more engaged in the writing task itself.

Hypothesis 3. Cognitive motivational affordance (detailed product information, writing hints and word count feedback) is positively associated with online review engagement.

User engagement is associated with positive outcome of online system across different contexts. For example, higher user engagement leads to better user performance in online product understanding, and higher intention to the website [35]. Cognitive absorption is positively related with task participation and learning satisfaction in virtual world context [37]. Besides, recent study on online review has found that online reviewer engagement characteristic improve the prediction of online review helpfulness [1]. Therefore, when online reviewers are more engaged in online review writing task, they are more likely to write online review of higher quality.

Hypothesis 4. Online review writing engagement is positively associated with online review writing quality.

4   Method

We design lab experiments to test the hypothesis. In the experiment, we will explore whether the design of motivational affordances can offer social presence and engage users. Four designs will be implemented: social affordance group, cognitive affordance group, social-cognitive affordance group and control group.

4.1   Procedures

First, participants are invited to read and signed the informed consent and notified the basic steps of the experiments. Second, participants need to finish a questionnaire about their online review experience. Third, participants are led to a web page to watch a short film and write an online review on it after watching it. There are four manipulated online review writing interfaces: social affordance interface, cognitive affordance interface, interface including both social and cognitive affordance, and the control interface. Forth, after submitting the online reviews, they will fill in a questionnaire about their experience on the online review-writing page. Perceived social presence and engagement adapted from [30, 39] will be measured. Manipulation check will be provided to see if the participants have noticed such design elements.

4.2 Dependent Variables

The dependent variables are the online review quality. According to previous research, we will consider the review quality from the review depth, review helpfulness and other dimensions. We will use Amazon mechanic Turk to credit the quality index the online reviews. In our study, we will exam the online review writing performance from two important factors of online review adoption: online review quality and online review helpfulness. Online review quality is framed as argument quality "the strength or plausibility of persuasive argumentation" [40, 41], and can be evaluated in terms of the information content, accuracy, format, and timeliness [42]. In terms of helpfulness, we will adopt the measurement of online review helpfulness in [21, 43].

5 Contribution

This study contributes to the literature of online review and motivational affordance theory. First, this study designs experiment to investigate the mechanism of motivation to online review writing while previous studies on online review motivation use survey method to explore the general determinants of online review generation [9]. How the social motivation and cognitive needs can be satisfied during review writing process can be examined through the experiment design. Second, compared with online review consumption activities, review writing behavior has been received less attention from IS literature. This study offers insights on the locus of review writing behavior, and enriches the repertoire of behaviors studied by IS community. Thirdly, this study is an application of motivation affordance theory in information system artifact design. More empirical evidence of motivational affordance theory is needed towards a stronger design theory [27]. Future study may look at how to generalize the design process of motivational affordance design, and such attempts may offer practical significance to guide the industry.

References

1. Ngo-Ye, T.L., Sinha, A.P.: The influence of reviewer engagement characteristics on online review helpfulness: a text regression model. Decis. Support Syst. **61**, 47–58 (2014)

2. Yu, J., Zha, Z., Wang, M., Chua, T.: Aspect ranking: identifying important product aspects from online consumer reviews. In: Proceedings of the 49th Annual Meeting of the Association for Computational Linguistics: Human Language Technologies, vol. 1, pp. 1496–1505 (2011)
3. Luca, M., Zervas, G.: Fake it till you make it: reputation, competition, and yelp review fraud. Harvard Business School NOM Unit working paper, No. 14–006 (2013)
4. Dellarocas, C., Gao, G., Narayan, R.: Are consumers more likely to contribute online reviews for hit or niche products? J. Manag. Inf. Syst. 27(2), 127–157 (2010)
5. Huang, A.H., Yen, D.C.: Predicting the helpfulness of online reviews a replication. Int. J. Hum. Comput. Interact. 29(2), 129–138 (2013)
6. Mudambi, S.M., Schuff, D.: What makes a helpful online review? A study of customer reviews on amazon.com. Manag. Organ. Rev. 34(1), 185–200 (2010)
7. Cheung, C.M.K., Lee, M.K.O.: What drives consumers to spread electronic word of mouth in online consumer-opinion platforms. Decis. Support Syst. 53(1), 218–225 (2012)
8. Baumeister, R.F., Leary, M.R.: The need to belong: desire for interpersonal attachments as a fundamental human motivation. Psychol. Bull. 117(3), 497–529 (1995)
9. Hennig-Thurau, T., Gwinner, K.P., Walsh, G., Gremler, D.D.: Electronic word-of-mouth via consumer-opinion platforms: what motivates consumers to articulate themselves on the internet? J. Interact. Mark. 18(1), 38–52 (2004)
10. Hars, A., Ou, S.: Working for free? Motivations for participating in open-source projects. Int. J. Electron. Commer. 6(3), 25–39 (2002)
11. Constant, D., Kiesler, S., Sproull, L.: What's mine is ours, or is it? A study of attitudes about information sharing. Inf. Syst. Res. 5(4), 400–421 (1994)
12. Park, D.-H., Lee, J.: eWOM overload and its effect on consumer behavioral intention depending on consumer involvement. Electron. Commer. Res. Appl. 7(4), 386–398 (2008)
13. Baek, H., Ahn, J., Choi, Y.: Helpfulness of online consumer reviews: readers' objectives and review cues. Int. J. Electron. Commer. 17, 99–126 (2012)
14. Mudambi, S.M., Schuff, D.: What makes a helpful online review? A study of customer reviews on amazon.com. Manag. Inf. Syst. Q. 34(1), 185–200 (2010)
15. Korfiatis, N., García-Bariocanal, E., Sánchez-Alonso, S.: Evaluating content quality and helpfulness of online product reviews: the interplay of review helpfulness vs. review content. Electron. Commer. Res. Appl. 11(3), 205–217 (2012)
16. Tsur, O., Rappoport, A.: RevRank: a fully unsupervised algorithm for selecting the most helpful book reviews. In: International Conference on Weblogs and Social Media (2009)
17. Li, M.X., Huang, L.Q., Tan, C.H., Wei, K.K.: Helpfulness of online product reviews as seen by consumers: source and content features. Int. J. Electron. Commer. 17(4), 101–136 (2013)
18. Lee, E.-J., Shin, S.Y.: When do consumers buy online product reviews? Effects of review quality, product type, and reviewer's photo. Comput. Human Behav. 31, 356–366 (2014)
19. Krestel, R., Dokoohaki, N.: Diversifying product review rankings: getting the full picture. In: 2011 IEEE/WIC/ACM International Conferences on Web Intelligence and Intelligent Agent Technology, pp. 138–145 (2011)
20. Michael, L., Otterbacher, J.: Write like i write: herding in the language of online reviews. In: Proceeding of 8th International AAAI Converence on Weblogs and Social Media, pp. 356–365 (2014)
21. Yin, D., Bond, S.D., Zhang, H.: Anxious or angry? Effects of discrete emotions on the perceived helpfulness of online reviews. Manag. Inf. Syst. Q. 38(2), 539–560 (2014)
22. Zhang, P.: Toward a positive design theory: principles for designing motivating information and communication technology. In: Avital, M., Boland, R.J., Cooperrider, D.L. (eds.) Designing Information and Organizations with a Positive Lens, pp. 45–74. Elsevier, Amsterdam (2008)

23. Jones, K.S.: What is an affordance? J. Ecol. Psychol. **15**(2), 37–41 (2010)
24. Norman, D.A.: The Design of Everyday Things. Basic books, New York (2002)
25. Zhang, P.: Motivational affordances: reasons for ICT design and use. Commun. ACM **51** (11), 145–147 (2008)
26. Sia, C.-L., Tan, B.C.Y., Wei, K.-K.: Group polarization and computer-mediated communication: effects of communication cues, social presence, and anonymity. Inf. Syst. Res. **13**(1), 70–90 (2002)
27. Jung, J.H., Schneider, C., Valacich, J.: Enhancing the motivational affordance of information systems: the effects of real-time performance feedback and goal setting in group collaboration environments. Manag. Sci. **56**(4), 724–742 (2010)
28. Hamari, J., Koivisto, J., Sarsa, H.: Does gamification work?—a literature review of empirical studies on gamification. In: 2014 47th Hawaii International Conference on System Sciences, pp. 3025–3034 (2014)
29. Williams, E.: Experimental comparisons of face-to-face and mediated communication: a review. Psychol. Bull. **84**(5), 963 (1977)
30. Biocca, F., Harms, C., Burgoon, J.K.: Toward a more robust theory and measure of social presence: review and suggested criteria. Presence **12**(5), 456–481 (2003)
31. Hassanein, K.S, Head, M.: Building online trust through socially rich web interfaces. In: Proceedings of the 2nd Annual Conference on Privacy, Security and Trust, pp. 15–22. Fredericton, New Brunswick, Canada (2004)
32. Kumar, N., Benbasat, I.: Research note: the influence of recommendations and consumer reviews on evaluations of websites. Inf. Syst. Res. **17**(4), 425–439 (2006)
33. Deci, E.L., Ryan, R.M.: Intrinsic Motivation and Self-determination in Human Behavior. Springer, New York (1985)
34. Severin, W.: Another look at cue summation. Av Commun. Rev. **15**(3), 233–245 (1967)
35. Jiang, Z., Benbasat, I.: The effects of presentation formats and task complexity on online consumers product understanding. MIS Q. **31**(3), 475–500 (2007)
36. Bettman, J.R.: Memory factors in consumer choice: a review. J. Mark. **43**(2), 37–53 (1979)
37. Goel, L., Johnson, N.A., Junglas, I., Ives, B.: How cues of what can be done in a virtual world influence learning: an affordance perspective. Inf. Manag. **50**(5), 197–206 (2013)
38. Liu, C.-L., Lee, C.-H., Ding, B.-Y.: Intelligent computer assisted blog writing system. Expert Syst. Appl. **39**(4), 4496–4504 (2012)
39. O'Brien, H.L., Toms, E.G.: Examining the generalizability of the user engagement scale (UES) in exploratory search. Inf. Process. Manag. **49**(5), 1092–1107 (2013)
40. Cheung, C.M.K., Thadani, D.R.: The impact of electronic word-of-mouth communication: a literature analysis and integrative model. Decis. Support Syst. **54**(1), 461–470 (2012)
41. Eagly, A.H., Chaiken, S.: The Psychology of Attitudes. Harcourt Brace Jovanovich College Publishers, San Diego (1993)
42. McKinney, V., Yoon, K., Zahedi, F.M.: The measurement of web-customer satisfaction: an expectation and disconfirmation approach. Inf. Syst. Res. **13**(3), 296–315 (2002)
43. Sen, S., Lerman, D.: Why are you telling me this? An examination into negative consumer reviews on the web. J. Interact. Mark. **21**(4), 76–94 (2007)

Topic-Based Stance Mining
for Social Media Texts

Wei-Fan Chen[✉], Yann-Hui Lee, and Lun-Wei Ku

Institute of Information Science, Academia Sinica, Taipei, Taiwan
{viericwf,lwku}@iis.sinica.edu.tw, andycyrus@gmail.com

Abstract. Recent techniques of opinion mining have succeeded in analyzing sentiment on the social media, but processing the skewed data or data with few labels about political or social issues remains tough. In this paper, we introduce a two-step approach that starts from only five seed words for detecting the stance of Facebook posts toward the anti-reconstruction of the nuclear power plant. First, InterestFinder, which detects interest words, is adopted to filter out irrelevant documents. Second, we employ machine learning methods including SVM and co-training, and also a compositional sentiment scoring tool CopeOpi to determine the stance of each relevant post. Experimental results show that when applying the proposed transition process, CopeOpi outperforms the other machine learning methods. The best precision scores of predicting three stance categories (i.e., *supportive*, *neutral* and *unsupportive*) are 94.62 %, 88.86 % and 10.47 %, respectively, which concludes that the proposed approach can capture the sentiment of documents from lack-of-label, skewed data.

1 Introduction

Opinion mining has drawn much attention for both research communities and industries for its high relevance to knowledge mining applications. In the web environment, opinions are largely provided by users, especially in the form of texts. In the past, opinions have been classified into several categories, e.g., positive, neutral and negative. In some researches, scores which show the degree of valence for text segments were also determined [13].

The successful results of applying opinion mining in business encourages the attempt at automatically collecting opinions from the Internet for government or political parties to make decisions. However, it is more challenging either from the perspective of relevance judgment for posts or from telling the standpoint, compared to the review analysis of products, movies or travel experience, which is considered a success in business. As to the relevance, real controversial posts need to be identified from all posts related to the issue. The pure introductions, descriptions, and the facts about the issue should be excluded, which are usually separated from real comments in review forums but mixed up in media like Facebook, blogs and political forums where opinions towards public issues are found. As these issues are usually very specific, performance of finding relevant posts tends to report high recall but low precision. In addition, typical decision making involves telling supportive instances from

© Springer International Publishing Switzerland 2015
F.F.-H. Nah and C.-H. Tan (Eds.): HCIB 2015, LNCS 9191, pp. 22–33, 2015.
DOI: 10.1007/978-3-319-20895-4_3

unsupportive ones, which is considered more easily prone to errors than telling positive instances from negative ones. A typical example could be a post which criticizes (negative content) the behavior of the unsupportive party and makes the standpoint of the whole post supportive.

At least three requirements need to be fulfilled for support determination. First, opinions that government is keen to know are usually towards new issues that trigger a heat debate. As these issues are new, data analytics usually have difficulties to find sufficient labeled data to create their models. Therefore, we need an approach which can easily start from a small set of labeled data. Second, data collected from the Internet are very often highly skewed. However, the minority opinions are of vital importance as they are challenging to be retrieved but valuable for decision making. Therefore, the proposed approach should be able to retrieve the minority. Third, as there will be many supportive and unsupportive documents, precision is very important for the proposed method when reporting evidence to the decision makers.

In this paper, we aim to extract supportive and unsupportive evidence from Facebook data of two characteristics: highly skewed but with little labeled training data. Hence, the public issue "Anti-reconstruction of Lungmen Nuclear Power Plant[1]", is selected in order to demonstrate the challenge of this research problem. The fate of the power plant is to be decided in a future country-wide referendum, and whether having the referendum or not is a government decision. Successfully analyzing opinions on Internet can definitely help government to make a right decision. However, there is no labeled data for experiments. Moreover, from the testing data we generate, we know the unsupportive evidence is only about 1.25 % of the whole, which is quite little. Here "supportive" denotes the "support" of "anti-construction" and having this literally unsupportive topic title implies that it might be unlikely to extract evidence by only determining the polarity of documents.

To meet the requirements of this research problem, we propose models which can start from a very small set of seed words, i.e., no more than 5 words. Working with these few seed words, we illustrate how to find supportive and unsupportive evidence based on an existing sentiment polarity determination tool or the SVM models. Then their performances are compared with each other. Results show that seed words working with the sentiment analysis tool together with a transition process from polarity to standpoint significantly outperforms the commonly adopted SVM models, i.e., pure SVM model or SVM co-training models, when having little and skewed training data.

2 Related Work

As we mentioned, researchers have been applying sentiment analysis techniques on political, social or public issues. For example, some researches tried to predict the results of American president election, analyze the aspects of candidates [12], or more specifically, show the influence of the speech of Obama on the election [5]. Wang et al.

---

[1] http://en.wikipedia.org/wiki/Lungmen_Nuclear_Power_Plant.

[16] adopted the Naïve Bayes model to analyze people's attitude towards DOMA (Defense of Marriage Act). However, most of them were working on existing balanced data or a certain amount of balanced data generated for experiments, which is not cost effective when many different issues are to be analyzed.

Both content based and knowledge based approaches have been tested for sentiment analysis, and we propose one approach for each of them. The knowledge based approaches usually have issues acquiring necessary resources or being applied to data of different languages. In this paper, we adopted a Chinese sentiment analysis tool CopeOpi [7], which provides sentiment scores for words, sentences and documents. As to the content based approach, we adopt the commonly used SVM model to solve the proposed research problem. SVM model has been adopted from the very beginning of the history of tackling sentiment analysis problems [10]. It has served as a good baseline. However, requiring labeled data for training makes it difficult to be applied on a large amount of various unlabeled Internet data.

This paper focuses on unsupervised or semi-unsupervised methods as it is usually difficult to find stance labels for web posts. Bollen et al. [2] used Profile of Mood States (POMS), which detected each tweet's emotion on six dimension without machine learning technique. The results on the timeline matched the global social, political and economic events happened in this time period. Hu et al. [4] used post-level and word-level models to detect the polarity of a tweet. This unsupervised method can be considered as an alternative of LSA or word vector. On the other hand, Blum and Mitchell [1] proposed co-train algorithm to utilize labeled and unlabeled data together when training models, and it is also widely used for sentiment analysis [8, 15]. It seems that the co-training model can decrease the pain of having too little labeled training data. Recently, Gao et al. [3] used co-training to build models to construct bilingual sentiment lexicon. Their co-training process is modified and utilized in this paper.

3   Materials

We collected a total of 41,902 Facebook documents from related fans groups in one year period of time for experiments. Each document contains the post time, title, message, number of likes, number of shares and number of comments. From them, we randomly selected 4,000 documents and labeled them as supportive, neutral or unsupportive for testing, while the other 37,902 unlabeled documents were left for training. Documents are classified into 5 types as shown in Table 1 when they are collected, where documents of the *status* type are from the status or shared post of Facebook users, and question is a function of Facebook fans groups. Testing data were labeled by four annotators and results are shown in Table 2. From Table 2, we can also see that the unsupportive documents are less than one tenth of supportive documents.

We select some example testing documents shown in Table 3 to give a brief view of the material. The *title* field could be a website address of in a *link* type post or the context of the shared (*status* type) post. The *message* written by the author is then listed, which may show a complete different sentiment to the context in the title (e.g., the supportive one, the author argued that the *title*'s author, who supported nuclear power, is an idiot). For the neutral ones, it could be a piece of news that reported the

Table 1. Five types of Facebook documents

Type	Photo	Link	Video	Status	Question	Total
Testing	1,264	1,806	556	594	0	4,000
Training	12,286	14,024	3,755	7,836	1	37,902

Table 2. Testing dataset

Sentiment	Supportive	Neutral	Unsupportive
Number	652	3,297	51

Table 3. Examplar documents

Sentiment	Post time	Type	Title	Likes	Shares	Comments
Supportive	2014/6/25 08:52:12 PM	Photo	台灣能源短缺，…要面臨電價成本提高及…的問題。 (There is a shortage of energy in Taiwan… will face the problems of higher electricity rate and some other problems.)	146	0	0

廢話+笨蛋！問題是：經長無腦，不知「能源金字塔」，不知再生能源不需燃料費、成本低、而且持續降低。

(Rubbish + Idiot ! The problem is that they know nothing about Energy Pyramid and don't know renewable energy needs no fuel cost and the c ost is decreasing continuously.)

Sentiment	Post time	Type	Title	Likes	Shares	Comments
Un-supportive	2014/5/17 10:33:30 AM	Status	No content	0	0	0

請問你們能提出比核能發電廠更適合當基載的發電廠嗎？
(Could you propose other base load power plant which is better than the nuclear power plant?)

Sentiment	Post time	Type	Title	Likes	Shares	Comments
Neutral	2014/6/23 12:07:44 AM	Video	No content	0	0	0

搶救新營最美好的 溼地
(Saving the most beautiful wetlands in Hsinying.)

event related to the nuclear power without showing the stance, a political event that prompted to these fans groups to ask for supporting, or something just unrelated to the nuclear power (the listed neutral one). As a result, it is hard to determine the stance only by surface information while documents of the same stance may contain similar context and sentiment. Moreover, even though these documents were collected from related fans groups, many unrelated posts from social movement groups asking for support still bring a lot of noise.

4 Method

From all documents, keyterms are extracted first and utilized to find relevant, or even supportive documents. Then the SVM models or CopeOpi will report supportive, neutral, and unsupportive documents from the relevant ones. All related modules are introduced in this section.

4.1 Keyterm Extraction

Keyterms and their ranks are given by InterestFinder [6], a system which proposes terms to indicate the focus of interest by exploiting words' semantic features (e.g., content sources and parts of speech). The approach adopted by InterestFinder involves estimating topical interest preferences and determining the informativity of articles. InterestFinder estimates the topical interest preferences by TFIDF, a traditional yet powerful measure shown in formula (1). Then semantic aware PageRank in formula (2) is used on candidates to find keyterms. In this paper, we hope to find keyterms related to certain seed words. Therefore, we only keep terms which are within the window of 6 words to the seed words in the article. Then we let InterestFinder propose keyterms of each article for us.

$$tfidf(art, w) = freq(art, w)/artFreq(w) \qquad (1)$$

$$\mathbf{IN}'[1,j] = \lambda \times \left(\begin{array}{l} \alpha \times \sum_{i \in v} \mathbf{IN}[1,i] \times \mathbf{EW}[i,j] + \\ (1-\alpha) \times \sum_{k \in v} \mathbf{IN}[1,k] \times \mathbf{EW}[k,j] \end{array} \right) + (1-\lambda) \times \mathbf{IP}[1,j] \qquad (2)$$

4.2 Co-training Process

As mentioned, our dataset is highly skewed and lacking of labeled instance dataset. In addition, as experimental documents are collected from Facebook, each document contains two types of information: content and metadata. Content information contains post title and the post itself, while the metadata information contains the number of comments, likes and shares. With all these properties of the dataset, we propose a co-training approach which can build two classifiers, the content classifier and the metadata classifier, and train each other by starting from a small set of labeled data. The co-training process then iterates to finish the labeling of the whole dataset.

4.2.1 Detailed Steps

The main idea of the co-training is to use the classifier trained by labeled data of one aspect to predict unlabeled data of another aspect. Instances predicted with confidence are then added into the labeled data and this updated labeled data are used to train the new classifier. The whole process is described as follows. We apply several context features to be the first independent feature set, including bag of words and combinations of word vector, detailed description of the features will be introduced in next section. Numbers of likes, shares and comments are included in the second independent feature set.

All. The whole dataset
Feature *F1*: Context Features
Feature *F2*: Numbers of likes, shares and comments (LSC)

Step 1: Find an initial labeled dataset, which contains supportive and unsupportive documents. It is usually a small set. Two labeled datasets, *L1* and *L2*, are both set as the initial labeled dataset. Two unlabeled dataset, *U1* and *U2* are both set as the complement of the initial labeled dataset, i.e., *U1 = All-L1*, *U2 = All-L2*.

Step 2: Build the content classifier *C1* using features *F1* extracted from the content information of *L1*. Here the first independent feature set is utilized. Use *C1* to label *U2*.

Step 3: Build the metadata classifier *C2* using features *F2* extracted from the metadata information of *L2*. Here, the second independent feature set is utilized. Use *C2* to label *U1*.

Step 4: Move highly confident labeled instances from *U2* to *L2* and set *U2* to All-L2; Move highly confident labeled instances from *U1* to *L1* and set *U1* to *All-L1*.

Step 5: Iterate from Step 2 to 4 until no confident labeled instances can be added into *L1* or *L2*, or the number of iteration exceeds a threshold *k*. Here *k* is set to 100.

4.2.2   The Context Features

For the context features used in the co-training process, we considered the following three types:

Bag of Words. This feature consider the words using in a post, which is widely used in the information retrieval domain and they are often the baseline in related work [14, 17]. Post representation by BOW is:

$$PR_{BOW} = [x_1, x_2, \ldots x_L], PR_{BOW} \in R^L, \tag{3}$$

where $x_i \in \{0, 1\}$ and L is the size of vocabulary in the corpus.

BOW with Word Vector. As the dimension of BOW feature is usually very large, and the feature is very sparse, we combine the idea of using BOW and the word vector. The word vector is able to represent every word as a feature vector with user-defined, reasonable number of feature dimensions. We use Glove [11] to generate word vectors for all words in the vocabulary, noted as W where $W \in R^{d \times L}$, d is the feature dimension and L is the size of vocabulary. Then we calculate the average of feature vectors of post words. Finally, the post representation by BOW with word vector then is defined as:

$$PR_{WV} = \frac{W \cdot PR_{BOW}}{|N_{WV}|}, PR_{WV} \in R^d, \tag{4}$$

where N_{WV} is the set of words of one post. The idea of averaging the word vectors was introduced in Maas's work [9].

Dependency Tree with Word Vector. Some words (like verbs) carry more information than other words (such as *a/an, the*) in one sentence. To capture this, we extract words that strongly related to the "root word" reported by the Stanford dependency parser. Then we extract all words that directly depended on the root word in the dependency tree and the root word to form a dependency vector, dep_s:

$$dep_s = [x_{s,1}, x_{s,2}, \ldots x_{s,L}],\tag{5}$$

where $x_{s,i} \in \{0, 1\}$ and s is the sentence index in a post. For example, in the sentence "*My dog also likes eating sausage.*", the root word is *likes*, and other extracted words are *dog, also, likes* and *eating*. Then the vectors of these words in the *s-th* sentence are averaged to get a sentence representation, $SR_{dep,s}$, defined as:

$$SR_{dep,s} = \frac{W \cdot dep_s}{|N_{dep_s}|}, SR_{dep,s} \in R^d,\tag{6}$$

where N_{dep_s} is number of dependency relations of the *s-th* dep_s. Finally, the post representation by dependency tree with word vector, PR_{dep}, is the average of $SR_{bin,s}$ of all sentences in a post as the Eq. (7), where S is all sentences in a post and $|S|$ is the size of it.

$$PR_{dep} = \frac{\sum_{s \in S} SR_{dep,s}}{|S|}\tag{7}$$

4.3   Using CopeOpi

CopeOpi [7] is selected as our sentiment analysis tool. CopeOpi can determine the sentiment score of Chinese words, sentences and documents without training. It not only includes dictionaries and statistic information, but also considers shallow parsing features such as negations to enhance the performance. The results it generates indicate sentiment polarities like many other similar tools. However, the polarities cannot directly be mapped to the standpoint. Therefore, we utilize CopeOpi together with the seed words to calculate the SUP, NEU, and UN_SUP to represent the sentiment comments on these seed words. First we categorize seed words into supportive, neutral and unsupportive classes. If we find any supportive seed word in a sentence, we calculate the score of this sentence. Then scores (could be positive, zero, or negative) of all sentences containing supportive seed words are added up to SUP, and neutral seed words and unsupportive seed words to NEU and UN_SUP, respectively. Note that it is important that the score of the seed word is not included to exclude its sentiment. As a result, having positive sentiment to the SUP and NEU seed words means supportiveness while having positive sentiment to the UN_SUP seed words means unsupportiveness. The final standpoint STD_PT of each document is calculated as formula (8).

Since the polarity of UN_SUP seed words differ from SUP and NEU seed words, we reverse it by multiplying a negative sign to UN_SUP to contribute to the determination of the stance

$$STD\_PT = SUP - UN\_SUP + NEU \qquad (8)$$

Generally, if STD_PT is greater than 1, the document is considered as supportive; if it is less than -1, the document is considered as unsupportive; otherwise the document is neutral. However, if the topic itself already bears an unsupportive concept (like in this paper, anti-construction), a STD_PT value greater than 1 identifies unsupportive documents, and vice versa.

5 Experiments and Results

We first test the performance of the relevance judgment. We generate relevant document sets using two seed word sets in four settings. The seed word set for setting **(Unsup)**$_{all}$ only contains the word "擁核" (embracing nuclear power plant). We believe documents containing keyterms generated from it would not support the reconstruction of the nuclear power plant as the word "embracing" here is ironic pragmatically. The seed word set for setting **(Sup+Unsup)**$_{all}$ includes five seed words "擁核" (embracing nuclear power plant), "廢核" (abandon nuclear power plant), "反核" (anti-nuclear), "核能" (nuclear power), "核電" (nuclear power electricity). Keyterms generated from this setting should contain most documents related to the nuclear power plant, including supportive, controversial, unsupportive and fact-describing ones. Setting **(Unsup)**$_{contained}$ finds those documents found by setting **(Unsup)**$_{all}$ but containing its one seed word, whereas setting **(Sup+Unsup)**$_{contained}$ finds documents found by setting **(Sup+Unsup)**$_{all}$ but containing one of its five seed words. According to the experimental result, the documents of the score greater than 15 found by setting **(Sup+Unsup)**$_{all}$ are treated as relevant in the training and testing data, and then the support and unsupportive document detection is performed on them.

Next the performance of support detection is evaluated. Results of random selection are here reported as the baseline: the f-score for Unsupportive, Neutral and Supportive is 2.40 %, 49.58 %, and 22.23 %, respectively. The results of adopting pure SVM as features are also reported as another baseline: the f-score for Unsupportive, Neutral and Supportive is 1.36 %, 84.55 %, and 28.76 %, respectively. Here SUP, NEU, and UN_SUP together with BOW are utilized as features. Only 20 supportive and 20 unsupportive documents are used for training as generating the SVM model needs labeled data but we have only 51 documents labeled as unsupportive. Note that as 40 labeled documents are selected for training, only 3,960 documents are tested in this experiment. The low performance of the pure SVM experiment could be due to the small and highly skewed training set. Compared to the random selection results, only the performance of the supportive class is improved. We try to train by more instances to decrease the effect of a small training set. However, the problem of lacking labeled data remains. Therefore, the co-train process is adopted to utilize both labeled and unlabeled documents in the training phase.

Before the co-train process starts, setting **(Sup+Unsup)**$_{all}$ is applied on the training data to first find the relevant document set, i.e., labeled and unlabeled data for co-training. Documents found by setting **(Unsup)**$_{contained}$ are the initial labeled supportive data and by setting **(Sup+Unsup)**$_{contained}$ are all initial labeled data for co-training. Table 4 shows the results of using these supportive and unsupportive documents as the two initial sets for SVM co-training with the BOW feature. Compared to the pure SVM, the performance improves a lot, but still it is not satisfactory. Tables 5 and 6 show the results of using word vector features. However, the results of identifying unsupportive posts in Table 5 are all zero, which means the unsupportive ones are all classified as supportive. The results in Table 6 are slightly better than Table 4, which suggests when compositing word vector as features, considering dependency relations is better than adding up BOW.

Table 4. Co-training performance by BOW post representation

Metric	Supportive	Neutral	Unsupportive
Precision	32.78 %	86.74 %	0.71 %
Recall	30.37 %	81.95 %	3.92 %
F-score	31.53 %	84.28 %	1.20 %

Table 5. Co-training performance by BOW with word vector post representation

Metric	Supportive	Neutral	Unsupportive
Precision	31.11 %	86.74 %	0.00 %
Recall	42.18 %	81.95 %	0.00 %
F-score	35.81 %	84.28 %	0.00 %

Table 6. Co-training performance by dependency tree with word vector post representation

Metric	Supportive	Neutral	Unsupportive
Precision	30.32 %	86.74 %	1.14 %
Recall	32.98 %	81.95 %	3.92 %
F-score	31.59 %	84.28 %	1.76 %

Next, we try to keep the same quantities of supportive and unsupportive labeled data during the co-training process to decrease the influence of the unbalance of data. In each iteration in step 4 of co-training, only a maximum number 10, an equal number of highly confidently labeled instances are moved to L1 or L2. The results are shown in Tables 7, 8 and 9, and the performance of finding the unsupportive evidence drops a lot compared to those reported in Tables 4, 5 and 6, respectively.

So far we have tested the performance of using SVM and SVM co-training in different settings but achieved limited improvements. Experimental results show that learning from small and skewed data is challenging, and the precision is too low to fulfill our requirements. Therefore, we try the other proposed method involving the

Table 7. Co-training performance by BOW post representation

Metric	Supportive	Neutral	Unsupportive
Precision	47.78 %	86.74 %	1.63 %
Recall	14.72 %	81.95 %	21.57 %
F-score	22.22 %	84.28 %	3.04 %

Table 8. Co-training performance by BOW with word vector post representation

Metric	Supportive	Neutral	Unsupportive
Precision	31.11 %	86.74 %	0.00 %
Recall	42.18 %	81.95 %	0.00 %
F-score	35.81 %	84.28 %	0.00 %

Table 9. Co-training performance by dependency tree with word vector post representation

Metric	Supportive	Neutral	Unsupportive
Precision	26.16 %	86.74 %	0.22 %
Recall	17.33 %	81.95 %	1.96 %
F-score	20.85 %	84.28 %	0.40 %

sentiment analysis tool. We keep the assumption that documents containing the key-terms generated from five seed words, setting **(Sup+Unsup)**$_\text{all}$, are relevant and adopt CopeOpi to calculate the sentiment scores, which determine the sentiment of each document. If it is greater than the threshold, the document is positive; if it is less than the threshold multiplied by −1, the document is negative; otherwise the document is neutral. Negative documents are labeled as supportive (support anti-reconstruction), while positive documents are labeled as unsupportive. We then set the threshold to 1, which achieved the highest performance than other value and results are shown in Table 10.

Table 10. Using CopeOpi directly for supportive/unsupportive determination

Metric	Supportive	Neutral	Unsupportive
Precision	18.68 %	86.32 %	1.60 %
Recall	45.71 %	51.50 %	13.73 %
F-score	26.56 %	64.51 %	2.86 %

The performance in Table 10 is worse than the results of the best SVM co-training model so far shown in Table 6. After analysis, we find that an additional transition process is necessary to tell the standpoint from the reported polarity. Again, the relevance judgment depends on keyterms generated from seed words. However in the transition process, seed words are also viewed as aspects to be commented on, i.e., people, organizations, events, etc. In addition, we categorize seed words into three

Table 11. Seed words for polarity to standpoint transition

Aspect	Value	Seed word
Positive	SUP	Embracing nuclear power plant
Neutral	NEU	Nuclear power, nuclear power electricity
Negative	UN_SUP	Anti-nuclear, abandon nuclear power plant

Table 12. Performance of CopeOpi followed by a transition process for support determination

Metric	Supportive	Neutral	Unsupportive
Precision	94.62 %	88.86 %	10.47 %
Recall	18.87 %	99.67 %	35.29 %
F-score	31.46 %	93.95 %	16.14 %

aspect categories to calculate the SUP, NEU, and UN_SUP values as shown in Table 11. Results of adding this transition are shown in Table 12. The performance is boosted up and better than the SVM and SVM co-training models, especially the precision. However, the minority, the unsupportive class, is still difficult to be identified.

6 Conclusion

Finding supportive and unsupportive evidence usually encounters the issues of lacking labeled data and data skewness. In this paper, we have proposed two methods which can start from very few predefined seed words to find relevant supportive and un-supportive evidence. Results show that as the support determination module in the proposed methods, adopting the sentiment analysis tool together with a polarity to standpoint transition significantly outperforms using SVM or SVM co-training models.

Several aspects of our approach can be further improved. Sharing posts in Facebook may bring us many identical or very similar posts. Removing these redundant posts may give more reliable evaluation results. For a controversial topic that people pay attention to, data grow quickly in time. Some learning mechanisms can be injected into the CopeOpi-like sentiment analysis tool to enable the adaptation and improve the performance.

References

1. Blum, A., Mitchell, T.: Combining labeled and unlabeled data with co-training. In: Proceedings of the Eleventh Annual Conference on Computational Learning Theory, pp. 92–100. ACM (1998)
2. Bollen, J., Mao, H., Pepe, A.: Modeling public mood and emotion: twitter sentiment and socio-economic phenomena. In: Proceedings of ICWSM 2011 (2011)

3. Gao, D., Wei, F., Li, W., Liu, X., Zhou, M.: Co-training based bilingual sentiment lexicon learning. In: AAAI (2013)
4. Hu, X., Tang, J., Gao, H., Liu, H.: Unsupervised sentiment analysis with emotional signals. In: Proceedings of the 22nd International Conference on World Wide Web, WWW 2013. ACM (2013)
5. Hu, Y., Wang, F., Kambhampati, S.: Listening to the crowd: automated analysis of events via aggregated twitter sentiment. In: Proceedings of the Twenty-Third International Joint Conference on Artificial Intelligence, pp. 2640–2646. AAAI Press (2013)
6. Huang, C., Ku, L.-W. Interest analysis using semantic pagerank and social interaction content. In: Proceedings of the IEEE International Conference on Data Mining, SENTIRE Work-shop (2013)
7. Ku, L.-W., Ho, X.-W., Chen, H.-H.: Opinion mining and relationship discovery using CopeOpi opinion analysis system. J. Am. Soc. Inf. Sci. Technol. **60**(7), 1486–1503 (2009)
8. Li, S., Wang, Z., Zhou, G., Lee, S.Y.M.: Semi-supervised learning for imbalanced sentiment classification. In: Proceedings of International Joint Conference on Artificial Intelligence (IJCAI 2011), vol. 22, No. 3, p. 1826 (2011)
9. Maas, A.L., Daly, R.E., Pham, P.T., Huang, D., Ng, A.Y., Potts, C.: Learning word vectors for sentiment analysis. In: Proceedings of the 49th Annual Meeting of the Association for Computational Linguistics: Human Language Technologies, vol. 1, pp. 142–150. Association for Computational Linguistics (2011)
10. Pang, B., Lee, L., Vaithyanathan, S.: Thumbs up? Sentiment classification using machine learning techniques. In: Proceedings of EMNLP, pp. 79–86 (2002)
11. Pennington, J., Socher, R., Manning, C.D.: Glove: global vectors for word representation. In: Proceedings of the Empiricial Methods in Natural Language Processing (EMNLP 2014), p. 12 (2014)
12. Ringsquandl, M., Petkovic, D.: Analyzing political sentiment on twitter. In: AAAI Spring Symposium: Analyzing Micro-text (2013)
13. Yohei, S., Lun-Wei, K., Le, S., Hsin-Hsi, C., Noriko, K.: Overview of multilingual opinion analysis task at NTCIR-8: a step toward cross lingual opinion analysis. In: Proceedings of the 8th NTCIR Workshop Meeting on Evaluation of Information Access Technologies: Information Retrieval, Question Answering, and Cross-Lingual Information Access, pp. 209-220, Tokyo, Japan 15–18 June 2010
14. Socher, R., Pennington, J., Huang, E.H., Ng, A.Y., Manning, C.D.: Semi-supervised recursive autoencoders for predicting sentiment distributions. In: Proceedings of Conference on Empirical Methods in Natural Language Processing (EMNLP 2011), pp. 151–161 (2011)
15. Wang, X.: Co-training for cross-lingual sentiment classification. In: Proceedings of the Joint Conference of the 47th Annual Meeting of the ACL and the 4th International Joint Conference on Natural Language Processing of the AFNLP, vol. 1, pp. 235–243. Association for Computational Linguistics (2009)
16. Wang, Y., Clark, T., Agichtein, E., Staton, J.: Towards tracking political sentiment through microblog data. In: ACL 2014, p. 88 (2014)
17. Yang, Y.H., Liu, J.Y.: Quantitative study of music listening behavior in a social and affective context. IEEE Trans. Multimedia **15**(6), 1304–1315 (2013)

What Do Patients of Different Medical Illness Say About Their Doctors Online? An Analysis of Online Physician Reviews

Ming-Hsin Phoebe Chiu[✉] and Chia-Lin Chang

National Taiwan Normal University, Taipei, Taiwan, R.O.C.
phoebechiu@ntnu.edu.tw, lin38538@gmail.com

Abstract. This study aims to understand the role and function of online physician reviews as a process of health information communication, as well as the applications on medical practice and patients and caregivers' medical decision-making process. It collected online physician reviews from two Taiwan-based health information websites - Good Doctor and Health and DocHos. The analysis framework comprised four aspects: (1) length of reviews; (2) moment in the medical encounter process is reviewed; (3) themes of the reviews; and (4) review intents. In addition to analyzing the structural and textual characteristics of online physician reviews, this study took a step further to identify the relationship between patients of different medical and how they evaluated a medical encounter. In this paper, findings were reported and implications in improving physician-patient communication and patients' empowerment were discussed.

Keywords: Online physician review · Content analysis · Physician-patient communication · Physician selection information

1 Background

The Internet increases information transparency and symmetry in several ways, and one way is to allow patients and caregivers access to needed information without having to consult the physicians. It promotes the autonomy of the patients' role in medical decision-making, creates better physician-patient communication, and further improves health and healthcare quality. Past research suggests that among those who use the Internet for health care information, about 60 % access "user-generated" information, including reading others' health experiences, and consulting ratings or reviews of healthcare facilities or healthcare providers (Fox and Jones 2011). Half of all health care consumers relied on word of mouth referrals and recommendations from relatives and friends when choosing a primary care physician (Tu and Lauer 2008). Online physician reviews or a word-of-mouth referral, as a type of popular medical and health information, increases patients and caregivers' understanding of doctor selection and supports proactive medical decision-making. Online reviews of physicians may provide valuable insights about patient perceptions of medical care, as they represent public perspective and input from patients and caregivers (López et al. 2012). From the

F.F.-H. Nah and C.-H. Tan (Eds.): HCIB 2015, LNCS 9191, pp. 34–40, 2015.
DOI: 10.1007/978-3-319-20895-4_4

patients and caregivers' perspective, online physician reviews increase patient empowerment to take proactive actions by supporting useful information on selection of physicians (Hay et al. 2008; Sciamanna et al. 2003). From the health care providers' ｐｅｒｓｐｅｃｔｉｖｅ, ｔｈｅ ｒｅｖｉｅｗｓ ｃａｎ ｂｅ ｃｏｎｓｉｄｅｒｅｄ ａｓ ａ ｆｏｒｍ ｏｆ ｑｕａｌｉｔｙ ｅｖａｌｕａｔｉｏｎ, ｓｏ ｔｈａｔ improvement can be made based on the review results in order to provide better health care services (Strech 2011).

This study aims to understand the role and function of online physician reviews as a process of health information communication, as well as the applications on medical practice and patients and caregivers' medical decision-making process. The online physician reviews were collected from two Taiwan-based health information websites - Good Doctor and Health (http://health.businessweekly.com.tw/GSearchDoc.aspx), and DocHos (http://www.dochos.com.tw). The analysis framework comprised both structural and textual aspects, each with distinct analytical focuses. The structural analysis included length of reviews. The textual analysis included moment in the medical encounter process reviewed, intent of the reviews, and themes of the review. In addition to analyzing the structural and textual characteristics of online physician reviews, this study took a step further to identify the relationship between patients of different medical and how they evaluated a medical encounter, by conducting statistical tests on the data sets.

This study hopes to understand the role and function of the online physician reviews in the process of health information communication, as well as the applications on physicians' practice of clinical medicine and patients and caregivers' medical decision-making process. It may provide insight into developing patient-centered rather than institution-centered evaluation criteria for evaluating healthcare quality, while the institution-centered evaluation criteria often focuses on physicians' performance data (e.g. number of malpractice payment) which is hidden from public. Furthermore, the results from the statistical analysis may inform the weight assigned to each evaluation criterion in online physician rating service.

2 Research Methods

This study collected online physician reviews from two Taiwan-based health information websites, Good Doctor and Health (http://health.businessweekly.com.tw/GSearchDoc.aspx), and DocHos (http://www.dochos.com.tw). Good Doctor and Health was funded and established by Business Weekly Media Group- Good Doctor and Health. DocHos was developed and owned by an internal medicine physician; however, the service was closed due to unforeseen circumstances. These two sites are by far believed or used to be the largest and most popular online physician review sites in Taiwan. Both sites were operated in Traditional Chinese, but were also opened for international users.

The online reviews posted by users can be divided into reviews of doctors, practices and medical centers, and pharmacies. The reviews are rated on a scale of one to five, as well as are given in written comments, and are searchable by medical specialties and practice locations. Fifty pieces of physician reviews for each of the 24 medical disciplines are collected, resulting a total of 1,200 reviews for data analysis, and the 24 medical disciplines under investigation were neurology, dermatology, dentistry, obstetrics and gynecology, psychiatry, pediatrics, gastroenterology and hepatobiliary, ophthalmology, traditional Chinese medicine, pulmonology, urology, hematology and oncology, physical medicine and rehabilitation, general surgery, general medicine, orthopedics, family medicine, nephrology, cardiovascular medicine, otolaryngology, rectal digestive surgery, plastic and reconstructive surgery, endocrinology and metabolism, and rheumatoid allergy and immunology.

The analysis framework inspired by Pollach (2006) was adapted and comprised four aspects: (1) length of reviews; (2) moment in the medical encounter; (3) intent of the reviews; and (4) themes of the reviews. The 1,200 reviews were first analyzed as aggregate to form the fundamental understanding of the characteristics of online doctor's reviews, and then were examined specifically for 24 distinct medical disciplines to determine the similarity and differences that existed across medical disciplines. It was this study's assumption that patients of different medical illness may experience the medical encounter differently, and may evaluate such experience with different criteria and different attitude.

Privacy is considered one of the utmost necessary prerequisites for medical research. This study is highly related to a profession that is dependent on professional knowledge as well as trust, and could be damaging to physicians' reputation or patients' privacy. For ethical reason, information that was identity sensitive, such as a doctor's name and practice information or a patient's personal information, was concealed in the reporting of study results.

3 Preliminary Findings

Table 1 shows that average length of all 1,200 reviews is 68.24 words, but review length varies between medical disciplines. Reviews of Neurology (135.6 words), Dermatology (89.6 words), and Dentistry (87.8 words) are the three longest ones. Reviews of Rheumatoid Allergy and Immunology (51.0 words), Endocrinology and Metabolism (51.3 words), and Plastic and Reconstructive Surgery (51.7 words) are the three shortest ones.

Regarding moment in the medical encounter process is reviewed, the research findings mimic the patients' experience and identifies nine critical moments that are addressed in the reviews. According to Table 2, this study conceptualizes the medical process into seven sequential moments and two general remarks: (1) Prior to the medical encounter (5.8 %); (2) making an appointment (1.3 %); (3) waiting for appointment (3.1 %); (4) during examination and diagnosis (34.3 %); (5) receiving prescription and medical advice (5.1 %); (6) during treatment (27.5 %); (7) after treatment (25.8 %). Two general remarks are physician-patient interaction in general (17.1 %) and unrelated to medical encounter process (23.8 %).

Themes of the review can be categorized into physician-related, system-related, clinical-related, and patient-related. The themes mentioned in the physician reviews can be reasoned as the evaluation criteria that patients acknowledged and perceived as important. Physician-related aspects can be broken into a physician's medical ethics (22.5 %), reputation (12.1 %), medical competence (45 %), appearance (2.6 %) and

Table 1. Average length of online physician reviews by medical disciplines

Medical disciplines	Average length
Neurology	135.6
Dermatology	89.6
Dentistry	87.8
Obstetrics and gynecology	76.1
Psychiatry	75.1
Pediatrics	73.7
Gastroenterology and hepatobiliary	71.0
Ophthalmology	69.0
Traditional Chinese medicine	68.9
Pulmonology	67.2
Urology	66.5
Hematology and oncology	66.3
Physical medicine and rehabilitation	65.1
General surgery	63.2
General medicine	62.4
Orthopedics	60.8
Family medicine	60.1
Nephrology	59.5
Cardiovascular division	58.0
Otolaryngology	55.3
Rectal digestive surgery	53.7
Plastic and reconstructive surgery	51.7
Endocrinology and metabolism	51.3
Rheumatoid allergy and immunology	51.0
Average	68.24

Table 2. Moment in the medical encounter process is reviewed by medical disciplines

Medical Disciplines	Prior to medical encounter		Making an appointment		Waiting for appointment		During examination and diagnosis		During treatment		Receiving prescription and medical advice		After treatment		Physician-patient interaction in general		Unrelated to medical encounter process	
General Medicine	2	4.0%	0	0.0%	0	0.0%	27	54.0%	12	24.0%	1	2.0%	13	26.0%	9	18.0%	9	18.0%
General Surgery	2	4.0%	0	0.0%	2	4.0%	16	32.0%	18	36.0%	0	0.0%	20	40.0%	13	26.0%	6	12.0%
Pediatrics	2	4.0%	1	2.0%	2	4.0%	27	54.0%	13	26.0%	8	16.0%	9	18.0%	7	14.0%	9	18.0%
Cardiovascular Division	2	4.0%	0	0.0%	1	2.0%	15	30.0%	14	28.0%	2	4.0%	11	22.0%	7	14.0%	17	34.0%
Dentistry	8	16.0%	3	6.0%	3	6.0%	24	48.0%	27	54.0%	0	0.0%	16	32.0%	1	2.0%	9	18.0%
Dermatology	8	16.0%	3	6.0%	7	14.0%	26	52.0%	17	34.0%	6	12.0%	18	36.0%	13	26.0%	2	4.0%
Otolaryngology	5	10.0%	1	2.0%	1	2.0%	24	48.0%	21	42.0%	6	12.0%	15	30.0%	4	8.0%	7	14.0%
Hematology and Oncology	0	0.0%	0	0.0%	2	4.0%	13	26.0%	13	26.0%	1	2.0%	6	12.0%	8	16.0%	22	44.0%
Traditional Chinese Medicine	4	8.0%	2	4.0%	4	8.0%	20	40.0%	17	34.0%	18	36.0%	21	42.0%	1	2.0%	9	18.0%
Gastroenterology and Hepatobiliary	2	4.0%	0	0.0%	0	0.0%	16	32.0%	7	14.0%	0	0.0%	3	6.0%	13	26.0%	14	28.0%
Chest Medicine	1	2.0%	0	0.0%	0	0.0%	18	36.0%	14	28.0%	3	6.0%	13	26.0%	9	18.0%	10	20.0%
Urology	1	2.0%	0	0.0%	0	0.0%	21	42.0%	12	24.0%	1	2.0%	10	20.0%	8	16.0%	12	24.0%
Rectal Digestive Surgery	3	6.0%	0	0.0%	1	2.0%	12	24.0%	24	48.0%	0	0.0%	15	30.0%	7	14.0%	13	26.0%
Rheumatoid Allergy and Immunology	0	0.0%	1	2.0%	2	4.0%	26	52.0%	7	14.0%	5	10.0%	5	10.0%	7	14.0%	13	26.0%
Endocrinology and Metabolism	1	2.0%	0	0.0%	3	6.0%	13	26.0%	10	20.0%	0	0.0%	6	12.0%	7	14.0%	21	42.0%
Family Medicine	3	6.0%	1	2.0%	2	4.0%	15	30.0%	11	22.0%	5	10.0%	11	22.0%	13	26.0%	8	16.0%
Orthopedics	1	2.0%	0	0.0%	0	0.0%	14	28.0%	14	28.0%	2	4.0%	16	32.0%	3	6.0%	16	32.0%
Obstetrics and Gynecology	0	0.0%	1	2.0%	3	6.0%	23	46.0%	16	32.0%	1	2.0%	13	26.0%	6	12.0%	10	20.0%
Ophthalmology	7	14.0%	1	2.0%	2	4.0%	5	10.0%	11	22.0%	3	6.0%	25	50.0%	1	2.0%	17	34.0%
Physical Medicine and Rehabilitation	4	8.0%	0	0.0%	0	0.0%	13	26.0%	11	22.0%	2	4.0%	18	36.0%	10	20.0%	14	28.0%
Nephrology	2	4.0%	1	2.0%	0	0.0%	10	20.0%	10	20.0%	0	0.0%	5	10.0%	22	44.0%	12	24.0%
Neurology	4	8.0%	0	0.0%	1	2.0%	11	22.0%	15	30.0%	3	6.0%	13	26.0%	18	36.0%	8	16.0%
Psychiatry	4	8.0%	1	2.0%	1	2.0%	17	34.0%	8	16.0%	6	12.0%	9	18.0%	11	22.0%	9	18.0%
Plastic and Reconstructive Surgery	3	6.0%	0	0.0%	0	0.0%	6	12.0%	8	16.0%	1	2.0%	18	36.0%	7	14.0%	19	38.0%
Total	69	5.8%	16	1.3%	37	3.1%	412	34.3%	330	27.5%	74	6.2%	309	25.8%	205	17.1%	286	23.8%

Table 3. Themes of the review by medical disciplines

	Physician's personality		Medical competence		Treatment outcomes		Medical ethics		Diagnostic process		Service attitude		Personal opinion		Physician's reputation		Clinical encounter process in general		Other service staff		Prescription and medical advice		Medical equipment and devices		Physician's appearance		Clinical environment	
General Medicine	38	76.0%	29	58.0%	5	10.0%	26	52.0%	10	20.0%	7	14.0%	1	2.0%	3	6.0%	6	12.0%	2	4.0%	1	2.0%	0	0.0%	0	0.0%	0	0.0%
General Surgery	25	50.0%	38	76.0%	13	26.0%	22	44.0%	6	12.0%	5	10.0%	6	12.0%	5	10.0%	8	16.0%	3	6.0%	0	0.0%	0	0.0%	0	0.0%	0	0.0%
Pediatrics	34	68.0%	30	60.0%	9	18.0%	23	46.0%	5	10.0%	7	14.0%	3	6.0%	5	10.0%	8	16.0%	5	10.0%	5	10.0%	2	4.0%	2	4.0%	1	2.0%
Cardiovascular Division	28	56.0%	30	60.0%	10	20.0%	23	46.0%	6	12.0%	7	14.0%	5	10.0%	8	16.0%	7	14.0%	2	4.0%	1	2.0%	1	2.0%	2	4.0%	0	0.0%
Dentistry	26	52.0%	32	64.0%	19	38.0%	8	16.0%	5	10.0%	8	16.0%	4	8.0%	12	24.0%	8	16.0%	6	12.0%	1	2.0%	6	12.0%	3	6.0%	6	12.0%
Dermatology	36	72.0%	34	68.0%	18	36.0%	11	22.0%	6	12.0%	7	14.0%	4	8.0%	15	30.0%	2	4.0%	7	14.0%	1	2.0%	0	0.0%	3	6.0%	2	4.0%
Otolaryngology	41	82.0%	25	50.0%	15	30.0%	10	20.0%	17	34.0%	15	30.0%	7	14.0%	5	10.0%	2	4.0%	3	6.0%	4	8.0%	1	2.0%	1	2.0%	1	2.0%
Hematology and Oncology	38	76.0%	22	44.0%	2	4.0%	12	24.0%	11	22.0%	19	38.0%	4	8.0%	5	10.0%	3	6.0%	3	6.0%	1	2.0%	2	4.0%	0	0.0%	1	2.0%
Traditional Chinese Medicine	27	54.0%	18	36.0%	17	34.0%	9	18.0%	15	30.0%	19	38.0%	4	8.0%	5	10.0%	4	8.0%	4	8.0%	14	28.0%	0	0.0%	0	0.0%	2	4.0%
Gastroenterology and Hepatobiliary	28	56.0%	16	32.0%	6	12.0%	11	22.0%	10	20.0%	3	6.0%	16	32.0%	3	6.0%	0	0.0%	0	0.0%	2	4.0%	3	6.0%	0	0.0%	0	0.0%
Chest Medicine	31	62.0%	26	52.0%	9	18.0%	15	30.0%	16	32.0%	9	18.0%	2	4.0%	2	4.0%	6	12.0%	3	6.0%	1	2.0%	0	0.0%	1	2.0%	0	0.0%
Urology	38	76.0%	17	34.0%	12	24.0%	19	38.0%	14	28.0%	7	14.0%	6	12.0%	9	18.0%	3	6.0%	4	8.0%	2	4.0%	0	0.0%	1	2.0%	1	2.0%
Rectal Digestive Surgery	34	68.0%	16	32.0%	13	26.0%	9	18.0%	11	22.0%	9	18.0%	2	4.0%	5	10.0%	3	6.0%	3	6.0%	0	0.0%	2	4.0%	3	6.0%	0	0.0%
Rheumatoid Allergy and Immunology	40	80.0%	4	8.0%	5	10.0%	7	14.0%	27	54.0%	19	38.0%	9	18.0%	3	6.0%	1	2.0%	2	4.0%	5	10.0%	2	4.0%	0	0.0%	0	0.0%
Endocrinology and Metabolism	38	76.0%	16	32.0%	8	16.0%	11	22.0%	8	16.0%	11	22.0%	8	16.0%	3	6.0%	3	6.0%	2	4.0%	2	4.0%	1	2.0%	0	0.0%	1	2.0%
Family Medicine	37	74.0%	10	20.0%	8	16.0%	7	14.0%	18	36.0%	11	22.0%	5	10.0%	4	8.0%	3	6.0%	5	10.0%	5	10.0%	3	6.0%	3	6.0%	1	2.0%
Orthopedics	33	66.0%	17	34.0%	14	28.0%	6	12.0%	15	30.0%	10	20.0%	7	14.0%	6	12.0%	3	6.0%	4	8.0%	3	6.0%	1	2.0%	1	2.0%	0	0.0%
Obstetrics and Gynecology	36	72.0%	16	32.0%	10	20.0%	6	12.0%	19	38.0%	10	20.0%	13	26.0%	2	4.0%	6	12.0%	4	8.0%	2	4.0%	1	2.0%	1	2.0%	0	0.0%
Ophthalmology	14	28.0%	13	26.0%	25	50.0%	1	2.0%	6	12.0%	3	6.0%	10	20.0%	13	26.0%	2	4.0%	8	16.0%	4	8.0%	3	6.0%	1	2.0%	1	2.0%
Physical Medicine and Rehabilitation	37	74.0%	12	24.0%	16	32.0%	7	14.0%	9	18.0%	8	16.0%	16	32.0%	7	14.0%	3	6.0%	9	18.0%	2	4.0%	3	6.0%	3	6.0%	0	0.0%
Nephrology	35	70.0%	12	24.0%	5	10.0%	9	18.0%	6	12.0%	5	10.0%	12	24.0%	6	12.0%	1	2.0%	2	4.0%	3	6.0%	0	0.0%	2	4.0%	0	0.0%
Neurology	32	64.0%	19	38.0%	11	22.0%	7	14.0%	6	12.0%	3	6.0%	11	22.0%	7	14.0%	7	14.0%	4	8.0%	2	4.0%	0	0.0%	0	0.0%	0	0.0%
Psychiatry	36	72.0%	10	20.0%	8	16.0%	4	8.0%	8	16.0%	7	14.0%	13	26.0%	5	10.0%	3	6.0%	3	6.0%	7	14.0%	1	2.0%	3	6.0%	2	4.0%
Plastic and Reconstructive Surgery	24	48.0%	24	48.0%	15	30.0%	7	14.0%	3	6.0%	3	6.0%	9	18.0%	7	14.0%	6	12.0%	2	4.0%	3	6.0%	1	2.0%	1	2.0%	2	4.0%
Total	786	65.5%	486	40.5%	273	22.8%	270	22.5%	257	21.4%	212	17.7%	177	14.8%	145	12.1%	98	8.2%	90	7.5%	71	5.9%	33	2.8%	31	2.6%	21	1.8%

personality (65 %). System-related reviews deal with clinical environment (1.8 %), medical equipment and devices (2.8 %), office service staff (7.5) and service attitude (17.7 %). Medical-related reviews tend to focus on the diagnostic process (21.4 %), medical advice and prescription (5.9 %), and treatment outcomes (22.8 %). Patient-related aspect focuses on patients' personal opinion (14.8 %) on the overall medical encounter experience (Table 3).

This study uncovered ten types of intent that corresponded to the reviews posted. As shown in Table 4, these intents included (1) showing praise (86.6 %); (2) acknowledging previous comments (28.0 %); (3) asking questions (20.0 %); (4) describing health situations (16.7 %), (5) describing treatment process (16.3 %); (6) making recommendation (12.8 %); (7) showing gratitude (11.6 %); (8) addressing criticism (4.8 %); (9) refuting previous comments (1 %); and (10) others (4 %). It further calculated the number of intent that reviews of each medical discipline communicated, in order to examine the relationship between medical disciplines and the variety of intent. On average, each review had 1.6 intents, while reviews of dentistry (2.0) and ophthalmology (1.9) demonstrated the most number of intents, and reviews of rheumatoid allergy and immunology demonstrated the least number of intents (1.2). The results may suggest that when patients engaged in uninsured medical services, such as jaw reconstruction or laser vision correction, they would evaluate the medical encounter with even higher standard not only as patients, but also as consumers who paid to receive services.

In addition to the descriptive statistics, this study further conducted three statistical tests. To investigate how patients of different medical illness may demonstrate different rating behaviors on the medical encounter, three sets of Chi-square tests were conducted on medical specialties and the categorical variables of three research themes.

Table 4. Intent of the review by medical disciplines

	Showing praise		Describing health situation		Describing treatment process/Treatment		Making recommendation		Showing gratitude		Addressing criticism		Acknowledging previous comments		Refuting previous comments		Asking questions		other	
Medicine	47	94.0%	1	7.0%	1	7.0%	4	8.0%	9	18.0%	1	7.0%	0	0.0%	0	0.0%	0	0.0%	2	4.0%
General Surgery	39	78.0%	8	16.0%	4	8.0%	4	8.0%	7	14.0%	3	6.0%	1	2.0%	0	0.0%	0	0.0%	4	8.0%
Pediatrics	44	88.0%	3	6.0%	7	14.0%	8	16.0%	5	10.0%	3	6.0%	1	2.0%	0	0.0%	0	0.0%	1	2.0%
Cardiovascular Division	44	88.0%	3	6.0%	9	18.0%	5	10.0%	6	12.0%	3	6.0%	0	0.0%	1	2.0%	1	2.0%	3	6.0%
Dentistry	40	80.0%	18	36.0%	19	38.0%	12	24.0%	4	8.0%	2	4.0%	0	0.0%	3	6.0%	0	0.0%	0	0.0%
Dermatology	40	80.0%	14	28.0%	13	26.0%	9	18.0%	5	10.0%	3	6.0%	0	0.0%	0	0.0%	1	2.0%	4	8.0%
Otolaryngology	42	84.0%	10	20.0%	10	20.0%	10	20.0%	4	8.0%	4	8.0%	0	0.0%	2	4.0%	0	0.0%	2	4.0%
Hematology and Oncology	44	88.0%	5	10.0%	4	8.0%	6	12.0%	6	12.0%	2	4.0%	0	0.0%	0	0.0%	0	0.0%	2	4.0%
Traditional Chinese Medicine	39	78.0%	12	24.0%	14	28.0%	9	18.0%	4	8.0%	1	2.0%	3	6.0%	0	0.0%	1	2.0%	1	2.0%
Gastroenterology and Hepatobiliary	41	82.0%	4	8.0%	6	12.0%	10	20.0%	8	16.0%	2	4.0%	0	0.0%	0	0.0%	0	0.0%	5	10.0%
Chest Medicine	45	90.0%	10	20.0%	5	10.0%	4	8.0%	10	20.0%	2	4.0%	0	0.0%	1	2.0%	0	0.0%	1	2.0%
Urology	47	94.0%	9	18.0%	9	18.0%	7	14.0%	6	12.0%	1	2.0%	1	2.0%	0	0.0%	0	0.0%	0	0.0%
Rectal Digestive Surgery	47	94.0%	8	16.0%	8	16.0%	5	10.0%	7	14.0%	1	2.0%	0	0.0%	1	2.0%	1	2.0%	1	2.0%
Rheumatoid Allergy and Immunology	44	88.0%	3	6.0%	2	4.0%	4	8.0%	3	6.0%	3	6.0%	0	0.0%	0	0.0%	0	0.0%	1	2.0%
Endocrinology and Metabolism	45	90.0%	5	10.0%	5	10.0%	2	4.0%	6	12.0%	2	4.0%	0	0.0%	0	0.0%	1	2.0%	1	2.0%
Family Medicine	45	90.0%	6	12.0%	10	20.0%	5	10.0%	5	10.0%	2	4.0%	2	4.0%	0	0.0%	1	2.0%	1	2.0%
Orthopedics	37	74.0%	11	22.0%	8	16.0%	6	12.0%	4	8.0%	5	10.0%	1	2.0%	1	2.0%	2	4.0%	5	10.0%
Obstetrics and Gynecology	47	94.0%	15	30.0%	11	22.0%	7	14.0%	4	8.0%	3	6.0%	0	0.0%	0	0.0%	1	2.0%	0	0.0%
Ophthalmology	42	84.0%	13	26.0%	16	32.0%	4	8.0%	14	28.0%	3	6.0%	1	2.0%	0	0.0%	1	2.0%	3	6.0%
Physical Medicine and Rehabilitation	44	88.0%	13	26.0%	11	22.0%	7	14.0%	4	8.0%	3	6.0%	0	0.0%	2	4.0%	0	0.0%	2	4.0%
Nephrology	46	92.0%	3	6.0%	2	4.0%	3	6.0%	1	2.0%	1	2.0%	1	2.0%	1	2.0%	0	0.0%	1	2.0%
Neurology	45	90.0%	14	28.0%	6	12.0%	8	16.0%	7	14.0%	4	8.0%	1	2.0%	0	0.0%	0	0.0%	2	4.0%
Psychiatry	39	78.0%	5	10.0%	7	14.0%	5	10.0%	8	16.0%	4	8.0%	2	4.0%	0	0.0%	0	0.0%	4	8.0%
Plastic and Reconstructive Surgery	46	92.0%	7	14.0%	9	18.0%	10	20.0%	2	4.0%	0	0.0%	0	0.0%	0	0.0%	0	0.0%	1	2.0%
Total	1039	86.6%	200	16.7%	196	16.3%	154	12.8%	139	11.6%	58	4.8%	14	1.2%	12	1.0%	10	0.8%	47	3.9%

The results show that the intents of "describing health situation ($\chi^2(df) = 55.755$)" and "describing treatment process ($\chi^2(df) = 59.925$)" are significant at the 5 % level ($p < .001$), meaning patients of different illness may show different patterns in indicating these two intents. Regarding moments in the medical encounter is reviewed, the results indicate that medical discipline is a strong factor when the medical encounter moments under review are "during examination and diagnosis($\chi^2(df) = 56.12$)," "after treatment ($\chi^2(df) = 56.90$)," and "physician-patient interaction in general ($\chi^2(df) = 70.47$)." Last set of chi-square test attempted to confirm that medical discipline would be a factor in affecting patients' priority of the evaluation criteria. This study identified 14 themes of the review, physician's personality is the most mentioned theme. However, the Chi-square test reveals that patients of different medical illness don't show any difference in focusing on physician's personality. When a Chi-square test was further carried out to test the relationship between medical disciplines and each of the review themes mentioned, only themes on "medical competence ($\chi^2(df) = 86.148$)," "treatment outcomes ($\chi^2(df) = 58.692$)," "medical ethics ($\chi^2(df) = 90.178$)," "service attitude ($\chi^2(df) = 61.962$)," and "personal opinion ($\chi^2(df) = 59.339$)" were significant.

4   Implications of the Study

Further analysis regarding the characteristics of the reviews by 24 distinct medical specialties will be reported. Online reviews of physicians provide unfiltered and unedited feedbacks, not only on physician-patient relationship, but also on quality of healthcare in general. Themes of the reviews generated from this study may propose an alternative multi-dimensional patient satisfaction measure that is patient-focused instead of doctor or institution-centered. In addition, the intent behind the reviews reveals that fact that the majority of the reviews are demonstrating a positive attitude toward the medical encounter by showing praise and gratitude, or recommending the physicians. Description of health situation and treatment process may be informative and useful for other patients in comparing their own situation to the described situation, and in determining how a physician being rated can be ultimately selected.

References

Fox, S., Jones, S.: The social life of health information. Pew Internet & American Life Project, Washington, D.C. (2011). http://www.pewinternet.org/2011/05/12/the-social-life-of-health-information-2011/

López, A., Detz, A., Ratanawongsa, N., Sarkar, U.: What patients say about their doctors online: a qualitative content analysis. J. Gen. Intern. Med. **27**(6), 685–692 (2012)

Pollach, I.: Electronic word of mouth: a genre analysis of product reviews on consumer opinion web sites. In: System Sciences, 2006. HICSS 2006. Proceedings of the 39th Annual Hawaii International Conference on System Sciences, vol. 3, p. 51c. IEEE (2006)

Tu, H.T., Lauer, J.R.: Word of mouth and physician referrals still drive health care provider choice. Res. Brief (9):1–8 (2008)

Hay, M.C., Strathmann, C., Lieber, E., Wick, K., Giesser, B.: Why patients go online: multiple sclerosis, the Internet, and physician-patient communication. Neurologist **14**(6), 374–381 (2008)

Sciamanna, C.N., Clark, M.A., Diaz, J.A., Newton, S.: Filling the gaps in physician communication: the role of the Internet among primary care patients. Int. J. Med. Inform. **72**(1), 1–8 (2003)

Strech, D.: Ethical principles for physician rating sites. J. Med. Int. Res. **13**(4), e. 113 (2011)

Privacy by Design: Examining Two Key Aspects of Social Applications

Ben C.F. Choi[✉] and Joseph Tam

School of Information Systems, Technology and Management, UNSW Australia Business School, UNSW Australia, Sydney, Australia
chun.choi@unsw.edu.au, joseph.tam@student.unsw.edu.au

Abstract. Social applications do not only acquire users' personal information but potentially also collects the personal information of users' social networks. Despite considerable discussion of privacy problems in prior work, questions remain as to how to design privacy-preserving social applications and how to evaluate its effect on privacy. Drawing on the justice framework, we identify two key aspects of social, namely information acquisition and exposure control and examine the effects on user evaluation of social applications. Furthermore, we investigate the impact of this evaluation on usage intention. In doing so, we provide new insight into embedding privacy in technology development.

Keywords: Social applications · Online social networks · Information privacy

1 Introduction

Recently, in an attempt to expand the functionality of their social platforms, online social networks such as Facebook, Twitter and LinkedIn, have begun opening their platforms to allow third party developers to create social applications to improve the experience of users online. Social applications are essentially software programs that are developed to enhance social interactivity on online social networks. These applications have fundamentally augmented the online social networks experience by creating a spectrum of new, functional and entertaining software that have become a new paradigm of social interaction [1]. There are over 200 million users currently using social applications, with that number expected to double within the next 5 years [2]. The surge in the popularity of social applications has also become a significant revenue stream for these online social networks with platforms such as Facebook Platform, yielding revenues of 1.96 Billion dollars.

Despite the increasing popularity of social applications, the concern of users over privacy appears to be the biggest obstacle when individuals are deciding to use these applications [3]. As identified by prior privacy research, these may include but are not limited to, accidental information disclosure, damaged reputation and image, and identity thieves [e.g., 4, 5]. The advancement of technologies embedded and used in the social environment can further raise users' perception of privacy risk because these applications do not only threaten personal privacy but also invade the privacy of users'

© Springer International Publishing Switzerland 2015
F.F.-H. Nah and C.-H. Tan (Eds.): HCIB 2015, LNCS 9191, pp. 41–52, 2015.
DOI: 10.1007/978-3-319-20895-4_5

online social network friends. For example, Angwin and Singer-Vine [6] analyzed 100 of the most-used applications on Facebook and found that users did not only expose their own profile information, such as name, profile photo, and gender, but also reveal their friends' profile information (i.e., friends' profile photos, names, and genders). Overall, this extended scope of profile information collection has stirred concerns among users.

The objective of this research is to enrich understanding of information privacy in the context of social application usage. Specifically, we aim to enhance the literature by developing and testing a model that explains social application usage. Drawing on the justice framework, we examine how extended information collection (such as the collection of network information) and control over profile exposure (such as the ability to deny disclosure) can influence user evaluation, which in turn, influence their usage intention. By doing so, we seek to provide new insight into embedding privacy proactively into the core of social application designs.

The remainder of the paper is organized as follows. The next section reviews previous literature and discusses the theoretical foundation for this study. The research model and hypotheses are then proposed, followed by the introduction of research methodology and the report of the data analysis results. This paper concludes with the discussion of theoretical and practical contributions, limitations, and avenues for future research.

2 Literature Review

2.1 The Justice Framework

The justice framework has been vastly accepted as an important framework in understanding privacy issues [7, 8]. Indeed, ample scholarly efforts have been devoted to theoretical development for analyzing privacy through a justice theoretical lens. For example, Son and Kim [8] examined internet users' information privacy protective responses and found that individuals' perceptions of justice powerfully drove their privacy-related behavior. Overall, a general conclusion from this stream of research is that individuals' justice perceptions of a firm's information practices can have a major positive effect on their privacy decision making [9].

In the context of information privacy, two key types of justice are found to be imperatively important, namely distributive justice and procedural justice [10]. Distributive justice refers to the evaluation of fairness of economic and socio-emotional outcomes [11]. Distributive justice is promoted when outcomes are coherent with implicit norms for distribution. In particular, past research found that perceptions of outcome fairness were largely developed based on the equity principle [12, 13]. The equity principle posits that outcomes should be distributed in accordance to the cost incurred on individuals. This concept is consistent with the privacy calculus or a psychological tradeoff that is widely established in privacy research, which suggests that individuals evaluate the exchange outcome when their personal information is concerned.

Procedural justice typically manifests in the structural aspects of procedures, such as process control and fair allocative procedures [14]. Past research suggests that procedural justice can be enhanced when the decision processes enable the correction of wrong decisions, represents the needs and values of all parties in the exchange, and meets the ethical and moral values of the social system. More importantly, recent studies highlight the importance of individuals' ability to voice their opinions through the decision process in ensuring procedural justice. Collectively, these studies demonstrate the viability of procedural justice in explaining behavioral outcomes across a broad range of contexts.

2.2   Challenges to Distributive Justice – Information Acquisition

Consistent with the justice framework, in the context of social application usage, distributive justice can be challenged when individuals' profile information is acquired by social applications. This study focuses on local and global profile acquisition, which is particularly prevalent when individuals evaluate social applications. Local information acquisition is about the collection of users' own profile information. When local information is acquired, a user's personal information, which resides on his or her personal profile, is revealed to the social applications. Local information acquisition often involves the collection of an extensive range of profile information, such as profile names, email addresses, genders, and birthdays [15].

Global information acquisition does not only involve the collection of a user's own profile information but also entails information collection that involves the profiles of his or her online social networks [15]. When global information is acquired, in addition to the user's profile information, it collects friends' profile information, such as his or her list of friends, their profile names, email addresses, genders, and birthdays. Since users are entrusted with their friends' profile information, users often assume to have a stake of ownership over such information and expect to exercise some control over the exposure of the shared information.

2.3   Challenges to Procedural Justice – Exposure Control

Exposure control refers to the design feature that enables users to regulate who can access and use their personal information when they use social applications. In the context of information privacy, fair information practice (FIP) principles serve as global normative standards that reflect procedural justice, which include the stipulations that users should be given control with regard to the use of their information [16]. Indeed, according to contemporary choice theory, in privacy situations, users evaluate attributes of choice alternatives, which may comprise both economic and psychological factors, to make privacy decisions [17].

Consistent with contemporary choice theory, exposure control can be challenged when users' profile information is compulsorily acquired by social applications. This study focuses on optional exposure and compulsory exposure of users' profile information. When optional exposure is available, a user might choose the specific profile information to reveal to the application provider. Past privacy research indicates that users' privacy concerns can be addressed by providing users with more control over their information [e.g., 9, 18]. By retaining control over information provision, users could protect their personal information and hence become less concerned about their privacy.

Compulsory exposure makes revelation of profile information mandatory for application usage. With compulsory exposure, users do not only lose control over their own profile information, but often at times lose control over their friends' profile information as well. This lack of control over information engenders mistrust in the technology and induces the perceptions of risks of data extraction.

2.4 Privacy Calculus

Whereas the justice framework sheds light on the two privacy aspects of the social application, past work on privacy calculus helps understand individuals' cognitive evaluation processes. In particular, previous research suggests that when individuals' personal information is concerned, they undergo a privacy calculus to evaluate the cost and benefit of the exchange [17]. Prior IS research on privacy calculus have examined this concept in a variety of contexts, such as online commerce, location-aware marketing, and online social interactions [e.g., 19]. Yet little is known about the role of privacy calculus in social application usage. In this study, individuals' cost and benefit evaluations are represented by perceived privacy risk and perceived application value. Perceived privacy risk refers to the degree to which an individual believes that a high potential for loss is associated with social app usage [20]. Prior privacy literature has identified aspects of privacy situations that induce privacy risk, including information collection and information control. Individuals often estimate privacy risk by considering the types of information collection as well as their ability to control information after revelation.

Usage of technology is typically driven by the value the technology can provide to users [21]. Accordingly, we examine perceived application value, which refers to the extent to which the social application fulfills user's personal needs [22], as a major benefit that individuals derive from using social applications. Research on value evaluation theorizes that individuals' perception of application value is highly dependent on the types of information acquisition, which allows users to evaluate the relevance and importance of information collection [23, 24]. Usage of social applications typically involves information collection, which is commonly considered relevant when individuals' personal information is acquired by an application.

Past studies examining value evaluation also suggests that subsequent control over revealed information is an important consideration in assessing application value [20]. The value of technologies related to personal information disclosure has often been discounted when individuals are denied control over their information [25]. Without proper control, the information collected for one purpose can be used for another, secondary purpose. Control is especially important in social application usage context because users take higher risks in the submission of profile information. Several studies have suggested that in reality, individuals want to have the ability to control information exposure.

3   Research Model and Hypotheses Development

We present our research model in Fig. 1 below.

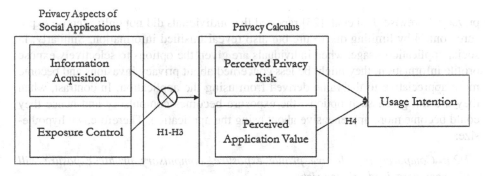

Fig. 1.   Research model

3.1   Information Acquisition and Privacy Calculus

Usage of social applications may involve a local scope of information acquisition or a global scope of information acquisition. When a local scope of information acquisition is performed, individual users' profile information is acquired by the social application. As a result, the decision to use the application predominately challenges users' personal privacy. In contrast, a global scope of information acquisition extends the extent of information collection beyond users' profile information by acquiring the profile information of their online social network friends. Consequently, a global information acquisition scope does not only challenge individual personal privacy but also confronts the collective privacy [26].

Previous research has shown that the relevance of information collection influences users' evaluation of application value [23, 24]. In particular, when the specific information collected is vital in enriching technology usage experience, users would believe the information collection is relevant and hence enhance their perception of application value [27]. However, when the information collected is deemed unnecessary in enabling usage experience, users would deem the information collection inappropriate and hence reduce their application value perception. Therefore, compared to a local scope of information acquisition, a global scope of information acquisition would escalate threats to the privacy of individuals' entire online social network and reduce the value of using the application. Thus, we posit:

H1a: Compared to a local scope of information acquisition, a global scope of information acquisition will increase perceived privacy risk.
H1b: Compared to a local scope of information acquisition, a global scope of information acquisition will reduce perceived application value.

3.2 Exposure Control and Privacy Calculus

Past IS research has identified exposure control as a key privacy consideration in individuals' evaluation of technology. For example, Son and Kim [8] revealed that online consumers typically reduced disclosure of personal information to protect privacy. Likewise, Hui et al. [25] reported that individuals did not only exercise exposure control by limiting disclosure but also reveal falsified information. Similarly, in social application usage, when individuals are given the options to selectively expose profile information, they might be less concerned about privacy invasions and become more appreciative to the value derived from using the application. In contrast, when they are not given such options, the exposure becomes compulsory and hence they could become more apprehensive about using the application. Therefore, we hypothesize:

H2a: Compared to selective profile exposure, compulsory profile exposure will increase perceived privacy risk.
H2b: Compared to selective profile exposure, compulsory profile exposure will reduce perceived application value.

3.3 Interaction Between Exposure Control and Information Acquisition

Referent cognitions theory (RCT) offers an explanation for the joint effect of information acquisition and exposure control on perceived privacy risk and perceived application value [28]. Specifically, this theory states that individuals tend to evaluate outcomes (i.e., information acquisition) based on whether fair procedures are followed (i.e., exposure control). When users have a high degree of control over their information, they would be less sensitive to information acquisition in using social applications. However, if they perceive a lack of control over their information, they are more likely to focus on attaining an equitable outcome. Thus, according to RCT, the question of whether exposure control was faithfully facilitated moderates the way users cognitively evaluate information acquisition.

In the case of selective profile exposure, users are allowed control over subsequent use of their profile information, thereby reducing their sensitivity toward information acquisition. However, in the case of compulsory profile exposure, equitable outcome for using the application cannot be guaranteed; hence, users' sensitivity toward information acquisition is likely heightened. Taken together, in the context of social application usage, customers who are satisfied with exposure control tend to perceive the application to be less privacy threatening and more valuable; therefore, exposure control could complement information acquisition in affecting perceived privacy risk and perceived application value. Thus,

H3a: The effect of information acquisition on perceived privacy risk is weaker in the selective profile exposure condition than in the compulsory profile exposure condition.
H3b: The effect of information acquisition on perceived application value is stronger in the selective profile exposure condition than in the compulsory profile exposure condition.

3.4 Privacy Calculus and Usage Intention

Usage of social applications not only exposes individuals' profile information to the provider but also makes them vulnerable to further privacy invasions. Past studies suggests that individuals' perception of privacy invasion reduces usage intention in the online environment. For instance, Youn [29] examined online privacy-protective behavior and revealed that Internet users coped with privacy invasions by limiting participation in online transactions. Accordingly, we propose that usage is essential in realizing the value provided by the social application. For example, Grosser et al. [30] revealed that users who found social application valuable would be motivated to use the application. Specifically, usage was found to be determined by value, such as social connectivity and image gain. Usage can also be understood as a manifestation of commitment in online exchange, in that individuals acknowledge the value provided by the application. Therefore, individuals who perceive high application value will engage in usage behavior. This leads us to posit:

H4a: Higher perceived privacy risk will reduce usage intention.
H4b: Higher perceived application value will increase usage intention.

4 Research Methodology

4.1 Experimental Design

A laboratory experiment with 2 (Information Acquisition: Local Scope vs. Global Scope) $\times$ 2 (Exposure Control: Selective Profile Exposure vs. Compulsory Profile Exposure) factorial design was conducted to test the proposed hypotheses. Information acquisition was manipulated by the type of profile information collected by the application. Exposure control was facilitated by manipulating the availability of selective revelation.

4.2 Sample and Experimental Procedures

Subjects in this experiment were students at a large public university. Prior to the experiment, subjects were asked to provide information about demographics, Internet experience, Facebook experience, Facebook application experience, and dispositional privacy concerns.

5 Data Analysis

5.1 Subject Demographics and Background Analysis

Among the 130 subjects participating in the study, 62 were females. The age of the subjects ranged from 18 to 24, with average Internet experience an average Facebook experience being 8.2 years and 3.3 years, respectively. The average Facebook application experience was 2.41 years. In average, a subject spent 25.23 min to complete the entire experiment.

5.2   Measurements

The manipulation checks were performed. Results suggest that the manipulation for information acquisition and exposure control were successful.

Four items measuring perceived privacy risk were adapted from Folger and Konovsky [28] (Cronbach's alpha = 0.83) (see Table 1). Four items measuring perceived application value were adapted from Folger and Konovsky [28] (Cronbach's alpha = 0.89). Four items measuring usage intention were developed based on Mathieson [31] (Cronbach's alpha = 0.88). Exploratory factor analysis shows that, in general, items load well on their intended factors and lightly on the other factor, thus indicating adequate construct validity.

Table 1. Internal consistency and discriminant validity

	CR	CA	M	PPR	PAV	UI
PPR	0.85	0.83	5.23	0.85		
PAV	0.91	0.89	4.91	0.23	0.89	
UI	0.90	0.88	5.23	−0.19	0.26	0.87

Notes: CR = Composite Reliability; CA = Cronbach's Alpha; M = Mean

ANOVA with perceived privacy risk as dependent variable reveals the significant effects of information acquisition $(F (1, 126) = 55.89, p < 0.01)$ and exposure control $(F (1, 126) = 34.50, p < 0.01)$. Therefore, H1a and H2a are supported. The significant interaction effect $(F (1, 126) = 26.18, p < 0.01)$ suggests that the effect of information acquisition on perceived privacy risk is moderated by exposure control. Simple main effect analysis reveals that (1) a global scope of information acquisition is associated with significantly higher perceived privacy risk than a local scope of information acquisition under the compulsory profile exposure condition $(F (1, 66) = 67.23, p < 0.01)$, and (2) a global scope of information acquisition and a local scope of information acquisition are not different from each other in affecting perceived privacy risk under the selective profile exposure condition $(F (1, 60) = 1.68, p = 0.20)$. Therefore, H3a is supported.

5.3   Results on Perceived Application Value

ANOVA with perceived application value as dependent variable reveals the significant effects of information acquisition $(F (1, 126) = 12.56, p < 0.05)$ and exposure control $(F (1, 126) = 85.48, p < 0.01)$. Therefore, H1b and H2b are supported. The significant interaction effect $(F (1, 126) = 22.24, p < 0.01)$ suggests that the effect of information acquisition on perceived application value is moderated by exposure control. Simple main effect analysis reveals that (1) a global scope of information acquisition is associated with significantly lower perceived application value than a local scope of information acquisition under the selective profile exposure condition $(F (1, 60) = 32.04, p < 0.01)$, and (2) a global scope of information acquisition and a local scope of information acquisition are not different from each other in affecting perceived application value under the compulsory profile exposure condition (F $(1, 66) = 0.73$, $p = 0.57$). Therefore, H3b is supported.

5.4 Results on Willingness to Profile Information Provision

PLS was used to test the structural model proposed on the right-hand side of Fig. 1. Results indicate that perceived privacy risk has a significant and negative effect on usage intention ($p < .05$). Thus, H3a is supported. In line with our expectation, perceived application value also positively affects usage intention ($p < .05$), thereby supporting H3b.

6 Discussion of Results

The results are in support of our hypotheses. We seek to provide a more holistic understanding of individuals' usage of social applications by examining their privacy tradeoff when evaluating social applications. Whereas the cost in the tradeoff is subsumed in privacy risk, the benefit is embodied in application value. We establish that social application usage intention is negatively driven by privacy risk and positively motivated by application value. We also hope to achieve a more comprehensive understanding of privacy tradeoff in this context of social application usage by examining two antecedents: information acquisition and exposure control, which are derived based on the justice framework. Our findings show that these two antecedents powerfully predict both privacy risk and application value.

7 Contributions

We enrich information privacy studies on several grounds. First, we contribute to the IS literature by identifying antecedents of privacy tradeoff in the context of social application usage. While past studies have identified a myriad of factors pertinent to privacy issues, rarely have researchers put forth a coherent framework of antecedents. Drawing on the justice framework, we offer two antecedents, namely information acquisition and exposure control. Specifically, information acquisition accounts for the important role of distributive justice in privacy issues. The procedural aspect of justice is reflected by exposure control in social application usage. Overall, the justice framework offers a coherent perspective for future privacy research.

Furthermore, this study examines the interactions between information acquisition and exposure control that are unique to our context of social application usage. As hypothesized, exposure control somewhat complements information acquisition. Users with the ability to control the extent of profile information exposure tend to perceive information acquisition more acceptable than those without the ability to regulate exposure. To this end, our study offers a concrete account of how information acquisition and exposure control jointly shape users' evaluations of social applications.

This study also offers several important practical contributions. We recommend that social application designers enhance existing technical features to effectively mitigate the impact of exposure control. This study reveals that privacy risk powerfully inhibits usage intention. To this end, we advocate that social application designers should allow individuals to exercise some control over the types of information exposure in using social applications.

Recall that, in our study, exposure control moderates the effects of information acquisition on privacy risk and application value. The results show that information acquisition is a critical attribute of social app evaluation. To help manage the impact of information acquisition, social application providers should exercise prudence in collecting profile information which is relevant to ensuring usage experience.

8   Limitations and Future Directions

We acknowledge some limitations in this study. First, our findings may also be limited by using an application evaluation scenario. While the mock-up application presented in the scenario resembled those of a real social application, the application may not completely reflect the actual environment. However, in the actual social networking environment (i.e., Facebook App Center), it would be impossible to manipulate the experimental conditions (i.e., controlling the number of friends using the application). Therefore, despite the limitation, the employment of scenarios is necessary. We encourage researchers to verify the impact of information acquisition and exposure control on social application in a more natural setting.

Furthermore, it could be possible that our findings are specific to the student samples and not necessarily generalized to other populations. For instance, our respondents might feel that they had little to "lose" economically or socially in terms of their profile information and displayed more willingness to use social applications. Despite this concern, university students are reported to represent a huge portion of the actual population engaging actively in social application usage. More importantly, university students are found to be vulnerable to privacy loss and become targets for physical and psychological threats.

This study opens up a number of exciting directions worthy of further pursuit. For example, this study examines individuals' initial evaluation and usage of application apps. It is likely that individuals may behave differently if they have actual usage experience. We believe our theoretical perspective can be instrumental to these potential future studies.

Additionally, this study has focused on willingness usage intention. In a real setting, users might engage in other behaviors. For example, users might complain to friends about the usage of the application in physical interactions. Likewise, users might resign from using online social networks entirely. Hence, future research could investigate how users react to information collection by social applications in the offline environment.

References

1. Besmer, A., et al.: Social applications: exploring a more secure framework. In: Proceedings of the 5th Symposium on Usable Privacy and Security. ACM (2009)
2. Markets, R.A.: Global Online Gaming Market 2014. Research and Markets (2014)
3. Smock, A.D., et al.: Facebook as a toolkit: a users and gratification approach to unbundling feature use. Comput. Hum. Behav. **27**(6), 2322–2329 (2011)
4. Boyd, D.M., Ellison, N.B.: Social network sites: definition, history, and scholarship. J. Comput. Mediated Commun. **13**(1), 210–230 (2007)
5. Debatin, B., et al.: Facebook and online privacy: attitudes, behaviors, and unintended consequences. J. Comput. Mediated Commun. **15**(1), 83–108 (2009)
6. Angwin, J., Singer-Vine, J.: Selling you on facebook (2012). http://online.wsj.com/articles/SB10001424052702303302504577327744009046230
7. Culnan, M.J., Bies, R.J.: Consumer privacy: balancing economic and justice considerations. J. Soc. Issues **59**(2), 323–342 (2003)
8. Son, J.-Y., Kim, S.S.: Internet users' information privacy-protective responses: a taxonomy and a nomological model. MIS Q. **32**(3), 503–529 (2008)
9. Culnan, M.J., Armstrong, P.K.: Privacy concerns, procedural fairness, and impersonal trust: an empirical investigation. Organ. Sci. **10**(1), 104–115 (1999)
10. Xu, H., et al.: The role of push-pull technology in privacy calculus: the case of location-based services. J. Manag. Inf. Syst. **26**(3), 135–174 (2010)
11. Cropanzano, R., Ambrose, M.L.: Procedural and distributive justice are more similar than you think: a monistic perspective and a research agenda. Adv. Organ. Justice **119**, 151 (2001)
12. Deutsch, M.: Equity, equality, and need: what determines which value will be used as the basis of distributive justice? J. Soc. Issues **31**(3), 137–149 (1975)
13. Schwinger, T.: The need principle of distributive justice. In: Bierhoff, H.W., Cohen, R.L., Greenberg, J. (eds.) Justice in Social Relations, pp. 211–225. Springer, New York (1986)
14. Thibaut, J., Walker, L.: Procedural Justice: A Psychological Analysis. Erlbaum, Hillsdale (1975)
15. Wang, N., Xu, H., Grosslags, J.: Third-party apps on facebook: privacy and the illusion of control. In: CHIMIT'11 Proceedings of the 5th ACM Symposium on Computer Human Interaction for Management of Information Technology (2011)
16. Smith, H.J., Milberg, S.J., Burke, S.J.: Information privacy: Measuring individuals' concerns about organizational practices. MIS Q. **20**(2), 167–196 (1996)
17. Dinev, T., Hart, P.: An extended privacy calculus model for e-commerce transactions. Inf. Syst. Res. **1**(17), 2006 (2006)
18. Phelps, J., Nowak, G., Ferrell, E.: Privacy concerns and consumers willingness to provide personal information. J. Public Policy Mark. **19**(1), 27–41 (2000)
19. Jiang, Z., Heng, C.S., Choi, B.C.F.: Privacy concerns and privacy-protective behavior in synchronous online social interactions. Inf. Syst. Res. **24**(3), 579–595 (2013)
20. Malhotra, N.K., Kim, S.S., Agarwal, J.: Internet users' information privacy concerns (IUIPC): the construct, the scale, and a causal model. Inf. Syst. Res. **15**(4), 336–355 (2004)
21. Lee, Y.E., Benbasat, I.: The influence of trade-off difficulty caused by preference elicitation methods on user acceptance of recommendation agents across loss and gain conditions. Inf. Syst. Res. **22**(4), 867–884 (2011)
22. Komiak, S.Y.X., Benbasat, I.: The effects of personalization and familiarity on trust and adoption of recommendation agents. MIS Q. **30**(4), 941–960 (2006)
23. Tam, K.Y., Ho, S.Y.: Web personalization as a persuasion strategy: an elaboration likelihood model perspective. Inf. Syst. Res. **16**(3), 271–291 (2005)

24. Ho, S.Y., Bodoff, D., Tam, K.Y.: Timing of adaptive web personalization and its effects on online consumer behavior. Inf. Syst. Res. **22**(3), 660–679 (2011)
25. Hui, K.L., Teo, H.H., Lee, S.Y.T.: The value of privacy assurance: an exploratory field experiment. MIS Q. **31**(1), 19–33 (2007)
26. Petronio, S.: Boundaries of Privacy: Dialectics of Disclosure. State University of New York Press, Albany (2002)
27. Awad, N.F., Krishnan, M.S.: The personalization privacy paradox: an empirical evaluation of information transparency and the willingness to be profiled online for personalization. MIS Q. **30**(1), 13–28 (2006)
28. Folger, R., Konovsky, M.A.: Effects of procedural and distributive justice on reactions to pay raise decisions. Acad. Manag. J. **32**(1), 115–130 (1989)
29. Youn, S.: Teenagers' perceptions of online privacy and coping behaviors: a risk-benefit appraisal approach. J. Broadcast. Electron. Media **49**(1), 86–110 (2005)
30. Grosser, T.J., Lopez-Kidwell, V., Labianca, G.: A social network analysis of positive and negative gossip in organizational life. Group Org. Manag. **35**(2), 177–212 (2010)
31. Mathieson, K.: Predicting user intentions: comparing the technology acceptance model with the theory of planned behavior. Inf. Syst. Res. **2**(3), 173–191 (1991)

To Believe or Not to Believe a Call to Action: An Empirical Investigation of Source Credibility

Craig Claybaugh[✉]

Missouri University of Science and Technology, Rolla, USA
claybaughc@mst.edu

Abstract. How well can individuals detect deception from information sources? This study examines consumer evaluations of a real CRM product brochure and a fraudulent one that imitates it. The forged brochure contains malicious manipulations designed to decrease trust in the product and oversell the abilities of the CRM system. This study seeks to see how manipulations of the material are perceived by the individuals and how that impacts their willingness to believe the source credibility of a message.

Keywords: Source credibility · Deception · Trust · Media assurance

1 Introduction

Individuals acquire information from a variety of sources every day. These sources of information vary considerably with respect to reliability and credibility of their content [31]. For example, the *Wall Street Journal* might be considered a more credible provider of information on business matters than *National Geographic*. Views about credibility also develop based on the sources mentioned by or associated with sources of information [33]. Knowledge about an individual source (e.g., a respected multinational corporation vs. a small regional corporation) and the quality of its presentation have been found to influence whether readers trust on or ignore the propositions provided by that source [38].

This paper explores the following research question: Are individuals able to detect deceptions of printed technical advertisements from a trusted source? More specifically, this study aims to see if deceptive manipulations of a print media's quality and layout can be detected if the source of the information is trusted by the individual. To address this research question an experimental design using eye tracking will be conducted to examine how elements of print material are used to assess credibility. One of the contributions of this study, made feasible by the use of eye tracking, is to open the black box of information assimilation and to study the visual cues used by subjects to make a determination of credibility.

© Springer International Publishing Switzerland 2015
F.F.-H. Nah and C.-H. Tan (Eds.): HCIB 2015, LNCS 9191, pp. 53–63, 2015.
DOI: 10.1007/978-3-319-20895-4_6

2 Conceptual Background

The conceptual background in this paper draws on marketing and IS literature to look at an understanding of how subjects may detect instances of deception that are found in printed media (pdf file displayed on a computer screen). The theoretical approach here looks at the concepts of perceived source credibility and deception. The model proposed here looks at how perceived deception, trust, and risk influence a participant's attitude towards a particular source.

2.1 Source Credibility

Perceived source credibility is defined as judgments made by a perceiver on the believability of the communicator of information [38]. Credibility is important in creating effective information dissemination and acceptance by the subjects. In measuring source credibility, several researchers have utilized the three dimensions of expertise, trustworthiness and attractiveness [27]. Other dimensions, such as believability, likability and attractiveness, have also been used as dimensions of credibility [1, 10]. For the purposes of this paper, credibility is comprised of expertise (the degree to which a perceiver believes a source to know the truth), trustworthiness (the degree to which a perceiver believes a source will provide the truth), and goodwill (the degree to which a perceiver believes the source to act in good faith). Research has found that increasing source credibility positively influences a business, or brand, in several ways. For example, credible information elicits a greater attitude change within the viewer of the material than less credible information sources [7]. Marketing research has shown consumers are more likely to discount communications from spokespersons that they perceive to have low credibility [27].

Research also has demonstrated that source credibility also has a strong relationship with brand and company reputation [19]. Consumers use reputation as a means of inferring quality of a product offering and in surmising information being sent from a company. Credibility is whether a company can be relied on to do what it says it will do which is based on the firm's track record of success. Firms which value their reputation should not engage in deception due to the potential impact that deception will have on their public image [9]. By using a firm's positive reputation in communication a firm is able to deliver a strong message and make an impact on the recipient. At the same time a third party might try to use the positive reputation of a firm to their own advantage through deception. Types of manipulations and their implications on perceptions of credibility are described next.

2.2 Deception

Deception is an act in which individuals incorrectly infer that a product (or other object) possesses certain attributes due to an information source (i.e. advertisement or other communication medium) [30]. Within this domain, researchers have examined four related but distinct paradigms: deception, deceptiveness, misleadingness, and legal deception [37]. In general, academic scholars tend to take different viewpoints from practitioners about what a deceptive claim is and why deception matters. The Federal Trade Commission (FTC), for example, has found deception to occur if there is a misrepresentation, omission, or practice that is likely to mislead the consumer acting reasonably in the circumstances, to the consumer's detriment. Marketing researchers have looked at deceptive claims in advertising ranging from incomplete or partial information, false information, manipulative claims, ambiguous information, and a variety of customer testimonials [18]. Deception in an information source leads to a risk on the part of the individual as they face adverse consequences from believing the source [2].

As communication media has become more impersonal the individuals are left with fewer methods of establishing trust in a particular source. Uncertainty increases when the person cannot observe the real quality of the product or the verify performance and is therefore dependent on information that is provided by the information source [17]. As individuals try to deal with an information source they will use certain heuristics when interpreting actions or motives of the source of information. Past research has looked at ways to increase trust in communication in different contexts such as internet transactions or social interactions [38]. Detecting deception is not automatic and can be a daunting task for the cognitive processes of individuals. Insight into how individuals use inference and context to establish source validity will demonstrate how these beliefs are formed.

Figure 1 presents a model of source credibility that relates deception, perceived risk, and trust. The model draws on the theory of reasoned action [15] and assumes that an individual's beliefs about a source of information affect the individual's attitude towards the source. These attitudes are either favorable or unfavorable evaluations of information being presented. These attitudes towards the information source in turn influence the behavioral intention (willingness to believe a source of information is credible).

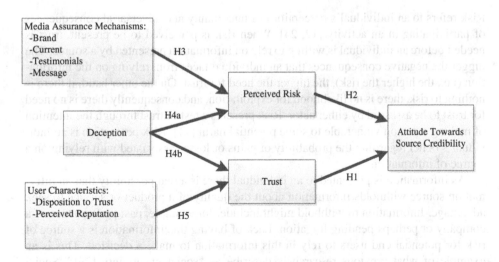

Fig. 1. Model of source credibility and deception

2.3 Trust

Trust and trust building are key components of trying to inform an audience on how to proceed. Kramer [24] provides a definition of trust: "a state of perceived vulnerability or risk that is derived from individual's uncertainty regarding the motives, intentions, and prospective actions of others on whom they depend." Although acknowledging that trust can comprise emotional and social elements, the focus here is on the cognitive processes of trust and view trust as a choice process based on how an individual approaches the choice. Choice can depend on a calculative justification or can be grounded on heuristics familiar to the individual [3].

The trustworthiness of a source is expected to have a significant impression on an end user's attitude toward the message [21]. Past studies have shown that highly trustworthy sources' arguments are more eagerly accepted than that of low trustworthy sources [5] and that the trustworthy sources are presumed to provide truthful message information. Priester and Petty [32] propose that messages from untrustworthy sources come under greater inspection than those from their trustworthy counterparts. When we consider information which is from a known source with an established reputation in the market (SAP in this study) individuals will feel the source is able to be relied upon. This favorable trust formation should influence the individual's attitude towards establishing if the source is credible. Hence, the following hypothesis is proposed:

H1:   Perceptions of trust in the information source will have a significant effect on the individual's attitude towards the source's credibility.

2.4 Perceived Risk

Risk refers to an individual's perceptions of uncertainty and adversarial consequences of participating in an activity [12, 24]. When risk is perceived to be present, trust is needed before an individual is willing to rely on information presented by a source. The bigger the negative consequences that an individual faces from relying on the information (i.e., the higher the risk), the higher the need for trust. On the other hand, if there is nothing to risk, there is no likelihood for exploitation, and consequently there is no need for trust to be assessed by either actor. Risk presents a test of trust through the intention of making a person vulnerable to some potential harm [11]. Risk perception is an individual's belief regarding the probability of gains or losses associated with relying on a source of information.

As information is presented to an individual there is a real possibility that an information source withholds information about the quality of a product or service to seek advantage. Information to withhold might include, for example, past performance of a company or perhaps pending litigation. Lack of having this information is a source of risk for potential end users to rely in this information to make a decision. This is an example of what previous researchers describe as "social uncertainty [39]." Social uncertainty exists when (1) an information provider has an incentive to act in a way that inflicts costs (or harm) on the information consumer; and (2) the information consumer does not have enough evidence to predict if the information provider will in fact act in way to cause harm. Uncertainty increases when the individual cannot observe the quality of the product directly (as is the case for printed information) and is therefore dependent on information that is provided by the information source. To that end the following hypothesis is proposed:

H2:   Perceptions of risk in the information source will have a significant effect on the individual's attitude towards the source's credibility.

2.5   Media Assurance Mechanisms and Deception

A number of methods are available to manipulate media to improve assurance of quality and build trust. These mechanisms are designed to reduce the appeal of the source being valid. Assurance mechanisms act as signals of behavior which should reduce the probability of there being a risk of relying on the information [17, 37]. Here we examine four forms of media assurance mechanism: brand, current (copyright), testimonials, and message.

Brand has had an impact on credibility of a message as the believability of the information contained in a message accompanied by a brand has been shown to decrease risk perception [14]. Brands can function as indications of a promise since brand equity will erode if and/or when they do not deliver what is expected [13]. Brands, and the equity embedded within, are long term signals from the firm used to create a higher perception of expected performance and quality [13]. When a brand holds a higher perception by an individual this can lower the cost of information assessment and lower risks of relying on a source with the brand. Firms build their brand reputation to increase their performance in the marketplace. This implies a recognized brand would have a strong incentive to provide accurate and current information. Conversely, an unrecognized brand might imply less of a promise to adhere to the same standards.

More traditional sources of information (library books, newspapers, magazines for example) provided organizational structures and publication dates. New trends of media and the information contained within tend to provide fewer assurances of the currency of their information [34]. More current information sources have been shown to increase the perception of information trust [29]. Information media being distributed by a corporation has a few qualifiers to signal currency namely in the form of a copyright date. These copyright dates provide a reference point to which the information was compiled and can be used in comparison to date the information is viewed. Including an older copyright date or none appearing at all will increase the risk of the individual relying on information which is not current.

Information media provide customers testimonials to help convey to the individuals the firm's ability to execute and achieve a stated goal. These customer testimonials also serve to demonstrate the firm's willingness and ability to transact in a trustworthy manner [28]. These testimonials act as an independent verification of the claims being made by the firm and being included in the media. These customers are providing their name to the media such that they provide validation to the success they have enjoyed [17]. Providing the customer testimonial from a recognized third party (large multinational firm) can further increase the trust one places in the information provided. At the same time if the customer is not recognized or has a negative image in the mind of the information evaluator the sense of trust in the information decreases. This will also impact the risk perceived from relying on the source.

Messages contain a variety of claims that convey material information about product or service attributes [4]. A substantial stream of research has derived a variety of typologies for messages to be considered to be deceptive [37]. The claims contained within a message can be intentionally crafted in a way to mislead individuals to read beyond the literal statements and to infer erroneous information about a product or service being offered by the firm. When a message contains statements that appear too good to be true they indicate a willingness of the information source to stretch the truth. This implies that relying of the information is a risk for the individual.

In this study the expectation is that perceived deception will increases the strength of the relationship between media assurance mechanism and reduced risk. This is consistent with past studies on confirmation bias that suggests that people tend to allow their past beliefs influence their attitude towards information [16]. The higher the level of perceived deception a person has the more attention they will pay to assurance mechanisms. The expectation is that perceived deception will trigger the individual to seek cues about the safeguards of relying on the information source. The higher the perception of the media assurance mechanisms the less likely they are to perceive there to be a risk relying on the information source. Formally the following is proposed:

H3: Perceptions of risk in the information source is determined by the presence of media assurance mechanisms.

H4: Perceptions of deception in the information source will have a significant effect on risk perception of the information source.

H5: Perceptions of deception in the information source will have a significant effect on trust of the information source.

2.6 Participant Characteristics

A number of individual differences have been found to influence the ability of a person to detect deception [25]. Two of these user characteristics are examined in this study: disposition to trust and perceived reputation.

Disposition to Trust. Disposition to trust, also called trust propensity, is an indication of an individual's overall willingness to depend on others within a wide variety of social contexts [22]. This general disposition of the individual to have a trusting attitude impacts his or her specific formation of trust towards an object (information source in this context). Many studies have looked at disposition to trust and how different settings influence its significance in trust formation [8, 20]. Following these other studies example this study sees the disposition to trust having a direct effect on the formation of trust in the information source.

Perceived Reputation. Reputation is defined as "the extent to which buyers believe a seller is professionally competent or honest and benevolent [35]". Past studies have documented that a firm's reputation is a valuable intangible asset that necessitates a long-term investment of resources, efforts, and attention to ensure success [6]. Reputation, similar to brand, is an intangible, strategic asset that can be easily tarnished or damaged If̶ ̶m̶m̶ ̶c̶o̶m̶e̶r̶c̶i̶l̶l̶y̶ ̶p̶r̶o̶m̶o̶t̶e̶d̶.̶ ̶A̶ ̶f̶i̶r̶m̶ ̶w̶i̶t̶h̶ ̶a̶ ̶h̶i̶g̶h̶ ̶p̶e̶r̶c̶e̶p̶t̶i̶o̶n̶ ̶o̶f̶ ̶r̶e̶p̶u̶t̶a̶t̶i̶o̶n̶ ̶i̶s̶ ̶g̶e̶n̶e̶r̶a̶l̶l̶y̶ ̶r̶e̶l̶u̶c̶-̶ tant to jeopardize their reputation through opportunistic behavior. A firm has a high perception of reputation from the individual is expected to have a higher perception of trust as well.

H5. The user's characteristics (disposition to trust, perceived reputation) will have a significant effect on trust of the information source.

3   Method

This section introduces the proposed subject sample, the experimental design, the measures, and the methods used to test them.

3.1   Subjects and Experimental Task

Undergraduate student subjects will be recruited to participate in the experiment. All subjects are asked to read a set of print advertising for a CRM software system from SAP. The subjects are instructed the task is focused on reading comprehension. The subjects performed the task using University computers and also had the eye tracker attached to their person. Once the subjects had read the print material they instructed to minimize the material and perform three additional tasks: (1) fill out the first part of a questionnaire; (2) go back to the printed material and examine five specific features of the material (copyright, corporate logo, customer testimonial, pictures in the advertisement, and facts presented); (3) fill out the rest of the questionnaire.

3.2   Design and Manipulations

Participants will be assigned one of two conditions. Half the subjects assessed a real print advertisement and the other half accessed a copy of the material forged by the researcher. The forged material contains several malicious manipulations designed to increase distrust and increase the risk of believing the source as being credible.

The forged material was built from a copy of an original print material from a real vendor selling CRM software, SAP CRM. The five modifications were made to the real material for the purpose of including a variety of mechanisms to see if the source credibility of a print advertisement from an established company can be found to be uncredible. The specific modifications were developed from previous research [17, 37].

(1) Copyright – The copyright was created blurry and of small font.
(2) Corporate logo – The corporate logo was blurry and was also slightly tilted.
(3) Customer testimonial – Existing endorsements from customers were inflated by adding hyperboles and were from firms not internationally known.

(4) Pictures in the advertisement – Created blurry and also slightly tilted.
(5) Facts presented – Facts from the original were created with speculative that implies superiority without evidence to verify the claim.

3.3 Measures

The potential measures and their sources are shown in the appendix.

4 Discussion

This study has the potential to validate how individuals approach the task of validating the source of information as being valid. Depending on whether individuals have the ability and motivation to detect the deception contained in the study they may or may not recognize the manipulation. Some individuals are more susceptible to deceptive claims. Even if they detect the deception they still might not question the information if the source is from a firm they trust and has a good reputation in the market.

Appendix: Items to Use in Study

Attitude Towards Source Credibility - The following items are answered on a 1–7 scale of strongly disagree to strongly agree [23].

I have a favorable opinion of the information source.
I believe the information source is credible.
I believe the information source is competent.

Trust - The following items are answered on a 1–7 scale of strongly disagree to strongly agree [17].

This information source is trustworthy.
This information source keeps customers' best interests in mind.
The information source can be relied upon.

Perceived Risk – The following items are answered on a 1–7 scale of strongly disagree to strongly agree [36].

I feel relying on this source of information is risky.
How would you characterize the decision of whether to believe the information from this information source? (Anchors: Very significant risk to Very significant opportunity)

Deception - Please evaluate the quality of information provided by the source. To what extent do you believe that the information provided by the store is (1–7) [17].

Accurate
Misleading
Truthful

Deceptive
Factual
Distorted

Media Assurance Mechanisms [17]: Testimonial (1–7)

How convincing are the customer testimonials?
Convincing - Unconvincing
How believable are the customer testimonials?
Believable - Not believable
How impartial are the customer testimonials?
Impartial - Partial

Media Assurance Mechanisms: Message (1–7) –

How convincing are the messages in the information source?
Convincing Unconvincing
How believable are the messages in the information source?
Believable Not believable
How impartial are the messages in the information source?
Impartial Partial

Media Assurance Mechanisms: Brand (1–7) –

This information source has a good brand.
This information source has a positive perception in the market.
This information source has a good name.

Media Assurance Mechanisms: Current (1–7) –

The information provided in the source is current and up to date.

User Characteristics: Disposition to Trust [22] (1–7) –

It is easy for me to trust a person/thing.
I tend to trust a person/thing, even if I have little knowledge of it.
Trusting someone or something is not difficult.

User Characteristics: Perceived reputation [35] (1–7) – I believe this information source:

Is well known
Has a good reputation in the market
Has a reputation for being fair
Has a reputation for being consumer-oriented

References

1. Arora, R., Stoner, C., Arora, A.: Using framing and credibility to incorporate exercise and fitness in individuals' lifestyle. J. Consum. Mark. **23**(4), 199–207 (2006)
2. Bond, G.D.: Deception detection expertise. Law Hum. Behav. **32**(4), 339 (2008)

3. Brockner, J.: Making sense of procedural fairness: how high procedural fairness can reduce or heighten the influence of outcome favorability. Acad. Manag. Rev. **27**(1), 58–76 (2002)
4. Burgoon, J.K., Buller, D.B., Guerrero, L.K., Afifi, W.A., Feldman, C.M.: Interpersonal deception: XII. Information management dimensions underlying deceptive and truthful messages. Commun. Monogr. **63**(1), 50–69 (1996)
5. Cheung, C.M., Thadani, D.R.: The impact of electronic word-of-mouth communication: a literature analysis and integrative model. Decis. Support Syst. **54**(1), 461–470 (2012)
6. Chopra, S., Sodhi, M.S.: Managing risk to avoid supply-chain breakdown. MIT Sloan Manag. Rev. (Fall 2004) (2012)
7. Clark, J.K., Wegener, D.T., Habashi, M.M., Evans, A.T.: Source expertise and persuasion the effects of perceived opposition or support on message scrutiny. Pers. Soc. Psychol. Bull. **38**(1), 90–100 (2012)
8. Claybaugh, C.C., Haseman, W.D.: Understanding professional connections in linkedin–a question of trust. J. Comput. Inf. Syst. 54(1) (2013)
9. Claybaugh, C.C., Srite, M.: Factors contributing to the information technology vendor-client relationship. J. Inf. Technol. Theory Appl. (JITTA) **10**(2), 3 (2009)
10. Clow, K.E., James, K.E., Kranenburg, K.E., Berry, C.T.: The relationship of the visual element of an advertisement to service quality expectation and source credibility. J. Serv. Mark. **20**(6), 404–411 (2006)
11. Colquitt, J.A., Scott, B.A., LePine, J.A.: Trust, trustworthiness, and trust propensity: a meta-analytic test of their unique relationships with risk taking and job performance. J. Appl. Psychol. **92**(4), 909 (2007)
12. Dowling, G.R., Staelin, R.: A model of perceived risk and intended risk-handling activity. J. Consum. Res. **21**(1), 119–134 (1994)
13. Erdem, T., Swait, J.: Brand equity as a signaling phenomenon. J. Consum. Psychol. **7**(2), 131–157 (1998)
14. Erdem, T., Swait, J., Valenzuela, A.: Brands as signals: a cross-country validation study. J. Mark. **70**(1), 34–49 (2006)
15. Fishbein, M., Ajzen, I.: Belief, Attitude, Intention and Behavior: An Introduction to Theory and Research. Addison-Wesley, Reading (1975)
16. Fiske, S.T., Taylor, S.E.: Social Cognition: From Brains to Culture. Sage, Beverly Hills (2013)
17. Grazioli, S., Jarvenpaa, S.L.: Perils of Internet fraud: An empirical investigation of deception and trust with experienced Internet consumers. IEEE Trans. Syst. Man Cyber. Part A Syst. Hum. **30**(4), 395–410 (2000)
18. Hastak, M., Mazis, M.B.: Deception by implication: a typology of truthful but misleading advertising and labeling claims. J. Public Policy Mark. **30**(2), 157–167 (2011)
19. Herbig, P., Milewicz, J.: The relationship of reputation and credibility to brand success. J. Consum. Mark. **12**(4), 5–10 (1995)
20. Jarvenpaa, S.L., Tractinsky, N., Saarinen, L.: Consumer trust in an internet store: a cross-cultural validation. J. Comput. Med. Commun. **5**(2), 0–0 (1999)
21. Johnston, A., Warkentin, M.: The influence of perceived source credibility on end user attitudes and intentions to comply with recommended IT actions. In: Dwivedi, A., Clarke, S. (eds.) End-User Computing, Development, and Software Engineering: New Challenges: New Challenges, p. 312. Information Science Reference, Hershey (2012)
22. Kim, M., Ahn, J.: Comparison of trust sources of an online market-maker in the E-marketplace: buyer's and seller's perspectives. J. Comput. Inf. Syst. **47**(1), 84–94 (2006)
23. Ko, D.-G., Kirsch, L.J., King, W.R.: Antecedents of knowledge transfer from consultants to clients in enterprise system implementations. MIS Q. **29**(1), 59–85 (2005)

24. Kramer, R.M.: Trust and distrust in organizations: emerging perspectives, enduring questions. Annu. Rev. Psychol. **50**(1), 569–598 (1999)
25. Kuhn, G., Tatler, B.W., Findlay, J.M., Cole, G.G.: Misdirection in magic: implications for the relationship between eye gaze and attention. Vis. Cogn. **16**(2–3), 391–405 (2008)
26. Lafferty, B.A., Goldsmith, R.E.: How influential are corporate credibility and endorser attractiveness when innovators react to advertisements for a new high-technology product? Corp. Reputation Manag. **7**(1), 24–36 (2004)
27. Lafferty, B.A., Goldsmith, R.E., Newell, S.J.: The dual credibility model: the influence of corporate and endorser credibility on attitudes and purchase intentions. J. Market. Theor. Pract. **10**(3), 1–12 (2002)
28. Li, X., Hess, T.J., Valacich, J.S.: Why do we trust new technology? a study of initial trust formation with organizational information systems. J. Strateg. Inf. Syst. **17**(1), 39–71 (2008)
29. Metzger, M.J., Flanagin, A.J., Zwarun, L.: College student web use, perceptions of information credibility, and verification behavior. Comput. Educ. **41**(3), 271–290 (2003)
30. Oh, H., Jasper, C.R.: Processing of apparel advertisements: The extension of the elaboration likelihood model. Clothing Text. Res. J. **24**(1), 15–32 (2006)
31. Pornpitakpan, C.: The persuasiveness of source credibility: a critical review of five decades' evidence. J. Appl. Soc. Psychol. **34**(2), 243–281 (2004)
32. Priester, J.R., Petty, R.E.: Source attributions and persuasion: perceived honesty as a determinant of message scrutiny. Pers. Soc. Psychol. Bull. **21**(6), 637–654 (1995)
33. Sparks, J.R., Rapp, D.N.: Readers' reliance on source credibility in the service of comprehension. J. Exp. Psychol. Learn. Mem. Cogn. **37**(1), 230 (2011)
34. Teacy, W.L., Patel, J., Jennings, N.R., Luck, M.: Travos: Trust and reputation in the context of inaccurate information sources. Auton. Agent. Multi-agent Syst. **12**(2), 183–198 (2006)
35. Teo, T.S.H., Liu, J.: Consumer trust in e-commerce in the United States, Singapore and China. Omega **35**(1), 22–38 (2007)
36. Van Slyke, C., Shim, J.T., Johnson, R., Jiang, J.: Concern for information privacy and online consumer purchasing. J. Assoc. Inf. Syst. **7**(6), 415–444 (2006)
37. Xie, G.X., Boush, D.M.: How susceptible are consumers to deceptive advertising claims? a retrospective look at the experimental research literature. Mark. Rev. **11**(3), 293–314 (2011)
38. Westerman, D., Spence, P.R., Van Der Heide, B.: Social media as information source: recency of updates and credibility of Information. J. Comput. Med. Commun. **19**(2), 171–183 (2014)
39. Zinn, J. (ed.): Social Theories of Risk and Uncertainty: an Introduction, pp. 18–49. Blackwell Publishing, Oxford (2008)

Understanding the 'Quality Motion' of Wikipedia Articles Through Semantic Convergence Analysis

Huijing Deng[✉], Bernadetta Tarigan, Mihai Grigore, and Juliana Sutanto

Department of Management, Technology, and Economics, ETH Zurich, Zürich, Switzerland
{huijingdeng,btarigan,mgrigore,jsutanto}@ethz.ch

Abstract. To better inform the users of the articles quality, Wikipedia assigns quality labels to the articles. While most of the existing studies of the Wikipedia phenomenon took the quality ratings provided by Wikipedia as the outcome variable of their research, a few yet growing number of studies ask expert raters to rate the quality of selected Wikipedia articles because of their doubts in Wikipedia's ratings. This study aims to check if Wikipedia's ratings *really* reflect its stated criteria. According to Wikipedia criteria, having abundant and stable content is the key to article's quality promotion; we therefore examine the content change in terms of quantity change and content stability by showing the semantic convergence. We found out that the quantity of content change is significant in the promoted articles, which complies with Wikipedia's stated criteria.

Keywords: Wikipedia · Article quality · Quality motion · Content change · Semantic convergence

1 Introduction

Since its advent in 2001, Wikipedia has become the most sought after online encyclopedia; its free distribution and wide coverage radically changed the way people approach knowledge. By 2014, there are more than 4 millions English articles in Wikipedia ranging from natural science to social science. Moreover, Wikipedia provides a gold mine for researchers of various disciplines. For researchers in the social science field, Wikipedia serves as a prominent exemplar of using wiki technology for crowdsourcing; it offers a great source of data for researches on online collaboration, open innovation, etc.

Typically researchers utilizing Wikipedia data would analyze the predictors of the quality of Wikipedia articles. Ironically, the quality of Wikipedia has been a debatable issue for long time; drawing much attention not only from the regular users who simply

This research received financial support from SNSF Grant No.: 100018_146444.

F.F.-H. Nah and C.-H. Tan (Eds.): HCIB 2015, LNCS 9191, pp. 64–75, 2015.
DOI: 10.1007/978-3-319-20895-4_7

use its content as knowledge sources but also from researchers who are interested in the study of Wikipedia. There are two main streams of researches related to the quality of the Wikipedia articles: one stream is modeling of the articles quality, which propose methods to help identify or distinguish article quality levels [1, 2]; another stream is to use quality as a dependent variable for the studies of collaboration, conflicts, or virtual teams in general [3, 4]. The studies from both streams basically rely on some sample articles which are already rated to different quality levels. The typical ways to derive the quality ratings are either directly making use of Wikipedia internal ratings or hiring outer expert raters to evaluate the quality of randomly selected articles. Based on the quality rating criteria provided by Wikipedia, about 1 million out of 4 million articles were ever assigned one or more quality labels, moreover, many of the articles have experienced quality promotion or demotion or both over their development history. Kittur and Kraut [5] found significant correlation between Wikipedia's article quality ratings and the article quality ratings assigned by external raters. The study indicates the high consistency in the evaluating criteria from within and outside of Wikipedia. The main limitation of this study is that it is based on only a small number of articles. So the question remains: Does the rating assigned by Wikipedia to around 1 million articles really reflect the criteria in Wikipedia's evaluation system?

We first refine this question before attempting to answer it. We notice that constant change made to articles distinguishes Wikipedia from traditional encyclopedia; therefore the quality rating in Wikipedia is a dynamic process. Kane et al. [6] suggests two stages of online collaboration, namely, the creation stage when the information is developed and shaped, and the retention stage when the created information gets preserved and refined through ongoing collaboration. Similarly, the development of Wikipedia articles can also be divided into these two stages; accordingly, the improvement for Wikipedia articles would have different focuses in these two stages. In the creation stage, content completeness is the priority while elaboration and minor details like having reliable references would be looked after later. In Wikipedia's criteria, the complete, accurate content and detailed requirements in citations and writing styles are all taken into consideration. In our study of examining the mapping between quality and criteria, we focus on the content change since the complete content formed the mainframe of the articles on which any other minor changes are based. Content change is therefore the critical factor for a significant quality improvement.

There are seven quality scales in Wikipedia, for each scale there is a corresponding rating criterion. Observing the content-related rule in the criterion of each scale, we noticed that splitting the seven quality scales into two groups would facilitate a better alignment of the content rule and the article quality, since these two groups have significant distinguishable content requirements, which only slightly differ within the groups. This quality scales grouping is also adopted in some recent study which propose a model to evaluate the article quality [7]. We define quality promotion as the change of quality scale from the lower-level group to the higher-level group, and quality demotion as the change of quality scale from the higher-level group to the lower-level group. Having collected almost all of the English Wikipedia articles that have experienced quality promotion and demotion in their first two quality ratings, noted as promoted and demoted articles, we subsequently conduct a longitudinal analysis of the content change by examining the semantic convergence during the time period of quality change. Semantic convergence is a measurement of content change by computing the semantic similarity of each version with the last version of the article.

2   Quality Promotion and Demotion

According to Wikipedia quality rating system, articles' quality level ranges from Stub, Start, C-class, B-class, Good Articles (GA), A-class, to Featured Articles (FA) in ascending order. Wikipedia provides guidelines for assessing the articles in a multi-dimensional measure. For instance, a Featured Article needs to be: (1) well written; (2) comprehensive; (3) well-researched by including appropriate references; (4) neutral; (5) stable (no ongoing edit wars); (6) compliance with Wikipedia style guidelines, like consistent citation and appropriate structure; (7) having appropriate media mostly in the form of images with acceptable copyright status; and (8) having appropriate length and focusing on the main topic.

Wikipedia has developed various mechanisms for quality rating centering around two principles: relying on consensus of most reviewers and constraining the influence of major contributors. To promote an article to GA or FA, it first needs to be nominated by at least one registered editor, and all other editors excluding the significant contributors can review the article and give their comments based on the corresponding criteria, after then vote for the nomination. For a nomination to be promoted to GA or FA, a consensus among most reviewers must be reached. But for GA assessment, nominator is not allowed to participate in the review. The quality assessments for other levels (e.g. B-class, C-class) are normally performed by members of WikiProject. A WikiProject is composed of a collection of articles of the same domain or on a specific topic, and a group of editors who collaborate in these articles. Similarly, a consensus among WikiProject members is required for the rating.

In general, an article changing from any level to a more superior level is considered to have been promoted or demoted in reverse. Nevertheless, instead of exhausting all the possible changes, we simplify the problem by firstly grouping quality levels and then adjusting the definition of promotion and demotion accordingly. We cluster GA, A and FA as advanced group while B, C, Start and Stub as underdeveloped group. The reason beyond this grouping is primarily based on the reader's experience and the Wikipedia editing suggestions. According to Wikipedia, readers tend to perceive FA articles as professional, outstanding, and thorough; A-class articles as very useful and fairly complete; and GA articles as useful, without obvious problems and approaching the quality of professional encyclopedia articles. For FA articles, no further content is needed unless new information becomes available. Some style problems may need solving in GA and A-class articles. GA articles may need some editing by subject and style expert.

Moving down to B-class articles, the content is probably not be enough to satisfy a serious researcher, which means a few aspects of content and style need to be addressed, the inclusion of supporting materials as well as a better style should also be considered. It is worse in C-class articles as there is no complete picture for a detailed study, and considerable editing is needed. In Start-class articles, users can find some meaningful content, but most readers will need more; these articles are suggested to provide reliable sources and substantial improvement in content and structure.

From the above descriptions of each quality class provided by Wikipedia, there seemingly exists a line to distinguish GA, A, and FA articles from B, C, Start and Stub articles. That is, the considerable content changes. In GA, A and FA articles, an expert-level elaboration and minor updates are needed, while the articles of the other three lower levels require more content. This distinction matches the two dimensions of our study: content change and quality motion. Based on the grouping, we characterize the promotion as the change from any level in the underdeveloped group (B or C or Start or Stub) to one in the advanced group (GA, A, FA), and the demotion as the change from advanced group to the underdeveloped group.

As aforementioned, around 1 million Wikipedia articles have ever received quality rating; many of them have had more than two quality assessments. In our research, we only focus on the articles' first quality motion. For example, when one article has assessment history like "B → GA → FA", we conduct the study on the content change during the time period from B to GA. We align the promoted and the demoted articles by their first quality motion, regardless of their age and birth date. In the following section, we provide the details of collecting and preparing the data. We then describe the method of semantic convergence and present the semantic convergence for the different groups of quality motion.

3 Data Collection

We extract the data from the recent English Wikipedia as of January 2014. It includes over 4 million articles, out of which 3,799 articles are labeled as FA, 18,616 articles are categorized as GA, and 674 articles as A-class. There are also 64,021 B-class articles and 118,906 C-class articles. We did not consider the articles currently rated as Start or Stub class, since we only focus on articles that have already undergone one creation stage.

Each Wikipedia article has its own talk page where the discussions on the article editing take place among the editors. Wikipedia not only stores the most recent version of the articles and their talk pages but also records every effective change made to them in the form of revision through its lifecycle. A revision of Wikipedia article is a version of the article and the changes made to the current revision is based on its last revision. When a revision is submitted, in addition to the updated article content, Wikipedia would also record the information of the editor who creates the revision and the submission time. The same recording procedure applies for talk page. Additionally, each version of the talk page contains new comments and new meta information about the article. The meta information includes which WikiProject the article belongs to, suggestions on improving the article and the current quality level of the article. We retrieve the quality information of the articles from their talk pages.

To get articles that have been promoted or demoted, we first retrieve the quality rating history for all the 205,987 articles, covering all articles which are presently labeled as C-class, B-class, Good, A-class and FA. We derive the quality ratings by checking the meta information through all the revisions of each article's talk page.

We finally get the quality rating history for around 201,500 articles out of 205,987 articles. About 5,000 articles were dropped because of missing information in the talk page. The quality ratings' are recorded in the form: $q_1(t_1)...q_n(t_n)$; where q_i is the ith quality rating at timestamp t_i. An article is considered at q_i level from t_i until a different quality level is assigned, i.e., q_i is different from its adjacent quality ratings.

Next, we collect all articles that have at least two quality assessments over their histories. By checking their first two quality levels, regardless of their present quality level, we select the articles which meet the condition that one of the two quality classes is from advanced group (GA, A, FA) and another one is from underdeveloped group (B, C, Start, Stub). We then cluster them as promoted articles (PA) and demoted articles (DA) according to the quality change order. Finally, we get 7,653 promoted articles and 525 demoted articles; both of the two clusters contain articles that are presently assessed as C-class, B-class, GA, A-class or FA. This is our base dataset on which we check the relation between the pattern of the first quality motion and the present quality of these articles.

Interestingly, from all the promoted articles and demoted articles, we found out that the first quality motion pattern indeed has an impact on its present quality status: (1) more than 95 % of the promoted articles (7,399 out of 7,653) stay at the advanced group and less than 5 % suffered demotion after having been promoted; (2) only about 40 % of the demoted articles (213 out of 525) get promoted to advanced group after having experienced a demotion, while the rest (60 %) stay at underdeveloped group. The finding in (1) shows that if an article gets promoted to advanced group from underdeveloped group in their first quality motion, it is more likely that it will stay as at least a Good article. Hence, this initial finding further implies the importance of the change made in the time period between the first two quality assessments.

For all the promoted and demoted articles, we do the following: given the timestamps t_1 and t_2 corresponding to the first quality rating q_1 and the second quality rating q_2, to capture the content changes in the article between t_1 and t_2, we extract every revision of the article which was issued during this time period for the computation of semantic convergence.

4 Semantic Convergence to Measure Content Change

Semantic convergence measure applied in Wikipedia research was first designed to assess stability of Wikipedia articles, in order to automatically judge their maturity [8]. In our research, we adopted the similar method to measure the content change during the time from the first quality assessment to the second assessment. The detail of the method and the validity of using this method for measuring content change are stated as follows.

4.1 Vector Space Model

"Semantic" is a commonly used term in natural language processing domain. It is normally referred in a context when comparing the similarity of two documents in terms of their topic and content. When two documents are matched in their contents, they are considered to be semantically similar to each other. If a vector is used to represent an article, then the similarity degree is typically computed by the cosine measure of the two vectors having values from -1 to 1. The value of 1 indicates that the two documents are the same or very highly matched, while the value of -1 tells the opposite relation. Among all the type of vectors representing document, Term Frequency (TF) vector is used in our study, which will be explained in the following.

We take any revision of an article as one single document. Suppose an article has N revisions issued during the first quality motion time. This article is composed into a set of N documents, denoted by:

$$D = \{d_k | k \in 1\ldots N\}, \tag{1}$$

with d_k is the kth document or k^{th} revision. We then establish a vocabulary from all the documents in D, i.e., a list of all the distinct words appeared in D. Let $w_1, w_2, \ldots, w_m$ be the words in the vocabulary. The (sparse) representation of the TF value of the words in d_k is denoted by the vector

$$\overrightarrow{d_k} = \{TF(w_{1,k}), \ldots, TF(w_{m,k})\}, \tag{2}$$

with $TF(w_{i,k})$ is the Term Frequency value of word w_i ($i \in 1\ldots m$) in document d_k, i.e., the number of occurrence of word w_i in document d_k. For some words listed in the vocabulary but not appeared in this document, the TF value of those words in the document is zero. Suppose there is a different document d_l with its vector representation as $\overrightarrow{d_l} = \{TF(w_{1,l}), \ldots, TF(w_{m,l})\}$, then the semantic similarity between d_l and d_k is computed by the cosine value of the two vectors:

$$\cos\left(\overrightarrow{d_k}, \overrightarrow{d_l}\right) = \frac{\overrightarrow{d_k} \cdot \overrightarrow{d_l}}{|d_k||d_l|}, \tag{3}$$

where the nominator is the dot product of the two vectors:

$$\overrightarrow{d_k} \cdot \overrightarrow{d_l} = \sqrt{TF(w_{1,k}) \times TF(w_{1,l}) + \ldots + TF(w_{m,k}) \times TF(w_{m,l})} \tag{4}$$

and in the denominator "$|d_k|$" denotes $\sqrt{TF(w_{1,k})^2 + \ldots + TF(w_{m,k})^2}$.

Following the above way, a matrix is built for every Wikipedia article with the rows representing the different revisions in order of the date they were issued and the columns representing words in the vocabulary, such as:

$$Article\,Matrix = \begin{pmatrix} TF(w_{1,1}) & \cdots & TF(w_{m,1}) \\ \vdots & \ddots & \vdots \\ TF(w_{1,N}) & \cdots & TF(w_{m,N}) \end{pmatrix} = \begin{pmatrix} \overrightarrow{d_1} \\ \vdots \\ \overrightarrow{d_N} \end{pmatrix}. \tag{5}$$

The reason that we think the above vector model is appropriate for measuring the content change lies in the type of actions leading to the change. Similar to any other text revise, the primary editing actions in Wikipedia article include [4]: (1) insertion or deletion of a sentence; (2) modification or rewording of an existing sentence; (3) linking a existing word to another Wikipedia article to external Internet articles; (4) change the URL of the name of an existing link; (5) deletion of an existing link; (6) adding or deleting of a reference; (7) modification of an existing reference; (8) reverting an article to a former version. Basically all these actions, to more or less extent, caused the change in word frequency. For example, inserting a new sentence means the vector representing the new revision will have bigger values in some of its entries. The more the value changes, the more it varies from the previous revision. In prior work [9], the distance of two revisions was represented by the count of inserted and deleted words. This count is computed by a complex algorithm, which would become quite time-consuming when the article is long and has a large number of revisions. In our study, we firstly index the words of each revision using Lucene, and then build the vectors using the indexing. This way, the matrix computation is much faster than the word-counting methods and it can be even improved by using some optimal algorithm for sparse vectors. Thus, we consider vector space model more robust and efficient as compared to other models measuring the document distance.

4.2   Revision Milestone

After we get the article matrix that is composed of the vectors representing all the requested revisions of the article, we start to compute the semantic similarity between any two revisions. However, before computing the semantic similarity, there are still some problems that need to be addressed. First, vandalism is commonly seen in Wikipedia. Since this action was also recorded as a revision, this will add noise to the analysis of effective content change. Second, to explore the characteristics in content change of a group of articles, such as promoted group and demoted group, we need to align the articles in some way, because these articles vary in the number of revisions and timestamps for each revision.

Inspired by the work of Thomas and Sheth [8], we use revision milestone to address the above stated problems. Revision milestone is an abstract revision that is representative for the content change made through a cluster of real revisions. Since revision milestone is considered as a "revision", it then can be represented as a vector. Given one article matrix as in Eq. (5) where each row is the vector representing one revision and chronologically ordered by the timestamp of the revision. We now cluster the revision vectors from top to bottom of the matrix using a one-week timeframe. That is, the revisions belonging to one cluster are issued within one week starting from the timestamp of the first revision in this cluster. For example, we derive the first cluster matrix from the article matrix as:

$$Cluster_1 = \begin{pmatrix} \mathrm{TF}(w_{1,1}) & \cdots & \mathrm{TF}(w_{m,1}) \\ \vdots & \ddots & \vdots \\ \mathrm{TF}(w_{1,i}) & \cdots & \mathrm{TF}(w_{m,i}) \end{pmatrix}, \tag{6}$$

where $1 \leq i \leq N$; $t_{rev_1} \leq t_{rev_i} \leq (t_{rev_1} + 1week)$. The revision milestone vector of the first cluster, denoted by $\overrightarrow{RM_1}$, is defined as:

$$\overrightarrow{RM_1} \quad median(Cluster_1), \tag{7}$$

where the "median" is to get the median value of entries in each column of the cluster matrix.

Using revision milestone vector, we can align the articles regardless of their different developing time. Moreover, taking the median value as entry of the revision milestone helps to eliminate the impact of revert wars and random vandalism. Hence, we represent for each article by its revision milestone vectors instead of revision vectors; the rows of the new article matrix are the vectors of the revision milestones in the order of the weeks and the columns are the words from the vocabulary.

4.3   Semantic Convergence

The next step is to measure the content change using the new article matrix composed of the revision milestone vectors. Given an article having L revision milestones, we display its semantic convergence by computing the cosine similarity, as showed in Eq. (3), between each $\overrightarrow{RM_l}(l \in 1...L)$ and the last vector $\overrightarrow{RM_L}$. In this way, we can track the major content change towards the last version that dynamically leads to a quality motion.

The same semantic convergence computation is applied to each article, after then we align the articles by grouping the cosine similarity value with the same index (correspond to the index of their revision milestones from the 1st week to the last week).

5   Comparison of Semantic Convergence

By displaying the semantic convergence over the revision milestone index, we examine the pattern of the content change of the promoted and demoted articles during the period between the times of their first and second quality assessments. The promoted articles have had their first quality level from the *underdeveloped group* (B, C, Start, Stub) upgraded to one level in the *advanced group* (GA, A, FA), while the demoted articles have the quality motion in the opposite direction.

In addition, when we look back to our quality levels grouping and the definition of quality motion, we recall that (according to Wikipedia's statements): (a) considerable content change distinguishes the articles belonging to the *underdeveloped group* and the *advanced group*; (b) meanwhile, the quality motion within advanced group should be caused by other minor updates instead of significant content change. In order to confirm these two statements computationally, we also display the process of the semantic convergence of the articles having their first quality motion within advanced group. We cluster the articles by their motion pattern: (1) promotion_GA → A; (2) promotion_GA → FA; (3) promotion_A → FA; (4) demotion_A → GA;

(5) demotion_FA → GA; (6) demotion_FA → A, and show their semantic convergence process separately.

5.1 Semantic Convergence of Quality Motion Across Groups

As aforementioned, we have 7,653 promoted articles and 525 demoted articles in our dataset. In order to balance the sample quantity in the two groups, we randomly select 600 promoted articles and take all 525 demoted articles. We filter out the articles having less than 3 revision milestones, since we assume that content change would be more stable and effective after at least three weeks. Further, to better align the articles, we split the selected articles into 3 subgroups according to the number of their revision milestones, the range of the number in first subgroup is from 3 to 20, in second subgroup is from 21 to 50, and in the third subgroup is from 51 to 100. Finally we have in total 358 promoted articles and 187 demoted articles. Notice that about 60 % of the demoted articles have less than 3 revision milestones. This phenomenon already indicates that remarkable content change should not be the main reason for quality demotion. We further check the semantic convergence of the sampled articles.

In Fig. 1, the blue curve shows the mean of semantic similarity values of each revision milestone to its final revision milestone. We see that, in each subgroup, the similarity distance from the first revision milestone to the final revision milestone for promoted articles are larger than that for demoted articles. This can be interpreted as that much editing efforts made to the content improvement for quality promotion, even though it might experience some fluctuations during the process. In contrast, the semantic convergence for demoted articles is faster, without noticeable distance in semantic. In general, the semantic convergence patterns computationally reflect Wikipedia's rating

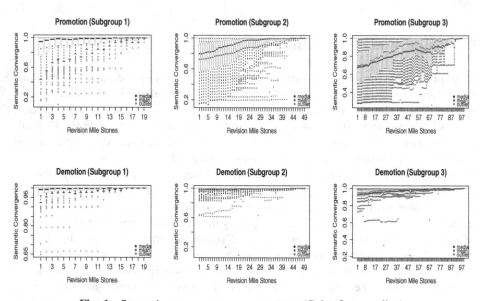

Fig. 1. Semantic convergence across groups (Color figure online)

mechanism. On one hand, considerable improvement in content is needed for the underdeveloped articles to be promoted to an advanced quality level; specifically it means complete coverage of the specific topic with abundant facts and resources as well as the professional writing style. On the other hand, there is no strong evidence that content issue is critical for quality demotion; it is probably caused by outdated references, problems in article structure, or writing style. For the promoted articles, we see that the more number of revision milestone the articles have, the larger the similarity distance is.

In terms of content stability, for the demoted articles, we don't see turbulence in all the three subgroups, same for the first two subgroups of promoted articles. There is some fluctuation seen in the third promoted subgroup after 55 revision milestones, this is mostly due to the drop in the number of articles which have more than 55 revision milestones.

5.2 Semantic Convergence of Quality Motion Within Advanced Groups

Now we are going to show the semantic convergence of the quality motion within *advanced group* to compare with the quality motion across groups. From our original dataset, we extract all the articles matching the motion patterns within the advanced group; Table 1 shows the number of sampled articles, since the number of articles are less, instead of divide the articles by the number of revision milestones as did in Sect. 5.1, we simply filtered out the articles which have far more revision milestones than the average revision milestones of each case.

From the result in Fig. 2, we see that all demotion and promotion cases within the *advance group* do not show significant semantic change over the period of quality motion. This phenomenon seems to be consistent with Wikipedia's suggestion on how to improve the article quality when the current quality level is already high: instead of content change, some knowledge from expert is needed.

5.3 Tests on the Distribution of Means Across

Now that we see the difference in the semantic convergence patterns of promotion and demotion across groups, we are going to test the distribution discrepancy of the means in the two groups. The mean of the semantic convergence throughout the first revision to the final revision represents an effort needed to be either promoted or demoted.

Table 1. Sampled articles within group quality motion

		Number of articles	Samples which have at least 3 revision milestones	Final samples after filtering
Promotion	GA → A	67	41	37
	GA → FA	182	139	139
	A → FA	49	21	19
Demotion	FA → GA	4	4	3
	FA → A	14	12	11
	A → GA	41	28	27

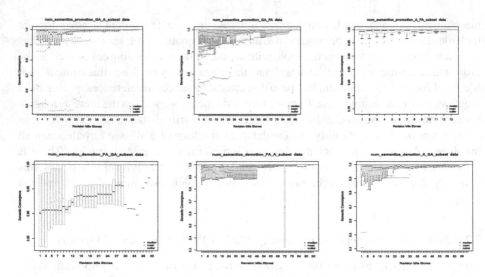

Fig. 2. Semantic convergence within advanced group

A smaller mean shows a larger effort. As Fig. 1 depicts that the mean of promoted articles across group is smaller than of demoted article, we performed the non-parametric Kolmogorov-Smirnov (KS) test and confirmed that the mean in the promotion cases is statistically smaller than the mean in the demotion cases for each subgroup, with "p-value = 0.0003892" for the first subgroup, "p-value = 6.715e-15" for the second, and "p-value < 2.2e-16" for the third.

6 Conclusion

Some prior studies on Wikipedia phenomena are conducted using its internal quality ratings of the articles. Though Wikipedia provides a set of criteria and implements voting mechanism for quality evaluation, the validity of the internal ratings is yet to be examined. Our study is one of the first that shows the mapping between the stated evaluation criteria and the quality rating of the Wikipedia articles. We investigate one of the most important evaluation criteria, i.e. the content rule, in a computational way. We check to what extent the content in terms of quantity change and stability affects quality change in both directions (promotion and demotion) and if the result is consistent with the criteria stated by Wikipedia. We measure the content change by computing the semantic similarity of every revision of the article until the final revision, starting from the first quality rating until the first quality motion occurs to see how the semantic converges. We define quality promotion as the change of quality scale from the *underdeveloped group* to the *advanced group*, and quality demotion as the reverse. In order to show the semantic convergence of a group of articles, namely a group of promoted or demoted articles, we align the semantic convergence of the articles by their revision milestones.

By showing the aligned semantic convergence of the articles, we found out that the quantity of content change is significant in the promoted articles, which complies with Wikipedia's stated criteria. We also saw slight content instability in some demoted articles though the phenomenon is not as clear at the group level. We thereby conclude that there could be other major issues which cause quality demotion instead of content instability, such as the outdated references and the missing links. Overall our findings suggest that Wikipedia's evaluation for promotion is significantly influenced by content change whereas the evaluation for demotion is influenced by other factors stated in Wikipedia's evaluation criteria. Wikipedia's assigned quality rating may thus be a reliable outcome variable for research provided that the researchers are comparing articles from the lower-quality group (articles with B-class, C-class, Start, and Stub ratings) with the higher-quality group (articles with Featured, A-class, and Good ratings). A more fine-grained outcome variable is not suggested, as there are only slight different content requirements' evaluation criteria within the advanced group. Nevertheless, for the articles that experience quality promotion within *underdeveloped group*, for example, from Start-class to B-class, we expect larger content change to take place.

Acknowledgments. The authors gratefully acknowledge the financial support from SNSF Grant No.: 100018_146444.

References

1. Hu, M., Lim, E.-P., Sun, A., Lauw, H.W., Vuong, B.-Q.: Measuring article quality in Wikipedia: models and evaluation. In: Proceedings of the sixteenth ACM conference on Conference on information and knowledge management, pp. 243–252. ACM, New York (2007)
2. Xu, Y., Luo, T.: Measuring article quality in Wikipedia: lexical clue model. In: Web Society (SWS) 2011. In: 2011 3rd Symposium on Web Society (SWS), pp. 141–146. IEEE (2011)
3. Arazy, O., Yeo, L., Nov, O.: Stay on the Wikipedia task: When task related disagreements slip into personal and procedural conflicts. J. Am. Soc. Inf. Sci. Technol. **64**, 1634–1648 (2013)
4. Liu, J., Ram, S.: Who does what: collaboration patterns in the Wikipedia and their impact on article quality. ACM Trans. Manag. Inf. Syst. **2**, 23 (2011)
5. Kittur, A., Kraut, R.E.: Harnessing the wisdom of crowds in wikipedia: quality through coordination. In: Proceedings of the 2008 ACM Conference on Computer Supported Cooperative Work, pp. 37–46. ACM (2008)
6. Kane, G.C., Majchrzak, A., Johnson, J., Chen, G.L.: A lifecycle model of perspective making and perspective taking in fluid online collectives. In: International Conference on Information Systems (2009)
7. Warncke-Wang, M., Cosley, D., Riedl, J.: Tell me more: an actionable quality model for Wikipedia. In: Proceedings of the 9th International Symposium on Open Collaboration, p. 8. ACM (2013)
8. Thomas, C., Sheth, A.P.: Semantic convergence of Wikipedia articles. In: Web Intelligence, IEEE/WIC/ACM International Conference on, pp. 600–606. IEEE (2007)
9. Wöhner, T., Peters, R.: Assessing the Quality of Wikipedia Articles with Lifecycle Based Metrics. ACM (2009)

Social Media in Health Care

Brenda Eschenbrenner[1(✉)] and Fiona Fui-Hoon Nah[2]

[1] University of Nebraska at Kearney, Kearney, NE, USA
eschenbrenbl@unk.edu
[2] Missouri University of Science and Technology, Rolla, MO, USA
nahf@mst.edu

Abstract. To identify existing streams of research and develop an agenda for future research, we reviewed and synthesized the existing literature relevant to social media in health care. In particular, our review encompassed two themes - Patient Use of Social Media and Healthcare Organization/Professional Use. Within these overarching themes, we focused on four subthemes (i.e., two under each main theme): community/public health and patient support/use, as well as medical litigation & compliance risk and health education & information sharing. From this review, we have also proposed future research topics and questions to further cultivate this salubrious research domain.

Keywords: Social media · Health care · Patient social media use · Healthcare organization social media use

1 Introduction

Social media provides new prospects for the healthcare industry and new avenues for research. Social media is unique in that the content can be shared in real-time masses, and is user-generated as well as organization facilitated. Social media is present on many organizations' lists of strategic media to achieve its goals and provide new channels of interacting with relevant stakeholders. Social media has also developed a noticeable presence in the healthcare industry and is an important domain for research [1]. In this paper, we will review and synthesize the literature relevant to social media in health care into thematic areas, as well as provide suggestions for future research.

Social media is being utilized by a variety of healthcare institutions. For example, it is estimated that more than 1,500 hospitals are utilizing various types of social media [2]. Examples of social media use include collaboration among healthcare professionals to share information and consult with one another regarding complex or unique cases. Healthcare organizations are also leveraging social media to support internal operations such as providing a platform for employees to communicate. Hospitals have utilized social media to recognize employee achievements and announce employee-related activities [3]. Providing a new channel to connect with patients or potential patients, social media also offer opportunities for healthcare professionals to educate the public and healthcare institutions to extend their branding and marketing efforts [2, 4]. For example, hospitals have promoted patient wellness activities [3].

F.F.-H. Nah and C.-H. Tan (Eds.): HCIB 2015, LNCS 9191, pp. 76–85, 2015.
DOI: 10.1007/978-3-319-20895-4_8

The amount of potential could be considered equivalent to the amount of uncertainty surrounding social media usage in health care. Healthcare organizations are contemplating managing and growing social media usage while also considering risks and legal implications [2, 3]. Although most or all hospitals have an established Facebook page, only approximately 19 % have been identified as actively managing it [3]. Some healthcare providers are using Twitter and Youtube, or social media specifically dedicated to health care such as PatientsLikeMe and Inspire [2]. However, given their limited usage, weighing the advantages and disadvantages, as well as evaluating social media's contribution to health care, will be pivotal and an important domain for research. Therefore, our research objective is to explore the existing streams of social media in healthcare research through a literature review, and identify meaningful agendas for future research.

2 Review of Literature

During our literature review, we identified two key themes: Patient Use of Social Media and Healthcare Organization/Professional Use, and will focus on these two themes in the paper. Within the Patient Use of Social Media theme, we focused on two key subthemes: Community/Public Health and Patient Support/Use. For the Healthcare Organization/Professional Use theme, we focused on two key subthemes: Medical Litigation & Compliance Risk and Health Education & Information Sharing.

2.1 Patient Use of Social Media

Community/Public Health. Research has found that patients utilize the Internet to address information shortfalls which can help to improve self-efficacy as well as coping abilities [5]. However, other research found information inaccuracies to be prevalent in websites that were studied. Additional research suggests that some social media channels, e.g., Twitter, could be used to foster behavioral changes. For example, healthcare organizations may alert patients who are at risk of being infected with a disease based on their data on social media [6]. Social media can also be used to alert or notify the public of a disease epidemic. Social media not only can be used to monitor health-related events for public wellness, but can also be used to notify the public or specific individuals about health-related risks. Hence, social media is a powerful means for monitoring and managing health-related events [6].

In addition to connecting patients with their physicians and subscribing institutions, social media also connect patients to the online medical community. For example, they can be used to offer support for specific health related problems or solutions such as obesity [7] and smoking cessation [8]. In the event of a health-related crisis, the public can receive advice from healthcare organizations to manage the crisis, which could include assistance to find the right drugs or the nearest treatment center. Social media provide a channel for patients to share challenges and achievements in dealing with diseases, so others can learn and benefit from them as well as contribute to them [9].

Crowdsourcing can also be used to share knowledge and information about drug safety and allergies, thus empowering patients in diagnosing health-related issues [6].

Patient Support/Use. Social media can be used by physicians or healthcare providers to assist, reach out to, and offer support to their patients [10]. There are many potential benefits to patients including conveying information or opportunities for better health and keeping patients up-to-date on health-related information [9]. Patients may participate in social media that are either publicly available, such as by subscribing to a specific healthcare provider on Facebook or Twitter, or dedicated specifically to health care, such as PatientsLikeMe and Inspire [4]. For example, healthcare providers can maintain a fan page on Facebook to post information and updates, and manage communications and discussions with their "fans" or current and potential patients. PatientsLikeMe provides a communication channel for patients, doctors and healthcare institutions to discuss health issues, where patients can also learn from other patients who have the same disease or illness. Inspire, on the other hand, provides a platform where patients, families, friends, caregivers, and health professionals can stay connected and provide support to one another. Support groups are available in Inspire, where patients have control over their personal information in terms of what information they choose to share and who they share it with.

Norton and Strauss [9] reported on a study by PricewaterhouseCoopers LLP (PwC) Health Research Institute indicating that consumers are willing to have their conversations on social media monitored if it can help them to improve their health [11]. Norton and Strauss [9] also reported that, in the same study involving adult consumers, 28 % indicated that they supported health-related causes, 27 % commented on others' health experiences, 24 % posted about health experiences, 20 % joined health forums and communities, 18 % tracked and shared symptoms/behaviors, 17 % posted reviews of doctors, 16 % posted reviews of medications/treatments, 16 % shared health-related videos/images, and 15 % posted reviews of health insurers. Hence, social media have significant implications for health care. An example of a successful social media for health care is Angieslist.com where it offers reviews on healthcare institutions and providers. Other forms of social media, including Twitter and Facebook, have been used by patients to share or comment on their health experiences. Social media not only can support health management of patients, they can also influence patients' choices of physicians, doctors, medical facilities, and hospitals [10].

Privacy is a relevant consideration and concern for patients and healthcare organizations [9]. Patients may hold back from sharing information due to privacy concerns, or friends and family members may post protected information about a patient on social media. There are risks involved in the use of social media that will need to be carefully monitored by patients and social media providers, and some of the information are protected by the Health Insurance Portability and Accountability Act (HIPAA) and cannot be shared on social media. The high sensitivity of healthcare information and protection by HIPAA may have been a reason for the limited success of social media in health care to date. The Health Information Technology for Economic and Clinical Health (HITECH) Act, however, is in place to promote the adoption of health information technology in compliance with HIPAA.

2.2 Healthcare Organization/Professional Use

Medical Litigation and Compliance Risk. Based on a review of the literature, topics and objectives included reviews of applicable legislation and specific cases of violations; suggestions for mitigating risks; and discussions of social media policies, monitoring, inappropriate use, adoption, additional risks associated with mobile device use, and inability to track communications and control information transmissions with certain social media [2, 9, 12–14]. Recommendations put forth included implementing, communicating, and updating social media policies; utilizing administrative controls; monitoring social media usage and posts; correcting inaccurate information; implementing security measures; training; posting disclosure statements; making professionalism a priority; and holding users accountable. Also, suggestions were made regarding considerations of potential litigation or evidence for litigation, healthcare professionals' online relationships and communications, leadership and proactive use of social media, security of mobile devices, data encryption, protecting privacy, and conducting risk analysis/assessment of social media use/tools.

A previous exploratory study identified concerns with social media use by hospitals in Spain including data security, privacy, and compliance issues with applicable regulations [15]. Challenges noted have been categorized into three areas: reputation, productivity, and privacy [16]. For example, individual employee postings on social media can lead to negative perceptions of the institution [9]. Privacy issues can encompass patient and organizational information. Productivity challenges include reduced cognitive focus on work-related tasks as well as cyberbullying in the workplace.

As mentioned earlier, privacy and HIPAA are key concerns for healthcare organizations. Not only must policies on social media be in place, employees need to be trained on appropriate usage versus inappropriate usage, as well as the implications that go along with them [9]. A healthcare organization that maintains a social media presence needs to ensure that its social media usage is compliant with HIPAA, regardless of the source of the posts. Hence, careful monitoring is required for protection from HIPAA violations. HITECH also imposes rigid requirements for reporting and violations [2]. Not only do social media need to be monitored carefully, timely actions are needed to fix issues or problems such as negative or inappropriate posts on social media [9].

The literature has identified specific and potential unintended consequences from negative social media use [1, 14, 17–19]. Some examples include the lack of filtering information leading to frauds, issues with billing and insurance reimbursements for social media based communication and care, questions regarding quality of care via social media versus in-person visits, distractions from social media messages being the impetus for errors during medical care, and losing the trust of stakeholders.

Health Education and Information Sharing. The literature has identified benefits that social media can provide to the healthcare industry including real-time access to health and medical information, the ability to share or collaborate (e.g., pictures as well as text), mass communication of health- or wellness-related instructions or information concerning health-related debates or conditions, educational opportunities (e.g., posting educational videos, and podcasts), assisting with treatment and supporting patients managing certain health conditions and diseases using various methods (e.g., games), and increased speed of information sharing or transfer as well as more rapid collaboration and knowledge acquisition [4, 10, 19, 20]. To successfully utilize social media for public health initiatives, the literature has identified the importance of engaging content and interactivity (e.g., games) [21]. However, in a study that analyzed hospitals' social media pages' posts and tweets, the majority were made by the hospital indicating a greater unilateral dialogue versus an interactive exchange [22].

Social media has been viewed as a tool to accumulate patient experiential knowledge such as effects of or reactions to medication as well as educate patients on medication management [23]. In a case study of a medication review site, the study identified the vetting process that occurred with the information patients submitted. The process entailed the site developers restricting some information from being posted but was done for quality control purposes and information integrity. The study proposed that social media sites can help educate patients which can facilitate greater compliance with medication regimens, but can also be shared with other stakeholders such as pharmaceutical companies. Social media has also been viewed as a data collection tool for healthcare research and monitoring [24]. However, potential ethical issues have been associated with this practice such as protecting identities as well as differentiating public and private spaces regarding privacy expectations.

Social media has been used by physicians to collaborate with or garner opinions from other physicians, gain different perspectives on a healthcare topic, become educated on recent healthcare advances and issues, and provide advice to patients [17, 25]. Social media has also been used by healthcare organizations to provide health-related information such as information regarding illnesses and treatments [14]. An exploratory study of social media use and impact in a public healthcare context found social media use to facilitate productivity and efficiency improvements for physicians and healthcare employees, and improve access to quality and quantity of information for patients [26]. Also, information on social media was noted as being used to identify potential epidemics, as well as facilitate patients sharing information with one another leading to additional questions to be addressed and interactions with their healthcare provider. Concerns, however, were identified regarding expanding the impact of the digital divide for those unable to access social media in health care to benefit from it. In another exploratory study, findings suggest that hospitals promoting health education and quality performance outcomes on their websites are more likely to be engaged in social media use [27]. Also, hospitals are more likely to distribute information versus facilitate engagement.

In one study of Twitter usage regarding the topic of childhood obesity, suggestions were made to utilize social media tools such as Twitter to provide evidence-based information from credible or expert sources to educate individuals on healthcare topics [7]. Applying the persuasion knowledge model in another study of perceptions of commercial websites as sources of health information, results indicate that adolescents are *less* likely to trust and rely on commercial websites in comparison to other websites (e.g., government) even after receiving eHealth literacy training [28]. Therefore, even if commercial or brand websites are providing reliable information or engaging in corporate social responsibility initiatives, adolescents may still not trust or rely on the Web site for health information.

In a descriptive research study of health organizations' (i.e., government, healthcare institutions, educational institutions, corporations, community, and others) use of social media, it was found that photo sharing was the most salient interactive tool utilized by all health organizations studied [29]. The interactive tool utilized the least was e-news-letters. From a literature review of Web 2.0 in the health domain (e.g., impact on atti-tudes), the commentaries reviewed indicate that social media is instrumental in enhanced interactivity, extended engagement, personalization, and cost efficiencies [30]. However, it was also noted that social media's impact may be inconsistent. For instance, variations may exist due to different socioeconomic statuses. Also, assessing the effec-tiveness of health-related interventions facilitated by social media was noted as a chal-lenge. The descriptive studies that were reviewed suggest that social media has the potential to facilitate health improvements. Intervention studies varied in topics (e.g., behavior changes, training employees) and included methods such as competitions and providing patient support.

Although social media research in a healthcare context has become a proliferating topic, additional research is vastly needed and has much potential for practical and theoretical contributions. Based on the findings from our literature review, we propose directions for future research next.

3 Directions for Future Research

3.1 Community/Public Health

Given the many positive implications and benefits of using social media for monitoring and managing health-related events and crises, more research is needed to understand how the process and results of social media usage can be managed efficiently and effec-tively. For example, how could we use existing social media and their associated data to make accurate predictions on health-related risks and to control or mitigate the risks? Can social media be used more effectively to manage health-related crises and public health, and if so, how? We also need to assess and evaluate the reliability and accuracy of using crowdsourcing for supporting health-related issues or problems. Are there reli-able mechanisms that can be used to gauge or assess the degree of trustworthiness or accuracy of information on crowdsourcing sites and to discount those that are not reliable or accurate? How can trust be assessed on crowdsourcing sites and what are their impli-cations (both positive and negative) on health care? Would offering trust ratings on healthcare social media and crowdsourcing sites be helpful? If so, what are the appro-priate sources for such ratings? An important overarching research question relates to the need to assess the effectiveness of social media in supporting public health in order to identify the areas for improvements.

3.2 Patient Support/Use

Future research may explore patient use of social media in which inappropriate amounts or types of uses generates negative consequences. For example, patient overuse of social media may lead the patient to become more stressed about a condition, side effects of a medication, or risks associated with a medical procedure. This stress may result in the patient experiencing anxiety or hypertension. Hence, research can identify effective use of social media to address a patient's health questions or concerns to avoid possible negative outcomes.

Research is also needed to examine how to reach out to remote patients who need immediate attention in times of crises and how assistance can be offered in the most effective way. Given the power of collective knowledge and intelligence, it would be particularly helpful to create an online community or environment where healthcare experiences can be shared across a critical mass. Research on the critical success factors (e.g., needs and desired functionality) of such an online community is also warranted.

Given the privacy concerns of patients and the protection of patient information by HIPAA, what is the best or appropriate mechanism for protecting such information in social media? Can users be prompted about or prevented from carrying out an action when they attempt to share protected information on social media? Would the system be able to detect such violations and warn the user or prevent him or her from taking the action? Would the social media provider be liable for such violations? The next section will discuss this issue further.

3.3 Medical Litigation and Compliance Risk

In the domain of social media and health care, there is a paucity of medical litigation and compliance risk research which generates a future research agenda replete with opportunities. For example, the existing literature supports the creation and implementation of social media policies which provides a rich area for research. For example, research questions to be pursued may include: What specific policy or guidance is appropriate for social media use by healthcare organizations, healthcare providers, and employees? A previous study indicated inappropriate use of social media by medical students at 60 % of U.S. medical schools [12]. Policies that are too restrictive will inhibit the use of social media to foster relationships with patients and other healthcare providers, but too little restriction could create legal or ethical ramifications or hinder employee productivity.

Issues of privacy continue to challenge healthcare organizations and professionals, and the use of social media presents another consideration for compliance risk. Considering the pervasiveness of individuals accessing social media content and sites with mobile devices, additional risks are introduced. Research can explore appropriate risk assessments of social media use and controls to mitigate the risks. Future research may pursue appropriate methods of monitoring social media and mobile device use by employees. Also, studies regarding accountability that can be fostered in employees using social media, as well as embedding accountability within the IT infrastructure can be undertaken. Studies can be conducted in which software applications are utilized to monitor relationships and behaviors on social media using data mining and analytics. Future research can also evaluate the use of nondisclosure statements or reminder messages regarding protection of personal health information, for example, to evaluate the effectiveness of increasing intentions to use social media professionally and reducing noncompliant behavior. Related questions include: What are the risks for a healthcare organization to offer social media? Would the benefits outweigh the risks? Can health-care providers implement mechanisms to increase patients' comfort in using social media by eliminating the risks associated with them? To what degree do patients trust social media? Factors that impact trust and behavioral intentions also need to be accessed.

3.4 Health Education and Information Sharing

Providing patients with information needed to comprehend, treat, or manage a health condition or issue is essential, and social media may be a potentially effective tool to do so. Future research may explore the potential of patients to trust information that is provided through social media channels. The literature has proposed that many patients make health care decisions based on individuals' opinions they trust (e.g., family members) [4]. Research studies may explore methods of instilling a sense of trust in healthcare organizations' or professionals' social media posts, tweets, or blogs.

Social media provides a platform for rich and extensive dialogue regarding health-care matters, such as becoming a parent or managing diabetes, in which patients can share their experiences and opinions. Albeit with the best of intentions, patients may provide information that is idiosyncratic or not completely accurate. Hence, future research may explore appropriate methods of evaluating information shared by patients for content accuracy while still encouraging open sharing of patient information and experiences.

Future studies may explore individual tendencies or factors influencing acceptance and use of social media among healthcare professionals. These studies may identify contributory factors to acceptance as well as aversion. Factors to be explored may be studied at the individual, organizational, societal or environmental level.

4 Conclusion

The categories that have emerged in the literature review accentuate the efforts that healthcare organizations are making to connect with patients to provide information and support. It also notes the concerns that healthcare organizations have regarding compliance with regulations and addressing the risks posed by social media. The literature has viewed multiple participants' social media use in health care, e.g., healthcare providers/professionals, patients, and support groups. Future research can explore the various themes and questions that we have identified in this review using a variety of research methodologies including action research, case studies, and experiments.

References

1. Fichman, R.G., Kohli, R., Krishnan, R.: The role of information systems in healthcare: current research and future trends. Inf. Syst. Res. **22**(3), 419–428 (2011)
2. Moses, R.E., Chaitt, M.M., Jones, D.S.: Social media in health care: lessons from the field. J. Health Care Compliance **16**(5), 17–24 (2014)

3. Miller, A.R., Tucker, C.: Active social media management: the case of health care. Inf. Syst. Res. **24**(1), 52–70 (2013)
4. Hackworth, B.A., Kunz, M.B.: Health care and social media: building relationships via social networks. Acad. Healthc. Manag. J. **7**(2), 1–14 (2011)
5. Gill, H.K., Gill, N., Young, S.D.: Online technologies for health information and education: a literature review. J. Consum. Health Internet **17**(2), 139–150 (2013)
6. Boyce, N.: The lancet technology: March, 2012. Lancet **379**, 1187 (2012)
7. Harris, J.K., Moreland-Russell, S., Tabak, R.G., Ruhr, L.R., Maier, R.C.: Communication about childhood obesity on Twitter. Am. J. Public Health **104**(7), e62–e69 (2014)
8. Lowe, J.B., Barnes, M., Teo, C., Sutherns, S.: Investigating the use of social media to help women going back to smoking post-partum. Aust. NZ. J. Public Health **36**(1), 30–32 (2012)
9. Norton, A., Strauss, L.J.: Social media and health care – the pros and cons. J. Health Care Compliance **15**(1), 49–51 (2013)
10. Waxer, N., Ninan, D., Ma, A., Dominguez, N.: How cloud computing and social media are changing the face of health care. Phys. Exec. **39**(2), 58–62 (2013)
11. Memmott, S., Clarke, J.L.: The proposed rule on transparency reports: shedding light on the sunshine act. An overview of the most important aspects of the proposed regulations. J. Health Care Compliance **14**(2), 13–20 (2012)
12. Bottles, K., Kim, J.: Evolving trends in social media compliance in medicine. Phys. Exec. **39**(5), 96–98 (2013)
13. Burke, T.R., Goldstein, B.: A legal primer for social media. Mark. Health Serv. **30**(3), 30–31 (2010)
14. Dinh, A.K.: Privacy and security of social media in health care. J. Health Care Compliance **13**(1), 45–46, 72 (2011)
15. Bermùdez-Tamayo, C., Alba-Ruiz, R., Jimènez-Pernett, J., Garcìa-Gutièrrez, J.F., Traver-Salcedo, V., Yubraham-Sànchez, D.: Use of social media by Spanish Hospitals: perceptions, difficulties, and success factors. Telemed. e-Health **19**(2), 137–145 (2013)
16. Cain, J.: Social media in health care: the case for organizational policy and employee education. Am. J. Health-Syst. Pharm. **68**(11), 1036–1040 (2011)
17. Anikeeva, O., Bywood, P.: Social media in primary health care: opportunities to enhance education, communication and collaboration among professionals in rural and remote locations. Aust. J. Rural Health **21**(2), 132–134 (2013)
18. Hawn, C.: Take two aspirin and Tweet Me in the morning: how Twitter, Facebook, and other social media are reshaping health care. Health Aff. **28**(2), 361–368 (2009)
19. Piscotty, R., Voepel-Lewis, T., Lee, S.H., Annis-Emeott, A., Lee, E., Kalisch, B.: To Tweet or not to Tweet? Nurses, social media, and patient care. Nurs. Manag. **44**(5), 52–53 (2013)
20. Johnson, C.: Games patients play. Physician Executive **38**(3), 6–10 (2012)
21. Kilaru, A.S., Asch, D.A., Sellers, A., Merchant, R.M.: Promoting public health through public art in the digital age. Am. J. Public Health **104**(9), 1633–1635 (2014)
22. Huang, E., Dunbar, C.L.: Connecting to patients via social media: a hype or a reality? J. Med. Mark. **13**(1), 14–23 (2013)
23. Adams, S.A.: Maintaining the collision of accounts: crowdsourcing sites in health care as brokers in the co-production of pharmaceutical knowledge. Inf. Commun. Soc. **17**(6), 657–669 (2014)
24. McKee, R.: Ethical issues in using social media for health and health care research. Health Policy **110**(2/3), 298–301 (2013)
25. Bottles, K., Kim, J.: How physician leaders can use social media to crowdsource. Phys. Exec. **40**(1), 82–84 (2014)

26. Andersen, K.N., Medaglia, R., Henriksen, H.Z.: Social media in public health care: impact domain propositions. Gov. Inf. Q. **29**(4), 462–469 (2012)
27. Richter, J.P., Muhlestein, D.B., Wilks, C.A.: Social media: how hospitals use it, and opportunities for future use. J. Healthc. Manag. **59**(6), 447–460 (2014)
28. Hove, T., Paek, H.J. Jeansson, T.: Using adolescent eHealth literacy to weigh trust in commercial web sites. J. Advertising Res. **51**(3), 524–537 (2011)
29. Park, H., Rodgers, S., Stemmle, J.: Health organizations' use of Facebook for health advertising and promotion. J. Interact. Advertising **12**(1), 62–77 (2011)
30. Chou, W.S., Prestin, A., Lyons, C., Wen, K.: Web 2.0 for health promotion: reviewing the current evidence. Am. J. Public Health **103**(1), e9–e18 (2013)

The Value of Expert vs User Generated Information in Online Health Communities

Jie Mein Goh[1(⊠)] and Elena Yndurain[2]

[1] Beedie School of Business, Simon Fraser University, 8888 University Drive,
Burnaby, BC V5A1S6, Canada
jmgoh@sfu.ca
[2] IE Business School, Maria de Molina 11, Madrid 28006, Spain
elena_yndurain@yahoo.com

Abstract. Online health communities are becoming an important source of information whereby users of these platforms, especially patients, participate for knowledge sharing and emotional support. This research examines the perceived value of expert generated information and user (patient) generated information and how it is influenced by different types of information that a user seeks. First, we propose a framework to classify the types of information based on the different types of information patients typically seek out on online health communities using a knowledge based perspective. Then based on this framework, we provide a set of propositions on the perceived value of expert generated versus user driven responses derived by patients. We expect that expert generated responses to have greater perceived value by patients as compared to community driven responses depending on the type of information patients are asking. Specifically, information uncertainty requiring tacit knowledge and high affect such as treatment experiences has greater value when generated by other patients. On the other hand, information uncertainty requiring explicit knowledge and low affect such as understanding the nature of diseases has greater value when generated by expertise. The proposed framework can help to extend the line of research on online health communities and inform health professionals, health organizations or developers of such communities.

1 Introduction

Online communities serve as an important platform that can have significant impact on health care and health care organizations. Patients can gain access to health information from a larger group of people than ever before (Viswanath et al. 2007). In many websites of health care organizations, message boards, messaging, mailing lists and chat rooms are provided, allowing individuals and patients to forge online communities through their platform. Prominent examples of online health communities include those offered by digital businesses such as WebMD and non-profit health care organizations such as American Cancer Society.

There are several reasons why patients participate in online communities. Previous studies have documented the main functions of Internet use for health such as searching for information about the disease, for coping and social support (Kalichman et al. 2003).

© Springer International Publishing Switzerland 2015
F.F.-H. Nah and C.-H. Tan (Eds.): HCIB 2015, LNCS 9191, pp. 86–95, 2015.
DOI: 10.1007/978-3-319-20895-4_9

Some studies have shown that the World Wide Web is an important channel for patients to source information on health conditions (Berland et al. 2001; DeGuzman and Ross 1999; Loader et al. 2002). This is made possible because increased access to health information allows patients or individuals who are concerned with their health to gain knowledge about symptoms, treatments and conditions.

In addition to fulfilling information needs, the social fabric of the Internet enabled through online communities has increased the possibility of fulfilling emotional needs required by patients or individuals who are concerned about their health. Leimeister et al. (2008) corroborated that virtual relationships formed among social networks of cancer patients indeed provide informational and emotional support. They also showed that Internet usage behavior, motives and perceived advantages of computer mediated communication affect virtual relationships positively.

Patients are linked to similar others who encourage each other, provide social support, share and evaluate treatment options, and build effective coping strategies. Cohen et al. (1985) found that social networks have a direct effect on reducing physical symptoms. Previous studies on online support groups have corroborated the notion that online support is beneficial to patients through empathetic support and supportive communication. Mickelson (1996) has found that individuals from electronic support groups perceive their electronic friends with similar problems higher than their family and non-electronic friends. Other studies have shown that technology is an important channel for patients to source information on health conditions (Maloney-Krichmar and Preece 2003; Berland et al. 2001; DeGuzman and Ross 1999). Access to these communities is twenty-four hours by seven days, making it convenient and flexible for users (Maloney-Krichmar and Preece 2003). Additionally, diversity of the communities is also valued by users of such communities (Maloney-Krichmar and Preece 2003).

The way information is delivered through these technological platforms has also seen tremendous changes from purely informational websites to user-driven websites where patients themselves interact and provide information with one another via online message boards (or forums). This in part drives one of the major problems faced by patients that is the credibility of information they received via online communities. This is especially true when the information is provided by anonymous others who participate in the community as it is difficult to verify the identity of the users of the community. This problem is compounded because patients try to hide their identity under the veil of anonymity to avoid the stigma of suffering from a disease. At the same time, people who intend to market their health products use these platforms as a way to disseminate product information and this could be harmful when misinformation is generated. To ameliorate these problems of user-generated information, some online web portals engage medical experts (e.g. physicians) to moderate the communities. Health sites such as WebMD provide a solution to this problem by introducing medical experts on their technological platform to allow medical experts to respond to patients' queries.

Korp (2006) suggested that the Internet has the potential to displace experts and professional interests and that it is imperative to examine how expert versus user (patient) generated knowledge relate to each other. However, previous studies have not investigated the comparative value of expert generated information versus user-generated information in online health communities. Furthermore the impact of medical experts on these communities has not been explored in previous research and a comparison between the perceived value from medical experts versus peers has not been examined. Thus, the goal of this paper is to tease out the value of expert and user-generated information in online health communities. While the provision of medical knowledge in the real world is largely dependent on experts like medical experts, technology provides a platform where knowledge is generated and transferred between different types of users. Although this bottom up generation and transfer of knowledge may have less credibility, it poses an interesting research question: What is the value of the information provided by experts compared to user (patient) generated information? We propose a comprehensive framework to link the major types of online health discussion (expert or user) generated information to the perceived value of information to patients. Results from testing the proposed hypotheses can help to inform health professionals and organizations or online community developers.

2 Theoretical Lens

Drawing from literature across different disciplines, we attempt to examine the question of whether expert generated or user generated information is more valuable for online health communities using a knowledge based lens.

Uncertainty. To understand the value of online health communities to patients, we first need to understand that one of the fundamental reasons for patients to visit online health communities is to seek information. The relationship between information seeking behavior and uncertainty has been well established (Berger and Calabrese 1975). Dosi and Egidi (1991) define "substantive uncertainty" as lack of information and introduce the notion of "procedural uncertainty" which reflects the gap between the complexity of the situation and the agents' competence in processing information. This gap can be addressed with greater knowledge.

Uncertainty exists when there is inadequate, inconsistent or unavailable information arising from complex, ambiguous and volatile circumstances (Brashers 2001). In the health context, patients often feel uncertain about their situation with respect to their disease condition. Individuals may have questions about verifying symptoms, their ability to manage illness, making sense of medication, treatment and even their health care provider's skills and abilities. These questions are usually resolved through a search for answers and then employing certain heuristics to make sense of the information provided.

In the literature on cognitive processing, it has been suggested that judgment under uncertainty is driven by heuristics. Some of the heuristics identified in the notable work of Tversky and Kahneman (1974) are: (1) representativeness, (2) availability and (3) anchoring.

1. Representativeness refers to the stereotypical impression of types that people use to make judgments.
2. The availability heuristic refers to the number of times a class or the probability of an event by the ease with which instances or occurrences can be recalled and brought to mind.

3. Anchoring refers to heuristic where people judge the new probability with respect to the original value.

These heuristics suggest that people tend to err in their judgments because of the fundamental flaws inherent in these heuristics and will be used to explain our hypotheses.

Knowledge Based View. Nonaka and Takeuchi's (1995) knowledge creation model has been widely cited in previous literature. They popularized two different types of knowledge: explicit knowledge and tacit knowledge. In this knowledge creation model, the authors propose that human knowledge is created and expanded through social interaction between tacit knowledge and explicit knowledge. This interaction is the knowledge conversion process whereby one state (explicit or implicit knowledge) is converted from one form to another.

In this paper, we propose a knowledge based lens on online health communities and suggest that the value of the expert generated information versus user-generated information depends on the type of knowledge the patients seek for. Specifically the perceived value of knowledge generated will depend on what type it is: explicit or tacit, as this will change the associated uncertainty gap. The organizational literature is replete with attempts to distinguish tacit knowledge from explicit knowledge. We use the definitions of the various types of knowledge following Grant's model (1996).

Explicit knowledge is objective and refers to the knowledge about "facts and theories". It is rational and has some form of sequential processing involved. Typically, explicit knowledge refers to knowledge that can be easily codified and transferred. Therefore, uncertainty that needs to be addressed by explicit knowledge tends to rely on experts or top management in providing explicit knowledge to bridge the gap. Instructions and guidelines (e.g. medications to treat high blood pressure) will fall into this category of knowledge. An alternative conceptualization to explicit knowledge is that it is somewhat like declarative knowledge, which includes factual knowledge.

On the other hand, tacit knowledge refers to the "know-how", about how to do something. This can refer to the way tasks are carried out or the methods involved. This knowledge manifests itself in the doing of something. This type of knowledge is not easily transferable. Tacit knowledge cannot be articulated easily and often creates a large uncertainty gap. This knowledge is embedded in the engagement and exchanges between individuals that includes the interactions between the patients seeking for information and the medical expert, or patient seeking for information and other patients. Tacit knowledge is knowledge gained from experience that cannot be found in manuals or books. To a certain extent, tacit knowledge requires personal judgment and skilful action. However, the individual performing the action may not be even aware of the details and how he has performed the action. Tacit knowledge transfer is an emergent process where the knowledge comes from coordination and self-organizing of individuals. These individuals can be both experts and non-experts. Thus, tacit knowledge is linked to procedural knowledge where important differences of opinions exist.

Uncertainty can be managed through articulation (Afifi and Burgoon 2000). To reduce uncertainty that needs to be addressed with tacit knowledge, individuals can benefit from exchanges with one another collating diverse opinions and options.

Because tacit knowledge may not be captured easily and may even be missed by the individual with tacit knowledge, pooling knowledge from many individuals may reduce uncertainty further by building on top of existing knowledge. A similar notion of "collective intelligence" or user-generated information has been suggested in the community of practice literature. In communities of practice, people come together as a group to share knowledge, learn together and create common practices. Thus, it has been suggested that in these communities, the complexity of knowledge requires that no one expert can provide the "best" answer and thus, collective intelligence is a better alternative in giving this answer.

Information Needs. We propose that the perceived value of information generated by experts or users is contingent on the information needs of the information seeker. In the information science literature (Wilson 2006), there are three types of information needs which interrelate with one another: physiological, affective and cognitive. Physiological needs refer to basic needs like need for water, air and other essentials. Affective needs refer to the needs related to emotional and psychological needs such as the need for attainment and support. Cognitive needs refer to the need to plan and learn a certain skill. However, this approach is limited when applied to domains such as health information seeking.

Context is an important factor for information seeking (Johnson 2003). In the marketing health literature, Moorman (1994) defines health information acquisition as a process where consumers obtain and assimilate "knowledge relevant to physical and mental well-being" and it involves "[…] decision making and the implementation and confirmation of health related behaviors". From the previous studies, there is a need to fill this gap of information seeking in the health context. Thus, we will integrate the above literature and formulate a framework for classifying health information needs. In the information seeking literature, Graydon et al. (1997) has identified five information needs categories—(1) nature of disease, its process and prognosis, (2) treatments, (3) investigative tests, (4) preventive, restorative, and maintenance physical care, and (5) patient's psychosocial concerns. A recent study (Medlock et al. 2015) identified similar topics by examining the information seeking behavior and the types of information seniors seek online. The first four types of information needs can be categorized according to the uncertainty framework except for the last dimension of affective needs.

There are two dimensions of information need that we used to classify the types of information users seek in online health communities. Firstly, information can be classified based on the type of knowledge is used to fill the uncertainty gap. Explicit knowledge and tacit knowledge are the different types of knowledge that are required to fill an uncertainty gap. Secondly, the affective need refers to the type of information that invokes emotions such as supportive information. Based on the two different dimensions, we classify four different types of information needs (Fig. 1): (i) information needs that require explicit knowledge and low affective need, (ii) information needs that require tacit knowledge and low affective need (iii) information needs that require explicit knowledge and high affective need and (iv) information needs that require tacit knowledge and high affective need. Patients with illnesses experience high uncertainty about their prognoses, potential treatments, social relationships and identity concerns.

3   Proposed Theoretical Model

Based on the framework in Fig. 1, we propose the hypothesized relationships in the research model shown in Fig. 2.

Expert generated information. Studies have found that cues to assessing credibility for web sites include the site's identity, currency and authoritativeness of its information, its sponsors, business partners and privacy practices. Expert knowledge is usually judged as having greater credibility (Stanford et al. 2002). Since greater credibility instills confidence in the information that is being read, experts can positively influence the perceived value of information received.

P1: The presence of expert is positively associated with the value of information generated within the online community.

User (patient) generated information. The value of user (patient) generated information in online health communities can increase with the diversity of the patients' back-grounds and the sheer quantity of peer patients. This prediction is in line with the theory of weak ties of Granovetter (1973) and that of Friedkin (1982). Granovetter (1973) suggests that weak ties can provide more useful information as opposed to strong ties because diverse set of people provides different information. Weak ties serve as a way to bridge across different groups of people thereby increasing access to different resources. Additionally, Friedkin (1982) attributed the success of weak ties through the sheer number of ties. Quantity is a major factor to increased availability of resources because as more people see the request, the chances that there is somebody who has the knowledge will be able to provide a helpful response. The number of users is likely to be positively associated with the value of information generated by the community because of the higher levels of social support that can be garnered. This means that more responses will be provided to an information seeker.

P2: The number of users is positively associated with the value of information generated by the community.

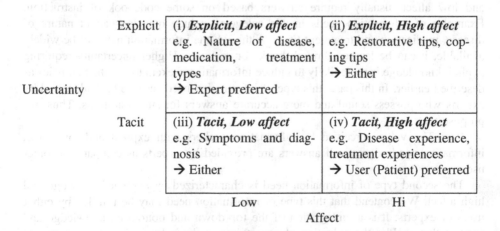

Fig. 1. Dimensions of information needs and examples

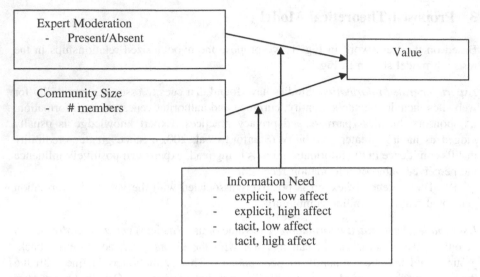

Fig. 2. Proposed model

Information Need. The value of information provided by experts or users (peer patients) can differ as a result of differences in terms of information needs. Certain types of information provided by medical experts will be perceived as having greater value compared to those provided by other patients. As suggested in the proposed framework in Fig. 1, this information need could be categorized into four types. Each of these four types of information needs affect the perceived value of expert generated information versus user (patient) generated information.

The first type of information need, i.e. explicit knowledge, is required to fill the uncertainty gap when affective need is low, expert opinions are judged as having greater value. This is because users regard an expert opinion as more credible because of the specialized knowledge held by the experts. Information needs that are explicit and low affect, usually require answers based on some codebook of instruction. Examples of information needs in this category include questions about nature of disease, medication and treatment types. Although the information may not be widely available, it can be learned through books or manuals. Higher uncertainty requiring explicit knowledge is more likely to induce information seekers to use the heuristics as described earlier. In this case, this type of information needs can be best addressed by experts who possess sound and more accurate answers for such questions. Thus, we propose that:

P3a: The value perceived by information seekers with explicit and low affect information need is greater if answers are provided by experts as compared to other users.

The second type of information need is characterized by explicit knowledge and high affect. We contend that this type of information need may be fulfilled by either users or experts. It is an integration of the top-down and bottom-up knowledge and support that enables the reduction of uncertainty at the individual level. Experts can provide value by providing information based on their knowledge and both experts and users can provide social support. Social support can be used to assist in uncertainty management. In general, when affective needs are high, both expert and user generated social support can fill the information need of the individual. For instance, social support is often requested in online health communities by patients or family of patients. There are two reasons: first, the user will share a common attribute such as an illness and invoke some form of empathy, which is not present when the user is dealing with the experts. Second, the mass of users as compared to a single expert can create a greater amount of social support.

Similarly, it has been argued that to reduce uncertainty, knowledge does not need to be entirely accurate (Brashers 2001). As long as the knowledge is coherent, it can reduce uncertainty to a certain extent. Kahneman and Frederick (2002) argued that attribute substitution happens when one attribute which is usually used as the judgmental criteria is not available, another more readily accessible attribute is used in the assessment. Thus, in this case when the expert is not available, other users who provide information becomes important. Thus, we posit that:

P3b: There is no difference in value perceived by information seekers, on explicit and high affect information needs, between the answers provided by experts and users.

The third type of information need requires tacit knowledge and low affect. We argue that there is no difference between the perceived value of the information generated by the experts of users. The reasoning is similar to hypothesis 3b. In this case, just as tacit knowledge creation is enabled through a "spiral conversion process" (Nonaka and Takeuchi 1995), tacit knowledge elicitation is enabled through the exchanges between information seeker, expert and users. Thus, this knowledge not only helps the user to reduce uncertainty, it also helps the user to make sense of a circumstance such as interpreting an unknown symptom that others have experienced (Brashers et al. 2000). Thus, we posit that

P3c: There is no difference in value perceived by information seekers with tacit knowledge and low affect information need between the answers provided by experts and users.

On the other hand, when affect is high and tacit knowledge is required, user is judged as having greater value than experts. In a previous study, it was shown that online social network helps patients manage uncertainty through information provision (Brashers et al. 2004). Representativeness, one of the judgment heuristics that people use, plays a central role for information need requiring tacit knowledge and high affect. This judgment heuristic refers to the impression of others being similar to the object of interest (Tversky and Kahneman 1986). Based on implications, people view the value of information on treatment experiences and psychosocial support provided by users similar to themselves, to have greater value when the information sourced are treatment experiences and psychosocial support as compared to an expert. The diverse opinions across many different individuals create a pooled intelligence resulting in substantial value. Users are more valuable in answering such information needs because they have undergone similar experiences. The affective need is provided through the mass of users.

P3d: The perceived value tacit and high affect information (such as treatment experiences) is greater if it is user generated as compared to expert generated.

4 Conclusions

This study attempts to tease out the value between user (in this case the patient) generated information and expert generated information. Starting with an information needs framework, we provide an integrative information need framework and proposed a research model that suggests that the perceived value of expert generated or user generated content by patients is contingent on information need of the patient.

A recent study finds that 59 % of US adults look online for health and medical information (Fox and Duggan 2013). As such, the findings from this study will be highly relevant as it will help to answer the question of when user generated information may be a better approach than expert generated information and vice versa when individuals seek health information in online health communities. Further, this study provides a theoretical basis for future research on online health communities and has practical implications such as informing health professionals, health organizations or online health communities' developers in the use of technological platforms.

Acknowledgement. The first author is grateful for generous financial support from Simon Fraser University's President's Research Startup Grant and Foundation Ramon Areces.

References

Afifi, W.A., Burgoon, J.K.: Behavioral violations in interactions: The combined consequences of valence and change in uncertainty on interaction outcomes. Hum. Commun. Res. **26**, 203–233 (2000)

Berger, C.R., Calabrese, R.J.: Some explorations in initial interaction and beyond: toward a developmental theory of interpersonal communication. Hum. Commun. Res. **1**(2), 99–112 (1975)

Berland, G.K., Elliott, M.N., Morales, L.S., Algazy, J.I., Kravitz, R.L., Broder, M.S.: Health information on the internet: accessibility, quality, and readability in English and Spanish. JAMA **295m**, 2612–2621 (2001)

Brashers, E.: Collective AIDS activism and individuals' perceived self-advocacy in physician-patient communication. Hum. Commun. Res. **26**(3), 372–402 (2000)

Brashers, D.E.: Communication and uncertainty management. J. Commun. **51**(3), 477–497 (2001)

Brashers, D.E., Neidig, J.L., Goldsmith, D.J.: Social support and the management of uncertainty for people living with HIV or AIDS. Health Commun. **16**(3), 305–331 (2004)

Butler, B.S.: Membership size: communication activity, and sustainability. Inf. Syst. Res. **12**(4), 346–362 (2001)

Cline, R.J.W., Haynes, K.M.: Consumer health information seeking on the internet: the state of the art. Health Educ. Res. **16**, 671–692 (2001)

DeGuzman, M.A., Ross, M.W.: Facilitating coping with chronic physical illness. In: Zeidner, M., Endler, N.S. (eds.) Handbook of Coping: Theory, Research, and Applications, pp. 640–696. Wiley, New York (1999)

Dosi, G., Egidi, M.: Substantive and procedural uncertainty: an exploration of economic behaviours in changing environments. J. Evol. Econ. **1**(2), 145–168 (1991)

Fox, S., Jones, S.: The Social Life of Health Information. Pew Internet & American Life Project, Washington, D.C. (2009)

Fox, S., Duggan, M.: Health Online. Pew Internet & American Life Project, Washington, D.C. (2013)

Grant, R.M.: Toward a knowledge-based theory of the firm Strateg. Manag. J. 17, 109–122 (1996)

Graydon, J., Galloway, S., Palmer-Wickham, S., Harrison, D., Rich-van der Bij, L., West, P., et al.: Information needs of women during early treatment for breast Cancer. J. Adv. Nurs. 26, 59–64 (1997)

Johnson, J.: On contexts of information seeking. Inf. Process. Manag. 39, 735–760 (2003)

Kalichman, S.C., Benotsch, E.G., Weinhardt, L., Austin, J., Luke, W., Cherry, C.: Health-related internet use, coping, social support, and health indicators in people living with HIV/AIDS: preliminary results from a community survey. Health Psychol. 22, 111–116 (2003)

Korp, P.: Health on the internet: implications for health promotion. Health Educ. Res. 21(1), 78–86 (2006)

Kulthau, C.C.: Inside the search process: information seeking from the user's perspective. J. Am. Soc. Inf. Sci. 42(5), 361 (1991)

Maloney-Krichmar, D., Preece, J.: An ethnographic study of an online health support community. In: Duquense Ethnography Conference, Philadelphia, pp. 10–12 (2003)

Medlock, S., Eslami, S., Askari, M., Arts, D.L., Sent, D., de Rooij, S.E., Abu-Hanna, A.: Health information–seeking behavior of seniors who use the internet: a survey. J. Med. Internet Res. 17(1), e10 (2015)

Nonaka, I., Takeuchi, H.: The Knowledge-Creating Company: How Japanese Companies Create the Dynamics of Innovation. Oxford University Press, New York (1995)

Leimeister, J.M., Schweizer, K., Leimeister, S., Krcmar, H.: Do virtual communities matter for the social support of patients?: Do virtual communities matter for the social support of patients? Inf. Technol. People 21(4), 350–374 (2008)

Steginga, S.K., Occhipinti, S., Gardiner, R.A., Yaxley, J., Heathcote, P.: Making decisions about treatment for localized prostate cancer. BJU Int. 89(3), 255–260 (2002)

Tapscott, D., Williams, A.D.: Wikinomics. Tantor Media, Connecticut (2006)

Tversky, A., Kahneman, D.: Rational choice and the framing of decisions. J. Bus. 59(4), S251–S278 (1986)

Viswanath, K., Ramanadhan, S., Kontos, E.Z.: Mass media and population health: a macrosocial view. In: Galea, S. (ed.) Macrosocial Determinants of Population Health, pp. 275–294. Springer, New York (2007)

Wilson, T.: On user studies and information needs. JDOC 62(6), 658–670 (2006)

A Study of the Uses of Instant Messaging in the Government Offices

A Case of the Macau Government Offices

Rachael K.F. Ip[✉] and Akina K.W. Ho

School of Business, Macau University of Science and Technology, Macau, China
{kfip,1209853abp20011}@must.edu.mo

Abstract. In recent decades, the pervasiveness of information and communication technologies (ICTs) has changed the communication patterns of the majority of the Internet users. This phenomenon is further intensified by the popularity of instant messaging (IM) chat. IM-chat has not only impacted on personal social communication, but also has significantly changed the way organizations communicate internally and externally. This study aims at examining the impact of three personal level factors on workplace IM uses and the associated communication satisfaction. Our findings reveal that *habit* and *boundary crossover* have positive impact on workplace IM uses and *communication inhibition* has a positive influence on the relationship between workplace IM uses and the associated communication satisfaction. Based on our findings, implications for research and practices are discussed.

Keywords: Instant messaging · Habit · Boundary crossover · Spiral of silence · Communication satisfaction

1 Introduction

Information and communication technologies (ICTs) had existed in the workplace over a century. One of the oldest and most popular telecommunication devices, telephone was introduced to the public in the 1890s. Emails appeared in the business since the 1990s, and more recently, instant messaging (IM) starts to play an important role for business to communicate internally and externally. Although the concept of instant messaging has existed since mid-1960s, it does not become ubiquitous until the popularity of the Internet, especially the emergence of social networking sties.

It is almost undeniable that communication is a very important component in organization operations [1–4]. More and more enterprises, including governments, are using emergent ICTs to create participation, transparency and accountability [5]. Being the anchoring of regions, governments should understand how ICTs can be used effectively and efficiently within and beyond the government offices. We believe that internal business process is the base for a government to provide services to her citizens, therefore, it is important for a government to realize the benefits brought by certain type of ICTs.

© Springer International Publishing Switzerland 2015
F.F.-H. Nah and C.-H. Tan (Eds.): HCIB 2015, LNCS 9191, pp. 96–105, 2015.
DOI: 10.1007/978-3-319-20895-4_10

This study aims at studying how ICTs in general, with instant messaging (IM) in particular, are used in government offices for work-related purposes. We targeted at the employees working in Macau government offices. Government offices are believed to have their unique organizational culture, for instant, bureaucratic and conservative culture. Such culture, first, may not encourage the uses of emergent technologies in their enterprise telecommunication network. Second, management may have skepticism toward the fruitfulness of adopting emergent social communication technologies in the workplace because such kind of technologies is originally designed for social interaction. Thirdly, the worry about security is another major hurdle. Although governments may be able to ban the implementation of social communication technologies in the enterprise network, it is almost impossible to forbid the uses because civil servants are able to bring their own devices to the workplace. Such BYOD (Bring your own device) or BYOA (Bring your own apps) phenomenon allows users to perform communication without the restriction of devices provided by organizations. BYOD phenomenon encourages IM users to use their own mobile phone to perform personal communication in the workplace. Furthermore, many instant messaging users have already built up their habit of using IM tools for social communication and the uses become automatic even the action is performed in the workplace. To understand the IM workplace uses, IM habitual uses and the perceived boundary crossover between workplace and social domains could be the exogenous factors influencing the workplace uses. Furthermore, we want to examine whether IM uses can encourage communication inhibitors to gain communication satisfaction through IM uses.

The rest of this paper is structured as follows: first, we describe the building blocks of our research model and hypotheses, followed by the research method. Findings and discussion are then presented, and the paper is concluded with implications and future research direction.

2   Background

Communication is inevitable in any organizations. It involves information collecting, disseminating, sharing, decision making, coordination and motivation [6]. Communication process starts when the message sender encodes the message, transmits it to the message recipient through a communication channel. The recipient then decodes the message and provides feedback through the same or other channel [7]. Organizational communication can be multiple directional – vertical (upward or downward) and lateral. Robbins and Judge [7] point out the downward communication usually is the message sent from the superior to assign tasks, explain policies, give instructions, or provide feedback to the subordinates. Upward communication is mainly reporting to the senior or seeking clarification. Lateral communication is mainly the collaboration with peers. Communication in organizations can be verbal, non-verbal (e.g. body language) or written [7]. In government offices, lateral communication may occur within or beyond departments, while, cross departmental vertical communication is rare.

Email can be considered as the most important business communications tool since the 1990s. However, after the first Internet-based free IM, ICQ, was introduced in 1996, the daily IM uses has grown dramatically [8, 9]. Although the original design of IM was for social personal communication, it has now entered the business territories, and is adopted in many organizations for internal and external communication. Not only for social interaction, IM has already been widely used in the business environment [10]. IM is a real time communication system, allowing two or more people to communicate with test, audio, video or file transfer. Because of its low cost and high reward attributes, IM has grown significantly popular in business [11]. Its real time communication and online presence further promotes its uses by greatly reducing the time for communication because instant reaction can be expected [12]. In addition, its emoticons can reduce the negligence of facial cues and be able to show friendliness as if the communication is performed F2F [8]. IM also provides a soundless communication channel for co-workers to communicate without the notice of other colleagues [11]. Although IM is almost universally accepted as one major communication medium in the business world, it may not be the case in government offices. In a bureaucratic and conservation environment, IM may still be considered as an informal communication tool and should not be used for official purposes. Despite the bright sides of using IM in the workplace, the draw-backs which catch the management's attention include: the not-organized messaging will increase the communication loads, the increase of polychromic communication, and IM provides a seedbed for hackers and virus attack.

2.1 Habit

Habit is a learning process [13, 14] and a practice of the prior behavior [14]. For any habitual reaction, it is not necessary for an individual to exert much effort for that action or behavior. The higher the proficiency of mastering that behavior, the higher it becomes automatic. Repeating actions will result in habit [15] and the majority of habitual behavior is efficient, effortless, unconsciousness [15] and sometimes cannot be controlled [16].

Habit in using information systems is defined as "the extent to which people tend to perform behavior (use IS) automatically because of learning" [13]. We believe that the majority of Internet users, especially the younger generations, would have already built up their habit of using IM for social communication purposes. To understand how instant messaging is used in government offices, it is essential for us to know whether habitual IM uses will encourage civil servant to bring IM to the workplace for work-related purposes. We, therefore, hypothesize,

H1:   The higher the habitual uses of instant messaging in the social environment, the higher the uses of instant messaging in the workplace.

2.2 Perceived Boundary

Boundary theory helps to explain how an individual switches across the boundary between the workplace and the family and manage a balance between work and family lives [17]. Boundary permeability allows an employee to perform other role or behavior in the workplace [18], for example, an employee is able to accept personal calls and visits in his workplace [19, p. 474]. Boundary permeability helps employees to manage their time between work and social (including family) domains, resulting in the increase of the quality of life [20]. If an individual has more power on controlling his own work, his intention to leave, work/family conflict and depression will be decreased as well [21].

Instant messaging can increase the boundary permeability between work and social domains because individuals can easily communicate with anyone if they have brought their own devices. Senarathne and his colleagues [22] find that if ICT uses in organization is effective, the uses in social environment is effective as well, and vice versa. We, therefore, believe that IM, besides being used for social interaction, can also be a good tool being used in the workplace for work-related purposes. Although Avrahami and Hudson [10] find that communication patterns in workplace and non-work environment has significant differences, we think that such uses will contribute to increase the harmony of the domains shifting. To understand how civil servants bring social-oriented IM to the government offices for work-related purposes, we hypothesizes,

H2: The higher the crossover between workplace and non-work, the higher uses of instant messaging in the workplace.

2.3 Instant Messaging Uses and Communication Satisfaction

Workplace communication plays an important role in influencing employee productivity and workplace satisfaction [23]. Gregson [24] finds that communication satisfaction has impact on overall job satisfaction because better communication brings need satisfaction, expectation fulfillment and decreases uncertainty. Better communication helps to increase knowledge management, more accurate prediction, understanding better the environment and resulting in the reduction of uncertainty [25]. Clampitt and Downs [26] also point out that the higher the communication effectiveness, the lower complaints and absenteeism happened in the workplace. Flanagin [27] highlights the positive relationship between interpersonal relationship with IM and evidence IM users are more satisfied while carrying on multiple simultaneous conversation. Therefore, we hypothesize,

H3: The higher the uses of instant messaging, the higher the communication satisfaction in the workplace.

2.4 Spiral of Silence

When individuals sense that their opinions are the majority within a group, they tend to voice out their opinions. On the contrary, people tend to hide their opinions if they sense that their opinions are at the side of the minority [28]. Individuals rely on their quasi-statistical organ to sense the climate of opinion to see whether their opinion is on the majority or the minority side, so as to decide whether they voice out or suppress their ideas [28, 29]. When an individual sense his opinion is at the minority side, he will further hide his own opinions which result in the deeper he falls into the spiral of silence (SoS) [29]. One of the reasons people keep silence in the group is the fear of being isolated [30] or considered as aliens [31].

With the willingness to self-censor [30], individual will measure the climate of opinion to decide whether to voice out. Self-censorship does not imply obedient to the majority, just keep quiet to protect them from being isolated. However, even when an individual's opinion sinks to the bottom of the spiral, it doesn't imply they give up their own belief, they just don't want to express the ideas publicly [28]. Although keeping silence may lead to the reduction of conflict and increase seeming harmony, it is not health to the overall benefit. In the working environment, silence can be the symptom of low employee morale. Liu and Fahmy [32] find that individuals tend to voice out their own ideas in the online environment compare to offline situation. We believe that IM provides a good channel for civil servants to express their ideas to their friends in a safer way without being noticed by the third person in the workplace, which ultimately will increase the communication satisfaction with IM, we therefore, hypothesize,

H4:   The relation between IM uses in the workplace and communication satisfaction will be stronger for communication inhibitor than non-inhibitor.

3   Research Method

Our research model was tested with a sample of civil servants working in multiple Macau government offices. The Macau SAR is one of the special administrative regions of the People's Republic of China. There are around 30,000 civil servants working in the 81 Macau government offices (source: 2013 MSAR Public Administration Human Resource Report).

3.1   Data Collection

Data were collected from respondents through paper-based and online questionnaires. A referral sample was used through the connection of one of the authors. Paper-based questionnaires were sent through the chain of our acquaintance and the online one was posted to several social networking sites to invite Macau civil servants to participate.

3.2   Measures

Our questionnaire items were mostly adopted from established measures from prior studies. All constructs were measured with at least two items by a five-point Likert scale, ranging from strongly disagree (1) to strongly agree (5). *Habit* items were adopted from [13] scale with SmartPLS composite reliability (CR) of the items of 0.8733; *Perceived Boundary crossover* items came from [21] and *Work-related IM uses in the workplace* were adopted from [21, 33] with CR of the items 0.8504 and 0.8235 respectively. The *SoS* items had been measured in [30]. Composite reliability of the items is 0.7508. *IM-based communication satisfaction* items came from [34] and [35] with CR of 0.8733. In addition, the outer loading of almost all variables are all above 0.707, with one SoS item scores 0.5605 and one Work-related IM uses 0.6101. The AVE values of all constructs are between 0.6006 and 0.7753. Since all AVE values are higher than 0.5, convergent validity are guaranteed. Furthermore, the AVE values are all higher than the latent variable correlation with other variables, discriminant validity is also confirmed.

3.3 Sample Profile

A total of 141 valid questionnaires were collected, with 106 paper-based and 35 online. Response rate of paper-based questionnaires (excluded invalid ones) was 85 %. It is not possible for us to get the response rate of the online questionnaires because the link was posted to different social networking sites and the click rate could not be obtained. Among the respondents, 56.7 % was male and 43.3 % was female. Almost 80 % of the respondents had an education level of university or above. Around 48 % of the respondents had more than 10 years working experience in the government offices.

4   Data Analysis and Results

To perform the path analysis of our research model, with moderating and mediating effect being measured, we adopted Structural Equation Modeling (SEM) technique. We used SmartPLS 2.0 to test our research model. The results of the measurement model have been discussed in the previous section. Figure 1 shows the results of the hypothesized structural model test. All hypotheses are supported. The R^2 value demonstrates that the model explains 24.9 % of the variance in IM-based Communication satisfaction. The results of the structural model will be explained in the following section.

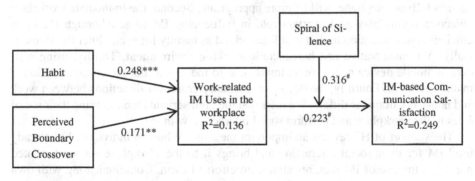

(Note: $^\#$p<0.10,* p<0.05, **p<0.01. ***p<0.001)

Fig. 1. Results of the proposed research model

5   Discussion and Conclusion

The objective of our study is to explain the impact of three individual level variables, namely *habit, perceived boundary crossover,* and *SoS,* on IM-based communication satisfaction. First, we consider habit and perceived boundary crossover as two independent variables and examine whether they have impact on workplace work-related

IM uses. Results show that these two independent variables have positive impact on the mediating variable, with habit stronger than perceived boundary crossover. Instant messaging has been widely used by the majority of mobile device users and many of them have already built up the habit of using this tool for daily communication. Therefore, it is not surprise that Macau civil servants also have built up similar habit and carry this habit to the workplace of using IM for work-related communication. However, from the responses, we find that 54 % of the respondents mentioned there was less than 20 % of their IM content was job-related. It implies that although IM is used in the workplace for communication, the communication was still mainly social-oriented. The proportion of work-related content was comparatively very small.

Bring-your-own-device (BYOD) or bring-your-own-application (BYOA) phenomenon strengthens the flexibility and permeability of the boundary between work and non-work domains. Although it is not officially mentioned that Macau civil servants are allowed to use their own mobile devices in the workplace, mobile devices uses are not banned. Almost all of this group of public servants can use their own devices for external and internal communication. Because of BYOD and BYOA, the boundary permeability greatly allows government office workers to switch their roles between work and non-work domains.

Although both path coefficients are significant, the R^2 value of workplace work-related IM uses is relatively low. There are many possible explanations. First, the nature of tasks assigned influences the use of IM in the workplace. IM is good for quick interaction, so, when the tasks are relatively simple, IM is one of the best choices. However, when the tasks are complicated and need detail explanation, other communication tools, such as F2F or telephone, will be more appropriate. Second, the immediate workplace objective norms play an important role in influencing IM uses. Although IM is an efficient communication tool, it is still perceived as mainly for social interaction, especially in a conservative and bureaucratic working environment. Thirdly, using self-owned mobile device may give an impression to the senior that the communication is mainly personal. Fourthly, the degree of boundary crossover directions between work and non-work domains differs. We infer that the civil servants tend to bring their social roles to the workplace and perform social interaction with IM.

The support of H3 reveals an important message. When an individual has already used IM for their social interaction and brings it to the workplace for work-related purposes, the use of IM requires almost no effort to them. Communicating with own device and using a familiar tool for communication may also imply communication effect can be optimal. Finally, IM provides a very efficient and effective channel for employees to seek help from their peers without the notice of others. Quick answers to questions would result in a quick job completion. All of the above provide explanations to why workplace work-related IM uses has a positive relationship with IM-based communication satisfaction. This message is important because communication satisfaction is positively related to job satisfaction [24] and negatively related to complaints, absenteeism and turnover [26].

According to the spiral of silence theory, an individual falls in the spiral of silence is not necessary a person who is afraid of expressing himself in front of others [29]. When an individual senses that his idea is in the minority side, being afraid of breaking the harmonious atmosphere and therefore be isolated [30], he will swallow his words and remains silence. The more he swallows his words, the higher degree he perceives himself as the minority and then to the lower the bottom of the spiral he is sinking. With IM, his ideas may have an outlet to be released to the persons this individual trusts. Fear of being isolated may be reduced accordingly. When his ideas are agreed by more people, this individual may rise in the spiral of silence. When it comes to the situation that a lot of people accept his ideas, his ideas may become the majority, and he may have the confidence to voice out his opinions. Based on this logic, we believe that IM can increase the level of an individual's voice being heard, and therefore, is able to increase the communication satisfaction. The support of H4 reveals that IM is one of the potential vehicles to promote balance of an office's various opinions.

In most government offices, bureaucracy is not uncommon. Individuals tend to keep silence so as not to break the harmony. Discussing about different opinions and heard by other colleagues may create disturbance in the office. But, if agreement has been made through IM conversations, individuals will have more confidence to voice out because support has already gained. For communication inhibitors, using IM in the offices would therefore increase higher communication satisfaction.

6   Implications and Future Research

The contribution of this study is two-folded. Theoretically, this study integrates spiral of silence theory into the explanation of IT-based communication effectiveness. Practically, this study provides evidences to the government that allowing social communication tools in the workplace will increase employee communication satisfaction and ultimately will bring higher productivity to the government. Since it is difficult for any organizations to ban IM uses in the workplace, governments should impose policies to regulate the uses so as to grasp the benefits brought by this emergent technology.

To keep the model parsimonious, we only include the factors of habit and the boundary crossover as independent variables. However, the R^2 of workplace work-related IM uses demonstrates that there should be other uncontrolled variables influencing this mediating variable. Possible constructs are nature of assigned tasks or immediate workplace objective norms. Our future research aims at considering more group level and organizational level factors in influencing workplace IM uses. The second limitation comes to the referral sampling. Due to the nature of referral, respondents might share similar traits and behavior characteristics because they were recruited by the chain of friends. Finally, to further increase the external generalization of the research result, employees working in other nations' government office will be our research targets.

References

1. Muchinsky, P.M.: Organizational communication relationships to organizational climate and job satisfaction. Acad. Manage. J. **20**(4), 592–607 (1977)

2. Pettit, J.D., Goris, J.R., Vaught, B.C.: An examination of organizational communication as a moderator of the relationship between job performance and job satisfaction. J. Bus. Commun. **34**(1), 81–98 (1997)
3. Roberts, K.H., O'Reilly, C.A.: Failures in upward communication in organizations; three possible culprits. Acad. Manage. J. **17**(2), 205–215 (1974)
4. Cooren, F., Kuhn, T., Cornelissen, J.P., Clark, T.: Communication, organizing and organization: an overview and introduction to the special issue. Organ. Stud. **32**(9), 1149–1170 (2011)
5. Majchrzak, A., Markus, M.L., Wareham, J.: ICT and societal challenges. MISQ special issue call for papers (2012)
6. Miller, K.: Organizational Communication: Approaches and Processes. Wadsworth Cengage Learning, Boston (2009)
7. Robbins, S.P., Judge, T.A.: Organizational Behavior, 15th edn. Pearson Education, New York (2013)
8. Lancaster, S., Yen, D.C., Huang, A.H., Hung, S.Y.: The selection of instant messaging or e-mail: college students' perspective for computer communication. Inf. Manage. Comput. Secur. **15**(1), 5–22 (2007)
9. Osterman, M.: Instant messaging in the enterprise. Bus. Commun. Rev. **33**(1), 59–62 (2003)
10. Avrahami, D., Hudson, S.E.: Communication characteristics of instant messaging effects and predictions of interpersonal relationships. In: The 2006 20th Anniversary Conference on Computer Support Cooperative Work, pp. 505–514. ACM (2006)
11. Rennecker, J., Godwin, L.: Theorizing the unintended consequences of instant messaging for worker productivity. Sprouts: Working Pap. Inf. Syst. **3**(14), 138–168 (2003)
12. Li, D., Chau, P.Y., Lou, H.: Understanding individual adoption of instant messaging: an empirical investigation. J. Assoc. Inf. Syst. **6**(4), 102–129 (2005)
13. Liyamem, M., Hirt, S.G., Cheung, C.M.: How habit limits the prediction power of intention: the case of information systems continuance. MIS Q. **31**(4), 705–737 (2007)
14. Ouellette, J.A., Wood, W.: Habit and intention in everyday life: the multiple processes by which past behavior predicts future behavior. Psychol. Bull. **124**(1), 54–74 (1998)
15. Aarts, H., Verplanken, B., Knippenberg, A.: Predicting behavior from actions in the past: repeated decision making or a matter of habit? J. Appl. Soc. Psychol. **28**(15), 1355–1374 (1998)
16. Aarts, H., Dijksterhuis, A.P.: The automatic activation of goal-directed behavior: the case of travel habit. J. Environ. Psychol. **20**(1), 75–82 (2000)
17. Clarks, S.C.: Work/family border theory: a new theory of work/family balance. Hum. Relat. **53**(6), 747–770 (2000)
18. Matthews, R.A., Barnes-Farrell, J.L., Bulger, C.A.: Advancing measurement of work and family domain boundary characteristics. J. Vocat. Behav. **77**(3), 447–460 (2010)
19. Ashforth, B.E., Kreiner, G.E., Fugate, M.: All in a day's work: boundaries and micro role transitions. Acad. Manage. Rev. **25**(3), 472–491 (2000)
20. Greenhaus, J.H., Collins, K.M., Shaw, J.D.: The relation between work-family balance and quality of life. J. Vocat. Behav. **63**(3), 510–531 (2003)
21. Kossek, E.E., Lautsch, B.A., Eaton, S.C.: Telecommuting, control, and boundary management: correlates of policy use and practice, job control, and work-family effectiveness. J. Vocat. Behav. **68**(2), 347–367 (2006)
22. Senarathne Tennakoon, K.L., Da Silveira, G.J., Taras, D.G.: Drivers of context-specific ICT use across work and non-work domains: a boundary theory perspective, information and organization. Inf. Organ. **23**(2), 107–128 (2013)

23. Downs, C.W., Hazen, M.D.: A factor analytic study of communication satisfaction. J. Bus. Commun. **14**(3), 63–73 (1977)
24. Gregson, T.: Communication satisfaction; a path analytic study of accountant affiliated with CPA firms. Behav. Res. Acc. **2**, 32–49 (1990)
25. Hecht, M.L.: Toward a conceptualization of communication satisfaction. J. Speech **64**(1), 47–62 (1978)
26. Clampitt, P.G., Downs, C.W.: Employee perceptions of the relationship between communication and productivity: a field study. J. Bus. Commun. **30**(1), 5–28 (1993)
27. Flanagin, A.J.: IM online: instant messaging use among college students. Commun. Res. Rep. **22**(3), 175–187 (2005)
28. Griffin, E.A., McClish, G.A.: A First Look at Communication Theory, 8th edn. McGraw-Hill, New York
29. Noelle-Neumann, E.: The spiral of silence: a theory of public opinion. J. Commun. **24**(2), 43–51 (1974)
30. Hayes, A.F., Glynn, C.J., Shanahan, J.: Willingness to self-censor: a construct and measurement tool for public opinion research. Int. J. Pub. Opin. Res. **17**(3), 298–323 (2005)
31. Janis, I.L.: Groupthink. Psychol. Today Mag. **5**, 84–90 (1971)
32. Liu, X., Fahmy, S.: Exploring the spiral of silence in the virtual world: individuals' willingness to express personal opinions in online versus offline settings. J. Media Commun. Stud. **3**(2), 45–57 (2011)
33. Xu, B., Zhang, W., Li, D.: Copresence and its social-relational antecedents in computer-mediated communication: the case of instant messenger. Inter. J. Hum. Comput. Interact. **27**(10), 991–1009 (2011)
34. Spector, P.E.: Measurement of human service staff satisfaction: development of the job satisfaction survey. Am. J. Community Psychol. **13**(6), 693–713 (1985)
35. Dhammika, K.A.S., Almad, F.B., Sam, T.L.: Job satisfaction, commitment and performance: testing the goodness of measures of three employee outcomes. South Asian J. Manage. **19**(2), 7 (2012)

Leveraging Social Media for the Fishing Industry: An Exploratory Study

Azrin Shah Ismail and Haliyana Khalid[✉]

Putra Business School, UPM, Seri Kembangan, Malaysia
`azrin.mbal3@grad.putrabs.edu.my`,
`haliyana@putrabs.edu.my`

Abstract. One of the main challenges in the fishing industry today is the art of connecting buyers and sellers effectively so that information about products, price, quantity and location is synchronized. A lack of communication and technology skills has forced fishermen and fishing industry authorities to depend on intermediaries to market their products, leading to higher prices for consumers. This paper explores the potential use of social media to reduce intermediaries in the fishermen market supply chain. It also aims to understand the critical success factors in using social media as a platform to promote the market.

Keywords: Fishing industry · Fishermen · Social media · Social media marketing · Intermediaries · HCI · Business · Human wellbeing

1 Introduction

In Malaysia, the Fisheries Development Authority of Malaysia (FDAM) is an authorized body that is responsible for developing the fishing industry. FDAM continually strives to create a developed, independent and progressive fishermen community nationwide. Unfortunately, the marketing of marine produce in Malaysia still relies heavily on a large number of intermediaries. From traditional landing sites to vendors or consumers, there are auctioneers, agents, exporters, wholesalers and other agents who play specific roles in the marketing of fish. The price differences between what the fishermen receive at landing sites and what the consumers pay is due to the handling, transportation and marketing costs of intermediaries. This price spread may be largely due to the vagaries of supply and demand, or even due to profiteering. The existence of many intermediaries in the supply chain ultimately influences the higher price of fish to the consumer. In a study conducted by Haque [1], fishermen were found to be the poorest actors in the supply chain due to the failure to enhance their bargaining power and access to market information. This dilemma is also happening in the fish marketing channel in Malaysia.

To improve the wellbeing of fishermen, new fishermen markets have been developed by the government in certain seafood landing sites in Malaysia. This initiative hopes to reduce the number of intermediaries, thus reducing fish and seafood market prices.

© Springer International Publishing Switzerland 2015
F.F.-H. Nah and C.-H. Tan (Eds.): HCIB 2015, LNCS 9191, pp. 106–117, 2015.
DOI: 10.1007/978-3-319-20895-4_11

However, to date, there is no coordinated mechanism to promote, create awareness, or educate consumers on these new markets in remote landing sites. As a result, people are currently not aware of the existence of fishermen markets. We believe there is a lack of information online to persuade people to visit these fishermen markets.

Thus, this study aims to explore the use of social media marketing in helping government initiatives to promote the new fishermen market program. It also aims to understand the critical success factors in using social media as a platform to promote the market. This study combines both qualitative and quantitative approaches to answer the research questions. For the purpose of this paper presentation, only findings from our quantitative study will be elaborated. This research hopes to contribute to the growing literature on social media marketing. Although many studies have been conducted on the usage of social media as marketing tools, there are hardly any that focus on the fisheries industry. Thus, this research hopes to fill this gap in the literature.

2 Literature Review

This section presents the proposed research framework and hypotheses constructed for the study. The four variables being studied are: perceived knowledge about fish, type of content sharing in social media, credibility of information, and purchasing decision in the fishermen market. Previous research and studies will also be discussed to provide better insights on the factors that influence consumers to purchase their fish supply at the fishermen market.

2.1 Perceived Knowledge About Fish

One of the crucial elements in the thinking process is the relationship between perceived knowledge about products and the consumers' motivation to make a purchasing decision. Many researchers that studied the fishing industry found a positive relationship between knowledge and need for cognition (NFC) [2, 3]. Need for cognition is the tendency of people to engage in and enjoy thinking by using the richness of information they gather from a variety of sources [4]. Therefore, using a rich medium of communication enhances the efficiency of the thinking process [5]. A similar study by Aurier asserts that the knowledge of consumers affects their personal search behaviour to acquire information regarding products [6]. According to the cue utilization theory [7], assessing the quality of products is carried out in terms of identifying and defining the information cues that consumers use as indicators. A recent study by Gaviglio et al. [8] classifies product information cues into two categories, which are intrinsic and extrinsic cues. Intrinsic cues are those inherent in the product, such as taste, smell or colour, while extrinsic cues include external features of the product, such as price, brand, or packaging. Both information cues are perceived as important knowledge about fish [8]. Hence, the following hypothesis is drawn:

H1: There is a positive relationship between the perceived knowledge about fish and purchasing decision in the fishermen market.

2.2 Type of Content of Social Media

Consumers are turning more frequently to various types of social media to conduct their information searches and to make their purchasing decisions [9]. The contents of information must be objective, trusted, and relevant to be shared on the social media platform. Richer media have significantly positive impacts on decision quality when consumers have sufficient knowledge about the products/services [10]. This argument confirms the study conducted by Verbeke et al. [11], which found that less confident consumers need to seek more knowledge about quality of fish before they purchase the right species. Therefore, they tend to search for trustworthy information to build their confidence before finalizing their purchasing decision. This is consistent with the media richness theory (MRT) introduced by Daft and Lengel [12] whereby the communication efficiency between people is affected by the fitness of the media and the characteristics of the communication task. When more information is communicated in the online medium, the richer the medium will be. It is important to determine whether the type of content shared in social media has a relationship with purchasing decisions at the fishermen market. Hence, the following hypothesis is drawn:

H2: There is a positive relationship between the type of content sharing in social media and purchasing decision in the fishermen market.

2.3 Credibility of Information in Social Media

Kautsar et al. [13] define credibility of information as how consumers view information as a source of knowledge which is trustworthy, objective, relevant, and free of biasness. In this research, the subject of credibility refers to the information sought with regard to apparel and not the trusts or beliefs about an individual or an organization. Consumers will be more willing to accept information when the information source has high credibility. As a result, consumers' attitudes become more positive [14]. A recent study by Neti [15] concluded that social media is probably the only marketing platform that encourages fool proof communication and accountability among sellers as well as consumers. Yoon [16] strongly agreed that credibility is closely linked to trust and satisfaction. When consumers feel the information can be trusted, they will secure that information as knowledge that intrigues their desire to purchase products. In a study conducted by Abraham [17], information was found to be a crucial element to manage fish supply chains from producers (fishermen) to consumers. The entire supply chain involves different roles of market players who need to make instant decisions on purchasing fish. This is because fish is a perishable item and fish quality drops with its price [17]. Thus, consumers' purchase decisions at the fishermen market may be influenced by whether or not they believe the information in social media to be credible. Hence, the following hypothesis is drawn:

H3: There is a positive relationship between the credibility of information in social media and purchasing decision in the fishermen market.

2.4   The Theoretical Framework of the Research

Figure 1 below depicts the theoretical framework proposed in this research. This theoretical framework is to introduce and describe the theories and hypotheses explained in the earlier section. Thus, it helps the researcher understand the underlying research objectives of this study. On the left of the diagram there are three (3) independent variables. These independent variables comprise perceived knowledge of fish, type of content sharing in social media, and credibility of information in social media.

The variable on the right of the diagram is the dependent variable. This variable represents the purchasing decision at the fishermen market, which is determined by the independent variables mentioned earlier. The relationships between the three (3) independent variables and the dependent variable are denoted as H1, H2 and H3 respectively. This theoretical framework was adapted from studies by [18, 19, 20].

The researcher is therefore compelled to explore how the perceived knowledge of fish, type of content sharing in social media, and credibility of information in social media influences consumers to buy fresh fish at the fishermen market.

3   Research Methodology

The previous section has deliberated and presented the conceptual model and hypotheses of the study based on prior research. This section will focus on the methods of research, including data collection methods, instrument design, sampling, and data analysis.

3.1   Quantitative Method

In this study, questionnaires were used as the data collection instrument. The designed questionnaire combined closed questions and interval questions, and was made up of

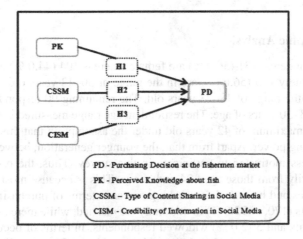

Fig. 1. Proposed theoretical framework

five (5) parts, namely Section A, B, C, D, and E. Section A covered the socio-demographic profile of the respondents. In Section B, respondents were asked about the existence of fishermen markets developed by FDAM. Section C posited five (5) close-ended questions and four (4) interval questions. It solicited data on fish consumption and consumers' perceived knowledge about fresh fish that may influence their purchasing decision in the fishermen market. To understand the usage of social media in promoting the fishermen market, Section D and Section E covered the type of content sharing in social media and credibility of information in social media, respectively, as variables that may influence consumers' purchasing decision in the fishermen market.

After the questionnaire was constructed, it was then pre-tested, checked and rectified to ensure that the items will help the researcher answer the research questions and achieve the research objectives.

3.2   Participants and Data Analysis

Questionnaires were distributed to 235 Malaysian consumers who are regular eaters of fish, live in urban areas and are social media users. The sample is relatively homogenous in terms of its demographics, and thus has high internal validity. This study undertakes convenience sampling, which is based on the availability of respondents for the study. A computer program for statistical analysis, Statistical Package for Social Sciences (SPSS) Version 20 was used to process data collected from the questionnaires. Using this software, descriptive analysis, reliability and validity testing, and Pearson Correlation analysis were conducted.

4   Findings

This section will present the results of the data analysis as well as discussions following those results.

4.1   Demographic Analysis

Of the 235 respondents, 131 (56.0 %) are female whereas 104 (44.0 %) are male. Most respondents, namely 133 (56.6 %), are in the range of 30–42 years old, while only 12 (5.1 %) were in the range of 18–23 years old. The remaining 90 respondents (38.3 %) were between 23–30 years of age. The respondent age range measured in this study was determined at a maximum of 42 years old under the assumption that this range has the highest purchasing power. Apart from that, the younger generation, between the ages of 18 and 23, is less motivated to participate in this survey. Thus, the response of this survey is primarily from those aged 24 and above. This is because most of them have their own families and have decision-making power in terms of purchasing food items. Most respondents (170, or 72.0 %) in this study are married, while there are 60 (26.0 %) single respondents and 5 (2.0 %) widowed respondents. In terms of occupation status, 191 (81.3 %) respondents are full time workers, whereas 26 (11.1 %) are students.

Self-employed respondents comprise 10 (4.3 %), followed by 7 (3.0 %) part-time workers and 1 (0.4 %) retiree. These numbers indicate that most of the participants in the survey are people who are currently working and have purchasing power.

4.2 Social Media: An Alternative to Communicate Information

The dominant Social Media communication devices used by the respondents to search for online information were identified. The data shows that a majority of 192 (81.7 %) respondents prefer to use their Smart Phones to gain online information, whereas only 17 (7.2 %) of respondents prefer to use their PC/Desktops. Meanwhile, other devices such as tablets are dominantly used by 12 (5.1 %) respondents, while Laptops are used by 9 (3.8 %) respondents and iPads are only dominantly used by 5 (2.1 %) respondents. The results indicate that respondents feel more at ease searching for online information through smart phones compared to other devices. This trend is an opportunity for marketers to disseminate information to target consumers on a 24–7 basis.

Additionally, the dominant Social Media networks used by the respondents were also investigated. The data shows that 113 (48.1 %) respondents use Facebook as a dominant social media network, while Google+ is a close second with 94 (40.0 %) respondents. Other social media networks show lesser value to consumers, as less than 10 respondents prefer to use these networks. For example, Email is preferred by 8 (3.4 %) respondents, followed by Instagram being preferred by 7 (3.0 %) respondents and YouTube being preferred by 6 (2.6 %) respondents only. The least preferred social media network is Twitter, which recorded only one (0.4 %) respondent who dominantly used the application. Thus, Facebook is at the top of the popularity list for respondents to seek online information. Therefore, FDAM should consider developing their digital marketing strategy by creating new FDAM Facebook pages. This Facebook page is to disseminate information to Malaysian consumers, especially information about the fishermen market.

Table 1 below shows five (5) statements that measure the type of content sharing in Social Media. All five (5) statements are viewed as important, as they have mean scores that are greater than 3.00. With a sample of 235, the highest mean score is 4.03, while the second highest is 3.48. Based on these scores, it can be surmised that most respondents agree that content on criteria to determine the freshness of fish should be shared in social networks. A recent study by [9] has classified product information cues into two categories, intrinsic or extrinsic. Intrinsic cues are those inherent in the product, such as taste, smell or colour, while extrinsic cues include any external features, such as price, brand or packaging. Both information cues are perceived as important knowledge about fish [9]. Thus, freshness is one example of an intrinsic cue to consumers. This cue is important because it helps the consumer choose fish that offer value for money. Usually, people learn this cue through experiences of consuming many different types of fish over the course of their lives.

Therefore, content sharing on how to measure freshness is important in this subject matter. Neti [15] and Golden [21] describe that content sharing includes media such as internet forums, message boards, weblogs, wikis, podcasts, pictures, and videos.

Table 1. Type of content sharing in social media

Statements	N	Mean	Std deviation
I need to look at the customer reviews, testimonials and recommendations to motivate me prior buying fresh fish at the fishermen market	235	3.43	0.982
I need to view at the pictures to see the ambience to motivate me prior buying fresh fish at the fishermen market	235	3.48	0.975
I need to acquire information on location, landing time and personal contact number to convince me prior to buying fresh fish at the fishermen market	235	3.41	1.019
Information on species and price is not important prior to buying fresh fish at the fishermen market	235	3.09	1.074
Criteria on determining the freshness of fish should be as part of content sharing	235	4.03	0.776
Valid N (listwise)	235		

Providing respondents with more input using these media channels, gives them an opportunity to review comments, seek testimonials and browse through recommendations before they buy fresh fish at the fishermen market.

This affirms the idea of Daft and Lengel [12] that when more information is communicated in the online community, the richer the medium used will be. Consequently, [10] concluded that the richness of media has significant positive impacts on decision quality when consumers have sufficient knowledge about the products/services.

Table 2 below illustrates the credibility of information in social media. All five (5) statements are viewed as important as they have mean scores that are greater than 3.00. The data shows that the highest mean score is 3.78, indicating that respondents will ensure the contents of information sought are reliable, trustworthy and correct before they make any purchasing decision at the fishermen market. This finding is similar to [9] recent study, which stated that consumers have a perception that social media is a more trustworthy source of information. Meanwhile, according to Yoon [16] credibility is closely linked to trust and satisfaction.

Table 3 below shows five (5) statements regarding purchasing decision at the fishermen market. All statements that are viewed as important have a mean score greater than 3.00. The data reports that the highest mean score is 4.13. This shows that most respondents agree that distance and time is the most influential factor for consumers in selecting where to buy fresh products. Therefore, points-of-differentiation (POD) or unique selling points (USP) are necessary as new motivating factors to make consumers feel the worth of buying fresh fish at the fishermen market despite its distance.

Meanwhile, the second highest mean score of 3.85 was recorded by two (2) statements. These statements suggest that consumers with knowledge and interest in browsing attractive online information regarding fish are those who might be interest in visiting fishermen markets. Further, this finding indicates that to be successful in social

Table 2. Credibility of information in social media

Statements	N	Mean	Std deviation
Video sharing about the landing site activities clarify my perception on fishermen market	235	3.64	0.812
I need to ensure that the information sought is relevant and related to my needs prior to buy fish at the fishermen market	235	3.73	0.806
I need to ensure that the contents of information sought are reliable, trustworthy and correct prior to buy fish at the fishermen market	235	3.78	0.802
I need to ensure that the information is unbiased and free from emotion prior to motivation to purchase fish at fishermen market	235	3.70	0.850
I believe that well-presented information reflects the believability of the information	235	3.66	0.813
Valid N (listwise)	235		

Table 3. Purchasing decision in fishermen market

Statements	N	Mean	Std deviation
Knowledgeable consumer on fish products is motivated to seek information on fishermen market	235	3.85	0.721
I feel that information in social media generating exposure to fishermen market and attract people to buy fish	235	3.85	0.767
Distance and time is the most influence factor to buy fresh and quality products	235	4.13	0.748
I do not feel confident that information search in social media will improve purchasing decision in fishermen market	235	3.16	1.105
I will recommend others to search for information on fishermen market to assist them in making purchasing decision	235	3.79	0.732
Valid N (listwise)	235		

media marketing, marketers must be able to handle two-way communication between consumers and their brand. Marketers must respond quickly to increase the credibility of their information, as that information will determine the consumers' decision to visit fishermen markets.

4.3   Testing the Pearson Correlation Between the Variables

To investigate whether the three independent (3) variables used in this study are correlated to the dependent variable, Pearson analysis was conducted to assess the relationship between perceived knowledge about fish, type of content sharing, credibility of information and purchasing decision at the fishermen market. The hypotheses to be tested using the Pearson correlation analysis are as follows:

H1: There is a positive relationship between the perceived knowledge about fish and purchasing decision in the fishermen market.

H2: There is a positive relationship between the type of content sharing in social media and purchasing decision in the fishermen market.

H3: There is a positive relationship between the credibility of information in social media and purchasing decision in the fishermen market.

Figure 2 represents the results of the Pearson correlation analysis in detail. The analysis shows that for H1, the correlation coefficient r = .084, N = 235 and the significance level at 5 %, p = .201. Thus, there was a positive but weak correlation between perceived knowledge about fish and purchasing decision. However, the p-value = .201 is more than the acceptable value of .05. Therefore, H1 is statistically not significant. There is no significant relationship between perceived knowledge about fish and purchasing decision at the fishermen market and H2 is rejected.

Meanwhile, the data shows that the correlation between the type of content sharing in social media and purchasing decision at the fishermen market is significant at 0.000 (p < .05). There is a positive correlation between the two variables, as r = .527. Therefore, there is a strong positive relationship between the type of content sharing in social media and purchasing decision at the fishermen market. Thus, this analysis supports the H2, so it can be deduced that the type of content sharing in social media will influence the purchasing decision at the fishermen market.

There is also a strong positive correlation between the credibility of information in social media and purchasing decision at the fishermen market, where r = .600, N = 235 and p-value = .000. Since the p-value is less than .05, it can be concluded that there is a statistically significant correlation between those two variables. Hence, H3 is supported. As mentioned by [14] credibility of information is defined as how consumers view the information as a source of knowledge which is trustworthy, objective, and relevant to the consumers as intrinsic and extrinsic types of information. Based on this finding, this study suggests that consumers who believe that the information they seek

Variables	Coefficient, r	Scale of Effect Statistics Correlation Coefficient (Hopkins,2002)	Correlation Direction (Positive +ve or Negative _ve)	Significance level, p	
Perceived knowledge about fish (CPK)	0.084	Small	Positive (+ve)	Yes, CPK and EPD are positively correlated	Reject H1
Type of content sharing in social media (DSM)	.527**	Large	Positive (+ve)	Yes, DSM and EPD are positively correlated	Accept H2
Credibility of information in social media (DCI)	.600**	Large	Positive (+ve)	Yes, DCI and EPD are positively correlated	Accept H3

Fig. 2. Summary results of Pearson correlation analysis based on the relationship between independent and dependent variables.

is reliable, unbiased, and believable will be reaffirmed to make their purchasing decisions.

The results of this study also show that two independent variables, type of content sharing in social media and credibility of information, (DSM and DCI) have the strongest and most significant positive correlations with purchasing decisions of the respondents. This shows that the credibility of information and type of content sharing in social media are the most important elements that need to be paid particular attention to in influencing the consumers' purchasing decision at the fishermen markets.

However, the variable 'perceived knowledge about fish' was found to have a small and non-significant correlation to purchasing decision at the fishermen market. Thus, this variable is a weak predictor of purchasing decision on fresh fish at this market. In conclusion, the most significant variables with the highest correlations are as follows: credibility of information in social media (DCI) and type of content sharing in social media (DSM). Thus, the two hypotheses tested are accepted. However, the variable perceived knowledge about fish (CPK) is not statistically significant. Thus, the hypothesis is rejected.

5 Discussion

The results of this study are consistent with Stoke [20], who asserted that customer reviews, testimonials and recommendations posted in social media open a huge opportunity for marketers to create intention to buy. In the context of this study, consumers may share information about the fresh fish or fishermen markets if they are provided with social media platforms that are reliable and trustworthy. According to Golden, social media needs to be transparent and honest [21] to ensure that the messages and information are credible and reliable to the online community. Marketers need to monitor and respond to the reviews, testimonials, or recommendations of consumers as quickly as possible, perhaps using a 3-h rule of thumb as a good social media response rate. Hence, two-way communication will increase consumer awareness and promote the exchange of ideas and perceptions. When marketers, especially in the fishery industry, decide to use social media as a promotion tool, they need to stimulate consumers by enhancing their content strategy in marketing. A study by Drury [22] also supports this view of marketing as no longer one-dimensional; instead, it is now a two-way process engaging a brand and an audience. By implementing the usage of social media, businesses are not just limited to giving messages, but also benefit from receiving and exchanging perceptions and ideas [22]. This proves that consumers may rate the content of social media in evaluating the credibility of information to help them in the decision-making process.

6 Conclusion

The explosion of mobile Internet connectivity and social media has given the Malaysian fishing industry wider access to new marketing tools to reduce the dependency on intermediaries. Social media is a vital tool to promote, educate, and create awareness among consumers about the new fishermen markets. This study posits that to make the initiative a successful one, FDAM must adhere to information credibility, frequency of information updates, and sharing of informative articles in their social media channel. A high level of product awareness may influence consumers' purchasing behaviour, and thus could lead them to the fishermen market -no matter how remote the location is.

References

1. Haque, M.A.: Fish-market chain and fishres' income in Sherpur district, Bangladesh (2010). Accessed 10 Sept 2014
2. Pieniak, Z., Verbeke, W., Scholderer, J., Brunsø, K., Olsen, S.O.: European consumers' use of and trust in information sources about fish. Food Qual. Prefer. **18**(8), 1050–1063 (2007)
3. Tidwell, P.S., Sadowski, C.J., Pate, L.M.: Relationships between need for cognition, knowledge, and verbal ability. J. Psychol. **134**(6), 634–644 (2000)
4. Cacioppo, J.T., Petty, R.E.: The need for cognition. J. Pers. Soc. Psychol. **42**(1), 116–131 (1982)
5. Saeed, N., Yang, Y., Sinnappan, S.: Media richness and user acceptance of Second Life. In: Proceedings of Ascilite (2008)
6. Aurier, P., Ngobo, P.: Assessment of consumer knowledge and its consequences: a multi-component approach. Adv. Consum. Res. **26**, 569–575 (1999)
7. Olson, J.C., Jacoby, J.: Cue utilization in the quality perception process. In: Proceedings of the Third Annual Conference of the Association for Consumer Research, pp. 167–179 (1972)
8. Gaviglio, A., Demartini, E., Mauracher, C., Pirani, A.: Consumer perception of different species and presentation forms of fish: an empirical analysis in Italy. Food Qual. Prefer. **36**, 33–49 (2014)
9. Mangold, W.G., Faulds, D.J.: Social media: the new hybrid element of the promotion mix. Bus. Horiz. **52**(4), 357–365 (2009)
10. Kahai, S., Cooper, R.: Exploring the core concepts of media richness theory: the impact of cue multiplicity and feedback immediacy on decision quality. J. Manage. Inf. Syst. URL http://portal.acm.org/citation.cfm?id=1289809
11. Verbeke, W., Vermeir, I., Brunsø, K.: Consumer evaluation of fish quality as basis for fish market segmentation. J. Food Qual. Prefer. **18**, 651–661 (2007)
12. Daft, R.L., Lengel, R.H.: Organizational information requirements, media richness and structural design. J. Manage. Sci. **32**(5), 554–571 (1986)
13. Kautsar et al. (2012)
14. Negara, V.A.,: Pengaruh kredibilitas perusahaan dan kredibilitas endoser pada sikap terhadap iklan, sikap terhadap merek, dan intensi membeli (2004)
15. Neti, S.: Social media and its role in marketing. Int. J. Enterp. Comput. Bus. Syst. **1**(2), 1–15 (2011)
16. Yoon, S.J.: The antecedents and consequences of trust in online-purchase decisions. J. Interact. Market. **16**(2), 47–63 (2002)
17. Abraham, R.: Mobile phones and economic development: evidence from the fishing industry in India. In: Information and communication technologies and development, 2006, ICTD'06, pp. 48–56. IEEE, May 2006

18. Burger, J., Gochfeld, M., Batang, Z., Alikunhi, N., Al-Jahdali, R., Al-Jebreen, D., Aziz, M.A.M., Al-Suwailem, A.: Fish consumption behavior and rates in native and non-native people in Saudi Arabia. J. Environ. Res. **133**, 141–148 (2014)
19. Batzios, C., Moutopoulos, D.K., Arampatzis, G., Siardos, G.: Understanding consumer's attitude on fish quality and marketing aspects in the Greek market. Agric. Econ. Rev. 6(1), 18 (2005)
20. Stokes, R.: EMarketing: The Essential Guide to Marketing in a Digital World, 5th edn. Quirk eMarketing, Cape Town (2013)
21. Golden, M.: Social Media Strategies for Professionals and Their Firms: The Guide to Establishing Credibility and Accelerating Relationships. Wiley, Hoboken (2011)
22. Drury, G.: Opinion piece: social media: should marketers engage and how can it be done effectively? J. Dir. Data Digit. Market. Pract. **9**(3), 274–277 (2008)

The Design of IdeaWorks: Applying Social Learning Networks to Support Tertiary Education

Lele Kang[1], Shaokun Fan[2(✉)], and J. Leon Zhao[1]

[1] Department of Information Systems, City University of Hong Kong,
Kowloon Tong, Hong Kong, China
Lele.Kang@my.cityu.edu.hk, jlzhao@cityu.edu.hk
[2] College of Business, West Texas A&M University, Texas, USA
sfan@wtamu.edu

Abstract. Online education has progressed from having students passively read and watch materials to having them proactively engage in interactions with other students and teachers. Social network technologies enable students to interact with each other, leading to a new platform for online education. Based on the social learning theory, we design a new social learning network system, named IdeaWorks. Two empirical studies, a usability study and an impact study, were conducted to examine how the social learning network system (i.e., IdeaWorks) has an impact on students' learning activities. The results of the usability study show that IdeaWorks' design performs well on user interface, functionality, and process. Generally, users have a high level of usage intention towards Idea-Works. The results of the impact study show that learning via IdeaWorks, as well as learning in traditional classrooms, enables users to perceive a high level of social presence, cognitive presence, satisfaction with the course, and satisfaction with the group. However, the impact study also showed that we should enhance IdeaWorks to support instructional communication and group communication in the context of online education.

Keywords: IdeaWorks · Social learning networks · Online education · E-learning

1 Introduction

The advance of information technologies has lead to new education systems that extend traditional classroom teaching. The concept of blended learning describes courses in which the learning activities take place partly in the classroom and partly on the internet. Studies of blended learning explore how to maximize the advantages of both face-to-face learning and electronic learning by combining various learning delivery methods (Alonso et al. 2005; Osguthorpe and Graham 2003; So and Brush 2008). Though these studies discuss the advantages and disadvantages of blended learning, we still have little knowledge about how learning activities are influenced by the social networks that are becoming more and more popular. Powered by Web 2.0 technologies, social networking is penetrating all sectors of society, including tertiary education,

© Springer International Publishing Switzerland 2015
F.F.-H. Nah and C.-H. Tan (Eds.): HCIB 2015, LNCS 9191, pp. 118–129, 2015.
DOI: 10.1007/978-3-319-20895-4_12

to transform the way that we connect and communicate, leading to unprecedented changes in the way social ties are formed and understood (Park et al. 2014). A social learning network is defined as the online social network platform that supports university learning by connecting students and instructors beyond class-centric activities. As social network sites such as Facebook and Twitter are becoming increasingly popular among learners, the social learning platform will enable connections with other social networks to achieve a broader impact. Guided by pioneering thinking in educational theories, this research strives to investigate and demonstrate how social learning networks (SLN) can be incorporated into tertiary education with the end goal of enhancing students' learning performance.

In order to achieve this goal, we develop a SLN platform, called IdeaWorks, to support learning activities in the online environment. Blended learning, social learning theory, and innovation-centered learning are used to support the design of IdeaWorks. IdeaWorks is built on Web 2.0 technologies, particularly social networking and instructional techniques. This platform implements the "learning through socialization" approach among the partner universities to facilitate courses that require individual and group projects. Three groups of essential features of social learning networks are developed in this platform. First, the system provides exploration functions for the users to find students/advisors and build their social learning networks; explore projects/groups and join projects/groups of interest; and search for relevant events. Second, collaborative learning management functions are also offered by IdeaWorks to help users store important information (e.g., ideas), develop and conduct group projects; and manage social networks with their friends, team/project members and advisors. Third, additional collaboration tools such as Skype and GoogleDocs are also integrated into the system. Figure 1 shows the interface of IdeaWorks.

Two empirical studies were conducted to evaluate IdeaWorks. A usability study was conducted to evaluate the usefulness and ease of use of the system from the perspective of the system users. Undergraduate students, who are the potential users of the system, were invited to participate in the study to experience the system and give their feedback on its usability. We find that the major feature of IdeaWorks (i.e., conveniently explore and extend social networks for learning) is recognized by users. An impact study was conducted to compare the learning outcomes of using IdeaWorks and learning outcomes via face-to-face teaching. A foreign language (i.e., English) learning program was organized for experiment participants, who were randomly assigned into two study groups. While the experimental group had online sessions using IdeaWorks, the control group had face-to-face classroom sessions. By comparing students' perceptions under two different environments, we found that there is no significant difference in students' perceptions of social presence, cognitive presence, satisfaction with the course, and satisfaction with the group. However, the analysis results show that instructional communication and group communication are better supported by classroom teaching.

The objective of this study is to contribute to previous research and to provide useful guidance to education practitioners on how to facilitate students' learning activities via social learning networks. This IdeaWorks research makes two significant contributions that we believe are worth highlighting. The first important contribution of our research is our designed social learning network platform - IdeaWorks. Though

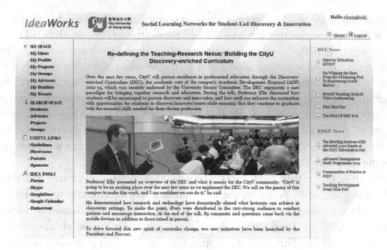

Fig. 1. An illustration of the social learning network platform – IdeaWorks

scholars and practitioners have noticed the value of social networks for education, there is little research on designing a social learning network platform to support students' learning activities. In this research, social connection functions, collaborative management functions, and additional collaborative tools are integrated to assist social-oriented learning. The usability study shows that students are satisfied with the functionality and interface design of IdeaWorks. Second, the impact study shows that IdeaWorks can effectively support students' learning activities as well as classroom learning. Our empirical study shows that students' perceptions of social presence, cognitive presence, satisfaction with the course, and satisfaction with the learning group have no significant difference under the two different contexts, namely learn in classroom and learn through IdeaWorks. Such findings contribute to current literature of e-learning by demonstrating that facilitating social connections via SLNs also enables students to perceive social presence and cognitive presence in the learning process. Additionally, students' are still satisfied with the course and learning groups after they move from the classroom to IdeaWorks.

2 Theoretical Foundation

Social learning networks are designed based on several key domains that are particularly relevant to the requirements of students and instructors: blended learning, social learning theory, and innovation-centered learning. Blended learning, which combines online technologies with traditional face-to-face teaching methods, has emerged as an alternative mode of traditional classroom teaching. Social learning theory emphasizes social interactions among people in the teaching and learning process. Innovation-centered teaching cultivates creativity, motivation, and knowledge among students in their learning processes.

2.1 Blended Learning

As the "third generation" of distance education systems, blended learning maximizes the best advantages of face-to-face learning and multiple technologies to deliver learning. It is particularly suitable to the process of transforming from traditional forms of learning and teaching towards e-learning (Hoic-Bozic et al. 2009). It combines many different learning delivery methods, such as face-to-face instruction and electronic learning methods (So and Brush 2008). Blended learning could facilitate learners to have both online and offline interactions with their classmates and teachers. This is effective in encouraging the process of online collaborative learning. So and Brush (2008) found that this collaborative learning could improve student perceptions of satisfaction and social presence in the learning process. The effectiveness of blended learning is confirmed in the research of (Al-Qahtani and Higgins 2013).

Osguthorpe and Graham (2003) suggested that three types of mixing could be identified in blended courses, namely online and face-to-face learning activities, online and face-to-face students, and online and face-to-face instructors. Importantly, they also identified six goals which are expected in the blended environments: (1) pedagogical richness, (2) access to knowledge (3) social interaction (4) personal agency (5) cost effectiveness and (6) ease of revision. For instance, Hoic-Bozic et al. (2009) developed a learning management system (LMS) to make a mixture of different learning activities, including collaborative learning, problem-based learning and independent learning. Their evaluation results show that students were satisfied with the pedagogical approach, and had a better academic performance. Schnurr et al. (2013) also integrates three education delivery methods-preparatory learning, face-to-face learning, and online collaborative learning-to simulate negotiation.

2.2 Social Learning Theory

Bandura's (1977) Social Learning Theory proposed that people learn from others via observation, imitation, and modeling. The theory emphasizes the importance of observing and modeling the behaviors, attitudes, and emotional reactions of each other. *"Most human behavior is learned observationally through modeling: from observing others, one forms an idea of how new behaviors are performed, and on later occasions this coded information serves as a guide for action"* (Bandura and McClelland 1977). An important point of this theory is that learning occurs in a social context, which is a weakness of our current online systems design.

There are three major arguments in his social learning theory. (1) Observation learning includes live model, verbal instructional model, and symbolic model. Live model is when an actual person demonstrates a behavior; verbal instruction is when an individual describes and explains a behavior; symbolic model is when a real or fictional character demonstrates the behavior through media, such as television and internet. (2) Intrinsic reinforcement, as well as environmental and external reinforcement, influence learning behavior. (3) Four steps are involved in the modeling process. First, attention should be paid to observational learning. Second, retention (i.e., the ability to remember) is necessary to reproduce the behavior. Third, reproduction makes people improve their learned behavior with practice. Fourth, individuals have to be motivated to imitate the behavior which has been modeled. There are many studies and guidelines on the learning process. We are interested in how this concept supports blended learning in our IdeaWorks design.

In the blended learning context, Wu and Hwang (2010) found that intrinsic reinforcement (e.g., learning attitude) influences the effectiveness of e-learning for blended courses. Hill et al. (2009) further analyzed different social learning perspectives and discussed how they could be adopted in the design and implementation of e-learning. Three general directions are proposed for future research and practice: (1) examine students' personal characteristics through e-learning; (2) identify strategies for encouraging social interaction in e-learning systems; (3) develop effective design principles for e-learning. In addition, Vassileva (2008) identified that the new learning technologies should perform three main roles to support social learning: (1) enable the learners to find the appropriate content; (2) support them to connect with the right people; (3) motive individuals to learn.

Based on a blended and eclectic view of different learning theories, Alonso et al. (2005) designed e-learning mechanisms following different approaches: (1) look at the content structure; (2) focus on the cognitive process of understanding how the mind works during the learning process and what factors determine and condition the success of the process; (3) understand that human learning is constructed not only by interacting with the content but also by working together with colleagues and instructors.

2.3 Innovation-Centered Learning

The goal of innovation-centered learning is to improve learners' innovation ability through a series of methods. Numerous training programs were developed to improve learners' innovation ability in the last half century. Scott et al. (2004) conducted a meta-analysis of the program evaluation efforts and found that more successful programs were likely to emphasize development of cognitive skills and the heuristics involved in skill application, using realistic exercises appropriate to the domain at hand. Three components are the sources of innovation, namely knowledge, creative thinking, and motivation (Adams 2005). (1) Knowledge is all the relevant understanding an individual brings to bear on a creative effort; (2) creative thinking relates to how people approach problems and depends on personality and thinking/working style; and (3) motivation is generally accepted as key to creative production, and the most important motivators are intrinsic passion and interest in the work itself. Innovation-centered learning tries to improve these three components of the individual learning process.

Innovation is not so much an individual trait but rather a social phenomenon involving interactions among people within their specific group or cultural settings (DeHaan 2009). For instance, brainstorming methods are used to improve group innovation. Groups of interacting individuals were better at solving complex, multipart problems than single individuals. Many scholars acknowledge that creative discoveries in the real world, such as solving the problems of cutting-edge science—which are usually complex and multipart—are influenced or even stimulated by social interaction among experts. By integrating social learning theory, six techniques are suggested to improve student innovation in the classroom: model creativity, cross-fertilize ideas, repeatedly encourage idea generation, build self-efficacy, constantly question assumptions, and imagine other viewpoints. Clements (1991) investigated the effects of information technology usage on creativity improvement. The results showed that computer-based training could improve learner innovation. This is also confirmed by Benedek et al. (2006).

3 Design of IdeaWorks

IdeaWorks is a web-based collaborative group learning system which aims to facilitate discovery-enriched teaching and learning by using social network functions. The system is designed for users to conveniently explore and extend their social networks for learning; efficiently manage their ideas, interest groups, projects, and events; facilitate group learning efficiency; and support innovative thinking.

Key functions in IdeaWorks can be found in MY SPACE and SEARCH SPACE, which help students manage and explore their resources. Under MY SPACE, students can store and manage their ideas in My Ideas. My Projects shows a list of projects that a student has joined. Project-related information (introduction, members, milestones, and outcomes) is shown to provide students a platform to interact with other project members and advisors. Students can also initiate new projects and invite other students to join. My Groups shows a list of groups that the student has joined. Students are able to manage their group resources, submit their individual or group assignments, and communicate with group members and teachers under My Groups. They can also manage their social learning networks and events related to their projects or groups in MY SPACE. Under SEARCH SPACE, students can further explore and extend their social learning networks in IdeaWorks by searching for learning buddies and advisors and inviting them to join their social learning networks. Public projects and groups can also be found in SEARCH SPACE. Other functions in USEFUL LINKS and IDEA TOOLS are designed to provide students with important information to facilitate collaborative group learning. For instance, Skype and Google Calendar are embedded in IDEA TOOLS to encourage student interaction. We conducted usability and impact studies to evaluate IdeaWorks.

4 IdeaWorks Usability Study

The goal of the IdeaWorks usability study is to invite users to evaluate the usefulness and ease of use of this system. Eight first and second year students from four departments at one university were invited to participate in the study. We believe that students with different backgrounds can better evaluate the usability of the system, since they will complete multi-disciplinary tasks to highlight the collaborative feature of the system.

The usability study is comprised of two stages: online tutorial and offline tasks. During the online tutorial, which takes one hour, students are gathered in a lab to learn how to use the IdeaWorks system. We assign small tasks for them to complete. Before each task, we teach them relevant functions and basic operations of the system. After finishing each task, they are required to complete a portion of the questionnaire based on their experiences on the system. The questionnaire is designed to test three aspects of the system: user interface, functionality, and process (Chin et al. 1988; Lewis 1995). The first two aspects (i.e., user interface and functionality) are evaluated in the lab, while the system process is tested offline. Seven-point scales are used to measure the usability, with 7 indicating the greatest user satisfaction (Fig. 2).

First students were asked to register and browse the system, which gave them a general understanding and some user experience on the system. They then gave feedback (i.e., give scores) on the relevant user interface questions on the question-naire. These questions ask for users' overall reaction to IdeaWorks, followed by questions on screen, terminology and system information, learning, and system capa-bilities. Then, the students explored each key function of IdeaWorks (i.e., functions under My SPACE, Search SPACE, Useful Links, and Basic Tools) and completed the functionality relevant questions in the questionnaire. Functionality relevant questions are designed to evaluate user satisfaction with the system functions. Usefulness, ease of use, and reliability are the key criteria for user satisfaction (Segars and Grover 1993). Students completed the assigned tasks successfully in the lab.

At the end of the lab experience, we assigned an offline task for the students that simulated the group forming and group project development process. This is a common process for university students. We expect that experiencing this process will increase students' understanding of the usability of the IdeaWorks system. Each student was required to create an interest group, search other interest groups, join interest groups after communication with these interest group members through the forum, discuss ideas with group members via a message board that is only visible to members, and

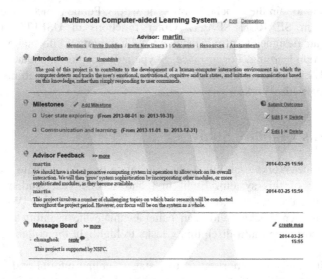

Fig. 2. Project Module in IdeaWorks

develop projects based on the ideas. Using IdeaWorks, students successfully created interest groups and developed projects through cooperation. Questions on the system process were answered after they finished the task. Process relevant questions ask about user experience regarding smoothness, consistency, and ease of use. Overall assessment of IdeaWorks and usage intention are also included in the questionnaire. In addition to the Likert questions, there's also an open question on the advantages and disadvantages of the system.

Table 1 summarizes the results of the Likert questions. As suggested in the table, mean values of all dimensions are above average (i.e., 3.5 points), which suggests a satisfying result on the prototype system in general. Based on the average values of the constructs, we conclude that the users are satisfied with the user interface design and the functionality of our system. System capabilities and the functionality of search space achieved notably high scores (i.e., 5.94 and 5.38 respectively). The results also demonstrate that the functionality is recognized by the users. Generally, the users agree that MY SPACE AND SEARCH SPACE are convenient for them to use. The results for the open question were similar. From the perspective of users, advantages of the system include *"easy to contact buddies," "easy to find projects done by others for reference," "encourage innovative ideas," "user-friendly,"* and *"easy to find friends with similar interests."*

Compared with user interface, functionality, and overall assessment, the scores of process relevant questions are not high, indicating the ease of use of IdeaWorks could be further improved to meet user requirements. Feedback from the open question on the disadvantages of the system also shows that the convenience of using the system is questioned. Some users also feel that the system is dull and not attractive enough. This user feedback helps us identify needed improvements. In the following, we summarize the areas of improvement for IdeaWorks based on user feedback from the usability study. (1) Improve system robustness by consummating basic functions (e.g., enhancing core features and fixing bugs). (2) Simplify and smooth the operation process to improve the ease of use of the system. (3) Add more attractive features to make the system more fascinating. (4) Enhance the security of the system through advanced access control mechanism (e.g., multilevel privacy control), data protection, and communication security maintenance.

To summarize, we achieved a satisfying result from the usability study. The undergraduate student participants recognized the core features of the system and found the social network expansion useful for learning, group collaborative learning, and innovative idea generation. However, the system still needs improvements on robustness, ease of use, attractiveness, and security to achieve higher user satisfaction.

5 IdeaWorks Impact Study

The impact study is intended to evaluate how IdeaWorks influences students' learning process. We propose that learning in IdeaWorks is as useful as learning through classroom-centric courses. The education research shows that perception of presence, communication, and satisfaction are important for students' learning activities. The experiment is designed to compare students' perceptions in the context of IdeaWorks and traditional classrooms.

Table 1. Measurement items

Construct	Item	
Social presence (SP)	SP1	I formed distinct impressions of some students
	SP2	I felt comfortable participating in course discussions
	SP3	I felt comfortable interacting with other students
	SP4	I felt comfortable with other students while still maintaining a sense of trust
	SP5	I felt my point of view was acknowledged by other students
Cognitive presence (CP)	CP1	Problems posed increased my interest in course issues
	CP2	Course activities piqued my curiosity
	CP3	I felt motivated to explore content related questions
	CP4	I utilized information sources to explore problems
	CP5	Brainstorming and finding relevant information helped me resolve content related questions
	CP6	Discussions were valuable in helping me appreciate various perspectives
	CP7	Combining new information helped me answer questions in course activities
	CP8	Learning activities helped me construct explanations/solutions
Instructional communication (IC)	IC1	I can easily ask questions and get answers
	IC2	I freely discussed with instructor
	IC3	The instructor provided answers to my questions
	IC4	I can understand the focus of the content
	IC5	I can frankly tell my thoughts to the instructor
	IC6	Q&A with instructor about learning content helped me
	IC7	I can understand the content of the class
Group communication (GC)	GC1	Communication with group members helps me to learn more knowledge
	GC2	Communication with group members enhances my understanding of the knowledge
	GC3	Communication with group members corrects my miss-understanding of teachers' delivered knowledge
	GC4	Generally, communication with group members helps me to learn in this course
Satisfaction with the course (SC)	SC1	I am satisfied with the teaching method in this course
	SC2	I am satisfied with student-to-faculty interaction
Satisfaction with the group (SG)	SG1	I am glad to be part of the group
	SG2	I am satisfied with the learning in this group so far
	SG3	I like to learn with this group
	SG4	I would like to work with this group again in future
	SG5	I am satisfied with the decision of the group

An English learning program was designed for the experiment and divided into two equal sessions. An experienced instructor was invited to teach this course. Thirty-three undergraduate students from the department of information systems were invited to learn business report writing. They were randomly assigned into two different groups

(16/17). Conducting the t-tests of demographics in two groups of students enabled us to determine that the assignment process is appropriate. The 16 students in the first group was taught the first session of the course through traditional classroom learning and the second session via IdeaWorks. The other 17 students learned the first session via IdeaWorks and the second session in a traditional classroom. After each session, the students were required to evaluate the courses on the following constructs: social presence, cognitive presence, instructional communication, group communication, satisfaction with the group, and satisfaction with the course.

Students were asked to respond to a questionnaire based on a 7-point Likert scale (1 = strongly disagree; to 7 = strongly agree) at the end of each session. The validity of the questionnaire was reviewed by a panel of 4 educational technology experts and adopted items were revised based on their comments and recommendations. The questionnaire items are presented in Table 2.

T-tests were conducted to compare students' perceptions under two different environments. The results are shown in Table 3. Our results reveal that there was no

Table 2. IdeaWorks usability study results

Construct	Dimension	Mean	St. D.
User Interface (Mean: 5.25)	Overall reaction to IdeaWorks	5.06	0.34
	Screen	5.38	1.21
	Terminology and system information	4.81	0.95
	Learning	5.05	1.35
	System capabilities	5.94	0.68
Functionality (Mean: 4.82)	MY SPACE	4.66	1.18
	SEARCH SPACE	5.38	0.67
	Useful links and basic tools	4.42	0.94
Process (Mean: 4.13)	Easy to learn	4.20	1.30
	Consistency	4.20	1.48
	Smoothness and efficiency	4.00	1.22
Overall assessment and usage intention (Mean: 4.53)	Usefulness	4.60	1.67
	Satisfaction	4.60	1.14
	Usage intention	4.40	0.89

Table 3. IdeaWorks impact study results

Construct	Learn in classroom	Learn through IdeaWorks	T-value
Social presence	5.70 (0.77)	5.33 (0.94)	1.74
Cognitive presence	5.65 (0.77)	5.32 (1.02)	1.43
Instructional communication	5.90 (0.66)	5.26 (0.94)	3.21
Group communication	5.93 (0.71)	5.17 (1.00)	3.60
Satisfaction with the course	5.74 (0.88)	5.29 (1.02)	1.94
Satisfaction with the group	5.70 (0.91)	5.32 (0.93)	1.68

difference in students' perceptions of social presence, cognitive presence, satisfaction with the course, and satisfaction with the group under the two different environments. Using the social media functions in IdeaWorks, students can perceive a high level of social presence (mean = 5.33) and cognitive presence (mean = 5.32). The analysis results also show that students are satisfied with the course (mean = 5.29) and the group (mean = 5.32) when they learn with IdeaWorks. Unfortunately, the communication support is still limited in IdeaWorks. Students perceive a higher level of instruction communication ($p < 0.01$) and group communication ($p < 0.001$) in the context of a traditional classroom.

6 Conclusions

Building on the social learning theory, we designed a new online education system, called IdeaWorks, to support students' online learning activities. IdeaWorks functions include idea management, project management, and group management, which support learning activities through interaction with students and instructors. The system is evaluated by a usability study and an impact study. The results of the usability study show that students are satisfied with the user interface and functionality of IdeaWorks and would like to use it in their learning activities. Impact study results showed that IdeaWorks could help students achieve a high level of social presence and cognitive presence. Additionally, students are satisfied with the course and group when they learn via IdeaWorks. In the future, IdeaWorks will be further improved to help fulfill students' growing networking needs and, thus, improve their social learning effectiveness.

Acknowledgement. The work was partially supported by a grant from City University of Hong Kong (Project No. 6980108), and a grant from NSFC (Project No. 71471157).

References

Adams, K.: The Sources of Innovation and Creativity, pp. 1–59. National Center on Education and the Economy, Washington (2005)

Alonso, F., López, G., Manrique, D., Viñes, J.M.: An instructional model for web-based e-learning education with a blended learning process approach. Br. J. Educ. Technol. **36**(2), 217–235 (2005)

Al-Qahtani, A.A.Y., Higgins, S.E.: Effects of traditional, blended and e-learning on students' achievement in higher education. J. Comput. Assist. Learn. **29**(3), 220–234 (2013)

Bandura, A., McClelland, D.C.: Social Learning Theory, pp. 217–235. General Learning Press, New York (1977)

Benedek, M., Fink, A., Neubauer, A.C.: Enhancement of ideational fluency by means of computer-based training. Creativity Res. J. **18**(3), 317–328 (2006)

Chin, J.P., Diehl, V.A., Norman, L.K.: Development of an instrument measuring user satisfaction of the human-computer interface. In: Proceedings of the SIGCHI Conference on Human Factors in Computing Systems - CHI 1988, pp. 213–218 (1988)

Clements, D.H.: Enhancement of creativity in computer environments. Am. Educ. Res. J. **28**(1), 173–187 (1991)

DeHaan, R.: Teaching creativity and inventive problem solving in science. CBE-Life Sci. Educ. **8**(3), 172–181 (2009)

Hill, J.R., Song, L., Wang, D.: Social learning theory and web based learning environments: a review of research and discussion of implications. Am. J. Distance Educ. **23**(2), 88–103 (2009)

Hoic-Bozic, N., Mornar, V., Boticki, I.: A blended learning approach to course design and implementation. IEEE Trans. Educ. **52**(1), 19–30 (2009)

Lewis, J.R.: IBM computer usability satisfaction questionnaires: psychometric evaluation and instructions for use. Int. J. Hum. Comput. Interact. **7**(1), 57–78 (1995)

Osguthorpe, R.T., Graham, C.R.: Blended learning environments: definitions and directions. Q. Rev. Dist. Educ. **4**(3), 227–233 (2003)

Park, S.Y., Cha, S.-B., Lim, K., Jung, S.-H.: The relationship between university student learning outcomes and participation in social network services, social acceptance and attitude towards school life. Br. J. Educ. Technol. **45**(1), 97–111 (2014)

Schnurr, M.A., De Santo, E., Craig, R.: Using a blended learning approach to simulate the negotiation of a multilateral environmental agreement. Int. Stud. Perspect. **14**(2), 109–120 (2013)

Scott, G., Leritz, L.E., Mumford, M.D.: The effectiveness of creativity training: a quantitative review. Creativity Res. J. **16**(4), 361–388 (2004)

Segars, A.H., Grover, V.: Re-examining perceived ease of use and usefulness: a confirmatory factor analysis. MIS Q. **17**(4), 517–525 (1993)

So, H.-J., Brush, T.A.: Student perceptions of collaborative learning, social presence and satisfaction in a blended learning environment: relationships and critical factors. Comput. Educ. **51**(1), 318–336 (2008)

Vassileva, J.: Toward social learning environments. IEEE Trans. Learn. Technol. **1**(4), 199–214 (2008)

Wu, W., Hwang, L.: The effectiveness of e-learning for blended courses in colleges: a multi-level empirical study. Int. J. Electron. Manage. **8**(4), 312–322 (2010)

Contribute Knowledge Continuously or Occasionally?

Determining the Continuous Contributors in Opinion-Sharing Communities

Yi-Cheng Ku[1]([⊠]), Chih-Hung Peng[2], Chih-Ping Wei[3], and Yin-An Chen[3]

[1] Providence University, Taichung, Taiwan
ycku@pu.edu.tw
[2] City University of Hong Kong, Kowloon Tong
Hong Kong, People's Republic of China
chpeng@cityu.edu.hk
[3] National Taiwan University, Taipei, Taiwan
cpwei@ntu.edu.tw

Abstract. This study focuses on continued knowledge contribution. We hypothesize that continued knowledge contribution of members in opinion-sharing communities is influenced by five factors: the number of reviews written, the average of helpfulness scores received from other members, the average of helpfulness scores given to other members, the ratio of the number of negative reviews to the total number of reviews, and the number of trustors. We collect data from Epinions.com and find that these five factors have significant impacts on continued knowledge contribution. These findings have significant theoretical and practical implications for knowledge sharing.

Keywords: Knowledge contribution · Knowledge contributor · Online community · Trust network

1 Introduction

Knowledge is power. People leverage knowledge to solve problems and make decisions. Because of the Internet, people can rely on online communities to find out knowledge needed and solve problems, such as evaluating products and learning domain knowledge. Substantial studies and reports have offered evidences supporting the idea that electronic word-of-mouth (eWOM) has a significant impact on consumers' purchase decisions and their perception of product value [21, 35]. For instance, eMarketer has found that 61 % of consumers read online reviews and other kinds of online customer feedbacks before their purchasing [11]. On the other hand, a nationwide survey conducted in 2012 by the Pew Internet & American Life Project found that 72 % of U.S. adults who use the Internet have searched online for health information in the past year [16]. Hence, online knowledge has been an important reference for consumers when they are making decisions.

© Springer International Publishing Switzerland 2015
F.F.-H. Nah and C.-H. Tan (Eds.): HCIB 2015, LNCS 9191, pp. 130–141, 2015.
DOI: 10.1007/978-3-319-20895-4_13

The purpose of opinion-sharing communities is to facilitate knowledge sharing. However, researchers argued that the creation of an online social platform does not guarantee that knowledge exchange will actually take place [10]. These scholars suggested that the success of an online community depends on whether members use the online community persistently and contribute their knowledge to the online community continuously [10, 23, 26]. Specifically, because knowledge shared in an online community is generally public goods, its members can easily free-ride on the efforts of other contributors [33]. Therefore, it is a critical challenge for practitioners and scholars to understand how to facilitate social interaction and encourage knowledge contribution in opinion-sharing communities [29]. Despite a significant growth in the number of opinion-sharing communities, recent studies show that limited online communities are successful in terms of retaining their members and motivating future contributions of knowledge [14]. Joyce and Kraut [24] described that the high turnover rate in online communities is because most newcomers (56 %) only contributes their knowledge once in their online community. It implies that the most members who did initial knowledge contribution in an online community will not contribute knowledge continuously. Thus, how to encourage members to contribute and update current knowledge within online communities is one of the biggest challenges [18], which justifies the importance of investigating continued knowledge contribution in online communities.

Cheung et al. [12] summarized 35 studies related to knowledge-sharing behavior in online communities to explore the factors influencing knowledge contribution. They found that 29 out of 35 studies collected data by survey, 3 studies adopted case study, and the rest adopted an interview study or mixed method. The findings of these recent studies have important implications for both research and practice. However, most of these studies investigated sample members' opinions directly. These empirical surveys suffer from some limitations. Since a survey measures respondent's psychological status and subjective intentions rather than actual continuation, the results of the studies might not be sufficiently representative of the actual knowledge contribution behaviors. Although behavior intention is an appropriate proxy to understand the beliefs and actual knowledge contribution behavior, we argue that it will be more robust to measure the actual behavior than behavior intention in order to understand the consumers' knowledge contribution behaviors. Furthermore, most of the previous studies adopted a belief-based view to understand how continued knowledge contribution is associated with a variety of individual users' beliefs [19]. However, it's almost impossible for a practical website to ask all members' beliefs to predict their intention to share knowledge continuously.

To address these limitations of the previous research, we determine the continued knowledge contributors in opinion-sharing communities based on users' profiles and actual behaviors. We propose a prediction model to discriminate the continued knowledge contributors from the others. Since a practical website can record all users' profiles and usage behaviors, our method is more applicable to practitioners to predict whether a member will continue sharing knowledge in an online community or not. We collected archival data and examine our research model from Epinions.com. Epinions. com is a third-party product review website which facilitates the exchange of consumer reviews about a variety of products. Our findings reveal that a continued knowledge contributor could be predicted by her/his profiles and online behaviors, i.e., number of reviews, average helpfulness score received, average helpfulness score given to other members, number of trustors, and ratio of negative reviews.

The remainder of this study is arranged as follows. Prior works on knowledge contribution are reviewed in Sect. 2. We describe the hypotheses and research method in Sect. 3. The findings are discussed in Sect. 4. Finally, some research and practical implications are discussed in Sect. 5.

2 Literature Review

Knowledge contribution has been investigated at different levels. Some studies investigated knowledge contribution behaviors from the perspective of institutional-level [2, 17]. Since our study investigates how individuals contribute their knowledge into their online community, we focus on summarizing the findings of the knowledge contribution at the individual level in this section.

2.1 The Value of Continued Knowledge Contribution

Because an online community usually involves a large number of participants with different social backgrounds and perspectives, it is more difficult to establish mutual understanding and share valuable information in an online community than traditional face-to-face communication group [14]. In particular, knowledge in online communities is public goods [7]. Many people read or use knowledge accessible in an online community without contributing to the community. Hence, how to enhance knowledge contribution in an online community is an important research topic. Although knowledge sharing includes knowledge seeking as well as knowledge contribution [8, 25], some previous studies used "*knowledge sharing*" to denote the knowledge contribution behavior [12, 26, 32]. Following the prior studies, we focus on knowledge contribution instead of knowledge seeking because rich knowledge capital drives knowledge seeking and enhances the value of the online community. Therefore this study reviews the previous studies which focused on knowledge contribution behaviors.

Knowledge contribution occurs in an online community when individuals contribute useful, valuable, and practice-related knowledge that can be accessed and reused by other individuals [19, 33]. Knowledge contribution accumulates knowledge and, in turn, makes value (even revenue) for an online community. For example, Kim et al. [26] indicated that "*knowledge contribution is one of the essential factors behind the success of blogging communities* (p. 1760)". Travel information sharing website— Tripadvisor, an practical example, successfully capitalizes on its traveler forum, which has accumulated more than 150 million reviews and opinions covering more than 3.7 million accommodations, restaurants and attractions in 2013. These valuable reviews and opinions attract travelers to seek useful travel information and become a source of revenue for Tripadvisor. Knowledge contribution may take on a variety of forms. This study focuses on product reviews that evaluate a variety of products or answer questions related to products in a third-party review website. While knowledge contribution will create value for an online community, one of the basic requirements for a successful online community is that contributors have to continuously make active contribution [15]. Therefore, understanding the factors influencing continued knowledge sharing behavior is an important research issue and critical challenge to administrators of virtual communities

2.2 Factors Influencing Continued Knowledge Contribution

Researchers have put considerable attention to factors that motivate people to share knowledge in online communities [5, 9, 10, 20, 22, 23, 28]. Some studies proposed their research model based on IS adoption models or social psychology theories, such as expectation-confirmation theory [12–14] and the theory of reasoned action [6], and social exchange theories [25], to investigate the factors influencing knowledge contribution intention or continued knowledge contribution behaviors. For instance, Chen [9] investigated the impacts of members' expectation confirmation on continuance intentions in professional virtual communities. In particular, both extrinsic motivation and intrinsic motivation are two dimensions which were frequently adopted to explain members' sustained participation in virtual communities [30]. Other studies investigate the specific factors influencing continued knowledge sharing behavior. For example, from the perspective of justice, trust, and organizational citizenship behaviors, Fang and Chiu [15] found that the knowledge-sharing continuance intention in VCoPs (virtual communities of practice) is affected by altruism and conscientiousness. We summarized the research findings and methodologies of recent studies related to continued knowledge contribution in Table 1.

3 Hypotheses and Research Method

3.1 Hypotheses Development

Previous studies enrich our understanding of continued knowledge contribution. The success of an online community depends primarily on the extent to which members use their community as well as the extent to which members continue to contribute knowledge in the community. Therefore, it is more critical to understand how to encourage online community members to contribute knowledge continuously than how to attract a crowd. Cheung et al. [12] have defined *"intention to continue sharing knowledge"* as *"the likelihood a member will continue sharing knowledge in an online community of practice* (p. 1360)." Since our study focuses on a continuance behavior, the "continued knowledge contribution" can be defined as "users' repeated act of contributing what they know in an online community."

Self-efficacy can motivate members to contribute knowledge with other members [25]. Prior research on cognitive theory has suggested that people act on a certain behavior based on their judgment on the likely consequences [4]. Knowledge self-efficacy is typically manifested in people believing that their knowledge can help others to solve specific problems. A member will be more likely to contribute knowledge continuously in an online community when she/he has a high level of

Table 1. Factors influencing continued knowledge contribution

1. He and Wei [19] • Theoretical foundation: belief-based IS continuance model • Methodology (method/community): a web-based survey in an international IT company with 161 participants • Significant predictor variables: contribution intention which is significantly affected by contribution belief (second-order construct) and contribution attitude, facilitating conditions • Knowledge contribution measurement: The actual continuance behavior was measured via the usage time spent in the system which was transferred into 5-point scales ranging from rarely used (1) to extensively used (5)
2. Fang and Chiu [15] • Theoretical foundation: justice, trust, and organizational citizenship behaviors (OCB) • Methodology: survey (a sample with 142 members of JavaWorld@TW) • Significant predictor variables: altruism (affected by trust in members which was affected by distributive justice and interpersonal justice) and conscientiousness (affected by trust in management which was affected by procedural justice and informational justice) • Continuous knowledge contribution measurement: continuance intention was assessed with items adapted to reflect the likelihood that an individual will continue sharing knowledge in the future
3. Sun et al. [30] • Theoretical foundation: expectancy-value theory and a social learning process • Methodology (method/community): survey (a sample with 205 subjects in a transactional virtual community, Taskcn.com website in China) • Significant predictor variables: extrinsic motivation (which is contingent on task complexity) and intrinsic motivation • Continuous knowledge contribution measurement: Sustained participation was measured using the instrument of continuance intention adopted from Bhattacherjee [5].
4. Cheung et al. [12] • Theoretical foundation: expectation disconfirmation theory/social cognitive theory • Methodology (method/community): online survey with 124 contributors in an online community of practice, Hong Kong education city (hkedcity.net) • Significant predictor variables: (1) knowledge self-efficacy which was affected by disconfirmation of helping others and (2) satisfaction which was affected by disconfirmation of reciprocity, disconfirmation of helping others, and knowledge self-efficacy • Continuous knowledge contribution measurement: intention to continue sharing knowledge was defined as the likelihood a member will continue sharing knowledge in an online community of practice. Two items modified from [3] were adapted to measure the degree of intention to continue sharing knowledge

knowledge self-efficacy [12]. In other word, knowledge contributors who are confident in their ability to provide valuable knowledge will develop more positive attitudes and intentions toward knowledge contribution. Therefore, if a member contributed more reviews in previous period, she/he is expected to be more confident in her/his ability to provide valuable knowledge and consequently to be more likely to contribute knowledge continuously. Hence, we hypothesize:

H1:   Knowledge contributors who have contributed more reviews will be more likely to continue contributing knowledge in an online community.

Knowledge contributors' behaviors are influenced not only by contributors' characteristics, but also the interactions among the members in an online community. Since community members' positive feedbacks will encourage knowledge contributors to enjoy helping others, community members' helpfulness votes will encourage knowledge contributors to contribute knowledge continuously [12, 19]. After receiving positive feedbacks from some knowledge seekers, knowledge contributors are likely to have a high level of enjoyment of helping other knowledge seekers. Such enjoyment leads to continued knowledge sharing [12, 19]. In the context of a knowledge sharing website, a helpfulness vote is one type of positive feedback. Therefore, we hypothesize:

H2:   Knowledge contributors who received higher average helpfulness score from others will be more likely to continue contributing knowledge in an online community.

Kankanhalli et al. [25] investigated the effects of cost factors, benefit factors, and contextual factors on knowledge contribution behavior based on social exchange theory and social capital theory. Their results show that EKR (electronic knowledge repository) usage by knowledge contributors is positively associated with intrinsic benefits (e.g., knowledge self-efficacy and enjoyment in helping others) and extrinsic benefits (e.g., reciprocity and organizational reward). A member learns product knowledge from the introduction of products provided by opinion-sharing websites and product reviews written by other members. If members found that the products introduced by an opinion-sharing website are not useful for their decision making, they have lower intention to stay or contribute knowledge in the website. Therefore, a knowledge contributor who has a high ratio of negative reviews will be dissatisfied with the products introduced by the website. Moreover, based on social exchange theory, individuals will contribute knowledge because of the expectation of obligation and reciprocity from the receivers. Knowledge contributors will contribute more if they can reciprocally learn knowledge from others. Since a member will vote positive helpfulness score to a useful review provided by another member, knowledge contributor will be benefited if she/he gave higher average helpfulness score to others, and vice versa. Therefore, we propose hypothesis 3 and hypothesis 4 here,

H3:   Knowledge contributors who gave higher average helpfulness score to others will be more likely to continue contributing knowledge in an online community.

H4:   Knowledge contributors who had a higher ratio of negative reviews will be less likely to continue contributing knowledge in an online community.

Previous studies have used social capital and social ties to investigate the continuous contributing behaviors of knowledge contributors. For example, Wasko and Faraj [32] examined intention to contribute knowledge in electronic networks of practice and found that both reputation and individual network centrality have positive effects on the helpfulness of contribution and the volume of contribution. From the perspective of social capital, the structure of ties within a social network is an important predictor of collective action and knowledge change [34]. Individuals occupying central positions in an organization have the high degree of work reputation and performance [32] and have high intention toward helping others [1]. Since a member who has higher trust density implies that she/he is a more reputable reviewer [27], we argue that a member who has the higher number of trustors will has the higher likelihood of contributing knowledge continuously. Hence, we propose hypothesis 5 as follows,

H5:   Knowledge contributors who have a higher number of trustors in a community will be more likely to continue contributing knowledge in an online community.

3.2   Data Collection

We collected data from Epinions.com. To examine our hypotheses, we retrieved the profiles of 3,298 members with Most Popular Author badge from 2007 to 2011, such as Web of Trust, review history, and membership history. Table 2 provides the details of variable operationalization.

Epinions.com is a product review website for people to obtain information about products of their interest for supporting their purchase decision. Reviews typically are composed of a review title, review content, product's pros and cons, and a product rating (1–5 stars). Other members can rate reviews as 'not helpful,' 'somewhat helpful,' 'helpful,' 'very helpful,' and 'off topic.' In addition, Epinions.com provides a unique mechanism, Web of Trust, to allow all members to indicate whether a focal member is trustworthy or not. Specifically, if a focal member is trusted by other members, they can follow the focal member. On the other hand, a focal member can trust other members.

4   Findings and Discussions

Since our dependent variable (continued knowledge contribution) was converted into a categorical scale, this study adopted logistic regression to discriminate contributors who will continuously contribute knowledge in a virtual community from those contributors who may share knowledge occasionally. Although some of our variables (e.g., number of trustors) do not follow the normal distribution, it's valid to develop a logistic regression model to discriminate continued contributors from the others. The logistic regression model is as follows,

$$Logit_i = b_0 + b_1 X_1 + b_2 X_2 + b_3 X_3 + b_4 X_4 + b_5 X_5,$$

where
$Logit_i =$ The logit value as the dependent measure,
$X_1 =$ Number of reviews,
$X_2 =$ Average helpfulness score received,
$X_3 =$ Average helpfulness score given to other members,

Table 2. Operational definitions of all variables

Variable	Operational Definition
Continued knowledge contribution (dependent variable)	Assume that member i has contributed some product review(s) in period $t-1$ (in this study, each time period covers three months). If member i writes any review in period t, this variable will be coded 1 which means that member i contributes knowledge continuously. Otherwise, this variable will be coded 0 which means that member i did not contribute knowledge continuously
Number of reviews	The number of reviews written by member i in period $t-1$
Average helpfulness score received	The average helpfulness score given to the reviews written by member i in period $t-1$. This variable measures, on average, the helpfulness level of a review written by member i during period $t-1$. We convert the helpfulness levels into a numerical scale as follows: "Very Helpful" = 3, "Helpful" = 2, "Somewhat Helpful" = 1, "Not Helpful" = -2, "Off Topic" = -4. Because a review may receive several helpfulness votes from other members, we take the macro-average helpfulness score for the reviews written by member i. The formula for this variable is: (Σ average helpfulness score for each review written by member i in period $t-1$)/(number of reviews written by member i and received some helpfulness vote(s) from other members)
Average helpfulness score given to other members	The average helpfulness score given by member i to the reviews written by other members in period $t-1$. The formula for this variable is: (Σ helpfulness score that member i gave to a review written by other member in period $t-1$)/(number of times that member i give helpfulness scores)
Ratio of negative reviews	The ratio of negative reviews across all reviews written by member i in period $t-1$. A positive or negative review is determined by that review's product rating score, which is normally between 1 to 5 stars. Reviews with 5 or 4 stars of product rating are considered positive reviews, those with 2 or 1 stars are negative reviews, and those with 3 stars are regarded as neutral reviews. The formula for this variable is: (negative reviews written by member i in period $t-1$)/(number of reviews written by member i in period $t-1$)
Number of trustors	The number of member i's trustors in period $t-1$. Trustors of member i refer to the members who trust member i. Since the number of trustors follows a power law function, this variable was transformed into log (the number of trustors + 1) when we test our research model to avoid bias

$X_4 =$ Ratio of negative reviews, and
$X_5 =$ Log (number of trustors + 1).

Then the logistic regression model was tested by the sampling dataset. The statistical results show that the omnibus test is highly significant (χ^2 = 1003.406, p < 0.001) and the Hosmer and Lemeshow measure of overall fit is not significant (χ^2 = 5.488, p = 0.704), which jointly indicate that the goodness of fit of the model is acceptable. The Cox and Snell R^2 and Nagelkerke R^2 values are 0.316, and 0.437, respectively, suggesting a satisfactory explanatory power of the logistic regression model. We therefore use this logistic regression model to test the research model and attain the results in Table 3.

We also analyze the classification accuracy of the logistic regression model. The overall classification accuracy is 78.5 %. Our evaluation result thus suggests that the logistic regression model we propose is capable of predicting the continued knowledge contributors in an online community. As illustrated in Table 3, the significance level for the Wald statistic and the value of Exp (β) show that all five hypotheses are significantly supported. Especially the number of trustors is a powerful predict variable. This result supports our argument that the number of trustors reflects knowledge contributors' social capital and benefits. The members who have a greater number of trustors will be more likely contribute their knowledge continuously in online communities.

In addition, the ratio of negative reviews is a significant but negative predictor. It implies that knowledge contributors are more likely feel discouraged and disappointed when they found the products presented in the website are not good enough so that they may not contribute knowledge in the future. Our analysis also shows that the number of reviews has a significant effect on members' continued knowledge contribution, which coincides with the findings in prior studies, which indicate that members who have confidence in contributing knowledge are more likely to devote themselves to the community. Furthermore, our analysis results also show both the average helpfulness score received from and the average helpfulness score given to other members are two

Table 3. The result of logistic regression analysis

Variables	Logistic coefficient (S.E.)	Wald statistic	Exp (β)	Hypothesis test
Number of reviews	.086 (.008)	110.715***	1.090	H1 is supported
Average helpfulness score received	.334 (.079)	17.718***	1.397	H2 is supported
Average helpfulness score given to other members	.095 (.043)	4.929*	1.099	H3 is supported
Ratio of negative reviews	−.635 (.199)	10.160**	.530	H4 is supported
Log (number of trustors + 1)	.750 (.069)	116.736***	2.117	H5 is supported
Constant	−1.796 (.205)	76.569***	.166	

*: $p < 0.05$; **: $p < 0.01$; ***: $p < 0.001$

significant predictors. It implies that knowledge contributors will be encouraged to contribute knowledge continuously if more members consider their contributions helpful. On the other hand, knowledge contributors will continue to contribute knowledge if they find that the other members' reviews are helpful.

5 Implications and Conclusions

This article makes two major research contributions. First, this study adopted longitudinal data to define and test continued knowledge contribution. Although the behavioral intention is a reliable proxy to actual behavior, there is still a gap between behavioral intention and actual behavior. For example, the knowledge contribution behavior was explained or predicted by behavioral intention construct in several previous studies [19, 31], but the R-squares are not high enough (lower than 0.25). Prior studies also suggested that future research can address the connection of psychological intention and actual knowledge sharing behavior even behavior intention is a reliable proxy to actual human behavior [14, 36]. This study measured continued knowledge contributing behavior by longitudinal data instead of users' behavioral intention or cross-sectional data. The results of this study provide robust evidence on the knowledge contributing behavior in a third-party opinion sharing website. Second, all variables in our model were measured by the members' profiles and online behaviors in Epinions.com. We adopted objective behavioral data instead of self-reported data, e.g., online survey. This method is more appropriate to practitioners to implement, because all users' profiles and behavioral data can be accessed via the database of website. It's unnecessary to ask members to answer online survey to obtain self-reported data.

The findings of this study also provide significant insights for practitioners. First, we found that knowledge contributor's behavior is influenced by the knowledge seekers' feedbacks. Therefore, the results of this study are consistent with the findings of previous studies which indicated that supporting social interaction among members will encourage knowledge contribution in an online community [15, 29]. Hence, building a reputation system and trust mechanism will enhance knowledge contributors to contribute their knowledge continuously. Furthermore, an online community can adopt our prediction model to find out the members who may contribute knowledge continuously. It would be beneficial to provide incentive benefits to enhance these members' loyalty to enrich the value of community. An online community should have a group of valuable knowledge contributors who can continuously contribute their opinions, experiences, and knowledge. Otherwise, this online community will lose their reliability [23] and lose its value – updated knowledge.

Acknowledgements. This work was partially supported by the Ministry of Science and Technology of the Republic of China under the grant NSC101-2410-H002-041-MY3 and MOST 103-2410-H-126-010-MY3.

References

1. Ahuja, M.K., Galletta, D.F., Carley, K.M.: Individual centrality and performance in virtual R&D groups: an empirical study. Manage. Sci. **49**, 21–38 (2003)
2. Alavi, M., Leidner, D.E.: Review: knowledge management and knowledge management systems: conceptual foundations and research issues. MIS Q. **25**, 107–136 (2001)
3. Bagozzi, R.P., Dholakia, U.M.: Intentional social action in virtual communities. J. Interact. Mark. **16**, 2–21 (2002)
4. Bandura, A.: Social Foundations of Thought and Action: A Social Cognitive Theory. Prentice-Hall, Englewood Cliffs (1986)
5. Bhattacherjee, A.: Understanding information systems continuance: an expectation-confirmation model. MIS Q. **25**, 351–370 (2001)
6. Bock, G.-W., Zmud, R.W., Kim, Y.-G., Lee, J.-N.: Behavioral intention formation in knowledge sharing: examining the roles of extrinsic motivators, social-psychological forces, and organizational climate. MIS Q. **29**, 87–111 (2005)
7. Cabrera, A., Cabrera, E.F.: Knowledge-sharing dilemmas. Organ. Stud. **23**, 687–710 (2002)
8. Chen, C.-J., Hung, S.-W.: To give or to receive? Factors influencing members' knowledge sharing and community promotion in professional virtual communities. Inf. Manage. **47**, 226–236 (2010)
9. Chen, I.Y.L.: The factors influencing members' continuance intentions in professional virtual communities - a longitudinal study. J. Inf. Sci. **33**, 451–467 (2007)
10. Cheung, Christy M.K., Lee, Matthew K.O.: What drives members to continue sharing knowledge in a virtual professional community? The role of knowledge self-efficacy and satisfaction. In: Zhang, Zili, Siekmann, Jörg H. (eds.) KSEM 2007. LNCS (LNAI), vol. 4798, pp. 472–484. Springer, Heidelberg (2007)
11. Cheung, C.M.K., Lee, M.K.O.: What drives consumers to spread electronic word of mouth in online consumer-opinion platforms. Decis. Support Syst. **53**, 218–225 (2012)
12. Cheung, C.M.K., Lee, M.K.O., Lee, Z.W.Y.: Understanding the continuance intention of knowledge sharing in online communities of practice through the post-knowledge-sharing evaluation processes. J. Am. Soc. Inform. Sci. Technol. **64**, 1357–1374 (2013)
13. Chiu, C.-M., Wang, E.T.G., Shih, F.-J., Fan, Y.-W.: Understanding knowledge sharing in virtual communities: an integration of expectancy disconfirmation and justice theories. Online Inf. Rev. **35**, 134–153 (2011)
14. Chou, S.-W., Min, H.-T., Chang, Y.-C., Lin, C.-T.: Understanding continuance intention of knowledge creation using extended expectation-confirmation theory: an empirical study of taiwan and china online communities. Behav. Inf. Technol. **29**, 557–570 (2010)
15. Fang, Y.-H., Chiu, C.-M.: In justice we trust: exploring knowledge-sharing continuance intentions in virtual communities of practice. Comput. Hum. Behav. **26**, 235–246 (2010)
16. Pew Research Center. http://www.pewinternet.org/Reports/2013/Health-online.aspx
17. Grover, V., Davenport, T.H.: General perspectives on knowledge management: fostering a research agenda. J. Manage. Inf. Syst. **18**, 5–21 (2001)
18. Hashim, K.F., Tan, F.B., Andrade, A.D.: Continuous knowledge contribution behavior in business online communities. In: CONF-IRM 2011 (2011)
19. He, W., Wei, K.-K.: What drives continued knowledge sharing? An investigation of knowledge-contribution and -seeking beliefs. Decis. Support Syst. **46**, 826–838 (2009)
20. Hsu, M.-H., Ju, T.L., Yen, C.-H., Chang, C.-M.: Knowledge sharing behavior in virtual communities: the relationship between trust, self-efficacy, and outcome expectations. Int. J. Hum. Comput. Stud. **65**, 153–169 (2007)

21. Jabr, W., Zheng, Z.E.: Know yourself and know your enemy: an analysis of firm recommendations and consumer reviews in a competitive environment. MIS Q. **38**, 635–654 (2014)
22. Jin, X.-L., Cheung, C.M.K., Lee, M.K.O., Chen, H.-P.: Factors affecting users' intention to continue using virtual community. In: The 9th IEEE International Conference on E-commerce Technology and The 4th IEEE International Conference on Enterprise Computing, E-commerce and E-services (CEC-EEE 2007), pp. 239–246. IEEE Computer Society, (2007)
23. Jin, X.-L., Lee, M.K.O., Cheung, C.M.K.: Predicting continuance in online communities: model development and empirical test. Behav. Inf. Technol. **29**, 383–394 (2010)
24. Joyce, E., Kraut, R.E.: Predicting continued participation in newsgroups. J. Comput. Mediated Commun. **11**, 723–747 (2006)
25. Kankanhalli, A., Tan, B.C.Y., Wei, K.-K.: Contributing knowledge to electronic knowledge repositories: an empirical investigation. MIS Q. **29**, 113–143 (2005)
26. Kim, H.-W., Zheng, J.R., Gupta, S.: Examining knowledge contribution from the perspective of an online identity in blogging communities. Comput. Hum. Behav. **27**, 1760–1770 (2011)
27. Ku, Y.-C., Wei, C.-P., Hsiao, H.-W.: To whom should I listen? Finding reputable reviewers in opinion-sharing communities. Decis. Support Syst. **53**, 534–542 (2012)
28. Oreg, S., Nov, O.: Exploring motivations for contributing to open source initiatives: the roles of contribution context and personal values. Comput. Hum. Behav. **24**, 2055–2073 (2008)
29. Shen, K.N., Yu, A.Y., Khalifa, M.: Knowledge contribution in virtual communities: accounting for multiple dimensions of social presence through social identity. Behav. Inf. Technol. **29**, 337–348 (2010)
30. Sun, Y., Fang, Y., Lim, K.H.: Understanding sustained participation in transactional virtual communities. Decis. Support Syst. **53**, 12–22 (2012)
31. Tsai, H.-T., Bagozzi, R.P.: Contribution behavior in virtual communities: cognitive, emotional and social influences. MIS Q. **38**, 143–163 (2014)
32. Wasko, M.M., Faraj, S.: Why should I share? Examining social capital and knowledge contribution in electronic networks of practice. MIS Q. **29**, 35–57 (2005)
33. Wasko, M.M., Faraj, S., Teigland, R.: Collective action and knowledge contribution in electronic networks of practice. J. Assoc. Inf. Syst. **5**, 493–513 (2004)
34. Wasko, M.M., Teigland, R., Faraj, S.: The provision of online public goods: examining social structure in an electronic network of practice. Decis. Support Syst. **47**, 254–265 (2009)
35. Yin, D., Bond, S., Zhang, H.: Anxious or angry? Effects of discrete emotions on the perceived helpfulness of online reviews. MIS Q. **38**, 539–560 (2014)
36. Zhang, Y., Fang, Y., Wei, K.-K., Chen, H.: Exploring the role of psychological safety in promoting the intention to continue sharing knowledge in virtual communities. Int. J. Inf. Manage. **30**, 425–436 (2010)

The New Way of Social Connecting for the Elderly Through Smart Home Applications

Rich C. Lee[✉]

National Sun Yat-Sen University, Kaohsiung, Taiwan
richchihlee@gmail.com

Abstract. An emerging elder-living centric concept has brought a new category of potential business opportunities into the needs of aging and aged societies. This emerging concept is nourished by the diverse applications of information and communication technologies; Smart Home is one of the killer applications integrating the technologies of the Internet-of-Things and the Social Network to facilitate a better elder-living and to maintain the family values and traditions. This article identifies the needs of various types of the elderly and elaborated what applications can facilitate the elder-living, and thus a new concept of Smart Home is positioned.

Keywords: Social media · Smart home · Open innovation model · Service science · Strategic planning

1 The Aged Society Is Coming

The aging and aged societies, according to the definitions from the WHO (World Health Organization), the population proportion of the aged over 65 exceeds 7 % is classified as the "aging society" and classified as the "aged society" if the proportion exceeds 14 %, have been more and more common in the globe. There are two major reasons behind this, one is the fertility rate is declined and reaches a stable level, at the meantime the other is the life expectancy is increasing. This aging trend will impose major social and economic consequences against the societies from various perspectives (Department of Economic and Social Affairs Population Division 2013). Taiwan is inevitably moving toward an aged society rapidly and will be a hyper-aged society—20 % of the population will be the age over 65 years old—by 2025, predicted by the *Council for Economic Planning and Development* of Taiwan. However, this paper argues that many elderly are not disable and can still lively pursue their meaningful lives such as taking care of the youngsters of the family, maintaining their social connections, doing the physical-appropriate jobs, learning new skills, or exploring the philosophic spiritual world.

Based on the Employment Analytic Data prepared by *Taiwan National Statistics* from the year 1993 to 2013, this paper has found that the workforce of age over 45 is increasing from 23.88 % to 37.27 % with 2.25 % year-to-year growth illustrated in Fig. 1; and furthermore, the workforce of age between 50 and 64 contributes more

© Springer International Publishing Switzerland 2015
F.F.-H. Nah and C.-H. Tan (Eds.): HCIB 2015, LNCS 9191, pp. 142–152, 2015.
DOI: 10.1007/978-3-319-20895-4_14

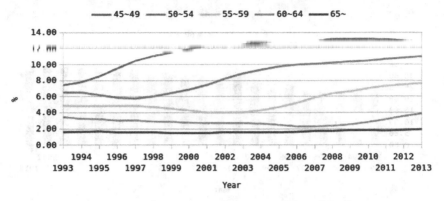

Fig. 1. Taiwan annual employment rate trend

growth of the proportion illustrated in Fig. 2. This implies that the age of retirement is delayed and should be a strong employment market demand for the senior workforce in Taiwan (Directorate General of Budget 2014). In this senior population, a concern of Digital Divide—the gap between the underprivileged members of society, who do not have the access, or reluctantly approach, the computers or the internet—will restrict the capability of seniors from taking advantage of technologies and information to interact with the innovating world as the new generation do.

According to the report of *World Knowledge Competitiveness Index* 2008, Taiwan was top ranked the 6th of broadband access and the 9th of Internet hosts, per thousand users (Centre for International Competitiveness 2008). This implies that the population of using the Internet is considerably high; the digital divide is on the way of closing the gap at least in the metropolitans of Taiwan. On the other hand, the population of higher

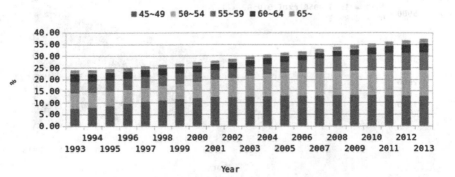

Fig. 2. Taiwan annual employment rate stacks

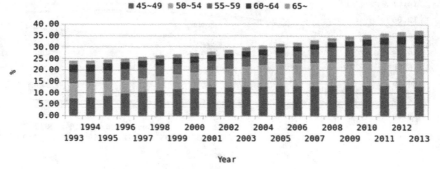

Fig. 3. Taiwan annual employment rate stacks

education (above the college graduated) is annually increasing illustrated in Fig. 3; another interesting finding is that more elderly of Taiwan are using the mobile devices and the apps to reach out their connections. This means that the aging and aged people should be more capable to apply the new services brought by the information and communication technologies to facilitate their works and living than before (Directorate General of Budget 2014) (Fig. 4).

In the Confucius world such as Taiwan or China, a society that is honoring and paying the respect to the family value—taking care of the youngsters and look after the elderly (Zhengkun 2012), most of these family structures can be understood from various perspectives: (1) having/no children, (2) having/no elders or disabled, (3) single parent/both parents, (4) living with/without children, (5) living with/without elders or disabled, (6) single/both income, (7) leased/own premises, or (8) living in city/rural; the family types can have up to 2^8 combinations. It is almost impossible to design or

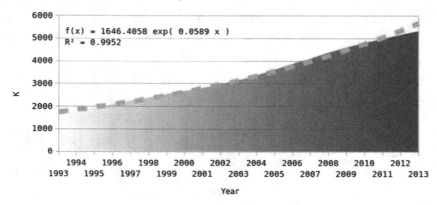

Fig. 4. Taiwan higher education/k graduation trend

explore the requirements of specific services without aiming the target family structure first. On the other hand, there are core values centered in the Confucius families; therefore, despite of the numerous structure combinations, exploring the needs from any particular structure will result the similar essence of family needs. Observing from such a social reality, among these family structures, this paper argues that, it is very common that the elders, usually the grand-parents assist in taking care of children and doing the miscellaneous chores for the family; the adults always care about the elderly and their youngsters when they are out for working.

Based on the aforementioned viewpoints—the aging and aged less-digital-divided-population trend, the increasing educated people, and the ubiquitous computing environment—this paper argues that the technologies related to maintaining the family value can fulfill the social needs of nowadays families from the perspective of the elderly.

2 Smart Home Versus Digital House

The definition of Smart Home is still under developing; it is very vague between the differences of the terms of Smart Home and Digital House. These terms are used alternatively in various occasions. There is a common definition about the smart home or smart house that incorporates advanced automation systems to provide the inhabitants with sophisticated monitoring and control over the building's functions (Smart Home Energy 2014). This paper looked up the abstracts of the first 50 of the 170 published articles collecting total 73,691 words in 2014 from Google Scholar by using the keywords of "Smart Home" and "Elderly" surveyed on 21st, Dec., 2014. Most frequent words occurred in these abstracts were about the concepts of: (1) video, sensors, tool, robot, technologies; (2) patients, adults, citizens, persons, users, people; (3) products, design, development; (4) falls, assistive, prevention, health, medical, care, environment: (5) settings, activities, detection, monitoring, living: (6) need, requirements, project, platform, system; (7) process, service, industry; and (8) issues, challenges, social. It is worth noted that the term of *Gerontechnology*—an interdisciplinary field of scientific research in which technology is directed towards the aspirations and opportunities for the older persons and aiming at good health, full social participation and independent living, development or design of products and services to increase the quality of life for the elderly (Bouma 2014)—plays significant role in the concept of Smart Home. The *Tag Cloud*—a visual representation of context driven tags or keywords based on their occurrences—illustrated in Fig. 3 explains the most frequently addressed words among these abstracts.

It is obvious that the meaning of "home" and "house" should be with two different concepts; the "house" refers to a premises or a building while the "home" is more toward spiritual belongingness. This paper argues that the concept between the Smart Home and the Digital House is a different idea. The Digital House applies the technologies to automate the command-and-control activities to provide a more convenient living and accommodated environment to the people; while the Smart Home is not just about automation but more toward human-centric concept that connects to people and brings meaningful social values to the family (Fig. 5).

Fig. 5. The tag cloud of Smart Home for the elderly

3 Lifestyle and Daily Activities of the Elderly

In order to design the potential required services of Smart Home to the elderly, this paper identified two metropolitan but with different aspects about lifestyle as the sample, Taipei and Kaohsiung, to conduct a series of interviews to understand whether the elderly would accept and be willing to adopt the concept of Smart Home to retain their family value by taking advantage of technologies. These interviews collected the information of family structure from the interviewees and inquired them about what the common daily activities are. The interviewers chose the elderly, one hundred samples of each metropolitan, from the city parks, the elderly communities, and the apartment builders.

This paper prepared a structure questionnaire in the Mind-map form as the basis for the interviewers. The survey team used the mobile pad-device and a shared folder over the Internet to facilitate the interview. The interviewer denoted the competence score from 1 to 5 for each links between nodes and could also develop a customized questionnaire from the basis to collect the unplanned information. For example, "Do you wish to have the parents to watch the children home activities remotely?" the interviewer recorded the proper score on the link between the nodes "Children" and "Remote Care" on mind-map questionnaire, based on the confidence of the interviewee's answer. Each interviewee had his/her own questionnaire file stored on the shared folder. This paper consolidated all questionnaire files, derived a superset mind-map to cover various aspects, and aggregated the scores between nodes to imply the degree of need about the concept represented by the nodes respectively (Fig. 6).

The questionnaire consisted of four concepts namely: (1) Digital Devices—to understand the degree of digital product manageability of the interviewee; (2) Living—

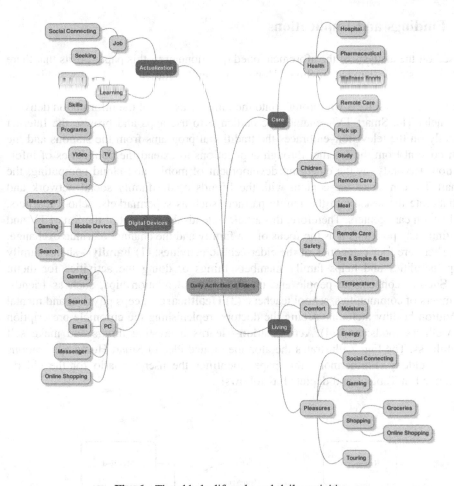

Fig. 6. The elderly lifestyle and daily activities

to understand the degree of adoptability of the digital house appliances; (3) Care—to understand how the interviewee manage his/her health related activities; and (4) Actualization—to understand the need of learning and employment. The interviewer introduced the potential Smart Home services during the survey; for example, when asking the attitude about "Remote Care" under "Health", the interviewer explained the features of video surveillance and how they can be used to re-exam the reasons causing the elderly falls; when asking whether the interviewee uses popular instant messenger such as LINE or Hangout to chat with their friends, the interviewer explained how these features could help in extending the social connections. Therefore, the training of the interviewer took quite some time and practiced what was the better way of eliciting the information from strangers in the field. Some of the elderly were very protective and not willing to share their daily activities.

4 Findings and Implications

Based on the analysis of the aforementioned questionnaires, this paper posits that there will be a strong demand of Smart Home services for the elderly. First watching the television is still a part of the daily family life; the television has been in the focus of the living room since it was brought into the families as one of the information delivery channels. The Smart TV—enables the audience to use apps and browse the Internet directly on the television–embraces the traditional programs from the stations and the rich content from the Internet through applications to extend the boundaries of information. Recently, as the emerging development of mobile and cloud computing, the Smart TV can share the content with the friends of the family social network and collaborate the tasks with the family partners such as supermarkets, school teachers, and health care centers. Therefore, this article extends the concept of the Smart TV and continuously positions it as the focus of the family and the channel of value exchange.

There are four categories of the elder-centric activities: (1) **Family**—shares family responsibilities and helps family members things or doing the activities for them; (2) **Social**—connects to people and maintains social relationships, such as friends, members of communities, school teachers; (3) **Healthcare**—keeps physical and mental condition healthy including seeing the doctors, replenishing the chronicle prescription or wellness foods; and (4) **Actualization**—learns interesting things and make self usefulness. The Fig. 7 illustrates the aforementioned idea of Smart Home applications for the elderly. Furthermore, this paper identifies the user scenario for the elderly illustrated in Table 1 and depicted as follows:

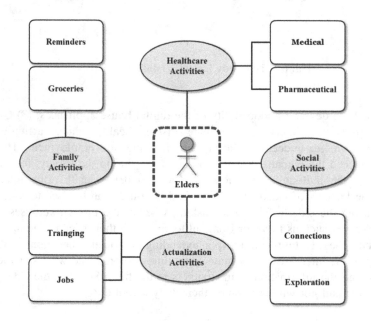

Fig. 7. Smart Home activities of the elderly

Table 1. The user scenario for elderly

Activity	Explanation
Reminders	• Check the to-do list of a day.
	• This to-do list can be input by the members of the family.
	• Environment hazard checks such as from gas, CO_2, and fire.
	• Safety monitoring through surveillance cameras at home.
Gathering	• Watch the TV news.
	• Read the headlines of major newspapers from the Internet, collected by the news delivery predefined application.
	• Comment on the interesting topics.
	• Initiate a virtual conference, picnic, with the family members not nearby.
Medical	• Make a reservation to see the doctor.
	• Invite the friends who are also going to the same hospital.
	• Check the waiting-list of the reservation.
	• Read the patient instructions from the doctor.
	• Update family expenditure records.
Pharmaceutical	• Order the prescription medicines or the wellness foods.
	• Check the waiting-list of the orders.
	• Receive the goods from the purchased stores.
	• Update family expenditure records.
Grocery	• Read the promotion items from the neighbor supermarkets.
	• Share the item information with the friends.
	• Order the desired items.
	• Check the waiting-list of the orders.
	• Receive the goods from the purchased stores.
	• Update the to-do list if the items were on the reminder.
	• Update family expenditure records.
Connections	• Read the status updates of friends through the social network application.
	• Chat with the friends about the interests.
	• Join the virtual organizations and share thoughts.
Exploration	• Enjoy the sightseeing, update the status and upload photos throughout the journey for the sharing.
	• Read the promotion from various exhibitions and the travel agents.
	• Share the information and hear the comments from the friends.
	• Make a reservation and travel plan.
	• Check the travel status and the weather condition.
	• Update family expenditure records.
Training	• Participate in the spiritual or philosophic gatherings, the trainings for new skills of interests.
	• Initiate a virtual classroom to make contribution to the society.
	• Share the knowledge and experience to virtual attendees.
Jobs	• Seek the appropriate jobs for the elderly.
	• Check the hiring status from the employment agencies.
	• Receive the hiring recommendations from the agencies.

5 Service Realization and Business Potentials

The Smart TV is emerging as an important medium for advertisements to reach out to the target audiences—family members—by grabbing their attention through multi-screens, driving the market growth not just of the Smart TV but also of the applications and the associated content providers business (Wood 2014). This trend implies that more applications running on the Smart TV can get revenue from the associated advertisements, which is similar to the mobile business model for the applications. There are many existing applications for reminders running on the Smart TV and the mobile devices—similar to the "TODO list"—such as the "*24me*" (Pozin 2014) which is a task-management and able to send-and-receive notes for family and social events. To link the frequently contacting friends or groups of shared interests, it is very common to gather the people using the instant messenger applications such as "*Ekiga*" providing the video conferencing and text messaging features. The Fig. 8 illustrates the holistic concept of Smart Home applications from the elders' perspective. Many concepts of Smart Home for the elderly have been already realized by the existing business applications.

The healthcare is one of the major concerns of the elderly; using the sensors to monitor the living safety—such as the surveillance camera can be used for detecting the location of the sound source where the special events occurred (Ou et al. 2013)—and the functional status—such as for fever thermometers, skin sensors, blood analyzers, etc. (GE Sensing 2007)—; using the online hospital reservation application—such as the one offered by the "Taipei Medical University Hospital"—to book the regular health examinations, will significantly alleviate the stress of the caregivers (Tomita et al. 2010). Selling the wellness foods and the prescribed medicines from the online drug stores such as "Drugstore" and "Walgreen" has been a mature business model—retail clinic—for years. The role of these ubiquitous "retail clinic" is expected to exchange of health information among the medical specialists and hospitals to let the

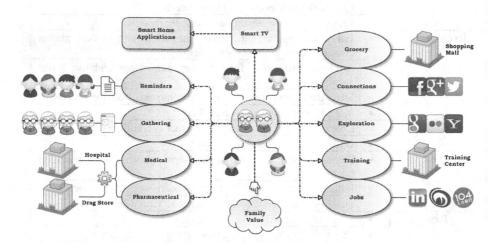

Fig. 8. Potential business opportunities of smart home from the elderly perspective

relevant clinician to access the patient's health information by taking advantage of the convenience brought by the information technologies (Cassel 2012).

Grocery shopping is one of the important daily family activities, has been addressed in many literatures (Hollywood et al. 2013; Nilsson et al. 2015). An interesting finding was that many people at work agreed to the convenience—access, search, evaluation, transaction, possession, and post-purchase (Jiang et al. 2013)—could be brought by the online shopping but not had the enough time to shop online purposely (Noor et al. 2011). This implies that the elderly can take the advantage of the convenience of online grocery shopping with less time constraint.

It is evident that the elderly using the social media tool to connect people and to explore the interests are increasing. The social media is also widely used to promote products and services by the business owners. This hybrid element of the promotion mix gives a new way of communication directly to the customers and the potential influencers through their social network (Mangold and Faulds 2009). The social media can bring much benefit for the elderly such as: (1) keeping in touch with friends, (2) learning new things, (3) asking questions especially the health related, (4) entertaining themselves through multimedia contents and online games, (5) finding jobs, (6) entrepreneuring the existing or a new business, and (7) seeking the opportunities of big sales (Ng 2012).

Based on the aforementioned elaboration from the existing applications and the literatures, the potential business cases of Smart Home for the elderly are solid. The technical challenge will be the integration of these applications as the Smart Home service portal for the elderly on a single Smart TV.

6 Conclusion

The Smart Home services base on the top of Digital House to provide environment sensing and appliances control capabilities to offer a new lifestyle for the elderly, not just taking care of themselves but also making contribution to the family, most of all, retaining the family value through the daily activities that bind the family members in more interactive and concerning way by taking advantage of technologies. The aforementioned findings can be served as guidance of the service design in the Smart Home industries. Considering time-to-market, the vendors of Smart Home service industries should apply the Open Innovation Model—to collaborate with other vendors, to share the resources, and bring the tangible services to the market—would be sooner and effective than trying to reinvent-the-wheel or replicate less competitive me-too by oneself.

References

Bouma, H.: What is Gerontechnology? Retrieved from Herman Bouma Fund for Gerontechnology (2014). http://gerontechnologie.nl/what-is-gerontechnology

Cassel, C.K.: Retail Clinics and Drugstore Medicine. J. Am. Med. Assoc. **307**(20), 2151–2152 (2012)

Centre for International Competitiveness. World Knowledge Competitiveness Index (2008)

Department of Economic and Social Affairs Population Division: World Population Ageing. United Nations, New York (2013)

Directorate General of Budget, A. a.: Taiwan National Statistics. Executive Yuan (2014)

GE Sensing: Sensors for Healthcare-Temperature, Gas, Humidity and Pressure Solutions (2007)

Hollywood, L.E., Cuskelly, G.J., O'Brien, M., McConnon, A., Barnett, J., Raats, M.M., et al.: Healthful grocery shopping. Perceptions and barriers. Appetite **70**, 119–126 (2013)

Jiang, L., Yang, Z., Jun, M.: Measuring consumer perceptions of online shopping convenience. J. Serv. Manage. **24**(2), 191–214 (2013)

Mangold, W.G., Faulds, D.J.: Social media: The new hybrid element of the promotion mix. Bus. Horiz. **52**(4), 357–365 (2009)

Ng, D.: 11 Reasons why seniors should care about social media. Retrieved from Social Media Scoop for Seniors. http://seniornet.org/blog/11-reasons-why-seniors-should-care-about-social-media/. Accessed 5 Mar 2012

Nilsson, E., Gärling, T., Marell, A., Nordvall, A.C.: Who shops groceries where and how? The relationship between choice of store format and type of grocery shopping. Int. Rev. Retail Distrib. Consum. Res. **25**(1), 1–19 (2015)

Noor, A.M., Zaini, Z.M., Jamaluddin, M.R., Zahari, M.S.: Exploratory studies on online grocery shopping. In: The 3rd International Conference on Information and Financial Engineering, pp. 423–427. IACSIT, Singapore (2011)

Ou, Y.-Y., Shih, P.-Y., Chin, Y.-H., Kuan, T.-W., Wang, J.-F., Shih, S.-H.: Framework of ubiquitous healthcare system based on cloud computing for elderly living. In: Signal and Information Processing Association Annual Summit and Conference (APSIPA), pp. 1–4. IEEE (2013)

Pozin, I.: 7 Great apps to simplify your life. Retrieved from Forbes Entrepreneurs (2014). http://www.forbes.com/sites/ilyapozin/2014/09/12/7-great-apps-to-simplify-your-life

Smart Home Energy. What is a "Smart Home"? Retrieved from Energy Saving Products and News for Smart Homes (2014). http://smarthomeenergy.co.uk/what-smart-home

Tomita, M.R., Russ, L.S., Sridhar, R., Naughton, B.J.: Smart Home with Healthcare Technologies for Community-Dwelling Older Adults. InTech (2010)

Wood, L.: Global Smart TV Market Opportunities 2014-2018: LG Electronics, Panasonic Samsung Electronics & Sony Dominate. Research and Markets (2014)

Zhengkun, G.: Confucian family values as universal values in the 21st century family-nation-world. Globalization Confucius Confucian. **41**, 43–62 (2012)

The Effect of Structural Holes on Social Capital and Individual Performance Within Social Media Networks

Yoanna Long[✉] and Roberto Mejias

Colorado State University-Pueblo, Pueblo, CO, USA
{yoanna.long, roberto.mejias}@csupueblo.edu

Abstract. The increasing use of social media has transformed the way that individuals interact with each other and has accelerated the exchange of information and knowledge. Social media has also created the phenomenon of social capital defined as the expected collective or economic benefit derived from the cooperative interaction between individuals and groups. Our research paper explores the effect on structural holes on social capital and participant performance. Structural holes have been defined as weak links to other social media groups outside the primary social network group. Research posits that weak links generate more alternate sources of new information and knowledge than strong links and thus, create more social capital and affect individual performance within a social network. Our results discuss the effect of frequency of user logins, posts counts and hierarchy (as a measure of structural hole) on experience and activeness as a measure of individual performance.

Keywords: Social media networks · Social capital · Structural holes · Hierarchy · Virtual community

1 Introduction

Social media (e.g., Facebook, Twitter, and LinkedIn, etc.) represents one of the most influential forces in our society and impacts all aspects of IT and information sharing [3]. Social media provides interaction among individuals in virtual communities and social networks which are created to share or exchange information, ideas and knowledge [1]. Social media has also been defined as a group of Internet-based applications that build on the ideological and technological foundations of Web 2.0 technologies which include social networks, blogs, wikis, video sharing, and web-based applications to create user-generated content [13].

The increasing use of social media has transformed the ways that individuals interact with each other [3]. Additionally, social media has accelerated the exchange and the transfer of knowledge and information to further create "social capital" [6]. Social capital has been defined as the expected collective or economic benefit derived from the preferential treatment and cooperation between individuals and groups [18]. Although different social sciences may emphasize different aspects of what constitutes social capital, these disciplines agree that social networks generate "value" and social

© Springer International Publishing Switzerland 2015
F.F.-H. Nah and C.-H. Tan (Eds.): HCIB 2015, LNCS 9191, pp. 153–164, 2015.
DOI: 10.1007/978-3-319-20895-4_15

contacts which may positively affect the productivity of individuals [18]. The development of social capital engenders competitive advantages similar to the benefits derived from financial and human capital. The social capital embedded within social networks may engender more information and knowledge sharing, career opportunities, and other intrinsic rewards.

A widely accepted social capital metaphor is that people who are successful are somehow better connected [8]. But how does one define a "better" connection? Burt [6–8] posits that the "structural" position of a participant within a social media network determines his/her access to social capital. Therefore, a better structural position within a social media network may lead to "better" connections. Our research paper explores the effect of structural holes on social capital and individual performance. We begin with a brief review of the literature and propose hypotheses to be tested. Next, we describe the empirical data used for our study using the Social Network Analysis (SNA) tool to analyze the social structure of our data set. We then test our hypothesis using structured equation modeling (SEM) techniques. Finally, we discuss our results, their implications for future research and conclusions from our findings.

2 Literature Review

Social capital exists where individuals exert a competitive advantage because of their relative location within a social structure [7]. The relationship between social capital and success was observed as early as the 19th century by Alexis de Tocqueville. The proliferation of various social media networks has created new social capital applications which generate new and interesting trends and developments. The link between social capital and success has been related to the structural "position" of a particular individual within a social media network [6]. Individuals whose social networks bridge across different and external sources of information appear to have a competitive advantage in detecting new and rewarding opportunities [7]. These individuals are better positioned to broker new information and translate it into a "vision" [7].

However, researchers differ with regard to what constitutes a "better" position within a social network. The "*Strong Link*" theory posits that opinions and behavior are more complete and homogeneous *within* groups than across different groups [7]. Additionally, social media groups with dense internal connections facilitate the rapid spread of key information [8]. However, while individuals within strong link social media groups may efficiently regenerate the same information, new or incremental knowledge is not being distributed. Additionally, members from "strong link" groups often require higher "maintenance" in the form of continued communication and periodic "touching base" with other group members. Subsequently, "strong link" social media may not be effective in disseminating new information or new knowledge [7].

Conversely, the "*Weak Link*" theory posits that while participants within the same social media group may efficiently disseminate existing information, connections that span across different social media networks are more effective in generating new sources of information. Alternative viewpoints are the mechanism by which social capital is created [7]. Weak links or sparse connections between heterogeneous social media participants facilitate the diversity of information diffusion across different groups. Additionally, weak links do not require the same level of communication maintenance as strong links do. Weak links to social media groups outside a primary group are referred to as "structural holes" [6]. Prior empirical evidence supports the effectiveness of structural holes in disseminating new information and knowledge that creates social capital and enhances individual performance [7].

Researchers propose different measures of *structural holes*. Among them are *ego* and *constraint*. Ego is defined as the smallest unit of analysis (as an individual "focal point") in a social network node [12]. An individual (i.e., ego) possesses high bargaining power if other participants within a particular social network are restricted to trade or interact only with that particular individual. Conversely, such individuals will have low bargaining power if other individuals are not constrained to a particular individual network and can interact with other participants. *Constraint* measures the extent to which *ego* is restricted by its the relationships to participants [8, 9, 11].

Another measurement of structural holes is *hierarchy*. Hierarchy measures whether structural constraint is concentrated on certain users or if it is distributed evenly among other participants [8, 9, 11]. The value of hierarchy indicates dependency (of ego on the social network neighborhood) and inequality (of the distribution of constraints across the social network neighborhood). The higher the value of hierarchy, the more unequal the strength of the relationships distributed across a particular social network, creating a greater probability that new information and will more easily diffuse among heterogeneous participants.

Research suggests that individual performance within social media networks may be approximated by the *quantity* and the *quality* of interaction between users and the information shared on a website [15]. For our study, *experience* is defined as the frequency a user accessed and interacted with the MITBBS website. The more frequently a user accessed a website, the more experienced a user becomes with the website and related virtual community of that particular discussion forum. *Activeness* is an indicator of the quality and frequency of meaningful posts and replies to queries by a user within a particular discussion forum. The value of activeness for example, is increased if the user actively replies to other posts and queries and created discussion threads that were, for example, selected as "top ten threads" on a certain day.

3 Research Model and Hypotheses

Prior research supports the fact that information brokers whose social networks span across diverse sources of information can provide critical information and knowledge to organizations [7]. Individuals whose social network span across structural holes have easier access to diverse information and knowledge which may provide them with a competitive advantage in generating new ideas and innovations. Individuals with a "better" structural position such as *hierarchy* within a social media network may engender better performance in the form of experience value and activeness value.

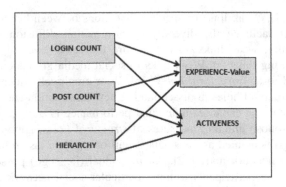

Fig. 1. Preliminary research model

Based upon the previous discussion and prior research findings relating to social capital, structural holes and individual performance within social network communities we propose the following research model (see Fig. 1) and related hypotheses.

H1. The higher the value of hierarchy, the higher the user experience value.
H2. The higher the value of hierarchy, the greater the extent of user activeness.

We propose that the frequency of online behavior on social network websites affects individual performance. For example, the more frequently a user logs on to a particular discussion forum, the more experienced that user becomes with that website and the related virtual community of that particular discussion forum. Additionally, the more frequently a user logs onto a particular discussion and maintains interaction with other forum users, the higher the activeness value of that user. Therefore, we propose the following hypotheses:

H3. The more frequently a user logs on to a website, the higher the experience value of the user.
H4. The more frequently a user logs on to a website, the greater the extent of activeness of the user.

We also propose that the frequency of user posts comments within a particular social network website affects individual performance. For example, the more frequently a user posts comments, replies or opinions to queries and threads on a particular discussion forum, the higher the experience value of that user with that particular social website. Additionally, the more frequently that a user maintains interaction with other users by posting comments, opinions and replies to other users, the higher the activeness value of that user Therefore, we propose the following hypotheses:

H5. The more frequently a user posts comments on to a website, the higher the experience value of the user.
H6. The more frequently a user posts comments on to a website, the greater the extent the activeness of the user.

4   Data Collection

We selected the social network website MITBBS (www.mitbbs.com), a Chinese bulletin board system to explore how structural position (i.e., structural holes) affects social capital and individual performance. The MITBBS website was built in 1997 by Chinese students from the Massachusetts Institute of Technology. MITBBS provides the most popular discussion forums for Chinese students studying abroad with a large variety of bulletin board topics such as entertainment, sports, literature, career advice and employment opportunities.

Data from the MITBB was selected for our study for the following reasons. First, MITBBS is an active discussion forum with intensive social interactions. Second, while the users of MITBBS are primarily Chinese students studying abroad, these students are located throughout the world and have varied backgrounds and interests. Our sample data sample therefore, was diversified and the social media networks they formed demonstrated various configurations. Third, the MITBBS website maintains records of all online discussions for several years and publishes usage data (e.g., actual posts, log times) by individual user account. These archival features provided researchers the opportunity to collect and mine data from the MITBBS website.

MITBBS possess hundreds of thousands of registered users which does not include guest users who may browse in and out without posting comments or replies to threads. MITBBS hosts over 300 discussion forums which are classified into 13 major categories. Table 1 displays the range of discussion forums hosted on the MITBBS website. Chinese students studying abroad and away from their families often must become self-sufficient within a completely new environment. Websites like MITBBS become a valuable virtual community where users can share and search for information, find friends and obtain news and entertainment. Within virtual communities such as MITBBS, social interaction occurs extensively online. Once a discussion "thread" is posted, an ID (i.e., registered user of the website) will receive responses from other IDs within that discussion forum. ID users become familiar with each other by posting and replying to discussion queries and threads.

As the purpose of our research was to explore how the structural position of users within social media networks would enhance social capital and individual performance, our study focused on analyzing interactions from those discussion forums that exchanged information and knowledge instead of forums that supported sports or pure entertainment. We selected "Academic Disciplines" from the major categories in Table 1 and then selected the "Business" discussion forum under this category. Within the Business discussion forum we analyzed IDs (users) that focused on school ranking, major areas of study, career development, professional licenses, job interviews and topics related to the study of business and business career opportunities.

5   Data Measurement

Two types of data were collected to empirically test our hypotheses. First, we collected data which recorded the behavior and the performance of individual users. This data was found via the user's personal page posted on the MITBBS website. Each MITBBS

Table 1. Discussion forums on MITBBS

Primary discussion forum category	Examples of specific forums under each category	No. of forums in each category
News	Overseas News, Business News, China News, Salon, etc.	32
Life	Living, Parenting, Food, Family, Money, Investment, etc.	50
Regional discussion	USA, Canada, Europe, and Australia, etc.	70
Sports and fitness	Football, Baseball, Swimming, Outdoors, and Travel, etc.	44
Entertainment	Music, Movie, TV, Gardening, Fashion, and Photo, etc.	43
Love and emotion	Dreamer, Lover, Les, Rainbow, and Piebridge, etc.	21
Literature	Arts, Chinese Classics, Comic, Poetry, and Prose, etc.	24
Alumni	Beijing University, Fudan University, Etc.	62
Hometown	Beijing, Shanghai, and Hubei, etc.	25
Computers and networking	Computer Science, Database, Linux, and Apple etc.	26
Academic disciplines	Business, Biology, Psychology, and Engineering, etc.	41
BBS system maintenance	Announcement, Complaints, and Tests, etc.	19
Clubs	A Variety of Clubs (Hobby, Technology, Games)	2000

user has a personal webpage which lists how frequently the user logged in, the number of comments posted and user status (e.g., regular user, system admin or forum host, etc.). Additionally and more importantly, MITBBS website offers information on performance measures such as *experience* and *activeness* (the dependent variables in our study). Second, data was collected on "social interaction". Social Network Analysis (SNA) was used to collect social interaction data from the Business discussion forum data sample and was used to analyze the related social structures. SNA uses network theory to analyze social networks and social relationships [17]. Relationships between participants such as friendship, kinship, organizations and sexual relationships are depicted in a "social network diagram" where nodes are represented as points and ties are represented as lines [17]. SNA is a distinctive methodology that encompasses techniques for data collection, statistical analysis and visual representation [14]. To analyze the interactive data from the MITBBS Business forum, the researchers followed a three-step procedure as detailed in Table 2 [16].

Step 1. Thread Downloads

The MITBBS website archives all threads posted since May 2001. Each thread may include more than one message (e.g., the original message and several replies to that message). Each message contains both the content and the sender of the message. The

Table 2. Social network analysis process

Steps	Summary	Software	Input	Output
Step 1. Threads download	Download all the threads from Business forum from May 2001 to May 2014	Web spider program[a]	Business forum on MITBBS	Threads with sender and replier
Step 2. Threads analysis	Generate a matrix revealing the interaction among users IDs (*i.e.*, *who replied to messages from whom*)	Web parsing program[a]	Threads	Matrix showing interaction between each pair of user IDs
Step 3. Statistical analysis	Calculate network structure indices	Ucinet[b]	Matrix	Social network index indicator (e.g., *hierarchy*)

[a]Programs were developed by the author. [b]Software was developed by Borgatti et al. [9]

data was analyzed to determine the interaction between IDs, specifically, who sent message to whom. Starting from May 2001 to May 2014, there were approximately 5000 threads with over 30,000 messages posted by 350 different users. A web spider program was developed to download all these threads across 13 years, which then generated the data for our analyses.

Step 2. Thread Analyses

After threads were downloaded, the SNA process generates a matrix displaying the social interaction between each pair of user IDs. A Web parsing program was developed to produce the matrix as shown in Fig. 2. The rows and columns of the matrix

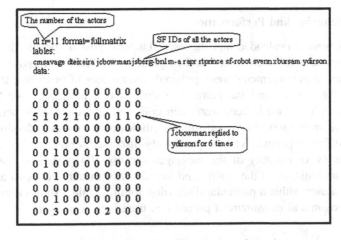

Fig. 2. An example of the generated matrix

represent participants in the social network, which are identified as the unique user IDs who posted messages on the MITBBS Business forum. The cells represent the interactions between each pair of IDs which are determined by the number of messages sent from row A to column B. The matrix is asymmetric since the reply message determines the direction; A may reply B more times than B replies A.

Step 3. Statistical Analysis

The matrices generated from step 2 served as input for the SNA software program. A SNA (see Fig. 3) was generated by UCINET [9], a widely-used software to measure and analyze social networks. A particular structural social network index such as "hierarchy" therefore, could then be calculated for each user ID to measure the structural hole for the ego index (i.e., the individual "focal" node) in this social network.

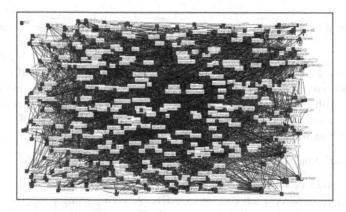

Fig. 3. Social network of the MITBBS; business forum for hierarchy variable

Individual Behavior and Performance

Once threads were downloaded and the user IDs who posted specific threads were identified, those user IDs were traced to their personal MITBBS homepage. Then two user IDs behavior measurements were gathered: the number of times that the user ID logged onto the website and the number of threads that particular user ID posted comments or replies. Two indices were then collected as indicators of performance: *experience* and *activeness*. Each performance indicator measures individual performance from different perspectives. As previously discussed, *experience* value focuses on the frequency or quantity of the messages the user ID posted on the website. *Activeness* is an indicator of the quality and frequency of meaningful posts and replies to queries by a user within a particular discussion forum. Table 3 shows a summary of the data collection and measurement procedures used for our analysis.

Table 3. Summary of data collection and measurement

Data type	Data source	Measurement
Online behavior (Login times, No. of posts)	Personal webpage	Content analysis
Social network (Hierarchy)	Threads from business forum	Social network analysis
Individual performance (Experience, Activeness)	Personal webpage	Content analysis

6 Results

Structural equation models were developed to test the research model depicted in Fig. 1. In assessing the research model, the Chi-square statistic (X^2), p values and the following fit indices were used: relative fit index (RFI), incremental fit index (IFI), Tucker-Lewis index (TLI) comparative fit index (CFI) and the root mean square error of approximation (RMSEA). Our initial structural model generated poor to moderate fit statistics and negative error variances. In cases where model refinement was required model paths were assessed and deleted one at a time and the fit of the refined model was reassessed, reflecting logical model building and purification [2, 10]. The final structural model (see Fig. 4) indicated no negative error variances and no unacceptable correlations (i.e., ≥1.00) [5]. Our final model generated good to very good fit indices (see Table 4) with a RMSEA of .044 which was below the recommended 0.10 threshold [4]. Standardized path coefficients from all independent variables (i.e., *login count, posts count, hierarchy*) to the two dependent variables, *experience* and *activeness* and were significant at p < .05.

As shown in Fig. 4, the path coefficient from *login count* to *experience* ($\beta = .24$) was significant at the p < .05 level. The path coefficient from *posts count* to *experience* ($\beta = .82$) was substantial and significant at the p < .05 level. The path coefficient from *posts count* to *activeness* ($\beta = .80$) was also was substantial and significant at the

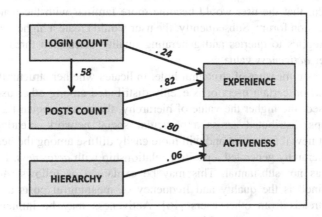

Fig. 4. Final structural model results

Table 4. SEM analysis result

Fit Statistic	(X^2)	p value	X^2/df	NFI	RFI	IFI	TLI	RMSEA
	8.335	.001	1.667	.995	.990	.998	.996	.044

p < .05 level. Finally, the path coefficient from *hierarchy* to *activeness* (β = .06) was significant (p < .05) but was not substantial. There was no relationship between *hierarchy* and *experience*. Our final structural equation model was stabilized by the addition of a path between Login Count and Post Count as these two variables we intrinsically related; *post count* could not occur without a user ID first logging (i.e., *login count*) into the MITBBS website.

7 Discussion of Results

Login count, which measures the number of times a user logs onto the MITBBS website, generated a significant relationship with *experience* but did not generate a relationship with *activeness*. This may be explained as follows. When a particular user accessed the MITBBS website numerous times it, of course, created a higher value for Login Count. Subsequently, the more frequently a user accessed a social media website, the more familiar the user became with the website features of that particular virtual community, thus creating a higher "experience" value. However, merely logging in and cruising a particular social media website did not guarantee that a particular user also posted replies to queries or created discussion threads which would increase the "activeness" value of the user.

Posts Count generated a significant and substantial relationship with both *experience* and *activeness*. This may be explained as follows. A higher post count would assume at least a minimum frequency of login count (hence the relationship between login count and post-count in Fig. 4). That is, if a user logged in numerous times and also posted numerous replies to queries and discussion threads, that particular user would generate both a high a higher experience value and a higher activeness value. Conversely, as a user would post more replies and initiate new discussion threads it would be logical that the user would become more familiar with the features of that particular discussion forum. Subsequently, the user would create a higher probability of posting more replies to queries and generating quality discussion threads thus, generating a higher *activeness* value.

Hierarchy, as a measure of structural hole, indicates whether structural constraints are concentrated on certain users or is evenly distributed among other users. As previously discussed, the higher the value of hierarchy, the more unequal the strength of the relationships distributed across a particular social network, creating a greater probability that new information and will more easily diffuse among the heterogeneous participants. Hierarchy generated a positive relationship with *activeness*. However this relationship was not substantial. This may be explained as follows. *Activeness* as previously defined is the quality and frequency of meaningful posts and replies to queries and threads from other users [16]. Activeness may be influenced by the diversity of user information (i.e., hierarchy) and *hierarchy* may be affected by other factors such as user personal user traits. While the heterogeneous information (received from a unevenly distributed network) may have exposed the user to new information, it may not have been substantial enough for the user to feel empowered to further share (i.e., post) this new information with others in his social media network.

However, this same dynamic did not apply to the relationship between hierarchy and experience. *Hierarchy* did not generate any relationship with *experience*. This may be explained as follows. Since the relationship between hierarchy and activeness was already low, we could assume that the frequency of user posts that shared new information with other users was also low. Subsequently, the availability of new, heterogeneous information may not have affected the relative experience value of the user who may have been accessing or cruising a particular website without posting replies, disseminating knowledge or creating discussion threads.

8 Implications for Future Research

The results of our research emphasize the value of maintaining heterogeneous networks outside an immediate social media group. Participants that are connected across a span of different social media groups are exposed to alternative sources of new knowledge which generates social capital [7]. The greater the number of weak links or structural hole connections between these heterogeneous social media groups, the more diverse new information may be linked to various groups and individuals thus generating new ideas, knowledge and social capital.

Our research results generated several implications for future research studies. First, the analysis of other structural hole factors such as density, centrality, and core/periphery could provide researchers with different perspectives on the social structure characteristics of social media networks. These factors could influence social capital and individual performance. Second, studying the effects of different structural hole factors could be compared across different discussion forum categories (see Table 1). As previously stated MITBBS hosts hundreds of different discussion forums. For the current study, data from the Academic-Business category provided a casual social media community that discussed issues relating to the business discipline in general. Social media network data from other discussion forums which focus on sharing new ideas and innovations could provide different results. Finally, future research studies could analyze data from entirely different social media outlets (e.g., Facebook, Twitter, LinkedIn) to test how different social structural factors within different social media networks affect social capital and individual performance.

9 Conclusion

This research investigated the relationship between the effect of one structural hole factor (*hierarchy*) on the creation of social capital and its effect on individual performance within a social network. Our results indicate that while the frequency of user Logins (i.e. *login count*) affected the *experience* value of individual performance, it did not affect the *activeness* value of individual performance. Conversely, the number of posts (i.e. *posts count*) submitted by a particular user significantly affected both the *experience* value and the *activeness* value of individual performance. Finally, *hierarchy* (as a measure of structural hole) generated a small relationship with the *activeness* value but no relationship with the *experience* value. Our research results suggest the possibility that connections or weak links with heterogeneous groups or other individuals outside of a particular social network media group may facilitate the generation of new ideas and useful knowledge. We encourage future research in this direction.

References

1. Ahlqvist, T., Bäck, A., Halonen, M., Heinonen, S.: Social media road maps exploring the futures triggered by social media. VTT Tiedotteita – Valtion Teknillinen Tutkimuskeskus (2454):13 (2008). Accessed 9 Dec 2012
2. Anderson, J.C.: An approach to confirmatory measurement, structural equation modeling of organizational properties. Manage. Sci. **33**(4), 525–541 (1987)
3. Aral, S., Chrysanthos, D., Godes, D.: Introduction to the special issue social media and business transformation: a framework for research. Inf. Syst. Res. **24**(1), 3–13 (2013)
4. Browne, M., Cudeck, R.: Alternative ways of assessing model fit. In: Bollen, K.A., Long, J. S. (eds.) Testing Structural Equation Models. Sage Publishing, Newbury Park (1993)
5. Byrne, B.: Structural Equation Modeling with AMOS: Basic Concepts, Applications, and Programming, 2nd edn. Routledge, Taylor and Francis Group, New York (2001)
6. Burt, R.S.: Structural Holes. Harvard University Press, Cambridge (1992)
7. Burt, R.S.: The network structure of social capital. In: Sutton, R.I., Staw, B.M. (eds.) Research in Organizational Behavior, pp. 345–423. JAI Press, Greenwich (2000)
8. Burt, R.S.: The social capital of structural holes. In: Guillén, M.F., Collins, R., England, P., Meyer, M. (eds.) The New Economic Sociology, pp. 148–192. Russell Sage Foundation, New York (2002)
9. Borgatti, S.P., Everett, M.G., Freeman, L.C.: Ucinet for Windows: Software for Social Network Analysis. Analytic Technologies, Harvard (2002)
10. Hair, J., Anderson, R.E., Tatham, R.L., Black, W.C.: Multivariate Data Analyses. Prentice Hall, Englewood Cliffs (1995)
11. Hanneman, R.A., Riddle, M.: Introduction to Social Network Methods. University of California, Riverside, Riverside, CA (2005) http://faculty.ucr.edu/~hanneman/
12. Jones, C., Volpe, E.H.: Organizational identification: extending our understanding of social identities through social networks. J. Organ. Behav. **32**, 413–434 (2011)
13. Kaplan, A.M., Haenlein, M.: Users of the world, unite! The challenges and opportunities of social media. Bus. Horiz. **53**(1), 61 (2010)
14. Katz, N., Lazer, D., Arrow, H., Contractor, N.: Network theory and small groups. Small Group Res. **35**(3), 307–332 (2004)
15. Long, Y., Siau, K.: Impacts of Social Network Structure on Knowledge Sharing in Open Source Software Development Teams. In: The 14th Americas Conference on Information Systems, Toronto, ON, Canada. 14–17 Aug 2008
16. Long, Y., Jin, L.: A Longitudinal Study on Member Contributions in Open Source User Oriented Community. In: AMCIS 2009, p. 388 (2009)
17. Pinheiro, C.A.R.: Social Network Analysis in Telecommunications, p. 4. Wiley, New York (2011). ISBN 978-1-118-01094-5
18. Putnam, R.: Bowling Alone: The Collapse and Revival of American Community. Simon and Schuster, New York (2000)

Serving the Social Customer: How to Look Good on the Social Dance Floor

Nicola J. Millard[✉]

British Telecommunications PLC, Adastral Park, Ipswich, Suffolk, UK
nicola.millard@bt.com

Abstract. Customers are increasingly coming to expect brands to deliver customer service on the social media dance floor. The dilemma is that brands don't always understand the mechanics of the dance. The first step to looking good on the social media dance floor is to watch and listen to the dancers – so this study investigates what customers are actually engaging with on social media (primarily Twitter, Facebook and forums) with respect to brands. It takes two 1 week snapshots of customer (not brand) activity on social media for 13 brands in 6 vertical sectors across 2 time periods (one sample during 2011 and one in 2014). We discovered that customers were actively engaging with brands on a number of levels – from complaints to complements and beyond – that different sectors had different challenges, that saying sorry wasn't necessarily enough to satisfy customers and that social dancing often requires brands to do a coordinated conga through multiple channels and complex internal processes.

Keywords: Social media · Customer experience · Omnichannel · Customer relationship management · Contact center

1 The Shape of the Social Dance Floor

Customers now expect major brands to have not only an online presence but a social media one. The challenge is how brands appropriately use this social dance floor. Too much sales talk or blatant attempts to control communication can lead to corporates dancing by themselves. Ignoring the social dance floor can also get them a slap in the face. The challenge and opportunity for corporates is to allow customers to interact and participate with them in order to influence trust, reputation, loyalty and propensity to buy [1–4]. Social media also potentially provide a cost effective channel for customer service alongside more established (and less public) channels like the phone, webchat and email.

Although social media's effectiveness in influencing purchase and loyalty has been questioned [5], one thing this research wanted to address was the appetite for customers to engage with brands, rather than just with each other [6].

To do this, we decided to take a snapshot approach and sample 1 week's customer (not corporate) activity on social media for 13 brands in 6 vertical sectors. We also did a small survey of social customers using Twitter, Facebook and LinkedIn asking about their experiences of engaging with brands on social media. The initial snapshot study was done in 2011 and the second one in 2014.

© Springer International Publishing Switzerland 2015
F.F.-H. Nah and C.-H. Tan (Eds.): HCIB 2015, LNCS 9191, pp. 165–174, 2015.
DOI: 10.1007/978-3-319-20895-4_16

The approach we took was to use a social mining tool developed by BT called Debatescape [7]. Using keyword analysis, we looked at content on key forums and social media sites (principally Facebook and Twitter because they are the overwhelmingly dominant channels, comprising 47 % and 51 % of the research content respectively in 2014).

Specific brand and customer names and content have been anonymized to protect the innocent, so the brands will be referred to under a code name. The sample encompassed retail (SuperCo & DepartStore), banking (BrandBank & GlobeBank), travel (Hi-Flyer, Lo-Flyer & TrainCo), logistics (LogistiCo), central government (GovCo), local government & police (CopShop & LocalGov) and utilities (EnergyCo & WaterCo). The selection included a number of brands that have a substantial presence on social media as well as some who have yet to engage significantly to see if this made any difference to the conversations.

In the 2014 study, we collected 44,336 customer interactions in total. We then took out retweets of the same story, tweets generated by the brands themselves and content that wasn't specifically about the brand but featured a keyword. We were then left with 12,553 social media conversations with brands (compared to 2986 in 2011 – over 4 times the amount of traffic).

Interactions were then *manually* classified into 5 categories. This was mainly because irony and sarcasm tends to bypass most analytics tools, e.g. *"A whole 2p off my next shop. Thank you @SuperCo, I know where to come for a good bargain"*; *"I'm really glad TrainCo have installed saunas in their rolling stock. It's doing wonders for my skin"*. These would probably be classified as compliments using analytics but are, in fact, veiled complaints.

The 5 categories we used were:

1. **Comment/Opinion** – Expressing a personal viewpoint about a brand. Not generally something a company would necessarily feel the need to reply to, e.g.

   - *"Anyone know how to open a SuperCo plastic bag? It's just I have things to do tomorrow"*;
   - *"Signed up for the gym and this was considered such unusual activity for me that GlobeBank blocked my card. Trying not to be too offended"*.

2. **Complaint/Criticism** – Reporting specific problems, issues or complaints with products or services, e.g.

   - *"Telephone robots that don't understand Scottish accents, vomit-inducing hold music; the GovCo helpline experience is awful"*;
   - *"@SuperCo thanks for my "luxurious" lillies - what they lacked in flower heads they made up for in slugs"*.

3. **Compliment/Recommendation** – Positive comments and promoters, e.g.

   - *"One small step for GovCo, one large step for convenience. Just did everything online. Brilliant!"*;
   - *"I'm just in love with SuperCo's Cinnamon and Apple tea, it smells like Christmas and tastes like heaven"*.

4. **Suggestion** – Constructive recommendation about how to improve a product or service, *e.g.*

   - *"@GlobeBank it would be good to be able to create travel plans that span multiple countries instead of one for each journey. A bit like Google maps. Create a plan, then add countries with an "add country" button".*

5. **Question/Answer** – Customer asking a question or answering one, e.g.
   1. *"@SuperCo hi lovely peeps! Pls can you tell me nearest store to Derby that stocks coconut yoghurt? Thx"*;
   2. *"@AnoYmouse Good afternoon Mr A, we missed you last week! Can you share how you got GlobeBank to answer your tweets?"*

2   What Customers Are Talking About on the Social Dance Floor

Analysis of the reasons that customers used social media across all brands and channels can be seen in Fig. 1.

It is unsurprising that the bulk of the content was simply comment or opinion (36 % in 2014, up from 27 % in 2011). Brands should probably just accept this and listen because customers may express surprise if they get a response, e.g.

- *"Seriously @BrandBank, I'm flattered you ask but haven't you got better things to do than reply to my idle twitterings?"*;
- *"I'm sorry but why has SuperCo replied to my tweet?"*

Questions and answers were the major category where things had grown since 2011 (from 13 % in 2011 to 22 % in 2014). Questions were often firmly directed at the brand in question (along with their Twitter handle or Facebook tag, although many brands

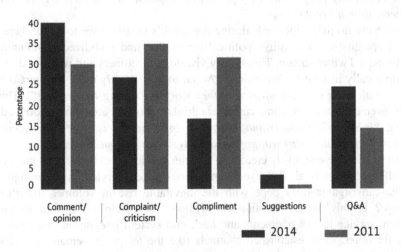

Fig. 1. Analysis by social category

cause confusion by having multiple social identities [8]). They were sometimes directed at the world in general either because the user was unaware of how to use handles and tags or in the expectation that someone out there might have an answer.

As in 2011, there were surprisingly high levels of compliments and recommendations (15 %, down from 28 % in 2011). Unsurprisingly, there were more negative comments in the form of complaints and criticisms about products and services (24 %, down from 31 % in 2011) than positive (a trend documented in numerous other studies of social media engagement with brands [1, 9]).

Of these complaints and criticisms, 9 % of these were about primary contact channels (i.e. the face-to-face, contact center, email or web experience). This has also shifted since 2011, when 84 % were about contact channels.

This seems to indicate that social media have shifted from channels that people go to in order to complain about other channels, to channels they complain on. In other words, they are now primary rather than secondary channels for contact. A typical comment from a social customer we interviewed was: "*I don't even bother ringing the contact center any more. I get faster and better service on social media.*"

Many reinforced this view:

- "*@DepartStore - funny that weeks of going into different stores and calling I get lack of help, I tweet and within minutes I hear back!*";
- "*I'd like to apologize to all followers about my on-going LoFlyer rants. It seems to be the only way I get any response from them Much love x*";
- "*@LoFlyer 7-10 WORKING days? That's long for such a simple question; besides I see people using Twitter/Facebook and it is being solved faster*".

This is a challenging trend because, if customers believe that the only way to get service is to blast the brand on social media, they are going to increasingly blast the brand on social media [10]. Social breeds social – volumes can rise rapidly, especially if customers are inciting similar others in their network to complain. The sudden flooding of the social dance floor can prove problematic – as one social customer noted: "*Twitter is training people that they get faster response in that mode. Thus everyone goes there, thus it breaks*".

There were no major incidents during the week's snapshot we took but there were social campaigns about sensitive political issues that had mobilized communities to blitz a brand's Twitter stream. This is very visible to customers and was noted in some (fairly politically incorrect) Tweets, e.g. "*No chance of a reply from @SuperCo today. Too busy with nobs who are upset that they stock the wrong type of veg!*". This can provoke even more anger if some customers think that others are being prioritized over them, e.g. "*@SuperCo I understand that you're busy but tweets posted after mine were being answered while I was waiting for a reply. Poor customer care*".

If companies are effectively creating a two tier service level with social media users being offered preferential, faster or more personalized service than through other channels, can organizations cope with the inevitable rise in volumes that this will encourage? Is this, indeed, sustainable without the discipline around resourcing, escalation, service level agreements and back end system integration that tends to be present for other, more established channels like the telephone, email and webchat? Social channels are often used in addition to these channels rather than as replacements for them. This is would strongly suggest that the ability to easily and seamlessly switch between channels is highly desirable, as well as the ability to track customer activity across these channels.

3 Not All Dance Floors Are the Same

The appetite for customers to dance also varies by sector (see Fig. 2):

Retailers were lords of the dance with 74 % of traffic – topping the table in 2014 (from its position in 2nd place at 32 % in 2011). They had an almost equal split between complaints (20 % in 2014; 25 % in 2011) and compliments (18 % in 2014; 32 % in 2011). Retailers had the highest number of compliments of any sector. Typical content ranged from criticism about deliveries, inability to get through to the contact center, ignoring feedback and staff attitudes.

Retailers were also engaging back on a more personal level with customers on social media – which implies that social service breeds increased social engagement amongst the community [1]. However, being a good conversationalist can provoke some somewhat surprising content that brands may not have anticipated (or may want to engage with), e.g.:

- "@SuperCo if you were a salad, what salad would you be?";
- "@SuperCo tell me a rude joke";
- "@SuperCo what do I do if my friend's having a bad day?"

Travel earned second place in terms of volume (down from 1st in 2011 when it gained 41 % of the traffic) with 12 %. This is largely thanks to a combination of a very well established set of social travel forums plus delayed and grumpy travelers armed with smart phones. They had the most active dance floor for complaints of any other

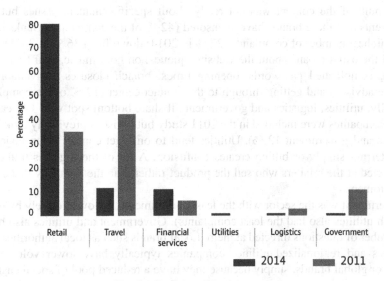

Fig. 2. Social activity by sector

sector (34 % in both 2011 and 2014) as well as one of the lowest levels of compliments and recommendations (10 % in 2014; down from 26 % in 2011).

Again there was evidence that social contact breeds more social contact – especially in the case of LoFlyer who had a very high volume of questions coming through (31 % of questions directed at LoFlyer, verses 16 % directed at HiFlyer). These included customers asking why flights are delayed and for how long, where bags are, baggage allowances and boarding cards.

The challenge for travel is to ensure that everyone is operating from the same information set. If the social media stream contradicts the app or website and the customer service person at the airport, station or in the contact center, the result is often frustration and confusion, e.g.

- "@LoFlyer why doesn't the app sync up with the website? They're showing different things";
- "Flight delayed by 5 h. Google knows more than airport staff, who don't seem to know much…"

Rising from 6 % in 2011, financial services took third place with 11 %. This is despite the fact that, for regulatory and compliance reasons, social media and finance are not comfortable dance partners. Financial services companies can't provide unregulated financial advice on a public channel, which potentially makes responding to customer queries a legal minefield.

This has understandably meant that banks have been late entrants onto the social dance floor – very few were on Twitter or Facebook in 2011. Customers don't always talk about their finances in public either. However, it is clear that social media are becoming increasingly popular mechanisms to engage with banks as they have risen from near the bottom of the table in 2011 to third place in terms of social activity in 2014 (and top of the table for questions and answers at 27 % in 2014; up from 17 % in 2011).

The bulk of the content was not really about specific financial issues but about major events that these brands have sponsored (42 % of the comments). Banks had the second highest number of complaints (27 % in 2014; down from 36 % in 2011). These included the usual moans about the website, queues, on hold music, staff training and attitudes, complicated passwords, opening times, branch closures, unavailability of mortgage advisors and getting through to the contact center (17 % of the complaints).

Finally, utilities, logistics and government all share bottom spot with 1 % each (no utilities companies were included in the 2011 study but logistics previously took 3 % of the traffic and government 12 %). Utilities tend to only get contact when major incidents interrupt supply or billing creates confusion. A lot of the logistics traffic often gets directed at the retailers who sell the product rather than the company that delivers it to customers.

Government was the sector with the least compliments, followed closely by utilities (although utilities also had the least complaints). Government and utilities also had the least number of questions directed at them. Local brands such as local authorities/police authorities and regionalized utilities companies typically have lower volumes than national or global brands, simply because they have a reduced pool of social customers to start from.

This sample suggests that each sector has different challenges for social media engagement. Understanding how and why customers want to be served over social channels and how they fit alongside other channels is vital. Getting onto the dance floor "because everyone else is" is not a great strategy.

4 Boogie Wonderland or Murder on the Dance Floor?

Social media's real value, and its challenge, is around the immediacy of engagement. Customers seem to believe that they will get a faster response on social media than through other more traditional channels like the phone or email [10] – with recent BT research suggesting that 70 % expect a response within 15 min of posting [11].

Our evidence shows that response times from brands can vary hugely – from 15 min (an average for one "best practice" retailer under study), to 8–10 h (especially if posts arrive outside standard office hours), to no response at all. The impatient social customer is very ready to note this:

- "@GlobeBank I finally got a response to my question but then they went quiet again. Three days for each reply is not acceptable";
- "@SuperCo I hope SuperCo answer my previous tweet towards them. Easy to ignore something they can't answer #RubbishCustomerService";
- "@SuperCo feeling sad, you still haven't responded to my stock question from 4 h ago";
- "Well, pretty #BadCustomerService from the Twitter bods at @LoFlyer today. Four hours to respond to first query and then silence afterwards".

This lack of response can cause customers to channel shift multiple times – "Brandbank website won't let me update phone number as site link doesn't work & their customer service is engaged. Let's try online web chat".

This means that they frequently phone, email and post on social media about the same issue and wait to see which responds first – sometimes with contradictory results: "TrainCo customer service is amongst the worst I have encountered. The station staff argue with info provided to me by their Twitter team and telephone customer service team despite having the information in front of me. In future I will avoid them at all cost".

Some companies tend to apologize but then direct customers to another more private channel such as email, as this frustrated customer's retweet shows: "RT: unfortunately we are unable to follow you. If you send an email to GlobeBank-help@GlobeBank.com, I can assist you". "#useless". This is not ideal from the customer perspective as they are given the corporate channel shunt and often have to repeat themselves every time they switch.

It's also not ideal from a corporate perspective because it can substantially increase cost to serve. This is because customers are effectively being double or triple handled by the agents dealing with social media, the phone or email channel. It is more effective and efficient if the agent handling the social interaction can seamlessly pick the conversation up through chat or phone from social media itself, e.g. using click-to-call or click-to-chat.

This shift from public to private channel is essential for any company actually wanting to know the real identity and personal details of @fuzzyduck567, without he or she publishing everything publically. Customers are also often more than aware of the public nature of social media:

- "@SuperCo you are deluded if you think I am going to reply on Twitter with my details";
- "@GlobeBank I wouldn't put my bank details on here but a phone number is ok no? If a weirdo calls I can just hang up!"

If the only way to solve these issues is to take them from a public channel to a private one by solving the issue "offline", the resolution then becomes invisible to the social customer. It is, therefore, important to close the loop with the customer in public once things have been resolved.

Another issue is around the limitations of social media itself – especially Twitter where customers are extremely limited in the number of characters that they can use:

- "@GlobeBank- Not sure I can do that in 126 characters...";
- "@LoFlyer Hi, thank for the response. Think I'll need an email add to make a complaint – not enough characters in a DM! Thanks".

And sometimes there is the occasional slap in the face because of 'inappropriate' dancing (often because of the informality of the conversation):

- "@CEOSuperCo have you looked at your @SuperCo feed recently. Several men staffing it are incredibly rude and dismissive. #customercare?";
- "@SuperCo since this is a legitimate complaint, perhaps you could reserve the emoticons for when you're texting your mates...?".

The single biggest issue that emerged is that saying sorry isn't enough for many customers. It rapidly becomes apparent what questions and issues companies are unwilling or unable to respond to. Process flaws that probably exist quietly in other channels become the source of very public frustration on social media. Customers often want some of these fundamental problems solved rather than an apology with no action – and they can often rapidly find allies in other customers who have had similar experiences. As Frank Eliason, one of social customer service's pioneers, puts it: "customers never wanted social customer service, they want to be treated right the first time" [12].

There are many examples of customers wanting organizations to solve their issues, not simply pass them on or ignore them:

- "@TrainCo An apology is pointless unless measures are taken to prevent the problem recurring. Love from ALL your customers";
- "HighFlyer Customers don't expect you to be perfect. They do expect you to fix things when they go wrong";
- "@GlobeBank: my social media tirade will continue, Including colourful derogatory language!! Until I receive a personalised solution";
- "@LoFlyer "hi Phil, we don't know what we are doing so we will keep sending the same reply. If you send us this we will do this "blah blah blah"";

- "*@SuperCo I can't fault you, you always reply to my tweeted complaints – if only they went beyond simply being passed on*";
- "*@LoFlyer I have had so many tweets telling me how sorry everyone is and to send in my booking ref in. It's been done but still nothing!*"

This inevitably exposes the inadequacies of back end processes and the limitations of internal silos – especially when one brand has multiple, and entirely functionally or geographically separated, social media feeds:

- "*@SuperCo Can you please explain what is going on, lots of conflicting information coming from various departments*";
- "*RT reply from @Brandbank: "Hi there. I'm sorry I can only help with Globe-Bank UK queries. I don't have contact details for India. Please contact them directly*".

The dilemma for brands is that (a) these are often very difficult, systemic failures to solve and (b) the weaknesses in their customer service delivery processes become extremely transparent to all. It can, indeed, be murder on the dancefloor.

5 Social Media and the "Omni-Channel" Waltz

It is clear from this snapshot study that social media needs to have a defined role in a brand's overall "omni-channel" customer experience journey [13, 14]. Customers need to be guided as to what is or isn't likely to get a response. They also need to have an expectation as to how long will it take to get something back (some brands are now publishing waiting times and service levels on their social media sites [8]).

Some organizations are doing this well. However, strategies vary hugely. Some answer pretty much everything (even if it isn't entirely appropriate to do so). Some direct everything to other, less public channels like email. Some don't engage at all - which is fine as a strategy, as long as you state upfront that you aren't dancing.

What isn't good are inconsistent strategies, no indications of what customers can or can't expect in terms of service levels, multiple disconnected branded streams who don't (or can't) pass customers to the right place to get their issue addressed or a lack of signposting as to which channel is the most likely to get customers to their goal [8]. Action truly does speak louder than words – and the responsiveness of organizations is not simply judged by how quickly they respond to demands on social media.

The challenge on social media is to learn how (and if) it is appropriate to dance with customers. Engaging in social media with no intention to create dialogue is liable to get organizations a virtual slap in the face – they may just as well stick to broadcast channels. However, engaging in uncoordinated dialogue, especially if it isn't linked in to overall strategies for customer experience is likely to get the same outcome. Not having adequate policies on staff intervening on social can also be a recipe for disaster.

In reality, social media cannot be regarded as a discrete or separate channel for customer contact. It is part of an intricate waltz between channels as customers weave around in an attempt to reach their goals. Although most companies recognize the need to be on the dance floor, they frequently don't understand how to measure it effectively or integrate it in with established channels like the contact center. Treating social as part of a coordinated "omni-channel" contact strategy and integrating it into a universal queue, along with appropriate service level measures, is best practice in brands that do social contact well [8, 12, 13].

Acknowledgments. This paper couldn't have been written without the help of Dr. Hamid Gharib from BT TSO Research.

References

1. Schweitzer, L.: Planning and social media: a case study of public transit and stigma on Twitter. J Am. Plann. Assoc. **80**, 218–238 (2014). (Routledge)
2. Canhota, A.I., Clark, M.: Delivering effective social customer service 140 characters at a time. J. Mark. Manage. **29**(5), 522–544 (2013). (Taylor & Francis)
3. Colliander, J., Dahlen, M.: Following the fashionable friend: the power of social media: weighing publicity effectiveness of blogs verses online magazines. J. Advertising Res. **51**, 313–320 (2011)
4. Laroche, M., Habibi, M.R., Richard, M.O.: To be or not to be in social media: how brand loyalty is affected by social media. Int. J. Inf. Manage. **33**(1), 76–82 (2013)
5. Phan, M.: Do social media enhance customer perception and purchase intention of luxury fashion brands? Vikalpa J. Decis. Mak. **36**(1), 81–84 (2011)
6. Ritson, M.: Hard Evidence of Social Media's Failings, p. 58. Marketing Week, London, 24 Nov 2011
7. Orlikowski, W., Thompson, S.: Leveraging the web for customer engagement: a case study of BT's debatescape. MIT Sloan working paper, 4935-11 (2010)
8. Blunt, C., Hill-Wilson, M.: Delivering Effective Social Customer Service. Wiley, New York (2013)
9. Hu, M., Liu, B.: Mining and summarizing customer reviews. In: Proceedings of the ACM SIGKDD International Conference on Knowledge Discovery & Data Mining (KDD-2004, full paper), Seattle, WA (2004)
10. Schrage, M.: A Better Way to Handle Publicly Tweeted Complaints. Harvard Business Review, Watertown, 21 Nov 2011
11. Davies, J., Hickman, M.: Serving the autonomous customer, BT/Avaya white paper (2015)
12. Stephens, G: Five years of social customer care: the pig puts on some lipstick and the fish come out to play, future care initiative white paper (2014). http://futurecare.today/
13. Hanna, R., Rohm, A., Crittenden, V.: We're all connected: The power of the social media ecosystem. Bus. Horiz. **54**(3), 265–273 (2011)

Are Spectacles the Female Equivalent of Beards for Men? How Wearing Spectacles in a LinkedIn Profile Picture Influences Impressions of Perceived Credibility and Job Interview Likelihood

Sarah F. van der Land[1](✉), Lotte M. Willemsen[2], and Suzanne A.J. Unkel[3]

[1] Erasmus University Rotterdam, Rotterdam, The Netherlands
vanderland@eshcc.eur.nl
[2] University of Amsterdam, Amsterdam, The Netherlands
[3] Google, Dublin, Ireland

Abstract. This study builds on our previous work on beardedness [1] and explores whether wearing spectacles in a LinkedIn profile picture affects a female candidate's prospects of being invited for a job interview and whether this is contingent on the type of job vacancy. Results of a 2 (spectacle use: spectacles versus no spectacles) × 3 (job type: expertise, trustworthiness, attractiveness) experiment conducted among 139 participants show that bespectacled candidates are perceived as having more expertise and –to our surprise- also being more attractive than candidates not wearing spectacles. Moreover, a candidate's perceived credibility is a significant predictor of the intention to invite the candidate for a job interview. Theoretical and practical implications of these findings are discussed.

Keywords: Personal branding · Strategic social media · Impression management · Recruitment · Spectacles · Credibility · Job interview success · LinkedIn

1 Introduction

Today's employers are increasingly using Social Network Sites (SNSs; e.g., Facebook and LinkedIn) to screen potential job applicants before inviting them to a job interview [2]. Because most employers have limited time and information processing capabilities to search among the large online pool of potential job candidates on LinkedIN [2], they often resort to heuristic inferential strategies, as elicited in the Elaboration Likelihood Model, to economize their judgments [3]. Therefore, judgments about a candidate's *credibility* are likely to be guided by very minimal visual cues displayed in a profile picture such as gender, ethnicity, spectacles and facial hair [4, 5]. Credibility refers in this study to perceived positive characteristics of a potential candidate that affect the receiver's (e.g. employer) acceptance of a message, and is viewed as a multifaceted construct [6, p. 48]. Thus, the cues a potential job candidate displays on their online profile may determine first interpersonal impression formation [7], credibility and, evidently, job interview success.

© Springer International Publishing Switzerland 2015
F.F.-H. Nah and C.-H. Tan (Eds.): HCIB 2015, LNCS 9191, pp. 175–184, 2015.
DOI: 10.1007/978-3-319-20895-4_17

This study explores whether one specifically salient visual cue in a LinkedIn profile picture, namely wearing spectacles, affects a candidate's prospects of being invited for a job interview. The research design of this study builds on, and partially replicates, our prior work on the effects of bearded candidates on job interview success [1]. Moreover, it extends Guido, Peluso, and Moffa's study [8] on the effects of bearded endorsers in advertising, to the context of job recruitment. Spectacles were chosen as a visual manipulation in this study because prior research indicated that the stereotype of spectacles is to decrease a persons' level of attractiveness [9], but increase intelligence ratings [10]. In other words, spectacles in your LinkedIN profile picture may make you less attractive, but you look more intelligent. Moreover, based on our earlier work [1] we were curious to investigate whether spectacles are the female equivalent of beards in terms of expertise and intelligence perceptions. As there is a lack of empirical knowledge on effective online personal branding [11] we've formulated the following research question: *"Does wearing spectacles in a LinkedIN profile picture affect a female job candidates' likelihood of obtaining a job interview, and to what extent is this contingent on the type of job vacancy?"*

2   Theoretical Framework

In everyday life, when we get acquainted with previously unfamiliar people, we base our first impressions of others on very minimal visual cues of information such as race, height and attractiveness [7, 12, 13]. Particularly in the context of applying for a job, a strong first impression is vital because the minimal cues displayed in a job candidates' self-presentation, may impact employers' hiring decision [14]. In an ideal world, when searching for a suitable candidate, recruiters and employers would engage in a rational cost-benefit analysis of all available information on potential candidates, and not be tempted to be guided by first impressions and stereotypes. However, fact is that most recruiters have limited time and information processing capabilities and therefore must resort to heuristic inferential strategies to economize their judgments, as elicited in the Elaboration Likelihood Model [3] and the Heuristic-Systematic Model [4]. More important: once a first impression is made of the candidate, recruiters are reluctant to change them, as they are inclined to be consistent in their decisions [15].

In an online setting, research has shown that a profile picture is one of the first things people notice when they view someone's Social Network Site (SNSs) [16]. Therefore, it receives the most attention from those to whom the profile picture belongs [16], as well as those who observe the SNS profile [17]. SNS users carefully select their profile pictures to present and "brand" themselves in the best possible way [18]. Observers attend to the profile picture to draw inferences of the profile picture's owner [19]. Profile pictures are especially relevant when information is exchanged between unknown contacts, as people are not able to rely on other social cues (e.g., voice intonation, non-verbal communication, facial expressions etc.). Indeed, according to Social Information Processing theory, the few available cues present in this profile picture (e.g. spectacles, hair color) are prone to be magnified and stereotyped by those who form judgments of the profile picture [5]. Thus, the cues a potential job candidate displays on their LinkedIN

profile picture may determine interpersonal impressions, including credibility perceptions, and, evidently, job interview success. In this study, perceived credibility is a
multifaceted construct, which is generally believed to consist of expertise, trustworthiness and attractiveness perceptions [see 6 for a review].

In our previous research on impression formation [1], we found that wearing a beard
in a LinkedIn profile pictures was a salient cue for men that enhanced perceptions of
expertise and affected and job interview likelihood for *expertise-jobs*. In this study, we
perceive spectacles as the female equivalent of the male beard and expect that spectacles
arouse the same associations of intelligence, trust and wisdom for women as beards do
for men. An additional reason to focus on spectacles as a cue is that putting on a pair of
spectacles is a simple act that may have a major impact on a person's face and how the
person is perceived [20], and therefore is a suitable cue to study 'personal branding'.

Traditionally, spectacles are first and foremost functional objects, helping people
with impaired sight to improve their vision [21]. However, nowadays spectacles are
increasingly turning into fashion accessories [20], which has been sparked by
popular culture as celebrities and famous models are more frequently seen wearing
spectacles with noticeable frames [22, 23]. The stereotypical association of bespectacled people is that they are considered to be more intelligent [24], often associated
with the "nerd stereotype". In an experiment by [20], it was found that individuals
wearing spectacles (both rimless and full-rim) were rated as more successful and
more intelligent than individuals not wearing spectacles. Therefore, we hypothesize
that spectacles may serve as a cue to enhance expertise perceptions for women, in a
similar vein as beards do for men.

An important indicator of trust is the ability to look someone in the eye [25]. The
eye region is very informative part of the human face, which gives important information
about people's current focus of attention and intentions [26]. Spectacles were found to
significantly enhance perceptions of trustworthiness in an experiment in comparison to
faces without spectacles [20].

Many studies have demonstrated that most people tend to be rated as less attractive
with spectacles on [9, 27]. Yet for women's ratings of attractiveness, this effect seems
to be particularly negative [28, 29]. Therefore, we hypothesize the following:

H1: Wearing spectacles in a LinkedIn profile picture interacts with job type, such that
wearing spectacles (vs. not wearing spectacles) in a LinkedIn profile picture (a) positively affects credibility perceptions for the expertise-job, (b) positively affects credibility perceptions for the trustworthiness-job, but (c) negatively affects credibility
perceptions for the attractiveness-job

In the context of persuasive communication, higher levels of perceived credibility
have been linked to various positive outcomes [6, 30]. For instance, the rich body of
credibility research demonstrates that more credible sources produce more attitude
change than less credible sources [see 31, for a review]. Moreover, [30] found that
salesmen who were perceived more credibly are able to gain a significantly higher
number of customer purchases for their product than salesmen who were not perceived
as such. Therefore, we argue that the perceived credibility of a job candidate will affect
the intentions to invite him for a job interview and offer the following hypothesis:

H2: Candidates with a higher perceived credibility are more likely to get a job interview invitation than candidates with a lower perceived credibility.

3   Method

To test these hypotheses graphically displayed in Fig. 1 a 2 (spectacle use: spectacles versus no spectacles) × 3 (job type: attractiveness, trustworthiness, expertise) between subject factorial design was conducted.

Fig. 1.   Facial stimuli used as job candidates

3.1   Sample

In total, 139 participants, between 18 and 55 years old (52.2 % female, $M_{\text{age}} = 25.53$, $SD = 7.27$) participated in this online experiment. Participants were selected based on a convenience sample of the social networks of the students who participated in a Master's level Media and Communication course at a high-ranked University in the Netherlands. Thus, the sample consisted of some recruiters, but also friends, colleagues and acquaintances were invited to fill out the online survey.

3.2   Research Design

To manipulate job type, three job vacancies were created to represent Ohanian's [6] three sub-dimensions of credibility—i.e., attractiveness, trustworthiness, and expertise. In line with previous research [cf. 1], the expertise-job comprised a position as an architect at an architectural firm, and the trustworthiness-job comprised a position as a back office cashier at a bank. The attractiveness-job comprised a vacancy for a promotion model at a promotion agency. Participants (n = 38, of which most in the age category between 19 and 30 years of age, 65.8 % female) were randomly shown one of three job vacancies. Participants were asked to imagine they were a recruiter and to indicate on 15-items of Ohanian's perceived credibility what kind of candidate would be most suitable for this job vacancy (1 = strongly disagree; 7 strongly agree). An example item corresponding with the attractiveness vacancy was "the candidate should be elegant", for the expertise vacancy "the candidate must be knowledgeable", and for the trust vacancy "the candidate must be reliable". Perceptions about required qualities matched with the intended sub dimensions of credibility. Respondents perceived attractiveness an important quality for the promotion model vacancy ($M_{attractiveness}$ = 5.45, SD = 1.19), trustworthiness an important quality for the cashier vacancy ($M_{trustworthinesss}$ = 5.20, SD = .40), and expertise an important quality for the architect vacancy ($M_{expertise}$ = 5.20, SD = .57). This was also confirmed by one-sample t-tests; each quality scored significantly higher than the mid category of the scale (all ps < .01). Therefore, the analyses verified that the selected job vacancies were valid representations of the intended subdimension.

To manipulate the facial stimuli, *spectacle use,* respondents were exposed to a Linkedin profile picture, showing a female candidate who did or did not wear spectacles. The design of the spectacles was a modern style consisting of a thick full-rim and a black frame, as this corresponds to current fashion for eye spectacles [20]. The thick rim was chosen in order to make sure that participants would notice them. The hairstyle of the model was put up in a bun, in order to avoid unwanted effects of increasing female attractiveness due to long and medium hairstyles [19]. The model was a relatively young female (31 years of age), because candidates in this age category are rewarded more positive replies to their job application by recruiters than older candidates [12]. To control for unwanted effects of familiarity with the model [35], we asked: "Are you familiar with the model?" Only (n = 3) participants indicated being familiar with the model, which were then eliminated from the dataset.

The model wore a black blazer because employers prefer candidates to wear dark, conservative clothing during job interviews [36, 37]. The model expressed a neutral but pleasant face (by holding her lips together and directing the corners of her mouth upwards), in order to avoid unwanted interpersonal effects of smiling [38]. To ensure that the spectacles were the only manipulation cue, the picture of the model was photo shopped by a graphical designer, creating two identical pictures in terms of facial expression. Thus, apart from this manipulation, these two LinkedIn profile pictures were identical. Finally, the LinkedIN logo was added to increase the photo's likeness to a real LinkedIN profile picture (see Fig. 2).

3.3 Procedure

The procedure was similar to our prior study [1]. Participants were led to a Qualtrics survey website after having clicked on the online link they received via email, Facebook or LinkedIN. The first page of the survey presented a welcome message and stated that the general purpose of this study, provided background information on the researchers and offered instructions. Subsequently, participants were randomly assigned to one of the six experimental conditions (e.g. with spectacles versus without spectacles in combination with one of the three designed jobs). Respondents were forced to look at the job

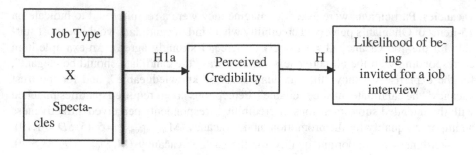

Fig. 2. Conceptual model of this study

description for at least 20 s first (a timer only activated the "next" button after 20 s) and at least twelve seconds at the LinkedIn profile picture, after which the post experiment questionnaire was activated.

3.4 Measures

Ohanian's [6] 15-item semantic differential scale was used to measure the *perceived credibility of the candidate,* with five items representing each of the three sub–dimensions. The scales for the three sub dimensions proved sufficiently reliable as *attractiveness* formed a one-dimensional scale (Cronbach's $\alpha = .84$), and so did *expertise* (Cronbach's $\alpha = .90$), and *trustworthiness* (Cronbach's $\alpha = .89$). *Perceived invitation intention* (Cronbach's $\alpha = .81$) of the female job candidate, was measured via a two-item rating scale based on Fishbein and Ajzen [39]. One item measured the strength of the likeliness to invite the job candidate, and the other item measured the subjective probability that the inviting behavior will be effectively performed within the next three months. All of the items discussed above were measured on a seven-point semantic differential scale ranging from 1 (strong negative evaluation) to 7 (strong positive evaluation).

4   Results

A check for gender effects was carried out and the results from a difference analysis showed that participants' gender has no significant effect on female candidates' perceived credibility, its sub dimensions, and the intention to invite applicants to a job interview $p = .17$.[1] This finding supports that gender has no role in the model; relationships among independent and dependent variables are not affected by gender.

To test the research hypotheses, a factorial ANOVA analysis was performed with spectacle use and job type as independent variables and perceived credibility as dependent variable. The results reveal a main effect of spectacle use, $F(1,133) = 5,657$, $p < .05$, $\eta^2 = .04$). A candidate who wears spectacles in a LinkedIN profile picture is

---

[1] All our results are presented one-tailed, due to predicted directional effects of our hypotheses [45].

perceived to be more credible ($M = 4.80$, $SD = .58$) than a candidate who wears no spectacles ($M = 4.55$, $SD = .70$). Importantly, and more germane to the hypotheses, the results revealed a spectacle use by job type interaction, $F(1,133) = 5,657$, $p < .05$, $\eta^2 = .04$). Planned comparisons demonstrate that for expertise jobs wearing spectacles ($M = 4.80$, $SD = 50$) versus no spectacles ($M = 4.32$, $SD = .74$) significantly increases a candidate's perceived credibility, $F(1,41) = 6.163$, $p < .05$, $\eta^2 = .13$. Hence, the analyses provide support for 1a, stating that spectacle use positively affects credibility perceptions for the expertise-job.

Hypotheses 1b posed that wearing spectacles in a LinkedIN profile picture would positively affect credibility perceptions for the trustworthiness jobs as well. However, results showed that wearing spectacles ($M = 4.62$, $SD = .58$) or not wearing spectacles ($M = 4.73$, $SD = .44$) didn't seem to help or hinder the perceived credibility levels elicited by candidates' physiognomies, $F(1,46) = .529$, $p = .41$, $\eta^2 = .13$ for the trustworthiness job. Hence, hypothesis 1b is not confirmed. Hypothesis 1c stated that wearing spectacles would negatively affect credibility perceptions for the attractiveness-job. To our surprise, we found that the picture of our female job candidate was perceived as more credible for the attractiveness job *with* spectacles ($M = 4.96$, $SD = .63$) than *without* spectacles ($M = 4.56$, $SD = .84$), $F(1,46) = 3.539$, $p = .06$, $\eta^2 = .07$, thus hypothesis 1c was rejected.

To test our second hypothesis, a regression analysis was carried out. Results show that candidates' *perceived credibility* is a significant predictor of *invitation intention* for a job interview, $F(1, 137) = 21.59$, $p < .001$, which explained 14 % on the ($R2 = 0.14$). In line with our expectations, perceived credibility was positively related to invitation intention, $b* = 0.37$, $t = 4.65$, $p < .001$. Therefore, hypothesis H2 was confirmed.

5 Discussion

Our study contributes to research and practice in the following ways. As indicated in [1], first, although prior research shows that SNSs are increasingly popular recruitment tools, there has been very little empirical research into effective *personal branding* of job candidates on SNSs [11].

Second, in contrast to the attention that Facebook has received from marketing and computer-mediated communication scholars, very little research has been dedicated to *professional* SNSs such as LinkedIn [cf. 41]. Third, from a practical perspective, for jobs seekers today, it is important to know which visual cues in an online profile picture can help create positive impressions on employers, and how these self presentation mechanisms work in relation to different job categories. For instance, depending on the type of job one aims for, it may be wise or unwise to wear a colourful shirt, put on a bow tie – or wear spectacles.

The present study shows that LinkedIn profile pictures of bespectacled candidates are perceived as more *credible* than candidates without spectacles only when the job vacancies was an *expertise-job* (H1a). For the *trustworthiness-job*, there was no significant difference in wearing spectacles or not (H1b). Moreover, our results indicated that bespectacled candidates are perceived as *more credible* for the *attractiveness-job*, than non-bespectacled candidates (H1c). This finding is in contrast to our expectations and inconsistent with the existing body of literature that supports that spectacle wearers are perceived as unattractive [9, 28]. Regarding our final hypothesis (H2), as expected, a higher degree of *perceived credibility* indeed resulted in a greater likelihood to obtain *a job interview* than candidates with a lower perceived credibility. This implies that candidates' *perceived credibility* can be considered an explanatory variable of their *invitation intention*. In other words, the more credible candidates are perceived to be, the more likely they will be invited for a job interview.

An explanation for our findings regarding spectacles and attractiveness may be that this type of spectacles with a thick rim induced symmetry, and therefore attractiveness [9]. Second, this specific pair of spectacles may have magnified the model's eyes, and big 'puppy' eyes have always been a biological indicator of attractiveness [40]. Lastly, this finding might be related to the current trend of wearing spectacles-without-lenses, which entails that people wear spectacles as a fashion accessory. This turnaround has been initiated by popular culture as celebrities and famous models are increasingly wearing spectacles with noticeable frames [22, 23]. An explanation for our finding regarding trust could be that for trustworthiness-jobs people want to look job applicants in the eyes. It has been shown that narrow eyes raise suspicion whilst round eyes are perceived as a sign of trust [41], moreover, adults make attributions about competence based on eye gaze patterns [42].

As for practical implications, people managing their personal brand [43] should carefully choose a profile picture when they are applying for a specific job category. Applicants incorrectly upload profile pictures that are inconsistent with the offered job vacancy (for example, a woman without spectacles who applies for an expertise-job) as it is so much harder to get the approval of recruiters and persuade them to invite the applicants to a job interview. Another field of interest is advertising, where the presence of spectacles on the face of product endorsers could boost their credibility as perceived by consumers, with positive effects on purchase intention. Moreover, politics is yet another domain where wearing spectacles could boost candidates perceived credibility; this will positively affect the voting intention [44].

A limitation of this study with respect to its external validity relates to the type of spectacles and the model as manipulation material. Further research should verify whether different styles of spectacles (flamboyant with noticeable colors, modest with a slim frame, etc.), paired with different models (e.g. ethnicity, age, degrees of attractiveness) have similar results when it comes to *perceived credibility*. Ohanian's [6] construct of credibility could be used for this purpose to test the ability of the selected photos to elicit the three credibility sub dimensions in participants' minds. Second, the role of culture and fashion trends in self-presentation needs to be considered in regard to wearing spectacles. Third, future research could investigate the combination of men wearing a beard and spectacles on perceived credibility.

In conclusion, based on this research's findings, an optimist would state that it seems women can have it all: spectacles may enhance perceptions of credibility for jobs related to 'beauty' and 'brains'. However, further research is necessary to investigate whether these effects hold for all types of spectacles, all "types" of women and in all types of cultures.

References

1. Van der Land, S., Muntinga, D.G.: To shave or not to shave? In: Nah, F.F.H. (ed.) HCIB 2014, LNCS, vol. 8527, pp. 257–265. Springer, Heidelberg (2014)
2. Khremper, D.H., Rosen, P.A. Future employment selection methods: evaluating social networking web sites. J. Manag. Psychol. **24**(6), 567–580 (2009)
3. Chaiken, S.: Heuristic versus systematic information processing and the use of source versus message cues in persuasion. J. Pers. Soc. Psychol. **39**(5), 752–766 (1980)
4. Petty, R.E., Cacioppo, J.T., Schumann, D.: Central and peripheral routes to advertising effectiveness: the moderating role of involvement. J. Consum. Res. **10**(2), 135–146 (1983)
5. Walther, J.B.: Computer mediated communication: impersonal, interpersonal and hyperpersonal interaction. Commun. Res. **23**(1), 3–43 (1996)
6. Ohanian, R.: Construction and validation of a scale to measure celebrity endorsers' perceived expertise, trustworthiness, and attractiveness. J. Advertising **19**, 39–52 (1990)
7. Goffman, E.: The Presentation of Self in Everyday Life. Doubleday, New York (1959)
8. Guido, G., Peluso, A.M., Moffa, V.: Beardedness in advertising: Effects on endorsers' credibility and purchase intention. J. Mark. Commun. **17**(1), 37–49 (2011)
9. Edwards, K.: Effects of sex and spectacles on attitudes toward intelligence and attractiveness. Psychol. Rep. **60**, 590 (1987)
10. Thornton, G.R.: The effect upon judgments of personality traits of varying a single factor in a photograph. J. Soc. Psychol. **18**, 127–148 (1943)
11. Labrecque, L.I., Markos, E., Milne, G.R.: Online personal branding: processes, challenges, and implications. J. Interact. Mark. **25**(1), 37–50 (2011)
12. Duck, S.W.: Interpersonal communication in developing acquaintance. In: Miller, G.R. (ed.) Explorations in Interpersonal Communication, pp. 127–148. Sage, Beverly Hills (1982)
13. Wang, S.S., Moon, S.I., Kwon, K.H., Evans, C.A., Stefanone, M.A.: Face off: implications of visual cues on initiating friendship on Facebook. Comput. Hum. Behav. **26**(2), 226–234 (2010)
14. Caers, R., Castelyns, V.: LinkedIn and Facebook in Belgium: the influences and biases of social network sites in recruitment and selection procedures. Soc. Sci. Comput. Rev. (2010)
15. Dougherty, T.W., Turban, D.B., Callender, J.C.: Confirming first impressions in the employment interview: a field study of interviewer behavior. J. Appl. Psychol. **79**(5), 659 (1994)
16. Hum, N.J., Chamberlin, P.E., Hambright, B.L., Portwood, A.C., Schat, A.C., Bevan, J.L.: A picture is worth a thousand words: a content analysis of Facebook profile photographs. Comput. Hum. Behav. **27**(5), 1828–1833 (2011)
17. Utz, S.: Show me your friends and i will tell you what type of person you are: how one's profile, number of friends, and type of friends influence impression formation on social network sites. J. Comput. Mediated Commun. **15**(2), 314–335 (2010)
18. Ellison, N., Steinfield, C., Lampe, C.: The benefits of Facebook "friends:" socialcapital and college students' use of online social network sites. J. Comput. Mediated Commun. **12**, 1143–1168 (2007)
19. Tong, S.T., Van Der Heide, B., Langwell, L., Walther, J.B.: Too much of a good thing? The relationship between number of friends and interpersonal impressions on Facebook. J. Comput. Mediated Commun. **13**, 531–549 (2008)
20. Leder, H., Forster, M., Gerger, G.: The spectacles stereotype revisited. Swiss J. Psychol. **70**(4), 211–222 (2011)
21. Terry, R.L., Krantz, J.H.: Dimensions of trait attributions associated with eyespectacles, men's facial hair, and women's hair length. J. Appl. Soc. Psychol. **23**(21), 1757–1769 (1993)

22. Cochrane, L.: Glasses – the latest must-have accessory. In: The Guardian. http://www.theguardian.com/fashion/2012/oct/31/glasses-latest-must-have-accessory. Accessed 31 Oct 2012
23. Tschorn, A.: Eyeglasses a new fashion essential? In: Los Angeles Times. http://articles.latimes.com/2012/apr/29/image/la-ig-eyeglasses-20120429-1. Accessed 29 Apr 2012
24. Argyle, M., McHenry, R.: Do spectacles really affect judgments of intelligence? Br. J. Soc. Clin. Psychol. **10**, 27–29 (1971)
25. Acker, S.R., Levitt, S.R.: Designing videoconference facilities for improved eye contact. J. Broadcast. Electron. Media **31**(2), 181–191 (1987)
26. Bayliss, A.P., Tipper, S.P.: Predictive gaze cues and personality judgments: should eye trust you? Psychol. Sci. **17**, 514–520 (2006)
27. Lundberg, J.K., Sheehan, E.P.: The effects of spectacles and weight on perceptions of attractiveness and intelligence. J. Soc. Behav. Pers. **9**, 753–760 (1994)
28. Terry, R.L., Hall, C.A.: Affective responses to eye spectacles: evidence of a sex difference. J. Am. Optom. Assoc. **60**, 609–611 (1989)
29. Harris, M.R.: Sex differences in stereotypes of spectacles. J. Appl. Soc. Psychol. **21**, 1659–1680 (1991)
30. Woodside, A.G., Davenport, J.W.: The effect of salesman similarity and expertise on consumer purchasing behavior. J. Mark. Res. **11**(2), 198–202 (1974)
31. Pornpitakpan, C.: The persuasiveness of source credibility: a critical review of five decades' evidence. J. Appl. Soc. Psychol. **34**(2), 243–281 (2004)
32. NSMBL: nsmbl x specsavers de leukste brilmonturen gecombineerd met 5 verschillende kapsels. http://www.nsmbl.nl/nsmbl-x-specsavers-de-leukste-brilmonturen-gecombineerd-met-5-verschillende-kapsels/. Accessed 21 Jan 2014
33. Mesko, N., Bereczkei, T.: Hairstyle as an adaptive means of displaying phenotypic quality. Hum. Nat. **15**(3), 251–270 (2004)
34. Jackson, W.C., Bendick, M., Romero, H.J.: Employment discrimination against older workers. J. Aging Soc. Policy **8**(4), 25–46 (1997)
35. Reis, H.T., Maniaci, M.R., Caprariello, P.A., Eastwick, P.W., Finkel, E.J.: Familiarity does indeed promote attraction in live interaction. J. Pers. Soc. Psychol. **101**(3), 557–570 (2011)
36. Wilson, E.: The return of the interview suit. In: The New York Times. http://www.nytimes.com/2008/11/13/fashion/13INTERVIEW.html?pagewanted=all&_r=0. Accessed 12 Nov 2008
37. Grimaldi, L.: The job hunt: Part 3 acing the interview. Meet. Conventions **67–68** (2010)
38. Martin, W.W., Gardner, S.N.: The relative effects of eye-gaze and smiling on arousal in asocial situations. J. Psychol. **102**(2), 253–259 (1979)
39. Fishbein, M., Ajzen, I.: Belief, Attitude, Intention, and Behavior: An Introduction to Theory and Research. Addison-Wesley, Reading (1975)
40. Cunningham, M.R.: Measuring the physical in physical attractiveness: quasi experiments on the sociobiology of female facial beauty. J. Pers. Soc. Psychol. **50**(5), 925–935 (1986)
41. Zebrowitz, L.A.: Reading faces: Window to the soul? Westview Press, Boulder (1997)
42. Kleinke, C.L.: Gaze and eye contact: a research review. Psychol. Bull. **10**, 78–100 (1986)
43. Shepherd, I.D.: From cattle and coke to Charlie: meeting the challenge of self marketing and personal branding. J. Mark. Manage. **21**(5–6), 589–606 (2005)
44. Todorov, A., Mandisodza, A.N., Goren, A., Hall, C.C.: Inferences of competence from faces predict election outcomes. Science **308**, 1623–1626 (2005)
45. Field, A.: Discovering Statistics Using SPSS. Sage Publications, Thousand Oaks (2009)

Mining Social Media for Enhancing Personalized Document Clustering

Chin-Sheng Yang$^{(\boxtimes)}$ and Pei-Chun Chang

Department of Information Management, and Innovation Center for Big Data
and Digital Convergence, Yuan Ze University, Chung-Li, Taiwan, ROC
csyang@saturn.yzu.edu.tw, s996202@mail.yzu.edu.tw

Abstract. Social media is nowadays an excellent platform for gathering user
intelligence for supporting business intelligence applications. Social tagging
system (aka. folksonomy) is a critical mechanism for collaboratively creating,
organizing and managing the wisdom of crowds. The knowledge gained from
social tagging system should be tremendous assets for conducting and
improving various business intelligent applications. Consequently, the purpose
of this study is to examine the values of folksonomy on an important business
intelligent task, namely personalized document management. Specifically, we
employ Delicious, a pioneered social bookmarking service, to construct a
statistical-based thesaurus which is then applied to support personalized document clustering. According to our empirical evaluation results, social tagging
system indeed improve the quality of the statistical-based thesaurus in comparison with that constructed on the basis of a general-purpose search engine in
generating personalized document clusters.

Keywords: Social media · Business intelligence · Social tagging · Social
bookmarking · Personalized document clustering

1 Introduction

Social media is nowadays the most popular platform that allows the creation and
exchange of user generated content [15]. According to the research results by the Pew
Research Center [24], over 70 % of internet users use social media sites as of January
2014. Another report by eMarketer [12] reveals that, by the end of 2013, 163.5 million
people in U.S.-more than two-thirds of internet users-will be social media users.
Moreover, Facebook, the global leading social networking service provider, has 1.35
billion monthly active users as of the third quarter 2014 [13]. 4.5 billion "Likes" were
generated and 4.75 billion pieces of content was shared daily as of May 2013. These
statistics indicate the social appeal associated with social media and user-generated
content and the value of acquiring information from social media to facilitate the
development of novel and the improvement of existing products and services.

   Various social media websites, such as wikis (e.g., Wikipedia), blogs and microblogs (e.g., Twitter), media sharing (e.g., YouTube, Flickr), social news (e.g., Digg,
Reddit), social bookmarking (e.g., Delicious, CiteULike), and social networking
(e.g., Facebook, Google+), have been established. The knowledge (aka "wisdom of

© Springer International Publishing Switzerland 2015
F.F.-H. Nah and C.-H. Tan (Eds.): HCIB 2015, LNCS 9191, pp. 185–196, 2015.
DOI: 10.1007/978-3-319-20895-4_18

crowds") gained from social media sites can not only meet the objectives of businesses offering them but also help the development of novel and effective services that are better tailored to users' needs. In this study, we focus on analyzing a specific mechanism, i.e., social tagging system (aka folksonomy), commonly supported by numerous social media sites, e.g., YouTube, Flickr, Delicious, etc., for enhancing the effective of personalized information management. A folksonomy is a system of classification [29] which allows users to attach self-defined keywords (or tags) to describe resources [21], [27]. Folksonomy generally consists of a set of users, a set of self-defined tags, a set of resources, and a set of tag assignments (i.e., a set of user-tag-resource triple relationships) [8]. Semantically, tags in a folksonomy reflect users' collaborative cognition on information. They can reveal both the users' behavior and resources' properties [34].

The knowledge gained from folksonomy is valuable for supporting various applications, such as Web page classification [1], recommendation [22, 37], and information retrieval [3, 6]. In this study, we attempt to apply the wisdom of crowds of folksonomy to a novel document management task, namely personalized document clustering. Specifically, we adopt the CAC technique proposed by Yang and Wei [36] as our underlying personalized document clustering algorithm. The CAC technique takes into consideration a user's categorization preference (expressed as a list of anchoring terms) and subsequently generates a set of document clusters from this specific preferential perspective. Furthermore, the CAC technique exploits the world wide web as an information source to construct a statistical-based thesaurus, which then serves to expand the set of anchoring terms which is then applied to represent the source documents and then performs clustering to generate document clusters in accordance with the input preferential context (i.e., initial set of anchoring terms provided by the target user). Alternatively, we want to understand the effectiveness of folksonomy, in comparison with a general-purpose search engine (i.e., Google in Yang and Wei's study), on constructing a statistical-based thesaurus for supporting personalized document clustering. We select delicious (https://delicious.com/), a leading social bookmarking site, as the folksonomy for our social-tagging-based CAC technique (ST-CAC). We also conduct some experiments to evaluate the effectiveness of the ST-CAC technique and its benchmark approaches.

The remainder of this paper is organized as follows. Section 2 reviews existing document clustering techniques relevant to this study. In Sect. 3, we describe the detailed design of the proposed ST-CAC technique. Subsequently, we depict our experimental design and discuss important evaluation results in Sect. 4. Finally, we conclude with a summary and some future research directions in Sect. 5.

2   Literature Review

Document clustering entails the automatic organization of a large document collection into distinct groups of similar documents that reflect general themes hidden within the corpus [23, 32]. The documents in the resultant clusters exhibit maximal similarity to those in the same cluster and, at the same time, share minimal similarity with documents in other clusters. However, according to the context theory of classification, document clustering behaviors of individuals not only involve the attributes (including contents) of documents but also depend on who is performing the task and in what context [2, 7, 17]. As a result, document clustering is an intentional act that should reflect individuals' preferences with regard to the semantic coherency or relevant categorization of documents [26] and should conform to the context of a target task under investigation.

Most of existing document clustering techniques are anchored in document content analysis. The overall process of a content-based document clustering technique generally comprises three main phases: feature extraction and selection, document representation, and clustering [14, 32, 33]. The purpose of feature extraction and selection is to extract and select from the target document corpus a set of representative features to represent the documents in the document representation phase. Subsequently, the clustering phase applies a clustering technique to group the target documents into distinct clusters.

Feature extraction begins with the parsing of each source document to produce a set of nouns and noun phrases and exclude a list of prespecified "stop words" that are non-semantic-bearing words. Subsequently, representative features are selected from the set of extracted features. Feature selection is important for clustering efficiency and effectiveness, because it not only condenses the size of the extracted feature set, but also reduces the potential biases embedded in the original (i.e., nontrimmed) feature set [25, 35]. Commonly used feature selection metrics include: TF, TF × IDF, and their hybrids [4, 19].

On the basis of a particular feature selection metric, the k features with the highest selection metric scores then are selected to represent each source document in the document representation phase. Based on the chosen representation scheme, each document is described in the k-dimensional space and represented as a feature vector. Commonly employed document representation schemes include binary (presence or absence of a feature in a document), within-document TF, and TF × IDF [4, 19, 23, 25, 32].

In the final phase of document clustering, source documents are grouped into distinct clusters on the basis of the selected features and their respective values in each document. Common clustering approaches include partitioning-based [4, 9, 19], hierarchical [11, 25, 30, 32], and Kohonen neural network [18, 20, 25].

As mentioned, content-based document clustering techniques rely on an objective feature-selection metric (e.g., TF or TF × IDF) that merely considers document content. As a result, existing content-based techniques generate for all users an identical set of document clusters from a given document collection and, thus, is unable to support personalized document-clustering. In response to the limitation of existing content-based document clustering techniques, prior research has proposed several extended approaches that might support personalized document clustering. For example, Deogun and Raghavan [10] propose a user-oriented document clustering technique that considers only document relevance to user queries. Kim and Lee [16] propose a semi-supervised document clustering technique to improve clustering effectiveness. Their approach essentially is a hybrid one that considers not only content similarity but also a user's perception of the document similarity using a relevance-feedback mechanism. Wei et al. [32] instead propose a personalized document clustering (PEC) approach to support personalization in document categorization.

In addition to the contents of the documents to be clustered, the PEC approach includes a target user's partial clustering as input, because it reflects his or her categorization preference. Last, Yang and Wei [36] propose a context-aware document-clustering (CAC) technique that takes into consideration a user's categorization preference (expressed as a list of anchoring terms) and subsequently generates a set of document clusters from this specific preferential perspective.

The abovementioned extended document clustering techniques in some degree can support the desired personalized document clustering task. Accordingly to Yang and Wei's study [36], the CAC technique outperforms other extended approaches in terms of supporting personalized document clustering. Thus, we adopted the CAC technique as the underlying algorithm for personalized document clustering. The CAC technique adopt a general-purpose search engine (i.e., Google) to construct a statistical-based thesaurus which serves as the basis for generating a set of document clusters which fits the categorization preference of a specific user. In this study, we adopt social media (more specifically, social tagging system) as an alternative information source for statistical-based thesaurus construction. The rational is that the information in folksonomy has been processed by crowds and reflects users' collaborative cognition. Such collaborative wisdoms should be better in supporting personalized document clustering.

3 Proposed Method

The context-aware document-clustering (CAC) technique, proposed by Yang and Wei [36], takes into consideration a user's categorization preference (expressed as a list of anchoring terms) and then generates a set of document clusters from this specific preferential perspective. For example, given a set of research articles related to "data mining," a person interested in developing new data mining techniques may prefer document categories anchored on the techniques under discussion and thus provides some anchoring terms as classification analysis, clustering analysis, association rules, sequential patterns, and so on. On the other hand, another person, who is working on data mining techniques to real world business applications, may prefer a different set of categories based on the application domains involved (e.g., banking, retailing, health care, telecommunications, etc.). Given the set of user-provided anchoring terms which represent the specific user's categorization preference, the CAC technique first constructs a statistical-based thesaurus and subsequently expands the given set of anchoring terms by adding their relevant terms. The expanded set of anchoring terms is adopted as the representative features for performing personalized document clustering.

The major difference between the CAC technique and our extended social-tagging-based CAC technique (ST-CAC) is the way of constructing statistical-based thesaurus. As shown in Fig. 1, the ST-CAC technique consists of five main phases: (1) feature extraction and selection; (2) statistical-based thesaurus construction; (3) anchoring term expansion; (4) document representation; and (5) document clustering. The detailed design of each phase is described in this section.

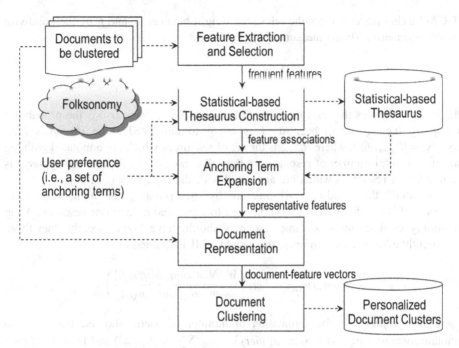

Fig. 1. Overall process of the ST-CAC technique

3.1 Feature Extraction and Selection

This phase aims at extracting and selecting a set of meaningful features (specifically, nouns and noun phrases) from the target document corpus. We adopt the part-of-speech (POS) tagger developed by Brill [5] to syntactically tag each word in the target documents and then employ Voutilainen's approach [31] to implement a noun-phrase parser for extracting noun phrases from each tagged document. Furthermore, we remove features that infrequently appear in the target document corpus. Particularly, we only retain those features whose document frequency (*df*) is no less than a prespecified threshold δ_{DF}.

3.2 Statistical-Based Thesaurus Construction

The purpose of this phase is to automatically construct a statistical-based thesaurus that will be used for expanding the user-provided anchoring terms. We adopt the folksonomy of Delicious website as the corpus for constructing a statistical-based thesaurus. Folksonomy generally is consisted of a set of users (U), a set of self-defined tags (T), a set of resources (R), and a set of tag assignments $A \subseteq U \times T \times R$ (i.e., a set of user-tag-resource triple relationships). A bookmark in Delicious website is a triple (u, T_{ur}, r) with $u \in U$, $r \in R$, and a set of tags $T_{ur} = \{t \in T \mid (u, t, r) \in A\}$.

For each anchoring term q_i pertaining to the categorization preference of a target user and every feature f_j representative to the target document corpus, the proposed

ST-CAC technique calculates the relevance weight between q_i and f_j by the pointwise mutual information (PMI) measure [28] as follows:

$$rw_{q_i,f_j} = log_2\left(\frac{p(q_i \wedge f_j)}{p(q_i)p(f_j)}\right) = log_2\left(\frac{N \times \text{hits}(q_i \wedge f_j)}{\text{hits}(qi)\text{hits}(f_j)}\right), \tag{1}$$

where $rw_{qi,fj}$ denotes the relevance weight between q_i to f_j, $p(query)$ is the probability that $query$ (i.e., q_i or f_j) been used as a tag to annotated some resources (i.e., $p(query) = |R_{query}|/|R|$, where R_{query} is the set of resources which are annotated with tag $query$), N is total number of resources in the folksonomy (i.e., $|R|$), and $\text{hits}(query)$ is the number of resources which are annotated with the tag $query$ (i.e., $|R_{query}|$).

We extend the standard PMI measure by incorporating the number of users $U_t = \{u \in U \mid (u, t, R) \in A\}$ who use the tag t to annotated at least one resource. A tag commonly used to annotate same resources should have higher weight than those infrequently adopted. Accordingly, the weight PMI is defined as:

$$weighted\_rw_{q_i,f_j} = log_2\left(\frac{W\_N \times sum\_u(q_i \wedge f_j)}{sum\_u(q_i)sum\_u(f_j)}\right), \tag{2}$$

where $sum\_u(query)$ is the summation of number of users who use tag $query$ to annotate some resources (i.e., $sum\_u(query) = \sum_{query \in Rquery} |U_{query}|$) and W_N is the total number of tag assignments (i.e., $|A|$). We employ the weighted PMI measure for our proposed ST-CAC technique.

3.3   Anchoring Term Expansion

On the basis of the constructed statistical-based thesaurus, this phase expands a given set of anchoring terms AT by including additional relevant terms. An anchoring term q_i in AT is expanded with a set of terms E_{qi} whose relevance weights, measure by weighted PMI values, to q_i need to be greater than a prespecified threshold α. The expanded set of anchoring terms $RF = \left(\bigcup_{q_i \in AT} E_{q_i}\right) \cup AT$ is formed for the succeeding document clustering task.

Because RF consists of the anchoring terms originally provided by the target user and relevant terms expanded from the anchoring terms, the importance of the terms in RF should not be identical when they are used to represent each document to be clustered. Accordingly, a TF × IDF-like scheme is adopted to estimate the weight of each expanded term f_j (i.e., in RF but not in AT) as:

$$w_j = \sum_{q_i \in ET_j} rw_{q_i,f_j} \times log\left(\frac{|AT|}{|ET_j|} + \varepsilon\right), \tag{3}$$

where $ET_j \subseteq AT$ is the set of anchoring terms that expand f_j and ε is a small positive value to avoid the log component being 0. On the other hand, if $f_i \in AT$, w_j is the largest weight across all expanded terms derived previously.

3.4 Document Representation

Subsequently, each document to be clustered is represented using the expanded set of anchoring terms RF. ST-CAC employs the weighted TF $\times$ IDF scheme for document representation. Specifically, each document d_l is described by a feature vector $\vec{d_l}$ as:

$$\vec{d_l} = \langle v_{l1} \times w_1, v_{l2} \times w_2, \ldots, v_{lm} \times w_m \rangle, \tag{4}$$

where m is the total number of terms in RF, v_{lj} is the standard TF $\times$ IDF value of f_j in d_l, and w_j is the weight of the term f_j in RF.

3.5 Document Clustering

Finally, the target documents are grouped into distinct clusters on the basis of the expanded set of anchoring terms (i.e., RF) and their respective representation values in each document. ST-CAC adopts the hierarchical clustering approach (specifically, the HAC algorithm with the cosine measure for the similarity estimation between two documents and the group-average link method for similarity measurement between two clusters) as the underlying clustering algorithm.

4 Empirical Evaluation

This section reports our empirical evaluation of the proposed ST-CAC technique using a traditional content-based document clustering technique and the CAC technique as performance benchmarks. In the following, we discuss the evaluation design (including data collection and evaluation criteria), parameter tuning experiments, and important evaluation results.

4.1 Data Collection

The collection of document corpus for our evaluation purpose consists of 434 research articles related to information systems and technologies that were collected through keyword searches (e.g., XML, data mining, robotics) from a scientific literature digital library website (i.e., CiteSeer, http://citeseerx.ist.psu.edu/). For each article in our literature corpus, only the abstract and keywords were used in this evaluation study.

To evaluate the effectiveness of a personalized document clustering technique, we need to categorize our literature corpus from different users' preferential perspectives. We developed a system to collect individuals' preferred clustering for the literature corpus. Each experimental subject was asked to subjectively categorize the entire

Table 1. Summary of subjects' categories for the literature corpus

	Number of clusters (i.e., anchoring terms)	Number of documents in a cluster
Maximum	67	125
Minimum	10	1
Average	26.12	16.64

literature corpus manually on the basis of his/her own preference. After clustering, the subject was asked to assign a label for each category. These category labels are then considered as the set of anchoring terms of the subject which will be used as the input to the ST-CAC technique. A total of 33 subjects accomplished the manual clustering of the literature corpus. According to the self-reported estimates of the subjects, each subject spent a minimum of eight hours performing manual document clustering. A summary of the document categories generated by the subjects is provided in Table 1.

4.2   Evaluation Criteria

We employ cluster recall and cluster precision [25], defined according to the concept of associations, to measure the effectiveness of the ST-CAC technique and its benchmark techniques. An association refers to a pair of documents that belong to the same cluster. Accordingly, the cluster recall (CR) and cluster precision (CP) from the viewpoint of a subject u_a is defined as:

$$CR = \frac{|CA_a|}{|T_a|} \quad \text{and} \quad CP = \frac{|CA_a|}{|G_a|}, \tag{5}$$

where T_a is the set of associations in the categories manually produced by the subject u_a, CA_a is the set of correct associations that exists in both the clusters generated by a document-clustering technique and the categories produced by u_a, and G_a is the set of associations in the clusters generated by the document-clustering technique.

To address the inevitable trade-offs between cluster recall and cluster precision, precision/recall trade-off (PRT) curves are employed. A PRT curve represents the effectiveness of a document clustering technique with different intercluster similarity thresholds.

4.3   Parameter Tuning

We randomly select 10 users from the 33 subjects to determine the appropriate value of each parameter involved in the three document clustering techniques (i.e., a traditional content-based approach, the CAC approach, and our proposed ST-CAC approach) examined. The overall clustering effectiveness of each technique in the tuning experiments is calculated by averaging the cluster recall and cluster precision obtained from the ten subjects.

The traditional content-based document clustering (TCC) approach involves the parameter of number of features (k) for document representation. We range k form 200 to 2000 in increments of 200 and obtain the best performance when k is equal to 2,000. On the other hand, both CAC and ST-CAC techniques include the parameters δ_{DF} (the threshold to remove infrequent features in the feature extraction and selection phase) and α (the threshold to determine whether a term should be expanded in the anchoring term expansion phase). We first investigate α from 1 to 10 in increments of 0.5. The best values of α for CAC and ST-CAC are 2.5 and 2 respectively. Subsequently, we examine δ_{DF} from 3–10 in increments of 1 and get the best δ_{DF} values of 10 and 9 for CAC and ST-CAC respectively.

4.4   Comparative Evaluation Results

Using the parameter values determined previously, we evaluate the effectiveness of the ST-CAC technique and its benchmark techniques. In this experiment, all of the 33 subjects are used for evaluation purpose. The comparative evaluation result is shown in Fig. 2. The proposed ST-CAC technique achieves better clustering effectiveness than do the TCC and CAC techniques. Moreover, the CAC technique also outperforms the TCC technique. These results suggest that both ST-CAC and CAC techniques indeed have the ability to generate personalized document clusters according to the target user's personalized preference expressed as a set of anchoring terms. Furthermore, using social media for statistical-based thesaurus construction has better performance than that constructed from a general-purpose search engine.

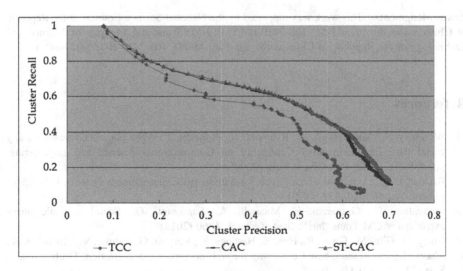

Fig. 2. Comparative evaluation results

5 Conclusion and Future Research Directions

Social media is nowadays an excellent source for gathering user intelligence to support various business intelligence applications. Motivated by the observation, this paper attempts to investigate the effectiveness of social tagging system (aka. folksonomy) in enhancing an important document management task, i.e., personalized document clustering. Specifically, we adopt the CAC technique proposed by Yang and Wei (2007) as our underlying algorithm and incorporate a leading social bookmarking site (i.e., Delicious) to design the ST-CAC technique which uses the folksonomy in Delicious to construct a statistical-based thesaurus for personalized document clustering. According to our empirical evaluation results, the ST-CAC and CAC techniques definitely have the ability to generate personalized document clusters than a traditional content-based approach. Moreover, the statistical-based thesaurus constructed from social media also slightly outperforms that generated from a general-purpose search engine.

Some ongoing and future research directions are briefly discussed as follows. First, Delicious, which is a social bookmarking service for webpages, is adopted as the social media for statistical-based thesaurus construction. Since our document corpus for evaluation purpose is collected from a scientific literature database, it is essential to evaluate the performance of an alternative social bookmarking service (i.e., CiteU-Like), which allows users to share citations to academic papers, on our proposed ST-CAC technique. Second, only the PMI measure is applied for statistical-based thesaurus construction. It should be interesting to implement and test empirically other measures for statistical-based thesaurus construction.

Acknowledgments. This work was supported by the National Science Council of the Republic of China under the grant NSC 100-2410-H-155-013-MY3 and the Ministry of Science and Technology of the Republic of China under the grant MOST 103-2410-H-155-027-MY3.

References

1. Aliakbary, S., Abolhassani, H., Rahmani, H., Nobakht, B.: Web page classification using social tags. In: International Conference on Computational Science and Engineering, pp. 588–593. IEEE Press, New York (2009)
2. Barreau, D.K.: Context as a factor in personal information management systems. J. Am. Soc. Inform. Sci. **46**, 327–339 (1995)
3. Biancalana, C., Gasparetti, F., Micarelli, A., Sansonetti, G.: Social semantic query expansion. ACM Trans. Intell. Syst. Technol. **4**, 60 (2013)
4. Boley, D., Gini, M., Gross, R., Han, E., Hastings, K., Karypis, G., Kumar, V., Mobasher, B., Moore, L.: Partitioning-based clustering for web document categorization. Decis. Support Syst. **27**, 329–341 (1999)
5. Brill, E.: A simple rule-based part of speech tagger. In: Third Conference on Applied Natural Language Processing, pp.152–155. Association for Computational Linguistics, Stroudsburg, PA (1992)

6. Cai, Y., Li, Q., Xie, H., Min, H.: Exploring personalized searches using tag-based user profiles and resource profiles in folksonomy. Neural Netw. **58**, 98–110 (2014)
7. Case, D.O.: Conceptual organization and retrieval of text by historians: the role of memory and metaphor. J. Am. Soc. Inform. Sci. **42**, 657–668 (1991)
8. Cattuto, C., Benz, D., Hotho, A., Stumme, G.: Semantic grounding of tag relatedness in social bookmarking systems. In: Sheth, A.P., Staab, S., Dean, M., Paolucci, M., Maynard, D., Finin, T., Thirunarayan, K. (eds.) ISWC 2008. LNCS, vol. 5318, pp. 615–631. Springer, Heidelberg (2008)
9. Cutting, D., Karger, D., Pedersen, J., Tukey, J.: Scatter/gather: a cluster-based approach to browsing large document collections. In: 15th Annual International ACM SIGIR Conference on Research and Development in Information Retrieval, pp. 318–329. ACM Press, New York (1992)
10. Deogun, J., Raghavan, V.: User-oriented document clustering: a framework for learning in information retrieval. In: 9th Annual International ACM SIGIR Conference on Research and Development in Information Retrieval, pp. 157–163. ACM Press, New York (1986)
11. El-Hamdouchi, A., Willett, P.: Hierarchical document clustering using ward's method. In: 9th Annual International ACM SIGIR Conference on Research and Development in Information Retrieval, pp. 149–156. ACM Press, New York (1986)
12. eMarketer.: US social network users 2013: smartphone usage drives mobile-social growth (2007). https://www.emarketer.com/Coverage/SocialMedia.aspx
13. Facebook.: Facebook reports third quarter 2014 results (2014). http://investor.fb.com/releasedetail.cfm?ReleaseID=878726
14. Jain, A.K., Murty, M.N., Flynn, P.J.: Data clustering: a review. ACM Comput. Surv. **31**, 265–323 (1999)
15. Kaplan, A.M., Haenlein, M.: Users of the world, unite! the challenges and opportunities of social media. Bus. Horiz. **53**, 59–68 (2010)
16. Kim, H., Lee, S.: A semi-supervised document clustering technique for information organization. In: 9th International Conference on Information and Knowledge Management, pp. 30–37. ACM Press, New York (2000)
17. Kwasnik, B.H.: The importance of factors that are not document attributes in the organization of personal documents. J. Doc. **47**, 389–398 (1991)
18. Lagus, K., Honkela, T., Kaski, S., Kohonen, T.: Self-organizing maps of document collections: a new approach to interactive exploration. In: 2nd International Conference on Knowledge Discovery and Data Mining, pp. 238–243. AAAI Press, Menlo Park (1996)
19. Larsen, B., Aone, C.: Fast and effective text mining using linear-time document clustering. In: 5th ACM SIGKDD International Conference on Knowledge Discovery and Data Mining, pp. 16–22. ACM Press, New York (1999)
20. Lin, C., Chen, H., Nunamaker, J.F.: Verifying the proximity and size hypothesis for self-organizing maps. J. Manage. Inform. Syst. **16**, 57–70 (1999–2000)
21. Milicevic, A.K., Nanopoulos, A., Ivanovic, M.: Social tagging in recommender systems: a survey of the state-of-the-art and possible extensions. Artif. Intell. Rev. **33**, 187–209 (2010)
22. Movahedian, H., Khayyambashi, M.R.: Folksonomy-based user interest and disinterest profiling for improved recommendations: an ontological approach. J. Inform. Sci. **40**, 594–610 (2014)
23. Pantel, P., Lin, D.: Document clustering with committees. In: 25th Annual International ACM SIGIR Conference on Research and Development in Information Retrieval, pp. 199–206. ACM Press, New York (2002)
24. Pew Research Center: Social networking fact sheet (2014). http://www.pewinternet.org/fact-sheets/

25. Roussinov, D.G., Chen, H.: Document clustering for electronic meetings: an experimental comparison of two techniques. Decis. Support Syst. **27**, 67–79 (1999)
26. Rucker, J., Polanco, M.J.: Siteseer: personalized navigation for the web. Commun. ACM **40**, 73–75 (1997)
27. Suchanek, F.M., Vojnovic, M., Gunawardena, D.: Social tags: meaning and suggestions. In: 17th ACM Conference on Information and Knowledge Management, pp. 223–232. ACM Press, New York (2008)
28. Turney, P.D., Littman, M.L.: Measuring praise and criticism: inference of semantic orientation from association. ACM Trans. Inform. Syst. **21**, 315–346 (2013)
29. Vander Wal, T.: Folksonomy (2005). http://vanderwal.net/folksonomy.html
30. Voorhees, E.M.: Implementing agglomerative hierarchical clustering algorithms for use in document retrieval. Inform. Process. Manage. **22**, 465–476 (1986)
31. Voutilainen, A.: Nptool: A detector of english noun phrases. In: Workshop on Very Large Corpora, pp. 48–57 (1993)
32. Wei, C., Chiang, R., Wu, C.: Accommodating individual categorization preferences: a personalized document clustering approach. J. Manage. Inform. Syst. **23**, 173–201 (2006)
33. Wei, C., Hu, P., Dong, Y.X.: Managing document categories in e-commerce environments: an evolution-based approach. Eur. J. Inform. Syst. **11**, 208–222 (2002)
34. Wu, C., Zhan, B.: Semantic relatedness in folksonomy. In: International Conference on New Trends in Information and Service Science, pp. 760–765. IEEE Press, New York (2009)
35. Yang, Y., Chute, C.G.: An example-based mapping method for text categorization and retrieval. ACM Trans. Inform. Syst. **12**, 252–277 (1994)
36. Yang, C.S., Wei, C.: Context-aware document-clustering technique. In: 11th Pacific Asia Conference on Information Systems (2007)
37. Yang, C.S., Chen, L.C.: Personalized recommendation in social media: a profile expansion approach. In: 18th Pacific Asia Conference on Information Systems (2014)

The Influence of Individual Affective Factors on the Continuous Use of Mobile Apps

Yi-Hsuan Yeh[1(✉)], Belinda Chen[1], and Nien-Chu Wu[2]

[1] Innovative DigiTech-Enabled Applications and Services Institute,
Institute for Information Industry, Taiwan, Republic of China
celesteyeh@iii.org.tw
[2] Service Systems Technology Center, Industrial Technology Research Institute,
Taiwan, Republic of China

Abstract. Mobile apps have attracted a substantial amount of attention in mobile commerce. Usage behavior of consumers is always an important issue in this research area. The objective of this study is to explore what factors will affect an individual's continuance intention to use mobile apps. We proposes a research model that integrates the Task-Technology Fit (TTF) and Theory of Reasoned Action (TRA), which are augmented with concepts of affective factors. We conduct an online survey and the results show that a higher degree of TTF and VTF (Value-Technology Fit) resulted in a more positive attitude towards using the mobile app. SN and attitude had strong significant impacts on users' continuance intention to use the app. However, TTF and VTF had no significant effect on the continuance intention to use the app.

Keywords: Mobile apps · Task-Technology Fit · Value-Technology Fit · Subjective norm

1 Introduction

Recent years have seen an explosive growth in the number of mobile devices such as smart phones and tablets. There are hundreds of thousands of mobile apps out there for iOS and Android users. According to Gartner's report, it indicates that mobile apps revenues tipped to reach 26 billion dollars in 2013, and estimates that 103 billion mobile apps will be downloaded [20]. Gartner also predicts future trends in the market, claiming that by 2017, annual app downloads will reach 268.7 billion, and in-app purchases will generating 48 % of revenues. Due to the great potentials, users' behavior of mobile apps is always an important issue both in the research area and practical area.

To date, many theories and the antecedents of consumer adoption in mobile marketing have been discussed, such as theory of reasoned action, theory of planned behavior, task-technology fit, trust, flow, playfulness, decision-making, and perceived usefulness etc. Most previous literature focuses on treating new service/technology adoption as a rational decision based on the functional needs of an individual. In many cases, however, new service/technology adoption is not due to functional needs but affective reaction. Gartner points out that five simple attributes into mobile apps to

© Springer International Publishing Switzerland 2015
F.F.-H. Nah and C.-H. Tan (Eds.): HCIB 2015, LNCS 9191, pp. 197–206, 2015.
DOI: 10.1007/978-3-319-20895-4_19

better engage our customers are as follows: recognize your customer, demonstrate that you value your relationship with your customer, create interactions that are inviting and fun, provide information sufficient for making a buy decision, and make payment easy. That is, mobile commerce apps should emphasize on the entire customer experience and satisfy their individual needs. Users with different motivations for adoption may lead to different outcome. In addition, we found there are few articles that can include functional factors and affective factors into consideration. Therefore, this study tries to understand what factors will affect an individual's continuance intention to use and whether different perceived value (functional value vs. mental value) will affect the continuance intention to use of the new app.

In this paper, we aim to investigate affective factors that may affect the continuance intention to use of mobile apps. In order to provide a solid theoretical basis for examining the use of mobile apps, this paper proposes a research model that integrates the Task-technology Fit (TTF) and Theory of Reasoned Action (TRA), which are augmented with concepts of affective factors. TTF and TRA have been used in many studies to predict and understand user intention to adopt new information systems. Hence, they are also appropriate for analyzing the continuance intention to use mobile apps. The purposes of this paper are specified as:

1. To investigate whether affective factors significantly impact a user's continuance intention to use mobile apps.
2. To evaluate whether the augmented technology adoption model can provide a better predictive power for the continuance intention to use mobile apps.

This paper proceeds as follows. Section 2 reviews related literature and describes our research framework. Section 3 outlines research method and instruments. Section 4 provides data analysis and results. Finally, Sect. 5 summarizes our findings and discusses potential implications.

2   Theory and Hypotheses

2.1   Fit

In recent years the fit concept has been widely predicted individual and organizational technology adoption and performance. Fit reveals different kinds of match in social science. For example, Task-Technology Fit (TTF) proposed by Goodhue and Thompson is more likely to have a positive impact on individual performance in organization and is used if the capabilities of the IT match the tasks that the user must perform [8–10, 24]. Fit-Appropriation Model (FAM) extended from TTF considers organizational context and argues a TTF is a necessary but not sufficient condition to improve performance. That is, TTF affects performance, but is moderated by appropriation [6]. Technology-Organization-Environment framework (TOE) identifies three aspects of an enterprise's context that influence the process by which it adopts and implements a technological innovation [23]. Fit-Viability Model (FVM) proposed by Liang and Wei [16] combines TTF with the general notion of organizational viability of information technology. Viability refers to the extent to which the organizational environment is ready for the application. Fit refers to the extent to which the capabilities of IT meet the requirement of task. As mentioned above, besides TTF can both be used in the organizational and individual context, other theories are standing on organizational level.

In this research, we focus on the study of individual continuance intention to use under the mobile commerce context. The satisfaction of Individual needs deriving from the unique features of mobile apps (such as customization, personalization, and social integration etc.) becomes more and more important. Therefore, TTF which is one of appropriate theories will be considered in our research. Although TTF effectively uses a user evaluation perspective to explain individual performance after information technology/service adoption, it neglects user's attitudes and intention in its model. To some extent, it is the concept of "cognitive fit", because whether task and technology fit for each other depends on individual's personal perception. If user perceived task and technology are fit for each other, it would affect user's intention of technology adoption. Meanwhile, if user perceive task and technology are fit for each other, it would also positive affect user's attitude toward technology usage. Therefore, factors affecting users' attitude and intention to use IT will be both considered in our theoretical model. In the use of mobile commerce context, the cognitive dimension, fit, measures the whether mobile app fits for the tasks that the individual needs to perform. Therefore, we propose our first two hypothesis.

Hypothesis 1: Task-Technology Fit positively affect user's attitude toward using mobile apps.

Hypothesis 2: Task-Technology Fit positively affect user's continuance intention to use mobile apps.

Most previous literature focuses on treating new service/technology adoption as a rational decision based on the functional needs of an individual. In many cases, however, new technology/service adoption is not due to functional needs but affective needs. That is, the other individual perception we concerned in this research. We have thought that a user who adopts a service was desire to gain a reward or avoid a negative outcome. However, we found an alternative behavior occur while people have other particular needs [11, 13, 15, 20]. For example, people are playing a game because they find it exciting, joining a charity event due to increase social status, and participating in a sport to gain a social identity [12]. It is called perceived intangible value. On the contrary, people are participating in a sport in order to win awards, and competing in a contest for winning a scholarship. This means perceived tangible value. Therefore, Value-Technology Fit is defined by this study as the extent that technology functionality matches perceived value of individual. If technology functionality and perceived value of individual fit for each other, it will affect individual attitude and intention to use new technology. Thus, the followings are our hypothesis.

Hypothesis 3: Value-Technology Fit positively affect user's attitude toward using mobile apps.

Hypothesis 4: Value-Technology Fit positively affect user's continuance intention to use mobile apps.

2.2   Theory of Reasoned Action

TRA was derived from social psychology and proposed by Ajzen and Fishbein [1, 7]. It is a models that have been used to interpret and predict the intention of technology use in the information systems area. The components of TRA are three general constructs: behavioral intention, attitude, and subjective norm. Behavioral intention measures a person's relative strength of intention to perform a behavior. Attitude consists of beliefs about the consequences of performing the behavior multiplied by his or her evaluation of these consequences. Subjective norm (SN) refers to the social pressure exerted on an individual to perform or not perform a particular behavior [7]. Consequently, the social pressure causes the relevant behavior to become the individual's normative beliefs with which he/she would comply. Motivation to comply refers to he/she wanting or being willing to comply with these beliefs. That is, a user may exhibit different motivations for complying with the opinions of relevant people on the adoption of mobile apps. This theory has been applied to study many information technology applications and is certainly appropriate for investigating the continuance intention to use mobile apps.

Hypothesis 5: Attitude toward mobile apps positively affect user's continuance intention to use mobile apps.

Hypothesis 6: Subjective Norm positively affect user's continuance intention to use mobile apps.

2.3   Research Model

To summarize, our theoretical model examines effects of (1) task-technology fit to user attitude, (2) task-technology fit to continuance intention to use, (3) vale-technology fit to user attitude, (4) value-technology fit to continuance intention to use, (5) user attitude to continuance intention to use, and (6) subjective norms to continuance intention of using mobile apps. Figure 1 shows the theoretical framework.

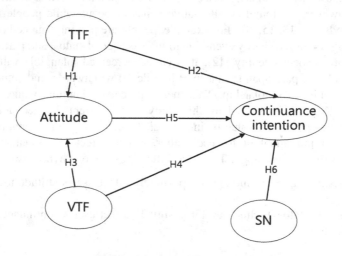

Fig. 1. Theoretical framework

3 Instrument Development and Research Methodology

3.1 Instrument Development

Existing measures from previous studies were adapted with slight modifications to fit our context. The measures used five-point Likert scales. All measures are listed as follows (Table 1).

3.2 Measure and Data Collection

The targets of this research are office workers in Taiwan. The voluntary users were invited to join the Project 2 weight-loss challenge. Each volunteer had to record his/her daily exercise and food via a health-related app, JustFit. JustFit is one of the most popular apps in Taiwan. It not only can help people to record daily food, exercise and mood easily, but also provide over 120,000 local food data. An online survey was conducted to gather data after using the app for three months (from 11 July to 31 October in 2014). Finally, a total of 278 volunteers (170 females and 108 males) were recruited. Their ages ranged from 31 to 45 years old (43.5 %). 70.2 % of the subject had at least a master degree, and 75.2 % of them were sitting at their desks for over 5 h per day. There were over 120 people (50.4 %) who think his/her body type is a little fat, and over 123 people (44.3 %) who don't satisfy their body (shown in Table 2).

4 Analysis of Results

4.1 Measurement Model

A confirmatory factor analysis using the Partial Least Squares (PLS) was conducted to assess the validity and reliability of our data. Reliability and convergent validity of the factors were estimated by composite reliability and average variance extracted (AVE). The acceptable composite reliability value is suggested to exceed 0.7, and the AVE value to exceed 0.5. Discriminant validity verifies whether the squared correlation between a pair of latent variables is less than the AVE for each variable. As can be seen in Tables 3 and 4, all constructs satisfies the criteria, thus requiring no changes to the constructs.

4.2 Structural Model

The results show that the combined model can interpret user attitude toward mobile apps and users' continuance intention of mobile app. The model indicates that Task-Technology Fit and Value-Technology Fit can explain 46.5 % of the variance in attitude and the attitude along with subjective norm can explain 50.3 % of the variance in continuance intention. Attitude was affected by Task-Technology Fit and Value-Technology Fit, and continuance intention to use was affected by attitude and subjective norm. However, Task-Technology Fit and Value-Technology Fit had no

Table 1. Measures of constructs

Construct	Items	References
Task-technology fit (TTF)	Information/Data needs	5, 10
	1. The APP provides me with up-to-date health information	
	2. The APP provides the consistency of information from a variety of information resources to me	
	3. The APP allows me to deliver, access and storage a large amount of information	
	4. The APP provides me with accurate health information	
	5. The APP allows me to quickly access health information	
	6. The APP provides me with understandable information	
	Ubiquitousness needs	
	7. The APP allows me to use on the move	
	8. The APP allows me to use in different place	
	9. The APP allows me to use at any time	
	EOU needs	
	10. Learning to use the APP is easy for me	
	11. It will be impossible to use the APP without the manual	
	12. It takes too much time to learn to use the APP	
	13. Using the APP requires a lot of mental effort	
	Importance	
	14. Information/Data needs is important to weight management	
	15. Ubiquitousness needs is important to weight management	
	16. EOU needs is important to weight management	
Value-technology fit (VTF)	Intangible value	14, 19
	1. I use the APP to improve personal exposure and visibility	
	2. I use the APP to increase the chance of interacting with others	
	3. I use the APP to obtain social identity	
	4. In sum up, using the APP can bring me an intangible value	
	Tangible value	
	5. I use the APP to control eating habits efficiently	
	6. I use the APP to record exercise habits	
	7. I use the APP to remind me to take care of my health	

(*Continued*)

Table 1. (*Continued*)

	8. In sum up, using the APP can bring me an tangible value	
Social Norm (SN)	1. My partners/close friends support me to use the APP	
	2. Generally speaking, how much do you care what your partners/close friends think you should do?	
	3. My boss/my parents support me to use the APP	
	4. Generally speaking, how much do you care what your boss/your parents think you should do?	
	5. My colleagues/my classmates support me to use the APP	
	6. Generally speaking, how much do you care what your colleagues/your classmates think you should do?	
Attitude (ATT)	1. Using the APP to manage weight is a good idea	7
	2. Using the APP to manage weight is a wise idea	
	3. Using the APP to manage weight is a pleasant idea	
Continuance intention to use (CI)	1. For me, it is worth using the APP	5
	2. I will continue using the APP in the future	

significant influence on the continuance intention to use mobile app. Therefore, hypotheses 1 to 6 are partially supported. That is, the integrated model can predict 50.3 % of the continuance intention to use mobile app (Fig. 2).

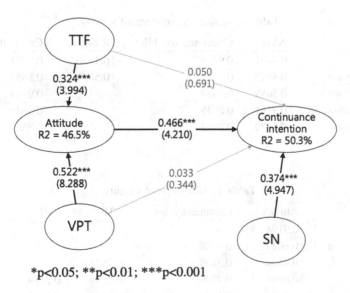

*p<0.05; **p<0.01; ***p<0.001

Fig. 2. Path analyses of mobile app

Table 2. Demographic characteristics of participants

Characteristics	Item	Frequency	Percent
Gender	Female	170	61.2
	Male	108	35.8
Age	16–30 years	64	23
	31–45 years	121	43.5
	46–60 years	73	26.3
	61–75 years	20	7.2
Education	High school	13	4.7
	College	70	25.2
	Master	184	66.2
	Upper Master	11	4
Sitting time	3–4 h	29	10.4
	4–5 h	40	14.4
	Upper 5 h	209	75.2
Body type	Thin	9	3.2
	A little thin	42	15.1
	Fit	87	31.3
	A little fat	120	43.2
	Fat	20	7.2
Do you satisfy your body	Very dissatisfied	26	9.4
	Dissatisfied	97	34.9
	Neutral	58	20.9
	Satisfied	57	20.5
	Very satisfied	40	14.4

Table 3. Reliability, convergent validity

	AVE	Composite reliability	R Square	Cronbach's alpha
Attitude	0.8461	0.9428	0.4650	0.9087
Continuance use	0.8813	0.9369	0.5029	0.8653
Task-technology fit	0.5659	0.9437		0.9345
Value-technology fit	0.5161	0.8945		0.8645
Subjective norm	0.5779	0.8913		0.8559

Table 4. Discriminant validity

	Attitude	Continuance use	TTF	VPT	SN
Attitude	0.9198				
Continuance use	0.6024	0.9388			
TTF	0.4594	0.3639	0.7523		
VTF	0.6068	0.4026	0.2594	0.7184	
SN	0.2506	0.5099	0.2438	0.1992	0.7602

5   Conclusion

Mobile devices such as mobile phones and tablets have become a part of human life. The mobile apps market seems have the feeling of a gold rush. Juniper Research claimed that 80 billion mobile apps will be downloaded in 2013, rising to 160 billion by 2017, but only around 5 % of apps will be paid by 2017 [21]. That is why many researchers attempted to investigate the issue of factors affecting users' adoption behavior. Given that the adoption of mobile app is purpose-sensitive, this paper aims to analyze user's continuance usage of mobile apps by providing an integrated TTF and TRA model and augmented the model with affective factors. Using a health-related mobile app as example, our specific goal is to examine to what extent our model can explain the continuance usage of mobile apps. After the empirical study and data analysis, we have obtained the following findings.

TTF and VTF both had significant impact on attitude towards using the mobile app. However, the coefficients of variation of VTF is higher than TTF's. It indicates that people had more positive attitudes toward using a new technology while their affective needs were satisfied [20]. SN and attitude had strong significant impacts on users' continuance intention to use the app. However, TTF and VTF had no significant effect on the continuance intention to use the app. The further analysis, we found most of people are not satisfied with their bodies even they have a standard body shape. Any app which could help them to manage and control their weight is viewed as a good app. It will increase users' positive attitude toward the app. Furthermore, some of people who use the lose-weight app are trying to connect with others, or gaining a sense of identity. They expect to have more confidence via increasing opportunities of communication with other people. This implies that a good app should not only provide the right technical services, but also satisfy the mental needs. Besides, those people who care about other people's opinions, especially colleagues and friends, are more willing to continue using the app. The research findings have suggestions for the mobile apps and future research studies.

One potential limitation of this research surrounds the size of the sample collected. Also, the convenient sampling used to solicit respondents for the survey may not be as perfect as random sampling. Another measurement limitation is that only two affective effects were investigated in this study. Other affective factors may affect users' intentions and future research could usefully identify and explore the effects of these factors.

Acknowledgements. This study is conducted under the Smart LOHAS Service Development/ Technology Applications and Multi-field Validation Project (2/4)" of the Institute for Information Industry which is financially supported by the Ministry of Economy Affairs of the Republic of China.

References

1. Ajzen, I., Fishbein, M.: Understanding Attitudes and Predicting Social Behavior. Prentice-Hall, Englewood Cliffs (1980)
2. Bohlen, J.M.: The adoption and diffusion of ideas in agriculture. In: Copp, James H. (ed.) Our Changing Rural Society: Perspectives and Trends, pp. 265–287. Iowa State University Press, Ames (1964)

3. Bohlen, J.M.: Research needed on adoption models. In.: Diffusion Research Needs. Columbia: Missouri Agricultural Experiment Station, North Central Regional Research Bulletin, vol. 186, pp. 15–21 (1968)
4. Clarke, I.: Emerging value propositions for M-Commerce. J. Bus. Strat. **18**(2), 133–147 (2001)
5. Davis, F.D.: Perceived usefulness, perceived ease of use, and user acceptance of information technology. MIS Q. **13**(3), 319–342 (1989)
6. Dennis, A.R., Wixom, B.H., Vandenberg, R.J.: Understanding fit and appropriation effects in group support systems via meta-analysis. MIS Q. **25**(2), 167–193 (2001)
7. Fishbein, M., Ajzen, I.: Belief, Attitude, Intentions and Behavior: An Introduction to Theory and Research. Addison-Wesley, MA (1975)
8. Goodhue, D.L.: Understanding user evaluations of information systems. Manage. Sci. **41**(12), 1827–1844 (1995)
9. Goodhue, D.L.: Development and measurement validity of a task-technology fit instrument for user evaluations of information systems. Decis. Sci. **29**(1), 105–138 (1998)
10. Goodhue, D.L., Thompson, R.L.: Task-technology fit and individual performance. MIS Q. **19**(2), 213–236 (1995)
11. Govers, P.C.M.: Product Personality. Unpublished doctoral dissertation, University of Delft, Delft (2004)
12. Gotzsch, J.: Managing product expressions: Identifying conditions and methods for the creation of meaningful consumer home products. Unpublished doctoral dissertation, Brunel University, London (2003)
13. Kandinsky, W.: Concerning the Spiritual in Art. Online Distributed Proofreaders. Retrieved from Project Gutenberg, Oxford (1977)
14. Klonglan, G.E., Coward, E.W.: The concept of symbolic adoption: a suggested interpretation. Rural Sociol. **35**(1), 77–83 (1970)
15. Kreitler, H., Kreitler, S.: Psychology of the Arts. Duke University Press, Durham (1972)
16. Liang, T.P., Wei, C.P.: Introduction to the special issue: a framework for mobile commerce applications. Int. J. Electron. Commer. **8**(3), 7–17 (2004)
17. Lin Y.L., Liang, T.P., Ho, S.C., Yeh, Y.H.: The impact of situation influences on the intention to use mobile value-added services. In: Paper Presented at the 6th Workshop on e-Business (WeB2007), Montreal, 9 December 2007
18. Penny, G.: Use Mobile Apps to Provide Customer Value, and Revenue Will Follow. Gartner (2014)
19. Rogers, E.M.: A communication research approach to the diffusion of innovations. In: Diffusion Research Needs, Columbia: Missouri Agricultural Experiment Station, North Central Regional Research Bulletin, vol. 186, pp. 27–30 (1968)
20. Shiau, W.L., Liou, T.R.: Understanding the effects of consumer's value technology fit on a mobile shopping website: the case of Rakuten Ichiba. In: Pacific Asia Conference on Information Systems (PACIS 2014)
21. Stuart, D.: Mobile apps revenues tipped to reach $26bn in 2013. the guardian (2013). http://www.theguardian.com/technology/appsblog/2013/sep/19/gartner-mobile-apps-revenues-report
22. Sian, R.: Over 160 Billion Consumer Apps to be Downloaded in 2017, Driven by Free-To-Play Games. Juniper Research (2013). http://www.juniperresearch.com/viewpress release.php?pr=383
23. Tornatzky, L.G., Fleischer, M.: The Processes of Technological Innovation. Lexington Books, Lexington (1990)
24. Wang, W.T., Wang, B., Wei, Y.T.: Examining the impacts of website complexities on user satisfaction based on the task-technology fit model: an experimental research using an eye-tracking device. In: Pacific Asia Conference on Information Systems (PACIS 2014)

Identifying Appraisal Expressions of Online Reviews in Chinese

Pei Yin[1(✉)], Hongwei Wang[2], and Wei Wang[2]

[1] Business School, University of Shanghai for Science and Technology,
516 Jungong Road, Shanghai, China
evawater@163.com
[2] School of Economics and Management, Tongji University, 1239 Siping Road,
Shanghai, China

Abstract. With the development of Web2.0 technology, an increasing number of consumers are giving comments on products over the Internet, thus opinion mining rises in response to the requirement of retrieving valuable information in speed. After thoroughly analyzing the style of language and the ways of expression in Chinese, this paper proposes a semantic lexicon-based method to identify the appraisal expressions in Chinese online reviews. A comparative experiment based on cellphone online reviews in Chinese is conducted in this research, and the result indicates that the proposed method is quite promising and outperforms the two baselines (a statistic orientation method and a semantic orientation method). Moreover, the method is applied to a comparative evaluation of two popular cellphones, demonstrating the theoretical significance and the practical value of this research.

Keywords: Online reviews · Appraisal expressions · Product feature · Review feature · Semantic lexicon · Consumers' opinions

1 Introduction

With the rapid development of online social media like Weibo and Weixin in China, consumers' opinions on products are being exchanged in unprecedented scale and detail. This online word of mouth (WOM) has the potential to influence both firms' product design strategies and consumers' purchasing decisions (Chen and Xie, 2008) (Zhang etc., 2009) (Lau etc., 2014). Therefore, techniques of opinion mining rise in response to the requirement of retrieving useful information in speed.

Consumers always give comments on specific features of a given product in online reviews, thus the collocation of a product feature (such as '屏幕(screen)' and '外观 (appearance)' of a cellphone) and its corresponding opinion (such as '好(good)' and '差(poor)') can be considered as the key component for extracting consumers' feedbacks on the product from online reviews. The pair < feature, opinion > is seen as the basic appraisal expression unit of online reviews, and hence its identification is the basic object and the fundamental task in opinion mining. Different from English language, Chinese online reviews are characterized by their terseness in language, vagueness in semantics and complexity in syntax. The style of language and the ways

F.F.-H. Nah and C.-H. Tan (Eds.): HCIB 2015, LNCS 9191, pp. 207–218, 2015.
DOI: 10.1007/978-3-319-20895-4_20

of expression in Chinese greatly increase the difficulty of opinion mining. Therefore, this paper aims at identifying appraisal expressions in Chinese online reviews.

The remainder of this paper is organized as follows. We review the literatures in 'Literature review' section and introduce the method of appraisal expressions identification in 'Proposed Approach' section. We conduct comparative experiment on cellphone online reviews in Chinese and apply the method to a comparative evaluation of two cellphones in 'Experiment and Application' section. We conclude the paper with possible further research in 'Conclusions' section.

2 Literature Review

In the extant researches of appraisal expressions identification, there are mainly two kinds of methods: statistic orientation and semantic orientation.

The statistic orientation method extracts features at first, and identifies opinions occurred in the vicinity. For example, Hu and Liu (2004) utilized Association Rules to extract frequent nouns and noun phrases as product features, and identified the adjectives closest to each feature as its opinions. Su, etc. (2008) proposed a mutual reinforcement method to analyze the hidden sentiment association between noun features and adjectival opinions. Zhang, etc. (2010) identified product features based on conditional random fields (CRFs) and identified the corresponding opinions based on syntactic tree. With the rapid development of techniques in statistics and probability theory, some researches brought the state-of-art probabilistic modelling into opinion mining, and the polarity of text is detected at a much finer-gained word level by computing the probabilistic measures of word association. For example, Titov and McDonald (2008) proposed a Topic-Sentiment Model (TSM) along with Lin and He (2009) presented a Joint Sentiment/Topic (JST) model to jointly detect topic and predict sentiment at document level. Jiang, Meng and Yu (2011) analyzed the change of topic sentiment based on Probabilistic Latent Semantic Indexing (PLSI).

However, the statistic orientation method only identifies high-frequent nouns and noun phrases as product features, and neglects low-frequent terms and phrases in other parts-of-speech (e.g. verbs). Moreover, a product feature and the corresponding opinion are not always close to each other and the opinion identified may not be the one holding toward the feature, due to missing punctuation mark or an implicit feature not showing in the text, thus this method is somewhat heuristic.

The semantic orientation method explores linguistic knowledge, such as language pattern, syntactic relationship and sentiment lexicon, to identify appraisal expressions in online reviews. For example, Popescu and Etzioni (2005) extracted nouns and noun phrases as product features at first, and then utilized 10 extraction rules to identify opinions based on the syntactic dependencies. Wilson, etc. (2005) developed an Opinion Finder system to identify opinion and its targeted feature based on hand-crafted sentiment lexicon. Zhuang, Jing and Zhu (2006) manually selected features and opinions in movie reviews from WordNet, and used dependency grammar graph to detect appraisal expressions. Bloom, Garg and Argamon (2007) extracted adjectival opinions based on a hand-built lexicon, and identified their corresponding features according to the predefined 31 syntactic rules. Yao, etc. (2008) manually

created 278 product features and took an opinion as a chunk of information consisting
of three slots < subject, attribute, value >. Miao, Li and Zeng (2010) took the
high-frequent Nouns as product features and the high-frequent Adjectives, Adverbs and
Verbs as opinions at first, and then identify appraisal expressions based on manually
pre-defined syntactic rules. Zhao, etc. (2010) applied automatically selected syntactic
paths to detect appraisal expressions, with the help of edit distance based path matching
method. Vu et al. (2011) extracted product features and opinions based on Vietnamese
syntax rules and synonym in VietSentiWordnet dictionary. Qiu et al. (2009, 2011)
proposed a semi-supervised method that began with an initial opinion lexicon consisting of manually selected opinion word seeds, and extracted new sentiment words
based on the relations between opinions and features described in dependency trees.
Somprasertsri and Lalitrojwong (2010) also built a domain knowledge base to save the
information like synonyms of features and sentiments of opinions within a certain
domain. Lee and Bradlow (2011) applied a constrained-logic program to simultaneously cluster phrases referring to the same product feature and to discover the
underlying properties of a given product feature.

Compared with the statistic orientation method, syntactic rules contained more
useful linguistic knowledge than the association rules used in the statistic orientation
method, thus the semantic orientation method gets better precision. However, since
these rules are always applied to the text with simpler and regular grammars, the
method is low in recall rate, especially in the scenario of Chinese online reviews with
complex syntax.

Therefore, this paper proposes a semantic lexicon-based method to identify
appraisal expressions in Chinese online reviews by thoroughly analyzing the ways of
expression and the style of language in Chinese.

3 Proposed Approach

3.1 Basic Procedure of the Proposed Approach

The proposed approach follows the trend of the semantic orientation method, but from
a different perspective. Unlike previous methods utilizing language patterns or syntactic rules to identify appraisal expressions, this approach semi-automatically built
semantic lexicons by analyzing the words and their semantic relationships like synonyms in the manually labeled corpus. In this way, the various verbal expressions of
product features are identified correctly, the semantic ambiguity is removed efficiently
and the missing subjects are supplemented by the semantic lexicons. The basic procedure of the proposed approach is shown in Fig. 1.

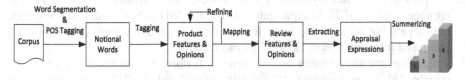

Fig. 1. Basic procedure of appraisal expressions identification

3.2   Step 1: Word Segmentation and POS Tagging

Traditional document pre-processing procedures such as stop word removal, word segmentation and Part-of-Speech (POS) tagging are invoked to pre-process product online reviews. This process is to split text into sentences and to produce the part-of-speech tag for each word (whether the word is a noun, verb, adjective or adverb). The following shows a sentence with POS tags.

"外观/n时尚/a,/w全/a触摸/v屏/n,/w用/v的/u方便/a。/w" (Fashionable/a appearance/ n,/w all/a touch/v screen/n,/w convenient/a for/u use/v./w).

Each sentence is saved in the review database along with the POS tag information, and a transaction file is then created to save notional words only including nouns, verbs, adjectives and adverbs in the sentence.

3.3   Step 2: Labeling Product Features and Opinions

Product features are the words and phrases describing the components, the functions and the properties of a given product (Ding, Liu and Yu, 2008). Unlike the previous researches only take nouns and noun phrases as product feature (e.g. Popescu & Etzioni, 2005), this paper asserts that product feature not only includes the nouns representing component, appearance, function or performance of a given product, but also contains the verbs describing behaviors in the use of the product. For example, in cellphone reviews, the verb '操作(operate)' is a behavior of using cellphone.

Opinions are the words and phrases used to evaluate subjectively particular product features. It is believed that sentiment words include not only Adjectives and Adverbs but also Nouns, Verbs and etc. (Pang and Lee, 2008). Thus this paper takes adjectives, nouns, verbs or adverbs as opinion words. Therefore, the semantic lexicon containing product features and opinion words is established to identify appraisal expressions in the set of notional words. Keep the candidate word if a match is found in the lexicon and mark it with F (Feature) or O (Opinion).

3.4   Step 3: Refining Product Features and Opinions

1. Reducing Redundancy. In Chinese online reviews, product features have various verbal expressions, thus this paper proposes four rules to reduce the redundancy of the feature set.

1. Integrating semantic synonyms. For example, in cellphone reviews, '价格(price)', '价值(value)', and '价钱(expense)' have the same meaning, thus they are integrated into one feature '价格(price)';
2. Integrating contextual synonyms. For example, in cellphone reviews, '存储卡 (storage card)', '扩展卡(expansion card)' and 'SD卡(SD card)' are semantic homonyms but refer to the same feature '记忆卡(memory card)', thus they are integrated into one feature '记忆卡(memory card)'.
3. Integrating specific features as one general feature. For example, in cellphone reviews, '触屏(touch screen)', '主屏(main screen)' and '电容屏(capacitive screen)'

all belong to the general feature '屏幕(screen)', thus they are integrated into one feature '屏幕(screen)'.

4. Integrating function features and their corresponding behaviors as one feature. For example, in cellphone reviews, '播放(broadcast)' is the behavior of '音响(loud-speaker)', thus they are integrated into one feature '音响(loudspeaker)'.

2. Removing Ambiguity. Some components or functions of a given product may share the same attribute, such as each part of a cellphone has the '质量(quality)' attribute. These common attributes usually appear in a sentence without the specific determiner to describe their hosts, thus cause semantic ambiguity. For instance, if a review only states '质量好(quality is good)' may lead to a question: which quality is it? Therefore, in order to remove semantic ambiguity in Chinese online reviews, this paper presents a matching rule based on the co-occurrence of the attribute and its determiner.

In the field of information retrieval (IR), mutual information (MI) is commonly-used to compute the co-occurrence of two words. However, this algorithm ignores the implicit relationships between the two words. Therefore, this paper introduces the variant of the expected mutual information from the research of Lau et al. (2009a, 2009b), the balanced mutual information (BMI), to calculate the co-occurrence of word W_i and word W_j, which considers both words' presence and absence as the evidence of an implicit association. Furthermore, a windowing process is conducted to filter noisy terms, for the attribute and its determiner is usually near each other, and the closer word W_i and word W_j is, the stronger relationships they have.

$$
\begin{aligned}
BMI(w_i, w_j) = & \\
\beta \times & \left[Pr(w_i, w_j) \times \log_2\left(\frac{Pr(w_i, w_j)}{Pr(w_i)Pr(w_j)}\right) + Pr(\neg w_i, \neg w_j) \times \log_2\left(\frac{Pr(\neg w_i, \neg w_j)}{Pr(\neg w_i)pr(\neg w_j)}\right) \right] - (1-\beta) \times \\
& \left[Pr(\neg w_i, w_j) \times \log_2\left(\frac{Pr(w_i, \neg w_j)}{Pr(w_i)Pr(\neg w_j)}\right) + Pr(\neg w_i, w_j) \times \log_2\left(\frac{Pr(\neg w_i, w_j)}{Pr(\neg w_i)pr(w_j)}\right) \right]
\end{aligned}
\tag{1}
$$

A virtual window of σ words is moved from left to right one word at a time until the end of each document. According to previous researches (Lau et al., 2009a, 2009b), a text window of 5 to 10 terms is effective. Due to the long and colloquial expressions in Chinese product reviews, we take 8 terms as the size of the text window ($\sigma = 8$). In Eq. (1), $(Pr(w_i)(Pr(w_i)) = \frac{N(\sigma_{w_i})}{N(\sigma)}$, where $N(\sigma_{w_i})$ is the number of windows containing the word W_i and $N(\sigma)$ is the total number of windows obtained from a document) denotes the probability that word w_i appears in the text window. Similarly, $Pr(\neg w_i)$ denotes the probability that word W_i doesn't appear in the text window. $Pr(w_i, w_j)$ $(Pr(w_i w_j) = \frac{N(\sigma_{w_i,w_j})}{N(\sigma)}$, where $N(\sigma_{w_i,w_j})$ is the number of windows containing both W_i word and W_j word) denotes the joint probability that both words are present in the text window. Similarly, $Pr(\neg w_i, w_j)$ denotes the joint probability that both words are absent in the text window, and $Pr(\neg w_i, w_j)$ or $Pr(w_i, \neg w_j)$ denotes the joint probability that only one of them appears in the text window. The parameter $\beta \in [0.5, 0.7]$ was used to adjust the relative weight of positive and negative evidence respectively. After computing the co-occurrence of word W_i and word W_j, a linear normalization ($ass_{normal} = \frac{ass-ass_{min}}{ass_{max}-ass_{min}} \in [0, 1]$) is carried out to maintain all values in the interval of 0 and 1.

3. Solving Word Deficiency. In Chinese online reviews, the subjects are sometimes missing but implied in the context. These missing subjects are regarded as implicit features of the product (Ding, Hu and Yu, 2008). For example, a review states '有点重 (a little heavy)', the missing subject '重量(weight)' is implicitly indicated by '重 (heavy)'. This paper identifies and supplements the implicit features with the help of the contexts. There are two kinds of opinions words. The ones with clear and definite meanings are regarded as feature indicator (Ding, Hu and Yu, 2008), which are used to evaluate only a finite number of product features, such as '便宜(cheap)' indicates '价 格(price)' and '重(heavy)' indicates '重量(weight)'. While the others with general meaning are regarded as general opinion, which are used to appraise all features, such as '好(good)' and '差(bad)'. Based on these kinds of opinion words, the word deficiency will be solved by matching the implicit features with the indicators and the general opinions with the closest feature in the same clause.

3.5   Step 4: Mapping Product Features to Review Features

In order to summarize all customer reviews of a product, product features are further gathered and mapped to review features, which are the high-profile features being mentioned a lot in online reviews. The mapping rules between product features and review features are determined by their semantic relations. Three semantic relations are analyzed in this paper, attribute-to-host, part-to-whole and event-to-role.

1. Attribute feature is mapped to its corresponding host feature. For example, in cellphone reviews, '颜色(color)', '分辨率(resolution)' and '亮度(brightness)' are attributes of '屏幕(screen)', and the comments on these attributes are equal to the comments on screen, thus these features are all mapped to '屏幕(screen)'.
2. Component feature is mapped to its corresponding whole feature. For example, in cellphone reviews, '耳机(earphone)', '记忆卡(memory card)' and '数据线(data line)' all belong to '配件(accessory)' (they are the accessories of cellphone), and the comments on these components are equal to the comments on accessory, thus these features are mapped to '配件(accessory)'.
3. Some feature representing user's perception of using product is mapped to its corresponding behavior feature. For example, in cellphone reviews, '实用性(utility)' and '操作性(operability)' are both the perceptions of operating cellphone, thus they are mapped to '操作(operate)'.

3.6   Step 5: Identifying Appraisal Expressions

After labeling product features and opinions in step 2, four types of appraisal expressions are recognized as follows.

FO/OF represents a single product feature and a single opinion word. For example, the appraisal expression of "屏幕/F大/O" is < screen/F, big/O >.

FFO represents a group of multiple product features and a single opinion word. There are two kinds of relation among these product features. (1) Father-child relation. The meaning of a Father-child phrase is conveyed by the child feature, such as "手机/F 操作/F方便/O (cellphone/F operates/F conveniently/O)", where 'operates' is a behavior of using cellphone, so the appraisal impression is < operates/F, conveniently/O >. (2) Coordinating relation. For example, "外观/F和操作系统/F都不错/O (appearance/F and operating system/F are good/O)", where the preposition 'and' indicates a coordinating relation between 'appearance' and 'operating system', so the appraisal expression are < appearance/F, good/O > and < operating system/F, good/O >.

FOO represents a group of multiple opinion words and a single product feature, and each opinion word can be regarded as the evaluation of the product feature. For example, "屏幕/F大/O而清晰/O (the screen/F is big/O and clear/O)", where 'big' and 'clear' are both appraising 'screen', so the appraisal expressions are < screen/F, big/O > and < screen/F, clear/O >.

FFOFOO represents a combination of FFO pattern and FOO pattern, so we take the longest sequence starting with 'F' and ending with 'O', and divide the sequence into several FFO and FOO.

4 Experiment and Application

4.1 Corpus

The experiment is designed based on cellphone's online reviews, in order to test and verify the effectiveness of the proposed approach. The corpus is obtained from the most popular E-commerce website in China, Taobao.com, in which 1000 pieces of reviews are taken as training corpus for lexicon establishing, and the other 1000 pieces of reviews are taken as the testing corpus.

In this experiment, a natural language processing tool, ICTCLAS (Chinese Lexical Analysis System researched by Institute of Computing Technology, Chinese Academy of Sciences) is employed for word segmentation and POS tagging of each review. And we replace all the punctuation mark with the comma.

Two researchers manually identify and label the product features, opinion words and appraisal expressions in training corpus. In order to reduce the subjectivity deviations in the labeling process, 20 pieces of corpus are selected randomly and the value of statistic Kappa are computed to test the consistency of labeling results. The Kappa value is 0.72, higher than 0.7, demonstrating an acceptably stable result. The labeling result is shown in Table 1.

Table 1 demonstrates that about 96.3 % of online reviews contain appraisal expressions, indicating that appraisal expressions are the key component of online reviews. Besides that, the amount of opinion words is bigger than that of appraisal expressions, indicating the existence of implicit features, which are the product features (subjects) missing in reviews. And the amount of product features is much bigger than that of opinion words, indicating that the type FFO (multiple product features with a single opinion word in one sentence) is much more popular than other types of appraisal expressions. Furthermore, the average numbers of product features, opinion

Table 1. Labeling result of training corpus

Item	Result
Amount of reviews	1000
Amount of reviews that contain FOP	963
Amount of FOP	2009
Amount of features	2991
Amount of opinions	2308
FOP/sentence	2.0
Feature/sentence	3.0
Opinion/sentence	2.3

Table 2. Result of features and opinions

Item	Result
Amount of features (non-repeated)	242
Amount of opinions (non-repeated)	221
Amount of features appearing more than twice	235
Amount of opinions appearing more than twice	213

words and appraisal expressions are more than 2 in each sentence, illustrating that the training corpus contains relatively rich information and is suitable for establishing semantic lexicons.

After labeling, the repeated product features and opinions words have to be deleted to build lexicons and the final result of features and opinions are shown in Table 2.

Table 2 demonstrates that over 95 % of product features and opinion words repeat in all online reviews, indicating that users prefer using regular words in their reviews of a particular product, thus the number of product features and opinion words are limited and the lexicons established upon these reviews are useful in appraisal expressions identification.

4.2 Evaluation

In this paper, recall rate (R), precision rate (P) and F-score (F) are employed to measure the performance of the proposed approach: $P = |A \cap B|/|A|$; $R = |A \cap B|/|B|$; $F = 2*P*R/(P + R)$, Where A denotes the set of appraisal expressions being identified by the algorithm, and B denotes the set of appraisal expressions being labeled by hand.

4.3 Comparative Experiment

A comparative experiment is conducted based on the cellphone online reviews in Chinese and among the approach proposed in this paper and two baselines including a statistic orientation method and a semantic orientation method.

Baseline 1: method based on Association Rules and Nearest Principle (Hu and Liu, 2004b): at first, Association Rules are applied to identify the frequent items in the set of nouns and noun phrases as product features. Then for each feature, extract the adjectives closest to the feature as opinion words. At last, use the identified opinion words to find and extract the low-frequent features.

Baseline 2: method based on syntactic rules (Popescu and Etzioni, 2005): firstly, extract high-frequent nouns and noun phrases as product features. Then 10 extraction rules are used to find the heads of potential opinion phrases, and each head word together with its modifier is returned as a potential opinion phrase. At last, calculate the sentiment orientation of each candidate opinion based on HowNet, and these with distinct polarity are determined as opinion words.

Table 3 lists the comparative performances between our semantic approach and the two baselines, which shows that an obvious improvement in obtaining a more accurate result is achieved by our approach.

Table 3. Comparison on the performances of proposed approach and two baselines

Methods	Precision Rate (%)	Recall Rate (%)	F-score (%)
Baseline 1	67.45	69.63	68.52
Baseline 2	79.18	73.24	76.09
The proposed method	79.44	87.62	83.33

Table 3 demonstrates that the performance of the first baseline is the lowest in all three measurements. That's because the procedure of obtaining features and opinions is empirical and random, without any deep syntactic or semantic analysis. In contrast, the two semantic orientation methods (the second baseline and our approach) perform better, indicating that extracting deep syntactic and semantic relationships between features and opinions are more useful than simply considering the frequency and the location of them.

In addition, our approach outperforms the second baseline, especially in the recall rate, due to the following three reasons: (1) only high-frequent product features are extracted by the second baseline, omitting features with low-frequency; (2) these frequent nouns and nouns phrases may include non-product features like '配送速度 (delivery speed)'; (3) the syntactic rules are not suitable for review mining in Chinese, for Chinese online reviews are short, vaguely semantic and lack of syntactic standardizations.

4.4 Application

Moreover, the proposed approach is further applied to a comparative evaluation of two popular cellphones on Taobao.com, iPhone 5S and Nokia 1050. 100 pieces of online reviews are selected respectively and the sentiment polarity of each appraisal expression is determined manually. The comparative evaluation of the two cellphones is shown in Fig. 2.

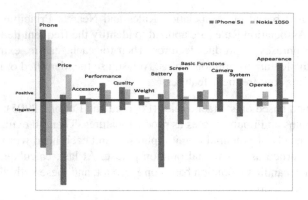

Fig. 2. Comparative evaluations of the two cellphones

Figure 2 illustrates the following conclusions: (1) iPhone 5S gets remarkably more positive comments on phone, screen, camera and appearance than those of Nokia 1050, thus gains more favor from younger people. This conclusion consists with the fact that iPhone 5S is an entertaining mobile. (2) Nokia 1050 gets remarkably more positive comments on price, battery and operating than those of iPhone 5S. This conclusion consists with the fact that Nokia 1050 is a practical cellphone and more suitable for aged population compared to iPhone 5S.

5 Conclusions

In the perspective of the ways of expression and the style of language in Chinese, this paper presents an approach based on semantic lexicon to extract appraisal expressions in Chinese online reviews. The proposed approach overcomes the difficulties in mining short, vaguely semantic and complicated syntactic Chinese online reviews, by establishing semantic lexicons to identify the various verbal expressions of product features, remove the semantic ambiguity and supplement the missing subjects. A comparative experiment based on cellphone online reviews in Chinese is conducted in the research, and the result illustrates that the proposed approach outperforms the two baselines including a statistic orientation method and a semantic orientation method. Moreover, the method is applied to a comparative evaluation between two cellphones, indicating that opinion mining will help customers as well as manufacturers to know the strengths and weaknesses of products without manually going through reviews.

Further research will be conducted in the following aspects: (1) study the knowledge structure in online reviews and explore the deeper semantic relations among features and opinions with the help of ontology; (2) classify the sentiment polarity of the identified appraisal expressions automatically; (3) integrate opinion mining with statistic method to analyze consumers' needs.

Acknowledgments. This work is partially supported by the Natural Science Foundation of China [70971099, 71371144], the Fundamental Research Funds for the Central Universities [1200219198], and Shanghai Philosophy and Social Science Planning Projects [2013BGL004].

References

Chen, Y., Xie, J.: Online consumer review: word-of-mouth as a new element of marketing communication mix. Manage. Sci. 54(3), 477–491 (2008)

Zhang, Z., Ye, Q., Law, R., Li, Y.: The impact of e-word-of-mouth on the online popularity of restaurants: a comparison of consumer reviews and editor reviews. Int. J. Hospitality Manage. **28**, 180–182 (2009)

Lau, R., Li, C., Liao, S.: Social Analytics: Learning Fuzzy Product Ontologies for Aspect-Oriented Sentiment Analysis. Decision Support Systems (2014)

Zhuang, L., Jing, F., Zhu, X.: Movie review mining and summarization. In: Proceedings of the 15th ACM International Conference on Information and Knowledge Management, Arlington, VA, USA, pp. 43–50 (2006)

Shi, B, Chang, K.: Mining chinese reviews. In: Proceedings of Sixth IEEE International Conference on Data Mining, Hong Kong, China, pp. 585–589 (2006)

Hu, M., Liu, B.: Mining and summarizing customer reviews. In: Proceedings of the 10th ACM SIGKDD, Seattle, WA, USA, pp. 168–177 (2004b)

Scaffidi, C., Bierhoff, K., Chang, E., Felker, M., Ng, H., Jin, C.: Red Opal: product-feature scoring from reviews. In: Proceedings of the 8th ACM Conference on Electronic Commerce. San Diego, California, USA, pp.182–191 (2007)

Su, Q., Xu, X., Guo, H., Guo, Z., Wu, X., Zhang, X., Swen, B.: Hidden sentiment association in chinese web opinion mining. In: Proceedings of the 17th International Conference on World Wide Web, Beijing, China, pp. 959–968 (2008)

Zhang, S., Jia, W., Xia, Y., Meng, Y., Yu, H.: Extracting product features and sentiments from chinese customer reviews. In: Proceedings of the 7th LREC, pp. 1142–1145 (2010)

Titov, I., McDonald, R.: A joint model of text and aspect ratings for sentiment summarization. In: Proceedings of ACL-HLT, Columbus, Ohio, USA, pp. 308–316 (2008)

Lin, C.H., He, Y.L.: Joint sentiment/topic model for sentiment analysis. In: Proceedings of the 18th ACM Conference on Information and Knowledge Management, Hongkong, China, pp. 375–384 (2009)

Jiang, Y., Meng, W.Y., Yu, C.: Topic sentiment change analysis. In: Proceedings of the 7th International Conference on Machine Learning and Data Mining in Pattern Recognition. New York, USA, pp. 443–457 (2011)

Popescu, A.M., Etzioni, O.: Extracting product features and opinions from reviews. In: Proceedings of HLT/EMNLP, Vancouver, Canada, pp. 339–346 (2005)

Wilson, T., Hoffmann, P., Somasundaran, S., Kessler, J.: Opinion Finder: a system for subjectivity analysis. In: Proceedings of HLT/EMNLP, Vancouver, Canada, pp. 347–354 (2005)

Bloom, K., Garg, N., Argamon, S.: Extracting appraisal expressions. In: Proceedings of HLT-NAACL 2007, Rochester, NY, USA, pp. 308–315 (2007)

Yao, T., Cheng, X., Xu, F.: literature reviews on text opinion mining. Chin. Inf. J. **3**, 71–80 (2008)

Zhao, Y., Qin, B., Che, W.X., Liu, T.: Appraisal expression recognition with syntactic path for sentence sentiment classification. Int. J. Comput. Process. Orient. Lang. **23**(1), 21–37 (2010a)

Miao, Q., Li, Q., Zeng, D.: Fine-grained opinion mining by integrating multiple review sources. J. Am. Soc. Inf. Sci. Technol. **61**(11), 2288–2299 (2010)

Zhao, Y., Qin, B., Che, W., Liu, T.: Appraisal expression recognition with syntactic path for sentence sentiment classification. Int. J. Comput. Process. Orient. Lang. **23**(1), 21–37 (2010b)

Vu, T.T., Pham, H.T., Luu, C.T., Ha, Q.T.: A feature-based opinion mining model on product reviews in vietnamese. Stud. Comput. Intell. **381**, 23–33 (2011)

Qiu, G., Liu, B., Bu, J., Chen, C.: Expanding domain sentiment lexicon through double propagation. In: Proceedings of the 21st International Joint Conference on Artificial Intelligence. Pasadena, California, pp. 1199–1204 (2009)

Qiu, G., Liu, B., Bu, J., Chen, C.: Opinion word expansion and target extraction through double propagation. Comput. Linguist. **37**(1), 9–27 (2011)

Somprasertsri, G., Lalitrojwong, P.: Mining feature-opinion in online customer reviews for opinion summarization. J. Univers. Comput. Sci. **16**(6), 938–955 (2010)

Lee, Y.T., Bradlow, T.E.: Automated marketing research using online customer reviews. J. Mark. Res. **48**(5), 881–894 (2011)

Lau, R.Y.K., Song, D., Li, Y., Cheung, C.H., Hao, J.X.: Towards a fuzzy domain ontology extraction method for adaptive e-Learning. IEEE Trans. Knowl. Data Eng. **21**(6), 800–813 (2009)

Lau, R.Y.K., Lai, C.C.L., Ma, J., Li, Y.F.: Automatic domain ontology extraction for context-sensitive opinion mining. In: Proceedings of International Conference on Information Systems. Phoenix, Arizona, pp. 60–79 (2009b)

Ding, X., Liu, B., Yu, P.: A holistic lexicon-based approach to opinion mining. In: Proceedings of the International Conference on Web Search and Web Data Mining, pp. 231–239 (2008)

Dong, Z., Dong, Q.: HowNet and the computation of meaning. World Scientific Publishing Co. Pte.Ltd, Singapore (2006)

Electronic, Mobile
and Ubiquitous Commerce

The Impact of Usability on Patient Safety in Long-Term Care

Fuad Abujarad[1]([X]), Sarah J. Swierenga[2], Toni A. Dennis[3], and Lori A. Post[1]

[1] Yale School of Medicine, New Haven, CT, USA
{fuad.abujarad,lori.post}@yale.edu
[2] Usability/Accessibility Research and Consulting Michigan State University,
East Lansing, MI, USA
sswieren@msu.edu
[3] Department of Licensing and Regulatory Affairs, State of Michigan, Lansing, MI, USA
dennist@michigan.gov

Abstract. Our best practice approach to pre-employment Real-Time Screening (RTS) demonstrates how health information technology positively impacts organizational communication practices, which is essential for effective public health management. Using user-centered design methodologies has improved the effectiveness of the background check system in a complex organizational environment under challenging time constraints. Using cutting edge technology and a user-focused design process the research team has developed a system that allows users to seamlessly move highly-sensitive, complex information swiftly, efficiently and securely.

Keywords: Criminal background checks · Real-time screening · Long-term care health information technology · Usability · User-centered design · Patient safety

1 Introduction

Population growth in the U.S. is slowing and the population is aging and becoming more diverse. According to U.S. Census projections, the population aged 65 years and older will increase by 55 % from 2015 to 2030 and by 2050 will comprise 20 % of the population [1]. The group most likely to need long-term care–people over age 85–is estimated to grow from 5.3 million in 2006 to nearly 21 million by 2050. The methods of providing services to this aging population have evolved over the past two decades to deinstitutionalize care for the elderly and people with disabilities, and includes more options for home and community based services. The U.S. Bureau of Labor Statistics reports that the fastest growing occupations include personal care workers and home health aides, and the need is projected to increase by 50 % by 2025 [2]. Additionally, elderly and disabled persons in long-term care (LTC) settings are vulnerable to abuse, neglect, and exploitation necessitating special protective measures by criminal justice, social services, and healthcare agencies [3, 4]. In 2006, 28.6 % of Michigan households with a family member in LTC reported that person having experienced one or more forms of abuse including physical, caretaking, verbal, emotional, neglect, sexual and material exploitation [3, 5, 6].

© Springer International Publishing Switzerland 2015
F.F.-H. Nah and C.-H. Tan (Eds.): HCIB 2015, LNCS 9191, pp. 221–231, 2015.
DOI: 10.1007/978-3-319-20895-4_21

Pre-employment background screening of workers plays a significant role in maintaining a safe and stable healthcare system [7, 8]. Recently, local and national legislation has reflected these themes and demanded a broader and stronger pre-employment noncriminal background checks (Sect. 6201 of the U.S. Patient Protection and Affordable Care Act Pub. L. 111–148, 124 Stat. 119–124, Stat. 1025, enacted March 23, 2010; Michigan Compiled Laws §§ 330.1134a, 333.20173a, and 400.734b). More specifically, the legislation highlights the importance of performing noncriminal background checks on applicants who have direct contact with vulnerable populations.

Fingerprint-based background checks are the most accurate method of linking criminal history records to an individual. While turnaround time for performing a comprehensive employment fingerprint-based background checks has decreased dramatically from several weeks to a few days in most cases, often employers face critical staffing shortages that require immediate action. The decreasing number of workers available and the increase in the number of people requiring services creates pressure on employers to meet the demand. While waiting on the fingerprint results and the final employability determination, Michigan employers can conditionally hire workers for period of 60 days if they pass an online registry checks, which can be completed in a matter of minutes. Given that these healthcare workers would then be taking care of vulnerable adults until the fingerprint results come back, it is crucial that the registry checking process be straightforward, intuitive, and easy to use to help ensure patient safety. Real-time screening, designed with significant involvement of the providers conducting the background checks, would enhance this process by providing the employers with convenient, automated, and centralized access to a comprehensive set of online background registries.

2   Program Background

Currently, most states require pre-employment background checks for workers who have direct access to residents in nursing homes or who provide services to beneficiaries of federal funding in long-term care. Section 307 of the United States Medicare Prescription Drug, Improvement, and Modernization Act (MMA) of 2003 (PL 108–173) directed the Secretary of Health and Human Services to establish a program to identify efficient, effective and economical procedures to conduct background checks on prospective employees of long-term care facilities and providers of services in recipients' homes.

Michigan was one of seven states that received funding in 2004 from the U.S. Department of Health and Human Services, through the Centers for Medicare & Medicaid Services (CMS), to design and implement an economical, effective and efficient program of background checks for direct care workers. The Michigan Workforce Background Check (MWBC) system was developed based on the CMS requirements. Using the $5.1 million grant award from CMS, Michigan implemented a statewide training program to prevent abuse and neglect and a statewide background check program that expanded the existing background check requirements by adding more facility types, collecting digital fingerprints for all prospective employees, requesting a state and federal criminal history check, and creating a process for notifying the employer in the case of a subsequent arrest or conviction. The MWBC system launched in 2006 and has remained active since the pilot phase with support from the Michigan Department of Licensing and Regulatory Affairs in collaboration with Michigan State University and Yale University. The State continues to provide funding for the MWBC program. Additionally, Michigan was awarded $1.5 million from CMS under the Patient Protection and Affordable Care Act (P.L. 111–148) Title IV Subtitle C, Sec. 6201, in May 2013 to enhance the MWBC system to address issues related to adding personal care workers, piloting a FBI rap back, designing a national Nurse Aide Abuse registry, and delivering electronic criminal history records.

3   Michigan Workforce Background Check (MWBC) System Overview

The MWBC system is designed to improve the process of conducting background checks by reducing unnecessary costs (waste) and increasing efficiency, while maintaining easy to use and user-friendly interface. MWBC centralizes the fragmented screening process for prospective employees in long-term care facilities into a single web-based system. This system integrates abuse and neglect registries, the Office of Inspector General's Medicare/Medicaid exclusion database and state criminal records archives, while providing secure communication with the fingerprint vendor, the Michigan State Police (MSP), the Department of Licensing and Regulatory Affairs (LARA) analysts, and the Department of Human Services (DHS) analysts. (See Fig. 1.) In the initial design of the MWBC system and subsequently when incorporating new functionality, our research team utilized systems engineering, humans factors methods, and user experience methodologies to guide the implementation. Specifically, we conducted multiple focus groups, heuristic user interface reviews, usability testing sessions with the long-term care providers and State analysts, in addition to accessibility compliance inspections to provide valuable input into the design and development process, which was critical for deploying an efficient, effective, and usable system [9–11].

The Real-Time Screening (RTS) process includes name-based searches in relevant databases, which contain information that may disqualify a candidate from health care employment according to federal regulations or local policy, such as the Michigan Public Sex Offenders Registry (PSOR) and the Michigan Nurse Aide Registry (NAR) abuse list. Checking applicant names allows for quick and initial assessment that identifies persons with potential disqualifying convictions in Michigan. Such immediate response gives employers timely information that may result in discontinuing the hiring process for that applicant. Provided the applicant successfully completes the initial assessment, the employer then initiates the more comprehensive fingerprint-based state and federal (FBI) criminal history checks.

The MWBC system provides a single data entry point for Michigan employers to check registries for potentially disqualifying information, request fingerprinting appointments for a state and federal fingerprint-based check of criminal history records, automatically import results of federal and state fingerprint checks, and download and print system-generated employment authorization letters from the regulatory agencies.

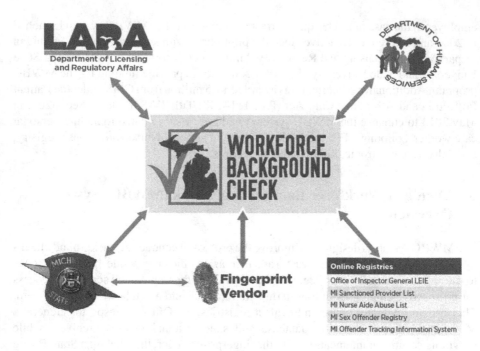

Fig. 1. MWBC system overview

Since April 1, 2006, long-term care healthcare employers have used the MWBC system to screen 949,117 candidates. Of these, 12,236 were immediately screened out due to criminal convictions involving abuse, illegal delivery and manufacture of controlled substances, criminal sexual conduct, health care fraud and numerous types of felony offenses from conditional employment in nursing homes, home health care and other long term care facilities.

4   Real-Time Screening Process (RTS)

A key feature of the MWBC system is the real-time screening process that combines data streams from various databases and online registries in an easy-to-use dashboard decision process (see Fig. 2). The background check begins with entering the applicant's demographic data. This is usually done by a human resources specialist or administrator designated by the employer, who records the applicant's Social Security Number and date of birth (having already receiving applicant's written consent to conduct the background check for employment). The MWBC system immediately alerts the provider that the applicant is ineligible to work when there is a disqualifying record already in the system from a previous request, which saves the employer time and resources. If the applicant is not "flagged" by the system as unfit for employment in long term care, the provider completes a demographic form that collects all the information necessary for the various registry checks. Having several online registries, which require different search criteria, integrated into a single system where the demographic information is passed to an internal search form that is customized for each data source eliminates redundant data entry and reduces data entry errors associated with checking each registry separately manually.

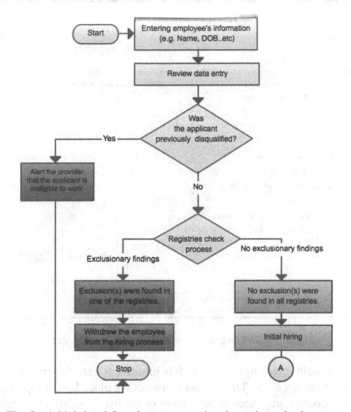

Fig. 2. A high-level flowchart representing the registry check process

Employers then check the results on each of the registries to look for possible matches (see Fig. 3). The registries include the US Office of Inspectors General's (OIG) HHS Medicare/Medicaid Exclusion List, Michigan Sanctioned Provider List, Michigan Nurse Aide Registry (NAR), Offender Tracking Information System (OTIS), and the Michigan Public Sex Offender Registry (PSOR). The results of those queries can collectively be used to make an informed initial hiring decision. The MWBC passes the required parameters to the registry being searched. The number and the type of parameters depend on the registry search engine requirements. As each registry is being checked, the system records the date and time. If an applicant match is found, the system will display and store the appropriate information for that registry. At this point, the employer reviews the results and determines whether to end the search. Otherwise, the employer proceeds until all registries have been checked.

The results of the registry queries can collectively be used to make an informed initial hiring decision. The employer may decide to conditionally hire the applicant, wait for the results of the background check, or withdraw the applicant from the hiring process.

Fig. 3. MWBC registry checks screen from the system

This simple "red light, green light" approach is intuitive for employers, many of whom have limited technology skills. The no-cost registries are placed at the top of the list and the fee-based registries are placed at the bottom of the list. Similarly, the registries that are easier to analyze and understand are listed at the top.

After successfully passing the registry checks, applicants must submit fingerprints (a set of ten rolled live scan images) for a State and FBI records search. When the responses are received, an electronic notification of a "hit" or "no hit" is sent to the background check system. If no record is found, the MWBC generates a letter notifying the employer that is sent by email, letting him or her know that results are available for review and that a final hiring decision is needed. The employer then indicates whether the applicant was hired or withdrew from the hiring process. If a criminal history record is found, a "hit" notice is sent to the system and the applicant record status indicates that the case is pending analysis. The Department of State Police sends a hard copy of the criminal history record to the requesting department, where an analyst reviews the record and makes an employability determination. At that point, the process mirrors the "no hit" process. An applicant or employee has the right to appeal the decision of the department.

Once a record is established in the system, a compliance officer can track and monitor the records through rap back system alerts, creating a means of communicating the results of a search of those records immediately to the State background check unit and to the employer(s). Taken together, the real-time screening process, the fingerprint-based criminal history checking process, and the continuous monitoring after employment through the rap back, which provides employers with updated information that allows for informed hiring and employment decisions.

5 User Experience Approach to Redesign

During the redesign of the Michigan Workforce Background Check (MWBC) system the team adopted a user-centered design approach, gathering user experience feedback throughout the iterative development process. Usability experts conducted in-depth interviews with a few experienced users responsible for conducting background checks at provider agencies on a regular basis. They discussed what was working well and where improvements would increase the efficiency of the process. Participants expressed the for a quick preliminary check based on Social Security Number and date of birth to find out if the applicant is currently ineligible to work in long-term care before filling out the full demographic form. They also wanted a quick way to access the registries without creating a new record, e.g. the OIG needs to be checked every month.

The usability researcher also used a structured walkthrough approach of the concept user interface design prototype. The recommendations resulting from the interviews were incorporated into user interface requirements for the redesign, as well as a user interface specification document. For example, these subject matter experts recommended that the applicant profile page include all actionable information, demographic information, and documentation related to their employment status at the facility.

After the development team implemented the redesign, the State analysts were encouraged to test out various use scenarios and their feedback was folded into the redesign in an iterative fashion. Usability experts also conducted an accessibility inspection of the new functionality; ensuring its compliance with Web Content Accessibility Guidelines, level AA. Finally, before releasing the redesigned system into production, a formal usability evaluation was performed with representative users from provider agencies who conducted pre-employment background checks.

5.1 Usability Evaluation Strategy and Methods

The goal of the usability research was to identify usability issues with the MWBC system before the redesigned web application was released to 7,000 long-term healthcare providers in Michigan. Usability, as defined by the International Standards Organization (ISO), refers to how easily a specific task can be accomplished with a specific tool in a specific context of use. The ISO defines effectiveness as "accuracy and completeness with which users achieve specified goals," efficiency as "resources expended in relation to the accuracy and completeness with which users achieve goals," and satisfaction as "freedom from discomfort, and positive attitudes towards the use of the product [12]."

The evaluation was designed to address the following questions:

- What do users like and dislike about the flow of the MWBC user interface, e.g., navigation, organization of task flows, and grouping of content?
- Which aspects of the user interface are hard to understand?

- What are user expectations regarding where the information should be found in the menus and on the site?
- Which aspects of the process need to be enhanced?

5.2 Procedure

Each one-on-one usability session lasted approximately one hour and included several components:

- **Overview and consent**: A description of the study and the order of activities were read to participants. Each participant was asked to sign the consent form before participating in the study.
- **Demographic questionnaire:** A questionnaire was administered to gather background information on participants' age, education level, computing platform, Internet use, and experience with the MWBC system.
- **Task scenarios and ratings:** Participants were given six representative tasks, such as creating new applications, determining employment eligibility for applications with and without hits, and managing the account. Participants were asked to think aloud and describe any confusion while performing tasks to aid researchers in identifying areas of difficulty, as well as patterns and types of participant errors. Participants were also asked to rate the difficulty of each task before beginning the following task.
- Post-study questionnaire: At the conclusion of a session, each participant completed a post-study questionnaire to assess their experience.
- **Post-study debriefing:** Participants were debriefed at the end of the session and given a hard copy of the usability-evaluation information.

Usability was evaluated in terms of its three constituent components: effectiveness, efficiency, and satisfaction (defined previously). Effectiveness was measured as the percentage of tasks completed successfully. Efficiency was measured as the average time to perform a task and assessed based on issues observed during performance of the tasks. Satisfaction was measured by user satisfaction ratings (i.e., from post-task and post-study questionnaires) written feedback on the questionnaires, and verbal comments from each session. While effectiveness and efficiency measures were quantitative, satisfaction was measured qualitatively.

5.3 Participant Profile

Research literature suggests that at a minimum 4–5 users from each group are needed for conducting a valid usability test [13–15]. It has been shown, for example, that using five people (from one type of group) for a usability test will uncover approximately 85 % of a website's usability issues. However, more recent literature suggests that 10–12 participants are generally more appropriate for studies related to problem discovery [16–18].

The current study included six participants, five females and one male, with varying levels of experience in conducting background checks. Four participants were in human resources; one was a background check specialist; and one was a licensee of an adult foster care facility. All participants worked at long-term care facilities in mid-Michigan, including skilled nursing, hospice, adult foster care, assisted living, and psychiatric facilities. All participants conducted applicant background checks as part of their job responsibilities: Three conducted background checks every day, two participants did them 1–2 times or less per week, while one rarely performed them

5.4 Usability Results

Overall, the users were successful in completing the tasks and they had a favorable impression of the MWBC system. They had little difficulty understanding how to perform registry checks, locate existing records in the system, updating hiring decisions for employees or applicants that did not work at the facility anymore. However, they had some difficulty making the correct eligibility determination when there was a non-disqualifying hit in a registry, tending to incorrectly mark the findings as non-disqualifying and then continuing with the next registry check. As a result, some applicants would have been sent for fingerprints when they might have been excluded based on the registry findings alone. After attempting all of the task scenarios, participants were asked to use the System Usability Scale (SUS) to rate their experience with the MWBC system. The SUS, created by John Brooke, is an industry standard used as a quick and reliable tool for measuring usability that can be used for small sample sizes [19–21]. The SUS score for the MWBC system was 94.6, which is considered a very high score. Overall, participant responses were favorable for the redesigned provider user interface, which has been upgraded to HTML5 coding standards.

Recommendations from the usability evaluation for improving the user experience included using more on-screen messaging to let users know how to proceed in the system and what will happen when the system flags an applicant as ineligible, in addition to the instructions to call their regulatory agency; providing more guidance using on-screen instructions and/or a link to the Help system to assist providers in interpreting the registry results correctly; and redesigning the applicant profile page to display all actionable items near the top of the page. Our user-focused development approach resulted in a product that is usable, accepted, comprehensive, and efficient.

6 Impact of Pre-Employment Real-Time Screening Process

Our research identified areas for improvement in the existing long-term care workers hiring process, mainly by automating the name-based background check of relevant registries to quickly provide a comprehensive view of the worker's background, and provide a single and unified interface for employers. Our best practice approach to pre-employment real-time screening via the Michigan Workforce Background Check system decreases the risk of conditionally hiring applicants without realizing that they have a publicly known criminal or abuse history; it helps employers immediately identify individuals who present a risk to vulnerable citizens, with minimal impact on the employer's workflow. Also, pre-employment screening eliminates the ability to circumvent the process through data entry errors, deception, identity theft, and fraud, while protecting the applicant's privacy as much as possible.

For patients and recipients of long term care services, the pre-screening of applicants online registries and subsequent digital fingerprinting speeds up the hiring process, which reduces risks and enhances patient safety. Staffing shortages in the long term care workforce are common, and can place patients in these facilities at higher risk. For workers, the decreased turnaround time and immediate results of registry checks increases the opportunity for employment. For employers, the MWBC system reduces costs by providing a reliable and accurate alternative to the more expensive biometric-based background checks to conduct the initial screening of potential employees. For state governments, automating these tasks increases productivity by requiring fewer resources and allows for real-time reporting.

7   Conclusion

The experience of the MWBC program shows that users are willing to make an initial investment of time to learn the background check process because they recognize that decreasing turnaround time for background checks helps to mitigate risk related to patient safety, since many healthcare workers are conditionally hired. A centralized automated process that is user-friendly also makes it easier to comply with regulatory requirements, especially when cost of compliance is an ongoing concern. A deep under-standing of the impact of a new system on the diverse group of end users persuaded the system design team to be flexible in its approach The user-centered design approach facilitated interfacing with multiple players, bringing disparate entities together. The resulting RTS system benefits thousands of patients and employers in Michigan, but could benefit millions of patients, healthcare workers and employers, as well as hundreds of state government agencies.

Acknowledgments.   This research was funded through a grant between Michigan Department of Licensing and Regulatory Affairs and Michigan State University, Usability/Accessibility Research and Consulting: Michigan Department of Licensing and Regulatory Affairs (U.S. Department of Health and Human Services – Center for Medicare and Medicaid Services). *Michigan Workforce Background Check – Enhancement.* Grant # 1A1CMS331188-0-00. Principal Investigator: Toni Dennis (Prime), 5/20/13–05/19/16, $1,500,000. MSU Subaward Grant # BHCS/MSU-CMS NBCP 2013-2016. Principal Investigator of MSU Subaward: Sarah J. Swierenga. Yale University Subaward from Grant # (1A1CMS331188-0-00). Principal Investigator of Yale Subaward: Fuad Abujarad.

We sincerely appreciate the contributions of Thi Nguyen for creating the test scenarios in the system and providing technical support, as well as Tim Decloniemaclennan and Phil Deaton for assistance with the tagging the video recordings.

References

1. US Census Bureau: The Older Population: 2010 Census Briefs (2011). http://www.census.gov/content/dam/Census/library/publications/2011/dec/c2010br-09.pdf
2. U.S. Bureau of Labor Statistics: Occupational Outlook Handbook – Fastest Growing Occupations, January 8, 2014. http://www.bls.gov/ooh/fastest-growing.htm

3. Department of Health and Human Services, Office of Inspector General: Nursing Facilities' Employment of Individuals with Criminal Convictions. Report OEI-07-09-00110, March 2011
4. Cooper, C., Selwood, A., Livingston, G.: The prevalence of elder abuse and neglect: a systematic review. Age Ageing **37**, 151–160 (2008)
5. Post, L.A., Salmon, C.T., Prokhorov, A., Oehmke, J.F., Swierenga, S.J.: Chapter 6 - Aging and elder abuse: projections for Michigan. In: Murdock, S.H., Swanson, D.A. (eds.) Applied Demography in the 21st Century, pp. 103–112. Springer Science and Business Media B.V. (ISBN: 1402083289) (2008)
6. Post, L.A., Swierenga, S.J., Oehmke, J., Salmon, C., Prokhorov, A., Meyer, E., Joshi, V.: The implications of an aging population structure. Int. J. Interdisc. Soc. Sci. **1**(2), 47–58 (2006)
7. Galantowicz, S., Crisp, S., Karp, N., Accius, J.: Safe at Home?. Developing Effective Criminal Background Checks and Other Screening Policies for Home Care Workers. AARP Public Policy Institute, Washington (2010)
8. Blumstein, A., Nakamura, K.: Redemption in the presence of widespread criminal background checks. Criminology **47**(2), 327–359 (2009)
9. Swierenga, S.J., Abujarad, F., Dennis, T.A., Post, L.A.: Real-world user-centered design: the Michigan Workforce Background Check system. In: Salvendy, G., Smith, M.J. (eds.) HCII 2011, Part II. LNCS, vol. 6772, pp. 325–334. Springer, Heidelberg (2011)
10. Abujarad, F., Swierenga, S.J., Dennis, T.A., Post, L.A.: Rap Backs: continuous workforce monitoring to improve patient safety in long-term care. In: Marcus, A. (ed.) DUXU 2013, Part III. LNCS, vol. 8014, pp. 3–9. Springer, Heidelberg (2013)
11. Swierenga, S.J., Abujarad, F., Dennis, T.A, Post, L.A.: Improving patient safety through user-centered healthcare background check system design. In: Proceedings of the International Symposium of Human Factors and Ergonomics in Healthcare HFES 2013. Human Factors and Ergonomics Society, 2(21), pp. 21–26 (2013)
12. International Organization for Standardization: Ergonomic Requirements for Office Work with Visual Display Terminals (VDTs) – Part 11: Guidance on Usability. (ISO Reference No. 9241-11:1998) (1998)
13. Nielsen, J.: Estimating the number of subjects needed for a thinking aloud test. Int. J. Hum Comput Stud. **41**, 385–397 (1994)
14. Nielsen, J.: Why You Only Need to Test with 5 Users, March 19, 2000. http://www.useit.com/alertbox/20000319.html
15. Virzi, R.A.: Refining the test phase of usability evaluation: how many subjects is enough? Hum. Factors **34**, 457–468 (2002)
16. Hwang, W., Salvendy, G.: Number of people required for usability evaluation: the 10±2 rule. Commun. ACM **53**(5), 130–133 (2010)
17. Macefield, R.: How to specify the participant group size for usability studies: a practitioner's guide. J. Usability Stud. **5**(1), 34–45 (2009)
18. Molich, R.A.: A commentary of "How to specify the participant group size for usability studies: a practitioner's guide". J. Usability Stud. **5**(3), 124–128 (2010)
19. U.S. Department of Health & Human Services: System Usability Scale (SUS). usability.gov (n.d.). http://www.usability.gov/how-to-and-tools/methods/system-usability-scale.html
20. Bangor, A., Kortum, P.T., Miller, J.T.: An empirical evaluation of the System Usability Scale. Int. J. Hum. Comput. Interact. **24**(6), 574–594 (2008)
21. Brooke, J.: SUS: a retrospective. J. Usability Stud. **8**(2), 29–40 (2013)

The Knowledge Gap: Providing Situation-Aware Information Assistance on the Shop Floor

Mario Aehnelt[✉] and Bodo Urban

Fraunhofer IGD, Joachim-Jungius-Str. 11, 18059 Rostock, Germany
{mario.aehnelt,bodo.urban}@igd-r.fraunhofer.de

Abstract. Situation-aware information assistance strongly depends on the quality of available contextual background knowledge for an application domain and on its automatic processing. In this paper we present a conceptual approach towards using cognitive architectures to provide information assistance and allow complex decision making based on expert knowledge. We transfer our approach into a technical concept which was finally implemented as part of the *Plant@Hand* assembly assistance system within a mobile workshop trolley. The paper gives insights into our work on formalizing knowledge and providing ad-hoc mechanisms for planning, assisting and controlling assembly tasks on the manufacturing shop floor.

1 Introduction

Evaluations show that people with a detailed work plan complete their tasks faster than without it, even if they did not carry out the planning themselves [6]. This is a key motivation for intelligent systems which assist the worker by creating work plans autonomously and guide through single tasks aiming to improve both efficiency and effectiveness of work. Such intelligent systems will help in manufacturing to ensure a high product quality even when working with insufficiently qualified personnel. They need to provide the missing knowledge which is required to fulfill even complex work tasks on the shop floor. Although, manufacturing industries already use powerful data management systems, there is still a lack of methods and technologies which allow an automated processing of the lion's share of domain dependent background knowledge. It is still hidden in unstructured information sources (e.g. standards, guidelines) or simply maintained by experts, thus not available for the average worker.

The paper introduces an abstract model of work related background knowledge. It shows how cognitive architectures are used to bridge the knowledge gap by modeling, applying, and learning domain dependent context knowledge in order to provide situation-aware information assistance at the workplace. Finally, the theoretical approach is implemented in and illustrated with the mobile *Plant@Hand smart assembly trolley*, which guides manufacturing workers through their daily work tasks and assists them at the assembly workplace with detailed situation-dependent task knowledge.

© Springer International Publishing Switzerland 2015
F.F.-H. Nah and C.-H. Tan (Eds.): HCIB 2015, LNCS 9191, pp. 232–243, 2015.
DOI: 10.1007/978-3-319-20895-4_22

2   Related Work

Although, smart factories establish digitalization and automation to streamline manufacturing processes and quality, there is still the need for manual assembly operations. However, we find there a majority of specialized and simple high solutions focusing on quality assurance and information transfer. Mayer et al. introduce the usage of intelligent systems to resemble human decision making and problem solving for complex assembly tasks [10]. They use a *cognitive control unit* which ensures the numerical planning of robot behavior backed by a cognitive architecture. Cognitive architectures can be understood as a mean to implement intelligent and autonomous behavior in assistance applications. They have proven capable of supporting even complex problem solving tasks, e.g. for the mission management for unmanned aircrafts [5].

Our own work contributes to the growing demand of information assistance for manual work operations in manufacturing which underlies human flexibility and failures as motivated in [1,3]. In particular, we focus on assistance that can be generated automatically from existing knowledge sources in order to manage todays growing complexity and heterogeneity of extremely small lot sizes.

3   Approach

Similar to formal education processes, information assistance can be understood as an informal way of mediating and *learning facts* (what), *procedures* (how) and *concepts* (why) required for a specific work task. In [2] we showed how assistance artifacts - e.g. embodied by an interactive smartwatch - are used to mediate this work related knowledge depending on a specific *assistance goal* (e.g. remember, understand, apply). However, a technological system which is able to operate the contextual background knowledge in a situation-aware manner was still missing. In our approach (see Fig. 1) we address this knowledge related gap now on three levels:

- on *conceptual level* we establish a relationship between abstract work situations, assistance goals and required knowledge types along the generalized information process,
- on *information level* we map domain dependent context knowledge into formal information rules which control the collection, filtering, and provision of work related knowledge in specific work situations, and
- on *technical level* we use a cognitive architecture to integrate intelligent and situation-aware information assistance with the already existing information infrastructure at the workplace.

We will explain each level carefully in the next sections by introducing the main rationale illustrated with examples from the assembly work domain.

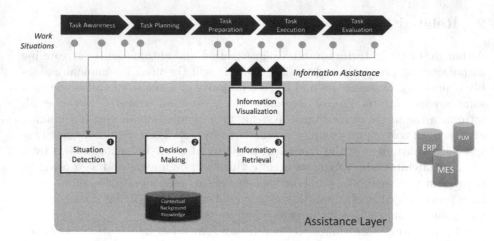

Fig. 1. Conceptual architecture of situation-aware information assistance on the shop floor

3.1   Conceptual Level

Task related information assistance aims at providing the required information needed to understand, carry out, evaluate, or reflect on a specific work task. This means to establish a continuously information process in parallel to the work process as described in [2]. Finally, it is an upcoming information demand during planning, preparing, executing, or evaluating a task which connects work and information processes. Such a demand arises from work situations in which provided information does not satisfy the worker's expectations as well as needs, or the information given is incomplete and even contradictory. What we require here is an ad-hoc mechanism to analyze work situations with respect to the knowledge needed by the worker to carry out tasks without interruptions. We can achieve this by conceptually connecting the work with the information process. This requires the modeling:

- of *work situations* in which knowledge related information demands arise,
- of *knowledge*, which satisfies the information demand,
- of an *information assistance strategy*, which connects the required knowledge with situation dependent assistance objectives to be achieved, and
- of a technical *relationship between knowledge and information sources* which finally maintain and provide the required information pieces in form of structured or unstructured data.

The basis for our further exploration on the conceptual relationship between work situations, assistance goals and knowledge types will be the worker's knowledge-based *control of action* process [12]. Summarizing this process, a conscious perception of information leads to its' interpretation and cognition based remembering in order to actively plan own actions. By the observation and evaluation of action outcomes a learning sub process is triggered.

For our approach we basically simplify the control of action into three phases: action planning, acting, and reflecting. The *planning phase* includes all cognitive steps to get aware of the current situation and plan own actions accordingly. During the *acting phase* the beforehand developed action plan is realized. Afterwards, during the *reflecting phase* the outcomes of own actions are compared against expectations which lead to further learning. The worker requires for each phase specific knowledge in order to plan, execute, and evaluate work tasks efficiently. In Fig. 2 we propose an information assistance strategy which considers this individual knowledge demand by providing small information pieces along the workers own control of action respectively work process. The order and depths of information to be provided to the worker follows an iterative sequence of assistance goals as described in [2] which consequently addresses the increasing knowledge demands of the work process.

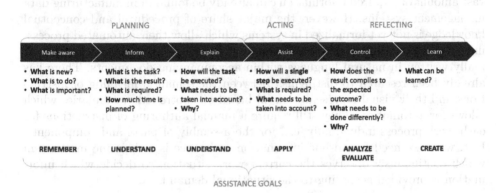

Fig. 2. Conceptual relationship between assistance process, knowledge types and process dependent assistance goals

Once a new situation occurs, e.g. a new work task which was scheduled from the manufacturing execution system shortly before, the information assistance makes the worker *aware* of this new task and provides help in remembering this information. Before executing the new task the worker requires in depths knowledge to understand what and how to do. We propose here a two-staged information assistance based on *informing* first in general and *explaining* details on demand. Once the task was understood, information assistance comes into the role of assisting the task execution, e.g. by monitoring and visualizing task parameters, showing step-by-step guidance, or similar [1], to ease the application of provided information. Finally, it is again the information assistance which provides required information pieces when the work result is controlled. It then supports the *analysis* and *evaluation* as well as *creation* of new insights and knowledge.

On conceptual level we link with this approach work situations, which require a new action strategy, with an accompanying information process delivering the required knowledge in parallel to the progressing control of action process of the worker. However, information sources in manufacturing, such as manufacturing execution systems or product lifecycle management systems, normally do not provide all information as required for systematically assisting the worker. A lion's share of *contextual background knowledge* which is needed to plan, execute and evaluate work tasks are domain dependent and subject to individual expertise. The next section addresses this very specific challenge when providing ad-hoc and situation-aware information assistance.

3.2   Information Level

The previous section explains our conceptual considerations with respect to acquiring knowledge on actual work situations as well as to providing information assistance at the workplace. Looking at the manufacturing shop floor, a vast amount of required information can already be found in manufacturing data management systems. However, the major share of procedural and conceptual knowledge is not yet formalized in systems which allow their automated processing (see Fig. 3). We find work instructions, standards, or assembly guidelines normally written in natural language within accompanying documents. There has already been research to distinguish between the semantic meaning of instructions and their visual representation [9] based on controlled vocabularies which allows for automation. They still require a manual authoring of instructions for each work process individually, e.g. for the assembly of parts and components. But, what we need for ad-hoc information assistance is a dynamic mechanism which continuously observes the current work situation to decide which information is provided according to the situational demand.

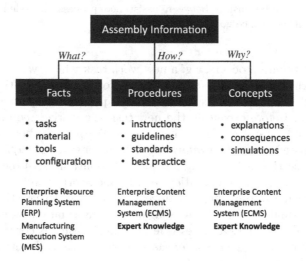

Fig. 3. Required information is contained in different enterprise resources. Partly it is individual expert knowledge which is not externalized in any management system [1].

On information level, we distinguish three major types of work related contextual background knowledge which needs to be provided by information assistance (see Fig. 3). *Facts* contain objective data with respect to tasks, material or tools to be used or a machine configuration for example. Specific work orders or step by step instructions are encoded in *procedures* while further explanations are contained in *concepts*. But how can we enable the machine processing of such contextual background knowledge in order to improve the quality of information assistance?

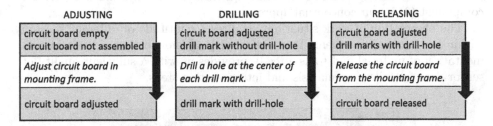

Fig. 4. Contextual background knowledge is modeled in information rules. The example describes very simple the order of assembly steps combined with a textual information for the worker. At the top of each rule are characteristic states of the work environment and at the bottom a target state which will be reached once the assembly step was successfully executed.

In our approach we model knowledge with formal *information rules*. An information rule encodes required knowledge as processable information in dependency of a specific work situation. The situation is identified by characteristic conditions or states of the work environment, e.g. materials, parts, or tools. This helps us for example to formalize even the hitherto missing procedural or conceptual knowledge. Thus, knowledge related to specific work procedures and routines can be expressed within modular rules. In our example (see Fig. 4), we formalized parts of the German industrial standard VDI 2860:1990 [4] in very simple information rules which declare the structure and sequence of assembly steps in case of a drilling operation. We can now use the same rules to model more complex knowledge, e.g. possible solution strategies in case of assembly issues or even the selection and filtering of information sources which provide further operational data (planned figures, construction details, etc.). The modularity of information rules guarantees knowledge modeling in very different granularities. New knowledge can simply be added in a new rule declaring the situational dependencies and thus extending the existing knowledge base.

But, the more information rules with the same or even similar situational conditions are modeled, the more complex grows the decision making for valid and applicable rules in a specific work situation. Therefore, the next section will take a look at the technical perspective of situation aware information assistance.

3.3   Technical Level

In Fig. 1 we developed a conceptual view onto the integration of intelligent and situation-aware information assistance with the existing technological infrastructure on a shop floor. Basically, we have to deal here with a heterogeneity of available information sources and technical systems including their native interfaces and protocols. *Enterprise service bus* technologies reduce the effort of connecting all system components on technical level by providing an universal messaging bus which interconnects each system on data and procedural level as well. This component can be understood as functional equivalent of the *information retrieval* component (3) in our conceptual approach.

The observation of work situations requires a multitude of different *sensors* within the work environment. Previous work [1,3] showed that a basic instrumentation of material and tools already provides us with a sufficient quality of sensor data for following analysis and interpretation steps.

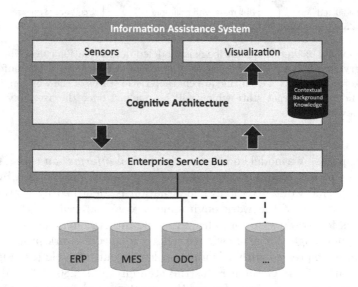

Fig. 5. The technical architecture of an information assistance systems shows a layered layout of interaction, logical and data related components. The system uses an enterprise service bus approach to connect with existing shop floor management systems, such as enterprise resource planning (ERP), manufacturing execution (MES), operational data collection (ODC), as well as other information sources (...).

The cornerstone of our technical architecture (see Fig. 5) is represented by a logical component, the *cognitive architecture*. It is responsible for the functional elements *situation detection* (1) and *decision making* (2) in Fig. 1. As of today, a cognitive architecture transfers the mental structure for human information processing into a technical system, which specifically includes the representation and organization of knowledge within these structures as well as the functional processing required to acquire, use, and modify knowledge [8]. Cognitive architectures can be traced back to Newell's early hypothesis that any artificial intelligence is based on a symbol system and related rules [11]. Hence, they establish technical equivalents for long-term and short-term memories as well as for cognitive processes, such as learning or remembering which are required for an intelligent information assistance system. Cognitive architectures represent and interpret knowledge in a similar formal way as introduced in Sect. 3.2. Within our approach we use it specifically for:

- *situation detection* based on sensorical observations of the physical work environment,
- the *formalization and processing* of contextual background knowledge (e.g. procedures, explanations), as well as for
- *decision making* in order to structure and control the work process itself based on knowledge and data from the work domain, and for
- *learning* new knowledge and practices from observation.

Finally, a *visualization* component communicates the previously selected knowledge as visual information embedded in the ongoing work process.

The following section explains how this still abstract conceptual and technical approach has been implemented in an industrial application which supports assembly workers on the shop floor.

4 Industrial Application

The proposed approach has been implemented within the *Plant@Hand* assembly assistance system which was already introduced in our previous work [1–3]. We used *Soar* as cognitive architecture which enables us now to analyze the specific work situation and to make decisions on missing information which an assembly worker needs to plan, execute, and evaluate his work accordingly.

The whole system was developed to provide mobile information assistance for the assembly part of the manufacturing shop floor. It is required to support there assembly work on complex special units which require a great amount of worker flexibility and mobility. The next sections describe the technological setup as well as our use of Soar for automatic knowledge processing.

4.1 Technological Setup

The assembly of partly large and complex special units requires from the worker a high degree of flexibility and mobility. Components need to be assembled in varying complexities at different locations of the special unit. This makes it difficult to instrument the work environment with activity recognizing sensors. An instrumentation of the worker is also limited due to safety reasons. Because of this challenging conditions we use a standard mobile workshop trolley (see Fig. 6) as technical basis for our assembly assistance application. Such a unit is normally used to store and transport tools as well as material during an assembly.

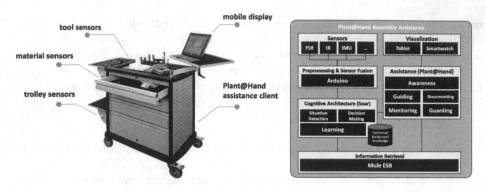

Fig. 6. Hardware and software components of the industrial *Plant@Hand smart assembly trolley* prototype.

The trolley provides shelves and drawers for different sorts of assembly tools or small to medium sized work materials. All hardware and software components of the *Plant@Hand* assembly assistance system are built into the mobile workshop trolley:

- **Sensors:** We use different sensor types to monitor the ongoing assembly activities of the worker. *Force sensitive resistors* (FSR) and *infrared sensors* (IR) provide data on material and tool usage, e.g. the removal of screws from a material container. *Inertial measurement units* (IMU) give us information on the trolley movements.
- **Preprocessing and Sensor Fusion:** An *Arduino Uno* board is used to make a first preprocessing (filtering) and fusion of incoming sensor data. It generates activity events for further interpretation in the Soar cognitive architecture.
- **Cognitive Architecture:** The cognitive architecture *Soar* provides the functional subcomponents for situation detection out of the incoming trolley events, decision making on required assistance actions and information to be provided as well as learning from observed activities.
- **Information Retrieval:** For the connection with external manufacturing data systems the enterprise service bus system *Mule ESB* is used. Based on information flows, data is continuously exchanged which guarantees a provision of the latest information.
- **Assistance:** The main implementation of assistance functions can still be found within the *Plant@Hand* assembly assistance system. Functional blocks, such as raising the workers awareness, the step-by-step guiding of assembly works, or the documentation of work results are part of the *Plant@Hand* assistance client.
- **Visualization:** The mobile workplace requires also a mobile visualization of information for the worker. We use here mobile displays which are still available during the assembly task execution. Provided displays are tablets and even smartwatches [2].

With this setup we are independent from specific or stationary workplaces. The workshop trolley is positioned close to the assembly site and by observing the worker's activities with respect to material, tools and trolley, we obtain a sufficient overview on the ongoing work process to provide required knowledge with the Plant@Hand assistance system.

4.2 Knowledge Processing with Soar

In Sect. 3.3 we described the cognitive architecture as cornerstone component of our technical approach. It provides us with the functional abilities to add intelligent behavior to a static assistance system. In the following, we will explain the role of Soar for situation-aware knowledge processing in relationship to assisting the assembly worker. We use the generation of step-by-step instructions for novel assembly units as illustrating example. In general, processes in Soar are related to the gradual alternation of information and states in working or long-term memory [7]. Here, a situation is formalized as a state in working memory, which is modified by evaluating and applying *operators* until an intended final state is reached. The operator definition consists of required conditions and actions on the working memory. It inherits procedural and conceptual knowledge from the corresponding knowledge domain. New operators can also be derived by observation of decision making and through learning processes (*chunking*).

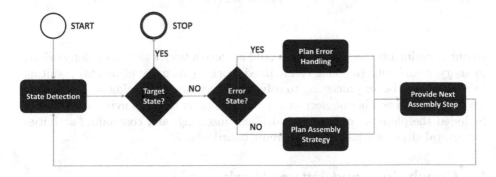

Fig. 7. Working cycle of Soar for the assembly sequence problem space.

Traditionally, the work instructions for an assembly are manually prepared by an expert. Based on the geometric model of the unit to be assembled, predefined production sequences and expert knowledge, each assembly step is textually and pictorially described including dependencies to a bill of materials as well as tools to be used. Soar helps us now to automate this time-consuming authoring process. Explaining our approach briefly, we first store expert knowledge related to the structuring and sequencing of assembly tasks in Soar's procedural memory (long-term memory). Additionally, we define a target state (unit assembled) as well as error states (wrong material, wrong tool, etc.) and leave it up to

Soar finding a valid solution for the *assembly sequence problem* (see Fig. 7). Soar uses now its operational decision making based on the previously stored assembly knowledge in order to plan an assembly strategy which finally leads to an assembled unit. Each assembly step is then visualized to the worker including all information required to understand, execute and control the step. In parallel Soar learns new knowledge through observing the decision making itself as well as the work environment. This knowledge is used in a similar situation to improve the decision quality. This has the positive effect, that during decision making the working memory complexity of Soar dramatically decreases in comparison to the same situation without the previously learned knowledge chunks.

Table 1. Comparison of two experiments without additionally learned production rules (*chunks*) and with using this additional knowledge for solving a small subassembly problem.

Category	1st Run	2nd Run (with learning)
required decisions	169	22
elaboration cycles	650	67
production firings	2.548	163
working memory changes	9.097	761
CPU time	0,047 sec	0,005 sec

In our experiments (see Table 1) we could achieve a twelve times smaller working memory complexity (amount of modified working memory elements) resulting in a nine times faster processing to solve the assembly sequencing problem. Here we used a subassembly of electronic components as testing environment which included the planning of handling, drilling, inserting, and controlling activities for several electronic parts into a circuit board.

5   Conclusions and Future Work

In this paper we introduced a threefold approach of bridging the knowledge gap when providing situation-aware information assistance. Based on the conceptual linking between work situations, assistance goals and knowledge types, we focused on the autonomous processing of contextual background knowledge with a cognitive architecture on information as well as on technical level. Finally, we presented the implementation of our approach within the *Plant@Hand* assembly assistance system which was integrated into a mobile workshop trolley. Here we used Soar for the autonomous planning and problem solving of assembly sequences.

Although, we could achieve with comparatively little modeling efforts good results in solving even complex assembly sequencing problems, the authoring of contextual background knowledge as production rules of a cognitive architecture is still one of the remaining major issues for the automation of information assistance. Here we need to investigate further into alternative authoring as well as learning approaches in the future in order to make it suitable for everyday use.

Acknowledgements. This research has been supported by the German Federal State of Mecklenburg-Western Pomerania and the European Social Fund under grant ESF/IV-BM-B35-0006/12.

References

1. Aehnelt, M., Bader, S.: Information assistance for smart assembly stations. In: Loiseau, S., Filipe, J., Duval, B., van den Herik, J. (eds.) Proceedings of the 7th International Conference on Agents and Artificial Intelligence (ICAART 2015), vol. 2, pp. 143–150. SciTePress, Lisbon (2015). http://dx.doi.org/10.5220/0005216501430150
2. Aehnelt, Mario, Urban, Bodo: Follow-me: smartwatch assistance on the shop floor. In: Nah, Fiona Fui-Hoon (ed.) HCIB 2014. LNCS, vol. 8527, pp. 279–287. Springer, Heidelberg (2014)
3. Bader, S., Aehnelt, M.: Tracking assembly processes and providing assistance in smart factories. In: Duval, B., van den Herik, J., Loiseau, S., Filipe, J. (eds.) Proceedings of the 6th International Conference on Agents and Artificial Intelligence, ESEO, Angers, Loire Valley, France, 6–8 March 2014, vol. 1, pp. 161–168. SciTePress, S.l. (2014). http://dx.doi.org/10.5220/0004822701610168
4. German Engineers' Association: Vdi 2860:1990–05 assembly and handling; handling functions, handling units; terminology, definitions an symbols (1990)
5. Gunetti, P., Dodd, T., Thompson, H.: Simulation of a soar-based autonomous mission management system for unmanned aircraft. J. Aerosp. Inf. Syst. **10**(2), 53–70 (2013)
6. Kokkalis, N., Köhn, T., Huebner, J., Lee, M., Schulze, F., Klemmer, S.R.: Taskgenies: automatically providing action plans helps people complete tasks. ACM Trans. Comput. Hum. Interact. **20**(5), 1–25 (2013)
7. Laird, J.E.: The soar cognitive architecture. Artif. Intell. Simul. Behav. Q. **134**, 1–4 (2012)
8. Langley, P., Laird, J.E., Rogers, S.: Cognitive architectures: research issues and challenges. Cogn. Syst. Res. **10**(2), 141–160 (2008)
9. Mader, S., Urban, B.: Creating instructional content for augmented reality based on controlled natural language concepts. In: Proceedings of 20th International Conference on Artificial Reality and Telexistence (ICAT 2010) (2010)
10. Mayer, Marcel Ph, Odenthal, Barbara, Wagels, Carsten, Kuz, Sinem, Kausch, Bernhard, Schlick, Christopher M.: Cognitive engineering of automated assembly processes. In: Harris, Don (ed.) Engin. Psychol. and Cog. Ergonomics, HCII 2011. LNCS, vol. 6781, pp. 313–321. Springer, Heidelberg (2011)
11. Newell, A.: Physical symbol systems*. Cogn. Sci. **4**(2), 135–183 (1980)
12. Reason, J.T.: Human Error. Cambridge University Press, Cambridge, New York (1990)

An Interactive Assessment Instrument to Improve the Process for Mobile Service Application Innovation

Karen Carey$^{(\boxtimes)}$ and Markus Helfert

Dublin City University, Gasnevin, Dublin 9, Ireland
karen.carey6@mail.dcu.ie,
markus.helfert@computing.dcu.ie

Abstract. In recent years, the adoption and use of new mobile service applications have not proliferated, consequently many applications fail to generate a profit [1, 2]. One reason for this is poor decision making in the process of mobile service innovation [1, 3, 4]. This paper details the construction of an interactive assessment instrument to improve decision making in this innovation process. To design the interactive assessment instrument, we follow a Design Science Research Methodology (DSRM) - a methodology which is new to HCI [5]. Adhering to the DSRM, the paper details the iterative design and evaluation cycles required to build and evaluate the instrument. The paper concludes that the designed assessment instrument improves the innovation process, by providing transparency, while also facilitating communication and understanding amongst team members. Additionally, the paper demonstrates that the DSRM can be of great use to design and evaluate interactive IT artifacts within the HCI field.

Keywords: Mobile service applications · Innovation process · Interactive assessment instrument · Design science research methodology · Design science in HCI

1 Introduction

Mobile service applications are essential in both business and avocation. They make user actions and activities more effective, productive and simplify routines [1]. Although valuable, their adoption has been much slower than expected [1]. This may be due to poor decision making in the process for mobile service innovation, as a result of a lack of structured and transparent activities [2–4]. Research suggests, the mobile service innovation process lacks structure and transparency [4, 7]. Furthermore, it has been suggested that poor understanding in this innovation process has resulted in problems flowing into the later development and deployment stages [6, 7]. Understanding within this research refers to decision maker's perceptions of particular factors that can influence the adoption of the mobile concept. Finally, poor communication is also a challenge for this process [7, 8]. Research suggests, the terminology used by different members of the development team can be contradictory (due to their diverse

© Springer International Publishing Switzerland 2015
F.F.-H. Nah and C.-H. Tan (Eds.): HCIB 2015, LNCS 9191, pp. 244–255, 2015.
DOI: 10.1007/978-3-319-20895-4_23

backgrounds) and can result in misunderstandings in relation to elements of the mobile concept.

Providing transparency and facilitating understanding and communication amongst team members is vital for rational decisions to take place [7]. These challenges are taken into account as important problems that must be solved with the proposed research. Consequently, the underlining research question addressed includes the following: how can the process of mobile service application innovation be improved to cater for transparency, understanding and communication challenges?

To address the aforementioned challenges, prescriptive knowledge must be provided to the process for mobile service application innovation, [5, 10–15]. Design science is a promising research approach that makes it possible to scientifically study the human experience as it relates to IT artifacts, while simultaneously creating new and powerful interactive experiences [5]. It facilitates the creation of prescriptive design knowledge through building and evaluating IT artefacts that can change the world. Despite this, the use of design science in HCI is rare [5]. Due to its prescriptive and practical suitability this paper follows the Design Science Research Methodology (DSRM) proposed by [16]. By doing so, this work provides comprehensive insight for the knowledgebase and practice while also demonstrating the applicability of the design science research methodology for HCI.

To address the issue of transparency the 'decision situation' is logically structured into a new calculative space and quantified [19, 20]. This involves defining the decision situation (e.g. concept definition and evaluation in the innovation process), and structuring its key elements (e.g. influencing factors scales and adoption scales) and quantifying this (e.g. aggregating the data to quantify the adoption for each alternative levels of influencing factors present). Specifically, we propose to do this is in the form of an interactive assessment instrument, namely: The Mobile Concept Assessment Instrument. To address the issue of poor understanding the instrument represents and structures the parameters of the decision in a graphical form (e.g. visual aid). Providing a visual aid helps decision makers to filter relevant dimensions of the context. Consequently, the visual aid can enable a deeper understanding of key factors and how they can influence the adoption of the mobile concept. Finally, communication can be improved by structuring the decision situation into traceable units of analysis, providing clear and consistent descriptions. This will encourage collective discussions on the important parameters of the decisions [21].

The following section provides an overview of the existing literature on the process for mobile service application innovation. Following this, section three describes the research methodology in more detail. Section four, describes the development of the assessment instrument and the ex-ante evaluation. The ex-ante evaluation involved interviews with industry experts which resulted in improvements to the initial design. Following the design improvements, section five describes the ex-post evaluation. This involved the implementation of the refined assessment instrument in a real world case study organization. Section six, discusses the findings from the ex-post evaluation and finally, section seven concludes the paper and summarizes the main contributions.

2 Literature Review

Since the 1950s, a lot of research has been done in relation to the phases and activities of the innovation process. Despite the vast research in this area, no one model, of the innovation process, has proved superior to others. Within this research, we discuss the innovation process in the context of mobile service applications.

Koen et al. [17], developed a theoretical construct, defined as the New Concept Development (NCD) model in order to provide common language and insight to the front end activities of innovation. Their model consists of three key parts: five front end elements; the engine that powers the elements, and external influencing factors. The engine represents senior and executive-level management support, which powers the five elements of the NCD model. The outer area denotes the influencing factors which affect the decisions of the two inner parts. The five front end elements (which can be conducted in an iterative manner) include the following activities:

- Opportunity Identification: this is where the organization, by design or default, identifies the opportunities that the company might want to pursue.
- Opportunity Analysis: this is where additional information is used to translate the identified opportunity into specific business and technology opportunities and where technology and market assessments are conducted.
- Idea Generation: This represents an evolutionary process in which ideas are built upon, torn down, combined, reshaped, modified, and upgraded.
- Idea Selection: this involves choosing which ideas to pursue in order to achieve the most business value.
- Concept Development: This involves the development of a business case based on estimates of market potential, customer needs, investment requirements, competitor assessments, technology unknowns, and overall project risk.
- Concept Evaluation: concept evaluation is the final 'go-no/go' decision point prior to moving into the planning and development stage. Here the results of the concept development case are evaluated.

The NCD model [17] best reflects the innovation activities of 'real world', mobile service application development organizations. Consequently, this research uses the NCD model [17] to describe the innovation activities for mobile service applications. In particular, this study focuses on the final two activities concept definition and evaluation.

While there has been a shift in thinking about service innovation over the years, challenges still exist, particularly for mobile service innovations. In recent years, it has been argued, that too many mobile service innovations fail, or do not achieve their inventors expectations, [18]. One reason for this is due to poor decision making in the mobile service innovation process [1, 3, 4]. Research suggests, the mobile service innovation process still lacks structure and transparency [7]. Furthermore, poor understanding and communication in the innovation stage can result in problems flowing into the later development and deployment stages [8]. Providing transparency and facilitating understanding and communication among team members is vital for rational decision making to take place [9]. Little published research or industry initiatives have been carried out to improve decision making in the mobile service innovation process. The area can be improved by adding transparency to the process, facilitating communication and understanding among members. This research is based on this identified gap and suggests that the facilitation of these elements can improve overall decision making in the mobile service innovation process.

3 Research Methodology

Design science is a promising approach that makes it possible to scientifically study the human experience as it relates to IT artifacts while simultaneously creating new and powerful interactive experiences [5]. Despite its advantages, the use of design science in HCI is rare [5]. Due to its prescriptive and practical suitability we follow the DSRM proposed by [16] to design an interactive assessment instrument and to evaluate user's experiences with it during the process of mobile service application innovation. By doing so, this research makes a contribution to both theory and practice while also demonstrating the applicability of the DSRM for HCI.

The six DSRM steps were followed which include: problem identification and motivation, objectives of a solution, design and development, demonstration, evaluation (ex-ante & ex-post) and communication [16]. The lack of transparency poor understanding and communication in the innovation process represent the first DSRM phase of problem identification and motivation. The objectives of a solution are derived from the three step process model: crafting rational decisions in practice [9]. The model was reviewed and selected for use during the design and development of the artefact (see Fig. 1). The three steps in the model (contextualization, quantification and calculation) are used as principles for the assessment instrument design and development. Following this, an ex-ante evaluation was conducted via interviews with practitioners, which resulted in improvements to the design. Further details of the tools design and development are outlined in Sect. 4.

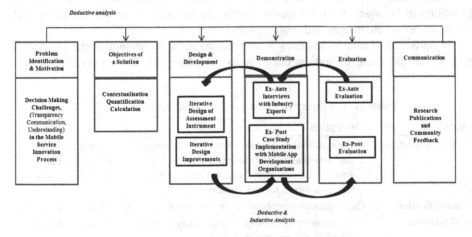

Fig. 1. The research methodology based on [9, 16]

Once the design was refined, a case study organization (mobile app development organization, Galway, Ireland) was selected as the test site to execute the demonstration and ex-post evaluation. The ex-post evaluation captures the participant's experiences with the assessment instrument and the change to the mobile service innovation process as a result of using the assessment instrument. The method of evaluation is a qualitative investigation through semi-structured interviews with the development team members at the case study organization. The interview data analyzed using a comprehensive thematic analysis approach [22]. Particularly, the researchers will investigate if elements of decision theory are replicated [9].

4   Assessment Instrument Design and Ex-ante Evaluation

This research has outlined the existing challenge of poor decision making in the mobile service innovation process as a result of a lack of transparency, communication and understanding. This section details the iterative design of a solution to these challenges, in the form of an interactive assessment instrument, namely: The Mobile Concept Assessment Instrument.

Firstly, the researchers gathered the requirements needed to address the aforementioned challenges. These requirements were gathered via interviews with industry experts and are summarized in Table 2. In addition, a further review of relevant literature was required to discover suitable theories that could be used to design a solution to the mentioned challenges and to meet the outlined requirements. This resulted in the theory of crafting rational decisions in practice [9] being incorporated as the kernel theory to assist the design and development. The choice of this theory is justified by the core focus of our research which, is to improve decision making in the mobile service innovation process. Their theory [9] includes a three step process model which illustrates how decision analysts perform rational choice theory in practice. Their model includes 'contextualization', 'quantification' and 'calculation'. Descriptions of these are outlined in Table 1 below.

These three steps (contextualization, quantification and calculation) form the principles of the assessment instrument design and are included in Table 2 along with the summarized challenges and requirements.

In particular, Table 2 illustrates how structure must be present in the innovation process, if the 'lack of transparency' is to be addressed. Consequently, 'process

Table 1. The theory of rational decision making in practice [9]

Activity	Description
Contextualization	Contextualisation consists of turning an unstructured situation into a decision-analysable problem. In essence it is about "getting the decision context right" and structuring the elements of the decision situation into a logical framework".
Quantification	Quantification simply refers to making the decision context calculable.
Calculation	Calculation involves applying calculative and statistics techniques to calculate the rational decision.

Table 2. Tool requirements and design principles

Challenges	Requirements	Tool Design Principles		
Transparency	Process Structur-ing	1. Contextualisation		Select and define key ele-ments
Communication	Consistent Termi-nology	2. Quantification		Aggregate necessary in-formation (past percep-tions/experiences with mobile services)
		3. Calculation		
Understanding	Visual Aid			Represent relevant infor-mation in a visual aid
User Experience	User Experience	Provide a valuable, easy to use and appropriate tool.		Automate assessment ac-tivities in a user friendly way.

structuring' is the first requirement. In order to add structure it is critical to ingrain the 'contextualisation' step outlined by [9] while developing the tool. This involves turning the unstructured situation into a decision-analysable problem. Thus 'contextualisation' is the first design principle. To contextualize the decision situation, the researcher conducted an in-depth content analysis and a focus group with practitioners (as part of a larger research project) to identify and select factors that should be considered during the innovation process. This resulted in thirteen (adoption) factors prioritized and selected for inclusion in the assessment instrument.

Table 2 also illustrates that to address the issue of 'poor understanding' relevant dimensions of the decision context must be filtered. Consequently, the second design principle is 'quantification' which allows factors to be filtered and for the decision to become calculable. To filter the data, the assessment is divided into three scales. Firstly, the development team must select the particular type of mobile concept out of six categories (communication, information, transaction, learning, social media, context sensitive). This will filter the aggregated data in the background. The second part of the assessment instrument involves answering questions in relation to the characteristics of the mobile service. For example, service complexity and intuitiveness. Finally, the third part involves answering questions in relation to the context of use of the service. For example the environment and use situations. The team answer each question applicable to them and allocate a score to the scale. For the team to be able to allocate a score to each question, they must discuss the factor that the question is addressing in detail. While this forces the team to consider adoption factors they would not have previously considered the structured list of questions acts as a guide during the meeting, helping them to stay focused. It was also important at this stage to use consistent terminology to facilitate communication flow.

Finally, Table 2 illustrates that the activities of allocating a score and calculating the user adoption must be automated, to ensure a positive user experience (UX). Addi-tionally, the decision situation must be represented in a graphical form therefore a 'visual aid' is required. To do so, it was necessary to apply 'calculative tools' to automate the assessment and represent the results in a visual aid (bubble-chart). The mobile service concept will be classified based on the scores that have been allocated to the questions for each of the scales. For example, the type of service, the service characteristics and the intended context of use of the service are classified. Following this, the 'potential' adoption score is calculated and visually represented. This is based on existing adoption that has been classified and aggregated in the background of the assessment instrument.

4.1   Ex-ante Evaluation and Design Improvements

By understanding the impact the designed assessment instrument has on its users, we can identify issues with the design and areas for improvement. This is referred to as the ex-ante evaluation.

A series of interviews were conducted with industry experts to identify areas for improvement. The assessment instrument was demonstrated to practitioners and they were then asked if they recommended any areas to be refined. The practitioners emphasized some issues with the initial design while also suggesting areas for refinement. The identified issues, suggestions and refinements are summarized in Table 3.

Specifically, Table 3 illustrates that the practitioners suggested that some of the questions were confusing. As a result, the questions were refined to reflect industry standard definitions. They highlight that the scales used to categorize the mobile concepts were also confusing, (e.g. the descriptions of scale categories were unclear). Consequently, all scales were clearly defined using industry standard definitions. Additionally, they suggested that the scales should be adjusted, that the visual-aid did not emphasize much of a difference between categories on the scale 1 to 5. For example, there was little visual difference between 3.5–5 %. As a result the scale was adjusted; the new scale categorizes factors between 0 and 100 % as opposed to 1 to 5 %.

The potential adoption score is divided into three parts; low, moderate and high adoption. Within this research adoption is based on intention to use. Low intention to use is captured as any score under the threshold of 50 %. Any score above 50 % represents a moderate to high intention to use. Moderate would move to high once past 60 %. This information is represented in a three dimensional bubble chart. The practitioners highlighted, the difference in bubble charts (adoption scores) were difficult to distinguish. As a result, the bubble chart was refined to have various sizes depending on the score. The smaller the bubble the lower the score (and vice versa), thereby indicating low adoption. The bubble is also colour coded for a deeper visual effect. A traffic-light colouring system is in place with red indicating poor adoption and green indicating high adoption. Providing this information in a bubble chart, can assist team members understating in relation to how these factors will positively or negatively affect adoption. This visual aid also provides necessary information which they can later use to justify their decisions for including/not-including certain elements in the mobile service.

Finally, they suggested that automating the process would be useful as some applications have a 'fast-to-market' need. To automate the process instant feedback is provided. Scores are allocated using a 'scroll-bar' and the bubble chart data automatically adjusts to the scores allocated. The suggestions provided by industry experts as well as recommendations in the literature were used to make the refinements to the

Table 3. Design issues, practitioner suggestions and refinements

Design Issues	Design Suggestions	Initial Design Refinements
Terminology: Some of the questions terminology is confusing.	Providing definitions with examples for each of the questions would prevent confusion.	Questions were re-worded to reflect industry standard definitions.
Scales: The bubble chart does not emphasize much of a difference between categories on a scale 1–5.	A larger scale between 0–100 could visually be more beneficial as the difference between categorizes would be emphasized more.	The scale was adjusted to categorize factors between 0–100 % as opposed to 1–5 %. As a result the difference between categories is clear as the larger scale results in a larger visual difference in the bubble chart.
Visual Aid: The different bubble graphs are difficult to distinguish between.	A 'traffic light' color system could be very beneficial as green could indicate good/high adoption and red could indicate bad/low adoption.	A traffic light color system along with different size bubbles is used to represent the different values of adoption.
Appropriateness: Some applications are 'fast to market' - need a speedy process.	As some applications are 'fast-to-market' they have a speedy design process and not too much time can be spent in the 'innovation stage' automating this would be useful.	To automate the process instant feedback is provided. Scores are allocated using a 'scroll-bar' and the bubble chart data automatically adjusts to the scores allocated.
Ease of Use: Where to allocate the scores (low or high) is confusing.	To which category the concept should fit is confusing, clearly defining the scales and providing examples would be useful.	Each of the scales are clearly defined with descriptions and examples for all categories using industry standard definitions.

assessment instrument. Several iterations of refinement to the design were conducted until the researchers were satisfied.

5 Case Study Demonstration and Ex-Post Evaluation

The ex-post evaluation involved the use of the assessment instrument in a case study organization. Following this, interviews were conducted to investigate the participants experience with the assessment instrument and the changes to the innovation process. Specifically, we investigated if a change occurred to transparency, understanding or communication in order to claim 'replication' (i.e. replicate the logic of decision theory [9] in the process of mobile service application innovation).

An agreement was reached with a mobile application development organization in Galway, Ireland, to trial the M-Concept Assessment Instrument. The organization is one of the leading app development organizations in Ireland. They provide cutting edge applications to both large and small scale clients and also develop in-house applications. Using the categorization of company size proposed by the European Commission, the organization fits between the categories, Micro-Entity (< 10 employees) and Small Company (< 50 employees) as they have nine employees on-site and five other employees working overseas. Their development team consisted of six members; a project manager, a UX designer, a business analyst, two software developers and one member from marketing. All members participated in this study. A mobile transaction service, which permits the payment of products (e.g. food at a grocery store) on your Smartphone, anytime any-where, was selected as the mobile concept. The end users need to create a profile and purchase online tokens which they can use as credit for their products. The supplier of the products can approve payment of the products by selecting an option 'approve' when the customer notifies them of the products they wish to purchase.

The study was carried out on-site at the organization. A presentation demonstrating the console of the assessment instrument was given to the development team. After this, a workshop was held where the assessment was conducted by the development team. The assessment instrument questions were answered by all team members together. During the workshop they read the questions out loud and discussed each point. The discussion began with one member suggesting their opinion, this continued until each member in the group had voiced their opinion. The team then debated which score to allocate to each question. This continued until all questions were answered. Based on the scores allocated to each question, the instrument calculated the potential user adoption score automatically. Specifically, the instrument classified the mobile service at (82 %) and the mobile service context at (82 %) and indicated that the potential user adoption between these scores was (90 %). This means that the mobile concept fitted into the category 'high intention to adopt'. A high adoption score indicates that the user has a high intention to use the service. The participant's experiences with the assessment instrument are summarized in Sect. 6 'study findings'.

6 Study Findings

To gather data for the ex-post evaluation, semi-structured interviews were conducted with the case study participants after the use of the assessment instrument. The interviews sought feedback about the participants experience with the assessment instrument and the changes to the innovation process. Specifically, we were investigating if a change occurred to transparency, understanding or communication in order to claim 'replication'. The interview data was examined using a comprehensive thematic analysis approach [22]. The findings from this analysis are briefly summarized under the following themes:

Transparency: There is strong evidence that the assessment instrument has added transparency. For example, one member suggested that it helped them to scope the concept: *"I think that if we used this, there would be more structure because from the beginning you are starting to determine the scope of the project and peoples roles in the project"*.

Another member suggested that it assisted with documenting the process and keeping focused: *"It adds transparency because it is more easily documentable, when everyone is together and answer specific questions, you can go back and see who said what... Also the more structure there is the more transparent the process becomes, because we had a list of questions today, we knew we couldn't leave anything out"*.

Communication: There is also evidence from the interviews that the assessment instrument can improve communication in the innovation process. For example, one member suggested: *"Using this tool we are more equal, we all talked about each point and everyone expressed their opinions and ideas it wasn't just one or two members of the team, with the team leader. It was more integrated"*.

Another member mentioned that it can help the team members communicate the extent to which particular elements of the app exist: *"It defiantly promotes communication because you are scoring each question, it means that there may be a broad agreement among the team that yes maybe we are on this factor but they may not agree on the extent to which we are covered"*.

Understanding: The interviews also indicated that the assessment instrument can improve understanding among team members. One member felt that it helped them to recognize factors that they would not have previously considered: *"I do think that using the assessment instrument brought up some conversations that would not have come up otherwise"*.

Another team member mentioned that it helps, not only to consider adoption factors but also to understand each member's role better: *"This helps us to understand the roles in the project and what is expected for each member...like for example after our discussions... I know the person in the marketing role might have a much bigger role in the project than we would have originally thought, because the project might be very depended on branding and that is something that we would not have discovered if we did not use this tool"*.

Along with capturing the changes to the innovation process the interviews sought feedback about the participant's experience of the use of assessment instrument. The outcomes of this are summarized under the following themes:

Appropriateness: One member mentioned that they were originally apprehensive about using the assessment instrument; however after using it they found that it was very useful and appropriate for this stage. *"When we started I thought that this wouldn't be the best project to use this with but when we actually did the assessment I thought that this made us think a lot more about the concept... so yes in this stage it is very useful"*.

Ease of use: Finally, the findings from the analysis suggested that the participants found the assessment instrument easy to use. One participant mentioned: *"The way it was structured with the scroll bar was useful... it was easy and well presented. The* *graph shows you your score so you get immediate feedback that was presented in a very straightforward way".*

7 Conclusions

In summary, the aim of this paper was to describe the construction and evaluation of an interactive assessment instrument to improve the process for mobile service innovation, following the DSRM. The ex-post evaluation has confirmed the potential of the M-Concept Assessment Instrument to address transparency, communication and understanding challenges within the innovation process. Naturally, the proposed assessment instrument needs further evaluation before 'replication' can be claimed. Consequently, further case study investigations are currently being undertaken. Nonetheless, the results of the evaluation provided comprehensive insight for the knowledgebase in terms of decision making in the mobile service application innovation process. Along with this, a significant achievement is the incorporation of the tool in the industry, thus providing strong evidence of industry relevance of the research outcome, [23]. Finally, the paper also demonstrates that (DSRM) provides a clearly defined step-by-step set of actions to design and evaluate an interactive IT artefact within the HCI field and therefore, it can serve as reference for other researchers who wish to use design science in HCI.

Acknowledgments. This research is funded by the Irish Research Council (IRC). The authors would like to acknowledge their support. Additionally, the authors would like to extend their appreciation to the participating organization for their commitment to this research.

References

1. Nikou, S., Mezei, J.: Evaluation of mobile services and substantial adoption factors with analytic hierarchy process (AHP). Telecommun. Policy **37**(10), 915–929 (2013)
2. Constantiou, I.D., Damsgaard, J., Knutsen, L.: Exploring perceptions and use of mobile services: user differences in an advancing market. Int. J. Mobile Commun. **4**(3), 231–247 (2006)
3. Fitzsimmons, J., Fitzsimmons, M.J.: New Service Development: Creating Memorable Experiences. Sage, Thousand Oaks (1999)
4. Menor, L.J., Tatikonda, M.V., Sampson, S.E.: New service development: areas for exploitation and exploration. J. Oper. Manage. **20**(2), 135–157 (2002)
5. Prestopnik, N.: Design science in human-computer interaction: a model and three examples. (2013)
6. Carlsson, C., Rossi, M., Tuunainen, V. K, et al.: In: Introduction to Mobile Value Services, Mobile Business and Mobile Cloud Minitrack, pp. 1323–1323 (2012)
7. Bouwman, H., De Vos, H., Haaker, T.: Mobile Service Innovation and Business Models, vol. 2010. Springer, Heidelberg (2008)
8. Simons, L.P., Bouwman, H.: Multi-channel service design process: challenges and solutions. Int. J. Electron. Bus. **3**(1), 50–67 (2005)

9. Cabantous, L., Gond, J., Johnson-Cramer, M.: Decision theory as practice: crafting rationality in organizations. Organ. Stud. **31**(11), 1531–1566 (2010)
10. Ghaoui, C.: Encyclopedia of Human Computer Interaction. IGI Global, Hershey (2005)
11. Carroll, J.M., Rosson, M.B.: Getting around the task-artifact cycle: how to make claims and design by scenario. ACM Trans. Inf. Syst. (TOIS) **10**(2) 181–212 (1992)
12. Norman, D.A., Draper, S.W.: User Centered System Design. CRC Press, Hillsdale (1986)
13. Norman, D.A.: The Design of Everyday Things. Basic books, New York (2002)
14. Shneiderman, B.: Designing the User Interface: Strategies For Effective Human-Computer Interaction, vol. 2. Addison-Wesley, Reading (1992)
15. Vredenburg, K., Mao, J., Smith, P.W., Carey, T.: A survey of user-centered design practice: 471–478 (2002)
16. Peffers, K., Tuunanen, T., Rothenberger, M.A., Chatterjee, S.: A design science research methodology for information systems research. J. Manage. Inf. Syst. **24**(3), 45–77 (2007)
17. Koen, P., Ajamian, G., Burkart, R., et al.: Providing clarity and a common language to the. Res. Technol. Manage. **44**(2), 46–55 (2001)
18. Gao, S., Krogstie, J., Siau, K.: Developing an instrument to measure the adoption of mobile services. Mob. Inf. Syst. **7**(1), 45–67 (2011)
19. Callon, M., Muniesa, F.: Peripheral vision economic markets as calculative collective devices. Organ. Stud. **26**(8), 1229–1250 (2005)
20. Porter, T.M.: Quantification and the accounting ideal in science. Soc. Stud. Sci. **22**(4), 633–651 (1992)
21. Schwandt, T.A.: The Sage Dictionary of Qualitative Inquiry. Sage, Thousand Oaks (2007)
22. Fereday, J., Muir-Cochrane, E.: Demonstrating rigor using thematic analysis: a hybrid approach of inductive and deductive coding and theme development. Int. J. Qual. Methods **5**(1), 80–92 (2008)
23. Kuechler, B., Vaishnavi, V.: Promoting relevance in IS research: an informing system for design science research. Informing Sci. Int. J. Emerg. Transdiscipline **14**(1), 125–138 (2011)

The Influence of Location and Social Network on Customers' Acceptance of Mobile Marketing: Evidence from Group Buying Field Experiment

Xi Chen[1]([✉]), Ruibin Geng[1], and Chee Wei Phang[2]

[1] Zhejiang University, Zhejiang, Peoples Republic of China
{tigychen, grace.binl207}@gmail.com
[2] Fudan University, Shanghai, Peoples Republic of China
phangcw@fudan.edu.cn

Abstract. With the rapid development and widespread popularity of smart phone devices, location-based social networking service (LBSNS) creates an era of GeoLife2.0 where people can share life experiences and connect to each other with their location histories. Previous academic studies have also realized the crucial role of location and social network on mobile marketing. However, many of them have been conceptual work using structural equation modeling, and the effects of these two factors are never considered at the same time. In our study, mobile marketing is exemplified as a time-limited, group-based "two for the price of one when you get a friend to buy together" promotion campaign advertised via mobile devices. Field experiment was conducted to explore the influence of location and social network on consumers' decision to accept mobile promotions. We then conducted follow-up surveys that revealed users' personality features and psychological states as supporting materials to explain our field experiment observations.

Keywords: Location-based social networking service · Field experiment · Mobile marketing · Distance · Social relationship

1 Introduction

With the rapid development and widespread popularity of smart phone devices, mobile applications play increasingly important role in marketing campaigns, especially location-based social networking service (LBSNS). The emerging LBSNS creates an era of GeoLife2.0 where people can share life experiences and connect to each other with their location histories (Zheng et al. 2009). Famous mobile applications using LBSNS include Yelp, Foursquare, and Dianping in China. These services provide an access to a valuable source of data on the geographic location of users as well as the online social connections among them. As a consequence, it offers a great opportunity to better understand individuals' behaviors by taking into account both spatial and social factors.

LBSNS provides merchants an efficient and effective approach to advertise and promote their products to individual consumers, and also to engage the consumers in

© Springer International Publishing Switzerland 2015
F.F.-H. Nah and C.-H. Tan (Eds.): HCIB 2015, LNCS 9191, pp. 256–266, 2015.
DOI: 10.1007/978-3-319-20895-4_24

product information dissemination. Such applications take advantage of location and social network information to enhance the interaction between buyers and sellers and to strengthen customer loyalty on brands. Previous academic studies have also realized the crucial role of location and social network on mobile marketing. However, the effects of these two factors are never considered simultaneously. In practice, many companies have been making use of mobile social media to leverage on location-based and social-based communications in their commercial pursuits. For example, the famous mobile marketing application, Foursquare, allows users to notify others about their location by 'checking-in' at a certain place. A company could spontaneously decide to launch a sales promotion that is only valid for 1-2 h and broadcast this information to all mobile devices within a certain range. This kind of location-sensitive and time-sensitive marketing practices will result in a unique route of propagation via social connections (Scellato et al. 2011). Combining this information with sophisticated data-mining techniques will give traditional merchants the ability to make efficient customized sales promotion (Kaplan 2012).

In our study, mobile marketing is exemplified as a time-limited, group-based "two for the price of one when you get a friend to buy together" promotional campaign advertised via mobile devices. Field experiment was conducted to explore the influence of location and social network factors on consumers' decision to accept mobile promotions. In the designed field experiment situation, consumers face a dilemma of whether to invite a stranger nearby or to insist on waiting for their friends to enjoy the deal. We are interested in how consumers make the decision when their purchase is constrained with both location and social relationship. First, whether the location of customers plays significant role on the consumption of promoted goods? Second, whether the strength of social ties influence the consumption of promoted goods? Third, what is the priority of customers' choice, spatial-dependent or social-dependent? We then conducted follow-up surveys that revealed users' personality features and psychological states as supporting materials to explain our field experiment observations.

The reminder of the paper is organized as follows. Section 2 outlines previous findings on the effects of location and social network on consumers' acceptance of mobile marketing. Section 3 describes the design of field experiment and the supporting survey study. Section 4 illustrates data analysis results based on field experiment observations and survey findings. Section 5 makes discussion about the empirical results and draws conclusions.

2 Literature Review

Although a number of academic studies have been conducted on consumers' acceptance of mobile marketing and related issues, many of them have been conceptual work using structural equation modeling (Leppaniemi & Karjaluoto 2005; Merisavo et al. 2007). Technology acceptance model (TAM) suggests that perceived usefulness and perceived ease-of-use are two fundamental factors to determine consumers' adoption behavior, which is the basic theoretical framework applied in empirical studies. These empirical studies explored the effectiveness of various types of mobile marketing practices, such as mobile emailing and messaging (Barwise and Strong 2002), and mobile couponing (Wehmeyer and Müller-Lankenau 2005). Shankar et al. (2010) reviewed some key factors that enable or hinder the acceptance of mobile marketing in the retail environment. The enablers included networking, prices of mobile device and applications, the utility of mobile application, and trust with the application. The inhibitors are such as consumption inertia, economic barriers, limited knowledge, and distrust of marketing.

To better understand how mobile marketing works and to make it more effective, we focus on two advanced mobile services, that is, location-sensitive function and social network management. Prior studies suggested that location-relevant information and social network connections may increase consumers' willingness to accept mobile marketing practices. Location-based service is positively associated with consumers' perceived usefulness of mobile advertising, and social networking service enables the social-context awareness of mobile marketing. The influence of location and social network on consumers' acceptance of mobile marketing are examined independently in the extant literature.

The increasing utility of mobile applications benefit from location-based services to a great extent. According to Bauer et al. (2005), delivering a store's information via SMS advertising to consumers are effective and desirable only when they are within the physical vicinity of that store. Pura, M. (2005) examined the fundamental value of location-based mobile services from six dimensions: monetary, convenience, social, emotional, conditional, and epistemic value. Results showed that both commitment and behavioral intentions to use location-based services are strongly influenced by conditional value of getting customized information based on users' location. Mobile marketing is defined by Scharl, Dickinger, and Murphy (2005) as using a wireless medium to provide consumers with time- and location-sensitive, personalized information that promotes goods, services and ideas. They addressed the underlying importance of location to personalized mobile marketing. The study of Ho (2012) provided empirical evidence of the effectiveness of location personalization in mobile marketing and explored factors that not only attract individuals to mobile services but also keep them engaged in the services in the long term.

Social media applications including microblogs, blogs, virtual communities, and content communities, etc. have already become part of the standard communication repertoire in marketing campaigns. The combination of social media applications and mobile devices amplifies individual's urge to share opinions with friends at anytime and anywhere. Mobile social media has two forms communication, company-to-consumer communication and user-generated content (UGC) (Kaplan 2012). Due to homophily and contagion in social networks, advertisements and promotions will be well spread through social ties once companies accurately target potential customers (Rana et al. 2009). According to (Hill et al. 2006), marketing campaigns based on social network will significantly increase customers' trust, and then contribute to adoption by word-of-mouth.

The conceptual work in previous literature revealed that location and social network are both important drivers of consumer acceptance of mobile marketing. However, existing studies regard location and social network as two independent factors that may affect consumers' acceptance of mobile marketing. Seldom or never have research explored the interaction effect of these two factors on consumers' decision. Furthermore, papers focusing on adoption intention and satisfaction based on mobile applications and services are evidently insufficient compared with that based on social networking sites. In terms of research methodology, studies in this field are mainly conceptual work combined with survey investigations. In our paper, we conduct field experiment to observe the real reaction of consumer in designed experiment situation in which location and social network may simultaneously affect consumer's decision.

3 Methodology

We designed a time-limited, group-based "two for the price of one when you bring a friend to buy together" sales promotion situation for our field experiment. We posted an APP testing invitation to the BBS forum of a large public university in China and uploaded our mobile marketing application for free downloading. 99 subjects successfully installed our mobile promotion application and performed registration. We did not reveal the experiment objective to the subjects, and we collected real usage data in a natural, unobtrusive environment.

The mobile promotion application was developed specifically for the purpose of this study. It enables location-based service (LBS) as well as social network management. The main interface of the application includes six modules: my friends' list, import of mobile phone contact, discovery of someone nearby, historical records, and latest promotions. The friends list of each subject was obtained from their self-reported social connections. Subjects could get the list of people who is currently around him within a distance of 1.5 miles by clicking 'someone nearby'. Friends and strangers are distinguished in the nearby list by background color as it is shown in Fig. 1. The order of users appearing in the nearby list is randomly arranged. The ranking would be updated once user refresh the list. The latest promotion details would be pushed to inform all the subjects once a promotion was launched. As the promotion plan in our experiment was group-based, the subjects were required to invite a friend to redeem the promotional coupon together. The mobile application provided a function for subjects to make such invitations. The communication involved two actors, inviter and invitee. As an inviter, he should decide whether to invite a friend or someone nearby (the second interface in Fig. 2). Once the invitation is sent out, the invitee will receive a notification. The invitee should decide whether to accept this invitation (the third interface in Fig. 2). The specific invitation processes are demonstrated in Fig. 2.

We cooperated with one of the most popular bakery shop outside the university campus. Customers may be sensitive to the promotion price of the product. In order to avoid this unexpected effect, we manipulated one control factor, the price of promoted goods, in our field experiment. We made a within-subject design across two dessert packages, providing 10 RMB set and 30 RMB set. The sales promotions of these two packages were launched in two separate weekends with the same group of subjects, and subjects could spontaneously decide whether to participate in the promotions. Within the limited available time of the promotion, subjects had to make a decision about whether to invite a friend who may not be able to show up at that time or someone nearby who may not be an acquaintance. The invitation behaviors of subjects were recorded by our mobile applications. Subjects could make invitations several times to different people, but the deal could be redeemed only when at least one invitee accepted

Fig. 1. The interface of "someone nearby" module (Grey background indicates a friends nearby and white background indicates a stranger nearby) (Color figure online).

Fig. 2. Invitation processes

the invitation. Throughout the experiment, only the cashiers of the bakery shop (but not the authors of this paper) could interact with the inviter and invitee who came to buy and redeem the deal, therefore their responses should reflect their true decisions.

Regardless of whether subjects successfully invite someone to buy and redeem the deal, a follow-up survey was posted to elicit some necessary information. The questionnaire consists of four parts. First part was the personality test about the propensity to engage in social relationship exploratory and exploitative behavior (Mom et al. 2007). Second part measured the perceived time pressure of subjects during the two experiments. Third part inquired the subjects about the daily usage of location-based services and social network services in mobile applications, the spending habits of the goods promoted in our experiment, and the attitudes to group buying and mobile promotion. The last part gathered the demographical information of the subjects, such as, age, sex, and major. The complete questionnaire of the follow-up survey is shown in Appendix A. The results of follow-up survey serve to supplement the field experiment observations.

4 Results

Table 1 describes all the variables and their transformation form used in the data analysis below

Table 1. Description of field experiment variables and transformations

Variable	Description	Type	Value
Deal	Whether the invitation was approved by both inviter and invitee	Binary	0-not a deal 1-deal
Price	The value of promoted goods in each experiment	Binary	1- lower price 2-higher price
Relation	Whether there exist social ties between the inviter and invitee	Binary	0- not friends 1-friends
Distance	The geographic distance between inviter and invitee when the invitation was made	Continuous	
Distance_norm	The nominal scale of distance between inviter and invitee	Nominal	1- $(d < \mu - \sigma)$ 2- $(\mu - \sigma \leq d < \mu + \sigma)$ 3- $(\mu + \sigma \leq d)$
Inviter_shop_distance	The geographic distance between inviter and the shop when the invitation was made	Continuous	
Invitee_shop_distance	The geographic distance between invitee and the shop the invitation was made	Continuous	
Inviter_degree	The degree centrality of the inviter in the social network	Continuous	
Invitee_degree	The degree centrality of the invitee in the social network	Continuous	
Inviter_betweenness	The betweenness centrality of the inviter in the social network	Continuous	
Invitee_betweenness	The betweenness centrality of the invitee in the social network	Continuous	

The social network graph of 99 subjects and the directed graph of invitation relationship in the two field experiments are shown in Figs. 3, 4, and 5. In the field experiment of low-price product, 51 invitation relationships are overlapped with the social connections among the total 138 invitation trials involving friends as well as strangers. The overlapping rate of the two networks is 37.0 %. In the field experiment of high-price product, 40 invitation relationships are overlapped with the social connections among the total 103 invitations. The overlapping rate of the two networks is 38.8 %. The overlapping connections of social ties and invitation relationships are colored red in the graphs shown in Figs. 4 and 5.

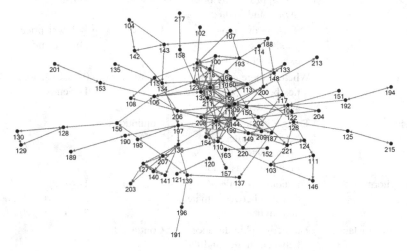

Fig. 3. Harel-Koren fast multiscale graph of social network among 99 subjects

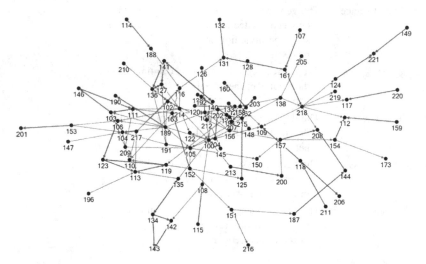

Fig. 4. Harel-Koren fast multiscale graph of invitation relationship in low-price product promotion experiment (red lines indicates overlapping with social ties) (Color figure online).

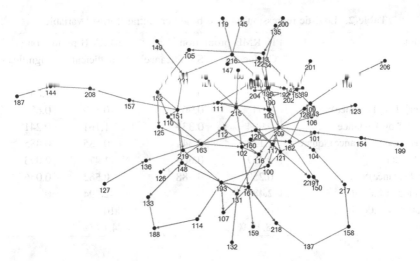

Fig. 5. Harel-Koren fast multiscale graph of invitation relationship in high-price product promotion experiment (red lines indicates overlapping with social ties) (Color figure online).

We applied two sample t-test and two-way ANOVA statistics to examine the effects of location and social network. At first, we ignore the price difference between the cases of two experiments and conduct two sample t-test based on the aggregated data. Two sample t-test on populations of Deal = 0 and Deal = 1 indicates the distance between inviter and invitee in successful invitation group is significantly different from that in failing invitation group. T-test on populations of Relation = 0 and Relation = 1 indicates that the successful rate of social relationship based invitation is significantly larger than invitation between strangers. Then we conduct two-way ANOVA in which price is taken as one factor that may decide whether the invitation will be accepted (Deal) and whether the inviter will choose a friend or a stranger (Relation). As the influence of price factor is controlled in two-way ANOVA, distance range between inviter and invitee (Distance_norm) and social network embededness (Relation) demonstrate significant influence on the response variable (Deal), that is, whether the invitation will be accepted.

In order to figure out factors that affect subject's decision on whether to accept the promotion invitation, we conducted logistic regression on the dependent variable "Deal". Table 2 and 3 depict the coefficient estimation results based on untransformed and transformed data sets. In low-price promotion setting, social relationship take significant effect but the influence of distance is not significant. When the value of promotion product increases, distance is regarded as a significant factor that may influence subject's decision as well as social relationship.

In addition to the acceptance of mobile marketing, we are also interested in the

Table 2. Logistic regression on deal based on untransformed variables

Variable	10 RMB promotion		30 RMB promotion	
	Coefficient	Significance	Coefficient	Significance
Intercept	**1.298**	0.035	**1.978**	0.006
Inviter_Log Distance	0.019	0.981	-0.137	0.848
Inviter_(Log Distance)Square	-0.04	0.965	-0.369	0.687
Invitee_Log Distance	-0.904	0.335	1.161	0.241
Invitee_(Log Distance)Square	-1.133	0.344	0.185	0.885
Log Distance	0.457	0.609	**1.47**	0.093
(Log Distance)Square	0.259	0.388	**0.582**	0.056
[Relation = 0.000]	**-2.485**	0	**-2.394**	0
[Relation = 1.000]	0		0(b)	
accuracy	78.45 %		74.19 %	

Table 3. Logistic regression on deal based on transformed variables

Variable	10 RMB promotion		30 RMB promotion	
	Coefficient	Significance	Coefficient	Significance
Intercept	**0.606**	0.675	**1.025**	0.509
[Inviter_Shop_Distance_Norm = 1]	-0.482	0.718	1.711	0.361
[Inviter_Shop_Distance_Norm = 2]	-0.28	0.826	1.243	0.429
[Inviter_Shop_Distance_Norm = 3]	0		0	
[Invitee_Shop_Distance_Norm = 1]	1.238	0.283	0.882	0.524
[Invitee_Shop_Distance_Norm = 2]	0.549	0.567	1.22	0.353
[Invitee_Shop_Distance_Norm = 3]	0		**0**	
[Relation = 0]	**-2.445**	0	**-2.41**	0
[Relation = 1]	0		0	
[Distance_Norm = 1]	1.374	0.234	-0.869	0.584
[Distance_Norm = 2]	0.311	0.739	**-2.42**	0.093
[Distance_Norm = 3]	0		0	
accuracy	77.59 %		73.12 %	

decision of inviters who should determine whether to invite a friend or a stranger. Thus logistic regression on variable Relation was made. Except for centrality properties such as degree and betweenness, the distance between invitee and shop and the distance between inviter and shop are found to be significant factors to influence the choice of friend or stranger. Furthermore, we find that the personality measurement scale in follow-up survey has significant association with subject's choice of friend or stranger. Social relationship exploitative scores are positively related to the intention to choose strong social ties while social relationship exploratory scores are negatively related to strong tie dependency (Table 4 and 5).

Table 4. Logistic regression on relation based on experiment dataset

	10 RMB promotion		30 RMB promotion	
Variable	Coefficient	Significance	Coefficient	Significance
Intercept	1.930	0.004	-1.242	0.120
Inviter_Degree	0.007	0.043	0.532	0.002
Inviter_Betweenness	0.263	0.032	-0.003	0.623
Inviter_Log Distance	-1.183	0.268	-1.284	0.279
Invite_(Log Distance)Square	-1.666	0.17	-3.684	0.011
Invitee_Degree	0	0.944	0.08	0.617
Invitee_Betweenness	0.063	0.642	-0.002	0.566
Invitee_Log Distance	0.272	0.785	-1.639	0.116
Invitee_(Log Distance)Square	1.911	0.15	0.199	0.882
Log Distance	1.12	0.209	0.646	0.309
(Log Distance)Square	0.409	0.124	0.073	0.458
accuracy	75.86 %		82.80 %	

Table 5. Logistic regression on relation based on personality assessment score

Variable	Coefficient	Significance
Intercept	-2.323	0.073
Exploratory score	-0.621	0.011
Exploitative score	1.048	0.008

5 Disscussion and Conclusion

The exploratory field experiment examines the significant influence of geographic location and social network on individual's acceptance of mobile marketing. Based on experiment data analysis and follow-up survey investigation, we obtain the following interesting findings. In terms of the acceptance of promotion invitation, we find that social relationship always plays significant role to affect the acceptance of invitation regardless of the price of promoted product. Logistic regression on Deal indicates that the effect of geographic location becomes significant when the price of promoted product is high. With regard to the choice of strong social tie or weak social tie, we find that geographic location has significant influence on inviter's choice of friend or stranger only when the price of promoted product is high. Social network centrality of the inviter is positively associated with the intention to invite a friend, no matter how much the promoted price is. The personality test of subjects indicated that the intention to invite friend or non-friend was influence by the social types of inviters as well. Social relationship exploratory individuals tend to invite non-friends while social relationship exploitative individuals are inclined to invite friends.

Managerial implications of the field experiment should be highlighted as well. For mobile advertising application developers, they should recognize users' demand for group-based mobile promotions, and their willingness to mobilize social resources, both of exploitative (existing friends) and explorative (strangers) nature, to obtain group-based deals. LBSNS' social network function can aid in this aspect to enhance mobile promotion effects, but the convenience of communication between individuals who are proximate in location but having weak social tie needs be improved for such social resources to be mobilized. As for merchants, location of target consumers should be the priority consideration when launching high-price promotions. Merchants should take advantage of word-of-mouth effect through social ties when designing their sales promotion scheme.

References

Barwise, P., Strong, C.: Permission-based mobile advertising. J. Interact. Mark. **16**(1), 14–24 (2002)

Hill, S., Provost, F., Volinsky, C.: Network-based marketing: identifying likely adopters via consumer networks. Stat. Sci. **21**(2), 256–276 (2006)

Ho, S.Y.: The effects of location personalization on individuals' intention to use mobile services. Decis. Support Syst. **53**(4), 802–812 (2012)

Kaplan, A.M.: If you love something, let it go mobile: mobile marketing and mobile social media 4x4. Bus. Horiz. **55**(2), 129–139 (2012)

Leppaniemi, M., Karjaluoto, H.: Factors influencing consumers' willingness to accept mobile marketing: a conceptual model. Int. J. Mob. Commun. **3**(3), 197–213 (2005)

Merisavo, M., Kajalo, S., Karjaluoto, H., Virtanen, V., Salmenkivi, S., Raulas, M., Leppäniemi, M.: An empirical study of the drivers of consumer acceptance of mobile marketing. J. Interact. Mark. **7**(2), 41–50 (2007)

Mom, T.J.M., Van, F.A.J., Volberda, H.W.: Investigating managers' exploration and exploitation activities: the influence of top-down, bottom-up, and horizontal knowledge inflows. J. Manage. Stud. **44**(6), 910–931 (2007)

Pura, M.: Linking perceived value and loyalty in location-based mobile services. Managing Serv. Qual. **15**(6), 509–538 (2005)

Rana, J., Kristiansson, J., Hallberg, J., Synnes, K.: Challenges for mobile social networking applications. In: Mehmood, R., Cerqueira, E., Piesiewicz, R., Chlamtac, I. (eds.) Europe-Comm 2009. LNICST, vol. 16, pp. 275–285. Springer, Heidelberg (2009)

Scellato, S., Noulas, A., Lambiotte, R., Mascolo, C.: Socio-Spatial properties of online location-based social networks. ICWSM **11**, 329–336 (2011)

Scharl, A., Dickinger, A., Murphy, J.: Diffusion and success factors of mobile marketing. Electron. Commer. Res. Appl. **4**(2), 159–173 (2005)

Shankar, V., Venkatesh, A., Hofacker, C., Naik, P.: Mobile marketing in the retailing environment: current insights and future research avenues. J. Interact. Mark. **24**(2), 111–120 (2010)

Soroa-Koury, S., Yang, K.C.: Factors affecting consumers' responses to mobile advertising from a social norm theoretical perspective. Telematics Inform. **27**(1), 103–113 (2010)

Wehmeyer, K., & Müller-Lankenau, C.: Mobile couponing–measuring consumers' acceptance and preferences with a limit conjoint approach. In: Proceedings of the 18th Bled eConference". Bled, Slovenia (2005)

Dishonest Behavior at Self-Service Checkouts

Susan Creighton[1] Graham Johnson[2] Paul Robertson[1] Ian Law[1]
and Andrea Szymkowiak[1(✉)]

[1] Abertay University, Dundee, UK
0804355@live.abertay.ac.uk,
{p.robertson,j.law,a.szymkowiak}@abertay.ac.uk
[2] NCR Discovery Centre, Dundee, UK
graham.johnson@ncr.com

Abstract. Self-service technology could be argued as creating less personal transactions when compared to traditional checkouts involving a sales assistant for the entire transaction process, which may affect customer behavior. The aim of our study was to investigate the perceived influence of social presence at self-service checkouts by staff and its perceived effect on dishonest customer behavior. Twenty-six self-service checkout staff took part in a series of semi-structured interviews to describe customer behaviors with self-service. With respect to actual physical social presence, staff reported that more customer thefts occurred when the self-service checkouts were busy and their social presence was reduced. Staff also reported that *perceived* and *actual* social presence is likely to reduce thefts. Future research will elaborate to which extent the perceived social presence via technological systems might support staff in their task to assist customers and reduce dishonest behavior.

Keywords: Self-service · Social presence · Dishonest behavior

1 Introduction

The wide implementation of self-service technology (SST) in retail provides a growing area of interest to assess social and psychological effects on consumers and staff. Retailers are replacing many traditional service delivery positions, usually conducted by a sales clerk, with self-service technology [21]. Such SSTs comprise technological interfaces that enable customers to engage in service transactions independent of direct employee involvement [9]. Self-service technologies can assist transactions such as placing an order, and scanning or paying for items [23], and can reduce costs and raise productivity, as they utilize the consumers as co-producers [14]. Examples of such SSTs include multimedia kiosks, express order terminals and self-service kiosks within retail [17, 31]. Self-service checkouts (SSCOs) within supermarkets (see Fig. 1) typically involve a customer scanning or weighing their selected items, bagging them and paying for them, without the assistance of a store employee. Supermarkets within the UK tend to have designated areas for self-service terminals, usually within close proximity to the store exit, containing between 4 and 10 self-service terminals and one member of staff

© Springer International Publishing Switzerland 2015
F.F.-H. Nah and C.-H. Tan (Eds.): HCIB 2015, LNCS 9191, pp. 267–278, 2015.
DOI: 10.1007/978-3-319-20895-4_25

supervising them. In the following sections we briefly review the role of SST use, followed by a discussion of the role of social presence in technology and a brief review of theories of dishonest behavior, before describing our study.

Fig. 1. Showing self-service checkouts (SSCOs) designed by NCR

1.1 Retailers and Consumers

Kallweit et al. [17] investigated why customers choose to use SSTs within retail, focusing on the technology acceptance model (TAM) [10]. An essential component of TAM is the notion that the perceived usefulness and perceived ease of use influences customer decisions to use technology, which, in the case of SST, is associated with perceived service quality. The perceived likelihood of requiring assistance in the absence of staff is a critical variable influencing perceived service quality and has an effect on customer attitudes towards using or the intention to use SST. Convenience perceptions, defined as the perceived time and effort to complete a transaction, are the strongest influence on the potential use for users and non-users of SSTs according to Collier and Kimes [8]. If customers' perceptions and expectations are not met when using SST then they will be less likely to use them in the future [8]. This theory is consistent with the Resource Matching Perspective, which suggests the expected resources needed to complete a transaction must be met during execution in order for the behavior to reoccur [1, 8]. As customer benefits are crucial to technology acceptance [17, 19], it is important for retailers to promote the convenience that the SSTs can provide, which may include quicker transactions with easy to use interfaces that employ well-known control elements and gestures.

While many studies have focused on the identification of factors that influence consumers' use of SSTs, such as convenience, ease of use and satisfaction [8, 21], there is a dearth of research on the perceptions of employees who work with the SST. Pietro, Pantano and Virgillo [27] noted that employees and consumers are the effective users of SSTs, thus, it is important for research to consider both perspectives. Using a qualitative approach, Pietro et al. [27] investigated employees' views on the use of self-service technology; self-service checkouts (SSCOs) were reported to have resulted in an increased number of sales, and do a faster job than the traditional checkout, which enhances the service for the customer. Staff also reported enjoyment with increasing their knowledge and personal skills associated with the use of the technology, resulting in better support of customers in their interactions, which in turn provides benefits for the quality of the final service. This is also consistent with the work by Meuter [22, 23] who described staff's personal growth in their abilities as intrinsic motivation, resulting from the use of SST. Interacting with customers at self-service checkouts is a good way of maintaining the personal interaction that was a fundamental part of the traditional sales clerk role. However, if self-service checkouts are busy, then this might affect how employees can interact with customers. This may result in reduced customer service and/or reduced level of social presence – a variable which may influence customer behavior at self-service checkouts.

1.2 Social Presence

Social presence is a sense of being with another [7] and creates the illusion in the mind of the perceiver that another intelligence, be it human or artificial, exists within the environment [30]. A review of the research literature suggests that the presence (real or imagined) of others could elicit thoughts that one is being evaluated [24]. Bateson, Nettle and Roberts [2] explored the effects of social presence on behavior by alternating a picture next to an honesty box in which office staff placed money for tea and coffee. In the high social presence condition there was an image of a pair of eyes presented next to the box; in the low social presence condition, an image of a bunch of flowers was shown next to the box. High social presence induced people to behave less dishonest compared to the low social presence condition: there was three times more money in the box when the poster with the eyes was shown compared to when the poster of a bunch of flowers was shown next to the box. Thus, even a perceived social presence in the form of eyes on a poster is sufficient to modify dis/honest behavior and it is reasonable to suggest that this effect might transfer to interaction with technology, as people treat computers as social actors [29], i.e., as if it were human. The perception of social presence can enhance human computer interaction and is especially important for technology that is designed to have limited human contact, while still maintaining a high standard of customer service [18]. The quality of quasi-social interactions is often measured in terms of perceived social presence, which may modify an individual's behavior [33] to, for example, communicate a positive self-impression [3]. Thus, customer perceptions of social presence may be a useful way for reducing potential dishonest behaviors occurring at SST.

1.3 Dishonest Behavior

Goodenough and Decker [12] discuss theories behind what makes good people steal with respect to the nature/nurture debate. Nature theories suggest people steal as a result of innate motives that encourage them to enhance their property; nurture theories suggest that people learn social behaviors, moral values and laws and it is their learning that influences how they behave. They suggest that emotions, such as empathy, play a part in the consideration of property, as we foresee how we would feel if our property were to be taken from us. Wispé [32] described empathy as "the process whereby one person feels her/himself into the consciousness of another person" (p42). Lower levels of empathy have been linked to an increase in dishonest behaviors such as vandalism and theft [16]. There is a vast amount of research which suggests empathy is an essential component within customer service [20, 26, 28]. However, it is not clear whether the customer experiences empathy when using SST, especially when perceived social presence of the technology (or staff) is low. This may impact on dis/honest behaviors at self-service checkouts.

Harmon-Jones and Mills [13] suggested that creating a sense of personal responsibility results in people modifying their behavior to align with their attitudes. Customers may feel less accountable for dishonest behavior at SSCOs, as they are not interacting with a sales assistant (a social presence), but instead are relying on technology to confirm they have paid for their shopping. Mohr et al. [25] state that there must be a social presence in order for there to be accountability; thus, incorporating a social presence within SST may reduce the likelihood of dishonest behaviors occurring, as social presence may induce similar feelings to those experienced during a typical sales assistant interaction, i.e., personal responsibility for payment.

As part of a wider study into the investigation of dishonest customer behavior, we conducted an exploratory study to assess staff perceptions on social presence, as perceived social presence appears to be a critical factor in customer behavior, which has as yet not been explored in detail at self-service checkouts (SSCOs) typically found in supermarkets. We were particularly interested in how staff perceive their own presence and its effect upon customers, but also how supported staff would feel in their ability to supervise checkouts with the incorporation of an additional social presence, for example, induced by technology. Specifically, the aim of the present study was to investigate the perceived influence of a social presence at self-service checkouts by staff, and its perceived effect on dishonest customer behaviors.

2   Method

An ethnographic approach was adopted involving prolonged immersion within four supermarkets. Semi-structured interviews provided the flexibility of working with the key themes as interviews allowed participants' insights and attitudes to emerge, allowing for inductive thematic analysis to take place. Interviews with self-service checkout staff explored their views on the effect of actual and perceived social presence on customer behavior. Responses were grouped into two categories, i.e. regarding actual, physical staff presence at self-service and perceived social presence as created by technology, e.g., via cameras. Ad -hoc observations were made to create a fuller picture of behaviors at self-service checkouts.

2.1   Participants

Twenty-six self-service checkout staff, with an age range of 18-63 (8 male, 18 female, with 7 years to 6 months experience in supervising SSCOs) from four supermarkets in the UK were interviewed during June-September 2014.

2.2   Materials and Apparatus

An Olympus VN-713PC Voice Recorder and an Olympus LS-20 M HD Recorder were used to record participants' responses. A semi-structured interview was used to guide the interview. Verbatim transcription of all interviews was conducted enabling detailed inductive analysis. The supermarkets had designated self-service checkout areas, positioned in a rectangular layout. Two of the supermarkets had six SSCOs and the other two had ten SSCOs.

2.3   Procedure

Ethical Approval was received from Abertay University's ethics committee. Before conducting the study, store managers from four major supermarkets within the UK were contacted via telephone, to request permission to access their store for the research to take place. Several meetings took place with various members of staff including personnel, managers and supervisors in order to explain what the research was about and permission to interview self-service checkout staff was granted. In the actual interviews, participating staff were also given the opportunity to pose questions to the researcher to explore the context of the study. All volunteering participating staff were asked to read and complete the information and informed consent forms before being interviewed. Participants were initially asked about general customer behaviors at self-service checkouts for example, "What are the most common mistakes made by customers at self-service checkouts" or "Do you feel self-service checkouts have affected customers at all"? Specific questions on dishonest behavior were then asked such as "Have you noticed whether or not people steal at SSCOs?" and "Do you feel various factors affect the likelihood of thefts occurring at SSCOs?". Interviews took place in staff rooms, medical rooms, store cafes, and customer service desks or areas within their works premises in-line with the ethnographic approach, collecting data within the setting of our group of participants. Interviews were paused if customers approached the area where the staff member was being interviewed. Participants were debriefed at the end of the interview. With the permission of participants, interviews were recorded; a typical interview lasted about 20 min.

3   Results

The findings are described in relation to actual (physical) and perceived social presence in relation to dishonest customer behavior. The findings for generic questions relating to customer behavior at self-service are to be reported elsewhere. For each category, the relevant questions are listed in the graphs with frequencies of mentions by staff and shop.

3.1   Physical Social Presence

Figure 2A shows responses to the question "Have you noticed whether people steal at self-service checkouts?". The majority of the staff had noticed people stealing even when there is an actual social presence of the staff member. Most staff spontaneously added that busyness at SSCOs is one major component for the likelihood of thefts occurring. Typical comments were that staff are "too busy watching other checkouts" (male, 25), and that it was "too hard for one person to watch all self-service checkouts when it is busy" (female, 52). Another participant stated "only one member of staff present at the self-service checkout, it can be hectic and can affect theft because you can only look after 2 at most" (male, 65). This indicates that staff feel the task attention demanding, and are aware of the gap in customer supervision – or lack of social presence - related to the likelihood of thefts occurring.

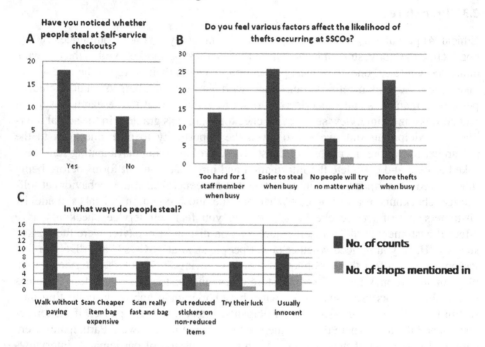

Fig. 2. (A, B, C) Clustered bar charts showing the number of counts of themes from staff and shops, to questions regarding actual social presence.

When asked "Do you feel various factors affect the likelihood of thefts occurring at self-service checkouts?", the majority of responses reflected busyness as the most critical factor (Fig. 2B), consistent with the answers to the previous questions. All staff interviewed said that it was "easier for customers to steal when the shop is busy" even when there was an actual social presence and most stated that "more thefts occur when it is busy". It was suggested that it is "too hard for one person to watch all of the self-service checkouts when it is busy" (male, 23). Staff also reported feeling pressured when the SSCOs are busy as their attention is engaged elsewhere, for example, when helping an individual customer, thus, they are unable to watch for potential thefts occurring and this "creates opportunity for theft" (female, 22).

We also wanted to explore the observed methods customers applied to steal items at self-service (Fig. 2C). While most of the listed methods clearly indicate customer intent to be dishonest, the last method "usually innocent", points to thefts occurring without intent from the customer. Figure 2C shows that the most common reported method of stealing was customers walking away without paying for their items. It was reported that many of the customers walking away without paying have initially put their payment card in the card terminal within the SSCO, either in an attempt to pay or to deceive the staff member into thinking they were paying. Staff reported being distracted by other customers and state that it is "impossible to watch them all at the same time" (male, 45). The second most common method of theft reported by staff was customers scanning cheap items but bagging expensive items in their place. Customers were reported to be scanning items really fast in attempt to steal items so that their weights would not be detected. Customers also put reduced stickers from one item onto a more expensive item that has not been reduced.

Staff also reported that some innocent mistakes were made by customers in relation to weighing products at SSCOs; for example, one comment was that stealing was committed "not on purpose - it was caused by weight issues" (female, 24).

To summarize, three major components are reflected in the data: staff perceive most but not all customer thefts as intentional, even in the actual presence of staff; staff are aware that attending many customers imposes attentional limitations on their ability to meet the supervisory or customer assistance demands, due to a lack of social presence; and finally, staff perceive a grey area where customers are not intentionally stealing; instead their behaviors are explained as being a result of the SSCO's technological setup.

It could be suggested, that identified attempts to steal items with intent suggests that customers do not feel they will be accountable, which is consistent with the various theories [11, 25] on the occurrence of dishonest behavior that explain thefts, not only at SSCO, but also during traditional sales interactions [16]. It is noteworthy that staff acutely perceive that their actual presence is insufficient to deter thefts.

Staff were also asked "Do you feel you can tell when someone is going to steal at a self-service checkout?". This highlighted some behaviors shown by customers which staff associate with an increased likelihood of thefts occurring. For example, some staff members reported certain customers' "body language is an indicator", as people can "become shifty, looking around the SSCOs" (female, 26). Some staff members stated that if a customer were to go to the furthest checkout away from the staff member that it would make them more aware of that customer's behavior, and more likely to keep a closer eye on them. Customers who state that they no longer want an item after there has been a weight issue, due to an item not being scanned properly and then bagged, were reported by staff to have been likely to have been trying to act dishonestly. Staff reported that they can ask to check customers' shopping bags if they suspect dishonest behavior, however, if the customer has not left the shop with an unpaid item then it is not considered to be theft and they cannot be prosecuted without clear evidence of an intent to behave dishonestly.

3.2 Perceived Social Presence

In order to gauge how staff would assess the effect of a perceived social presence on customers they were initially asked "Do you feel that if customers felt they were being watched it would have any effect on the likelihood of thefts occurring?" (Fig. 3A).

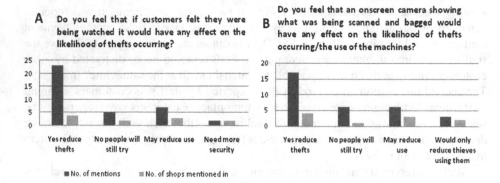

Fig. 3. (A, B) Clustered bar charts showing the number of counts of themes from staff and shops to questions regarding perceived social presence.

The majority of staff reported that this might reduce thefts. More specifically, staff reported that if customers felt they were being watched then it would reduce thefts occurring as they would feel "less likely to get away with it" (female, 46) or "would feel paranoid they will get caught" (female, 26). This suggests that staff perceive customers' perceptions of being watched can modify behavior to reduce the likelihood of thefts occurring, and raises questions as to how this social presence can be induced – either by the presence of more staff, or via technological implementations.

To explore the latter, staff were asked "Do you feel that an onscreen camera showing what was being scanned and bagged would have any effect on the likelihood of thefts occurring?" (Fig. 3B). The majority of staff reported that they felt an onscreen camera would reduce thefts at SSCOs, which was illustrated by the comment that "if customers could see it and were more aware they were being watched it definitely would reduce thefts" (male, 53).

To summarize, there were two major components reflected in the data: staff believe that the general perception of being watched (social presence) can modify behavior to reduce the likelihood of thefts occurring; staff also perceived a potential for the technological implementation of social presence at SSCO to be helpful, for example, via an onscreen camera.

4   Discussion

Although there is always an actual social presence with a member of staff at SSCOs, the present study found that staff perceive themselves to be limited in their capacity to create the same sense of social presence when SSCOs are busy, which they perceive leads to a greater risk of thefts occurring. Staff also reported feeling under pressure when self-service checkouts are busy as they are impaired in their ability to watch for thefts and customer problems occurring, and maintain a high level of social presence at the same time, assisting customers. Pietro et al.'s [27] study found staff reporting feeling more satisfied at work when working with SSCOs as they could provide a "better" final service. This may not be possible if staff are feeling pressured due to the perceived high risk of thefts at SSCOs when they are busy. Implementing a social presence within a self-service interface may increase the sense of social presence but also maintain a high level of customer service, as the customers can feel supported throughout their trans action by it providing the impression that help is at hand. This may also enhance the likelihood of staff feeling satisfied with their work and increase levels of employee job performance, as they may feel supported in giving assistance to customers.

Most staff agreed that theft would be reduced if customers felt they were being watched generally. This is consistent with Baumeister's [3] theory which stated feeling the presence of others can lead individuals to alter their behavior in a manner that communicates a positive self-impression. This view was underlined when the majority of staff agreed that an onscreen camera on SSCOs would reduce the likelihood of theft. Thus, staff perceive that they could be assisted by a social presence implemented in technology. It is noteworthy that a social presence may be created via CCTV in stores and, thus, should already be perceived by customers. However, only two members of staff made references to CCTV in relation to the question "Do you feel that if customers felt they were being watched it would have any effect on the likelihood of theft occurring?", although all participating stores in this study used CCTV supervision. This suggests that most staff do not perceive CCTV to induce an effective social presence on customers. There is considerable research to suggest that CCTV has become over-familiar to customers and that it no longer upholds its crime reduction effects [4, 15]. An onscreen camera at self-service checkouts may be a more effective way of reminding people that they are under direct, i.e., one-to-one, surveillance and create an effective sense of social presence to result in less theft occurring.

Within this context it is also important to point out that the perception of one's own presence can affect behavior. The self-focused attention theory refers to an individual considering their internal standards and making sure their behavior is consistent with these standards [5]. Beaman et al. [5] conducted an experiment on Halloween whilst children were trick-or-treating. Children were asked to take only one sweet and were then left alone with the sweets. Children were significantly more likely to only take one sweet when there was a mirror placed behind the sweet bowl than without the mirror. This suggests that their reflection increased their self-awareness and perhaps sense of social presence, encouraging them to behave in a manner that was consistent with the standards associated with the setting [5]. An onscreen camera at SSCOs displaying the customer's interaction with the SSCO via its interface may likewise enhance customers' self-awareness and sense of social presence.

Staff reported that some thefts were actually innocent mistakes made by the customer due to the interactions with the SSCO, mainly weighing items. Genuine mistakes can happen when using SSCOs, perhaps due to lack of experience with the system, thus clear instructions on how to use SSCOs may prevent this from happening. The potential for more challenging transaction processes at SSCOs may be encouraging thefts, however, as the customer can blame any un-scanned items on the technology, masking their intention to steal, and reducing the feeling of responsibility. Frustration may be experienced by the customer if the SSCOs are not operating in a straightforward manner, which may lead to dishonest behavior such as bagging un-scanned items, consistent with the "frustration factor" (p14) stated by Beck [6]. It is reasonable to assume that frustration potentially provides the customer with a reason to justify their dishonest behavior, which Beck [6] defines as the "self-scan defence" (p14). It could be argued that customers who do not pre-plan to act dishonestly at self-service checkouts, but may be influenced by frustration, would be likely to be guided by a social presence, as it would encourage them to behave in a socially accepted manner, reducing the likelihood of thefts [13]. A social presence in the form of an onscreen camera at SSCOs may result in customers feeling accountable for their actions, as social presence induces a sense of accountability [25]. Future research will address the aspects of social presence and possible manifestation in the context of technology.

4.1 Conclusions

The findings from this study suggest that the effect of social presence on customer behaviors deserves more exploration. Actual staff presence should consistently induce a sense of social presence, however, this is not perceived by staff to be sufficient within self-service. The present study found that the presence of numerous customers increases the perceived likelihood of theft. Arguably, it can be suggested that a greater number of staff members would reduce the likelihood of thefts occurring. Therefore, the effects of staff density and perceived identity (staff or customer) within a SSCO area on social presence require to be further investigated. There is also uncertainty as to whether or not customers are intentionally stealing at SSCOs or whether thefts occur due to aspects of the technological setup, providing justification for dishonest behaviors. Future research will elaborate to what extent the perceived social presence via technological systems might support staff in their task and will explore customer views. This may benefit future interactions for the retailer, staff and customers, and encourage businesses to obtain SST to enhance their productive potential.

Acknowledgements. We would like to thank all of the participating supermarkets and their staff for accommodating and agreeing to participate in this research. We would also like to thank NCR for their on-going support with our research.

References

1. Anand, P., Sternthal, B.: Ease of message processing as a moderator of repetition effects in advertising. J. Mark. Res. **27**(3), 345–353 (1990)
2. Bateson, M., Nettle, D., Roberts, G.: Cues of being watched enhance cooperation in a real-world setting. Biol. Lett. **2**, 412–414 (2006)
3. Baumeister, R.F.: A self-presentational view of social phenomena. Psychol. Bull. **91**, 3–26 (1982)
4. Beck, A., Willis, A.: Context-specific measures of CCTV effectiveness in the retail sector. In: Surveillance of Public Space: CCTV, Street Lighting and Crime Prevention. Crime Prevention Studies Series, pp. 251–269 (1999)

5. Beaman, A.L., Klentz, B., Diener, E., Svanum, S.: Self-awareness and transgression in children: two field studies. J. Pers. Soc. Psychol. **37**(10), 1835–1846 (1979)
6. Beck, A.: Self-scan checkouts and retail loss: understanding the risk and minimising the threat. Secur. J. **24**(3), 199–215 (2011)
7. Biocca, F., Harris, C., Burgoon, J.K.: Towards a more robust theory and measure of social presence: review and suggested criteria. Presence: Teleoperators Virtual Environ. **12**(5), 456–480 (2003)
8. Collier, J.E., Kimes, S.E.: Only if it is convenient understanding how convenience influences self-service technology evaluation. J. Serv. Res. **16**(1), 39–51 (2013)
9. Chen, K.J.: Technology-based service and customer satisfaction in developing countries. Int. J. Manag. **22**(2), 307–318 (2005)
10. Davis, F.D.: Perceived usefulness, perceived ease of use and user acceptance of information technology. MIS Q. **13**(3), 319–340 (1989)
11. Dooley, J.J., Pyżalski, J., Cross, D.: Cyberbullying versus face-to-face bullying. J. Psychol. **217**(4), 182–188 (2009)
12. Goodenough, O.R., Decker, G.: Why do Good People Steal Intellectual Property? The Social Science Research Network Electronic Paper Collection (2008). http://papers.ssrn.com/sol3/papers.cfm?abstract_id=1518952
13. Harmon-Jones, E., Mills, J.: Cognitive Dissonance: Progress on a Pivotal Theory in Psychology. American Psychological Association, Washington, DC (1999)
14. Hilton, T., Hughes, T., Little, E., Marandi, E.: Adopting self-service technology to do more with less. J. Serv. Mark. **27**(1), 3–12 (2013)
15. Honess, T., Charman, E.: Closed Circuit Television in Public Places. Home Office, London (1992). (Police Research Group Crime Prevention Unit Series Paper, #35.)
16. Jolliffe, D., Farrington, D.P.: Examining the relationship between low empathy and self-reported offending. Leg. Criminological Psychol. **12**(2), 265–286 (2007)
17. Kallweit, K., Spreer, P., Toporowski, W.: Why do customers use self-service information technologies in retail? The mediating effect of perceived service quality. J. Consum. Serv. **21**, 268–276 (2014)
18. Kang, M., Gretzel, U.: Differences in social presence perceptions. In: Fuchs, M., Ricci, F., Cantoni, L. (eds.) Information and Communication Technologies in Tourism 2012, pp. 437–447. Springer, New York (2012)
19. Kinard, B.R., Capella, M.L., Kinard, J.L.: The impact of social presence on technology based self-service use: the role of familiarity. Serv. Mark. Q. **30**(3), 303–314 (2009)
20. Korczynski, M.: The contradictions of service work: call centre as customer-oriented bureaucracy. In: Customer Service: Empowerment and Entrapment, pp. 79–101 (2001)
21. Lee, H.J., Yang, K.: Interpersonal service quality, self-service technology (SST) service quality, and retail patronage. J. Retail. Consum. Serv. **20**(1), 51–57 (2013)
22. Meuter, M.L., Bitner, M.J., Ostrom, A.L., Brown, S.W.: Choosing among alternative service delivery modes: an investigation of customer trial of self-service technologies. J. Mark. **69**(2), 61–83 (2005)
23. Meuter, M.L., Ostrom, A.L., Roundtree, R.I., Bitner, M.J.: Self-service technologies: understanding customer satisfaction with technology-based service encounters. J. Mark. **64**(3), 50–64 (2000)
24. Miller, R.S., Leary, M.R.: Social Sources and Interactive Functions of Emotion: The Case of Embarrassment (1992)
25. Mohr, D.C., Cuijpers, P., Lehman, K.: Supportive accountability: a model for providing human support to enhance adherence to ehealth interventions. J. Med. Internet Res. **13**(1), e30 (2011)

26. Parasuraman, A., Berry, L.L., Zeithaml, V.A.: Understanding customer expectations of service. Sloan Manag. Rev. **32**(3), 39–48 (1991)
27. Pietro, L., Pantano, E., Virgillo, F.: Frontline employees' attitudes towards self-service technologies: threats or opportunity for job performance. J. Retail. Consum. Serv. **21**(5), 844–850 (2014)
28. Siddiqi, K.O.: Interrelations between service quality attributes, customer satisfaction and customer loyalty in the retail banking sector in bangladesh. Int. J. Bus. Manag. **6**(3), p12 (2011)
29. Reeves, B., Nass, C.: The Media Equation: How People Treat Computers, Television, and New Media like Real People and Places. Cambridge University Press, New York (1996)
30. Romano, D.M., Sheppard, G., Hall, J., Miller, A., Ma, Z.: BASIC: A believable, adaptable socially intelligent character for social presence. In: PRESENCE 2005, The 8th Annual International Workshop on Presence, 21–22, September, 2005. University College London, London (2005)
31. Wang, M.C.H.: Determinants and consequences of consumer satisfaction with self-service technology in a retail setting. Managing Serv. Qual. **22**(2), 128–144 (2012)
32. Wispé, L.: History of the concept of empathy. In: Eisenberg, N., Strayer, J. (eds.) Empathy and its Development, pp. 17–37. Cambridge University Press, New York (1987)
33. Zhao, S.: Toward a taxonomy of copresence. Presence **12**(5), 445–455 (2003)

Consumer Adoption of Social Commerce

Nick Hajli[1](✉) and Xiaolin Lin[2]

[1] Newcastle University Business School, Newcastle upon Tyne, UK
Nick.hajli@ncl.ac.uk
[2] Department of Management, IS, and Entrepreneurship, College of Business,
Washington State University, Pullman, USA
xiaolin@wsu.edu

Abstract. The paper considers the emergent, so called, 'social commerce' imperative which enables consumers to generate active WEB content and engage commercially with providers through social networking systems. It is apparent that little research currently addresses the need for an understanding of consumer adoption in this respect and therefore further critical issues involved in contemporary consumer research. Our contribution relates to a consideration of adoption behaviour through the formulation of the technology acceptance model (TAM), social commerce constructs and trust. We consequently present specific insights into consumers 'intention to buy' through social commerce engagement. The results of our research also inform providers with an initial important awareness of the impact of social media within a commercial context.

Keywords: Social commerce · TAM · Intention to buy · SEM-PLS

1 Introduction

Electronic commerce has emerged mainly from the information systems (IS) literature, which integrates factors from the marketing discipline into information technology (IT) adoption. The current perspective of e-commerce adoption generally divides into two main streams, ie Technology Acceptance Model (TAM) (Davis, 1989) and the Theory of Planned Behavior (TPB) (Ajzen, 1985). However, e-commerce has now developed into, so called, social commerce facilitated by new advances in Web 2.0 technologies (M. Hajli, 2013). Social commerce is a new stream in 'commerce' integrating social networking sites (SNSs) particularly in electronic media platforms (Liang, Ho, Li, & Turban, 2011). The increasing application of SNSs provides an opportunity for researchers to rethink consumer adoption of e-commerce (Cooke and Buckley, 2008). Traditionally in e-commerce, consumers interact with online vendors and base their decisions on information provided by the vendors' websites (Gefen & Straub, 2004) but in social commerce, customers rely on the information produced by their peers (Hajli, Lin, & Hajli, 2013). Social commerce has changed the nature of online consumer activity and has enabled users to interact with other consumers before making any purchasing decisions (Hajli & Lin). This raises critical questions such as; does social commerce bring any new aspects to the market?; if so, does this impact on a consumer's e-commerce adoption? In addition, the question of trust, a vitally important

F.F.-H. Nah and C.-H. Tan (Eds.): HCIB 2015, LNCS 9191, pp. 279–287, 2015.
DOI: 10.1007/978-3-319-20895-4_26

factor in e-commerce (Ono et al., 2003), is also apparent. Trust is a fundamental element in trading in an online context (Morid & Shajari, 2012). In the social commerce era, there are now new facilities in e-commerce platforms to establish trust through the social interaction of individuals in SNSs (Hajli et al., 2013).

The purpose of this paper is to explain and empirically test e-commerce adoption from a social commerce perspective at the consumer level. More specifically, our research seeks to integrate the underlying constructs of social commerce - forums and communities, ratings and reviews, recommendations and referrals (N. Hajli, 2013) - with e-commerce constructs into TAM. Although TAM is a traditional theoretical framework, its adoption within consumer research makes a useful contribution to the new stream of social commerce. Most importantly, TAM has been proven to be a successful theory in predicting acceptance behaviour (Cheng & Yeh, 2011). In addition, the study of consumer behaviour in SNSs by integrating TAM and social commerce constructs is believed to be another contribution to the area. The main objective is to propose and formulate a comprehensive adoption model, from the social commerce perspective, thus contributing to a new paradigm of consumer behavior research.

2   Literature Review

Electronic (e)-commerce has been well studied in the IS discipline (Ba & Pavlou, 2002; Pavlou & Dimoka, 2006) and focuses on online consumer engagement in online transactions with vendors (Pavlou & Fygenson, 2006). Purchasing intentions and information acquisition about product are the two main components of established online consumer behaviour. Online activity extends beyond purchasing a product, it is also about acquiring product information before making any purchasing decisions (Gefen & Straub, 2000; Pavlou & Fygenson, 2006). Consequently, acquired product information is a critical element for any consumer purchasing decision. However, via the applications of Web 2.0 technologies, consumers now have more resources and can easily obtain all the relevant product information they may need (Huang & Benyoucef, 2013). The social communication between consumers and the interconnectivities through SNSs have developed e-commerce into social commerce (Liang et al., 2011). Social commerce provides consumers with a host of platforms and opportunities to communicate with other experienced consumers before they purchase a product.

Social commerce is a new concept which enables customers to have an active position in cyber space. It is a development in e-commerce based on a network of buyers and sellers. It is more commonly found in social and interactive forms of e-commerce (N. Hajli, 2013).

The process of acquiring product and shopping information is similar to window shopping (Gefen & Straub, 2000), transferring product information from an e-vendor's website to consumers (Pavlou & Fygenson, 2006). Previously, the internet was less involved in the relationship of buyer and seller (Deeter-Schmelz & Kennedy, 2004) but now Web 2.0 has introduced a more interactive environment between two parties intent on trading. Social commerce moves consumers from traditional e-commerce websites to social commerce websites and to share shopping information amongst consumers.

The era of social commerce is becoming better established and is becoming more influential than traditional systems of depending on business websites for information (Owyang, 2009).

3   Consumer Behavior Research Model

Within our proposed model nine constructs were determined and analyzed, as follows:

H1: Learning and training positively affects consumers' intention to use an e-vendor's website for shopping.

H2: Perceived ease of use is positively associated with a consumer's online learning and training.

H3: A consumer's computing and internet experience positively affects his/her trust in an e-vendor's website.

H4: A consumer's computing and internet experience is positively associated with his/her perceived ease of use.

H5: A consumer's computing and internet experience is positively associated with his/her social presence.

H6: The level of social presence embedded in an e-vendor's website is positively related to consumer trust in that website.

H7: An increased degree of familiarity with an e-vendor's website is positively associated with consumer trust in that website.

H8: Social commerce constructs will increase a user's familiarity with an e-vendor's website.

H9: Social commerce constructs are positively associated with social presence.

H10: A consumer's perceived usefulness is positively related to his/her intention to use an e-vendor's website.

H11: A consumer's perceived ease of use is positively related to his/her perceived usefulness of an e-vendor's website for shopping.

H12: A consumer's perceived ease of use is positively related to his/her intention to use an e-vendor's website.

H13: A consumer's perceived ease of use is positively related to his/her trust in an e-vendor's website.

H14: Social commerce constructs are positively related to a consumer's perceived ease of use.

H15: A consumer's trust in an e-vendor's website is positively related to his/her intention to use that website for shopping.

4   Research Methodology

The main sample of this research is based on the cooperation of 215 internet users with 1200 emails and paper questionnaires issued. Respondents were asked to use their previous online shopping experiences to answer the questions. In total 226 samples were received with a response rate of 19%. The usable sample was 215, comprising of 65% female and 35% male. In the administration of the online-survey, different issues that might affect people's participation were considered. For instance, a webpage with helpful graphics and an easy to navigate email were provided for participants in the survey. In an invitation letter email, respondents were asked to take part by simply clicking on a 'link' and completing the survey. A pre-test was conducted with a total of 30 students, 20 female and 10 male, mostly postgraduate students, to enhance the measurement scales. This was good practice as useful comments on the questionnaire were received, helping with face validity. This pre-test data was excluded from the main dataset.

5 Measurements

Most of the measurement items were adapted from the existing literature in e-commerce adoption and social commerce. Social commerce constructs are forums, communities, ratings, reviews and recommendations (N. Hajli, 2013). Learning and training were not used in e-commerce adoption models but the author is proposing this to assess the influence of this variable on user behaviour. Trust, PU and intention to use were adapted from Gefen et al, (Gefen, Karahanna, & Straub, 2003). Familiarity was based on Gefen (Gefen, 2000). PEOU was adopted from Gefen, Karahanna and Straub (Gefen et al., 2003). User experience was adopted from Crobitt et al. (Corbitt, Thanasankit, & Yi, 2003) and social presence was based on Gefen and Straub (Gefen & Straub, 2004).

6 Results of Measurement Model Testing

Construct validity can be checked by discriminant and convergent validity (Chin, Gopal, & Salisbury, 1997). To test convergent validity, AVE is considered. This should be at least 0.50 (Wixom & Watson, 2001). The results are shown in Table 1. AVE in all constructs is more than 0.50, indicating that the research has achieved this criterion. PLS for discriminant validity was also carried out. Details of correlation matrix among constructs are shown in Table 2.

7 Results of Structural Model Testing

The model (Fig. 1.0) validity is assessed by R square value and the structural paths (Chwelos, Benbasat, & Dexter, 2001). This was undertaken using bootstrapping to test the statistical significance of construct path coefficient by means of t-tests. In this model, user experience path coefficients of its causal links with social presence and trust are not significant. This means that user experience does not influence social presence and trust in this model. However, all other constructs are significant and the finding supports the hypotheses at $p < 0.05$ level.

In Fig. 1.0, the R square values are shown, indicating that almost 40% of the variance in the intention to buy was accounted for by the constructs in the model. This means that intention to buy was, as hypothesized, affected by PU, PEOU, learning and

Table 1 PLS Quality Criteria Overview

Constructs	AVE	Composite Reliability	Familiarity	Intention to buy	Learning & Training	PEOU	PU	Social Commerce Constructs	Social Presence	Trust	User Experience
Familiarity	0.619549	0.828736	0.78								
Intention to buy	0.564577	0.710052	0.338347	0.76							
Learning & Training	0.546566	0.778358	0.281665	0.28408	0.74						
PEOU	0.550301	0.830307	0.432856	0.529019	0.172742	0.75					
PU	0.606145	0.859794	0.703996	0.428998	0.293058	0.46834	0.78				
Social Commerce Constructs	0.529498	0.755532	0.368791	0.310725	0.30481	0.35453	0.33542	0.73			
Social Presence	0.661446	0.886382	0.095263	0.3085	0.232043	0.22345	0.08501	0.159671	0.82		
Trust	0.535672	0.821271	0.400998	0.537355	0.214943	0.56975	0.5311	0.270012	0.239739	0.74	
User Experience	0.759978	0.904738	0.51103	0.364354	0.240072	0.44213	0.43856	0.104499	0.146271	0.32635	0.88

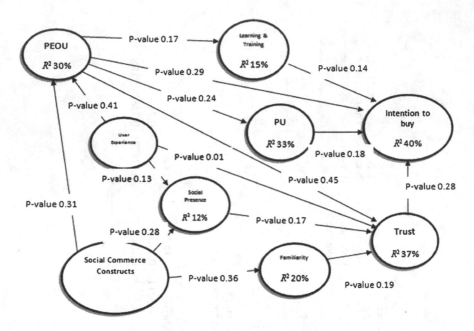

Fig. 1. Consumer behavior model

trust. Trust also has a notable R square value. The results show that 37% of the variance in this construct was accounted for by familiarity, social presence and PEOU. The other construct with a good R square value is PU, where almost 33% of the variance was accounted for by trust and PEOU in the model. PEOU has an R square value of 30%, accounted for by social commerce constructs and user experience. Familiarity, with an R square value of 20%, learning and training, with an R square value of 15%, and finally social presence, with an R square value of 12%, are the results obtained for the other constructs (Fig. 1).

8   Discussion

The aim of this paper is to provide a further understanding of consumer e-commerce adoption from a social commerce perspective thus illumination current and relevant consumer behaviour. A comprehensive model integrating e-commerce and social commerce constructs has been proposed. More specifically, this study investigates the impact of social commerce constructs on a technology acceptance model and trust, leading to intention to buy. It is seen that social commerce constructs could be incorporated into an e-commerce adoption model. The results of this structural model analysis show that social commerce constructs, namely, forums, communities, ratings, reviews and recommendations influence social presence and familiarity of e-commerce platforms leading to trust. The trust established through social commerce constructs will affect a customer's intention to buy. In addition, social commerce constructs influence perceived ease of use and indirectly perceived usefulness, which together affect intention to buy. These results show that consumers are using social commerce constructs, which in turn make them more likely to use e-commerce platforms successfully due to the information gathered from these social commerce constructs. This positively increases their trust in e-commerce platforms and helps them in their purchasing journey. Moreover, social commerce constructs make e-commerce platforms easy to use through social media. This also affects their decisions regarding shopping online.

9   Theoretical Implications

The key constructs of the model - perceived ease of use, perceived usefulness, and intention to use - come from the domain of information systems. This confirms the important role of information systems in predicting consumer behaviour in an online context. The impact of these constructs highlights the fact that information systems can be a reference discipline for future study of online customer behaviour. There has also been an emergence of social media and social commerce in the business studies sector. The other contribution made by this research is to demonstrate that e-commerce studies mainly use two main streams, TRA and TAM. However, social commerce is a new stream in e-commerce, highlighting the role played by social media and social networking sites in e-commerce platforms. Therefore, using social commerce constructs and integrating these constructs with TAM theory can provide a model for a new theoretical framework for e-commerce adoption studies. Considering social commerce constructs in B2C e-commerce adoption not only extends e-commerce adoption models but also gives a more holistic understanding of the behaviour of online customers. The importance of a positive social online environment in adoption processes is emphasized. This is a new integrated model in e-commerce adoption to date. This also improves the predictive power of the e-commerce adoption model since this model considers all of the main aspects related to the adoption process of e-commerce. Finally, trust as a key element of an online transaction is highlighted as a crucial factor in this research. The research argues that social commerce constructs influence trust, leading to intention to buy.

10   Conclusion

To better understand e-commerce adoption, a new model based on the technology acceptance model, social commerce constructs and trust is proposed. Through empirical research, data has been analyzed by SEM-PLS to validate the model. The results show that trust is still a central factor in an online context; this significantly impacts on intention to buy. Results also show that social commerce constructs increase a user's familiarity and trust; this affects intention to use. By integrating the technology acceptance model, social commerce constructs and trust in an e-commerce adoption model, this research has shown that social interaction of individuals in social networking sites has significant economic value which influence perceived ease of use and indirectly affect trust and intention to buy.

References

Ajzen, I.: From intentions to actions: A theory of planned behavior. Springer, Heidelberg (1985)

Ba, S., Pavlou, P.A.: Evidence of the effect of trust building technology in electronic markets: price premiums and buyer behavior. MIS Q. 26(3), 243–268 (2002)

Cheng, Y.-H., Yeh, Y.-J.: Exploring radio frequency identification technology's application in international distribution centers and adoption rate forecasting. Technol. Forecast. Soc. Chang. 78(4), 661–673 (2011). doi:10.1016/j.techfore.2010.10.003

Chin, W.W., Gopal, A., Salisbury, W.D.: Advancing the theory of adaptive structuration: the development of a scale to measure faithfulness of appropriation. Inf. Syst. Res. 8(4), 342–367 (1997)

Chwelos, P., Benbasat, I., Dexter, A.S.: Research report: empirical test of an EDI adoption model. Inf. Syst. Res. 12(3), 304–321 (2001). doi:10.1287/isre.12.3.304.9708

Corbitt, B.J., Thanasankit, T., Yi, H.: Trust and e-commerce: a study of consumer perceptions. Electron. Commer. Res. Appl. 2(3), 203–215 (2003). doi:10.1016/s1567-4223(03)00024-3

Davis, F.D.: Perceived usefulness, perceived ease of use, and user acceptance of information technology. MIS Q. 13(3), 319–340 (1989)

Deeter-Schmelz, D.R., Kennedy, K.N.: Buyer-seller relationships and information sources in an e-commerce world. J. Bus. Ind. Mark. 19(3), 188–196 (2004)

Gefen, D.: E-commerce: the role of familiarity and trust. Omega 28(6), 725–737 (2000). doi:10.1016/S0305-0483(00)00021-9

Gefen, D., Karahanna, E., Straub, D.W.: Trust and tam in online shopping: an integrated model. MIS Q. 27(1), 51–90 (2003)

Gefen, D., Straub, D.: The relative importance of perceived ease of use in is adoption: a study of E-Commerce adoption. J. Assoc. Inf. Syst. 1, 1–30 (2000)

Gefen, D., Straub, D.W.: Consumer trust in B2C e-Commerce and the importance of social presence: experiments in e-Products and e-Services. Omega 32(6), 407–424 (2004). doi:10.1016/j.omega.2004.01.006

Hajli, M.: A Study of the Impact of Social Media on Consumers. International Journal of Market Research, forthcoming (2013)

Hajli, M., Lin, X.: Developing tourism education through social media. Tourism Plan. Dev. doi:10.1080/21568316.2014.883426

Hajli, M., Lin, X., Hajli, M.M.: Social word of mouth: how trust develops in the market. Int. J. Market Res., accepted for publication (2013)

Hajli, N.: A research framework for social commerce adoption. Inf. Manage. Comput. Secur. 21(3), 144–154 (2013)

Huang, Z., Benyoucef, M.: From e-commerce to social commerce: a close look at design features. Electron. Commer. Res. Appl. 12(4), 246–259 (2013). doi:10.1016/j.elerap.2012.12.003

Liang, T.-P., Ho, Y.-T., Li, Y.-W., Turban, E.: What drives social commerce: the role of social support and relationship quality. Int. J. Electron. Commer. 16(2), 69–90 (2011)

Morid, M.A., Shajari, M.: An enhanced e-commerce trust model for community based centralized systems. Electronic Commerce Research, 1–19 (2012)

Ono, C., Nishiyama, S., Kim, K., Paulson, B.C., Cutkosky, M., Petrie, C.J.: Trust-based facilitator: handling word-of-mouth trust for agent-based e-commerce. Electron. Commer. Res. 3(3), 201–220 (2003)

Owyang, J.: The Future Of The Social Web (2009). www.forrester.com/

Pavlou, P.A., Dimoka, A.: The nature and role of feedback text comments in online marketplaces: implications for trust building, price premiums, and seller differentiation. Inf. Syst. Res. 17(4), 392–414 (2006). doi:10.1287/isre.1060.0106

Pavlou, P.A., Fygenson, M.: Understanding and prediction electronic commerce adoption: an extension of the theory of planned behavior. MIS Q. **30**(1), 115–143 (2006)

Wixom, B.H., Watson, H.J.: An empirical investigation of the factors affecting data warehousing success. MIS Q. **25**(1), 17–41 (2001)

Helping Customers Help Themselves – Optimising Customer Experience by Improving Search Task Flows

Sue Hessey[✉]

BT Plc Research and Innovation, Adastral Park, Ipswich, UK
Sue.hessey@bt.com

Abstract. Large consumer-facing enterprises can offer a wide range of products and services to their customers. In parallel, often the quantity of information offered online to customers to support these services is similarly large in scale – so how can an enterprise optimize online support to improve customer satisfaction and lower support costs to the business? To address this problem we have used quantitative and qualitative methods to identify the most significant topics concerning customers over a 14-week period. These analyses in turn informed our user test design, which investigated individual search-for-help behaviors. The output from these analyses was used to form recommendations for high-priority, low cost interventions in the User Interface design of the support website, so that customers are more willing and able to help themselves.

Keywords: Customer service · User Interface · Information search · Information retrieval

1 Introduction

There is a growing desire by commercial enterprises and customers to conduct transactions digitally, where possible [1]. For enterprises, this requirement is usually driven by cost reduction objectives. For customers, the convenience of online service support - available at all times and via multiple devices - is important in an increasingly complex and time-poor world, provided it does not cause them extra effort [2].

Effective online service support enables customers to find answers to service problems, and where possible to diagnose and fix them themselves, meaning that – if it works well - they may never need to come into direct contact with helpdesks. However, there is the risk of a trade-off between 100 % self-service and good customer experience, if for example online support information is hard for the customer to find, or where their expectations are not met. To offer a satisfactory self-support experience to customers, the enterprise needs to understand:

– How customers' need for support is expressed in their own language.
– The contexts of where, when and how customers seek support.
– What customers consider reliable sources of online information.

© Springer International Publishing Switzerland 2015
F.F.-H. Nah and C.-H. Tan (Eds.): HCIB 2015, LNCS 9191, pp. 288–299, 2015.
DOI: 10.1007/978-3-319-20895-4_27

- When customers abandon online help and seek assistance from a helpdesks.
- How navigation and presentation of information can be optimized for self-support.

The objective of this paper is to present findings of research conducted to (a) identify the highest priority customer support issues, and (b) to identify the Information Seeking and Retrieval (IS and IR) strategies [3] customers adopt to resolve these issues, within the context of the five "areas of understanding" listed above, leading to recommendations for improving the search process, to help customers help themselves and reduce customer support costs consequently.

2   Business Rationale and Context for Project

British Telecommunications Plc has around 10 million residential customers, and offers hundreds of products individually and combined as packages. Consequently it has a significant customer service division to support these customers and their diverse needs, handling 10 billion minutes of inbound voice calls per year [2]. The help section of its online web presence is intended to be the first port of call for customers seeking help with service problems, so that customers can diagnose and fix their own service issues without them needing to contact these helpdesks.

The customer support site we researched receives around half a million hits per week. Around 6000 searches are made per day via the specific search engine for the site. Some 2500 customer support articles are available and any can be returned based on the search terms entered. Articles are also accessible via the navigational structure of the site via a series of tabs and drop-down menus. These are also accessible from search engines operating from outside the site (Google.com for example). With respect to these figures, prioritization needs to occur as to where the most significant interventions can be made for the lowest cost. The first step to achieve this was identifying the most significant topics for which customers were searching for help and accessing support articles on. We did this by analyzing the following data inputs: Most-Searched Keywords, Article Ratings, Verbatim Feedback, and Click-Throughs.

3   Quantitative Analysis of IS and User Feedback Behaviors

Most Searched Terms. Using a prototype dashboard created in R Shiny [4], daily data feeds from web analytics were processed to present graphically, via the GUI, the searches made by customers over a 14-week period between October 2014 and January 2015. (The search engine only functioned within the boundary of the support section of the enterprise's website). This was used to define the key issues customers were seeking support for in their own language.

The top ten single keywords and their associate search terms over this period were found to be (in descending order): Password, Change, Email, Number, Phone, Hub, Line, Broadband, Account, Mail.

This dashboard was also used to detect when most searches were conducted. Results show that most searches take place on Mondays, followed by Wednesdays, with the least number of searches conducted on Sundays. This infers that days where the majority of customers are at work are chosen to sort out service issues. This is explored further in the user tests.

Ratings Against Returned Articles. Currently, customers are asked the following at the end of each support article:

After clicking on the stars (Fig. 1), a free-text box opens, offering customers the opportunity to provide verbatim feedback (see below).

Fig. 1. Ratings and Feedback box presented to customers at the foot of support articles

All articles that were rated overwhelming received poor ratings (71 % of all ratings given were "1" compared to 18 % given "5". It was observed through manual analysis of the verbatim that comments are very often negative even when an article has a high rating, suggesting customers pay less attention to giving representative ratings when they want to express an opinion via free text).

Therefore we inferred the most rated articles represented the most significant customer topics. The articles with the most ratings were ranked over the same 14-week period to achieve an average ranking (where articles were in very similar topic areas we grouped these together). In summary, the most poorly-rated article topic areas were, in order:

1. Fixing phone line faults.
2. Parental controls.
3. How to deal with Email security.
4. Broadband problems and fixes.

This list broadly matches the search terms top ten, with the exception of "Parental controls".[1]

Verbatim Feedback Against Returned Articles. In conjunction with the above analysis all verbatim feedback given against articles rated "1" were input into "Debatescape" [5] (a text and sentiment analytics tool), to generate simple word clouds. This gave a visual representation of the most frequently used words in the free text comments box. According to Debatescape, during the 14-week period, the ten most

---

[1] "Parental Controls" are service improvements which were introduced part-way through the 14-week period. Although generating customer comments, this reflected a specific event. We prioritized continuous key customer topics across the entire timeframe, so Parental Controls was excluded from this study.

used words entered in the comments box were (in descending order): Email, password, answer, account, phone, problem, service, work, broadband and mail.

Again, these results reflect the search term top ten (broadly relating to email, password, phone), with some discrepancies which relate to general experiences (e.g. service, answer, work).

Click-Throughs. Click-through data was the final input considered to understand key customer topics. These are specifically recorded when a user accesses the "Contact Us" page after reading an article, inferring that users are not satisfied with the support article returned and that they now wish to contact a helpdesk.

Using data feeds from web analytic tools, over the 14-week period four articles which generated the highest click-throughs were:

1. "Help with usernames and passwords".
2. "Compromised email accounts".
3. "How to change or cancel an account"[2].
4. "I've got no broadband connection".

Again, there are similarities between the search terms, ratings and verbatim feedbacks in terms of topic areas (passwords, email, broadband problems).

In summary the key customer topics thus distilled from these four analyses are:

- Needing help with email and password problems
- Needing help with broadband connection problems
- Needing help with phone service

4 User Experience Testing

Qualitative User Experience Testing was carried out to explore the participants' Information Seeking and Retrieval strategies [3] within scenarios based on the three topic areas identified, reflecting the original objective to understand:

- How customers express their need for support in their own language.
- The contexts of where, when and how users seek support.
- What customers consider reliable sources of information.
- When online help is abandoned and helpdesk assistance is needed.
- How the navigation and presentation of information be optimized to minimize calls to helpdesks.

Participants. Participants were selected as being users of broadband, email and telephony services but were not BT customers, so they had no pre-knowledge of the navigation of the site. There were five male and five female users, ranging in age from 31 to 55. All were computer users to some degree. None had IT or HCI-based

---

[2] This article contains a direct instruction for the customer to contact a helpdesk, thus generating high levels of click-throughs. For this reason this article was excluded from the study.

occupations (occupations included accountancy, university lecturer, full-time child carer, musician, HGV driver). All user tests were conducted using a laptop computer (while we acknowledge users will use phones and tablets as well we aimed to provide consistency in this test, to ensure we are evaluating the entire journey rather than the differences presented via different access devices).

User Test Design. We followed Marchionini and White's framework [6] for IS as a reference, giving consistency to the user tests but with slight adaptations, i.e.:

- The Recognise and Accept phases were given to the participants when the scenario was described.
- The Formulate, Express, Examine, Re-formulate and Use phases were participant-driven with prompts from the researcher where necessary.

The tests were conducted sequentially, with each participant following their own journey against the following scenarios:

Scenario 1: "Imagine you are having problems accessing your email account, although your Internet connection seems to be OK. What would you do to solve this problem?"

Scenario 2: "Imagine you are experiencing poor service from your broadband connection. What would you do to solve this problem?"

Scenario 3: "Imagine you've picked up the phone and there is noise on the line. What would you do to solve this problem?"

Participants were asked to put themselves in the position of a BT customer. BT's homepage was open on the laptop, although it was not a requirement for the participant to start their journey there, or to use it at all (until prompted). All user tests were conducted in a home environment and video recorded so that notes could be made after. Results were collated according to the five key points of the original objective.

Results

How customers express their need for support in their own language. When prompted, most participants entered what they considered general search terms because *"if you're more general with your search you can find what you want"*. (In reality, the terms used are more closed-task type searches [7]). Re-formulation of the query is rare, with participants more likely to follow other paths for IR than re-entering search terms.

There is variety in the "formulate" and "express" phases of IS within the tests. Requests were expressed predominantly via:

(a) short experiential statements e.g.: "Email account blocked", "email not working", "broadband keeps cutting out", "no dial tone", "phone fault".
(b) full experiential statements e.g.: "My username is no longer working and I can't access account", "There is crackling on the phone line".
(c) implicit requests for help: "Unblocking my email account".

(d) explicit requests for help: "I have no connection, what can I do?" "I need help with my connection", "I have a terrible crackle on my line, please help".
(e) Searching directly for diagnostic tools: "Line fault check".

For the phone line self diagnostic in Scenario 3 there is a gap between customer language and how we ask them to define their own problem. Of the available options in self-diagnosis, *"some make sense, some not so – "ring trip" – I don't know what that means, ….you've also got "unable to trip ringing", I'm not really sure what that means…."*. For the same scenario, one participant attempted to input a full telephone number into the line checker tool, including a space between the area code and the number. The box cannot contain this number of characters so an error message is returned, but with no indication of why it was wrong or what would be the correct way to enter numbers.

When, Where and How Users Seek Support. Self-support is already embedded behavior for half the participants who would conduct their own diagnostic tests before seeking support online. The search for support in this context involves drawing on previous experiences of dealing with the issues in the scenarios (e.g. checking PC, router and security settings, pop-ups and ad blockers, re-setting passwords and using line speed checkers), commenting: *"I'd always try to fix a problem myself rather than get someone else to do it"*. For in-home-broadband connection issues, workarounds by using 3G and 4G compatible devices to access support are widely used. While this is encouraged, there is also a risk of following poorly-formed procedures and increasing the problem, but this risk is mitigated by avoidance of calling helpdesks for those who were so inclined.

After accessing support articles, all apart from two would go through the diagnostic and fixing steps (wizards, desktop help, check my line etc.) suggested before contacting a helpdesk - or they would ask their partner or a friend to help them.

Two participants went straight to Google.com for help as a habit - *"that's what I tend to search everything with…you stick with one thing and you trust it"*. These same participants would not start their journey on the BT homepage, *"assuming it* [Google] *would take me there anyway"*. Another participant commented that they would use Google if the BT website did not yield satisfactory responses, without re-formulating the search terms used.

Participants expressed they wanted to find solutions to problems as soon as possible, especially during a working day (for those who work at home this is especially important). This was reflected in the search trends outlined earlier, regarding preferred days of week for searching. Additionally, instant useful responses to searching are expected - currently over 1000 articles are returned on average after a search, which can be overwhelming. Two participants commented that they expect the answer to their question immediately, and not on the next page of 20 or so answers.

For those who cannot resolve issues during work-time the choice of support depends on *"what I've got available to me at the time"*. This participant is a driver and does not have ready access to Internet-connected devices during the day. His workaround is that he has support phone numbers stored in his mobile phone.

Time of day may also have an impact on the motivation of the customer to self-support: *"I'm lazy* [at the end of the day] *and I'm not going to do the whole* [self-diagnosis] *thing….this is all very irritating, why can't I just ring somebody…I'm bored now, I'm really tired."*

Reliability of Information - Forums. There was variability in the reliance and trust placed on forums. The two participants who went straight to Google.com preferred to use community forums to check if others had solved similar problems. This is based on previous positive experiences – one participant commented that forums had been used successfully for advice on fixing his car. Forums were considered more reliable *"because it's based on other people's direct experience, and if they've had the same problem they might have come up with solutions or explanations which are slightly different to what the service provider suggested".* Another comments, *"techy people put stuff on there because they know what they're doing – I don't".*

However, the immediacy of the need for information forms a barrier to using forums – it is unknown how long it may take for an answer to be made to a post. Dates and times of postings are important details for trusting forum posts.

Six participants however did **not** trust forums, preferring to rely on what their service provider suggests, fearing they would *"blow up their computer"* if they did anything else: *"you're the guys with the know-how…why wouldn't I work through your advice before I tried* [forums]*?".* Lack of trust in forum contributors is also pervasive: *"I don't believe other people….Forums are usually full of people just talking rubbish."*

Reliability of Information – Ratings. Although customers are invited to give ratings to articles there is no indication as to why this is useful to them. It informs the "Answers others found helpful" (see Fig. 2) but this is not obvious to participants. Rating stars are given next to forum posts but often these are not populated. As a result there is a general reluctance to actively engage in the rating process. Apart from the lack of noticeable benefit to the customer, this is also due to: lack of time available, not expecting to see ratings for support content, being unaccustomed to give ratings to support content, and general apathy.

Participants commented that it appeared no-one else had rated articles either – this is especially true for the forums where stars appeared mostly blank - *"For some reason I didn't think it was asking me…it's like when you're reviewing a product and the stars are blank it's because no-one's reviewed it, so it's almost as if I'd thought other people hadn't reviewed it…".*

When ratings are given, they are highly polarized (this is supported by the quantitative analysis). This was observed by participants and underlines potential unreliability. One user commented he would **only** rate useful articles (positively) while another said he would **only** give poor ratings saying *"if you get what you want, you very rarely report that".* Assumptions were expressed that all online ratings are only ever very negative or very positive: *"usually you only get the extreme."*

The purpose of providing ratings was misinterpreted by two participants who assumed the rating system was for overall customer service, and again would only give very high or very low ratings.

Another participant comments: *"I wouldn't ever look to see a rating to help me decide that* [reliability] *so I don't think it's relevant to give my opinion to help other people."* His choice of what to trust is based on the relevance of the article title.

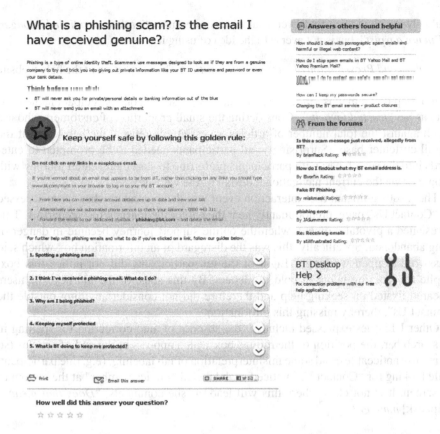

Fig. 2. Screenshot of example article return screen

For those who favored the contribution of the forums there is also a perceived lack of trust of ratings on the provider website.

Abandoning online help and using helpdesks. Three out of ten participants would go straight to a helpdesk to resolve the issues presented by the scenarios, without considering other alternative solutions.

The other seven referred to phoning the helpdesk as a *"last resort"*, preferring if needed a "web-chat" with a helpdesk agent. These users assume that, via this route, they will make contact with an agent immediately rather than having to go through IVR queues, hold the call or submit a form (for which the response timescale is unknown), commenting, *"in this day and age you want to solve your problems right away, everyone at least expects to"*.

Previous positive experience of other support sites' web-chat facilities helps with acceptance: *"I had a problem with Amazon and there was a little person* [pop-up box] *saying can I help you and he sorted it out straight away...which was good rather than having to talk to them on the phone."*

Additionally, a significant advantage of web-chat is that any language barriers – particularly when dealing with off-shore call centres are avoided. However the participant who would always phone first finds web-chat a barrier because, "*it takes me a little bit longer, as I'm not a typist*", but is not averse to the idea of using it.

Navigation and Presentation of Support Information. The navigation of the help website is clear. All participants used the navigational tabs (predominantly "Help") and the related drop-down menus - indeed by the end of the user test one participant named this route as her "*trusted favorite*". Considering the small proportion of customers who use search against the total number of articles accessed this reflects the behaviors of the overall customer base. (Surprisingly, all participants needed to be prompted to enter words into the search bar; with participants preferring to start their search journey with Google or via the current navigational design of the website).

The most significant user interaction event was demonstrated when users accessed the "Contact Us" page, predominantly near the end of the journey for Scenario 1. This represented a pivotal moment, when the online support journey became in danger of being abandoned. Specifically, this was the disregard of an information box which said "Password stopped working?" Eight of the ten participants did not notice this box, despite the lettering being in bold red letters. By this stage of the journey, the users appeared fixated on seeking help and therefore did not consider anything outside the "Contact Us", thereby missing this information.

Other UI issues expressed included: the absence of auto-correction for spelling in the search bar, the position of the ratings box which appears at the end of articles (so not readily noticeable), and some misinterpretation of tab labeling. (e.g. one participant, while looking for "Contact Us" noticed a tab labeled "Find a Number" at the bottom of the screen. It is not clear where this will lead, as she comments, "*Does that mean a* [helpdesk] *number?*"

5   Recommendations

Supporting customers in their own language – Semantic Search. Due to the variety in how search terms are expressed (see "Results") it is suggested that a semantic search capability [8] is implemented to address not only this but user intent and context. For example, the search terms that were entered as requests for help should return information which reflect these.

Query expansion and spell-checking of search terms may also help with filtering searches, ensuring accuracy and reducing the number of returned articles.

Supporting customers in their own language – editorial changes. Some simple changes to the content can be effective – 3 are outlined here. First, from the user tests and from the verbatim analysis, it was clear that some users were using both the search bar and the comments box to enter direct requests for help. Two options are possible to resolve this: (a) provide a fuller explanation of the purpose of the boxes and what to expect as a result of entering information, and (b) present an alternative box where users can enter requests for help, at an earlier stage in the journey to the observed arrival at the "Contact Us" page. Second, for the phone line fault check example (see page 7), a simple but effective change would result from changing the words given in the options available for diagnosing faults into customers' language (and not presenting words by which the enterprise categorizes faults, which is currently the case). Finally, when asking customers to enter a phone number into the phone line fault checker, make allowances for how they normally read and use phone numbers – e.g. allow enough space for these permutations within the tool and if errors are still experienced, explain why it is not working [9].

Reliability of information - Ratings. Many returned articles give instructions which may take customers away from the website or indeed the computer (if it involves checking cables), meaning they are unlikely to go back to the online article at a later stage to rate it as useful or not (most will find what they want and leave, or will forget or not notice the ratings box). So, it is recommended to rate usefulness of the **entire** experience (some assume this is what the ratings box is for anyway). This is currently done via other survey methods for overall customer experience and could be extended to include the online experience.

Ratings given are either very good or very poor, with little in between. Users assume this, and therefore may disregard them as they only reflect "the extreme". In turn, for analysis, they are not reliable indicators of how well articles meet user needs. Depending on the article (i.e. not those with lists of actions – as above), the recommendation is to remove the request for numerical (star) ratings and present only a text feedback box which is (a) presented more prominently, (b) worded in a way which outlines the purpose and benefit of doing so to the customer and (c) use text analytics to distill the keywords and expressions raised. Text analytics and click-through data can then inform the content designer of which articles work for customers using qualitative data, and in turn support content can be confidently presented back to customers as "Answers others found helpful". Conversely, articles which are not useful can be identified and re-worked as needed.

Reliability of Information - Forums. The test participants who valued the contribution of forums found them after searching on Google. For those who did not value them, they would never have looked to them for advice in the first place. As a result, there may be a case for not including forums on the support site. There is an element of risk in this, in that customers may look to un-moderated forums on the external Internet for solutions, but as this is a tried and tested method for some, it can be argued that customers will locate what is useful to them via trial and error. In this regard, space on the website can be used for provider-generated content only, which for many participants appeared to be the only trustworthy content available.

Changes in the UI to Minimize Online Journey Abandonment. Several minor changes to the UI can be recommended. However the most significant change recommended regards the following example:

This recommendation is based on the probability that the customer is (by this stage) fixated on contacting their provider, (see Results, page 9), and reflects a participant's comment that *"If the message had been in the "Contact Us" box I probably would have clicked on it"*. Eight of the ten participants missed this box in the Current UI (see Fig. 3. left), so theoretically 80 % of customers are more likely to notice this box in the Recommended UI (Fig. 3, right), and take action accordingly. Again theoretically this could lead to a potential 80 % reduction of helpdesk contacts as a result. (This of course would need further testing, with success measured through web analytics).

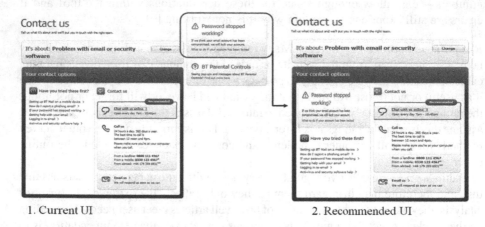

1. Current UI   2. Recommended UI

Fig. 3. Recommended change to position of "Password Stopped Working?" box

6 Conclusions

Our first conclusion is that an enterprise's understanding of, at a macro-level, the IS and IR strategies of its user base, is a vital first step in prioritizing where to concentrate efforts for improvement. For our research, this was based on manually analyzing four sets of quantitative data to identify this. In future these inputs should be integrated and automated for efficiency - although the manual approach is workable for a research project, for continuous business operations it is too labor and time-intensive.

Our second conclusion is that not all customers will want to, or be able to, help themselves by accessing all their support information online. With a diverse customer base and product range it is a worthy ambition to aim for a high percentage of support transactions to be conducted online without but in practical terms this may not always be possible. However, many of the recommendations from the user tests for minor content-based changes (e.g. matching article language to customer language) and more significant changes (e.g. introducing more sophisticated semantic search engine capabilities) can enable the enterprise to maximize the expertise which users already demonstrate in dealing with their own problems, and their willingness to do so.

Our final conclusion is that, theoretically, by reducing operational costs for the vast majority of self-helpers, investment can be made to enhance customer support for the minority – e.g. for dealing with complex issues and to support more vulnerable and less confident customers. In conjunction with making interventions in the customer journey as above, this could result in customer support being optimized for all, with seamless integration between channels where needed [2]. This is a long-term opportunity and one which could be considered for all large enterprises.

References

1. Hirt, M., Willmott, P.: Strategic principles for competing in the digital age. McKinsey Quarterly (2014) http://www.mckinsey.com/insights/strategy/strategic_principles_for_competing_in_the_digital_age
2. Davies Hickman Partners: The Autonomous Customer 2013, p. 6 (2013). www.avaya.com/usa/documents/the_autonomous_customer_survey_2013.pdf
3. Ingwersen, P., Jarvelin, K.: The Turn, Integration of Information Seeking and Retrieval in Context. Kluwer International Series on Information Retrieval, pp. 23–24. Springer, New York (2005)
4. RStudio and Inc. Shiny: Web Application Framework for R. R package version 0.10.2.1 (2014). http://CRAN.R-project.org/package=shiny
5. Thompson, S., Orlikowski, W.: Leveraging the web for customer engagement: a case study of BT's debatescape. MIT Sloan School Center for Information Systems Research Working Paper 380 (2010)
6. Marchionini, G., White, R.: Find what you need, understand what you find. Int. J. Hum. Comput. Interact. **23**(3), 205–237 (2010)
7. Lee, H.-E., Yoon, W.C.: Types of document search tasks and users' cognitive information seeking strategies. In: Yamamoto, S. (ed.) HCI 2014, Part I. LNCS, vol. 8521, pp. 449–460. Springer, Heidelberg (2014)
8. Ceri, S., et al.: Semantic Search. In: Web Information Retrieval, Data-Centric Systems and Applications, Chap. 12, pp. 181–206. Springer, Heidelberg (2013)
9. Nielsen, J.: 10 Usability Heuristics for User Interface Design (1995). http://www.nngroup.com/articles/ten-usability-heuristics/

Digital Rights Strategies in a Virtual World Marketplace

Yuanrong Hu, Si Fan, and Qiuhong Wang[(✉)]

School of Management, Huazhong University of Science and Technology,
Wuhan, China
qhwang@mail.hust.edu.cn

Abstract. This paper adopts the Heckman two-step model to analyze the impact of copyright strategy on sales performance of digital product, using the panel data comes from online virtual goods transaction website Xstreet.com. The results show that (1) significant relationship exists between sales performance and copyright strategy of digital product, but the influence of each copyright strategy on sales performance are different; (2) A seller's copyright structure within same product line can also affect sales performance of a digital product, thus in order to optimize the copyright combinations, a seller should fully consider the copyright strategy within the whole product line.

Keywords: Copyright strategy · Digitial products · Virtual products

1 Introduction

Rapid advances in Web2.0 and digital technologies now enable end-users to create and share digital contents through Internet. A large amount of user generated content (UGC) are created on social networks such as wikis, blogs, Twitter feeds, as well as in virtual worlds such as Second Life [1]. The proliferation of UGC greatly enhances the production and consumption of digital content, and thus offers a great business chance for content providers. Meanwhile, concerns were raised about digital rights violations. To protect their benefit, Many right-holders adopt technological methods, i.e. DRM (Digital right management system), to deterring rights piracy. However, copyright control technologies make them confronted with a digital dilemma [2]. On the one hand, the copyright protection technologies allow rights-holders well control the permissions granted to end-users (i.e. View, Copy, edit, move, etc.). On the other hand, it may in turn decrease demand due to the possible restriction on user rights. Prior researchers have done a lot of works on copyright protection strategy (either technological or administrative) to compete with piracy [3–6] and impact of the piracy on digital product sales performance [7–10]. Some find that both the legal demand and the willingness to pay for digital content will increase without DRM due to the increased consumer utility [6]. Therefore, in order to maximize profits, the rights-holders must find the optimal copyright strategies to keep balance between copyright protection and the legal use of end-users [5]. This study investigates the relationship between digital rights strategy and digital products' sales. Our main objectives is to (1) examine how copyright strategies affect sales performance of digital contents; (2) examine how the

© Springer International Publishing Switzerland 2015
F.F.-H. Nah and C.-H. Tan (Eds.): HCIB 2015, LNCS 9191, pp. 300–311, 2015.
DOI: 10.1007/978-3-319-20895-4_28

rights-holders set copyright strategies optimize copyright strategies under multi-product sales and different market structure.

We base our research on the online virtual goods transaction website www.Xstreet. com. Xstreet is the official transaction marketplace of Second Life. More than two million items and 22 categories of user created virtual goods are for sale on Xstreet SL. These virtual goods have many similarities to digital products. Firstly, they are digital and can be sale and distributed though Internet. Secondly, creators of virtual goods in Second Life own entire copyright of the product. To maximize benefits, sellers in Xstreet adopt different copyright strategies for virtual goods [11]. The three basic right permission (i.e. copy, modify, and transfer) are very similar to the three main rights of digital content illustrated in DRM system (i.e. render, transport, and derivative right) [12]. Thirdly, Different copyright strategy can affect user's perceived utility and thus have impact on demand [11, 13]. These similarities provide the probability of applying our findings based on virtual goods to general digital products. Furthermore, Xstreet has tens of thousands of active buyers and sellers. According to Second Life statistics, the daily transactions for virtual goods are 1.2 million in 2013.[1] So it provides us a favorable research platform to study the relationship between the copyright strategy and digital content sales performance.

Our findings suggest that (1) Sales performance of digital content significantly correlates to its copyright permission. Relative to no right permission strategy, the only modify strategy and the only transfer strategy will decrease the product's probability of entering into top 1000 sales ranking list, while other four strategies can increase the probability. (2) Other things being equal, digital contents with completely open copyright (e.g. Copy &modify& transfer) will cannibalize the market share of seller's other products in same category or with same function. The right-holders shall optimize his copyright strategies by taking into consideration the permission setting of other similar goods in his own product line or even the whole market.

The rest of this paper is organized as follows. Next section reviews the related literatures. Section 3 presents research date and some theoretical assumptions. Section 4 presents the estimation results and research findings. Section 5 concludes the paper.

2 Related Literatures

Our paper is directly related to four streams of literature, including the literatures about (1) virtual goods consumption; (2) Digital Rights Management (DRM); (3) information goods pricing and versioning; (4) open source product.

2.1 Virtual Goods Consumption

Various studies focus on consumer's virtual item purchasing behavior in virtual world [14–18]. Guo et al. (2009) provides us the empirical evidence that factors such as social

---

[1] http://community.secondlife.com/t5/Featured-News/bg-p/blog_feature_news

influence, trust, perceived profit-making opportunities are most concerned by purchasers [16]. Therefore, except the function of virtual item, players also compare prices and seller's credit ratings before purchasing. Guo et al (2011) further find that the higher degree of customization will significantly increase the consumer's purchase intention [17]. Yee (2005) also find consumers can get satisfaction with customizing their avatar appearance and using unique accessories [18].

These literatures about consuming behavior in virtual world constitute solid theoretical basis for our study. In SecondLife, Modify permission can increase the customization degree by enabling purchasers to change the original design. Transfer permission can increase buyers' profit-making opportunity in the future. Thus, different right permissions can definitely affect user's purchasing behavior. However, prior literatures do not identify the right permission of virtual items as an important factor influencing sales performance. Basulin et al. (2009) recognize the problem and conduct an empirical study to examine the relationship between price and permission of virtual items in Second Life. the results show the positive effect of "copy" permission on virtual goods pricing strategy [11].

Our paper is closest to the research of [11] but differs from it in four aspects. First, we consider right permission in our model as a copyright strategy, not as one of the product attributes. Second, we aim to test the relationship between copyright strategies and sales performance (not price) of virtual product. Third, we also examine how sellers optimize copyright strategies under multi-product sales condition and different market structure. Fourth, we view virtual goods as one special form of digital content and thus extend our conclusions to digital product area.

2.2   Digital Rights Management (DRM)

DRM, which is defined as technologies, tools and processes to protect intellectual property during digital content business, can help right holders well control the use and distribution of the digital content and effectively prevent piracy [4]. Rosenblatt et al. describe the three main rights granted to users in DRM: render (including view, print and play), transport (including copy, move and loan) and derivative rights (including extract, edit and loan) [12]. The rights description in [4] and [12] are similar to the main three types of rights (i.e. COPY, MODIFY, and TRANSFER) in our setting. [19] and [20] find evidence about the role of DRM in enhancing producer's control ability in movie industry. However, Sinha et al. [6] empirically demonstrate that the revenue of music producers will increase as they supply DRM-free rather than DRM music in the market. DRM-free environment can increase the demand and consumers' willingness to pay for legal product [6]. Foroughi (2002) consider that, in order to maximize the profits, the rights-holders must seek to find the optimal copyright strategies to keep a delicate balance between copyright protection and the legal accessibility of end-users [5]. Our paper is different from [5] and [6] in that it presents a more specific model involved eight different copyright permissions and investigate how these permissions affect sales performance. Thus, our work contributes this literature by quantifying the influence of different copyright strategy on sale.

2.3 Information Goods Versioning

From copyright perspective, virtual goods share some similar features with information goods. Free-trial software is analogous to virtual goods with copy and transfer permissions. Customized information goods are similar to the modified virtual item. While online sharing music and open source software are in common with transferable virtual product. The versioning of information goods has attracted considerable interest in the literature. Shapiro proposes that content provider can execute price discrimination by supplying different version in the market to satisfy consumer demand of different level. By this way they can gain more consumer surplus [21]. Chen et al.(2007) and Bhargava et al.(2008) indicate versioning is optimal for the seller when there is multiple outside option for customers and high-end customers would not be attractive by lower-quality version [22, 23]. In our paper, we consider copyright permission as a method of versioning. Virtual goods seller can set different copyright permission for similar products to meet different needs and thus attract more potential consumers. Meanwhile, our results suggest some permission strategy may not necessarily increase sales. Rather, it could lead to cannibalization effect in same category. This paper adds to the existing literatures a delicate analysis of cannibalization effect occurring in similar products with different copyright permissions.

2.4 Open Source Software (OSS) and License

OSS is software that is subject to a particular type of license. The OSS licenses ranges from very permissive to more restrictive [24]. Conversely, Proprietary software normally restricts user's rights to copy, redistribute, or modify. Sen et al. (2011) suggest that more restrictive license will decrease user's perceived value from two aspects: (1) limit the commercial use in the future; (2) lack of compatibility with other software with less restrictive license. Thus, the less restrictive (more permissive) the license is, the more the user OSS can attract [25]. Subramaniam et al. (2009) find that if great efforts are needed to improve OSS, the following developer would prefer less restrictive license [26]. The situation is similar for digital product, especially in an age of UGC. UGC is usually created based on the existing digital products. For the creative work requiring more professional technology, users want more permission to copy, share or resell the product so that they can gain revenue. In virtual world Second Life, modifying a virtual good such as Script products is difficult for common users, so only-modify permission cannot positively affect user interest and sales performance. By contrast, full permission will attract more users and developers due to the possibility to sell the improved products in the future.

3 Hypothesis and Research Model

In this section, we outline the main hypothesis addressed in this paper and discuss the theoretical rationale underlying each hypothesis.

Different copyright permission would affect user's expected utilities and purchasing decision. From this perspective, Second Life provides us a rich date pool to study the relationship between the copyright strategy and digital product sales performance. Different from other virtual world, Second Life users are an important part of the largest user-generated 3D virtual goods economy in the world. They create, merchandise, and sell virtual goods for Linden dollars, which is exchangeable for real currencies such as U.S. dollars. Furthermore, Creators of virtual goods in Second Life own entire copyright of their creations and can set different copyright permissions to protect their intellectual property and limit the usage rights of next owner. Though combination of the three basic permissions, there are eight permission strategies seller can set: Copy-only, Modify-only, Transfer-only, Copy & Modify, Copy & Transfer, Modify & Transfer, Copy & Modify & Transfer (full-permission), and No-permission. If a consumer gets a product with Copy & Modify permission, he can revise the original design of the product according his own preference (modify permission) and make a lot of copies of this product (copy permission). However, resell and redistribute the original product and the duplicates are not allowed without Transfer permission.

3.1   The Impact of Copyright Permission on Sales Performance

Basulin (2009) points out consumers in virtual world may tend to use many same products at the same time [11]. For example, consumers may need more than one of same virtual chairs to decorate his virtual kitchen. Copy permission ensure consumer legally own and use the copies of the virtual product without any additional cost, thus can increase the utility of consumer and encourage the purchasing behavior. The existing literature revealed that, customized products and service become the important competitive advantage of online commerce [27, 28]. Compared with traditional products, customized goods can meet consumer's special preference and increase purchasing willingness. Modify permission enable purchasers to change the product's original design, thus can satisfy the different demand of individual customer. Therefore, we consider copy permission and modify permission have positive impact on sales.

Berry et al (2002) consider convenience as a method to measure the level of time and effort saving in buying and using the product [29]. The more convenient the purchasing process is, the stronger the consumer's willingness to purchase due to the decreased transaction cost. Thus, convenience is positive correlated with purchase willingness. Transfer permission grants consumer the legal right to resell and redistribute the virtual product to others in the future, which can reduce the decision complexity. If the product is not satisfactory, purchaser can resell it to minimize his lost. Additionally, Transfer permission can increase buyers' profit-making opportunity in the future. Thus, we consider transfer permission have positive impact on sales.

Based on the above analysis, we hypothesize as follows:

Hypothesis 1.1(H1.1): COPY, MODIFY, TRANSFER permission all have positive impact on sales performance.

If the three permissions all have positive impact on sales performance, we can further assume that product with more-than-one permissions would be more popular than which with single permissions. We further state the hypothesis as follows:

Hypothesis 1.2(H1.2): Any combination of the three permissions has a larger impact on sales performance than single permission.

3.2 The Cannibalization Effect of the Copyright Permission on Sales Performance of Products Within the Same Product Line

In general, multiple product manufactures tend to provide a wide range of products under same product line so that consumers have more choice to meet their individual preference and budget constraint. For instance, Hyundai produces advanced limousines XG for wealthy customers, Accent for consumers of small cars, and Santa Fe for consumers favor multi-purpose vehicle. A lot of researches have shown that product variety strategy can effectively promote sales and expand market share [30–32]. Similar to conventional product producer, many digital companies like Borland sold different versions of their programs—one was low priced and could not be copied and the other was high priced and could [21]. Shapiro and Varian (1998) suggest that digital information goods can be differentiated though granting different rights for user to store, duplicate, print or otherwise manipulates the digital product [21]. Thus, copyright permissions can be used as important method of distinguishing digital products. However, product variety also leads to the cannibalization effect within same product line. If digital product producer provide different versions so as to induce consumers to self-select, the cannibalization may occur within same product line. Considering the dual role copyright permission paly, it is important for profit-maximizing right-holders to decide whether they should set same copyright permission within product line or not. We state our hypothesis as following:

Hypothesis 2 (H2): The cannibalization effect exists between products within same product line when different copyright permissions assigned to them.

4 Data and Econometric Specifications

4.1 Data and Variables

The panel data used in this paper comes from online virtual goods transaction website www.Xstreet.com. We focus on products in 5 categories: Animations, Arts, Audio and Video, Business, Scripts. During the study period starting from January 2011 to May 2011, we collect the detailed information of all products in focused categories, including item ID, item name, seller name, price, right permission, the highest history rank, current rank, number of reviews, number of discussions, and number of votes, score and item category. Thus the final panel data have 20-weeks.

4.1.1 Dependent Variable

Given Linden Lab did not officially publish transaction date such as cumulative transaction volume, we use sales rank as a proxy for the number of products sold in XStreet market. XStreet.com lists the Top 1000 best-selling products, with 1 corresponding to the highest selling product. Literatures related to economics and marketing revealed that sales and sales rank follows a Pareto distribution [33, 34]. The higher the rank is, the more the sales, and vice versa. Thus we use RANK and RANK_YN as an indicator of digit product sales performance in second life. RANK_YN is a 0-1 variable to denote that whether the products enter into the TOP 1000 ranks (equal to 1) or not (equal to 0). RANK is the actual ranking of the product on the TOP list.

4.1.2   Independent Variables

In Second Life, The combination of three basic permissions (Copy, Modify, and Transfer) forms eight copyright permission strategies. We create a set of copyright dummy variables to represent seller's copyright setting: CRC, CRM, CRT, CRCM, CRMT, CRCT, CRCMT, and CRN. CRC, CRM, CRT represent Copy, Modify, Transfer permission only respectively. CRCM represent Copy & Modify permission, CRMT represent Modify & Transfer permission, CRCT represent Copy & Transfer permission, CRCMT represent full permission, CRN represent No permission.

4.1.3   Control Variables

In our study, we control for other factors that could affect sales performance but are not explored in this research: price, score, category, market competition factors, and total number of products sold by seller.

Prior research shows that online scoring system play a very important role in establishing consumer trust and thus is a crucial factor affecting seller's success [35]. We incorporate seller's score into our model, denoted by SCORES. In order to control the impact of business scale on sales performance, we incorporate the total number of product of a seller into our model, represented by TOL. Two variables (WEEK, WEEKS) are introduced to control the change of market factors, such as the total number of products for sale in XStreet, the total weekly transaction volume, WEEK reflect the linear impact of linear factors, and equal to $0 \sim 19$. WEEKS reflect nonlinear impact of unobserved factors, and equals to $0^2 \sim 19^2$. Finally, we create four dummy variables (ANI, ARTS, AUVI, BUZ) that control the impact of category on sales performance. The ANI=1 when the product is in animation category, otherwise ANI=0. Similarly, ARTS=1, AUVI=1, BUZ=1 when the virtual product is in arts, Audio and Video, Business category respectively. Script is benchmark group.

The summary statistics of all variables discussed above is given in Table 1.

Table 1. Summary Statistics (N=1,360,483)

Variables	Mean	Std.dev.	Min	Max
PRICE	416.6456	18887.21	0	10000000
RANK	486.9281	282.9132	1	1000
RANK_Y	0.0013598	0.0368506	0	1
SCORES	4.10082	0.667001	1	5
TOL	176.3738	461.7694	1	2936
CRC	0.107036	0.309159	0	1
CRM	0.062512	0.242084	0	1
CRT	0.147555	0.354658	0	1
CRCM	0.20795	0.405841	0	1
CRMT	0.219565	0.413952	0	1
CRCT	0.042979	0.20281	0	1
CRCMT	0.122365	0.327707	0	1
CRN	0.079822	0.271018	0	1

4.2   Results

4.2.1   Copyright Strategy Impact on Sales

In order to eliminate selection bias, we adopt the following Heckman two-step model to examine the impact of copyright strategy on sales performance of digital products. In step 1, we estimate the relationship between the copyright strategy and the probability of a product entering the TOP 1000 rank. In step 2, we incorporate the inverse Mills ratio (calculated from step 1) into the equation and further analyze the impact of copyright strategy on product's sales performance (RANK). In order to reduce the disturbance of numeric volatility, we take the log form of RANK_YN, RANK and TOL. Due to many sellers provide freebie goods (price=0), PRICE is transferred to In (price+1). The coefficient estimates ($\beta 1$-$\beta 7$) for CRC, CRM, CRT, CRCM, CRMT, CRCT, CRCMT are of our interest. CRN is benchmark variable. Table 2 reports the main results of the econometric estimation.

Table 2. Estimats for Heckman two-step model (N=1,360,483)

VARIBLE	RANK_YN	log(RANK)
CRC	-0.0271	0.1805
CRM	-0.4605***	0.8326+
CRT	-0.2473***	0.1511
CRCM	0.3852***	-0.4175+
CRMT	0.1590**	-0.0789
CRCT	0.1349+	0.2386
CRCMT	0.1703**	-0.1072
ANI	0.4164***	-0.3356
ARTS	-0.4953***	0.0326
AUVI	0.2325***	-0.5478***
BUZ	-0.2058***	0.3551**
log(PRICE+1)	0.2140***	0.1294*
SCORE	0.3339***	-0.2628
log（TOL）	-0.1226***	0.1433***
WEEK	-0.0071	0.0165
WEKKS	0.0003	-0.0004
Invers Mills ratio		-0.3876
R^2	0.1741	0.1045
Chi^2/F	3325.95***	10.54***

$$\text{probit}(\text{RANK}_{YN_{it}}) = \beta_0 + \beta_1 \text{CRC}_{it} + \beta_2 \text{CRM}_{it} + \beta_3 \text{CRT}_{it} + \beta_4 \text{CRCM}_{it} + \beta_5 \text{CRMT}_{it} +$$
$$\beta_6 \text{CRCT}_{it} + \beta_7 \text{CRCMT}_{it} + \beta_8 \text{ANI}_i + \beta_9 \text{ARTS}_i + \beta_{10} \text{AUVI}_i + \beta_{11} \text{BUZ}_i + \beta_{12} \log(\text{PRICE}_{it} + 1) + \beta_{13} \text{SCORES}_{it} + \beta_{14} \log(\text{TOL}_{it}) + \beta_{15} \text{WEEK}_t + \beta_{16} \text{WEEKS}_t + \varepsilon_{1it}$$

(step 1)

$$\log(\text{RANK}_{it}) = \beta_0 + \beta_1 \text{CRC}_{it} + \beta_2 \text{CRM}_{it} + \beta_3 \text{CRT}_{it} + \beta_4 \text{CRCM}_{it} + \beta_5 \text{CRMT}_{it} +$$
$$\beta_6 \text{CRCT}_{it} + \beta_7 \text{CRCMT}_{it} + \beta_8 \text{ANI}_i + \beta_9 \text{ARTS}_i + \beta_{10} \text{AUVI}_i + \beta_{11} \text{BUZ}_i + \beta_{12} \log(\text{PRICE}_{it} + 1) + \beta_{13} \text{SCORES}_{it} + \beta_{14} \log(\text{TOL}_{it}) + \beta_{15} \text{WEEK}_t + \beta_{16} \text{WEEKS}_t + \beta_{17} \lambda_{it} + \varepsilon_{2it}$$

(step 2)

Note that the coefficient of CRC, CRM, and CRT in RANK_YN model is all negative, though the coefficient of CRC is not significant. That means that products with single permission have lower probability of entering TOP 1000 rankings than those with no permissions. Thus, hypothesis H1.1 is not approved. Instead, the coefficient for CRCM, CRCT, and CRCMT in RANK_YN model is significant and positive. The coefficient of CRMT is positive but not significant. The results indicate that the probability of entering TOP 1000 rankings is higher for goods with multiple permissions than those with single and no permissions. Thus, hypothesis H1.2 is approved.

In general, the estimates for RANK_YN indicate that the multiple permission strategy is superior to single permission strategy. Among all copyright strategies, the copy&modify work best. However, we should also note that all coefficient of our interest are not significant in RANK model (step 2). This indicates that the promotion effect of copyright strategy only exists before the products entering the TOP ranks. Thus at the early stage of promotion, the seller should optimize the copyright strategy to gain market share rapidly. Once the product list in Top 1000 ranking, right permission is not a primary factor for consumer's purchasing decision.

4.2.2 Cannibalization Effect

Generally, product variety strategies can be effective in expanding market share [30–32]. However, Prior research has generated substantial evidence that extensive differentiation can lead to significant cannibalization within the firm's product line [36, 37]. On SL virtual product market, a lot of products with similar function are sold with different copyright permission. In a particular category, if a seller grants his products with varies permission, the cannibalization may exist between these products. In this part we will further analyze how the seller's copyright distribution in his product line affects sales performance.

Consider a seller have many products on sale with varies permissions. We construct a set of variables CR_k/CR_j (k,j=1,2....7, and $k{\neq}j$) to identify sellers copyright distribution (i=1 for copy, 2 for modify, 3 for transfer, 4 for copy&modify, 5 for modify&transfer, 6 for copy&transfer, 7 for copy&modify&transfer). If a product is granted CRM permission, then j=4. CR_j represents the number of products with CRM strategy the seller provides. CR_k represents the number of products with other 6 permissions respectively. Thus we totally get 42 variables. For each $j{\neq}4$, we set $CR_k/CR_j=0$. We use these variables to measure the impact of other products' permission strategy on a products' probability of entering the TOP 1000 list (Table 3).

We use the following Probit model to test our hypothesis H2.

$$\text{probit}(RANK_{YN_{it}})=\beta_0+\beta_1CRC_{it}+\beta_2CRM_{it}+\beta_3CRT_{it}+\beta_4CRCM_{it}+\beta_5CRMT_{it}$$
$$+\beta_6CRCT_{it}+\beta_7CRCMT_{it}+\beta_8ANI_i+\beta_9ARTS_i+\beta_{10}AUVI_i+\beta_{11}BUZ_i$$
$$+\beta_{12}\log(PRICE_{it}+1)+\beta_{13}SCORES_{it}+\beta_{14}\log(TOL_{it})+\beta_{15}WEEK_t$$
$$+\beta_{16}WEEKS_t+\gamma CR_{kit}/CR_{jit}+\varepsilon_{1it}$$

Note that, $\gamma=[\gamma\_1, \gamma\_2,..., \gamma\_42]$.

Table 3. Impact of copyright distribution on sales performance

i \ k	1	2	3	4	5	6	7
1		+	+	-	+	+	-
2	+		-	-	-		
3	-	-		-	-		-
4	-	-	+		+	-	-
5	+	-		-		-	-
6	+		-	+	+		-
7	-	-	-	-	-	-	

The estimation results show that only some coefficients are statistically significant. Therefore we adopt the non-parameters symbols test to focus on the signs of the estimated regression coefficients.The results are reported in Table 7. The signs in line 3 and line 7 are all negative, indicating that a produts' sales would be cannibalized by produts with CRT and CRCMT permissions.

5 Strengths and Weaknesses of the Study

This paper is one of the first steps in examining the impact of copyright permission strategy on digital products transaction in a virtual market. Applying Heckman models, we are able to find that virtual goods' copyright permission settings on Second Life are not random rules, but strategic in this user-generated virtual word. Price strategy and copyright permission of virtual goods in Second Life is a leverage of selling virtual. Some results of our initial data analysis are consistent with prior research work.

This paper has its limitations. As for the great volume data, it takes a quite long time to download the whole dataset and the Linden Lab strategically makes a fast and complete download impossible. So we cannot get the whole dataset from XStreet; meanwhile, sellers do adjust their item settings along the time, but we cannot capture how, when and what they change, which lower our dataset's accuracy. We also can see from our data collection that a great amount of items in XStreet have never been paid attention or even been purchased, i.e. items without Votes records. There are quite a few missing values for a certain number of items. We do not have virtual goods transaction volume data; even though we use XStreet sales rank as proxy of buyers' demand, the result still contains bias. In addition, definition of "similar-item" is not accurate. Given the varieties of subcategories, we think items within same category can be totally different, which will result in biased and inconsistent parameter estimations.

In this paper, we discuss the impact of copyright strategies on virtual goods transaction in Second Life Marketplace. These virtual goods bear certain similarities with other information goods, i.e. e-book, software and online music. Prior research on copyrights of information goods focus on a market structure with few vendors and mass consumers, while our study focus on an online market with many creators and sellers. Some of our conclusions can be extended to other digital goods. We hope this paper will shed light on users of virtual world and attract practitioners and researchers to explore the general or universal optimal permission strategy that can be taken by all digital goods.

Acknowledgements. We thank for the financial support from the Natural Science Foundation of China (71371082) and the innovation research funding (2013TS088) from the Huazhong University of Science and Technology.

References

1. Halbert, D.: Mass culture and the culture of the masses: a manifesto for user-generated rights. In: Vand. J. Ent. & Tech. L., 11, 921(2008)
2. Aichroth, P., Hasselbach, J.: Incentive management for virtual goods: about copyright and creative production in the digital domain. Virtual Goods **2003**, 70–81 (2003)
3. Jamkhedkar, P.A., Heileman, G.L.: Digital rights management architectures. Comput. Electr. Eng. **35**(2), 376–394 (2009)
4. Fetscherin, M.: Digital rights management: what the consumer wants. J. Digit. Asset Manage. **2**(3–4), 143–149 (2006)
5. Foroughi, A., Albin, M., Gillard, S.: Digital rights management: a delicate balance between protection and accessibility. J. Inf. Sci. **28**(5), 389–395 (2002)
6. Sinha, R.K., Machado, F.S., Sellman, C.: Don't think twice, it's all right: Music piracy and pricing in a DRM-free environment. J. Mark. **74**(2), 40–54 (2010)
7. Chen, Y.N., Png, I.: Information goods pricing and copyright enforcement: Welfare analysis. Inf. Syst. Res. **14**(1), 107–123 (2003)
8. Khouja, M., Park, S.: Optimal pricing of digital experience goods under piracy. J. Manage. Inf. Syst. **24**(3), 109–141 (2007)
9. Khouja, M., Smith, M.A.: Optimal pricing for information goods with piracy and saturation effect. Eur. J. Oper. Res. **176**(1), 482–497 (2007)
10. Khouja, M., Rajagopalan, H.K.: Can piracy lead to higher prices in the music and motion picture industries&quest. J. Oper. Res. Soc. **60**(3), 372–383 (2009)
11. Ba, S., Ke, D., Stallaert, J., Zhang, Z.: Why give away something for nothing? Investigating virtual goods pricing and permission strategies. In: ACM Transactions on Management Information Systems (TMIS), 1(1), p. 4 (2010)
12. Rosenblatt, W., Trippe, W., Mooney, S.: Digital Rights Management: Business and Technology (2002)
13. Ba, S., Ke, D., Stallaert, J., Zhang, Z.: An empirical analysis of virtual goods pricing strategies in virtual worlds. In: PACIS, p. 86 (2010)
14. Lehdonvirta, V.: Virtual item sales as a revenue model: identifying attributes that drive purchase decisions. Electron. Commer. Res. **9**(1–2), 97–113 (2009)
15. Martin, J.: Consuming code: use-value, exchange-value, and the role of virtual goods in second life. J. Fosr Virtual Worlds Res. **1**(2), 1–21 (2008)
16. Guo, Y., Barnes, S.: Virtual item purchase behavior in virtual worlds: an exploratory investigation. Electronic Commer. Res. **9**(1–2), 77–96 (2009)
17. Guo, Y., Barnes, S.: Purchase behavior in virtual worlds: an empirical investigation in second life. Inf. Manage. **48**(7), 303–312 (2011)
18. Yee, N.: Motivations of play in MMORPGs. In: DiGRA. Vancouver, Canada (2005)
19. Waterman, D., Ji, S.W., Rochet, L.R.: Enforcement and control of piracy, copying, and sharing in the movie industry. Rev. Ind. Organ. **30**(4), 255–289 (2007)

20. Kuchinskas, S.: Mazingo: DRM plus content could equal handheld movies. Econtent-Wilton-**26**(3), 52–53 (2003)
21. Shapiro, C., Varian, H.R.: Versioning: the smart way to. Harvard Bus. Rev. **107**(6), 107 (1998)
22. Chen, Y.J., Deshadri, On Product development and pricing strategy for information goods under heterogeneous outside opportunities. Inf. Syst. Res. **18**(2), 150–172 (2007)
23. Lee, C.Y.: When is Versioning Optimal for Information Goods? (2010)
24. Sen, R., Subramaniam, C., Nelson, M.L.: Determinants of the choice of open source software license. J. Manage. Inf. Syst. **25**(3), 207–240 (2008)
25. Sen, R., Subramaniam, C., Nelson, M.L.: Open source software licenses: strong-copyleft, non-copyleft, or somewhere in between? Decis. Support Syst. **52**(1), 199–206 (2011)
26. Subramaniam, C., Sen, R., Nelson, M.L.: Determinants of open source software project success: a longitudinal study. Decis. Support Syst. **46**(2), 576–585 (2009)
27. To, P.L., Liao, C., Lin, T.H.: Shopping motivations on Internet: a study based on utilitarian and hedonic value. Technovation **27**(12), 774–787 (2007)
28. Franke, N., Schreier, M., Kaiser, U.: The "I designed it myself" effect in mass customization. Manage. Sci. **56**(1), 125–140 (2010)
29. Meuter, M.L., Ostrom, A.L., Roundtree, R.I., Bitner, M.J.: Self-service technologies: understanding customer satisfaction with technology-based service encounters. J. Mark. **64**(3), 50–64 (2000)
30. Bayus, B.L., Putsis Jr, W.P.: Product proliferation: an empirical analysis of product line determinants and market outcomes. Mark. Sci. **18**(2), 137–153 (1999)
31. Chong, J., Ho, T., Tang, C.S.: Product structure, brand width and brand share. In: Research Advances in Product Variety, Kluwer Academic Publishers, Boston, MA (1998)
32. Kekre, S., Srinivasan, K.: Broader product line: a necessity to achieve success? Manage. Sci. **36**(10), 1216–1232 (1990)
33. Sundararajan, G.O.S.A.: Are Digital Rights Valuable? Theory and Evidence from eBook Pricing (No. 06-01). CeDER Working Paper (2006)
34. Devi, J.I.: Estimating the helpfulness and economic impact of product reviews. Int. J. Innovative Res. Dev. **1**(5), 232–236 (2012)
35. Qu, Z., Zhang, H., Li, H.: Determinants of online merchant rating: Content analysis of consumer comments about Yahoo merchants. Decis. Support Syst. **46**(1), 440–449 (2008)
36. Hui, K.L.: Product variety under brand influence: an empirical investigation of personal computer demand. Manage. Sci. **50**(5), 686–700 (2004)
37. Moorthy, K.S.: Market segmentation, self-selection, and product line design. Marke. Sci. **3**(4), 288–307 (1984)

UX and Usability on Smart TV: A Case Study on a T-commerce Application

Andrea Ingrosso[1(✉)], Valentina Volpi[1,2], Antonio Opromolla[1,2], Eliseo Sciarretta[1], and Carlo Maria Medaglia[1]

[1] Link Campus University, Via Nomentana 335, 00162 Rome, Italy
{a.ingrosso,v.volpi,a.opromolla,e.sciarretta,
c.medaglia}@unilink.it
[2] ISIA Roma Design, Piazza della Maddalena 53, 00196 Rome, Italy

Abstract. Smart TVs offers new possibilities of interaction, due to the peculiarity of the device and the presence of apps. However, more usability studies on Smart TV apps are needed in order to improve the quality of the user interfaces. So, in this paper the authors focus on the interaction between user and Smart TV through remote control. In detail, they test with the users an e-commerce (or more specifically, t-commerce) application on Smart TV.

Keywords: T-commerce · Smart TV · User experience · Usability · Interfaces

1 Introduction

For over 50 years, the television has been one of the main tools for home entertainment and information [1] in most Western countries. As "entertainment furniture" it has greatly influenced the home environment, setting the type of interaction and relations among the room's elements. The greater influence occurred in the arrangement of the living room, where the television found a place of honor.

However, over the years the television has significantly changed, changing as well the type of interaction between the users and the medium itself. New devices (e.g. cable or satellite receiver, videocassette or digital video recorder, DVD player, audio amplifier) and controller (e.g. different kinds of remote controls, gesture recognition systems) were attached and integrated by television, up to the so-called Smart TV. Moreover, the succession of some technological innovations gave the television new looks and new capabilities: full colors images, lager screen sizes, less case thickness, LAN or Wi-Fi broadband connections, media sharing, smartphone connectivity (second screen), etc. A new offer in contents corresponds to the enhancement of the device. So, the Smart TV gives access to app stores, games, videos playback, social networks, web browser, streaming movies. However, the TV apps available today are not so much different from smartphone apps, while they should take advantage of the fact that they are located on a TV and make use of TV specific content [2].

In details, the Smart TV is a television including components for network connectivity, which make it able to communicate and to synchronize with other devices

© Springer International Publishing Switzerland 2015
F.F.-H. Nah and C.-H. Tan (Eds.): HCIB 2015, LNCS 9191, pp. 312–323, 2015.
DOI: 10.1007/978-3-319-20895-4_29

connected into the home network. Beside to Ethernet cable and Wi-Fi network card, a Smart TV generally consists of some other elements that make it similar to a personal computer, such as Operating System and USB ports, through which connecting various devices (e.g. keyboards) and interfaces, which greatly facilitate navigation and writing on the Internet.

However, Smart TV models differ in interaction modes and personalization features. The latest models, for example, allow an interaction through gesture or voice recognition, while a third more typical way of interaction is through remote control. A separate analysis should be done on the evolution of the remote control devices, since the lack of common guidelines on the implementation of the interfaces of these remote controls created an extremely confusing and varied set of devices [3].

In this paper the authors focus on the interaction between user and Smart TV through remote control. In detail, they test with the users an e-commerce (or more specifically, t-commerce) application on Smart TV, since there is a lack in the related literature about usability of Smart TV apps, due to the yet moderate diffusion of Smart TV devices and the recent interest in the debate about interaction guidelines for Smart TV. Moreover, the test of an application for buying products and services through television is useful as such type of services, i.e. e-commerce services, has been the drive motor for the main spread of Internet and are expected to give costumers a more complete purchase experience through Smart TV. So, in this paper the authors intend to contribute to the research on usable applications for Smart TVs by deducing some considerations from the usability test on a Smart TV application for T-commerce.

2   Related Work

Smart TV devices are a recent product on the mass market and they look promising in increasing much more in the next years [4]. Indeed, although they present well-known schemes of human-computer interaction, such as "app" (largely used on smartphone, tablet, etc.) and web sites, there are substantial changes in the user interface (hereafter, UI) and in the user experience (hereafter, UX), due to the peculiarity of the Smart TV device. So, usability studies on Smart TV apps are needed in order to improve the quality of the UIs.

However, Smart TV is the last form of a series of similar technologies, often considered as the basis for its evolution, such as Digital TV, Connected TV, Interactive TV (iTV), Internet TV, Internet Protocol TV (IPTV), etc., and discussed in usability and UX related literature. First of all, Chorianopoulos [5] drew attention to the lack of specific UI principles for the unique characteristics of iTV applications. He sustained that the usability mentality of efficiency and task completion (*effectiveness*) may not be suitable for design and expert evaluation of iTV applications, since the latter gratifies entertainment needs and leisure activities in a relaxed domestic context, rather than productivity. So, he recommended two categories of design principles: the first refers to which are the most suitable features for interactive TV applications, the second to how to design UX that supports the novel features. However, applications that involves more information processing than enjoyment could be modeled after a list of high-level principles and generic design factors. However, Chorianopoulos mainly refers to a class of TV services, such as Electronic Program Guide (EPG), Digital Video Recorder, and applications related to the broadcast TV program. Miesler et al. [6] observed that, because of the rapid growth of Smart TVs, it has been hard to establish any standards concerning UI and interaction modes. However, the identification of user-centered design, as well as the consideration of UX, is an important precondition for service adoption. According to Shin et al. [4] Smart TV is considered a very promising connecting device among different home systems (computers, telephones, electricity, security, entertainment, etc.), but its contents and services are still limited and there are many usability problems to overcome, too. So, they examined consumer's perceptions of Smart TVs and provided practical insights into developing a user-centered Smart TV interface in order to develop effective Smart TV services. In detail, designers should consider that although people turn increasingly to Smart TV for services they formerly got from other sources, however the expectations for those services change. So, the system characteristics impact on perception of enjoyment and usefulness. Moreover, perceived usability can influence behavioral intentions through attitude.

In general, many studies that concern the analysis of factors affecting consumers' adoption of Smart TVs used the Information Technology Acceptance Model (TAM) or other derived models [4, 7, 8]. It emerged that a possible reason for low service usage of Smart TVs could be the insufficient service usability and UX, mostly due to the lack of dedicated contents, competing services, and high service quality. So, the development of specialized contents for Smart TVs is expected to strengthen the differentiation from other form of similar technologies and to provide stable service quality, promoting, as a consequence, the usage of Smart TV services [8]. Also well-designed functions are capital for the acceptance of the Smart TV by users. In detail, without a proper and convenient way to control Smart TV functions all other advanced features are useless [9].

With regard to this, in studying the usability of the Smart TV the presence of different interaction modes, mainly gesture recognition and remote control, which differently influenced the usability and UX of the Smart TVs services, has to be considered. The remote control is used to navigate between different types of content, more or less interactive, since Smart TV offers a greatest number of options to the user in respect of the traditional TV. Consequently, also the number of actions performed by remote control multiplies (in addition to the channel selection and the management of basic functions, there is the interaction with different apps). Nevertheless, in the past decade the user has been accustomed to this growing complexity, firstly because of the use of various remote controls to manage the home electronics connected to the TV (video recorder, home theater, etc.), and secondly because of the use of a universal remote control with an increasing number of buttons (in order to control all the features of the electronics mentioned above). In their study on usability and usage of iTV services, Bernhaupt et al. [10] revealed that users had difficulty in text-inputs with the remote control keypads and pushed arrow buttons more than the color buttons. Liang et al. [11] conducted a usability analysis of a Smart TV music service, but, identified some usability problems that can affect also other kind of services: system response lag, difficulty in using the remote control, possibility to exit the system by accident. In investigating the usability of remote controls in regards to the currently prevalent interfaces, Lim et al. [12] found that the general remote controller had a better performance in channel selection and simple navigation composed of low-depth tasks, while the motion remote controller facilitated the ubiquitous information communication between the TV and user (especially for more advanced functions such as web browsing and entertainment factors). Moreover, the motion remote controller reduced visual distraction and was relatively preferred in subjective ratings. Nilsson Helander [2] conducted an in-depth analysis about the different ways to interact with a Smart TV (i.e. remote control, keyboard, mouse, smartphone and tablet) during the performance of different activities (i.e. TV watching, texting, menu browsing, Internet browsing, video watching, gaming) by using Natural Goals, Operations, Methods and Selection Language Test (NGOMSL) usability model. Since the interaction through remote controller might turn to be clumsy, unnatural, and unsuitable to the requirements on functions and applications of Smart TV, Li et al. [13] proposed some design and usability parameters for a hand-wave Smart TV Control Mode through Kinect. In addition, Jeong et al. [14], considered as capital to minimize user efforts while interacting with multimedia contents. So they proposed a system able to improve the speed and accuracy of the contents search in Smart TV environment by inferring user's search intent trough movement patterns.

The increasing market penetration of Smart TVs brings on these devices some services traditionally accessible through others, offering new possibilities to engage customers in a smarter way. In this sense, T-commerce (here considered as a new kind of market available for the user/customer through iTV or Smart TV applications) could create new business models [15]. According to McGuigan et al. [16], the television's marketing capability can be optimally applied in T-commerce experience. Indeed, people can use the remote control to make purchases in a new kind of shop or directly interacting with advertisements [17]. According to Omar et al. [18], T-commerce is a tool in iTV advertising that purposely facilitates the purchase of services and goods at home using a remote control through TV, instead of a telephone, PC, or PDA. As a result, it will eliminate the constraints in terms of time and space always experienced by buyers in traditional commerce experience. Omar et al. state that since iTV, provides more vivid images, words, video, and audio, the TV audience is led to consider it more attractive than traditional TV or Internet.

3   The Usability Test on the Smart TV App

In this section, the authors present the main findings from the usability study on the prototype of a Smart TV application (described in Sect. 3.1), focusing both on the description of the followed methodology (Sect. 3.2) and on the collected results (Sect. 3.3).

3.1   Description of the System

The prototype of the Smart TV application tested in the study described by the authors of this paper is part of a digital platform for electronic commerce designed for Samsung Smart TV and controlled through remote control. In detail, the platform includes a set of interactive channels for the individual merchants, who can customize contents (catalogues of products and services, company information, etc.), images, icons, menus, etc. of their own channel.

The platform provides to the final consumer a set of basic features to finalize the purchase: creating an account, adding and visualizing the products in the cart, paying the added products or services, adding one or more address, adding one or more payment card, checking the order history. So the user can surf among the different commercial channels adding the products he/she likes and then make a single purchase process.

3.2   Methodology of the Usability Test

The authors conducted a usability test on a Smart TV application for T-commerce in order to define and evaluate the usability problems of the app. Beside this, the test was also useful in order to study the general factors that may affect the interaction between user and Smart TV.

The performance of the application was evaluated against a set of criteria, defined according to the studies of Nielsen [19, 20], Norman [21], and Polillo [22]. In detail, the authors were mainly interested in evaluating: the suitability for the task (*the dialogue supports the user in the effective and efficient completion of the task*); the self-descriptiveness (*each dialogue step is immediately comprehensible through feedback from the system or is explained to the user on request*); the conformity with user expectations (*the dialogue is consistent and corresponds to the user characteristics, such as task knowledge, education, experience, and to commonly accepted conventions*); the error tolerance (*despite evident errors in input, the intended result may be achieved with either no or minimal action by the user*); the learnability (*users can easily accomplish basic tasks the first time they use the system and the dialogue supports and guides the user in learning it*); the subjective satisfaction (*the system is pleasant to use*). Generally, these criteria are applied to different kinds of devices, first of all, web sites and tablet or mobile app, while there is not a common specific methodology for evaluating the usability of T-commerce applications on Smart TV. However, since the system tested was an application as well and the mentioned criteria are general principles for Human-Computer Interaction, the authors considered them suitable for evaluating the usability of Smart TV apps, too.

The whole test was organized in 3 phases: filling the entry questionnaire, performing the required tasks, and filling the exit questionnaire.

So, first of all, the user completed an entry questionnaire consisting of a first part (identical for all) designed to know the participants habits in using digital devices (smartphone, PC, tablet, TV) and in purchasing products and services through them, and a second part that focuses on the use of Smart TV and on the purchasing of products and services through it. The authors prepared two version of the latter part, one for users that know what a Smart TV is (so they were asked to give the definition) and one for users that do not know what a Smart TV is (so they were given a definition).

Then, the authors conducted an in-person lab testing involving 10 users (5 male and 5 female) that, one by one, have to complete a purchasing process and some additional tasks by interacting with Smart TV by remote control. The group of participants was consistent with the age range of the main target audience of Smart TV (20-49 years old) [23]. Moreover, from the entry questionnaire it emerged that they also have a high educational level (they have at least bachelor's degree). During each test session, the user was performing tasks and was thinking aloud to explain what he/she was doing, why and how he/she was feeling, as he/she did it (*task walkthrough method*). A scenario approach was adopted, instead of a list of specific tasks. Two test supervisors and observers introduced basic instructions of the usability test session and took notes regarding events, activities and thinking aloud that were occurring while the user was performing the test. In addition, a camera operator recorded the test session.

Lastly the participant completed an exit questionnaire designed to evaluate the usability of the application and the UX on the basis of the mentioned criteria. The questionnaire consisted of 4 5-point Likert scale questions, 2 open-ended questions, and 1 matrix question.

Since the task walkthrough usability inspection method was adopted, the authors did not measured metrics such as the task completion rate (*effectiveness*) and the task completion time (*efficiency*) in accomplishing the purchase through the Smart TV application. As a consequence, it was not possible to evaluate the usability according to the definition given by the ISO 9241-11 [24]. Instead, the authors evaluated how easy it is for new users to accomplish tasks with the system and noticed which usability problems emerged from each test session. Moreover, the whole interaction and UX with the system was studied by considering some general usability criteria and by observing the participant's reactions (e.g. facial gestures, body language, tone of voice, verbatim comments, etc.) and expressed emotion while performing the required tasks.

3.3 Results of the Usability Test

In this paragraph, the authors present the main finding of the described usability study. In details: the first three sections show the results of the entry questionnaire and the following five sections present the results of the exit questionnaire.

Respondents' Habits in Using Digital Devices. The 10 respondents used at least once the digital devices the authors investigated (smartphone, PC, tablet, TV). The most used device is the smartphone, whereas the less used one is the tablet. In detail, during a typical day, the use of smartphones and PCs decreases with the passing of hours, whereas the use of TVs and tablets increases.

Respondents also indicated the activities carried out more frequently through these devices. In details: smartphones are mainly employed to call, to send/receive SMS, and to listen music; PCs to access Internet for various activities; tablets to play; TVs to watch films/videos.

Respondents' Habits in Purchasing Products and Services through Digital Devices. The PC is the most used device during almost all the different stages of a purchasing process, from the "search for information on products/services of interest" to the "evaluation of the purchased products/services". The exception is for the "check of shipment status", during which the smartphone is the most employed device. However, the "search of physical stores" is the task more frequently carried out through the smartphone. Finally, the TV is not used at any stages of the purchasing process. The respondents affirm that the PC meets their main needs during these processes (e.g.: comfort in visualizing information and in data entry). The PC is also the device most used for the impulse purchases.

Moreover, concerning the frequency of use of these devices during the purchasing processes, the most part of the participants declare to use the PC more than six times a year, the smartphone less than once a year or never, and tablets and TVs never.

Use of the Smart TV. 9 respondents out of 10 declare to know what a Smart TV is. The authors asked them to offer a definition of it. In general, they consider the Smart TV as a device with added features in relation to the traditional TV, making it similar to a PC. Considering that, the respondents identify as main feature of a Smart TV the Internet access, followed by the use of *ad hoc* applications that allow "to enjoy of various services". 2 respondents point out that Smart TV are equipped with a specific OS.

7 of the 9 respondents who declare to know what a Smart TV is say they had already used a Smart TV. The remote control is the device employed for the interaction with this type of television; only 1 respondent declares to have used also a gesture recognition system. The most part (5 respondents) used the Smart TV to watch films/videos, 3 respondents to access to the Internet, and 3 respondents to use apps. The frequency of use of the Smart TV apps is low. Moreover, 2 respondents used them at home and 1 respondent in a store and during an event; the part of the day most affected is the evening. None of the 3 respondents who used Smart TV apps have purchased products/services through a TV app. The provided reasons are: "I do not have a Smart TV", "I never thought of that", and "I am not interested".

The 4 respondents who used a Smart TV without interacting with app have not used them because they prefer other devices (e.g.: smartphone, PC, etc.) rather than Smart TV. They suppose that the interaction with these applications is uncomfortable.

Finally, the 3 respondents who never used a Smart TV declare that they don't have this device.

Suitability for the Tasks. The participants in the usability test consider the app they analysed more focused on the technology rather than on the tasks to perform. This consideration emerges, for example, in the inability to save data useful to perform the consecutive tasks, in the lack of basic features (e.g.: retrieving the lost password), in requiring data not useful in order to complete a specific task, in the lack of visibility of central features, in the high number of steps to perform a task, etc.

The remote control is considered a not suitable and intuitive input device. It is considered complicated, uncomfortable, not ergonomic, laggard in the response on the screen, not controllable, not tolerant in case of a not totally correct position. The participants affirm that the buttons of the remote control were too many, difficult to push, and too close to one another (with the risk of pressing no correct buttons). Their position in the remote control is not totally intuitive, as well as the employed icons and labelling (e.g.: Fig. 1.a - "TTX", used to switch on the keyboard letters/numbers or capital/small letters; Fig. 1.b - "PRE-CH" to delete letters), by obligating users to randomly push buttons. Moreover, some icons on the remote control are inconsistent with the operations required on the screen (e.g.: Fig. 1.c - "Press OK", but the remote control has not an "OK" button, but a "sending" button) or they are similar to each other (e.g.: Fig. 1.d "source" button similar to the "sending" button).

1.a   1.b   1.c   1.d

Fig. 1. Icons on some of the remote control buttons.

Then, the remote control is considered too long. Indeed, the participants need to move from the top to the bottom of it, a sequence considered inconvenient.

The alphanumeric keyboard, through which data are entered (Fig. 2), resembles the keyboard of the feature phones. For this reason, it is considered not suitable to the Smart TV, since the interaction is hard (e.g.: inserting two letters on the same button). Moreover, during a data entry operation both the hand are used on the remote control, and users need at the same time to see both the screen and the remote control. So, the users require added/alternate input devices (e.g.: a physical keyboard, a controller, a smartphone, etc.), mainly based on gesture and voice recognition systems.

Fig. 2. Alphanumeric keyboard

The potential of the TV screen, used as output device, is not fully exploited. Also for this reason, the users tend to give more importance to the remote control rather than the contents on the screen (e.g. one of the respondents searches "add to cart" as a button of the remote control).

Self-Descriptiveness. The self-description of the system is low. In details, the users have little information about what they can do and how to move. One of the main problems of the system is to understand that, in order to add a product to her/his cart, he/she needs to register. Furthermore, the users do not receive feedback about specific actions or choices (e.g.: the stability of the chosen password) or they receive them too late (e.g.: the needed elements for registration).

Moreover, on the one hand, in some cases the selected interface elements are not clear (e.g.: the type of payment card, the channel, etc.); on the other hand, the selectable elements are not clear, or, if clear, users do not know how to select them.

The elements useful for navigation are not evident. Indeed, the menus at the bottom of the interface (Fig. 3) and the messages at the top are not very visible and, in some cases, the labelling is not present.

Fig. 3. Menu at the bottom of the interface

Finally, there is a lack not only of the aid to suggest users how to fill out a form or that help to fill it, but also of use guides and tutorials. It entails a random user interaction.

Conformity with User Expectations. The users pointed out a lack of conformity from different points of view: with familiar modes of interaction (e.g.: the users expect to be able to add a product to cart without be logged, in accordance with a traditional procedure of e-commerce); with data usually required (e.g.: during the registration phase or a purchase procedure); with familiar icons; with the expected position of specific icons (e.g.: "add a new card/address", "sig in"); with the different modes to insert data in this application (letters are inserted only through the alphanumeric keypad whereas numbers are inserted both through the alphanumeric keypad and directly through the numeric keypad remote control; in some cases to insert data the form needs to be activated, in other cases not); with the modes used to refer to the same elements in this application (e.g.: "country" and "nation"); among remote control buttons and screen icons or commands. Moreover, the users understand with difficulty the labelling used on the remote control or on the screen (the "return" and "exit" button/icons are not clear).

Error Tolerance. The app is not tolerant to the errors. If, by mistake, the user presses a button instead of another, unexpected and irreversible things can happen (e.g.: exit the app). Moreover, the app presents a low possibility to avoid or retrieve the error. Finally, when it reports an error, it does not give additional and useful information (e.g.: during the registration phase).

Learnability. The participants declare that the prolonged use of the devices allows them to faster interact and to gradually understand the app mode of interaction. However, they have had many difficulties in understanding how to interact with the app (e.g.: the sequence of tasks to achieve a goal) and what data (and data format) are required to perform a task.

Satisfaction. Overall, the interaction with the Smart TV was unsatisfactory and hard, especially for the users who had never interacted with it. Their most frequent moods were: agitation, irritation, anger, frustration, fear, and boredom. Considering that, 2 of the participants abandoned the tasks they were doing. In addition, they were overly focused on understanding how to interact rather than carry out the task.

In general, the users consider that the Smart TV should communicate with other devices (e.g.: smartphone, PC, tablet) and that it is important to identify its real added value. Indeed, since the interaction with the Smart TV is considered complex, currently it is still uncompetitive compared with other devices. Figure 4 shows the devices that the participants would use as an alternative to the Smart TV in the different phases of a purchasing process. Inserting the shipping address and the registration process are considered the most inconvenient procedures on a Smart TV.

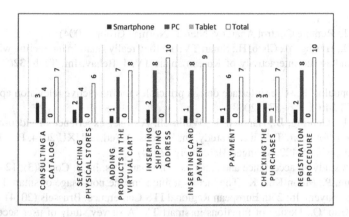

Fig. 4. Exit questionnaire. Summary of the question: "Please indicate which of the following procedures you would have preferred to carry out through other devices". Total: 10 participants.

Moreover, the perception of the security of a Smart TV is low. Finally, the users consider as necessary added features: unique login for the different app, social activities, multimedia contents, etc.

4   Conclusions

In this paper, the authors present the main findings of a usability test on a Smart TV application for T-commerce. By evaluating the usability problems of the app, they also identified the general factors that may affect the interaction between user and Smart TV.

Mainly, the usability test participants consider the remote control an inappropriate input device. They point out that it is little ergonomic, its icons and labelling are not only difficult to understand but also risk to be inconsistent with the commands on the screen. These elements confuse the user and prevent him/her to interact effectively and efficiently with the Smart TV. On the contrary, the use of gesture/voice recognition systems could improve the interaction.

In conclusion, currently this device is considered uncompetitive with the others digital devices (smartphone, PC, tablet), both concerning the UX and usability, and the usefulness. Indeed, it is necessary to find a practical use of the Smart TV within a consistent multi-channel strategy, which represents an added value for the user (together with the traditional characteristics of the television, e.g.: home context, broadcasting contents, social use, etc.). Moreover, it is important to give the user more support in order to get him/her familiar with the device and with their modes of interaction.

References

1. Zillmann, D.: The coming of media entertainment. In: Zillmann, D., Vorderer, P. (eds.) Media Entertainment: The Psychology of its Appeal, pp. 1–20. Erlbaum, Mahwah (2000)
2. Nilsson Helander, K.: Smart TV: a more interactive way of watching TV. Thesis, Umea University (2013)
3. Nielsen, J.: Remote Control Anarchy. Nielsen Norman Group (2004)
4. Shin, D.H., Hwang, Y., Choo, H.: Smart TV: are they really smart in interacting with people? Understanding the interactivity of Korean smart TV. J. Behav. Inf. Tech. **32**(2), 156–172 (2013)
5. Chorianopoulos, K.: User interface design principles for interactive television applications. Int. J. HCI **24**(6), 556–573 (2008)
6. Miesler, L., Gehring, B., Hannich, F., Wüthrich, A.: User experience of video-on-demand applications for smart TVs: a case study. In: Marcus, A. (ed.) DUXU 2014, Part IV. LNCS, vol. 8520, pp. 412–422. Springer, Heidelberg (2014)
7. Lee, S.: A study on acceptance and resistance of smart TVs. Int. J. Con. **8**(3), 12–19 (2012)
8. Jong Hyun, P., Moon Koo, K.: The factors influencing the non-usage of smart TV services by Korean buyers. In: 25th European Regional ITS Conference, Brussels (2014)
9. Ma, H., Guo, Q.: Design of functions in smart TV. A survey study of user acceptance on Smart TV functions. Thesis, University of Gävle (2014)
10. Bernhaupt, R., Obrist, M., Tscheligi, M.: Usability and usage of iTV services: lessons learned in an Austrian field trial. J. Comput. Entertain. **5**(2) (2007)
11. Liang, S.-F.M., Kuo, Y.-C., Chen, S.-C.: Identifying usability problems in a smart TV music service. In: Rau, P. (ed.) HCII 2013 and CCD 2013, Part I. LNCS, vol. 8023, pp. 306–312. Springer, Heidelberg (2013)
12. Lim, Y., Park, J., Jung, E.S., Chung, D.H., Kim, T., Choi, K., Lee, S.: Comparative study on advanced TV interface types in the smart media world. In: 9th International Conference on Autonomic & Trusted Computing and Ubiquitous Intelligence & Computing, pp. 342–348. IEEE Press (2012)
13. Li, H., Qiu, J., Gao, L.: A study of kinect-based smart TV control mode. In: Rau, P. (ed.) CCD 2014. LNCS, vol. 8528, pp. 174–183. Springer, Heidelberg (2014)
14. Jeong, J.W., Lee, D.H.: Inferring search intents from remote control movement patterns: a new content search method for smart TV. J. IEEE Trans. Cons. Elect. **60**(1), 92–98 (2014)
15. Blasco-Arcas, L., Ortega, B.H., Martínez, J.J.: Adopting television as a new channel for e-commerce. The influence of interactive technologies on consumer behavior. J Electron. Commer. Res. **13**(4), 457–475 (2013)
16. McGuigan, L.: Direct marketing and the productive capacity of commercial television t-commerce, advanced advertising, and the audience product. J. Telev. New Media **16**(2), 196–214 (2015)
17. Yu, J., Ha, I., Choi, M., Rho, J.: Extending the TAM for a t-commerce. J. Inform. Manag. **42**(7), 965–976 (2005)
18. Omar, A.C., Shiratuddin, N., Sarif, S.M., Mutalib, A.A., Rashid, S.M.: Identification of research gap: t-commerce impulse purchase for iTV advertising. In: International Conference on Informatics and Creative Multimedia, pp.119–122. IEEE (2013)
19. Nielsen, J., Loranger, H.: Web Usability 2.0 - L'usabilità che conta. Apogeo, Milan (2006)
20. Nielsen, J.: Usability Engineering. Academic Press, Boston (1993)
21. Norman, D.A.: The Psychology of Everyday Things. Basic Book, New York (1998)
22. Polillo, R.: Facile da usare. Apogeo, Milan (2010)

23. Smart TV Ad Effectiveness: a pilot study about the impact of Smart TV Advertising. Whitepaper, Smartclip (2013)
24. ISO 9241-11:1998 Ergonomic requirements for office work with visual display terminals (VDTs) - Part 11: Guidance on usability

Research on Virtual Item Purchase Intention in Taking Part in Mobile Device Games: Taking the Middle and Old Aged Players for Example

Chia-Yu Kao[1(✉)] and Chenwei Chiang[2]

[1] Department of Information and Communication, Master Degree Student,
Yuan Ze University, Taoyuan City, Taiwan
pomeloyu025@gmail.com
[2] Department of Information and Communication Assistant Professor,
Yuan Ze University, Taoyuan City, Taiwan
chenwei@saturn.yzu.edu.tw

Abstract. This study targets middle and old aged players' mobile game participations, as well as their purchase intention of virtual items, and an internet-based survey is conducted. Results show that when players are in the flow channel, motivations such as competition and self-assurance, game playability, artistry, and sociability, increase players' purchase intention for virtual items. On the other hand, entertainment of motivation and mobility of playability, decrease players' willingness to purchase virtual items. Younger players demonstrate significant difference than middle and old aged players on mobile games. However, gaming market of middle and old aged players shouldn't be overlooked. More in depth investigation of middle and old aged players' needs for mobile games is helpful for designing better games and campaigns attracting middle and old aged players, and increase their purchase intention for virtual items.

Keywords: Mobile game · Game motivation · Game playability · UX

1 Introduction

Demographics keep changing globally, and recently aging society has become a key issue. Taiwan has been an aging society since 1993 - in Taiwan, citizens aged between 45 and 65 are defined as middle and old aged by Employment Service Act [1].

Technology improves rapidly, and mobile devices are now a part of our life. For instance, smartphone and tablet both change our life dramatically. In Taiwan, more than 60 % of people own a mobile device. They use the device to make phone calls, take photos, chat with friends, and play games. Mobile devices now are also key instruments for information communication and entertainments [2]. Moreover, choices for digital games are increasing as well. Mobile devices also boost developments of mobile games that utilize multiple technologies, such as touch screen and gyroscope

© Springer International Publishing Switzerland 2015
F.F.-H. Nah and C.-H. Tan (Eds.): HCIB 2015, LNCS 9191, pp. 324–334, 2015.
DOI: 10.1007/978-3-319-20895-4_30

that create a new way of gaming. People can interact with friends, and buy virtual items to make game progressing easier.

Before maturity of mobile devices' developments, there are relatively fewer middle and old aged players. However, without specific gaming platform, recent survey shows number of players older than 15 increase significantly compared to 2013 [3]. It's assumed that as mobile devices become more popular, number of middle and old aged people use mobile games for entertainment also increase. Huang's report [4] mentions that when playing mobile games, middle and old aged players prefer to purchase virtual items for achievements or self-assurance.

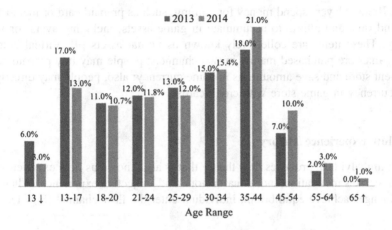

Fig. 1. 2013 & 2014 Yahoo 2014 Yahoo! game White Paper, players' age comparison

In summary, this study focuses on middle and old aged players' purchase intention for virtual items in mobile games. In questionnaires all ages are surveyed, and results lay groundwork for future interview questionnaire design. Companies may utilize the result to design games and campaigns that encourage players to purchase virtual items.

2 Literature Review

2.1 Middle and Old Aged Player

Taiwan has officially been an aging society since 1993. According to Employment Service Act, Ministry of Justice, middle and old aged are citizens aged between 45 and 65 [1]. In digital era, middle and old aged may face digital disorders, including psychological disorder, physiological disorder, societal disorder, and lack of experience. However, due to recent mobile devices and mobile games craze, middle and old aged treat mobile games as a new way of entertainment. They can interact with relatives and friends, or purchase in game virtual items for self assurance [4, 5].

2.2   Mobile Game and Virtual Items

Mobile Game. As technology improves, communication and game industries gradually move into same mobile game industry. Mobile games utilize mobile devices with wireless connectivity, and they can be played anytime [6]. Take smartphone as an example, Lin, Chen & Kuo [7] state that smartphone integrates several technologies, including touch screen and sensors, and users can operate intuitively and create new ways of gaming. Lin [8] points out that smartphones revolutionize mobile games; touch screen enables user to operate intuitively; sensors including gyroscope, G-sensor, and GPS, allow players to feel presence and receive feedbacks.

Virtual Items. Players spend money for gaming, such as prepaid card or membership, and spend time and efforts to accumulate in game assets, including avatar or virtual currency. These items are collectively known as virtual assets [9]. Virtual items for mobile games are purchased mainly in two channels: people may buy prepaid card in convenient store and save amounts as in game currency; also, people may directly buy virtual currency in game store with credit cards.

2.3   Flow Experience Theory

Csikszentmihalyi [10] proposes flow theory that is also known as flow experience. The theory integrates motivation, individual factors, and subjective experience. When skills and challenges achieve equilibrium, individual enter the flow channel (Fig. 1).

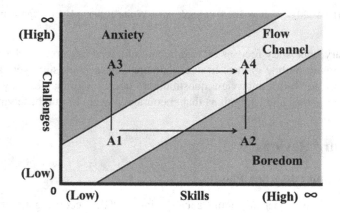

Fig. 2. Flow theory model

Csikszentmihalyi [11] summarizes that there are eight characteristics when individual enters flow channel: clear goals and immediate feedbacks, balance between challenges and skills, actions and awareness merge, concentration on the task, a sense of potential control, loss of self-consciousness, altered sense of time, and experience becomes autotelic. Based on past literatures, this study classifies flow experiences into two states (flow level): partial flow state, and complete flow state.

2.4 Game Motivation

Game motivation affects players' behavior to participate games. Characteristics of players' game motivation are studied for player participation increase [12]. Lepper & Malone [13] categories game motivation into individual motivation and interpersonal motivation; individual motivation includes challenge, curiosity, control, and fantasy; interpersonal motivation includes competition, cooperation, and recognition. Based on past studies, Tsai [14] categorizes motivation of mobile games participation into entertainment, curiosity, self-assurance, social interaction, and attribution avoidance. Summarized from past literatures, this study categorizes game motivation into five types: challenges and curiosity, cooperation and social interaction, competition and self-assurance, fantasy, and entertainment.

2.5 Game Playability

Playability derives from the concept of usability; when usability is adopted in game environment, game designer identifies it as playability. Clanton [15] classifies game playability into three sections: game interface, game mechanics, and game play. For mobile games, Korhonen and Koivsto [16] classify it as game usability, mobility, and gameplay. Based on past literatures, this study classifies playability as four types: usability, mobility, artistry, and sociability.

2.6 Satisfaction and Purchase Intention

Woodside, Frey and Daly [17] point out that customer satisfaction is the overall behavior after purchases and reflects customers' fondness of the product. Cronin & Taylor [18] state that satisfaction is a key factor for customer's decision to repurchase. Kotler [19] states that if customers are very satisfied with the product or service, their purchase intention is also higher. They will repurchase relevant product or service, and inform others benefits of the product or service.

3 Method

This study adopts quantitative method, and the survey is conduct for players of all ages. Only people with mobile games experience can be qualified for survey subjects. The survey is conducted through internet questionnaires with 15 days duration, and 1,283 replies are received. After 148 invalid replies are removed, final effective sample size is 1,035 and effective response rate is 80.6 %. Afterward, analytical software, SPSS 20, is used to conduct analysis, including reliability, correlation, regression, and variance. Based on analysis results, players' views of all age can be understood, including perspectives of participation motivation, playability for mobile games, satisfaction impact due to flow level, and purchase intention of virtual items. Results inferred above can be adopted for questionnaire improvement and used for future individual interview of middle and old aged players.

4 Analysis and Discussion

Participants. The number of total effective survey subjects is 1,035 players. Based on Erikson's stages of development [20], Employment Service Act [1], and studies of Lin [21], this study categorizes subjects into four groups by ages (Fig. 3), (A) 239 teenagers aged between 13 and 18, 23 %; (B) 591 youths aged between 19 and 30, 57 %; (C) 133 middle-aged aged between 31 and 44, 13 %; (D) 72 old-aged aged between 45 and 65, 7 %.

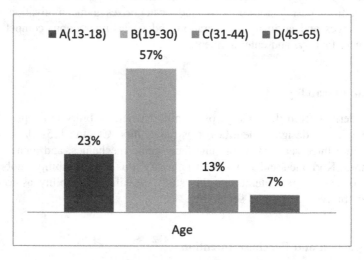

Fig. 3. Participants' age in this study

Reliability Analysis. This analysis focuses on consistency of each dimension for mobile games, including participation motivation, playability, flow level, and purchase intention. When Cronbach's α is higher, internal consistency and correlation are also higher, which is insightful for reliability of each dimension. In this study, Cronbach's α

Table 1. Reliability analysis in this study

Dimension factor		Dimensions' Cronbach's α value
Game motivation	Challenges and Curiosity	.812
	Cooperation and social interaction	.844
	Competition and self-assurance	.859
	Fantasy	.815
	Entertainment	.778
Game playability	Usability	.824
	Mobility	.726
	Artistry	.786
	Sociability	.821
	Flow level	.812
	Purchase intention	.958

of each dimension is larger than .70 (Table 1). After removing items, Cronbach's α is still mostly larger than .70. Therefore it's concluded that questionnaire hold good reliability, and survey subjects' views are consistent.

Correlation Analysis. This study aims to understand correlation of game motivation, flow level, purchase intention, as well as game playability, flow level, and purchase intention; thus Pearson correlation coefficient analysis is conducted. According to results (Tables 2 and 3), coefficient of game motivation and flow level is .555, which shows they are moderately correlated; coefficient of game motivation and purchase intention is .328, which shows they are modestly correlated; coefficient of game playability and flow level is .572, which shows they are moderately correlated; coefficient of game playability and purchase intention is .187, which shows they are modestly correlated; coefficient of flow level and purchase intention is .239, which shows they are modestly correlated.

Analysis results infer that game motivation and flow level, as well as game playability and flow level, are moderately correlated. This means the higher players' participation motivation, and game provide varieties for playability, the better players are in flow channel; although game motivation and purchase intention, as well as game playability and purchase intention, are modestly correlated, different game motivation or game playability may produce different purchase intention of virtual items. Flow level and purchase intention are modestly correlated, so that players in flow channel are not correlated to purchase intention. Additional game features may be needed to increase purchase intention when players are in flow channel and increase their correlation.

Table 2. Correlation Analysis of game motivation, flow level and purchase intention in this study

	Game motivation	Flow level	Purchase intention
Game motivation	1	.555**	.328**
Flow level	-	1	.239**
Purchase intention	-	-	1

Table 3. Correlation Analysis of game playability, flow level and purchase intention in this study

	Game playability	Flow level	Purchase intention
Game playability	1	.572**	.187**
Flow level	-	1	.239**
Purchase intention	-	-	1

Regression Analysis. This study conducts multiple regressions for all effective samples. Purchase intention of virtual items is dependent variable; dimensions of game motivation and game playability are independent variables; flow level is the intervening variable. Results of correlation are shown in Tables 4 and 5.

According to Table 4, it can be inferred that each dimensions of game motivation affects flow level (A1) positively and significantly, so the survey subject will achieve flow channel for all game motivations. For each dimension of game motivation and purchase intention (A2), only competition and self-assurance affect it positively and significantly, and entertainment affects it negatively and significantly. This denotes survey subject may seek self-assurance by succeeding in competition. Using virtual items will increase chance of succeeding, therefore purchase intention for virtual items increase as well. However survey subject will not increase purchase intention of virtual items because of entertainment - mobile games are only a recreation of life. If flow level is intervening variable (A3) of game motivation to purchase intention, flow level affects purchase intention positively and significantly. When affected by flow level, competition and self-assurance affects purchase intention positively and significantly; entertainment affects purchase intention negatively and significantly. Summarized from A1 to A3, it's clear that whether flow level is intervening variable, competition and self-assurance and entertainment affects purchase intention significantly. Therefore this study concludes that albeit flow level does not hold significant mediating effect for competition, self-assurance, and entertainment, it does indirectly increase flow level and increase purchase intention.

Table 4. Regression analysis of game motivation, purchase intention and flow level in this study

	Flow level (A1)		Purchase intention (A2)		Purchase intention (A3)	
	Beta	p	Beta	p	Beta	p
Challenges and curiosity	.151	.000***	.044	.247	.030	.437
Cooperation and social interaction	.111	.001**	.071	.060	.060	.110
Competition and self-assurance	.227	.000***	.288	.000***	.267	.000***
Fantasy	.084	.011*	.071	.059	.063	.093
Entertainment	.155	.000***	-.093	.011*	-.107	.003**
Flow level	-	-	-	-	.094	.007**

Moreover, according to Table 5, it can be inferred that each dimension of game playability affect flow level (B1) positively and significantly so survey subjects achieve flow channel for all game playability. Each dimensions of game playability affect purchase intention (B2) and mobility negatively and significantly; it affects artistry and sociability positively and significantly. This denotes survey player will not increase purchase intention if virtual items can be purchased anytime and anywhere. On the contrary, if artistry design is favorable, such as avatar, scenario, and visual effects, they are more likely to increase purchase intention of virtual items. If games also provide social interaction, and achievements can be accomplished by interactions such as chatting, cooperation, or competition, this will also increase purchase intention for virtual items. If flow level is intervening variable (B3) for game playability to purchase intention, flow level affects purchase intention positively and significantly. Affected by flow level, mobility affects purchase intention negatively and significantly. It affects artistry and sociability positively and significantly. Summarized from B1 to B3, whether flow level is intervening variable or not, mobility, artistry and sociability affect purchase intention positively and significantly. Therefore this study concludes that albeit flow level does not hold significant mediating effect for mobility, artistry and sociability of game playability, it does increase purchase intention by indirectly increasing flow level.

Table 5. Regression analysis of game playability, purchase intention and flow level in this study

	Flow level (B1)		Purchase intention (B2)		Purchase intention (B3)	
	Beta	p	Beta	p	Beta	p
Usability	.257	.000***	-.010	.777	-.053	.146
Mobility	.117	.000***	-.097	.005**	-.116	.001**
Artistry	.226	.000***	.161	.000***	.123	.000***
Sociability	.213	.000***	.264	.000***	.229	.000***
Flow level	-	-	-	-	.166	.000***

Variance Analysis. This study categorizes survey subjects into four groups: (A) teenagers aged between 13 and 18, (B) youths aged between 19 and 30, (C) middle-aged aged between 31 and 44, (D) old-aged aged between 45 and 65. Each group is analyzed to check if each dimension holds significant difference with one-way ANOVA. Moreover, Scheffé Method is used to understand difference among each group. Analysis result (Table 2) shows that overall gaming motivation achieves level of significance (p=.004*); group A and B are more significant than group D. Game playability achieves level of significance (p=.000***); group A, B, and C are more significant than group D. Game mobility also re achieves aches level of significance (p=.000**); group B and C are more significant than group D. Therefore, younger groups (A, B & C) are more significant than group D in game motivation or game playability. This study concludes that players in group A, B, and C are grown up during matured digital gaming era. Overall participation motivation is high due to increasing number of mobile devices, as well as craze of mobile games, Their game perspective for mobile games is also more significant than group D, especially game mobility. This study concludes that younger groups (A, B & C) tend to accept mobile games that can be played anytime, anywhere. Old group (D) holds no significant difference in each dimension. This may be due to the sample size is fewer than younger groups', and old group (D) may be new to video game and lack of gaming experience. Therefore there are significant difference of game motivation and game playability among younger and old groups (Table 6).

Table 6. Variance Analysis in this study

Dimensions	Age								p	Scheffe
	A		B		C		D			
	M	SD	M	SD	M	SD	M	SD		
Game motivation	3.61	.53	3.64	.51	3.58	.50	3.41	.66	.004*	A>D B>D
Game playability	3.95	.51	3.98	.46	3.96	.46	3.70	.53	.000***	A>D B>D C>D
Mobility	4.09	.67	4.22	.59	4.26	.59	3.99	.72	.001**	B>D C>D

5 Conclusion

As digital technology advances, smart mobile devices have become part of our life, and mobile games are now popular entertainments. This study discovers that albeit there is big sample size difference among groups, youth group aged between 19 and 30 contains the most players, and there are relatively fewer players with age over 45. However according to survey in 2014, players aged over 45 have already accounted for 14 % of all players; albeit this study only focus on mobile games on smart devices, players aged over 45 still accounts for 7 % of all players. This infers that number of players aged over 45 gradually increase. Past reviews [4] also denote that middle and old aged players prefer to buy virtual items to achieve objectives and self assurance and posses huge potentials for mobile game industry. It will be beneficial for companies if behaviors of middle and old aged players are studied in depth. Moreover, regression analysis results show that if companies increase competition and self-assurance of game motivation, as well as artistry and sociability of game playability, players will be in higher flow level and increase purchase intention of virtual items. They can share those topics with friends, and increase self assurance due to their game skills. On the contrary, increasing entertainment will decrease purchase intention, because some players only view mobile games as a recreation and do not pay for virtual items. In variance analysis, younger players have more significant difference than middle and old aged players. This is due to two reasons: the difference of sample sizes, and middle and old aged players may be lack of gaming experience. Finally, based on these data, companies can design games that attract players to increase purchase intention of virtual items, and increase market share for middle and old aged players. They may design campaigns for players of all ages to increase their desire to purchase virtual items, increase company profit, and please those players.

6 Future Work

Some areas in this study can be improved. Firstly, there is big difference in sampling size among each age group that cause incomplete analysis result. It's recommended that future researchers should keep each group similarly sized. Also, number of video games can be shortlisted to increase accuracy of survey results.

Secondly, interviews are needed to understand middle and old aged players in depth. To design suitable interview questionnaire, results in this study can be utilized. Interviews should be based on motivation and playability, as well as flow theory that affects purchase intention of virtual items. Interviews can provide players' first hand data that reflect their ideas. They are also helpful for mobile games companies to design contents that attract players to purchase virtual items; players can also enhance abilities in game by purchasing virtual items. Both companies and player acquire benefits from each other and achieve a win-win situation.

References

1. Employment Service Act. http://law.moj.gov.tw/LawClass/LawAll.aspx?PCode=N0090001
2. MIC FIND: The first half of 2014 released survey of consumer behavior. http://www.iii.org.tw/service/3_1_1_c.aspx?id=1367
3. Yahoo! Game White Paper. http://img1.37wanimg.com/file/2014yahoo.pdf
4. Game app consumer behavior survey. http://life.trendgo.com.tw/epaper/page/5
5. Danesh, A., Inkpen, K., Lau, F., Shu, K., Booth, K.: GeneyTM: designing a collaborative activity for the palmTM handheld computer. In: CHI 2001 Proceedings of the SIGCHI Conference on Human Factors in Computing Systems, pp. 388–395. ACM Press, New York (2001)
6. Lu, Y.N., Wang, C.C.: A study of the consumer behavior on mobile game service–a case study of college students in Taipei. J. J. Commun. Manage. 5(3), 21–41 (2004)
7. Lin, T.-M., Chen, S.-C., Kuo, P.-J.: Motivations for game-playing on mobile devices – using smartphone as an example. In: Chang, M., Hwang, W.-Y., Chen, M.-P., Müller, W. (eds.) Edutainment 2011. LNCS, vol. 6872, pp. 101–105. Springer, Heidelberg (2011)
8. Refurbished hardware specifications Mobile game get into smartphones. http://www.mem.com.tw/article_content.asp?sn=1002100005
9. Chen, C.C., Hung, C.Y., Ke, C.H., Chen, Y.C.: Design and implementation of a virtual property description language——By example of protecting virtual properties of online games. J J. Inf. Technol. Soc. 8(1), 21–41 (2008)
10. Csikszentmihalyi, M.: Flow: The Psychology of Optimal Experience. Harper Perennial, New York (1990)
11. Csikszentmihalyi, M.: The Evolving Self: A Psychology for the Third Millennium. HarperCollins Publishers, New York (1993)
12. Shen, J.Y.: Multi-user interactive situated learning games on WWW. Master thesis, Department of Computer Science and Information Engineering, National Central University, Taoyuan (1997)
13. Lepper, M.R., Malone, T.W.: Making learning fun: a taxonomy of intrinsic motivation for learning. In: Snow, R.E., Farr, M.J. (eds.) Aptitude, Learning, and Instruction 3, pp. 223–253. MIT Press, Cambridge (1987)
14. Tsai, C.H.: Motivation And Playability On Satisfaction And Use Behavior Effects Of Smartphone Mobile Games. Master thesis, Department of Radio & Television, Nation Taiwan University of Arts, Taipei (2012)
15. Clanton, C.: An interpreted demonstration of computer game design. In: CHI 1998 Cconference Summary on Human Factors in Computing Systems, pp. 1–2. ACM Press, New York (1998)

16. Korhonen, H., Koivisto, E.M.: Playability heuristics for mobile games. In: Proceedings of the 8th Conference on Human-Computer Interaction with Mobile Devices and Services, pp. 9–16. ACM Press, New York (2006)
17. Woodside, A.G., Frey, L.L., Daly, R.T.: Linking service quality, customer satisfaction, and behavioral intention. J. J. Health Care Mark. 9(4), 5–17 (1989)
18. Cronin Jr, J.J., Taylor, S.A.: Measuring service quality: a reexamination and extension. J. J. Mark. 56(3), 55–68 (1992)
19. Kotler, P.: Marketing Management: Analysis, Planning, Implementation, and Control. Prentice-Hall Press, New Jersey (2000)
20. Erikson, E.H.: Childhood and Society. Norton, New York (1950)
21. Lin, Y.H.: A Study of the Motive of Playing Digital Games for the Mid-aged and Elder People. Master thesis, Department of Multimedia and Entertainment Science, Southern Taiwan University of Science and Technology, Tainan (2009)

Key Factors in Developing Omnichannel Customer Experience with Finnish Retailers

Satu Peltola[1], Harri Vainio[2(✉)], and Marko Nieminen[1]

[1] School of Science and Technology, Aalto University, Espoo, Finland
{satu.peltola,marko.nieminen}@aalto.fi
[2] Palmu Evolution Oy, Helsinki, Finland
harri.vainio@palmu.fi

Abstract. Change in consumer behavior towards increased use of digital services throughout the buying process drives retailers to rethink their services. Contemporary shoppers engage in a mixture of real-life and digital activities combining events in brick-and-mortar stores with online and mobile browsing. Our interviews with seven Finnish retailers show that the changing consumer behavior affects not only services but also other operations including organizational structure and supply chains. For analysis purposes, we modified customer journey maps to record and illustrate user activity. We conclude that a good omnichannel customer experience lies in the unity of retailer's organizational culture, pricing, operations, and communications. Instead of full-range digital and physical service offering, seamless and intuitive linking of consumer touch-points appears as a promising path. Our results contribute to better understanding of omnichannel customer experience indicating the need for a more profound approach in omnichannel development to more traditional channel and customer interface development.

Keywords: HCI · Human-computer interaction · Omnichannel · Development · Customer experience · Customer journey

1 Introduction

Digitalization has changed the retail industry permanently. Today, many retail companies operate in multiple online and offline channels. A new form of retail, where all the channels of the company are seamlessly integrated has emerged. This is referred as omnichannel retail [14]. In omnichannel retail the aim is to make the customer experience as seamless as possible [3, 6, 11, 13]. Customer can choose to use any of the available channels during any phase of their buying process depending on their needs.

In order to distinct between various concepts in e-commerce, on-line commerce, m-commerce, as well as multi-channel and omnichannel retail, Huuhka [8] outlines omnichannel as three waves:

First wave started in the mid-90 s. The development of online sales was driven by new technological solutions that made it possible for retail companies to build first online sales channels. Majority of consumers had not yet grown accustomed to new technologies and consumer adoption of online stores stayed low. The first online stores lacked proper strategies and most of them disappeared when dot-com bubble bursted [14].

© Springer International Publishing Switzerland 2015
F.F.-H. Nah and C.-H. Tan (Eds.): HCIB 2015, LNCS 9191, pp. 335–346, 2015.
DOI: 10.1007/978-3-319-20895-4_31

Second wave emerged when consumers started to use more and more digital solutions in their day-to-day lives. Online stores with high usability interfaces were built to answer the ever growing consumer demand. Traditional offline retailers built their own online channels, but these channels remained often separated from the original offline channels.

Third and current wave emerged as smart mobile devices became more common with consumers. New breed of technologically native consumers do not recognize anymore separate channels but they expect seamless experiences across all channels. A new concept called omnichannel retail [14] was introduced to describe retail environment where all channels, both in online and offline are seamlessly integrated.

A constant change in consumer behavior drives the transformation of retail. Consumers are connecting more and more with companies through web, mobile and offline channels, and in very diverse ways. According to Deloitte [3] already 86 % of consumers use computer or mobile devices for shopping related activities. Consumers view different channels just as different ways to access same information and products, not as separate services. And as consumers get used to utilizing multiple channels effectively throughout their buying process, companies need to find more diverse ways to interact with their customers and at the same time evolve their business in the omnichannel environment.

Frazer and Stiehler [4] recognize that even though the early research of omnichannel retailing focuses on the challenges posed by integrating channels, retailers should recognize that the aim of omnichannel retailing is to create a seamless customer experiences. The interviewed companies find the omnichannel approach as a phenomenon that eventually changes their business more profoundly and at the same time enables them to express their competitive advantages in new ways.

In this paper we focus on how retailers in Finland have noticed and reacted to omnichannel behavior in their customers.

2 Developing Omnichannel Customer Experience

2.1 Omnichannel Consumers

Consumers' buying behavior is more complicated than one would expect [7]. From company's point of view, consumers switch erratically between channels and even between companies depending on their needs in different points of buying process. This opportunistic behavior, where customers first find information from one company and then buy the product from another company is further enhanced by the increased usage of mobile devices while in store. Price is a major influence for consumers switching between companies, but also other factors such as service quality and availability can sometimes override price as the deciding factor [5]. With social media, recommendations from friends or reviews in blogs can also be a major influence.

2.2 Omnichannel Strategy

Moving into omnichannel business can be a major investment with various challenges. Bagge [1] recognizes that a successful transition to omnichannel strategy and business requires a transformation in organizational culture, operations and processes, and underlying technologies. Huuhka et al. [8] point that, along with changes within the company, there are also new challenges in selecting strategic partners. For instance, the more dependent businesses are on external partner's digital e-commerce platforms, the more effort they should be in choosing these long term partners.

Even if technology can often be the first and seemingly most logical step into omnichannel transformation for a retailer, it can be argued that the most relevant changes lie in organizational culture [1]. Strategies for doing business with tightly-coupled physical and digital aspects differ from traditional brick-and-mortar retail as well as from pure web-based shops. With the transformation, businesses need to develop ways to integrate omnichannel thinking into how they measure success and how their employees are motivated. Traditionally, businesses have built their processes, information, and reporting into separate channels, with employees encouraged to maximize the profit in their own channel or product group. Bagge [1] underlines that even if processes and operations are changed to match the omnichannel customer behavior, it is crucial to see that the transformation also reaches the employees in their everyday actions. For many companies, the consumer behavior is considered as unstructured and erratic. It can pose major challenges for traditionally structured approach of running businesses.

In our interviews we studied how businesses have embraced this consumer transition into omnichannel buying processes, and in which ways they approached their own transformation into running omnichannel business.

2.3 Research Question

Piotrowicz, W., and Cuthbertson, R. [12] recognize a clear conflict in customer expectations and retailers ability to respond to transition to omnichannel business. Also, Lazaris, C., and Vrechopoulos, A. [10] calls for research and investigation in strategic impact of omnichannel consumer behavior on retailers.

In this paper we study the state of omnichannel development of retailers in Finland, and interview retailers to find out the key factors they consider most important in their transformation.

The resulting research question is: "What key factors should retailers in Finland consider when developing the omnichannel customer experience?"

3 Methods and Data

3.1 Semi-structured Interview

The research method is based on semi-structured interview. This form of qualitative research is widely used in business research. Interview is an appropriate method when one tries to collect meanings and interpretations around a specific subject [9]. Since the goal of this research was to collect perceptions and experiences of the interviewees, qualitative interview was selected as the research method.

The interviews were facilitated and conscripted with the help of a customer journey map tool based on Deloitte's [3] buying process, and modified for the research

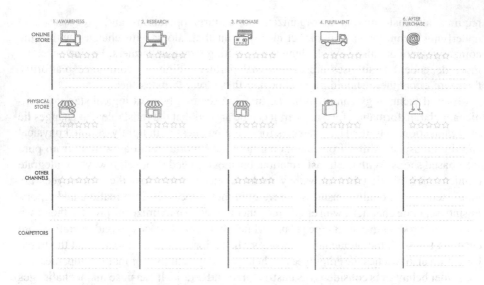

Fig. 1. A modified customer journey map tool used in interviews

purposes (Fig. 1). Customer journey maps are used to visualize the sequence of touch-points where the customer interacts with the service. Typical customer journey map is time-based and multi-channel by nature. Customer journey maps allow analysis on two levels: on the touch-point level and on the overall experience level. This allows both more detail driven approach and more overview type of approach for recognizing general advantages and challenges [15].

Our applied version of customer journey map was primarily targeted to study the relationship between online and offline functions in a company. In our application of the method, the rows represent different sales channels while the columns represent different stages of consumer buying process. Just as customer journey maps, our tool combines two viewpoints, namely the company's channel oriented viewpoint and the consumer buying process viewpoint. As each interview was documented with the same tool, a conscription device, the results were easily comparable (Fig. 2).

3.2   Data

The qualitative research was conducted through seven interviews with top-level managers from small-to-medium sized to large sized retail companies operating in the Finnish market. All interviewed companies had experience operating in both online and offline channels. The companies vary in terms of product categories, such as electronics, clothes and furniture. The interviews are listed in the Table 1.

Each interview lasted approximately an hour. Interviews were recorded to ensure easy processing and analysis of the data. Interviews 2, 3, 4 and 7 were held at the company's premises. Interview 1 was held through video call service Skype.

It appeared in the interviews that there were several factors influencing the companies approach and responses to omnichannel transformation:

Table 1. Interviews conducted in this study

Interview	Role of interviewee(s)	Product category	Company size	Starting point
1	Head of Digital Commerce	Home electronics	Big	Offline
2	CIO	Home electronics	Big	Online
3	e-commerce Manager	Furniture	Big	Offline
4	Deputy CEO	Outdoor equipment	Mid-sized	Offline
5	CEO CFO (two interviewees)	Eco products	Small	Offline
6	COO	Children's clothes	Small	Offline
7	CEO	Motor sports	Small	Offline

Role of the interviewee has an effect on the topics of interest for the interviewee. CEOs had a different perspective on omnichannel business compared to a more detailed approach of e-commerce managers.

Product category made a big difference: some of the selected product categories have a natural need for touching and experiencing during the buying process.

Company size influences the way how omnichannel development is approached. Bigger companies often have more resources for developing new solutions. However smaller companies might be more agile when big changes are implemented.

Starting point is used here to indicate whether the company started in e-commerce or in traditional retail before expanding to other channels. Starting point has significant effect on what kind of challenges company faces in multi-channel retail [2].

4 Results

4.1 Customer Behavior Change

In all the interviews, the companies had noticed definite changes in consumer behavior (see Table 2 for common statements). The increased interactions with digital services in all phases of customer buying process have forced the companies to rethink their services. All the interviewed companies had recognized that a growing number of customers visit company's online channels before coming to the physical store. Five of the seven companies had recognized this omnichannel behavior becoming more common among their customers. This flexible moving between channels and situations can be visualized by combining the recognized customer behavior in the interviews to a single journey mapping diagram (Fig. 2). The resulting journey map with transitions indicates that there is no single customer behavior pattern that would be easily distinguishable.

Companies had noticed a significant increase in use of mobile services. Five of the companies had noticed that consumers use mobile technologies while in their physical store. Two of the companies also mentioned that customers usually search products first on their mobile devices as they become aware of the need for the product.

Table 2. Common statements (amount indicated in column 2) from interviews

OMNICHANNEL	
Have noticed omnichannel behavior becoming more common among their customers.	5/7
Consider omnichannel approach vital for improving customer experience	5/7
See underlying technology as major influence for channel integration and unity	5/7
Have difficulties in measuring channel crossing behavior	3/7
CHANNELS	
Have noticed that customers had browsed products online before visiting a physical store	7/7
Recognize different strengths of various channels according to product types	6/7
Consider presenting product availability in online to strengthen the link to offline channels	5/7
Predict the increase of mobile use in consumer buying processes	5/7
PERSONNEL	
View the attitude of personnel as a major contributor to seamless customer experience	5/7
Recognize a demand for growing expertise in response to more information available online, e.g. social media	5/7

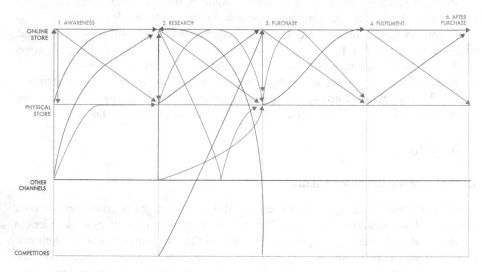

Fig. 2. Combined observations from the interviews in journey mapping tool

4.2 Business and Service Development

All interviewed companies were familiar with the term omnichannel, and had goals in developing their business and services towards it. In general, omnichannel was seen as a new, more customer centric approach, where operations are flexible and happen on customer's terms. At the same time, the relationship between physical stores and online channels was strong in all of the companies. One of the companies even stated that their physical stores would close in an instant if their online channel would be closed.

All companies noted that changes to service or business models are needed when companies transform into omnichannel retail. Especially the smaller companies had noticed new business opportunities along with omnichannel development, including consumer engagement and loyalty services, and countering seasonal demand with dexterity in product offering brought by e-commerce solutions. Larger companies were developing new ways of logistics and deliveries for both changing consumer behavior, but also to cut their costs by storing goods in physical stores.

Five of the seven companies stated that different channels have various benefits depending on the type of product the customer is buying. For example, touching or fitting products can be important for the purchase decision. However, while keeping a large assortment of products might provide a good customer experience, it also increases operating costs since large assortment requires a larger space for the store. Also, if the product is extremely expensive, the customer might be more inclined to seeing it in person.

Five companies stated that cultural change is needed inside the company in order to make the transformation to omnichannel retail happen. It is critical that the personnel understand the benefits of integrating all channels, and this requires also new ways to measure sales success over channels, not by each channel.

Because of the amount of information commonly available online, customers are very well informed about the products. This poses a challenge for sales personnel: customers might expect that the salesperson should have a very deep knowledge of each product. Companies need to educate their sales personnel thoroughly or recruit people who have deep knowledge of their products. Companies also recognized that one way to fix the knowledge gap between the sales personnel and the customer is to use company's online channels as additional information resource for the personnel.

Three of the seven companies had a catalog that complimented other sales channels. The main challenge with catalogs is its static nature in comparison to digital services. However, printing out an official catalog makes the company seem more credible since physical catalogs requires certain amount of resources that small companies might not be able to afford.

4.3 Technology in Omnichannel

In the responses, the role of technologies behind omnichannel services was focused on unifying customer information, product availability, product information and pricing in all touch-points over all channels. In this way, technology integrates all touch-points by enabling similar information to be used every time consumers are met in any channel.

The importance of the decision of engaging in partnership with e-commerce platform and development companies was evident in the interviews. Two companies had a clear opinion on the risks of ready-made e-commerce platforms. One of the companies had the development of their online channel technologies in-house, and was extremely satisfied with the decision. They felt that having their own e-commerce platform allowed more possibilities regarding customization of the business development. One of the companies had experienced critical difficulties with their selected e-commerce partner. They felt that the company was not contributing enough towards the development of the e-commerce platform.

5 Conclusions and Discussions

Every interviewed company had noticed that majority of their customers have omni-channel behavior. Most prominent change is the increase in the interactions with digital channels during the consumer journey. Many of the customers visit online services before physical stores, or use mobile services while in store.

Along with the constant availability of new digital channels, most of the interviewed companies have reasoned that complete consumer journeys or paths cannot be predetermined or managed. Rather, the emphasis should be in making every existing customer touch-point as good as possible, and supporting smoothly guided proactive transition between relevant touch-points.

When the same experience and message is conveyed in all channels and customer touch-points, it will reduce the risk of losing the customer during their omnichannel customer journey. This notion of unified and integrated experience is also supported by previous articles. According to Bagge [1], it is impossible to understand or predict how and in which order the customer will use different channels and touch-points. Also, according to Yohn [16], common tools like predefined customer journeys, are also incomplete because multiple customer journeys usually exist for a single company. Most companies target more than one customer segment with more than one need or driver, and today's customers engage in more than one channel or sequence of channels.

This varying customer behavior, prominent also in this study, cannot be modeled with predictable paths. None of the interviewees were able or willing to outline a single predictive and occurring customer path in the journey mapping tool. For them, the lack of predictability is best resolved by developing rich, flexible and unified omnichannel services, leaving the consumer with the freedom of engaging in any touch-point in any channel - in their preferred order.

According to Frazer and Stiehler [4], the unity and integration of channels and touch-points is just the first step in creating a good omnichannel experience. Their study emphasizes the seamless experience by studying the consumer's channel switching behavior. In our interviews, the emphasis for creating a seamless customer experience was pointed out as understanding various customers' needs in a touch-point, as well as past actions, and then providing intuitive services and functions in most logical channels to complement customer needs. The customer is not assumed to get the best experience only by continuing on a predetermined path to buy as quickly as possible on this channel, but rather offered a selection of actions in various channels resolving issues in the way of proceeding towards the purchase decision.

In conclusion, according to our study, providing a good omnichannel experience has two key factors:

1. Reducing the risk of losing the customer during customer journey by providing a unified and integrated services and customer experience
2. Encouraging the customer to proceed in the customer journey with the company by providing seamless and intuitive transitions across channels in each touch-point to match customer preferences, needs, and behavior

5.1 Unified and Integrated Customer Experience

In our study, unified customer experience is a key factor for success in omnichannel services. Along with the change from channel oriented thinking into omnichannel approach, this unity has a profound meaning in the interviewed companies. Where unity in channel based development is often associated with more external factors such as user interfaces and branding, unity in omnichannel means strategic and concrete changes in all levels of operations.

From the interviews we conclude four factors in operations influencing unity in omnichannel customer experience: organization and culture, product information and pricing, systems and logistics, and customer communications.

The importance of organizational and cultural unity was clearly emphasized as a prerequisite for unified customer experience. If the company measures its success and sales per channel, the personnel in all levels have no incentive to utilize all of the omnichannel service potential. Unity also requires a new structural approach, where service channels do not set limits within organization for flexible omnichannel development.

Unified pricing and product information across channels is a fundamental requirement for unified customer experience according to our interviews and previous studies. If prices or information vary from one channel to another, it is very difficult to offer customer a unified and intuitive links between channels. Pricing and product information variation decrease the predictability for the customer, and might cause the customers to reconsider their purchase decision. Also, without a clear statement of unified channels, an unbeneficial price competition between channels can occur within the company.

Flexibility in systems and logistics is vital in omnichannel development. Some of the companies stated that they were too dependent on software product development of external e-commerce partners in their own service development. On the other hand, companies able to develop their own e-commerce platform or CRM solutions feel that they have a competitive edge in omnichannel development, with the ability to develop digital services in line with the unified omnichannel experience. E-commerce platform integrated with logistics systems should also comply with intuitive omnichannel service, where customer can freely choose and change on the fly their preferred delivery or pickup method from any service channel. Logistics-wise this requires integrated logistics processes across all channels, where storage and shop availabilities, delivery options and pricing, possibilities to test a product in store etc. create a truly unified service experience.

Unified communications to customers have a significant impact on unified customer experience. With new channels and communications processes with e.g. social media and email, the unity in especially marketing messages in emphasized.

Some of the interviewed companies had recognized that campaigns originally designed in email newsletter or social media marketing should be clearly visible and in line with campaigns in physical and online stores. This requires also marketing personnel to adopt omnichannel approach instead of channel specific activities.

5.2   Seamless Connections Between Customer Touch-Points

In all the interviews, the companies had noticed definite changes in consumer behavior towards a more free movement across channels. Along with this seemingly unpredictable or erratic omnichannel customer behavior, the approach of the companies for developing seamless customer experience had changed. The approach can be argued to have moved along with Huuhka's [8] three waves of omnichannel retail presented in the introduction of this paper:

1. From per-channel oriented process design in **first wave**
2. To multi-channel oriented customer path modelling in **second wave**
3. To the design of supporting free and intuitive customer movement in omnichannel environment in the **third and current wave**

By default, the companies had fewer channels in which the actual sales transactions take place, as compared to all channels in which they are present e.g. in marketing communications. This makes it mandatory to link various touch-points in customer journey across channels in order to convert marketing into sales without losing customers on the way. This logical and intuitive linking of touch-points was considered as far more important area of development, compared to developing channels as individual entities.

In addition, the interviews revealed an ambition to use omnichannel approach as a competitive advantage. In most interviews, "seamless" does not mean the shortest and easiest way to buying, but rather ways to expose customers to company's competitive advantages, without losing the customers at any point along the journey.

It can be argued that companies having adopted omnichannel approach have at the same time moved from developing usability with seamless customer interactions in multi-channel environment into developing business with seamless customer experience in omnichannel environment.

5.3   Reliability and Validity

This study took the commonly acknowledged method of qualitative interviews as the primary way of collecting data. We focused on finding the depth and variety within each question in each interview to overcome the quantitative application and strengthen the qualitative benefit of this study.

In order to validate the approach to interviews, we carried out a substantial theoretical study in order to avoid any problems in validity of the terms used. Also, a preliminary interview was carried out in order to ensure the content validity of the selected questions.

All interviews were recorded and transcribed, and analyzed in TAMS Analyzer. This made it possible for a much more thorough and reliable analysis of the interviews, as well as gave the interviewer more freedom in the interview situation to follow and elaborate the discussion.

In order to get more useful results, the interviewed companies were selected from various business areas. As the results were common and applicable over each business area, it can be argued that these results can be applied to various business areas.

Some of the questions required answers that could be classified as business secrets. This can cause a lack of details in some answers, in order not to reveal future actions in business development. Also, there might be a motivation to give out a more positive estimate on company's readiness to omnichannel development, and not to expose weaknesses. However, there is no clear indication of these aspects distorting the overall results.

As the interviews were restricted to companies with business in Finland, the validity in market areas with major differences in consumer readiness to omnichannel behavior can be questioned. This can be especially visible in the use of online channels, where Finland has a high availability and usage among all population.

5.4   Future Work

To complement this study, a similar study from consumer behavior perspective would give more depth and validity to the decisions made by these companies to respond to the changes in consumer behavior.

A study on the effect of businesses omnichannel strategy to "free-riding" or "showrooming" phenomenon would provide insight as to whether a company can actually lower the probability of losing a customer during buying process to a competitor by adopting an omnichannel strategy.

A study of clear dependence of seamless omnichannel behavior and buying can give more validity on the assumption that proactively supported seamless transition between channels results in better customer experience. This, in turn, may result in customers buying more often and bigger volumes.

References

1. Bagge, D.: Multi-channel retailing: the route to customer focus. Eur. Retail Dig. **53**, 57–70 (2007)
2. Bell, D.R., Galliano, S., Moreno, A.: How to win in an omnichannel world. MIT Sloan Manage. Rev. **56**(1), 45–53 (2014)
3. Deloitte. The omnichannel opportunity - Unlocking the power of the connected consumer (2014). http://www2.deloitte.com/content/dam/Deloitte/uk/Documents/consumer-business/unlocking-the-power-of-the-connected-consumer.pdf. Accessed
4. Frazer, M., Stiehler, B.E.: Omnichannel retailing: the merging of the online and offline environment. In: Proceedings of the Global Conference on Business and Finance, vol. 9, issue no. 1, pp. 655–657, January 2014
5. Gensler, S., Verhoef, P.C., Böhm, M.: Understanding consumers' multi-channel choices across the different stages of the buying process. Mark. Lett. **23**(4), 987–1003 (2012)
6. Griffiths, G.H., Howard, A.: Balancing clicks and bricks-strategies for multi-channel retailers. J. Glob. Bus. Issues **2**(1), 69–76 (2008)
7. Heitz-Spahn, S.: Cross-channel free-riding consumer behavior in a multi-channel environment: an investigation of shopping motives, sociodemographics and product categories. J. Retail. Consum. Serv. **20**(6), 570–578 (2013)

8. Huuhka, A., Laaksonen, M., Laaksonen, P.: The evolution of new systemic forms in retailing and digital business. In: Contributions to International Business, Acta Wasaensia, vol. 303, pp. 239–249 (2014)
9. Koskinen, I., Alasuutari, P., Peltonen, T.: Laadulliset menetelmät kauppatieteissä (2005)
10. Lazaris, C., Vrechopoulos, A.: From multi-channel to "omnichannel" retailing: review of the literature and calls for research. In: 2nd International Conference on Contemporary Marketing Issues, (ICCMI), June 2014
11. Müller-Lankenau, C., Wehmeyer, K., Klein, S.: Strategic channel alignment: an analysis of the configuration of physical and virtual marketing channels. Inf. Syst. e-Bus. Manag. 4(2), 187–216 (2006)
12. Piotrowicz, W., Cuthbertson, R.: Introduction to the special issue information technology in retail: toward omnichannel retailing. Int. J. Electron. Commer. 18(4), 5–16 (2014)
13. Regalado, A.: It's All E-Commerce Now. MIT Technology Review, 3 November 2013. http://www.technologyreview.com/news/520786/its-all-e-commerce-now/. Accessed
14. Rigby, D.: The future of shopping. Harv. Bus. Rev. 89(12), 65–76 (2011)
15. Stickdorn, M., Schneider, J.: This is Service Design Thinking: Basics, Tools, Cases. Wiley, Hoboken (2011)
16. Yohn, D.L.: 7 Steps to Deliver Better Customer Experiences. Harvard Business Review, 3 Feburary 2015. https://hbr.org/2015/02/7-steps-to-deliver-better-customer-experiences. Accessed

The Role of Brand Loyalty and Social Media in E-Commerce Interfaces: Survey Results and Implications for User Interfaces

Dimitrios Rigas$^{(\boxtimes)}$ and Hammad Akhtar Hussain

University of West London, London W5 5RF, UK
{Dimitrios.Rigas,Hammad.Hussain}@uwl.ac.uk

Abstract. This paper explores the role of brand loyalty and social media in e-commerce interfaces. A survey consisting of 118 respondents was contacted to address the questions relating to online shopping and brand loyalty. The issues investigated included the link between the frequency of access and time spent on an e-commerce user interface, and brand loyalty, gender and age profile differences, and the role of social media to branding and on-line shopping. It was found that online loyalty differs from offline loyalty and loyalty also differed across genders, showing that males may develop loyalty easier than females when shopping online. Information shared about products on social media by friends and family played an important role in purchase decision making. Website interface and ease of navigation were also key aspects for online shopping. The research concluded with some pointers towards multimodal interfaces that aid loyalty with the use of interactive multimodal social media.

Keywords: On-line consumer behavior · Brand loyalty · E-commence interfaces · Social media interfaces · User interface guidelines

1 Introduction

E-commerce interfaces has become common with the advancement of technology and user friendly devices such as smartphones and tablets. According to the UK Office of the National Statistics [1], £678.8million was spent online in February 2014. Alba et al. [2] suggest that online purchase follows different rules to traditional face-to-face shopping because it is 'virtual'. Therefore it can be asserted that the dynamics of online purchase may be different from the face-to-face shopping experience.

A brand name is often the first point of contact between the customer and the product [3]. Lee and Carter [4] define brand as a differentiator amongst competitors in the market. Moreover, a brand gives out information about the price, performance, quality and the content of a product or service [4]. Rigas et al., [31–33] suggest that the use of multimodal metaphors in e-commerce interfaces is an effective mode of communication to deliver the required information. Extending the idea of Brand, the ideology of Brand Loyalty comes into context where Dick and Basu [5] define Brand Loyalty as a commitment from the consumer to repurchase or keep on using the same

© Springer International Publishing Switzerland 2015
F.F.-H. Nah and C.-H. Tan (Eds.): HCIB 2015, LNCS 9191, pp. 347–357, 2015.
DOI: 10.1007/978-3-319-20895-4_32

product or services. However, it is very hard to achieve loyalty from consumers. Goldscher [6] explains that today's consumers are 'frighteningly disloyal'. This raises the question of the interactivity needed so that online customers become loyal. The online e-commerce user may be affected by several factors during the development of brand loyalty [7, 8]. Loyalty is complex, intriguing, multidimensional, and needs to be maintained [9]. Evans et al. [10] suggest that 'user satisfaction' leads to brand loyalty.

2 Literature Review

2.1 Technology Acceptance Model (TAM)

There is no definitive model that can fully explain the acceptance or rejection of a system [11]. The Technology Acceptance Model (TAM) was proposed by Fred Davis [12] and was based on previous models created by Fishbein and Ajzen [13]. TAM has become a leading model to predict whether user will use or reject the system [14]. Figure 1 shows the latest version of TAM as illustrated by Venkatesh and Davis [26].

2.2 Decision Making Process

Convenience is one of the reasons that users access e-commerce interfaces [7, 15–17]. The question of convenience comes when a consumer analyses all the options prior to a purchase. The decision making model in Fig. 2 shows the stages that consumers take during purchase. Although made for offline consumers but the model is applicable to both online and offline consumers.

A problem occurs when there is a significant difference between what a consumer has and what they desire [27] which results in a gap between the actual state and the desired state [28]. The desired stage on the context of buying online can be a recommendation from a friend, family or even a picture on a social networking website.

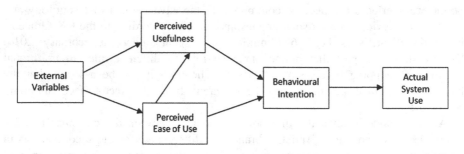

Fig. 1. Technology acceptance model (Venkatesh and Davis, 1996, [26])

Fig. 2. Decision making model (Engel, Kollat, Blackwell, 1968)

But on the other hand another reason for the trigger of this need can be a change in the circumstance of the consumer which has led to the creation of this need [27].

Consumers, with intermediate or advanced knowledge of the Internet, prefer to be kept updated on the marketplace and they often are involved in a so-called *ongoing search* [29]. According to Solomon [27], consumers seek information for a product in a specific category through social networking so that they can eliminate the items/brands with lower ratings. However, if a consumer is brand loyal and makes habitual decisions, then the processes 1 to 4 (see Fig. 2) may not even be carried out [27]. In this case, the transaction would be carried out instantly (*re-purchase*, 5th step) given the previous experience and preference for the brand. The e-commerce interfaces play an important role in the re-purchase. An excellent user experience with good ease-of-use of the interface is likely to gravitate the user to the ecommerce interface for all user purchases.

2.3 Theory of Reasoned Action and Planned Behaviour

The Theory of Reasoned Action (TRA) and Theory of Planned Behaviour (TPB) take user attitudes and social influences into account [13]. TRA in Fig. 3. shows that actions are the direct results of a person's 'intentions' and these actions are taken under 'volitional' control [18]. However, Warshaw [19] suggests that behaviour is not completely under the control of the actor.

As a result the TPB was formed, which is the extended version of the TRA [20, 21]. According to Evans et al. [10], the TPB model, as shown in Fig. 4, takes into account the 'influence' of other people (e.g. parents, partner, friends or other users) to a user's e-commerce decision-making.

These models were challenged [22, 23] as they assume that an e-commerce user goes through this '*comprehensive cognitive processing*' prior to completing a purchase.

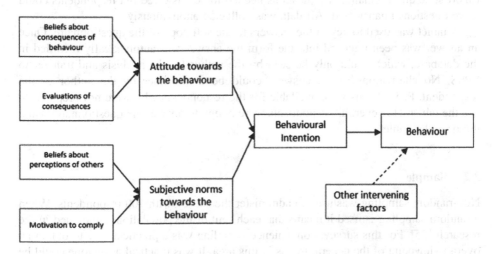

Fig. 3. Theory of reasoned action (Fishbein and Ajzen, 1975; Loudon and Bitta, 1993)

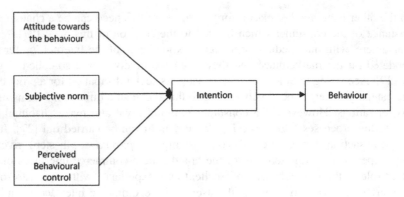

Fig. 4. Theory of planned behaviour (Ajzen, 1991)

They also do not take into account possible emotional, habitual, spontaneity and user cravings [24]. Other factors that may affect on-line user behavior include lack of finance, motivation, and change of circumstances Evans et al. [10].

3   Methodology

3.1   Survey

The data was collected through a self-completion questionnaire in various shopping locations around London, UK. The reason it was administered in various shopping locations in London was because it would give better opinions from the shoppers who select to shop offline rather than shopping online. A large number of people head towards shopping in markets, and they have experience of shopping in store and online. The questionnaire comprised of 31 closed end questions of which 11 were using a Likert-style questionnaire. All questions needed to be answered but respondents could leave questions unanswered. All data was collected anonymously.

A tablet was used to key in the answers to the soft copy of the questionnaire. Once an answer was been punched into the form the answer was automatically recorded in the database, which could only be seen by the author for the analysis and transfer to SPSS. No alternations to the answers could be done either by the author or the respondent. Paper forms were available for the respondents who were not prepared to use the tablet. However, all respondents were happy to answer the questionnaire using the provided tablet.

3.2   Sample

Non-random sampling was used to administer the survey with 100 respondents. When a random sampling is used it means that each unit of the population is included in the research [25]. For this survey, convenience sampling was a practical way to obtain an overall viewpoint of the general trends in this area. It was practical as anyone could be approached irrespective of their traits to fill out the questionnaire. If a different type of non-probability sample was used it would be difficult to gather data and the element of biasness would be higher. In convenience sampling the response rate is also high but it will be more difficult to generalise the results [25].

3.3 Response Rate

A total of 117 respondents were asked to carry out the questionnaire. 115 (98.3 %) valid responses were received back. There were two missing cases which accounted to 1.7 % of missing or invalid responses. Two respondents did not fill in their gender. Therefore the number of males who participated in the research was 60 (52.2 %) and 55 (47.8 %) for females.

4 Findings and Analysis

From the questionnaire, eight different factors were selected and divided across genders to compare and contrast their effect on the Purchase Decision. These findings are discussed according to:

1. *Proficiency on the Internet:* The Internet proficiency of the respondents was important in order to better understand their predisposition to online loyalty.
2. *Online vs Offline Brand Loyalty:* The results would demonstrate some difference between online and offline brand loyalty and relate this to gender.
3. *Important Factors to Online Shopping:* This is to obtain an overall viewpoint of the factors that motivate users to shop online.
4. *Time Spend on Websites and Brand Loyalty:* The possible linking time spent on e-commerce websites to brand loyalty.
5. *Frequency of Visit and Brand Loyalty:* In traditional face-to-face shopping, consumers visit their favorite retailers more often than other shops. This question would show whether this is correct in online shopping.
6. *Role of Social Media in Brand Loyalty:* The influence of social media to online users that predisposes to the development of brand loyalty.
7. *Factors Which Keep Consumers Away from Online Shopping:* This was to identify some of the reasons that could prevent users from online shopping.

4.1 Online Experience of the Sample

Figure 5 shows that 53.8 % of the people were using Internet for eight years or more and 50.4 % people described themselves as advanced users of the Internet. By advanced they meant that they were very good, very confident and experienced users of the internet. These results not only show the time since people have been using internet or their proficiency but also it shows that these days people have become technology friendly and use the Internet more than ever before. Therefore confirming ease of use of technology of the TAM.

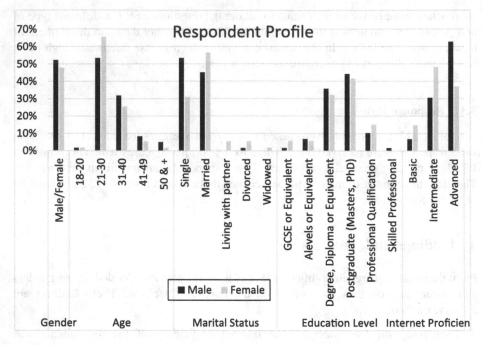

Fig. 5. Profile of the respondents

4.2 Online Vs Offline Brand Loyalty by Gender

Figure 6 shows that 28.7 % of the males regarded themselves as brand loyal and 23.5 % of the females regarded themselves as not loyal when they shopped in store. 21.7 % females were brand loyal which is 7 % less than males. 26.1 % females agreed that they are not brand loyal when they shop in store. However, when it came to online shopping 36 % of males considered themselves as brand loyal as compared to only 25.4 % of female agreeing that they are brand loyal when shopping online.

4.3 Important Factors to on-Line Shopping

The first set of most important factors, as shown in Fig. 7, for shopping online are *brands* (26.1 %), *price* (16.2 %) and *convenience* (14.4 %). The reason for price being a factor is that there are so many people who have no specific loyalty. Their main aim is to acquire cheaper products. This can be easily achieved online, as there are low costs for the online businesses. It is not surprising that convenience is a factor as people to shop online.

In the second set of most important factors was *time-saving* (24.1 %), which was almost a quarter of respondents. It was followed by convenience (19.4 %) and price (15.7 %). Brand came at number four with only 14.8 % people selecting it as an option. This may be because they have selected this option in the previous question.

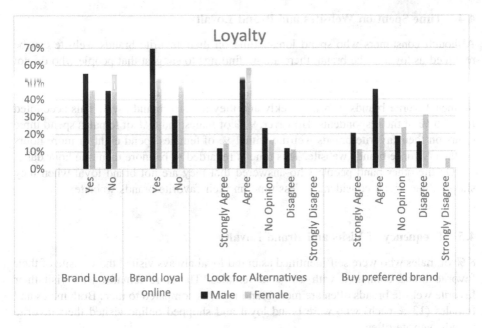

Fig. 6. Brand loyalty online and offline

Fig. 7. First and Second most important Factor to Shop Online

4.4 Time Spent on Websites and Brand Loyalty

Although consumers who spend longer time on their favorite brands website can be regarded as loyal to the brand, there are no findings to suggest that people who do not spend time on their favorite brands website are not loyal.

The results show that 28 % of males and 22 % of females spend two to three hours on their favorite brands website weekly and they are also brand loyal. This accounted for 72.5 % of the respondents. However, 9 % of males and 6 % of females spend three hours on their favorite brands website with 1 % of females spend eight or more hours on their favorite brands website. This time is regarded to be more than one hour daily.

On the other band people who answered that they are not brand loyal when they shop online, spend considerably less time on their favorite brands website.

4.5 Frequency of Visits and Brand Loyalty

8 % of males who were self-identified as brand loyal always visited the website of their favorite brand compared with 10 % of females. Therefore females who visit their favorite website brands often are more brand loyal as compared to men. Both males and females (13 % each) who were brand loyal and shopped online visited their favorite brands website often.

This number significantly drops for females to 4 %. However, the opposite happened with male respondents. The percentage increased to 17 % when it came to visit their favorite brands website. A total of 26.1 % respondents always visited their favorite brands website whereas this number jumps to 37.5 % who say that their visit their favorite brands website sometimes. With regard to the frequency of respondents visiting their preferred brand website sometimes, a high percentage of 30.4 % was found. Surprisingly there were 5.8 % respondents who never visited their preferred brand website.

4.6 Role of Social Media in Brand Loyalty

38.5 % respondents agreed that they followed social networking recommendations and also a 45.7 % of respondents agreed that they tried to purchase an item following a social influence. Respondents strongly agreed (7.8 %) to search online to purchase similar items that have been previously bought by their friends. However, 13.7 % strongly agreed to follow social media recommendation from their friends and family.

4.7 Factors Preventing Consumers from On-line Shopping

Consumers were enquired about factors which keep them away from online shopping. Results showed that online shoppers were concerned about the value of the product for the price paid. 17 % of the respondents raised alarms of not receiving the item whereas 37 respondents (16 %) were worried about credit card frauds.

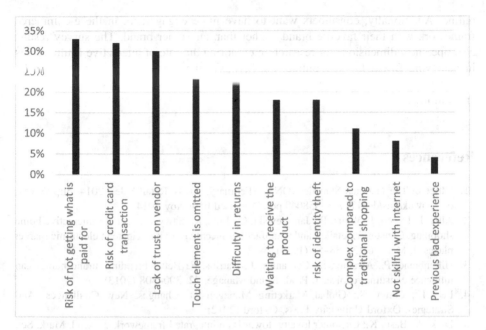

Fig. 8. Factors which keep away from shopping online

The third most important factor identified by the respondents was the lack of trustworthiness of vendors, which accounted for 15 % of the respondents. This is a difference between online and offline shopping as there is no physical interaction between the customer and the vendors. This is a trust related issue. The results are shown in Fig. 8.

5 Conclusion: Implications for E-Commerce Interfaces

The results from the survey carried out showed directions and areas of improvements in the e-commerce interfaces. The top five reasons why people do not shop online are the areas for further development in the e-commerce sector. The top three issues that prevent consumers from shopping online can be eliminated through appropriate interaction between the consumer and the vendor. Interactive multimodal websites and applications shall be created to provide better overall experience and satisfaction to consumers which also leads to loyalty online. Interactive multimodals not only convey messages but also build 'trust' on the vendors which is a major weaknesses in current e-commerce interfaces framework.

Social media also plays an important role not only for businesses to market their products and services but also to collect valuable feedback from consumers to improve the products. The research findings inform the online user interface industry about the importance of presence within the social media and user engagement which is more likely to lead to purchase and online brand loyalty. This is derived from how consumers follow their friends lead on social media and look for similar items to buy online. Additionally, consumers want to have more engagement in the e-commerce framework with their favorite brands rather than any other brand. The survey results also open new dimensions for research in exploring the role of interactive Multimodals in achieving Brand Loyalty online. Furthermore, the survey results also trigger the importance to research why female gender is less brand loyal when they shop online and offline.

References

1. Office of The National Statistics (ONS). (February, 2014). Retail Sales, 2014. http://www. ons.gov.uk/ons/dcp171778_358049.pdf. Accessed 05th Nov 2014
2. Alba, J., Lynch, J., Weitz, B., Janiszewski, C., Lutz, R., Sawyer, A., et al.: Interactive home shopping: Consumer, retailer, and manufacturer incentives to participate in electronic market places. J. Mark. 61(3), 38–53 (1997)
3. Hillenbrand, P., Alcauter, S., Cervantes, J., Barrios, F.: Better branding: brand names can influence consumer choice. J. Prod. Brand Manage. 22, 300–308 (2013)
4. Lee, K., Carter, S.: Global Marketing Management: Changes, New Challenges, And Strategies. Oxford University Press, Oxford (2012)
5. Dick, A., Basu, K.: Customer loyalty: towards an integrated framework. J. Acad. Mark. Sci. 22(2), 99–113 (1994)
6. Goldscher, S.: Count the ways to loyalty, part 1. BNP Media, Northbrook (1998)
7. Degeratu, A.M., Rangaswamy, A., Wu, J.N.: Consumer choice behavior in online and traditional supermarkets: the effects of brand name, price, and other search attributes. Int. J. Res. Mark. 17, 55–78 (2000)
8. Emmanouilides, C., Hammond, K.: Internet usage: predictors of active users and frequency of use. J. Interact. Mark. 14(2), 17–32 (2000)
9. Kalauz, Maja, Vranesevic, Tihomir, Trantnik, Miroslav: The clothing brand loyalty of teenagers: differences between loyalty and desire to be loyal. Int. J. Manage. Cases 13(4), 156–164 (2011)
10. Evans, M., Foxall, G.R., Jamal, A.: Consumer behaviour. Wiley, Chichester (2009)
11. Davis, F.: Perceived usefulness, perceived ease of use, and user acceptance of information technology. MIS Quartely 13(3), 319–340 (1989)
12. Davis, F.: A Technology Acceptance Model for empirically testing new end-user information systems: theory and results. Unpublished Doctoral Dissertation, MIT Sloan School of Management, Cambridge, MA (1985)
13. Fishbein, M., Ajzen, I.: Belief, Attitude, Intention and Behaviour: An Introduction to Theory and Research. Addison-Wesley, Reading (1975)
14. Lee, Y., Kozar, K.A., Larsen, K.R.T.: The Technology acceptance model: past, present, and future. Commun. AIS 12(50), 752–780 (2003)
15. Beauchamp, M.B., Ponder, N.: Perceptions of retail convenience for in-store and online shoppers. Market. Manage. J. 20(1), 49–65 (2010)
16. Colwell, S.R., Aung, M., Kanetkar, V., Holden, A.L.: Toward a measure of service convenience: multiple-item scale development and empirical test. J. Serv. Mark. 22(2), 160–169 (2008)
17. Reimers, V., Clulow, V.: Retail centres: it's time to make them convenient. Int. J. Retail Distrib. Manage. 37(7), 541–562 (2009)

18. Fishbein, M., Stasson, M.: The role of desires, self-predictions, and perceived control in the prediction of training session attendance. J. Appl. Soc. Psychol. **20**, 173–198 (1990)
19. Warshaw, P.R.: Predicting Purchase and other behaviors from generally and contextually specific intentions. J. Mark. **17**, 26–33 (1980)
20. Ajzen, I.: Attitudes, personality, and behavior. Harvey Press, Chicago (1900)
21. Ajzen, I., Madden, T.J.: Prediction of goal-directed behavior: Attitudes, intentions, and perceived behavioral control. J. Exp. Soc. Psychol. **22**, 453–474 (1986)
22. Bagozzi, R.P.: Atttudes, intentions, and behavior: A test of some key hypotheses. J. Pers. Soc. Psychol. **41**, 607–627 (1981)
23. Gürhan-Canli, Z., Ahluwalia, R.: Understanding processes underlying consumer inferences. In: Broniarczyk, S., Nakamoto, K. (eds.) Advances in Consumer Research, vol. 29, p. 489. Association for Consumer Research, Provo (2002)
24. Hale, J.L., Householder, B.J., Greene, K.L.: The theory of reasoned action. In: Dillard, J.P., Pfau, M. (eds.) The Persuasion Handbook: Developments in Theory and Practice, pp. 259–286. Sage, Thousand Oaks (2002)
25. Bryman, A., Bell, E.: Business Research Methods. Oxford University Press, Oxford (2011)
26. Venkatesh, V., Davis, F.D.: A model of the antecedents of perceived ease of use: development and test. Decis. Sci. **27**(3), 451–481 (1996)
27. Solomon, M., et al.: Consumer Behaviour: A European Perspective, 3rd edn. Prentice Hall, Harlow (2006)
28. Bruner, I.I., Gordon, C., Pomazal, Richard J.: Problem recognition: the crucial first stage of the consumer decision process. J. Consum. Mark. **5**(1), 53–63 (1988)
29. Bloch, P.H., Sherrell, D.L., Ridgeway, N.M.: Consumer search: an extended framework. J. Consum. Res. **13**, 119–126 (1986)
30. Engel, J.F., Kollat, D.T., Blackwell, R.D.: Consumer Behavior. Holt, Rinehart & Winston, New York (1968)
31. Rigas, D.I., Alty, J.L.: Using sound to communicate program execution. In: Proceedings of the 24th EUROMICRO Conference, vol. 2 pp. 625–632 (1998)
32. Rigas, D., Hopwood, D.: The role of multimedia in interfaces for on-line learning. In: 9th Panhellenic Conference on Informatics (PCI 2003), Thessaloniki, Greece (2003)
33. Rigas, D.I.: Guidelines for Auditory Interface Design: An Empirical Investigation. Ph.D thesis, Loughborough University of Technology (1996)
34. Rigas, D., Almutairi, B.: An empirical investigation into the role of avatars in multimodal e-government interfaces. Int. J. Sociotechnology Knowl. Dev. (IJSKD) **5**(1), 14–22 (2013)

The Mediating Role of Perceived Security:
An Empirical Study of Mobile Wallet Adoption
in USA

Norman Shaw[✉]

Ryerson University, Toronto, ON, Canada
norman.shaw@ryerson.ca

Abstract. Because the USA is introducing 'chip and pin' card standards in 2015, payment terminals are being implemented that have the capability of reading plastic cards that are simply waved in proximity to the terminal. With the aid of a 'mobile wallet' app, smartphones are able to substitute for the physical card and complete contactless payments. The transaction flows through an ecosystem that is comprised of the smartphone manufacturers, software developers, mobile network providers and financial institutions. However, consumer adoption has been slow and, in order to help practitioners with their investment decisions, this study seeks to explain the factors that influence intention to use. Theory extends the technology acceptance model with the constructs of perceived security and personal innovativeness. An empirical study supports the hypotheses and explains the mediating role of perceived security.

Keywords: Mobile wallet · Technology acceptance · Perceived security · Personal innovativeness · PLS

1 Introduction

In order to counter credit card fraud, a new card payment technology, 'chip and pin' is being introduced into the USA in 2015. This new card payment standard has been developed by EMVCo, whose member organizations are American Express, Discover, JCB, MasterCard, UnionPay and Visa [1]. At the same time that merchants are upgrading their payment terminals, consumers are being encouraged to upgrade their payment cards. The Aite Group estimates that 75 % of the credit cards in the USA will be chip enabled by the end of 2015 [2].

The EMV standard includes contactless payments using Near Field Communications (NFC). Many smartphones also have NFC capability, which enables them to replace the physical wallet with a 'mobile wallet' [3]. With the physical card, consumers are aware of the organizations that assure the security of the payment transaction, but with the mobile wallet, the ecosystem is more complex, with the addition of smartphone manufacturers, app developers and mobile network providers [4]. As examples, Google Wallet is a partnership with Sprint and Citi MasterCard [5] and Isis Mobile Wallet is a partnership between the US wireless companies, Verizon, T-Mobile

© Springer International Publishing Switzerland 2015
F.F.-H. Nah and C.-H. Tan (Eds.): HCIB 2015, LNCS 9191, pp. 358–369, 2015.
DOI: 10.1007/978-3-319-20895-4_33

and AT&T [5]. On 9 September 2014, Apple, who was the last major smartphone supplier not supporting NFC, added NFC to its iPhone 6, with the introduction of ApplePay [6].

In order to advance acceptance of the mobile wallet, companies that make up the extended ecosystem must consider additional investments in the infrastructure to overcome any adoption barriers, such as security concerns. In order to assist practitioners with their investment decision, our research question is how does perceived security influence consumers' intentions to use a mobile wallet.

This paper is organized as follows. The next section is the literature review, in which we develop our research model. The third section is the research methods where we introduce the scales that will measure each construct. We analyze the results in the fourth section. In the fifth section we discus the results and include the limitations of the current research and suggestions for future research. Our conclusions are presented in the final section.

2 Literature Review

2.1 Technology Acceptance

TAM was originally designed by Davis [7] to help software designers design applications for an organization that would be adopted by its employees. It has since been applied to the adoption of personal computing, such as Internet shopping [8, 9] and mobile commerce [10, 11]. The model is parsimonious with two independent variables that predict intention to use: perceived usefulness (PU) and perceived ease of use (PEOU).

Designers of the wallet are emphasizing the usefulness of the mobile wallet when compared to the physical card. It is also easy to use by just waving the phone over the terminal. Our first two hypotheses are:

Hypothesis 1:   Perceived usefulness positively influences intention to use a mobile wallet.

Hypothesis 2:   Perceived ease of use positively influences intention to use a mobile wallet.

2.2 The Role of Perceived Security

Chellappa and Pavlou [12] define the security of a payment as 'the flow of information originating from the right entity and reaching the intended party without being observed, altered or destroyed during transit and storage'. When making a payment, consumers' prime concern is security [13, 14]. In a study by Linck et al. [15], consumers stated that their concerns were confidentiality, authentication, integrity, authorization and non-repudiation. Mobile payments decrease the sense of security because personal data is stored on the smartphone, which can be lost or stolen. We therefore add perceived security to our model:

Hypothesis 3:   Perceived security positively influences perceived usefulness.
Hypothesis 4:   Perceived security positively influences perceived ease of use.

2.3   Personal Innovativeness

In Roger's study of the theory of diffusion and innovations [16], he found that innovations diffuse at different rates depending, amongst other characteristics, on the attitude of the individual. Although there is less information available from the trials and
observations of the innovation, early adopters are willing to take more risks. They are
more comfortable with uncertainty [17] and tend to seek out stimulating experiences
[18]. Agarwal and Prasad captured this concept with the construct of personal innovativeness, which they defined 'as the willingness to try out a new information technology' [19]. We follow their practice and extend TAM by hypothesizing:

Hypothesis 5:   Personal innovativeness positively influences perceived usefulness.
Hypothesis 6:   Personal innovativeness positively influences perceived ease of use.

2.4   Perceived Security as a Mediating Variable

Innovators are willing to take risks [17], but when it comes to payments they still
require that the transaction is processed securely. If the new mobile payment ecosystem
is perceived to be less secure than the current means of payment, early adopters might
hesitate until they are persuaded that more security is in place. Following Baron and
Kenny's description that mediation is the mechanism where 'an active organism
intervenes between stimulus and response' [20], we hypothesize that perceived security
is a mediating variable.

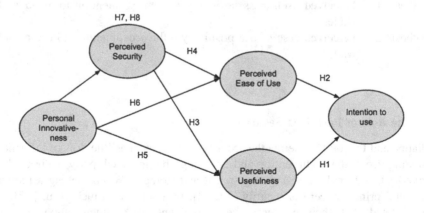

Fig. 1. Research model for acceptance of mobile wallet

Hypothesis 7:   Perceived security mediates the influence of perceived usefulness on intention to use the mobile wallet.

Hypothesis 8:   Perceived security mediates the influence of perceived ease of use on intention to use the mobile wallet.

2.5 Research Model

The research model is shown in Fig. 1.

3 Research Methods

Data from an online survey was analysed using PLS. The survey questions used indicators for the constructs that were borrowed from the extant literature. For perceived ease of use, perceived usefulness and intention to use, we turned to Chandra et al. [21] whose study was focussed on the use of a mobile payment system. We adopted the scale for perceived security from D. Shin [3] and for ppersonal innovativeness we went to the original study by Agarwal and Prasad [22].

The content of the questionnaire was developed with the help of experts. Then tested against a small sample. Finally, with the help of a sampling company that had panels of consumers, we sent the survey to 800 participants in the United States who were eighteen years old or over and who owned a smartphone. 597 completed questionnaires were received and further analyzed with the help of Partial Least Squares (PLS) using the SmartPLS software.

Following the recommendations of Hair et al. [23], we first evaluated the measurement model for internal consistency by calculating Cronbach's alpha and evaluating composite reliability. The convergence of indicators on their constructs was tested by calculating the average variance extracted. In addition, the Fornell-Larcker criterion was used to test the discriminant validity of all the constructs in the model.

After completing the analysis of the measurement model, we evaluated the structural model [23]. The coefficients of determination (R^2) were calculated for all endogenous variables. For each path in the model, the size of the path coefficients were calculated and bootstrapping was used to determine their significance. f^2 was calculated to measure the effect size for each construct. To test the role of perceived security as a mediating variable, we calculated the Variance Accounted For (VAF) factor, following Preacher's method of multiplying the indirect effects [24].

4 Results

4.1 Descriptive Statistics

In the sample, there were 296 males (49.6 %) and 301 females (50.4 %). Almost half the sample (4 %) was between 18 and 40 years of age and remaining 52 % was 41 and above, with the oldest participant 75. The median length of ownership for those who

Table 1. Ownership by type of phone

Type	Number	%
Android	392	66 %
Apple	207	35 %
Microsoft	28	5 %
Blackberry	21	4 %

*Note: some participants have more
than one phone, so the total is
greater than 100 %*

possessed a smartphone was 3.5 years with 50 % having owned a smartphone for three years or more. Table 1 shows the ownership by type of phone.

4.2 The Measurement Model

The cross loadings of the measurement model were calculated by the SmartPLS software and the indicators were shown to be collinear. All correlation coefficients were greater than the threshold value of 0.708 [25]. By running a Bootstrap within SmartPLS with 5,000 samples using the replacement method, the t statistic for each cross loading was calculated and in every case, the significance was $p < 0.001$.

The internal consistency of each construct was assessed via Cronbach's alpha [26], where values above 0.8 indicate reliability. The Average Variance Extracted (AVE) for each construct further confirmed the reliability of the model, where the AVE was above the guideline of 0.5. In addition, the Composite Reliability was above the guideline of 0.6 [25].

Discriminant validity was tested using the Fornell-Larcker score, where the AVE must be greater than the square of the correlations [27]. Table 2 compares the correlations with the square root of AVE (shown in italic bold along the diagonal).

Table 2. Values for Fornell Larcker test

Construct	ITU	PEOU	PI	PU	PS
Intention to use	**0.893**				
Perceived ease of use	0.628	**0.853**			
Personal innovativeness	0.527	0.556	**0.92**		
Perceived usefulness	0.782	0.719	0.527	**0.887**	
Perceived security	0.724	0.658	0.45	0.699	**0.912**

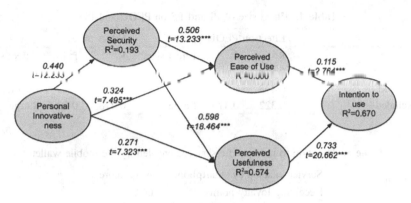

Fig. 2. Results of analysis of structural model

Table 3. Effect Size on Intention to Use

	R^2	f^2	Effect size
All constructs R^2 included	0.621		
PI excluded	0.621	–	
PEOU excluded	0.612	0.02	Small
PS excluded	0.621	–	
PU excluded	0.395	0.60	Large

4.3 The Structural Model

The SmartPLS algorithm calculated the R^2 measures for each endogenous variable and the path coefficients for each path within the model. R^2 for intention to use was 0.670, which is considered moderate [28]. All hypotheses were supported. Results are shown in Fig. 2.

The effect size was calculated in a series of steps, where each exogenous variable was removed from the model in turn and the new R squared calculated. The effect size is represented by f squared, where values between 0.02 and 0.14 are small, between 0.15 and 0.34 are medium and 0.35 and above are large [25]. Table 3 shows that PU has a large effect size and PEOU has a small effect size.

We also evaluated the effect size of personal innovativeness and perceived security on the intervening variables, PEOU and PU. Personal innovativeness had a large effect and personal security had a medium effect. See Table 4.

4.4 Intention to Use

In the questionnaire, participants were asked about their intention to use other features that would be enabled by a mobile wallet. See Table 5.

Table 4. Effect size of PI and PS on PEOU and PU

	Effect on PEOU			Effect on PU		
	R^2	f^2	Effect size	R^2	f^2	Effect size
All constructs R2 included	0.518			0.545		
PI excluded	0.433	0.18	Medium	0.489	0.12	Medium
PS excluded	0.322	0.41	Large	0.278	0.59	Large

Table 5. Intention to use specific services enabled by the mobile wallet

Service enabled by smartphone	Avge score
Receiving loyalty points	66.0
Paying by credit	64.5
Receiving digital receipts	64.3
Receiving e-coupons	61.7
Paying by debit	61.1
Paying with loyalty points	60.4
Paying by pre-paid card	45.4
Using for transit	44.1
Exchanging $ with a friend	40.5

Participants indicated their preference to use their smartphone for the convenience of handling loyalty points and for managing receipts and coupons. Unlike payments, these are features that are enabled by the mobile wallet innovation.

4.5 Perceived Security as a Mediator

In order to evaluate the effect of perceived security as a mediating variable, we evaluated the indirect paths: personal innovativeness to perceived security to perceived ease of use; and personal innovativeness to perceived security to perceived usefulness. From running a bootstrap, all paths were significant with p > 0.001. We also ran the model without perceived security. The paths are illustrated in Figs. 3 and 4.

The indirect effect was calculated as the product of a and b [24]. The Variance Accounted For was derived from the formula

$$VAF = a * b / (a * b + c')$$

Table 6 shows the results. In both cases, the mediation is partial. VAF can have values from 0 % to 100 %, where 100 % represents full mediation. A value of 41 % is a moderate VAF level [23, 29, 30]. Our conclusion is that perceived security as a mediator has a moderate effect on perceived ease of use and a moderate effect on perceived usefulness, accounting for 41 % and 49 % of the variance respectively.

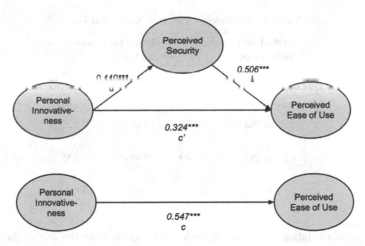

Fig. 3. Mediation of perceived security on the effect of personal innovativeness on perceived ease of use.

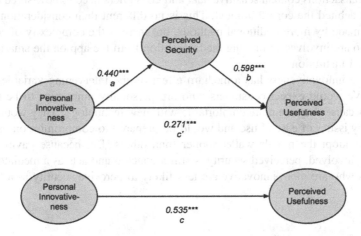

Fig. 4. Mediation of perceived security on the effect of personal innovativeness on perceived usefulness.

5 Discussion

PU has a large effect on intention to use, consistent with other studies of TAM [31, 32]. This also confirms Roger's conclusion that adopters perceive a relative advantage of the innovation over the current process [16]. As Table 5 shows, consumers see advantages, over and above just the payment, such as the handling of loyalty points and the reduction of paper receipts.

In our empirical setting, the effect of PEOU on intention to use is small, which is consistent with past studies [31]. The explanation here is that using a smartphone to

Table 6. Mediation - Variance Accounted For

	Effect on perceived ease of use		Effect on Perceived usefulness	
	Path	Coeff.	Path	Coeff.
a	PI to PS	0.440	PI to PS	0.442
b	PS to PEOU	0.506	PS to PU	0.598
c'	PI to PEOU	0.324	PI to PU	0.271
c	PI to PEOU	0.549	PI to PU	0.535
	VAF	41 %	VAF	49 %

pay is a simple operation and does not differ very much from the use of the physical payment card. Consequently learning to use the mobile wallet is perceived to be easy.

Perceived security has a large effect on the intervening variables, PEOU and PU. Payment transactions contain sensitive data and consumers need to be assured that their account is debited the correct amount. This is no different than considerations around payments made by more traditional methods, but there is the complexity of additional parties who are involved in moving the transaction from the app on the smartphone to the financial institution.

Personal innovativeness has a medium effect on the intervening variables, PEOU and PU. We would expect consumers who are personally innovative to be the early adopters because they are more comfortable with new technology. They would be less inhibited by issues of ease of use and would be prepared to compromise on usefulness in order to adopt the mobile wallet sooner than others. But because payment transactions are involved, perceived security is still a concern and acts as a mediator. Those consumers who are more innovative are less likely to perceive security as a barrier to adoption.

5.1   Theoretical Contribution

Our theoretical contribution is to add to the theory that has extended TAM in the context of consumer acceptance of the mobile wallet. Past studies have evaluated personal innovativeness and perceived security, but they have not been combined in the same model with an evaluation of the mediation effect of perceived security. It is the challenge of the researcher to construct a parsimonious model that explains phenomena minimizing confounding effects [33]. Our model has only five constructs, but with the added path of mediation, it is able to explain which consumers are more likely to adopt the mobile wallet.

A further contribution to theory is the comparison of the influence of PU to that of PEOU. Meta-analysis of the TAM literature has indicated that PU has a stronger influence than PEOU [31] and we confirm these findings and agree with Geffen and Straub, who proposed that PEOU relates to the 'intrinsic characteristics of the IT artefact...whilst PU is a response to user assessment of its extrinsic outcomes' [34]. These results suggest that if the IT artefact is simple to use and its use is similar to current actions, PEOU has a small effect on intention to use.

5.2 Limitations and Future Research

Our sample was from a panel conducted by a professional organization experienced in conducting surveys with selected audiences. Panel members have voluntarily offered their services and receive some form of compensation for taking a survey. The results reflect the responses of the panel population, which may be different than the general population. A further limitation is that the research was conducted with residents of the USA, and the findings may not be applicable to other geographical or cultural groupings.

Our theoretical contribution lays the groundwork for future researchers. The model can be tested across a broader cross section of the general population. The data can be segmented to determine whether age and income are moderating factors. Given the dominance of PU as an influencing factor, future researchers could explore other antecedents of PU. In addition, perceived security has been the subject of past studies and more detailed research could seek to decompose this construct. Because offerings and infrastructure vary by country, research could be further extended by comparing acceptance in different countries.

6 Conclusion

The mobile wallet, defined as an app on the smartphone to be used for face-to-face payment transactions, is relatively new. For the USA, with more NFC-enabled terminals becoming available because of the impending chip and pin standard, the capability of making contactless payments at retail outlets is growing. Consequently there is an increased opportunity for the smartphone to initiate payment instead of a physical card.

The development of these mobile wallet apps depends upon providers investing further in the software and the infrastructure, and their decision to invest depends upon the acceptance by consumers of this new technology. In order to understand the factors that influence guests, we have applied the Technology Acceptance Model, which is a seminal theory for an individual's acceptance of a new IT artefact. For payment transactions, security is a primary concern. We have added the construct of perceived security and investigated how it mediates personal innovativeness.

The results of our empirical study confirm that perceived usefulness is the most important influencing factor, and that personal innovativeness and perceived security are significant antecedents. A further contribution of this paper is how perceived security is a mediating factor, mediating personal innovativeness. Consumers are willing to use the mobile wallet if they perceive it to be secure. Practitioners are in a position to influence consumer acceptance of smartphone apps and, given the importance of security, they should emphasize the security of their solutions.

References

1. EMVCo: About EMV (2013). http://www.emvco.com/
2. Aite Group: Seventy Percent of U.S. Credit Cards to be EMV Enabled by the End of 2015 (2014). http://aitegroup.com/seventy-percent-us-credit-cards-be-emv-enabled-end-2015
3. Shin, D.: Towards an understanding of the consumer acceptance of mobile wallet. Comput. Hum. Behav. 25(6), 1343–1354 (2009)
4. Kemp, R.: Mobile payments: current and emerging regulatory and contracting issues. Comput. Law Secur. Rev. 29(2), 175–179 (2013)
5. Ross, P.E.: Phone-y money. IEEE Spectr. 49(6), 60–63 (2012)
6. Apple: Apple Announces Apple Pay (2014). http://www.apple.com/pr/library/2014/09/09Apple-Announces-Apple-Pay.html
7. Davis, F.D.: Perceived usefulness, perceived ease of use, and user acceptance. MIS Q. 13(3), 319–340 (1989)
8. Gefen, D., Karahanna, E., Straub, D.W.: Trust and TAM in online shopping: an integrated model. MIS Q. 27(1), 51 (2003)
9. Ingham, J., Cadieux, J., Berrada, A.M.: e-Shopping acceptance: A qualitative and meta-analytic review. Inf. Manag. 52(1), 44–60 (2015)
10. Shin, S., Lee, W.-J.: The effects of technology readiness and technology acceptance on NFC mobile payment services in Korea. J. Appl. Bus. Res. 30(6), 1615–1626 (2014)
11. Lopez-Nicols, C., Molina-Castillo, F.J., Bouwman, H.: An assessment of advanced mobile services acceptance: contributions from TAM and diffusion theory models. Inf. Manag. 45(6), 359–364 (2008)
12. Chellappa, R.K., Pavlou, P.A.: Perceived information security, financial liability and consumer trust in electronic commerce transactions. Logist. Inf. Manag. 15(5/6), 358–368 (2002)
13. Dahlberg, T., et al.: Past, present and future of mobile payments research: a literature review. Electron. Commer. Res. Appl. 7(2), 165–181 (2008)
14. Hartono, E., et al.: Measuring perceived security in B2C electronic commerce website usage: a respecification and validation. Decis. Support Syst. 62, 11–21 (2014)
15. Linck, K., Pousttchi, K. Wiedemann, D.G.: Security issues in mobile payment from the customer viewpoint (2006)
16. Rogers, E.M.: Diffusion of Innovations. Free Press, New York (1995)
17. Kirton, M.: Adaptors and innovators: a description and measure. J. Appl. Psychol. 61(5), 622 (1976)
18. Hurt, H.T., Joseph, K., Cook, C.D.: Scales for the measurement of innovativeness. Hum. Commun. Res. 4(1), 58–65 (1977)
19. Agarwal, R., Prasad, J.: Are individual differences germane to the acceptance of new information technologies? Decis. Sci. 30(2), 361–391 (1999)
20. Baron, R.M., Kenny, D.A.: The moderator-mediator variable distinction in social psychological research: conceptual, strategic, and statistical considerations. J. Pers. Soc. Psychol. 51(6), 1173–1182 (1986)
21. Chandra, S., Srivastava, S.C., Theng, Y.-L.: Evaluating the role of trust in consumer adoption of mobile payment systems: an empirical analysis. Commun. Assoc. Inf. Syst. 27(1), 561–588 (2010)
22. Agarwal, R., Prasad, J.: A conceptual and operational definition of personal innovativeness in the domain of information technology. Inf. Syst. Res. 9(2), 204 (1998)
23. Hair, J.F., et al.: A Primer on Partial Least Squares Structural Equations Modeling (PLS-SEM). SAGE Publications, Thousand Oaks (2014)

24. Preacher, K.J., Hayes, A.F.: SPSS and SAS procedures for estimating indirect effects in simple mediation models. Behav. Res. Methods Instrum. Comput. 36(4), 717–731 (2004)

25. Henseler, J., Ringle, C.M., Sinkovics, R.R.: The use of partial least squares path modeling in international marketing. In: Sinkovics, R.R., Ghauri, P.N. (eds.) Advances in International Marketing (AIM), vol. 20, pp. 277–319. Emerald Group Publishing Limited, Dingle, (2009)

26. Cronbach, L.J., Meehl, P.E.: Construct validity in psychological tests. Psychol. Bull. 52(4), 281–302 (1955)

27. Fornell, C., Larcker, D.F.: Evaluating structural equation models with unobservable variables and measurement error. J. Mark. Res. 18, 39–50 (1981)

28. Hair, J.F., Ringle, C.M., Sarstedt, M.: PLS-SEM: indeed a silver bullet. J. Mark. Theory Pract. 19(2), 139–152 (2011)

29. Shrout, P.E., Bolger, N.: Mediation in experimental and nonexperimental studies: new procedures and recommendations. Psychol. Methods 7(4), 422 (2002)

30. Helm, S., Eggert, A., Garnefeld, I.: Modeling the impact of corporate reputation on customer satisfaction and loyalty using partial least squares. In: Vinzi, V.V., Chin, W.W., Henseler, J., Wang, H. (eds.) Handbook of partial least squares, pp. 515–534. Springer, Heidelberg (2010)

31. Legris, P., Ingham, J., Collerette, P.: Why do people use information technology? A critical review of the technology acceptance model. Inf. Manag. 40(3), 191–204 (2003)

32. Turner, M., et al.: Does the technology acceptance model predict actual use? A systematic literature review. Inf. Softw. Technol. 52(5), 463–479 (2010)

33. Easterby-Smith, M., Thorpe, R., Jackson, P.: Management Research, 3rd edn. SAGE, London (2008). xvi, 351

34. Gefen, D., Straub, D.W.: The relative importance of perceived ease of use in IS adoption: a study of e-commerce adoption. J. AIS 1, 1–30 (2000)

Productpedia – A Collaborative Electronic Product Catalog for Ecommerce 3.0

Wee-Kek Tan[✉] and Hock-Hai Teo

Department of Information Systems, National University of Singapore,
Computing 1, 13 Computing Drive, Singapore 117417, Singapore
{tanwk, teohh}@comp.nus.edu.sg

Abstract. Despite the advancements made in ecommerce technologies over the past years, the inability to define and exchange semantically rich and accurate product information among ecommerce websites/applications has continued to intrigue researchers. This problem has taken on greater urgency because it impedes the realization of the full benefits of Ecommerce 3.0. The present research conceptualizes, designs and implements a cloud computing-based platform that enables global merchants to maintain a collaborative Electronic Product Catalog (EPC) known as Productpedia. This collaborative EPC platform addresses numerous shortcomings of prior researches by (1) maintaining a single centralized EPC database; (2) negating the need to synchronize and convert data; (3) creating an integrated meta-model ontology for merchants to define previously unclassified product information without the involvement of domain experts; and (4) enabling an Open Application Programming Interface based on RESTful web services to facilitate direct modification of the EPC database by even third-party applications.

Keywords: Electronic product catalog · Ecommerce · Web 3.0 · Web service · Design science

1 Introduction

An enduring and intriguing problem in ecommerce is the defining and exchanging of semantically rich and accurate product information [1–4]. Specifically, unstructured product information (e.g., product categories, descriptions, attributes and attribute values) that are readily understandable by human buyers and sellers cannot be automatically processed by ecommerce websites and applications easily [3]. Even when structured product information is available, it is at best an arduous if not impossible endeavor to exchange them among different ecommerce websites and applications [4]. For instance, even though major ecommerce websites such as Amazon.com and CNET Shopper have their own structured product information catalogs, these are closed catalogs that cannot be shared and modified outside of the respective website.

The lack of common and sharable structured product information impedes the development of ecommerce in the Web 3.0 era of semantic web, which is characterized by automated software agents that are capable of performing tasks on behalf of users using structured sharable data. This problem requires urgent attention as proponents of

© Springer International Publishing Switzerland 2015
F.F.-H. Nah and C.-H. Tan (Eds.): HCIB 2015, LNCS 9191, pp. 370–381, 2015.
DOI: 10.1007/978-3-319-20895-4_34

Ecommerce 3.0, a loose term for describing the third generation of ecommerce in the Web 3.0 era, have noted its huge potential. For instances, Ecommerce 3.0 is expected to enable data-driven interactions across multiple devices and touch points [5], and extensible ecommerce web services [6].

This research applied the design science framework and guidelines put forth by Hevner and his colleagues [7] to conceptualize, design and implement a cloud computing-based platform that enables global merchants to maintain a collaborative Electronic Product Catalog (EPC) known as Productpedia. Whereas a standard EPC caters only to a single standalone ecommerce application, the envisioned collaborative EPC potentially allows the merchants of a large number of ecommerce applications on a global scale to contribute product information with a common ontology for describing products and services as well as facilitating ecommerce sales transaction. The choice of a cloud computing-based architecture allows the collaborative EPC platform to be dynamically scalable and highly reliable [8]. In gist, Productpedia possesses the ability to help ecommerce merchants and service providers to realize the full potential of Ecommerce 3.0.

2 Theoretical Background

2.1 Ecommerce and Structured Product Information

The late 1990 s to early 2000 saw the rise of the integrative ecommerce web-era [1]. This era was characterized by an emphasis towards integration and interoperability of various electronic business processes such as electronic supply chain management and electronic customer relationship management among different websites. The integrative web-era is only possible if information can be shared among ecommerce websites [1]. To achieve information sharing, it is necessary to have a standardized way of representing information, e.g., Extensible Markup Language (XML), such that it may be readily extracted, used and reused. In particular, XML-based web services hold the promise towards enabling online business processes that facilitate sharing and reuse of information among websites. The proposed collaborative EPC platform, i.e., Productpedia, will primarily consist of a shared database of product information constructed using a XML-based data standard. A set of RESTful web service-based Open Application Programming Interface (API) will be provided by the collaborative EPC platform for developers to build new tools around it, i.e., any ecommerce applications or websites, such that anyone can easily contribute to the collaborative EPC.

The typical functionalities provided in an ecommerce website may be classified into seven categories [9]. Several of these functionalities may be directly or indirectly supported by an EPC. Content management from a seller's perspective involves managing information about the product items that are sold on an ecommerce website. This is the key focus of Productpedia, which not only includes a standardized ontology for describing products but also how the product information will be stored and assessed via the cloud, and reused by sellers across multiple ecommerce websites/ applications. From the buyers' perspective, content management may refer to the browsing of product information and aggregating information from multiple sources for comparison. In a standard EPC context, a buyer may only browse the product offerings in an EPC of a particular ecommerce website but is not aware of other similar offerings from other websites. A structured and sharable collaborative EPC allows service providers adopting Productpedia to provide recommendation agents that will help consumers to search for product information across multiple websites [10]. Merchandising refers to the placement of online advertisements, launching of up-sell or cross-sell promotions, and making product recommendations to consumers. Product-pedia provides an avenue for sellers to implement multiple forms of negotiation across multiple websites using a single set of product information obtained from Productpedia.

2.2   Prior Works on Collaborative Electronic Product Catalog

The concept of a collaborative EPC such as Productpedia has been explored by prior researchers to varying extent. Schubert put forth the idea of a Participatory Electronic Product Catalog (PEP) to transform standard EPCs into trust-building entities that allow different stakeholders to leverage the social benefits in a virtual community of transaction [3]. The core component in Schubert's PEP architecture consists of a mediating EPC that is capable of combining different single merchant catalogs into one integrated EPC [3]. The PEP thus contains the aggregated product information of multiple merchants, which can then be utilized to provide value-added services to customers of these merchants. Collectively, the merchants, other service providers and customers form the virtual community of transaction.

Within this virtual community of transaction, the PEP architecture facilitates the provision of sophisticated value-added services such as enhanced recommendation service that returns aggregated results from different websites when customers search for desired items matching certain criteria. These advanced features are made possible by the mediating EPC of the PEP architecture, which provides an integrated source of structured sharable product information aggregated from multiple merchants.

However, Schubert's PEP architecture suffers from several problems [3]. First, the PEP architecture relies on an intermediate software component to integrate product information from multiple sources into the mediating EPC. This process requires continuous periodic synchronization between the single merchant catalogs and the mediating EPC. Second, the structured product information is not truly sharable because each merchant that wants to utilize production information from the mediating EPC must perform two-way conversion between its internal data format and the mediating EPC's data format. Third, the PEP architecture does not cater to the direct definition and modification of product information thus hampering the collaborative construction of the mediating EPC. Fourth, the PEP architecture is a conceptual one that lacks implementation details.

Yoo and Kim proposed a concrete web-based knowledge management system for sharing product information among application systems within a design and production environment [4]. The authors based their work on the notion that product information inherently possess complex semantics and thus are difficult to share among application systems [11]. Consequently, the authors defined product information carefully as three different types of knowledge – namely metadata, ontology and mapping relationships.

A knowledge base system using software agents is then created to share the knowledge using XML-based technologies. This approach enables effective search of product information, and automatic translation and reuse of product information. For instance, product information encoded in one data format, e.g., STEP, may be converted into business data encoded in another data format, e.g., EDIFACT, for use in electronic data interchange.

Although Yoo and Kim's approach provides a viable solution for sharing structured product information, it involves highly specialized data formats, software technologies and business processes that are not suitable for adoption in a general ecommerce environment [4]. The present research on Productpedia adopts an approach that is similar to Yoo and Kim's but one that is more lightweight and can be readily adopted in any ecommerce environment.

Lee and his colleagues also observed that even though having a database of well-defined products and services is essential for collaborative ecommerce processes, scant research has focused on developing and deploying a workable technology in a real-world commercial environment [2]. The authors proposed and developed an ontology-based EPC system that adopts a multi-layered software architecture consisting of (1) an EPC database; (2) the ontology-based EPC system itself; as well as (3) interoperability with different external ecommerce websites that can download and synchronize updated product information automatically. The most noteworthy feature of the entire platform is the use of meta-modeling approach for capturing the product ontology, which enables a highly extensible and flexible product ontology model [12, 13]. A meta-model product ontology does not predefine the actual categories, relationships among categories or the attributes describing product items in the same category. Rather, it specifies the notion of product categories and attributes and how instances of categories and attributes may be created and associated with each other.

The ontology-based EPC system does not rely on specialized data formats and enable interfacing with external websites. However, it is essentially a closed catalog that is maintained by internal domain experts and cannot be modified by external stakeholders. In this regard, it is not suitable for a generic ecommerce environment characterized by heterogeneous marketplace participants. Productpedia builds upon the works done by prior researchers [2–4] but addresses their limitations.

3 Requirements Analysis and Design of Productpedia

3.1 Collaborative Electronic Product Catalog Architecture

Schubert's PEP architecture is largely based on a mediating EPC that integrates different single merchant catalogs together [3]. The Productpedia collaborative EPC differs significantly from the PEP architecture. In the case of Productpedia, there exists only a single EPC that contains the original definitions of all product information directly contributed by different stakeholders in a collaborative manner. An overview of the proposed architecture of the Productpedia collaborative EPC is shown alongside the PEP architecture in Fig. 1. Productpedia's architecture addresses the shortcomings of the PEP architecture. In particular, structured product information is directly defined in a single source using a common data standard and can be shared without any conversion. This approach resembles Yoo and Kim's knowledge base system architecture [4], and Lee and his colleagues' ontology-based EPC system architecture that both feature centralized metadata and ontology management [2].

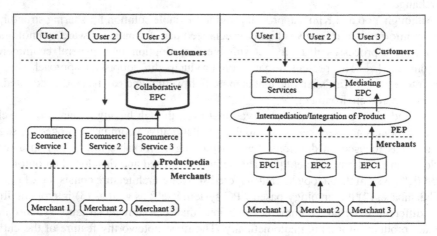

Fig. 1. Overview of the Productpedia collaborative EPC architecture (left) and Schubert's PEP architecture [3, p. 231] (right).

Productpedia's collaborative EPC will be exposed to external stakeholders via a multi-layered software architecture similar to Lee and his colleagues' ontology-based EPC system architecture [2]. A multi-layered software architecture is chosen because it enables greater flexibility, extensibility and scalability in adding new software components to provide new services in the future [14]. For instance, recommendation, collaborative filtering and data analytics components may be layered on top of the collaborative EPC to realize the full potential of Ecommerce 3.0 as envisioned by researchers and practitioners, e.g., [5, 6]. Specifically, Productpedia will follow a multi-layered web service architecture to provide a user-centered, interactive and collaborative EPC ecosystem. In addition, it adopts a semantic web approach to enable third-party software tools to be built around the structured product information residing in the cloud.

A complete architecture of the Productpedia collaborative EPC platform is shown in Fig. 2. At the core of the Productpedia platform are the meta-model ontology and the EPC database for describing the semantics of the product information and the actual product information using XML. The database is maintained by a core backend system. The core backend system handles critical functional logic and operations of the entire information system platform.

There are two non-trivial differences between Productpedia's architecture and those of prior researchers [2, 4]. First, Productpedia will be made open-source so that it may be maintained by all stakeholders in a collaborative fashion. A set of Open API based on RESTful web services, a type of software architecture for distributed systems using

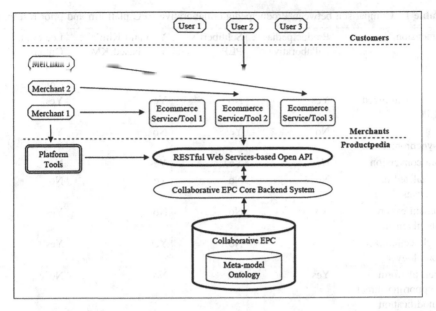

Fig. 2. Complete architecture of the Productpedia collaborative EPC platform

the Hypertext Transfer Protocol and the concept of representational state transfer, will be used to expose the meta-model ontology and EPC database to stakeholders. The Open API will contain a set of web service methods that enable websites and software tools to retrieve product schema and manipulate product information. Individual and organizational stakeholders can choose to interact with the collaborative EPC using a set of primary platform tools, or create their own software tools using the Open API. The latter approach allows the collaborative EPC to be seamlessly integrated into any new or existing ecommerce applications, including lightweight mobile devices, social networking applications and mashup applications.

Second, Productpedia's collaborative EPC includes an open meta-data ontology that allows any stakeholders to create and maintain the product ontology and relationships. The notion of internal domain expert does not exist and stakeholders operate collaboratively as peers to define the ontology. The differences between Productpedia' architecture and those of prior researches are summarized in Table 1.

3.2 Collaborative Electronic Product Catalog Design

Providing consumers with online tools to search and filter product information has long been highlighted as a critical success factor for ecommerce. Unfortunately, this is a non-trivial task because online merchants use vastly different product descriptions, albeit rich in information, and nonstandard formats to present these descriptions. Consequently, designing and implementing useful online tools to help consumers find products and services that meet certain attributes or for merchants to locate potential buyers of a particular trait has proven to be an elusive challenge [15].

Table 1. Comparison between Productpedia collaborative EPC platform and prior research

Dimension	Productpedia collaborative EPC	Schubert's PEP	Yoo and Kim's Web-based KM system	Lee et al.' Ontology-based EPC
Architecture	Concrete	Conceptual	Concrete	Concrete
Single centralized EPC	Yes	No	Yes	Yes
Data synchronization	No	Yes	No	Yes
Data conversion	No	Yes	Yes	No
Specialized data formats	No	No	Yes	No
Domain experts involvement	No	No	No	Yes
Single centralized ontology	Yes	No	Yes	Yes
Open platform supporting direct modification	Yes	No	No	No

Researchers acknowledging product information heterogeneity as a major imped-iment factor to business information exchange have proposed two general approaches to resolve this problem [16]. The first approach is standardization, which involves creating common vocabulary and protocol to be adopted by all parties involved in a business exchange. The United Nations Standard Product and Services Codes (UN-SPSC) (http://www.unspsc.org) provide a global standard to classify products and services in a hierarchical fashion. However, it does not define the attributes for describing each commodity. eCl@ss (http://www.eclass.de) is a competing standard for product classification and description. Similar to UNSPSC, eCl@ss aims to facilitate information exchange between customers and their suppliers. eCl@ss is better because it attempts to provide a set of attributes to describe each product class. However, when compared to commercial shopping websites such as CNET Shopper.com (http://shopper.cnet.com), the predefined set of attributes is often less rich in details. The second approach is integration [16], which involves building mappings among product attributes from different product descriptions. In the context of integration, heteroge-neity among different product schemas can be classified as either attribute naming conflicts or missing attributes. These problems are further complicated if the product schemas are multi-level trees [16].

Productpedia attempts to resolve the product information heterogeneity problem by adopting a standardized approach towards meta-model product ontology. A set of XML-based web service methods will be used by its community of stakeholders to define and maintain structured product information in an open and collaborative fashion similar to how articles on the Internet's largest free encyclopedia Wikipedia (http://www.wikipedia.org) is created and maintained. That is, to build upon the col-lective wisdom of Productpedia's community to create and maintain a useful collaborative EPC just like how Wikipedia's volunteers have come together to maintain the hundreds of thousands of quality articles [17]. Neither domain experts nor a central authority is required to predefine the product categories, schemas and items. Productpedia's primary website as well as all third party websites and applications developed with its Open API will utilize this common set of XML based product schemas to exchange product information. The added benefit of an open and collaborative approach is to allow the Productpedia community of stakeholders to create a rich set of attributes for each product category of interest to them, and presumably one in which they possess the relevant expertise. Ultimately, Productpedia collaborative EPC may become as comprehensive as global standards such as UNSPSC and eCl@ss, and as rich in details as private product schemas.

Productpedia's collaborative EPC ontology will be based on a single-level tree product schema model. Design provisions will be made to enable integration with users' existing product schemas or descriptions, if necessary, by making all attributes optional and allowing the definition of aliases for each attribute.

4 Design Science Artifacts of Productpedia

The design science research guidelines prescribed by Hevner, March, Park and Ram (HMPR) [7] have often been used by scholars to analyze and evaluate design science research [18]. In accordance with HMPR's design as an artifact guideline, "design science research must produce a viable artifact in the form of a construct, a model, a method or an instantiation" [7, p. 83]. Constructs are the concepts that form the research domain's vocabulary. Models are a set or propositions or statements expressing relationships among constructs. Methods are a set of steps used to perform a task. Instantiations are realized information systems built according to the specification of the three preceding artifacts.

Each higher-level artifact builds upon the lower level artifacts in an implied linear hierarchical manner [18]. In particular, the instantiation artifact involves a fully functional prototype of the Productpedia collaborative EPC platform together with the primary website that was developed with the Open API. Collectively, the instantiation artifact demonstrates the viability of Productpedia's community of stakeholders collaboratively maintaining the EPC, and also embodies all the lower level artifacts.

4.1 Construct

Ontology development is an approach commonly used in design science research that focuses on construct artifact [19, 20]. Ontology is a formal representation of knowledge as a set of related concepts within a domain. It is intended to facilitate interoperability among various information processing applications [21].

In our context, we attempt to define a meta-model ontology for a collaborative EPC platform. This is focused on the two major dimensions of ecommerce functionalities [9], namely content management and merchandising. The ontology is depicted in Fig. 3. A detailed vocabulary specification for the ontology has also been defined. For instance, a product category "represents a classification of related product items exhibiting a common set of properties". This model follows the basic meta-model [2, 12, 13]. The inclusion of product category and product schema allows merchants to define new product items that are currently not categorized in the EPC.

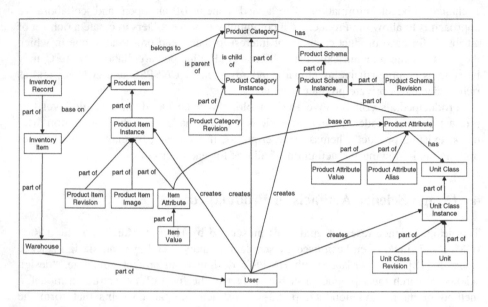

Fig. 3. Ontology for content management and merchandising ecommerce functionalities provided for by the Productpedia collaborative EPC platform.

4.2   Models

The ontology that has been described in the preceding sub-section forms the foundation to define the relationships among the constructs for a collaborative EPC. Unified Modeling Language (UML) is chosen to depict the models as it is the industry standard for object-oriented modeling [22]. UML class diagram is also more intuitive for depicting superclass and subclass concepts as compared to enhanced entity relationship diagram since it is (1) congruent with the objected-oriented programming paradigm; and (2) independent of the underlying data storage. Object-oriented programming itself is ideal for developing large and complex software system such as the platform proposed in this research.

The UML class diagrams represent both the solution to the information requirement analysis of the preceding chapter and the problem definition for the information system design task of the instantiation artifact. It essentially serves as reference logical data models for the development of the proposed platform. In accordance with the design characteristics discussed in the preceding section, the corresponding model for the subset of the ontology on product category shown in Fig. 3 is depicted in Fig. 4.

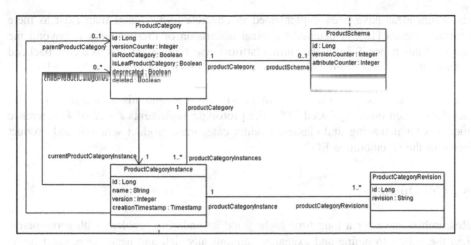

Fig. 4. Model for the product category ontology

4.3 Methods

The logical data models produced in the preceding sub-section form the basis for prescribing how various product information management tasks should be performed in the Productpedia collaborative EPC platform. Since the platform is based on an Open API architecture using RESTful web services, a series of API web service methods are carefully defined that allow an ecommerce application to interact with the collaborative EPC. This approach is similar to major commercial services such as eBay API (http://developer.ebay.com/common/api) and Amazon Marketplace Web Service (https://developer.amazonservices.com). In conjunction with the API methods, complementary processes are formulated to provide a reference implementation blueprint. Essentially, merchants contribute to the EPC by defining unit classes, product categories, product schemas for leaf product categories and product items. These components collectively constitute a shared EPC that community stakeholders can easily tap on to perform various ecommerce tasks such as creating a sales listing.

Since the collaborative EPC is a shared and distributed resource, the platform features several design characteristics to provide for an efficient and orderly management process. For example, each unique data record manifests as multiple instances and all revisions made to each instance of a unique data record are tracked and saved into the EPC database.

4.4 Instantiations

Instantiations operationalize the constructs, models and methods into the actual artifact that is used in the intended environment [7]. As part of this research, the constructs, models and methods defined in the preceding sub-sections were used to create a fully functional prototype of the proposed Productpedia collaborative EPC platform. It epitomizes the best practice recommended by design science scholars to the extent that its design ideas have been implemented in concrete forms rather than exist as mere abstract entities [18]. A detailed technical discussion of Productpedia is beyond the scope of this paper. Briefly, the entire platform essentially manifests as a core backend system that is developed using Java Platform Enterprise Edition (Java EE) with component-based software engineering architecture for extensibility and scalability. This implementation approach is similar to how Lee and his colleagues' [2] had developed their ontology-based EPC. The prototype implements a total of 47 reference methods for managing unit classes, product categories, product schemas and product items in the collaborative EPC.

5   Conclusion

Researchers have for a long time highlighted an enduring problem with ecommerce, i.e., the ability to define and exchange semantically rich and accurate product information [1–4]. This research adopts a design science strategy to solve the problem by conceptualizing, designing and implementing a fully functional prototype of a collaborative EPC platform, i.e., Productpedia. This platform addresses the shortcomings of prior researches by (1) maintaining a single centralized EPC database; (2) negating the need to synchronize and convert data; (3) creating an integrated meta-model ontology for merchants to define previously unclassified product information without the involvement of domain experts; and (4) enabling an Open API based on RESTful web services to facilitate direct modification of the EPC database by even third-party applications. Productpedia holds the promise of empowering merchants to realize the full benefits of Ecommerce 3.0. For instance, its Open API is an example of an extensible ecommerce web service [6] that allows a merchant to define and share structured product information.

Acknowledgements. This paper was supported by a grant from the Academic Research Fund sponsored by the Ministry of Education of Singapore of project number R-253-000-094-112.

References

1. Chu, S.C., Leung, L.C., Hui, Y.V., Cheung, W.: Evolution of E-Commerce web sites: a conceptual framework and a longitudinal study. Inf. Manag. **44**(2), 154–164 (2007)
2. Lee, I.-H., Lee, S., Lee, T., Lee, S.-G., Kim, D., Chun, J., Lee, H., Shim, J.: Practical issues for building a product ontology system. In: 2005 International Workshop on Data Engineering Issues in E-Commerce, pp. 16–25, Tokyo, Japan (2005)
3. Schubert, P.: The pivotal role of community building in electronic commerce. In: 33rd Hawaii International Conference on System Sciences, Maui, Hawaii (2000)
4. Yoo, S.B., Kim, Y.: Web-based knowledge management for sharing product data in virtual enterprises. Int. J. Prod. Econ. **75**(1–2), 173–183 (2002)
5. Walker, L.: 2013 and the Rise of Ecommerce 3.0. Get Elastic Ecommerce Blog. http://www.getelastic.com/2013-and-the-rise-of-ecommerce-3-0
6. Cabage, N., Zhang, S.: Web 3.0 has begun. Interactions **20**(5), 26–31 (2013)

7. Hevner, A.R., March, S.T., Park, J., Ram, S.: Decision science in information systems research. MIS Q. **28**(1), 75–105 (2004)
8. Vaquero, L.M., Rodero-Merino, L., Caceres, J., Lindner, M.: A break in the clouds: towards a cloud definition. ACM SIGCOMM Comput. Commun. Rev. **39**(1), 50–55 (2009)
9. Ihingran, A.: Anatomy of a real E-commerce system. In: 2000 ACM SIGMOD International Conference on Management of Data, pp. 571–572, Dallas, Texas (2000)
10. Xiao, B., Benbasat, I.: E-commerce product recommendation agents: use, characteristics, and impact. MIS Q. **31**(1), 137–209 (2007)
11. McKay, A., Bloor, M., de Pennington, A.: A framework for product data. IEEE Trans. Knowl. Data Eng. **8**(5), 825–838 (1996)
12. Atkinson, C., Kühne, T.: The essence of multilevel metamodeling. In: 4th International Conference on the Unified Modeling Language, Modeling Languages, Concepts, and Tools, Toronto, Ontario, Canada (2001)
13. Shim, J., Lee, S.-J., Wu, C.: A unified approach for software policy modeling: incorporating implementation into a modeling methodology. In: Song, I.-Y., Liddle, S.W., Ling, T.-W., Scheuermann, P. (eds.) ER 2003. LNCS, vol. 2813, pp. 118–130. Springer, Heidelberg (2003)
14. Garlan, D., Shaw, M.: An introduction to software architecture. In: Ambriola, V., Tortora, G. (eds.) Advances in Software Engineering and Knowledge Engineering, vol. I. World Scientific Publishing Company, New Jersey (1993)
15. Adam, N., Yesha, Y., Awerbuch, B., Bennet, B., Blaustein, B., Brodsky, A., Chen, R., Dogramaci, O., Grossman, B., Holowczak, R., Johnson, J., Kalpakis, K., McCollum, C., Neches, A.L., Neches, B., Rosenthal, A., Slonim, J., Wactlar, H., Wolfson, O., Yesha, Y.: Strategic directions in electronic commerce and digital libraries: towards a digital agora. ACM Comput. Surv. **28**(4), 818–835 (1996)
16. Ng, W.K., Yan, G., Lim, E.P.: Heterogeneous product description in electronic commerce. ACM SIGecom Exchanges **1**(1), 7–13 (2000)
17. Liu, J., Ram, S.: Who does what: collaboration patterns in the wikipedia and their impact on article quality. ACM Trans. Manag. Inf. Syst. **2**(2), 1–23 (2011). Article 11
18. Arnott, D., Pervan, G.: Design science in decision support systems research: an assessment using the hevner, march, park, and ram guidelines. J. Assoc. Inf. Syst. **13**(11), 923–949 (2012)
19. Nazir Ahmad, M., Badr, K.B.A., Colomb, R.M., Ibrahim, R.: Ontology-based applications in information systems research: through the lens of design science research methodology. In: 16th Pacific Asia Conference on Information Systems, Paper 177, Ho Chi Minh City, Vietnam (2012)
20. Wales, R.C., Shalin, V.L., Bass, D.S.: Requesting Distant Robotic Action: An Ontology for Naming and Action Identification for Planning on the Mars Exploration Rover Mission. J. Assoc. Inf. Syst. **8**(2), 75–104 (2007)
21. Colomb, R.M.: Formal versus material ontologies for information systems interoperation in the semantic web. Comput. J. **49**(1), 4–19 (2006)
22. Tan, X., Siau, K., Erickson, J.: Design science research on systems analysis and design: the case of UML. In: 13th Americas Conference on Information Systems, Paper 351, Keystone, Colorado (2007)

The Moderating Role of Perceived Effectiveness of Provider Recommendations on Consumers' Satisfaction, Trust, and Online Repurchase Intention

Hongpeng Wang[✉], Rong Du, Shizhong Ai, and Zhe Chi

School of Economics and Management,
Xidian University, Xian 710126, Shaanxi, China
wanghongpeng@stu.xidian.edu.cn,
{durong, shzhai}@mail.xidian.edu.cn, lenovel23@163.com

Abstract. Despite the importance of online provider recommendations in e-commerce transactions, there is still little understanding about how provider recommendations impacts on customer retention. Addressing this gap, this study introduces a key construct, perceived effectiveness of provider recommendations (PEPRs) to investigate the differential moderating effects of PEPRs on the relationships between satisfaction, trust and repeat purchase intention. The research models are designed based on a research model and an online survey is conducted with 130 respondents. We draw conclusions that (1) PEPRs negatively moderate the relationship between satisfaction with vendor and trust in vendor and (2) PEPRs positively moderate the relationship between trust in vendor and repurchase intention. These findings are important theoretical contributions to know that first-hand experience can be to some extent replaced by supplementary information. In addition, we give some managerial countermeasures towards the new situation.

Keywords: Provider recommendations · Satisfaction · Trust · Online repurchase intention

1 Introduction

As e-commerce institutional mechanisms have been improved and more mature trust within vendors and consumers has been generated, online retailing has become more prosperous and competitive [20]. In this circumstance, how to retain existing consumers to make repeated purchases is considered to be an important concern for online firms [15].

Prior studies have long acknowledged that trust is a key factor for online repurchase [27, 31]. To meet for the requirement of trusting beliefs, a large number of online vendors offer provider recommendations (PRs) to promote their transaction intentions and purchasing behaviors. Despite the effects of provider recommendations on initial online purchase intention having already been examined, there is still little understanding about how they affect consumers satisfaction, trust and especially repurchase intention.

© Springer International Publishing Switzerland 2015
F.F.-H. Nah and C.-H. Tan (Eds.): HCIB 2015, LNCS 9191, pp. 382–391, 2015.
DOI: 10.1007/978-3-319-20895-4_35

PRs are divided into content-based filtering recommendations and collaborative-filtering recommendations in which they are based on explicit interests of the users or past buying behaviors of the affinity groups to extract recommendations for a specific buyer [24, 29]. For instance, regardless of whether the customer logs in, Amazon.com can track their browsing histories through using cookies and automatically provide personalized recommendation service as they move around the web. In order to analyze these two objects, we introduce a construct - the perceived effectiveness of provider recommendations (PEPRs). They are referred to as online shoppers' perceptions that provider recommendations provided is a sense of identification and agreement with an accurate and reliable information regarding to the transaction history of vendors and online experience with similar preferences [26].

2 Research Model and Hypotheses Development

In this Section, we present a research model to explore the influence of PEPRs on the relationship between satisfaction, trust and online repurchase as shown in Fig. 1.

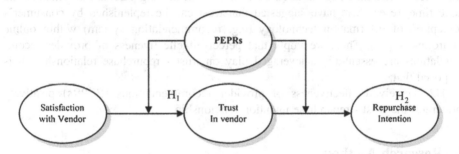

Fig. 1. Research model

2.1 The Moderating Role of PEPRs Between Satisfaction and Trust

Although extant researches support that successful, satisfying transactions will increase online customers' confidence they have in vendors toward future exchanges in online context [19], they tend to rely on other details instead of specific experience [6]. Satisfaction with vendor seems to be not enough for forming their trust perception. Those customers who use the internet have a special approach to making assessment towards sellers' trustworthiness: they mainly concern about the top sources of information - online ratings and reviews [8]. Provider recommendations provide more comprehensive details that compensate for their lack of experiential knowledge. In addition, a broad concept of online repurchase intention is online buyers' repeat intention for buying a products or services (same, similar or different) from a web-based store (same, similar or different) [5], which indicates that people will have largely dependence on collecting second-hand information. Therefore, perceived effectiveness of provider recommendations serves to migrate the role of customer's satisfaction inherent in the process of trust transfer. This is a negatively moderating role of PEPRs on the impact of his or her satisfaction with vendor on trust in vendor. Thus, it is proposed that:

H1: Perceived effectiveness of provider recommendations (PEPRs) negatively moderates the satisfaction - trust relationship in repurchase situation.

2.2   The Moderating Role of PEPRs Between Trust and Online Repurchase

Trust is a core factor of both initial purchase or repeat purchase because it can reduce worries of uncertainties and promote transaction success [14, 29]. When trustees fulfill trusters' expectation through their ability, credibility and benevolence, customers will be retained [3]. E-commerce platforms create a secure environment to assure trusting party's requirements of integrity by applying feedback mechanisms (e.g. PRs) [16], which boosts customers' trusting beliefs to form repurchase intentions. Previous studies also revealed that there are other factors at play in the relationship between trust in vendor and repurchase intention. Reference [18] demonstrated that consumers' trusting beliefs are more significantly influence their online purchase intentions when using online recommendation agents as an assistant tool for making purchase decision. At the same time, researchers have suggested that trust can be replenished by consumer's perception of information technology (e.g. recommendation system) within online environment [28]. Thus, we imply that perceived effectiveness of provider recommendations are essentially a leveraged play on trust - repurchase relationship. It is proposed that:

H2: Perceived effectiveness of provider recommendations (PEPRs) positively moderates the trust - repurchase intention relationship.

3   Research Method

We used all constructs from validated scales in the extant literature. To validate the instrument [29], we followed the guidelines on validation proposed by [30], and took the recommendations proposed by [23]. The adapted items contained words and sentences are adjusted to improve subjects' understanding [25]. This study measured them with 7-point Likert scales (1 = "strongly disagree"; 7 = "strongly agree"). A number of control variables incorporated into the research models to ensure the empirical results.

Data was collected by using online survey through a top research institution (sojump.com) in China. A total of 326 questionnaires distributed, 300 were returned for a response rate of 92.02 %. Then, we examine all surveys and dropped some surveys of same or contradictory answers, which resulted in 130 usable responses.

The PLS-SEM algorithm was used to estimate the path coefficients and other model parameters (e.g. internal consistency reliability, discriminant validity and so on) [22]. Path significance was determined by bootstrap technique. As a rule, 5000 bootstrapping samples contained 130 cases are recommended [12]. Moderating effects were modeled using the product indicator approach [7]. The method involves multiplying each (mean-centered) indicator of the predictors with each (mean-centered) indicator of the moderator variables.

4 Data Analysis and Results

To access the reliability (internal consistency reliability and indicator reliability), we examine composite reliability scores for every constructs and the indicator's outer loading [2, 6]. All composite reliabilities in Table 3, ranging from 0.87 to 0.94, are above the cutoff value of 0.70. Each indicator's loading on its respective factor exceed 0.70 (Table 2). These results are considered as good reliability. Convergent validity assessment builds on average variance extracted (AVE) values as the evaluation criterion that should be met the threshold value (> 0.50) [13]. Table 1 shows that the AVE of each construct are well above 0.50, satisfying this requirement, which demonstrate high levels of convergent validity. Discriminant validity is assessed by confirming (1) outer loadings, (2) cross loadings and (3) the relationship between inter-construct correlations and the square root of AVEs [6, 11]. First, items' outer laodings on their corresponding constructs (in Table 2) are greater than their cross loadings on any other constructs. Second, the square of AVEs of each construct are larger than their correlations among other constructs (as shown in Table 1). Therefore, these test results report adequate discriminant validity.

Table 1. Internal consistency reliability, correlations and the square root of AVE among constructs.

	ICR[a]	EX	FV	PEPRs	SP	SV	RI	TV	VR	WQ
Expertise (EX)	0.87	**0.79**[b]								
Familiarity with vendor (FV)	0.94	0.43	**0.91**							
PEPRs	0.92	0.42	0.51	**0.89**						
Satisfaction with online purchasing (SP)	0.88	0.52	0.54	0.53	**0.84**					
Satisfaction with vendor (SV)	0.89	0.46	0.56	0.55	0.59	**0.86**				
Repurchase intention (RI)	0.88	0.48	0.66	0.54	0.58	0.78	**0.84**			
Trust in vendor (TV)	0.91	0.60	0.53	0.62	0.70	0.76	0.67	**0.85**		
Vendor's reputation (VR)	0.94	0.45	0.65	0.53	0.52	0.74	0.75	0.70	**0.91**	
Website quality (WQ)	0.91	0.49	0.43	0.55	0.50	0.71	0.62	0.68	0.71	**0.82**

Note: [a] ICR is internal consistency reliabilities; [b] diagonal elements are the square roots of AVE.

Results of research model are shown in Fig. 2. The model explains 73.38 percent of variation in returning customers' trust in vendor and accounts for 56.47 percent of variation in repurchase intention. As hypothesized, exposed PEPRs negatively moderate the relationship between satisfaction with vendor and trust in vendor (H1: $\beta = -0.204$, $t = 3.581$, $p = 0.000$, two-tailed) and exposed PEPRs positively moderate the relationship between trust in vendor and repurchase intention (H2: $\beta = 0.393$, $t = 2.805$, $p = 0.005$, two-tailed). Figure 3 further illustrate these two moderating effects. At high levels of PEPRs, trust in vendor increases slowly when satisfaction with vendor increases and repurchase intention increases rapidly as trust in vendor

Table 2. Item loadings and cross loadings

Construct	Items	EX	FV	PEPRs	SP	SV	RI	TV	VR	WQ
Expertise (EX)	EX1	0.78	0.19	0.31	0.26	0.24	0.28	0.37	0.23	0.36
	EX2	0.87	0.35	0.33	0.42	0.36	0.40	0.46	0.33	0.35
	EX3	0.78	0.48	0.26	0.57	0.38	0.42	0.46	0.32	0.25
	EX4	0.74	0.29	0.45	0.36	0.43	0.39	0.58	0.52	0.59
Familiarity with vendor (FV)	FV1	0.35	0.90	0.41	0.50	0.52	0.64	0.49	0.57	0.38
	FV2	0.45	0.94	0.49	0.48	0.51	0.59	0.51	0.63	0.40
	FV3	0.38	0.90	0.49	0.51	0.50	0.57	0.45	0.58	0.40
PEPRs	PEPRs1	0.33	0.46	0.88	0.47	0.49	0.49	0.49	0.46	0.48
	PEPRs2	0.38	0.39	0.90	0.44	0.47	0.46	0.54	0.42	0.46
	PEPRs3	0.42	0.50	0.89	0.51	0.52	0.51	0.62	0.54	0.53
Satisfaction with Online purchasing (SP)	SP1	0.51	0.46	0.54	0.88	0.56	0.52	0.67	0.46	0.47
	SP2	0.43	0.45	0.41	0.88	0.55	0.49	0.60	0.43	0.41
	SP3	0.36	0.47	0.38	0.76	0.34	0.44	0.46	0.41	0.38
Satisfaction with vendor (SV)	SV1	0.37	0.45	0.49	0.56	0.88	0.65	0.68	0.64	0.66
	SV2	0.39	0.56	0.46	0.49	0.84	0.69	0.60	0.62	0.50
	SV3	0.41	0.45	0.47	0.45	0.85	0.67	0.67	0.63	0.65
Repurchase Intention (RI)	RI1	0.42	0.47	0.45	0.38	0.58	0.79	0.55	0.62	0.58
	RI3	0.47	0.61	0.53	0.54	0.72	0.91	0.63	0.67	0.54
	RI5	0.31	0.58	0.38	0.53	0.66	0.83	0.49	0.60	0.45
Trust in vendor (TV)	TV1	0.53	0.42	0.57	0.59	0.61	0.52	0.82	0.50	0.59
	TV2	0.46	0.45	0.53	0.60	0.72	0.60	0.90	0.68	0.63
	TV3	0.45	0.46	0.48	0.55	0.74	0.55	0.86	0.63	0.59
	TV4	0.61	0.47	0.52	0.63	0.51	0.60	0.80	0.54	0.50
Vendor's reputation (VR)	VR1	0.38	0.57	0.45	0.41	0.68	0.67	0.56	0.88	0.56
	VR2	0.41	0.59	0.51	0.50	0.67	0.70	0.70	0.92	0.68
	VR3	0.44	0.62	0.50	0.49	0.68	0.69	0.64	0.94	0.68
Website quality (WQ)	WQ1	0.44	0.22	0.50	0.35	0.58	0.45	0.55	0.55	0.82
	WQ2	0.48	0.35	0.43	0.44	0.57	0.49	0.55	0.56	0.84
	WQ3	0.39	0.22	0.43	0.32	0.56	0.41	0.52	0.57	0.85
	WQ4	0.40	0.46	0.42	0.42	0.56	0.56	0.56	0.57	0.78
	WQ5	0.30	0.46	0.47	0.50	0.63	0.61	0.60	0.62	0.79

increases. But the contrary is the case at low levels of PEPRs. Additionally, the main effects of PEPRs (PEPRs $\rightarrow$ trust; PEPRs $\rightarrow$ repurchase intention) are not significant ($\beta_1 = 0.117$, $t_1 = 1.544$; $\beta_2 = 0.120$, $t_2 = 1.247$). Nevertheless, satisfaction with vendor has a positive influence on trust in vendor ($\beta = 0.272$, $t = 2.801$, $p = 0.005$, two-tailed). Trust in vendor is also positively effected repurchase intention ($\beta = 0.444$, $t = 3.300$, $p = 0.001$, two-tailed). Moreover, two control variables, vendor's reputation ($\beta = 0.203$, $t = 2.051$, $p = 0.041$, two-tailed) and satisfaction with online purchasing ($\beta = 0.292$, $t = 4.154$, $p = 0.000$, two-tailed), have a significant influence on trust in vendor. Only one control variable, that is website quality, is found to be significant affecting repurchase intention ($\beta = 0.356$, $t = 3.361$, $p = 0.001$, two-tailed).

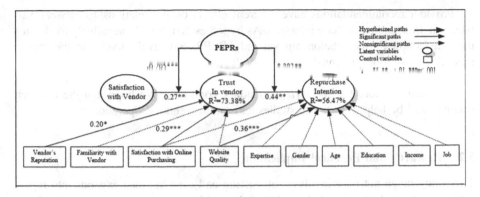

Fig. 2. Research model

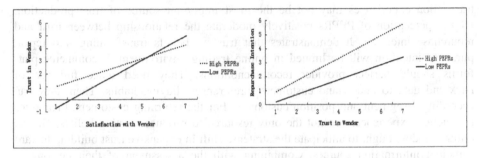

Fig. 3. The moderating effect of PEPRs

In order to evaluate whether the moderating effects of PEPRs have a substantive impact on endogenous variables (i.g. trust in vendor and repurchase intention), the change in R^2, f^2 effect size and F-test are examined [1, 4, 9]. When interaction term with PEPRs are added into Model 3, R^2 of trust in vendor increased by 2.08 % (F Change = 10.08, p = 0.002) and f^2 effect size is 0.10 that indicates a medium effect. Respectively, R^2 of repurchase intention increased by 7.1 % from Model 2 to Model 3 (F Change = 18.91, p = 0.000), indicating a medium effect (f^2 effect size = 0.12). Thus, the addition of interaction effects of PEPRs improved the explanatory power of the Model 3, which verifies the significance of moderating effects.

5 Discussion

5.1 Summary and Discussion of Results

How perceived effectiveness of provider recommendations (PEPRs) influence the casual link (satisfaction $\rightarrow$ trust $\rightarrow$ repurchase intention) have been put forward. We answer these questions by correspondingly verifying the moderating effects of PEPRs on the relationship between satisfaction and trust or the relationship between trust and repurchase intention.

Provider recommendations have different effects on the relationship between satisfaction, trust and repurchase intention. As hypothesized, PEPRs negatively moderates the satisfaction - trust relationship yet only PEPRs positively moderate the trust - repurchase intention relationship. These findings confirmed that not only PRs are the other source of trust production but also the impact of trust on repeat purchase intention have limitation under the specifying boundary condition. We hope that the research findings will be helpful to future studies and online vendors' operation.

5.2   Research and Practical Implication

This study range not only involves satisfaction and trust but also expands into repeat online purchase. In order to fully understand provider recommendations, we develop a new constructs, PEPRs. Additionally, we find that high level PEPRs can migrate the effect of satisfaction with vendor on trust in vendor. This finding reveals previous transaction experiences may not be the most important source of trust production. Higher perception of PEPRs positively moderate the relationship between trust and repurchase intention. It demonstrates that trusting beliefs transforming into repeat purchase intention will be limited in online trading environment. E-commerce platforms should perfect provider recommendations. They need make full use of back-end data to understand customers' preferences, buying habits. Then, they can accordingly segment and position customers. For the returning customers, their prior transaction experiences are not the only resource to produce trusting beliefs. Hence, online vendors ought to anticipate the strategic shift in expensive trust building toward sufficient information sources. Combining with the assessment of their customers' perceptions of PEPRs, they are able to design effective marketing strategies.

5.3   Limitations and Future Research Directions

As with any research, some potential limitations should be further studied in the future research. First, this study needs to be extend to more general areas that can be any e-commerce platforms or a wider range of individuals. Because a larger sample size will improve our statistical power to predict the significance of effects. Second, although a number of control variables are added into research model, we think that controlling for priority allocation of information in website would be helpful to validate the moderating role of PEPRs. Since some websites display provider recommendations prominently and some are the opposite, these features may not be equally effective influencing perceived effectiveness of PEPRs. Third, we only focus on repurchase intention and ignore investigating online repurchase behavior. Thus, an additional dependent variable, repeated purchase behavior, can be explored to enhance our model's persuasiveness.

Acknowledgments. This research is supported in part by the National Natural Science Foundation of China through grant 71271164 and Program for Advisors of Doctorial Students in University in China through grant 20120203110021.We are grateful to the editors and the reviewers for their insightful comments and invaluable guidance. We appreciate all other members in our research team for their contribution.

Appendix A

Table 3. Appendix A

Variables	Trust in vendor			Repurchase intention		
	Model 1	Model 2	Model 3	Model 1	Model 2	Model 3
Control variables						
Vendor's reputation	0.30**	0.18	0.20*	–	–	–
Familiarity with vendor	−0.03	−0.06	−0.02	–	–	–
Satisfaction with online purchasing	0.37***	0.31***	0.29***	0.23	0.16	0.10
Website quality	0.21*	0.11	0.09	0.37***	0.29**	0.36***
Expertise	–	–	–	0.11	0.06	0.04
Gender	–	–	–	0.03	0.00	0.02
Age	–	–	–	0.03	0.01	0.01
Education	–	–	–	0.06	0.05	0.08
Income	–	–	–	-0.06	-0.05	-0.03
Job	–	–	–	0.03	0.01	0.06
PEPRs	0.17	0.15	0.12	0.18	0.13	0.12
Direct effects						
Satisfaction with vendor		0.32**	0.27**			
Trust in vendor					0.25*	0.44**
Interaction effects						
Satisfaction with vendor × PEPRs			-0.20***			
Trust in vendor × PEPRs						0.40**
R^2	69.23 %	72.75 %	74.83 %	52.02 %	53.80 %	60.18 %
R^2 Change	–	3.52 %	2.08 %	–	1.78 %	7.10 %
Model F	55.80***	54.73***	51.81***	14.46***	13.86***	16.21***
Model F Change	–	15.89***	10.08**	–	4.58*	18.91***
Effect Size (f^2)	–	0.13	0.10	–	0.04	0.12

References

1. Aiken, L.S., Stephen, G.W.: Multiple regression Testing and Interpreting Interactions, pp. 75–87. Sage, Newbury Park (1991)
2. Barclay, Donald, Higgins, Christopher, Thompson, Ronald: The partial least squares (PLS) approach to causal modeling: personal computer adoption and use as an illustration. Technol. Stud. **2**(2), 285–309 (1995)

3. Yakov, B., et al.: Are the drivers and role of online trust the same for all web sites and consumers? A large-scale exploratory empirical study. J. Mark. **69**(4), 133–152 (2005)
4. Carte, T.A., Russell, C.J.: In pursuit of moderation: Nine common errors and their solutions. MIS Q. **27**, 479–501 (2003)
5. Chen, Y.-Y., et al.: Confirmation of expectations and satisfaction with the Internet shopping: the role of internet self-efficacy. Comput. Inf. Sci. **3**(3), 14 (2010)
6. Chin, W.W.: Commentary: Issues and opinion on structural equation modeling. MIS Q. **22**, vii–xvi (1998)
7. Chin, W.W., Marcolin, B.L., Newsted, P.R.: A partial least squares latent variable modeling approach for measuring interaction effects: results from a monte carlo simulation study and an electronic-mail emotion/adoption study. Inf. Syst. Res. **14**(2), 189–217 (2003)
8. Cisco internet business solutions group, catch and keep digi-tal shoppers (2013). http://www.cisco.com/web/about/ac79/docs/retail/Catch-and-Keep-the-Digital-ShopperPoV.pdf
9. Cohen, J., Cohen, P.: Applied multiple regression/correlation analysis for the behavioral sciences (84). Erlbaum, Hillsdale (1983)
10. Floyd, K., et al.: How online product reviews affect retail sales: a meta-analysis. J. Retail. **90** (2), 217–232 (2014)
11. Fornell, C., Larcker, D.F.: Evaluating structural equation models with unobservable variables and measurement error. J. Mark. Res. **18**, 39–50 (1981)
12. Hair Jr, J.F., Hult, G.T.M., Ringle, C., Sarstedt, M.: A primer on partial least squares structural equation modeling (PLS-SEM). Sage Publications, Thousand Oaks (2013)
13. Hu, X., et al.: Hope or hype On the viability of escrow services as trusted third parties in online auction environments. Inf. Syst. Res. **15**(3), 236–249 (2004)
14. Hoffman, D.L., Novak, T.P., P, M.: Building consumer trust online. Commun. ACM **42**(4), 80–85 (1999)
15. Johnson, D., Grayson, K.: Cognitive and affective trust in service relationships. J. Bus. Res. **58**(4), 500–507 (2005)
16. Jøsang, A., Ismail, R., Boyd, C.: A survey of trust and reputation systems for online service provision. Decis. Support Syst. **43**(2), 618–644 (2007)
17. Nanda, K., Benbasat, I.: Research note: the influence of recommendations and consumer reviews on evaluations of websites. Inf. Syst. Res. **17**(4), 425–439 (2006)
18. Komiak, S.Y.X., Benbasat, I.: The effects of personalization and familiarity on trust and adoption of recommendation agents. MIS Q. **30**(4), 941–960 (2006)
19. Li, D., Browne, G.J., Wetherbe, J.C.: Why do internet users stick with a specific web site? a relationship perspective. Int. J. Electron. Commer. **10**(4), 105–141 (2006)
20. Li, X., Hitt, L.M., John Zhang, Z.: Product reviews and competition in markets for repeat purchase products. J. Manag. Inf. Syst. **27**(4), 9–42 (2011)
21. Lim, K.H., et al.: Do I trust you online, and if so, will I buy? an empirical study of two trust-building strategies. J. Manag. Inf. Syst. **23**(2), 233–266 (2006)
22. Lohmoller, J.-B.: The PLS program system: latent variables path analysis with partial least squares estimation. Multivar. Behav. Res. **23**(1), 125–127 (1988)
23. MacKenzie, S.B., Podsakoff, P.M., Podsakoff, N.P.: Construct measurement and validation procedures in MIS and behavioral research: Integrating new and existing techniques. MIS Q. **35**(2), 293–334 (2011)
24. Montaner, Ml, López, B., De La Rosa, J.L.: A taxonomy of recommender agents on the internet. Artif. Intell. Rev. **19**(4), 285–330 (2003)
25. Moore, G.C., Izak, B.: Development of an instrument to measure the perceptions of adopting an information technology innovation. Inf. syst. Res. **2**(3), 192–222 (1991)
26. Pavlou, P.A., Gefen, D.: Building effective online marketplaces with institution-based trust. Inf. Systems Res. **15**(1), 37–59 (2004)

27. Israr, Q., et al.: Understanding online customer repurchasing intention and the mediating role of trust–an empirical investigation in two developed countries. Eur. J. Inf. Syst. **18**(3), 205–222 (2009)

28. Senecal, S., Nantel, J., Sivakumar, K.: Online peer and editorial recommendations, trust, and choice in virtual markets. J. Interact. Mark. **19**(4), 1–9 (2005)

29. Straub, D.W.: Validating instruments in MIS research. MIS Q. **13**(2), 147–169 (1989)

30. Straub, D., Boudreau, M.-C., Gefen, D.: Validation guidelines for IS positivist research. Commun. Assoc. Inf. Syst. **13**, 63 (2004)

31. Wei, Y.Z., Moreau, L., Jennings, N.R.: A market-based approach to recommender systems. ACM Trans. Inf. Syst. (TOIS) **23**(3), 227–266 (2005)

32. Zboja, J.J., Voorhees, C.M.: The impact of brand trust and satisfaction on retailer repurchase intentions. J. Serv. Mark. **20**(6), 381–390 (2006)

An Exploratory Study of Website Localization Strategies: The Effect of Exogenous Factors

Tailai Wu[✉], Chih-Hung Peng, Yani Shi, and Choon Ling Sia

City University of Hong Kong, Kowloon Tong, China
Lncle2012@yahoo.com,
{chpeng,Yanishi2,iscl}@cityu.edu.hk

Abstract. This paper explores the relationship between website localization and their exogenous factors. Three exogenous factors are studied: online transaction availability, product types and history length. Based on the previous studies, this paper distinguishes website localization design strategies from website localization degree. Through a content analysis of Fortune 1000 companies' websites, this paper finds that website localization strategies are positively related to website localization degree and that product types positively associate with website localization degree. Besides, all the exogenous factors are relevant to some specfic website localization strategies.

Keywords: Website localization · Exogenous factors · Strategies · Content analysis

1 Introduction

By leveraging the Internet, many firms are able to introduce and sell their products to customers all over the world through their websites. Global e-commerce is increasingly important for not only firms but also consumers. The sales of global B2C e-commerce is estimated around \$1.5 trillion and accounts for nearly 6.7 % of worldwide retail in 2015 (Rueter 2014). Correspondingly, more and more consumers are engaging in global e-commerce. According to the reports (Miglani 2012; Nielsen 2008), the world online users will reach 3.5 billion by 2017 and more than 85 % of the world's online population have purchased online in 2008.

There are two general ideas for designing websites for different countries: standardization and localization. First, website standardization refers to using same website content with only language translation for every country (Singh and Pereira 2005). In contrast, website localization refers to customizing a website for a specific country. Website localization makes a website seem natural or "local" to their users (Singh et al. 2009). Emerging studies have investigated the effectiveness and importance of website localization (Chen et al. 2009; Singh et al. 2004; Tixier 2005; Vyncke and Brengman 2010) and we think that website localization is significant trend for global e-commerce and more research of website localization is necessary for successful global e-commerce.

Website localization has received attention from researchers. Although previous international marketing literature also has discussed adaptation or localization strategies,

© Springer International Publishing Switzerland 2015
F.F.-H. Nah and C.-H. Tan (Eds.): HCIB 2015, LNCS 9191, pp. 392–402, 2015.
DOI: 10.1007/978-3-319-20895-4_36

they focus on marketing mix(Solberg 2000), resource allocation (Szymanski et al. 1993), environmental and market determinants (Yip 1997), advertising and communication (Solberg 2002) and performance measurement (Lages et al. 2008). Some of studies on website localization literature have focused on establishing website localization frameworks and validating them through comparing and analyzing different countries' websites localization (Baack and Singh 2007; Gibb and Matthaiakis 2007; Singh and Matsuo 2004; Singh et al. 2009). Moreover, some of studies have explored the related factors which influence website localization. The factors studied include immigrants or minorities' acculturation level (Singh et al. 2008), culture, geography and infrastructure (Shneor 2012), managerial attitudes (Singh et al. 2010). There are also a few studies that identify and discuss several localization elements for website localization practice, like symbols and graphics, color preferences, links, maps, search functions, page layout, language, and content (Cyr et al. 2005), presentation of human image and environment types (Singer et al. 2007), access to product, logical presentation of product information, and information professional design (Cyr et al. 2005).

Although some related factors have been explored in previous literature, other exogenous factors, such as history length, online transaction availability and product types, have not been discussed. These factors provide a way to predict the usage of website localization strategies and decide the degree of website localization. For example, the longer history the foreign companies operate business in local countries, the more knowledge and motivation the foreign companies may have to localize their websites. Therefore, studying these factors into more detail could further our understanding of website localization. Besides, compared with other exogenous factors, information about history length, online transaction availability and product types is easier to access through public reports and foreign companies' websites. Thus, the objectives of this study are:

What exogenous factors influence website localization? How?

To achieve the objectives of this study, we structure the rest of this paper as follows. In the second section, we discuss the theoretical background and develop the hypotheses about the relationships among website localization strategies, website localization degree and their exogenous factors. In the third section, we empirically test the hypotheses through a content analysis. In the fourth section, we report the analysis results. In the fifth section, we discuss the implication, limitation and future research of this study.

2 Theoretical Background and Hypothesis Development

2.1 Website Localization Strategies

Previous literature discusses the specific localization strategies mainly based on a culture framework (Baack and Singh 2007; Singh et al. 2008; Singh and Matsuo 2004). The website localization strategies are proposed according to the definitions of different cultural dimensions like Masculinity for quizzes and games or Uncertainty avoidance for customer service (Singh and Matsuo 2004). The studied cultural dimensions included: individualism–collectivism, uncertainty avoidance, power distance, masculinity- femininity (Hofstede 1980), high/low context (Hall 1976), intellectual autonomy, hierarchy and affective autonomy (Schwartz 1994). Although several strategies have been put forward based on cultural frameworks, very few studies have actually tested the effectiveness of strategies.

Wu et al. (2015) also identified several website localization strategies to localize foreign companies' websites based on social identity perspective. In line with the social identity perspective, website localization strategies can localize foreign companies' websites through creating similarities between foreign companies' websites and local consumers or through providing information about foreign companies' beneficial actions towards local consumers or their communities. We do further investigation based on Wu et al.'s (2015) website localization strategies. Given website localization strategies (e.g., Local Symbol and Corporate Social Responsibility) involve local group's features or attributes to make the websites be similar to the local group, or convey foreign companies' kindness and benefit to local group through the websites, they could increase websites' localization degree. Therefore, we can hypothesize as:

H1: Website localization strategies associate with website localization degree positively.

2.2   Exogenous Factors of Website Localization

Global marketing literature revealed that companies which produced the different types of products localized their businesses differently. The literature suggested that industrial and high-tech products were more appropriate for standardization rather than consumer products because industrial and high-tech products tended to meet universal needs and consumers were more rational in purchasing such products. Compared with industrial and high-tech products, consumer products are more suitable for localization because they appeal to consumers' hard-to-change tastes, habits, cultures and customs and foreign companies should adapt their marketing mix to be consistent with local consumers' characteristics (Cavusgil et al. 1993; Jain 1989). Similar to the relationship between consumer and industrial products, non-durable products require higher adaptation rather than durable products in consumer products (Malhotra 1993). Given that companies which produce different product types localize their marketing activities differently and website localization strategies are likely to help localize foreign companies' website, we can hypothesize that:

H2a: Product types associate with website localization degree positively.
H2b: Product types associate with usage of website localization strategies positively.

In e-commerce era, many companies do the transaction through their websites and trust is a widely accepted essential ingredient for developing successful business relationship between companies and consumers (Gefen et al. 2003). Previous studies have revealed consumers' willingness to accept vulnerability if the consumers trust the website and its vendor. The acceptance of vulnerability facilitates consumers' engagement in the online transaction (Mayer et al. 1995). According to Kramer et al. (1996), trust can be built on shared features or common values between consumers and the website vendors in e-commerce context. Meanwhile, localized website makes consumers feel that the foreign companies' website is naturalized to them and helps to identify foreign companies and their websites as local ones. In other words, website localization can develop and establish commonalities between local consumers and website vendors (Singh et al. 2009). Therefore, website localization strategies and high website localization degree can promote trust and improve the usage of online transaction. Thus, we can hypothesize that:

> H3a: Online transaction availability associates with website localization degree positively.
> H3b: Online transaction availability associates with website localization strategies positively.

Strategic choice perspective suggests organizations respond to the external environment changes by adapting their strategies (Chaffee 1985). Such adaptation seeks for a balance between organizations' behavior systems and their external environment (Alderson 1965). Boeker (1989) studied the effect of organization history on organization's strategies' change and uncovered its significant role. To be specific, the external conditions or events in an organization history limit or encourage organization's strategy choice. As an important channel of companies' global business, the choice of website design method is an important strategic decision. Given history impacts organizations' strategy choice, more adaptation in their websites will be done and more website localization strategies will be used in line with longer history length. Therefore, we can hypothesize that:

> H4a: History length associates with website localization degree positively.
> H4b: History length associates with website localization strategies positively.

3 Methodology

In this study, we test the relationships among website localization strategies, website localization degree and their three exogenous factors. Website localization strategies are from Wu et al. (2015) and the designed website features to localize foreign companies' websites, while website localization degree is the extent to which local people perceive the localization of foreign companies' websites. Towards the three exogenous factors, product types are about main products provided by foreign companies to consumers and contain two types: consumer product and industrial product, online transaction availability is about whether foreign companies' websites provide the channel to do online business, and history length is the length foreign companies do business in local countries. The sample of this study and the ways to measure the variables are described as follows.

3.1 Sample

For this study, we choose foreign companies' (Fortune 1000) websites in China as the object of our research. The local people are Chinese people. To do the analysis, the first step is to sort out companies that have Chinese websites/pages and companies that do not have Chinese websites/pages. Among the Fortune 1000 American Companies, 729 companies do not have specific websites/pages for the Chinese market and only 271 companies have Chinese websites/pages. Thus, the final sample for this study is the 271 companies that have Chinese websites/pages.

3.2   Measurement

To measure each websites' localization degree, several measurement frameworks are proposed in previous literature. Among the measurement frameworks established in previous studies, Singh (2012) comprehensively covered and tested the dimensions of website localization. To apply this framework in our context, we adapted it according to our sample's traits in this research. The adapted framework contains four dimensions: *Translation quality* (How will the foreign language translate into Chinese), *Content localization* (How the content in website can be understood by local people), *Cultural customization* (How the website reflect local culture) and *Local Gateway* (Whether there're links to Chinese pages from English home pages) would be primarily considered to compose the measurement framework in this research. Each dimension has different items and totally ten items are included in the framework. Every item is ranked on a scale of 1 to 5, based on the level of localization degree. We add up all the scores of certain website obtained in each item to reflect its website localization extent.

To decide whether the websites make use of website localization strategies, we analyze Fortune 1000 companies' Chinese websites and code the website as "1" if it leverages some specific website localization strategy and "0" if it does not utilize it. We choose four website localization strategies proposed in Wu et al. (2015) for the purpose of this study. They are *Special Plan* (Information about a special plan of product/services provided for local people by foreign companies), *Corporate Social Responsibility* (Information about how the foreign companies undertake their social responsibilities for the local people), *Local History* (Information which depict the development history of foreign companies in the local country) and *Local Authentication* (Symbols denoting that the website is authenticated by a local organization as a trusted, safe and legal website).

Regarding the product types being marketed by the companies, we analyze the public financial information of companies and decide the product type based on their main revenue sources. If the companies' revenue mainly comes from producing and selling consumer product, we code the companies' website as "1". If the main revenue sources are industrial product, we code their websites as "0". Because some of the companies are service companies, we do not consider them for this variable and 181 websites are included in this variable. Similarly, for availability of online transaction channel, we code the websites as "1" if we can do online transaction with the companies through websites and "0" if not. With regard to how long Fortune 1000 companies operate in China, we also search the public information of the companies and compute the history length by using the number of current year minus the number of year they entered into China.

3.3 Data Analysis

This paper uses content analysis to judge the localization extent of websites in our sample by using a measurement scale, analyze whether the websites contain some specific website localization strategies and figure out whether there are transaction channels in their websites. The reason why we use content analysis is because the data of this study is limited to the content of foreign companies' website and language of website is crucial (Kassarjian 1977). Meanwhile, one type of content analysis is to quantify or index the content according to some principles and this study belongs to this type (Neuendorf 2002). To test the quality of content analysis, two bilingual raters who have website localization and design related knowledge and background analyzed the 271 American companies' Chinese websites. The inter-rater reliability test among raters is used to check to judge whether the analysis is reliable. The percentage of agreement of identifying website localization strategies and three exogenous factors is 79.5 %.

Given website localization strategies are binary variables, binary logistic regression technique is adopted to analyze their relationships with product types, online transaction availability and history length. As the data of website localization degree is continual, multiple linear regression technique is utilized to analyze its relationship with website localization strategies, product types, online transaction availability, and history length. Both regressions are implemented by PASW 18.0.

The descriptive statistics of variables in this study are listed in Table 1.

Table 1 Descriptive Statistics of Variables

Binary variables	Mean	Std. Dev.	Number of "0"	Number of "1"
Local history	0.33	0.47	181	90
Corporate social responsibility	0.35	0.48	177	94
Special plan	0.08	0.27	249	22
Local authentication	0.08	0.27	250	21
Online transaction availability	0.22	0.42	211	60
Product type	0.28	0.45	130	51
Continual variables	Mean	Std. Dev.	Min.	Max.
History length	18.34	9.15	0	43
Website localization degree	27.44	6.66	10	42

4 Results

4.1 Regression Analysis of Website Localization Degree

To test the relationships between the exogenous factors, website localization strategies and website localization degree, we analyze the data by using Multiple Linear Regression technique. The estimation results are in Table 2, which show the regression coefficients and standard errors. In model 1, we find that website localization strategies: Local History, Local Authentication, Corporate Social Responsibility and Special Plan are all significantly and positively associated with website localization degree. Thus, the regression results support H1. In model 2, we find that only product type is significantly associated with website localization degree, while history length and availability of online transaction channel are not significantly associated with website localization degree. Thus, H2a is supported, while H3a and H4a are not supported.

Table 2. Regression results of website localization degree

Variables	Model 1	Model 2
Local history	2.151**	1.119
	0.805	0.959
Corporate social responsibility	3.457***	2.514**
	0.789	0.900
Special plan	5.608***	2.017
	1.310	1.743
Local authentication	5.451***	3.316*
	1.351	1.621
Online transaction availability		0.489
		1.284
Product type		6.096***
		1.132
History length		0.030
		0.049

Note: * $p < 0.05$, ** $p < 0.01$, *** $p < 0.001$.

4.2 Regression Analysis of Website Localization Strategies

Given the important role of website localization strategies, to know the relationships between exogenous factors and website localization strategies can provide valuable guidance to enhance websites' localization degree. Considering the nature of data of

Table 3. Regression Results of Website Localization Strategies

	Local history	Corporate social responsibility	Special plan	Local authentication
Online transaction availability	−0.715 (0.205)	0.476 (0.338)	−0.104 (0.891)	2.262(0.005)
Product type	1.675 (0.001)	0.851 (0.046)	2.204 (0.005)	−0.109(0.889)
History length	0.096 (0.000)	0.083 (0.000)	0.051 (0.146)	0.008(0.818)
-2 log-likelihood ratio	195.521	217.176	70.558	80.668
Nagelkerke's R square	0.256	0.187	0.180	0.170

website localization strategies, we utilize Binary Logistic Regression to analyze the relationships. The results are in Table 3 which exhibit the regression coefficients and P-values. The results indicate that availability of online transaction channel only positively associates with Local Authentication significantly, while product types positively associate with Local History, Corporate Social Responsibility and Special Plan significantly. History length also positively associates with Local History and Corporate Social Responsibility. Thus, H2b, H3b and H4b are all partially supported.

5   Discussion and Conclusion

5.1   Discussion

In this study, we explore the relationships between website localization and their exogenous factors. The exogenous factors contain product types, online transaction availability and history length, while we distinguish website localization design strategies from localization degree of each website. Based on the nature of data of different variables, we analyze the relationships by employing multiple linear regression and binary logistic regression. The results imply that the more we leverage website localization design strategies, the higher website localization degree is, while websites which belong to consumer product companies require higher website localization degree than the other websites.

To provide more insights to design a highly localized website, we also discuss the relationships between exogenous factors and specific website localization strategies. Online transaction availability only associates with Local Authentication which is used to endorse websites as safe and secure websites. The result implies that the utmost variable for online transaction is security. Product types link to more website localization strategies than other exogenous factors. Given consumer product companies need to interact with local consumers online and website localization strategies can raise positive attitude of local consumers, consumer product companies have stronger motivation to localize their websites as much as possible rather than industrial product companies. Although history length does not relate to website localization degree directly, it still associates with two website localization strategies: Local History and Corporate Social Responsibility. Taking full advantage of these two strategies needs a deep understanding of local culture and accumulation of interactions with local consumers. History length is a precondition of the understanding and accumulation.

The unsupported hypotheses include the relationships between history length, online transaction availability and website localization degree. Although organizations should be adaptive to the environment as time passes based on strategic choice perspective, the current result shows their websites design do not follow this practice. We explain this result in that the role of websites in different companies' strategies is different. For some companies, websites are an important channel to communicate with local consumers and building brand image, while websites are just a way to deliver basic information for other companies. For online transaction availability, the utmost and essential concerns for people are privacy and security (Belanger et al. 2002), may not be website localization. Although website localization can convey some quality information about the website, it may still not be enough to ensure the security.

5.2 Limitations and Future Research

Although we explore the relationships among exogenous factors, website localization strategies and website localization degree, we still have some limitations which provide many opportunities for the future research. First of all, we demonstrate the positive relationship between website localization strategies and website localization degree, but empirical experiments which test consumers' response towards website localization strategies directly will help us understand the effectiveness of website localization strategies deeper. Therefore, future research can conduct experiments that emphasize rigor to test the effectiveness of website localization strategies.

Secondly, we do not explore the underlying working mechanisms of different website localization strategies. As we can see from the discussion of this study, different website localization strategies work through different underlying mechanisms and these mechanisms may determine their effectiveness. To explore such mechanisms could be the key to understanding why some website localization strategies are more effective than the others. It may also lead to substantial theoretical contribution through addressing this research question because it can open the "black box" and establishes an opportunity for theory building. Therefore, future research also can explore the underlying processes of different website localization strategies through implementing controlled experiments.

Thirdly, since the study target is Chinese consumers who are collectivistic, consumers who belong to other cultures like individualistic culture may value website localization differently from Chinese consumers. We think this difference will make individualistic consumers focus on different website localization strategies from collectivistic consumers. For example, previous studies revealed that individualistic culture treats in-groups and out-group more equally than collectivistic culture (Lee and Ward 1998), and strategies which involve in-group features like Local Symbol for individualistic culture may not be as effective as it is for collectivistic culture. Therefore, future research can analyze the effectiveness of website localization strategies in individualistic context and compare the results in this study, which is in the collectivistic context.

5.3 Implications

This study contributes to the literature in several ways. Firstly, we explore and confirm the relationship between exogenous factors and website localization strategies/degree. The exogenous factors make us understand and predict the usage of website localization strategies and website localization design. Secondly, we understand the effect of different website localization strategies on website localization degree. This could trigger further studying of the website localization strategies. At last, we adapt and validate the measurement framework of Singh (2012) in our study context, and develop measurement framework of website localization furtherly. To establish an appropriate website localization measurement instrument is always meaningful for improving effectiveness of website localization.

Meanwhile, our study also contributes to website localization practice. At first, we investigate the current extent of website localization of Fortune 1000 companies. This result can help the companies to check whether their websites' localization degree help or impede achieving their strategic goal in China. Second, exogenous factors of website localization we explored can be applied directly to predict the usage of website localization strategies and decide website localization degree. These three factors are quite operable and practical. Last but not the least, we validate the effectiveness of website localization strategies and foreign companies can better understand how to design their websites when they decide to promote the localization of their websites.

References

Alderson, W.: Dynamic Marketing Behavior: A Functionalist Theory of Marketing. Richard D. Irwin Inc., Homewood (1965)

Baack, D.W., Singh, N.: Culture and web communications. J. Bus. Res. **60**(3), 181–188 (2007)

Belanger, F., Hiller, J.S., Smith, W.J.: Trustworthiness in electronic commerce: the role of privacy, security, and site attributes. J. Strateg. Inf. Syst. **11**(3), 245–270 (2002)

Boeker, W.: Strategic change: the effects of founding and history. Acad. Manag. J. **32**(3), 489–515 (1989)

Cavusgil, S.T., Zou, S., Naidu, G.M.: Product and promotion adaptation in export ventures: an empirical investigation. J. Int. Bus. Stud. **24**(3), 479–506 (1993)

Chaffee, E.: Three models of strategy. Acad. Manag. Rev. **10**(1), 89–98 (1985)

Chen, J.V., Ross, W.H., Yen, D.C., Akhapon, L.: The effect of types of banner ad, web localization, and customer involvement on internet users' attitudes. CyberPsychol. Behav. **12**(1), 71–73 (2009)

Cyr, D., Bonanni, C., Bowes, J., Ilsever, J.: Beyond trust: web site design preferences across cultures. J. Global Inf. Manag. **13**(4), 25–54 (2005)

Gefen, D., Karahanna, E., Straub, D.: Trust and tam in online shopping: an integrated model. MIS Q. **27**(1), 51–90 (2003)

Gibb, F., Matthaiakis, I.: A framework for assessing web site localisation. Electron. Libr. **25**(6), 664–678 (2007)

Hall, E.T.: Beyond Culture. Doubleday, Garden City (1976)

Hofstede, G.: Culture's Consequences: International Differences in Work-Related Values. Sage, Beverly Hills (1980)

Jain, S.C.: Standardization of international marketing strategy: some research hypotheses. J. Mark. **53**(1), 70–79 (1989)

Kassarjian, H.H.: Content analysis in consumer research. J. Consum. Res. **4**(1), 8–18 (1977)

Kramer, R.M., Brewer, M.B., Hanna, B.A.: Collective trust and collective action. In: Tyler, T.R. (ed.) Trust in Organizations: Frontiers of Theory and Research, pp. 357–389. SAGE Publications, Thousand Oaks (1996)

Lages, L.F., Abrantes, J.L., Lages, C.R.: The stratadapt scale: a measure of marketing strategy adaptation to international business markets. Int. Mark. Rev. **25**(5), 584–600 (2008)

Lee, L., Ward, C.: Ethnicity, idiocentrism-allocentrism, and intergroup attitudes1. J. Appl. Soc. Psychol. **28**(2), 109–123 (1998)

Malhotra, I.B.B.N.K.: Marketing management bases for international market segmentation: an alternate look at the standardization/customization debate. Int. Mark. Rev. **10**(1), 19–44 (1993)

Mayer, R.C., Davis, J.H., Schoorman, F.D.: An Integrative Model of Organizational Trust. Acadamy Management Review **20**(3), 709–734 (1995)

Miglani, J.: Forrester Research World Online Population Forecast, 2012 to 2017 (Global). Forrester Research, Cambridge (2012)

Neuendorf, K.A.: The Content Analysis Guidebook. Sage Publications, Thousand Oaks (2002)

Nielsen, : Over 875 Million Consumers Have Shopped Online. The Nielsen Company, New York (2008)

Rueter, T.: Global e-commerce will increase 22 % this year (2014). https://www.internetretailer.com/2014/12/23/global-e-commerce-will-increase-22-year. Accessed 9 March 2015

Schwartz, S.H.: Beyond individualism/collectivism: new cultural dimensions of values. In: Kim, U., Triandis, H.C., Kagitcibasi, C., Choi, S.-C., Yoon, G. (eds.) Individualism and Collectivism: Theory, Method, and Applications, pp. 85–119. Sage Publications Inc., Thousand Oaks (1994)

Shneor, R.: Influences of culture, geography and infrastructure on website localization decisions. Int. J. Cross Cult. Manag. **19**(3), 352–374 (2012)

Singer, D.D., Baradwaj, B., Avery, A.E.: Web localization in international online banking. J. Internet Bus. **4**, 1–23 (2007)

Singh, N.: Localization strategies for global e-Business. Cambridge University Press, Cambridge (2012)

Singh, N., Baack, D.W., Bott, J.P.: Are multinationals localizing their web sites? the link between managerial attitudes and mne web content. Int. J. Commer. Manag. **20**(3), 258–267 (2010)

Singh, N., Baack, D.W., Pereira, A., Baack, D.: Culturally customizing websites for US Hispanic online consumers. J. Advertising Res. **48**(2), 224–234 (2008)

Singh, N., Furrer, O., Ostinelli, M.: To Localize or to Standardize on the Web: Empirical Evidence from Italy, India, Netherlands, Spain, and Switzerland. Multinatl. Bus. Rev. **12**(1), 69–88 (2004)

Singh, N., Matsuo, H.: Measuring cultural adaptation on the web: a content analytic study of us and japanese web sites. J. Bus. Res. **57**(8), 864–872 (2004)

Singh, N., Pereira, A.: The Culturally Customized Web Site. Routledge, Burlington (2005)

Singh, N., Toy, D.R., Wright, L.K.: A diagnostic framework for measuring web-site localization. Thunderbird Int. Bus. Rev. **51**(3), 281–295 (2009)

Solberg, C.A.: Standardization or adaptation of the international marketing mix: the role of the local subsidiary/representative. J. Int. Mark. **8**(1), 78–98 (2000)

Solberg, C.A.: The perennial issue of adaptation or standardization of international marketing communication: organizational contingencies and performance. J. Int. Mark. **10**(3), 1–21 (2002)

Szymanski, D.M., Bharadwaj, S.G., Varadarajan, P.R.: Standardization versus adaptation of international marketing strategy: an empirical investigation. J. Mark. **57**(4), 1–17 (1993)

Tixier, M.: Globalization and localization of contents: evolution of major internet sites across sectors of industry. Thunderbird Int. Bus. Rev. **47**(1), 15–48 (2005)

Vyncke, F., Brengman, M.: Are culturally congruent websites more effective? an overview of a decade of empirical evidence. J. Electron. Commer. Res. **11**(1), 14–29 (2010)

Wu, T., Sia, C. L., Shi, Y., Peng, C.-H., Lu, Y.: An exploration study of website localization strategies: a perspective from fortune 1000 (2015)

Yip, G.S.: Patterns and determinants of global marketing. J. Mark. Manag. **13**(1–3), 153–164 (1997)

Consumers' Purchase Intention of Online Product Customization Using Different Terminals with/without Default Template

Jiaheng Xie, Wangsheng Zhu, and Kanliang Wang[✉]

School of Business, Renmin University of China, Beijing, China
{aaron.xiejh,kanliang.wang}@gmail.com,
zhuwsl992@163.com

Abstract. To provide more personalized products, many vendors allow consumers to design their products by selecting attribute by attribute, a technology commonly called customization. Complexity of customizing process has been a concern for consumers, and default template was introduced to solve this dilemma. With the rapid development of mobile internet, mobile terminals, such as tablets and smart phones, play ever vital roles in conducting e-commerce. The shift from desktop computers to mobile terminals may generate changes in the response of consumers viewing identical content as digital interfaces fundamentally change the experience of the content they access. However, little attention has been paid to the impacts of different terminals on consumers' purchase intention. This research aims to find out the impact of default template on consumers' purchase intention, and the interaction effect that terminal and need for uniqueness have on the relationship. A lab experiment was conducted to test the proposed hypothesis. The result shows that default template increase consumers' intention to buy. Besides, terminal and need for uniqueness have moderating effect on the relationship.

Keywords: Default template · Terminal · Need for uniqueness · Intention to buy · Interaction effect · Customization

1 Introduction

Mass customization (MC) is a production strategy focused on the broad provision of personalized products and services (Davis 1989; Pine et al. 1993). It is the method of "effectively postponing the task of differentiating a product for a specific customer until the latest possible point in the supply network." (Chase, Jacobs and Aquilano 2006, p. 419). To meet the personal needs of customers, vendors provide consumers with a wild range of choices, which leads to higher task complexity (Dellaert et al. 2005). Since increased complexity requires greater consumer effort to generate the same mass customized product (Johnson and Payne 1985), and, all else equal, consumers like to minimize decision effort (Wright 1975), some vendors offer consumers default template to help consumers customize products. Prior research showed that customizing with a default product template reduces task complexity and increases mental simulation (Hildebrand, Häubl, and Herrman 2014), which affects consumer's perceived

© Springer International Publishing Switzerland 2015
F.F.-H. Nah and C.-H. Tan (Eds.): HCIB 2015, LNCS 9191, pp. 403–413, 2015.
DOI: 10.1007/978-3-319-20895-4_37

ownership to the customized product (Peck, Barger, and Webb 2003). By customizing from scratch, consumers may find it hard to design the product they want, while a default template gives them a prototype to customize their products. Under the default provision scenario, consumers can firstly choose a product template from a choice set, and then modify the chosen product to meet their final needs. In this way, consumers may find it easier to customize the product and create mental images of the product, a process that may also affect consumers' customizing experience. When consumers are given a default product template, they are more likely to create the vivid mental simulation, and the mental simulation increases perception of ownership (Peck, Barger, and Webb 2003). Thus, default template is very likely to affect the customizing process and consumers' decision making.

Previous MC researches mainly focus on four areas: namely, economics of MC, MC success factors, MC enablers and C-M interaction (Fogliatto et al. 2012), while few studies have focused on the interface perspective. With the rapid development of mobile internet, mobile terminals play ever vital roles in conducting e-commerce. Industry research suggests that over 8 % of e-commerce website visits come from tablets, and the 2012 Black Friday weekend saw almost 20 % of online sales from tablets and smart phones (IBM 2012).As computer usage has shifted from desktop computers to laptops and tablets, interfaces have shifted from computer mice to touch pad and touch screen (Brasel and Gips 2014).These interface changes may, in turn, generate changes in the response of consumers viewing identical content as digital interfaces fundamentally change the experience of the content they access (Rokeby 1998). Since touch interface often leads to better shopping experiences, mobile terminals have the salient advantage over PCs. In the context of online customization, however, little attention has been paid to the impacts of different terminals on consumers' purchase intention. Previous research has shown that touching a product increases consumers' psychological ownership (Peck and Shu 2009), in a way to result in higher endowment effect (Pierce, Kostova, and Dirks 2003;Reb and Connolly 2007). Even imagining touch can generate perceived ownership similar to actually touching an object (Peck, Barger, and Webb 2003). When consumers use mobile tablet, they have to touch the product on the screen. At the same time, they may imagine touching the real product. When consumers customize products, they have to devote efforts to the customizing process, so that endowment effect is created, which causes consumers to overvalue items that they perceive they own (Franciosi et al. 1996). As a result, when consumers use configurator on mobile tablet, the value generated from the customizing process and the purchase decision may be different from those on PC. Since terminal affect mental simulation, terminal may affect default template's influence on consumers' purchase intention.

Default template not only provides convenience for consumers by giving a prototype, it also depresses consumers' expression of personalization. Different people may perceive the usefulness of default template differently, so personality trait is introduced to explain the mechanism. Need for uniqueness reflects an individual's desire to be different from other people (Ho et al. 2008). Need for uniqueness may moderate default template's effect as well.

This article aims to find out the effect that default template have on purchase intention. Besides, we also explore the moderating effect of terminal and need for uniqueness. A 2 by 2 factor lab experiment was conducted to test the hypothesis. All subjects were asked to customize a pair of shoes using www.idx.com.cn. Our study illuminates the impacts of different terminals and default template on consumers' decision making, and finds out the moderating effect of the terminal and need for uniqueness. Based on the result, vendors can also determine whether or not to provide default template and how to design their website on different terminals.

This paper is constructed as follows. In the following section, we review prior literature and discuss theoretical model and hypothesis. We then present analysis and result, followed by a discussion and implication. Finally, we conclude the paper with directions for future research.

2 Literature Review

In this study, consumers' intention to buy (ITB) denotes consumers' intention to buy a customized product. Need for uniqueness (NFU) is introduced as a moderating variable. Need for uniqueness reflects an individual's desire to be different from other people; it is a "counter-conformity motivation" (Nail 1986).

2.1 Default Template

To provide more personalized products for customers, vendors give consumers the opportunity to configure their own product by individually choosing each of its attributes. However, customizing a product by specifying each attribute individually tends to be onerous for consumers (Hildebrand et al. 2014). Too many choices in the customizing process increase the task complexity for consumers, and, in turn, depress consumers' purchase intention. As mass customization becomes more complex, it becomes more likely that consumers need to resort to simplifying decision heuristics (Newell and Simon 1972). To solve the dilemma, some vendors provide a set of default templates to give consumers some inspires to design their own products. In the default template provision scenario, consumers' customizing process is divided into two steps. Firstly, they can choose a template that is most similar to their preferences. Secondly, they can refine any small element on the template if they are not satisfied with some parts of the template.

In the case of customizing with default template, the configuration process begins with the presentation of fully specified products, from which consumers select one as their starting point. So customizing with default templates is a top-down process. According to neurophysiologic studies, top-down processing is more strongly associated with the dorsal region of the human brain, which is responsible for motor behavior and visual control (Engel, Fries, and Singer 2001; Goodale and Milner 1992; Norman 2002).Activation of brain regions that are associated with motor behavior should be conducive to mental simulation (Hildebrand et al. 2014). Social psychology research has demonstrated that mental simulation can lead to higher assessed probability estimates of simulated events and positive changes in attitudes, brand evaluations, and actual behavior, particularly if the simulation is self-relevant and repeated (Anderson 1983; Carroll 1978; Gregory, Cialdini, and Carpenter 1982).

In addition, insights from prior work on problem solving suggest that partitioning a problem into a number of smaller, more manageable ones can mitigate the perceived difficulty of solving the overall problem (Von Hippel 1994; Lau, Yam, and Tang 2011). Since the task is less difficult, consumers may be more willing to buy the customized product. Therefore, we propose:

H1: *Customizing with default template results in a higher level of intention to buy (ITB) than customizing without default template.*

2.2   Terminal

As computer usage has shifted from desktop computers to laptops and tablets, interfaces have shifted from computer mice to touch pads and touch screens (Brasel and Gips 2014). Touch in consumer behavior is a recent area of inquiry (Jansson-Boyd 2011; Peck and Childers 2003). Since most mobile terminals, such as smart phones and tablets, are equipped with touch interfaces, research on mobile terminals calls for special attention. Peck and Shu (2009) found that merely touching a product increases psychological ownership, and touching is employed in social contexts to communicate temporary territorial ownership over public goods (Werner, Brown, and Damron 1981). Other research has shown that imaging touching a product also increases psychological ownership (Peck, Barger, and Webb 2003), and object interactivity increases the vividness of mental product images (Schlosser 2006), so mental simulation is created. When consumers customize products on mobile terminals, they have to touch the product on the screen. As a result, they would be more likely to create mental simulation and perceive that they own the product.

Since terminal affects the customizing process, terminal may moderate the effect that default template has on consumers' ITB. When customizing on tablet, consumers will perceive a higher level of mental simulation, so the positive effect of default template will be more obvious. Besides, when consumers customize on PCs, they are skillful enough to use the configurator, so they may feel less complex about the task. As a result, the difference between with default template scenario and without default template scenario will be narrowed on the PC terminal. Therefore, we propose:

H2: *Terminal will moderate the effect that default template has on consumers' intention to buy (ITB).*

2.3   Need for Uniqueness

Although default template offers consumers a prototype to design their own products, it may also depress consumers' uniqueness expression. To better understand the mechanism of the effect of default template, personality trait should also be considered. Need for uniqueness (NFU) reflects an individual's desire to be different from others; it is a "counter-conformity motivation" (Nail 1986). Individuals with a high need for uniqueness have a higher tendency to develop and enhance their personal identity through the acquisition, utilization, and disposition of consumer goods (Tian et al. 2001). Individuals with a high need for uniqueness are less likely to choose

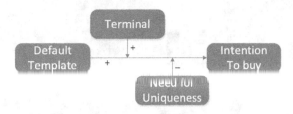

Fig. 1. Theoretical model

compromise options and tend to make unconventional choices (Simonson and Nowlis 2000). Individuals with a high need for uniqueness prefer unusual choices because they want to use non-obvious grounds and reasons that are novel to express their distinctiveness and uniqueness and to demonstrate their intellect (Ho et al. 2008).In the customization settings, people with a high level of need for uniqueness tend to seek for their own design element. Even given a default template, they would find default template less useful, because they will design their own product anyway. As a result, need for uniqueness will moderate the effect of default template. Therefore, we propose:

H3: *Need for uniqueness (NFU) will moderate the effect that default template has on consumers' intention to buy.*

The theoretical model is shown in Fig. 1, where terminal: 0 for PC; 1 for tablet; default template: 0 for without default template and1 for with default template.

3 Methodology

3.1 Experimental Design

We employed a 2 by 2 factorial design. Two types of terminal, namely PC and tablet, were used to conduct the experiment. Two different task scenarios were exposed to the subjects in the experiment: with default template and without default template. A total of 40 subjects (65 % female) were recruited from a national university in China to participate the experiment. Since woman is more likely than man to customize product, female ratio is a little bit higher. All the subjects were asked to customize a pair of shoes for themselves using the configurator: www.idx.com.cn. According to configurator-database report (2013), shoes are listed the top 10 products across over 900 product configurators, so shoes were used as a typical customization product in the experiment. At first, subjects were shown a video introducing customization, and were given a piece of paper introducing their tasks. Then subjects are randomly assigned to one of the four treatments: namely, PC/with default template, PC/without default template, tablet/with default template, tablet/without default template. After the experiment, they were asked whether they felt comfortable when they were customizing the shoes, whether the default template was helpful, and how did they like the tablet. To ensure the quality of the experiment, we informed all subjects that they had one out of eight chances to get the pair of shoes they customized during the experiment.

For subjects using PC terminal, they were given a desktop computer with a mouse to customize the shoes. For subjects using tablet terminal, they were given a Windows

Fig. 2. With default template(left) versus without default template(right)

Fig. 3. PC condition (left) versus tablet condition (right)

Surface with touch interface to finish the task. All the web design on the PC terminal and tablet terminal was the same. In the with default template scenario, a set of finished designs was shown on the screen, and subjects were told that they can choose designs from the set and refine the designs. In the without default template scenario, subjects were given a pair of white shoes. All other irrelevant elements on the original webpage were concealed by changing the source code. Screen snapshots of "with default template" and "without default template" were shown in Fig. 2. PC and Tablet experiment conditions are shown in Fig. 3.

3.2   Instrument

To measure consumers' intention to buy, we asked subjects to what degree they would like to buy the customized shoes. Need for uniqueness is measured using the scale in Ho et al.'s (2008).

4   Result and Analysis

4.1   Sample and Assumptions Tests

The sample used for this study consists of 40 subjects. The demographics of our sample can be seen in Table 1.

Table 1. Subject demographics

Variable	Frequency (%)	Variable	Frequency (%)
Gender		Age	
Male	35.0 %	18	2.5 %
Female	65.0 %	19	2.5 %
Education		20	30.0 %
Undergraduate	82.5 %	21	30.0 %
Master	17.5 %	22	35.0 %

The age of our subjects ranges from 18 to 22. The subjects include 65 % female and 82.5 % undergraduate students.

To confirm that the subjects were randomly assigned to the four treatments, we conducted a multivariate analysis of variance (MANOVA). Test result showed no significant differences in gender (F = 0.347, P = 0.792), age (F = 2.604, P = 0.067), and education (F = 1.891, P = 0.149) among the four experimental conditions. Also, since there are more women than men and more undergraduate students than master students in our sample, we used analysis of variance (ANOVA) to test whether there are any significant differences in the dependent variable between genders and education, and result shows that the dependent variable has no significant differences.

In order to test the validity of the constructs, we performed reliability analysis. The Cronbach's alpha values and descriptive statistics of all constructs can be seen in Table 2. As seen in Table 2, the scales show good convergent validity. The Cronbach's alpha value for need for uniqueness is above the recommended 0.7, indicating good reliability (Nunnally 1967).

Table 2. Reliability and validity

Dependent variable	Cronbach's α	AVE	Mean	St. Dev.
Need for uniqueness (NFU)	0.710	0.550	18.180	4.107

To test the convergent validity, average variance extracted (AVE) was assessed. As seen in the Table 2, AVE is above the threshold of 0.5 (Chin 1998). Thus, this construct demonstrated satisfactory convergent validity.

4.2   Results

In order to test the model, we conducted analysis of variance (ANOVA). The results of the effects that default template, terminal and NFU have on ITB can be seen in Table 3.

Table 3. ANOVA (Dependent variable: ITB)

Variables	F	Sig.	Results
Default template	4.482	0.041	**
Terminal	0.352	0.556	–
Need for uniqueness	2.155	0.046	**

** sig. < 0.05; *sig. < 0.1

Default template and need for uniqueness have significant influence on ITB. So H1 is supported.

The interaction effects are shown in Table 4. As the result indicates, terminal moderates the effect that default template has on intention to buy. Thus, H2 is supported. Need for uniquessness also moderatesthe positive effect that default template has on intention to buy. H3 is supported. As seen in Fig. 4, PC terminal will narrow the gap between the ITB with default templates and that without default templates.Individuals with a high level of need for uniqueness tend to be less affected by default template.

Table 4. ANOVA (Dependent variable: ITB)

Variable	F	Sig.	Results
Default template * Terminal	3.203	0.082	*
Default template * NFU	2.622	0.047	**

** sig. < 0.05; *sig. < 0.1

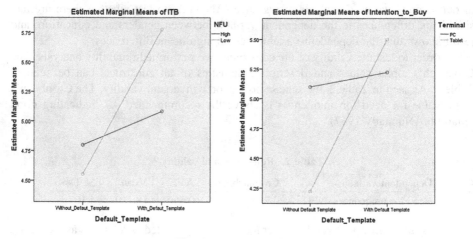

Fig. 4. Interaction effect

5   Discussion

This study examined the effect that default template has on consumers' purchase decision, and the moderating effect of terminal and need for uniqueness on the relationship. We reexamined the role of default template in the study of Hildebrand et al.

(2014), and we introduced a new dependent variable: intention to buy. As per our study, default template increases consumers' intention to buy. To demonstrate the mechanism in the model, we introduced two new moderating variables: terminal and need for uniqueness. Test result showed that on PC condition the positive effect that default template has on consumers' intention to buy is alleviated, and individuals with a high level of need for uniqueness are less affected by default template.

Theoretically, our study illuminates the role of default template in the customization settings. Moreover, moderating effect of terminal and need for uniqueness were also illustrated in this paper.

Practically, vendors can learn how to design their configurators on PC and tablet, respectively. Since mobile terminals have the salient advantage over PCs, vendors should pay more attention to the design and promotion of the site on mobile terminal. However, our research has some limitations. Firstly, more types of products can be examined to illustrate this issue. Secondly, smart phones can be also studied to explore the difference on three terminals: PC, tablet and smart phone. For future studies, similar studies can be carried on more products, such as T-shirts. To test all terminals, customizing on PC, tablet and smart phone can also be studied.

6 Conclusion

In the context of customization, too many choices are given to consumers. To solve the problem that consumers may find it difficult to customizing the most wanted products facing a wide range of choice set, many vendors provide default template for consumers. We found that default template increases consumers' intention to buy the customized products. Contrary to prior studies, we introduced two moderating variables to demonstrate the mechanism. As mobile terminals become vital devices in conducting e-commerce, vendors should better understand the difference between mobile terminals and desktop computers. We also found that terminal have moderating effect on default template, and consumers' need for uniqueness moderates default template's effect as well. Default template shows minor effect on desktop computer, while it shows significant positive effect on tablet. When need for uniqueness is high, the positive effect of default template is alleviated.

Acknowledgement. This research was supported by the National Natural Science Foundation of China with grant # 71331007.

References

Anderson, C.A.: Imagination and expectation: The effect of imagining behavioral scripts on personal influences. J. Pers. Soc. Psychol. **45**(2), 293 (1983)

Brasel, S.A., Gips, J.: Tablets, touchscreens, and touchpads: how varying touch interfaces trigger psychological ownership and endowment. J. Consum. Psychol. **24**(2), 226–233 (2014)

Carroll, J.S.: The effect of imagining an event on expectations for the event: an interpretation in terms of the availability heuristic. J. Exp. Soc. Psychol. **14**(1), 88–96 (1978)

Chase, R.B., Jacobs, F.R., Aquilano, N.J.: Operations Management for Competitive Advantage, 11th edn. McGraw-Hill/Irwin, New York (2006)

Chin, w.w.: The partial least squares of structural equation modeling. *Modern methods for business research*, 295–336 (1998)

Configurator-Database. Configurator Database Report 2013 (2013) (accessed from http://www.configurator-database.com/report2013)

Davis, S.M.: From "future perfect": Mass customizing. Strategy Leadersh. **17**(2), 16–21 (1989)

Dellaert, B.G., Stremersch, S.: Marketing mass-customized products: striking a balance between utility and complexity. J. Mark. Res. **42**(2), 219–227 (2005)

Engel, A.K., Fries, P., Singer, W.: Dynamic predictions: oscillations and synchrony in top–down processing. Nat. Rev. Neurosci. **2**(10), 704–716 (2001)

Fogliatto, F.S., da Silveira, G.J., Borenstein, D.: The mass customization decade: An updated review of the literature. Int. J. Prod. Econ. **138**(1), 14–25 (2012)

Franciosi, R., Kujal, P., Michelitsch, R., Smith, V., Deng, G.: Experimental tests of the endowment effect. J. Econ. Behav. Organ. **30**, 215–226 (1996)

Goodale, M.A., Milner, A.D.: Separate visual pathways for perception and action. Trends Neurosci. **15**(1), 20–25 (1992)

Gregory, W.L., Cialdini, R.B., Carpenter, K.M.: Self-relevant scenarios as mediators of likelihood estimates and compliance: does imagining make it so? J. Pers. Soc. Psychol. **43**(1), 89 (1982)

Hildebrand, C., Häubl, G., Herrmann, A.: Product customization via starting solutions. J. Mark. Res. **51**(6), 707–725 (2014)

Ho, S.Y., Davern, M.J., Tam, K.Y.: Personalization and choice behavior: the role of personality traits. ACM SIGMIS Database **39**(4), 31–47 (2008)

IBM. Black Friday Research Report 2012. IBM Digital Analytics Benchmark (2012) (accessed from www-01.ibm.com)

Jansson-Boyd, C.V.: The role of touch in marketing: An introduction to the special issue. Psychol. Mark. **28**, 219–221 (2011)

Johnson, E.J., Payne, J.W.: Effort and accuracy in choice. Manage. Sci. **31**(4), 395–414 (1985)

Lau, A.K., Yam, R., Tang, E.: The impact of product modularity on new product performance: Mediation by product innovativeness. J. Prod. Innov. Manage. **28**(2), 270–284 (2011)

Nail, P.R.: Toward an integration of some models and theories of social response. Psychol. Bull. **100**(2), 190 (1986)

Newell, A., Simon, H.A.: Human Problem Solving. Prentice Hall, Englewood Cliffs, NJ (1972)

Norman, J.: Two visual systems and two theories of perception: an attempt to reconcile the constructivist and ecological approaches. Behav. Brain Sci. **25**(1), 73–96 (2002)

Nunnally, J.C.: Psychometric Theory. McGraw-Hill, New York (1967)

Peck, J., Childers, T.: To have and to hold: The influence of haptic information on product judgments. J. Mark. **67**(2), 35–48 (2003)

Peck, J., Shu, S.: The effect of mere touch on perceived ownership. J. Consum. Res. **36**, 434–447 (2009)

Peck, J., Barger, V., Webb, A.: In search of a surrogate for touch: the effect of haptic imagery on perceived ownership. J. Consum. Res. **23**(2), 189–196 (2003)

Pierce, J.L., Kostova, T., Dirks, K.T.: The state of psychological ownership: Integrating and extending a century of research. Rev. Gen. Psychol. **7**, 84–107 (2003)

Pine II, B.J., Victor, B.: Making mass customization work. Harvard Bus. Rev. **71**(5), 108–117 (1993)

Reb, J., Connolly, T.: Possession, feelings of ownership and the endowment effect. Judgment Decis. Making **2**(2), 107–114 (2007)

Rokeby, D.: The construction of experience: Interface as content. In: Dodsworth Jr., C. (ed.) Digital Illusion: Entertaining the Future with High Technology. ACM Press, New York (1998)

Schlosser, A.: Learning through virtual product experience: The role of imagery on true versus false memories. J. Consum. Res. 33(3), 377–503 (2006)

Simonson, I., Nowlis, S.M.: The role of explanations and need for uniqueness in consumer decision making: unconventional choices based on reasons. J. Consum. Res. 27(1), 49–68 (2000)

Tian, K.T., Bearden, W.O., Hunter, G.L.: Consumers' need for uniqueness: Scale development and validation. J. Consum. Res. 28(1), 50–66 (2001)

Von Hippel, E.: "Sticky information" and the locus of problem solving: implications for innovation. Manage. Sci. 40(4), 429–439 (1994)

Werner, C.M., Brown, B.B., Damron, G.: Territorial marking in a game arcade. J. Pers. Soc. Psychol. 41(6), 1094–1104 (1981)

Wertenbroch, K., Skiera, B.: Measuring consumers' willingness to pay at the point of purchase. J. Mark. Res. 39(2), 228–241 (2002)

Wright, P.: Consumer choice strategies: simplifying vs. optimizing. J. Mark. Res. 12(1), 60–67 (1975)

An Empirical Study of User Decision Making Behavior in E-Commerce

Dongning Yan[1(✉)] and Li Chen[2]

[1] Design Department, Politecnico Di Milano, Milano, Italy
Dongning.yan@polimi.it
[2] Computer Science Department, Hong Kong Baptist University,
Kowloon Tong, Hong Kong
lichen@comp.hkbu.edu.hk

Abstract. The large number of customer reviews and inconsistent writing style make it difficult for users to digest information and make online purchasing decisions. In light of human decision making theory, an in-depth understanding of user decision making behaviors serves as the foundation of effective information displays. In this paper, we conduct a formative study to empirically investigate user decision making behaviors in online hotel booking, in particular, with respect to customer reviews. Through analysis of the results, we identify the information decision makers are inclined to seek and the decision strategies they utilize to process information in three stages of online purchasing.

Keywords: Customer review · E-commerce · Human decision making · User study

1 Introduction

Customer reviews in E-commerce are playing an important and unique role; a staggering 90 % of people use and monitor reviews in their online purchasing process. However, the overwhelming number of reviews and inconsistent writing style require significant effort to read and tend to let important information slip by. To help users effectively and efficiently glean information from reviews, a number of systems have summarized customer reviews by extracting features and associate sentiments. From the perspective of customers, online purchasing can be viewed as a decision making process. In light of human decision-making theory, we learn that the foundation of effective information displays for user decision improvement is gaining a deep understanding of user decision-making behavior. However, no clear picture exists to systematically elaborate on how consumers make purchase decisions in E-commerce, in particular, with respect to customer reviews. In this paper, we take online hotel booking as an example to investigate customer decision-making behaviors in three stages of online purchasing: (1) screening out interesting alternatives, (2) evaluating alternatives in detail, and (3) comparing candidates for final choice. Interfaces that aggregate information from customer reviews are developed to support the three alternative stages. Through analysis of the results, we identity the decision strategies

© Springer International Publishing Switzerland 2015
F.F.-H. Nah and C.-H. Tan (Eds.): HCIB 2015, LNCS 9191, pp. 414–426, 2015.
DOI: 10.1007/978-3-319-20895-4_38

users utilize to process information and the information they are inclined to seek at each stage. These findings lay solid groundwork for designing E-commerce interfaces to improve consumer purchase decisions.

2 Related Work

2.1 Literature Research on the Summary of Customer Reviews

Most E-commerce websites, such as Amazon, provide an overall review score for each entity to help users make purchase decisions. However, given that people evaluate whether a product fits their desire in an attribute-driven manner [9], a number of systems have summarized customer reviews by extracting features and associate sentiment toward each feature. Liu et al. (2005) and Carenini et al. (2009) used bar charts to visualize the sentiment toward each feature [4, 10]. Carenini et al. (2006) summarized reviews in the form of a Tree map by representing a feature as a rectangle with nested rectangles corresponding to the descendants of the feature [3]. In addition to numerical ratings, Yatani et al. (2011) used adjective-noun word pairs to summarize the sentiment (adjective) towards each feature (noun) to help users explore reviews in greater detail. Huang et al. (2013) developed a system that can automatically highlight sentences that are related to relevant features to make a balance between reducing information overload and providing the original review context [8].

2.2 Three-Stage Decision Making Process of Online Purchasing

In most conditions, customers identify the need for a product or service without specific requirements on which one to buy [13]; accordingly they need to select interesting one (s) from a range of options that satisfy their desire. Chen (2010) interpreted online purchasing as a precise, three-stage decision-making process: (1) screening out interesting alternative(s) for further consideration, (2) evaluating alternatives in detail, and (3) comparing candidates to confirm the final choice [5]. The transition between the three stages does not follow a rigorous linear order; it is iterative in nature. However, on the whole, the process does follow an approximate sequence.

2.3 Human Decision Making Theory

In classical decision theory, decision makers are assumed to properly process all relevant information and explicitly consider trade-offs among values to choose an optimal alternative on the basis of an invariant strategy. However, human decision-making behaviors in reality often violate the prescription of classical decision theory. One the one hand, decision makers do not process all available information, but devote attention to perceptually salient information or information that they believe to be helpful [2]. On the other hand, they use a wide variety of strategies depending on the relative weight they place on making an accurate decision versus saving cognitive effort, because the accuracy and effort characteristics are different across strategies for a given decision environment and different across environment for a given strategy [2].

The adaptive nature of decision making behavior provides the insight that information display can impact not only information acquisition but also information combination, leading to higher/lower decision accuracy and less/more cognitive effort. For example, an insufficient information display can blind a decision maker to myopic, uninformed decision [15]. Moreover, merely presenting all necessary information is not enough. Decision makers tend to ignore important information simply because the most salient information is not diagnostic or important for decision makers [12]. Thus, the match between the relative importance of information and the salience of information display is important. In addition, decision effort can be reduced by improving the congruence between the format and organization of information and the way that users process information to make decisions. If the decision strategy adopted is not efficient or proper for a task, reducing the effort needed to execute certain operations can direct decision makers toward the use of compensatory processing [17].

To recap, in light of human decision-making theory, an in-depth understanding of customers' decision making behaviors serves as the foundation of effective information displays for user decision improvement.

3 Formative Study

3.1 Research Questions

A central distinction among strategies is the extent to which they make trade-offs among attributes. Decision strategies that explicitly consider trade-offs are called compensatory strategies, whereas strategies that do not make trade-offs are called non-compensatory strategies. RQ1: which kind(s) of decision strategies do customers adopt to process information, compensatory or non-compensatory strategies?

In an E-commerce environment, each entity is described by diverse information. In general, the information can be classified into two types: static features (such as price and specifications) and customer reviews. RQ2: which kind(s) of information do decision makers seek, static features or/and customer reviews?

The format in which the sentiment towards each attribute extracted from customer reviews is presented can also be different. Numerical values provide an easy proxy for opinions, whereas verbal values provide reasons underlying the scores. RQ3: which kind(s) of values do decision makers refer to concerning the sentiment of attributes extracted from customer reviews, numerical or/and verbal?

3.2 Tasks

To examine decision-making behavior in an E-commerce environment, we took online hotel booking as the test domain for two reasons. First, it is feasible to recruit appropriate and sufficient subjects to participate in the study. Second, the hotel domain contains abundant online customer reviews that are written with multiple attributes in mind. All hotel information and corresponding customer reviews used in the formative study were crawled from Tripadvisor.com in May, 2014.

Three tasks were implemented corresponding to the three-stage decision making process. Task 1: imagine that you will have a trip to Beijing in the summer holiday and need to book a hostel online. The top 10 Beijing Bed and Breakfast are presented. Please choose interesting one(s) for further consideration. Task 2: please read detailed information of the hotel you selected in the preceding task and decide whether to save it as a candidate. Task 3: compare the candidates to choose one as the final choice.

3.3 Research Methods

Two process-tracing methods that have proven especially valuable in decision research are verbal protocols and information acquisition methods [14]. Verbal protocol method asks subjects to "think aloud" while performing decision tasks. As to different information acquisition techniques, the process underlying eye tracking is most similar to real-world process. Computerized process tracing tool (CPT) is done by setting up a decision task so that all relevant information is hidden in boxes until a subject moves mouse to click. Considering that we do not have eye tracking equipment and there is no substantial influence on our research questions by using CPT [11], we employed CPT in our study, which is fairly straightforward in data collection but cannot directly observe internal cognitive process. In contrast, verbal protocols can measure information processing directly but are difficult to analyze formally. Thus, verbal protocols and CPT are concurrently used to complement each other.

3.4 Interfaces for the Formative Study

The feature-sentiment summary of customer reviews has proven to be an effective way to help users digest the massive quantity of customer reviews [4, 10]. However, the variances in other elements of reviews are not taken into account. In our study, we provide a multiple-level exploration of customer reviews, which incorporates post date, usefulness and reviewer into review summary, in addition to feature and associate sentiment. For example, when users learn that there are 23 5-star reviews for location, they can inspect the usefulness, time, and reviewer distribution of the subset of reviews, as shown in the red boxes of Fig. 1. There is evidence that subjects tend to use non-compensatory strategies when faced with complex decision tasks [18]. Thus, in the interface for task one, in addition to static features and review summary for each hotel, there are sorting and filtering to facilitate users selecting an alternative with the best value on the most important attribute and eliminating alternatives with values for an attribute below a cut-off. In addition, attributes extracted from customer reviews are incorporated in sorting and filtering (see Fig. 1).

With respect to the interface for evaluating alternatives in detail, Sinha and Swearingen (2002) used a music system as an example and noted that the information that comes into play during this stage can be classified into three categories: basic item information, social opinion and item sample [16]. In the hotel system, hotel name, price, address and facilities are included as basic information. Social opinion is customer reviews from a large community of travelers. Traveler photos are taken as the item sample to enable hotel preview (see Fig. 2).

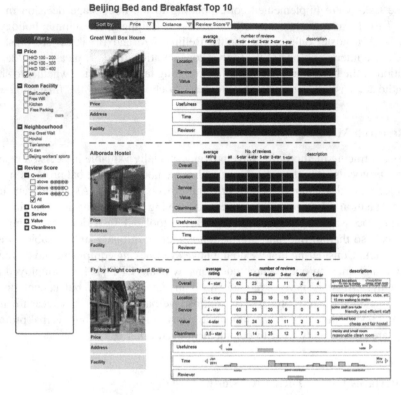

Fig. 1. Screenshot of the interface for task one with one review summary uncovered

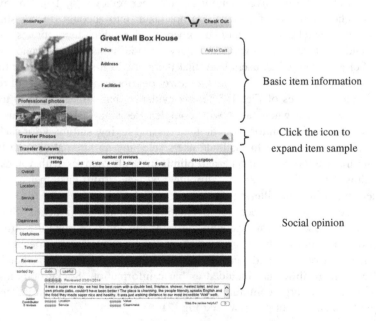

Fig. 2. Screenshot of the interface for task two

The shopping cart provides a comparison matrix in the form of alternatives (columns) and attributes (rows), with which users can perform feature-by-feature comparison between products. This method has been demonstrated to improve decision quality compared with its absence [7]. Moreover, the attributes (rows) are not limited to brief static features; the {opinion attribute, sentiment} pairs extracted from customer reviews are embedded to complement {static feature, value} pairs (see Fig. 3).

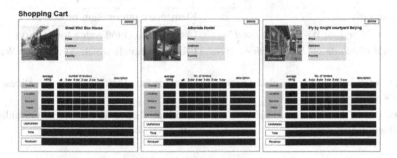

Fig. 3. Screenshot of the interface for task three

3.5 Procedure and Participants

The main procedure for the formative study can be divided into three steps. Step 1: Each participant was required to fill in his/her personal background and E-commerce experience. Then, we gave a brief introduction on the experiment and explained the interfaces to participants. All boxes within a given screen were uncovered. Step 2: Before conducting the task, we asked participants several testing questions to make sure that they understand the hidden content of each box and would not randomly click. Step 3: Participants were asked to perform the three tasks and verbalize their thinking processes. All mouse click and verbal protocols were recorded automatically.

50 participants were recruited to take part in the experiment. They are students at Hong Kong Baptist University pursuing Bachelor, Master or PhD degrees, from different departments, such as Computer Science, Chemistry, Education and Management. In the pre-study questionnaire, they specified their frequency of Internet use (on average 4.96 'daily/almost daily', S.D. = .23), E-commerce shopping experience (on average 3.5 '1–3 times a month', S.D. = .56), and online hotel booking experience (on average 2.42 '1–3 times', S.D. = .45). Thus, most of them are frequent E-commerce users and target customers of online hotel booking.

4 Analysis of the Results

We transcribe individual cases by coding each observed behavior in terms of Elementary Information Processes (EIPs) [1] and corresponding verbal protocols (i.e., supporting commentary). In turn, based on a specific collection and sequence of EIPs, the decision strategy participants adopted can be inferred. An example of formally coded data transcript is recorded in Table 1. To guarantee the reliability of coding, two coders were employed to independently transcribe all the cases. The measure of agreement of Kappa for each variable is above 0.7, suggesting a good level of consistency between the two coders. Disagreements in the coding were solved by discussion.

Table 1. An example of formally coded data transcript

Verbal protocols	Elementary information processes
"There should be free Wi-Fi in the hotel"	(Acquire the cutoff value for facility)
"So I would eliminate all hotels without Wi-Fi"	**Eliminate** hotels which do not have Wi-Fi
"I prefer hotels with values on cleanliness above 4-star"	(Acquire the cutoff value for cleanliness)
"So eliminate all hotels with scores on cleanliness below 4-star"	**Eliminate** hotels whose score on cleanliness is lower than 4-star

4.1 Stage 1: Screening Out Interesting Alternatives

Decision Strategy. 3/50 (6 %) participants adopted Lexicographic, 9/50 (18 %) participants made use of Eliminate-by-aspect plus Lexicographic, 18/50 (36 %) participants screened out alternatives by Eliminate-by-aspect, and 20/50 (40 %) participants used Eliminate-by-aspect plus Additive difference. In the following, we elaborate on the four types of decision strategies and use LEX, EBA + LEX, EBA, EBA + ADDIF to denote participants who adopted the corresponding decision strategy.

Eliminate-by-aspect. Decision makers eliminate alternatives with values for an attribute below a cut-off. The process continues with the second attribute, and then the third, until a smaller set of alternatives remains.

Lexicographic. Decision makers determine the most important attribute and then select the alternative with the best value on that attribute.

Eliminate-by-aspect plus Lexicographic. Firstly, users eliminate alternatives to a smaller set in terms of Eliminate-by-aspect. Then, they select the alternative with the best value on the most important attribute.

Eliminate-by-aspect plus Additive Difference. Decision makers begin by narrowing down the set of alternatives in terms of Eliminate-by-aspect. Then, they compare the remaining alternatives by summing the differences between alternatives on multiple attributes. Finally, they select the alternative with the best overall value.

Information Acquisition in Eliminate-by-aspect. 47 participants began by narrowing down the range of options in terms of Eliminate-by-aspect to simplify the complexity of choice. As shown in Fig. 4 (left), significantly more users eliminated alternatives by both static features and customer reviews (26/47) compared to those merely using static features (16/47) or customer reviews (5/47); $\chi^2(2) = 14.09, p < .05$.

In greater detail, Fig. 4 (right) lists the specific information of static features and customer reviews to which participants referred. On average, 2.62 attributes (S.D. = 1.22) were utilized, to which static features and customer reviews respectively contribute 1.5 and 1.12. Moreover, significantly more participants eliminated alternatives by attributes extracted from reviews (denoted by opinion attributes) compared to those referring to an overall review score (26/47 vs. 5/47), $\chi^2(1) = 14.23$, $p < .05.(1) = 14.23$, p < .05.

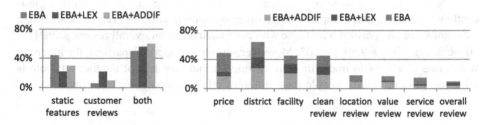

Fig. 4. Information acquisition in Eliminate-by-aspect

The process of generating cut-offs is adaptive in nature, determined by the value distribution of an attribute and correlation among attributes, in addition to stable preference. Participants referred to the value distribution to avoid invalid filter, such as too many/few options available due to loose or strict cut-offs. Moreover, participants who explicitly considered trade-offs among values frequently referred to attribute correlation to determine cut-offs. For example, one might explore a hotel with price above original price limit to see how much better it is. If its rating greatly exceeds expectations, the cut-off of price may be shifted, otherwise the cut-off is reinforced.

Information Acquisition in Lexicographic. 12 participants selected alternatives by Lexicographic (3 with LEX, 9 with EBA + LEX). 58.3 % (7/12) of subjects chose the entity with the best value on some static feature, and 41.7 % (5/12) chose based on customer reviews (see Fig. 5(left)). The frequency of each attribute considered the most important is listed in Fig. 5 (right). As to sorting by customer reviews, the proportion of participants who selected hotels in terms of an opinion attribute is not significantly different from that using an overall rating (2/12 vs.3/12), $\chi^2(1) = .20$, $p > .05$.

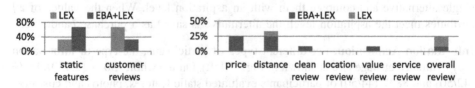

Fig. 5. Information acquisition in Lexicographic

The weight of an attribute is determined not only by stable preference but also by the value range of an attribute. In other words, the weight given to an attribute is a function of attribute ranges. As the variance in the values on one attribute across alternatives increases, the importance weight on that attribute becomes higher [6].

Information Acquisition in Additive Difference. Because price and quality are generally thought to be negatively correlated (i.e., higher-quality hotels tend to have higher rents), all 20 participants who compared alternatives on multiple attributes (i.e., EBA + ADDIF) referred to both price and customer reviews to make decisions. In addition, 45 % of participants added address into comparison (see Fig. 6 (left)). Considering the information of customer reviews, as shown in Fig. 6 (right), significantly more participants compared alternatives by opinion attributes (e.g.., location and cleanliness) in comparison with those who compared using an overall review score (17/20 vs. 3/20), $\chi^2(1) = 9.80$, p < .05. Moreover, during product comparison, the extent to which one is willing to trade off more of one attribute for less of another attribute is different. In other words, people gave different relative importance to attributes.

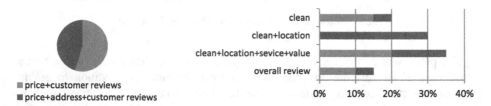

Fig. 6. Information acquisition in Additive Difference

The format in which the sentiment of an opinion attribute is evaluated can be different. The majority of participants (10/20) made their decisions based on both numerical values (i.e., the average rating and number of reviews) and verbal values (i.e., adjective-noun word pairs), followed by just numerical values (9/20). The smallest proportion relied on only verbal values (1/20).

4.2   Stage 2: Evaluating Alternatives in Detail

Decision Strategy. In this stage, only one alternative is considered at a time. Participants use alternative-based manner, which means users evaluate multiple attributes of a single alternative and compare them with an aspiration level. When the values of all attributes meet the aspiration level, the alternative is saved as a purchase candidate.

Information Acquisition. For different types of participants, the type of information they evaluated at stage two is shown in Fig. 7 (left). On the whole, 50 % (25/50), 84 % (42/50) and 88 % (44/50) of participants evaluated static features, photos and customer reviews, respectively. More specifically, Fig. 7(right) shows which aspects of customer reviews that participants would inspect. The number of participants reading reviews in a feature-driven manner was significantly larger than the number of participants doing so in a holistic manner (38/50 vs. 6/50), $\chi^2(1) = 23.27$, $p < .05$. For example, people mentioned "*I mainly concern about cleanliness and location, while others are indifferent... (reading reviews)... but I cannot find content on cleanliness, most of them are about location and service*".

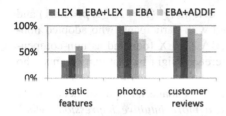
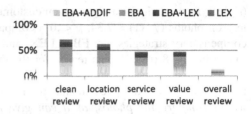

Fig. 7. Information acquisition at stage two

Concerning the numerical values of customer reviews, 24 % and 39 % of participants evaluated the average rating and average rating plus the number of reviews, respectively, whereas the other 37 % also read the time distribution of all and the 5-point customer reviews to examine whether there is a download trend for customer reviews. For example, people noted "*the trend of customer reviews often change over time, like the hotel may improve its service, so that the recent reviews may be opposite to old reviews in which people complained about the service*".

In addition to the numerical values, 7 %, 56.5 % and 36.5 % of participants referred to the verbal values in terms of summarized adjective-noun word pairs, raw reviews and both, respectively. Overall, 93 % of participants read raw reviews to assist in the context understanding. Due to the large quantity of raw reviews, participants performed two types of behavior: inspecting the latest and/or the most negative customer reviews. Participants who sorted customer reviews by date mentioned that "*I would like to read the newest reviews... especially the reviews written by those who just lived in there last night... I think it will be closer to the real condition and more credible*". More than half of the participants clearly indicated that they favored negative comments compared with positive ones. For example, people said "*I would like to read negative ratings and learn the reasons why other customers gave lower rating to see if I have the same concern*", and "*The reason of adding it in shopping cart is not only how good it is, but also whether I can stand its drawbacks*".

4.3   Stage 3: Comparing Candidates for Final Choice

Decision Strategy. 43 participants who saved more than one option engaged in this stage. The decision strategy can be interpreted as calculating the value difference between alternatives on one attribute. The process repeats with other attributes. Then, the differences are summed to obtain an overall relative evaluation for each entity. Finally, the alternative with the best evaluation is retained as the final choice

Information Acquisition. Figure 8 (left) lists the type of information that participants compared at stage three. Through statistical analysis, there is no significant difference in the static feature comparison between participants $\chi^2 (3) = 1.32, p < .05$; while, there are significant associations between the types of participants and whether they compare customer reviews ($\chi^2 (3) = 8.21, p < .05$) and whether they compare photos ($\chi^2 (1) = 11.87, p < .05$). More notably, we found that participants who adopted a compensatory strategy at stage one, i.e. EBA + ADDIF (denoted as compensatory in Fig. 8

(right)), focused significantly more on customer reviews (χ^2 (1) = 16.59, $p < .001$) and less on photos (χ^2 (1) = 7.34, $p < .01$) compared with participants who adopted non-compensatory strategies, i.e. EBA, LEX, and EBA + LEX (denoted as non-compensatory in Fig. 8 (right)). The reason for the difference might be that participants who prefer non-compensatory strategies more greatly emphasized minimizing effort, rather than referring to extensive amount of information to make an optimal decision: "*I would compare the photos, as it can give me a more intuitive impression, which facilitates choosing the most attractive one*".

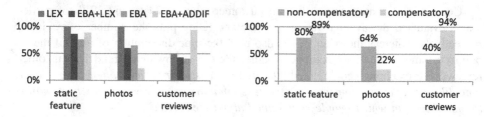

Fig. 8. Information acquisition at stage three

Figure 9 (left) illustrates the frequency of each attribute utilized in the product comparison. For all types of participants, price is most frequently compared, which means that people treat price as a crucial factor in online purchasing. Moreover, significantly more participants used {opinion attribute, sentiment} pairs extracted from reviews to perform feature-by-feature comparison between products compared to those merely referring to an overall review score (22/43 vs. 5/43), $\chi2$ (1) = 10.7, p < .001.

Out of the 27 participants who compared customer reviews, 13/27 participants made their decisions based on numerical values, 3/27 participants relied on adjective-noun word pairs, and 11/27 participants referred to both, as shown in Fig. 9 (right).

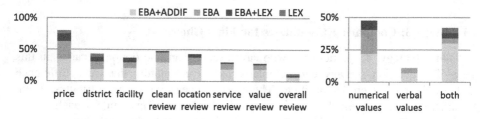

Fig. 9. Attributes in product comparison

5 Conclusion

The results of the formative study provide practical implications on E-commerce interface design. For the interface of screening out interesting alternatives, we propose that: (1) including both static features and opinion attributes in filter, (2) visualizing the value distribution of each attribute and the correlation among attributes, (3) enabling users to sort alternatives by multiple attributes and giving different weight to attributes, and (4) in addition to static features, integrating opinion attributes in sorting. For the detail page, the following advices are concluded: (1) categorizing customer reviews by features, (2) in addition to the average rating and number of reviews, representing time distribution for opinion attributes to support the analysis of temporal evolution, (3) coupling numerical values with verbal values (i.e., adjective-noun word pairs and raw reviews), and (4) facilitating users to inspect the latest and most negative raw reviews. As to comparison interface, we suggest that: (1) decreasing the difficulty in calculating value difference on each attribute across alternatives, (2) summarizing customer reviews in the form of {feature, sentiment}, and (3) representing both numerical and verbal values toward each opinion attribute.

References

1. Bettman, J.R., Johnson, E.J., Payne, J.W.: A componential analysis of cognitive effort in choice. Organ. Behav. Hum. Decis. Process **45**(1), 111–139 (1990)
2. Bettman, J.R., Luce, M.F., Payne, J.W.: Constructive consumer choice processes. J. Consum. Res. **25**(3), 187–217 (1998)
3. Carenini, G., Ng, R.T., Pauls, A.: Interactive multimedia summaries of evaluative interfaces text. In: Proceedings of the 11th International Conference on Intelligent User Interfaces (IUI 2006), pp. 124–131. ACM 2006
4. Carenini, G., Rizoli, L.: A multimedia interface for facilitating comparisons of opinions. In: Proceedings of the 14th International Conference on Intelligent User Interfaces (IUI 2009), pp. 325–334. ACM (2009)
5. Chen, L.: Towards three-stage recommender support for online consumers: implications from a user study. In: Chen, L., Triantafillou, P., Suel, T. (eds.) WISE 2010. LNCS, vol. 6488, pp. 365–375. Springer, Heidelberg (2010)
6. Goldstein, W.M.: Judgments of relative importance in decision making: global vs. local interpretation of subjective weight. Organ. Behav. Hum. Decis. Process. **47**(2), 313–336 (1990)
7. Haubl, G., Trifts, V.: Consumer decision making in online shopping environments: the effects of interactive decision aids. Mark. Sci. **19**(1), 4–21 (2000)
8. Huang, S.-W., Tu, P.-F., Fu, W.-T., Amamzadeh, M.: Leveraging the crowd to improve feature-sentiment analysis of user reviews. In: Proceedings of the 2013 International Conference on Intelligent User Interfaces (IUI 2013), pp. 3–14. ACM 2013
9. Lee, Y.E., Benbasat, I.: Interaction design for mobile product recommendation agents: supporting users' decisions in retail stores. ACM Trans. Comput. Hum. Interact. **17**(4), 1–32 (2010)
10. Liu, B., Hu, M., Cheng, J.: Opinion observer: analyzing and comparing opinions on the Web. In: Proceedings of the 14th International Conference on World Wide Web, pp. 342–351. ACM (2005)
11. Lohse, G.L., Johnson, E.J.: A comparison of two process tracing methods for choice tasks. Organ. Behav. Hum. Decis. Process **68**(1), 28–43 (1996)
12. MacGregor, D., Slovic, P.: Graphical representation of judgmental information. J. Hum. Comput. Interact. **2**(3), 179–200 (1986)

13. Miles, G.E., Howes, A., Davies, A.: A framework for understanding human factors in web-based electronic commerce. Int. J. Hum. Comput. Stud. **52**(1), 131–163 (2000)
14. Payne, J.W., Bettman, J.R., Johnson, E.J.: The Adaptive Decision Maker. Cambridge University Press, Cambridge, UK (1993)
15. Payne, J.W., Bettman, J.R.: Measuring constructed preferences: towards a building code. J. Risk Uncertainty **19**(1–3), 243–270 (1999)
16. Sinha, R., Swearingen, K.: The role of transparency in recommender systems. In: CHI 2002 Extended Abstracts on Human Factors in Computing Systems, pp. 830–831. ACM (2002)
17. Todd, P., Benbasat, I.: The influence of decision aids on choice strategies: an experimental analysis of the role of cognitive effort. Organ. Behav. Hum. Decis. Process. **60**(1), 36–74 (1994)
18. Tversky, A.: Elimination by aspects: a theory of choice. Psychol. Rev. **79**(4), 281–299 (1972)

Enterprise Systems, Business and Gamification

Exergames for Older Adults: Towards Sustainable and Transferrable Health Benefits

Young Anna Argyris$^{(\boxtimes)}$ and Taiwoo Park

Department of Media and Information,
School of Communication Arts and Sciences, Michigan State University,
404 Wilson Road, East Lansing, MI 48823, USA
{yelee, twp}@msu.edu

Abstract. This study presents an exergame called Pressure-Ball game that is designed to increase health among institutionalized older adults. As many older adults develop sedentary lifestyle in which their physical activities are reduced, it is important to engage them in a mild exercise activity. The mild exercise activity can increase their confidence in fitness levels and reduce fear of injuries; thereby building active lifestyle that can be sustainable and transferrable to other domains of life. To assess health benefits brought about by Pressure-Ball game, we propose a longitudinal study that employs a series of experiments in retirement homes in Midwest. The completed research has potential to provide health benefits to aging population.

Keywords: Exergame · Flow · Continued use of IS · Older adults · Healthcare IT

1 Background and Motivation

Exercise- and physical activity-based games (exergame, henceforth) have recently received much attention from a variety of healthcare fields due to the game's potential health benefits. Commercial exergame consoles requiring increased amount of physical activities, such as Nintendo Wii, Microsoft Kinect, and Sony Move, have been developed and occupied a significant share of worldwide video game market. Also, exergames have frequently been employed for rehabilitation and exercise purposes, including isometric muscle training [8], body balance training [2], as well as, exercise for adults with cerebral palsy [7] and for elderly [10]. Researchers have also designed and evaluated customized exergames in various usage contexts such as rehabilitation [4–6] and elderly socialization [9].

Among many potential beneficiaries of exergames, this study focuses on institutionalized older adults. According to the Center for Disease Control and Prevention statistics in 2010,[1] one out of three older adults falls. These falls often lead to severe disabilities, injuries, impaired function; more importantly, falls cause fear of falling

---

[1] Centers for Disease Control and Prevention (CDC), National Center for Injury Control and Prevention Web-based injury statistics query and reporting system (WISQRS) [Internet]. Atlanta: CDC; 2010 [cited 2010 April 8]. Available from:
http://www.cdc.gov/injury/wisqars/index.html

© Springer International Publishing Switzerland 2015
F.F.-H. Nah and C.-H. Tan (Eds.): HCIB 2015, LNCS 9191, pp. 429–436, 2015.
DOI: 10.1007/978-3-319-20895-4_39

among survivors, who as a result develop sedentary life-styles and lower quality of life. Sedentary lifestyle refers to a lifestyle that lacks physical activities or involves only irregular and infrequent activities, and is often called as "sitting disease."[2] Although sedentary life style is not limited to institutionalized older adults, this lifestyle can be aggravated among institutionalized older adults, since they experience social isolation and a lack of resources to pursue physical activities (e.g., limited facilities for activities in the institution). Therefore, the benefits of exergames can be augmented for this population.

Despite the important health benefits exergames can provide, only a handful of previous researchers have investigated exergames [4, 5]; and none of them has employed systematic investigations. The previous studies employed small, cross-sectional experiments, each with less than 10 participants and focused on whether participants were able to play games in the same ways intended by developers. However, the previous researchers did not investigate whether playing exergames actually bring any health benefits to the players. As such, the primary motivation of this research is to examine whether exergames bring any health benefits to players, especially, institutionalized older adults to whom exergames may bring greater health benefits.

We suggest that the answer to our research is contingent upon the *sustainability* of physical activities that the exergames promote among older adults. Like any other physical activities that can potentially increase health among older adults, such as light walking and gentle stretching, health benefits of exergames will increase when individuals get engaged in the physical activities continuously and regularly rather than having a sudden surge in the activity level and quitting shortly thereafter. In addition, if health benefits of exergames will increase if the exergame increases the player's confidence in his/her fitness level and thereby reduces the fear of falling/injuries, and, as a result, becomes **transferrable** to other activities in their real lives. In this case, the player will be able to overcome sedentary life style and may be able to lead more active lifestyle that has a long-term health benefits. As such, our second objective is to design exergames that promote sustainable and transferrable physical activities.

To increase sustainability and transferability of the exergames, we propose two factors: (1) game design that optimizes players' flow states and (2) social features embedded in an exergame that increases players' loyalty to the exergame. We suggest flow states because older adults, like any others, may be interested in playing exergames, for a few months due to the game's novelty but they may lose their interests gradually. A commercial exergame, Wii Fit, for example, is well known for causing boredom among players after a few months. One of the primary factors that prevents boredom and increases enjoyment is flow state [1]. We suggest that the game should be designed in such ways that the difficulty levels get adjusted as a player progresses his/her activity level. In so doing, the exergame will be able to create and maintain flow statues among players. Also, social influence has been recognized as a positive influence on continued use of any information systems, according to UTAUT (Unified Theory of Acceptance and Use of Technology) [11]. Also, recent studies on social media has suggested a social feature embedded in a website creates a sense of

---

[2] Fields, "Do you have sitting disease?" WebMD, available from:
http://www.webmd.com/fitness-exercise/do-you-have-sitting-disease

community and thereby gravitates users' voluntary participation and contribution [3]. Accordingly, we include a social feature to the exergame so that players can play the game together, which is postulated to increase their continued use of the exergame.

2   Research Questions and Model

2.1   Research Questions

The above motivations are manifested in the following research questions:

R1. What factors increase the continued use of exergames?
- Flow state (immersion and engagement in games)
- Social influence (created by the social feature embedded in the exergame)

R2. Do the exergames increase physical activities sustainably among institutionalized older adults?

R3. Is the physical activity level increased by exergames transferrable to other daily activities of institutionalized older adults?

R4. What health benefits do exergames bring to institutionalized older adults?

2.2   Research Model

We use a conceptual framework integrating UTAUT (Unified Theory of Acceptance and Use of Technology) and Flow. UTAUT explains factors that lead to continued use of technology above and beyond the initial acceptance [11]; one of the factors is social influence, which fits well with one of our research question. Flow explains user engagement and immersion in gaming experiences [1]. We integrate the two theories in order to identify the factors, such as social influence and flow state, which leads to continued use of the exergame (Fig. 1).

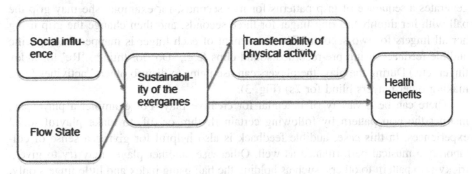

Fig. 1. Research model

3 Game Design

3.1 Exergame and Interface Design

We adopt a ball squeezing play as a medium of online social-physical interaction (see Fig. 2). Ball squeezing is usually employed for arm and finger muscle rehabilitation, as well as considered as a habitual play. For a similar example in East Asian countries, walnut playing is a popular and widespread hand exercise for acupressure therapy. We intended to give players a positive and healthy sense through utilizing this inherently health-related activity.

The design and implementation of the ball play consist of two parts: (1) Game interface and in-game social interaction and (2) Ball-based game controller.

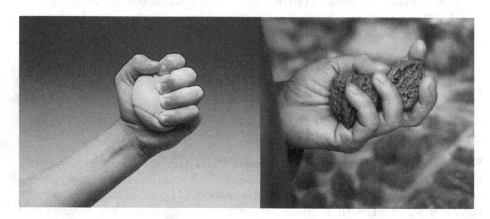

Fig. 2. Ball squeezing (left) and walnut play (right)

3.2 Exergame Interface and Social Interaction Design

While playing the game, each player alternately takes a role of instructor. Instructor generates a sequence of grip patterns for five seconds, for example, she may grip the ball with her thumb and ring finger for three seconds, and then change the grip using her all fingers for two seconds. The movement of each finger is mapped into specific audible feedback using pre-recorded sound clips (e.g., 'Do' for thumb, 'Re' for index finger, etc.) During the play, the players can use items to disturb others' activities (e.g., making other players blind for 2s) (Fig. 3).

There can be a variety of potential for creative play. For example, a player can instruct the grip pattern by following certain rhythm or riff, to make playful social experiences. In this case, audible feedback is also helpful for giving a sense of collaborative musical performance as well. Otherwise, another player may try to give a tricky grip pattern to others, such as holding the ball using index and little fingers only.

In the background, the gaming interface plays a cheerful and rhythmical music. The players can talk together online while playing the game, to share their emotions, as well as their everyday life. This social and physical interactive play naturally helps players overcome extremely inactive condition.

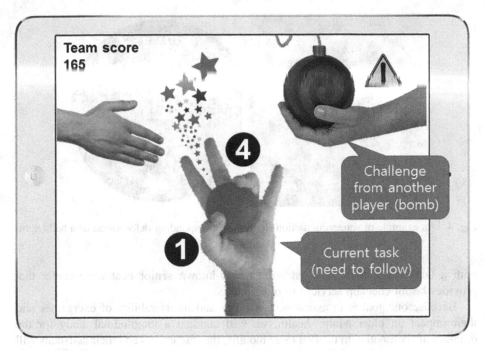

Fig. 3. Game play screenshot

3.3   Game Controller Design

We design a squeeze ball game controller, featuring intuitive hand squeeze gameplay by incorporating sensors to monitor changes of shape and external force. It is able to connect to players' mobile devices, such as smartphones and tablets, and role as a physical gaming interface for mobile games. We combined a soft form outside with a set of flexure sensors inside, and the sensors monitor the current shape of the ball (i.e., deformation, as shown in Fig. 4) and force from outside. A microcontroller and a wireless communication component with Bluetooth technology are in the ball, and we develop software logic to analyze data from the sensor and transmit it to players' mobile devices.

4   Experiment Design

In order to examine health benefits that the above exergame has on institutionalized older adults, we will conduct a longitudinal study that involves series of experiments.

4.1   Data Collection Sites

Three-four retirement homes for senior citizens in Midwest region of the US will be our data collection sites. Also, in order to check their health indicators, we will collaborate

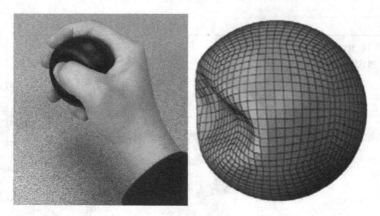

Fig. 4. An example of squeezing motion (left) and corresponding deformation of a ball (right)

with a large hospital in Midwest with a well-known senior healthcare center that provides health checkup services to older adults.

Because our goal is to assess sustainability and transferability of exergames and their impact on older adults' health, we will conduct a longitudinal study for the duration of six months. In the first three months, the researchers and their assistants will visit selected retirement homes, ask older adults to play exergames once a week, and repeat this session once/week for three months (12 sessions in total). In the first 12 sessions, their health indicators, such as blood pressure, subjective pain levels, and depression/anxiety levels, will be constantly measured and recorded.

Upon completion of the first 12 weeks of data collection, we will observe whether participants continue to play the exergames (i.e., sustainability) and whether they get engaged in any other activities (i.e., transferability), for the other 12 weeks. During the second half of data collection, we will continue to measure their health indicators.

4.2 Experimental Design

The experiment employs 2 × 2 factorial design with a control group. Two factors are physical activity and social influence. Physical activity has two levels – non-adjusted activity level and adjusted activity level. These two levels are devised to text the impact of flow states on players. Specifically, the exergame we propose will have physical activity levels that are being adjusted depending on players' progress. The more they play, the game will present a slightly more challenging activity level for the players to fulfill. Completion of one level will allow the player to move on to the next level. The second factor is social influence, which has two levels—no social influence (solo play) vs. social influence (co-play). In addition, we employ a control group in which participants are not asked to play any exergames (Fig. 5).

Physical activity level

Social influence		Non-adjusting	Adjusting
	No social feature	Plain exergame	Exergame with automatically adjusted activity levels
	With social feature	Exergame that allows for co-play	Exerga that allows for co-play and provide automatically adjusted activity levels and

Control group	No exergame

Fig. 5. Experimental design

5 Summary and Conclusion

In this study, we propose a pressure-ball exergame as a means to improve health among institutionalized older adults who are most susceptible to sedentary lifestyles due to their social isolation and high likelihood of falls and physical injuries. As sedentary lifestyle causes severe health issues, such as high blood pressure, high cholesterol, weight gain, and depression and anxiety, it is important to keep these susceptible population engaged in mild physical activities regularly and constantly. The purpose of the proposed pressure-ball games, in this sense, is not to drastically increase their activity levels, which could potentially cause further injuries, but to motivate them to lead an active lifestyle by building their confidence in their fitness levels and by alleviating fear for physical activities. To measure benefits of the pressure-ball game, we propose two factors—sustainability and transferability of physical activities promoted by the pressure-ball game. In order to increase sustainability and transferability, we propose also two factors—players' flow states and social feature. The former will be operationalized by equipping the game with an automatic level adjustment feature that tracks a player's progress and increases or decreases the next level. The ever-changing difficulty level and the resultant challenges are postulated to create and maintain players' flow states. The latter will be operationalized by a social feature embedded in the game that allows players to enjoy the game with others. Social interaction is known to be a significant influence on continued use of IS [11]. We will conduct a longitudinal study that involves a series of experiments over the six months period at retirement homes located in the Midwest region of the US with the help of senior healthcare team from a large hospital in the region. The experiment employs an incomplete factorial design with two factors—social influence and physical activity, each of which has two levels, and finally a control group to which no exergame will be provided.

As aging population in the US is growing rapidly, it is important than ever before to keep this growing population in good health. One of the most accessible yet challenged way to increase their health is to increase their activity level mildly to prevent them from developing sedentary lifestyle. The pressure-ball we propose involves a very mild exercise yet is equipped with automatically adjusted challenge levels and social features that have a high possibility to achieve this goal.

References

1. Csikszentmihalyi, M., Abuhamdeh, S., Nakamura, J.: Flow Flow and the Foundations of Positive Psychology, pp. 227–238. Springer, Netherlands (2014)
2. Deutsch, J.E., Robbins, D., Morrison, J., Bowlby, P.G.: Wii-based compared to standard of care balance and mobility rehabilitation for two individuals post-stroke. In: Virtual Rehabilitation International Conference, pp. 117–120. IEEE, June 2009
3. Dholakia, U.M., Bagozzi, R.P., Pearo, L.K.: A social influence model of consumer participation in network- and small-group-based virtual communities. Int. J. Res. Mark. **21** (3), 241–263 (2004)
4. Gerling, K., Livingston, I., Nacke, L., Mandryk, R.: Full-body motion-based game interaction for older adults. In: Proceedings of the SIGCHI Conference on Human Factors in Computing Systems, pp. 1873–1882. ACM, May 2012
5. Gerling, K.M., Mandryk, R.L., Kalyn, M.R.: Wheelchair-based game design for older adults. In: Proceedings of the 15th International ACM SIGACCESS Conference on Computers and Accessibility, p. 27. ACM, October 2013
6. Hernandez, H.A., Graham, T.C., Fehlings, D., Switzer, L., Ye, Z., Bellay, Q., Stach, T.: Design of an exergaming station for children with cerebral palsy. In: Proceedings of the SIGCHI Conference on Human Factors in Computing Systems, pp. 2619–2628. ACM, May 2012
7. Hurkmans, H.L., van den Berg-Emons, R.J., Stam, H.J.: Energy expenditure in adults with cerebral palsy playing Wii Sports. Arch. Phys. Med. Rehabil. **91**(10), 1577–1581 (2010)
8. Sohnsmeyer, J., Gilbrich, H., Weisser, B.: Effect of a six-week-intervention with an activity-promoting video game on isometric muscle strength in elderly subjects. Int. J. Comput. Sci. Sport **9**(2), 75 (2010)
9. Theng, Y.L., Chua, P.H., Pham, T.P.: Wii as entertainment and socialisation aids for mental and social health of the elderly. In: CHI 2012 Extended Abstracts on Human Factors in Computing Systems, pp. 691–702. ACM, May 2012
10. Wollersheim, D., Merkes, M., Shields, N., Liamputtong, P., Wallis, L., Reynolds, F., Koh, L.: Physical and psychosocial effects of Wii video game use among older women. Int. J. Emerg. Technol. Soc. **8**(2), 85–98 (2010)
11. Venkatesh, V., Morris, M.G., Gordon, B.D., Davis, F.D.: User acceptance of information technology: toward a unified view. MIS Q. **27**(3), 425–478 (2003)

Reimagining Project Management Applications via Gamification

Charles Butler[✉]

Westerdals – Oslo School of Arts, Communication and Technology,
Faculty of Technology, Oslo, Norway
charlesabutler@gmail.com

Abstract. The objective of this paper is to present a prototype design of a project management application which has been designed to leverage the power of gamification. The specific set of gamified features contained within the prototype follow the model set forth in previous work which attempted to aid gamification designers in the selection and implementation of the most effective mechanics for whatever the intended purpose. This was done by mapping a number of gamification mechanics to existing effects in behavioral economics, which allows designers an unconventional insight into the behavioral reasons as to why various methods of gamification affect a user-base. It should also be noted that unlike some gamification implementations which can, at times, be seen in a negative light by being excessively *game-like*, the focus here is on bringing gamification into the business setting in a serious and professional manner in order to ease adoption among all users.

1 Objective

The objective of this paper is to present a prototype design of a project management application which has been designed to leverage the power of gamification. The specific set of gamified features contained within the prototype follow the model set forth in previous work which attempted to aid gamification designers in the selection and implementation of the most effective mechanics for whatever the intended purpose. This was done by mapping a number of gamification mechanics to existing effects in behavioral economics, which allows designers an unconventional insight into the behavioral reasons as to why various methods of gamification affect a user-base. It should also be noted that unlike some gamification implementations which can, at times, be seen in a negative light by being excessively *game-like*, the focus here is on bringing gamification into the business setting in a serious and professional manner in order to ease adoption among all users.

2 Significance

Gamified mechanics are increasingly being integrated into the software that we use every day, both in subtle and more obvious ways. While these tactics often hold the power to affect our behavior, it can be difficult to predict the exact change that such mechanics will have on a system or its user-base. Unintended consequences can be very serious at

F.F.-H. Nah and C.-H. Tan (Eds.): HCIB 2015, LNCS 9191, pp. 437–445, 2015.
DOI: 10.1007/978-3-319-20895-4_40

times, and a gamification designer must recognize that there is typically a tradeoff when encouraging any behavior. This isn't necessarily to say that these tradeoffs should be avoided (or that it would even be possible to do so), but it is certainly necessary to recognize the potential consequences and to plan for them. However, by working with a model based on existing behavioral economic theory, the presented product intends to improve on typical gamified implementations through theory-based design. By using such a framework, the designer would ideally be better at both eliciting the desired behavior as well as recognizing the tradeoffs involved. If proven successful, this could inform future attempts at gamification, especially in the business software area.

3   Method

This paper draws on previous work which analyzed a number of the core concepts within behavioral economics through the lens of gamification, attempting to create a mapping of gamified mechanics to behaviors that a designer may want to elicit within a user. This essentially created a behavioral model of gamification which was used to design a prototype of a project management application which attempts to leverage a theory-based design and implementation of a set of gamified mechanics. In order to accomplish this, the design took into consideration the typical outcomes desired from the use of project management tools and then considered the employee behaviors likely to optimize the chances of those desirable outcomes. The behavioral model of gamification was then used to identify and develop the specific gamified mechanic implementations best suited to support the intended behaviors.

3.1   Supporting Concepts

As detailed and categorized in previous work, here are nine behavioral economic concepts which are common in game mechanics and gamification and were selected for their potential impact in non-game products and business environments (Butler 2015).

Loss Aversion. This is the tendency of people to exhibit an aversion to loss which overpowers a desire to acquire a disproportionate amount of gain (Kahneman and Tversky 1984).

Maintaining Intrinsic Focus. This concept contends that the addition of a tangible reward to an activity previously performed for its own enjoyment replaces that enjoyment with a form of payment (Heyman and Ariely 2004).

Pseudocertainty. This is the tendency of people to make decisions that treats an uncertain outcome with undue certainty (Tversky and Kahneman 1986).

The Paradox of Choice. This is the tendency of people to almost universally see an increase in the number of available choices as a positive change even though making a choice becomes much more difficult as the number of choices increases (Iyengar and Lepper 2000).

Scarcity/Urgency. This is the tendency of people to irrationally value an item seen as having limited availability or when the time available to act is limited (Cialdini 2006).

Variable Reinforcement Schedules. Rewarding a user for a certain action or behavior, but doing so in an irregular pattern (Lee and Fields 2007).

Commitment. The tendency of people to want to fulfill agreements that they have made in order to avoid the cognitive dissonance that occurs when breaking these commitments (Cialdini 2006).

IKEA Effect. This is the concept that one's valuation of an item is disproportionately increased by the personal labor one has invested into its creation (Ariely 2010).

Sunk Costs. This concept implies that even though money or effort invested in the past has no bearing on future decisions, these past investments still carry significant weight when considering those decisions (Arkes and Blumer 1985).

3.2   Relevant Mechanics

The following is a list of the previously defined concepts with a description of how these are leveraged in the following product design discussion.

Loss Aversion

- Decreasing the value of a task if the time to complete it exceeds the estimate (thus losing both the expected points as well expending additional time to do so)
- Losing a potential bonus by breaking a streak of desired actions
- Losing a top leaderboard slot
- Losing in-app benefits such as task selection order
- Losing potential points if your feature is cut or incomplete

Maintaining Intrinsic Focus

- Non-monetary rewards are implemented and suggested, such as social rewards or status rewards
- If monetary rewards are to be given, it is suggested that they be team-based

Pseudocertainty

- Giving users rewards that are likely to be minor but which have a small chance of being very significant

The Paradox of Choice

- Ensuring that the user always has a choice in how to proceed but minimizing the available options or complexity in order to help the user focus and prevent them from being overwhelmed

Scarcity/Urgency

- Using a countdown timer to keep the user aware of the time left before a task exceeds its estimate
- Ensuring that the user is aware of the sprint or milestone progress
- Ensuring that the user is aware of the number of days left before the project deadline

Variable Reinforcement Schedules

- Giving the user a random chance at a reward each time a task is completed

Commitment

- Giving the user ownership of a feature
- Allowing the user to create and design the tasks for that feature
- Allowing users to place estimates on their potential tasks
- Allowing the user to choose their own tasks to work on

IKEA Effect

- Giving the user ownership of a feature
- Allowing the user to create and design the tasks for that feature

Sunk Costs

- Points and progression accumulate over the course of a project
- Investing considerable time and energy into the design and implementation of features

4   Product

In designing the product features around the behavioral economic principles outlined above, the features were broken into functional segments based on the workflow anticipated in a project management scenario. The planning segment is primarily concerned with the development of the various tasks that a project requires, the estimation of the complexity or time requirements for the tasks, and the selection of tasks by team members. The progression section deals mainly with the points system, which is core to the gamification of the product. Finally, the status segment deals with continuous feedback to the team members about the current state of the project and the tasks therein.

It should be noted, however, that these features are focused around the interactions that a team member would be expected to have with the project and a project management tool. There would also be significant additional functionality that would be required at the management or supervisor level, including but not limited to configuration, initial setup and population, and reward structuring. This management interaction is largely outside the scope of this paper as its goal is to focus on the behaviors of the end users of project management software, namely the individual team members. This also means that the functionality described below is largely tactical in nature. The more strategic issues are expected to happen largely outside the realm of a project management tool.

4.1 Planning

The planning stage is among the most crucial of times in any project, and any errors made here can manifest themselves in a myriad of ways throughout a project's development. The suggestions here, while not too far removed from that of typical project management software, are intended to impart ownership of the project as a whole, as well as its tasks, to the team members. This is somewhat conflicting with agile methodologies, though it should be noted that the intent is not to prevent a user from working on the most useful task available but simply to give each part of the product an internal stakeholder who feels personally responsible for it.

Preliminary Preparations. An initial planning phase would be assumed to have already taken place with the client or product owner to determine the scope and the features that the project in question should encompass. An initial priority level should have also been set for each feature. The project management tool would have also been pre-populated with these along with user accounts for each team member, with each member being responsible for a certain set of features. Ideally, this would be a process of self-selection in order to impart the greatest sense of ownership to the team members. Afterwards, the members would each assume an informal stakeholder role in the design and development of these features. Ideally, the number and difficulty or complexity of features would be evenly distributed between members, though that could be difficult in practice due to the available feature-set and the varying levels of experience and skill-sets of the team members.

Task Creation. After the creation of the initial feature set the feature owners would be responsible for taskifying all work required to fully implement the feature. This likely requires considerable cooperation among the team, especially in multidisciplinary environments where any one person would be unable to implement an entire feature themselves. This is likely to cause friction initially, but it encourages communication and collaboration within the team. Ideally, the feature owners would also have access to the client or product owner in order to ensure that the features being developed are actually the features that are needed or desired. Maintaining sufficient client communication is a commonly cited problem in project management, and this would ensure that the client is kept involved (to the extent that the client is available or willing).

In addition, it moves some degree of organizational responsibility onto the team members, which serves to help them understand the project from a management perspective and gives them the room to grow professionally. Obviously, this phase would necessitate considerable supervision with all but the most competent and experienced teams, though once through this phase, the management overhead would likely be reduced considerably.

Estimation. Once all tasks are created, team members should review the tasks for all features and put a time estimate on each. If a team member would be unable to complete a task due to a difference in expertise, that member should abstain from estimating. Each task would then have the estimates and the estimator openly listed, and discussion and revisions could occur if desired. The appropriate typical and maximum task estimates are likely to vary with the type of project and the experience of the team members though it is suggested that tasks taking long than one-third or half of a working day be broken down into smaller tasks. Larger tasks may more easily hide unforeseen risk or complexity, and even in best case scenarios, multi-day tasks may not provide sufficiently granular progression data.

4.2 Progression

Progression, both of the project and of each team member's effectiveness, is tied to an integrated points system which comprises the core of the gamification of the project management tool. The exact values and weightings should be configurable by the project managers, but we will discuss the intent of the values in general terms.

Point Accumulation. Though a team member may gain points in a number of ways, completion of tasks is the core driver of the points system. A team member essentially gains a certain number of points based on the time required to complete a task versus the average time estimate. It should also be possible to modify the value based on feature or task priority in order to encourage team members to work on the highest priority tasks first. Additionally, the further solidify a team member's ownership over the features they have purview over, a member could receive a bonus percentage of any points earned on that feature's tasks, regardless of who completed it.

As another way to progress, awarding bonus points for repeated performance of desired behaviors should be supported. For example, one might track the number of days in a row that a team member has completed a task. This might provide an increasingly desirable points bonus as the successful instances accumulate, while at the same time providing additional encouragement to continue the desired behavior.

Aligning Incentives. Of course, team members will seek to use any incentive system to their advantage, so the onus is on the designer of the system (and potentially the manager who is configuring the values) to ensure that the incentives offered to the team members are aligned with the success of the project. The overarching goal for a project management tool should be the efficient utilization of a team's resources, and so the team should be rewarded for working quickly and effectively together towards the completion of the project. Again, while there are strategic issues that likely complicate this overly-simple explanation, at the tactical level, a project management tool should encourage team members to complete the most important remaining tasks as quickly as possible while still achieving whatever quality level that the client desires.

To reduce opportunities for abusing the points system via intentionally faulty estimates, all team members capable of completing a task enter their own estimate, and the effective value of a task is based the average of those estimates. However, after selecting a task, the team member's effectiveness is judged based on that member's own estimate. Additionally, any team member is able to choose any available task to work on, so if a task ends up overvalued, it may be any member who can take advantage of it. Furthermore, completing a task ahead of schedule shouldn't impart much more of a bonus, if any at all, than completing it exactly on time. The real bonus from completing a task early is essentially in optimizing the points earned per unit of time. However, exceeding the estimate could cause a considerable reduction in the awarded points, which causes an effective double loss due to the task taking longer than anticipated and earning the member fewer than the anticipated number of points.

Rewards. It may be natural to assume some level of monetary reward when discussing incentives, but it is suggested to find non-monetary means of rewarding team members for performance in the vast majority of cases to help keep them focused on the intrinsic value in what they are doing. In addition, yearly or end-of-project bonuses are often so far away that hyperbolic discounting comes into play and causes the reward to be valued far less than a manager might anticipate. To further complicate this type of reward structure, once a project starts to go off-track, the members may begin to think that the bonus is a lost cause, causing it to actually have the opposite effect.

As an alternative to using cash bonuses or similar monetary rewards based directly on a member's performance, it is suggested that other means be used on a much more frequent basis. The goal is to keep the member focused on the work instead of on the money. (If monetary rewards are to be used, it is suggested that they be team-based in order to promote teamwork and cooperation instead of competition.) The project management application should maintain overall and weekly leaderboards as a display of status and effectiveness. The leaders of these lists gain recognition simply from being at the top of the list, but management could go further and publicly recognize their effectiveness and contribution periodically.

Some types of rewards can even be implemented directly into the project management tool. For example, the point leader at the end of a week could get first choice of tasks each day the following week, and task selection could continue in that order (though this could encourage a positive feedback loop). To go even further, a variable reinforcement schedule could be created by randomly giving out a reward when completing a task. These bonuses could also leverage pseudocertainty by having a very small change to be a very large reward. The project management tool could incorporate a point bonus with adjustable values and weighting, but it could also allow for manager created rewards which could extend the potential bonuses outside of the system.

4.3 Visibility

Status. A key point to the effectiveness of this proposed project management tool would be keeping the team members aware of the status of the system at any given time. They need some indication of how the project as a whole is doing, how well the current sprint or milestone is progressing, and how much time is remaining on their current task. They also need some degree of visibility on the performance of their teammates, both to gauge their relative performance and to see if any of their teammates are having problems or need assistance.

In order to accomplish this, the project management tool should have a main view which keeps the member informed of the project's status but also serves to impart a sense of urgency. The weekly and overall leaderboard leaders should be displayed (likely the top three positions) along with the viewer's weekly and overall score. In addition the following should be displayed to offer a sense of progress at all levels of the project: the number of days left in the project, a timeline of the progress remaining in the current sprint or milestone, and a countdown timer showing the amount of time remaining on the viewer's currently selected task. In addition, a user should be able to easily find a list of all tasks currently being worked on as well as a list of tasks remaining in the sprint or milestone sorted by priority.

Control. The amount of control to give to a team member at any given time is a difficult design decision. A user may want to have complete control over the environment, but given the paradox of choice, that may not be the most effective approach. It is suggested that each screen of the project management tool should be kept very simple with only the options that are absolutely needed by the user. Some popular project management tools can be initially overwhelming to users due to the number of options presented to them, even though many of those options are only commonly needed by managers or supervisors. By keeping the end user view as minimalistic as possible, the adherence to the project management tool is expected to increase. Even for those members who dutifully engage in the project management process, the less time that it takes them to use the software effectively, the more time they will have to spend working on their tasks.

5   Conclusion

5.1   Implications

The end result of this research is a well-documented example of product prototype developed via theory-based design which can inform future attempts at gamifying other software within the business setting. As gamification becomes more prevalent, similar products will begin to emerge in any spot where performance needs to be optimized. By paving the way with research and testing, it could be possible to improve future attempts, increasing the pace of progress in this area.

5.2   Potential Issues

By its nature, gamification capitalizes on our innate reward centers and encourages us to perform certain actions while discouraging us from performing others. This can, at times, cross into territory that many find uncomfortable or even unethical, where designers may be, intentionally or not, toying with the compulsions of people. Gamification designers must keep this in mind and, when appropriate, ensure that stakeholders are aware of the issues. In addition, certain techniques are likely to be more effective on some people than others, so implementing a gamified process in a workplace may unintentionally select for employees who are most susceptible.

5.3   Future Work

Future work would involve further testing and development of the application including its introduction to a real-world environment where its results could be compared to industry-standard applications.

References

Ariely, D.: The Upside of Irrationality: The Unexpected Benefits of Defying Logic at Work and at Home. Harper Collins, New York (2010)

Arkes, H., Blumer, C.: The psychology of sunk cost. Organ. Behav. Hum. Decis. Process **35**, 124–140 (1985)

Butler, C.: Applied behavioral economics: a game designer's perspective. In: Wood, L., Reiners, T. (eds.) Gamification in Education and Business. Springer, New York (2015)

Cialdini, R.B.: Influence: The Psychology of Persuasion. Harper Business, New York (2006)

Heyman, J., Ariely, D.: Effort for payment: a tale of two markets. Psychol. Sci. **15**(11), 787–793 (2004)

Iyengar, S.S., Lepper, M.R.: When choice is demotivating: can one desire too much of a good thing? J. Pers. Soc. Psychol. **79**(6), 995–1006 (2000)

Kahneman, D., Tversky, A.: Choices, values, and frames. Am. Psychol. **39**(4), 341–350 (1984)

Lee, R., Sturmey, P., Fields, L.: Schedule-induced and operant mechanisms that influence response variability: a review and implications for future investigations. Psychol. Rec. **57**(3), A7 (2007)

Tversky, A., Kahneman, D.: Rational choice and the framing of decisions. J. Bus. **59**, S251–S278 (1986)

A Study on Mobile Fitness Application Usage

Ben C.F. Choi[✉] and Nathaniel T. Lee

School of Information Systems, Technology and Management, UNSW Australia
Business School, UNSW Australia, Kensington, Australia
chun.choi@unsw.edu.au,
nathaniel.lee@student.unsw.edu.au

Abstract. Although the importance of physical activity in a healthy lifestyle is well known, little attention has been paid thus far to systematically understand users' continued usage of mobile fitness applications. The objective of this paper is to understand the determinants of usage of mobile fitness applications beyond initial adoption. The research model is tested with data collected from fifty users of mobile fitness applications. The results indicate that expectation confirmation is the key predicator of attitudes towards the application, such as perceived usefulness, perceived enjoyment, and satisfaction. Furthermore, users' attitudes are found to determine continued usage intention. Overall, this paper contributes by integrating intrinsic motivation into the expectation-confirmation model for mobile fitness application usage.

Keywords: Expectation-confirmation · Satisfaction · Perceived usefulness · Perceived enjoyment · Continued usage · Mobile fitness applications

1 Introduction

Increasing evidence suggests that physical activities help form the foundation of healthy living [1]. Despite the health benefits of engaging frequent physical exercises, studies show that the majority of the population is not benefited because people are simply physically inactive in general. More importantly, ample evidence shows that physical inactivity is a major risk factor to health in modern society. The engagement of physical activity typically constitutes a complex interaction between biological, environmental, social, and psychological influences [2]. Past research examining exercise psychology reveals that human motivations are important determinants of exercise behavior [e.g., 3, 4]. More important, emerging evidence suggests that Information Systems (IS) could play an important role in sustaining the impact of motivations on behavior.

Past IS research has drawn on a variety of theoretical perspectives to understand motivations in the context of IS continual usage [e.g., 5, 6]. In particular, the expectation-confirmation model is shown to be particularly useful in understanding individuals' continued usage of technology. Extending the traditional expectation-confirmation model, Bhattacherjee [7] put forth the IS continuance model that continued usage of technology can be determined by perceived usefulness, which represents the consequences of technology usage, and satisfaction, which denotes

© Springer International Publishing Switzerland 2015
F.F.-H. Nah and C.-H. Tan (Eds.): HCIB 2015, LNCS 9191, pp. 446–457, 2015.
DOI: 10.1007/978-3-319-20895-4_41

individuals' affective attitude toward a technology. The IS continuance model has been widely adopted in IS research [e.g., 8, 9].

Despite the popularity of the IS continuance model, very few studies have tried to apply the model to understand IS continuance beyond utility-based systems. Furthermore, extant studies have primarily focused on investigating the relationships between system quality and satisfaction. This is a crucial omission and an important topic to be investigated since individuals' attitude in sustained mobile fitness applications usage is likely to differ from that in the pre-adoption process. Sustained usage is distinct from pre-adoption because individuals have prior physical experience to draw upon and has formed a level of satisfaction that is likely to influence continued usage. Therefore, additional theoretical insights are needed to understand the sustained usage process, and how factors that predict pre-adoption decisions combine with physical outcomes to influence continued usage decisions.

2 Theoretical Background

2.1 Expectation-Confirmation Framework

The expectation-confirmation framework has been utilized to examine behavior prior to adoption (i.e., deliberation) and post-adoption (i.e., evaluation). Specifically, as described by Oliver [10], individuals first formed expectations of a technology prior to actual usage. Subsequently, individuals' actual usage resulted in experienced-based perception, which was influenced by these expectations. Substantial differences between deliberation and evaluation would either confirm or refute expectation formed prior to purchase. Overall, the expectation-confirmation framework posits that expectations and level of confirmation affect satisfaction, which ultimately drive individuals' repeated usage intention.

Ample IS research has built upon the expectation-confirmation framework. In particular, Bhattacherjee [7] proposed a modified expectation-confirmation framework, which is extended to explain continued IT usage. To explain continued IT usage, Bhattacherjee [7] emphasized several important differences with past research examining expectation-confirmation. For instance, past expectancy-confirmation research has predominately focused on the importance of pre-usage expectation in influencing confirmation, which in turn affects individuals' satisfaction in using technologies. MacInnis and Price's [8] study, as an example, found that imagery processing influenced consumers' expectation formation, which subsequently interacted with actual experience, to derive satisfaction with their spring vacations. In contrast, Bhattacherjee [7] emphasized the importance of post-adoption expectations. In particular, it is posited that individuals' actual technology usage experience should shape their usage expectation.

Furthermore, past research drawing upon the expectancy-confirmation paradigm have predominately focused on expectation in terms of individual beliefs about the levels of attributes possessed by a technology. For example, in a study examining brand loyalty, Yoon and Kim [9] revealed that consumers derived expectations based on several brand attributes (such as image, economy, and sensory). The authors also reported that these expectations were typically subjected to a confirmation process, which was the key determinant of overall satisfaction and loyalty. On the contrary, to reflect the unique technological attributes of IS, Bhattacherjee [7] postulates perceived usefulness as the key manifestation of expectation.

In essence, past research suggests that the expectation-confirmation model is a relevant and integral theoretical framework to explain continued IS usage.

2.2   Organismic Integration Theory (OIT)

Among the many theoretical perspectives advanced to address motivations of technology usage, the Organismic Integration Theory (OIT) proposed by Ryan and Deci [11] is particularly useful in predicting fitness-related technology usage behavior. OIT focuses on how a user's internal psychological perceptions about autonomy shape his or her intentions and behaviors. In particular, it posits that endogenous motivations are important determinants of user intentions and behaviors.

In contrast to OIT, past IS studies typically view technology usage behavior as being driven by extrinsic motivations, such as perceived usefulness and rewards. For example, Venkatesh and Goyal [12] examined the usage of an internal electronic human resource information system and found that continued usage intention decreased at a faster rate as pre-exposure perceived usefulness increased and post-exposure perceived usefulness decreased. Similarly, Limayem et al. [13] examined university students' usage of the Internet and reported that perceived usefulness was a significant predictor of satisfaction and IS continuance intention. In essence, extant research mostly focused on the essentiality of extrinsic motivations in explaining continued IS usage. As such, OIT provides an important theoretical complement by underscoring the importance of intrinsic motivations.

According to OIT, individuals are volitional and tend to utilize stimuli to satisfy their individual needs. In particular, the theory centers on the unique role of locus of causality, which refers to individuals' ability to enact autonomy by initiating and endorsing behavior as they desire. More importantly, OIT formally posits that locus of causality helps facilitate individuals' intrinsic motivations in performing sustained activities, such as engaging in prolonged physical exercise and participation in strenuous fitness programs. Furthermore, past research has identified a myriad of intrinsic motivations which might drive continued IS usage. In particular, perceived enjoyment has been identified as the key form of intrinsic motivation in using hedonic IS. In the context of mobile fitness application usage, enjoyment is particularly relevant in determining satisfaction. Evidence suggests that enjoyment is a key driver of sustained fitness activities. For instance, Murcia et al. [14] revealed that enjoyment was an important form of self-determined motivation in driving sports engagement. Similarly, Waterman [15] demonstrated that hedonic enjoyment was the major affective state that influenced the extent to which activities were seen as facilitating the realization of an individual's best potential. Overall, past research highlights enjoyment as a key intrinsic motivation which drives sustained fitness-related behavior.

3   Research Model and Hypotheses

By integrating the expectation-confirmation model and OIT, the research model is proposed (see Fig. 1). Specifically, this study importantly examines expectation confirmation, which refers to the consistency between a user's expected experience of augmented fitness activities and his or her actual fitness activity experience with the mobile fitness application [16].

Consistent with the expectation-confirmation model and OIT, we consider the impact of expectation confirmation on two forms of motivations, namely extrinsic motivation and intrinsic motivation. Corresponding to the important role of extrinsic motivation, this study considers perceived usefulness, which is defined as the degree to which an individual believes that using the mobile fitness application would enhance his or her fitness activity performance [17]. In this study, in terms of intrinsic motivation, we center on perceived enjoyment, which is defined as the extent to which fun can be derived from using the mobile fitness application [18]. Furthermore, in line with the expectation-confirmation model, this study considers satisfaction with the application, which is defined as the user's emotion-based response about the application, to capture the overall evaluation of the application.

Past IS research typically focused on continued IS usage as the behavioral outcome of expectation-confirmation. This study draws on this view by examining continued mobile fitness application usage, referring to a user's intention to continue using the mobile fitness application [35].

3.1   The Effects of Expectation Confirmation

Ample evidence suggests that expectation confirmation enhances individuals' perceptions of usefulness in using technology [e.g., 19–21]. For instance, prior to actual

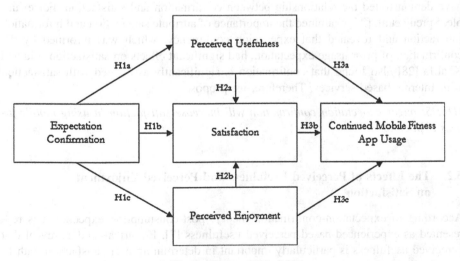

Fig. 1.   Research Model

usage, users may be uncertain about what to expect from using the mobile fitness application and hence develop low initial usefulness perceptions. Consequently, given the low initial perceived usefulness, users' expectation can be easily confirmed. Having a strong confirmation of initial expectation, users would be induced to elevate their perceptions of extrinsic utility in using the mobile fitness application. Indeed, theoretical evidence suggests that individuals might experience cognitive dissonance if their elaborative usefulness perceptions are disconfirmed in actual experience [22, 23]. More importantly, individuals typically try to resolve this inconsistency by adjusting their usefulness perceptions to more accurately match their experience. Therefore, we posit

H1a: stronger expectation confirmation will increase perceived usefulness in using mobile fitness applications.

Deci and Ryan [24] suggested that sustained behaviors are driven by both extrinsic motivation and intrinsic motivation. In this study, extrinsic motivation is considered in terms of perceived usefulness whereas intrinsic motivation is represented by perceived playfulness. According to the expectation-confirmation model, confirmation is the key determinant of experienced-based motivation.

In the context of mobile fitness application usage, since individuals' perceptions of usefulness and enjoyment are common motivations, it is reasonable to expect that confirmation would impact on perceived enjoyment. Indeed, past research suggests that individuals might experience cognitive dissonance or psychological tension if their pre-usage enjoyment perceptions are not congruent with their usage experience [25, 26]. Hence, we posit

H1b: Stronger expectation confirmation will increase perceived enjoyment in using mobile fitness applications.

Individuals form expectations about technologies prior to actual usage. When lower expectation meets with higher performance, users typically develop a stronger sense of confirmation, which in turn drives satisfaction in using the technology. Past studies have demonstrated the relationship between confirmation and satisfaction. For example, Spreng et al. [27] examined the importance of attribute satisfaction and information satisfaction and revealed that expectation congruency, which was informed by the confirmation of prior usage expectation, had significant effects on satisfaction. Liu and Khalifa [28] also found that confirmation is significantly associated with satisfaction with Internet-based services. Therefore, we propose

H1c: Stronger expectation confirmation will increase satisfaction in using mobile fitness applications.

3.2   The Effects of Perceived Usefulness and Perceived Enjoyment on Satisfaction

According to expectation-confirmation theory, post-consumption expectation is represented as experienced-based perceived usefulness [7]. Empirical studies reveal that perceived usefulness is particularly important in determining user satisfaction with IS

[17, 29]. For instance, Mawhinney and Lederer [30] reported that users who perceived a technology useful, were more likely to be satisfied with the technology than those who did not.

Additionally, past research suggests that perceived enjoyment is an important precursor of satisfaction in using technology. Specifically, users who report a higher perceived enjoyment in use of a technology tend to be associated with more creative and innovative usage. Consequently, they are more likely to develop insights through exploratory behaviors, hence resulting in an enhanced usage experience. For example, Van Dolen et al. [31] examined online commercial group chat and found that technology attributes which facilitated perceived enjoyment influenced satisfaction directly. In a study examining the role of an IT artifact in online service continuance, Kang and Lee [32] reported that hedonic motivational factors, such as perceived enjoyment, were important antecedents to customer satisfaction.

In summary, we hypothesize the following

H2a: Higher perceived usefulness will increase satisfaction in using mobile fitness applications.

H2b: Higher perceived enjoyment will increase satisfaction in using mobile fitness applications.

3.3 Determinants of Intention to Continue Using Mobile Fitness Applications

The technology-acceptance model (TAM) underscores the importance of perceived usefulness in driving technology usage. In this model, perceived usefulness is considered the basic extrinsic motivation in driving consumers' repurchase behavior. Recently, researchers noted that TAM, which focused on explaining initial technology adoption, could be extended to predict continued technology usage. Indeed, ample research drawing upon the expectation-confirmation model has demonstrated the positive effect of perceived usefulness on continued usage [e.g., 19, 22, 33].

Past research examining intrinsic motivation reveals that positive subjective experience is an important reason for continuing an activity [34]. To illustrate, when an individual is interested in or enjoys performing an activity, he or she will be intrinsically motivated by the process of the activity, and hence he or she will be more likely to undertake the activity in a prolonged manner. In the context of mobile fitness application usage, users who experience enjoyment are more absorbed and appealed by the augmented exercising experience.

Satisfaction is an individual's feelings of pleasure which is the outcome of evaluating his or her expectation with actual experience. According to the expectation-confirmation model, satisfaction determines intentions to use or not to use a technology in the future. Indeed, in a study examining mobile internet, Hong et al. [33] found that users' satisfaction with mobile internet was the principal determinant of continued usage.

In summary, we hypothesize the following

H3a: Higher perceived usefulness will increase intention to continue using mobile fitness applications.

H3b: Higher perceived enjoyment will increase intention to continue using mobile fitness applications.

H3c: Higher satisfaction will increase intention to continue using mobile fitness applications.

4   Research Method

4.1   Operationalization of Constructs

We adopted existing validated scales with known psychometric properties as far as possible. To assess expectation confirmation in augmented fitness activities, we adapted scales from Bhattacherjee [7] by considering our research context of mobile fitness applications. We also adapted items from previous literature [12, 18, 27] to measure perceived usefulness, satisfaction, and perceived enjoyment. To measure continued mobile fitness application usage, we adapted items from Mathieson [35]. The questionnaire employed a seven-point Likert scale (1 = strongly disagree, 7 = strongly agree).

4.2   Sample and Experimental Procedures

Fifty users of mobile fitness applications participated in the online survey over two weeks. The descriptive statistics of the sample indicate that the majority of respondents were between 18 and 25 years of age.

Nonresponse bias was assessed by comparing early and late respondents (i.e., those who responded in the first two days and those who took part during the last two days). T-tests performed on each group of respondents did not differ significantly in terms of age, Internet experience, or application usage experience. Therefore, nonresponse bias is not a serious concern.

5   Data Analysis

Data analysis was conducted using the partial least squares (PLS) technique.

5.1   Instrument Validation

Convergent validity and discriminant validity were assessed. Convergent validity can be established by examining composite reliability (CR), Cronbach's α, and the average variance extracted (AVE) of constructs. The CR and Cronbach's α for all constructs

Table 1. Descriptive Statistics and Correlations

	Mean	S.D.	CON	PU	PE	SAT	C-USE
CON	4.78	1.45	*0.91*				
PU	4.89	1.32	0.46	*0.88*			
PE	4.22	1.56	0.43	0.33	*0.82*		
SAT	4.97	1.89	0.45	0.42	0.41	*0.81*	
C-USE	4.54	1.09	0.28	0.35	0.39	0.47	*0.79*

Notes: S.D. = Standard Deviations; CON = Confirmation; PU = Perceived Usefulness;
SAT = Satisfaction; PE = Perceived Enjoyment; C-USE = Continued Mobile Fitness Application
Usage

exceeded 0.7. The AVE for each construct was greater than 0.5. Since the results
met all threshold criteria, the convergent validity for the constructs was supported.

Discriminant validity of a measurement model can be established when the square
root of AVE for each construct is greater than the correlations between that construct
and other constructs. As shown Error! Reference source not found., this requirement
was met. We also tested for common method bias based on the guidelines suggested by
Liang et al. [36]. Results showed a small magnitude of method variance and insignificant method factor loadings, and hence method bias was unlikely a concern in this
study (Table 1).

5.2   Hypotheses Testing

Path coefficients and significance values are reported in Fig. 2. As hypothesized,
expectation confirmation has significant effects on perceived usefulness ($\beta = 0.41$,
$\rho < 0.01$), perceived enjoyment ($\beta = 0.38$, $\rho < 0.01$), and satisfaction ($\beta = 0.35$,
$\rho < 0.01$). Thus, H1a, H1b, and H1c are supported.

Furthermore, as expected, perceived usefulness is found to have a significant and
positive effect on satisfaction ($\beta = 0.32$, $\rho < 0.05$). Likewise, perceived enjoyment also
positively affects satisfaction ($\beta = 0.28$, $\rho < 0.05$). Hence, H2a and H2b are supported
(Fig. 2).

Finally, perceived usefulness ($\beta = 0.34$, $\rho < 0.05$), perceived enjoyment ($\beta = 0.29$,
$\rho < 0.05$), and satisfaction ($\beta = 0.26$, $\rho < 0.05$) are found to have significant and positive
effects on continued mobile fitness application usage. Therefore, H3a, H3b, and H3c
are supported.

6   Discussion and Concluding Remarks

6.1   Discussion of Results

The results supported all our hypotheses. There are several important findings obtained
from our study. Firstly, this study reveals that both satisfaction and perceived usefulness act as key motivators for continued application usage. This finding is consistent
with past research examining expectation-confirmation, which claimed that satisfaction

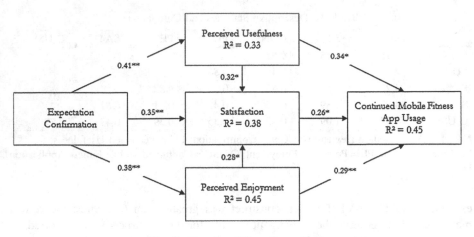

Fig. 2. Results of Hypotheses Tests

and perceived usefulness are two major determinants of sustained behavior. Further, perceived enjoyment is found to have substantial influence on continued usage. As hypothesized, an individual with high level of perceived enjoyment has a greater desire to maintain the intrinsic benefit, confirming the effect of self-determination on sustained behavior. Also, the significant effects of perceived usefulness and perceived enjoyment on satisfaction are consistent with and extend previous research on experience-based motivations that explains the effects of intrinsic and extrinsic benefits on satisfaction associated with fitness activities.

Additionally, consistent with the expectation-confirmation paradigm, expectation confirmation is found to be the key predictor of perceived usefulness, perceived enjoyment, and satisfaction in the context of mobile fitness application usage.

6.2   Contributions

This study makes several important contributions. First, we establish that extrinsic benefit evaluation (i.e., perceived usefulness) is not the only consideration in individuals' expectation-confirmation in using mobile fitness applications. Past IS research examining expectation-confirmation in technology usage has predominately focused on the importance of extrinsic benefits (i.e., perceived usefulness and perceived ease of use) in driving continued usage behavior. The interesting role of intrinsic benefit evaluation has been largely neglected. In this study, we enrich this stream of research by positing and empirically demonstrating that perceived enjoyment is a major experienced-based intrinsic benefit that individuals evaluate.

Secondly, this study adds to the literature by extending expectation-confirmation theory. This concept has previously been used to explain continued IS usage [e.g., 9, 37, 38]. In this study, the theory is used to model and understand the motivations behind the continued usage of mobile fitness applications. Further, a salient contribution is made by showing how various perspectives, such as technology acceptance framework and flow theory, can be integrated to explain sustain usage of technology. While the expectation-confirmation framework serves as the overarching perspective for our explanation of continued usage of mobile fitness applications, technology acceptance framework and flow theory elucidate the specific effects of extrinsic and intrinsic motivations on satisfaction and continued usage.

This study additionally contributes to the broader line of research on technology acceptance that has mainly been conducted in workplace settings [e.g., 12, 38]. Previous research [e.g., 13] has also explained how voluntary continued internet usage could be predicted by confirmation and satisfaction. Our study adds to this literature by examining confirmation as the key determinant of satisfaction in using mobile fitness applications.

6.3 Limitations and Future Research

The interpretation of our findings is subject to certain limitations. First, our results are largely consistent with past IS research examining expectation-confirmation. Yet to test the robustness of our findings, it would be useful to replicate this study across a variety of mobile applications. Second, it may be possible to identify additional antecedents of satisfaction in using mobile fitness applications. For example, individuals who have been physical active may derive greater satisfaction in using the application than those who are less active. Thus, future studies could explore various personal characteristics that may influence expectation-formation in the context of mobile fitness application usage.

References

1. Organization, W.H. Physical Activity - Fact Sheet N. 385 (2014). http://www.who.int/mediacentre/factsheets/fs385/en/
2. Biddle, S.J., Mutrie, N.: Psychology of physical activity: Determinants, well-being and interventions. Routledge, London (2007)
3. Thomas, J.L., Côté, J., Deakin, J.: Youth sport programs: an avenue to foster positive youth development. Phys. Educ. Sport Pedagogy 10(1), 19–40 (2005)
4. Pelletier, L.G., Dion, S.C.: An examination of general and specific motivational mechanisms for the relations between body dissatisfaction and eating behaviors. J. Soc. Clin. Psychol. 26(3), 303–333 (2007)
5. Hsu, C., Lee, J.-N., Straub, D.W.: Institutional influences on information systems security innovations. Inf. Syst. Res. 23(3-part 2), 918–939 (2012)
6. Karahanna, E., Straub, D.W., Chervany, N.L.: Information technology adoption across time: a -sectional comparison of pre-adoption and post-adoption beliefs. MIS Q. 23, 183–213 (1999)
7. Bhattacherjee, A.: Understanding information systems continuance: an expectation-confirmation model. MIS Q. 25, 351–370 (2001)
8. MacInnis, D.J., Price, L.L.: An exploratory study of the effects of imagery processing and consumer experience on expectations and satisfaction. Adv. Consum. Res. 17(1), 41–47 (1990)

9. Yoon, S.-J., Kim, J.-H.: An empirical validation of a loyalty model based on expectation disconfirmation. J. Consum. Mark. **17**(2), 120–136 (2000)

10. Oliver, R.L.: Effect of expectation and disconfirmation on postexposure product evaluations: an alternative interpretation. J. Appl. Psychol. **62**(4), 480 (1977)

11. Ryan, R.M., Deci, E.L.: Self-determination theory and the facilitation of intrinsic motivation, social development, and well-being. Am. Psychol. **55**(1), 68 (2000)

12. Venkatesh, V., Goyal, S.: Expectation disconfirmation and technology adoption: polynomial modeling and response surface analysis. MIS Q. **34**(2), 281–303 (2010)

13. Limayem, M., Hirt, S.G., Cheung, C.M.: How habit limits the predictive power of intention: the case of information systems continuance. Mis Q. **31**, 705–737 (2007)

14. Murcia, J.A.M., et al.: Peers' influence on exercise enjoyment: a self-determination theory approach. J. Sports Sci. Med. **7**(1), 23 (2008)

15. Waterman, A.S.: Two conceptions of happiness: contrasts of personal expressiveness (eudaimonia) and hedonic enjoyment. J. Pers. Soc. Psychol. **64**(4), 678 (1993)

16. Hayashi, A., et al.: The role of social presence and moderating role of computer self efficacy in predicting the continuance usage of e-learning systems. J. Inf. Syst. Educ. **15**, 139–154 (2004)

17. Davis, F.D.: Perceived usefulness, perceived ease of use, and user acceptance of information technology. MIS Q. **13**, 319–340 (1989)

18. Davis, F.D., Bagozzi, R.P., Warshaw, P.R.: Extrinsic and intrinsic motivation to use computers in the workplace1. J. Appl. Soc. Psychol. **22**(14), 1111–1132 (1992)

19. Brown, S.A., Venkatesh, V., Goyal, S.: Expectation confirmation in information systems research: a test of six competing models. MIS Q. **38**(3), 729–756 (2014)

20. Brown, S.A., Venkatesh, V., Goyal, S.: Expectation confirmation in technology use. Inf. Syst. Res. **23**(2), 474–487 (2012)

21. Xiao, B., Benbasat, I.: E-commerce product recommendation agents: use, characteristics, and impact. MIS Q. **31**(1), 137–209 (2007)

22. Lin, C.S., Wu, S., Tsai, R.J.: Integrating perceived playfulness into expectation-confirmation model for web portal context. Inf. Manag. **42**(5), 683–693 (2005)

23. Brown, S.A., et al.: Expectation confirmation: an examination of three competing models. Organ. Behav. Hum. Decis. Process. **105**(1), 52–66 (2008)

24. Deci, E.L., Ryan, R.M.: A motivational approach to self: integration in personality. In: Dienstbier, R. (ed.) Nebraska Symposium on Motivation: Perspectives on motivation, pp. 237–288. University of Nebraska Press, Lincoln (1991)

25. Kang, Y.S., Hong, S., Lee, H.: Exploring continued online service usage behavior: the roles of self-image congruity and regret. Comput. Hum. Behav. **25**(1), 111–122 (2009)

26. Wu, X., et al.: A conceptual model of m-commerce customers' continuance intention based on the customers' perceived value. Int. J. Mobile Learn. Organ. **3**(3), 243–257 (2009)

27. Spreng, R.A., MacKenzie, S.B., Olshavsky, R.W.: A reexamination of the determinants of consumer satisfaction. J. Mark. **60**, 15–32 (1996)

28. Liu, V., Khalifa, M.: Determinants of satisfaction at different adoption stages of Internet-based services. J. Assoc. Inf. Syst. **4**(1), 12 (2003)

29. Venkatesh, V., et al.: User acceptance of information technology: towawrd a unified view. MIS Q. **27**(3), 425–478 (2003)

30. Mawhinney, C.H., Lederer, A.L.: A study of personal computer utilization by managers. Inf. Manag. **18**(5), 243–253 (1990)

31. Van Dolen, W.M., Dabholkar, P.A., De Ruyter, K.: Satisfaction with online commercial group chat: the influence of perceived technology attributes, chat group characteristics, and advisor communication style. J. Retail. **83**(3), 339–358 (2007)

32. Kang, Y.S., Lee, H.: Understanding the role of an IT artifact in online service continuance: an extended perspective of user satisfaction. Comput. Hum. Behav. **26**(3), 353–364 (2010)
33. Hong, S., Thong, J.Y., Tam, K.Y.: Understanding continued information technology usage behavior: a comparison of three models in the context of mobile internet. Decis. Support Syst. **42**(3), 1819–1834 (2006)
34. Chang, Y.P., Zhu, D.H.: The role of perceived social capital and flow experience in building users' continuance intention to social networking sites in China. Comput. Hum. Behav. **28** (3), 995–1001 (2012)
35. Mathieson, K.: Predicting user intentions: comparing the technology acceptance model with the Liang theory of planned behavior. Inf. Syst. Res. **2**(3), 173–191 (1991)
36. Liang, H., Xue, Y.: Avoidance of information technology threats: a theoretical perspective. MIS Q. **33**(1), 71–90 (2009)
37. Jung, Y.: Understanding the role of sense of presence and perceived autonomy in users' continued use of social virtual worlds. J. Comput. Mediated Commun. **16**(4), 492–510 (2011)
38. McKinney, V., Yoon, K., Zahedi, F.M.: The measurement of web-customer satisfaction: an expectation and disconfirmation approach. Inf. Syst. Res. **13**(3), 296–315 (2002)

Developing a Context Model of Process Variants for Business Process Integration

Jorge E. Giraldo[1,2(✉)], Demetrio A. Ovalle[1], and Flavia M. Santoro[3]

[1] Universidad Nacional de Colombia, Medellín, Colombia
{jegiraldp, dovalle}@unal.edu.co
[2] Politécnico Colombiano Jaime Isaza Cadavid, Medellín, Colombia
jegiraldo@elpoli.edu.co
[3] Universidad Federal del Estado de Rio de Janeiro, Rio de Janeiro, Brazil
flavia.santoro@uniriotec.br

Abstract. Since the integration of business process variants can be affected by contextual information the aim of this paper is to propose the development of a context model for Business Process Integration that considers the propagation of process changes towards process variants of the reference model. The method used to develop such a model focuses on following stages: (1) conceptualization of process variants, by building a related ontology, (2) identification of contextual elements, (3) definition of operational and organizational constraints; (4) formalization of contextual situations in the variants, and (5) construction of a reasoning mechanism for searching and retrieval of process variants. In order to validate the context model proposed we implemented both a prototype and a case study that consider each of the five stages proposed. The obtained results demonstrate the effectiveness of using this kind of approaches for business process integration.

Keywords: HCI in business · Context process model · Business process integration

1 Introduction

A business process is defined as the logical description of a specific business activities sequence being modeled through process models which allow new value to be added to their products or services [1]. Due to the rise of using business processes and their automation, process models generated can reach an amount of hundreds or even thousands. This fact allows them to be considered as model collections for searching, retrieval, and reuse [2, 3].

When a business process is executed, there may be domain-dependent situations, implying the need for configuration of reference process model variations. These variations are known as variants and constitute an adjustment of the reference model under specific requirements [4].

Updating a process reference model requires propagation of changes to the associated variants. Variant management can be individually performed or through a group mechanism by means of an integration process [5]. However, not all variants can

F.F.-H. Nah and C.-H. Tan (Eds.): HCIB 2015, LNCS 9191, pp. 458–468, 2015.
DOI: 10.1007/978-3-319-20895-4_42

support the propagation of changes due to following issues: (a) their close relationship with the domain, (b) the execution in a specific context, and (c) the associated events that generated the variant [6].

Since the integration of business process variants can be affected by contextual information [7], it is important to define a decision mechanism that determines the set of variants to be integrated wherein their execution will not be affected from variants updates that have been previously performed.

The aim of this paper is to propose the development of a context model for Business Process Integration that considers the propagation of reference model process changes towards process variants based on following stages: (1) conceptualization of process variants, by building an ontology, (2) identification of contextual elements, (3) definition of operational and organizational constraints; (4) formalization of contextual situations in the variants, and (5) construction of a reasoning mechanism for searching and retrieval of process variants.

The rest of the paper is organized as follows: Sect. 2 presents the conceptual framework of this research. Section 3 reviews some related works analysis. Section 4 describes the context model of process variants proposed for business process integration. In order to validate the proposed context model, a case study is described in Sect. 5, and finally Sect. 6 presents the conclusions and future work.

2 Conceptual Framework

Following are the main concepts related to business process integration and model process variants.

2.1 Definition of Business Process Integration

The Business Process Integration -BPI- is defined as *"the consolidation of a set of process variants partially or permanently, in order to analyze and propagate changes from its reference model, related to their structural, logical and organizational information"*.

The result of BPI is represented by the description of a process model, which should allow the propagation of changes and ensuring a minimum amount of change, which is considered as the similarity measure between the process involved and the variants generated.

Figure 1 presents an example of business processes integration wherein starting from two processes (Process A and Process B) a third process (Process C) is generated to be able to replace both A (solid lines) and B (dashed lines). The first is composed of two sequential activities and the second by two separate mandatory activities.

Therefore the process generated is composed of an activity 'A', a condition and an activity of the process B. In this case the activities 'A1' and 'B2' are selected because are appropriate for integration. Additionally, the process B contains a conditional C1 is selected because it enriches the description of the process model generated.

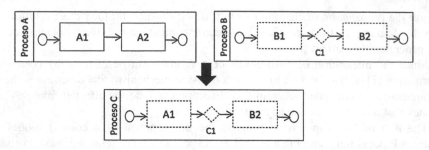

Fig. 1. Business process integration

2.2 Model Process Variants

A variant is considered as the change of the structure of a business process, specifically in instances of a reference model. Variants are classified into the following types:

Evolutions variants: Once a business process is in production, adjustments can be made in the structure, due to the recollected information during execution leading to perform redesign or optimization. Also changes may occur from the execution domain, involving an upgrade process, for example, during the merger of two companies, it may require two different versions of the same process.

Request variants: During process execution, situations can be generated by special customer requests, for which adjustments are necessary to make. For example the case making a sale to a corporate client, for which the company is prepared to do it only with small and medium enterprise, therefore requires modifying the structure of the process.

The main use of the variants is to allow the propagation of changes from a reference model. The propagation can be of two types as well: Single and Multi-modal [8], the first taken separately each of the variants and propagate the changes, while the multimodal approach obtains a single process model from consolidation variants. Each type has its advantages and disadvantages.

According to [9], change management involves three steps, (1) detection of differences, (2) analysis of their relations, and (3) resolution of differences.

3 Related Works

The propagation of changes from a reference model to its instances focuses its efforts in allowing the identification and alignment, either syntactic or semantic, among business process models [10].

Weidlich et al. present in [11] a mechanism to support the change propagation between models processes related. Basically from a given change, an abstract behavior is generated in order to identify the region of change in process instances. Thus alignment processes in inconsistent behavior is ensured.

Weber et al. define in [12] a process instance adaptation wherein common high-level changes have been classified as change patterns. Authors discuss how changes can be applied in a net system and in this way they introduce the notion of a change region.

For business process alignment, similarity metrics are often used [13] to measure the degree of difference between two processes. The main focus thereby consists in identifying their differences to attempt to minimize them.

Once processes are aligned then it is proceed to perform the integration. La Rosa et al. consider in [14] the construction of sets of multiple models (called merged models) as well as intersections. Merged models are intended for analysts who wish to create a model that subsumes a collection of process models, typically representing variants of the same underlying process.

Process variants exhibit a major challenge in story generation, search and retrieval of information from events. Ruopeng et al. present in [15] a tool for discovering of preferred variants through effective search and retrieval based on the notion of process similarity, where multiple aspects of the process variants are compared according to specific query requirements.

Ploesser et al. propose in [16] a model for the design of a context-sensitive process which highlight relevant issues such as context modeling, context learning, taxonomies of context and process operations associated with the business context.

Saidani and Nurcan propose in [17] a context model to delegate tasks based on skills and experience wherein an operation can be executed or not by a role, depending on changes in the requirements that have been previously expressed by the customers of the process.

Bernal et al. present in [18] a constraint-based model for implementation and invocation of activities in order to perform decomposition of objectives and thus to obtain rules related to own model activities. Tavares et al. propose in [19] an architectural approach for managing the flexibility of business processes considering contextual information being gathered from the environment and thus attempt to improve and automate adaptation mechanisms.

Mattos et al. show in [20] a formal background of business process models based on conceptual models approach. This formalization seeks to identify the status of an activity in order to support decision-making during the execution of a process.

It is important to develop solutions that provide the kind of contextual dependence when integrating process variants, since the spread of non-relevant changes to the structure and semantics of the model process integration could affect its performance and representation.

4 Model Proposed

The context model for Business Process Integration proposed considers the propagation of process changes from reference model towards process variants based on five stages that are described as follows. However, before developing all stages some useful definitions will firstly be presented.

4.1 Definitions

Some useful definitions for context model development such as reference model, activities, transition, domain, among others, appear as follow.

- **Reference Model.** Giving MR(A, Pr, Gw, T, Ev, Rv, D) the reference model is composed of A: Activities, Pr: Participants, Gw: Gateways, T: Transitions, Ev: Evolution Variants, Rv: Request Variant, and D: Domain.
- **Activity.** An activity is denoted by A(n, ctx, dom, pr, t), where n:Name, ctx: Context, dom: Domain, pr: Participant y t: Activity type, for instance 66:Begin, 99: End, 1:Activity.
- **Transition.** A transition is given by Tr(Ao, Ad, name). Ao: Activity Source and Ad: Activity Destination.
- **Domain:** A domain is composed of concepts and contextual tags. These tags determine the concept relevancy in a given context. Contextual tags are denoted by EtqCtx (concept).
- **Context:** It is denoted by Ctx (st, ent, c) where st are Situations, ent: Contextual Entities, c: Constraints. Note that it is necessary to determine what are the concepts that are affected by the context from the domain context labels.
- **Contextual Element:** A contextual element deals with aspects of each activity such as person, place, and applications involved in the implementation. Each contextual element also has contextual information, represented in its properties.
- **Situation:** A situation is given by S (Eve(A), eCtx, ICtx(eCtx), Ri), where Eve is the event that generated the variant by adding or removing activities, eCtx: Contextual Element, ICtx (eCtx): Contextual Information, and Ri: Restriction of associated information, either organizational or operational.
- **Structural Similarity:** This concept deals with the number of activities, participants (actors), gateways, transitions, and rules that make up each of the processes. In addition, a syntactic comparison is performed between process's name and its activity tags.
- **Semantic Similarity:** It seeks the degree of semantic similarity between the names of the processes and activities, which depends on the domain of execution and the context model.
- **Performance Similarity:** This concept refers to the execution time of activities and process variants. In addition, it determines the frequency with which activities are used.

4.2 Context Model Development

Five stages composing the context model development are presented as follows.

   • **Stage 1 - Conceptualization of variants.** In order to clarify the concept of variant and its relationship with contextual information associated with levels and situations of process changes, an ontology was developed using the methodology "*Ontology Development 101*" [21]. Figure 2 shows a class diagram fragment of the process variant ontology.

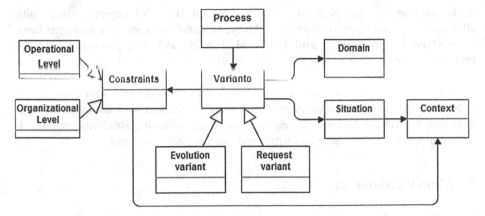

Fig. 2. Class diagram fragment of the business process variant ontology

It is important to highlight that a business process can generate several variants. Variants of a process have a relationship with execution domain information and contextual situations. In turn, depend on constraints levels, which can be operational and organizational type.

The definition of the levels and situations related to the context, can help to determine whether or not to incorporate a couple of variants to propagate. Then can be possible not propagate changes to process variants due to their constraint and contextual situations.

There are two kinds of constraint levels: (1) Operational levels of information, refer to the data that can be manipulated from the workflow process variants and its objects (activities, decision structures and actors) and (2) Organizational level, that takes into account information related to the organization and its units, which depend on internal rules and external.

• **Stage 2 – Identification of Contextual Elements.** The Stage 2 of the model proposed regards the identification of contextual elements. For doing so, a taxonomy of business process context is given by Saidani and Nurcan in [17], context elements related to constraints and levels of consolidation schemes must be defined such as availability, associated skills, experience, mental condition, physical condition, business rules, process location, affinity actors and government, and regions laws.

• **Stage 3 – Definition of Constraints.** The definition of operational and organizational constraints, useful for developing Stage 3, is associated with the levels of process execution. In this way, operational constraints must be defined in terms of the data manipulated from the workflow process variants, and also in terms of the process objects like activities, decision structures, and actors. On the other side, organizational constraints consider information related to the organization and its units that depend on internal and external rules.

• **Stage 4 – Formalization of Situations.** In addition, the levels of integration constraints can be affected by contextual elements represented by contextual situations in the variants that must be initially formalized as follows: (a) process objects and decision structures: availability, duration, execution date, frequency of use. (b) Actors:

skills, experience, age, physical condition, mental state. (c) Organizational units: affinity actors, execution location, availability, business rules and governmental laws.

• **Stage 5 – Reasoning and Retrieval.** Finally, and after process variants — represented through an ontology—, contextual elements, operational and organizational constrains, and contextual situations had been identified from Stage 1 to 4, the construction of a reasoning mechanism is needed to be developed within Stage 5 in order to search and retrieve every process variants generated. It is important to highlight that the variant retrieval process uses the three following similarity techniques: structural similarity, semantic similarity, and performance similarity.

5 Model Validation

The validation of the model is composed of two parts. The first one describes the case study and the second follows all the stages of the context model development.

5.1 Case Study Description

The model validation is applied to the process called "Academic Self-Assessment" — generally used in university scopes—, considers as a case study, which consists of the following activities: Starting, Awareness Development, Software Process Opening, Password Assignment, Weighting Development, Information Source Selection, Survey Application, Software Process Ending, Improvement Plan Design, and Accreditation Process Authorization.

There are 12 activities identified by codes as follows: 1 of Starting type (66), 1 of Ending type (99), 1 of Exclusive-Gateway type (1), 2 of Inclusive-Gateway type (2), and 8 of Normal Type (0). On the other hand, there are 20 process models among them 1 reference model and 19 variants (12 evolution variants and 7 request variants).

Table 1 exhibits the structural information of the reference model and its associated variants where P: Participants, A: Activities, G: Gateways, T: Transitions, EV: Evolution Variants, RV: Request Variants, and R: Rules.

The domain is composed of concepts and contextual tags. Concepts are the following: Committee, faculty, academic institution, self-assessment, awareness, weighting, information sources, improvement plans, high quality accreditation, tracking. On the other hand, Contextual tags are the following: Place (institution), location (awareness), person (weighting), location (surveys).

Figure 3 deploys the Reference Model of "Academic Self-Assessment".

5.2 Context Model Development Based on Stages

The context model is initially defined in terms of situations and restrictions, then the process integration objective is presented and finally the variant search and retrieval which are based on similarity criteria.

• **Stage 1 - Conceptualization of Variants.** From the previously modeled contextual ontology emerges 12 variants by evolution and 7 variants by request. Variants

Table 1. Structural information of the reference model

Code	P	A	G	T	R	EV	RV
RM01	3	12	0	11	12	12	7

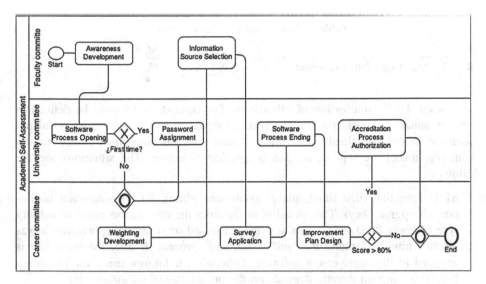

Fig. 3. Reference model of "Academic Self-Assessment"

by evolution only have events dealing with addition of activities. On the other hand, variants by request have both events corresponding to addition and elimination of activities.

Events refer to the action carried out on the process model structure, which did consider the generation of a variant. Adding events include activities and participants of the process. On the other hand, elimination events consider activities and transitions.

Table 2 gathers all the information of the variants.

• **Stages 2 and 3 - Identification of Contextual Elements and Definition of Constraints.** The following contextual elements are identified in the case study:

– eCtx1(place, institution), where the "place" is the contextual entity and "institution" is the contextual information.
– eCtx2(person, size), where the "person" is the contextual entity and "size" is the contextual information.

Constraints. From contextual properties following constraints are identified:

– R1: If eCtx1 (institution) == departmental => update (key). This constraint classifies as organizational type. It refers to whether the institution allows to "departmental" order the input key into the management system is automatically assigned each semester.
– R2: If eCtx2 (size) < 5 => activity (participant, teacher). Although the origin of the information is organizational, this constraint has a structural nature, since it directly affects the structure while adding a new participant to the process.

Table 2. Variants defined

Evolution	Request	Adding events	Elimination events
12	7	3	12

Table 3. Search and retrieval of variants

RM	V	NCF	CF
RM02 – "Academic Self-Assessment"	19	15	12

• **Stage 4 - Formalization of Situations.** The context model must be defined in terms of situations considering their contextual elements. In the case study considered situations are only identified for the MR2 – "Academic self-assessment", since starting from this model we will define the integration objective. The situations are the following:

- S1 (Elimination (first time), place, institution (place), R1: departmental institution => upgrade key). This situation arises from the elimination event of activity type Gateway "first time". This activity is focused on determining whether it was the first time performing the "self-assessment" process. If true, the input key is assigned to the management software. Otherwise, it follows using the preceding key. This situation directly depends on the organizational constraint "R1".
- S2 (addition (make tracking), person, size (person), R: Committee members < 5 - => do not track). This situation arises from the adding event of the activity 'Track' in charge of the Programme Committee and thus depends on the operational constraint "R2".

• **Stage 5 – Reasoning and Retrieval.** At first, the integration goal is defined, and then, the variant search and retrieval are performed by applying similarity criteria.

Integration Objetive. It is described in terms of the reference model structure to be affected and therefore it considers associated variants. For the case study an activity called "generate follow-up report" is attempted to be added in charge of the Programme Committee. However, it is expected that contextual model notifies that such an activity can be added, but only taking into consideration the contextual situation, related to the number of members of the Programme Committee.

Search and Retrieval of Variants. From similarity techniques and inference mechanisms those variants concerning the integration objective —that will not be affected by the change propagation— are retrieved. The retrieval process applies three types of similarity known as structural, semantic, and performance thus obtaining following results gathered in Table 3, where RM: Reference Model, V:Variants, NCF: No contextual filter, and CF: Contextual Filter.

From 19 variants of the reference model, 15 variants were retrieved accomplishing the minimum similarity degree. However, once the contextual filter was applied, 12 variants were finally obtained.

6 Conclusions and Future Work

The instance representation of reference models using both evaluation variants and variants-by-request allows determining whether generated changes are specific to the execution domain or even if they are related to the context.

The main issue of defining a context model for business process integration is to allow linking external and independent variables of the domain affecting the process performance once a change propagation has been performed starting from a reference model to its variants.

From the definition of a situation-based context model by using operational and organizational constraints the process of variant recovery is improved since contextual filtering prevents spreading unnecessary changes. However, the model presents some weaknesses that will be addressed in following issues as future work.

- Design a functional prototype that allows the interactive and automatic representation of the integration objective and process variants.
- Perform a comparative study of similarity metrics in order to select those appropriate for handling the context.
- Formalize and integrate evaluation criteria of similarity metrics to the functional prototype in order to determine minimum and maximum ranges that facilitate the evaluation among processes.

Acknowledgments. The research work presented in this paper was partially funded by the project entitled: "Método de integración inteligente de procesos de negocio sensible y adaptado al contexto" from the Universidad Nacional de Colombia through Postgraduate Supporting Program 2014 offered to Jorge Giraldo with code Quipu 200000013723.

References

1. Dumas, M., La Rosa, M., Mendling, J., Reijers, H.A.: Fundamentals of Business Process Management. Springer, Berlin (2013)
2. Zhiqiang, Y., Remco, M., Dijkman, M.: Business process model repositories - framework and survey. Inf. Softw. Technol. **54**(4), 380–395 (2012)
3. Li, C., Reichert, M., Wombacher, A.: Discovering reference models by mining process variants using a heuristic approach. In: Dayal, U., Eder, J., Koehler, J., Reijers, H.A. (eds.) BPM 2009. LNCS, vol. 5701, pp. 344–362. Springer, Heidelberg (2009)
4. Döhring, M., Reijers, H., Smirnov, S.: Configuration vs. adaptation for business process variant maintenance: an empirical study. Inform. Syst. **39**, 108–133 (2014)
5. Lohrmann, M., Reichert, M.: Modeling business objectives for business process management. In: Stary, C. (ed.) S-BPM ONE 2012. LNBIP, vol. 104, pp. 106–126. Springer, Heidelberg (2012)
6. Kumar, A., Yao, W.: Design and management of flexible process variants using templates and rules. Comput. Ind. **63**(2), 112–130 (2012)
7. Ploesser, K., Peleg, M., Soffer, P., Rosemann, M., Recker, J.: Learning from Context to Improve Business Processes. BPTrends (2009)

8. Li, C., Reichert, M., Wombacher, A.: Mining business process variants: challenges, scenarios, algorithms. Data Knowl. Eng. **70**(5), 409–434 (2011). ISSN: 0169-023X
9. Gerth, C., Küster, J.M., Engels, G.: Language-independent change management of process models. In: Schürr, A., Selic, B. (eds.) MODELS 2009. LNCS, vol. 5795, pp. 152–166. Springer, Heidelberg (2009)
10. Jason, J.: Semantic business process integration based on ontology alignment. Expert Syst. Appl. **36**(8), 11013–11020 (2009)
11. Weidlich, M., Mendling, J., Weske, M.: Propagating changes between aligned process models. J. Syst. Softw. **85**(8), 1885–1898 (2012). ISSN: 0164-1212
12. Weber, B., Reichert, M., Rinderle-Ma, S.: Change patterns and change support features – enhancing flexibility in process-aware information systems. Data Knowl. Eng. **66**(3), 438–466 (2008)
13. Becker, M., Laue, R.: A comparative survey of business process similarity measures. Comput. Ind. **63**(2), 148–167 (2012). ISSN: 0166-3615
14. La Rosa, M., Dumas, M., Uba, R., Dijkman, R.: Business process model merging: an approach to business process consolidation. ACM Trans. Softw. Eng. Meth. - TOSEM (2012)
15. Ruopeng, L., Shazia, S., Governatori, G.: On managing business processes variants. Data Knowl. Eng. **68**(7), 642–664 (2009). ISSN: 0169-023X
16. Ploesser, K., Peleg, M., Soffer, P., Rosemann, M., Recker, J.: Learning from Context to Improve Business Processes. BPTrends, January 2009
17. Saidani, O., Nurcan, S.: Context-awareness for adequate business process modelling. In: Proceedings of the Third IEEE International Conference on Research Challenges in Information Science, RCIS 2009, pp. 177–186 (2009). ISBN: 978-1-4244-2864-9
18. Bernal, J., Falcarin, P., Morisio, M.: Dynamic context-aware business process: a rule-based approach supported by pattern identification. In: Proceedings of the 2010 ACM Symposium on Applied Computing, Sierre, Switzerland, pp. 470–474, March 2010
19. Tavares, V., Lima, C., Santoro, F.: Dynamic process adaptation: a context-aware approach. In: Proceedings of the 15th International Conference on Computer Supported Cooperative Work in Design – CSCWD 2011 (2011)
20. Mattos, T., Santoro, F., Revoredo, K., Tavares, V.: Formalizing the situation of a business process activity. In Proceedings of CSCWD 2012, pp. 128–134 (2012)
21. Noy, N., McGuiness, D.: Ontology Development 101: A guide to creating tour first ontology (2001). http://www.ksl.stanford.edu/people/dlm/papers/ontology-tutorial-noy-mcguinness-abstract.html

Designing Enterprise System Information Architecture Using Task Data

Dawei Huang[(⋈)]

Microsoft Corporation, Redmond, WA, USA
whuang@microsoft.com

Abstract. Much of today's information architecture for enterprise tools is organized in a complex and feature oriented way – frustrating the users and requiring tons of learning to be efficient. We introduced a task taxonomy research project that studied a few hundred database users to understand their responsibilities, roles, and tasks. We created a task taxonomy model filled with large quantitative data on tasks. We found task hierarchy emerged from the model and it had a strong relationship with user roles – implying role-based workspace design principles. With the task hierarchy data, the degree of relevance of task hierarchy could be estimated and applied for enterprise information architecture designs.

Keywords: Task taxonomy · Information architecture · Enterprise · Database management tasks · Database users

1 Introduction

Much of today's information architecture (IA) for enterprise server tools was organized in a complex and feature oriented way. What the users were interacting with was arranged by features or objects, in a manner that was easy to make but hard to use. For years, customer feedback on our database management tools included features hard to find, too many tools with similar functions, tools not integrated, difficult to customize for different users, and unable to scale for managing thousands of servers.

In response, the 'Task Taxonomy' project was started in 2006. It was to present and codify a view of database users' entire task space and to discover user task patterns to inform enterprise IA designs. In the following years, data on user roles, responsibilities and tasks with task frequency, time on task, task difficulty and task importance measures were collected. The task data were analyzed and card-sorted into a rigorously defined Task Taxonomy Model, and loaded into an OLAP data cubes for further exploration.

2 Background: Task Taxonomy Project

After "Task Taxonomy" project was started, standardized data collection protocols and measures were formulated and used. Over 500 database users from 240 companies worldwide were interviewed with data collected on their roles, job responsibilities,

© Springer International Publishing Switzerland 2015
F.F.-H. Nah and C.-H. Tan (Eds.): HCIB 2015, LNCS 9191, pp. 469–480, 2015.
DOI: 10.1007/978-3-319-20895-4_43

tasks and pain points. For each task on which a user reported, measures on frequency with which the task was performed, average time that the task takes, and ratings of importance, complexity, and satisfaction (5-pt or 7-pt Likert scale) were collected during the interview. Example tasks and associated metrics are shown in Fig. 1.

1. Casemix_TSI ownership (Constantly being modified/added to - batch only DB, no real-time)

Task	Security
Description	HIPPA compliant - contains clinical data
Frequency	Once per day (4)
Time on Task	20 minutes
Importance	Very (5)
Satisfaction	Neutral (3)
	Person who created the original roles left the company and no one knew what anything meant - lack of knowledge transfer/documentation.

Task	Nightly/Daily update (batch process)
Description	Check to verify that they are running/automated. About 3 jobs.
Frequency	Once per day (4)
Time on Task	15 minutes (if problem, takes longer up to 6 hours)
Importance	Very (5)
Satisfaction	Satisfied (4)

Task	Recovery
Description	Doesn't happen often, but when it does it's critical
Frequency	Once per year (1)
Time on Task	Depends on complexity
Importance	Very (5)
Satisfaction	Satisfied (4)

Fig. 1. Example of a user reported responsibility and tasks

The task data collected from those 500 users was analyzed in two stages allowing us to derive fuller value. The first stage was to construct a rigorously defined Task Taxonomy model. The second was to use SQL Server's Analysis Services to place the data into OLAP cubes that could then be data-mined. As such, the project has gone through a few activities of taxonomy literature research, data cleansing and card sorting, and discussions with engineering program managers, architects and internal experts to refine the Task Taxonomy model, data cube creation and finally insight reporting.

3   Development of Task Taxonomy Model

A taxonomy is often simply defined as a "systematic classification of information" [1], which operates as experts' classification in industry practices. "Taxonomies can be defined as sets of rules and principles to ensure consistent classification of data and information into ordered categories, attempt to address the problem of information overload. A good taxonomy will bring order and cohesiveness to information portals, thereby speeding up relevant information retrieval and improving business efficiency"

[2]. "Taxonomies are the classification scheme used to categorize a set of information items. They represent an agreed vocabulary of topics arranged around a particular theme. ... we typically encounter hierarchical taxonomies such as in libraries, biology, or military organizations" [3] These definitions match well with the classification research found in library science [4].

In defining Task Taxonomy for this project, we combined those approaches as we relied on both experts' and users' knowledge to define the task hierarchy reflected in the database structure. We also set up rules and principles to ensure consistent classification of task information across various input sources.

3.1 Task Taxonomy Model

The database users' task taxonomy model composes of *task hierarchy, action-object map, and perspectives* (see Fig. 2). A user self-reported task is typically a node in the tree of the *task hierarchy* - a tree of different levels of tasks following a set of hierarchy rules [4]. A low level task can be mapped on to a database UI action-object map. Perspectives such as related technologies, features, job roles, and lifecycle processes are different angles of looking at (or associating with) certain parts of the task hierarchy.

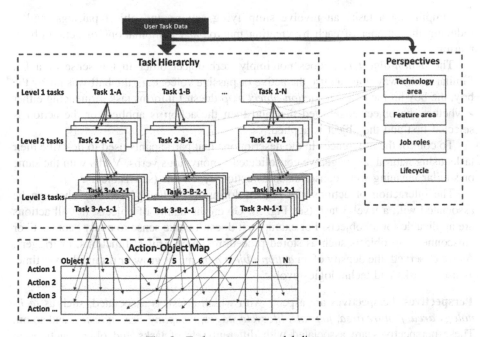

Fig. 2. Task taxonomy model diagram

Task Hierarchy. User's responsibility and task data were first categorized and mapped to a task hierarchy given a set of strong hierarchy rules [4]:

- *Inclusiveness*: The top class is the most inclusive class and describes the domain of the classification.
- *"Is A" relationship*: A sub-class task is a member of a top-class task.
- *Inheritance*: Attributes of top class tasks are inherited by the sub-class and sub-sub-class tasks.
- *Necessary and sufficient criteria*: To belong to a class, a task must have the necessary and sufficient attributes.

A few other strong hierarchy rules such as mutually exclusiveness were not followed in this model as many user tasks can fall under more than one category as database operational verbs were standardized to fewer common terms.

Action-Object Map. Each of the level 3 tasks in the task hierarchy can be mapped on to *an action-object map* to bridge user tasks to the set of operations entailed. It can be a one-to-one mapping or a one-to-many mapping if the task relates to more than one action or set of objects.

An atomic level of a user task can be expressed as:

$$If \text{ Action(s) X Object(s)} = \text{Operation,}$$

$$Then \text{ N (Operation)} = \text{A set or series of operations} = \text{Task}$$

Simplifying a task can involve simplifying actions and object pairings, and/or reducing the number of each by creating macros and combinations of action-object pairings.

The *action-object map* does not imply verb-object order in the sense of a UI. Similar to the way you can use the active or passive voice, e.g., the ball was hit by the boy, the boy hit the ball. The *action-object map* doesn't informs task sequencing either - whether the object is selected first and then the action is applied, or the action is selected first and the object is applied.

To control the differences in the descriptions that participants used to describe their tasks using natural language, we consolidated synonymous verbs. Verbs with the same or similar meaning were consolidated as action synonyms (see Table 1).

The interaction of actions and objects forms the *action-object map* that can be associated with a level-3 task (see Fig. 3). Given the nature of objects, not all actions are applicable for all objects. For example, it doesn't make sense to apply "connect" or "disconnect" to objects such as stored procedures, types, rules, functions, or triggers. As we observed, the density of an *action-object map* might grow or diminish over time, as users' tasks and technologies evolve.

Perspectives. Perspectives are aspects with which a task is associated, such as *technology area, feature area, job role, lifecycle stages, company size, industry*, and so on. These perspectives are associated with different sets of tasks and objects/actions at different levels, with different densities. For example, database administrator (DBA) is a *job role* perspective whose task space is associated primarily with database management tasks and database server objects. A developer role may be associated with database design, query, debugging, testing related tasks, actions and objects. Similarly,

Table 1. Example of consolidated actions

Action name	Action synonyms	Paired with
Browse	Drill down | Locate	Search/Browse
Copy	Replicate	
Create	Install | New | Design | Code	Create/Remove

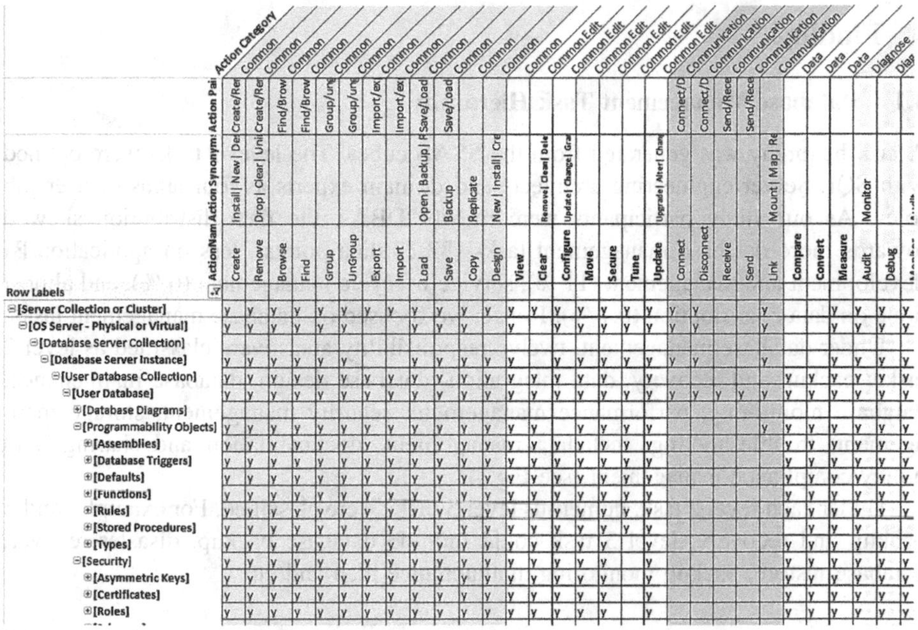

Fig. 3. A part of the Action-Object map

high availability is a *feature area* perspective and associates with database backup, recovery, monitoring, performance management, troubleshooting and other related tasks.

3.2 Task Taxonomy Data Cubes

The raw user task data were transformed into a set of standardized scales. For inconsistent rating scales used by different researchers in earlier data collections, 7-point Likert scale was used. The frequency data were converted to the number of occurrence for a year. Time on task were converted to hours. The raw data were then mapped onto the *task taxonomy* model through assigning each data record to the task hierarchy (if there is no existing record, a new level 1/2/3 task is created based on the hierarchy rule). Then the level 3 task data was mapped to the *action-object map*. In the meantime, the record was also tagged with perspectives. E.g., database backup was tagged with DBA role, Windows Server platform, high availability feature area etc.

After the mapping and tagging were complete, the entire database tables were loaded to SQL Server Analysis Services (SSAS) cubes. Task hierarchy, action-object map, and perspective data were defined as dimensions. The task measures such as ratings of importance, complexity, task frequency, and time on task were defined as measures. The SSAS would then enable us to create pivot tables in MS-Excel to explore the relationship among task measures and task dimensions.

4 Findings

4.1 Database Management Task Hierarchy

A task hierarchy was generated from the SSAS cubes. The level 1 tasks were defined with SQL Server engineering architects and domain experts as four areas of user job roles. As our study participants were mostly DBAs, the data distribution skewed towards more database management tasks (83 % data points), less on application/BI development and management (11 %), service lifecycle management (6 %), and almost none on data consumption (0.1 %). Hence, we focused on database management tasks.

Under database management, twelve responsibility areas were classified as level 2 tasks: backup and recovery, data integration, database design, database maintenance, database monitoring, performance management, security management, storage management, troubleshooting, metadata management, documentation and sharing, and policy/compliance management (see Fig. 4).

Under each level 2 task, numerous level 3 tasks were classified. For example, under backup and recovery, level 3 task could include database backup, disaster recover, database restore, backup monitoring, maintenance plan and etc.

Level 1: Database Management
  Level 2:
  - Backup, Recovery, High Availability
    Level 3:
    o Database backup
    o Disaster recovery
    o ...
  - Data Integration/DTS
  - Database Design
  - Documentation & sharing
  - Maintenance
  - Metadata Management
  - Monitoring
  - Performance Management
  - Policy/Compliance Management
  - Security Management
  - Storage Management
  - Troubleshooting

Fig. 4. Example of database management task hierarchy

4.2   Task Hierarchy and Roles

Our early user interviews found that database user roles are heavily overlapped in small businesses with a common notion of "I wear multiple hats – I do it all". In large and enterprise companies, user roles become more distinct, and they are created to meet the business workload needs. Research shows that in even in these environments, however, roles expand and change, overlap, get delegated across individuals, and differ greatly from company to company. This has implications for the way we construct our UIs, information architectures, roles and permissions, and delegation models.

Role Differentiation: Fig. 5 shows the responsibility areas that are covered by different roles. "DBA" as a general database role covers almost the entire responsibilities area. However, the general DBA role could split into multiple roles such as Application DBA, System DBA, Data Warehouse DBA, BI DBA in larger firms. The splitting of a big DBA role implies the shift of responsibility focuses - from covering the broad area of responsibilities to focusing on a smaller set of specialized responsibilities. For instance, System DBAs are responsible for troubleshooting, database deployment, and monitoring and maintenance tasks at the Operating System level. Many BI or Data Warehouse DBAs roles are generated (mostly from senior DBAs) in companies where large BI systems are deployed.

Role Stratification: DBAs at different tiers working at different tactical-strategic levels are common in many enterprise companies, especially in companies which have outsourced their tier-1 support. Indirectly, Fig. 5 provides comparative information on role-responsibility mapping among DBAs, DBA managers, and DATABASE Archi-

Responsibilities	DBA	DB Architect	DBA Manager	Developer or Programmer	DB Developer or Programmer	IT Pro	System Architect	DBA Application	Dev Manager	Program Manager	System Manager	Syst
Database Management												
Database Design	●	●	●	●	●	●	●	●	●	●	●	
Performance Management	●	●	●	●	●		●					
Backup, Recovery, High Availability	△		●			●		●				
Data Integration/DTS	●	●	●	●	●		●	●			●	●
Monitoring	●		●	●	●		●					
Maintenance	●		●		●				●		●	
Security Management	●							●				
Troubleshooting	●		●			●					●	
Storage Management	●		●	●			●					
Documentation & sharing	●		●	●	●							
Matadata Management	●											
Policy/Compliance Management	●				●							

Fig. 5. The coverage of responsibilities and tasks by database user roles

tects. As DBAs move up the ladder from senior DBA to DBA Managers, and to DBA Architects, their responsibilities shift from working at the tactical level to strategic planning, design, performance, and data quality and data integration related responsibilities.

4.3   Task Hierarchy and Degree of Relevance

The data cubes provides relevant measures on task hierarchy and perspectives from the task measures collected. The aggregated importance rating and frequency provided a good estimate of how relevant of a lower level task to its higher level task and to a particular perspective such as a job role (see Table 2). For example, under level 2 - performance management, relevant tasks include performance monitoring, performance tuning, profiler tracing, and troubleshooting. This could be further traced down to the action-object level. Relevant objects include performance data, performance plans, queries, stored procedures, user databases, and server instances. Relevant actions include tune, monitor, trace, debug, and check or review (see Table 3).

5   Implications and Applications

5.1   Information Architecture Design Constructs

The task taxonomy model has provided instruments for defining database enterprise system IA. The task hierarchy and its interaction with different perspectives such as job roles reflects the ways how the users structure, slice and dice their work towards achieving different goals. Level 1 tasks represent different job roles and therefore correspond to different tools or applications that are designed for those roles. Level 2 tasks of responsibilities represent the clustering of users' common goals in dealing with the same set of objects in the same context. They are the workspaces inside the tool for a particular user role. The responsibilities are similar to the user goals described in Goal-Directed Design by Cooper et al. [5].

Design Role-Based Workspace as Distinct Interface for Best Fulfilling Responsibilities. In UI design, a responsibility can be supported through a common workspace. For example, database design is a major responsibility for DBAs, DB Architects, and DB Developers. Database objects include servers, databases, tables, and foreign relationships. A database design workspace serves a common goal to monitor, create, and update all those objects. However, roles with the same responsibility may have different focuses. The workspace should be optimized for different tasks for each role. Of course, different roles may have different set of workspaces.

Optimize for Personalized Views to Support Role Differentiation. For database design tasks, DB architects care more about logical designs but DBAs care about how to implement it. DB architects are required of a deep understanding of business requirements, technology, and resources to create an appropriate logical design. In contrast, DBAs may care more about the physical implementation. Therefore, DB Architects and DBAs need different focal views when dealing with different forms of database design.

Table 2. Examples of tasks and task measures for degree of relevance

Task hierarchy	Importance	Frequency	Time on task	Satisfaction
Level 1 - Database Management	6.30	3.79	6.96	4.73
Level 2 - Policy/Compliance Management	7.00	5.00	2.00	1.00
Level 2 - Backup, Recovery, High Availability	6.83	3.76	7.48	5.39
Level 3 - Monitoring Backups	7.00	4.80	1.67	6.00
Level 3 - Test Or Check Backup	7.00	4.67	4.00	5.50
Level 3 - Review Backup/Recovery	7.00	3.50	2.25	3.25
Level 3 - Test Failover	7.00	3.00	3.00	7.00
Level 3 - Test Recoverability	7.00	3.00	3.00	3.63
Level 3 - Database Recovery	7.00	2.50	3.17	5.50
Level 3 - Log Shipping	7.00	2.00	6.00	5.50
Level 3 - Database Restore	6.86	3.55	2.17	5.00
Level 3 - Database Backup	6.84	4.35	1.80	5.45
Level 3 - Setup Backup/Maintenance Plan	6.83	2.78	28.56	6.00
Level 3 - Disaster Recovery	6.67	3.67	15.50	6.50
Level 3 - HA Maintenance	6.63	1.00	80.00	4.00
Level 3 - Maintain Backup Restore	4.00	4.00	0.17	5.50
Level 2 - Monitoring	6.65	4.23	2.38	4.81
Level 2 - Security Management	6.58	3.53	1.15	3.86
Level 2 - Maintenance	6.57	4.74	1.88	5.44
Level 2 - Data Integration	6.45	3.65	6.05	4.36
Level 2 - Database Design	6.37	3.82	11.13	4.70
Level 2 - Documentation & Sharing	6.20	3.33	6.59	3.68
Level 2 - Performance Management	5.92	3.69	5.48	4.78
Level 2 - Troubleshooting	5.40	3.82	2.64	4.26

Provide Relevant Task and Actions in the Context. In database administration, team communication, project versioning, documentation, guidelines, script library, and templates are critical for the job. These should be designed in the context of the corresponding workspace and tasks.

Balance the Focal Views and Context Using Relevance Measures. The task measures provide comparative weights for any workspace, tasks, and UI objects and actions. In performance monitoring workspace, database availability and response latency are the primary goals. They should be designed as the focal view whereas performance guidelines should be minimized in its context.

Table 3. Example of relevant tasks, objects and actions under L1 database management

L2 Responsibility	L3 Relevant tasks	Relevant objects	Relevant actions
Performance management	Performance monitoring	Performance data	Tune
	Performance tuning	Performance plan	Monitor
	Profiler tracing	Stored Procedure or query	Trace
	Troubleshooting	Server instance	Debug or troubleshoot
	Tuning codes	User databases	Check or review
	Maintain performance	Database server	Create
	Performance	Views	Design
	assessment	Indexes	Maintain
	Query performance	Programmability	Find
	File management	objects	Test
		Tables	Upgrade
		Design, models	Measure
			Run
			View

5.2 An Extended Framework to Goal-Directed Design

Goal-Directed Design [5] has a simple premise: "If we design and construct products in such a way that the people who use them achieve their goals, these people will be satisfied, effective, and happy and will gladly pay …, translate into business success" (page 3). It differentiates goals from tasks or activities that "a goal is an expectation of an end condition, whereas both activities and tasks are intermediate steps…" and goals are "driven by human motivation, they change very slowly … over time" (page 15). Goal-Directed Design draws a direct line between a user's initial state and the end state of the objectives he or she wants to achieve, eliminating the noise from other aspects such as activities, tasks, technologies, or solutions.

When come to IA design, the task taxonomy model leads us to focus on user goals using quantitative data – inducing user goals through the task hierarchy, action-object map, with relevance measures, and placing the user goals in the multi-user, multi-group, multi-purpose, and collaborative context. As shown in Fig. 6, the level 2 responsibilities in the task hierarchy represent clusters of users' common goals and should be designed as workspaces in the UI. The level 3 tasks represent the individual's long term goals within that responsibility. Therefore, when a large amount of user task data were collected and degree of relevance of each task were calculated, the workspaces could be organized and personalized as high level navigation nodes for each user role to better fulfill that responsibility. Within that workspace, the focal views could be designed as the evolving user needs for the most important and frequent tasks. Many supportive tasks would be designed as its context.

Fig. 6. Extended Framework of applying task taxonomy model in IA design

5.3   Design Illustration

To illustrate the idea, Fig. 7 shows the use of the task data to design a database management IA. For a DBA role such as a production DBA, the enterprise database management tool is customized with fewer workspaces that are optimized for his/her job. Within the Backup and Recovery workspace, a navigation structure with focal views and personalized views provides a quick access to the important backup jobs, backups and schedules. In the context, tasks/scripts, disaster recovery solutions, and others are designed as context views – context sensitive to the active focal view. Switching over to the performance workspace, he/she may see performance monitoring meters, gauges, alerts and recommended actions with backup and recovery tasks in its context.

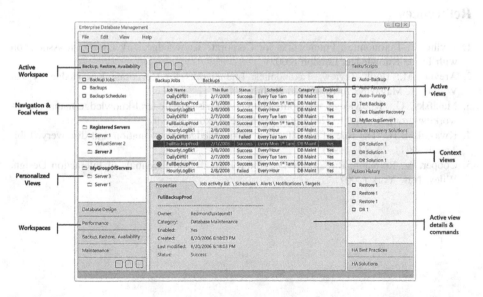

Fig. 7. Illustration of applying task taxonomy model and data to enterprise database management tool design. Note: the design was only an illustration of the extended task taxonomy design framework. It was not designed for any potential or future Microsoft products.

6 Summary

From features-driven to Goals-Directed design, from easy-to-make to easy-to-use, the shift into a user centered design culture is critical to user satisfaction, customer loyalty and product success. Such a shift requires a re-thinking of our product design and development processes, attention to the overall user experience, and the dedication to a comprehensive understanding of user's responsibilities, tasks and organizational context, as well as their personality and emotion aspects if possible.

In this project, the task taxonomy model and task data provide clear underpinnings for planning and designing an enterprise IA, and for sorting out the complex relationships among individual and team goals and responsibilities. It is an extension and quantification of Goal-Directed Design. Placing users in a goal-structured workspace can reduce the costs and shorten the time required for training during role shifts and transitions, and drive team collaboration. Our recent dashboard and role-based designs on enterprise management tools have shown greater usability and higher customer satisfaction – partially attributing to this project.

Acknowledgements. I'd like thank Dave Campbell, Dave Nettleton and Shawn Bice for project sponsorship, Mark Stempski, George Engelbeck, Candace Soderston, Lisa Mueller, Aimee Freeding, Nate Gunderson and Buck Woody for data collection and model discussions.

References

1. Wyllie, J.: Taxonomies: Frameworks for Corporate Knowledge. Ark Group, in association with Inside Knowledge, London (2003)
2. Arevuo, M.: Book Review: Taxonomies: Frameworks for Corporate Knowledge by Jan Wyllie. IK Magazine **7**(10), Posted 20 July 2004
3. Malafsky, G.: Knowledge taxonomy. http://wiki.nasa.gov/federal-knowledge-management-working-group-kmwg/files/2013/06/Knowledge_Taxonomy.pdf
4. Kwasnik, B.H.: The role of classification in knowledge representation and discovery. Libr. Trends **48**(1), 22–47 (1999)
5. Cooper, A., Reimann, R., Cronin, D.: About Face 3: The Essentials of Interaction Design. Wiley, New York (2007)

Kindle: How Gamification Can Motivate Jobseekers

Bart van der Kruys and Vassilis Javed Khan[✉]

Academy for Digital Entertainment, NHTV Breda University of Applied Sciences,
Breda, The Netherlands
Bartvanderkruys@gmail.com, khan.j@nhtv.nl

Abstract. Prolonged unemployment can lead to depression and a loss of self-esteem. Gamification is a strategy that engages and motivates groups of people by implementing game mechanics and dynamics in an existing non-gaming system. This paper studies the possibility of using gamification to motivate job seekers. To test the effectiveness of the ideas proposed in this paper, a between-subjects study was executed. Those results, although preliminary, do suggest the potential of including gamification features in job seeking systems.

Keywords: Gamification in business · Jobseekers · Unemployment

1 Unemployment in the Netherlands and Globally

Data from the Dutch institute for statistics state that in March 2014 there are a total of 691 thousand unemployed people in the Netherlands, which is 8.8 % of the Dutch labor force (CBS, 2014). This is the highest number of jobseekers in the Netherlands that was ever measured.

The high rate of unemployment does not only occur in the Netherlands, it is global. In fact, compared to other European countries, unemployment rate in the Netherlands is relatively low. In other countries it ranges from 6 % or below (Germany, Austria, and Luxembourg) to well above 17 % (Portugal, Spain, Greece) (Friedman, 2013). This data makes it evident that Europe is clearly struggling to recover from the economic crisis of 2008. The high unemployment rates and debts of some European countries have and will have effect on the recovery of other European countries due to the fact that all European countries financially depend on each other because of trade.

Nevertheless it is not just Europe struggling to recover from the global financial crisis. Estimates of the International Labour Organization (ILO) state that global unemployment increased by 5 million people in 2013 and that if it continues to follow this trend it will rise by a further 13 million people by 2018 reaching more than 215 million jobseekers (ILO, 2014). The areas with the largest slowdown of economic recovery are southern and eastern Europe, Latin America and South-East Asia. A lot of those people are young in age and have just entered the job market.

© Springer International Publishing Switzerland 2015
F.F.-H. Nah and C.-H. Tan (Eds.): HCIB 2015, LNCS 9191, pp. 481–492, 2015.
DOI: 10.1007/978-3-319-20895-4_44

1.1   The Causes

The World Economic Forum lists the causes of youth unemployment as: population growth, education that is often not adequately matched to what is needed on the job marked, discouraged youth, lack of national comprehensive policy framework and deficiencies of labor market institution and policies (World Economic Forum, 2013).

The cause that is particularly motivating our research is the discouraged youth. The ILO reports that in 2012 there were 75 million youth worldwide that were out of work and that an additional 6 million have given up looking for a job completely (International Labour Organization, 2014). In addition to the youth there are other demographic categories affected by discouragement. Older generations that have lost jobs also have trouble staying motivated to find a job. Reuters (Mukitani, 2013) quotes assistant professor of economics Peter McHenry: *"People are just giving up the search for work. A lot of them would like to work and they aren't, that is a serious sickness in the economy"*.

2   Integrating Jobseekers

This section will analyze the situation of the jobseeker. We first analyze the psychological effects of job loss and how they affect the motivation to actively look for a job. After we present some solutions that can help motivate the search for a job.

2.1   Job Loss

To understand why people are giving up searching for a job after losing a job, one needs to breakdown the effects of job loss. Job loss can be defined as an event where employment is involuntarily taken away from an individual. Job loss can have many negative psychological effects on people. De Witte (1993) describes that job loss causes activities to feel pointless, social contact to suffer, day-to-day life to be disrupted and deterioration of self-esteem and confidence can occur. After long-term unemployment, these symptoms may lead to depression.

These symptoms make it emotionally even harder for unemployed people to find a new job. Missing the structure of day-to-day life and missing the daily work commitment and time spent at the workplace causes the unemployed person to feel bored and unfulfilled.

More specifically, job loss can be broken down into seven emotional stages (Straits, 2014): denial, disbelief, outward anger, inward self-criticism, withdrawal, reflection, and acceptance. After denying, disbelieving and the blaming of third parties, a person who has just lost a job comes into stage four, inward self-criticism. At this point, confidence and self-esteem wane by overthinking past events and blaming the self. The next stage is withdrawal. After losing self-esteem and confidence, the person will hide and find excuses to avoid contact in the external world, which may (if the person does not receive enough social support) lead to depression.

2.2 Motivation

People are goal oriented. Everything we do is with an end goal in mind. We either perform activities because we enjoy the activity itself, or we perform activities for the reward it brings. As Deci and Ryan (2000, p. 60) describes "*Extrinsic motivation is a construct that pertains whenever an activity is done in order to attain some separable outcome. Extrinsic motivation thus contrasts with intrinsic motivation, which refers to doing an activity simply for the enjoyment of the activity itself, rather than its instrumental value*". When reading this description of extrinsic and intrinsic motivation one might think that for most people, job seeking is driven by extrinsic motivation. The act of looking for a job is generally not seen as a fun activity but rather the means for having a job. However, intrinsic motivation can be stimulated by making the activity in itself fun.

A common method for people to be intrinsically motivated is to approach a mundane activity not as work but as play. The classic example of this concept is demonstrated in Mark Twain's novel The Adventures of Tom Sawyer. In the book, Tom is asked to whitewash a fence (Twain 1876). When one of his friends shows up and teases Tom for doing a mundane activity, Tom tells his friend that he enjoys doing it – "*Like it? Well I don't see why I oughtn't to like it. Does a boy get a chance to whitewash a fence every day?*" (Twain 1876, p. 14). Tom's friend is convinced and asks if he can partake in the activity.

2.3 Setting Goals

A combination of short term and long term goals can have a significant effect on the motivation of job seekers. De Witte (1993) states that when setting a goal, the motivation for achieving that goal is determined by the confidence in achieving that goal. However, rarely, the motivation for achieving a goal is only determined by the close deadline. De Witte gives as example that studying for an exam is seldom motivating in itself, the possibilities that are opened for completing the exam are often motivation for completing it. It is known that people are not easily motivated for goals that are far off. Having a set of short term sub goals can help make a related long term goal more attractive if all sub goals lead to the realization of the long term goal. The short term sub goals serve as a bridge towards the long term goal. Job seekers need to create a plan that is filled with short term sub goals that help them focus on short term objectives. Next to the job seekers' benefit of having short term objectives, having a reachable array of sub goals can also improve their confidence towards the long term goal making it more motivating. An important reason for the success of having sub goals is that the job seeker has the possibility to receive feedback. De Witte (1993) suggests that feedback can keep job seekers focused on their goals, and gives them clarity over the correctness of the path they are taking "*Giving autonomy and informative feedback plays a key role in the development of intrinsic motivation, especially to people with self-development needs*". (De Witte, 1993, p. 7).

2.4 Social Support

Succeeding to make progress stimulates motivation, setbacks and failing to make progress can significantly lessen motivation. Studies have proven that providing social support to during these setbacks has a positive effect on the motivation to engage in job-seeking and the job-seeking self-efficacy. A rigorous experiment in 1989 split 928 recently unemployed adults randomly into an experimental group and a control group (Caplan et al. 1989). The experimental group were assigned trainers that supported the members with practical advice on job seeking as well as positive social reinforcement. The results were that the experimental group yielded higher quality reemployment in terms of earnings and job satisfaction, and higher motivation among those who were still unemployment.

3   Gamification

"Gamification is an informal umbrella term for the use of video game elements in non-gaming systems to improve user experience (UX) and user engagement." (Deterding, Dixon, Khaled, and Nacke 2011, p. 1) Gamification is a new strategy that can engage and motivate groups of people by implementing game mechanics and dynamics in an existing non-gaming system. Gamification is used to gain customer loyalty, educate children and adults alike, it is even used to motivate in doing everyday tasks. A successful gamification system is for example the iOS app called EpicWin created by Rexbox and Supermono that motivates people to do daily activities by turning them into quests in a simulated adventure. Another example of a different gamification system is Badgeville, a system that motivates team members in large companies to cooperate by giving rewards and short term objectives.

3.1 Mechanics of Gamification

Two common terms in gamification are game mechanics and game dynamics. Game mechanics are the elements that game designers put in place to engage gamers, while game dynamics represent the fundamental needs and desires that are satisfied by the game mechanics. Bunchball (2010) presents six of the most prominent game mechanics that are used in gamification: *points and levels, challenges, virtual goods, leader boards, and gifts and charities*. There are many variations of these mechanics, but all of them can be generalized to six core mechanics.

Points quantify the users' progress and quality of their engagement. People naturally enjoy collecting, and this makes distributing points for activities a very effective mechanic. Levels serve as milestones for the progress of the user. It is motivating to see your own progress and levels serve as an extra motivational boost by highlighting a certain milestone.

Challenges give the user a clear goal to strive for. As discussed in chapter 2.3, setting clear and attractive objectives can have a good effect on motivation. These objectives can also be used as an opportunity to entice the user to explore different parts of the system.

Virtual goods are non-physical objects that have value in the game world. They can be anything from badges and decorations to virtual clothing and accessories that are bought with the currency of the system or rewards for completing certain objectives in the system. Often virtual goods can be gifted to other users in the system.

Leader boards quantify the results of the competitions between users. It gives users a chance to compare themselves to other users in the system. This can also have positive and negative effects. Competitive participants can gain self-esteem by climbing the leader boards and set goals for them to improve. Non-competitive participants can become demotivated when they see that they are on a low position in the leader board. Some participants may not want to compete but just improve themselves; these are all valid reasons to never force participants to be placed on the leader boards unless the goal of the system is improve competition in users.

People can have a lot of different goals when *gifting* to others. They might want to gain a friend, win prestige or respect or simply want to feel better by enhancing their self-esteem by giving to others. Participants can use gifts in gamification systems to improve their relationships with other participants.

3.2   Dynamics of Gamification and Gamer Types

The reason that people are motivated by the game mechanics is because of the game dynamics. Bunchball (2010, p. 10) links the game dynamics to human desires – *"People have fundamental needs and desires. Game designers have known for years how to address these needs within gaming environments, and gamification now enables these precepts to be applied more broadly"*.

Figure 1 displays a table that links the game mechanics to game dynamics (named "human desires" in the image). Each game mechanic has a set of linked human desires represented by the blue dots, and one perfect match represented by a green dot. Not all people have the same personality and the same desires and this affects which is their most pursued game dynamic. The psychologist Richard Bartle proposed that players of video games can be divided into four different personality types; *Killers, Achievers, Socialites and Explorers* (Bartle. 1996) One can tell the personality type of gamers by analyzing what games they play and how they play them. *Killers* enjoy competition and like to compare themselves to other players and are mostly motivated by competition and challenges. *Achievers* are completionists at heart that enjoy collecting. This type of gamers will be most interested in the game mechanics that grant them status and achievement. *Socialites* like to co-operate and make friends. This type of gamers will be most attracted to engage in mechanics that grant them satisfaction in self-expression and altruism. *Explorers* are the free spirits that want to experience new things all the time. In traditional open world games, explorers would want to explore the environment, in gamification systems they would want to explore and experiment with all of the mechanics.

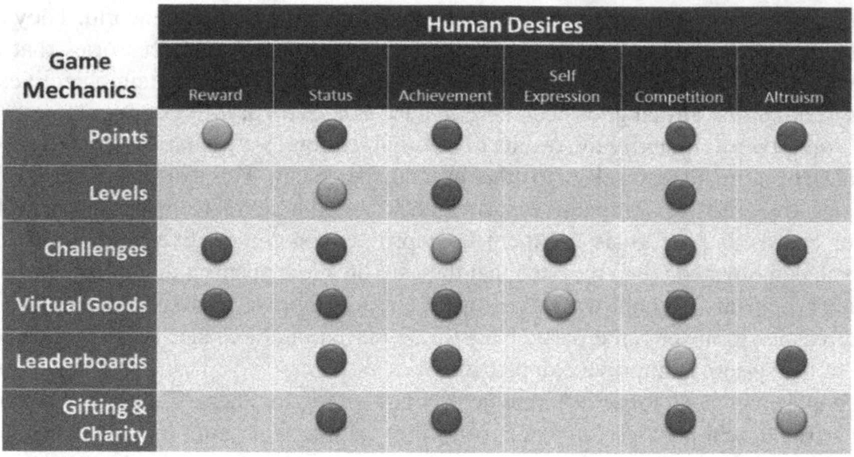

Game Mechanics	Human Desires					
	Reward	Status	Achievement	Self Expression	Competition	Altruism
Points	●	●	●		●	●
Levels		●	●		●	
Challenges	●	●	●	●	●	●
Virtual Goods	●	●	●	●	●	
Leaderboards		●	●		●	●
Gifting & Charity		●	●		●	●

Fig. 1. Human desires linked to game mechanics (Bunchball, 2010)

4 Gamification for Work Reintegration

To find an aspect that can be gamified, one needs to seek something that all jobseekers can identify with. An artifact that is common among all jobseekers is the CV. A CV is a testament of the professional progress that a person has gone through and is necessary for all people that want to find a job. The CV shall be used as the starting or main foundational focal point for the proposed gamification platform.

A CV can already be linked to three human desires presented in Fig. 1: status, achievement and self-expression. The system-concept we present in this paper is focused in improving the quality of the participant's resume. The CV is only the subject for entry into the system. After accessing the system, the user will enter into a community with fellow job seekers. The system is designed to motivate and guide the user into integrating or reintegrating into working life. There are many services that provide jobseekers help with improving the quality of their CVs, but many of them cost money and make the resume fall into a pre-defined template. Thus, the concept we present in this paper can be an alternative business model to the existing ones.

4.1 Core User Requirement of the System and System Description

The requirements of this system are in line with the desires of job seekers. Our system needs to create a daily structure and clear goals and sub goals for the job seeker. The system should also encourage and facilitate social contact and motivate the user to make new connections. The system should also make the activities of the jobseeker seem more meaningful and attractive.

The proposed gamification system is an online platform that encourages and facilitates (i) improving resume of job seekers and (ii) motivating them in the search for a job. In the system, users are rewarded credits to give feedback on the resumes of others.

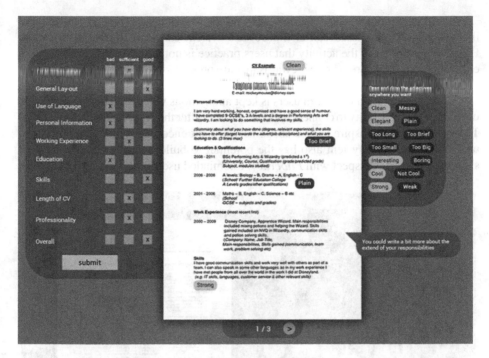

Fig. 2. A mock-up screen of the proposed system displaying the review system which is used to give feedback on the CVs of others.

They can then request feedback on their resume from other users by spending credits earned in the game. Users can also spend earned credits in "purchasing" other rewards like training courses, job magazines, etc. (Fig. 2).

Economy and Virtual Goods. The system features three different currencies that have different uses and different ways of obtaining them. *Activity points* represent the experience of the player and are gained with everything the player does in the system. They are mainly meant to give the user a sense of progression and a means for comparison with other users. *Reward points* represent the quality of the user's feedback. When a user has a lot of reward points it indicates to other players that his/her feedback is often appreciated. *Credits* are granted to the user when the user earns reward points. Users can use credits to request feedback from other players on their own CV or to purchase real life and virtual goods.

The user progresses through the game by earning activity points and reward points. By progressing through ranks, the user unlocks more features in the game. The reasoning behind this is to ease the player into the more advanced features like the standard pass feedback. A sense of progression will make the user feel more competent.

The goal of the challenge system is to provide the user with concrete short term objectives. These objectives can introduce users to unexplored parts of the system and motivate users to increase their effort. Completing an objective can give the player a boost in confidence and a sense of competence.

As aforementioned, users can use credit points to purchase virtual goods and real life rewards. As discussed earlier this reward system can lead to over-justification. However, in this case, the activity that users practice is not widely considered to be an enjoyable activity. Moreover, the rewards that are presented in the system are all means to achieve the same goal as the system motivates the users for.

Although interaction between users is kept anonymous when transferring feedback, users have the possibility to connect with one another after the completion of the transfer. The system does not aspire to be a social network but encourages interaction between users. However, this system also has the potential to build a strong community as it shares one important aspect with *Fitocracy*; likeminded users with same goals (Fig. 3).

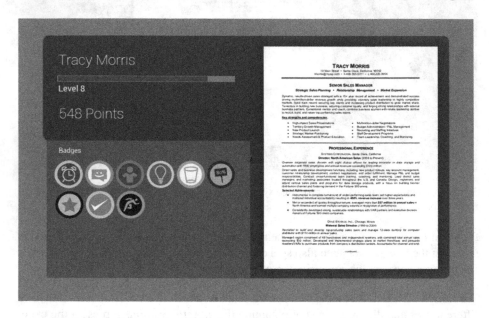

Fig. 3. Part of the concept UI displaying the user's progression and achievements

5   System Evaluation

To test the effectiveness of the proposed gamification system, two systems were designed and tested. One system represented the proposed gamification system with all of its game mechanics in place. The other represented the proposed system without any of the gamification elements. The research design was between-subjects and the measurement instrument an online questionnaire distributed to 34 jobseekers.

The questionnaire was created with the purpose of measuring the system's perception of use. It included seven-point Likert scale items such as: "*I think this system will motivate me to improve my CV*". Participants were requested to give their opinion on the review, feedback and overall system whereas the questionnaire for the gamified system had additional statements about the reward, profile, challenge and network system.

5.1 Results

T-Test Results. The two statements regarding motivation that were included in both questionnaires were: "*I think this system will motivate me to improve my CV*" and "*I think this system will help motivate me when looking for a job*". We filtered data captured by job seekers (N = 68).

Both aforementioned statements were analyzed using the T-test, nevertheless the results did not yield a statistically significant difference. We did observe though the mean values to be in the expected direction. For example, the question: "*I think this system will motivate me to improve my CV*" between the non-gamified questionnaire score yielded a mean value of M = 5.15 (SD = 1.019, N = 34) and the gamified questionnaire score M = 5.29 (SD = 1.404, N = 34), $t(66) = -.494$, $p = .623$.

The same observation was more obvious on the question: "*I think this system will help motivate me when looking for a job*" between the non-gamified questionnaire score (M = 4.47, SD = 1.331, N = 34) and the gamified questionnaire score (M = 5.00, SD = 1.633, N = 34), $t(66) = -1.465$, $p = 0.148$.

Descriptive Results. The questionnaire also included items beyond the system's evaluation and was answered by job seekers (N = 68) as well as participants not actively looking for a job (N = 62). One apparent finding is that 112 of the 130 participants believe that their CVs can be improved. This means the majority of the participants fit the target audience requirement.

Six participants used a review service before and most of them agreed that the service they used was useful. One of the services was an online tool that assisted in building their CV. Two of the services were private services. The remaining three were educational institutions. This means that none of the participants had ever used a service like the one proposed in this paper.

The first statement about the system was about the review system. Figure 4 displays the results for this statement from both questionnaires. The great majority of participants agreed or somewhat agreed that the review system would be useful to them.

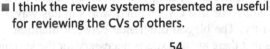

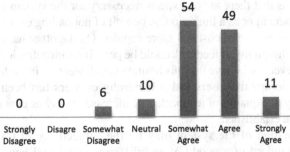

Fig. 4. Answers to the statement "I think the review systems presented are useful for reviewing the CVs of others".

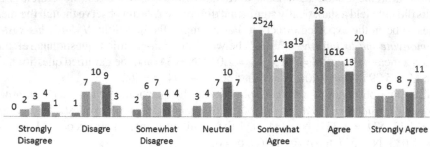

Fig. 5. Participants' opinion on the gamified elements demonstrated in the gamified survey.

The graph in Fig. 5 displays the survey results of the statements about gamification features in the gamified questionnaire. Overall, for each feature, most participants agreed or somewhat agreed that the feature would motivate them. However, it is clear that some features were more appreciated. The feedback system is especially well received. 54 out of 65 participants agreed or somewhat agreed to this feature being motivating. The reward system and network system are both well received as well, but the profile and challenge systems had mixed results.

6 Discussion

In both questionnaires, a great majority of the participants agreed that the proposed system would be useful and motivating and the data pointed preference towards the gamified system. As it is the first CV tool that works in this way, it might have a big impact on the industry. The biggest difference between traditional CV tools and the proposed system is that there are no experts necessary for the system to function. This can be seen as a benefit or as a limitation. A benefit of not having exclusively experts is that feedback is given free of cost and more rapidly. On the other hand, a limitation to this aspect is that the quality of feedback could be perceived unprofessional and therefore less useful. However, we believe that this limitation will wear off in the long-term. When the system has more active users and a hierarchy of users has been established by rewarding quality, the quality of feedback will increase greatly as examples are set and a culture has been established.

Another limitation of the system may be the subjectivity of CVs. There is no unique, single standard of a good CV and different users will have different ideas about the ideal CV. This may cause users to receive contradicting feedback and leave them clueless about which one to pursue. The system should encourage users to make their own independent decisions. Independence (having a clear individual stand) is a necessary value in a highly networked, self-organizing environment.

A reason for the mixed reviews of different gamification features may be the difference in personality types. As presented previously, there are four different gamer types that each has a different preference in game mechanics and experience. The challenge and progression systems would be attractive mechanics to *achievers* and *killers* as it gives the user something to collect and clear goals to complete.

7 Conclusion

The worldwide unemployment crisis has led to many people being unemployed for long periods of time, it has also made it harder for graduates to find employment. Long term unemployment can lead to the deterioration of self-esteem, a lack of day-to-day structure, a lack of social interaction and many more negative psychological effects which can all lead to depression. This paper has established that there is a great need for systems that motivate and support jobseekers. We presented the mechanics, dynamic and types of gamification. The dynamics of gamification are similar to the needs of jobseekers. This means that the use of gamification mechanics can solve the motivation problems if used in an effective matter.

Further, we presented a gamification system in which jobseekers improve the quality of their CVs. The system contains several gamification mechanics that satisfy the needs of jobseekers. The system contains a progression system that visualizes the improvements of the user, a challenge system that provides clear objectives to the player and rewards that give the player added extrinsic motivation.

To evaluate the effectiveness of the designed system online questionnaires with jobseekers compared two proposed systems for helping job seekers with improving their CVs: a system with gamification features and one without any gamification features. The results, although not statistically significant, point in favor of the gamified system for motivating job seekers. The feedback system, reward system and network system were perceived to be the most motivational gamified elements. The feedback system gives users the same short term and clear objectives as challenges do. We imagine this review and feedback system to be used effectively by governmental organizations.

References

Bartle, R.: Hearts, clubs, diamonds, spades: players who suit MUDs. J. MUD Res. **1**(1), 19 (1996)

Gamification 101: An Introduction to the Use of Game Dynamics to Influence Behavior. http://www.bunchball.com/sites/default/files/downloads/gamification101.pdf

Caplan, R.D., Vinokur, A.D., Prive, R.H., Ryn, M.V.: Job seeking, reemployment and mental health: a randomized field experiment in coping with job loss. J. Appl. Psychol. **74**(5), 759–769 (1989)

Deterding, S., Dixon, D., Khaled, R., Nacke, L.: For game design elements to gamefulness: defining "gamification". In: Proceedings of the 15th International Acedemic MindTrek Conference: Envisioning Future Media Environments. ACM, New York (2011)

Europe,   Unemployment   and   Instability.   http://www.stratfor.com/weekly/europe-unemploymentand-instability

Global Employment Trends 2014: The risk of a jobless recovery. http://www.ilo.org/global/research/global-reports/global-employment-trends/2014/lang–en/index.htm

Ryan, R.M., Deci, E.L.: Intrinsic and extrinsic motivations: classic definitions and new directions. Contemp. Educ. Psychol. **25**, 54–67 (2000)

Emotional Stages of a Job Loss. http://www.theladders.com/career-advice/emotional-stages-job-loss

Twain, M.: The Adventures of Tom Sawyer. American Publishing Company, Hartford (1876)

Witte, H.D.: Gevolgen van langdurige werkloosheid voor het psychisch welzijn: overzicht van onderzoeksliteratuur. Psychol. Belg. **33**(1), 1–35 (1992)

Enhancing User Experience of Enterprise Systems for Improved Employee Productivity: A First Stage of Case Study

Honglei Li[✉]

Department of Mathematics and Information Sciences, Faculty of Engineering and Environment, Northumbria University, NE2 1XE, Newcastle upon Tyne, UK
Honglei.Li@northumbria.ac.uk

Abstract. User experience has been regarded as the focus of technology design following the diffusion of information technology into the society level. There are many researches discussing user experience as a concept from the software testing and design perspective and seldom the specific dimensions of user experience are investigated. This research attempted to conduct a case study to explore the psychological dimensions of user experience from the interpersonal relationship theoretical perspective. Specifically, a case study on the usage of SAP ERP system has been conducted and 8 enterprise systems users have been interviewed to reflect on their interactions with the ERP system. The interpersonal relationship features is reported missing from the current enterprise systems design. Implications to both researchers and practitioners are provided.

Keywords: User experience · Interpersonal relationship · Case study · Enterprise systems

1 Introduction

User experience refers to the subjective, dynamic and emotional side of technology usage from users' perspective [1]. Originating from the practical side of interface design, user experience has recently been penetrating into the academic field, especially HCI discipline, mainly because of the recent design stream alongside burgeoning social computing devices such as iPad, tablet PCs and smartphones. The technology advancement has allowed the design of the computer devices to not only focus on the functional part of the product, but also the aesthetic, affect, or hedonic side of the product. At the same time, the information technology has diffused into the society level and the growth of user base demands for more interactive interface [1]. Following this trend in the industry, studies on user experience appears in main stream journals and recently becomes a main stream study in user interface design field. It has replaced the previous word interface design for it provides richer meaning and broader context. Given this fact, many new software product developments focus on holistic user experience from user's perspective to improve product quality as well as the overall business performance. Several studies have reported better performance of the company by focusing on user experience. For example, Suh and Chang [2] has investigated

© Springer International Publishing Switzerland 2015
F.F.-H. Nah and C.-H. Tan (Eds.): HCIB 2015, LNCS 9191, pp. 493–500, 2015.
DOI: 10.1007/978-3-319-20895-4_45

the role of telepresence in the online shopping environment and found that telepresence could directly or indirectly augment consumers' product knowledge, attitudes and purchase intentions, and reduces consumer perceptions of product risk and discrepancies between online product information and actual products.

With this wave of new user experience design, the software design has shifted from function-centred to user experience centred. However, the interfaces of most enterprise systems, such as ERP systems are still in its legacy state, i.e., the interfaces of these large systems are hard to change due to the scale of the software. The interface of many such systems could be traced back to at least ten years ago. The implementation of such systems involves huge investment and takes very long period of time. As reported in previous studies, there are many barriers in implementing such large systems in the organization [3]. At the same time, previous studies have also reported that hedonic or emotion factors such as affect [4] played an important role in determining information technology usage in workplace. The improvement of the social and emotional perspective of the enterprise systems should be able to improve employees' adoption rate of the information technology, leading to improved productivity. Study also report that user experience variables such as hedonic factor influence employee's continued adoption of enterprise systems [5]. We thus infer enterprise systems' adoption rate and performance could be improved greatly by focusing on improved user experience.

The aim of this research intends to investigate user experience of the current ERP system through a case study. During the study, ERP users from different stages will be interviewed for their experience of the existing ERP usage. Both the hedonic and functional experience will be investigated. To effectively represent the current ERP users, both early stage users and sophisticated users for SAP ERP systems have been selected for interview. The interview scripts and results will thus be analysed to give the guidance on the effectiveness of user experience on employee ERP system usage.

2 Literature Review

This section reviewed the state-of-the-art of user experience development and evolution followed by a review of user needs theory.

2.1 User Experience

User experience as a concept could be traced back to 1980s when PC when PCs were become more popular and software development processes started emphasizing the role of user involvement or user participation to successful implement and design information systems [6]. According to Hirschheim [6], users value high the participative design/implementation approach by which users are actively involved in the design/ implement process despite user experiences are subjective by nature. Meanwhile the negative experience such as frustration and fear are also identified during computer usage [7]. Although many systems developed in those times focuses more on the functionality of the system rather than user experience concepts we are discussing now days, a shift toward user-centred design can be observed in the information system development trend over years. Experience has been studied but does not play a central role before 2000s [8, 9]. User experience starts to gain popularity in 2000s when the mobile devices are enhanced to deal with picture, audio, and video information. The concept of technology as experience and design for experience are brought out [10–12], followed by a heated discussion [1, 13, 14] on user experiences from various perspectives under different virtual environments, especially virtual world [2, 15]. The concept of user experience evolved to include the subjective, emotional, and sensory perceptions from users' interactions with the information systems. The positive user experience will enhance the technology and the negative or the rejected experience results in decreased technology usage [7, 16]. User experience is regarded as an interaction process with technology and is influential in technology implementation.

Most user experience studies agreed that user experience is subjective [6] and related with emotional perspective of human needs [1, 2, 13, 17], sometimes highly related with the pleasure or hedonic factors [11, 18]. In Deng et al.'s [5] study on the role of user experience on continual intention to use mobile devices, the experience is discussed from the cognitive absorption perspective and measured as hedonic and utilitarian experience. According to the current explanation for user experience, it fluctuates with the situation and emotion [10]. It is also dynamic and interactive and focuses on the co-creation feelings with friends and colleagues [11]. Yet, it is linked with human needs [19]. In a metaphor, user experience sounds like a woman hard to be pleased and vague to figure out. It is capricious and changes with emotions and situation. It seems there is no logical and theoretical method to identify why user experience changes. We would like to point out that this is because most previous studies are from computer sciences perspective but a social psychological theoretical mechanism is neglected in the previous study by focusing too much on the functional dimension of user requirements. Like Freud's dream analysis method, experience and feelings links with social dimensions and spiritual dimensions covered in the subliminal. The surged user experience might be the manifestation of fulfilled or under fulfilled social or interpersonal needs [19]. From this perspective, the technology acts as the artefact for the social presence.

2.2 Social Needs and Interpersonal Needs

It has long been a tradition for social scientists to discover the human nature from various perspectives, among which Maslow's hierarchy needs theory [20] probably explained all fundamental needs as an individual, physiological needs, security needs, respect and esteem needs, and self-actualization needs. Taken the human needs into consideration, it's no hard to find that trust plays an important role in online shopping design because it satisfies security needs from Maslow's perspective [21]. There are also many other social psychological theories and this study will take the interpersonal needs perspective to discuss the user experience of software design because the social dynamic nature of the interpersonal relationship theory.

We will adopt the Fundamental Interpersonal Relationship Orientation (FIRO) developed by Schutz [22] to explain how the current enterprise systems meet the user experience requirements from the fundamental interpersonal needs. Schutz [22, 23] proposed that interpersonal relationships could be measured by a person's intention to interact with others. He argued that people's intention to interact with others can be measured by three dimensions—inclusion, control, and affection. Each of these three dimensions has two behavior directions—expressed and wanted behavior. In total, there are six dimensions in FIRO—expressed inclusion, wanted inclusion, expressed control, wanted control, expressed affection, and wanted affection. Based on this framework, the expressed behavior describes the extent of people's willingness to include, control, and loves others, whereas wanted behavior describes the extent of people's willingness to be included, controlled, and loved by others.

To be applied empirically, FIRO was operationalized as FIRO-B (FIRO behavior). Since the introduction of FIRO, its measures have been widely adopted in social psychology research. On average, FIRO has an average of twenty-five citations annually in the Social Science Citation Index [24]. Furnham [25, 26] indicated that the FIRO-B was one of the three most widely used questionnaires in occupational psychology.

The FIRO model can be applied to all situations in which interpersonal relationships are investigated [22]. There are three levels of the theoretical application of the model, based on the number of persons involved in the interpersonal relationship—the individual level (one person), family level (more than two persons), and group level (more than two people). While individual-level applications described mainly an individual's orientation in the three dimensions, which provide the foundation to analyze the individual's social behaviors, family-level applications mainly deal with how the orientations of family members in the three areas influences their relationships inside and outside the family, and group level applications deal mainly with how the match of the orientations of group members in the three dimensions, namely, the group's compatibility, affect the group's performance [27–29], effectiveness [30, 31], and efficiency [32]. We will adopt the individual level application of FIRO to guide the analysis of ERP user needs.

3   Research Methodology

A case study approach has been adopted for this study because of the explorative nature of user experience study for the enterprise systems. As for the user experience study is still in early stage theory building through qualitative analysis such as case study is essential for a subject [33]. As an exploratory case study, the research follows a set of classical qualitative research principles in information systems and some other social scientific fields [34].

Enterprise systems might refer to CRM system, supplier relationship management system but the core is the ERP system. We select SAP system as our case study software because SAP takes the largest market share for the ERP software. To objectively capture user experience, two groups of SAP ERP users from both sophisticated and early stage users are selected for focus group study. A strict research ethical procedure is followed before conducting the study. All the participants for the focus group study are voluntary and an informed consent form is provided to them before the study. 8 early stage users in the ERP class who have used SAP ERP software for assessment for one month have been invited to participate in a one hour focus group to discuss their experience with ERP systems. 2 skilled SAP ERP users agreed to give their opinions on SAP ERP user experience. Two focus group studies for these two groups are held independently.

The profile of these two groups of users is strikingly different. For the early stage ERP users, 7 are male and one is female and all of them are between 20-28 age groups except one between 28-35 age group. The first focus group participants are from multi-cultural background, with two of them from China, two from Thailand, one from Germany, one from Indonesia and one from Nigeria. Most of them have some work experience in business related area. They have full access to all modules in the ERP system. Each of them is required to describe their personality and most of them are outgoing and sociable. The skilled ERP user groups consist of two ladies above 36 years old and both of them are British. The first lady A has been working with SAP ERP system for 7 years and the second Lady B has been working with SAP ERP system for about 15 years. Both of them have been using accounting and financial accounting modules of SAP system. A semi-structured questionnaire with guided questions is adopted during the two focus group sessions. A set of questions is designed based on the characteristics of ERP systems and the FIRO theory.

4   Case Analysis and Results

After gathering all the data from the two rounds of focus groups, we analyse our data firstly by coding all the transcripts. In general we have classified our transcripts into three categories: experience, difficulty, and improvement. We will present our analysis on these three categories based on the FIRO framework.

4.1   Experience

The experience here refers to the experience with the ERP systems and users are given opportunities to describe their feelings and emotions with using ERP systems. Users from both groups have expressed the feeling of frustration during the usage process. Specifically, one typical user from focus group 1 described his feelings:

I feel really frustrated when I couldn't find anyone to help with using the system. It's so complicated and I am tired very soon. I feel isolated during this process.
Another member from the focus group 2 also mentioned the similar feeling:

The overall experience is very difficult because it's self-taught. You know have anyone to help you with the learning process although you will be given training.

However, after certain level of usage, some users will experience the positive feeling. For example, one user from focus group 1 reported that he feel happy after using it for a while. Another member from focus group 2 although mentioned that she feels the system is good because of all the functions it provides.

From the basic human needs or the FIRO perspective, it's not difficulty to find out that the current ERP system lacks social functions and makes users frustrated and helpless. The overall experience with the systems is difficulty and hard to follow because no human features are designed into the system. Features to fulfil human's basic interpersonal needs such as inclusion, control, and affect are missing in the current system. That's why users feel isolated and helpless with any control over the system. Although users feel happy after some level of usage, the positive emotions is more related with the fulfilment of need for security [20] or the flow theory [35].

4.2   Difficulty

The difficulty in the paper refers to the difficulty users experience during the usage process. Users are asked to recall all the difficulties they have experienced during using the ERP systems. Both focus group members reported similar difficulties. For example, one user from group 1 reported that "*it's very hard to correct the mistakes you have made while using the system. No functions to allow you to know what I have done wrong.*" Similarly, both members from group 2 reported that "because *the system is self-taught, it's very different to correct the mistakes.*"

There are more difficulties such as error messages are hard to be found and the colour of the system is too monotonous. There is no backward button etc.

From the human needs perspective, this is an extension of the experience users have been through. There are not enough human features in the system design which limits users' sense of inclusion and control during using the systems.

4.3   Improvement

Improvements refer to users' expectations to improve the system design so that they could use the system more efficiently. Both groups have expressed that they wish to have improved graphic interface with better colour scheme. At the same time, they expect to have improved audio functions for reminding etc. All these are related with human's perceptions about the world. Search functions all through the system is expected to improve so that users won't need to go through all the paths to get to the specific transactions. Search functions across different tables could also greatly improve the sense of control over the system, which is related with the need for control dimension of the FIRO framework.

5   Discussions, Implications and Conclusions

This paper is a first attempt to investigate the user experience of the ERP system from the interpersonal relationship perspective with FIRO framework. We have used the case study approach by analyzing data from two focus groups through three perspectives: experience, difficulty, and improvement. All focus group analysis showed that the human features are lack in the current ERP system. From the FIRO framework, most of human interpersonal needs are missing in the current system design. When human interact with the computer systems such as ERP system, the fulfilment of interpersonal needs dimensions in the system would greatly improve user experience. Need for inclusion could be embedded in the system by enabling users to send messages to each other and discuss the issues they encounter. Need for control could be improved by interface of the system so that users could operate more functions such as customization of the system. Need for affect is currently missing in the system but the future design shall consider this.

References

1. Hassenzahl, M., Tractinsky, N.: User experience – a research agenda. Behav. Inf. Technol. **25**(2), 91–97 (2006)
2. Suh, K.-S., Chang, S.: User interfaces and consumer perceptions of online stores: the role of telepresence. Behav. Inf. Technol. **25**(2), 99–113 (2006)
3. Amoako-Gyampah, K., Salam, A.F.: An extension of the technology acceptance model in an ERP implementation environment. Inf. Manag. **41**(6), 731–745 (2004)
4. Bereron, F., et al.: Determinants of EIS use: testing a behavioral model. Decis. Support Syst. **14**(2), 131–146 (1996)
5. Deng, L., et al.: User experience, satisfaction, and continual usage intention of IT. Eur. J. Inf. Syst. **19**(1), 60–75 (2010)
6. Hirschheim, R.A.: User experience with and assessment of participative systems design. MIS Q. **9**(4), 295–304 (1985)
7. Appelbaum, S.H.: Computerphobia: training managers to reduce the fears and love the machines. Ind. Commercial Train. **22**(6), 9–16 (1990)
8. Taylor, S., Todd, P.: Assessing IT usage: the role of prior experience. MIS Q. **19**(4), 561–570 (1995)
9. Shneiderman, B.: Designing trust into online experiences. association for computing machinery. Commun. ACM **43**(12), 57 (2000)
10. McCarthy, J., Wright, P.: Technology as experience. Interactions **11**(5), 42–43 (2004)
11. Battarbee, K.: Co-experience: the social user experience. In: CHI 2003 Extended Abstracts on Human Factors in Computing Systems, ACM (2003)
12. Hsu, C.-L., Lu, H.-P.: Why do people play on-line games? an extended TAM with social influences and flow experience. Inf. Manag. **41**(7), 853–868 (2004)
13. McNamara, N., Kirakowski, J.: Functionality, usability, and user experience: three areas of concern. Interactions **13**(6), 26–28 (2006)
14. Sánchez-Franco, M.J., Roldán, J.L.: Web acceptance and usage model: a comparison between goal-directed and experiential web users. Internet Res. **15**(1), 21–48 (2005)
15. Kohler, T., et al.: Co-creation in virtual worlds: the design of the user experience. MIS Q. **35**(3), 773–788 (2011)
16. Battarbee, K., Koskinen, I.: Co-experience: user experience as interaction. CoDesign **1**(1), 5–18 (2005)
17. Tolia, N., Andersen, D.G., Satyanarayanan, M.: Quantifying interactive user experience on thin clients. Computer **39**(3), 46–52 (2006)
18. Hackbarth, G., Grover, V., Yi, M.Y.: Computer playfulness and anxiety: positive and negative mediators of the system experience effect on perceived ease of use. Inf. Manag. **40**(3), 221–232 (2003)
19. Hassenzahl, M., Diefenbach, S., Göritz, A.: Needs, affect, and interactive products–Facets of user experience. Interact. Comput. **22**(5), 353–362 (2010)
20. Maslow, A.H.: Toward a Psychology of Being. Start Publishing LLC, New York (2013)

21. Kim, J., Jin, B., Swinney, J.L.: The role of e-tail quality, e-satisfaction and e-trust in online loyalty development process. J. Retail. Consum. Serv. **16**(4), 239–247 (2009)
22. Schutz, W.C.: The Interpersonal Underworld, p. 242. Science & Behavior Books. xi, Palo Alto (1966)
23. Schutz, W.C.: FIRO: A Three-Dimensional Theory of Interpersonal Behavior, p. 267. Rinehart, New York (1958)
24. Hurley, J.R.: Does FIRO-B relate better to interpersonal or intrapersonal behavior? J. Clin. Psychol. **46**(4), 454–460 (1990)
25. Furnham, A.: The fakeability of the 16 PF, Myers-Briggs and FIRO-B personality measures. Personality Individ. Differ. **11**(7), 711–716 (1990)
26. Furnham, A.: The FIRO-B, the learning style questionnaire, and the five-factor model. J. Soc. Behav. Pers. **11**(2), 285–299 (1996)
27. Ilgen, D.R., O'Brien, G.: Leader-member relations in small groups. Organ. Behav. Hum. Perform. **12**(3), 335–350 (1974)
28. Di Marco, N.J.: Supervisor-subordinate life-style and interpersonal need compatibilities as determinants of subordinate's attitudes toward the supervisor. Acad. Manag. J. **17**(3), 575–578 (1974)
29. Hill, R.E.: Managing Interpersonal Conflict in Project Teams. Sloan Manag. Rev. (pre-1986) **18**(2), 45–61 (1977)
30. Smith, P.B., Linton, M.J.: Group composition and changes in self-actualization in t-groups. Hum. Relat. **28**(9), 811–823 (1975)
31. Fisher, S.G., Macrosson, W.D.K., Walker, C.A.: FIRO-B: the power of love and the love of power. Psychol. Rep. **76**(1), 195–206 (1995)
32. Hewett, T.T., O'Brien, G.E.: The effects of work organization, leadership style, and member compatibility upon the productivity of small groups working on a manipulative task. Organ. Behav. Hum. Perform. **11**(2), 283–301 (1974)
33. Chen, W., Hirschheim, R.: A paradigmatic and methodological examination of information systems research from 1991 to 2001. Inf. Syst. J. **14**(3), 197–235 (2004)
34. Yin, R.K.: Case Study Research: Design and Methods. Sage publications, Thousand Oaks (2014)
35. Moneta, G.B., et al.: The effect of perceived challenges and skills on the quality of subjective experience. Journal of personality **64**(2), 275–310 (1996)

Designing Mobile Applications
for Organizational Routines

Kenny Lienhard, Thomas Boillat(⊠), and Christine Legner

Department of Information Systems, Faculty of Business and Economics (HEC),
University of Lausanne, Lausanne, Switzerland
{kenny.lienhard,thomas.boillat,
christine.legner}@unil.ch

Abstract. As tablet computers and smartphones have become widespread, organizations are increasingly using mobile applications for supporting routines, i.e., repetitive patterns of activity that occur throughout an organization. However, prior studies see user interactions mostly as a silo – able to help individual users perform better – but not embedded in an organizational context of a user group or company. In order to address this gap, the paper at hand looks into the roles of mobile applications in supporting routines, and the related principles for mobile application design. We present two mobile applications that support domain experts in two diverse contexts, automotive car dealerships and hospitals. Based on their analysis, we were able to identify patterns as well as a number of design principles for mobile applications supporting organizational routines.

Keywords: Mobile application design · Organizational routines · User interface · Healthcare · Sales and service

1 Introduction

With the increasing proliferation of mobile technologies, computing's traditional application areas have broadened and encompass a variety of mobile scenarios, such as m-commerce, mobile banking, and entertainment services (e.g., [1, 2]). Researchers often investigate consumer-oriented mobile services, but have paid less attention to mobile applications in organizational contexts. In this paper, we argue that mobile applications are particularly suited for supporting routines, i.e., repetitive patterns of activity that occur throughout an organization [3]. Since routines embed much organizational knowledge [4], they often rely on artifacts such as forms, checklists, written procedures, or rules [3, 5]. Mobile applications can replace or enhance traditional artifacts to improve the support for workers in the execution of routines. However, we are still lacking design guidelines for these applications. Prior studies mainly focus on user-centric design and adaptive mobile interfaces from the individual user's perspective [6, 7]. They see user interactions mostly as a silo – able to help individual users perform better – but not embedded in an organizational context of a user group or company.

© Springer International Publishing Switzerland 2015
F.F.-H. Nah and C.-H. Tan (Eds.): HCIB 2015, LNCS 9191, pp. 501–512, 2015.
DOI: 10.1007/978-3-319-20895-4_46

Since the performance of an organization is positively linked with the effectiveness of its organizational routines and its artifacts [8], we are interested in understanding: (1) What are the roles of mobile applications in organizational routines? (2) What are the design principles for mobile applications to support organizational routines? In view of our research goals, we analyzed two mobile applications that support domain experts in diverse contexts, automotive car dealerships and hospitals. Both are advanced and innovative examples of mobile applications that were created to support complex activity patterns and have been developed in close collaboration with end-users. From our involvement in the design process and collaborations with these applications' developers, we were able to identify patterns as well as five design principles for mobile applications supporting organizational routines.

The remainder of this paper is structured as follows: First, we review the literature related to organizational routines and their representations as IT artifacts. We then present our research methodology. After presenting the two case studies, we synthesize our findings related to the roles and design principles. The paper ends with a summary of our findings and provides an outlook on future research.

2   Organizational Routines and the Role of Artifacts

Organizational routines are repetitive patterns of activity that are functionally similar, but are not fixed and do not constrain to follow a strict sequence [3]. They capture and codify individuals' experience in order to increase knowledge transfer in an organization [9]. Organizations rely on different kinds of artifacts such as forms, checklists and written procedures to support the execution of organizational routines [10]. Interestingly, the roles of artifacts have evolved over time. In early contributions, artifacts were seen as an organization's external memory with the aim of helping people to solve complex problems [3]. Later, artifacts were considered an enabler for the evolution, transfer, and replication of routines [11]. More recently, artifacts are seen as central to organizational routines and as actively enhancing individuals' knowledge, skills, and competence [12]. With the democratization and evolution of technology, IT artifacts play an increasingly significant role in organizational routines. On the positive side, IT artifacts facilitate data sharing, enable tracking the progress of changes and swifter feedback exchange [13]. There are, however, also negative effects [12]: IT artifacts, specifically software applications, have their limits when it comes to adapting to individuals' routines. In practice, their adaptations often require the involvement of dedicated resources. This often results in users adapting their behavior [14], sometimes at the expense of an organization's performance and competitiveness. In short, organizational literature shows that artifacts play a strategic role in supporting and maintaining organizational routines. To date, researchers have focused on software applications as IT artifacts, but have not yet investigated mobile applications as an IT artifact in supporting organizational routines. However, mobile applications provide new opportunities for supporting routine work through their small touchscreens, gesture navigation, and integration of sensors [15, 16].

3 Methodology

Our research analyzes two mobile applications supporting complex activity patterns (see Table 1). Their goal is to support experts in two domains, customer service as well as healthcare, which are among the best representative domains for the use of mobile technology [17]. Our first case describes the Mobile Service Advisor (MSA), which guides mechanics in the interactive service reception routine in car dealerships. MSA is a mobile application developed by proaxia consulting group AG, a Swiss IT consulting company with expertise in innovative solutions for sales and service in the automotive and other technical industries. The mobile application has been co-developed with Autohaus Bald, a group of car dealerships in Germany with more than 20 000 customers, and is currently used by more than 20 of their mechanics in eight different locations. The second case describes the Legon Clinical Solution (LCS), a mobile application that guides physicians during routine patient care. This solution has been developed in collaboration between a rheumatology department of a Swiss cantonal hospital and Legon Informatik AG, a Swiss software company that specializes in the development of customized software solutions for healthcare. The LCS supports physicians' particular way of practicing and is currently being tested by rheumatologists in their daily work. Both cases can be considered as innovative examples of mobile applications and have been recognized as such by experts: The MSA was awarded best mobile application in November 2012 by a primary software vendor for its innovativeness, functionality, usability, and customer feedback [18]. The LCS is considered by senior physicians to be one of the most advanced and innovative mobile applications used in Swiss hospitals.

The authors were able to gain in-depth insights into the designs of these applications, since they were either part of or collaborated with these mobile applications' development teams. We participated in discussions with future users as well as with software developers and graphic designers, collecting valuable insights towards understanding the user requirements and organizational contexts, as well as their

Table 1. Factsheet case studies

	Mobile service advisor	Legon clinical solution
Routine	Interactive service reception	Routine patient care
Provider	proaxia consulting AG, Switzerland	Legon Informatik AG, Switzerland
Users and context	Mechanics/Car dealerships Here, Autohaus Bald	Physicians/Hospitals Here, rheumatology department
Usage	Approx. 15 000 inspections per year	Approx. 3000 patients per year; average consultations per patient are 2.7 per year
Mobile platform	Apple iOS: Native iPad application	Apple iOS: Native iPad application
Technology	SAP Mobile Platform	Hybrid: iOS SDK and HTML5

implications on mobile application design decisions. Thus, we argue that such an approach is far more valuable to understand the roles and the designs of mobile applications than simply analyzing existing solutions available in mobile app stores.

4 Case Studies

4.1 Case I: Mobile Application for Service Reception in Car Dealerships

Background and Motivation. This case focuses on customer interactions in the early phases of car inspection in automotive dealerships. Traditionally, when customers bring their cars to the dealership for service maintenance, they give the car keys to a mechanic, exchange few words about problems that they detected or specific parts that must be repaired, then leave. This approach is increasingly replaced by the so-called interactive service reception (ISR), which seeks to guide mechanics in a more professional way and establishes a dialogue with customers towards better satisfaction. ISR intends to overcome two main shortcomings centered around the lack of systematic car inspection and the lack of interaction between mechanics and customers. Existing studies in the automotive industry demonstrate that without a consistent service reception routine, only one quarter of cars' problems are detected and eventually repaired [19].

Many dealerships are currently introducing ISR by means of paper-based checklists as support to routines' execution. Despite listing the primary activities of the ISR routine, paper-based checklists have many drawbacks: They require one to re-enter the manually collected information after the inspection in the dealership's information system. Also, they do not prevent mechanics from looking for and copying a great deal of information related to a specific customer and vehicle, while they cannot adapt to specific situations (e.g., specific cars).

Mobile Application's Roles. MSA's primary role is to guide mechanics through the inspection process and to explicitly document the inspection results to ensure high work quality and full transparency for the customer. On the one hand, the mobile application can 'force' mechanics to perform specific activities – e.g., access current customer information to consider his or her wishes – before continuing the routine. On the other hand, the mobile application suggests a predefined sequence of activities, which mechanics can then decide to follow or not, depending on the context (e.g., interaction with a customer) and on their experience. With the MSA, mechanics have access to various kinds of information to successfully conduct the ISR routine, such as customer information and previous inspection outcomes, potential open points from previous inspections, and warranty and recall. This information is usually centralized in the dealership's enterprise systems, but is not necessarily available for the mechanic during customer interactions. Finally, MSA supports the documentation of activities that are traditionally performed manually at the end of the routine, avoiding much administrative work and reducing potential errors that can occur during manual post hoc reporting.

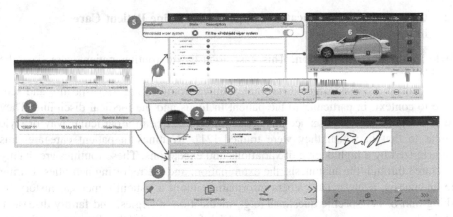

Fig. 1. Storyboard of MSA with customer selection, car inspection and validation

User Interface Design and Interaction Flow. MSA's storyboard consists of three main views: (1) Customer selection, (2) the current service order with access to detailed customer information and vehicle history, and (3) the detailed inspection checkpoints. Access to information is possible through the SAP Mobile Platform, which connects the mobile application and the dealership's enterprise systems. This data is copied locally on the mobile device, while the synchronization occurs at the end of the routine to ensure data consistency. The first view contains a list of fields used as a filter to find customers and access previous inspections (see Fig. 1. #1). The second screen allows mechanics to update customer information and access a vehicle's information and history and review the status of the current inspection. When previous inspections are opened, damages that were repaired are displayed. If it is a new inspection, the known customer wishes and issues are listed. The user interface contains a primary navigation element as a tab-based menu to access the third view (see Fig. 1. #2). A second navigation level, also as a tab-based menu, provides access to the closing activities, including notably the handover report and its customer validation (see Fig. 1. #3). The third view is dedicated to the car's inspection. In this case the second navigation level describes the car's different parts, following a physical structure [20] – the checkpoints are grouped based on their proximity e.g., inside, chassis, outside (see Fig. 1. #4). Each group's activities are presented along with a checklist approach that allows for the quick and systematic documentation of each activity. It is described with a number to facilitate its identification, a short text to describe the checkpoints, a checkbox to indicate the state of the activity (i.e., not checked, checked and no damage, checked and damage), a text field that provides predefined entry sets related to each checkpoint if damage is observed, and a switch button to indicate if the customer wants to repair the damage or not (see Fig. 1. #5). For activities that require specific documentation and that are also car-specific, MSA embeds different visual elements. This is notably the case for the chassis check that relies on a 3-D model of the customer's car to mark the potential damage (see Fig. 1. #6). At the end of the inspection, all the repair activities are listed in a report that a customer digitally signs to validate the inspection. The transfer of data into the dealership's enterprise systems terminates the routine.

4.2   Case II: Mobile Application Supporting Routine Patient Care in Hospitals

Background and Motivation. This case focuses on routine patient care, i.e., the activities that a physician performs to cure a patient's disease, at a rheumatology department of a Swiss cantonal hospital. Clinical routines are very specific and sensitive to context, in particular to the patient in focus and the medical discipline. They are also highly individual, since physicians often practice in a particular way or style similar to that in which they were trained [21]. Routines in patient care are thus characterized by a high degree of variations and exceptions. These routines are mainly structured through the anamnesis, the examination, and the reporting activities. During the anamnesis, a physician gathers information about a patient's medical history by asking him or her specific questions (e.g., medication, allergies, and family diseases). While the anamnesis seeks to provide useful information for the diagnosis and treatment, information gathering is limited to the fact that a patient or his or her family can only report symptoms that are known to them. The anamnesis is therefore complemented by an examination. Thereby, a rheumatologist gathers information by directly investigating a patient's body. Finally, rheumatologists document the routine to report the outcome (e.g., diagnosis and therapy plan) to various stakeholders such as the patient or other health professionals.

Previously, the routines at the rheumatology department were entirely supported by paper-based forms. The rheumatologists opted for mobile devices as a new artifact assisting their routines, because it allowed them to capture digital information during routine execution without disturbing face-to-face communication with patients.

Mobile Application's Roles. The mobile application represents the basic sequence of activities in routine patient care, i.e., anamnesis, examination, and reporting. Anamnesis and examination are codified in forms, which provide the stable and visible part of the routine. One of the mobile application's role is to provide a shared vocabulary among rheumatologists by means of forms. The latter are especially useful for less experienced physicians, who need more help and guidance during routine execution. The mobile application automates the creation of medical reports. When a physician activates a checkbox during a routine, a predefined text module is added to the medical report together with content of the free-text fields. During the routine, the medical report is updated in real time, providing the physician with an overview of his or her current activities. When a rheumatologist finishes a routine, the related medical report is immediately ready to be sent to the various stakeholders (e.g., patients and general practitioners).

In our first analysis, it was particularly interesting to observe how rheumatologists use the mobile application during their activities. Even though the item order in the primary and the secondary navigation was fixed, it was not perceived as a predefined structure to do a routine. For instance, during the anamnesis, there is a high variation in the information gathering process. A rheumatologist would limit the medical history to a minimum in an emergency case, and would focus on important details such as a patient's name or previous allergies. Thereby, the forms and the related navigation structure are perceived as a repository of activities that provides the basis to dynamically build the supporting mobile application for each instance of a routine.

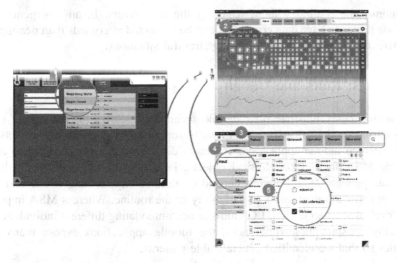

Fig. 2. Storyboard of LCS with patient selection and routine support

User Interface Design and Interaction Flow. The mobile application's storyboard is composed of two different screens. On the first screen (see Fig. 2. #1), a rheumatologist searches for a patient. Administrative data about patients is provided by a centralized clinical information system. Through the selection of a patient, the physician triggers a transition to the second screen, where the patient's medical history is accessible and where the actual routine is executed (see Fig. 2. #2). The navigation elements and the forms on the second screen constrain and guide the physician during the routine. An important paradigm when designing artifacts for routine patient care is the effort of switching from one patient to the other. For a rheumatologist, it must be highly visible to whom a medical history belongs, and in which patient's record he or she is documenting. Therefore, the mobile application clearly separates the patient selection from the routine.

A tab-based menu on the top of the screen is the primary navigation element (see Fig. 2. #3). This menu describes the physician's main activities during the routine, i.e., anamnesis, examination, and reporting. The list menu on the left is the secondary navigation element, and its items adapt to the selected primary navigation item (see Fig. 2. #4). Items in the secondary navigation are generally named after anatomic terms (e.g., skin, eyes, abdomen) and represent specific parts of the body. A form describes each item in the secondary navigation and provides details for asking questions during anamnesis and for investigating a patient's body (see Fig. 2. #5). Clinicians basically use checkboxes and free-text fields to document a routine. Rheumatologists also use anatomy sketches (e.g., joints or muscle groups) to draw in a patient's specific pain points and inflammations. The form elements are intelligent and listen to specific events. For instance, when a physician fills in a patient's height and weight, the form elements for body mass index and body surface area automatically calculate their value. Forms are validated during data input. A yellow background on the form element indicates a false data entry. However, the data is saved anyway, and the rheumatologist can continue the routine without handling the data errors. In an emergency case, physicians prefer to have data errors that can be corrected afterwards than dealing with alerts from the mobile application during stressful situations.

5 Findings: Roles and Design Principles

The analyzed cases illustrate how mobile technology allows for the use of digital devices during routines that were traditionally supported by paper-based artifacts. The two investigated mobile applications represent different domains and different actors. While the MSA focuses on physical objects, i.e., cars, the LCS centers on human beings, i.e., patients. Both domains depend on domain experts' knowledge and experience, but show different levels of variability of the routine. Whereas MSA imposes a higher level of standardization, LCS aims at accommodating different individual ways of working. Despite these differences, the mobile applications expose many commonalities so that we identified generalizable patterns.

5.1 Mobile Application's Roles in Supporting Organizational Routines

R1. Support experts in performing routines and reduce variation in routine execution.
    In the cases of the MSA and the LCS, mobile applications structure a routine and guide workers during routine execution. Their design constrains the number of possibilities, in which the experts can do their work. For instance, they might be "forced" to perform a group of activities, before they are allowed to access the next group of activities. Input validation ensures that outcome of an activity is correctly achieved. Such an approach standardizes the patterns of some activities and ensures quality and consistency of routines.

R2. Support experts in documenting their activities during execution.
    A key benefit of using mobile applications in routines is that they facilitate the documentation of a routine while executing it. Predefined forms and checklists assist an employee in documenting his or her activities. In both cases, documentation was enhanced through the use of visual input elements (e.g., 3-D models of a car, anatomy sketches).

R3. Support experts in reporting a routine's outcomes.
    The documentation provides the basis to automatically generate reports in order to summarize and communicate the routine outcomes. In the past, this work was typically done after a routine, when the domain expert wrapped up his or her activities in a written report. This process was cumbersome and prone to loss of information. In both cases, the automatically generated reports are also directly distributed or made accessible to other stakeholders.

R4. Support experts in accessing context-specific knowledge.
    Routines depend on context-specific knowledge. In our cases, we find that this knowledge is often related to the 'objects' (e.g., customer, car, patient) involved in a routine. A key role of mobile applications is to provide individuals with direct access to

relevant administrative and historical data about the context-relevant object when executing a routine.

R5. Enable transparent communication between domain expert and individual.

In both cases, the domain expert (service technician or physician) interacts with an individual (customer or patient) while executing his or her tasks. Here, the domain expert must adapt his or her language, as they do not share the same knowledge as the counterpart. Mobile applications can support these different communication styles. For instance, they can visualize information in order to make them understandable for non-experts. This endeavor enables transparency in documentation and seeks to create a shared understanding between the domain expert and the individual.

5.2 Design Principles for Mobile Applications Supporting Routines

From our analysis, we were able to synthesize five design principles:

DP1. Mobile applications need to implement a routine's context and boundaries. Each instance of a routine focuses on one specific object, which defines a routine's boundaries.

When experts define and formalize a routine, it is often not clear to them where a particular pattern of activities starts and ends. The storyboard for a mobile application must separate the selection of the physical 'object' (e.g., a customer, car, or patient), which defines both a routine's boundary and a routine itself. Once the routine has started, the mobile application must prevent an individual from changing an object in use – by mistake or unconsciously. For instance, in hospitals, an emergency might change a physician's priorities. In that case, switching from one patient to another in the mobile application must occur without confusion. This can be achieved via buttons, which trigger a transition from one screen (definition of boundaries and selection of physical object) to the other (support of routine). Thereby, a mobile application cannot efficiently support a routine without knowing about the context in which a routine takes place.

DP2. User interface elements, such as navigational elements, forms, and checklists, should guide domain experts with a predefined structure for routine execution.

Navigation elements, forms, and checklists are typical user interface elements, which allow for codifying the formalized routines built on an organization's existing knowledge and past experience. The latter elements guide and support a domain expert in taking actions and contribute to providing a shared understanding of a routine. They provide a predefined structure and represent the stable parts of a routine.

DP3. A mobile application's navigational elements should be flexible enough to cope with a specific routine executed by a specific actor at a specific time.

Mobile applications are highly customizable to an individual's needs, supporting the required stability and flexibility of routines. On the one hand, navigational elements must implement a clear structure, which defines the stable parts of a routine, while on the other hand they must also provide enough flexibility to adapt to the required actions in a specific routine by a specific actor at a specific time. As we have seen in the case of routine patient care, the higher the variation and the number of exceptions, the more freedom domain experts will require to effectively and efficiently perform their activities. Instead of prescribing fixed navigation sequences, the interfaces have to provide a certain flexibility, e.g., by creating groups of activities. Thereby, primary and secondary navigation elements provide a repository out of which a routine is dynamically created, rather than a predefined enforced structure.

DP4. Mobile applications should provide the functionality to create and formally approve reports in order to communicate the outcomes of a routine to stakeholders.

While the use of mobile technology allows one to document a routine during its execution, an application must provide the functionality to automatically generate a report based on this documentation. An automatically generated report allows one to communicate the outcomes of a routine right after a worker has completed his or her tasks. Report generation is typically complemented by a formal approval of the routine outcomes (e.g., via a signature) and by automated distribution to those who were directly involved in the routine (e.g., customers or patients) or need to know about the outcomes. In medicine, a specialist usually sends the report to the general practitioner, who will explain the outcomes of a routine to the patient. In a future scenario, one could imagine that the documented routine serves as a basis for communicating an outcome to various stakeholders (e.g., a patient, general practitioners, insurances), each of them with a different language to make the outcome understandable to a specific audience.

DP5. Mobile applications must provide ubiquitous access to data about context-relevant object.

While executing a routine, a domain expert needs access to administrative and historical data about the context-relevant object (e.g., customer, car, patient). This data is usually centralized and stored in an organization's enterprise system that is used across different departments. The connection and integration of mobile applications to organizations' information system is then essential. Since one can typically not ensure that internet connectivity is available throughout the conduct of a routine, data needs to be synchronized as soon as the routine is completed or internet connectivity is available. In our cases, a local database and document storage served as a cache to store the history about an object of interest. At the same time, one must ensure that an organization's privacy policies and security guidelines are taken into account. These rules might prevent the storage of certain data on a mobile device or the accessibility to certain information outside of a specific location or area.

6   Conclusion

This paper investigates the roles and designs of mobile applications that support organizational routines. Our main research contributions are the insights into the role of mobile applications in routines, as well a set of design principles that can guide software developers in developing mobile applications for routines. We find that mobile applications guide workers in routine execution by standardizing the sequence of activities and validating the outcome of activities. Moreover, they provide context-specific information and enable transparent communication between domain expert and individual. Our design principles highlight the relevance of identifying the routine's boundary and creating pre defined structures for routine execution, while leaving a certain degree of flexibility to the experts. The design principles further suggest providing reporting functionality for communication to stakeholders and access to context-specific information. By looking into mobile application design for organizational routines, we complement existing research on user-centered design [6, 22] with specific design principles for expert users working in organizational contexts. Our research is meant to be a first step towards extending the notion of user context in mobile application development to the broader context of organizational routines.

Among the obvious limitations of our study is the limited number of cases we analyzed. In this regard, it will be interesting to analyze how different types of organizational routines and different contexts influence the ways mobile applications are designed and used.

References

1. Bouwman, H., Carlsson, C., Walden, P., Molina-Castillo, F.J.: Reconsidering the actual and future use of mobile services. Inf. Syst. E-Bus. Manag. **7**, 301–317 (2009)
2. Lee, S., Shin, B., Lee, H.G.: Understanding post-adoption usage of mobile data services: the role of supplier-side variables. J. Assoc. Inf. Syst. **10**, 860–888 (2010)
3. Nelson, R.R., Winter, S.G.: An Evolutionary Theory of Economic Change. Harvard University Press, Cambridge (1982)
4. Argote, L.: Organizational learning research: past present and future. Manag. Learn. **42**, 439–446 (2011)
5. Pentland, B.T., Feldman, M.S.: Organizational routines as a unit of analysis. Ind. Corp. Change **14**, 793–815 (2005)
6. Wasserman, T.: Software engineering issues for mobile application development. In: Proceedings of the Foundation of Software Engineering, Santa Fe, New Mexico, USA (2010)
7. Dix, A.: Human Computer Interaction. Pearson Education (2004)
8. Cohen, M.D., Bacdayan, P.: Organizational routines are stored as procedural memory: evidence from a laboratory study. Organ. Sci. **5**, 554–568 (1994)
9. Becker, M.C.: Organizational routines: a review of the literature. Ind. Corp. Change **13**, 643–678 (2004)
10. Becker, M.C.: The concept of routines: some clarifications. Camb. J. Econ. **29**, 249–262 (2005)
11. Cohen, M.D., Burkhart, R., Dosi, G., Egidi, M., Marengo, L., Warglien, M., Winter, S.: Routines and other recurring action patterns of organizations: contemporary research issues. Ind. Corp. Change **5**, 653–698 (1996)
12. D'Adderio, L.: Artifacts at the centre of routines: performing the material turn in routines theory. J. Inst. Econ. **7**, 197–230 (2011)
13. Orlikowski, W.J.: Knowing in practice: enacting a collective capability in distributed organizing. Organ. Sci. **13**, 249–273 (2002)

14. Pentland, B.T., Feldman, M.S.: Designing routines: on the folly of designing artifacts, while hoping for patterns of action. Inf. Organ. **18**, 235–250 (2008)
15. Barnes, S.: Mbusiness: The Strategic Implications of Mobile Communications. Routledge, New York (2003)
16. Tarasewich, P.: Designing mobile commerce applications. Commun. ACM **46**, 57–60 (2003)
17. York, J., Pendharkar, P.C.: Human-computer interaction issues for mobile computing in a variable work context. Int. J. Hum.-Comput. Stud. **60**, 771–797 (2004)
18. Suter-Crazzolara, C.: Finalists of the "SAP Mobile App Challenge 2012 for Partners in EMEA & DACH," http://scn.sap.com/people/clemens.suter-crazzolara/blog/2012/10/22/announcing-the-three-finalists-of-the-sap-mobile-app-challenge-2012-for-partners-in-emea-dach
19. Koller, W., Mischner, R., Pawlowski, B.: Erfolgreicher Sanierung und Restrukturierung im Automobilhandel. Dekra Consulting GmbH (2010)
20. Ockerman, J., Pritchett, A.: A review and reappraisal of task guidance: aiding workers in procedure following. Int. J. Cogn. Ergon. **4**, 191–212 (2000)
21. Chau, P.Y.K., Hu, P.J.-H.: Investigating healthcare professionals' decisions to accept telemedicine technology: an empirical test of competing theories. Inf. Manage. **39**, 297–311 (2002)
22. Norman, D.A., Draper, S.W.: User Centered System Design. New Perspectives on Human-Computer Interaction. Erlbaum Associates Inc., Hillsdale (1986)

Infusing User Experience into the Organizational DNA of an Enterprise IT Shop

Faith McCreary[✉], Marla Gomez, and Derrick Schloss

Information Technology Group, IT User Experience, Intel Corporation,
Santa Clara, CA, USA
{Faith.A.McCreary,Marla.A.Gomez,
Derrick.J.Schloss}@intel.com

Abstract. This case study describes how an enterprise IT user experience (UX) group evolved from its genesis as a tactical, backend fixer of usability issues to a strategic partner within a large IT department. We share specifics as to how UX emerged as a skillset, how UX professionals evolved their methods to increase their effectiveness, and how operational changes facilitated the adoption of UX practices within the corporate IT shop. We detail how data-driven UX decision-making was essential in transforming the traditional IT shop into a more user experience driven organization that better understands their target workforce and uses this understanding to set product strategy for the organization and drive strategic improvement of IT solutions. Learnings and insights from this journey provides guidance to others wanting to maximize the value of enterprise UX investments.

Keywords: User experience · Enterprise IT · UX decision-making · Big data · Thick data · UX metrics · Organizational transformation

1 Introduction

Today's enterprise experience is increasingly complex both for users and the IT shops that support them. This experience is fragmented across multiple devices, platforms, new enterprise products, legacy systems, and a multitude of vendors. In the course of daily work, users must often switch between very different interfaces and often times serve as the human glue connecting disjoint information systems. The fragmented experience leaves users frustrated and less efficient while also slowing the speed of business.

This fragmentation of the enterprise experience also requires that IT shops support a great many more products than they have historically. IT shops often find themselves consumed by the day-to-day challenges of keeping their diverse product portfolios running and keeping up with the latest technology, leaving them little remaining bandwidth to even consider the experience of their users. This fragmentation is exacerbated by the number of IT teams that are needed to develop and manage the enterprise experience. In a large enterprise such as ours, it can take many dozens of

© Springer International Publishing Switzerland 2015
F.F.-H. Nah and C.-H. Tan (Eds.): HCIB 2015, LNCS 9191, pp. 513–524, 2015.
DOI: 10.1007/978-3-319-20895-4_47

teams around the globe. Often times despite the interdependent nature of these functions within the enterprise, the teams supporting different elements operate in deep silos, independently of each other, and with little awareness of how individual pieces fit together to shape the enterprise experience.

Today's enterprise users are increasingly expecting their enterprise experience to be as easy-to-use as their consumer experiences. They have easy access to a multitude of web-based, external products that allow them to bypass IT regardless of whether the externally offered product complies with corporate information or security policies – potentially putting the corporation and its intellectual property at risk. This practice is often costly, and corporate mandates do little to stem the tide of external products into the enterprise environment. As a result, IT shops are increasingly turning to user-centered approaches as a means of improving user productivity, increasing business velocity, and in general making enterprise solutions more appealing to users. However, these practices run counter to the technology-centric, one-size-fits-all, and business-centric approaches of traditional IT. Further, UX and IT professionals use very different languages to describe the enterprise and significantly different methods to evaluate enterprise health which hampers the adoption of these user-centered approaches within most IT shops.

This paper describes the journey of one enterprise IT user experience group from its genesis as a tactical, backend fixer of usability problems to a strategic partner within IT that is transforming the holistic enterprise experience (i.e., the cumulative experience that results from using the many IT products and services). Recent years have seen user-centered shifts in how the corporate IT department delivers products and services resulting in changes across the organization. We will share learnings and insights from our journey for others looking to transform the enterprise.

2   The Journey to Strategic UX

This work takes place within the context of a large corporate IT shop that employs over 6000 individuals at 59 different sites around the world and supports over 102 K employees in 63 countries using over 160 K devices including over 53 K handheld devices. Its mission is to grow the business through information technology by increasing employee productivity and driving business efficiencies and growth, while delivering IT efficiently, securely, and with agility.

The journey to UX began with the creation of a central UX function in 2005. At first, the UX function focused mainly on tactical "catch and save" activities with projects, such as usability testing and enhancement of existing applications. Typically, we worked alone on an individual project and were the sole proponent of UX within the project. Arguments for UX often centered around its inherent goodness rather than business value so while UX was seen as important, it was not considered essential nor did the UX professionals within the group have sufficient understanding of the "business" of IT to position themselves more effectively.

Before we could start carving out a space for UX within the larger IT landscape, we had to transform ourselves from a group of UX zealots to a team running a UX business. Fortuitously, we were led by a seasoned IT professional who, while not a UX expert, could clearly articulate the potential value of UX to broader IT and help the group more successfully articulate its value. This guidance helped the team gain greater credibility within IT as well as increased business acumen. Simultaneously, we were coalescing as a team and developing more efficient ways of working with each other. Outside of project work that made up the bulk of UX activities, we focused on defining robust internal processes that mapped UX deliverables against the product lifecycle, developing standard templates for UX deliverables, creating a central UX repository, and designing a group portfolio.

By iteratively refining our processes so that we could work more effectively together and better fit the larger IT organization, we were able to repeatedly demonstrate high quality, reproducible results that tied to our core value proposition. Namely, by adopting a user-centered approach to delivering IT services, IT solutions could be optimized to improve employee productivity and increase business velocity by

- Aligning products to actual usage,
- Increasing user adoption of solutions,
- Reducing development rework,
- Delivering a consistent user experience, and
- Increasing user flexibility and choice

These optimizations minimize user issues while reducing development and support costs. In the process and over time, we arrived at a core set of UX services that enabled us to influence all levels of service decision-making and demonstrate business value.

2.1   An Evolving UX Services Landscape

In the years since the team's original inception, the scope of UX services offered within IT have grown to include

- Project support focused on a specific product,
- Enablement work focused on growing UX skills within the larger IT shop (e.g., training) and UX governance (e.g. UI standards),
- Satellite UX capabilities that over time grew within IT as part of the central team's growth of UX capabilities across IT,
- Metrics development to better assess the extent to which users found IT products and services usable and useful,
- Research transformation to provide a deep dive, front-end look at what users need prior to project and program definition, and
- Design innovation to look at experience possibilities prior to program or project inception.

Figure 1 shows how staffing of these different UX activities evolved over time and highlights the evolution of the UX capability within the corporate IT shop. Specifics of how each helped weave UX into the corporate IT shop's organizational DNA will be discussed in greater detail in the following sub-sections.

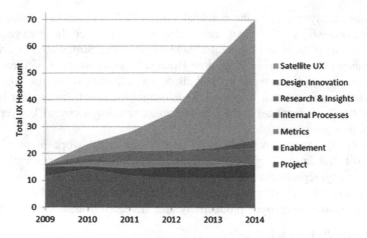

Fig. 1. Shifts in UX services staffing over time

2.2   Growing UX in the Workforce

Growing UX Skills. Faced with the reality that our numbers would never be sufficient to cover the plethora of enterprise products and projects, we tried to extend our reach by providing ad hoc training to members of the teams that we worked with. The training was targeted at a specific skill needed for a UX project deliverable (e.g., how to run a usability test). It helped us extend our resources and helped project teams gain new insights about what UX offered. As training was often developed on the fly and in response to a specific project need, it often required extensive updating for use in a different space. By 2011, our training approach had matured and we began

- Formally tracking ad hoc UX training,
- Standardizing training for common UX tasks (e.g., how to interview users), and
- Using foundational training to increase UX awareness and appreciation.

The training was mapped to corporate human resource competency areas for the UX job roles, which enabled job roles with skill affinities, such as software developers and system analysts, to target specific skill areas within our primary competency areas. Table 1 shows the evolution of IT job roles over time.

We also offered coaching by UX professionals and a "brown bag" series for practitioners that focused on topics related to the challenges of introducing UX methods into IT projects. To further speed the growth of UX within IT, a virtual Community of Practice was created to maximize IT engagement, foster UX collaboration, and cultivate emerging UX leaders. The online forum became the focal point for IT employees to learn more about how to integrate UX methods into their work practices and enable positive user experiences. With more than 3000 visitors in 2013, it provides one-stop access to IT UX resources and specialized UX communities (e.g., user research).

In 2012, we also began offering a formal apprentice program to train selected participants from IT groups with the aim of infusing UX practitioner skills across IT

Table 1. How IT roles transformed with the institutionalization of UX within the enterprise

IT Role	UX Focus Areas
Training, Quality Assurance	Usability evaluation of products and services
Business / Systems Analyst	Project UX practitioner on low to medium risk efforts
Program / Project Managers	Make UX part of decision-making, set UX goals, and plan for UX deliverables
Portfolio / Service Owners	Define UX roadmaps and make UX part of decision-making
Software Developer	UI design practitioner on low to medium risk efforts
UX Professionals	Business savvy UX architects and strategists on high risk efforts; UX coach for other roles

projects. In its original form, it was an intensive undertaking for the IT apprentices that required weekly classes and out-of-class work. Apprentices also had to pass a final exam. While those succeeding became successful UX practitioners, the drop-out rate was a whopping 61 %, largely due to competing job demands. To decrease the dropout rate, we shifted to self-paced learning and quarterly opportunities to demonstrate UX competency thru rigorous portfolio review, testing, and interviews. We also provided ongoing "office hours" where IT practitioners could just drop-in for advice and coaching from a UX professional.

We have found these approaches are successful at infusing UX into the workforce as long as there is the underlying UX skill affinity for the individual and organizational commitment within the parent IT group. However, even with that, it takes both time and money to grow UX skills as shown in Fig. 2.

Growing Satellite UX. With the increasing visibility and success of UX within IT, a hybrid staffing model emerged resulting in a distributed community of UX practitioners and professionals across the key IT divisions. These "teams" typically included a mix of local UX practitioners as well as UX resources from the central UX group. Often times, satellite UX was a by-product of previous large-scale UX initiatives that yielded significant business results. These initiatives were often a catalyst for the up-levelling of UX skills among local IT professionals who served as UX practitioners and took on more tactical UX responsibilities during the original work. The practitioners were typically used to supplement the skills of UX professionals. In a few cases, IT divisions hired UX professionals to drive UX strategic initiatives for their domains.

The growth in satellite UX was often accompanied by the emergence of a UX "champion" or evangelist within the division. Typically senior technical folks or mid-level managers, these champions were key allies for the central UX team and centers of gravity for UX work occurring in their area. In 2012, this loose network of UX champions was formalized and became an advisory council for the central IT group as well as local leaders of UX within their division.

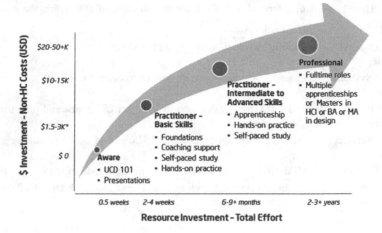

Fig. 2. Investment required to shift IT professionals to given levels of UX skill

2.3 Motivating with Metrics

Like many companies, as a way of motivating UX involvement and demonstrating the impact of UX activities, we developed a core set of metrics that could be applied across IT products and services [1]. They range from an upfront needs assessment to our Voice of the User survey, a yearly look at overall user satisfaction with delivered solutions. This common set of metrics allows the organization to reliably compare the UX of different components of the enterprise experience. Passing "grades" or scores are defined for each metric, providing shared UX expectations across the enterprise.

UX Risk Assessment. Earlier work found that re-framing usability in terms of risk management helps managers see the benefits of usability and helps usability gain traction in an organization [2]. This perspective speaks to core IT concerns and spurs IT to think about UX in terms of the "risk that the project will fail if you don't". The *UX Risk Assessment (UXRA)* looks at project risk relative to

- Number of users,
- Business criticality of user tasks,
- Magnitude of user experience change,
- Complexity of user workflow,
- Frequency of use,
- Level of ergonomic risk, and
- User satisfaction with existing solution

The UXRA generates both an overall risk score as well as prescriptive guidance for mitigating UX risks. It has evolved into a UX needs analysis for new projects, provides the UX organization with a way to compare projects, drives UX resourcing prioritization, and is mandatory for all new projects.

The IT Usability Scale. The IT Usability Scale (ITUS) is a four-item, Likert scale that assesses a solution's perceived usability [5] by having users rate whether

- [This solution's] capabilities meet my requirements.
- Using [this solution] is a frustrating experience.
- [This solution] is easy to use.
- I have to spend too much time correcting things with [this solution].

The ITUS was created to provide results similar to those obtained with the longer 10-item System Usability Scale [4], and was organized around the ISO 9241-11 definition of usability [9]. It is required for any project assigned UX resources and provides both a baseline and a post-deployment assessment of usability improvement.

Voice of the User. *Voice of the User (VoU)* is a yearly look at how well the collective IT experience satisfies employee day-to-day needs. It was originally conceived to connect user feedback to IT strategy and was designed to provide metrics to motivate experience improvement [7]. It assesses

- Overall satisfaction with the IT Experience,
- Overall satisfaction with how IT products and services enable core employee tasks (e.g., collaboration, information finding), and
- User satisfaction and perceived importance for individual products (e.g., employee portal, search, mobile apps).

Timed to coincide with the IT financial planning cycle, VoU became a tool for IT leadership to identify products and services that were most in need of UX improvement and funding in the coming year. We have linked responses of individual users back to their actual usage of IT products and services, which has allowed us to build models of how product and support use relate to satisfaction with a product and overall IT.

2.4 Infusing UX into IT Governance

While increasing UX awareness and skills within the parent IT organization and providing metrics helped improve individual products, it did little to help align the individual experience. Like many IT shops wanting to give users a more uniform experience, our group defined interface standards that prescribe color schemes, fonts, layouts, and the like. Built on a foundation of industry standards (e.g., ISO 9241-11), we increased their relevance by incorporating corporate brand standards and increased utility by combining them with re-usable interface assets (e.g., design patterns, re-usable code units). The resulting set of collateral cover

- General look and feel across platforms (*e.g.*, icon libraries, interface guidelines, design patterns)
- Platform specific guidelines (*e.g.*, Employee Portal, Business-to-Business portal)
- Application specific guidelines (*e.g.*, mobile apps, touch guidelines)
- Vendor specific guidelines (*e.g.*, SaaS solutions)

We increased their usage by making them part of IT governance and creating code libraries that streamlined development. While this governance was successful at taming the visual inconsistencies within the IT environment, they did little to address the functional inconsistencies between products or to ensure that the cumulative experience was a coherent one for our users.

2.5   Seeding Experience Transformation

While the previous efforts were instrumental in making incremental improvements in a product or service, they were insufficient to seed the entrepreneurial type thinking needed to transform the enterprise experience. Historically IT organizations focused on corporate total cost of ownership (TCO) often at the expense of the individual user efficiency. Conventional IT thinking was that there was always a trade-off; you could not have both and TCO would always trump in the long run making user-centric transformation unsustainable.

We recognized that any large-scale and sustainable transformation of the experience meant transforming organizational thinking about IT users. While we identified early on the potential transformative aspects of the large-scale UX work we discuss below, we didn't expend energy trying to talk about it in larger IT until we could demonstrate its impact. Instead we focused on engaging with organizations where there was pull and potential value in large-scale experience transformation.

Seeding Experience Transformation with Research. Most UX professionals perform user research in some form or another—typically at the start of a project or program. However, by waiting until project inception, user research often has little impact on larger IT strategy. So, early in 2008, we shifted our focus to transformative research that occurred before a project or program began and had the potential to transform both the experience and the enterprise. For instance, when creating new business-to-business services, or transforming core enterprise functionalities.

Collaborative Research to Seed Understanding and Empathy. Underlying our approach was a more collaborative, action research-based model [8]. In keeping with the tenets of process consultation [14] our approach was based on the belief that neither our IT clients nor the UX team knew enough initially to identify the "right" solution. Instead we partnered with the client to jointly identify the "real" problem and discover solutions that fit the client environment. Sociotechnical systems theory and macroergonomics served as the underlying theoretical model for understanding the data gathered through the collaborative process. They have been used successfully in earlier work to holistically assess how well a technology fits its users and their work environment in relationship to enterprise priorities [10, 12]. They are especially appropriate for examining the user experiences within the enterprise, as success requires IT to understand how their "technology" impacts other elements of the user's world.

We also focused on understanding the organizational beliefs and constraints that shaped the original experience. We spent substantial time packaging the user story in innovative ways to bring the story to life for the organization and help make it "sticky" to the organization. Success required organizations to think differently about the user and grow an organization-wide commitment to solving user problems.

We found that the collaborative process shifted the focus of power for the user experience, and often resulted in discomfort among key decision makers. The more collaborative approach was also often uncomfortable for some UX professionals who saw the process as ceding some of the power of their expertise and sometimes requiring them to give up something methodologically for success. By adapting our research methods to the situation at hand and carefully looking for opportunities that allowed us to influence IT strategy, this process seeded experience transformation, shifted organizational beliefs about the utility of UX, and shifted our own thinking about how to incorporate UX practices in the enterprise. It also typically spawned a series of impactful UX projects that brought the potential of the research to life.

Integrating Big Data and Thick Data to Frame Enterprise-wide Transformation. Corporations collect a wealth of operational data about enterprise users. IT organizations invest heavily in managing and storing this so-called "big" data, in hopes that it can be analyzed to reveal patterns, trends, and associations that might benefit the business. It can also be a rich source of information about user behavior. It excels at fine tuning the delivery of an enterprise experience. For instance, enterprises can use the data to identify problems by looking at support tickets and then fix the problems before a major escalation or serious user incident occurs. However, big data is fundamentally a backwards look at the enterprise; it lacks the qualitative insights that tell the organization why the behavior happened or the context in which it happened.

Fortunately, where big data falls short, more traditional UX methods excel. These methods yield qualitative information that provide the enterprise with granular, specific data about enterprise users that allows IT decision-makers to understand user behavior and adapt IT strategy to better meet user needs, and increase enterprise velocity. This so-called "thick" data is often in the form of user narratives or user observations [16]. These "stories" of use can come from many sources including interviews, observations, social media, participatory design sessions, or open-ended comments on surveys. Often times this data is elicited using small numbers of users using sample sizes that puts their generalizability in question in the eyes of IT decision makers. Further, even with careful curation and management, this data can be difficult to re-use outside of the context of the program or project in which it was gathered.

By growing connections between the massive amounts of operational big data in the enterprise and the thick data resulting from direct research with thousands of employees, we could blend the multiple types of data [11]. It required that we manually code the user stories to create a coding structure that represented the users' over-arching mental model of the enterprise experience [3, 15, 17]. We let the user stories guide the coding but made sure to code certain attributes related to our underlying sociotechnical model including specifics of the user activity, whether the story illustrated a positive or negative incident from the user perspective, underlying technology, environmental factors (e.g., workspace, location), and user characteristics (e.g., attitudes, motivators) that were not discernible from big data, and organizational factors (e.g. how work was organized). We then defined summary measures based on the coding framework that had emerged. These measures allowed us to connect the user stories with the big data in a way that allowed us to holistically examine the enterprise experience and discover patterns using the blended dataset. Mathematically best "fit" patterns were then identified in the blended dataset based on similarities in how employees used and responded to enterprises products and services [11].

These patterns became the foundation of our enterprise experience framework, which was composed of four main components.

- Core activities, or the high-level tasks, that all enterprise users engage in in order to accomplish work (e.g., find information, collaborate).

- Influencers, or core elements of the enterprise world, whose characteristics impact the user's ability to accomplish core activities (e.g., physical workspace)
- Themes, or the core experiences, that users wanted from the enterprise experience regardless of what product or service the user was interacting with.
- Segments, or groups of users, who interact or respond to IT products or services in a similar manner.

The experience framework became a conceptual model of the desired enterprise experience for product teams and provided a common vision to guide experience transformation. To help product teams use the framework to re-frame the experience of their product or service, we introduced large-scale, layered storytelling to unify the supporting framework collateral. Product teams used framework components to create their own stories that are relevant to what they are trying to accomplish; many stories are possible from the same data. The framework fuels UX roadmaps for portfolios by providing stories for agile teams. [11]

Agile Design Innovation Thru Design Thinking. In a world of package-based enterprise applications the concept of 'design' often gets lost. However, as IT shifts to delivering services, not just applications, design is increasingly playing a role. So in 2013, our UX group launched a new design service that focuses on taking what is known about the needs of enterprise users and generating innovative conceptual designs for enterprise services using design thinking and visualization techniques such as sketching or prototyping. Iterative in nature, the design process integrates stakeholders in the innovation process and seeks to co-create design concepts that are both feasible to implement and create value for the enterprise by increasing the pleasurability and efficiency of the products.

This agile-based approach used existing UX research and the previously discussed framework as a starting point for efforts to rapidly go from concept discussions to prototype. Previous UX work became the starting point for the team's "Vision Quest" activities and served as a catalyst to helping the team form a design hypothesis around core presumptions of what features and capabilities should be included in the solution [6]. A series of contextual scenarios were written from the design hypotheses which were then organized to form a high-level "narrative" or persuasive story of the product vision. These were then documented in a storyboard. To validate design presumptions, several intervals of presumptive design tests were conducted with end-users in tandem with design activities. Features not validated as "valuable" by users were removed from the storyboard and product vision. The vision iteratively became more defined and evolved into a 'lightweight' clickable prototype used to engage stakeholders and the technical team in feasibility discussions.

3   Conclusions

By seeking to transform the workforce, operational procedures, standards, and even ourselves as UX professionals, we have seeded transformation in individual enterprise products, the larger cumulative IT experience, and the larger IT shop. In the process, we have grown strong partnerships across IT that has further accelerated the infusion of

UX into the organizational DNA of our large corporate IT shop. We have found UX transformation can help corporate IT shops grow their strategic role within their enterprise and help re-frame their larger role in the corporation to. Our learnings along the way have implications for other IT groups looking to see a UX-centric transformation within their own organizations.

We have found that for UX to truly transform the enterprise experience, it must become part of the larger organization's DNA which means weaving UX into its culture, its standard operating procedures, and decision making. To do that, UX practitioners in IT shops must provide

- Easily consumable user insights to facilitate incorporation of UX into decision-making,
- UX training to shift the IT mind-set,
- UX tools and processes that are easy for non-UX professionals to leverage, and
- UX metrics to motivate change.

This "UX toolkit" must provide a holistic vision while at the same time provide insights at the product level to ensure that those responsible for individual products can work effectively together achieve the vision.

It's not enough for the UX professionals in the organization to act based on this information. Nor is it enough to get the buy-in of the CIO and senior leadership. Rather everyone right down to those who are "feet-on-the-ground" in the IT organization must work together in a well-coordinated fashion to achieve the vision. The road to a UX-centric transformation of an enterprise IT shop isn't necessarily easy, or straight, and is often fraught with ambiguity, but for those who persevere on this journey (and it is most certainly a journey), UX can seed a shared vision of the enterprise experience and focus actions on bringing the vision to life.

Acknowledgements. We give particular thanks to Deidre Ali, Shannon Morante, Linda Wooding, Judy Ossello, Brooke Castaneda, Candace Gilmore, Jayne May, Anne McEwan, Susan Michalek, Cindy Pickering, Pete Lockhart, Sri Canakapalli, Kraig Finstad, and the larger IT UX central organization. Their collective intelligence and persistence made this work possible.

References

1. Albert, W., Tullis, T.: Measuring the User Experience. Morgan Kaufmann, San Francisco (2010)
2. Altom, T.: Usability as risk management. Interactions **14**(2), 16–17 (2007)
3. Beyer, H., Holtzblatt, K.: Contextual design. Interactions **6**(1), 32–42 (1999)
4. Brooke, J.: SUS: A "quick and dirty" usability scale. In: Jordan, P.W., Thomas, B., Weerdmeester, B.A., McClelland, A.L. (eds.) Usability Evaluation in Industry. Taylor and Francis, London (1996)
5. Finstad, K.: The usability metric for user experience. Interact. Comput. **22**(5), 323–327 (2010)
6. Frishberg, L.: Presumptive design: cutting the looking glass cake. Interactions **13**, 18–20 (2006)

7. Gilmore, C.: Measuring worker expectations of information technology at the organizational level: identifying how end-user expectations influence productivity-enhancing behaviour. Unpublished dissertation (2012)
8. Greenwood, D., Levin, M.: Introduction to Action Research, 2nd edn. Sage Publishing, Thousand Oaks (2007)
9. ISO 9241-11: Ergonomic Requirements for Office Work with Visual Display Terminals (VDTs). Part 11: Guidance on Usability (1998)
10. Kleiner, B.: Macroergonomics as a large work-system transformation technology. Hum. Factors Ergon. Manuf. **14**(2), 99–115 (2004)
11. McCreary, F., Gómez, M., Schloss, D., Ali, D.: Charting a new course for the workplace with an experience framework. In: Nah, F.F.-H. (ed.) HCIB 2014. LNCS, vol. 8527, pp. 68–79. Springer, Heidelberg (2014)
12. McCreary, F., Raval, K., Fallenstein, M.: A case study in using macroergonomics as a framework for business transformation. Proc. Hum. Factors Ergon. Soc. Annu. Meet. **50** (15), 1483–1487 (2006)
13. Rosenfeld, L.: Seeing the elephant: defragmenting user research. A list apart, vol. 381 (2013). http://alistapart.com/article/seeing-the-elephant-defragmenting-user-research
14. Shein, E.: Process Consultation Revisited: Building the Helping Relationship. Addison Wesley Longman, Boston (1998)
15. Tuch, A., Trusell, R., Hornbaek, K.: Analyzing users' narratives to understand experience with interactive products. In: Proceedings of CHI 2013, pp. 2079–2088, ACM Press (2013)
16. Wang, T.: Big data needs thick data. Ethnography matters (2013). http://ethnographymatters. net/blog/2013/05/13/big-data-needs-thick-data/
17. Young, I.: Mental Models: Aligning Design Strategy with Human Behavior. Rosenfeld Media, New York (2008)

Effects of the Use of Points, Leaderboards and Badges on In-Game Purchases of Virtual Goods

Fiona Fui-Hoon Nah[1]([⊠]), Lakshmi Sushma Daggubati[1],
Amith Tarigonda[1], Raghu Vinay Nuvvula[1], and Ofir Turel[2]

[1] Department of Business and Information Technology,
Missouri University of Science and Technology, Rolla, MO, USA
{nahf, ldz98, atvdb, nrgy5}@mst.edu
[2] College of Business and Economics, California State University,
Fullerton, CA, USA
oturel@fullerton.edu

Abstract. Game design elements are major factors in gamification. In this study, we seek to examine the impact of game design elements on users' in-game purchases of virtual goods. The purchase of virtual goods due to players' intrinsic motivation has been studied but little is known about the purchase of virtual goods due to the use of game design elements (i.e., Points, Leaderboards and Badges) built into the games. Extending our knowledge to this realm can help researchers to better understand gamers' behaviors, and game designers and marketers to better promote and sell virtual goods in online games.

Keywords: Virtual goods · Gamification · Points · Leaderboards · Badges · Game design elements

1 Introduction

The purchase of virtual goods is progressively turning into a typical peculiarity of online games and virtual worlds [1–4]. Global revenue on the sale of virtual goods has been rapidly growing; assessments provided by business reports indicate an estimation of virtual goods revenues of \$14.8 billion in 2012 and an expected increase at a yearly rate of 12.5 % [5]. Even though a large percentage of users will never spend money in a game, the amount of spending from users who spend money is sizeable and significant [6]. The primary objective of the free-to-play or "freemium" model is to get more players into the game and provide desirable items or features that players can purchase. This revenue model, if successfully implemented, tends to increase profits from micro-transactions and can outweigh the profits from a one-time game purchase. Understanding the game elements that may lead to purchases of virtual goods is crucial because game developers have progressively become dependent on the sales of virtual products as their principle source of income [5].

Although past studies have explored motivations for the purchase of virtual goods [7–9], we have not come across a research study that has evaluated the impacts of

© Springer International Publishing Switzerland 2015
F.F.-H. Nah and C.-H. Tan (Eds.): HCIB 2015, LNCS 9191, pp. 525–531, 2015.
DOI: 10.1007/978-3-319-20895-4_48

specific game design elements on in-game purchases. Since Points, Leaderboards and Badges (PLBs) are rigorously deployed as game design elements in gamification, we are interested in studying their effects in the context of in-game purchases of virtual goods.

2   Research Objective

The following research question (RQ) is therefore proposed:
RQ: Does the use of PLBs have an impact on in-game purchases of virtual items? We will examine the above question in this research.

3   Points, Leaderboards and Badges (PLBs) in Online Games

In this research, we focus on studying the effects of the following game design elements:

Points. Points are numerical values which denote a measure of the ability of a player or the expendable resources still available in the game. Players are motivated when they are progressively being rewarded for their performance in a game [10].

Leaderboards. The leaderboard is a game element that displays the performance of individual players in comparison to other players. It lists the players in the order of the points they have achieved in the game and offers a form of metrics that players may strive to accomplish by showing their scores relative to what others have accomplished [11]. It can be motivating to players as they are able to compare their scores with others.

Badges. Trophies or badges are indications of virtual achievements awarded to players for accomplishing certain tasks. At the time when achievements were included as gaming elements in Xbox Live Platform [12], there was a vast scale usage of badges in online games. Since then, badges have been broadly implemented on other gaming platforms and have demonstrated a high degree of success, resulting in higher sales revenue and higher scores in reviews [13].

4   Literature Review

We reviewed the existing literature on the role of points, leaderboards and badges in games. PLBs are three of the most fundamental game design elements [14, 15]. Players who are short of points may purchase virtual items which enable them to do better or to survive in a game. Leaderboards can motivate players by providing a comparison of their scores with others. Badges are indications of achievements in a game.

Zagal et al. [14] classify PLBs as goal metrics, as all of them are utilized to track and give feedback on player accomplishments in games. Farzan et al. [15] examined the capability of a point-based reward system (i.e., "status" levels and a leaderboard) to enhance user activities on a social networking site. Although user activity was enhanced initially through the use of these features, it deteriorated back to the starting position, and after removing these game elements, the user activity dropped below what it used to be before introducing these rewards. A few users also indicated that the leaderboard has helped them to work harder toward keeping up with other users. Hence, the reward system has provided motivation to the users to keep up with the games, as after the removal of the reward system, they became less motivated and involved. While PLBs may also affect users' intrinsic motivation, we did not find any empirical studies that support this claim [16].

Virtual item purchases in online games are an emerging phenomenon that offers a unique business environment, where thousands of game users interact with one another, and they buy and sell virtual items in virtual worlds [7]. Although virtual items have no intrinsic value like physical items, virtual items satisfy users' intrinsic needs such as prestige, status, ego, uniqueness, and self-expression. Online users have the tendency or inclination to own virtual properties and rights, and can buy and sell properties [17, 18]. People not only value recognition, commendation and honor but they also command respect, show off their achievements as well as seek importance, social prestige, reputation and/or high office [19]. Hence, offering these features and opportunities in online games can satisfy users' needs in online gaming. The reward of being part of a gaming community and being recognized as a reputed name within the community is the most noticeable variation for players apart from the collaborative nature that helps in attaining shared experience [20].

The virtual world environment has generated a flood of creative virtual goods and properties which stimulated the exponential growth of virtual consumption [17]. Players are motivated to collect these virtual goods and utilize them at higher or more difficult levels when they strive harder to beat or accomplish a specific task. In a game-oriented virtual platform, virtual products are mainly used for increasing the offensive or defensive power of a character or to meet the requirements of quests. One study has demonstrated that users were extensively motivated towards multi-player online role-playing games (MORPG) because of the unique game playing experience, as well as the opportunity to earn rewards and collaborate with other players in the virtual world [20]. Reinforcement theory [21] and goal setting theory [22, 23], in similar lines, argue that positive feedback increases the likelihood of repeating a specific behavior. When reinforcement theory and goal setting theory are applied to online gaming, they suggest that positive feedback from the game and other gamers motivate users to stay engaged in the game and perform well in the game.

Game mechanics are constructs of rules or approaches intended for interaction with the game state by providing specific paths where players interact with the game. Game mechanics help users by encouraging them to explore the space available through feedback mechanisms [11]. Games are generally designed by applying game mechanics to attract users and engage them. Game mechanics can entice users to play continuously and make the game so engaging or addictive that they buy virtual goods [11, 24, 25].

Game experience and purchase of virtual items are highly dependent on the interactivity level generated by the gamers [26]. The level of interaction in a game can be enhanced by PLBs which allow players to compare their accomplishments against others. Oh and Ryu examined how game mechanics can be used to create and sustain the demand for virtual goods [27]. Hamari and Lehdonvirta [28] identified several mechanics that drive the desirability of virtual goods and examined how different types of game mechanics based on segmentation of players can generate repeated purchases or create settings for additional virtual goods. In this research, our focus is on assessing the impact of PLBs on virtual item purchases in online games.

5   Theoretical Foundation and Hypotheses

As mentioned earlier, reinforcement theory and goal setting theory can be used to explain the effects of PLBs on players' online gaming behavior. According to reinforcement theory [21], positive feedback or reinforcement invites a behavior to be repeated by the user. Hence, as players receive more points and badges in a game, they want to continue to perform well and advance in the game. Leaderboards, on the other hand, show the performance of players in a game. By comparing one's score with those of the leaders in the game, one begins to set a goal, which is typically a high achievement goal in line with the scores of the leaders in the game. Goal setting theory [22, 23] suggests that setting a high achievement goal causes one to strive for high performance in a game.

Points. Reinforcement theory [21] suggests that the use of points in online games serves as a form of positive feedback that reinforces one's game playing behavior. Feedback enables players to be aware of their progression or relapse, and makes it easier for players to assess the amount of effort needed to achieve the goal [29]. Points serve as a feedback mechanism in games by enabling players to maintain their commitment toward a goal. Goal setting theory [22, 23] suggests that the use of points can motivate a player to achieve a high goal in a game. In order to attain higher scores in a game to satisfy one's goal, players can purchase virtual items to increase their gameplay. Based on reinforcement theory, the use of points increases players' motivation to continue playing the game and increases their motivation to spend money on virtual items to progress faster in the game. Owning virtual goods allows players to enhance their points which help them to level up in the game in order to increase their progression in the game and achieve the goal they have set for themselves. Thus, we propose the following hypothesis:

H1: The use of the point system increases in-game purchases of virtual goods.

Leaderboards. Leaderboards offer various metrics for comparisons among players including other players' scores, leaderboard positions, and the number of levels that one has progressed relative to others. Hence, leaderboards can incentivize a player to set a higher goal in the game through comparing one's score with those of the leaders in the game. According to goal setting theory [22, 23], the use of leaderboards encourages a player to set higher goals in a game, which further increases their intention to perform well in the game. Players who want to be listed at the top of a leaderboard may purchase virtual items to improve their gameplay. Hence, players are motivated to make virtual item purchases to further strengthen their positions in the game. Thus, we propose the following hypothesis:

H2: The use of the leaderboard system increases in-game purchases of virtual goods.

Badges. Badges are offered to players as a means to showcase their accomplishments and achievements in a game. By offering badges to players for showcasing, it provides them the opportunity to set high goals for themselves in the game, such as to attain more badges or higher level badges. Goal setting theory [22, 23] suggests that when players set higher goals for themselves, they are willing to invest in the game, which can include purchasing virtual items to achieve their goal. One of the methods in which badges are regularly utilized is to encourage participation by distinguishing the players. Badges also serve a developmental purpose by offering consistent feedback and in keeping track of accomplishments. Badges increase recognition and reputation and hence, offer incentives for players to purchase virtual items to help them achieve their goal. Thus, we propose the following hypothesis:

H3: The use of the badge system increases in-game purchases of virtual goods.
    Figure 1 shows the research model.

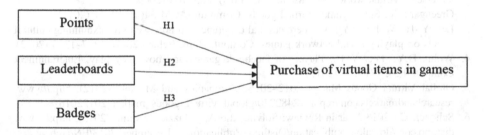

Fig. 1. Research model

6   Research Methodology

We plan to carry out both an experimental study and a questionnaire survey study to test our research model. For the experimental study, we will use a between-subject 2 × 2 × 2 factorial design to assess H1, H2 and H3. Hence, the experiment will have 2 levels for points (i.e., with and without the point system), 2 levels for leaderboards (i.e., with and without the leaderboard system), and 2 levels for badges (i.e., with and without the badge system). The experiment will be conducted in a laboratory setting. The questionnaire survey study will be administered to gamers over the Internet where we will survey their purchase behaviors in online games and whether PLBs influence their purchase of virtual items in the games.

7 Expected Contributions and Conclusions

Our research examines the effects of the use of game design elements – Points, Leaderboards and Badges (PLBs) – on users' in-game virtual item purchase behaviors. Drawing on reinforcement theory and goal setting theory, we hypothesize that PLBs will lead to users' purchases of virtual items in online games. The proposed studies will provide insights on specific game design elements that draw users into a game and entice users to purchase virtual goods. In other words, we are interested in assessing if PLBs increase users' in-game purchasing behavior of virtual goods.

In summary, the results of our studies will offer game designers a better understanding of the relevance and importance of game design elements in enhancing revenues through user in-game purchases of virtual goods, or more specifically, the efficacy of PLBs in doing so. Further studies will also be carried out to understand the motivations underlying users' in-game purchasing behavior with and without the presence of game design elements.

References

1. Castronova, E., Williams, D., Shen, C., et al.: As real as real? macroeconomic behavior in a large-scale virtual world. New Media Soc. **11**(5), 685–707 (2009)
2. Greengard, S.: Social games, virtual goods. Commun. ACM **54**(4), 19–21 (2011)
3. Lee, Y.-H., Wohn, D.Y.: Are there cultural differences in how we play? examining cultural effects on playing social network games. Comput. Hum. Behav. **28**(4), 1307–1314 (2012)
4. Wohn, D.Y., Lee, Y.-H.: Players of facebook games and how they play. Entertainment Comput. **4**(3), 171–178 (2013)
5. Global Virtual Goods Market 2012–2016. Companies and Markets (2012). http://www.researchandmarkets.com/reports/2482270/global_virtual_goods_market_20122016
6. Schoger, C.: 2013 Year in Review: Solving the App-Puzzle. Distimo (2013). http://www.distimo.com/download/publication/Distimo_Publication_-_December_2013/EN/archive
7. Guo, Y., Barnes, S.: Virtual item purchase behavior in virtual worlds. Electron. Commer. Res. **9**(1–2), 77–96 (2009)
8. Lehdonvirta, V.: Virtual item sales as a revenue model: identifying attributes that drive purchase decisions. Electron. Commer. Res. **9**(1–2), 97–113 (2009)
9. Lehdonvirta, V., Wilska, T., Johnson, M.: Virtual consumerism: case habbo hotel. Inf. Commun. Soc. **12**(7), 1059–1079 (2009)
10. Nah, F.F.-H., Zeng, Q., Telaprolu, V.R., Ayyappa, A.P., Eschenbrenner, B.: Gamification of education: a review of literature. In: Nah, F.F.-H. (ed.) HCIB 2014. LNCS, vol. 8527, pp. 401–409. Springer, Heidelberg (2014)
11. Galli, L., Bozzon, A.: On the application of game mechanics in information retrieval. In: Proceedings of the First International Workshop on Gamification for Information Retrieval. ACM (2014)
12. Jakobsson, M.: The achievement machine: understanding xbox achievements in gaming practices. Int. J. Comput. Game Res. **11**(1) (2011). http://gamestudies.org/1101/articles/jakobsson

13. Electronic Entertainment Design and Research. EEDAR Study Shows More Achievements in Games Leads to Higher Review Scores, Increased Sales. Press Release, October (2007). http://www.eedar.com/Uploads/57013c50-de91-4057-b3dc-9a55945860a2.pdf

14. Zagal, J.P., Mateas, M., Fernandez-Vara, C., Hochhalter, B., Lichti, N.: Towards an ontological language for game analysis. In: Proceedings of International DiGRA Conference: Changing Views – Worlds in Play, pp. 3–14 (2005)

15. Farzan, R., DiMicco, J.M., Millen, D.R., Brownholtz, B., Geyer, W., Dugan, C.: Results from deploying a participation incentive mechanism within the enterprise. In: Proceedings of the SIGCHI Conference on Human Factors in Computing Systems, pp. 563–572 (2008)

16. Mekler, E.D., Bruhlmann, F., Opwis K., Tuch, A.N.: Do points, levels and leaderboards harm intrinsic motivation? an empirical analysis of common gamification elements. In: Proceedings of the First International Conference on Gameful Design, Research, and Applications (Gamification 2013), pp. 66–73 (2013)

17. Jung, Y., and Pawlowski, S.: Consuming bits: an exploratory study of user goals for virtual consumption. In: Proceedings of the International Conference on Information Systems, paper 31 (2009). http://aisel.aisnet.org/icis2009/31/

18. Kim, Y.Y., Kim, M.H., Oh, S.: Emerging factors affecting the continuance of online gaming: the roles of bridging and bonding social factors. Cluster Comput. 17(3), 849–859 (2013)

19. Murray, H.A.: Explorations in Personality. Oxford University Press, New York (1938)

20. Yee, N.: Motivations for play in online games. CyberPsychology Behav. 9(6), 772–775 (2006)

21. Skinner, B.F.: Contingencies of Reinforcement: A Theoretical Analysis. Appleton-Century-Crofts, New York (1969)

22. Locke, E.A., Latham, G.P.: A Theory of Goal Setting and Task Performance. Prentice Hall, New Jersey (1990)

23. Locke, E.A., Latham, G.P.: Building a practically useful theory of goal setting and task motivation: a 35-year Odyssey. Am. Psychol. 57(9), 705–717 (2002)

24. Nah, F.F.-H., Telaprolu, V.R., Rallapalli, S., Venkata, P.R.: Gamification of education using computer games. In: Yamamoto, S. (ed.) HCI 2013, Part III. LNCS, vol. 8018, pp. 99–107. Springer, Heidelberg (2013)

25. Xu, Z., Turel, O., Yuan, Y.: Online game addiction among adolescents: motivation and prevention factors. Eur. J. Inf. Syst. 21(3), 321–340 (2012)

26. Davis, R., Sajtos, L.: Measuring consumer interactivity in response to campaigns coupling mobile and television media. J. Advertising Res. 48(3), 375–391 (2008)

27. Oh, G., Ryu, T.: Game design on item-selling based payment model in Korean online games. In: Proceedings of Digital Games Research Association (DiGRA), pp. 651–657 (2007)

28. Hamari, J., Lehdonvirta, V.: Game design as marketing: how game mechanics create demand for virtual goods. Int. J. Bus. Sci. Appl. Manage. 5(1), 14–29 (2010)

29. Sorrentino, D.M.: The SEEK mentoring program: an application of the goal-setting theory. J. Coll. Student Retention 8(2), 241–250 (2006)

Teleworkers and Their Use of an Enterprise Social Networking Platform

Daniel Weiss[1(✉)], Laurie E. Damianos[1], and Stan Drozdetski[2]

[1] Department of Collaboration and Social Computing, The MITRE Corporation,
Bedford, MA, USA
{dweiss,laurie}@mitre.org
[2] Department of Information Assets and Community Support,
The MITRE Corporation, Bedford, MA, USA
drozdetski@mitre.org

Abstract. This study surveyed teleworker usage of a social networking platform within an enterprise. Compared to on-campus employees, teleworkers exhibited earlier adoption, higher percentage of contributions, more variance in work hours, and lower membership in socially-oriented groups (versus work focused groups). The last result seems counterintuitive, and we propose two possible reasons for this phenomenon: the perceived need to cultivate an external perception of productivity, and lack of access to social events tied to specific geographic office locations. In addition, we provide insights, gleaned from interviews, into teleworker use of collaboration tools.

Keywords: Telework · Remote work · Social networking · Social software · Virtual teams · Teleworking · Enterprise · Collaboration

1 Introduction

As work teams become more distributed, and the Internet is more widely accessible, collaboration in the enterprise no longer happens exclusively in face-to-face meetings. Employees are commonly found to be working from diverse locations with non-traditional schedules. Additional classes of workers have emerged – from the teleworker who works from home one or more days per week to the mobile worker who works from coffee shops, airline terminals, and customer sites. Online communication and collaboration tools have greatly enhanced employee mobility by allowing them to stay in constant contact with their colleagues, but what can we learn from how teleworkers use these tools? In this case study, we delve into one company's teleworker population and how its usage of enterprise social media differs from populations that work from standard office locations.

2 Background

The MITRE Corporation is a not-for-profit organization with expertise in systems engineering, information technology, operational concepts, and enterprise modernization. In addition to managing multiple Federally Funded Research and Development

© Springer International Publishing Switzerland 2015
F.F.-H. Nah and C.-H. Tan (Eds.): HCIB 2015, LNCS 9191, pp. 532–541, 2015.
DOI: 10.1007/978-3-319-20895-4_49

Centers (FFRDCs), MITRE supports its own independent technology research and application development for solving sponsors' near-term and future problems. MITRE has over seven thousand scientists, engineers, and support specialists who work on hundreds of different projects across various sponsors and numerous domains. MITRE has two principal locations — one in McLean, VA and one in Bedford, MA – along with additional sites across the country and around the world. Over the past decade or so, MITRE has seen a shift of its working population from campus-based and site-based staff to mobile populations (those with no permanent, dedicated office space), tele-commuters (those working from home one or more days per week), and teleworkers (those working from home full time).

Because of the high level of technical, operational, and domain knowledge required, staff often seek out and consult with other MITRE experts on particular topics or seek assistance from in-house librarians in gathering resources. Much of MITRE's work involves collaboration across time and space, requiring virtual and mobile teams to share these resources and relevant research internally, but also to collaborate and share with external partners including government agencies, industry, academia, vendors, and other FFRDCs. Business and social connections formed during the duration of specific projects and programs often become hard to track and manage over time, and there is concern that knowledge may be lost between engagements.

To solve some of these problems and pressing business needs, the MITRE Corporation pioneered its exploration of enterprise social media in 2005 with research into social bookmarking tools, which were rapidly growing in popularity on the Internet at that time. MITRE developed and piloted its own internal version of a social bookmarking tool for resource management, information sharing and discovery, expert finding, and social networking [1]. Two years later, MITRE began to look at social networking tools as a means to track external relationships and to collaborate with external partners. In 2009, MITRE customized and launched Handshake [2], a social networking platform based on the open source Elgg platform [3]. The tool was made accessible outside of MITRE's network, so that the company could connect and engage with external partners while simultaneously enabling employees to collaborate with each other internally.

Handshake was initially released to just a small community of early adopters, but its user base quickly grew by word of mouth. Over the past five years, over 13500 members have joined Handshake, including 4000 invited external participants. Members have created more than 1500 Handshake project spaces, communities of practice, peer support groups, social groups, and more. Handshake enables users to participate in discussion forums, share documents, collaborate on wiki pages, and "connect" (or "friend") each other to keep abreast of what is happening in their network. Handshake also provides activity streams both within and outside the tool along with customizable email notifications to alert users to new content, comments, and updates.

3 Related Research

Much research has been done on the teleworker experience: the communication challenges imposed by the lack of common ground [4], factors like geographic separation [5], and even respect among peers [6]. Better collaboration tools make the mechanics of communication easier, but, as Olson et al. have put it, "Distance still matters" [7].

Despite the challenges, teleworking continues to appeal to employees seeking to improve their work/life balance, eliminate commuting hassle and expenses, and reduce stress. An analysis of existing research performed by Gajendran and Harrison [8] declared that the net effect on the employee is positive:

"Telecommuting has a clear upside: small but favorable effects on perceived autonomy, work–family conflict, job satisfaction, performance, turnover intent, and stress. Contrary to expectations in both academic and practitioner literatures, tele-commuting also has no straightforward, damaging effects on the quality of workplace relationships or perceived career prospects. However, there is a downside of higher intensity telecommuting in that it does seem to send coworker (but not supervisor) relationships in a harmful direction."

It is no surprise, then, that more people are choosing to work remotely: Forrester Research predicts that the ranks of telecommuters will swell to 63 million by 2016 in the US alone, with 11.7 million working from home full-time [9]. Today's teleworkers benefit from years of accumulated knowledge about working remotely. The United States Government even hosts a purpose-built web site, telework.gov, to provide tips to teleworkers and their managers.

A lot of theoretical knowledge about telework comes from studies of teams that use Information and Communication Technology (ICT) to collaborate over distance - what Olson et al. described as "hub to hub" communication [10] (where groups of people in two different locations collaborate with each other across distance). Each cycle of the ICT evolution, from email to video conferencing to instant messaging, is accompanied by research into the effect of that technology on remote collaboration. Enterprise social networking, in turn, has been explored by early adopters [11] as well as researchers surveying a developing technological landscape [12].

More recently, researchers have started taking a more nuanced look at the tele-worker experience, which traditionally follows the "hub and spoke" arrangement (where the teleworker is removed from the collocated team) [13].

This paper connects the two threads of research (enterprise social networking with teleworker experience) by evaluating the specific case of Handshake adoption and usage by MITRE's teleworker employees.

4   Methods

The Handshake platform was instrumented to collect usage data and statistics, which provided us with a rich set of data to analyze. For this study, we looked at tool adoption rates; login patterns and frequencies; contributions in the form of posts, comments (directly via browser and indirectly via reply-by-email), and edits – by volume, fre-quency, and pattern (i.e., time of day and changes in volume or frequency over time); number and type of group memberships; groups created and (co-) owned; and number of connections. We examined the data from the perspective of various user demo-graphics including job level, hire date, work unit (organization), time zone, location, and residency status (e.g., resident on campus, site-based, mobile, or teleworker).

By looking at the data across the different slices, we were able to detect patterns and differences, most notably by location and residency status. Due to the fact that the data lacked a normal distribution, we used non-parametric statistics such as Chi Square and Mann-Whitney U to analyze the data.

To complement the quantitative usage data, we reviewed and analyzed responses to a user survey first administered in September 2011 (333 respondents) and later repeated in November 2012 (409 respondents). Survey questions focused on aspects of usability, business value, knowledge management, situation awareness, collaboration support, and social connections. The survey snapshots represented user satisfaction over time for the general Handshake population. We were also able to take a closer look at changing satisfaction ratings for 99 users who participated in both surveys; we analyzed their rating changes with longitudinal changes in their usage patterns. Again, in the survey data, we were able to detect differences across the different populations. Respondents to both surveys were encouraged to write in comments, which helped us to better understand their responses and allow us to craft follow-up questions.

Based on our observations and analysis of usage patterns, survey data, and user comments, we developed several hypotheses about the differences we saw between the teleworker population and campus and site residents. We then developed a set of questions designed to probe the targeted group of teleworkers through structured interviews. We solicited volunteers who were willing to participate in a half-hour interview over an audio connection. Of those who responded, we selected 21, making sure that they represented all company centers and job levels and included new hires, more established employees, and long-term employees (over 15 years at the company). We also spoke to participants who were hired directly as teleworkers as well as those who transitioned to teleworking status after working on campus or on site. The interviews were transcribed and the data was later tabulated and analyzed.

5 Results

We analyzed both quantitative and qualitative data to understand our user population. In the course of our study, we observed the following differences between teleworkers and their office-based colleagues, based on our quantitative data:

- **Teleworkers are early adopters:** In our analysis of the data, we found that teleworkers have the oldest account age, i.e., they became members of Handshake earlier than other populations. Their median account age is ~ 130 days older than the campus-based populations, and the mean is ~ 160 days more than other locations ($p < 0.001$). When Handshake was initially launched, there was also a higher percentage of teleworkers who were members; 65 % of the teleworker population joined within the first year, compared to only 40 % of the rest of the company.
- **A higher percentage of teleworkers are contributors:** ~ 42 % of populations from principal locations contribute content and post comments while 35 % contribute from sites. In contrast, a whopping 61 % of teleworkers are contributors, a number significantly higher than other employee populations ($p < 0.001$).

- **Teleworkers are at least on par with other locations in all measures:** In all the data we analyzed, we did not find that teleworkers have lower usage statistics than any other population in the organization. In all measures (e.g., average number of groups, average number of connections, percentage of contributing population, average number of monthly contributions, etc.), they are either the same or higher. This speaks to the level of engagement of teleworkers; we found teleworkers to be either as active as or more active than other populations. The notable exception is that certain types of groups are not as popular with the teleworker population (see below); however, teleworkers do not join fewer groups than other populations, in general.

- **Teleworkers interact across more diverse hours:** Staff in main offices tend to work a conventional 8am-5pm schedule and post or interact on Handshake infrequently during after hours. Comparatively, teleworkers have a far more diverse interaction pattern even when accounting for time zones; they post to Handshake both earlier and later in the day, indicating they that are online for an extended work day. This may speak to the lesser boundary between work and home life that teleworkers talked about during our interviews.

- **Teleworkers are less likely to use networking tools for social uses:** We found that teleworkers are members of work-related groups more often than social groups. Other populations belong to a higher percentage of social groups ($p < 0.01$).

6   Discussion

There were a number of ways in which teleworkers engaged with our enterprise networking platform differently than employees at MITRE campuses. First, we discovered that teleworkers are earlier adopters of the enterprise networking platform, Handshake. We also found that a higher percentage of teleworkers post content and make comments. It is possible that both of these differences are attributable to teleworkers being remote and missing the rich communication of face-to-face interactions. During interviews, teleworkers stated that they found themselves using other communication mechanisms (such as instant messaging and e-mail) more than they had before; it therefore stands to reason that they may be more likely to adopt new communications tools early. This is supported by earlier findings showing that teleworkers are earlier adopters of technology that supports their work [15, 16] and that the willingness to become a teleworker is associated with a higher need for "innovativeness" [14].

In addition, we discovered that teleworkers tend to work more diverse hours than their non-teleworking colleagues. This was shown by our quantitative analysis, and a number of individuals spoke about this in the interviews as well. Some found their work extending into time with their family members. As one teleworker told us,

> *"Often I get in trouble with my wife when she finds me still at my desk and she thinks I should not be working."*

On the other hand, some teleworkers reported that they were now more strict with their working hours than they had been when they worked in one of the office locations. A teleworker explained his new working schedule since he transitioned to remote work:

"I am pretty strict about the hours I work... When I worked in the Bedford headquarters, I used to stay at the office until I finished what I was working on... I tried to keep work at work and not bring it home. Why the schedule difference [once I became a teleworker]? I... stop at a hard set time to see my grandmother, have dinner... [this routine] help[ed] me separate work and life because it would be too easy to work until 10 pm [when working from home]."

Others found that they had to shift the time they began their work earlier in the day in order to accommodate those in other time zones. One teleworker explained how being on the west coast of the US affects his interaction with his east coast colleagues:

"There is also the time difference. I have to get up at 4:30 am to have coffee to be awake for 5 o'clock meetings that someone schedules for 8 am on the east coast. It happens probably 10-15 times per quarter. I consider this part of the cost of being able to live where I want to live and still be able to support MITRE and our sponsors on the east coast."

Still others felt that they had more flexibility over the time they spent and could take time off in the middle of the day for a doctor's appointment or an errand. Regardless, we found that there was more variance in the times they started and ended their work.

Both our research, as well as the comprehensive review of best practices done by Koehne et al. [13], identified gaps in communication that are present in the teleworker environment and that some teleworkers do not feel as connected to co-workers as those in office locations. Teleworkers do not have the opportunity for "water cooler," or hallway, conversations and have to find other ways to engage with their co-workers. As two teleworkers put it:

"It's both an advantage and disadvantage. People don't just drop by and interrupt, but you miss that social engagement."

"You have to work harder to build relationships. You just want to jump in your car, shake their hands, and have lunch with them, but you just can't do that."

They also feel excluded from scheduled social events such as team lunches or office barbeques: one interviewee reminisced about door decorating contests as a seemingly insignificant activity that nevertheless brings people together. In addition, we found that teleworkers have to make an extra effort to keep in touch with people.

"It's harder to stay connected to people. Out of sight, out of mind. You have to take that extra effort to initiate chat or call someone. You don't run into people in the hallway or at lunch."

Because of lack of face-to-face communication and the fear of "out of sight, out of mind," teleworkers compensate by using online chat or picking up the phone more frequently than they might otherwise have had they been in an office location [9]. One person schedules what she calls "virtual teas," which are informal phone sessions where she meets with colleagues to "catch up" and socialize regardless of whether they are working together. She described the genesis of how it evolved out of a face-to-face gathering:

"There are a couple of ways I keep in touch with people. Virtual Tea – we meet once a month or every couple of months for a half hour or 45 min just to chat. It's like running into someone at the cafeteria but it's more intentional... At one of the Virtual Teas, there are 3 of us. Our first one was in person at the cafeteria, and we all agreed to do it again regularly."

When some teleworkers visit the office on business trips, they network heavily by scheduling informal lunches or making office "sweeps." In general, teleworkers reported that communication was much more difficult from remote locations and that they had to be very deliberate and proactive. As one interviewee put it:

"I need to meet people and get to know them. It's very difficult to do teleworking. I make a point to do office sweeps in the morning whenever I am visiting the office. The sweeps I do may be with people I have never met before. I might stop someone in the hallway. If I am working with someone I don't know, I will look at their picture on the MII [MITRE's intranet phonebook directory]. I like to see who they are so that I will recognize them when I see them. I never had to do this before but I found myself not knowing people I was working with."

Given this tendency for teleworkers to feel more disconnected from co-workers, we hypothesize that individuals who work remotely on a regular basis would be more likely to use an enterprise social networking platform as an added way to communicate with others and create an online presence. Indeed, we found that teleworkers adopted Handshake earlier than others and had a higher contribution rate (both in terms of volume and frequency of postings).

One intriguing finding was that teleworkers were in a lower percentage of social groups than they were in work-related groups in comparison to the other populations. This was counter-intuitive to us as we expected teleworkers, who have less opportunity to socialize, to use this medium to socialize more than other populations.

One hypothesis for the lower social group membership for teleworkers is that there may be more of a need for teleworkers to cultivate an outward perception of productivity. Previous research [13] found that teleworkers have to do more to make their work visible. Since others cannot observe them doing the work, it has to be explicitly called out and shared by the teleworker or their management. Since co-workers and management are not able to observe teleworkers conducting their work, the teleworkers may feel the need to project a persona of "productivity" and produce more indicators of work. Participating in social groups may work against this intended persona and may therefore be avoided to a higher degree by teleworkers. Alternatively, it is less about creating a persona and more about spending time creating observable work deliverables rather than social conversation. We did ask some of our interview participants whether they did anything specific to cultivate their professional image and whether they felt that their co-workers' perceptions of them had changed since they became teleworkers, but they did not specifically indicate that their lack of involvement in social groups had anything to do with maintaining their professional reputation at work.

Another potential explanation is that many social groups on Handshake are tightly connected to gatherings or location-specific activities, which require physical presence (e.g., softball or soccer teams, cycling enthusiasts, Frisbee players). Teleworkers, by virtue of the fact that they are not working from the same location as their co-workers, would naturally be left out of these organized activities. For example, while the cycling group on Handshake does contain general discussions about the safety of sharing the road or how to best ship a bike, there are frequently posts about planned group rides and local races in which a remote teleworker would not be able to participate. While this is a possible explanation, we would want to do further exploration to substantiate or refute it and understand why there is also lack of teleworker interest in other social groups that are not related to geographic location (e.g., gardening, vegetarianism, pet care, photography).

This study was a case study on a single company; therefore, the extensibility of the findings may be limited. In addition, The MITRE Corporation is unique in that it is not-for-profit and government-oriented, and most work is knowledge work which lends itself nicely to telework.

7 Future Directions

This study provided insight into the working lives of MITRE's teleworkers, and we plan on compiling relevant information into guidelines for teleworkers. With the aim of helping teleworkers maintain their productivity while retaining job satisfaction, we will focus on:

- Strategies for managing schedule and availability,
- Tips for keeping work life in balance,
- "Social" conventions for handling customer communication, work assignments, and meetings with remote participants.

We also plan on creating guidance and best practices for managers and project leaders who deal with teleworkers on a regular basis as to how to better foster a working environment that enables teleworkers to be productive and happy. In addition, we hope to continue partnering with MITRE's teleworkers to study challenges that ICT users face. Because of their reliance on collaboration tools, teleworkers have proven themselves to be valuable partners in our technology research program.

There are a number of areas that warrant further research. First, we observed a number of different types of teleworkers. While some literature [9, 17] does differentiate by frequency of telework (Full-Time, Regular, Occasional, etc.) and work location (home, office, field, etc.), we have not seen any differentiation in the literature for other dimensions of telework. For example, we interviewed some teleworkers who had spent many years in one of MITRE's headquarters and, only towards the end of their career, did they become teleworkers. This was in contrast to others who were hired directly as teleworkers. The former had developed extensive networks from interacting with co-workers face-to-face, but the latter did not have that initial face-to-face benefit. Another difference was that some teleworkers had other teleworking co-workers nearby, while others were completely isolated. It is clear to us that there are multiple, varying dimensions of telework. We believe that additional development of the types of teleworkers and their features may merit further exploration – particularly if we can discover differences in productivity or work satisfaction.

Work/life balance for teleworkers is another area that we would like to explore further. While we did see teleworkers working an extended range of hours, we do not know if this resulted in working more hours in total, or whether this was simply the result of their days being punctuated by other responsibilities (e.g., child care).

Lastly, our finding of social groups having lower teleworker membership raises a number of questions. We proposed two potential explanations for this: one that pondered whether social groups are more geographically based and are therefore less relevant for teleworkers, and a second that teleworkers are concerned about creating a persona that shows them as "business-like" rather than "social" and they therefore refrain from interacting in more social venues. Further research would be required to determine whether either of these theories explains this phenomenon – or to identify an altogether different explanation.

Acknowledgments. The authors would like to thank Donna L. Cuomo for her vision and continued support of Handshake-related activities. We would also like to thank Henry Amistadi, Mira Shapiro, and Kevin Gormley for their insights and assistance with statistical analysis. This research was funded by the MITRE Innovation Program and by MITRE's Center for Information and Technology.

References

1. Damianos, L.E., Cuomo, D., Griffith, J., Hirst, D.M., Smallwood, J.: Exploring the adoption, utility, and social influences of social bookmarking in a corporate environment. In: Proceedings of the Hawaii International Conference on Systems Sciences (HICSS-40) (2007)
2. Damianos, L.E., Cuomo, D.L., Drozdetski, S.: Handshake: a case study for exploring business networking for the enterprise, inside and out. In: Ozok, A., Zaphiris, P. (eds.) OCSC 2011. LNCS, vol. 6778, pp. 162–171. Springer, Heidelberg (2011)
3. Elgg. http://elgg.org
4. Olson, G.M., Olson, J.S.: Distance matters. J. Hum.-Comput. Inter. **14**(2), 139–178 (2000)
5. Gibson, C.B., Gibbs, J.L.: Unpacking the concept of virtuality: the effects of geographic dispersion, electronic dependence, dynamic structure, and national diversity on team innovation. Adm. Sci. Q. **51**(3), 451–495 (2006)
6. Bartel, C.A., Wrzesniewski, A., Wiesenfeld, B.M.: Knowing where you stand: physical isolation, perceived respect, and organizational identification among virtual employees. Organ. Sci. **23**(3), 743–757 (2012)
7. Bos, N., Buyuktur, A.G., Olson, J.S., Olson, G.M., Voida, A.: Shared identity helps partially distributed teams, but distance still matters. In: Proceedings of the 2010 International ACM SIGGROUP Conference on Supporting Group Work (GROUP 2010) (2010)
8. Gajendran, R.S., Harrison, D.A.: The good, the bad, and the unknown about telecommuting: meta-analysis of psychological mediators and individual consequences. J. Appl. Psychol. **92** (6), 1524–1541 (2007)
9. Schadler, T.: US telecommuting forecast, 2009 To 2016. Forrester Research (2009)
10. Olson, G.M., Olson, J.S., Venolia, G.: What still matters about distance? (2009). http://research.microsoft.com/pubs/78697/Olson9370.pdf
11. DiMicco, J.M., Geyer, W., Millen, D.R., Dugan, C., Brownholtz, B.: People sensemaking and relationship building on an enterprise social network site. In: Proceedings of the Hawaii International Conference on Systems Sciences (HICSS-42) (2009)
12. Leonardi, P.M., Huysman, M., Steinfield, C.: Enterprise social media: definition, history, and prospects for the study of social technologies in organizations. J. Comput.-Mediat. Commun. **19**(1), 1–19 (2013)
13. Koehne, B., Shih, P.C., Olson, J.S.: Remote and alone: coping with being the remote member on the team. In: Proceedings of Computer Supported Cooperative Work (CSCW 2012), pp. 1257–1266 (2012)

14. Lee, P.S., Leung, L.W., So, C.Y.: Impact and Issues in New Media: Toward Intelligent Societies. Hampton Press, New Jersey (2004)
15. Carey, J.: The first 100 years. Phys. World **24**(4), 17 (2011)
16. Donald, K., Webster, L. The Information Society in Europe: Work and Life in an Age of Globalization, p. 324. Werner Herrmann Rowman & Littlefield Publish (2000)
17. Garrett, R.K., Danziger, J.N.: Which telework? Defining and testing a taxonomy of technology-mediated work at a distance. Soc. Sci. Comput. Rev. **25**(1), 27–47 (2007)

Element Prioritization for Online Service Identity Management

Hoon Sik Yoo[1], Young Hwan Pan[2], Ping Shui[3], and Da Young Ju[1(✉)]

[1] School of Integrated Technology, Yonsei Institute of Convergence
Technology, Yonsei University, Seoul, Republic of Korea
{yoohs,dyju}@yonsei.ac.kr
[2] Graduate School of Techno Design, Kookmin University, Seoul, South Korea
peterpan@kookmin.ac.kr
[3] School of Journalism, Communication University of China, Beijing, P.R.China
pingshui2001@hotmail.com

Abstract. Services have taken the center stage over products in the industrial world. Thus, there have been many studies that focused on how to define and utilize service identity. The purpose of this study is to discover the elements of service identity that need to be managed with top priority when corporations manage their respective service identity. To discover the elements thereof and assess priorities, this study structured service identity based on the conventional theories. This study defined the specific elements of service identity through expert FGI. Also, this study deducted the priorities as the 14 experts of UI/UX/service design conducted AHP evaluation as to the elements thereof. As a result, this study found that those visual elements such as color, icon and layout had the highest priority. This study also found that the importance of the functional elements was relatively lower, whereas the operational elements had the lowest priority.

Keywords: Service identity · Identity management · Element prioritization · User experience design · Interface design

1 Introduction

As various types of devices like smart watch, smart phone, smart Pad and Smart Table are provided, service providers come to offer services which are suitable for display characteristics of various smart devices when they offer a service. Under this change in circumstances, the importance about the management of integrated service identity has emphasized. Main idea of this study is to draw the results which could help manage service identity by defining the structure and elements for the management of service identity and analyzing the importance between the elements (Fig. 1).

2 Previous Work

2.1 Identity

The definition for identity stems from philosophy. The identities in the field of management and economics which are being widely used at present are the theories that

© Springer International Publishing Switzerland 2015
F.F.-H. Nah and C.-H. Tan (Eds.): HCIB 2015, LNCS 9191, pp. 542–549, 2015.
DOI: 10.1007/978-3-319-20895-4_50

Service Identity Management

Fig. 1. Overview of main idea

were established with the emergence of corporations after the Industrial Revolution. These theories can be deemed as a result of applying the identity theory of psychology to corporations rather than people.

2.2 Corporate Identity

The definition of CI has changed variously with the development of the industry. It can be summarized into three stages. In the first stage that was the era of graphical design paradigm, visual elements were defined as a corporate symbol. Thus, it was defined that customers would recognize corporate images through visual elements. In the second stage that was the era of the integrated communication paradigm, not only visual elements but also communication methods were included as an important element of CI. In the third stage that was the era of the interdisciplinary paradigm, a comprehensive definition was established by including corporate characteristics and behavior in addition to visual elements and communication methods (Fig. 2).

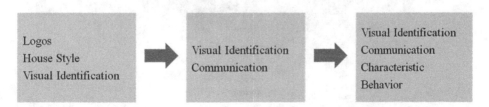

Fig. 2. The development of corporate identity

2.3 Brand Identity

Kapferer (1992) argues that brand is the essence, meaning and direction of a product. He also argues that brand define the identity of a product. Brand identity, which has many other definitions, can be seen as the most prominent communication strategy for a corporation to plant an awareness of its products in consumers.

2.4   Product Identity

Product image is an image that consumers have with respect to a certain product. It is also an overall feeling for the products of a corporation. Product identity is a strategy to express corporate images in products. It can be deemed as an integrated plan for a series of product images that create an improved value of design to meet consumers' needs and enhance corporate image through certain product families produced at a corporation.

2.5   Service Identity

Hwasun Kang (2013) defined service identity as follows. Service identity was to create an identity for corporate philosophy and brand identity in accordance with the properties of a given service. Thus, it is the methodology to manage all those mediating elements and activities in an integrated way, which would help form an ideal service image in terms of conveying customers consistent and differentiated service experience and value through services (Fig. 3).

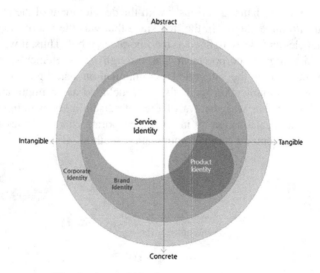

Fig. 3. Service identity model (Kang 2013)

Those identities that have been applied to people are now being applied to corporations. It can be concluded that the area thereof has been expanded into not only corporate image, brand image and product image but also services whose importance is gradually growing in recent years. The management and use of service identity has become a very important factor for strengthening corporate competitiveness.

3 Service Identity Frame and Elements

3.1 Service Identity Frame

Service types can be classified largely into online service and offline service. Additionally, experiences provided by services can be classified into functional elements, interactive elements and superficial elements. Using this classification system, structure of service identity is defined (see Fig. 4) and was used in the research. In order to manage service identity in this study, components of online service identity were identified first and subsequently.

	offline service identity elements	online service identity elements
function	function elements of offline service identity	function elements of online service identity
interaction	interaction elements of offline service identity	function elements of online service identity
surface	surface elements of offline service identity	function elements of online service identity

Fig. 4. Service identity frame

3.2 Elements of Online Service Identity

In order to materialize the elements for online service identity, FGI was conducted targeting online service experts. FGI was progressed with the following procedures and results are like Table 1.

Table 1. Expert profile

Number of experts	Average working experiences	Average age	Gender
6	7.5 years	33.8 years old	4 males/2 females

(1) Discussion and definition about Online Service Identity Elements
(2) Discussion and definition about the mapping of Online Service Identity Structure and Elements (Table 2).

Table 2. Elements of online service identity

Structure	Elements	Definition
Function	Main function & Sub function	Core functions and additional functions which are provided to products or services
	Function sequence	Necessary procedures to use functions
	Module	UI components which are classified according to functions
Interaction	Input interaction style	Input interaction methods to manipulate functions
	Feed-back & Feed-forward	Responses of the system to user's input
	Information architecture	Structural form of the information about products or services
	Label	Names of individual unit information
	Status indication	Elements which give the information about current conditions of products or service
Surface	Color	Classify with major colors and auxiliary colors which are applied in the products or services
	Shape	Morphological elements which are related with products or services
	Icon	Symbols which are expressed as characters or pictures with the commands to execute the functions
	Material	Material quality of products or services and superficial texture which are felt from them
	Font	Forms and size of the characters which are used in products or services
	Layout	Placement of objects which exist in products or services
	Sound	Sound elements which are provided to users from products or services

4   AHP Analysis for Service Identity

AHP (Analytic Hierarchy Process) is a calculation model which was designed by professor Thomas L. Saaty by understanding the truth that brain is using stepwise or hierarchical analysis procedures. This technique is one of the most appropriate methods to evaluate the expert's decision through quantification. AHP analysis to identify the priority in the components of online service identity was executed with the following methods and the composition and questions of the experts who participated in AHP analysis are like following Table 3.

(1) Produce the cases about individual elements of Online Service Identity
(2) Write questionnaires to compare individual elements of Online Service Identity
(3) Execution of AHP analysis targeting experts.

Table 3. Expert profile

Number of experts	Average working experiences	Average age
11	5.4 years	30.2 years old

Table 4. Part of AHP research sheet

Questions	Strongly disagree	Disagree	Undecided	Agree	Strongly agree
Do you think Color is more important than Icon to form identity?	-	-	-	-	-
Do you think Color is more important than Font to form identity?	-	-	-	-	-
Do you think Color is more important than Layout to form identity?	-	-	-	-	-
Do you think Color is more important than Shape to form identity?	-	-	-	-	-
Do you think Color is more important than Module to form identity?	-	-	-	-	-
Do you think Color is more important than Label to form identity?	-	-	-	-	-
Do you think Color is more important than Sound to form identity?	-	-	-	-	-
Do you think Color is more important than Material to form identity?	-	-	-	-	-
Do you think Color is more important than IA to form identity?	-	-	-	-	-

These are the questions to identify the priority in 14 elements and the investigation about 105 questions was conducted and the results could be obtained like below (Table 4).

Analysis results showed visual elements like color, icon, layout, font, shape and etc. These elements were identified to give the biggest effect to the identity, and the collection of provided functions and kinds of functions were identified to give second biggest influence. Elements which have high utilization in common like input methods

Table 5. Survey result of AHP analysis

Priority	Elements	Data
1	Color	0.111
2	Icon	0.080
3	Layout	0.076
4	Font	0.074
5	Shape	0.071
6	Module	0.069
7	Main function/Sub function	0.069
8	Label	0.068
9	Information architecture	0.068
10	Function sequence	0.066
11	Sound	0.064
12	Input interaction style	0.064
13	Feed-back/Feed-forward	0.061
14	Material	0.060

and feedback were analyzed to give relatively little influence to the creation of the identity (Table 5).

5 Conclusion and Discussion

In this research, we present service identity framework and element prioritization of online service identity. Results express research meaning in the respect they could be used as basic data to manage service identity. This study has a limitation in those arguments about the appropriateness. The reason why the definition of service identity has not be built though society yet. Future research should be conducted to identify the components and to study the priority about offline service.

Acknowledgement. This work was supported in part by the MSIP (Ministry of Science, ICT and Future Planning) under the "IT Consilience Creative Program" support program supervised by the NIPA (National IT Industry Promotion Agency) (NIPA-2014-H0201-14-1002).

References

Cees, B.M., John, M.T.: Corporate identity: the concept, its measurement and management. Eur. J. Mark. **31**(5/6), 340–355 (1997)

Erik, H.E., Joan, M.E.: The Life Cycle Completed. Norton and Company, New York (1998)

Kang, H.: A Study on Service Identity in a Changing Environment of Marketing and Communication. Graduate School of Techno Design, Kookmin University (2013)

Kapferer, J.N.: Strategic Brand Management: New Approaches to Creating and Evaluation Brand Equity. Kogan Page, London (1992)

LG Electronics : User First Design, LG Electronics Corporate Design Center Part 1-103

Locke, J.: An Essay Concerning Human Understanding. Penguin, Woolhouse, London (1997)

Rondeau, D.: For mobile applications, branding is experience. Mag. Commun. ACM **48**(7), 61–66 (2005). Designing for the mobile device CACM Homepage archive

Roto, V., Rautava, M.. User experience elements and brand promise. In: International Engagability and Design Conference (Idec4), in conjunction with NordiCHI 2008 conference, Lund, Sweden (2008)

Vyas, D., Veer, G.C.: Experience as meaning: some underlying concepts and implications for design. In: Proceedings of the 13th ECCE 2006, vol. 250 (2006)

Ji, Y.G., Jin, B.S., Mun, J.S., Ko, S.M.: Development of AHP model for telematics haptic interface evaluation. In: Jacko, J.A. (ed.) HCI 2007. LNCS, vol. 4550, pp. 517–526. Springer, Heidelberg (2007)

Gamification and Persuasion of HP IT Service Management to Improve Performance and Engagement

Yue Yuan[1(✉)], Ke Ke Qi[1], and Aaron Marcus[2]

[1] HP Software, Shanghai Hewlett-Packard Co.,Ltd, Building 6 #, Zhang Jiang
Mico-Electrical Port no.690 Bi Bo Road, Pu Dong New Area, Shanghai 201203,
People's Republic of China
{yue.yuan,ke-ke.qi}@hp.com
[2] Aaron Marcus and Associates, Inc, 1196 Euclid Avenue, Suite 1F, Berkeley,
CA 94708, USA
Aaron.Marcus@AMandA.com

Abstract. Currently, IT service management groups in many different companies are facing a common challenge: how to motivate IT service desks to perform more effectively and productively in order to reach desired customer service objectives/goals and promote customer satisfactions. Undoubtedly, IT service desks' performance and engagement will directly influence the delivered service, and the quality of the service will either enhance or degrade customer loyalty to a company's brand and business. Accordingly, we present an effective and feasible way to incorporate gamification and persuasion as the incentive mechanism into the current product, to socially reward IT service desks for their performances, and thereby to increase their motivation to contribute and to improve their performance.

Keywords: Business · Design · Enterprise software · IT service management · Gamification · Persuasion · Socal · Employee knowledge contribution · Employee engagement · Performance improvement · User interface · User experience

1 Introduction

Currently, IT services in companies handle issues from customers or users within certain response times and provide services to them. In daily work, they refer to knowledge stored in knowledge bases to solve different kinds of problems originating from customers or users. After they have solved problems, they write final solutions in ticket records, which become the primary assets used for future reference to solve similar problems.

However, most IT service desks prefer *consuming* knowledge content over *producing* it. Converting information into knowledge for the purpose of knowledge transfer is rather limited, because that conversion requires IT service desks to contribute extra effort and to invest their own precious time in creating content; they are *not* motivated sufficiently to overcome the impediments to knowledge transfer by themselves. As a result, IT service desks often cannot get the desired search results of

© Springer International Publishing Switzerland 2015
F.F.-H. Nah and C.-H. Tan (Eds.): HCIB 2015, LNCS 9191, pp. 550–562, 2015.
DOI: 10.1007/978-3-319-20895-4_51

solutions from knowledge bases. Consequently, IT service desks should spend more time to seek out and think out suitable solutions, whichWOULD influence their service delivery's speed and quality.

Likewise, IT service desks are required to record solutions in tickets, which will BECOME assets to a company or institution for future reference. IT service desks that are responsible for cases already have the knowledge about the issues with which they WORKED, so the case recorded is of less value and is time consuming for them. Thus, the case-study records often lack enough details and are unsuitable as good references for peers when peers are encountering similar problems.

Another point to be considered: Most IT service desks are concerned about service-response time, which is directly related to key performance indicators. As a result, the IT service desks try to deliver rapid service. However, not all services are of high quality and match the customers' expectations. Thus, customers or users sometimes are not satisfied with service quality. Many companies have realized that customer satisfaction is vital. Instead of looking at how quickly IT service desks close the ticket, they are moving from case closure to customer satisfaction.

2 Market Research

According to Gartner [1, 2], 70 % of business-transformation efforts fail due to lack of engagement. However, applying the right elements of gamification can address engagement, persuade employees to change behavior, and reach desired business outcomes. Therefore, companies *can* achieve transformation of business operations.

3 Our Solution

In order to improve IT service desks' performance and motivate them to deliver continually desirable services, we use the following objectives as guiding principles to encourage IT service desks to take positive changes when using enterprise software.

- Enable positively exchanging knowledge to improve the quantity of articles in the knowledge base.
- Enable actively reviewing and commenting on shared knowledge to help improve the articles' quality before publishing.
- Enhance case-record quality to benefit peers and the organization.
- Improve customer satisfaction through both the quality of service and the time of response, that is, balance the competing objectives of good service *versus* quick service.

According to the lessons learned from our user research, we propose to integrate gamification and persuasion mechanisms as incentives into the current HP Service Manager product. The incentive mechanism should fit into users' natural interactions, with minimal interruption during performing normal tasks.

In order to improve knowledge exchange quantity (article count) and quality (being easy to understand) in the groups, increase case record quality (cited count and helpfulness), and enhance customer satisfaction (good feedback from customer satisfaction surveys), we incorporate some gaming elements that are internal drivers for making progress, developing skills, and eventually overcoming challenges. Gaming elements include: dashboards, leaderboards, "high-fives," points, levels, badges, rewards, competitions, etc. Besides gamification, we also integrate persuasion and social influence, which are external drivers to increases employees' motivations to contribute personal knowledge and to improve service quality continuously through enterprise software application. Examples include: sharing, reinforcement, peer pressure, reciprocal liking, "power of because," etc.

Incentive System. In our concept, employees can earn reputation points by serving their work group with valuable contributions and gain positive customer feedback through the HP Service Manager. There are three ways for employees to collect reputation points.

- To contribute knowledge by submitting articles with high quality to the knowledge base.
- To provide high-quality ticket records, which can be cited by their peers.
- To gain good ratings or positive feedback from customer-satisfaction assessment.

Design Process. In order to explore the possibilities of the application, we created a process flow, user journey, and use scenario that explore how users might approach the application. The process-flow diagrams show the relationships among different parts of the application, with wire-frames showing basic content of key screens (see Fig. 1).

Users' Journey: Analogous to Maslow's Hierarchy of Needs. The user's journey contains elements that relate closely to Maslow's study of basic human needs.

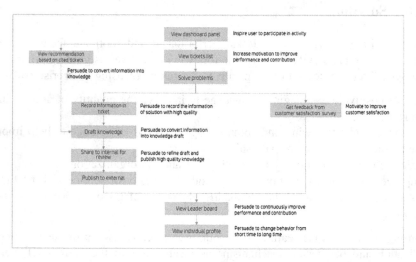

Fig. 1. Process flow diagram shows relationships among different parts and modules in the application

1. **Onboarding:** Once new members register, they can understand how to participate in activities and gain points.
2. **Contribution:** After they have engaged in activities, they can acquire and accumulate points.
3. **Recognition:** As they become known, they gain recognition and followers, earning higher levels of badges.
4. **Healthy competition:** They can see on leaderboards where they stand and how to surpass others' levels.
5. **Self express:** They gain a good reputation by sharing their knowledge and supplying high-quality service.
6. **Desire to do better:** Once they've achieved all of the preceding, they often have strong desires to do better and are encouraged to "pay it forward," giving to others beginning their journeys in the HP Service Manager.

Persona. We created a persona after considering demographic groups and behavioral segmentation: Tom Jones, 25, IT Service Desk, responsible for providing service to different customers in a medium-scale software company.

Use Scenario. We constructed a general use scenario based on the persona: As the IT service desk representative, Tom first registers in HP Service Manager without any reputation points. He notices a message about a performance comparison between himself and his peer through points. Playful competition incites him especially, due to the fact that his colleague is much better in the ranking. Tom is eager to know how he can quickly earn points. HP Service Manager gives him some advice to get points easily.

Tom effectively solves a customer problem the first time; the customer is very happy and gives Tom a "Good" rating as thanks. Within five minutes, Tom writes his solution about how to deal with the customer's problem in a case record as detailed as possible. Although he writes a high-quality case record primarily to get points, undoubtedly, his case record contains valuable information for other peers to reference. Based in part on this experience, he also starts to write articles regularly, which are shared in the knowledge base by the HP Service Manager. Within two weeks, Tom makes it from zero points to fifteen points, which helps him achieve rank number four, and his name appears in the leader board! The visibility of his good performance makes him have a sense of achievement. Therefore, he announces that he will continue contributing.

Tom quickly gains a considerable amount of points and becomes a "Hero of the Week"; dozens of "Congrats" and recognition from his peers are sent within seconds. Tom's boss is very happy with his outstanding performance, and gives him restaurant coupons as a reward, which reinforces his commitment to engage. One day, Tom meets Sonny at the end of the hallway when he leaves his office. Sonny takes the initiative to say hello: "Hey Tom, your sharing is very good. Today I encountered the same problem as well. You helped me to solve my problem!" Tom feels high appreciation and honest thanks from Sonny, which motivates him to behave even better in the long term.

User Interface Design. The user interface design is a mash-up of the original HP Service Manager user interface and additional gamification and persuasion mechanisms designed to enhance the original (see Fig. 2).

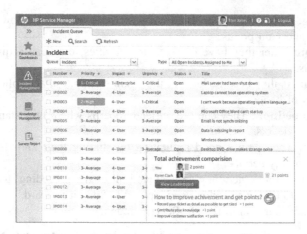

Fig. 2. Guideline for new user and occasional users

Guideline for new users and occasional users. In order to encourage IT service desks to participate actively, we designed a pop-up Guideline. Once the IT service desks access HP SM Incident Management, the Guideline appears in the corner of the screen and gives clear advice about what actions to take to gain points. We add comparison in here also. IT service desks can compare themselves with any other peer who achieves the highest score within the last week. Visualizing the gap helps motivate IT Service Desks to actively contribute.

Game mechanics used: step-by-step guideline, competition (See Fig. 2).

Record the information of the solution in a ticket. We use persuasion and gamification mechanics to motive IT service desks to contribute case records, and to convert that information into knowledge. In this step, the user interface displays the number of people who are drafting knowledge, which persuades the IT service desk person to take action for knowledge contribution (see Fig. 3).

Persuasion mechanics used.

Power of because [3]: According to a psychology study that appeared in the Journal of Personality and Social Psychology, giving a reason for a request can increase people's compliance from 60 % to 90 %.

Collective behavior: Collective behavior can often result in peer pressure, which compels people to conform to group behavior.

Peer pressure: Peer pressure is being used to urge people to do what peers are doing.

Social learning: People learn from watching others.

Automatically recommend IT service desks to draft knowledge once closed tickets are cited or recognized by peers. Another way to persuade IT service desk personnel to draft knowledge is to use feedback from peers. If previous closed tickets have been viewed or recognized by others, that means the problem resolved is similar to what others are facing. Hence, IT service desk personnel will be encouraged to draft knowledge and encouraged for doing so. We use progress bars to break down a task

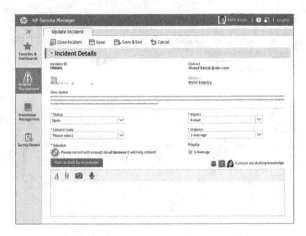

Fig. 3. Record the information of the solution in ticket.

Fig. 4. Recommend IT help desks to draft knowledge

into workable segments. Consequently, a time-consuming task is more manageable, because it is be split into smaller sub-tasks (see Fig. 4).

Persuasion Mechanics Used:

Reciprocal liking: People feel better about themselves knowing that they are liked and enjoy the company of those who give them positive feelings, which motivates them to do better.

Game mechanics used:

Progress bar: break goal into trackable activities.

Contribute Knowledge. We designed multiple small tasks to assist users to finish knowledge contributions. For example, there is a phase named "Share to Internal," which is reviewed by close colleagues. Because people will feel less pressure when facing close colleagues and more likely to refine knowledge according to their

Fig. 5. Contribute knowledge.

colleagues' feedback, IT service desks will feel more comfortable to move forward (see Fig. 5).

Game and persuasion mechanics used: Collective behavior, Social influence, Step-by-step

Share to Internal for Reviewing and Refining. The Default for sharing is that users' team members are selected to be reviewers. IT Help desk personnel, also, can select trust-worhty peers to review their contributions. (See Fig. 6)

Persuasion mechanics used:

"I need your help." This flips the roles of dominant and subordinate, engaging the other person and providing a transfer of power.

Social Influence.

Notification. As a close peer, users' colleagues will receive a request from the IT service desk personnel to review a draft. Under "close peer pressure," the reviewer is more likely to complete a review and give useful comments, which will help improve knowledge quality (see Fig. 7).

Persuasion mechanics used:

Power of people we like: people are most Influenced by people around us and take action under peer pressure.

Leaderboard (see Fig. 8). The incentive mechanism is visualized in three ways: level, ranking, and achievements, to make IT service desks and others aware of how much they have done for their group. IT service desks can review high-scoring individuals or teams, compare themselves to any other peers, or their teams to any other teams via the Leaderboard.

Points: The points will be rewarded when IT service desks perform valuable actions, such as contributing knowledge, closing tickets cited by peers, or getting positive feedback from customers. Our design seeks to motivate other IT service desks by highlighting individuals who contribute the most.

Fig. 6. Share to internal for reviewing and refining

Fig. 7. Notification

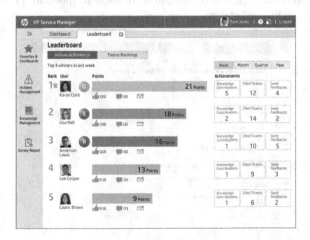

Fig. 8. Individual rankings in the Leaderboard

Ranking: The total number of points of the top five IT service desks through social comparison and competition is displayed in the Leaderboard. The visibility of good performance motivates all IT service desks to actively improve their behaviors.

Achievements: The achievement for the top five winners are public and visible to all IT service desks. Any IT service desk can drill down for more details. This mechanism rewards both short-term and long-term contributions.

We also highlight competition among teams by enabling IT service desks to switch to team rankings. Teams and their managers can compare themselves and other teams easily according to total scores.

User Profile. User profiles allow others to review an individual's performance and contribution, find where a user shines, highlighting recent contribution points, levels and badges earned, accessing hyperlinks of achievement, and drilling down for more details. People are concerned about their colleagues'and managers' opinions and attitudes, which will influence their behaviors. Thus, we use social influence to reinforce recognition and trigger IT service desks to perform improved behavior in both the short term and long term.

Game mechanics used:

Level: The default is to assign every IT service desk to a level in a hierarchy. IT service desks have to collect a certain amount of points before being promoted to a new level. This mechanism addresses the users' drive for achievement.

Points, Badges, Win Prize, Reward, Reinforcement, Sharing.

Survey Report about Customer Satisfaction. We designed a place to accumulate all customer feedback to which IT service desk personnel can refer. Feedback includes positive, neutral, and negative comments, so that the IT service desk personnel can know how to improve unsatisfied service and make things better (see Fig. 9).

Persuasion mechanics used:

Customer comments on Services: Using customer feedback to measure customer experience and improve customer satisfaction. It helps to motivate IT service desk to increase service quality and deliver more rapid service.

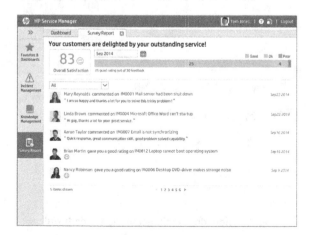

Fig. 9. Survey report about customer satisfaction.

4 Evaluation

We evaluated whether our concept was useful to improve the employee's contribution, performance, and engagement, as well as the employee's attitude and acceptance of gamification and persuasion used in a workplace. The evaluation served the purpose of finding out if the new concept design met our objecrtives. Therefore, the focus of our evaluation was explorative and concerns qualitative data.

We did A/B design evaluations, usinsg two different designs to see which design performed better. Design A was the current product without any gamification and persuasion mechanics; Design B was a new design using gamification and persuasion mechanics. We allocated two user groups to the different designs, half of all users reviewed Design A; they did not see any information about incentive mechanics. A second half of the users reviewed Design B; they could see points, the Leaderboard, and all social influence information. We respectively interviewed 16 employees in each group. Interviewees' age range were from 26 to 45 years old, and half of them were female.

During the process of reviewing designs, we interviewed employees, then asked the interviewees to fill out an attitudinal survey with a 10-point scale, which helped us to analyze the interviewee's opinions and feelings about the two different designs.

In evaluating the effect of the incentive mechanism on the employees' opinions, we set the research objective to answer the following questions:

- Does our incentive design encourage employees to invest time for recording information with enough details in ticket record?
- Do employees feel inspired to contribute knowledge?
- Do employees feel motivated to comment on articles and to improve knowledge quality from peers?
- What do employees think about the direct feedback of customer service?
- What do employees think about points, badges and leader board?
- Do employees consider gamification and persuasion in the enterprise software environment as a positive or negative factor?

4.1 Results of User Interviews and Future Design Recommendations

- **Does our incentive design encourage the employees to invest time for recording information with enough details in ticket record?**
  After interviewees saw the "Because" reminder when they were recording information in tickets, most interviewees seemed willing to record in detail to help their peers. However, some of them were not clear about how much detail should be written down; therefore, they suggested that a sample should be provided for reference next to the input field of the solution.
- **Do the employees feel inspired to contribute knowledge?**
  Because the system would automatically notify the interviewees about how many of their closed tickets have been cited by their peers, or any feedback from their peers about the recorded tickets, most interviewees stated that they would be encouraged

to contribute knowledge when they knew their recorded information was valuable and was helpful to others. As a result, they were more willing to convert information into knowledge. However, whether the status of how many employees were contributing knowledge should appear in the screen of the written solution in the ticket record seemed debatable. Some of the interviewees would be influenced by the number. If the system displayed that there were many employees contributing knowledge, the interviewee also would be inspired to consider contributing his/her knowledge; but, if the system told him/her that *few* peers were drafting articles, he/she might feel discouraged. The interviewees believed that the number of employees contributing knowledge should be shown in the screen of knowledge contribution, which was encouraging, because they felt their colleagues were accompanying them, and doing the same activity at the same time. In summary, which screen should display collective behavior needs to be researched further.

- **Do the employees feel motivated to comment on articles and to improve knowledge quality from peers?**
  Most interviewees believed that they definitely would review peer articles because a peer asked them to help reviewing articles, they would invest time to help improve the article's quality based on the request from *familiar* peers. Another factor was that the topic of an article was the interviewees' specialized field. Therefore, the interviewees felt confident and were willing to actively comment. Conversely, when the interviewees were asked who would be chosen to review their articles, over half of interviewees said they preferred to choose subject-matter experts to review their articles, because the experts' comments were trustworthy. Consequently, they suggested that the system should allow them to choose subject matter experts, in addition to choosing close colleagues who are familiar with the topic.

- **What do the employees think of the direct feedback of customer service?**
  Almost all interviewees stated they were concerned about customer feedback regarding their service, and they focused more on the neutral or bad comments from customers than positive feedback, because these comments would help them to understand where were problems and how to improve their future service.

- **What do the employees think about points, badges and Leaderboards?**
  Most interviewees claimed that they were concerned about the winners in Leaderboards in comparison to their own performances. They would like to learn more about the contribution from these winners, because the winners' performances were the invisible or informal benchmarks to motivate the interviewees to improve themselves. Similarly, once interviewees were the winners, they were more willing to continuously maintain great performance, so that they wouldn't become losers, because they cared about their self-image in front of others, wanting to make active, rather than passive, impressions. When talking about points and badges, the interviewees said that they paid attention to their points and status. Some of them suggested that the system could always indicate the current level and the next reachable level, which would be a clear goal to continuously stimulate them to move forward.

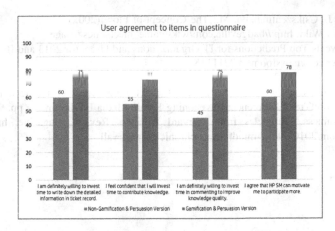

Fig. 10. Comparison of designs on users' attitudes.

- **Do the employees think of gamification and persuasion in the enterprise software environment as a positive or negative factor?**
  The interviewees thought the incentive system was encouraging positive, and could motivate them to perform better and to improve engagement.

4.2 Questionnaire Result About Users' Attitudes

Through user interviews and use of a user-attitudes questionnaire, we found that interviewees stated that the new design could motivate them to perform better and to exert a positive influence on them (see Fig. 10).

5 Next Steps

We have received valuable feedback from our user interviews, which gave us insights about how to improve our design. Therefore, in the next stage of our project, we shall continue to enhance, test, and validate our designs to further improve the user experience of enterprise software enhanced through gamification and persuasion techniques.

References

1. "Engagification" of the Enterprise – Gamification and Employee Engagement. http://blogs. gartner.com/elise-olding/2012/11/14/engagificationof-the-enterprise-gamification-and-employee-engagement/
2. Gartner Reveals Top Predictions for IT Organizations and Users for 2013 and Beyond. http://www.gartner.com/newsroom/id/2211115
3. Langer, E., Blank, A., Chanowitz, B.: The mindlessness of ostensibly thoughtful action: the role of "Placebic" information in interpersonal interaction. J. Pers. Soc. Psychol. **36**(6), 635–642 (1978)

4. Nakamura, J., Csikszentmihalyi, M.: The Concept of Flow (2002)
5. Gamification Wiki. http://badgeville.com/wiki/game_mechanics#usage
6. Gartner Reveals Top Predictions for IT Organizations and Users for 2013 and Beyond. http://www.gartner.com/newsroom/id/2211115
7. Deterding, S., Dixon, D., Khaled, R., Nacke, L.: From Game Design Elements to Gamefulness: Defining "Gamification". In: MindTrek 2011 Proceedings of the 15th International Academic MindTrek Conference: Envisioning Future Media Environments pp. 9–15 (2011)
8. The Mindfulness Chronicles from Harvard Business Review Magazine. http://harvardmagazine.com/2010/09/the-mindfulness-chronicles?page=all

Analytics, Visualisation
and Decision-making

Low Ambiguity First Algorithm: A New Approach to Knowledge-Based Word Sense Disambiguation

Dongjin Choi[1], Myunggwon Hwang[2], Byeongkyu Ko[1], Sicheon You[3], and Pankoo Kim[1](✉)

[1] Department of Computer Engineering, Chosun University, 375 Seoseok-dong, Dong-gu, Gwangju, Republic of Korea
{dongjin.choi84,byeongkyu.ko}@gmail.com, pkkim@chosun.ac.kr
[2] Korea Institute of Science and Technology Institute (KISTI), 245 Daehak-ro, Yuseong-gu, Daejeon, Republic of Korea
mgh@kisti.re.kr
[3] School of Informatics and Product Design, Chosun University, 375 Seoseok-dong, Dong-gu, Gwangju, Republic of Korea
scyou@chosun.ac.kr

Abstract. The Word Sense Disambiguation (WSD) problem has been considered as one of the most important challenging task in Natural Language Processing (NLP) research area. Even though, many of scientists applied the robust machine learning, statistical techniques, and structural pattern matching approach, the performance of WSD is still not able to bit human results due to the complexity of human language. In order to overcome this limitation, currently, the knowledge base such as WordNet has gained high popularity among researchers due to the fact that this knowledge base can extensively provide not only the definitions of nouns and verbs, but also the semantic networks between senses which were defined by linguists. However, knowledge bases are not fully dealing with entire words of human languages because maintaining and expanding the knowledge base is huge task which requires many efforts and time. Expanding knowledge base is not a big issue to concern however, a new approach is the major goal of this paper to solve WSD problem only based on limited knowledge resources. In this paper, we propose a method, named *low ambiguity first (LAF)* algorithm, which disambiguates a polysemous word with a low ambiguity degree first with given disambiguated words, based on the structural semantic interconnections (SSI) approach. The LAF algorithm is based on the two hypothesises that first, adjacent words are semantically relevant than other words far way. Second, word ambiguity can be measured by frequency differences between synsets of the given word in WordNet. We have proved these hypothesises in the experiment results, the LAF algorithm can improve the performance of traditional WSD results.

Keywords: Word sense disambiguation · Natural language processing · WordNet · Low ambiguity first

© Springer International Publishing Switzerland 2015
F.F.-H. Nah and C.-H. Tan (Eds.): HCIB 2015, LNCS 9191, pp. 565–574, 2015.
DOI: 10.1007/978-3-319-20895-4_52

1   Introduction

Word Sense Disambiguation (WSD) is one of the most important, complicated, and challenging task in the computational linguistics research area [1]. WSD is a task to find correct senses for the given words that have multiple senses but their appearances are the same (similarly, a polysemous type of word). For example, a noun *bat* represents not only for a *chiropteran*[1] but also *rackets* for squash, and *baseball bat*. When this polysemous word is appeared in a sentence, people are able to understand the meaning of the given polysemous word by referring co-occurrenced words but computers are not [8]. In order to compute human languages, many researchers have been studying for long time to discover the best approaches to obtain a good result, but it is still an ongoing problem.

Early approaches were started to make a corpus which was manually tagged senses of polysemous words from the small number of sentences [4]. After expanding and developing this small corpus, dictionaries had been lunched to public. It provided vast amount of definitions for the target language so, people started to apply the dictionaries to WSD task. The most famous dictionary-based approach is the *Lest* algorithm which was introduced by *Michael Lesk* in 1986 [2]. However, it has a limitation that WSD results are depended on the dictionaries.

A supervised and unsupervised method had been applied to overcome this limitation in WSD task. The supervised method can be considered as a classification task by using collocation, bag-of-words, n-gram[2], and context words a feature [5]. This method can apply many kinds of pattern recognition and machine learning approaches such as, Decision list, Naive Bayes classifier, k-Nearest Neighbors (kNN) algorithm, and Support Vector Machines (SVMs). However, it requires corpus which includes tagging information for words, but a problem is that tagging task has to be done manually, so it requires many times and costs. The unsupervised method is based on the assumption that the same sense of a words will occur in similar contexts. Therefore, it can be called as Word Sense Discrimination, in other words, this method is not able to distinguish specific senses for given words from a target sentence [6].

Currently, the most popular and powerful approach to WSD task is based on Knowledge dictionaries [7] such as WordNet[3]. Especially, Structural Semantic Interconnections (SSI) algorithm [3] is the most well-known approach to WSD task. This algorithm creates structural specifications of the possible senses for each target word to disambiguate in a context. And it selects the best hypothesis sense according to a grammar which describing relations between sense specifications. Even though, this SSI algorithm is powerful algorithm based on the strong knowledge-base, there is a limitation to overcome. This paper will be focusing on this limitation provide proposals to overcome this weakness.

---

[1] Nocturnal mouselike mammal with forelimbs modified to form membranous wings and anatomical adaptations for echolocation by which they navigate.

[2] is a contiguous sequence of n items from a given sequence of text or speech.

[3] is a lexical database for the human languages provides definitions and relations among synonyms developed by Cognitive Science Laboratory of Princeton University.

In this paper, we propose a new WSD algorithm, named *Low Ambiguity First (LAF)*, which is based on the hypothesises that it is able to calculate ambiguity of words by using WordNet, and the word with low ambiguity degree must be disambiguated first. Moreover, adjacent words are semantically relevant than other words far way. These hypothesises are the propposals to overcome weaknesses of the SSI algorithm. We believe that the LAF algorithm can improve precision performance of WSD.

The reminder of this paper is organized as follows: In Sect. 2, we describe the SSI algorithm in details and point out its weaknesses. Section 3 is the main part of this paper that we present the low ambiguity first algorithm and explain how it works with examples. Also, the word ambiguity measurement will be illustrated. Finally, Sect. 4 concludes this paper with future works.

2   Related Works

Structural Semantic Interconnections (SSI) algorithm is a method to disambiguate polysemous words by creating structural specifications of the candidate senses for each word and select the most appropriate sense by using the structural grammar. The structural grammar is a possible relevant relations between structural specifications precisely, semantic interconnections among graphs. This SSI algorithm can be described as following variables:

- $T = [t_1, ..., t_n]$ where, t is list of co-occurring terms to be disambiguated and n is a total number of noun types of word in the given sentence.
- $S_1^t, S_2^t, ..., S_k^t$ are structural specifications of the possible concepts for the given t, where k is a total number of the possible concepts.
- $I = [S^{t_1}, ..., S^{t_n}]$ is a list of the disambiguated senses (precisely, semantic interpretation of T), where S^{t_i} is the chosen sense for the given t or the null element that the t is not yet disambiguated.
- $P = [t_i | S^{t_i} = null]$, where P is a list of pending terms to be disambiguated.
- $G = (E, N, S_G, P_G)$, where G is a context-free grammar, E is edge labels to indicate semantic relations between possible senses. N is a path between concepts and S_G is a start symbol of G. P_G is set of productions includes about 40 productions.

The SSI algorithm only considers noun types of word as a term to be disambiguated. Therefore, the list of t will be initialized with noun types of words from the given sentence. The WordNet definitions for the given t will be considered as a possible concepts (S_j^t) for the t. If the target term t is a monosemous[4] word, I will be updated with S^{t_1}. If there are no monosemous terms nor initial synsets, the algorithm will choose the most probable sense based on the frequency of word senses. I will be updated as long as the SSI algorithm can find semantic relations between senses of I and possible senses of t in P by using G.

---

[4] having only single meaning or sense.

Let us assume that there is a sentence to be disambiguated as follows. *Sentence = Retrospective is an exhibition of a representative selection of an artists life work and art exhibition is an exhibition of art objects (paintings or statues).* The initial values of each variable will be updated as following:

T = [*retrospective, work, object, exhibition, life, statue, artist, selection, representative, painting, art*]
I = [*retrospective#1, -, -, -, -, -, -, -, -, -, -*]
P = [*work, object, exhibition, life, statue, artist, selection, representative, painting, art*]

At first, I will be updated with the senses of monosemous words in the list of P as follows:

I = [*retrospective#1, statue#1, artist#1*]
P = [*work, object, exhibition, life, selection, representative, painting, art*]

The I will be enriched until the senses of I and possible senses of t in P have semantic interconnections (such as, *kind-of, has-kind, part-of* and *has-part* relations). Therefore, the final statuses of the lists are as follows:

I = [*retrospective#1, statue#1, artist#1, exhibition#2, object#1, art#1, painting#1, life#12*]
P = [*work, selection, representative*]

As we can see in this SSI algorithm, there are two limitations to overcome. First, there are no criteria to measure which word needs to disambiguate earlier than others. P is a pending list to prepare terms to be disambiguated. However, the problem is that all the ambiguity of words is different from each other. Some words are mostly used by the first sense among other senses. Some words are uncertain due to their high ambiguities. Therefore, we need a method to measure the *Word Ambiguity (WA)* to decide which word has lower ambiguity than other words. So, we can reduce a possibility to make wrong choices in each disambiguation step.

Another limitation is based on the hypothesis that *the adjacent words are semantically relevant to each other.* In other word, a nearest word might have higher possibility to make strong semantic relations than a distant word. If this hypothesis is correct, we need to alter this SSI algorithm to consider structural locations of words in the given sentence.

In this paper, we demonstrate our hypothesis and prove that the SSI algorithm can be improved by concerning semantic relations among adjacent words. Also, we present the word ambiguity measurement by using WordNet sense frequency and propose Low Ambiguity First (LAF) algorithm in Sect. 3.

3 Low Ambiguity First Algorithm

This section presents the Log Ambiguity First algorithm (LAF), a knowledge-based Word Sense Disambiguation by applying the hypothesis that word ambiguity can be measured by frequency of senses in WordNet and the adjacent word are semantically relevant to each other. The variables of LAF algorithm is the same as the SSI algorithm as described in Sect. 2. However, items of pending list P will be ordered by their word ambiguity values.

3.1 A Measurement for Word Ambiguity

A word Ambiguity (WA) is a criteria to measure complexity of word senses in the pending list P. It is important to decide which words disambiguate earlier than other words due to the fact that the SSI algorithm disambiguates senses of t in P by using the senses in I which already have been founded in the previous step. In other word, in each step, the best senses are chosen according to the current I and P, therefore, the order in which senses are chosen may affect the final result.

Let us assume that we have pending list P as follow: $P = $ [group, Friday, investigation, Atlanta, primary_election, evidence, irregularity]. According to the SSI algorithm, the I will be enriched by the monosemous words from the P. Therefore, we've got $I = $ [-, Friday#1, -, -, primary_election#1, -, -] and $P = $ [group, investigation, Atlanta, evidence, irregularity] where,

$S^{group_3} = [(2350)group\#1, (9)group\#2, (3)group\#3]$,
$S^{investigation_2} = [(16)investigation\#1, (8)investigation\#2]$,
$S^{Atlanta_2} = [(7)Atlanta\#1, (1)Atlanta\#2]$,
$S^{evidence_3} = [(54)evidence\#1, (24)evidence\#2, (7)evidence\#3]$,
$S^{irregularity_4} = [(3)irregularity\#1, (2)irregularity\#2, (1)irregularity\#3, ()irregularity\#4]$

The word ambiguity can be measured by following Eq. 1 based on the frequencies of senses from each terms defined in WordNet.

$$WordAmbiguity(t) = \prod_{i=1}^{k-1} \prod_{j=i+1}^{k} \log \frac{frequency(S_i^t)}{frequency(S_j^t) + 1} \qquad (1)$$

where, $frequency(S_i^t)$ is the frequency of the ith sense of the given term t as illustrated in the previous paragraph. For example, the word ambiguity of term $(t = group)$ can be obtained as follow:

$$WordAmbiguity(group) = \log \frac{2350}{10} \times \log \frac{2350}{4} \times \log \frac{9}{4} \approx 2.312$$

If the word ambiguity value close to the zero, it means that the given term (t) has high ambiguity (semantic complexity). In contrast, if the value far apart from the zero, it means that the given term has low ambiguity. In other word, the term with low ambiguity will be disambiguated earlier than other words. Therefore, the pending list P will be updated by the order of word ambiguity as shown in the Fig. 1.

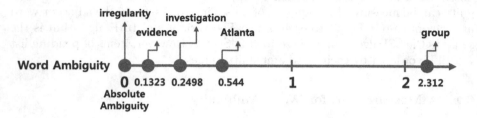

Fig. 1. Examples of Word Ambiguity corresponding to terms (t) in the pending list P.

Therefore, the pending list P will be configured as follows: $P = [group, Atlanta, investigation, evidence, irregularity]$. This is the major difference between the SSI and LAF algorithm that the LAF algorithm will disambiguate low ambiguity word first. Detailed algorithm and explanations will be described in the next section.

3.2 An Adjacent Word May Have Stronger Relations than Other Words

This section describes and demonstrates the hypothesis that an adjacent word of the target term (t) may have stronger semantic relations than other words which far apart from the target term. In order to discover an evidence to prove this hypothesis can be applied in the SSI algorithm, we defined a Morphological Distance (MD) and WordNet Hierarchical Distance (WHD) as shown in Fig. 2. The MD is a morphological distance between target term (t) and its adjacent words. And WHD is the shortest path distance between the target term and its adjacent words based on WordNet hierarchy.

Let us assume that we have a sentence as follows: $Sentence = [The\ Fulton\_County\_Grand\_Jury\ said\ Friday\ an\ investigation\ of\ Atlanta's\ recent\ primary\_election\ produced\ no\ evidence\ that\ any\ irregularities\ took\_place]$ which is the first sentence of the Brown1[5] of SemCor[6] data corpus. After preprocessing steps, we can obtain terms to be disambiguated as shown in Fig. 2. Therefore, the MD and WHD between the target term ($t = group$) will be calculated as follows:

- $MD(Group, Friday) = 1$, $MD(Group, investigation) = 2$, ... , $MD(Group, irregularity) = 6$
- $WHD(Group, Friday) = 8$, $WHD(Groupo, investigation) = 9$, ... , $WHD(Group, irregularity) = 8$

---

[5] The Brown University Standard Corpus of Present-Day American English.

[6] A SemCor corpus is a manually sense-tagged corpora created by the WordNet project research team in Princeton University.

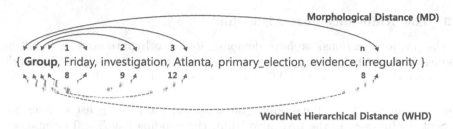

Fig. 2. Examples of the morphological distance and WordNet hierarchical distance between terms in pending list.

According to the examples in Fig. 2, the WHD was increased when the MD was getting bigger. However, the WHD was decreased even though the MD is getting bigger after certain point. Therefore, we need to discover this point that the tendency of WHD will be reversed, by comparing the MD and WHD from all sentences in Brown1 corpus. As a result, we obtained the average of WHD corresponding to the MD as shown in the following Table 1.

Table 1. Averages and Standard Deviations of WHD corresponding to MDs between terms in Brown1 corpus.

MD	Number of words	Ave. of WHD	Standard Deviation of WHD
MD = 1	5,161	10.16857	3.84991
MD = 2	5,133	10.32359	3.79279
MD = 3	4,330	10.41293	3.72705
MD = 4	3,420	10.19591	3.77212
MD = 5	2,661	10.24728	3.75285
MD = 6	1,983	10.29097	3.70380
MD = 7	1,436	10.03412	3.74383
MD = 8	1,068	10.08427	3.68752
MD = 9	752	9.98271	3.68088
MD = 10	531	10.45574	3.50725

As we can see in this table, the average value of WHD was increased until MD is equal to three. However, the average value of WHD was decreased when the MD is 4. These results can indicate that if the morphological distance between target term (t) and its adjacent words is less than 4, there will be a tenancy that morphologically close words have a high possibility to make strong semantic relations. The most of the words (more than 80 percent) in Brown1 corpus are located in condition that the MD is one to six. Because it is hard to find a sentence with more than six kinds of nouns in the natural human language.

We hereby have proved that the adjacent words of the target term are likely to have shorter WHD than a word with higher MD under the certain point.

3.3 Low Ambiguity First Algorithm

In the previous sections, we have demonstrated two hypothesises that will be applied in the LAF algorithm, in order to improve the traditional SSI algorithm. Before we start to apply the LAF algorithm, we need to initialize the variables which were required for saving co-occurring terms, structural specifications of the possible concepts, list of the disambiguated senses, and pending list as described in Sect. 2. However, in the LAF algorithm, the pending list P will be updated after measuring the word ambiguity followed by the Eq. 1, and weighting function will be applied to calculate semantic similarity between unknown senses and known senses, changed by the morphological distance.

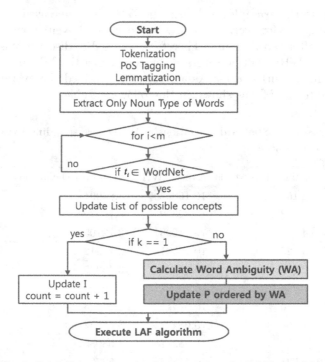

Fig. 3. Initializing processes for executing the LAF algorithm.

The proposed system will be developed by Python language and Pseudo-code for an implementation of the LAF algorithm described in the followings. This algorithm will take four kinds of list as input data which were the initialized list after preprocessing tasks shown in the Fig. 3. This algorithm will update list I and P until the system cannot find no further matching senses between items of P_C and I, by using the shortest path distance based on WordNet. The weighting function will be determined by the values of *alpha*, *beta*, and *theta*, respectively. These parameters are the constant values for applying the hypothesis that described in the Sect. 3.2.

```
Low Ambiguity First Algorithm(T, I, P_C, P){
    import nltk
    T[m] = list of co-occurring terms(t)
    T[m] = list of disambiguated senses for the given t
    P_C[m][k] = list of possible concepts for the given t
    P[m'] = list of pending terms to be disambiguated
    count = counting variable for items of list I

    for(i=1;i<m';i++){
        for(j=1;j<count;j++){
            for(x=1;x<k;x++){
                // similarity will be based on the shortest path
                // distance in WordNet
                find similarity(P_C[i][x], I[j])
                return the most semantically close sense P_C[i][x]
                        and its value.
            if count == 1:
                update I, P
                count = count + 1
                break
            else:
                continue
        // alpha, beta, and theta are the constant values to
        // apply adjacent words have strong semantic relations
        // where, alpha + beta + theta = 1
        alpha * similarity(P_C[i][x], I[j])
        beta * similarity(P_C[i][x], I[j'])
        theta * similarity(P_C[i][x], I[j''])
        find the most relevant P_C[i][x]
        update I, P
        count = count + 1
    return P_C[i][x]
```

In this proposed LAF algorithm, we are able to apply two hypothesises described in the previous Sects. 3.1 and 3.2, in order to overcome the limitations of traditional SSI algorithm. According to a base experiment[7] to verify reliability of the proposed algorithm, we have founded that our algorithm can improve the SSI algorithm. However, we are not going to describe experimental results in this paper due to the fact that the amount of testing data was not big enough. The major goal of this paper is the proposal of the LAF algorithm and demonstrations of the hypothesises. The experimental results will be introduced in the future works.

---

[7] We simply run a comparison test by using small amount of sentences.

4   Conclusions and Future Works

In this paper, we propose a new approach to overcome weaknesses of the traditional SSI algorithm which is the most popular knowledge-based WSD algorithm. People started to apply statistical approaches for disambiguating polysemous words however, the performance of these methods are still required improvements. Even though, knowledge base which is a machine readable knowledge database had been applied to WSD, there is a limitation that the current knowledge-base cannot cover entire senses of human language so far. The more we hold a rich knowledge base, the more we gained high performance for the WSD. However, enriching and maintaining knowledge base require many costs and time. Therefore we proposed a method only by using the limited current resources based on the two hypothesises. We demonstrated these hypothesises in this paper and proposed the Low Ambiguity First algorithm which is able to overcome weaknesses of the SSI algorithm. Experiments are still ongoing however, we believe that the proposed method can improve the performance of WSD.

Acknowledgments. This research was supported by SW Master's course of hiring contract Program grant funded by the Ministry of Science, ICT and Future Planning (H0116-15-1013) and the Human Resource Training Program for Regional Innovation and Creativity through the Ministry of Education and National Research Foundation of Korea (NRF-2014H1C1A1066494).

References

1. Ide, N., Veronis, J.: Introduction to the special issue on word sense disambiguation. Comput. Linguist. **24**(1), 2–40 (1998)
2. Lesk, M.: Automatic sense disambiguation using machine readable dictionaries: how to tell a pine cone form an ice cream cone. In: SIGDOC 1986: Proceedings of the 5th Annual International Conference on Systems Documentation, pp. 24–26. ACM, New York (1986)
3. Navigli, R., Velardi, P.: Structural semantic interconnections: a knowledge-based approach to word sense disambiguation. IEEE Trans. Pattern Anal. Mach. Intell. **27**(7), 1075–1086 (2005)
4. Weiss, S.F.: Learning to disambiguate. Inform. Storage Retrieval **9**(1), 33–41 (1973)
5. Jurafsky, D., Martin, J.: Speech and Language Processing: An Introduction to Natural Language Processing, Computational Linguistics, and Speech Recognition. Prentice Hall, Upper Saddle River (2000)
6. Pedersen, T.: Unsupervised corpus-based methods for WSD. In: Agirre, E., Edmonds, P. (eds.) Word Sense Disambiguation: Text, Speech and Language Technology, vol. 33, pp. 133–166. Springer, New York (2006)
7. Hwang, M., Choi, C., Kim, P.: Automatic enrichment of semantic relation network and its application to word sense disambiguation. IEEE Trans. Knowl. Data Eng. **23**(6), 845–858 (2011)
8. Choi, D. Kim, P.: Identifying the most appropriate expansion of acronyms used in wikipedia text. Softw. Pract. Experience (2014). doi:10.1002/spe.2006

A Data Visualization System for Considering Relationships Among Scientific Data

Jangwon Gim[1], Yunji Jang[1], Yeonghun Chae[2], Hanmin Jung[1], and Do-Heon Jeong[1(✉)]

[1] Korea Institute of Science and Technology Information, Daejeon, South Korea
{jangwon,yunji,jhm,heon}@kisti.re.kr
[2] Korea University, Sejong Campus, Sejong, South Korea
proin@korea.ac.kr

Abstract. With the recent explosive increase in the amount of web-based scientific data in big data environments, various researcher support systems have been developed to help discover desired scientific data and search insights. Scientific and researcher-related data are also applied to social networking services, thus promoting inter-researcher networking. However, much time and effort is put into big data mining to extract information customized to researchers' specific needs. Moreover, systems that facilitate information extraction by schematizing various inter-data relationships are absent. In this paper, we propose a system that facilitates relevant information extraction from scientific data and provides intuitive data visualization. Such data visualization allows efficient relationship expression between scientific data (relationships between researchers, acronyms and technical terms, and synonyms of a technology name), and provides an author disambiguation interface for authors with the same name. As a result, researchers can extract relevant information from big data with scientific data, and obtain significant information based on cleansed and disambiguated data.

Keywords: Visualization system · Scientific data · SOLR · Implicit relationships

1 Introduction

Recent years have seen an explosive increase in the number of web-based scientific data. Open Access (OA) is the representative platform of scientific data, in which they are distributed in the Open Archives Initiative (OAI) protocol format provided by OA repositories [1]. The number of OA scientific data marked a ten-fold increase in ten years from 19,500 in 2000 to 191,850 in 2009, and this rapid upward trend of online distribution of scientific data is expected to continue in coming years [2]. Against this background, a wide range of search engines for scientific data, such as Microsoft Academic Search, Google Scholar, and SciVal Experts have been developed for the purpose of collecting scientific data and providing them for users who seek scientific papers and insights. Of them, Google Scholar operates a freely accessible service by searching and collecting scientific data, indexing them according to data patterns, and expanding them [3]. Microsoft Academic Search service runs a pilot operation of a system for providing users with visualized display of inter linkages among scientific data. Yet, to the best of

© Springer International Publishing Switzerland 2015
F.F.-H. Nah and C.-H. Tan (Eds.): HCIB 2015, LNCS 9191, pp. 575–584, 2015.
DOI: 10.1007/978-3-319-20895-4_53

our knowledge, there is a lack of systems for visually displaying multifaceted inter-data relationships. Retrieval efficiency and system usability can be improved compared with currently available general search engines by revealing such variegated inter linkages among scientific data and analyzing them based on the attributes of respective extracted data [4, 5]. This paper presents a visualization system based on the Solr system for the purpose of expanding the usability of scientific data. First, we collected scientific data from the Digital Bibliography & Library Project (DBLP) website that publicizes computer science bibliographic lists. These basic data were enriched by an expanded search of related institutional data and researcher databases. Based on the researcher profiles thus collected, we constructed visualized presentations of not only researcher network status, but also data of the affiliated institutions and email addresses, and provided them in user interfaces such as Forced-Directed Graph, Timeline, and Facet Navigator, along with a system that retrieves such data.

This paper is organized as follows. In Sect. 2, we introduce previous researches into solutions to the visualization about scientific data. In Sect. 3, we explain the implementation system. Finally, we conclude this paper and discuss future work in Sect. 4.

2 Related Work

2.1 Analysis of Scientific Data

Along with the online distribution of scientific data, analytical research into the relationship of scientific data has been underway. Scientific papers distributed online provide information on key information related to the respective papers, such as year of publication and authors' names and affiliations, but no disambiguation data in the case of researchers with the same name. To address this problem, many studies have been conducted to establish and analyze methods for author name disambiguation [6–8]. One such method was investigated by a study using co-citation data. The co-citation data considered in this study were used by two other studies, which analyzed the co-citation patterns and disambiguated individual authors with the same name. In addition to mechanical analysis, a method of unique author identification was also presented, in which a unique identifier called Researcher ID is assigned to each scientific author. Researcher ID solves the problem of identifying authors with the same name by assigning an identifier to be linked to the academic papers produced by the corresponding author. Along with studies on author disambiguation, studies have been conducted on the relationships of researcher-related data that consider issues such as "similar researcher search" and "researcher recommendation" through similar entity search by extracting expertise profiles from the collected researcher-related data [9].

2.2 Data Visualization

The rapid increase in the amount of data caused by the rapid increase of Internet users has led to the intensification of research on new methods of data retrieval using multi-faceted information in addition to simple text search [10]. One such method is data visualization. As a result, a number of search engines have already presented visualized data service, and in turn, this has given rise to studies that evaluate the usability of such visualized data [11].

Researcher expertise profile retrieval systems, such as Google Scholar, Citeseer, Libra, and SciVal Experts, are useful tools for harvesting web-based academic papers. Users consult these search engines to find the materials related to their research. These systems provide data related to the objects queried by entering paper titles, author names, or technological domains [12]. Users can use them for launching queries and retrieving relevant papers, but cannot easily grasp what is contained in the papers and how retrieved papers relate to one another.

In order to overcome such limitations, search engines put much effort into the visualization of search results. Microsoft Academic Search, for example, shows researchers linked to a queried researcher in a graph (Fig. 1). This system can show co-authors, but output is limited to the identified researchers, so that the unidentified researchers cannot be reflected in the co-author graph. The identified data are then treated as uncertainty data, thus resulting in an analysis error in the data analysis process. In addition to graphic representation, the visualization of search results can provide users with more convenient intuitive views of search results with interactive features; for example, a facet navigation system offers a responsive interface that reflects the search terms entered by the user. In other words, users are provided with interactive data retrieval via faceted navigation. As a result, fact navigation-based search is more useful for users to retrieve relevant data than the best-first search method. Facet search is preferred not only for researcher database search, which is the object of this study, but also in other types of websites with high user accessibility, such as electronic commerce sites [13].

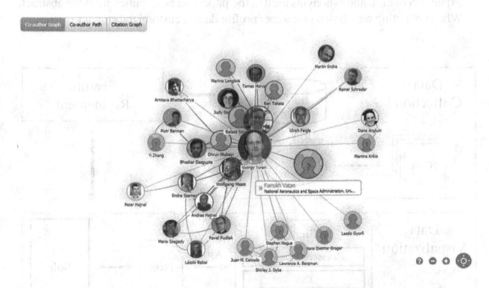

Fig. 1. Microsoft academic search - coauthor graph (http://academic.research.microsoft.com/ VisualExplorer#3317582)

This paper presents a data visualization system that allows the relationship analysis of scientific data and researcher disambiguation. The proposed system can be used efficiently to analyze research trends and harvest researcher disambiguation data by visualizing the inter-data relationships of search results capable of deriving the relationships among retrieved scientific data, irrespective of the results of researcher disambiguation, thus unaffected by data related to unidentified researchers.

3   Implementation System

3.1   Visualization Process

Figure 2 shows the system configuration proposed in this system, for which the process of visualizing researcher profile data comprises the three stages of data col-lection, data cleansing, and data visualization.

- **Data collection.** The first stage is the collection of researcher profile databases publicized on the Internet in the domain of computer science. To this end, the names of authors and co-authors, paper titles, and DOIs were extracted from the DBLP data published in the XML format. In order to solve the problem of author ambiguity with the same name, we used the DOI information of the concerned papers in order to collect additional author attributes leading to disambiguation, such as affiliated institutions and email addresses, from their respective websites. The DOI for a paper leads to the website on which the paper is published, and the corresponding page provides paper details, including the abstract, institution name, and email ad-dress. Acronyms, expansion names, and synonyms used in the paper can be obtained from the abstract. When collecting web-based researcher profile data, a customized crawler is required

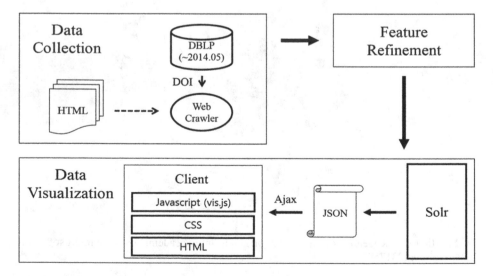

Fig. 2. System architecture

for each webpage, considering its structural pattern, because webpage structures are different from one website to another. Using such customized crawlers, acronyms and expansions are obtained from the papers collected. For this process, we applied an acronym and expansion extraction tool [14]. The extraction tool used contains a cleansing module for removing stopword, unnecessary punctuations, and typographical errors. In the data collection stage, a total of 30,672 acronyms and 512,587 expansions were collected from the data of the papers published online.

- **Data Cleansing and Processing.** Data retrieved by automated data collection should be subjected to data cleansing for the removal of unnecessary words and signs. In the case of the data provided by the DBLP, the sequential numbers added to author names or paper titles to avoid data double entries should be removed. For example, from the author name "Tomas Keller 0001," "0001" should be removed in order to enhance author disambiguation and retrieval accuracy. In addition, unnecessary abbreviations or academic degrees added to authors' names should be removed. Pages containing HTML tags retrieved by web crawlers often contain mixed upper and lower-case letters and signs, which should be cleansed.

- **Data Visualization.** We applied the Solr tool developed in the Apache Project to the visualization system in order to allow customized scientific data retrieval and facilitate detailed data retrieval. Solr, built on Apache Lucene, has the advantages of easily implementing facet navigation features used as an interactive user interface, and allowing high-speed and high-accuracy retrieval by indexing data. Therefore, we applied Solr for the implementation of an interactive user interface based on scientific data. We employed the Ajax technology to construct the interactive user interface, and applied vis.js library to visualize the graphic presentations based on data formatted using JavaScript Object Notation (JSON) [15].

3.2 Proposed System

The main search categories for the proposed system are author, acronym, and synonym to be selected according to the types of scientific data. The system is composed of Facet Navigator, Forced-Directed Graph, and Timeline.

- **Facet Navigator.** This feature is shown on the left side of the Fig. 3. Further search can be performed by clicking the links presented in the search results. Such a selected search within the presented search results induces simultaneous filtering of the data represented in the network graph and timeline, which is the main feature of the system. Facet Navigator allows users to pursue the search for data related to the search results and view only necessary data by targeted extraction, thus reducing the complicity of search results.

- **Forced-Directed Graph.** The Forced-Directed Graph represents each of the author's name, co-author, acronym, synonym, expansion, email, and affiliation by positioning it as a node on the graph. Nodes have different colors to facilitate visual differentiation. By the nature of a forced-directed graph, the higher the number of nodes, the harder the graph reading and the slower the visualization. To forestall this problem, we depicted only the core nodes that match the search terms

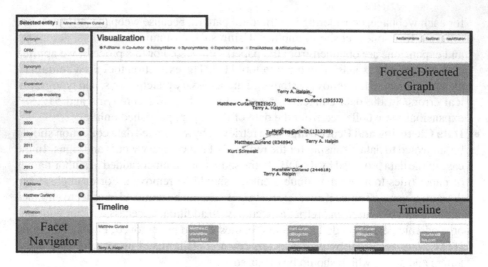

Fig. 3. Main interface to shows diverse scientific data

for the graph visualization. Users can choose additional nodes whenever additional information is required and renew the graph.

• **Timeline.** The Timeline shows the email addresses of the author and co-author(s) by year. The top line contains the email information of the author by year, and each line underneath contains that of a co-author. The lines have different colors, and ID values, with the exception of email addresses, were compared using the algorithm "Gestalt Pattern Matching" [16]; those showing similarities in excess of 60 % were marked with the same color.

3.3 Searching Scientific Data

• **Searching Authors.** This feature helps users disambiguate authors by providing affiliations and co-authors' email addresses. Result values related to authors are outputted as ID values, and users can disambiguate authors by reading graphs and timelines. Figure 4 show detail results about relationships among emails using Forced-Directed Graph. If the value yielded by the pattern-matching algorithm exceeds 60 %, the node is linked to the degree of similarity with a dotted line. The graph drawn within the quadrilateral marked in Fig. 4 displays three email addresses that match three authors, each with similarities that exceed 60 %, and thus connected with dotted lines. In this case, the probability of the three authors being the same person is considered high. The timeline can also help users disambiguate authors because it indicates the email addresses used in the papers by year. We decided the threshold of email similarity is 60 %, therefore if similarity value between ID of emails higher than the threshold then we can consider the authors who have the similar email ID can be the same author. In Fig. 5, four different emails are outputted from a paper authored by "Terry A. Halpin," of which those used in 2009 and 2011

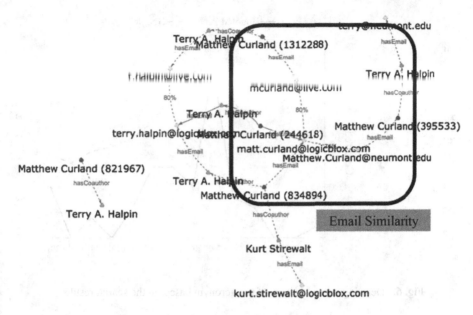

Fig. 4. Finding the same authors by email similarity

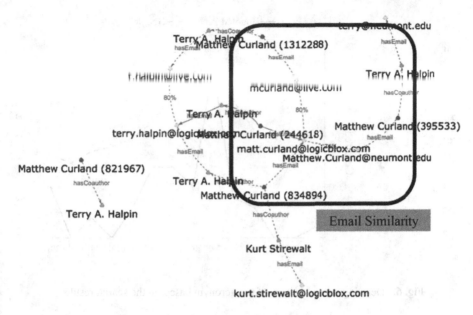

Fig. 5. Author identification interface with email timeline derived from scientific data (Color figure online)

are identical, and those used in 2013 are different, but with a high degree of similarity, and thus are depicted in the same color. The part grouped as "co-author" indicates that three authors prepared the paper together in the corresponding year. In the same fashion, it can be verified that "Matthew Curland" and "Terry A. Halpin" co-authored papers in other years as well. This information, in conjunction with the colors that express email similarities, leads to the assumption that the authors who appear in 2006, 2009, 2011, and 2013 can be considered to be identical.

- **Searching Acronyms.** In the proposed system, if an acronym has different expansions, the representative expansion is taken as the technology name. An acronym search can lead to obtaining detailed information regarding the concerned technology by launching queries based on the terms in the expanded form of the acronym.

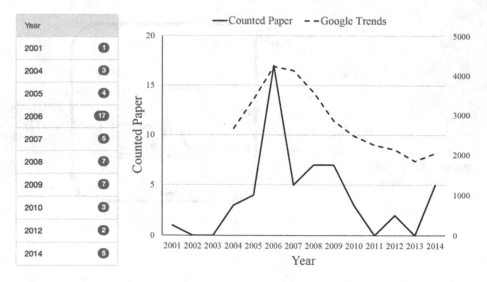

Fig. 6. Deriving a trend history of the acronym based on the search results

Fig. 7. Showing relationships between synonyms and their expansions

Figure 6 shows a graph derived from the trend observation regarding the corresponding technology by performing a detailed search with a further query on "Service-Oriented Architecture" from the search results yielded by the search term "SOA." The axis on the left side shows the number of papers by year yielded by the search results, and the axis on the right side shows the values of the "Service-Oriented Architecture" search results of the Google Trend Search, restructured by year. The graph derived via Facet Navigator reveals that the "Service-Oriented Architecture" technology began to be studied seriously in 2004, peaked in 2006, and has decreased since then. By comparing the corresponding data with the Google Trend Search results, we verified that the estimated (derived) trend was similar to the real trend. The corresponding graph is not outputted in UI, but users can derive it from the results outputted in the year item of the Facet Navigator.

- **Searching Synonyms.** Synonym search provides users with information by retrieving the words similar to, or translated from, the search terms by linking synonym data with expansion and acronym data. The examination of the part marked as "Synonym Group" in Fig. 7 reveals that the query of the term "cross-linguistic retrieval" leads to the information about the author who conducted research on its expansion and acronym data, namely, cross-lingual information retrieval, cross-language information retrieval, and CLIR.

4 Conclusion

In line with the recent progress of the Internet and the trend of publicizing open access academic papers, a wide variety and large amount of related research results have been produced. Services that support the research of those looking for collaboration partners, or probing the latest research trends, have been developed based on researcher profile databases. More recently, services based on predictive and prescriptive analytic methodologies have been developed to enhance researchers' competences. Amidst this trend, the need for accurate researcher profile data has become urgent to allow the accurate diagnosis and analysis of technological trends or researcher expertise. However, given that the currently available data have an unsolved problem of authors with the same name, constructing such services based on such data poses the issue of accuracy and reliability. This problem can be solved only by developing methods and systems for extracting data on the relationships of relevant researcher profile data from scientific data that can lead to author disambiguation. Therefore, this study presented a system that provides screens customized for users, helps them disambiguate researcher profiles by deriving inter-data relationships from researcher-related data, and visualizes them.

Researcher-related data could be disambiguated using the proposed system by comparing researchers' email addresses and research keywords. In addition, a time-line interface was developed that demonstrated the possibility of author disambiguation by tracking back individual attributes.

References

1. Choi, J.-H., Cho, H.-Y.: The recent trends of open access movements and the ways to help the cause by academic stakeholders. J. Korea Soc. Inf. Manage. **22**(3), 307–326 (2005)
2. Laakso, M., Welling, P., Bukvova, H., Nyman, L., Björk, B.-C., Hedlund, T.: The development of open access journal publishing from 1993 to 2009.PLoS ONE, **6**(6), 1–10 (2011)
3. Shim, W.: Big deal, open access, google scholar and the subscription of electronic scholarly contents at university libraries. J. Korea Soc. Inf. Manage. **29**(4), 143–163 (2012)
4. Lee, S.-H., Kwak, S.-J.: Development and evaluation of authority data based academic paper retrieval system. J. Korean Soc. Libr. Inf. Sci. **46**(2), 133–156 (2012)

5. Park, D.-J., Lee, S.-T., Choi, K.-S.: Conceptual design of metadata based research results information retrieval system. J. Korea Soc. Inf. Manage. **37**(2), 1–20 (2006)
6. Seglen, P.O.: Why the impact factor of journals should not be used for evaluating research. Br. Med. J. (BMJ) **314**(7079), 498–502 (1997)
7. Kang, I.-S.: Disambiguation of author names using co-citation. J. Korea Soc. Inf. Manage. **42**(3), 167–186 (2011)
8. Calsa, J.W.: Daniel kotza: researcher identification: the right needle in the haystack. Lancet **371**(9631), 2152–2153 (2008)
9. Gollapalli, S.D., Mitra, P., Giles, C.L.: Similar Researcher Search in Academic Environments. In: 12th ACM/IEEE-CS joint conference on Digital Libraries(JCDL 2012), pp. 167–170 (2012)
10. Jee, T.-C., Lee, H., Lee, Y.: Visualization method of document retrieval result based on centers of clusters. J. Korea Contents Soc. **7**(5), 16–26 (2007)
11. Kim, S.-H., Kim, M.-J.: A usability evaluation on the visualization techniques of web retrieval results. J. Korean Soc. Libr. Inf. Sci. **41**(3), 181–199 (2007)
12. Hwang, W.-S., Chae, S.-M., Kim, S.-W., Choi, H.J.: A ranking method for article search engines. J. Korean Inst. Inf. Sci. Eng. **40**(5), 345–357 (2013)
13. Tunkelang, D.: Faceted Search. In: Lectures on Information Concepts, Retrieval, and Services. Morgan & Claypool Publishers (2009)
14. Jeong, D.-H., Hwang, M.-G., Sung, W.-K.: Generating knowledge map for acronym-expansion recognition. U- E-Serv. Sci. Technol. **264**, 287–293 (2011)
15. VISJS. http://visjs.org/
16. Ratcliff, J.W., Metzener, D.: Pattern Matching: The Gestalt Approach. Dr. Dobb's Journal **13**, 46–72 (1988)

Design of Marketing Scenario Planning Based on Business Big Data Analysis

Seungkyun Hong[1,2], Sungho Shin[1], Young-min Kim[1],
Choong-Nyoung Seon[1], Jung ho Um[1], and Sa-kwang Song[1,2(✉)]

[1] Korea Institute of Science and Technology Information, Daejeon, South Korea
{xo,maximus74,ymkim,wilowisp,jhum,
esmallj}@kisti.re.kr
[2] Department of Big Data Analysis,
Korea University of Science and Technology, Daejeon, South Korea
{xo,esmallj}@ust.ac.kr

Abstract. As the amount and the type of data for business decision making are rapidly increasing, the importance of big data analytics is gradually critical for making effective business strategy. However, big data analytics based decision making systems basically requires distributed parallel computing capability in order to make timely business strategy recommendation via processing huge amount unstructured as well as structured business data. We introduce a big data analytics system for automatic marketing scenario planning based on big data platform software such as Hadoop and HBase. The analytics methodology for scenario planning is based on prescriptive analytics which is the most advance methodology consisting of generation of business scenarios and their optimization, among the three analytics of descriptive, predictive, and prescriptive analytics. Additionally, we developed a prototype of marketing scenario planning system and its graphical user interface, as well as the system architecture based on Hadoop eco-system based distributed parallel computing platform.

Keywords: Business intelligence · Prescriptive analytics · Big data · Marketing scenario · Scenario optimization

1 Introduction

With the advent of gigabit-level ultrafast Internet access to communication networks, and the subsequent development of financial information infrastructure, such as business transaction systems, businesses and entrepreneurs now possess a vast amount of sales-related databases. However, it is not simple for managers and business owners to use these data for detecting new business opportunities and attracting new clients to continue improving business performance. New clients can be either those who are already habitual consumers of their products and services, or those who visit their points of sale (POS) less frequently. Managers usually set business objectives that target these client clusters. Once the business objectives are established, concrete strategies should be set up, such as discounts and leaflet advertising, to achieve objectives.

© Springer International Publishing Switzerland 2015
F.F.-H. Nah and C.-H. Tan (Eds.): HCIB 2015, LNCS 9191, pp. 585–592, 2015.
DOI: 10.1007/978-3-319-20895-4_54

In most cases, decision makers are content with establishing objectives and strategies by manually analyzing the various business information resources they collect in their own ways, and using such information resources as check items for decision making regarding business actions. In some cases, decision makers do not even possess storage devices or analysis software for various POS data because of the financial burden of purchasing and operation. Such manual and unsystematic approaches to management have two problems in terms of accomplishing objectives: first, the decision makers can present a non-objective direction in the strategic planning processes; second, the expenditure saved from the costs of introducing automatic management data processing infrastructure can be easily outweighed by the costs of human resources and wasted time for manual data processing.

The present paper proposes a prescriptive analysis system that evaluates sales and logistical data in and around POS, and suggests marketing scenarios for management-related decision-making to business owners who cannot afford management information analysis systems. The proposed system stores general management information using HBase, which is a large-scale database management system (DBMS) based on a distributed/parallel database, performs high-speed computation of the stored data necessary for calculating strategic models for establishing marketing scenarios, and stores the output data. Users can then choose basic business information associated with their businesses, as well as additional business strategies interesting for their businesses, and apply them to the decision-making processes to finally find efficient marketing scenarios.

2 Related Works

Business Analytics (BA) refers to a series of analytic techniques used for identifying current problems by analyzing past business achievements or performing recurrent processes, such as simulation, in order to derive optimal strategies to overcome the problems. BA is largely divided into Descriptive Analytics, Predictive Analytics, and Prescriptive Analytics [1].

Descriptive Analytics is the basic data analysis technique in which past data are mechanically studied in order to learn the impact of past behaviors on future achievements, and thus anticipate future events. Management reports can be considered a representative example of Descriptive Analytics, given that they seek the clues that link different variables of past events that should be considered for achieving specific objectives in the future.

Predictive Analytics is the technique used for detecting in advance certain events or risk factors likely to occur in the future, and analyzing counterstrategies. It is applied in a variety of statistical techniques, such as machine learning, data mining, and game theory. In predictive analytics, numerical data that represents past transactions are generally used in order to capture significant relationships among various algorithms, statistical models, and patterns not contained in the collected data. It is one of the most widely used analytic techniques in processing big data, and it is essential to secure various analysis tools and a large amount of data to achieve high-accuracy and high-quality outcomes. In the field of financial services, predictive analytics is primarily used for customer credit rating.

Prescriptive Analytics is a brand-new analytic technique designed to predict the impact of a decision before implementing it. It aims not only at predicting the when and what of an event, but also at analyzing the why it occurs, and thus providing recommendations for optimized actions. From this strategic perspective, the goal of enhancing research competitiveness can also be interpreted as a business analytic perspective from which future actions should be predicted based on numerical data, given that the goal is analyzed based on numerical data, such as historical and changing trends regarding researchers and related technologies.

The business solutions from IBM and AYATA are representative examples of prescriptive analytics. AYATA is the worldwide unique company that analyzes data using prescriptive analytics. Mathematical sciences, machine learning, and computer science are some of the disciplines involved in the analytic techniques used by this company. Despite the great potential and promise that prescriptive analytics holds, organizations using prescriptive analytics account for only 3 % of all organizations worldwide, with the rest still using exclusively structured data.

3   Marketing Scenario Planning

Marketing scenario is a marketing tool that contains detailed and concrete plans for implementing intended strategic measures, e.g., to enlarge ongoing business projects or promote new products and services to potential customers via various media channels prior to launching. Given that business actions and ensuing results depend on the implementation of the marketing scenario, it necessarily occupies an important place in the phase of marketing goal setting. In particular, the scenario planning for small enterprises is of vital importance because of the great impact of the individual business components on the management environment. Nevertheless, the lack of data usable for small business owners poses difficulties in developing strategic plans for them.

When proposing marketing scenarios to small business owners, merely analyzing sales data and providing the results is not sufficient for helping them make proper decisions. In order to efficiently support small business owners, not only structured data that consists of sales and logistical data should be analyzed, but also unstructured data, such as Internet citizen (netizen) social networking service (SNS) feeds that represent consumer responses. Such integrated data analysis with regards to sales, logistics, and level of foot traffic can be applied for making customized sales predictions according to specific days of the week, time of day, age bracket, and gender.

In addition, SNS provides information on consumer responses to individual POS, and the trends of related business lines. By performing integrated analyses of such structured and unstructured data, marketing scenarios that reflect the current situations of small enterprises can be established, and finally, optimized marketing scenarios with the highest anticipated sales figures can be proposed. Small enterprises can thus be supported in marketing-related decision-making in the manner explained in the last part of the Introduction section.

The marketing scenario planning proposed in this paper to support decision makers of small enterprises can be divided into three stages. In the first stage, situation analysis, sales data from the POS under investigation are analyzed. The results provide managers and business owners with an overview of the sales trends and types in POS from multiple perspectives—for example, the types of customer clusters that bought what, when, and how. In the second stage, marketing goals are set, including target customer clusters and access strategies, in order to boost sales. In this goal setting stage, several goals can be considered, and correspondingly, many marketing approaches, such as a simple linear increase in sales at a specific rate or targeting a specific customer cluster. The third stage concerns deriving strategies for reaching the goals set in the previous stage by performing multi-dimensional analysis of various structured data, such as current management situations, foot traffic, and logistical data. The ultimate aim of this stage is to propose the optimal scenario that ensures accomplishment of the sales target or other specific goals.

In line with this aim, we designed a scenario proposal system for small business owners from the angles described above. Figure 1 shows the overview of the system architecture. The system consists of three modules: (1) data collection module in which multi-source structured and unstructured data are collected and converted to analysis-enabled formats; (2) prediction module in which various business models are derived from the data outputted from the data collection module; (3) prescriptive analytics module in which marketing strategies are designed and developed based on the prediction data outputted from the prediction module. In the data collection module, various types of data are collected from multiple sources (providers), processed in the pre-defined forms, and converted to data usable in the prediction module. In the prediction module, the incoming data from the data collection module are analyzed based on various business mind analysis techniques under aspects of product type, consumer types, and temporal elements, such as day of the week and time of day, and their correlations are established and predicted. In the prescriptive analytics module, based on the predicted data, a business scenario is derived that can be implemented in current business situations.

Figure 2 shows an example of a marketing scenario yielded by implementing the prescriptive analytics that reflect the business situations and goals in the last stage of Fig. 1. The result of prescriptive analytics can be largely divided into three parts: (i) anticipated future profit (in graph) shows the current prediction and profit increase rate as a result of implementing the marketing plan by business action; (ii) suggestions of various business actions to take in order to reach the sales target, including the period and manner of their implementation; (iii) numerical information related to the accomplished targets of various business actions integrated in the scenario.

In relation to the suggestions of various business actions, an endless number of combinations may be generated because of the discrepancies between baseline situations of business owners or managers, and POS and management objectives. Storing all these analysis results is a great challenge for conventional relational DBMS (RDBMS) models. This problem is addressed by constructing prescriptive analytics in business prediction models that consider only the elements and factors related to target accomplishment.

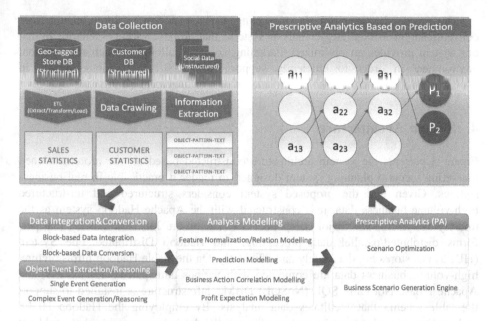

Fig. 1. System architecture for marketing scenario generation

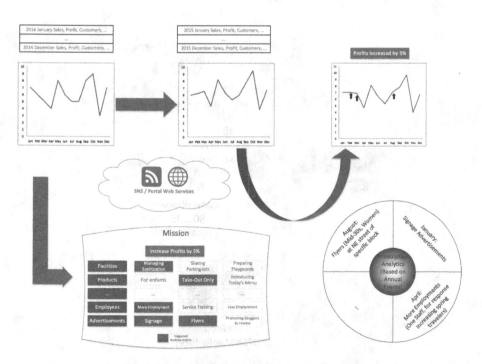

Fig. 2. Conceptual diagram of scenario planning

The proposed system for the marketing scenario design is differentiated from conventional business strategic analysis systems that propose various scenarios in that our system provides an optimized marketing scenario tailored to each management environment in order to efficiently support managers and business owners in decision-making to achieve their sales targets and management objectives.

4 System Architecture

Figure 3 presents the system architecture constructed based on the aforementioned marketing scenario planning system designed to render it practicable in real business settings. Given that the proposed system considers structured and unstructured high-volume business data, it is constructed with the Apache Hadoop system as the underlying system. The major components of Hadoop are Job/Task Tracker that performs distributed/parallel data processing, and Hadoop Distributed File System (HDFS) that stores big data safely and efficiently. On the stable Hadoop infrastructure, high-volume business data are computed with various anticipated-sales models, and Apache HBase Not Only SQL (NoSQL) DBMS infrastructure is installed to support the table schema that facilitates data analysis. By employing the Hadoop HDFS architecture, this infrastructure supports the parallel database processing that could not be implemented in conventional RDB, and adopts a distributed data storage approach for safe data storage. Thus, the data stores can be utilized by the client side for sales prediction through RESTful API supported by default in the HBase infrastructure.

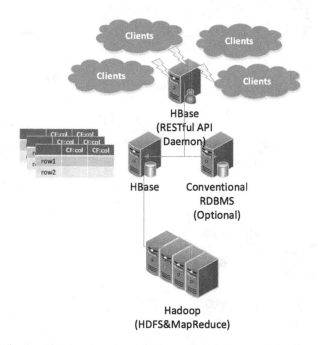

Fig. 3. Hadoop eco-system based architecture of marketing scenario planning system

RESTful API can receive data in the form of a simple ATTP protocol without the need for complicated wiring through the DB query GET/POST method similar to SQL. In particular, the RESTful interface can receive output data in the XML format, which does not require data parsing processes to render the incoming data usable by the client, and it has unlimited capacity for application and expansion without regard to client type.

Business big data have extremely variegated elements, and correcting the schema at each data input, as is the case with conventional RDB, is too complicated and time-consuming. HBase allows for unlimited column input pertaining to various elements once a column family is constituted by gathering the corresponding conceptual columns; furthermore, column family data are expandable, similar to the conventional RDB, via additional operation. The key advantage of the column family system is its simultaneous management of a set of different attributes, which allows the data analysis system architect and client developer to intuitively manage the data. Furthermore, in HBase, the challenge of managing records whose volumes range from millions to hundreds of billions of cases is efficiently addressed by distributed database storage of each node.

Figure 4 presents a design example of a client that suggests a final marketing scenario to a business owner using prescriptive analytics, as described above. A client can be basically divided into two parts: business operation and scenario analyses. In the business operation analysis, a detailed analysis is performed concerning the composition of POS and foot traffic volume according to gender and age distributions, as well as by time and weekday. In the scenario analysis, plausible scenarios that reflect the current sales situation, target sales volume, and the optimal scenario are generated. To facilitate decision-making, a ranking can be assigned to each suggested scenario, and the target achievement rate of the selected scenario can be viewed at one glance.

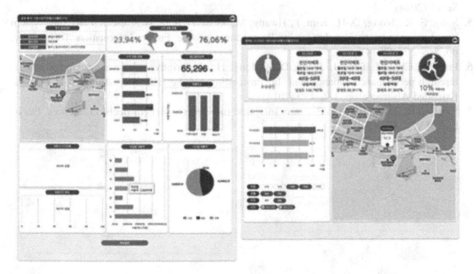

Fig. 4. Web based system UI providing trading area analysis and recommended scenarios

5 Conclusion

This paper presented a marketing scenario planning system that adopts prescriptive analytics on business big data in order to support business-related decision-making for managers or owners of small and medium-sized entrepreneurs. This system is constituted with the Hadoop/HBase-based data infrastructure capable of big data processing, and therefore multi-tiered business action recommendation could be established as a result of integrating structured and unstructured big data, such as sales, logistical information, and SNS feeds on top of various sales prediction models. At the end, it suggests a group of candidate marketing strategies expected to improve the current sales performance when the decision makers follow the business actions automatically recommended by the marketing scenario planning system.. As further research, we consider conducting a performance test of the proposed approach by evaluating the prediction accuracy of the marketing scenario suggested by the system, and by comparing its efficiency with that of previous methodologies in processing unstructured and/or structured business big data.

References

1. IBM: Descriptive, Predictive, Prescriptive: Transforming Asset and Facilities Management with Analytics (2014). http://www-01.ibm.com/common/ssi/cgi-bin/ssialias?infotype=SA&subtype=WH&htmlfid=TIW14162USEN
2. Li, Q., Wang, T., Gong, Q., Chen, Y., Lin, Z., Song, S.-K.: Media-aware quantitative trading based on public web information. Decis. Support Syst. **61**, 93–105 (2014)
3. George, L.: HBase: The Definitive Guide. O'Reilly Media Inc., Sebastopol (2011)
4. Jeong, H., et al.: Prescriptive analysis for enhancing research performance. In: Proceedings of the Symposium of the Korean Institute of Information Scientists and Engineers, pp. 486–488, Seoul (2014)
5. Song, S.-K., Jeong, D.-H., Kim, J., Hwang, M., Gim, J., Jung, H.: Research advising system based on prescriptive analytics. In: Proceedings of the Future Information Technology, pp. 569–574 (2014)
6. Lee, M., Cho, M., Gim, J., Jeong, D.-H., Jung, H.: Prescriptive analytics system for scholar research performance enhancement. In: Proceedings of the HCI International 2014-Posters' Extended Abstracts, pp. 186–190 (2014)
7. Evans, J.R., Lindner, C.H.: Business analytics: the next frontier for decision sciences. Decis. Line **43**(2), 4–6 (2012)

Applying the Rules of Image Construction to Graphical Representation of Infection Prevention Contextual Data in a Communicable Format

Valeriya Kettelhut[1(⊠)], Trevor Van Schooneveld[1], James McClay[1], and Ann Fruhling[2]

[1] University of Nebraska Medical Center, Omaha, NE, USA
vkettelhut@nebraskamed.com,
{tvanscho,jmccaly}@unmc.edu
[2] University of Nebraska at Omaha, Omaha, NE, USA
afruhling@unomaha.edu

Abstract. Antibiotic resistant infections are a serious threat for public health. Hospitals are accountable for preventing the infection transmission among patients. Situation awareness interface may improve healthcare workers' awareness about daily aberrations in infection burden and risks associated with infection transmission and underuse of preventive interventions. This study attempted to apply the rules for image contraction to furnish large amount of the electronic health record epidemiological data into a single image that would reduce informational overload and increase infection prevention situational awareness in a distributed group of healthcare workers. This research postulated that contextualization of the infection prevention data may provide critical cues for decision-making and detecting situations when prevalence and variety of antibiotic-resistant carriers reach dangerous thresholds.

Keywords: Image construction · Situation awareness system design · Information management · Antibiotic-resistance

1 Introduction

In 2013, The World Economic Forum reported that "the greatest risk of hubris to human health comes in the form of antibiotic-resistant bacteria" [1].

Every year, approximately 100,000 Americans, 80,000 Chinese and 25,000 Europeans die from hospital-acquired antibiotic-resistant infections. Hospitals are often characterized as infection transmission systems where a considerable proportion of patients are infected with antibiotic-resistant bacteria. Low compliance with infection prevention evidence-based practices is one reason that five to ten percent of patients admitted to hospitals acquire at least one healthcare-associated infection [2, 3]. The general goal of infection prevention is to "minimize the risk of individuals acquiring infections during the course of care by preventing the transmission of infectious

© Springer International Publishing Switzerland 2015
F.F.-H. Nah and C.-H. Tan (Eds.): HCIB 2015, LNCS 9191, pp. 593–604, 2015.
DOI: 10.1007/978-3-319-20895-4_55

agents" [4]. An important piece of information from the infection prevention perspective is awareness of patient's carriage of antibiotic resistant pathogens.

A situation awareness-oriented system design may improve healthcare workers' knowledge about daily aberrations in infection burden and the risks associated with infection transmission and underuse of preventive interventions. Studies have shown that situation awareness correlates with higher performance [5–7], better clinical sense-making and improved patient outcomes [8–11]. However, there is a large gap in the field of healthcare context representation as no recommendations are available about the functional needs of the context. There is also a gap between fundamental research on context representation and actual context awareness prototype [12].

The **objective** of this research is to create a graphical representation of the infection prevention contextual data by applying the Rules of Image Construction, grounded into Matrix Theory and the physiology of a retinal perception [13]. The goal of this construction is to enhance clinical sense-making in a distributed group about the changing risks of infection transmission and spatially-linked infection prevention activity at a hospital unit level. The study graphical model should answer the question "At a given location, what are the risks of infection transmission there?" in an instant of vision. This research postulated that contextualization of the infection prevention data may provide critical cues for health care workers' decision-making and detecting situations when prevalence and variety of antibiotic-resistant carriers reach dangerous thresholds. The study obtained the Institutional Research Board approval.

2   Effects of Data Representation on Human Performance

Ineffective data representation in electronic health records creates problems resulting in cognitive complexity [14–18]. Cognitive complexity is defined as activities related to identifying, perceiving, remembering, judging, reasoning, deciding, and planning [19]. In spite of years of research on human-computer interface, there is still a need to manage the information effectively in order to enable healthcare practitioners to gain a high level of understanding quickly. Representing information as a graphic is a form of information processing where a vast amount of data can be reduced to understandable and memorable information. Understanding of the graphically presented information can result in visual memorization, but there are the conditions of memorization; as the number of images and the amount of information increase, memorization becomes difficult. Cognitive psychology has described the difficulty with holding more than seven items in short-term memory [20]. Thus, effectively presented data will enable humans to interpret vast amounts of data, while ineffective data representation needs to be resolved.

A landmark study investigated memory for photographs and found that the performance on the recognition of 2,560 pictures, which were displayed for 10 s, exceeded 90 percent [21]. In healthcare, earlier studies explored that metaphor graphic offers a new form of medical knowledge representation [20, 22]. Metaphor graphic is defined as assemblies of icons for graphical representation of symptoms, signs, pathological situations, some components of diagnoses. A randomized trial on the effects of text, table, pie chart, and icon, on the efficiency of subjects' assimilation of information identified that icons were superior to the other formats in speed (p-value < 0.001) and accuracy (p-value = 0.02) [23]. The researchers concluded that icons are a valuable representation of medical information. Other studies found the icon-based graphics were more effective than numerical formats in increasing risk-avoidant behaviors in patients [24–27].

3 Matrix Theory and Visual Perception

Experimental psychology explains that human visual perception interacts with the ability to understand and memorize the forms within an image [13]. The matrix theory of graphics is the application of this property of visual perception [28]. An image has three independent dimensions, X, Y, and Z. The eye perceives two orthogonal dimensions X and Y, while a variation in light energy produces a third dimension in Z. The third component necessitates the use of visual variables, such as color, texture, shape, orientation, and symbol, to enable visual ordered perception. Transcribing a set of information into an efficient three-component image depends on the application of the factors that enable human associative, selective, ordered, or quantitative visual perception. While the plane possesses all of these properties, the retinal variables hold only some of them.

Bertin emphasizes that the retinal variables are physiologically different from the planar dimensions [13]. The knowledge of the eye physiology explains what makes visual perception instant or non-instant. The reader perceives the planar dimensions through the intermediary of eye movement, so-called "muscular response". In contrast, the retinal variables, inscribed "above" the plane, are independent of it. The eye perceives the retinal variation without eye movement. The retinal perception is called "retinal response." Therefore, the retinal variables, such as size, value, color, texture, orientation, and shape become indispensable in the creation of the efficient image.

4 The Rules of Image Construction

4.1 Graphical Information Processing

To choose the right graphic formula for a set of information, a designer should identify the purpose of graphics, consider the number of concepts (components), their nature, the presence of a geographic component, and determine the most efficient image construction. Efficiency of the image is defined as "the most efficient construction that enables a person to answer any question in a single instant of perception" [13]. When one construction requires a shorter observation time than another construction to answer a given question, this construction is more efficient. A graphic can furnish the means of retaining information with the help of visual memory. The primary graphical problem encountered is identifying the best degree of data simplification that will still provide the substance for decision-making. This problem links to issues of visual selectivity and conceptual complexity of a graphic: each additional component increases the conceptual complexity and requires a new visual variable leading to an increase in visual variability and reduction in memorability of the graphic.

In order to reduce a set of comprehensive information to a meaningful minimum, the information elimination and processing are required. Reducing the number of correspondences and keeping essential ones can simplify the information conceptual complexities to a degree when an individual is able to retain information with the help of visual memory. The process of elimination of some information makes the image less comprehensive but easier for inscribing information in the viewer's memory [13]. The mechanism of visual ordering and classing may decrease the overall information and increase the speed of discovering the groupings. Superimposing or overlaying several images in a figuration is the additional method of information reduction and simplification. Image construction involves the analysis of the transcribed information for identifying (1) an invariant defined as a component that is common to all the data, (2) the number of components, (3) the number of elements in each component, (4) the level of organization of each component (nominal, ordered, and quantitative), and (5) planar and visual variables that match these components.

4.2 Transcribing Information into Graphics, Length of the Component, and Graphic Processing of Information

The complexity of the image depends on the number of components and elements in each component. Short components, including up to four divisions, reduce visual variability and conceptual complexity of an image. "Long" components, when a number of divisions exceeds fifteen, not only increase the conceptual complexity of the image but also create a challenge for graphical representation. The visual perception is important for comparing the characteristics, discovering similarities and differences, and identifying areas of interest or exceptions. Therefore, the visual variables representing each component must permit visual selectivity, associativity, and ordering. The hierarchy of the visual variables that permit selectivity starts with the use of size and value, as the top choice, followed with color, texture, and orientation. Shape has no selectivity; however, it provides a base for symbolism. Selectivity is also enabled when characteristics are superimposed. The effectiveness of the chosen visual variables is measured by its capacity for enabling the reader to disregard everything else. In order to choose the most efficient retinal variables, it is important to determine the level of organization of each component and the length of each component. When the length of a visual variable matches the length of each component, diagrams and maps become visually retainable.

5   Methods

This paper is reporting research-in-progress. We present the first phase of our study: the conceptual model for infection prevention situation awareness model (IPSA). In phase two: the pertinent questions we intend to research are: To what extent can the 50-bed medical-surgical unit population IPSA information be graphically reduced? What is a meaningful minimum of information to be retained? What methods of information simplification can be used? The design process included: (1) development of an infection prevention conceptual model grounded in the epidemiology of nosocomial pathogens, (2) integration of the empirical data from the EHR for an analysis of the information complexity and the corresponding levels of visual variables, and (3) construction of the graphical interface.

5.1 A Conceptual Model for Situation Awareness Oriented System Design

In order to design a situation awareness-oriented (SA) system, it is important to develop a clear understanding as to what supporting SA means in a particular domain. Therefore, conceptualization was the first step in the image construction. Contextualization of the infection prevention data may provide critical cues that would capture health care workers' attention during serious situations when prevalence and variety of antibiotic-resistant carriers reach dangerous thresholds. For this, an interface designer can utilize the knowledge developed in the epidemiologic risk models for predicting the movement of infection through populations. During the first phase study, the knowledge from infectious diseases was synthesized and translated into a conceptual model consisted of the following: *Biological domain*-antibiotic resistant agent (bacteria), patient infection state, hazard zone for infection transmission, infection burden, member at risk of exposer to infection, and allergy; *Non-biological domain*-social (contact repetitiveness), structural (location, proximity); *Behavioral domain*- receipt of intervention; and *Temporal domain* - time to delivery of intervention (Fig. 1).

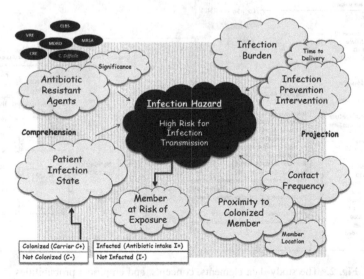

Fig. 1. The infection prevention situation awareness conceptual model

5.2   Study Setting and Data Sources

For the design phase, the study setting chosen is a 50-bed medical-surgical unit. The unit patient population consists of solid organ transplant patients (45 %), cancer patients (20 %), internal medicine patients (20 %), and general surgery patients (15 %). Each room is occupied with one patient. The first step to create a visualization was to abstract data elements from the distributed data sources. We have built the electronic report, an XLS file in the electronic health record system (EHR). The report abstracts patient's name, medical record number, date of admission, date of discharge, date and time of a patient hygiene note, authorship of the note, the note content, antibacterial medication administered to a patient, and the infection surveillance data recorded during a 24-hour period in the EHR. All patient personal data is de-identified. The EHR data was analyzed on availability of data that corresponds to the conceptual model informational needs. It is important to clarify that the model represents a "container" that can be filled with the varying "content" depending on available knowledge, technology, quality of data, and users' preferences. For example, "frequency of contacts" can be determined by using high radio-frequency wearable devices [29] or textual data indicating that a hospitalized patient requires maximum assistance. When the data was normalized, a decision tree (Fig. 2) was constructed to understand the daily aberrations in *patient infection states*, such as 1) the carriers of antibiotic resistant bacteria (ABR) who receive antibiotics IC + , 2) the ABR carriers who do not receive antibiotics I-C + , 3) the non-carriers who receive antibiotics I + C- , and 4) non-carriers who do not receive antibiotics IC-, for a period from June 7 through June 13, 2014.

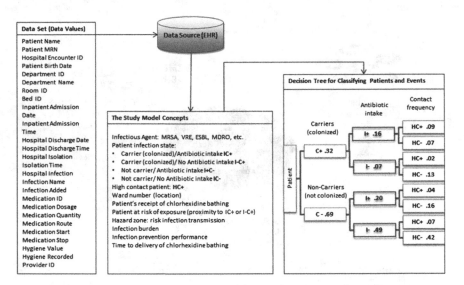

Fig. 2. The study data elements, concepts, and empirical probabilities

6   Image Construction Process: The Component Analysis

6.1   Defining the Number of Components and Invariant

Following the rules of image construction, we determined the components and invariant for the graphic. A process of data transcription requires a separation of "content", or the information to be transcribed, from the "container", which represents only the properties of the graphic system. In the first phase, the original content (context) included 16 concepts for the analysis of the data of interest. The presence of the geographic components, such as "location" and "proximity", and the spatially-linked concepts, such as "risk of exposure" and "hazard zone", informed the investigators that the most useful graphical construction would be a map that represents the unit's physical layout. In this study, the unit geographic order becomes the invariant. The geographical element (e.g., a distinct geographic space representing variation of the locations) is the ward of the unit. The second component is the "common circuit" - a common area where the doors of two wards open out. This component includes two elements: "contaminated circuit" when, for example, one of the wards is occupied by an ABR carrier. The second element is "not contaminated circuit". After a series of reviews, it was decided to keep the eleven essential components (Table 1). The elimination of some information would lead to constructing a graphic permitting visual memorization. This image can be customized to different interventions including various infection prevention and control activities.

6.2   Identifying Visual Variables Permitting Best Selectivity

The next step in our conceptual design process was the creation of the visual artifacts for the 11 components of the IPSA informational set and the continuous revision of the meaning of this information. By drawing different sketches and experimenting with the different visual variables, the investigators tried to identify the best variables that would reduce visual variability, permit visual selectivity and associativity, and reduce the conceptual complexity while preserving the original meaning. This analysis has conceptualized a set of the visual artifacts described in Table 1. It is recognized that "Patient Infection State" permitted a creation of an independent visual component "Colonized" (a carrier of ABR) consisted of two elements "C+" a carrier of ABR vs. "C-"non-carrier. To permit visual selectivity, the most clinically significant but least prevalent phenotype, "C+", was visualized with the use of red color, and the non-carriers "C-", with the gray color. Each ward occupied by "C+" vs. "C-"patients will be color-coded correspondingly. The concept "Infected" has originally included two elements: a receipt of antibiotics "I+" vs. no receipt "I-". The use of a texture for the element "I-", which would retain the background color of the component "Colonized", deems beneficial for several reasons.

First, such visualization reduced visual variability of the image, makes the most prevalent and a benign phenotype "I-" less salient, permitting a better selectivity for the phenotype "I+". In addition, the use of texture permits a perceptual associativity when a reader can easily associate the sub-groups "I+" or "I-" among the phenotypes "C+" and

Table 1 The summary of the graphic components and graphical information processing methods.

Map	Component	Elements of component	Length of component	Level of component	Retinal variable	Information processing methods
1	Geographic location	Unit layout	2 (X, Y)	INVARIANT		Ordered network
2	Ward number	50	50	Qualitative	SYMBOL: TEXT	
3	Common circuit	Not contaminated	2	Qualitative	SHAPE (brick)	Classing Ordering
		Contaminated			COLOR 1. Grey 2. Red	
4	Infectious agent	At least 8: MRSA, VRE, ESBL, C. Diff, etc.	8	Qualitative	SYMBOl (TEXT)	Superimposing
5	Colonized	1. Carrier of Antibiotic Resistance	2	Qualitative	COLOR: 1. Red 2. Gray	Classing Ordering
		2. No History of Antibiotic Resistance				
6	Infected	Not Infected: no receipt of antibiotics)	1	Qualitative	TEXTURE	Ordering Eliminating
7	Hazard Zone: Significance of Risk of Infection Transmission	IF "Carrier" THEN "Hazard Zone"	3	Qualitative	SIZE, SYMBOL	Classing Ordering
		1. High Risk (< 3 months ago)			1. Large glow	
		2. Moderate Risk (3-6 months ago)			2. Small glow	
		3. Low Risk (> 6 months ago)			3. No glow	
8	Patient at risk of exposure to infectious agent	This will be an interactive component, requires further development.				
9	High contact patient	Yes (maximum assistance or dependent on external assistance)	1	Qualitative	SHAPE, COLOR	Ordering Eliminating
					Yellow dot	Superimposing
10	Receipt of Infection Prevention	No receipt	1	Qualitative	SHAPE, COLOR	Ordering Eliminating
					Red ring	Superimposing
11	Allergy/intolerance to Chlorhexidine components	Yes	1		SHAPE, COLOR	Ordering Eliminating
						Superimposing

"C-". This approach reduced the original 4-division component "Patient Infection State" into two short components, including a two-division component for "Colonized" and a one-division component "Infected". The components that are spatially linked to the "Colonized" patient's location, such as "contaminated circuit" and "hazard zone", inherited the red color of "Colonized" patients in order to enhance the visual selectivity. The component "Hazard zone: significance of risk of infection transmission" includes the three elements, such as significant, moderate, and low. The use of the retinal variable depicting "size" enables selectivity. "Size" intuitively corresponds to the amount of bacteria produced by patients and, respectively, the significance of infection transmission risk. As a result, this visualization eliminates a need for the users to calculate this measure and increases the speed of their comprehension.

The component "High Contact Patient" denotes a group of patients who require maximum assistance and experience very frequent contacts with healthcare workers. Frequent contacts increase the risk for infection transmission among members of a population. This component has one element represented with a symbol, a yellow dot. This visual artifact is planned to be superimposed over the patient's location. In this study, "Receipt of an infection prevention intervention" is a component representing a receipt of chlorhexidine bathing. It includes only one element "No receipt of chlorhexidine bathing" and is represented with a symbol, a red circle. The red circle "informs" the reader about a lack of specific infection prevention intervention, allowing healthcare workers to recognize the underuse of the preventive intervention. The red circle and the yellow dot can be superimposed without overlapping each other. This information processing mechanism permits a visual selectivity for identifying a sub-group of patients who experience frequent contacts and lack infection prevention. When these two components are superimposed on the patient's phenotype "C+" they create a critical cue to healthcare workers that these particular patients may increase the risk of infection transmission. The combination of the patient's phenotype, contact frequency, and receipt of the infection prevention intention may provide a strong signal for actions, e.g., reinforcing the compliance with the existing policies or developing new tactics for specific situations. Finally, the concept "at risk of exposure" does not necessarily need visualization; a filter can be used to interactively present this group to

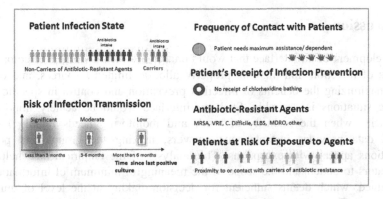

Fig. 3. The infection prevention situation awareness visual artifacts for user training

the users. Figure 3 presents the visual cues explaining the most important IPSA concepts developed for the graphical design discussed above.

7 Proposed Graphical IPSA Interface

As a result of the IPSA design process, a demonstrational unit for a given day is shown in Fig. 4. The infection prevention contextual information was transcribed into *a cartographic message* and implanted in the following structure: the invariant – a geographic order, which takes two orthogonal components (XY), and the nine components (Z) represented with the retinal variables, such as color, texture, size, shape, and symbol.

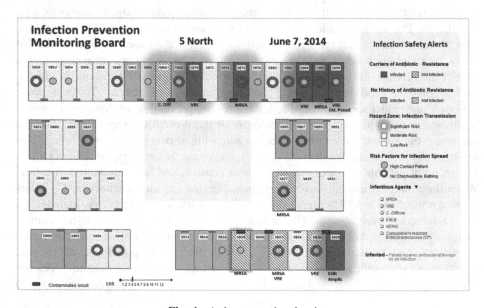

Fig. 4. A demonstrational unit

8 Discussion

The development of an interface that would enable healthcare workers to comprehend the risks of infection transmission, properly allocate limited resources, and develop tactics maximizing the benefits of infection prevention and control in specific epidemiologic situations is desirable. Such an interface would be acutely important in emergencies when the intensity of work and monitoring needs rapidly increase. Mapped data provides instantaneous answers, making the groups and potential explanations appear with exceptions. The analysis of the empirical data helped the investigators to understand the scope of the meaningful minimum of informational to be remained, which deems sufficient for decision-making at the level of unit daily management. The next step in this research project will evaluate if the healthcare workers' situation awareness increases with the use of the IPSA graphical interface in comparison with the current practice. The cartographic message aims at enabling the reader to locate high-risk for infection transmission patients, regarded as high priority for infection control services; to identify patients who are at high risk for exposure to pathogens, regarded as high priority for infection prevention services, to recognize the areas where the risk of infection transmission is significant, regarded as hazardous environments, and, ultimately, to assess the infection prevention needs in the context of these risks for work planning, patient arrangements, resources allocation, or targeted monitoring of compliance. The contribution of this research is the development of an innovative IPSA-oriented interface, a new form of medical knowledge representation where spatially-linked clinical data can be used for spatial decision-making in hospitals.

References

1. Howell, W.L.: Global risks 2013. World Economic Forum (2013)
2. Pittet, D., et al.: Considerations for a WHO European strategy on health-care-associated infection, surveillance, and control. Lancet. Infect. Dis 5(4), 242–250 (2005)
3. Pittet, D., et al.: 'Clean Care is Safer Care': the Global Patient Safety Challenge 2005-2006. Int. J. Infect. Dis. : IJID : Off. Publ. Int. Soc. Infect. Dis. 10(6), 419–424 (2006)
4. Dougherty, L., Lister, S.: The Royal Marsden Hospital Manual of Clinical Nursing Procedures. Wiley, Singapore (2011)
5. Locke, E.A., Latham, G.P.: New Developments in Goal Setting and Task Performance, vol. xxiv, p. 664. Routledge, New York (2013)
6. Endsley, M.R.: Theoretical underpinnings of situation awareness: a critical review. situation awareness analysis and measurement. In: Endsley, M.R., Garland, D.J. (eds.) Situation Awareness Analysis and Measurement, pp. 3–32. Lawrence Erlbaum Associates, Mahwah (2000)
7. Endsley, M.R., Jones, D.G.: Designing for Situation Awareness: An Approach to User-Centered Design, 2nd edn. CRC Press Taylor & Francis Group, Boca Raton (2012)
8. Hysong, S.J., et al.: Provider management strategies of abnormal test result alerts: a cognitive task analysis. J. Am. Med. Inform. Assoc. 17(1), 71–77 (2010)
9. Kawamoto, K., et al.: Improving clinical practice using clinical decision support systems: a systematic review of trials to identify features critical to success. BMJ 330(7494), 765 (2005)
10. Shojania, K.G., et al.: The effects of on-screen, point of care computer reminders on processes and outcomes of care. Cochrane Database Syst. Rev. 3, 1–68 (2009)
11. Hunt, D.L., et al.: Effects of computer-based clinical decision support systems on physician performance and patient outcomes: a systematic review. JAMA 280(15), 1339–1346 (1998)
12. Bricon-Souf, N., Newman, C.R.: Context awareness in health care: a review. Int. J. Med. Inform. 76(1), 2–12 (2007)
13. Bertin, J.: Semiology of Graphics: Diagrams, Networks, Maps. University of Wisconsin Press, Madison (1983)
14. Painter, D.: Cardiologist says EHR needs more custom features. A Georgia specialist finds it hard to jot life details about patients on stagnant EHR fields. Med. econ. 90(24), 61–63 (2013)

15. Farri, O.: Effects of time constraints on clinician-computer interaction: a study on information synthesis from EHR clinical notes. J. Biomed. Inform. **46**(6), 1136–1144 (2013)
16. Belden, J.L.: Making EHR notes more readable. Family pract. manag. **20**(3), 8–9 (2013)
17. Weir, C.R.: Direct text entry in electronic progress notes. An evaluation of input errors. Methods Inf. Med. **42**(1), 61–67 (2003)
18. Koppel, R., Lehmann, C.U.: Implications of an emerging EHR monoculture for hospitals and healthcare systems. J. Am. Med. Inform. Assoc. **22**(2), 465–471 (2014). doi:10.11.36/p. amiajnl-2014-003023
19. Klein, K.J., Conn, A.B., Sorra, J.S.: Implementing computerized technology: an organizational analysis. J. Appl. Psychol. **86**(5), 811–824 (2001)
20. Cole, W.G., Metaphor Graphics 8: Visual Analogy For Medical Data1. 1987
21. Standing, L., Conezio, J., Haber, R.N.: Perception and memory for pictures: Single-trial learning of 2500 visual stimuli. Psychon. Sci. **19**(2), 73–74 (1970)
22. Preiss, B., et al,: Concept graphics: a language for medical knowledge. In: Proceedings of the Annual Symposium on Computer Application in Medical Care. American Medical Informatics Association (1992)
23. Elting, L., Bodey, G.: Is a picture worth a thousand medical words? a randomized trial of reporting formats for medical research data. Methods Inf. Med. **30**(2), 145–150 (1991)
24. Stone, E.R., et al.: Foreground: background salience: explaining the effects of graphical displays on risk avoidance. Organ. Behav. Hum. Decis. Process. **90**(1), 19–36 (2003)
25. Zikmund-Fisher, B.J., et al.: Animated graphics for comparing two risks: a cautionary tale. J. Med. Internet Res. **14**(4), 1–13 (2012)
26. Galesic, M., Garcia-Retamero, R., Gigerenzer, G.: Using icon arrays to communicate medical risks: overcoming low numeracy. Health Psychol. **28**(2), 210 (2009)
27. Natter, H.M., Berry, D.C.: Effects of active information processing on the understanding of risk information. Appl. Cogn. Psychol. **19**(1), 123–135 (2005)
28. Novick, L.R., Hurley, S.M.: To matrix, network, or hierarchy: that is the question. Cogn. Psychol. **42**(2), 158–216 (2001)
29. Vanhems, P., et al.: Estimating potential infection transmission routes in hospital wards using wearable proximity sensors. PLoS ONE **8**(9), e73970 (2013)

Design on the BPEL Engine Generator for Adding New Functions

Donggyu Kwak[1], Jongsun Choi[1], Jaeyoung Choi[1(✉)], and Hoon Ko[2]

[1] School of Computer Science and Engineering, Soongsil University,
369 Sangdo-Ro, Dongjak-Gu, Seoul 156-743, Korea
kawk.coolman@gmail.com, {jongsun.choi,choi}@ssu.ac.kr
[2] The Department of Informatics Faculty of Science, J. E. Purkinje University,
Ceske Mladeze 8, Usti nad Labem 400-96, Czech Republic
hoon.ko@ujep.cz

Abstract. Business Process Execution Language (BPEL) is widely using in various domains because it describes the flow of works depending on their conditions, rules and the call of Web services in service-oriented computing environment, and many experts have been studying the BPEL to use, but still the high cost is required in existing systems. Also, the systems can only add a single function, and it is difficult to design and add new functions as necessary. To overcome this problem, it suggests the new function (?) to be low cost BPEL engine generator by defining XAS4B document that can extend the grammar function of BPEL through XML schema in order to add new functions as necessary and by processing the document. However, new functions, which cannot be found in BPEL grammar, are required in a specific domain. When a new function, which does not exist in the existing language, is required, the domain-specific language should be newly defined and developed in general. One more advantage of the proposed system is able to add new functions without modifying BPEL engine by AspectJ.

Keywords: Environmental impact assessment · Landscape visual impact assessment · Photo-manipulation · Photomontage

1 Introduction

Generally Business Process Execution Language (BPEL) calls a Web service to describe the flow of works and it describes the flow of the works according to the conditions and the rules [8]; however, an additional function can be required, when it is applied to and used in a specific domain. For example, when a business rule engine that made complicated conditions abstracted is necessary, or an applied program is called in the environment where an engine is executed, it is not easy to use the standard BPEL as it is [9]. A study on the method for adding functions using JWX (Java Weaving XML) document was conducted to add new functions to BPEL [10]. JWX has been proposed to describe the additionally required functions in BPEL on the JWX document with JAVA programming language and the additional program that described in JWX is executed together with BPEL. JWX system uses B2J (BPEL to JAVA) as a BPEL

© Springer International Publishing Switzerland 2015
F.F.-H. Nah and C.-H. Tan (Eds.): HCIB 2015, LNCS 9191, pp. 605–612, 2015.
DOI: 10.1007/978-3-319-20895-4_56

engine and this engine uses a method to convert from BPEL document to JAVA program, and next it executes the converted program [11]. JWX system weaves and executes using AspectJ and an implementation of aspect-oriented programming technique in order to execute the B2 J-generated JAVA program, and the added program draws up in the JWX document together [12, 13]. JWX offers a method that it adds the function which BPEL doesn't provide but it has a drawback that the new function to be drawn up together with BPEL should be described with JAVA program because of this; JWX is difficult for a domain expert, who is not good at computer programming. If the service is used by preparing it in an abstract way, the experts who have been studying about domains can easily use the added new functions depending on each domain. To this end, the study on the method for designing and developing language were conducted by many researchers. Simon proposed a language to provide pervasive computing services in a smart home [14]. Generally BPEL is used in the service-oriented structure based on Web service. The Web service interface of BPEL language needs to study to call the Web service using BPEL. So he proposed SOAL (Service Oriented Architecture Language) and also he suggested the system to convert from it to BPEL and WSDL. This method can be easily used because the proposed SOAL language is similar to JAVA but SOAL is more difficult than BPEL for a domain expert who is not a proficient in programming language. Moreover it is not easy to use the case in applications, in which another new function needs to be added. So, in this paper, it proposes new methods to extend the domain-specific language corresponding to new functions to XML-based BPEL language and add software to the BPEL engine to process the extended language function. To develop a new language, the language should be designed and developed by dividing it into grammar and semantic elements.

The grammar elements of the language can be processed with BNF (Backus-Naur Form) [16], and the semantic element of the language can be expressed with attribute grammar [17]. The grammar and semantic elements of the language can generate a complier or language processor using an automated tool such as YACC (Yet Another Compiler Compiler) [18]. YACC is widely used for designing and developing a new language and a complier for developing or a language processor. However, it is difficul to extend an already designed and developed language. The new language should be developed again by adding a grammar for the new function to extend BPEL using YACC. To do so, it developed XAS4B (XML Attribute Schema for BPEL), which can describe the new grammar and functions required for BPEL with XML schema and attribute grammar, respectively, by extending XML schema so as to add a new function to BPEL. A programmer describes new function's grammar of the element with XML schema and devises the functional element with attribute grammar form. The XAS4B is used together by organizing with XML schema that describes grammar information.

It consists of two parts: one part is to import classes necessary for additional functions and the other part is to describe semantic information. The part describing semantic information defines the variables of XML that describes a new function, and it also describes JAVA program using the attribute grammar. The method to process attribute grammar is similar to the YACC system. A developer designs the grammar of language with BNF and draws up a program using YACC grammar for semantics of the language, when the developer develops a language processor or complier using YACC. However this system does not design a new language operating independently, which is different from YACC but it is used to design the language operated together with BPEL.

2 XAS4B (XML Additional Schema for BPEL) to Describe Additional Functions

In this paper, we extend BPEL grammar by defining additional functions with XML schema, propose the document to draw up a program for the extended grammar, and show the processing engine for the document in order to add additional functions to BPEL.

The users of this system are divided into three layers as shown in Table 1. A programmer is the layer developing newly added functions. The programmer defines elements to describe the required functions with XAS4B document, and develops the JAVA program to process them. A domain expert describes the business flow required from the domain with BPEL document. To do so, the domain expert uses the elements developed by the programmer to add the new functions. An end user is offered the service, according to the business flow described by the domain expert. This paper proposes XAS4B, which can describe the program of the added function together with XML schema as the method to define the added function. Figure 1 shows XAS4B schema.

Table 1. Requirements, development scope, and used tools for 3 user layers

	Requirements	Development scope	Used tool
Programmer	Additional function	Program module	XAS4B JAVA program
Domain expert	Business flow	Work flow	BPEL language (additional element)
End user	User requirements	–	BPEL engine

As shown in Fig. 1, XAS4B consists of two parts: one is "javaImports",which imports JAVA classes required from the additional functions. And the other part is "semantics",which describes semantic information. This part is composed of the "variables"element and the "javaCode"element. The former is to assign the XML attribute for processing semantic information through attribute grammar in the XML schema, and the latter is to describe the new functions with programs.

3 System Architecture

This paper proposes a system to add new functions required for specific domains to BPEL at small cost. A programmer describes XML schema to intuitively use new functions, draws up semantic information of the elements using XAS4B document in terms of the new functions. The grammar for new functions developed by a programmer is used for a domain expert who does not familiar with program languages in order to draw up services, and this service is offered to the end user.

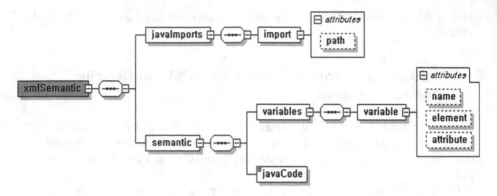

Fig. 1. Schema of XAS4B

The complier generator generate a new function compiler receiving as inputs the XML schema having the new function grammar information drawn up by the programmer, and the XAS4B document having semantic information. The generated new function compiler becomes part of the engine combined with B2J coordinator to execute the BPEL functions and the new functions, and it executes the BPEL document containing the new functions drawn up by the domain expert. This system uses B2J (BPEL to JAVA). B2J executes the service flow of BPEL document by converting BPEL documents to JAVA programs and then executing them.

The proposed system uses a method adding new functions to the program generated by B2J by using the aspect-oriented programming technique. The proposed system consists of a process to generate an engine for the new functions, and a process to execute a workflow added with the new functions. Figure 2 shows the engine generation of the proposed system.

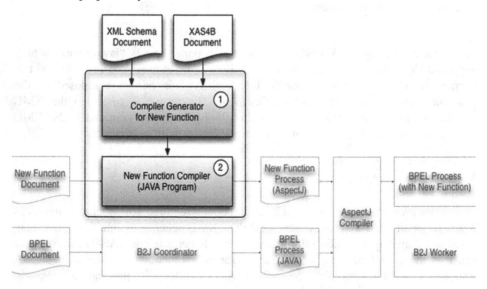

Fig. 2. Engine generation of the proposed system

The programmer defines the new XML grammar added to BPEL with XML schema, according to domain requirements, and draws up the functions with XAS4B document corresponding to grammar. The compiler generator for new functions (①) generates a new engine (② New Function Compiler) to process the new functions by receiving as the inputs of XML schema that defined the new functions, and XAS4B document. The generated engine is executed together with existing BPEL engine. Figure 3 shows the execution environment of the proposed system.

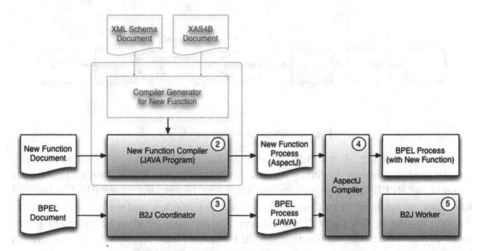

Fig. 3. Execution environment of the proposed system

The engine (②) generated through the compiler generator converts the document with the new functions to AspectJ program as shown in Fig. 3. The BPEL document is converted to JAVA program by B2J coordinator (③), which is the JAVA program generator of B2J engine. The AspectJ program and generated JAVA program are weaved together with the AspecJ complier (④), and the weaved program is executed in the B2J worker (⑤).

The compiler generator (①) consists of XML schema parser and XAS4B parser. The former analyzes grammar information of new functions, and the latter analyzes the location of the added function and then generates insertion rules. The generated compiler (②) generates the AspectJ program, which processes the new function document drawn up with new grammar through the added functions' grammar information and insertion rules. The BPEL document containing the new functions drawn up for service is converted to a Java program, and this program offers services to end users.

4 BPEL Added with Rule Function

This section shows the BPEL system added with rule functions as an application of the proposed system. Because BPEL offers an XML-based graphic compiler, a domain expert not familiar with computer programming languages can draw up workflow easily. However, it is required to describe complicated conditions using BPEL in order to process complicated and composite conditions. As conditions become complicated, it is difficult to describe them, and there is a high possibility to operate differently from the user's original intention. The rule engine [2] is generally used as a method to process complicated conditions; however, BPEL does not offer rule functions. Rules can simplify complicated and complex conditions, describe operations that can be executed when the conditions are satisfied, and thus, can provide modeling of service to users. Figure 4 shows a BPEL flow added with rules.

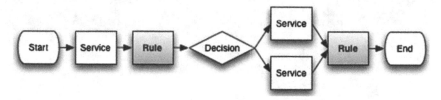

Fig. 4. BPEL flow added with rules

As shown in Fig. 4, the rule function added to BPEL has an effect to simplify complicated conditions by being drawn up between the BPEL flows. This paper extends the BPEL language so that the rules can be applied while BPEL's original functions are retained. A rule engine is needed to use rules, and we use Drools [2] as the rule engine in this paper. The elements for the rules need to be extended grammatically with XM, and the function should be defined with XAS4B document schema in order to extend the rules to the BPEL language. The XML schema and XAS4B document generate a new compiler through the complier generator. The generated compiler is used as a rule-based BPEL engine combined with B2J engine. Also it shows XML schema of the "drools-rule-set" element to use the rules of Drools among the elements to use the rules, and the "rule-execution" element to execute the rules, and Fig. 5 shows XAS4B document for rules.

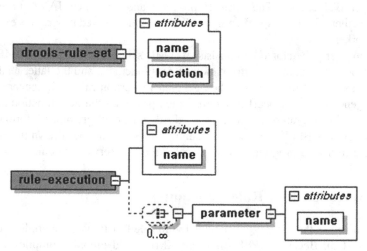

Fig. 5. XML schema for rules

5 Conclusion

I ⁄ililial⳺ ⳺ ⳺⳺⳺⳺⳺ not familiar with programming languages can easily draw up business flows with BPEL. Howẽvĕr, ⳺ĕw l⳺⳺⳺⳺⳺⳺ ⳺⳺⳺ ⳺⳺⳺⳺⳺⳺⳺ ⳺⳺ ⳺⳺⳺ ⳺⳺⳺⳺⳺⳺⳺ are required in some specific domains. For BPEL engine to process new functĩoñs, a ⳺⳺w ⳺⳺⳺⳺ engine needs to be developed, or the new functions needs to be added to the existing BPEL engine, which costs a lot. This paper proposes XAS4B document by extending XML schema, and shows a method to add new functions to the BPEL engine using the aspect-oriented programming technique. The aspect-oriented programming can add cross-cutting concerns without modifying core concerns by using weaving. We use B2J as the existing BPEL engine, which converts BPEL document to JAVA program, and executes it. This system adds the flow of new functions to the flow of BPEL by placing the JAVA program generated by B2J engine as core concerns, and by setting the program to process new functions as cross-cutting concerns, and thus weaving the two programs. This system provides a method to easily add new functions to existing BPEL engine, if the new grammar and functions are designed and developed well.

Acknowledgement. This research was supported by Basic Science Research Program through the National Research Foundation of Korea (NRF) funded by the Ministry of Education, Science and Technology (2013R1A1A2012118).

References

1. Wu, Z., Xiong, N., Han, W., Huang, Y.N., Hu, C.Y., Gu, Q., Hang, B.: A fault-tolerant method for enhancing reliability of services composition application in WSNs based on BPEL. Int. J. Distrib. Sens. Netw. **2013**, 11 (2013)
2. Nematzadeh, H., Motameni, H., Mohamad, R., Nematzadeh, Z.: QoS measurement of workflow-based web service compositions using colored petri net. Int. J. Distrib. Sens. Netw. **2014**, 14 (2014)
3. Bo, C., Peng, Z., Da, Z., Junliang, C.: The complex alarming event detecting and disposal processing approach for coal mine safety using wireless sensor network. Int. J. Distrib. Sens. Netw. **2012**, 12 (2014)
4. Tsalgatidou, A., Pilioura, T.: An overview of standards and related technology in web services. Distrib. Parallel Databases **12**(2–3), 135–162 (2002)
5. Koehler, J., Srivastava, B.: Web service composition: current solutions and open problems In: Proceedings of Workshop on Planning for Web Services (ICAPS 20003), pp. 28–35. ACM (2002)
6. Lanotte, R., Maggiolo-Schettini, A., Milazzo, P., Troina, A.: Design and verification of long-running transactions in a timed framework. Sci. Comput. Program. **73**(2–3), 76–94 (2008)
7. Nakajima, S.: Model-checking behavioral specification of BPEL applications. Electron. Notes Theoret. Comput. Sci. **151**(2), 89–105 (2006)
8. BPEL. http://www-128.ibm.com/developerworks/library/specification/library/specification/ws-bpel/
9. Drools. http://www.jboss.org/drools/

10. Kwak, D., Choi, J.: Design and implementation of a BPEL engine for dynamic function using aspect-oriented programming (in korean). J. Korean Inst. Inf. Scientists Eng. **37**(4), 205–214 (2010)
11. B2J. http://www.eclipse.org/stp/b2j/
12. Kiczales, G., Lamping, J., Mendhekar, A., Maeda, C., Lopes, C.V., Loingtier, J.-M., Irwin, J.: Aspect-Oriented Programming. In: ECOOP, pp. 220–242 (1997)
13. Eclipse AspectJ. http://www.eclipse.org/aspectj/
14. Simon, B., Goldschmidt, B., Kondorosi, K.: A human readable platform independent domain specific language for BPEL. Commun. Comput. Inf. Sci. **87**, 537–544 (2010)
15. Albreshne, A., Lahcen, A.A., Pasquier, J.: A framework and its associated process-oriented domain specific language for managing smart residential environment. Int. J. Smart Home **7** (6), 377–392 (2013)
16. Noam, C.: Syntactic Structures. Walter de Gruyter, Berlin (1957)
17. Knuth, D.E.: The genesis of attribute grammars. In: Proceedings of International Conference on Attribute grammars and Applications, vol. 461, pp. 1 – 12 (1990).
18. Levine, J., Mason, T., Brown, D.: Lex and Yacc. O'reilly Media, Sebastopol (1992)

A Dynamic Weighted Majority Algorithm for Dynamic Data Relationships Concept Drift Detection

Szu-Yin Lin[1](✉) and Chun-Hsian Lin[2]

[1] Department of Information Management, Chung Yuan Christian University,
Taoyuan, Taiwan
stan@cycu.edu.tw
[2] Institute of Information Management, National Chiao Tung University,
Hsin-Chu, Taiwan
brianmg60909@gmail.com

Abstract. In a dynamic environment, the data are changed almost instantly. It is difficult and time-consuming to find the correlation between data. At the same time, the concept drift might happen along with data change in the dynamic environment. In order to stimulate the highly correlated data to support better prediction and detected the concept drift, this study proposes a distributed dynamic data driven Application system (DDDAS)-based dynamic weighted majority (DWM) algorithm to solve the issue. The proposed algorithm tries to find the correlations between data by DWM. Moreover, it is capable of detecting concept drift. The simulation result shows the DDDAS-based DWM algorithm has up to 89 % accuracy in simulation case, and able to find the concept drift.

Keywords: Dynamic weight majority · Dynamic data driven application system · Concept drift

1 Introduction

In recent years, the techniques of data storage and processing (e.g. Big Data [1], and Cloud Computing [2]) have become more appropriate for sensor streaming; hence, the amount of the data accumulates quick and dynamically. In this situation, determining how to precisely make data prediction and evaluation by taking historical data as reference in data prediction problems in this dynamic, uncertain and complicated environment is a huge challenge. In addition, the existing prediction models mainly focus on processing static data; they are not appropriated for dynamic environments and cannot provide feedback regarding real time information into the model. Moreover, there are many sensor distributed in the sensor environment and each sensor stream may have high correlations [3], i.e. relationships with each other. The relationships of these sensor streams may change over time; if a data streams is highly dependent on another data stream; with time change the correlation might have change to another stream. We can recognized this situation as a Concept Drift-like [4] phenomenon; these kinds of correlation changes will raise the error rate of the model, making prediction results unusable.

© Springer International Publishing Switzerland 2015
F.F.-H. Nah and C.-H. Tan (Eds.): HCIB 2015, LNCS 9191, pp. 613–622, 2015.
DOI: 10.1007/978-3-319-20895-4_57

Hence, in this study we present a new solution which not only can dynamically detect and react to the concept drift between data streams with time changes, but also be appropriate in a real-time dynamic environment. Due to the problem discussed above, the objective is to propose an improved solution that can dynamically analyze concept drift and precisely predict results in a dynamic environment. A dynamic data driven application systems (DDDAS) [5] is a new concept which can use real time online or archival data dynamically integrated within other engineer models and instantly give feedback into a running model. The DDDAS concept offers a concept of dynamic data processing and feedback architecture, as well as enhancing the efficiency and effectiveness of data processing and model architecture. However, determining how to detect the concept drift between each sensor stream is a challenging topic in a dynamic environment. If we cannot solve this issue, the model will raise the error rate as time passes. The dynamic weight majority (DWM) [6] approach may help to solve the problem of concept drift. The DWM algorithm presents an ensemble method with a dynamic weighted voting mechanism. So that we can use multiple combinations of data streams and real-time prediction approaches to realize which data stream's prediction has the highest weight in each time step. This also means that it has the highest correlation.

In the next section, we describe the concept of dynamic data driven application systems, dynamic weighted majority, and concept drift. In Sect. 3, the modified dynamic weighted majority algorithm based on distributed dynamic data is proposed. In Sect. 4, we show the experimental designs, evaluation, and results. Finally, the conclusions are presented discussed in Sect. 5.

2   Related Works

2.1   Dynamic Data Driven Application System

A dynamic data driven application system (DDDAS) is a real time feedback control system. It is a new paradigm that was proposed by National Science Foundation (NSF) in order to solve the problem in traditional simulations, predictions and measurements. DDDAS provides a model with a more reliable outcome, stable data process and accurate prediction or analysis results. It also allows model dynamically receiving and responding [7]. However, the reason why NSF proposed the DDDAS concept is based on the two main topics: One, in January, $24 \sim 25$, 2000 a hurricane struck a major city New Orleans in America, unfortunately the relevant authority could not made the prediction precisely and in real-time. It caused a huge disaster. Second, scientists couldn't simulate the real wildfire which broke out beside the Los Alamos national lab. After the disaster, researchers found that most of the existing models were unable to capture the instantaneous reactions in a real environment, and that most of those model parameters were fixed and unchangeable. So, these model would cause unexpected errors and be unfit for handling on dynamic changing situations [7].

The DDDAS concept describes the dynamic capability of system processing and control. DDDAS shows real-time data coordination in a runtime system; hence, DDDAS not only provides more in-time statistics, but offer the feedback mechanism for dynamic model enhancing and experiment improving [8–11]. In recent years, thanks to the improvement in computing (e.g. Cloud Computing, Grid computing) and experiment (e.g. data storage technique), such enhancement speeds up the promotion of DDDAS architecture. The DDDAS architecture mainly includes: the user controller, dynamic visualization interface, dynamic computation and real-time dynamic data gathering modules [12]. These components integrate automatic feedback, measurement, simulation and a control mechanism and work in a dynamic way. Users could use the DDDAS concept model via the dynamic visualization module to interact with other components; real-time dynamic data gathering of responses by modules, and in time data gathering from measurement instruments (e.g. sensors, database); and dynamic computation modules dealing with mathematical models & prediction computation. Due to its architecture, DDDAS provides efficiency and stable ways to handle the real- time situation in real world.

In the past, when facing weather, agriculture and contaminant tracking, we used historical data as a prediction system's input. However there is a problem; if a model just relies on historical data, it cannot reflect the real situation or provide a real-time feedback mechanism. DDDAS proposed a real-time feedback mechanism to transfer data for a computing model, thereby enhancing the accuracy of the model. In regard to environmental science and agriculture (e.g. Greenhouse Gas emission, River Pollution monitoring, etc.) DDDAS offers the adjusting and changing of parameters; this feature makes the model more scalable [13]. Moreover, it can be used in hurricanes [14], rather than just using numerical data, also DDDAS can also use graphics and sensor data for real-time computing to raise the prediction success rate [15]. Frederica Darema who proposed the DDDAS concept, pointed out that the vision of the DDDAS encompasses more than real-time control. However, there are some challenges requiring future work; one is the uncertainty of computing, which will cause the prediction error. To deal with this problem, finding out how to establish the data correlation is a key to success; in this study we will try to solve the correlation problem and raise the efficiency.

2.2 Dynamic Weighted Majority (DWM)

The Weighted Majority Algorithm (WMA) is part of machine learning. WMA present a pool of prediction algorithms (e.g. a group of classifiers, a group of same or different approaches) without any prior knowledge. Unlike common prediction methods, the WMA makes decisions by group voting; the result is that because of its wider prediction approach to decisions, it makes fewer mistakes compare to a single prediction approach. The process of the algorithm is presented as follows in each trial: Same instance feeding to each prediction algorithm of the pool. Then each prediction is made and the WMA algorithm groups the results. The WMA will make a final prediction by selected most of the results. By running this algorithm, we can not only present a majority voting algorithm but also can know which prediction method best fits in this situation. The Dynamic Weighted Majority (DWM) is based on the Weighted Majority Algorithm (WMA). As discussed above, the WMA presents weighted voting based on the ensemble method. It combines a group of prediction approaches and takes each approach as an 'expert' with its own weight; it then compares the result to the single prediction approach, The superiority of this algorithm is that its use of group decision; with this mechanism, it provides more stable and accurate output. As discussed above, based on the foundation of WMA, DWM extends the advantage of WMA, and makes a dynamic change. DWM added a threshold (Θ) in the whole algorithm, and its weight is reduced by the multiplicative constant β (β is from 0 to 1).

2.3   Concept Drift

Concept Drift is a phenomenon that occurs a prediction model makes a prediction, but as the time passes, the characteristic or correlation of the data has been changed in unforeseen ways, causing the predictions to become less accurate as time passes [4]. The usually domains in which such changing concepts often happen are customers' preference and weather prediction. Here, we take weather rainfall prediction as an example. If the model has a good performance in the summer, when the season changes to autumn the parameters of the model will be unable to detect the change. By using the old parameters to predict the autumn rainfall, the model will often make wrong predictions. The types of concept drift can be distinguished either sudden, or gradual. In this study, we focus on the sudden concept drift and apply it in the experiments. The problem of concept drift has become a popular issue in data mining and weather domain and also in the dynamic environment it will happen more often.

3   A Dynamic Data Driven Application System-Based Dynamic Weighted Majority Algorithm

In a dynamic environment the running model will receive data from sensors or the database dynamically, but the traditional prediction algorithm currently lacks the capability of dealing with real time data. As discussed before, the data in the dynamic environment usually have highly correlation between data sets; it means that at each time step the relationship between data sets will changing. If we use some data sets as support predicting the main target data set, with time passing through the relationship between the target data set and the support data sets had changed and algorithm didn't detect it will cause the increase of prediction error rate. This situation also recognized as a concept drift problem. In the next section we proposed a dynamical algorithm to fit the environment and solve the concept drift problem, as well as determine the correlations between the target data set and each support data set.

3.1   Dynamic Data Driven Application System-Based Dynamic Weighted Majority Model

This study proposes a dynamic weighted majority prediction algorithm based on DDDAS, which comprises three parts. The modified DWM algorithm process will be first introduced. It provides a dynamic framework to control the whole system. Second, a dynamic weight voting, adjusting, and real-time feedback mechanism is proposed to choose the best support data stream at each time. The third part is the dynamic data stream prediction component. It provides a dynamic way to import the historical or real-time data stream nodes into model. For each sensor node, there has two prediction approaches. The data stream node provides dynamic data form the real world for the dynamic data driven approach, and then the prediction approach computes the combination of the historical and real-time data stream.

3.2   Modified Dynamic Weighted Majority Algorithm

The dynamic weighted majority provides a weighted based selection and feedback mechanism. In this section, we present a modified DWM for fitting the assumptions and dynamic environment. The proposed algorithm describes the whole processes of the algorithm. The modified DWM takes every data stream and approach as a combination and sees this combination as an 'expert' for making its own predictions. There are four main steps in the modified DWM procedure.

- Step1: At the initial stage, the algorithm will average all of the experts' weights and make the prediction.
- Step2: The algorithm will gather each expert's result and decide on the global result as the answer according to the highest weight expert.
- Step3: The modified DWM will make a comparison to the next time's real result. But if it is the first round of the algorithm, because the weight of each expert is equal, the algorithm will compare each expert's result to the real time result.
- Step4: Lastly, after comparing the results, if the result is close to real data, then the algorithm increase the expert's weight by formula (1); conversely, if the result is a mistake, then the algorithm decrease the expert's weight by formula (2). Here, $Weight_t$ represents the weight of the final result's expert's weight and α represents the speed of raising the weight. Also, β represents the speed of the decreasing weight.

$$Weight_{t+1} = Weight_t + Weight_t * \alpha \tag{1}$$

$$Weight_{t+1} = Weight_t - Weight_t * \beta \tag{2}$$

3.3   Threshold and Feedback Mechanism

By the explanation of the DWM in this section, the model we proposed also provides a feedback mechanism for suiting the dynamic environment. In the real-time situation there will be numerous correlations between data streams; in order to detect the phenomena, we take each stream as an individual expert and gave it a weight. Figure 1 shows the feedback process; θ represents a threshold: if an expert's weight is below this value, we consider it useless in this time period and make it sleep for a period; after the sleep period, it will return to the prediction pool with an average weight. Through the adjusting of the weight, the model can realize the changing of the weight in the previous loop of the model and provide feedback to the model. In this way, the model will know the correlation between the chosen data and the target data.

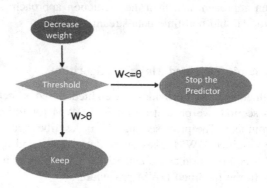

Fig. 1. Feedback process

3.4   Dynamic Data Stream Prediction Component

As Fig. 2 shows, each data stream can be seen as an independent part, and shows each part combining the input data stream with two approaches: the autoregressive approach and neural network approach. Then each date stream will face two methods: making its own local prediction and determining the weights. The component acts as a dynamic data driven way, which means if the model needs one of the data streams and prediction approach, the model will trigger the specific one by its weight and make the prediction. Through the data driven approach, the model will leverage the computed sources and times. In this study, we take each stream as a location; each location will have its own approach to make a prediction and have its own weight. If we have three locations, there will be three components like the object we described above. One will be set as the target; the other will be set as the support component.

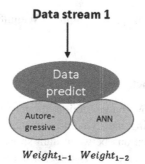

Fig. 2. Dynamic data stream prediction component

3.5 Summary

The advantage of the proposed method lies in the capability of dynamic driven specific data to enter into the running model, and its ability to recognize the correlations between the support data sets and target data set. A traditional prediction model only provides static data processing; if we put it in a dynamic environment, critical errors might happen in the runtime. Moreover, with time passing, the data relationship might have changed; if a prediction model only relies on specific data for supporting the target data prediction, it will increase the error rate of the model. It is necessary to find the link between data in each timestamp in a dynamic environment. In this study, we proposed a novel dynamic weight majority model based on a dynamic data driven application system to realize the data correlation and provide a solution in a dynamic environment. The proposed model not only provides the capability of real-time data processing, but also detects the data relationship dynamically.

4 Simulation Analysis

The proposed model is implemented in a real-time and dynamic environment, which fits a time flow concept. In the environment, at each time, new data will come through and the model will make the predictions with this new data, rather than just by historical data. In addition, we assume that the concept drift phenomenon could occur at each timestamp. On the other words, the relationship concept between the support data sets and the target data sets could change at each timeslot.

4.1 The Simulation Data Sets

A group of data sets are generated according to specific rules. The data sets are designed to eliminate the uncertainties and testing if the model works or not. We generate a rain data set to validate the model. The basic rule was introduced by MG Lawrence [23]. It provides a simple formula (3) to generate the relative humidity. T represents temperate; T_d represents dew point. The dew point is the water vapor in the air; we can know the probability of rainfall by judging this benchmark. We then use this formula to create a novel formula (4) to simulate the rainfall per hour. Here X means the timestamp increased in an arithmetic progression. C signifies clouds in the sky and W represents a random seed, to make the data irregular.

$$RH = 100 - 5(T - T_d) \tag{3}$$

$$Rainfall(R) = 100 - 5 * (T - T_d) * X + C + W \tag{4}$$

Based on the rule, we generate a data stream with 250 timestamps as the target data stream. Then other support data sets are created to have a correlation between target data sets in specific time periods. In these generated data sets, we presented four correlation transfer sections between $40 \sim 60, 90 \sim 110, 140 \sim 160$ and $190 \sim 210$ time periods. Here we can see generated target data which have suddenly value changes in the periods mentioned in this paragraph. Afterwards, we generate the other four data sets by also following formula (4)'s rule; moreover we create the time shift correlations between the target data stream and the four data streams. For example, in Fig. 3, the support stream1 we designed has a strong highly relationship with target data set in 40 ~ 60 time period. Therefore, after 30 time stamps, the highly relation shift from support stream1 to support stream 2 are in 90 ~ 110 time period. In these simulation data sets, the last two relationship changes will happened in the 30 time stamp periods.

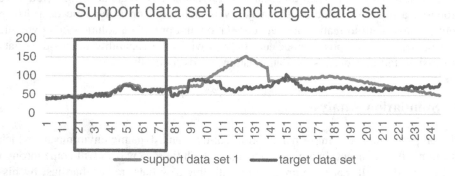

Fig. 3. Support data set 1 and target data set

4.2 Simulation Results

There are two metrics for evaluating the performance of prediction. The descriptions are as follows:

$$\text{Prediction Correct Rates (CR)} : \frac{\text{Total weight correct times}}{\text{Toatal Prediction Times}}$$

$$\text{Total Concept Drift detect Rates (CDR)} : \frac{\text{Total Relationship change Detected}}{\text{Toatal Realtionship Change}}$$

In this case, we set the parameters: $\alpha = 0.01$ and $\beta = 0.1$. As shown in Fig. 4, we can see that the target data set has a relationship with support streams 2-4, consecutively Fig. 4 shows the weight changing graphic. The result shows that, because of the relationship changing by time, the support stream 1's weight is raised first for it is generated by algorithm and makes no error. So the weight of the support data set is raised the same as the other support data sets. As previously mentioned, we have four relation changes, and the experiment shows the changing weights of four support streams. This means that the algorithm switches the support set to support the target data set's prediction and find the concept shift in each time period. It takes 25 mistakes out of 220 h for making predictions. As a result, the CR hits 89 % and the concept drift has been detected; the CDR comes in at 100 %.

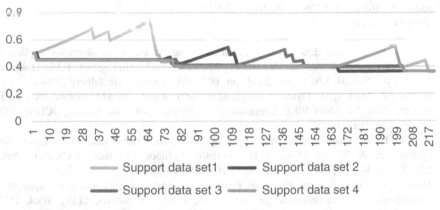

Fig. 4. Weight of each support data set

5   Conclusion

In this study, we proposed a Distributed Dynamic Data Driven Application System based on a Dynamic Weighted Majority using the dynamic data sets to construct the correlation and find the concept drift. The algorithm is based on DDDAS; it provides an algorithm with the capability of facing a dynamic environment and the ability to drive the specific data at each time to reduce the computation. Then DWM algorithm presents a dynamic voting way to give each data set a weight to dynamically adjust, in order to find the correlation between data sets and to support the prediction of target data sets. Moreover, this study presents the simulation experiments. The simulation presented that one target data set and four support data sets for supporting data prediction. Three concept drifts are designed between the target data set and the support data sets. This study proposed two metrics to measure the algorithm Prediction Correct Rates (CR) and Total Concept Drift detect Rates (CDR). The result shows that CR = 89 %, and it detected all of the concept drifts. It shows the capability of dynamic data handling and concept drift detecting of the algorithm, and provides a solution for dynamic environment prediction and concept drift detection.

Acknowledgment. This research work was supported by the Ministry of Science and Technology, Taiwan under the grant 103-2410-H-033-023.

References

1. McAfee, A., Brynjolfsson, E.: Big Data: The Management Revolution, pp. 60–62. Harvard business review, Boston (2012)
2. Mell, P., Grance, T.: The NIST definition of cloud computing. National Institute of Standards and Technology **53**, 50 (2009)

3. Aggarwal, C.C., Xie, Y., Yu, P.S.: On dynamic data-driven selection of sensor streams. In: Proceedings of the 17th ACM SIGKDD international conference on Knowledge discovery and data mining, pp. 1226–1234. ACM (2011)
4. Tsymbal, A.: The problem of concept drift: Definitions and related work. Computer Science Department, Trinity College Dublin, p.106 (2004)
5. Darema, F.: Dynamic data driven applications systems: a new paradigm for application simulations and measurements. In: Bubak, M., van Albada, G.D., Sloot, P.M., Dongarra, J. (eds.) ICCS 2004. LNCS, vol. 3038, pp. 662–669. Springer, Heidelberg (2004)
6. Kolter, J.Z., Maloof, M.: Dynamic weighted majority: a new ensemble method for tracking concept drift. In: Third IEEE International Conference on Data Mining, ICDM 2003, pp.123–130. IEEE (2003)
7. Darema, F.: Introduction to the ICCS 2007 workshop on dynamic data driven applications systems. In: Shi, Y., van Albada, G.D., Dongarra, J., Sloot, P.M. (eds.) ICCS 2007, Part I. LNCS, vol. 4487, pp. 955–962. Springer, Heidelberg (2007)
8. Darema, F.: Dynamic data driven applications systems: new capabilities for application simulations and measurements. In: Sunderam, V.S., van Albada, G.D., Sloot, P.M., Dongarra, J. (eds.) ICCS 2005. LNCS, vol. 3515, pp. 610–615. Springer, Heidelberg (2005)
9. Douglas, C.C., Efendiev, Y.: A dynamic data-driven application simulation framework for contaminant transport problems. Comput. Math Appl. 51, 1633–1646 (2006)
10. Rodríguez, R., Cortés, A., Margalef, T.: Data injection at execution time in grid environments using dynamic data driven application system for wildland fire spread prediction. In: Proceedings of the 2010 10th IEEE/ACM International Conference on Cluster, Cloud and Grid Computing, pp. 565–568. IEEE Computer Society (2010)
11. Douglas, C.C., et al.: DDDAS approaches to wildland fire modeling and contaminant tracking. In: Proceedings of the Winter Simulation Conference, WSC 2006, pp. 2117–2124. IEEE (2006)
12. Nsf DDDAS 2000 Workshop Report (2000)
13. Vodacek, A., et al.: Dynamic data-driven application systems for empty houses, contaminat tracking, and wildland fireline prediction. In: International Federation for Information Processing (2010)
14. Allen, G.: Building a dynamic data driven application system for hurricane forecasting. In: Shi, Y., van Albada, G.D., Dongarra, J., Sloot, P.M. (eds.) ICCS 2007, Part I. LNCS, vol. 4487, pp. 1034–1041. Springer, Heidelberg (2007)
15. Hirschfeld, R., Kawamura, K.: Dynamic service adaptation. In: Proceedings of the 24th International Conference on Distributed Computing Systems Workshops, pp. 290–297. IEEE (2004)

Enhancing the Explanatory Power
of Intelligent User Interfaces with Diagrams

Robbie T. Nakatsu[✉]

Loyola Marymount University, Los Angeles, CA, USA
rnakatsu@lmu.edu

Abstract. I describe techniques that can be used to enhance the explanatory power of intelligent user interfaces. I focus on advice-giving systems that provide recommendations to end-users on how to solve problems, or help end-users make the right decisions. By explanatory power I am referring to the ability of a system to "explain" its own actions. One approach to endowing a system with explanatory power is to develop some kind of diagram—a graphical model that shows how something works or makes something easier to understand. I explore, in particular, "dynamic" diagrams in which the end user can explore the diagrammatic structures in a variety of ways to aid in understanding and problem-solving.

Keywords: Explanatory power · System transparency · Intelligent user interfaces · Diagrammatic reasoning · Diagrams

1 Introduction

A typical user of computer technologies today must deal with a multitude of complex systems: a PC, a tablet, a smartphone, a television set, a printer, and a network to connect all these devices together. For many, it is difficult to feel comfortable with all of these myriad systems, beyond a rudimentary understanding of how to get basic tasks accomplished. Hence, when a system malfunctions, or when we wish to use a system in a novel way, it becomes a hugely difficult task to figure out how to get things done. Many of us will not even bother.

The problem with many of these technologies is that they lack what I refer to as "explanatory power." By this, I mean a black box system that is difficult to understand because its inner workings are not visible for inspection. In Nakatsu [1, 2], I more precisely define what I mean by explanatory power, and provide specific suggestions on how to enhance explanatory power. I describe two dimensions that are relevant to understanding this term: **system transparency**, or the ability to see the underlying mechanism of the system so that it is not merely a black box; and **flexibility,** or the ability of the user interface to adapt to a wide variety of end-user interactions, so that it is not merely a rigid dialogue, but, rather, an open-ended one that enables an end-user to explore the system more fully.

A long-standing problem with many systems today is that they can be difficult to modify, and extremely brittle when something goes wrong. In order to cope with

© Springer International Publishing Switzerland 2015
F.F.-H. Nah and C.-H. Tan (Eds.): HCIB 2015, LNCS 9191, pp. 623–632, 2015.
DOI: 10.1007/978-3-319-20895-4_58

technological complexity, what the average user needs is a mental model of how the system functions. I argue, therefore, that an appropriate diagram can go a long way toward explaining system actions and providing a deeper understanding of how a system functions. Furthermore, I demonstrate how a diagram can be used not only as a system aid, but also in more dynamic ways and serve as the user interface itself. (See Nakatsu [3] for a wide range of examples on how diagrams can be used as an intelligent user interface).

By diagram, I am referring to a graphical representation of how the objects in a domain of discourse are interrelated to one another. Unlike a linguistic or verbal description, a diagram is a type of information graphic that "preserves explicitly the information about topological and geometric relations among the components of the problem" [4].That is to say, a diagram indexes information by location on a 2-D plane— 3-D diagrams are also possible, but not, as yet, commonplace. As such, related pieces of information can be grouped together on a plane, and interconnections between related elements can be made explicit through lines and other notational elements. Indeed, diagrams are good at tapping into the very powerful visual information processing system that most humans possess, and can support a large number of perceptual inferences that are useful for problem-solving [4].

2   A Taxonomy of Diagrammatic User Interfaces

Most diagrams that we create are static, or are not intended to be modified by a user or updated by a system. Diagrams such as decision trees, basic flowcharts, semantic networks, and entity-relationship models help us understand systems better, but are usually not intended to be manipulated in any meaningful way. Other diagrams are intended to be used in more dynamic and interesting ways, and can serve as the graphical user interface of a system. In Fig. 1, a diagrammatic representation is classified by (1) **Modifiability of information**: Is the information in the diagram static or can information "propagate" in some way on the diagram (Information Static vs. Information Dynamic). (2) **Modifiability of structure**: Is the structure of the diagram static or can it be actively created and modified? (Structure Static vs. Structure Dynamic). (This framework is from Nakatsu [3]). Based on these two dimensions there are four types of diagrammatic user interfaces that are possible:

I. **Static Representations** (Information Static, Structure Static): These diagrammatic user interfaces are not intended to be modified. Because they are static, they can easily be inserted in a static medium such as in the pages of a book, or on a static web page.

II. **Propagation Structures** (Information Dynamic, Structure Static): While information on these diagrams can be modified and updated, the structures themselves are static. For example, a Bayesian network representing a network of causal associations may represent a static structure. Probabilities are assigned to each node and are updated based on the introduction of new evidence and data.

III. **Constructive Diagrams** (Information Static, Structure Dynamic): These diagrams are intended to be incrementally built: nodes and links can be actively added, deleted and modified.

IV. **Constructive Diagrams with Information Propagation** (Information Dynamic, Structure Dynamic): These diagrams are dynamic in a dual sense: both the structure itself can be modified and information can be updated and propagated through the structure.

	Structure Static	Structure Dynamic
Information Static	**I. Static Representations** Diagram and information cannot be modified.	**IIII. Constructive Diagrams** Diagram is actively constructed but no information propagation.
Information Dynamic	**II. Propagation Structures** Diagram is static but information propagates	**IV. Constructive Diagrams With Information Propagation** Diagram is actively constructed and information propagates.

Fig. 1. Types of diagrammatic user interfaces

3 Examples of Diagrammatic User Interfaces

Whereas Quadrant I diagrams are those in which both structure and information are static, Quadrant II, III, and IV diagrams are more dynamic, and, thus, can be the basis for a more dynamic graphical user interface. The future of diagrammatic user interfaces is really about discovering these more interesting uses.

To illustrate these ideas, in this Sect. 1 discuss and explore two possible intelligent user interfaces that employ dynamic diagramming techniques: (1) A propagation structures that allow for information propagation on a diagram, (2) An example of constructive diagramming in which end-users incrementally build the diagram to aid in problem-solving.

3.1 Quadrant II: Propagation Structures

Propagation structures are diagrams in which information on a diagram can be entered and modified by a user. Once entered, information propagates, or is updated, accordingly, throughout the diagram based on the values entered. Let us look at a simple example of a propagation structure. This prototype system was developed to better understand the benefits of diagrammatic user interfaces [1].

The hierarchic diagram above represents the situation in which a transportation broker must decide what type of transportation mode (air, trucking, rail, or small package service) to use in order to transport a client's shipment. The determination is made based on data inputs entered directly onto the diagram.

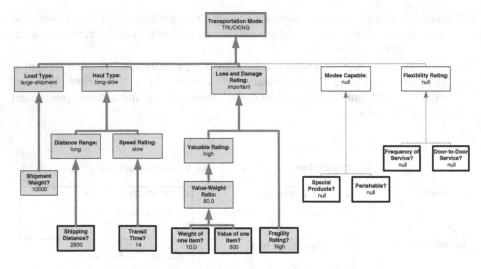

Fig. 2. Propagation structure

The hierarchy is composed of nodes (denoted by rectangles) and links among these nodes. There are three types of nodes in this diagram. The topmost node represents the goal of the decision-making problem, which is what transportation mode to choose. At the bottom of the hierarchy, the leaf nodes represent the unprocessed data inputs. They are represented by bold-faced rectangles—for example, shipment weight, shipping distance, and transit time. In between the root node and the leaf nodes are the intermediate nodes. These nodes read in values from the node(s) attached directly below it— their child node(s)—and process this input to produce an output, which, in turn, is passed to the node attached directly above it, the parent node. For instance, load type reads in the value passed to it by the shipment weight, its child node; the output from load type is then passed to transportation mode, its parent node.

A user can visually track a line of reasoning through the hierarchy to better understand how the system makes a recommendation. The upward-pointing arrows on the hierarchy signify that information moves from bottom to top. For example, the diagram above shows the following data inputs entered directly onto the hierarchy:

- Shipment weight: 10,000 (lbs)
- Shipping distance: 2,500 (miles)
- Transit time: 14 (days)
- Weight of one item: 10.0 (oz.)
- Value of one item: 500 (dollars)
- Fragility rating: high (denoting a highly fragile shipment)

By entering 10,000 as the *shipment weight*, *load type* is set to large-shipment. Similarly, when 10.0 is entered as *weight of one item* and 500 as *value of one item*, *value-weight ratio* is set to 50.0 (*value of one item* divided by *weight of one item*, or dollar value per ounce), which will, in turn, set *valuable rating* to high. When *fragility rating* is also set to high, *loss and damage rating* is set to important. In the diagram above some of the nodes are null, signifying that some information has not been entered—the hierarchic diagram will make a recommendation as soon as there is enough information to make a determination. That is to say, the three values from load type will will type, and loss and damage rating together, are sufficient to make a recommendation—in this case, trucking is the transportation mode selected As indicated in Fig. 2, all the nodes that have been activated are shaded and the associated links are boldfaced to show the user what part of the hierarchy is active at any given point in time.

The user can also request a "deeper" explanation for the trucking recommendation. In this particular instance, rail and trucking are the two suitable choices for large shipments between 5,000 and 15,000 lbs. (Air service is restricted by the physical dimensions of a cargo plane and, hence, cannot handle large shipments). However, rail is not as safe and secure as trucking, so for highly fragile, valuable cargo (loss and damage rating = high), trucking is the final recommendation.

3.2 Quadrant IV: Constructive Diagrams with Information Propagation

Diagrams that fall in this quadrant are dynamic in a dual sense: both the structure itself can be modified, and information can be updated and propagated through the structure. To illustrate such a diagram, I built a prototype system called LogNet (Nakatsu [5, 6] which supports a logistics network design task: how to configure a network of factories, warehouses, and customer zones interconnected by transportation links. See Fig. 3.

At the heart of LogNet is the network model. The problem of specifying the model would be one of specifying the network structure through which manufactured goods flow. To model this environment, three types of nodes are considered: first, the factories, where the products are manufactured; second, the warehouses, which receive the finished products from the factories for storage; and third, the customer zones, which place orders and receive the desired products from the assigned warehouse(s). Product moves through the logistics network via the transportation links between the nodes. There are two types of transportation links: inbound links move products from factories to warehouses, and outbound links move products from warehouses to customers. In Fig. 3, squares represent factories, circles represent warehouses, and triangles represent customer zones. Note that the number at the top of each node represents the number of items that moves through that node.

In essence, the network design task involves a tradeoff between consolidation (merging two or more warehouses into one) and decentralization (splitting warehouses into two or more separate locations so that they are closer to customers). On the one hand, consolidation results in lower costs primarily because of the fixed costs of operating a warehouse; on the other hand, consolidation can deteriorate customer service, in that warehouses are now located farther away from customers. LogNet allows you to assess these tradeoffs more systematically. The diagrams are constructive because they are meant to be actively modified by the user—different network configurations can be drawn (nodes can be added/deleted to the network, and transportation links can be added and deleted to connect and disconnect nodes). Furthermore, information propagates in the network, based on how the networks are configured. For example, the costs of operating the network, as well as customer service levels, are updated based on the network that you create.

Figure 3 illustrates how LogNet works. Before consolidation, in Fig. 3(a), the network is completely decentralized, costing $656,087 and resulting in perfect customer service—customer service is defined as the average distance between customer and warehouse. Because every customer zone is assigned own separate warehouse, the average distance is 0 miles. After consolidating the Washington DC warehouse into the New York warehouse, in Fig. 3(b), overall network costs decrease by $52,241 largely because operating a warehouse costs $50,000 (fixed network costs decrease from $250,000 to $200,000), but also because more consolidated inventories are cheaper (inventory costs are decreased from $101,868 to $98,928). Customer service deteriorates only by 1 mile, so shutting down this warehouse is probably a good idea.

Explanation of the Calculation of Benchmarks in LogNet. Details on the calculations are given in Table 1 (the table is annotated with specific comments given below—the numbered comments correspond to the numbered rows in the table).

(1) Outbound transportation costs are 0 before consolidation. This is because all customer zones have a warehouse located in the customer zone. By assumption, outbound transportation costs are based on the distance between the customer city and the warehouse city.

(2) Total transportation costs increase after consolidation. This is because the consolidation of Washington customers to the New York warehouse means that they are now located farther away. Because transportation costs are based on distance between warehouse and customer (for outbound costs) and factory and warehouse (for inbound costs), overall transportation costs are increased.

(3) It is assumed that each warehouse costs $50,000 to operate. After consolidation, one warehouse is shut down, resulting in $50,000 less in warehousing fixed costs.

(4) Inventory carrying costs are adjusted to reflect the fact that consolidated inventories are cheaper. This is because the more consolidated the logistics network becomes (i.e., the fewer warehouses used), the greater the inventory per warehouse. As a result, economies of scale are achieved, resulting in lower per-unit inventory carrying costs. In LogNet, these costs are estimated based on the square root rule (Ballou [7]). (More accurate functions may be used to estimate cost savings of consolidated inventories, but the square root rule is used to simplify the calculations). This rule can be used to estimate the cost of inventory when consolidating n stocking points. It states the following:

$$\text{Consolidated Inventory} = \frac{\text{Decentralized Inventory}}{\sqrt{n}}$$

For example, if previously a network utilized four warehouses at a cost of $50,000 each, for a total inventory investment of $200,00, after consolidation into one warehouse, inventory carrying costs are calculated as follows:

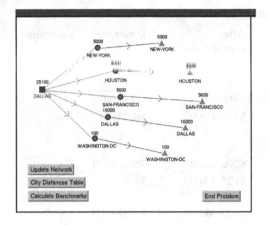

Transportation Costs	$ 178,719
Warehousing Costs	
Fixed (5 warehouses)	$ 250,000
Variable	$ 125,500
Total	$ 375,500
Inventory	$ 101,868
Total Costs	**$ 656,087**
Average Distance	
(Cust to Warehouse)	**0.0** miles
(% cust < 500 miles)	100%

(a) Before Consolidation

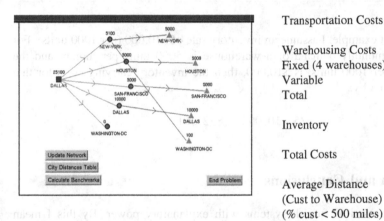

Transportation Costs	$ 179,418
Warehousing Costs	
Fixed (4 warehouses)	$ 200,000
Variable	$ 125,500
Total	$ 325,500
Inventory	$ 98,928
Total Costs	**$ 603,846**
Average Distance	
(Cust to Warehouse)	**1.0** miles
(% cust < 500 miles)	100%

(b) After Consolidation

Fig. 3. Designing a logistic network

$$\frac{200,000}{\sqrt{4}} = \$100,000$$

Inventory carrying costs, therefore, are decreased by half to $100,000. Based on this principle, LogNet calculates inventory carrying costs using the following function:

$$\text{Inventory Carrying Cost} = \sqrt{\frac{\text{Monthly Demand}}{1000}} * \text{Inventory Rate}$$

Table 1. Benchmark calculations of LogNet

	Before consolidation	After consolidation	Difference	Comments
Transportation costs				
Inbound	$178,719.00	$178,952.00	$(233.00)	
Outbound	$-	$466.00	$(466.00)	(1)
Total transportation costs	$178,719.00	$179,418.00	$(699.00)	(2)
Warehousing costs				
Fixed costs	$250,000.00	$200,000.00	$50,000.00	(3)
Variable handling costs	$125,500.00	$125,500.00	$-	
Total warehousing costs	$375,500.00	$325,500.00	$50,000.00	
Inventory carrying costs	$101,868.00	$98,928.00	$2,940.00	(4)
Total network costs	$656,087.00	$603,846.00	$52,241.00	

In the LogNet example, I assume an inventory rate of $10,000 (per 1000 units). For example, if the monthly demand of a warehouse is 5000 units per month, and the inventory rate (per 1000 units) is $10,000, then the inventory carrying costs for that warehouse is given by:

$$\sqrt{5} * 10,000 = \$22,361$$

4 Discussion and Conclusions

Diagrams can be used to furnish systems with explanatory power. By this I mean systems that provide both system transparency as well as system flexibility. A graphical user interface endowed with explanatory power may be one that contains a conceptual model describing how a system operates and works. It may, for example, be a causal model or influence diagram showing what variables affect a decision, like the diagram in Fig. 2 that shows how a transportation mode is selected. In terms of systems flexibility, these diagrams can be manipulated and updated to test out different problem-solving scenarios. In Fig. 2, for example, different scenarios can be tested out to determine how the transportation mode is affected. Likewise, in Fig. 3, a user to incrementally test out different network design configurations and LogNet will render its recommendations accordingly.

We have strong evidence in our own research lab that these diagrammatic user interfaces are beneficial. In one experimental study that I conducted on the transportation mode selection problem, participants were better able to understand and more accurately troubleshoot problems when using the hierarchic user interface, as opposed to using a regular "flat" user interface [1]. These participants overwhelmingly preferred using a diagrammatic user interface, citing such reasons as the ability to visualize relationships among variables in the system, increased comprehensibility, ease of use, and the cultivation in problem solving.

The future of diagrammatic user interfaces is promising. I have provided but a glimpse on some of its possibilities. Here are some more ideas on what future variations of diagrammatic user interfaces might look like:

- Diagrams that partition complex systems into meaningful chunks, and organize these chunks into hierarchic structures or some other organizational scaffold. Such diagrams can help users visualize the bigger picture of a complex system. Figure 2 is one such example.
- Venn diagrams that can be used to construct formal logic proof in a way that is much easier than using first order logic [8].
- Bayesian networks that illustrate a network of cause-and-effect associations can help us better understand mechanisms of cause and effect, and how they may be sensitive to different assumptions [9].
- Diagrams that illustrate problem-solving strategies and graphically show the methods that intelligent systems use to work through a problem. As a result, users have a rationale for why a system behaved the way that it did [10].
- Diagrams that help learners understand subject matter material at a deeper level, and help them form an appropriate mental model of a domain [11].
- Diagrams that foster a highly interactive dialog with a user. A user can update information on the diagram, test out different scenarios, and receive appropriate feedback from the user interface.

The systems of the future are likely to deal with increasingly complex tasks that will require some understanding of how they work. If users are to trust the advice and recommendations that these systems generate, the graphical user interface should be able to comfortably explain itself. A diagrammatic user interface can go a long way toward providing explanatory power for a user.

References

1. Nakatsu, R.T., Benbasat, I.: Improving the explanatory power of knowledge-based systems: an investigation of content and interface-based enhancements. IEEE Trans. Syst. Man Cybern. Part A Syst. Hum. **33**(3), 344–357 (2003)
2. Nakatsu, R.T.: Explanatory power of intelligent systems. Intelligent Decision-Making Support Systems, pp. 123–143. Springer, London (2006)
3. Nakatsu, R.T.: Diagrammatic Reasoning in AI. Wiley, London (2009)
4. Larkin, J.H., Simon, H.A.: Why a diagram is (sometimes) worth ten thousand words. Cogn. Sci. **11**(1), 65–100 (1987)
5. Nakatsu, R.T.: Designing business logistics networks using model-based reasoning and heuristic-based searching. Expert Syst. Appl. **29**(4), 735–745 (2005)

6. Nakatsu, R.T., Benbasat, I.: Designing intelligent systems to handle system failures: enhancing explanatory power with less restrictive user interfaces and deep explanations. Int. J. Hum. Comput. Interact. **21**(1), 55–72 (2006)
7. Ballou, R.H.: Business Logistics Management. Prentice-Hall, Englewood Cliffs (1992)
8. Nakatsu, R.T.: Using venn diagrams to perform logic reasoning: an algorithm for automating the syllogistic reasoning of categorical statements. Int. J. Intell. Syst. **29**(1), 84–103 (2014)
9. Nakatsu, R.T.: Inexact reasoning with certainty factors and Bayesian networks. Diagrammatic Reasoning in AI, pp. 264–301. Wiley, London (2009)
10. Nakatsu, R.T.: Rule based reasoning with diagrams. Diagrammatic Reasoning in AI, pp. 188–227. Wiley, London (2009)
11. Nakatsu, R.T.: Mental models: diagrams in the mind's eye. Diagrammatic Reasoning in AI, pp. 23–56. Wiley, London (2009)

A Comparison of Hybrid Neural Network Based Breast Cancer Diagnosis Systems

Hsine-Jen Tsai[1(⊠)], Hao-Chun Lu[1], Tung-Huan Wu[1],
and Chiang-Sheng Lee[2]

[1] Fu Jen Catholic University, New Taipei, Taiwan, ROC
{tsai.fju, bach0809}@gmail.com,
discgto@yahoo.com.tw
[2] National Taiwan University of Science and Technology,
Taipei, Taiwan, ROC
cslee@mail.ntust.edu.tw

Abstract. Breast cancer is the second leading cause of death among the women aged between 40 and 59 in the world. The diagnosis of such disease has been a challenging research problem. With the advancement of artificial intelligence in medical science, numerous AI based breast cancer diagnosis system have been proposed. Many researches combine different algorithms to develop hybrid systems to improve the diagnosis accuracy. In this study, we propose three artificial neural network based hybrid diagnosis systems respectively combining association rule, correlation and genetic algorithm. The effectiveness of these systems is examined on Wisconsin Breast Cancer Dataset. We then compare the accuracy of these three hybrid diagnosis systems. The results indicated that the neural network combining with association rule not only has excellent dimensionality reduction ability but also has the similar accurate prediction with correlation based neural network which has best accurate prediction rate among all three systems compared.

Keywords: Neural network · Association rule · Genetic algorithm · Medical artificial intelligence

1 Introduction

Breast cancer is the second leading cause of death among women in the United States according to the National Breast Cancer Foundation. The number of new cases of cancer in 2012 has reached around 14.1 million worldwide and 11.9 % (around 1.7 million) of these cases were diagnosed with breast cancer according to the WHO (World Health Organization). Breast cancer is a disease in which a malignant tumor forms in the tissues of the breast. A malignant tumor is a group of cancer cells that can grow into surrounding tissues in breast, but with early detection and treatment, most people continue to live a normal life. Early diagnosis is one of most significant steps in reducing the health and social complications of this disease. In the last decades, with increased emphasis towards cancer related research, new and innovative methods for

© Springer International Publishing Switzerland 2015
F.F.-H. Nah and C.-H. Tan (Eds.): HCIB 2015, LNCS 9191, pp. 633–639, 2015.
DOI: 10.1007/978-3-319-20895-4_59

early detection and treatment have been developed. Due to the use of electronic data capture and data management systems for both clinical care and biomedical research, the medical research has become toward quantitative research [9, 11, 14]. The abundance of data is strongly accelerating the trend. Data-driven study is becoming a common complement in medical diagnosis system. Many medical diagnosis systems use artificial neural networks (ANN) as a classification approach [2, 3, 5–8, 11, 12]. Artificial neural networks is a powerful tool which helps medical professionals to analyze, model and make sense of complex clinical data across a broad range of medical applications.

In this research, we proposed three artificial neural network (ANN) based hybrid diagnosis systems respectively combining association rule (AR), correlation and genetic algorithm (GA). The effectiveness of these systems is examined on Wisconsin Breast Cancer Dataset. The accuracy of these three hybrid diagnosis systems is compared. The main motivation behind this study is to use different approaches to minimize the number of features and then use the neural network to perform the prediction. By eliminating unnecessary features, we can save time and resource of computation during the prediction process.

In the next section we look at the literature review. Section 3 proposes three hybrid diagnosis systems which are artificial neural networks combining association rule, correlation and genetic algorithm respectively. Details of models and algorithm of these systems are described in this section as well. The experimental results are presented in Sect. 4. Finally, Sect. 5 provides the conclusions and future directions of research.

2   Literature Review

Breast cancer is the most common cancer in women both in the developed and less developed world. It is estimated that worldwide over 508,000 women died in 2011 due to breast cancer according to the WHO (World Health Organization) in 2013. Many research related to breast cancer have been reported and applied. They are prediction of breast cancer survivability [4, 13], reoccurrence rate and diagnosis of breast cancer [6, 10], etc. Many researchers have tried to use different methods to improve the accuracy of diagnosis system.

As the applications being developed in the data mining areas, researchers are still struggled with some challenges. Features selection is one of inevitable problems when there are significant amount of input features for a particular data mining applications. Limiting the number of input features has influence on the performance of data mining models in great part. Recently, many hybrid data mining systems have been put forward. Artificial neural network is one of the most common methods for prediction problems. Reference [5] proposed a hybrid model combing case-based reasoning and fuzzy decision tree and achieved 98.4 % forecasting accuracy for breast cancer. Reference [13] provided a diagnose model combing artificial neural network with genetic algorithm by processing patients' infrared thermal images to diagnose breast cancer.

3 Models and Algorithms

3.1 Database

The required data for this research was obtained from Wisconsin breast cancer database. They have been collected by Dr. William H. Wolberg at the University of Wisconsin-Madison Hospitals. There are 699 records in this database. Each record consists of nine features. These nine features detailed in Table 1 are graded on an interval scale from a normal state of 1–10, with 1 being the normal and 10 being the most abnormal state. 241 records out of 699 are malignant and 458 records are benign.

3.2 Models

Feature selection plays an important role in building a prediction model. By eliminating redundant input features that has no significant influence on the final outcome, we can build a prediction model with better efficiency and prediction accuracy. We propose three hybrid models that use different approaches, namely association rule (AR), genetic algorithm (GA) and correlation, to perform the feature selection task. Each model has two layers. First layer is the feature selector whose major task is to select significant features and lower the dimension of input vector. Second layer is the artificial neural network model to perform prediction. The general hybrid diagnosis system is shown in Fig. 1.

AR_Based ANN Model

Association rule is a method to discover relationship among items in large databases. A typical and well-known example of association rule is Market Basket Analysis [1]. That is, given a collection of items and a set of transactions, each transaction contains some number of items from given collection. An association algorithm can find rules such as 85 % of all the transactions that contain items A and B also contain items C and D.

Table 1. Descriptions of features in Wisconsin breast cancer database

Feature code	Feature description	Values of features	Mean	Standard deviation
A	Clump thickness	1–10	4.42	2.82
B	Uniformity of cell size	1–10	3.13	3.05
C	Uniformity of cell shape	1–10	3.20	2.97
D	Marginal adhesion	1–10	2.80	2.86
E	Single epithelial cell size	1–10	3.21	2.21
F	Bare nuclei	1–10	3.46	3.64
G	Bland chromatin	1–10	3.43	2.44
H	Normal nucleoli	1–10	2.87	3.05
I	Mitoses	1–10	1.59	1.71

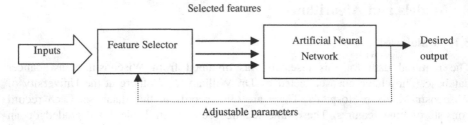

Selected features

Fig. 1. The block diagram of the hybrid diagnosis system

Apriori algorithm [1] is used in the feature selector of AR_based ANN model. Most of the association rule algorithms are somewhat variations of this algorithm. The Apriori algorithm [1] is given as follows:

```
Apriori()
L1 ={large 1-itemsets}
k = 2
while L_{k-1}≠φ do
begin
C_k = apriori_gen(L_{k-1})
for all transactions t in D do
begin
    C^t = subset(C_k, t)
    for all candiate c ∈ C^t do
    c.count = c.count+1
    end
    L_k ={ c ∈ C_k | c.count ≥ minsup }
    k = k + 1
end.
```

To run the Apriori algorithm, we use all input features and their all records to find some large itemset which has high confidence value and enough support value. For example, a large itemset [A, C, D, F] is obtained with 95 % of confidence and 80 % of support. Then feature A is selected as the representative of this itemset. The rest features in the itemset are redundant and eliminated. After several runs of such process with some sets of support and confidence, the input features of the second layer which is artificial neural network are obtained.

GN_Based ANN Model

Genetic algorithm is a common technique for optimization problems. In genetic algorithm, the population is associated with n chromosomes that represent candidate solution; each chromosome is an m-dimensional vector where m is the number of optimized parameters.

In our GA_based ANN model, the process of feature selection and prediction is stated as follows. At first, an input vector with a length of nine elements is created and feed into ANN model. Each element corresponds to the specific feature of the WBCD

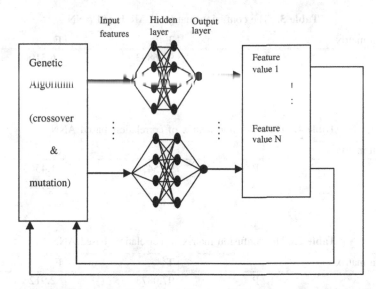

Fig. 2. A block diagram of GN_based NN diagnosis system

record. Output of ANN model is then feed into feature selector, genetic algorithm module in this case. Fitness value is calculated inside the feature selector. New generation of input features (chromosome) then are generated after crossover and mutation inside the feature selector. The process continues until stop criterion are satisfied. Figure 2 shows a block diagram of GN_based NN diagnosis system.

Correlation_Based ANN Model

Correlation is one the basic technique in statistic area. By discovering correlation between input features, redundant features can be located and eliminated. In this model, correlation is used as the feature selector. After features of WBCD records are feed into selector and calculated, the correlation of features are stored in the matrix. Redundant features are then eliminated according the threshold. Use the new feature set as the input of the second layer which is ANN model and perform training and testing.

4 Experimental Results

This experiment was conducted on the Wisconsin breast cancer database. In test stage, 10-fold cross validation method was applied. Experimental results are presented using confusion matrix to evaluate the accuracy of each approach. Table 2 shows the result using the ANN only without feature selection process. The result of these three hybrid

Table 2. The confusion matrix of ANN only without feature selection process

Confusion matrix		T	F
	P	97.5728	2.4271
	N	2.8169	97.1830

Table 3. The confusion matrix of AR_based ANN

Confusion matrix		T	F
	P	93.6893	6.3106
	N	3.9436	96.0563

Table 4. The confusion matrix of correlation_based ANN

Confusion matrix		T	F
	P	98.5436	1.4563
	N	2.5352	97.4647

Table 5. The confusion matrix of correlation_based ANN

Confusion matrix		T	F
	P	97.0873	2.9126
	N	3.9436	96.0563

Table 6. Accruacy rate comparison of ANN with three hybrid ANN model

	Feature	Accuracy
ANN	A ~ I	95.32 %
AR_based ANN(2)	B, F	94.10 %
Correlation_based NN(1) 90 %	A, B, D, E, F, G, H, I	95.88 %
GA_based ANN	B, C, G, H, I	94.73 %

models are shown in Tables 3, 4, and 5. A comparison of all four models is presented in Table 6.

The results show that correlation based neural network has the accurate prediction rate with 95.88 % which is the best among all three systems compared. With respect to dimensionality reduction, the result of AR_based ANN model is better than GA_based ANN and Correlation_based ANN.

5 Conclusion

A considerable amount of medical intelligence research has been conducted in the last decade. However, the researchers put more focus on diagnosis prediction systems. Many artificial intelligent techniques have been investigated to diagnose the breast cancer. This work has explored the accuracy of hybrid diagnosis models combining feature extraction with different classification techniques. Three artificial neural network based hybrid diagnosis systems respectively combining association rule, correlation and genetic algorithm. The effectiveness of these systems is examined on

Wisconsin Breast Cancer Dataset. The accuracy of these three hybrid diagnosis systems is compared.

The results indicated that the correlation based neural network has the best accurate prediction rate among all three systems compared. The artificial neural network combining with association rule not only has excellent dimensionality reduction ability but also has the similar accurate prediction with correlation_based ANN.

References

1. Agrawal, R., Srikant, R.: Fast algorithms for mining association rules in large databases. In: Proceedings of the 20th International Conference on Very Large Data Bases (1994)
2. Bishop, C.M.: Neural Networks for Pattern Recognition. Clarendon Press, Oxford (1996)
3. Choua, S.M., Leeb, T.S., Shaoc, Y.E., Chenb, I.F.: Mining the breast cancer pattern using artificial neural networks and multivariate adaptive regression splines. Expert Syst. Appl. **27**, 133–142 (2004)
4. Delen, D., Walker, G., Kadam, A.: Predicting breast cancer survivability: a comparison of three data mining methods. Artif. Intell. Med. **34**(2), 113–127 (2004)
5. Dybowski, R., Gant, V.: Clinical Applications of Artificial Neural Networks. Cambridge University Press, Cambridge (2007)
6. Er, O., Yumusak, N., Temurtas, F.: Chest disease diagnosis using artificial neural networks. Expert Syst. Appl. **37**(12), 7648–7655 (2010)
7. Fan, C.-Y., Chang, P.-C., Lin, J.-J., Hsieh, J.C.: A hybrid model combining case-based reasoning and fuzzy decision tree for medical data classification. Appl. Soft Comput. **11**, 632–644 (2011)
8. Floyd, C., Lo, J., Yun, A., Sullivan, D., Kornguth, P.: Prediction of breast cancer malignancy using an artificial neural network. Cancer **74**, 2944–2998 (1994)
9. Karabatak, M., Cevdet, M.: An expert system for detection of breast cancer based on association rules and neural network. Expert Syst. Appl. **36**, 3465–3469 (2009)
10. Mangasarian, O.L., Wolberg, W.H.: Cancer diagnosis via linear programming. SIAM News **23**(5), 1–18 (1990)
11. Owrang, O., Mehdi, M.: Association rules mining for breast cancer survivability prediction. http://www.siam.org/meetings/sdm06/workproceed/Scientific%20Datasets/bellaachia.pdf
12. Shortliffe, E.H.: Clinical Information Systems In the Era of Managed Care. Sea Island, GA (1993)
13. Zadeh, H.G., Haddadnia, J., Hashemian, M., Hassanpour, K.: Diagnosis of breast cancer using a combination of genetic algorithm and artificial neural network in medical infrared thermal imaging. Iran. J. Med. Phys. **9**, 265–274 (2012)
14. Vimla, L., Patel, A., Edward, H., Shortliffea, B., Stefanellic, M., Szolovits, D., Michael, R., Berthold, E., Bellazzic, R., Abu-Hanna, A.: The coming of age of artificial intelligence in medicine. Artif. Intell. Med. **46**, 5–17 (2009)

Rule-based Medical Decision Support Portal for the Emergency Department

I-Chin Wu[1(✉)], Tzu-Li Chen[1], Yen-Yi Feng[2], Ya-Ling Cheng[1], and Yung-Chih Chuang[1]

[1] Department of Information Management, Fu-Jen Catholic University,
510 Chung Cheng Road, Hsinchuang, New Taipei City 24205, Taiwan
`icwu.fju@gmail.com`
[2] Emergency Medicine, Mackay Memorial Hospital, Taipei, Taiwan

Abstract. Hospital Emergency Department (ED) crowding has led to an increase in patients' waiting times; thus, solving this problem requires a better understanding of a hospital's patient flow and the behaviors of patients. Existing research on ED crowding is sparse and has tended to focus on the present crowding state. Recent studies have addressed the importance of analyzing the length of stay (LOS) to understand the behaviors of patients in the ED. In this research, we proposed a rule-based data-mining approach to investigate the relationship between various types of patient behaviors and their LOS, and to build a model to predict patient LOS. The objective of this study is to build an interactive decision support system (DSS) for Mackay Memorial Hospital, which has the second-largest ED in Taiwan and is a representative institute. Accordingly, the aim of this study is twofold (1) building the DSS based on the proposed medical data-mining process in the ED and (2) visualizing the extracting rules and the statistical data in the proposed rule-based medical decision support (R-MDS) visualization portal. We introduce the system framework with associated modules in this study. We aim to integrate domain knowledge of the hospital ED with the data-mining technique to develop the system and provide interactive DSS using modern visualization techniques. We also believed that the qualified rules can be validated effectively and efficiently by experts with the aid of the proposed system.

Keywords: Data mining · Decision support · ED crowding · Length of stay · Rule-based

1 Introduction

The demand for emergency medical services has increased in recent years, and the emergency department (ED) has become the most important and busiest unit within most hospitals, providing emergency care and treatment to patients in need of immediate medical attention. However, EDs in Taiwan have not been able to accommodate the rapidly increasing patient demand in the past 14 years. This demand is attributed to the growth in the aging population and to influenza outbreaks caused by new variants of the virus. According to statistics of the Department of Health in Taiwan, the total

© Springer International Publishing Switzerland 2015
F.F.-H. Nah and C.-H. Tan (Eds.): HCIB 2015, LNCS 9191, pp. 640–652, 2015.
DOI: 10.1007/978-3-319-20895-4_60

number of people visiting EDs surged from 4,379,568 in 1998 to 6,730,946 in 2012. Figure 1 illustrates the growth rates of 53.7 % in total visits. Such increases cause an imbalance or a mismatch between supply and demand, ultimately creating long-term overcrowding in hospital EDs, also known as "ED crowding".

The Institute of Medicine recently noted that the problem of ED crowding is an obstacle to the safe and timely delivery of health care. Because EDs must always be available to provide emergency medical care to patients, ED resource management can be extremely complex and uncertain. Accordingly, ED overcrowding is a national problem that requires a promising approach to identify a solution or solutions. Hospital ED crowding has led to an increase in patients' waiting times; thus, solving this problem requires a better understanding of a hospital's patient flow and the behaviors of patients [10]. Existing research on ED crowding is sparse and has tended to focus on the present crowding state. Ding et al. [5] addressed the importance of analyzing the length of stay (LOS) to understand the behaviors of patients in the ED. Azari et al. [2] proposed a multi-tiered data-mining approach to predict patients' LOS by clustering and classification methods. This research provides good departure points for understanding patient behaviors based on the LOS factor.

In this work, we analyzed patients' lengths of stay (LOS) from the perspective of the behaviors of patients in the ED. That is, we extracted rules based on set of patient attributes and treatment processes (e.g., arrival to admission, examination pattern, transfer or discharge, etc.). Notably, the examination pattern denotes the frequency and usage order of medical resources such as X-rays, CTs, and the Lab, during the patient's stay in the hospital's ED. Then, we built up the model to predict LOS based on the rules. Accordingly, we proposed a novel rule-based data mining approach to investigate the issue of LOS prediction to tackle the problem of ED-crowding. Our aim was to find what kinds of patients and their associated behaviors would cause the overcrowding problem.

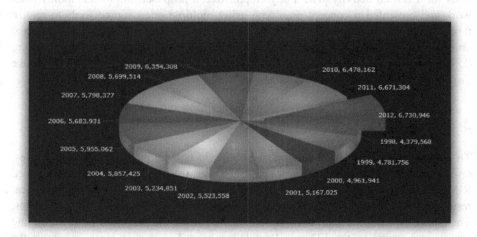

Fig. 1. Total and average daily number of patient visits to the emergency department at Taiwan from 1998 to 2012

The objectives with the associate procedures of this research are briefly addressed, as follows:

1. We conducted data preprocessing and then applied association rule mining to identify both frequent and infrequent ED behaviors of patients. Accordingly, two types of patient behavior (PB)—i.e., the regular and exceptional behaviors of patients—were identified, after which the rules for partitioning the dataset were extracted. In this research, we further partitioned data based on a five level triage scale, i.e. from level 1 (most urgent) to level 5 (least resource intensive) under different PBs, and LOS to analyze the correlation between various triage levels and ED crowding.
2. We constructed a prediction model with an explanation capability to assist the ED of a hospital in decreasing its overcrowding conditions. Then extracted rules from different groups of different LOS which may cause ED crowding and validated the accuracy of those rules.
3. We built a decision support system based on the proposed data-mining process in the ED and visualized the extracting rules and the statistical data in the proposed rule-based medical decision support (R-MDS) visualization portal.

The contributions of this research are, (1) to our best of knowledge, the idea of partitioning the unbalanced dataset by Apriori algorithm [1] to investigate different users' behaviors in the medical domain has not been reported; (2) as we know, the variants of patients' lengths of stay (LOS) in the ED are typically diverse; thus, collecting numerous patient records to conduct empirical study is another challenge in this work. We have collected 43885 medical records from Mackay Memorial Hospital representing the period from January 1, 2010 to June 30, 2010 to do this research; and (3) Yao and Kumar [9] proposed a novel CONFlexFlow (Clinical cONtext-based Flexible workFlow) approach to represent medical knowledge by a better understanding of clinical context through ontologies, and using them to activate the right rules for a certain activity. The study emphasized a proposed implementation framework and presented a concept prototype using multiple open source tools to realize flexible clinical pathways and to build the clinical decision support system. The optimal objective of this long-term research is to build an interactive decision support system (DSS) for Mackay Memorial Hospital to help doctors, nurses and clerks make just-in-time decisions.

2 The R-MDS Visualization Portal

To assist interactive decision support, we built a visualization portal. Doctors, nurses, or clerks can input patient attributes, i.e., triage, age, treatment, etc., via the developed R-MDS dashboard application, which can then graphically present the statistical results, rules, and other ED-related information for further interaction with the systems. The related patient data and the rules extracted based on the proposed ED data-mining process are stored in the ED rule knowledge base. For this research, we built the visualization portal using Silverlight. Then, using web services via a Silverlight application, we could elicit results from the ED rule knowledge base and the ED database. Figure 2 shows the system framework. We briefly introduce the deployment system as follows.

The EDDS Visualization Portal: We built a front-end interface using Rich Interactive Application (RIA) services with Silverlight and used the C# and the .NET framework to implement the back-end services. Silverlight is an application framework for writing and running RIAs that provides an interface that is faster and more responsive than traditional applications. The Microsoft .NET RIA services simplify n-tier application patterns and provide data validation and authentication by integrating with Silverlight components on the client and ASP.NET on the mid-tier. Several Silverlight visualization controllers can present data, e.g., the custom controller, dashboard controller,

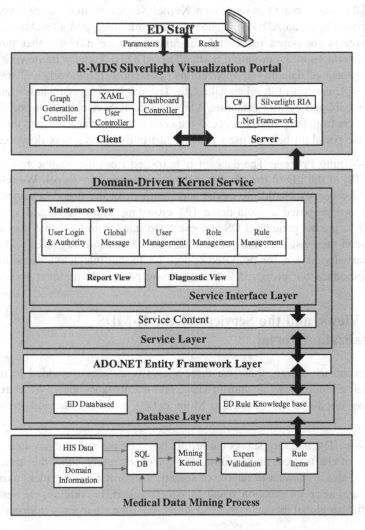

Fig. 2. The system framework of medical data mining and visualization

and graph generation controller. The user can then refer to the method on the domain context that corresponds to the domain service query method to retrieve the data. Technically, user interfaces are declared in Extensible Application Markup Language (XAML), a declarative XML-based language, to manipulate the controllers easily and efficiently.

Domain-Driven Kernel Service: Web or mobile applications developed by Silverlight are run on the client side; thus, we implement a domain-driven kernel service that adopts Windows Communication Foundation (WCF) RIA services to create a Silverlight client that uses simplified data validation and is aware of the application logic on the middle tier when interacting with data. That is, Silverlight controls will utilize classes that are automatically generated from codes in the middle tier. We can then use web services via a Silverlight application, i.e., the developed R-MDS visualization portal. In this work, our Domain-Driven Kernel Service includes three layers as follows: a service layer, an ADO.NET entity framework layer, and a database layer. The service layer is composed of several ED-related service modules that have corresponding interfaces in the proposed portal. The ADO.NET entity framework supports the development of data-driven applications. The entity framework will transform a LINQ or SQL entity to the relational SQL. The database layer includes an ED rule knowledge base and the ED database. When the R-MDS visualization portal receives the parameters from the portal, it will call the corresponding interface, and then pass the results to the portal for helping users provide just-in-time services or decision-making.

ED Data-Mining Process: The data set is extracted from the healthcare information system (HIS) of the ED of the Mackay Memorial Hospital in Taipei. We adopted the CRISP-DM process to build the model and then extract the users' behavior rules. In this work, we proposed a multi-tiered ED crowding data-mining and visualization framework to predict patients' LOS and extracted rules from LOS that may cause ED crowding and then visualize and validate the rules. The validating rules will be stored in the knowledge base in the proposed system for further interactive decision support. We will introduce our proposed ED data-mining process in the next section.

3   The Views, and the Services of the R-MDS Visualization Portal

In our preliminary design, there are three views (interfaces) provided in the developed portal: a report view, diagnostic view, and maintenance view. We introduce the three views briefly in the following. More details will be addressed in our future work.

Report View: The interface shows the results based on the user's input data. There are three kinds of charts used: line, column, and pie charts which show the statistical data of the ED. Table 1 shows an example of statistical information on patient attributes (in this case, age) as an information visualization (IV) chart. In addition, we designed the block to display global messages that can show real-time emergency information to the staff.

Table 1. Examples of attribute statistical information with IV charts

Information Visualization –Age			
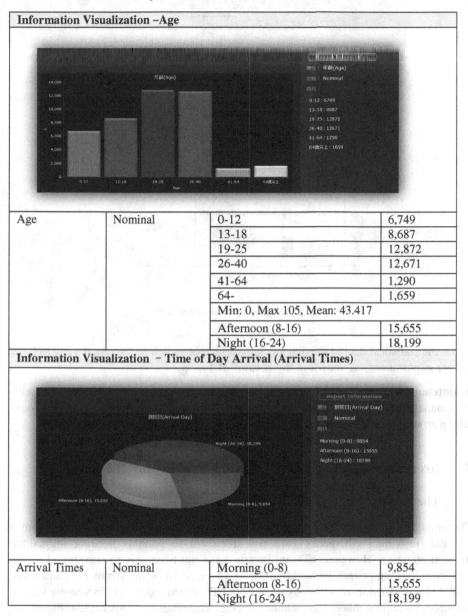			
Age	Nominal	0-12	6,749
		13-18	8,687
		19-25	12,872
		26-40	12,671
		41-64	1,290
		64-	1,659
		Min: 0, Max 105, Mean: 43.417	
		Afternoon (8-16)	15,655
		Night (16-24)	18,199

Information Visualization – Time of Day Arrival (Arrival Times)

Arrival Times	Nominal	Morning (0-8)	9,854
		Afternoon (8-16)	15,655
		Night (16-24)	18,199

Diagnostic View: This view allows users to append a new instance via the diagnostic view. In addition, the interface shows the matched inference rules based on the criteria set by users via the interface, as shown in Fig. 3. The rules will be ranked based on their scores, i.e., to what degree they match the user's setting criteria. The user can also

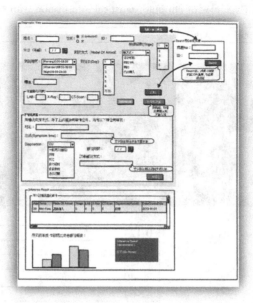

Fig. 3. Diagnostic view (interface)

check the statistical data in the diagnostic interface or switch to the report view to have further explorations, as shown at the bottom of Fig. 3.

Maintenance View: The maintenance view includes the role authority management, user management, global message management, and rule management. It helps system administrators to conduct basic but important system management tasks.

4   Three-Phase Medical Data Mining Process for the ED

4.1   The Process

The emergency department (ED) is the most important and the busiest unit within a hospital, providing emergency care and treatment to patients needing immediate medical attention. However, EDs in Taiwan have not been able to accommodate the rapidly increasing patient demand in the past 14 years. Hoot and Aronky [7] and Chan et al. [3] postulated three solutions to address ED overcrowding: (1) increasing supply resources by adding manpower, number of beds, equipment, and space; (2) controlling demand sources by implementing feasible strategies such as referrals to other departments, clinics, or hospitals; (3) exploiting management skills and operational research models for the efficient allocation of medical resources to reduce patient waiting time and alleviate ED overcrowding. In our ongoing work, we try to tackle the ED overcrowding problem by adopting a domain-driven decision support approach and by exploiting management skills for the efficient application of medical resources [4].

Basically, the main objectives toward building the medical data mining model are addressed as follows.

1. We conducted data preprocessing and then applied association rule mining to Identify frequent ED behaviors of patients and infrequent ED behaviors of patients. Accordingly, two types of patient behavior (PB)—i.e., regular and exceptional behaviors of patients—were identified.
2. We adopted a k-means clustering approach to classify the two types of PB based on different LOS and then labeled the cluster results by linguistic terms—i.e., long, medium or short LOS. Furthermore, we conducted correlation analysis between various groups of LOS and the ED crowding condition based on a five level triage scale, i.e. from level 1 (most urgent) to level 5 (least resource intensive).
3. We extracted rules from clusters of LOS of two types of PBs which have a positive correlation with ED crowding. We then used another data set to verify the rules in terms of precision and accuracy. Due to the limitation of pages, the validation results will be explained in our on-going work [4].

The procedure for three-phase data mining is introduced below briefly.

Phase 1. Data Preprocessing and Partitioning: First, we conducted data cleaning for dealing with noisy, incomplete, and inconsistent data Han and Kamber [6]. We then did data discretization for numerical data, e.g., age, numbers of varying medical equipment such as X-ray and CT machines, number of lab technicians, etc. Notably, the frequency for using medical resources will be combined into a treatment pattern and expressed as P(# of XRAYLevel, # of CTLevel, # of LABLevel) which form as a derived attribute, i.e., pattern. Accordingly, the attributes for data preprocessing includ: mode of arrival, triage, age, arrival day, arrival time, temperature, pattern (# of XRAY Level, # of CT Level, # of LAB Level), and disposition. After applying discretizing for the usage of medical resources, the pattern will be transformed into linguistic terms, i.e., high (H), medium (M) and low (L). Table 2 lists the basic demographic attributes of ED patients with descriptive statistical data from January 1, 2010 to July 31, 2010. The attributes are selected from the hospital's ED database treated as input variables of the association rule mining algorithm. We then adopted the Apriori algorithm to partition the dataset into frequent ED behaviors of patients and infrequent ED behaviors of patients. Accordingly, two types of patient behavior (PB)—i.e., the regular and exceptional behaviors of patients—were identified.

Phase 2. Data Clustering and Labeling: In this phase, we used k-means to cluster the separated dataset, i.e., regular PBs and exceptional into three groups based on the LOS and we extracted rules from each cluster in the next phase. We evaluated and compare the clustering results of three groups of two PBs. Then, analyzing the correlation between various ranges of LOS and ED crowding conditions based on the five- level triage scale respond to our research question: Which target group(s) caused the problem of ED crowding?

Phase 3. Rule Extractions and Validations: In the remaining phase, we adopted classification methods to build models and then extract the rules for future predictions. We evaluated the accuracy of the models to identify the one with the best predictive

Table 2. Basic demographic attributes with descriptive statistical data of ED patients

Attributes	Data types	Domain values	Instances
Mode of arrival	Nominal	Walk in/come	9,785
		Referral from other hospitals	953
		Referral from out-patient clinic	545
		Medical referral 119	4,369
		Escorted in to the hospital	28,056
Triage	Nominal	Level 1	539
		Level 2	6,034
		Level 3	21,788
		Level 4	12,980
		Level 5	2,367
Age	Nominal	0–12	6,749
		13–18	8,687
		19–25	12,872
		26–40	12,671
		41–64	1,290
		64 above	1,659
		Min: 0, max 105, mean: 43.417	
Arrival time	Nominal	Morning (12 midnight -8 am)	9,854
		Afternoon (8 am-4pm)	15,655
		Night (4 pm-12 midnight)	18,199
Arrival Day	Nominal	Weekday	29,691
		Weekend (monday to friday)	14,017
Temperature	Nominal	Fever(above 38 centigrade)	3,909
		Non-fever	39,799
Pattern	Nominal	P (XRAY_Level, CT_Level, LAB_Level)	
XRAY_Level	Nominal	Divided into three intervals:	
		Low (0–2)	42,861
		Medium (3–5)	840
		High (6–8)	7
		Min: 0, max 8, mean: 0.822	
CT_Level	Nominal	Divided into three intervals:	
		Low (0–1)	43,607
		Medium (2)	99
		High (3–4)	2
		Min: 0, max 4, mean: 0.089	
LAB_Level	Nominal	Divided into three intervals:	
		Low (0–5)	43,362
		Medium (6–10)	343
		High (11–15)	3
		Min: 0, max 15, mean: 1.093	

(*Continued*)

Table 2. (*Continued*)

Attributes	Data types	Domain values	Instances
Disposition	Nominal	Ward admission (intensive care unit [ICU] & cardiac catheterization room& surgery)	842
		Inpatient	5,482
		Discharge	33,812
		Death	27
		Nonadmission	738
		Against medical advice	2,460
		Refund and discharged	75
		Transfer to another hospital	272
Target	Nominal	Disposition	

capabilities that can explain the two types of PB based on triage. We will consult with the clinicians of the cooperating hospital to validate the rules. Finally, we will learn whether the rules can help the ED to decrease the problem of ED crowding.

4.2 The Preliminary Analysis Results

We first analyzed the correlation of patients with different LOS and ED crowding under various levels of triages, which based on the 5 level triage scale, are "Resuscitation", "Emergency", "Urgent", "Semi-Urgent", and "Nonurgent" (Level 1 to Level 5, respectively). Figure 4(a) and 4(b) show the results of Pearson's correlation analysis at different levels of triages in Mackay Memorial Hospital in the first six months of 2010. Apparently, no matter for regular PBs or exceptional PB, there is a positive relationship between each level of triage and ED crowding under the shortest LOS, i.e., cluster 0. On the other hand, for groups of medium or long LOS, there may be positive or negative relationship between different levels of triage and ED crowding conditions. In our ongoing work, we have consulted the attending physician to preliminarily confirm the value of the extracted rules. The attending physician has stated that the rules belonging to regular PB have higher value than those for exceptional PB. Accordingly, we will evaluate the prediction accuracy of the group with the shortest LOS for patients with regular behaviors.

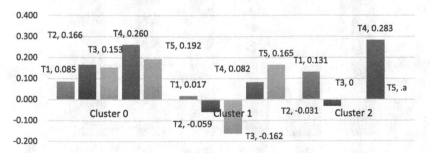

Fig. 4(a). Correlation of patients with different LOS and ED crowding under various levels of triage for regular PB

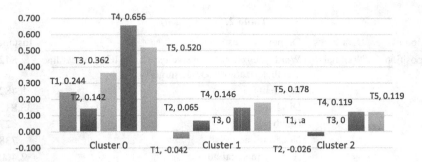

Fig. 4(b). Correlation of patients with different LOS and ED crowding under various levels triage for exceptional PBs

5 Experimental Setup and Preliminary Results

As mentioned earlier, we adopted classification methods to build the model and then extracted the rules for future predictions. Basically, *J48, CART* and *JRip* are selected as methods in this research. We conducted an experiment to investigate the effects of making prediction of patients' LOS by considering triage levels. First, the prediction is based on patients' behaviors without considering triage, named as either Regular or Exceptional. Then, the prediction takes into consideration the triage of the patients of regular behaviors, named as T_n_R. In this research, we adopted 10-fold cross validation to evaluate the accuracy of the prediction results.

In this research, we make a comparison between prediction results with or without considering triage levels for patients of regular behaviors. Note that we only focus on patients with the shortest LOS, due to its higher correlation with ED crowding as compared to a medium or long LOS. Figure 5 shows the prediction results with or without considering triage for patients with regular behaviors.

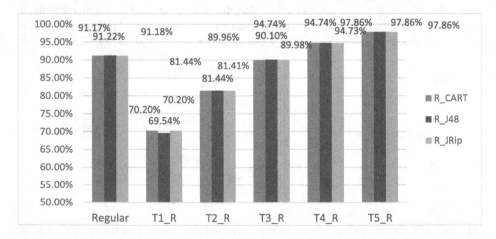

Fig. 5. Prediction results with or without considering triage for Regular PB

The results show that the three decision-tree methods can achieve similar results for each condition. If we partitioned data based on treatment behavior and triage, we find that we can achieve better prediction results for the regular-behavior patients who belong to triage 5 (T5) or triage 4 (T4) compared to the other conditions. Figure 5(a) shows regular behavior patients who belong to T4 with a positive conclusion with ED crowding and pass statistical test. Other ongoing work also shows that patients belonging to the nonurgent group lead to ED crowding. Thus, the results will be useful for analyzing the behaviors of patients who cause ED crowding and will be practical for medical decision support.

6 Conclusions and Future Works

In our work, we propose a novel framework for mining patients' behaviors in the ED related to different LOS, i.e., a multi-tiered ED crowding data mining and visualization framework for medical decision support. Accordingly, a rule-based medical decision support (R-MDS) visualization portal is presented in this work. We expect the future contributions of this research will be (1) to build a predictive model with the explanation capability to assist the ED of a hospital in decreasing its overcrowding conditions and improving the quality of health care; and (2) to accomplish the deployment of an interactive medical decision support system with information visualization tools to help doctors and clinical staff conduct analysis and make timely decisions. Keim and Kriegel [8] point out that developing visualization techniques that are adequate for exploring large amounts of multi-dimensional data is one of the research challenges. We would help users explore the multi-dimensional data by employing interactive techniques. Finally, we also believe that the proposed framework can be generalized to give rule-based decision support and include domain-driven knowledge discovery in the database.

Acknowledgments. This research was supported by the National Science Council of Taiwan under Grant No. 101-2221-E-195-001 and No. 102-2410-H-030-069-MY3.

References

1. Agrawal, R., Imielinski, T., Swami, A.: Mining association rules between sets of items in large databases. In: Proceedings of the ACM SIGMOD International Conference on Management of Data, pp. 207–216. ACM Digital Library, Washington, D.C. (1993)
2. Azari, A., Janeja, V.P., Mohseni, A.,: Predicting hospital length of stay (PHLOS): a multi-tiered data mining approach. In: 2012 IEEE 12th International Conference on Data Mining Workshops (ICDMW), pp. 17–24. Brussels, Belgium (2012)
3. Chan, C.L., Huang, H.T., You, H.J.: Intelligence modeling for coping strategies to reduce emergency department overcrowding in hospitals. J. Intell. Manuf. 23(6), 2307–2318 (2012)
4. Chen, T.Z., Wu, I.C., Feng, Y.Y., Yang, C.L.: An Empirical Study on Mining Behaviors of Patients Based on Their Length of Stay in the Emergency Department. A working paper (2015)

5. Ding, R., McCarthy, M.L., Lee, J., Desmond, J.S., Zeger, S.L., Aronsky, D.: Predicting emergency department length of stay using quantile regression. In: International Conference of Management and Service Science, pp. 1–4. Maryland, Baltimore (2009)
6. Han, J., Kamber, M., Pei, J.: Data Mining: Concepts and Techniques. Morgan Kaufmann, Los Altos (2011)
7. Hoot, N.R., Aronsky, D.: Systematic review of emergency department crowding: causes, effects, and solutions. Health Policy Clin. Pract. 52(2), 126–136 (2008)
8. Keim, D.A., Kriegel, H.P.: VisDB: database exploration using multidimensional visualization. IEEE Comput. Graph. Appl. 14(5), 40–49 (1994)
9. Yao, W., Kumar, A.: CONFlexFlow: integrating flexible clinical pathways into clinical decision support systems using context and rules. Decis. Support Syst. 55(2), 499–515 (2013)
10. Xu, M., Wong, T.C., Chin, K.S.: A medical procedure-based patient grouping method for an emergency department. Appl. Soft Comput. 14(Part A), 31–37 (2014)

Industry, Academia, Innovation and Market

Why Innovations of Capital Market IT Systems Fail to Diffuse into the General Public?

Sapumal Ahangama[✉] and Danny Chiang Choon Poo

Department of Information Systems, School of Computing, National University of Singapore, 13 Computing Drive, Singapore 117417, Singapore
sapumal@comp.nus.edu.sg, dannypoo@nus.edu.sg

Abstract. Capital markets represent an important component of the economy of any country. Yet, it has been found that in a majority of countries, participation of the general public in capital markets is at a low level even with the availability of online trading platforms. In this study, we integrate constructs of diffusion of innovation, technology acceptance and trust models to form a context specific model in order to identify the factors influencing the general public in using online trading systems. Implications of a survey study carried out among a diverse group of investors are presented in this paper.

Keywords: Financial systems · Diffusion of innovation · Capital markets

1 Introduction

Capital markets signify an important component of the economy of any country. Economic research has shown that the performance of the capital markets is a direct indicator of a country's economic performance [1]. Further, these authors conclude that stock market development along with the banking sector development is robustly correlated with current and future rates of economic growth, capital accumulation and productivity improvements of a country. In addition, capital markets are a key source to raise capital for many firms ranging from medium to large scale organizations. A well-developed capital market may be able to offer different kinds of financial services to these organizations and may, therefore, provide a different kind of impetus to investment and growth compared to a developed banking system [2]. During the past few decades, a many-fold increase in market capitalization and market activity around the world was observed [3, 4], proving the importance of capital markets.

Owners of stocks in a capital market can either be individuals or institutions. As mentioned before, the individual participation in capital markets is a better indicator of the economic development in any country. Interesting results could be observed from a study conducted by a compilation across 70 countries to estimate the capital market participation as a proportion of the population [5]. These results show (Table 1) that there is a high diversity among countries and that the participation in developed countries is also at a relatively low level.

© Springer International Publishing Switzerland 2015
F.F.-H. Nah and C.-H. Tan (Eds.): HCIB 2015, LNCS 9191, pp. 655–666, 2015.
DOI: 10.1007/978-3-319-20895-4_61

Table 1. Country percentage of population participating in capital markets in several countries [5]

Country	Percentage of population participating in stock markets
Argentina	0.52
Australia	31.88
China	5.9
Ghana	1.5
India	2.00
Romania	0.05
Singapore	11.97
Spain	2.22
Sri Lanka	1.53
United States	21.2

Traditionally, a capital market operation is broker-centric and stock market floor is a centre of high activity with the process of placing orders. Individuals will have to place orders on the capital market through a stock market broker. But in the past few years, technology has evolved to a level where individual participants can directly place orders online, either using a computer or mobile devices rather than relying on stock brokers. Such online trading systems have enabled individuals to obtain real-time financial updates, other analytic services and to reduce time taken to place orders. Further and more importantly, the cost of placing orders has been reduced and the control of market participation is taken to the individual level [6]. These could be stated as the main goals of incorporation of such technology which have resulted in easy access to the public and higher participation among populations. However, the latter of the two has been least achieved in many countries as shown in Table 1.

A similar example to capital markets would be the traditional auction environments. The traditional auctioning setup was similar to in-person participation with an auctioneer in charge of the process. However, with the introduction of online auctions, many tend to purchase even common household items from such systems now. Further, it is stated that online auctions attracted billions of dollars over the past years with a 10 % monthly growth rate [7]. This shows that the innovation diffusion in this sector has been successful.

In contrast, it is evident that although many technological innovations have taken place in financial markets making the trading process simpler and easily accessible, the population penetration has been poorly achieved. The innovation diffusion in the sector has been hampered due to various reasons and that will be investigated in this study. As mentioned previously the degree of population penetration of online stock trading systems are very low. In this study, the adoption of such online stock trading systems is analyzed based on a modified diffusion of innovation (DOI) model with other suitable constructs. Hence the research questions of the study are as follows.

- RQ1: Are the DOI model constructs significant predictors of user adoption of online stock trading systems?
- RQ2: What other factors influence the user's adoption of online stock trading systems?

Considering the dearth of studies related to online stock market adoption with trust models, this study provides few contributions, namely, an extended conceptual model for online stock markets is introduced and the findings will be useful to the developers as well as to implementers in introducing these systems successfully. In subsequent, sections the theoretical background, conceptual model and data analysis will be presented elaborately.

2 Theoretical Background

Electronic commerce (e-commerce) is the process of "sharing of business information, maintaining business relationships, and conducting business transactions by means of telecommunications networks" [8]. Hence online stock trading too can be viewed as a form of e-commerce. Due to the popularity, adoption, innovation diffusion and various other concepts of e-commerce have been evaluated in detail in prior research. For example Internet Banking is a field of e-commerce which is subjected to in depth studies [9, 10]. Yet, the depth of studies with regard to online stock trading systems dealing with capital markets can be considered to be inadequate.

The innovation diffusion of information and communication technology with regard to stock brokering industry has been studied in the past [11]. In such a study it is said that the stock brokering firms openly adapt to new information and communication technologies in order to maintain competitiveness and to be responsive to market conditions. Further studies on broker decision on adoption and strategies to motivate brokers on online stock trading systems have been carried out in different country contexts [12, 13]. Although the main focus of this study is on retail investors in stock trading, the technological advances of brokers in facilitating the technology for stock traders should be noted.

On a perspective of the retail investor, few studies have been carried out in various country contexts to understand retail investor interest on adoption and intention to use the new technology [14, 15]. The studies are based mainly on the Technology Acceptance Model (TAM) and the decomposed Theory of Reasoned Action (TRA) and not on the view of adapting to new technologies.

Since much technological advancement has taken place in online stock trading platforms of retail investors, Diffusion of Innovation (DOI) presented by Rodgers (1995) is utilized in this study in order to understand the technological adoption by retail investors [16]. The DOI model has been popular among many information systems research in the past in studying new technology adoption [17]. In addition, due to the relation of online stock trading to e-commerce, factors from Technology Acceptance Model (TAM) and trust worthiness models are used for the analysis. Previous research has found that these models play a significant role in assessing the user acceptance in e-commerce applications [18–21]. However due to the complexities of online stock trading process in contrast to common e-commerce scenarios such as online retailing, internet banking etc. more attention will be paid to make the model context specific with in-depth analysis of the stock trading process. The framework and guidelines proposed by Hong et al. will be utilized to generate context specific information systems research [22]. Hence it is intended to come up with a relevant and parsimonious model using the models of Diffusion of Innovation, Technology Acceptance and web trust.

2.1 Diffusion of Innovation (DOI)

According to the Diffusion of Innovations (DOI) theory, an innovation is "an idea, practice, or object that is perceived as new by an individual or other units of adoption" [23]. Further, the process of innovation diffusion can be explained as the "process by which an innovation is communicated through certain channels over time among the members of a social system" [16]. Based on the model, the rate of diffusion of an innovation is dependent on the factors such as relative advantage, compatibility, complexity, trialability and observability. Based on the model,

- Relative advantage: the degree to which an innovation is perceived as better than the idea it supersedes.
- Compatibility: the degree to which an innovation is perceived as being consistent with the existing values, past experiences, and needs of potential adopters.
- Complexity: the degree to which an innovation is perceived as difficult to understand and use.
- Trialability: the degree to which an innovation may be experimented with on a limited basis.
- Observability: the degree to which the results of an innovation are visible to others.

Apart from complexity, while the other constructs are generally positively correlated with rate of adoption, complexity is generally negatively correlated with rate of adoption [16]. However, according to published literature, compatibility, complexity and relative advantage are the most important antecedents to the adoption of innovations in the information systems domain [24]. Yet in this study trialability is retained, as consultation with stock brokers insisted that experimentation on a limited bias is an important factor for adoption by retail investors and also that such systems commonly exist.

In addition, Moore and Benbasat (1991) present two further constructs; image and voluntariness of use which is beyond Rodgers' classification [25]. In this study it is stated that image as "the degree to which use of an innovation is perceived to enhance one's image or status in one's social system". Although originally it was argued that image is an aspect of relative advantage, research has shown that image can be considered to be adequately different from relative advantage [24]. Given the popularity of stock trading within the social systems, image is included in our analysis. However voluntariness of use is not considered as a separate construct since the usage of online stock trading systems is an individual choice and hence would not show a significant variation [17].

2.2   Technology Acceptance Model (TAM)

The Technology Acceptance Model (TAM) [26] is a widely used model to understand the user acceptance of technologies. Although TAM model was introduced in the organizational context to understand software technology acceptance by employees, it has been widely tested in scenarios where e-commerce adoption was tested which is very much similar to online stock trading adoption [18–21]. According to TAM model, perceived usefulness (PU) and perceived ease of use (PEOU) influence the individual attitude of using a system. This in turn drives the behavioral intention to use. However TAM also provides a suitable theoretical foundation on intention to use based on ease of use and usefulness of the innovation [26]. Further complexity construct of DOI is similar to the PEOU construct from TAM in reverse direction [17].

2.3   Trust

Trustworthiness of a system may impact system adoption. For example, it has been shown that trustworthiness plays a significant role of citizens adapting to e-governance systems [17]. The importance of trust in e-commerce applications is well illustrated in previous research [27]. The study develops measures of trust suited for e-commerce scenarios based on previous studies and concludes that trust has many dimensions. The study states that "e-commerce consumers gauge web vendors not in broad, sweeping terms, but in terms of specific attributes". Further the study states four constructs, where one construct is with regard to institution based trust. It is stated that "Institution-based trust comes from sociology, which deals with the structures (e.g., legal protections) that make an environment feel trustworthy". Similar to e-governance study [17], as online stock trading is dealing with confidential information and electronic financial transactions, trust will play a key role and trust placed on the internet and trading systems are considered in the model.

3   Research Model and Hypotheses

The integrated research model of diffusion of innovation characteristics, technology acceptance and trustworthiness constructs is shown in Fig. 1. The hypotheses developed based on the background and theory presented in the previous section is given below.

- HYPOTHESIS 1 (H1): Relative advantage has a positive effect on the intention to use an online stock trading system.
- HYPOTHESIS 2 (H2): Compatibility has a positive effect on the intention to use an online stock trading system.
- HYPOTHESIS 3 (H3): Trialability has a positive effect on the intention to use an online stock trading system.
- HYPOTHESIS 4 (H4): Image has a positive effect on the intention to use an online stock trading system.

- HYPOTHESIS 5 (H5): Perceived usefulness has a positive effect on the intention to use an online stock trading system.
- HYPOTHESIS 6 (H6): Ease of use has a positive effect on the intention to use an online stock trading system.
- HYPOTHESIS 7 (H7): Trust of internet has a positive effect on the intention to use an online stock trading system.
- HYPOTHESIS 8 (H8): Trust of trading systems has a positive effect on the intention to use an online stock trading system.

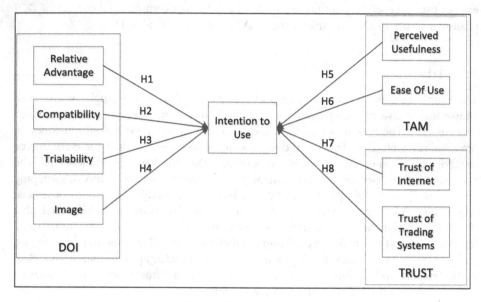

Fig. 1. Research model

4   Research Methodology

This study was carried out through a survey.[1] Sri Lanka was selected as the base country of study as the online stock trading penetration was reported to be at a very low level in Sri Lanka [5], although the country processed a stable and advanced stock trading platform [28, 29]. The survey questionnaires were distributed among employees at different levels of several organizations. However, the sample was selected such that the participants had prior investment experience and investment knowledge, without considering whether they have or have not invested in stock trading, engaged in online stock trading.

---

[1] The survey questionnaire is not attached to this paper due to the page limitations. Please contact authors should it be required.

4.1 Operationalization of Constructs

In order to develop survey instruments, previously validated scales were used. To measure innovation diffusion characteristics, items were adapted from Moore and Benbasat [23]. The scales for perceived usefulness and ease of use were adapted from Gefen and Straub [18]. Items for intention to use and items for trustworthiness on internet and stock trading systems were adapted from Carter and Belanger (2005) after modifying to suite the context [17].

A seven-point Likert scale ranging from 1 (strongly-disagree) to 7 (strongly-agree) was used in the questionnaire. Review of the survey questions were carried out with IS researchers prior to the actual survey, in order to validate the appropriateness of the questions. Further a separate pilot study was conducted among a sample of 30 suitable individuals in order to improve the validity and reliability of the instruments.

4.2 Data Collection

As mentioned previously individuals with background of investment were selected as samples for the survey study. In order to collect responses, online and paper based survey forms were used. Paper based survey was used for data collection carried out at organizations. However the participation of the survey was on a voluntary basis.

A total of 131 valid responses were collected. The sample had a range of 18 to 75 years of age (mean of 30.77 and standard deviation of 10.741). Other descriptive statistics are given in Table 2. As a general rule, in order to carry out a reliable survey the minimum number of responses has to be 10 times the number of constructs [30]. Since the study includes only 9 constructs, the sample size of 131 is adequate.

Table 2. Descriptive statistics of the sample

Sample Profile		Frequency	Percentage
Gender	Male	94	71.8 %
	Female	37	28.2 %
Investment Experience	Less than 1 year	24	18.3 %
	Less than 3 years	34	26.0 %
	Less than 5 years	24	18.3 %
	Less than 10 years	19	14.5 %
	More than 10 years	30	22.9 %
Stock market investment	Yes	66	50.4 %
	No	65	49.6 %
Use of online stock trading systems	Yes	44	33.6 %
	No	20	15.3 %
	Not applicable	67	51.1 %

5 Analysis and Results

The data analysis was carried out using partial least squares (PLS), a structural equation modelling technique with SmartPLS software package. PLS was selected to carry out the analysis as it enables to access the measurement model (relationship between items and constructs) within the context of the structural model (relationship among constructs) and also as it does not require large sample sizes of data [30]. Validity of the measurement instruments and results of hypothesis testing are presented below.

5.1 Instrument Validation

In order to demonstrate the construct validity, the convergent validity (the extent to which two or more items measured the same construct) and discriminant validity (degree to which items that measure different constructs differed) tests were carried out.

The convergent validity of the constructs was assessed using item reliability, composite reliability (CR) and average variance extracted (AVE). The generally accepted thresholds for item loading for constructs, CR and AVE are 0.5, 0.7 and 0.5 respectively [30]. The minimum item loading recorded was 0.81. The values of CR and AVE can be found in Table 3, where the values are within the accepted thresholds. Thus we concluded that the convergent validity is satisfactory.

The discriminant validity of constructs is satisfied if AVE for each construct is greater than its correlation with other constructs. This is shown in Table 3. Based on the results discriminant validity is also supported.

Table 3. Construct validity measures

	CT	IM	EU	PU	RA	TR	TRUST I	TRUST S	USEI	CR	AVE
CT	**0.93**									0.95	0.87
IM	0.25	**0.90**								0.93	0.82
EU	0.69	0.32	**0.88**							0.93	0.78
PU	0.72	0.25	0.75	**0.89**						0.94	0.79
RA	0.81	0.27	0.64	0.82	**0.90**					0.94	0.81
TR	0.39	0.22	0.36	0.49	0.49	**0.91**				0.91	0.84
TRUST I	0.48	0.25	0.45	0.42	0.44	0.15	**0.92**			0.94	0.84
TRUST S	0.62	0.23	0.62	0.57	0.58	0.23	0.71	**0.91**		0.95	0.83
USEI	0.82	0.19	0.73	0.82	0.82	0.4	0.53	0.64	**0.83**	0.91	0.69

Notes. Leading diagonal shows the squared root of AVE of each construct, CT = compatibility, IM = image, EU = ease of use, USEI = intention, PU = perceived usefulness, RA = relative advantage, TR = trialability, TRUST I = trust of internet, TRUST S = trust of trading systems

5.2 Hypotheses Testing

After validating the measurement model PLS was used to carry out the hypotheses testing. Demographic variables age and gender was used as control in the controls of the model.

Figure 2 shows the path coefficients of the significant results in the model. Relative advantage, compatibility, image, ease of use, perceived usefulness and trust of internet indicate a significant effect on the intention to use the model for analytics. However trialability and trust of trading systems doesn't indicate a significant relationship. In addition, the direction of relationship between image and intention to use is negative. Hence hypotheses H3, H4 and H8 are not supported. All the other significant relationships indicate a positive influence and as such H1, H2, H5, H6 and H7 are supported.

The explanatory power ($R2$) is 0.83 and it is above the threshold of 0.10 and hence is an indication of a substantive explanation power [30].

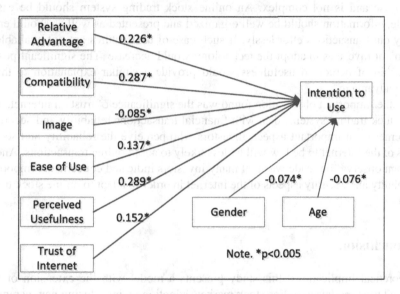

Fig. 2. Results of hypotheses testing

6 Discussion

Several important relationships were established from this study especially with DOI constructs relative advantage, compatibility and image being significant. It was found that relative advantage and compatibility are important factors affecting the intention to use online stock trading systems. Hence designers of online stock trading systems should design the system such that the online stock trading systems provide maximum advantage over traditional and other investment methods currently popular among investors. It is essential to explore all options that can be achieved from an online system. Further the significant positive relationship of compatibility shows that online stock trading systems should be designed for investors in such a form that they are compatible with their existing investment methods. For example for a stock market investor using traditional methods to place an order, the system should provide a compatible experience. An investor using other online investment systems would expect the online trading systems to be consistent with the existing systems.

However it was found that relationships between image and trialability were not as expected. It could be that since stock trading is a commonly found investment option for investors, use of an online trading platform will not result in added social status and image. In addition investors may not invest with the intention of improving their social status but merely to increase their income. Although experts in the industry viewed trialability as an important factor, since such a system provides only mock trading options and as it cannot be compared to a real transaction, the importance to investors may be low.

Significant positive relationship between ease of use and intention to use indicates that investor intention to use an online stock trading platform increase if the system is easy to use and is not complex. An online stock trading system should be easy to navigate, information should be well organized and presented as well as should enable to carry out transactions effortlessly. If such ease of use features are not available the intention of investors to adopt the technology would decrease. The significant positive relationship of perceived usefulness would provide a similar explanation to that of relative advantage.

Another important observation found was the significance of trust on internet. Since online stock trading systems deal with financial transactions reliability and security of the internet is an important aspect. Investors who perceive the reliability and security aspects of the internet to be low will be less likely to adopt online transactions. Another important observation made was that many investors indicated concerns on importance of reliability and security aspects of the internet in order to adapt to online stock trading systems.

7   Conclusion

As theoretical implications, this study presents a model with the extension of DOI, TAM and trust models to online stock markets adoption by introducing new parameters to consider. The study is carried out with a sample of investors with ample experience and knowledge on financial investments, as well as actual users of online stock trading systems from a country with low online stock trading penetration. Further, the sample was diverse in age, experience and financial ability. Hence the results of the study can be considered as highly valid in the context of online stock trading.

As practical contribution, we proved that relative advantage, compatibility, ease of use and trust are important constructs of online stock trading systems. The results can be used in the process of designing online stock trading systems in future leading to more user adoption of such systems.

Several limitations were encountered in carrying out this study. Firstly the limited sample size of 131 individuals should be pointed out as if a larger sample size was obtained, the results would have been more robust. In addition, during the study, no consideration was paid to mobility in accessing the online trading system and the study was conducted in general to all available online trading systems. Since mobile access of online stock trading systems would provide more interesting results, it is open for future research.

References

1. Levine, R., Zervos, S.: Stock market development and long-run growth. World Bank Econ. Rev. **10**(2), 323–339 (1996)
2. Arestis, P., Demetriades, P.: Financial development and economic growth: assessing the evidence. Econ. J. **107**(442), 783–799 (1997)
3. Demirgüç-Kunt, A., Levine, R.: Stock markets, corporate finance, and economic growth: an overview. World Bank Econ. Rev. **10**(2), 223–239 (1996)
4. Singh, A.: Financial liberalisation, stockmarkets and economic development. Econ. J. **107** (442), 771–782 (1997)
5. Grout, P.A., Megginson, W.L., Zalewska, A.: One Half-Billion Shareholders and Counting-Determinants of Individual Share Ownership Around the World. Available at SSRN 1364765 (2009)
6. Lee-Partridge, J.E., Ho, P.S.: A retail investor's perspective on the acceptance of internet stock trading. In: Proceedings of the 36th Annual Hawaii International Conference on System Sciences, 2003, p. 11. IEEE, Jan 2003
7. Lucking Reiley, D.: Auctions on the internet: what's being auctioned, and how? J. Industr. Econ. **48**(3), 227–252 (2000)
8. Zwass, V.: Electronic commerce: structures and issues. Int. J. Electron. Commer. **1**(1), 3–23 (1996)
9. Tan, M., Teo, T.S.: Factors influencing the adoption of Internet banking. J. AIS **1**(1es), 5 (2000)
10. Kolodinsky, J.M., Hogarth, J.M., Hilgert, M.A.: The adoption of electronic banking technologies by US consumers. Int. J. Bank Mark. **22**(4), 238–259 (2004)
11. Gharavi, H., Love, P.E., Cheng, E.W.: Information and communication technology in the stockbroking industry: an evolutionary approach to the diffusion of innovation. Ind. Manage. Data Syst. **104**(9), 756–765 (2004)
12. Huang, S.M., Hung, Y.C., Yen, D.C.: A study on decision factors in adopting an online stock trading system by brokers in Taiwan. Decis. Support Syst. **40**(2), 315–328 (2005)
13. Lau, A.S.: Strategies to motivate brokers adopting on-line trading in Hong Kong financial market. Rev. Pac. Basin Fin. Markets Policies **5**(04), 471–489 (2002)
14. Ramayah, T., Rouibah, K., Gopi, M., Rangel, G.J.: A decomposed theory of reasoned action to explain intention to use Internet stock trading among Malaysian investors. Comput. Hum. Behav. **25**(6), 1222–1230 (2009)
15. Lee, M.C.: Predicting and explaining the adoption of online trading: an empirical study in Taiwan. Decis. Support Syst. **47**(2), 133–142 (2009)
16. Rogers, E.: Diffusion of Innovations. The Free Press, New York (1995)
17. Carter, L., Bélanger, F.: The utilization of e-government services: citizen trust, innovation and acceptance factors*. Inf. Syst. J. **15**(1), 5–25 (2005)
18. Gefen, D., Straub, D.W.: The relative importance of perceived ease of use in IS adoption: a study of e-commerce adoption. J. Assoc. Inf. Syst. **1**(1), 8 (2000)

19. Moon, J.W., Kim, Y.G.: Extending the TAM for a World-Wide-Web context. Inf. Manage. **38**(4), 217–230 (2001)
20. Gefen, D., Karahanna, E., Straub, D.W.: Trust and TAM in online shopping: an integrated model. MIS Q. **27**(1), 51–90 (2003)
21. Pavlou, P.A.: Consumer acceptance of electronic commerce: integrating trust and risk with the technology acceptance model. Int. J. Electron. Commer. **7**(3), 101–134 (2003)
22. Hong, W., Chan, F.K., Thong, J.Y., Chasalow, L.C., Dhillon, G.: A framework and guidelines for context-specific theorizing in information systems research. Inf. Syst. Res. **25** (1), 111–136 (2013)
23. Rogers, E.M.: Diffusion of preventive innovations. Addict. Behav. **27**(6), 989–993 (2002)
24. Tornatzky, L.G., Klein, K.: Innovation characteristics and innovation adoption-implementation: a meta-analysis of findings. IEEE Trans. Eng. Manage. **EM-29** (1), 28–45 (1982)
25. Moore, G.C., Benbasat, I.: Development of an instrument to measure the perceptions of adopting an information technology innovation. Inf. Syst. Res. **2**(3), 192–222 (1991)
26. Davis, F.D.: Perceived usefulness, perceived ease of use, and user acceptance of information technology. MIS Q. **13**(3), 319–340 (1989)
27. McKnight, D.H., Choudhury, V., Kacmar, C.: Developing and validating trust measures for e-commerce: an integrative typology. Inf. Syst. Res. **13**(3), 334–359 (2002)
28. Gunasekarage, A., Pisedtasalasai, A., Power, D.M.: Macroeconomic influence on the stock market: evidence from an emerging market in South Asia. J. Emerg. Mark. Finance **3**(3), 285–304 (2004)
29. UPDATE 1-Sri Lanka stocks at fresh peak after doubling in 2009. http://in.reuters.com/article/2010/01/04/market-srilanka-idINSGE6030DU20100104?sp=true. Accessed 19 Feb 2015
30. Kankanhalli, A., Lee, O.K.D., Lim, K.H.: Knowledge reuse through electronic repositories: a study in the context of customer service support. Inf. Manage. **48**(2), 106–113 (2011)

A Critical Examination of the Causes of Failed IS Implementation: A Review of the Literature on Power and Culture

Hassan Aldarbesti[✉], Lazaros Goutas, and Juliana Sutanto

Department of Management, Technology and Economics,
ETH Zurich, Zürich, Switzerland
{ahassan, lgoutas, jsutanto}@ethz.ch

Abstract. As organizational life is becoming increasingly dependent on information systems (IS), proper IS implementation has become imperative. If it is not properly implemented, it may disrupt the organizations' daily operations and strategic decision-making, which can carry significant monetary consequences. Sometimes IS implementation is halted halfway, or at any stage of the implementation process, which may also carry significant monetary consequences to the organizations, especially when the size of the IS implementation projects is large. This paper focuses on the latter. Through our literature review, we discovered that it is the human aspect, instead of the technology aspect, that contributes to most of the failed IS implementations. To better understand how this could take place, our study highlights two possible reasons of failed IS implementation: (1) organizational culture complexity and (2) power and politics in the organization.

Keywords: IS implementation failure · Power · Politics · Organizational culture complexity

1 Introduction

Organizations invest heavily in technology projects in terms of money, manpower and time. IS guides the daily tasks of an organization and provides a competitive advantage. The study on IS implementation failure unearths the complexity in IS implementation, provides solutions and saves organizations the fear of investing in technology. IS implementation is arguably not a simple task as it initially seems. A survey of 5,400 large scale IS implementation projects (i.e., projects with the initial budgets greater than US$15 million) reported that 17 % of the projects were so bad that they threatened the very existence of the organizations [6]. The IS implementation projects may exceed the allocated budget, experience delays due to various reasons, or not deliver their expected value.

Most IS projects aim to improve or enhance an existing work process. The goals of technology projects are the visions that result from coordination and interaction of the actors involved. The actors include non-humans, for this case technology, and humans. This underscores the integral part that human behavior plays in the success of

© Springer International Publishing Switzerland 2015
F.F.-H. Nah and C.-H. Tan (Eds.): HCIB 2015, LNCS 9191, pp. 667–678, 2015.
DOI: 10.1007/978-3-319-20895-4_62

technology projects. Technology projects that do not take into account socio-technical factors such as diversity and plurality of actor groups, technology drift and interpretative flexibility result in miscalculations, costly delays and ultimately end up in failure [19, 28, 32]. Technical and social contingencies are of equal importance in the planning, formulation and implementation of technology projects.

There are inherent problems in IS implementation projects besides the technical problems encountered due to the diverse nature and culture of the employees and the management of the businesses for which they are being implemented. For a successful implementation, IS projects always require power realignments; understanding the impact of organizational culture, and a conducive environment within the organization [7, 44, 56].

The role of power in terms of IS failure has been highlighted in existing studies. In most cases, a wide gap between stakeholders' expectations enunciated in some ideal or standard project and its actual performance becomes the major cause of IS projects failure [36]. The stakeholders expect much more from the system whereas the actual outcome is far less than expected. Ultimately, the stakeholders are disappointed and the project fails. The failure of IS projects is also due to the vested interests of one or several groups of people called stakeholders. The interests originate from a personal, or a group advantage for controlling important material or organizational resources. These interests are symbolized in everyday situations through expectations expressing dynamic concerns of stakeholders with the IS projects [36, 44]. Various studies have been carried out to systematically identify the major factors associated to IS implementation failure.

Similarly, the role of culture has enjoyed a prominent role among instances of IS failure. The success of IS projects depend on the level to which values of subgroups of an organization merge with the values of embedded in the new technological innovation [28]. A mismatch between the values embedded in the process of software development and the values of the organization will lead to a complicated process of implementation. The IS systems are built with cultural assumptions in their process methodologies. If these cultural assumptions conflict with those of developers and users, the process of implementation will be increasingly difficult, thus leading to project failure [1, 14, 28].

Individuals with a culture of low uncertainty avoidance tend to have a lower perception of risks while those of high certainty avoidance culture have a high perception to risk [25]. Most technology projects involve high risks. The organizations involving people of low uncertainty avoidance culture venture into troubled technology projects with less opposition. Organization has participants of both low and high uncertainty avoidance cultures have complications in IS implementation since the participants with high uncertainty avoidance fear risks and opposes the projects.

The different occupational subcultures within an organization (e.g. those of engineers and operators) can impede the implementation of technology projects. The two groups hold entirely different cultural interpretations of technology projects that are proposed. Employees with individualistic cultures are more likely to report unfavorable news about troubled technology projects than those with collectivist cultures [37]. The technologies in such organizations experience conflict, leading to resistance to adopting and eventual failure. Overall, clashing values among institutional and organizational subcultures hinder collaboration and information sharing that is necessary for effective integration of technology such as development of component-based software. Such IS systems end up in a disaster.

The theory of values and culture in IS has for a long time been used to highlight the correlation between values and the ranges of social behavior. Studies on the adoption and diffusion of information technology in the organizations' subculture within the different groups found that these subgroups presented cultural differences, especially when it came to inception of the software component development and the methods to be applied [17]. These values did clash amongst the organizational subculture hindering the knowledge collaboration and flow necessary in integrating technology components and development of software efficiently [17, 28].

A number of studies have examined the link between IS project implementation failure and culture. The important role of social relations in project implementation and the group behavior has already been documented, as rich social relations can facilitate conflict resolution, increase interdependence among diverse group members and recognize the contribution of the minority [32, 58]. Shared ideologies have resulted to higher group cohesion, lower group conflicts, increased information exchange and greater commitment, thus leading to higher long-term group performance and IS project success [25, 59].

In sum, the effects of power, politics and culture appear to be important causes of IS failure. The main objective of the current study is to better understand how two main themes, namely (1) power and (2) culture can potentially impact the failure of IS projects. To this effect, we conducted an extensive literature review of the two topics. Our rationale was to identify the recent advances in these two streams of literature that can potentially shed additional light on the relationship between powers, culture and IS failure.

2 Literature Review

To serve the basis of our study, we conducted a literature review of published papers on power and culture until November 2014 from top-tier journals. In total, we reviewed 27 papers related to the organizational culture complexity literature, and 21 papers related to the literature on power and politics.

2.1 Organizational Culture Complexity (Theme 1)

As already discussed, the first stream of research on failed IS implementation has identified organizational culture complexity as a main reason for such negative outcomes. A substantial effort to discover cultural clashes prior to the implementation of an IS project is essential to avoid the project from being halted. Such clashes are extremely challenging to IS implementation success because it may remain undetected for an extended period of time [44]. Although an early detection can translate to fewer damages, it is unfortunately not possible to alter an organization culture [44] since culture is not constructed overnight. Towards this end, the newly planned IS has to match to the culture of an organization.

Lowry et al. [32] claimed that culture has a great effect on the technology supported decision-making group in the organizations and that in culturally homogenous groups, individualism is the factor which has a negative impact on the interpersonal trust on the information system technology. However, the excessive use of different virtual groups will help foster the trust of culturally diverse groups on the information technology systems [23].

Culture has an impact on the community manifestation as well as trust by the group when it comes to making decisions on technology grounds. Lowry et al. [32] conducted a study to understand the role of cognitive behavior in technology conceptualization. In their study, they realized that technology was likely to succeed once the culture attached to it is positive [32]. To understand the beliefs associated with information systems and technology in general, a study that was concluded by Koch et al. set out to find the implications of enabling social networking sites in a company since they happened to have certain implications on culture [26]. Culture has adverse effects that can lead to technology failure. However, if culture is designed in such a way that it fosters collaboration among the parties involved, it can boost their morale leading to technology development [48].

In our attempt to obtain a better understanding of the effects of organizational culture complexity on IS failure, we further scanned the recent literature on culture. Our literature review starts from June 2006, where Leidner and Kayworth [28] did an extensive literature review that examined most issues of each volume of the leading journals using IT culture and information systems keywords, dating back to the early 1990s. Leidner and Kayworth [28] categorized the studies by methodology across six themes: (1) culture and IS development, (2) culture, IS adoption, and diffusion, (3) culture, IS use, and outcomes, (4) culture, IS management, and strategy, (5) influence on culture, and (6) IS culture. In short, we tracked the related works that cite this study [28] and attempted to classify them under the prism of IS success/failure. In terms of the latter, we followed another group of scholars, namely Gordon and Gordon [15], who provide a framework that consists of four effective IS projects' success/failure stages: (1) Diagnosis (2) Evaluation, (3) Design, and (4) Implementation – the details will be described below.

Based on Leidner and Kayworth [28], Gordon and Gordon [15], and literature reviews from 2006 to November 2014, we have adopted the below four subthemes. And for our literature review, we examined 24 articles based on the roles of culture related to three levels: the national, organizational, and departmental levels of culture [28]. Of these, 16 articles are at the organizational level and 8 are at the national level. We did not identify any paper in the departmental level (Table 1). The structure of the table is based on the four stages of effective IS projects' success/failure developed by Gordon and Gordon [15], also referred to as subthemes. In short, these are the following:

Subtheme 0 – Diagnosis:

Diagnosis - Research; What other competitive companies are using; assess the situation and determine needs. The team will first assess an organization's need for information systems according to the existing situation facing it. The Diagnosis phase

requires a description of the existing problem, the context in which it occurs, opportunity, type of information available, the type of information required, and possible
ways of securing the required information. None of the papers that we reviewed were
classified under this subtheme.

Subtheme 1   Evaluation:

According to Gordon and Gordon [15], the evaluation phase has several steps:

1. Asses the current components of information technology and systems used to
   acquire, process, store, retrieve, or communicate information;
2. Compare these components to the available systems;
3. Determine what information needs are not or cannot be handled;
4. Examine and document any current initiatives currently being planned or implemented that involves IT resources.

We found that only two studies covered or examined the relationship between
culture and IS evaluation; both studies focused on organizational level of culture. It is
interesting for future research to assess this subtheme on the national level of culture in
the context of IS evaluation in multinational corporation.

Subtheme 2 – Design and Implementation:

The design phase includes correcting deficiencies in the existing systems or proposing new IS; integrate the state-of-the-art practices and technology into them and
involve making decisions about specific technology and their integration into the
existing IS.

This phase focuses on the issues associated with the implementation of the new
and/or altered systems. The focus is to answer the following question: how will the
implementation occur, what additional resources will be required for the IS implementation, what types of follow-up will occur, how will the changes affect other aspects
of an individual's or organization's functioning, what are the roles of different individuals (managers, IS staffs, specialists from outside the organization) for the IS
implementation, and how does the implementation timetable should look like [15, 28].
Six articles are related to this subtheme.

Subtheme 3: IS Use, Adoption, and Outcomes

16 of the studies fall into the subtheme of IS use, adoption and outcomes; nine at
the national level and nine at the organizational level of culture. Collectively, these
studies comprehensively examine the relationship between culture and the use of IS.

In sum, a number of studies have examined the link between technology project
implementation success/failure and culture since 2006. In any organization, the introduction of technology projects may be perceived as disruptive to the existing culture of
the organization and hence face opposition as people are more likely to resist changes
that make the users distress. As a result, it is necessary to better understand the concept
of culture, as it plays a very important role and can directly or indirectly influence
implementation of IT systems. However, defining, measuring, and understanding the
concept of culture remains a challenge [1, 26, 28, 58]. According to our literature
review, behaviors that result from introduction of information technology projects
define the success or failure of an IT project [58]. Social norms, which are part of the
organization culture, influence how members of the organization react to introduction of
IT and act as a means of social control by setting expectations and boundaries of

appropriate behaviors for members [55, 58]. Studies in culture and its effect on IT projects implementation were taken to another level when Kappos and Rivard [24] created a model that explains the relationships between culture and IS development. The authors identified three perspectives of the culture's modeling in information technology and their application; integration, differentiation, and fragmentation [24]. Culture has an impact on community manifestation, as well as on the degree of trust among group members when it comes to making decisions on technology initiatives. The role of cognitive behavior in technology conceptualization states that technology was likely to succeed once the culture attached to it is positive [32, 42, 58].

Table 1. Literature on organizational culture complexity and IS implementation

	Studies focusing on the national level of culture	Studies focusing on the organizational level of culture
Subtheme 1: IS evaluation	N/A	1. Bradley et al. [8]
		2. Hsu et al. [16]
Subtheme 2: IS design and implementation	1. Clemmensen [11]	1. Iivari and Huisman [18]
		2. Kappos and Rivard [24]
		3. Popovic et al. [39]
		4. Rai et al. [40]
		5. Schmiedel et al. [47]
Subtheme 3: IS use, adoption, and outcomes	1. Clemmensen [11]	1. Jackson [20]
	2. Im et al. [19]	2. Kappos and Rivard [24]
	3. Lowry et al. [32]	3. Koch et al. [26]
	4. Martinsons et al. [35]	4. Li and Mao [31]
	5. Sia et al. [49]	5. Ravishankar [41]
	6. Tan et al. [54]	6. Reinecke and Bernstein [42]
	7. Vance et al. [57]	7. Rizzuto et al. [43]
		8. Strong and Volkoff [53]
		9. Thomas and Bostrom [55]

2.2 Power and Politics (Theme 2)

A significant number of studies have provided evidence suggesting that failed IS implementation is due to the aspects of power and politics in the organization. Power is defined in terms of behavioral outcomes instead of the purposes or the professed legitimacy of the behaviors involved in power use [45]. Power has the potential to determine the success or failure of an IS implementation project. IS implementation projects have historically been halted through the misuse of power and politics. Power and politics complicate the process of implementing IS by constraining the process of constructing and setting up effective management models [3]. Power and politics in an organization may impact how the organization approaches the technology, recruit, and train project members, design the system, and support the project. Ironically, perhaps the existing IS in the organization nurtures the development of power in the organization since IS enable information to be disseminated in non-random ways, where some employees have better access to information compared to others [34]. To this end, failure of the IS implementation is essentially the embodiment of a recognized situation, instead of the actual failure of the system [3].

Our literature review starts from December 2002, where Jasperson et al [21] used the meta-triangulation method to explore the relationships between power and IS outcomes based on a sample of 82 articles from management and IS journals that were published between 1980 and 1999. We applied the framework of Jasperson et al. [21] to examine the literature in order to identify: (1) the casual structures between IS and organizational power based on Markus and Robey [33] 's concept, and, (2) the role of power and different IS outcomes based on Bradshaw-Camball and Murray's [9] concept.

We further classified the literature into three main IS disciplines: (1) the role and impact of IS when it comes to determining the most relevant decision-making to achieve competitive advantage, (2) IS development and deployment, and (3) IS use and implementation, which describes power and politics associated with IS management and implementation. Studies show that the conflict starts when IS staff acquire their power from their knowledge of and their access to technology, while the business users use their control of financial resources to guide the systems directions and implementation. The result is that everyone attempts to achieve some outcomes that favor their interests and/or increase their ownership of the resources.

In total, we examined 17 articles. Of these, 5 articles are related to the structure between IS and organizational power and 12 articles are related to role of power and (potential) IS outcomes. From the table, it is interesting to note the non-existent study that focuses on organization and management of IS resources to examine the role of power and potential IS outcomes although the two are closely related. This research gap should be investigated by future research (Table 2).

Our literature review revealed that power certainly has a strong influence on the failure/success of information technology projects. There are various perspectives of power and how they lead information systems implementation to success or failure; include; zero sum view of power, a processual view of power, an organizational view of power, and finally the social view of power [13, 21, 46].

A recent study was conducted to analyze how politics, power, norms, resistance and culture affect the implementation of an IT project by adopting Clegg's [10] framework of circuits of power, norms, resistance, power and cultural relationships to proof that implementation of IS often incurs problems and leads to failure due to of power relations and political games [10, 51]. Another empirical case study examined an IS project that lost its significance and finally failed due to political reasons and the practices that existed in the organization. The researchers adopted Michel Foucault's theoretical work on power, which states that every relationship is a power relationship. The existing power dynamics in the organization and the rationality in IS innovation greatly influenced how the interested parties judged the value of the new innovation. This in turn influenced their ability to corrupt or support the initiative [4, 12, 51]. A study by Attygalle et al. [3] explored the power and political aspects related to adoption of information systems. This study is in line with other works, which have concluded that power and politics complicate the process of implementing IS and may impact the ways in which an organization and its members approach technology, recruit and train members, design their systems and support projects [4, 45].

Table 2. Literature on power, politics, and IS implementation

	Studies focusing on the (potential) role and impact of IS	Studies focusing on IS development and deployment	Studies focusing on organization and management of IS resources
Subtheme 1: Structure between IS and organizational power	1. Silva et al. [51] 2. Xue et al. [61]	1. Dhillon [12] 2. Smith et al. [52]	1. Avgerou and McGrath [4]
Subtheme 2: Role of power and (potential) IS outcomes	1. Backhouse et al. [5] 2. Johnson and Cooper [22] 3. Silva and Fulk [50] 4. Williams and Karahanna [60]	1. Allen et al. [2] 2. Dhillon [12] 3. Doolin [13] 4. Lapointe and Rivard [27] 5. Levina [30] 6. Levina and Vaast [29] 7. Phang et al. [38] 8. Sabherwal and Gover [46]	N/A

3   Discussion and Future Research

Defining and measuring culture is one of the greatest challenges faced by researchers on the study of the relationship between information systems and culture. This can be attributed to that fact that it is difficult to decide what level of culture to study, as well as that fact that it is not possible to analyze culture objectively at a single level. There is therefore need for further research to unpack the levels of culture and identify the ones that are related to Information Technology. To have a conclusive and workable definition of culture in relation to information technology is a necessary point of study, so as to provide a formidable framework for the study of the IS phenomena [28]. Further studies should be focused towards identifying and creating a more realistic view of culture, so as to understand the individual simultaneously with the organization as well as other external factors, which have significant influence to functioning of the individual.

Other factors that influence the success of IT projects should be studied with bias towards IT related aspects such as the cost of the systems, complexity in use, interoperability among others, as those are some of the other factors which greatly impede project success. There is no data available on how such factors may influence organization culture as well as such affect the success of the projects. These are important areas where further research is need to provide answers to the many pending questions. The trend worldwide is that the uptake of information technology continues to increase despite the many challenges facing the sector. Providing the relevant data will thus help provide easy solutions so that projects can smoothly be integrated and Information Technology be integrated to organizations where they are required.

The previous studies concentrated on the influence of national and organizational cultures on the implementation of IS. However, offshore IS development practices are on the rise. Further research needs to be done on the influence of culture on culturally diverse, globally distributed software development teams. The future research should indicate how the values of these diverse team members contradict or complement each other in the process of IS development and implementation. It is important to indicate how such culturally diverse teams should reconcile their divergent value orientation and effectively develop and implement IS.

The research conducted on IS implementation and culture so far focuses on IS a construct rather than breaking it into the technology and informational aspects. This contradicts the study of culture on implementation. For example, the IS users of the uncertainty avoidance culture avoid technology for the fear of its cost. On the other hand, the culture may encourage them to seek more information for a deeper understanding. Future research should choose a categorically clear aspect of research on culture and IS, whether informational or technological.

One of the major gaps is related to diagnosis phase, where no studies dealt explicitly with the question of how culture and power influence IS initiatives during the Diagnosis phase (what other competitive companies are using; assess the situation and determine needs).

4   Conclusion

IS implementation projects often fail because of the vested interests of the stakeholders. If every stakeholder puts his/her personal interests on top of the common benefits, then the IS implementation projects are likely to be delayed, over-budget, or stopped. We posit that this seemingly common problem can be attributed to two factors: the organizational culture complexity, and the power and politics in the organization. Through systematic search and review of the literature, we classified the literature into different subthemes. It is important to note here that the two factors are by no means mutually exclusive. Instead, they are so much intertwined that the presence of any one of them may trigger the other.

To conclude, 'human-computer interaction' is indeed already present as early as in the initial planning of IS implementation. Right from the start, the decision to invest in a new IS is likely to be accompanied by cultural complexity and politics, which may be reflected through disagreement about the organizational goals and values, and the uncertainty about the means required to implement the IS. It is important for the organizations, especially the sponsors of the new IS, to be aware of these issues and prevent them from disturbing the successful implementation of IS projects.

References

1. Alavi, M., Kayworth, T., Leidner, D.: An empirical examination of the influence of organizational culture on knowledge management practices. J. Manage. Inf. Syst. **22**, 191–224 (2006)
2. Allen, D., Colligan, D., Finnie, A., Kern, T.: Trust, power and interorganizational information systems: the case of the electronic trading community TransLease. Inf. Syst. J. **10**, 21–40 (2000)
3. Attygalle, L., Hellens, L., Potter, L.: Information systems and intra-organisational power: exploring power and political aspects associated with the adoption of a knowledge sharing system in an IT services department. J. Inf. Inf. Technol. Organ. **5**, 1–23 (2012)
4. Avgerou, C., McGrath, K.: Power, rationality, and the art of living through socio-technical change. MIS Q. **31**, 293–315 (2007)
5. Backhouse, J., Hsu, C., Silva, L.: Circuits of power in creating de jure standards: shaping an international information systems security standard. MIS Q. **30**, 413–438 (2006)
6. Bloch, M., Blumberg, S., Laartz, J.: Delivering Large-Scale IT Projects on Time, on Budget, and on Value. Mckinsey & Company, New York City. From www.Mckinsey.com. Accessed Oct 31 2014
7. Boddy, D., Boonstra, A., Kennedy, G.: Managing Information Systems. Financial Times Prentice Hall, Harlow (2005)
8. Bradley, R., Pridmore, J., Byrd, T.: Information systems success in the context of different corporate cultural types: an empirical investigation. J. Manage. Inf. Syst. **23**, 267–294 (2006)
9. Bradshaw-Camball, P., Murray, V.: Illusions and other games: a trifocal view of organizational politics. Organ. Sci. **2**, 379–398 (1991)
10. Clegg, S.: Frameworks of Power. Sage Publications, London (1989)
11. Clemmensen, T.: Usability problem identification in culturally diverse settings. Inf. Syst. J. **22**, 151–175 (2011)
12. Dhillon, G.: Dimensions of power and IS implementation. Inf. Manage. **41**, 635–644 (2004)
13. Doolin, B.: Power and resistance in the implementation of a medical management information system. Inf. Syst. J. **14**, 343–362 (2004)
14. Dubé, L., Robey, D.: Software stories: three cultural perspectives on the organizational context of software development practices. Account. Manage. Inf. Technol. **9**, 223–259 (1999)
15. Gordon, S., Gordon, J.: Information Systems: A Management Approach. Wiley, New York (2004)
16. Hsu, C., Lee, J., Straub, D.: Institutional influences on information systems security innovations. Inf. Syst. Res. **23**, 918–939 (2012)
17. Huang, J., Newell, S., Galliers, R., Pan, S.-L.: Dangerous liaisons? Component-based development and organizational subcultures. IEEE Trans. Eng. Manage. **50**, 89–99 (2003)
18. Iivari, J., Huisman, M.: The relationship between organizational culture and the deployment of systems development methodologies. MIS Q. **31**, 35–58 (2007)

19. Im, I., Hong, S., Kang, M.: An international comparison of technology adoption. Inf. Manage. **48**, 1–8 (2011)
20. Jackson, S.: Organizational culture and information systems adoption: a three-perspective approach. Inf. Organ. **21**, 57–83 (2011)
21. Jeppesen, J., Carte, T., Saunders, C., Butler, B., Croes, H., Zheng, W.: Review: review and information technology research: a metatriangulation review. MIS Q. **26**, 397–459 (2002)
22. Johnson, N., Cooper, R.: Power and concession in computer-mediated negotiations: an examination of first offers. MIS Q. **33**, 147–170 (2009)
23. Kankanhalli, A., Tan, B., Wei, K.: Conflict and performance in global virtual teams. J. Manage. Inf. Syst. **23**, 237–274 (2007)
24. Kappos, A., Rivard, S.: A three-perspective model of culture, information systems, and their development and use. MIS Q. **32**, 601–634 (2008)
25. Keil, M., Tan, B.C.Y., Wei, K., Saarinen, T., Tuunainen, V., Wassenaar, A.: A cross cultural study on escalation of commitment behavior in software projects. MIS Q. **24**, 295–325 (2000)
26. Koch, H., Leidner, D., Gonzalez, E.: Digitally enabling social networks: resolving IT-culture conflict. Inf. Syst. J. **23**, 501–523 (2013)
27. Lapointe, L., Rivard, S.: A triple take on information system implementation. Organ. Sci. **18**, 89–107 (2007)
28. Leidner, D., Kayworth, T.: A review of culture in information systems research: toward a theory of information technology culture conflict. MIS Q. **30**, 357–399 (2006)
29. Levina, N., Vaast, E.: Innovating or doing as told? Status differences and overlapping boundaries in offshore collaboration. MIS Q. **32**, 307–332 (2008)
30. Levina, N.: Collaborating on multiparty information systems development projects: a collective reflection-in-action view. Inf. Syst. Res. **16**, 109–130 (2005)
31. Li, L., Mao, J.: The effect of CRM use on internal sales management control: an alternative mechanism to realize CRM benefits. Inf. Manage. **49**, 269–277 (2012)
32. Lowry, P., Zhang, D., Zhou, L., Fu, X.: Effects of culture, social presence, and group composition on trust in technology-supported decision-making groups. Inf. Syst. J. **20**, 297–315 (2010)
33. Markus, M., Robey, D.: Information technology and organizational change: causal structure in theory and research. Manage. Sci. **34**, 583–598 (1988)
34. Markus, M.: Power, politics, and MIS implementation. Commun. ACM **26**, 430–444 (1983)
35. Martinsons, M., Davison, R., Martinsons, V.: How culture influences IT-enabled organizational change and information systems. Commun. ACM. **52**, 118–123 (2009)
36. Mithas, S., Ramasubbu, N., Sambamurthy, V.: How information management capability influences firm performance systems. MIS Q. **52**, 118–123 (2011)
37. Peterson, D.K., Kim, C.: Perceptions on IS risks and failure types: a comparison of designers from the United States, Japan, and Korea. J. Glob. Inf. Manage. **11**, 19–38 (2003)
38. Phang, C., Kankanhalli, A., Ang, C.: Investigating organizational learning in eGovernment projects: a multi-theoretic approach. J. Strateg. Inf. Syst. **17**, 99–123 (2008)
39. Popovič, A., Hackney, R., Coelho, P., Jaklič, J.: Towards business intelligence systems success: Effects of maturity and culture on analytical decision making. Decis. Support Syst. **54**, 729–739 (2012)
40. Rai, A., Maruping, L., Venkatesh, V.: Offshore information systems project success: the role of social embeddedness and cultural characteristics. MIS Q. **33**, 617–641 (2009)
41. Ravishankar, M., Pan, S., Leidner, D.: Examining the strategic alignment and implementation success of a KMS: a subculture-based multilevel analysis. Inf. Syst. Res. **22**, 39–59 (2011)

42. Reinecke, K., Bernstein, A.: Knowing what a user likes: a design science approach to interfaces that automatically adapt to culture. MIS Q. **37**, 427–453 (2013)
43. Rizzuto, T., Schwarz, A., Schwarz, C.: Toward a deeper understanding of IT adoption: a multilevel analysis. Inf. Manage. **51**, 479–487 (2014)
44. Romm, T., Pliskin, N., Weber, Y., Lee, A.: Identifying organizational culture clash in MIS implementation. Inf. Manage. **21**, 99–109 (1991)
45. Rowlands, B.: Power and authority over systems professionals by the business client. In: Twenty Eighth International Conference on Information Systems. Montreal (2007)
46. Sabherwal, R., Grover, V.: A taxonomy of political processes in systems development. Inf. Syst. J. **20**, 419–447 (2009)
47. Schmiedel, T., vom Brocke, J., Recker, J.: Development and validation of an instrument to measure organizational cultures' support of business process management. Inf. Manage. **51**, 43–56 (2014)
48. Shang, S., Li, E., Wu, Y., Hou, O.: Understanding Web 2.0 service models: a knowledge-creating perspective. Inf. Manage. **48**, 178–184 (2011)
49. Sia, C., Lim, K., Leung, K., Lee, M., Huang, W.: Web strategies to promote internet shopping: is cultural-customization needed? MIS Q. **33**, 491–512 (2009)
50. Silva, L., Fulk, H.: From disruptions to struggles: theorizing power in ERP implementation projects. Inf. Organ. **22**, 227–251 (2012)
51. Silva, L.: Epistemological and theoretical challenges for studying power and politics in information systems. Inf. Syst. J. **17**, 165–183 (2007)
52. Smith, S., Winchester, D., Bunker, D., Jamieson, R.: Circuits of power: a study of mandated compliance to an information systems security de jure standard in a government organization. MIS Q. **34**, 463–486 (2010)
53. Strong, D., Volkoff, O.: Understanding organization-enterprise system fit: a path to theorizing the information technology artifact. MIS Q. **34**, 731–756 (2010)
54. Tan, C., Sutanto, J., Phang, C., Gasimov, A.: Using personal communication technologies for commercial communications: a cross-country investigation of email and SMS. Inf. Syst. Res. **25**(2), 307–327 (2014)
55. Thomas, D., Bostrom, R.: Building trust and cooperation through technology adaptation in virtual teams: empirical field evidence. EDPACS. **42**, 1–20 (2010)
56. Thong, J., Yap, C., Raman, K.: Top management support, external expertise and information systems implementation in small businesses. Inf. Syst. Res. **7**, 248–267 (1996)
57. Vance, A., Elie-Dit-Cosaque, C., Straub, D.: Examining trust in information technology artifacts: the effects of system quality and culture. J. Manage. Inf. Syst. **24**, 73–100 (2008)
58. Walsh, I.: A strategic path to study IT use through users' IT culture and IT needs: a mixed-method grounded theory. J. Strateg. Inf. Syst. **23**, 146–173 (2014)
59. Wei, K., Crowston, K., Li, N., Heckman, R.: Understanding group maintenance behavior in Free/Libre Open-Source software projects: the case of fire and gaim. Inf. Manage. **51**, 297–309 (2014)
60. Williams, C., Karahanna, E.: Explanation in the coordinating process: a critical realist case study of federated IT governance structures. MIS Q. **37**, 933–964 (2013)
61. Xue, Y., Liang, H., Boulton, W.: Information technology governance in information technology investment decision processes: the impact of investment characteristics, external environment, and internal context. MIS Q. **32**(67–96), 51 (2008)

HCI in Business: A Collaboration with Academia in IoT Privacy

Richard Chow[1(✉)], Serge Egelman[2], Raghudeep Kannavara[1],
Hosub Lee[3], Suyash Misra[3], and Edward Wang[4]

[1] Software and Services Group, Intel Corporation, Santa Clara, USA
{richard.chow, raghudeep.kannavara}@intel.com
[2] Electrical Engineering and Computer Sciences,
University of California, Berkeley, USA
egelman@cs.berkeley.edu
[3] Donald Bren School of Information and Computer Sciences,
University of California, Irvine, USA
{hosubl, suyashm}@uci.edu
[4] Electrical Engineering Department, University of Washington,
Seattle, WA, USA
ejaywang@uw.edu

Abstract. The Internet of Things (IoT) integrates communication capabilities into physical objects to create a ubiquitous and multi-modal network of information and computing resources. The promise and pervasiveness of IoT ecosystems has lured many companies, including Intel, to devote resources and engineers to participate in the future of IoT. This paper describes a joint effort from Intel and two collaborators from academia to address the problem of IoT privacy.

Keywords: Internet of things · Privacy · Notifications · Trust · Information disclosure · Design · User experience

1 Introduction

The Internet of Things (IoT) is the next great technology challenge that integrates communication capabilities into physical objects to create a ubiquitous and multi-modal network of information and computing resources. While IoT stands at the cusp of new technological possibilities, coupled with it are notions of tracking, surveillance, and concerns about personal privacy. This paper describes three cooperative but loosely coupled research efforts in the area of IoT privacy undertaken by Intel, UC Berkeley, and UC Irvine.

According to Weiser [11], *"The problem, while often couched in terms of privacy, is really one of control. If the computational system is invisible as well as extensive, it becomes hard to know what is controlling what, what is connected to what, where*

Edward Wang: work done while at Intel.

© Springer International Publishing Switzerland 2015
F.F.-H. Nah and C.-H. Tan (Eds.): HCIB 2015, LNCS 9191, pp. 679–687, 2015.
DOI: 10.1007/978-3-319-20895-4_63

information is flowing, how it is being used...and what are the consequences of any given action." Weiser is discussing ubiquitous computing over a decade ago, but he may as well have been talking about IoT today. In the first part of this paper, we describe research performed by Intel that focuses on this invisible nature of IoT. On our computers, we have at least a semblance of control because we can in principle determine what applications are running and what data they are collecting. For IoT, traditional methods of control are largely absent. Hence, we describe below communication mechanisms between the user and the IoT ecosystem that can inform the user of data collection practices (and perhaps offer the option to block these practices).

Even assuming user control and transparency of purpose and function of IoT devices in the environment, there remain thorny user interface issues. For example, when nearby devices are collecting personal data, under what conditions is the user notified? These could be devices in the environment, like street cameras or WiFi access points that track MAC addresses, or mobile devices belonging to others, like smart phones or wearables recording audio. Due to the expected density of IoT devices, communicating all privacy practices may result in notification fatigue. Privacy preferences vary widely among individuals [8], and data collection that may be worthy of notification for one person may be ignored by another. Also, since user privacy preferences are complex, it is a challenge for users to define them [7]. In the second part of this paper we describe research from UC Irvine which investigates user privacy preferences in IoT. (Figs. 1, 2 and 3).

While UC Irvine researchers are concentrating on the problem of when a user wants to be notified, the problem of how to notify a user is equally complex. As most IoT devices are "interface-less" entities that are meant to function unobtrusively, this posits a unique challenge to the design of the human-computer interface. We describe in the third part of this paper how UC Berkeley researchers have demonstrated the difficulty in relying on traditional IoT notification mechanisms such as LED lights and also how to make a modern IoT notification system more meaningful through a technique based on crowd-sourcing.

2 Intel: System Infrastructure

The Intel authors have been looking at some of the infrastructure problems related to IoT devices. Specifically, how to determine what IoT devices are nearby, how to get information on what data they are collecting, and how to deliver privacy notifications to the end user. For example, Alice has installed surveillance cameras in her home. She would like her guests to know about the surveillance cameras in case they feel uncomfortable about being captured on video.

We propose extending a system designed by the Auto-ID Center for RFID devices. The Auto-ID Center system, called Object Name Service (ONS), acts much like a Domain Name Service, except using Electronic Product Codes attached to devices instead of hostnames. For ONS, the focus is more on actual physical devices, but more relevant for privacy are the services running on the devices. Hence, we propose modifying ONS to provide a lookup for IoT software services. This lookup provides a communication mechanism to the user for presence of IoT devices and associated privacy notifications. We call the system Private.iot.

Basic Requirements.

- One Device, Many Services: Services may draw data from and control multiple devices, while an individual device may provide data to multiple services.
- Query Privacy: Queries made about individual IoT devices could result in a leak of a user's location. Here, the adversary is the operator of the lookup service, whose query logs might be examined by insiders or hackers.
- Transient Services: Many services will be statically installed. However, there is a class of services that is more transient. One prime example is a smartphone using a camera app. When the camera turns on, the phone becomes a sensor like any other device in the environment. This architecture aims to support these transient services in the same way as static ones, as long as the device is discoverable.

Private.iot relies on existing device discovery mechanisms. By definition, IoTs are physical "things" that are connected with each other, through the Internet or through other networks. To achieve this, the IoTs have to be able to discover and be discovered. For example, a *gateway* provides a portal for devices to access the internet through a central hub either through connecting via WiFi, Bluetooth, Zigbee, etc. A *beacon* actively broadcasts the device's presence and provides a point of access to gain information about the device and how to interface with it. A commercial example is the iBeacon from Apple, which employs BLE to broadcast a device UUID. Finally, a *tag* passively provides a device's information when being scanned. The barcode and QR codes are optically scanned while NFC and RFID tags are read by RF scanners.

Private.iot builds on top of the work of the Auto-ID Center. The Electronic Product Code(EPC) was designed by Auto-ID in 2003 and have since been maintained by GS1. The code consists, at a basic level, of a URI and a namespace identifier, up to 96 bits. The full specification of EPC is updated in the official EPC Tag Data Standard documentation [4]. The Auto-ID center is focusing specifically on RFID tagged objects by scanning for and using their EPC to perform a lookup on a name service (ONS) [9]. This name service acts much like a DNS for domain name resolving to an IP address. The result of the look up is a product description in the format of a physical markup language(PML). The strength in this lookup architecture is the flexibility and amount of information that can be retrieved through a simple DNS like query. The Physical Markup Language (PML) is a standardized format that is designed to describe physically manufactured objects such as manufacturer, expiration date, physical dimensions, and any other relevant information [1]. Over the last decade, additional categories to the descriptors have been added to accommodate more features provided by IoT.

System Description

Private.iot uses the ONS-PML architecture to serve privacy notifications that may be of concern to a user. The system can be broken into four components: (1) Device Discovery, (2) ONS, (3) PML, (4) Privacy Browser.

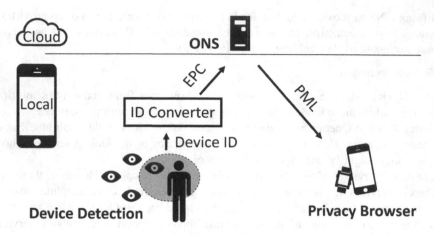

Fig. 1. ONS-PML architecture

(1) Device Discovery: Smartphones have become all-purpose communication protocol transceivers, including WiFi, Bluetooth, cellular, and NFC, all of which can be used to compose a list of device IDs that are in proximity. This is particularly true for beacons and tags. Note that devices connected through the gateway will not be discoverable directly through RF scanning. However, the gateway can control the discovery of devices connected to it. Because the proposed solution supports one-key-many-values, the gateway can register the services employed by the devices connected to it under its own device ID. In this way, the devices using gateways cannot be directly discovered but their services can. The final output from device discovery is a list of device IDs of devices around a person to be looked up in the ONS.

Different communication protocols present the issue that the lookup IDs are not all in the same format. In order to fit the current ONS infrastructure, the IDs can be reformatted to match the EPC format using a set of transformation functions done locally before the ONS query. This can be performed by constructing an EPC URI with the device ID type, device ID, and a namespace. This way, the ONS database schema will not have to be modified. To achieve this, a unique EPC is assigned to a device at the time of registration that encapsulates information about the device ID type, a device ID, and a corresponding namespace that matches the ID type broadcasted by the device (i.e. MAC, Bluetooth QPID). The device ID can then be extracted, assigned, and used by the device.

(2) Device-to-Service Lookup using ONS: A main goal of our system is to not modify the current ONS database. Given a device ID to EPC conversion, a user would be able to look up a device to retrieve a PML service description. One important criteria for the ONS lookup of this nature is the location privacy of the person querying. Unlike asking about a product, asking about a particular device could lead to exposing the location of the person. Fabian et al. describe various techniques to implement privacy preserving querying techniques for ONS [6]. The simplest is the adoption of a trusted server model where a server will purge the query data.

(3) Service Description using PML: The original ONS PML structure provided descriptions of objects belonging to physical categories. However, there have been additions to the original specifications over time as IoTs have become more capable. For example, objects that afford actuation have a "control" tag. In order to encapsulate services, we are proposing an additional tag category for services, which would include a privacy section. With this addition, the multiple service policies attached to a device can be captured in the following format:

```
<service>
<provider></provider>
<description></description>
<privacy>
<data raw="unprocessed sensor"
inference="processed sensor"/>
<notice>Human Readable Text</notice>
</privacy>
<optin></optin>
<optout></optout>
</service>
<service EPC="xxx.xxx...." />
```

Services may draw data from and control multiple devices, while an individual device may provide data to multiple services. In this way, the concept of a virtual EPC should still be applied for referencing services that is deployed on various devices.

(4) Privacy Browser: After fetching the service information from the PML, an application can extract the privacy policy and data types that are being collected by the service and present the notice to the user. Through this browser, the user can again discover services relevant to him and when he sees that there is a service doing something against his privacy preferences, he can walk away or potentially opt-in or out given the retrieved service hooks.

3 UC Irvine: User Reactions to IoT Scenarios

The UC Irvine authors are gauging people's attitudes, opinions and reactions to scenarios that involve IoT devices collecting potentially sensitive information. The specific goal of this project is to determine how the parameters of the scenarios influence participants' need for notification and control. In a pre-study, 10 participants were interviewed about 9 scenarios. These scenarios differed from each other in terms of the device that is tracking the information (parameter *who*), what information is being tracked (parameter *what*), the purpose of the tracking (parameter *reason*), and the place and time at which the tracking occurs (parameter *where* and *persistence*). Participants were asked whether they felt comfortable with the scenario, whether they wanted to be informed about it, and whether they wanted to control it. The main reasons to feel discomfort with the scenarios were disagreement with the purpose, or the belief that the purpose did not justify the tracking. The main reasons to feel comfortable were trust in the entity who collects the information (e.g. government), and/or that the purpose justified the tracking.

In a follow-up study, the researchers at UC Irvine more comprehensively tested scenarios with all possible combinations of parameters. This study is designed to more determine the relative importance of each scenario parameter, and explore the opportunity to learn users' preferences regarding notification and control. To this end, researchers recruited 200 participants through Amazon Mechanical Turk, and asked them seven questions related to their privacy preferences for a randomly generated scenario. Researchers assigned 14 scenarios to each participant, therefore they gathered 98 responses from a single participant and 19,600 responses in total. Statistical analysis on the dataset showed that *who* is the most significant scenario parameter influencing people's privacy preferences. To be specific, we calculated average responses for agreement to being monitored according to all individual scenario parameters, and confirmed that there is the largest difference between responses regarding the *who* and *what* scenario parameters. Relatively, *purpose*, *where* and *persistence* have less impact, in order of significance. The data also showed that most people (more than 50 %) think monitoring activities in an IoT environment is not comfortable, safe, or appropriate.

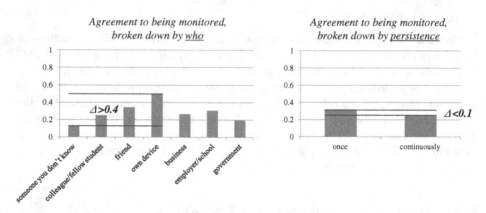

Fig. 2. Average responses of allow (1: allow, 0: not allow) for *who* and *persistence* scenario parameters.

To verify whether the *persistence* parameter is truly the most insignificant, we conducted an in-depth analysis using a matrix slicing technique. We constructed partial tables to study the conditional association between participants' binary responses (i.e., allow monitoring or not) and possible combinations of scenario parameters, conditional on the *persistence* parameter. For instance, we generated scenarios using combinations of the *who* and *what* parameters, and calculated the percentage difference between responses of allow according to whether the *persistence* parameter is true or not. The results showed that the *persistence* parameter has a noticeable influence on most of the responses in subspaces of the scenarios.

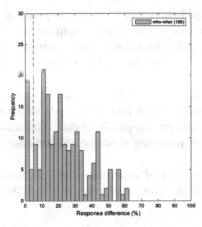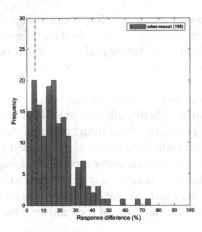

Fig. 3. Histogram of percentage differences between responses of allow for combinations of scenario parameters *who-what* and *what-reason*, conditional on the *persistence* parameter.

In summary, *who* and *what* scenario parameters affect people's privacy decisions globally, and the *persistence* parameter significantly interacts with subspaces of the scenarios, *who-what* and *what-reason* at least. In the future, we intend running additional live experiments to explore how people react to IoT notifications in realistic environments.

4   UC Berkeley: Communicating IoT Risks

IoT devices will capture a wide variety of data types, which will be accessible to numerous third-party applications. As a result, research is needed to understand the circumstances under which future users will want to be notified about an application's access to potentially-sensitive data. Providing too many notifications will lead to habituation, whereas providing too few notifications will lead to regret. Thus, in addition to studying *when* to notify, they are also examining *how* to notify.

As a precursor to designing privacy notifications for IoT devices, the UC Berkeley team studied an existing hardware privacy notification that has already been deployed for hundreds of millions of users: the webcam recording indicator. Popular media accounts suggest that many users fail to notice these indicators [2]. As a result, they performed a laboratory experiment to quantify this problem, as well as to uncover possible design improvements that could be applied to future privacy notifications [10]. They observed that fewer than half of their 98 participants noticed the indicators when performing computer-based tasks, and only 5 % noticed them when performing paper-based tasks within the computer's proximity. However, when redesigning the indicators to feature on-screen blinking glyphs, the rates at which participants noticed them increased to 93 % and 59 %, respectively.

As IoT devices become pervasive, they will need to communicate what data they are collecting (beyond raw video, as in the aforementioned experiments). We envision continuous sensing platforms employing trusted intermediaries to handle many of the sensing capabilities that third-party applications might require, similar to those described by D'Antoni et al. [3]. For instance, applications that use voice commands do not need to access recorded audio, which may contain identifiable information about the user or her surroundings. Instead, the trusted platform would process the audio so that only commands are shared with untrusted applications. One can imagine a plethora of system APIs that allow untrusted applications to benefit from audio and video input, while preventing them from collecting extraneous privacy-sensitive data. To facilitate this, users will need notifications, beyond simple recording indicators, to communicate the type of data an application is accessing.

The UC Berkeley researchers performed a series of experiments in collaborating with researchers at Intel to design these notifications for Intel's RealSense SDK [5], which performs some of the following functions:

- Age detection
- Emotion detection
- Gender detection
- Face detection (tracking)
- Face recognition
- Voice command
- Text to speech
- Language detection
- Gesture recognition
- Eye tracking
- Heart rate detection.

They conducted a series of experiments in order to create a set of intuitive icons that could be used to communicate to a user an application's use of these potentially sensitive functions. First, they described scenarios involving each of the above functions and asked participants to draw icons representing those functions, collecting a total of 240 pictograms. Through this process, they collected a wide variety of symbols representing each of the functions from participants of varying demographics and backgrounds. Next, multiple coders performed thematic analysis of the pictograms to determine the most prevalent themes. Based on the underlying themes, they iteratively created professional-looking icons and performed comprehension experiments. This iteratively improved set of icons is now going to be included in Intel's next RealSense SDK release.

5   Conclusion

The promise and pervasiveness of IoT ecosystems has lured many companies, including Intel, to devote resources and engineers to participate in the future of IoT. Privacy is part of the Internet of Things discussion because of the increased potential for sensitive data collection. This paper describes collaborative research undertaken in IoT privacy by Intel Corporation, UC Berkeley, and UC Irvine. We described some work by Intel on underlying communication protocols with an emphasis on enabling transparency with IoT devices. We saw how user studies by UC Irvine are determining which aspects of IoT are worrisome for end users. Finally, we described work by UC Berkeley researchers on the importance of the form of user notifications in IoT.

Acknowledgments. Work by UC Irvine supported by an Intel Software and Services Group Research Grant. Work by UC Berkeley supported by the Intel Science and Technology Center for Secure Computing (ISTC-SC).

References

1. Brock, D.L., Milne, T.P., Kang, Y.Y., Lewis, B.: The physical markup language core components: time and place. Auto-ID Center, Cambridge (2001)
2. Check Point Software Technologies Ltd: Are You Being Watched Through Your Webcam? http://www.zonealarm.com/blog/2013/10/are-you-being-watched-through-your-webcam/
3. D'Antoni, L., Dunn, A., Jana, S., Kohno, T., Livshits, B., Molnar, D., Moshchuk, A., Ofek, E., Roesner, F., Saponas, S., Veanes, M., Wang, H.J.: Operating system support for augmented reality applications. In: Proceedings of the 14th USENIX Conference on Hot Topics in Operating Systems, pp. 21–21 (2013)
4. EPC Tag Data Standard V1.9. GS1 (2014)
5. Egelman, S., Kannavara, R., Chow, R.: Is this thing on? Crowdsourcing privacy indicators for ubiquitous sensing platforms. In: Proceedings of the SIGCHI Conference on Human Factors in Computing Systems (2015)
6. Fabian, B.: Secure name services for the internet of things. Dissertation, Humboldt-University (2008)
7. Kelley, P.G., Cranor, L.F., Sadeh, N.: Privacy as part of the app decision-making process. In: Proceedings of the SIGCHI Conference on Human Factors in Computing Systems, pp. 3993–3402 (2013)
8. Knijnenburg, B.P., Kobsa, A., Jin, H.: Dimensionality of information disclosure behavior. Int. J. Hum. Comput. Stud. 71, 1144–1162 (2013)
9. Mealling, M.: Auto-ID object name service (ONS) 1.0. Auto-ID Center Working Draft 12 (2003)
10. Portnoff, R.S., Lee, L.N., Egelman, S., Mishra, P., Leung, D., Wagner, D.: Somebody's watching me? Assessing the effectiveness of webcam indicator lights. In: Proceedings of the SIGCHI Conference on Human Factors in Computing Systems (2015)
11. Weiser, M., Gold, R., Brown, J.S.: The origins of ubiquitous computing research at PARC in the late 1980s. IBM Syst. J. 38(4), 693–696 (1999)

The Smart Steering Wheel Cover Design: A Case Study of Industrial-Academic Collaboration in Human-Computer Interaction

Eleonora Ibragimova[1,2(✉)], Arnold Vermeeren[2], Peter Vink[2],
Nick Mueller[1], and Leanda Verboom[1]

[1] MOBGEN, Amsterdam, The Netherlands
{eleonora.ibragimova,nick,leanda.verboom}@mobgen.com
[2] Industrial Design Engineering,
Delft University of Technology, Delft, The Netherlands
{a.p.o.s.vermeeren,p.vink}@tudelft.nl,

Abstract. The transition to a knowledge-based economy has placed expertise and innovation rather than physical resources as the assets driving economic growth and international competitiveness [1]. The result is a relentless pursuit by businesses to innovate as a means to gain competitive advantage in their industry. However, with shorter product lifecycles, increasing product complexity and rising research and development costs, even large firms are struggling to develop new products on their own. Whereas there is a strong demand from businesses to obtain external research and development resources [2], academic institutions represent a large body of knowledge that often sees no practical implementations. This paper discusses the integration practices in new product development on the case study of The Smart Steering Wheel Cover design. A research team from Delft University of Technology collaborated with a mobile solution firm, MOBGEN, to design a system to enhance the safety and fuel-efficiency of drivers. Analyzing the risks and benefits, challenges and opportunities in industrial-academic collaborative projects, recommendations are presented on optimal collaborative practices in the field of human computer interaction.

Keywords: Industry-academia collaboration · Human-computer interaction · Automotive interfaces · Persuasive technologies · Internet of things

1 Introduction

The mobile industry has seen constant growth in the past decade. Mobile phones, especially smartphones, are now considered ubiquitous. In the majority of countries worldwide, personal handsets have become so well integrated in people's daily lives that they are found to be as essential when leaving home as keys and a wallet [3]. Added to this, the exponential advances in mobile computing power and the inclusion and accuracy of the sensors in these devices have broadened the potential use of smartphones. Such growth in the industry exposes mobile-oriented companies to a vast amount of opportunities along with challenges for these companies to keep up with the demand for innovation.

© Springer International Publishing Switzerland 2015
F.F.-H. Nah and C.-H. Tan (Eds.): HCIB 2015, LNCS 9191, pp. 688–698, 2015.
DOI: 10.1007/978-3-319-20895-4_64

Mobile innovations are the core business of MOBGEN, a leading mobile solutions specialist, headquartered in Amsterdam, the Netherlands [4]. MOBGEN leverages its expertise in the mobile space by extending its capabilities to disruptive technologies in various industries. MOBGEN:lab is the research division at MOBGEN, set up to investigate disruptive innovation with a focus on mobile technology and internet of things. The company's aim is to identify and map the trends across the design industry that will create changes in the way products and surroundings influence our behavior and performance. In these initiatives, MOBGEN:lab collaborates with universities to research and develop innovative products and services with the end-goal of creating enhanced user experiences.

The Smart Steering Wheel Cover Design project was an example of industry-academia collaboration, initiated by MOBGEN:lab in collaboration with the Faculty of Industrial Design Engineering (IDE), Delft University of Technology (TU Delft). With the research and development capabilities from Delft University of Technology [5] and the business-oriented designer mentality of MOBGEN we have the aim of designing interactive technology for drivers' safety and efficiency with the help of mobile solutions. Building on this case study, we analyze collaboration between academia and industry and its influence on the design project. The aim of the paper is to identify challenges and opportunities of such an approach to creating a product while providing practical recommendations for improvement.

The paper is organized as follows: In Sect. 2 we present previous literature on the topic of collaboration, and Sect. 3 describes the design process and approach implemented in the project. The design case study is introduced in Sect. 4 with results and evaluations. We present our reflections on the industrial-academic collaborations in Sect. 5 and conclude with Sect. 6.

2 Related Work

External research has played a critical role in firms' innovation process. The last two decades have seen a surge of collaborations between firms and its external partners. These external agents include sources as customers, suppliers, universities, research institutions, industry consortia, and even rival firms [6]. Particularly, a popular form of collaboration is the one between an industrial firm and an academic institution. While there are various reasons for firms to collaborate with universities, generally major motivations are access to complementary resources, speeding up of the process of innovation including market launch, and financial benefits [7]. As businesses want to capitalize on knowledge, obtaining the resources from academic partners is beneficial for processing their innovation. Accordingly, universities have their own interests in these collaborations, mainly consisting of intellectual capital sharing, knowledge dissemination, exposure to business problems and access to funding [8].

Current academic literature states that such complementary resources provide potential opportunities for the firms to explore new and different ideas about product design, concepts, and development, as well as to break away from previously specified rules and procedures [7]. This not only increases the efficiency, but also the effectiveness of the activities and tasks throughout the innovation process [6].

While these are significant benefits of such industrial-academic collaborations, these projects also face several challenges, such as:

Differences in the nature of projects. Academic research is focused on contribution to the community (process-oriented approach), whereas industrial firms base their research and development on achieving a product that can be capitalized (result-oriented approach) [8]. Literature suggests that academic research often does not directly translate into new products or services for industrial organizations [9].

Conflict of interests. Academics are concerned that too close a university-industry collaboration might affect their academic freedom and integrity [10]. University researchers prefer to choose their own research topics, which are often driven by what is perceived to be interesting and valuable in their field of work. Companies, however, prefer to research the fields that are trendy or profitable [11].

Knowledge Sharing. Academic success is often measured in the amount of publications [12]. University researchers often have to engage in 'status competitions' with their peers, based on publication records, institutional affiliations and prizes [8]. In contrast to the open nature of the science system, the knowledge creation process in the private sector is characterized by tendency to appropriate the economic value of firms' knowledge in order to gain competitive advantage [13]. Moreover, due to the high investment costs, unpatented innovation in asset-intensive, high-technological industries is kept under non-disclosure agreements [14].

Uncertainty of outcome. Particularly commercial companies have the pressure to deliver a certain viable product as a result of the project. With collaborative initiatives, there is a certain risk for them not to be able to do so, along with risks of possible spillovers [15].

The purpose of this paper is to analyze these and other challenges, along with benefits of industry-academia collaborations on the example of designing for automotive safety and efficiency.

3 Design Process

The design process of the project involved collaborative design, a process defined as co-operated efforts undertaken by multiple parties [16]. Co-creation was the main approach in the design process of this collaboration project. We define co-creation similar to Sanders and Stappers [17] to be the act of collective creativity of people working together in the product-service development process. The project team was comprised of a master program student, two academic supervisors from the IDE faculty of TU Delft, and an industry supervisor from MOBGEN. For the duration of the entire project, the student was stationed at MOBGEN for four days a week and a day a week at TU Delft. The complete team met once every two months for decision-making steps in the design process. Meetings with each of the supervisors were scheduled once every two weeks to report on the progress of the project. The project followed design process as illustrated below in Fig. 1 with multiple iterations within various phases.

ANALYSISSYNTHESIS

DEFINE	IDENTIFY	RESEARCH	INQUIRE	INVESTIGATE	NAVIGATE	IDEATE	DEVELOP	BUILD	EVALUATE	REFINE	FINALIZE
Understand where the problem comes from	Determine the target user and the context	Research the user and context, their needs and wants, and existing solutions	Create research questions based on what cannot be obtained through literature and needs to be investigated in the field	Conduct a field research with real users regarding their experiences, problems, needs and wants	Define the list of requirements the design needs to achieve	Brainstorm ideas together with stakeholders through participatory design methods	Generate solutions for design requirements and develop concepts holistically	Build prototypes and experiment various forms and contexts	Conduct usability testing. Verify with users all functions and properties	Modify the design according to user feedback. Make final adjustments	Deliver the final design to the client

START · ▶ ▶ END

Fig. 1. Detailed illustration of the design process of the current project

As suggested by Den Ouden and Valkenburg [18], as the first step of such collaborative innovation process it was important to define a suitable value proposition for future needs of the users. This step involved iterations of exploratory research observing and inquiring drivers to learn about problems and needs in their daily driving activities using contextmapping methods [19]. This process engaged participants from both the academic and industrial background, including colleagues at MOBGEN in either participating in context mapping sessions or inputting into the design of the research tools and materials.

The findings from the user research were translated into design goals that served as a basis for generating ideas and concepts. Both MOBGEN members and university partners participated in ideation sessions to generate concepts. This was to both ensure to get different perspectives on the topic, and to allow different stakeholders be involved in the design process. Creating value by enhancing experiences of all stakeholders and is proven to lead to higher productivity, creativity and lower costs and risks in the project [20]. Hence, this project's collaborative creative design process involved all stakeholders across the spectrum of the design process from concept generation to prototyping and embodiment. The ideation process went through various iterations until a concept that satisfied all the design criteria was developed. The final proof-of-concept prototype was created and evaluated to understand the effects of the design on the behavior of drivers.

4 The Case Study of an Industrial-Academic Collaboration

4.1 Design of the Smart Steering Wheel Cover

With increasing levels of traffic all around the world, more fuel is being consumed and more damage is caused to the environment. Commuters are spending increasing amounts of time in their vehicles as a result of the recent suburbanization process [21]. This results in an increased probability for road accidents, especially considering that 90 % of road traffic accidents is estimated to be caused by human factors [22]. These problems related to safety and fuel-efficiency of driving were recognized by

MOBGEN, who also saw an opportunity for enhancing driving experiences with the possibilities of mobile sensing and computing and internet of things.

The Smart Steering Wheel Cover was designed as a result of collaboration between MOBGEN and TU Delft and is an in-vehicle system to encourage safe and efficient driving using real-time feedback and customizable interface (Fig. 2). The system utilizes acceleration sensing technologies within the driver's smartphone to determine aggressive acceleration and braking behavior. The smoothness of the driving correlates with fuel saving, thus the less aggressive the driver's behavior is, the less fuel the vehicle consumes. Feedback is communicated to the driver in terms of vibration (as warning of poor behavior) and gradual change of light (as a reward to motivate continuous fuel-efficient behavior). Various kinds of in-vehicle tasks other than driving require a high level of hand-eye coordination, leading to an increase in driver distraction. Therefore, the design of the Smart Steering Wheel Cover incorporates tactile buttons that drivers can feel without having to look for controlling some of the most frequently accessed operations on their smartphones, such as (1) control of incoming and outgoing calls and (2) volume and control of a music application.

call controls

music controls

light feedback

haptic feedback

Fig. 2. The design of the smart steering wheel cover

The accompanying smartphone application records and summarizes the driver's journey in terms of driven distance, time, fuel efficiency and potential financial savings. The combination of The Smart Steering Wheel Cover with the post-analytics application is designed to offer positive reinforcement and influence on the driver's behavior to ensure safety and efficiency.

4.2   Evaluation of the Design

The design was evaluated with drivers, using a proof-of-concept prototype. The main objectives were to evaluate the characteristics of the design in the context of driving and the effects of ambient and haptic feedback on the driver's behavior. Results were analyzed to identify strong and weak points of the system and possible implications of each type of feedback on the drivers' behavior. Distinct groups, both comprised of members from TU Delft and MODOEN participated in devising the methodology, the user tests and the evaluation of the results. Both parties participated in analyzing the results, defining the benefits and challenges of the design, together with recommendations on improvements.

4.2.1   Methodology

A total of 10 drivers participated in the user tests with an age ranging from 25 to 49 and with at least two years of driving experience. The prototype mounted vibration motors and an LED-strip along the steering wheel cover. It included button straps as controls. Drivers were asked to drive for 20 min along a specified route and received feedback on their driving performance in the form of green light and vibrations. Their experiences were observed and interviewed after the drive.

4.2.2   Results

Iterative user testing of prototypes emphasized the proactive nature of the design to prevent poor driving as opposed to reacting to it. The gradual change of lights in terms of spatial arrangement and brightness worked in an engaging manner, forming an immediate connection between the driver's behavior and its effect on the steering wheel (Fig. 3). Users reported to be motivated to maintain the full green circle. All participants were observed to be more alert and with greater concentration when receiving the haptic feedback (Fig. 4). There was no universal hand placement position observed in the tests. Due to this diversity, we decided for controls to be fully customizable. Nevertheless, location of 2 and 10 o'clock on the wheel will be recommended, as researched to be the most natural position for thumb-controlled input areas [23] (Fig. 5).

4.2.3   Discussion

The team came together for discussing the results of the user validation and its implication on the design. TU Delft supported the analysis with theoretical information on automotive and persuasive technologies, along with knowledge on user behavior.

Fig. 3. The light feedback (color figure online)   **Fig. 4.** The haptic (vibration) feedback

MOBGEN, on the other hand, contributed in discussion with implications of mobile and peripheral technologies on the human behavior along with expertise on social and gamification components of the design. The user test showed that the real-time feedback of enlarging a green light area and increasing brightness was clearly understood as a reward for fuel-efficient driving, and the vibration feedback was interpreted as a warning. Our participants confirmed the need and preference towards the customizable controls to enhance their safety while being able to control their smartphones. Our work suggests that designing in-car persuasive technologies can help motivate drivers and contribute towards a safer and more efficient behavior. By adapting smart technologies in cars, we hope to encourage small changes in driving behavior in order to save on fuel efficiency and to decrease personal risk. Further research will include confirmation of long-term effects of the Smart Steering Wheel Cover on safety and fuel consumption.

5   Reflection on Industrial-Academic Collaboration

This project required an equally significant input from both the academic institution and the industry partner, as it deviated from the sole expertise of either party. With the complexity of the project involving challenges in information technology, human-computer interfacing, established vehicle driver behaviors and extensive user testing, the combined resources of both MOBGEN and TU Delft were required to achieve the end result.

TU Delft's goal in this project of designing the Smart Steering Wheel Cover involved enabling a positive educational experience for the student and enriching the research and product portfolio of the university. The industry partner, MOBGEN's goal in the project was to endorse the company's expertise in mobile solutions in the design of an innovative product. The project benefited from the collaboration of the research capabilities of the Industrial Design Engineering department of TU Delft, and the entrepreneurial acumen and IT expertise of MOBGEN. This complementary expertise and the two-way knowledge flows from both parties was the major benefit of this collaboration. Consequently, the availability of resources and facilities from both parties was an important factor influencing the outcome of the project. The thesis student bringing the two parties together played the role of a catalyst in the process, closely linked with both sides and ensuring smooth progress, efficient communication, minimal delays as a result to decision changes, coordination of efforts on either side, bringing together different groups to participate in the testing and evaluation project. The research community and prototyping facilities at TU Delft enabled the thesis student to receive assistance (in terms of both theoretical knowledge and practical skills) from faculty and staff at the university. Similarly, the mobile expertise of employees at MOBGEN helped in identifying the current trends, generating relevant ideas and utilizing the usability lab resources.

This and other benefits of the cooperation between TU Delft and MOBGEN were analyzed based on the industry-universities exchange framework by Balconi and Laboranti [24], and devised into the following framework of tangible and intangible information flow:

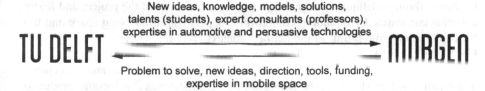

Fig. 5. Two-way knowledge exchange between the industrial and academic parties

Particularly, the following were identified as benefits for MOBGEN as an industrial partner:

- The fresh knowledge and ideas in the form of a thesis student from a university partner.
- Authenticated access to design tools, services and methodologies. This kind of collaboration facilitates a faster transfer of not only ideas, but also approaches and methodologies. Universities have a large database and knowledge of research tools, methodologies and approaches. During this project, the academic team introduced new methods for application within MOBGEN, such as ethnographic research, contextmapping and contextual inquiry. These methods, tools and approaches can benefit the company even in future projects.
- Improved focus on customers or users, such as better dissemination of findings about customers' or users' needs.
- Connections to qualified universities can create future opportunities for recruiting.
- Expertise in persuasive and automotive technologies in the form of professors.

In return, benefits of collaboration for TU Delft were:

- Exposure of students to the real-world problems and opportunity for them to become experts in their topics. The experience of conducting a project at a company gives the student an opportunity to learn about the business side of design projects and prepares them for their future careers, while expanding the research and product portfolio of TU Delft.
- MOBGEN's knowledge and expertise in the current trends in mobile space and information technologies provided necessary direction in the project.

However, such collaborations face challenges as were identified through literature earlier in the paper. As the purpose of this paper was to analyze the opportunities and challenges of such collaborative projects, we have addressed the identified challenges as follows:

Process-oriented vs. result-oriented nature of projects. Indeed, whereas the supervisors from TU Delft were interested in learning points of the design process and contribution to the research community, MOBGEN was interested in achieving results that had the highest potential to be implemented. Furthermore, due to the time pressure by the fast-changing industry and limited resources for research, MOBGEN was often inclined towards development of the first generated idea, whereas the educational background of the student was in favor of conducting thorough research and exploring various areas and directions to make the best idea selection. This challenge was overcome through defining a clear design process at the start of the project and finding a mutual consensus, by obtaining compromise of both sides: allowing space and time for exploration while fitting in the defined context and time restrictions.

Conflict of interests. The collaboration across different bodies of institutions did indeed mean that there were inevitable differences in the requirements and expectations of the partners. For TU Delft, the end-result of the project was a successful graduation of the student in the form of a thesis defense presentation and a proof-of-concept prototype, validating the function and experience of the concept by the use of prototypes and tests. However, MOBGEN as an industrial partner desired a result that is ready to go into a preliminary production phase. An important practice in this situation was to outline clear requirements and align each other's expectations at the beginning of the project for the collaboration to be mutually beneficial and successful.

Knowledge sharing. Both TU Delft and MOBGEN shared the common interest in sharing the obtained knowledge in terms of publication, which resulted in this conference paper. In fact, a considerable number of firms publish academic and technical papers to signal their competencies or to defend against others' attempts to control particular areas of technology [25]. Similarly, MOBGEN recognized the opportunity to publish results of their R&D to expose its work to the academic audience, which could potentially result in further collaborative projects with academic bodies.

Uncertainty of outcome. To face this challenge, various milestones were set and conducted at different stages of the project. The presentations of current findings at each of the milestones kept all parties updated with the progress and upcoming work, and decreased the uncertainty of outcome. As was recognized in the literature [15], breadth of interactions between parties helped to ease the barriers to collaboration.

As a general approach to overcome the challenges, we have found that consistent involvement of stakeholders in all decision making phases in the design process and keeping the process transparent proved to be important in achieving consensus on the design and the project results. These findings hope to contribute to the HCI community in conducting such projects of integration practices in new product and service development. The presented design process is assumed to be applicable as a framework for fellow researchers in other projects with similar nature.

6   Conclusions

In this paper we identified challenges and opportunities of the collaborative approach to creating the Smart Steering Wheel Cover. We have faced all four challenges (nature of projects, conflict of interest, uncertainty of outcome and knowledge sharing) that were identified in this paper, during this project. However we have learned that by identifying these challenges during the early stage of the project most of them can be overcome. To do so, all parties should align expectations early in the process and create clearly defined, mutually agreed objectives and a clear design approach at the start of the project. In addition, we recommend ensuring there is adequate room for flexibility within the process in order to be able to react to changes, but with a high level of importance placed on keeping all parties updated in order to achieve consensus on the design and the project results. Communication between all parties is the key to overcoming these challenges.

TU Delft and MOBGEN shared the common interest in obtaining knowledge and sharing that knowledge by publishing the results. Furthermore, this collaboration provided MOBGEN with the opportunity to explore new ideas about design. The ideation sessions not only resulted in different perspectives on the topic, but also helped MOBGEN employees to break away from previously specified workflows and procedures, creating both a motivating and stimulating environment. The complexity and the open character of the project involved technological challenges as well as challenges in human-computer interfacing that contributed to the self-development of all involved parties, taking mobile user experience to another level.

The industrial-academic collaboration provided a significant mutual advantage in design projects for both parties to benefit from complementary expertise and two-way knowledge flow in achieving successful results. Considering our work suggests that designing in-car persuasive technologies can help motivate drivers and contribute towards a safer and more efficient behavior, it is of interest to MOBGEN to further develop the current product, and to continue further research in collaboration with TU Delft. A longitudinal study will investigate whether there is a behavior change on safety and fuel consumption as a result of the use of the Smart Steering Wheel Cover. Additionally, it will be investigated whether positive reinforcement, or a social component, provided by the mobile application would strengthen the influence of the Smart Steering Wheel Cover on the users driving behavior.

The synergy between the automotive and persuasive technology expertise from TU Delft and mobile expertise on the side of MOBGEN made this project a success, with the result being a working prototype of the Smart Steering Wheel Cover that was successfully tested by potential end-users. Such success would not have been accomplished by either of the parties working independently.

References

1. Yarime, M., Trencher, G., Mino, T., Scholz, R.W., Olsson, L., van Ness, B.: Establishing sustainability science in higher education institutions: towards an integration of academic development, institutionalization, and stakeholder collaborations. Sustain. Sci. Policy Pract. **7**, 101–113 (2012)
2. Hagedoorn, J., Duysters, G.: External sources of innovative capabilities: the preferences for strategic alliances or mergers and acquisitions. J. Manag. Stud. **39**, 167–188 (2002)
3. Arase, Y., Ren, F., Xie, X.: User activity understanding from mobile phone sensors. In: Ubicomp 2010, pp. 391–392. ACM Press, New York (2010)
4. MOBGEN. http://mobgen.com
5. Industrial Design Engineering. http://www.io.tudelft.nl
6. Chesbrough, H.: Open Innovation: The New Imperative for Creating and Profiting from Technology. Harvard Business School Press, Boston (2003)
7. Das, T.K., Teng, B.S.: A resource-based theory of strategic alliances. J. Manag. **26**(1), 31–61 (2000)

8. Bruneel, J., D'Este, P., Salter, A.: Investigating the factors that diminish the barriers to university-industry collaboration. Res. Policy **39**, 858–868 (2010)
9. Pavitt, K.L.R.: Public policies to support basic research: what can the rest of the world learn from US theory and practice? (And what they should not learn). Ind. Corp. Change **10**, 761–779 (2001)
10. Bok, D.: Universities and the Future of America. Duke University Press, Durham (1990)
11. Nelson, R.R.: The market economy, and the scientific commons. Res. Policy **33**, 455–471 (2004)
12. Lee, Y.S.: 'Technology transfer' and the research university: a search for the boundaries of university-industry collaboration. Res. Policy **25**, 843–863 (1996)
13. Teece, D.: Profiting from technological innovation: implications for integration collaboration, licensing and public policy. Res. Policy **15**, 285–305 (1986)
14. Chiaroni, D., Chiesa, V., Frattini, F.: Unraveling the process from closed to open innovating: evidence from mature, asset-intensive industries. J. R&D Manag. **40**, 222–245 (2010)
15. Brandtner, P., Auinger, A., Helfert, M.: Principles of human computer interaction in crowdsourcing to foster motivation in the context of open innovation. In: HCII, ACM Press, New York (2014)
16. Wang, L., Shen, W., Xie, H., Neelamkavil, J., Pardsani, A.: Collaborative conceptual design: state of art and future trends. Comput. Aided Des. **34**, 981–996 (2002)
17. Sanders, E., Stappers, P.J.: Co-creation and the new landscapes of design. Co-Design **4**, 5–18 (2008)
18. Den Ouden, E., Valkenburg, R.: Balancing value in networked social innovation. In: Buur, J. (ed.) Participatory Innovation Conference (2011)
19. Sleeswijk Visser, F.S., Stappers, P.J., Lugt, R.V.D.: Contextmapping: experiences from practice. J. CoCreation Des. Arts **1**, 1–30 (2005)
20. Ramaswamy, V., Gouillart, F.: Building the co-creative enterprise. Harvard Bus. Rev. **88**, 100–109 (2010)
21. Hogan, D.J., Ojima, R.: Urban sprawl: a challenge for sustainability. In: Martine, G., et al. (eds.) The New Global Frontier: Urbanization, Poverty and Environment in the 21st Century, pp. 203–216. Earthscan, London (2008)
22. Lewin, I.: Driver training: a perceptual-motor skill approach. J. Ergon. **25**, 917–924 (1982)
23. Hirotaka, N.: Reassessing current cell phone designs: using thumb input effectively. In: CHI 2013, ACM Press, New York (2013)
24. Balconi, M., Laboranti, A.: University–industry interactions in applied research: the case of microelectronics. Res. Policy **35**, 1616–1630 (2006)
25. Hicks, D.: Published papers, tacit competencies and corporate management of the public/private character of knowledge. Ind. Corp. Change **4**, 401–424 (1995)

A Literature Review for Open Source Software Studies

Qiqi Jiang[1], Jianjun Qin[2(✉)], and Lele Kang[3]

[1] School of Economics and Management, Tongji University, Shanghai, China
jiangqq@tongji.edu.cn
[2] Shanghai Institute of Disaster Prevention and Relief, Tongji University,
Shanghai, China
lelekangnju@gmail.com
[3] Department of Information Systems, City University of Hong Kong,
Hong Kong, Hong Kong SAR

Abstract. In this work, we provided a comprehensive literature review of prior studies about OSS (open source software). In particular, we categorized those articles into three streams based on their research topics. In addition, the assessments of OSS success are also summarized. The future agenda and potential research gap are given in the end of the article.

Keywords: Open source software · Literature review · Assessment of OSS success

1 Introduction

Open source software (hereinafter OSS) is a user-driven, collaborative innovation produced by self-organizing teams of contributors dynamically formed through online interactions [1]. With the emergent development in the last decades, the OSS has become an important phenomenon in both economics and culture. Increasing number of IT giants has realized the value of OSS and created their own platforms for hosting the OSS projects. For instances, Google established Google Code on 2005 for providing fundamental tools for OSS developers to share their projects to the public; Microsoft subsequently set up the CodePlex for allowing the engineers and computer scientists to share their ideas and OSS projects although Microsoft used to strongly disagree the OSS campaigns [2].

Various benefits can be found with the emergence of OSS. We think three key benefits are predominantly important. First, OSS software can dramatically reduce the cost of development for IT company. Such cost does not only include the development cost but the innovation cost as well. The outstanding software received the effort and contribution from the talented developments throughout the world. Second, the OSS can facilitate the organizations to implement the information technology systems into their business process, especially for those small medium enterprise (hereinafter SMEs) or public institutes. There is no doubt that the IT can make the business better. However, due to the cost of IT implementations, the SMEs or public institutes may not implement the IT system due to their limited budget. Introducing the OSS systems can

© Springer International Publishing Switzerland 2015
F.F.-H. Nah and C.-H. Tan (Eds.): HCIB 2015, LNCS 9191, pp. 699–707, 2015.
DOI: 10.1007/978-3-319-20895-4_65

mitigate such dilemma. Last but not least, the information and knowledge can be diffused in terms of participating in OSS projects, which is beneficial for those people who want to have a good command of programming language since they can learn via practice.

To this end, great studies have been made to understand the OSS predominantly, with a focus on viewing OSS project as an organization for technological innovation. These investigations include the investigation of motivation to participate in the OSS development [3–6], the role of social network in promoting the OSS performance [7–10, 27], the governance and management of an OSS project [11, 12], and the influence of policy and legalization on OSS [13–15]. In addition, various measurements have been employed to assess to the extent the OSS success, such as number of downloads, frequency of CVS commits, extent of code reuse etc. Thus, it is imperative to provide a comprehensive extent of literature reviews on OSS studies. In this article, we surveyed the most representative OSS studies and summarized them into three streams based on their research topics. In addition, the assessments of OSS success are also summarized with their pros and cons. The future agenda and potential research gap are given in the end of the article.

2 Prior OSS Studies

In this section, a comprehensive extent of literature reviews is conducted. Based on the reviews, three subsections are listed by the research topics of prior OSS studies. In particular, the first stream includes the literatures studying the individual motivations to contribute or participate in the OSS projects. The second stream summarized the literatures discussing how the network characteristics influenced the OSS performances. In the third stream, we reviewed how the legalization, especially the OSS licenses, influences the OSS performances.

2.1 Individual Motivations

Thousands of individuals participate in OSS projects for diverse purposes. Their contributed product will be released to the public for free usage. Why are they willing to contribute to such OSS projects since their no economic returns from their contributed projects? What are their motivations? After surveying prior literatures, we found two key motivations, which can be concluded as intrinsic motivations and extrinsic motivations.

Intrinsic Motivation. The intrinsic motivations have been studied since 1970s. It is driven by an interest or enjoyment in the task itself and exists within the individual instead of depending on external pressure or desire for incentive reward [16]. The intrinsic motivation was widely regarded as a key motives for individuals to participate in the OSS projects. Previous literatures found more than half developers indicated that the enjoyment in programming and the sense of satisfaction originated form the participation in OSS software constantly motivate them to sustainably contribute to OSS projects. Besides the sense of enjoyment and satisfaction, Lakhani and Wolf [17] found the several individuals could show their creativity and new ideas in terms of implementing them into the OSS projects, which conferred great sense of accomplishment for them. Such sense was believed as another key motivation for constantly contribution. Although the intrinsic motivations were found as the original motives for breeding the OSS campaign, however, Roberts et al. [5] thought the intrinsic motivations had several defects, such as short effectiveness and strong self-direction, which might challenge the sustainability of OSS projects in future. Thus, it is imperative to unveil the extrinsic motivations for OSS participants.

Extrinsic Motivation. Extrinsic motivation denotes performing an activity is built upon the desired outcome like momentary incentives, reputations, and profits etc., which is the opposite of intrinsic motivation [16]. In other words, with the disappearance of external incentives, then the extrinsic motivations will decrease or even disappear. Von Krogh and his collaborators [18] investigated a large OSS project and interviewed several participants and summarized that the participation was built upon the pursuit of communal resources, which includes reputations, control of technology, and learning opportunities. The first dimension of extrinsic motivation is the acquisition of reputation. The reputation can be obtained in terms of (1) actively participating in the OSS projects, (2) providing solutions to the existing bugs or problems, (3) providing innovative revision or modification to the current OSS. With the increase of reputation, the participants will be conferred with higher authority, which will eventually enable him or her to dominate the entire project, such as the recruitment of developers or the decision power in the project management. To this end, the reputation in the OSS community is widely regarded as an extreme important extrinsic motivation for encouraging OSS developers to constantly contribute to OSS project. The second acquired communal resource is the "control over technology". Such extrinsic motivation is formalized from the demand of self-usage. It is found that the key reason to participating in OSS project is to customize such project for own usage [3]. Although the novel and creative ideas can be realized through OSS project, however, the overall quality of OSS project cannot reach the industrial standard due to the relaxed management system and software testing procedures. Thus, those experienced users may compile their revised OSS and incidentally update it. In terms of long-term investment, those users may have a good command of this technology, which would benefit them in the future. The third communal resource is the learning opportunities. The participants of OSS project do not only include those experienced developers but those users or fresh programmers. By joining in OSS project, these people were provided a very good opportunity to learn (1) programming by collaborating with talented programmers in the world, and (2) knowledge about project management in software engineering as well. Besides these three key extrinsic motivations, prior literatures also identified several other extrinsic factors motivating individuals to contribute to the OSS project such as sense of reciprocity and job opportunities. Sense of reciprocity is prevailing in the OSS user support community, in which those end-users proactively respond or answer other's questions in order to obtain the helps from others when they need in the future. In addition, prior literatures [19, 20] found some IT companies might recruit some talented programmers from the OSS community, which encourage some participants to diligently work on their contributed OSS projects.

Besides the explanation from motivation theory, several studies found institutional management or leadership also affected individual motivations. For instances, by interviewing the developers from Debian project, O'Mahony and Ferraro [12] found the democratic management style outperformed the bureaucratic one thought the later was found to be efficient. In addition, Li and her collaborators [11] found individuals preferred to join those OSS project which were employed the transformational leadership style. In other words, such leadership style signals that everyone could be conferred as a project leader in the future.

2.2 Network Characteristics

In second stream, prior studies investigated how network structures affected the OSS performances [7–10, 27]. The development of OSS project cannot be done without the collective actions. In this regard, prior literatures employed the social network analysis to articulate such collective actions, i.e. collaborative behaviors, which include inter-project individual-individual collaborative networks [7], project-affiliated networks [8, 9, 27], and intra-project communication or collaborative networks [10] etc. Thus, the social capital theory was mostly adopted as a theoretical underpinning to explicate such social relationships.

2.2.1 Inter-project Network

Due to the open nature of the OSS projects, the participants can freely contribute to multiple projects. In terms of such shared participants or concurrently contributed projects, two types of affiliated networks can be initialized. The first one is call project-affiliated network, in which the projects with shared participants are interconnected. The second one is called participant-affiliated network, in which the developers/project administrators who contributed to same projects are interconnected. Prior studies found the characteristics of participant-affiliated network, such as network distances or network density, had significant impact on the OSS performance [21]. After five-year observation on more than 2000 OSS projects hosted in Sourceforge.net, Singh and his collaborators [27] found internal collaborative cohesion had significantly positive impact on the OSS performances, manifested by the extent of CVS commits, but the external cohesion presented an inverted-U impact on the OSS performances. Hahn et al. [8] found the OSS developers preferred to join in those projects initialized by those who had collaborated before in terms of investigating the collaborative ties. Grewal et al. [7] argued the OSS performances was significantly influenced by the extent of network embeddedness in terms of studying the developer-affiliated network.

2.2.2   Intra-project Network

Besides the inter-project network, prior studies also found that the intra-project network also played a role on OSS performances [22]. Differing from the works studying OSS performances, the intra-project studies mainly discussed the individual collective behaviors. For instances, Conaldi et al. [10] established an analytical model for collaborative network and empirically verified it by using the debugging network from a large OSS project. Sowe et al. [23] categorized the participants from Debian (a leading Linux OS distributor) into three key roles, which included knowledge seekers, knowledge contributors, and knowledge brokers in terms of analyzing the emailing communication network, and argued that the knowledge brokers could facilitate the information flow and distribution. By studying the internal communication networks of two leading OSS projects, Singh and Tan [24] found the stability and efficiency cannot be concurrently reached, and advocated the OSS project administrators had to adjust the balance based on their key goals.

In sum, we can find the literatures on inter-project network mainly discussed how OSS projects could be outperformed in terms of network ties or vertex positions. The intra-project network studies mainly concentrated on particular behaviors or actions in OSS project development, such as debugging, communications, or collaborations. A brief summarization is given in Table 1.

2.3   Policy and Legalization

Comparing with the works studying individual motivations or network characteristics influencing the success of OSS project, the studies in third stream mainly discussed how external policy or legalization affect the OSS performances. In particular, two sub-streams in this domain can be found, i.e. the characteristics of OSS licenses and the intellectual property lawsuits enforcement [13–15].

The OSS supports encouraged the source codes could be shared, revised, and redistributed, however, the rights of the intellectual property of the creators cannot be overlooked. In this regard, several OSS licenses have been given to restrict the right of usage or revisions. There are more than 60 different OSS licenses prevailing throughout the world. The extent of restrictiveness of those OSS licenses is different. For instances, comparing with BSD whose restrictiveness is very low, the GNU license is widely known for its restrictive copyleft. Prior studies found OSS project administrators and users preferred the highly restrictive OSS licenses, but the OSS developers did not welcome such license [13]. In addition, Sen et al. [14] found the OSS project with moderately restrictive OSS license cannot attract the developers and users. Besides the effectiveness of OSS licences, Wen et al. [15] found the intellectual property lawsuits enforcement would increase the OSS usage cost, which would reduce the OSS participants' interests.

Table 1. Summarization of prior OSS studies using network analysis

Study	Dataset	Network measurement	Main results
Grewal et al. [7]	Randomly selected 10 projects in the "Perl" foundry and then identified another 98 projects also involving developers and owners from the 10 projects (total 108 projects hosted at Sourceforge; Nov 2005)	Network embeddedness	Developer network embeddedness is significantly related to number of CVS commits, and project manager (i.e., owner) network embeddedness is significantly related to number of downloads
Hahn et al. [8]	2349 Projects registered between September 30 and November 11, 2005 in Sourceforge	Tie (outcome and strength)	A developer is likely to participate in a project when this developer has prior collaboration tie with the project owner
Singh et al. [27]	2378 projects hosted at Sourceforge (Nov 1999 to Nov 2004)	Internal cohesion; direct and indirect ties; external cohesion	Teams with developers of greater internal cohesion and external cohesion could be significantly related (though differently) with project success
Singh [9]	5944 projects hosted at Sourceforge (Jan 2003 to Nov 2004)	Cluster coefficient ratio; Path length ratio	Clustering and average path length within the network affect the success of OSS projects
Conaldi et al. [10]	Single project; Epiphany's bug repository (March–Sep 2006)	Rate of network changes; Degree centrality (developers and bugs)	The intrinsic structure of bug-fixing network strongly affect the engagement of developers; A purposed methodology for analyzing the two-model network

3   Assessment of OSS Success

Several metrics have be employed to assess the OSS success, and such assessments were developed in consideration of the research propose and the audiences, such as number of subscribers, number of active developers, number of downloads, frequency of CVS commits, and the extent of code reuse etc. [25]. After comprehensively reviewing prior literatures, the number of downloads and the frequency of CVS commits were most widely used to assess the OSS project success. However, we though either number of downloads or frequency of CVS commits cannot best represent the performance of OSS, i.e. success of OSS success. The number of downloads can only serve as a proxy indicator of software exposure, but cannot represent the success of an OSS due to the unknown conversion rate [25]. For instances, end users can simply remove their downloaded OSS after a quick trial, which cannot be reflected in the number of OSS downloads. To reconcile such defect, some scholars advocated to use the frequency of CVS commit to assess the success of OSS projects. Comparing with the number of downloads which represent the extent to which OSS prevails in end-users, the frequency of CVS commit serves as a proxy indicator of development vitality. The higher frequency of CVS commit indicates the developers constantly contributed to the OSS project. However, the limitation of such indicator is also obvious. The higher frequency of CVS commit may also indicate the fundamental quality of this OSS project is not good, and the developers had to constantly fix the bugs found in the newly distributed versions.

Encouraging the literatures in innovation and strategic management, we thought the extent of code reuse could be a representative indicator to assess the success of OSS project. Haefliger et al. [26] found the qualified sources codes were extensively reused in other OSS projects. In innovation literatures, the innovation capability of an organization is measured by the extent to which their patents are cited. In similar vein, we argued the extent of code reuse could serve as an important indicator to assess the OSS project success, i.e. the innovation performance.

4   Conclusion and Future Agenda

In this article, we provide a comprehensive literature reviews on prior OSS studies. In particular, we categorized the previous literatures into three streams based on the research topics, which included individual motivations to contribute or participate in the OSS projects, the relationship between network characteristics and OSS performances, and the external factors like OSS licenses and policy influencing the OSS performances. In addition, we also surveyed the prior literatures and summarized several key indicators assessing the OSS project success, and found the pros and cons of the existing measurement. Encouraged by the innovation literatures, we expected the future research could use the extent of code reuse to indicate the innovation quality of OSS.

Acknowledgement. This work was supported by the Tongji Talented Youth Project (grant number 2014KJ002); National Natural Science Foundation of China [grant number 51408438]; the Scientific Research Foundation for the Returned Overseas Chinese Scholars, State Education Ministry of the People's Republic of China; and Shanghai Pujiang Program [grant number 14PJ1408300].

References

1. Von Krogh, G., Von Hippel, E.: The promise of research on open source software. Manage. Sci. **52**(7), 975–983 (2006)
2. Fitzgerald, B.: The transformation of open source software. Mis Q. **30**(3), 587–598 (2006)
3. Hertel, G., Niedner, S., Herrmann, S.: Motivation of software developers in open source projects: an Internet-based survey of contributors to the Linux kernel. Res. Policy **32**(7), 1159–1177 (2003)
4. Shah, S.K.: Motivation, governance, and the viability of hybrid forms in open source software development. Manage. Sci. **52**(7), 1000–1014 (2006)
5. Roberts, J.A., Hann, I.H., Slaughter, S.A.: Understanding the motivations, participation, and performance of open source software developers: a longitudinal study of the Apache projects. Manage. Sci. **52**(7), 984–999 (2006)
6. Lakhani, K.R., Von Hippel, E.: How open source software works:"free" user-to-user assistance. Res. Policy **32**(6), 923–943 (2003)
7. Grewal, R., Lilien, G.L., Mallapragada, G.: Location, location, location: How network embeddedness affects project success in open source systems. Manage. Sci. **52**(7), 1043–1056 (2006)
8. Hahn, J., Moon, J.Y., Zhang, C.: Emergence of new project teams from open source software developer networks: impact of prior collaboration ties. Inf. Syst. Res. **19**(3), 369–391 (2008)
9. Singh, P.V.: The small-world effect: the influence of macro-level properties of developer collaboration networks on open-source project success. ACM Trans. Softw. Eng. Methodol. (TOSEM) **20**(2), 6 (2010)
10. Conaldi, G., Lomi, A., Tonellato, M.: Dynamic models of affiliation and the network structure of problem solving in an open source software project. Organ. Res. Methods **15**(3), 385–412 (2012)
11. Li, Y., Tan, C.H., Teo, H.H.: Leadership characteristics and developers' motivation in open source software development. Inf. Manage. **49**(5), 257–267 (2012)
12. O'Mahony, S., Ferraro, F.: The emergence of governance in an open source community. Acad. Manage. J. **50**(5), 1079–1106 (2007)
13. Subramaniam, C., Sen, R., Nelson, M.L.: Determinants of open source software project success: a longitudinal study. Decis. Support Syst. **46**(2), 576–585 (2009)
14. Sen, R., Singh, S.S., Borle, S.: Open source software success: measures and analysis. Decis. Support Syst. **52**(2), 364–372 (2012)
15. Wen, W., Forman, C., Graham, S.J.: Research note-the impact of intellectual property rights enforcement on open source software project success. Inf. Syst. Res. **24**(4), 1131–1146 (2013)
16. Ryan, R.M., Deci, E.L.: Self-determination theory and the facilitation of intrinsic motivation, social development, and well-being. Am. Psychol. **55**(1), 68 (2000)
17. Lakhani, K., Wolf, R.G.: Why hackers do what they do: understanding motivation and effort in free/open source software projects (2003)
18. Von Krogh, G., Haefliger, S., Spaeth, S.: Collective action and communal resources in open source software development: the case of freenet. Academy of Management (2003)
19. Wu, C.G., Gerlach, J.H., Young, C.E.: An empirical analysis of open source software developers' motivations and continuance intentions. Inf. Manage. **44**(3), 253–262 (2007)
20. Zhou, M., Mockus, A.: What make long term contributors: willingness and opportunity in OSS community. In: Proceedings of the 34th International Conference on Software Engineering, pp. 518–528. IEEE Press (2012)

21. Long, Y., Siau, K.: Social network structures in open source software development teams. J. Database Manage. (JDM) **18**(2), 25–40 (2007)
22. Mockus, A., Fielding, R.T., Herbsleb, J.D.: Two case studies of open source software development: apache and Mozilla. ACM Trans. Softw. Eng. Methodol. (TOSEM) **11**(3), 309–346 (2002)
23. Sowe, S., Stamelos, I., Angelis, L.: Identifying knowledge brokers that yield software engineering knowledge in OSS projects. Inf. Softw. Technol. **48**(11), 1025–1033 (2006)
24. Singh, P.V., Tan, Y.: Developer heterogeneity and formation of communication networks in open source software projects. J. Manage. Inf. Syst. **27**(3), 179–210 (2010)
25. Crowston, K., Annabi, H., Howison, J.: Defining open source software project success. In: ICIS 2003 Proceedings, p. 28 (2003)
26. Haefliger, S., Von Krogh, G., Spaeth, S.: Code reuse in open source software. Manage. Sci. **54**(1), 180–193 (2008)
27. Singh, P.V., Tan, Y., Mookerjee, V.: Network effects: the influence of structural capital on open source project success. MIS Q. **35**(4), 813–830 (2011)

Cross-Cultural Research in IS: An Updated Review Since 2005

Yi Liu[✉], Bouchaib Bahli, and Hans Borgman

ESC Rennes School of Business, Rennes, France
{yi.liu,bouchaib.bahli,hans.borgman}@esc-rennes.com

Abstract. Culture has been found as an important factor in Information Systems studies and culture theory has been used to explain the IT behavior of the people across nations. In this paper, we review cross-cultural studies in Information Systems for the last decade. We choose the studies from senior scholar's basket of six journals in Information Systems. These studies are classified into two themes. The discussions of these studies and future research directions are presented in the paper.

Keywords: Cross-cultural · Cross-country · Information systems · Literature review

1 Introduction

Culture has been defined as "the collective programming of the mind which distinguishes the members of one human group from another" [1]. From Hofstede's study, four cultural dimensions are identified: masculinity/femininity, uncertainty avoidance, power distance, and individualism/collectivism, which are adopted by many cross-cultural studies. These identified dimensions facilitate cross-cultural researchers to explain human behavior in various disciplines. In Information Systems studies, culture has also been identified as an influencing factor concerning the IT behavior of the people. Leidner and Kayworth [2] conduct comprehensive review of IT/information systems culture for the studies till the fall of 2004. By analyzing eighty-two papers which examine IT culture in national and organizational levels, they develop the theory which indicates the effects of cultural conflict on system conflicts. In addition, culture has been largely investigated on the national level by conducting studies across countries [3]. In the last decade, information systems undergo radical changes due to the globalization and the introduction of social media. IT behavior of users across nations may converge by using the same information system platform (e.g., Facebook, LinkedIn, ERP, etc.) and this convergence perspective is mentioned previously [4] and partially investigated (e.g., [5]).

In this paper, we review the most recent culture studies in core Information Systems journals. We focus on cross-cultural studies which examine IT users across nations/countries. By analyzing these recent studies in Information Systems, we try to observe the current effects of culture on Information Systems. In the next section, we

© Springer International Publishing Switzerland 2015
F.F.-H. Nah and C.-H. Tan (Eds.): HCIB 2015, LNCS 9191, pp. 708–716, 2015.
DOI: 10.1007/978-3-319-20895-4_66

develop the literature review by introducing the review strategy and summarizing the studies. After presenting the papers, we discuss on research gaps.

2 Literature Review

The development of criteria for studies to be included, search strategy, and analysis scheme are required for literature review [2]. Concerning the studies to be included in our literature review, we chose senior scholar's basket of six journals in Information Systems (MIS Quarterly, Information Systems Research, Journal of Management Information Systems, Journal of the Association of Information Systems, European Journal of Information Systems and Information Systems Journal) which include the core research in Information Systems field. For the search strategy, in order to search for appropriate literature and ensure we have included all literature, we used three keywords "cross-cultural", "cross-nation" or "cross-country". Then, abstracts of the articles were examined to determine whether they were related to cross-cultural research, whether the studies targeted IT users across nations and whether the cross-country studies focus on cultural elements, instead of economics (e.g., developing countries vs. developed countries, etc.). Finally, we identified 16 published articles from 2005 to October 2014. Concerning the analysis method, we initially obtained the research objective, methodology, and key findings of each article (Table 1). Then we identified the relevant themes of the articles.

The 16 articles that we reviewed include 5 articles from Journal of Management Information Systems, 4 articles from both MIS Quarterly and Information Systems Journal, 2 articles from European Journal of Information Systems and 1 article from Information Systems Research. The following themes were observed: cross-cultural individual user behavior and cross-cultural IT management. Each theme is discussed in detail below. Before proceeding to the discussion, we summarize the methodologies employed by prior studies except Leidner & Kayworth's comprehensive literature review (Table 2). As the tables show, survey is the most employed methodology for examining the individual user behavior across nations and case study is widely used for investigating cross-cultural IT management.

2.1 Theme 1: Cross-Cultural Individual User Behavior

Diverse methodologies are used to examine the individual user behavior across nations, such as mixed methods (field experiment and survey) (e.g., [6]), think-aloud usability test (e.g., [7]), and survey (e.g., [8]) and various information technologies used by users across nations are compared. Clemmensen [7] conduct pilot study to illustrate how to conduct cross-country usability testing (e.g., topic, sample, data collection and analysis) by using the samples from Denmark, India and China. Tan et al. [6] compare the consumer response for the commercial messages disseminated via Email and SMS (Short Message Service) in Switzerland and China. Consumers from these two countries exhibit different attitudes towards these two technologies. Chinese consumers perceive greater value for the commercial messages via SMS and are more likely to redeem and

Table 1. Cross-Cultural Literatures

Author(s)	Cultures compared	Methodology	Key finding(s)
Tan et al. [6]	Switzerland and China	Field experiment, survey and focus group	Consumers in the environment of high context-cultural dimension (China) perceived digital product discount coupons as having a greater value, and exhibit a higher propensity to redeem and forward coupons sent to them via SMS than those sent by email. Swiss consumers perceive the coupon received via email as more valuable than that received via SMS, and are more inclined to forward them
Zhang et al. [18]	Chinese and US born-global firms	Survey	A comparative analysis of the Chinese and US born-global firms reveals a lack of a cross-cultural difference in the factors leading these firms to develop IT capability, therefore supporting the 'convergence' perspective in cross-cultural research
Clemmensen [7]	Denmark, India and China	Think aloud	The pilot study exemplifies themes to explore, who should be participants and where should the study be done, how to find examples of multiple-country usability testing, how to collect data and how to analyze that data and what kind of results and discussion of results that may be expected
Jain et al. [15]	American company and Indian vendors	Case study	Develop a process framework that illustrates how vendor silence may be mitigated in offshore outsourcing through various silence mitigation mechanisms. Cultural adaptation is likely to be positively related to vendor silence mitigation.

(Continued)

Table 1. (*Continued*)

Author(s)	Cultures compared	Methodology	Key finding(s)
Lowry et al. [2]	China and the United States	Survey	Cross-cultural dimensions are significant predictors of information privacy concerns and desire for online awareness, which are found to be predictors of attitude toward IM and, ultimately, intention to use IM and the actual use of IM
Posey et al. [8]	UK and France	Survey	French users have higher scores on horizontal individualism than British users. There is no difference in overall individualism or collectivism between the countries. British users have higher self-disclosure rates than French users
Sia et al. [11]	Australia and Hong Kong	Laboratory experiment	The impact of peer customer endorsements on trust perceptions was stronger for subjects in Hong Kong than Australia and that portal affiliation was effective only in the Australian site
Dinev et al. [9]	South Korea and the United States	Survey	Using antispyware technology as a representative of protective information technologies, South Korean users exhibit stronger relationship between subjective norm and behavioral intentions than American users. The role of awareness of negative consequences of spyware is much stronger in the US than in South Korea
Levina and Vaast [17]	The United States and Western European company and India and Russia vendors	Case study	Differences in country contexts (basis competencies in the financial services industry, software development discipline, the specific IS being developed, English language, computer science,

(*Continued*)

Table 1. (*Continued*)

Author(s)	Cultures compared	Methodology	Key finding(s)
			economic, social, and symbolic differences) gave rise to a number of boundaries that inhibit collaboration effectiveness
Dibbern et al. [14]	German company and Indian vendors	Multiple case study design	Cultural and geographic distance between client and vendor as well as personnel turnover are found to increase client extra costs
Kim [10]	The United States and South Korea	Survey	Transference-based trust determinants (perceived importance of third-party seal and perceived importance of positive referral) are more positively related to consumer trust in e-vendors in a collectivist culture than in a individualistic culture
Tiwana and Bush [16]	The United States and Japan	Conjoint analysis and interview	Project technical complexity is positively related to likelihood of outsourcing in the U.S. managers but not in the Japanese managers. Project requirements specifiability is positively related to the likelihood of outsourcing among Japanese managers but not U.S. managers. Requirements volatility was negatively related to the likelihood of outsourcing among Japanese but not U.S. managers
Zhang et al. [18]	The United States and China	Laboratory experiment	Minorities in Face-to-Face unsupported groups experience a higher level of majority influence than Face-to-Face computer-mediated communication groups and distributed computer-mediated communication groups. Majority influence is

(*Continued*)

Table 1. (*Continued*)

Author(s)	Cultures compared	Methodology	Key finding(s)
			manifested more strongly on Chinese minorities in heterogeneous groups than in homogeneous Chinese groups in a distributed computer-mediated communication setting.
Keil et al. [13]	The United States and South Korea	Laboratory experiment	The presence of a blame-shifting opportunity has a significant effect on American subjects' willingness to report bad news, but there is no effect on Korean subjects
Dinev et al. [12]	Italy and the United States	Survey	Italian society exhibit lower propensity to trust, institutional trust, privacy concerns, and higher perceived risk. The relationships between institutional trust and ecommerce use, privacy concerns and e-commerce use, and perceived risk and institutional trust are all weaker for Italy. The relationship between perceived risk and privacy concerns is stronger for Italy
Leidner and Kayworth [2]	N/A	Literature review	Propose the theory of IT-culture conflict

Table 2. Methodologies of the articles by themes

Methodology	Cross-cultural theme	
	Individual user behavior	IT management
Case study	0	3
Lab experiment	1	2
Think-aloud	1	0
Survey	5	1
Mixed	1	1

forward the coupon in the message. However, Swiss consumers perceive the messages via Email more valuable and are more likely to forward them. Besides Email and SMS, another communication technology, instant messaging, is also examined. Cross-cultural dimensions affect information privacy concerns and desire for online awareness which influence the actual use of instant messaging [3]. Uncertainty avoidance has been found to positively affect information privacy concerns and desire for online awareness in collectivism sample (Chinese users instead of American users). Privacy issue also affects online community behavior of users, since users may be reluctant to disclose personal and private information in online community. British working professionals have been found to have higher self-disclosure score in online community compared with French ones, who have higher score on horizontal individualism [8]. Concerning the use of antispyware to protect personal privacy, South Korean users exhibit stronger relationship between subjective norm and behavioral intentions than American users [9]. Regarding the trust and privacy concerns, Kim [10] finds that in online commercial transactions, transference-based determinants are more positively related to consumer trust for South Korean consumers (compared with American consumers) who have collectivist-strong uncertainty avoidance-high long term orientation-high context culture. In addition, the impact of peer consumer endorsement on trust perception is stronger for Hong Kong subjects than Australia subjects [11]. Besides the cross-cultural studies between America and Asia, cross-cultural study on privacy and trust issue has also been conducted between America and Europe. Dinev et al. [12] find that the relationships between institutional trust, privacy concerns and e-commerce use are weaker for Italian users than American ones.

2.2   Theme 2: Cross-Cultural IT Management

Besides the culture influence on IT behavior of individual users, culture also affects IT management across nations, such as project management, outsourcing and collaboration. Concerning software project management, the presence of a blaming-shifting opportunity has a significant effect on American subjects' willingness to report negative news on software projects than South Korean ones [13]. Regarding project outsourcing, project outsourcing decision and effectiveness are affected by culture across nations. Cultural distance between client and vendor is found to increase client extra cost by examining German company's offshore project to Indian vendors [14]. Cultural adaptation is found to be positively related to vendor silence mitigation which could reduce the extra cost [15]. Project technical complexity is positively related to outsourcing likelihood for American managers only and project requirements specifiability is positively related to outsource likelihood for Japanese managers only [16]. Levina and Vaast [17] investigate outsourcing projects from United States and Western Europe based multinational firm to Russia and India. It has been found that differences in country contexts give rise to a number of boundaries that inhibit collaboration effectiveness. Apart from project outsourcing, Zhang et al. [5] find that there is a lack of cultural difference in the factors leading Chinese and American born global firms to develop IT capability, which indicates the convergence of IT management culture. However, the decision making in a group via IT is still affected by culture. In culturally heterogeneous groups, majority influence on collectivistic minorities is stronger than that on individualistic minorities. Minorities in Face-to-Face unsupported groups experience a higher level of majority influence than Face-to-Face computer-mediated communication groups and distributed computer-mediated communication groups [18].

3 Discussions

Based on the review, we observe that cross-cultural (specifically cross-nation) studies in Information Systems have been well developed in the last decade. For the theme of cross-cultural individual user behavior, trust and privacy issues have been examined extensively across nations. Various communication technologies (e.g., SMS, Email, and Instant Messaging) are compared. However, there is a lack of study on cross-cultural comparisons on social media technologies. For the theme of cross-cultural IT management, project outsourcing is widely examined. European and American companies outsource IT projects to Asian countries and cultural elements affect the outsourcing effectiveness. The culture convergence perspective is also examined in IT management [5], which can be investigated in the future in a greater extent. Concerning the cultures investigated, Asian and American cultures are commonly used to compare IT behavior of users. Cross-cultural studies for intra-European nations and nations between Europe and America are needed for the future research.

4 Conclusion

Culture has been identified as influencing factor for IT use and management. The main objective of this paper is to review cross-cultural studies in the last decade in Information Systems and present a comprehensive overview of the existing knowledge in this research field. From the review, we perceive the future research topics which are not examined in the past. Moreover, we try to have a systematic view on the convergence of the culture in Information Systems field.

References

1. Hofstede, G.H.: Culture's Consequences: International Differences in Work-Related Values. Sage, Beverly Hills (1980)
2. Leidner, D., Kayworth, T.: A review of culture in information systems research: toward a theory of information technology culture conflict. MIS Q. 30(2), 357–399 (2006)
3. Lowry, P.B., Cao, J., Everard, A.: Privacy concerns versus desire for interpersonal awareness in driving the use of self-disclosure technologies: the case of instant messaging in two cultures. J. Manage. Inf. Syst. 27(4), 163–200 (2011)
4. Hofstede, G.H.: Culture's Consequences: Comparing Values, Behaviors, Institutions, and Organizations across Nations, 2nd edn. Sage, London (2001)
5. Zhang, M., Sarker, S., Sarker, S.: Drivers and export performance impacts of IT capability in 'born-global' firms: a cross-national study. Inf. Syst. J. 23(5), 419–443 (2013)

6. Tan, C.H., Sutanto, J., Phang, C.W., Gasimov, A.: Using personal communication technologies for commercial communications: a cross-country investigation of email and sms. Inf. Syst. Res. **25**(2), 307–327 (2014)
7. Clemmensen, T.: Usability problem identification in culturally diverse settings. Inf. Syst. J. **22**(2), 151–175 (2012)
8. Posey, C., Lowry, P.B., Roberts, T.L., Ellis, T.S.: Proposing the online community self-disclosure model: the case of working professionals in France and the U.K. who use online communities. Eur. J. Inf. Syst. **19**(2), 181–195 (2010)
9. Dinev, T., Goo, J., Hu, Q., Nam, K.: User behaviour towards protective information technologies: the role of national cultural differences. Inf. Syst. J. **19**(4), 391–412 (2009)
10. Kim, D.J.: Self-perception-based versus transference-based trust determinants in computer-mediated transactions: a cross-cultural comparison study. J. Manage. Inf. Syst. **24**(4), 13–45 (2008)
11. Sia, C.L., Lim, K., Leung, K., Lee, M., Huang, W., Benbasat, I.: Web strategies to promote internet shopping: is cultural-customization needed? MIS Q. **33**(3), 491–512 (2009)
12. Dinev, T., Bellotto, M., Hart, P., Russo, V., Serra, I., Colautti, C.: Privacy calculus model in e-commerce - a study of Italy and the United States. Eur. J. Inf. Syst. **15**(4), 389–402 (2006)
13. Keil, M., Im, G.P., Mähring, M.: Reporting bad news on software projects: the effects of culturally constituted views of face-saving. Inf. Syst. J. **17**(1), 59–87 (2007)
14. Dibbern, J., Winkler, J., Heinzl, A.: Explaining variations in client extra costs between software projects offshored to India. MIS Q. **32**(2), 333–366 (2008)
15. Jain, R.P., Simon, J.C., Poston, R.S.: Mitigating vendor silence in offshore outsourcing: an empirical investigation. J. Manage. Inf. Syst. **27**(4), 261–297 (2011)
16. Tiwana, A., Bush, A.A.: A comparison of transaction cost, agency, and knowledge-based theory predictors of IT outsourcing decisions: a U.S.-Japan cross-cultural field study. J. Manage. Inf. Syst. **24**(1), 259–300 (2007)
17. Levina, N., Vaast, E.: Innovating or doing as told? Status differences and overlapping boundaries in offshore collaboration. MIS Q. **32**(2), 307–332 (2008)
18. Zhang, D., Lowry, P.B., Zhou, L., Fu, X.: The impact of individualism - collectivism, social presence, and group diversity on group decision making under majority influence. J. Manage. Inf. Syst. **23**(4), 53–80 (2007)

Usage Diversity, Task Interdependence and Group Innovation

Yumei Luo[1], Cheng Zhang[2(✉)], and Yunjie Xu[2]

[1] School of Business Management and Tour Management, Yunnan University,
Yunnan, China
luoyumei@fudan.edu.cn
[2] School of Management, Fudan University, Shanghai, China
{zhangche,yunjiexu}@fudan.edu.cn

Abstract. Investments on information stems (IS) are costly. After the initial adoption of Information Systems, the value of IS to an organization depends on employees' innovative use of various features of IS in the infusion stage. Innovative use of IS, a key activity of technology infusion, depends not only on individual effort, but also on group effort of teams. Grounded on the research of individual-collective process, this paper seeks to build a situational contingency model of how individual innovative use of IS affects group innovative use.

Keywords: Individual innovative use · Group innovative use · Innovativeness diversity · Task interdependence

1 Introduction

Successful enterprise Information systems (IS) projects not only need to be accepted by users when they are first implemented, but also need to be fully utilized in the infusion stage [1]. With extended and creative use of system features, users' capacity is amplified, and their performance is significantly enhanced [2]. It has been found that organizations have high levels of success when users have a high level of expertise [3] and when systems are effectively used.

To encourage use, organizations conduct extensive IS training [4]. Some users also spontaneously engage in innovative self-exploration [5]. An important alternative to these is mutual sharing among users [6], such that group members get help from each other's innovative use of IS, and the whole group develop a climate for innovative use. Daft's (1978) dual-core model suggests that technology innovation is a bottom-up process initiated and supported by lower-level employees with expertise in the technical core activities of an organization. Although the importance of the bottom-up process of how individual innovative use of IS leads to group level innovative use in the infusion stage is strongly advocated in IS literatures, this process is unfortunately under-researched [3].

Our study is motivated by the research gap in the bottom-up process of innovative use of IS in the infusion stage. Our research question is: How does individual innovative use of IS, individual position in the group and group configural factors lead to group innovative use of IS? Individual innovative use of IS is the degree a user explores and uses

© Springer International Publishing Switzerland 2015
F.F.-H. Nah and C.-H. Tan (Eds.): HCIB 2015, LNCS 9191, pp. 717–726, 2015.
DOI: 10.1007/978-3-319-20895-4_67

system features that were not known to the user before [7]. However, group innovative use is a distinct notion from individual innovative use. Per Kozlowski and Klein [8] definition, group innovative use is emergent, to the degree that it originates in the innovative use behaviors of individual members, is amplified by their interactions (perhaps via intra-group sharing) and manifests as a group-level phenomenon [8].

Group members are more likely to have dissimilar contributions to group innovative use that result from differences in individual innovative use and individual position in the group. Thus, it will be important to consider how innovative use is distributed in the group to understand how group-level innovative use manifests individual abilities. We use centrality, a concept used to measure a node's importance in sharing network, where centrality usually indicates the importance of each individual in the overall pattern of information flow [9]. We also argue that a group's innovative use is impacted not only by the average level of innovative use but also by the distribution of innovative use relative to centrality. That is, the alignment between individual innovative use of IS and individual centrality in the group, called centrality-innovative use alignment (CI-Alignment), is likely to be positively related to group innovative use of IS.

Moreover, the effective interactions, as the core of bottom-up process, is influenced by group structural factors [8]. Group members have heterogeneous levels of innovativeness and task interdependence, both in degree and kind that stem from differences in individual characteristics and roles. We further argue that the impact of CI-alignment is conditional on group heterogeneity factors: innovativeness diversity and task interdependence. Innovativeness diversity refers to the degree to which group members differ in their innovativeness in IS use. Task interdependence refers to the extent to which group members' tasks depend on other members' job [10]. These two contingent factors serve to hamper or facilitate group innovative use, respectively.

This study bears important contributions. First, to the best of our knowledge, this is the first study to investigate the bottom-up process of IS use in the infusion stage. Second, we not only theoretically differentiate innovative use of IS at individual and group level, but also explicate the key antecedents to group innovative use. Innovative members with centrality in the group are likely to impact on group innovative use. Group innovative use hinges on the structural factors (e.g. task interdependence and innovativeness diversity) of the group. Finally, this work effectively melds structural perspective with resource theory. It also provides guidance to practitioners on how innovative individuals should be facilitated to spark the whole group into innovative use of IS.

We next introduce the key concepts and theoretical background. Then a research model is presented to describe the bottom-up process of IS innovative use.

2   Theoretical and Hypotheses Development

2.1   Individual and Group Level Innovative Use of IS

IS innovative use has been identified as an important user behavior in the infusion stage [7]. Innovative use can occur in two ways [11]. First, users engage in exploitative use of IS by making an endeavor to use more of the available IS functions to better support their work [12]. Exploitative use is similar to the notion of extended use [13]. Incorporation of IS features in more jobs usually lead to better individual performance. Second, users engage in explorative IS use by experimenting with new features and apply them innovatively to enhance their job performance [7, 14]. Notions similar to explorative use include emergent use [12], "innovate with IT" [14], and feature extension [7]. Explorative use further helps users leverage the potential value of the IS to a higher level [7]. The exploitative use and explorative use, however, could occur in parallel [1] and facilitate individual task accomplishment [13].

In many organizations, people often work with others to interact with IS to perform group-level tasks, but little research has investigated innovative use at the group level. In multilevel research, Burton-Jones and Gallivan [3] suggests that group innovative use cannot be a global construct [3]. This is because IS use occurs at the individual level and, as a result, the level of theory of group use (i.e., the group) will always be higher than its level of origin (i.e., the individual). Group innovative use is a configural construct because group members are likely to possess very different levels of innovative use. Differences in innovative use may result from users' personal characteristics (e.g., personality traits, demographics) and role characteristics (e.g., formal, informal).

These differences among members are extremely likely to develop various innovative use and different degrees of innovative use, and interaction processes among members are irregular, high in dispersion, and exhibit nonuniform patterns. Thus, group innovative use is complex combination of group member contributions. By interacting with each other, group member's innovative use contribute to group innovative use. Certain interactions, therefore, may be more contributions than others for group innovative use. For example, suppose two groups have the same average innovative use, but in one group members are frequent communication and willing and able to share their innovative knowledge, while in the other group members are little communication, resulting the lack of trust, and unwilling to share information. It seems reasonable to suggest that the first group will do a better job of making use of its members' innovative use.

To maximize emerging to group innovative use, these groups should be highly density in the sharing network, where the content of relationships focuses on information related to the innovative use of IS. Network density is important structural characteristics capturing patterns of social exchanges in an organizational unit [6]. Highly density has been associated with greater cooperation, information sharing, and accountability [15] and indicates the degree of information sharing and communication. Thus, we use the construct to help us model complex combination of group members' contributions and represent group innovative use.

2.2 The Individual-to-Group Process

The bottom-up process describes how the behaviors at individual level gives rise to group level IS use patterns and outcomes [8]. An examination of the literature shows some views to the bottom-up linkage in the IS research (see Table 1).

Table 1. The individual-to-group process in the IS research

Authors	Topic	Brief description of the individual-to-group process
Nan [21]	IT use	Individual assimilation of IS features contribute to group level assimilation. The impacts of employee learning, IT flexibility, and workplace rigidity that these factors in individual-level actions do not have a direct causal linkage with organizational-level IT use patterns and outcomes. Collective-level IT use patterns and outcomes are the logical and yet often unintended or unforeseeable consequences of individual-level behaviors
Kane and Borgatti [9]	IS proficiency	Effective group-level IS proficiency may also be a function of how a group's IS proficiency is distributed across its members
Sarker and Valacich [16]	IS acceptance	The individual a priori attitude towards technology affect the group level technology acceptance. Group configural features affect the group level technology acceptance through group member interaction
Aubert et al. [17]	IT implementation	IT implementation is influenced by individual variables, namely visions and impacts at the individual level, which can also lead to conflicts within the project
Lapointe and Rivard [18]	IS resistance	The bottom-up process by which group resistance behaviors emerge from individual behaviors is not the same in early versus late implementation. In early implementation, the emergence process is one of compilation, described as a combination of independent, individual behaviors. In later stages of implementation, if group level initial conditions have become active, the emergence process is one of composition, described as the convergence of individual behaviors
Tiwana and Mclean [19]	team creativity	Information systems development project teams creativity results primarily from integration of individually held expertise of team members at the team level
Racherla and Mandviwalla [20]	information infrastructure	How access to and use the Internet and the associated information infrastructure are influenced by both micro and macro factors. Universal use is a configural construce and has a mutual influence on individual use via interconnectedness

In the domain of technology acceptance, Sarker and Valacich [16] empirically found that the average individual attitude towards technology and configural factors affect the group level technology acceptance. While these configural factors are important in the acceptance stage, they are not necessarily in the infusion stage. For example, group innovative use is less likely to be affected by majority opinion or leaders' view, because IS innovative use is not a mandatory collective decision, but rather a voluntarily shared practice internalized by individuals. Nan [21] conceptualize the bottom-up process in IS feature learning as a complex adaptive system. Through agent based simulation, it was found that individual learning of IS features greatly facilitates the speed of group IS assimilation, but the workplace rigidity (i.e., a hierarchical or flat network structure among users) does not have a salient effect. In general, the limited investigations of the bottom-up process in both acceptance and infusion stage does not provide a clear and consistent picture of the IS infusion process.

How is the process from individual to group innovative use? First, it shall be recognized that group innovative use is emergent. Individual innovative use denotes elemental content, interaction denotes process. The form of the interaction process, in combination with the individual innovative use, comprises the group innovative use. Second, individual contributions to group innovative use are dissimilar. In group, there are various innovative use and different degree of innovative use, and the distribution of innovative use is non-uniform. To maximize contributing to group innovative use, the members with the innovative use should be interaction with others to give their help. Thus, it will be important to consider the alignment between innovative use and users' centrality in the group to more fully understand the impact individual innovative use will have on group-level innovative use.

Finally, the effective intra-group interactions is the hallmark of group innovative use. Group innovative use requires that individuals coordinate and dynamically combine distinct individual knowledge and innovative actions. Burton-Jones and Gallivan [3] suggest that the nature of the user and task, as contextual factors, may influence the interaction processes. These factors can impact on the construction of interdependencies-in-use that in turn lead to the emergence of group innovative use. At the group-level, the heterogeneous levels of group members' innovative use and task interdependence, as group structure factors, should be impact on the effective interactions processes. The research model and hypotheses are summarized in Fig. 1.

According to Kane and Borgatti's [9] suggestion, centrality-innovative use alignment (CI-Alignment) is alignment between centrality and innovative use within a

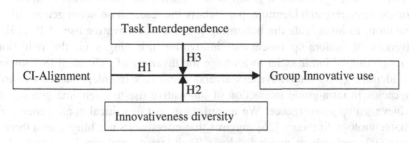

Fig. 1. Research model and hypotheses

group. CI-Alignment melds effectively structural perspective with individual innovative use. CI-Alignment is conceptualized as a continuum ranging form strong positive alignment to strong negative alignment. A strong positive alignment exists between node centrality and innovative use when the most innovative users tend to be the most central. A strong negative alignment exists between centrality and innovative use when the more innovative users tend to be the most marginal.

High CI-Alignment can affect group innovative use in several ways. First, central people may more directly contribute to a group's innovative use in terms of the innovative use they produce. People who are central in a social network occupy a more important position within the knowledge flows and work flows of a group [22]. Network centrality is the structural property most often associated with instrumental outcomes, such as power and influence in decision making. Thus, individual innovative use of key group members will have greater effects on group innovative use.

Second, central people may indirectly contribute to group innovative use in terms of their ability to help others. Group members may turn to other members for seeking and sharing innovative practices. Individuals who are central can exert more influence by virtue of being linked with a large number of people in the network. People will turn for help and advice to those with whom they are connected, so more central people are more likely to be approached for help. The knowledge of how others interact with a system may enable central users to provide better help on specific problems, as central users would better understand the contexts in which help was needed.

Third, high innovative users may influence how other group members innovative use the IS. Certain "master users," typically not the formal leaders of the group, often exert considerable influence over whether and how their peer use IS [23]. People in workgroups are also more likely to innovative use the IS if they perceive that coworkers have been well-trained to use it [24]. The actions and behaviors of central group members are typically more visible than the behavior of other members, so highly innovative central members may model innovative use behaviors and give others the confidence to innovative use a system themselves. Therefore, we state this formally as Hypothesis 1.

H1: Individual's centrality-innovative use will relate positively to group innovative use.

2.3 The Contingency Effect of Group Configuration

However, the synergy within a group is conditional on group structure factors. We draw on the team research literature, particularly the research on heterogeneity of group configuration, to investigate the bottom-up process of innovative use of IS [25]. The effectiveness of bottom-up process of innovative use hinges on the reduction of intra-group competition in order to leverage the diversity of individual IS knowledge.

We identify group innovativeness diversity and task interdependence as two key contingencies in intra-group interaction of innovative use to overcome group conflict and achieve group convergence. We regard them as two critical contingencies. First, the task-technology fit theory [26] suggests that effective IS use hinges on a three-way fit among task, technology, and individuals. Task interdependency is recognized as an important task factor [27], and individual absorptive such as innovativeness in IS use is an important individual trait factor [19]. Second, individual and inter-individual cognition of IS have been conceptualized as two routes to IS training effectiveness [27]. The former encompasses individual's IS application knowledge and the latter encompasses collaborative task knowledge. Group innovativeness diversity is a configural measure of individual absorptive capacity and knowledge in IS use, while task interdependence is a configural attribute of task that prescribes group interaction and cognition of both task and IS. As situational contingency factors, the two factors do not represent a complete list. Other contingencies include substantive conflict in the team, communication media used [16], workplace rigidity [21]. Similar to task interdependence, these factors constrains the interaction among group members.

Group innovativeness diversity could hamper intra-group interaction. A general finding in research on group heterogeneity is that homogeneous group is conducive to group performance. This process can be explained by the social categorization theory and the similarity or attraction perspective [28], suggesting that people prefer to work with similar others [29]. Group with homogeneous personal attributes is more likely to express similar rather than distinct viewpoints, and to develop feelings of being united by a shared group identity [30]. On the other hand, experience of dissimilarity has been found to result in factionalism, message distortion and other communication difficulties [28].

A group with a high level of average individual innovative use could be due to a few enthusiastic members who are extremely eager in IS use, while the rest of the group show little interest in it. This configural property, i.e., diversity in individual innovativeness, may hinder group interactive climate. First, when members differ in innovativeness in IS use, communication processes can be hindered due to the knowledge gap among them. Second, members could differ in their absorptive capacity. Diversity in individual innovativeness is likely to hinder the integration of knowledge. In the process of IS use, a highly innovative member is likely to propose new ideas of system use, while a less innovative member may not be able understand or accept. Third, they can also differ in terms of personal interests and preferences regarding the structural or cultural design of the work environment. Because innovative use of IS may bring about organizational change [31], more innovative individuals are likely to embrace IT-induced changes than less innovative ones do. As a result, high innovativeness diversity has been linked to destructive conflicts and miscommunication which hamper collaboration during creativity processes [32]. Therefore, we posit that:

H2: Individual innovativeness diversity dampens the impact of CI-Alignment on group innovative use, i.e. the effect of CI-Alignment on group innovative use is stronger with low innovativeness diversity than with higher innovativeness diversity.

Task interdependence is a formal configural property of task environment that could shape group interactions and cognition [33]. When tasks are interdependent, group members depend to a greater extent on each other for task performance [34]. This interdependence naturally promote communication and cooperation [35]. Researchers have proposed that the degree and nature of interdependence among group members moderate the relationship between work group diversity and outcomes. Information systems are complex and integrated systems that span many business functions and business processes. They are often characterized by high levels of task interdependence, and therefore require coordination among users.

In contrast with innovativeness diversity, task interdependence will facilitate group innovative use. High interdependence tasks require high levels of information exchange [36]. In this exchange process, in order to get job done, extensive sharing of knowledge and skills are likely to occur, even between members of very different IS innovativeness. In contrast, tasks of low interdependence can be coordinated effectively with low information processing mechanisms such as rules and procedures. With independent tasks, users are likely to adopt new IS features only for individual performance gains, and are less likely to be influenced by suggestions and ideas provided by other member [10]. As a result, in low interdependence groups, the positive effect of CI_Alignment on group innovative use will be reduced. We posit that:

H3: Task interdependence amplifies the impact of CI_Alignment on group innovative use, i.e. the effect of CI_Alignment on group innovative use is stronger in a high task interdependence condition than in a low task interdependence condition.

Acknowledgements. This research is supported by the National Natural Science Foundation of China (71402159, 71372112), Yunnan Science and Technology Fund (2014FB116) and Shanghai Social Science Fund (2013BGL003). The authors thank anonymous referees for their valuable comments and suggestions. Any remaining errors are the authors'.

References

1. Cooper, R.B., Zmud, R.W.: Information technology implementation research: a technological diffusion approach. Manage. Sci. **36**, 123–139 (1990)
2. Hsieh, J., Rai, A., Xu, S.X.: Extracting business value from IT: a sensemaking perspective of post-adoptive use. Manage. Sci. **57**, 2018–2039 (2011)
3. Burton-Jones, A., Gallivan, M.J.: Toward a deeper understanding of system usage in organizations: a multilevel perspective. Manage. Inf. Syst. Q. **31**, 657–679 (2007)
4. Sharma, R., Yetton, P.: The contingent effects of training, technical and complexity, and task interdependence on successful information systems implementation. MIS Q. **31**, 219–238 (2007)
5. Markus, M.L., Tanis, C.: The enterprise systems experience–from adoption to success. In: Zmud, R.W. (ed.) Framing the Domains of IT Research: Glimpsing the Future Through the Past, pp. 173–207. Pinnaflex Educational Resources, Cincinnati (2000)
6. Sykes, T.A., Venkatesh, V., Gosain, S.: Model of acceptance with peer support: a social network perspective to understand employees' system use. MIS Q. **33**, 371–393 (2009)
7. Jasperson, J., Carter, P.E., Zmud, R.W.: A comprehensive conceptualization of post-adoptive behaviors associated with information technology enabled work systems. MIS Q. **29**, 525–557 (2005)
8. Kozlowski, S.W.J., Klein, K.J.: A multilevel approach to theory and research in organizations: contextual, temporal, and emergent processes. In: Klein, K.J., Kozlowski, S.W.J. (eds.) Multilevel Theory, Research, and Methods in Organizations: Foundations, Extensions, and New Directions, pp. 3–90. Jossey Bass, San Francisco (2000)
9. Kane, G.C., Borgatti, S.P.: Centrality-IS proficiency alignment and workgroup performance. MIS Q. **35**, 1063–1078 (2011)

10. Van der Vegt, G.S., Janssen, O.: Joint impact of interdependence and group diversity on innovation. J. Manag. **29**, 729 (2003)
11. Burton-Jones, A.: Reconceptualizing system usage: an approach and empirical test. Inf. Syst. Res. **17**, 228–246 (2006)
12. Saga, V.I., Zmud, R.W.: The nature and determinants of IT acceptance, routinization, and infusion. In: Levine, L. (ed.) Diffusion, Transfer and Implementation of Information Technology, pp. 67–86. Software Engineering Institute, Carnegie Mellon University, Pittsburgh, PA (1994)
13. Hsieh, J., Wang, W.: Explaining employees' extended use of complex information systems. Eur. J. Inf. Syst. **16**, 216–227 (2007)
14. Ahuja, M.K., Thatcher, J.B.: Moving beyond intentions and toward the theory of trying: effects of work environment and gender on post-adoption information technology use. MIS Q. **29**, 427–459 (2005)
15. Sparrowe, R.T., et al.: Social networks and the performance of individuals and groups. Acad. Manag. J. **44**, 316–325 (2001)
16. Sarker, S., Valacich, J.S.: An alternative to methodological individualism-a non-reductionist approach to studying technology adoption by groups. MIS Q. **34**, 779–808 (2010)
17. Aubert, B.A., et al.: A multi-level, multi-theory perspective of information technology implementation. Inf. Syst. J. **18**, 45–72 (2008)
18. Lapointe, L., Rivard, S.: A multilevel model of resistance to information technology. MIS Q. **29**, 461–491 (2005)
19. Tiwana, A., Mclean, E.R.: Expertise integration and creativity in information systems development. J. Manage. Inf. Syst. **22**, 13–43 (2005)
20. Racherla, P., Mandviwalla, M.: Moving from access to use of the information infrastructure: a multilevel sociotechnical framework. Inf. Syst. Res. **24**, 709–730 (2013)
21. Nan, N.: Capturing bottom-up information technology use processes: a complex adaptive systems model. MIS Q. **35**, 505–532 (2011)
22. Borgatti, S.P., Cross, R.: A relational view of information seeking and learning in social networks. Manage. Sci. **49**, 432–445 (2003)
23. Spitler, V.K.: Learning to use IT in the workplace: mechanisms and masters. J. Organ. End User Comput. (JOEUC) **17**, 1–25 (2005)
24. Gallivan, M.J., Spitler, V.K., Koufaris, M.: Does information technology training really matter? A social information processing analysis of coworkers' influence on IT usage in the workplace. J. Manage. Inf. Syst. **22**, 153–192 (2003)
25. Carton, A.M., Cummings, J.N.: A theory of subgroups in work teams. Acad. Manag. Rev. **37**, 441–470 (2012)
26. Goodhue, D.L.: Development and measurement validity of a task-technology fit instrument for user evaluations of information system. Decis. Sci. **29**, 105–138 (1998)
27. Sharma, R., Yetton, P.: The contingent effects of management support and task interdependence on successful information systems implementation. MIS Q. **27**, 533–556 (2003)
28. Williams, K.Y., O'Reilly, C.A.: Demography and diversity in organizations: a review of 40 years of research. Res. Organ. Behav. **20**, 77–140 (1998)
29. Jackson, S.E.: Team Composition in Organizational Settings: Issues in Managing an Increasingly Diverse Work Force. Sage Publications Inc, California (1992)
30. Janssen, O.: Innovative behaviour and job involvement at the price of conflict and less satisfactory relations with co-workers. J. Occup. Organ. Psychol. **76**, 347–364 (2003)
31. Kim, H.-W., Kankanhalli, A.: Investigating user resistance to information systems implementation: a status quo bias perspective. MIS Q. **33**, 567–582 (2009)

32. De Dreu, C.K.W., Weingart, L.R.: Task versus relationship conflict, team performance, and team member satisfaction: a meta-analysis. J. Appl. Psychol. **88**, 741–749 (2003)
33. Majchrzak, A., et al.: Technology adaptation: the case of a computer-supported inter-organizational virtual team. MIS Q. **24**, 569–600 (2000)
34. Wageman, R.: Interdependence and group effectiveness. Adm. Sci. Q. **40**, 145–180 (1995)
35. Van Knippenberg, D., Schippers, M.C.: Work group diversity. Annu. Rev. Psychol. **58**, 515–541 (2007)
36. Andres, H.P., Zmud, R.W.: A contingency approach to software project coordination. J. Manage. Inf. Syst. **18**, 41–70 (2002)

Creating Greater Synergy Between HCI Academia and Practice

Fiona Fui-Hoon Nah[1(✉)], Dennis Galletta[2], Melinda Knight[3], James R. Lewis[4],
John Pruitt[5], Gavriel Salvendy[6,7], Hong Sheng[1], and Anna Wichansky[8]

[1] Missouri University of Science and Technology, Rolla, MO, USA
{nahf,hsheng}@mst.edu
[2] University of Pittsburgh, Pittsburgh, PA, USA
galletta@katz.pitt.edu
[3] Microsoft Corporation, Redmond, WA, USA
melinda.knight@microsoft.com
[4] IBM, Boca Raton, FL, USA
jimlewis@us.ibm.com
[5] Dell Corporation, Round Rock, TX, USA
john_pruitt@dell.com
[6] Purdue University, West Lafayette, IN, USA
salvendy@purdue.edu
[7] Tsinghua University, Beijing, China
[8] Oracle Corporation, Redwood Shores, CA, USA
anna.wichansky@oracle.com

Abstract. This paper presents perspectives from both academia and practice on how both groups can collaborate and work together to create synergy in the development and advancement of human-computer interaction (HCI). Issues and challenges are highlighted, success cases are offered as examples, and suggestions are provided to further such collaborations.

Keywords: Human-computer interaction · Synergy · Academia · Practice · Research · Industry

1 Introduction

According to Wikipedia, human-computer interaction (HCI) focuses on the design and use of computer technology. For a technology to be successful and be embraced by its users, the sociotechnical factors, which include not only the technology but also the users and their environments, must be taken into consideration. Hence, the field of HCI crosses many disciplines including information systems/science, computer science, psychology, sociology, organization science, communication, business administration, engineering, and ergonomics [1–3].

Academia and practice have long been concerned about the gap that exists between them [4–7]. In the context of this paper, we are focusing specifically on the field of HCI. Questions and issues that have arisen include: Are students today meeting the needs of

© Springer International Publishing Switzerland 2015
F.F.-H. Nah and C.-H. Tan (Eds.): HCIB 2015, LNCS 9191, pp. 727–738, 2015.
DOI: 10.1007/978-3-319-20895-4_68

the HCI and User Experience (UX) industry? Is academic research in HCI applicable and useful to HCI practice? Can HCI academia and practice work together to establish greater synergy in their profession and discipline, and if so, how?

2   Perspectives from HCI Academia

Four HCI academicians offer their perspectives on how the gap between academia and practice can be bridged and their suggestions on creating synergy between HCI academia and practice. They are: Dennis Galletta from University of Pittsburgh, Fiona Fui-Hoon Nah from Missouri University of Science and Technology, Gavriel Salvendy from Purdue University, and Hong Sheng from Missouri University of Science and Technology.

Perspective from Dennis Galletta (University of Pittsburgh). I believe that practice and the academy have synergies that provide great opportunities for interaction.

Innovations that are widely communicated have the best chance of further improvement over time, and eventually becoming mainstream. If innovations remain in academic journals, they merely remain as untested ideas or platforms for understanding the innovations. On the other hand, innovations that stay in an organization remain as proprietary technologies, and users are then forced to do painstaking research to discover which products have the best combination of unique and immature innovations. Innovations that are found through research (whether from the academy or from the corporate lab) and widely communicated and/or evaluated through academic journals and conferences will be on a quicker cycle to lead to further innovations that can be enjoyed by all.

In earlier days of our field, 30+ years back, research teams such as [8, 9] were pioneers of this interaction. Three examples from these two research teams should be helpful. I have chosen older examples because the world has had time to realize their value and extend their impact.

Gould and Lewis [8] provided a framework of three simple principles to design usable systems (through early focus on the users and task, testing, and iteration). Their survey revealed that surprisingly, very few designers describing their practices mentioned any of those principles. This disparity, and the simplicity of the framework, was appealing to researchers; as of this writing, Google Scholar reports 1,630 citations. Two years later, Gould et al. [10] reported how they applied their framework to a successful design of the Olympic Message System in 1984, attributing much of their success to those principles. In the following years, several practitioners set up usability labs. Some even have made available tools to support user testing and make it affordable. Examples of on-line tools in this area are Usertesting.com and Openhallway.com. Today we know much more about the sample size that is needed for testing, e.g., Hwang and Salvendy [11] has come up with the "10 ± 2 rule" indicating that designers should test with at least 8 to 12 subjects.

Card, Moran, and Newell [9] reported a hierarchy of models of expert user performance, which included the keystroke model. The first two authors were practitioner-researchers from Xerox's Palo Alto Research Center, and the third was an academic from Carnegie Mellon University. They pooled their resources to create a set of parameters and techniques for modeling error-free user behavior, which could predict the time it would take for highly experienced users to accomplish tasks using quantitative techniques rather than testing them in actual use. To date, not only have there been over 6,500 citations of that work, but in the 1980s, many devices and software packages were evaluated using that framework.[1]

There were two influential applications of the keystroke model. The first, "Project Ernestine," [13] saved NYNEX $2 million by avoiding the purchase of a "modern" GUI-based system; the keystroke model revealed an excessive amount of sequential operations for which operators had to wait, as compared to the faster but cruder-looking legacy system's parallel operations which could be performed while operators were doing other things. The second was IBM's "In-keyboard pointing stick," now known as the Track-point©, included on Lenovo's Thinkpad© line, as well as on many higher-end Dell, Toshiba, and HP laptops. Ted Selker of MIT's Media Lab, designed this red "eraser head," as some call it, a pointing device placed between the G, H, and B keys. Selker [14] found it to be 20 % faster in mixed keyboard and pointing tasks because users no longer needed 2 s to reposition the hands from the keyboard to a separate mouse and back. The efficacy of the pointing device was supported by the keystroke model as well as by performance of actual subjects, as depicted in a video by Rutledge and Selker [15].

The final example is again from Card, Moran, and Newell [9] in the foundational work that led to the development of the Xerox Star© workstation and the world's first graphical user interface (GUI) operating system. Many of its features led to the design of the first MacIntosh© and Windows© operating systems. Researchers at Xerox needed to painstakingly evaluate many alternative designs [16]. Tuck [17] reported that Apple refined the designs of their GUI by working with "psychologists, artists, teachers, and ordinary users." Tuck reports that they even used children in a California elementary school because kids "gave the truest reaction to basic interface issues." The innovations provided by the Xerox Star project were widely publicized in journals and conferences. This applied research resulted in innovations such as the mouse, Ethernet, Microsoft Word (a descendent of BravoX), laser printing, and other vital innovations that are still offered today, sometimes as hidden components of more well-known products (see [18]).

These examples demonstrate the synergy of practice and academia, suggesting a cycle of (1) innovations enjoyed by a firm, (2) widespread sharing of the innovation's concepts in academic literature, and then (3) further innovations derived from the academic concepts. Industry has benefited, demonstrated by the success of Apple's and Microsoft's operating systems, Ethernet and laser printing, the persistence of the Track-point©, and the savings enjoyed by NYNEX. The academy has also benefited our understanding of computer uses in new ways as we can now abstract across the successes and failures to extract general meaning and frameworks, and provide new building blocks for further research. Academics can study practice, widely communicate its innovations, and provide unique understanding across many products, companies, or applications. Practitioners who refer to analysis from the academy can integrate old and

---

[1] As an aside, one of my recent publications used the keystroke model and novice testing to demonstrate a vivid difference between ease of use and ease of learning. Comparing the four major smartphone platforms in terms of ease of use, Blackberry was first and iPhone was last. Comparing them on ease of learning, the order reversed [12].

new ideas and enhance the academy's work. An iterative cycle of this process can be considered as synergistic because the combination is more powerful than the sum of the two sides.

Perspective from Fiona Fui-Hoon Nah and Hong Sheng (Missouri University of Science and Technology). Being immersed and teaching in a department that integrates business and information science & technology, the field of HCI takes on high precedence in our curriculum and research agenda. As a STEM-oriented university where STEM stands for *S*cience, *T*echnology, *E*ngineering and *M*athematics, the Missouri University of Science and Technology places a strong focus on entrepreneurship to commercialize and roll out into practice the technological innovations and inventions that take place on campus. Hence, bridging research and practice is one important goal and a key success factor of the campus. However, collaborations with industry are still lacking and questions arise as to how we can better train and prepare our students for practice in the HCI/UX area.

From the perspective of providing better and more relevant HCI/UX training to our students, we find that internships, co-ops, and collaborations with industry on research projects offer valuable training and experiences to our students. With regard to collaborations with industry in the HCI/UX area, integrating such collaborations into classes is a powerful and effective way to bring practice-relevant training to students. Having HCI/UX practitioners as guest speakers in classes and serving on the advisory board of major programs can help to foster synergistic effects in bridging practice into academia. Having joint regional and international conferences/workshops/seminars involving academics, students, and practitioners is also desirable for creating and enhancing such synergy.

From the perspective of collaborating on HCI/UX research, there are mutual benefits for both parties to work together. As mentioned earlier, such research collaborations offer greater opportunities for students to work on practice-oriented research projects and apply what they have learned in the classroom to practice. It may also offer academics the opportunity to publish rigorous and practice-oriented research, all in one. Practitioners can benefit from the rigor of scientific research, from relatively inexpensive (or less expensive) labor from students to work on their projects, and from using the university environment to test and assess the HCI/UX aspects of their products and services (e.g., as a beta site).

Despite the many advantages and benefits, there are challenges that will need to be addressed, some of which include intellectual property rights and the somewhat different priorities and performance evaluation criteria of practitioners and academics. Having a mutual understanding of each party's goals and priorities, and striving for a mutual goal that is beneficial to both parties are keys to the success of collaborations.

Perspective from Gavriel Salvendy (Purdue University and Tsinghua University). Both industry and academia got their thrust and evaluation messed up. In industry, typically over 90 % of R&D function is allocated to short term developmental objectives that can germinate revenue for the corporation in the short term. Long term basic research which may have major impact on new products and services is typically downplayed or missing in the current industry objectives. In all or most university programs with the exception of business schools, the top priority is for faculty to bring in lots of research funding. For research output, less research oriented universities simply count the number of papers the faculty authored. The more research intensive universities look at the impact of the journal where a paper is published and the citation of the faculty but there is no emphasis on the impact of the research for societal needs. Based on the above observations, collaborations between industry and academia on basic research are warranted in order to design and produce far reaching high impact innovative products and services for the benefit of mankind. One way of springboarding such collaborations is by having industry sponsor a one full day meeting during a conference, such as HCII, that is attended by individuals from industry and academia in order to generate a white paper on the subject of interest to industry that would provide a road map for high impact international research.

3   Perspectives from HCI Practice

Four HCI practitioners who have received rigorous research training in their doctoral education offer their perspectives on how to address the gap between academia and practice and provide their suggestions on creating synergy between them. The HCI practitioners are: Melinda Knight from Microsoft, James Lewis from IBM, John Pruitt from Dell, and Anna Wichansky from Oracle.

Perspective from Melinda Knight (Microsoft). As the lead of a small team within a large organization, I have two primary objectives: finding and maintaining an outstanding team of world-class researchers, and ensuring that my team and I are providing the most action-able insights possible, activated towards current and future product opportunities in a timely way. We work in a format that roughly mirrors the scientific method: pose a research question, understand existing insights, form a hypothesis, determine the appro-priate method for the investigation of the research question (if that question has not already been answered by the broader HCI or Microsoft community), execute new research or interpret the existing research, frame up the set of insights derived from the investigation … and then activate it to produce real product change.

Activation — the translation of a finding, evidence, speculation, or certainty into a tangible, positive outcome for a customer — is the measure of success for us. Simply put, activation means getting insights into a product, and it includes much more than conducting and communicating research. While academia's culture is one of "publish or perish," for HCI practitioners in industry, the notion is "ship or sink." First, we must start from a research question that will have impact on the products our industry is shipping. We must manage time, budget, and scope of our research question to align with the product schedule in order to ensure that activation is even possible. Yes, our insights must be well-formed, our research plan sound, and our methods appropriate to the level of confidence needed to inform the decision. And yes, we strongly agree that documenting those insights is critical so that others who come after us can jump to the next activation point faster (or deactivate and redirect, as is sometimes the case). But our goal, and the measure of any body of research's true success — and our success as HCI practitioners — is activation.

This is a key point on which industry and academia, and by association, HCI education and training, differ. Conducting outstanding research is not a complete or sufficient outcome, but a step along a journey towards another goal. For my team, that journey also includes project management, leadership across interdisciplinary teams, and understanding how to interpret research results and recommendations in the context of a project timeline, technical constraints, market forces, and myriad other factors. Those are the skills I look for when I interview HCI grads and professionals. It is not the tools in their tool belt, or the number of citations they have produced. Knowledge of tools and number of citations indicate research potential, and are an important foundation for a great industry researcher. Strong qualitative and quantitative skills, mastery of statistical methods, and a background in experimental design are all valued as they are the foundation. The next layer up, however, is critical. I need colleagues with the ability to partner, frame, storytell, and prioritize a research insight to move a product forward.

Across industry and academia, *insight* is our common currency. As HCI practitioners, we share a goal to develop greater understanding of human needs, habits, beliefs and capabilities, and examine how new or existing technologies might best support and enhance these across diverse contexts. Ideally, industry would pause following the launch of a product to exhale those insights that led to (or away from) the customer outcomes embodied in a product solution. That broader sharing remains a challenge for us in many respects. Some revelations are becoming more common, as product teams put forth design language and human interface guidelines for developers of new technologies; however, the specific research findings that led to a piece of advice are not always revealed. I would ask academics to help your industry peers move further and faster by framing your research findings in ways that are actionable and accessible. Seek out and value the application of those findings as a measure of their success. Note product adoption in line with your peer-reviewed articles and publications, or consider it the ultimate citation. Doing so would increase the effective power of your work and afford experimentation and evaluation of your insight at scale.

Two practical barriers we have encountered to partnering with academia include IP and a focus on research funding. Greater partnerships could be facilitated by avoiding competition for IP on joint work, and leading with how existing and future insights could be activated in industry products and timelines vs. leading with the question of "What's in it for the university?" Where there is an opportunity for activation, money follows. Finally, I would implore us all to prepare the next round of HCI practitioners, be they targeting academia or industry, with those skills in project management, team management, and persuasive fortitude which will make them valued and valuable wherever they land.

Perspective from James Lewis (IBM). Given a goal of creating greater synergy between HCI academia and industrial practitioners, one question is, "What are the opportunities for synergy?" I joined IBM in 1981 as a human factors engineer with a master's degree in Human Factors Engineering from New Mexico State University. I haven't conducted research on this topic, but reflecting back on my personal history, here are some of the opportunities I've observed.

Internships. Internships bring students (and in similar but rarer programs, faculty) from academia and give them industrial experience – i.e., experience that can shape their future research activities as academicians in a way that also benefits industrial practice. Before I joined IBM as a regular employee, I interned in the summer of 1980, and that experience helped me decide to pursue industrial rather than academic work. Over the following decades, the Human Factors department in Boca Raton often had several interns (including John Pruitt, also on this panel) working side-by-side with seasoned professionals. Interns can be very influential on industrial practices in a given department given their up-to-date knowledge of applicable research and new analytical methods. Both academia and industry benefit from a robust internship program.

Doctoral Committees. I have twice had the opportunity to participate on the doctoral committees of interns with whom I have worked, one from the University of Central Florida and the other from the University of Miami. Both interns conducted research that had strong industrial value while also accomplishing the research goals required for their doctorates [19, 20].

Practical Courses. Some HFE and HCI professors teach practical courses in which they reach out to industrial practitioners to present design or research problems to the class. The students then, typically in teams, apply the design and research methods they've been learning to the problem. To complete the project they present their work to the practitioner.

Scientific Advisory Boards. Recipients of grant money often need to put together scientific advisory boards as part of their research process. When possible, board membership should be offered to qualified industrial practitioners. In addition to the collaboration via the board, there may also be opportunities for joint research or publication. Recently, I worked with one of the academic members of the Center for Research and Education on Aging and Technology Enhancement (CREATE) on a paper for the Journal of Usability Studies [21].

Professional Societies/Meetings. Membership in professional societies and participation in professional meetings can bring academic researchers and industrial practitioners together (e.g., this panel). Connections made through these activities sometimes result in collaboration. An inhibitor for industrial practitioners is a common lack of financial support for membership and attendance.

Publication. Participation in the publication process can bring academia and industry together. For this to happen there must be venues that are open to contribution by industrial practitioners and industrial practitioners need to be able to (1) recognize which aspects of their work are publishable and (2) work for companies that encourage (or at least don't actively discourage) publication. Ideally, journals in applied areas such as HCI should make an effort to include industrial practitioners on their editorial boards and as reviewers.

Continuing Education. Industrial practitioners can hone skills and connect with academic researchers through continuing education. These opportunities may take the form of short courses such as those offered by the University of Michigan or through tuition reimbursement benefits. For example, IBM essentially paid for my PhD in psycholinguistics, which I then applied for a number of years to help commercialize IBM's speech technologies.

Conclusion. There are a number of opportunities for synergy between HCI academia and practice, which requires investment from both sides. Academia should focus on increased outreach to practitioners, identifying good candidates for participation on committees and boards, providing opportunities for "reverse internships" (bringing qualified practitioners on campus or over the Web to teach a class/course or participate in a research activity), and creating venues for applied publication and presentation. Excellent examples of publication opportunities have been fostered by Gavriel Salvendy, who founded the International Journal of Human-Computer Interaction and the HCII conferences. Industry should create work environments that, while still supporting the goals of the company, provide incentives to practitioners to participate in the broader HCI community (e.g., reimbursing the membership fee for a professional society as a benefit, paying for conference attendance contingent on conference participation, awarding external publication, and seeking academic partners for R&D projects).

Perspective from John Pruitt (Dell). As we consider the question of how to improve the synergy between HCI academia and industrial practice, the first logical response is WHY? To what end do we desire to have better synergy? What is the requisite outcome for either party? For me, that question leads to the discussion of motivation and incentive. What truly motivates an individual practitioner, professor, student, department, team, or broader institution to devote time, energy, people and finances to collaborate across party lines? I posit that our motivations can be quite different and that acknowledging them upfront can lead to better collaboration, transparent negotiations, and win-win situations.

Let's consider first a corporate setting. What matters to almost any corporation is the bottom line. Is there a business case, product or process improvement, protectable and monetize-able intellectual property? For the practitioner in a corporate setting, practical innovation that can be productized and owned may be the primary outcome. In such a case, the specific institution (are they top 10 or lesser known) or individual (published and tenured or just establishing themselves) may matter less as long as they are an expert on the right topics, open to targeted collaborations toward a specific end, and willing to turn over ownership of the outcome to the sponsoring corporation. When considering longer term (promotions and careers), the skills and accomplishments gained in climbing the corporate ladder typically does not make an individual attractive to an academic institution and vice versa.

My own experience is that academic partnerships for HCI in usability and design related research often offers a less costly alternative to consulting agencies when needing to extend my team's capabilities and available resources. The relations are often less formal, more friendly and open. The difficulty typically lies in the fact that business timelines are typically condensed while project goals as well as product requirements can shift suddenly as organizational, industry and competitive changes occur. Agencies can turn on a dime, academic collaborations usually can't or don't. Further, project outcomes for the corporation need to be conclusive, actionable and perhaps show a visible return on investment. Academic collaborations can sometimes be satisfied with simply knowing the previously unknown and creating a call for further research. The research (and gained understanding) is the end, not necessarily a means to an end. For higher level research endeavors (understanding process, the larger system, a particular domain, uncovering innovative ideas), doing so may be fine. For more tactical or product specific work, it likely isn't. Finally, the research topic and findings for a business are largely held as private and protected. Publishing and conference participation is not typically encouraged in many organizations, or at least not explicitly supported. Patent protection, on the other hand, typically is encouraged and even financially incented for the practitioner.

As I consider the academic perspective, what matters might be the reputation of the target corporation, its ability to fund the collaboration, or the possibility of publishing the work (as opposed to being more secretive and protective). For the professor or research associate, will it further their line of investigation, improve their understanding of the domain, give access to certain valuable resources, or lead to further discovery? For the advisor or the student, will it give the student a better opportunity for employment later – real-world experience, connections, a fuller resume or portfolio? Again, for the corporation, not only is the intern's direct work important, but such a relationship allows for a long-term evaluation of a potential employee – a 3-month interview with benefits.

Of course, there is no single perspective or motivation that covers any institution or individual, in academia or industry. Motivations likely overlap some or even reverse in certain situations. They are complex and vary over time. I will also note that the specific motivational examples here revolve around my own primitive notions of traditional academic institutions to traditional businesses. There are many complexities and variations that could be called out in brilliant detail. On the academic side, there is likely a strong division between top tier universities focused on basic research and others that range from more applied research to mostly focused on education and training. On the business side, HCI and UX concerns (and the professionals who do this work) are no longer concentrated in tech companies. Banking, automotive, fashion, health care – you name the industry, and there are likely UX professionals working on interesting problems. The business objectives, processes and working environments must be all over the map. Still, the point here is that understanding motivations and being open about them may encourage new avenues of collaboration, or at least, more productive, mutually beneficial partnerships – a truly concerted effort. It is typically the case that motivations and deliverables are different between parties, but both sets of needs must be met in order for great collaborations to happen.

As James Lewis and others have pointed out, there exist today several good avenues of collaboration between these worlds – joint or one-party funded projects (corporate sponsorship), advisory boards, committees and standards bodies, sabbatical appointments, student internships, visiting/guest instructor/lecturer, targeted conferences, etc.

But, are these the only ones, the rights ones, or are there other, perhaps yet discovered alternatives? Perhaps joint goals, motivators and incentives can be created? Imagine a joint business endeavor or product line between a business and university, or the creation of a "corporate" university/campus or research institute. Imagine there being time-shared employees who spend part of their time in academic settings and part in corporate; students who move seamlessly between the two. The nature of education and business may need to evolve for greater HCI collaboration to happen.

Perspective from Anna Wichansky (Oracle). After receiving my Ph.D. in experimental psychology with concentration in human factors engineering, I felt I was not experienced enough in this very applied field to teach others; therefore, I embarked on an industry career which led to several jobs in high tech. I reasoned that after a long stint in industry (maybe up to 10 years!), I would have enough hands-on knowledge and practical skills to help guide young professionals in an academic setting. Now, after almost triple that time, I feel I might be able to articulate some of the attributes I wish for in a job candidate, particularly a fresh-out master's or doctoral grad who is anxious to get into high tech.

I will concentrate on two areas where I see regrettable lack of skills and knowledge in new HCI grads: product design, and experimental design and statistics. This may have to do with the university they come from, the survey nature of HCI academic programs, and the broad intellectual orientation of the individual who goes into any multidisciplinary field.

In the design area, most new grads come in without a working knowledge of a design process. From some programs, they understand design theory, but they have never started with a blank sheet of paper (or screen) and created a working product from start to finish. From other programs, they think that design is programming, so they start coding on the first day, and attempt to create a product "bit by bit." From still other programs, they attempt to test and analyze their way into product creation. While all of these approaches are complementary and play a role in the design process, they don't produce an actionable design. This is why high tech companies still hire most product designers from design schools granting BFA and MFA degrees, as they come in knowing a design process.

Professional designers understand that product architecture is a very advanced skill. Less experienced designers start in apprentice and journeyman roles, first creating smaller components such as icons and then whole workflows and features that merge into the grand design. Understanding what a design process is, how to follow it, where a project is in the process, and how to work with others to get it done, are things that could be taught through project workshops, design jams, hackathons, and internships, if the HCI program has faculty members who have this experience themselves.

Experimental design and statistics is truly an area of expertise where "what you don't know can hurt you." Many new HCI hires come in thinking they can do a brief survey on a product prototype with five of their colleagues and find out if it is usable. Or they just want to have "a conversation" with users about their product with no prepared questions. They do not have sufficient knowledge of experimental design, including techniques to minimize experimenter and subject biases, use of control conditions, or the effects of confounding, to prepare a methodologically sound study. They may not wish to conduct statistical tests, yet they do not understand that their results can be badly flawed and lead to the wrong design decisions if they do not test enough users. Their findings may not be representative of the user population, or may be merely anecdotal considering the small sample size. Yet companies make million dollar decisions based on these findings. If new grads cannot get enough depth in experimental design and statistics in their HCI programs, they should at least be made aware that this isn't one of their strengths, and how to recognize and support someone who is equipped to design and run a study. At the very least, they should know when they need to do a controlled behavioral study, and what type of study is needed based on the stage of the design process.

Two academic researchers from University of Dayton and Rochester Institute of Technology recently published results of surveys of new human factors professionals in their first jobs, hiring managers, and human factors students in academic programs about their expectations of HF/E programs. The results were keyed to the BCPE ergonomist formation model. While the details of the results differed based on whose perspective was being surveyed, there was common agreement on a couple of key areas [22]:

> The "take-home" message from the three surveys is quite clear: To better prepare new HF/E professionals for the demands of the workplace, their training should include practice in design, project management, working in interdisciplinary teams, and making persuasive arguments for human factors in all project phases. These are topics that could be incorporated into any college curricula on any topics, and we hope that educators hear this message loud and clear.

4   Conclusions

This paper offers perspectives from HCI practitioners and academics on ways in which greater synergy between HCI academia and practice can be achieved. The authors are the panelists at the 2015 HCI International Conference that is to be held in Los Angeles, California from August 2–7, 2015. The panelists will present their views at the conference and are looking forward to receiving comments, feedback and suggestions from the audience on how to achieve the mutual goal of closing the gap between HCI academia and practice, and, further, how to create greater synergy across them.

References

1. Galletta, D.F., Zhang, P., Nah, F.: AIS SIGHCI position paper. In: Proceedings of the Conference on Human Factors in Computing Systems (CHI). Portland, Oregon, USA, pp. 1080–1082 (2005). http://uxnet.org/devcon/DevCon-AIS.pdf
2. Zhang, P., Nah, F., Benbasat, I.: Human-computer interaction research in MIS. J. Manage. Inf. Syst. 22(3), 9–14 (2005)
3. Zhang, P., Nah, F., Preece, J.: HCI studies in management information systems. Behav. Inf. Technol. 23(3), 147–151 (2004)

4. Benbasat, I., Zmud, R.W.: Empirical research in information systems: the practice of relevance. MIS Q. **23**(1), 3–16 (1999)
5. Buhl, H.U., Fridgen, G., Konig, W., Roglinger, M., Wagner, C.: Where's the competitive advantage in strategic information systems research? Making the case for boundary-spanning research based on the German business and information systems engineering tradition. J. Strateg. Inf. Syst. **21**(2), 172–178 (2012)
6. Lyytinen, K.: Empirical research in information systems: on the relevance of practice in thinking of IS research. MIS Q. **23**(1), 25–27 (1999)
7. Mathiassen, L., Sandberg, A.: How a professionally qualified doctoral student bridged the practice-research gap: a confessional account of collaborative research practice. Eur. J. Inf. Syst. **22**(4), 475–492 (2013)
8. Gould, J.D., Lewis, C.: Designing for usability: key principles and what designers think. Commun. ACM **28**(3), 300–311 (1985)
9. Card, S.K., Moran, T.P., Newell, A.: The Psychology of Human-Computer Interaction. Lawrence Erlbaum Associates, London (1983)
10. Gould, J.D., Boies, S.J., Levy, S., Richards, J.T., Schoonar, J.: The 1984 olympic message system: a test of behavioral principles of system design. Commun. ACM **30**(9), 758–769 (1987)
11. Hwang, W., Salvendy, G.: Number of people required for usability evaluation: the 10±2 rule. Commun. ACM **53**(5), 130–133 (2010)
12. Galletta, D.F., Dunn, B.K.: Assessing smartphone ease of use and learning from the perspective of novice and expert users: development and illustration of mobile benchmark tasks. AIS Trans. Hum. Comput. Inter. **6**(4), 74–91 (2014)
13. Gray, W.D., John, B.E., Atwood, M.E.: Project Ernestine: validating a GOMS analysis for predicting and explaining real-world performance. Hum. Comput. Inter. **8**(3), 237–309 (1993)
14. Selker, T.: Fostering motivation and creativity for computer users. Int. J. Hum. Comput. Stud. **63**(4/5), 410–421 (2005)
15. Rutledge, J., Selker, T.: In-keyboard analog pointing device: a case for the pointing stick. In: Technical Video Program of the CHI'1990 Conference (1990)
16. Bewley, W.L., Roberts, T.L., Schroit, D., Verplank, W.L.: Human factors testing in the design of xerox's 8010 "star" office workstation. In: Proceedings of CHI. New York, NY pp. 72–77 (1983)
17. Tuck, M.: The real history of the GUI (2001). http://www.sitepoint.com/real-history-gui/. Accessed 8 Jan. 2015
18. Johnson, J., Roberts, T.L., Verplank, W., Smith, D.C., Irby, C.H., Beard, M., Mackey, K.: The xerox star: a retrospective. Computer **22**(9), 11–26 (1989)
19. Commarford, P.M., Lewis, J.R., Smither, J.A., Gentzler, M.D.: A comparison of broad versus deep auditory menu structures. Hum. Factors **50**, 77–89 (2008)
20. Millet, B., Asfour, S., Lewis, J.R.: Selection-based virtual keyboard prototypes and data collection application. Behav. Res. Meth. **41**, 951–956 (2009)
21. Sharit, J., Lisigurski, M., Andrade, A.D., Karanam, C., Nazi, K.M., Lewis, J.R., Ruiz, J.G.: The roles of health literacy, numeracy, and graph literacy on the usability of the VA'S personal health record by Veterans. J. Usability Stud. **9**(4), 173–193 (2014)
22. Rantanen, E.M., Moroney, W.F.: Employers' expectations for education and skills of new human factors/ergonomics professionals. In: Proceedings of the Human Factors and Ergonomics Society 56th Annual Meeting, pp. 581–585 (2012)

Ambient and Aesthetic Intelligence for High-End Hospitality

Daniela Alina Plewe[1(✉)], Rui An Ong[1], and Carsten Röcker[2]

[1] University Scholars Programme, National University of Singapore, Singapore, Singapore
{danielaplewe,ra}@nus.edu.sg
[2] Ostwestfalen-Lippe UAS and Fraunhofer IOSB-INA, Lemgo, Germany
carsten.roecker@iosb-ina.fraunhofer.de

Abstract. The core value proposition for most hospitality brands is to provide unique customer experiences; therefore we expect commercially viable opportunities for ambient intelligence systems in hospitality in general, and the high-end sector in particular. We believe that ambient intelligence systems paired with principles of Aesthetic Intelligence could facilitate such unique experiences and at the same time strengthen and differentiate the brands. This paper gives an overview of challenges in this field, reviews research and outlines future scenarios enhancing safety, economic optimisation and – especially - convenience for hotel guests.

Keywords: Smart hospitality · Business applications for home/leisure · Technology and branding · Smart environments · Personalized services · Aesthetic intelligence · Ambient intelligence

1 Introduction

Research in the field of ambient intelligence has covered a variety of applications, many centered on smart homes and offices, and rather little attention has been paid yet to its application in the hospitality industry. Most hospitality brands' value proposition is centered around creating unique customer experiences. We believe that strategies for "smart hospitality" based on ambient intelligence can offer commercially viable opportunities. Especially the field of aesthetic intelligence [3–6] with its focus on the conceptual and perceptional aspects of technologies may be able to contribute to shape such unique experiences. Aesthetics are also at the core, when it comes to strengthen brand value and differentiate brands from other competitors. The implications for "smart hospitality" are potentially huge with an annual volume of global travel accommodation sales in 2013 of US$670.861 billion [7] while the volume of global hotel sales in 2013 was recorded as US $488 billion [7]. Within this market, the hotel segment is expected to be the early adopters.

This paper first provides an overview of existing research in ambient intelligence for smart homes and hospitality, followed by a few examples of how concepts and technologies from aesthetic and ambient intelligence could be combined to provide new high-end hospitality services. We chose to concentrate on the high-end segment of the hospitality industry since innovations are often earlier adopted in the premium markets.

© Springer International Publishing Switzerland 2015
F.F.-H. Nah and C.-H. Tan (Eds.): HCIB 2015, LNCS 9191, pp. 739–747, 2015.
DOI: 10.1007/978-3-319-20895-4_69

2 Challenges for Hospitality

It is challenging to apply existing technology into the hospitality industry. The majority of ambient and aesthetic intelligence studies [see, e.g., 11, 12, 13 or 14] are designed for the use in homes and not in transit stays. Even though both settings may be considered as living environments, there are crucial differences between homes and hospitality rooms. For example, users as guests may have very different expectations towards a premium priced temporarily available space in a resort than to their daily living environment. They may rent a room, suite or villa more likely for its unique experiential value than for mere accommodation purposes. Unsurprisingly, guests pay higher for a unique level of service and expect an immersive experience.

A main challenge for all ambient technologies is the potential degree of intrusion and violation of privacy – in legal but perhaps for hospitality more importantly, in emotional terms. Hotel guests tend to be highly aware of details of the environment and services provided. Although they generally appreciate intelligence catering to their habits and preferences, such services need to be based on data obtained via non-intrusive methods [15–17]. Ambient intelligence should observe surrounding and aesthetically adapt to deliver personalized services [18] without crossing the line of intrusion to gain public support. In this respect, the European Union Information Society Technology funded a collective initiative that produced the European Privacy Design Guidelines for the Disappearing Computer [35]. This guidelines deal with amongst other things, privacy challenges of ambient intelligence. One of the guidelines includes applying the "privacy razor" that eliminates any information that is not "absolutely necessary".

Another challenge is that the time for configuration of devices is rather limited during temporary stays. Transit stays imply that there is short period of time for devices to learn about guests' environmental demands. Unlike smart homes where devices can use descriptive and predictive analytics to interpret, anticipate and respond to an individual's habits, transit stays do not allow for such predictive analytics. While in homes people generally are inclined to routines, this does not apply to tourist's use of hotel rooms. As such, identifying personal preferences becomes even more challenging in the hospitality sector, impeding the sufficient collection of data.

In addition, since hospitality environments are highly depending on the perception of their guests, there is a need to understand the relevance of beauty and aesthetic values for these ambient intelligence technologies. Aesthetically pleasing design for usability, technology acceptance, and well being in technology-enhanced spaces are likely to gain additional importance in the future. With the concept of "aesthetic intelligence" [34] we refer to the related conceptual, visual and methodological competencies required by designers and technology developers. Aesthetic intelligence highlights the "conceptual soundness" beyond the mere beautification of interfaces or designs. It stresses the importance of intersecting brand values, cultural values and an understanding of meaningfulness of the target audiences, for the creation of aesthetic systems. We will drill here not into the details of aesthetic intelligence as a set of methodological heuristics, but want to highlight its importance in relation to brand building in general and its applicability for the creation of user experiences in retail and hospitality environments.

3 Existing Research

To understand the applications of ambient intelligence in the hospitality sector, we consider existing studies in domains, smart homes, and hospitality. There have been extensive studies on ambient intelligence in smart homes; many of those findings seem to be transferrable to hospitality accommodation. We will highlight some of them in this section. We will refer also to some earlier ambient intelligence studies directed towards the hospitality sector; many of those could benefit from current technological developments.

3.1 Studies in Smart Homes Applicable to Hospitality

Since home and hospitality settings share common features, research findings on smart houses may be transferable. Granted, the tracking and sensing technologies in the Aware Home project [26] can assist hospitality industry in solving loss and theft scenarios. Using RF tags and long-range indoor position system, the Aware Home is able to locate misplaced items. Another research center, which could support studies for hospitality related scenarios, is the Assisted Living Laboratory [31]. Using basic technology and measurements of environment, it aims to assist elder living. It automates with ambient sensors based on European Installation Bus to keep track of the resident's activities. It also uses position-tracking solution such as radio frequency identification (RFID) tags mounted in the ceiling, ultrasonic and radio frequency based movement sensors.

The technologies used in the assisted living laboratory, while designed for the elderly, can be transferred into developing ambient intelligence in the hospitality industry, such as to collect data of guests' habits. In addition, by identifying repetitive patterns observed by sensors and predicting likely future activities with compression-based predictors, MavHome automated interactions with the environment by 76 %, on average [23]. Although limited in numbers, successful applications in smart homes such as those by MavHome might also be useful in the hospitality sector.

3.2 Studies in Hospitality and Tourism

While existing studies directed towards the hospitality industry provide an alternative perspective, not many seem to be informed by current ideas from Ambient and Aesthetic Intelligence. Leonides et al. [1] in their work on the Intelligent Hotel Room (iHR) seek to provide an ambient ecosystem that "observes its surroundings and adapts its behavior in real-time to deliver intelligent and personalized services to its guests" that contribute to a more seamless travelling experience. The suggested infrastructure includes a portable room controller, intelligent touch panel, universal remote, hotel explorer, doormat device and a digital room butler.

To control devices in the hotel room remotely, studies can tap into the test-bed of the University of Essex's intelligent dormitory (iDorm) [24], which allows any networked Java-enabled computer to access and control iDorm through its Universal Plug and Play (UPnP) [25]. However these researches seem still at its infancy and suggestions do not fully tap effectively into ambient intelligence. The concepts of the "disappearing computer" [19] proposed that users no longer need a "portable room controller" or "intelligent touch panel" [1]. Essentially, these slightly dated studies do not fully encapsulate today's potential that ambient and aesthetic intelligence possess.

4 Opportunities for Applications in Hospitality

The aesthetics [3–6] and "look and feel" of technological solutions are perhaps more important for hospitality than for many other commercial domains. Ambient and Aesthetic Intelligence can provide revitalized user experiences bolstering the brand. Due to social networks, consumer decision-making is highly informed by the opinion of others and viral effects can affect branding quickly and powerfully in both positive and negative ways [9]. Brands in the hospitality industry looking to improve their reputation management will be able to tap effectively on aesthetically sophisticated ambient intelligent solutions.

There are three major components for innovations in the field of Ambient Intelligent for hospitality environments: safety, economics and convenience. The first two components can be easily adapted from existing approaches. The main field for new applications we consider is in the category of convenience given its central role for hospitality brands.

4.1 Safety

A challenge in hospitality lies in providing safety in an environment filled with strangers. This poses a special emphasis on safety, though standard approaches seem to be applicable. As mentioned previously, non-invasiveness might have a higher priority than in private environments – finding an optimal combination of security and surveillance technologies without invading the guest's experience.

Non-invasive monitoring, through position-tracking solutions can elevate the security level in this sense effectively. The actions of guests having access to the room can be monitored and assistance can be given if a harmful situation is developing [29]. As compared to recording cameras, there is less intrusion using position-tracking solutions.

Apart from aiding physical accidents, harmful situations occur from unauthorized access of individuals. For example, in theft cases it might be difficult for the hotel management to make a judgment on staff theft and a guest's loss of items. Non-invasive monitoring can also identify if room attendants have unusual patterns or act differently from designated routines. Combined with tracking technologies that identify loss items, the confusion between theft and misplacement can be avoided. Security systems like this will have deterring effects.

4.2 Economical Optimizations

It has been well established, that ambient technology can help to optimize the use of resources. These approaches can easily be transferred to the hospitality environment. Optimization through customization is an obvious example: by using ambient intelligence integrated into the physical environment [20–22], the industry will be able to customize various facilities to individual guests and control energy usage at different times of day: ideal degree of light, position of curtains, frequency of changing sheets and towels, temperature of water in bath tub, television channels, music and radio channels.

Learning algorithms tracking the movement of guests allow the temperature of a room to be prepared in advanced, yet without having to leave the air-conditioners/warmers on throughout the day. Currently, travellers who wish to return to a room at a desirable temperature have to leave their conditioners/warmers on throughout the day.

In spite of cost-saving efforts by hotels to power electricity of rooms via key cards, travellers often circumvent this process with card substitutes to keep the air-conditioners running, causing inefficient uses of electrical energy in the hospitality sector. An example of a project outside of the hospitality sector that addresses intelligent use of energy is ambient lighting assistance for an ageing population (ALADIN) [30]. It translates the impact of lighting on wellbeing of older people into a cost-effective open solution.

Today commercial thermostats that track habits and adjust accordingly are available for homes such as those sold by Nest [27]. The improved interfaces and remote access of such devices tighten interactions between human and systems [28]. However, the necessary "learning" time of such devices is not always applicable to the hospitality industry due to the frequent occurrence of short stays. Nevertheless, with increasing connectivity [2], hotel chains might gather information through a series of stays and culminate collected information. This represents an opportunity to offer a higher value to guests while reducing costs through energy savings.

4.3 Convenience

Improving convenience in hospitality we consider the area with perhaps the highest potential for innovation. A variety of new applications can be envisioned around personalization, informational enrichment and atmospheric improvement.

Most guests, even in luxury hotels, do not have the privilege of receiving personalized services. Given the lack of information, housekeeping departments apply a general service for all clients. For example, a common practice in hotels and requirement for five-star rating is a "turn-down service" that includes entering a guest's room to close the curtains, turn on night-lights and prepare indoor footwear. This practice engenders privacy issues that can be ameliorated via ambient intelligence technologies.

Privacy can be bolstered when ambient intelligence supports or even substitutes tasks of room attendants, who might not necessarily have to enter a hotel room anymore to fulfill the various daytime service. This again represents an opportunity for customization through automatisation. Long-term guests of hotels or serviced apartments enjoy the privilege of having room attendants learn their preferences, such as guests preferring curtains opened throughout the day or otherwise. With ambient intelligence, these tasks can be customized to the guests taking into account their preferences for water temperature during bath and showers, sauna and spa [32] etc. Reminders for desirable routines such as health-related activities or medication can also be easily communicated.

Another scenario could include protection from environmental nuisances, such as insects: especially in tropical climates electronic insect deterrents could be automatically triggered during the dusk and dawn hours or after rain for the outdoor areas, private balconies and verandas without any intrusion.

Convenient for business guests and travellers requiring frequent communication should be a video-telephony system, such as the one embedded in the Assisted Living Laboratory [31]. As guests expect a higher level of technology and customization based on their stored preferences [10], the range of demands will expand and ambient intelligence provides a solution to quickly learn and meet individual needs. Or, one may envision voice recognition combined with a database so that when a guest hums a few bars of a song, the sound system of the room can retrieve and play the respective audio file [33].

Travelling implies – for most individuals - being in an unfamiliar environment. Therefore we spot opportunities for systems, which more or less explicitly offer educational information about the local culture, language, cuisine, flora and fauna etc., the immediate vicinity of the hotel, logistical support regarding travels and so on. For example, sensors in a guest room may recognize in real-time the exotic birds outside singing displaying some information about the bird. Basic language skills and gestures, the recipe of a dish conveyed as short media snippets might be nice "take-aways" from a stay. The collection of environmental data such as the cleanliness of air, clarity of water and timings of specific natural events will be also valuable to customers. Gamification, real time analysis of data, tapering into the pool of mobile and social media applications open a wide range for innovations.

We also identify opportunities for what we may call "atmospheric improvements". An interesting challenge could also be reconciling the apparent opposition of nature themed environments with high tech. Premium tropical resorts especially in Asia are designed with natural materials yet creating sophisticated aesthetically cozy environments often emphasizing health and wellness in a setting of tranquility.

Conveying atmospheric information between different parts within larger resorts such as private spaces, the hallways and the public areas could prove useful. For example, ambient displays may communicate crowd-sensing data from the buffets, the beach, the pools etc. Here video images would violate a sense of privacy, yet atmospheric displays [36] could provide helpful and anonymous atmospheric information. Especially in larger resorts this may help to avoid unwelcome over crowding during peak hours and let guest's make informed decisions. Such mechanisms may also attract attention for social events, tours or sites and may serve as a subtle real-time marketing channel.

Ambient displays and light dramaturgy are effective means for creating subtle atmospheres. They may display decorative or atmospheric visuals via video or still imagery, e.g. soothing landscapes. Real-time feeds from the region or vicinity of the hotel (beach, sunset etc.) might be of interest. Gentle light modulations imitating a sunrise can in future substitute the wake up call, if wanted [32].

Providing silence and the absence of noise could be a new feature for luxury environments, especially those targeting wealthy "silver" clientele. Audio profiling of rooms ("sound profiles" for the various room types, e.g. pool view, sea view, mountain view) could be new category of marketing different areas within a hotel. Guests may then be able to request particularly quiet rooms.

5 Conclusion and Further Work

In this paper we focused on three core aspects of ambient intelligence: safety, economical optimisation and convenience. We believe, there is significant potential in the hospitality industry to make use of ambient intelligent systems in combination with principles of aesthetic intelligence to create new customer experiences.

We offered a selection of proposals how ambient intelligence could be applied and consider the sector of convenience the most promising one. Ambient technologies can be used to enhance environments with information, education, and logistical explicit information. They may also be applied to create subtle atmospheres, through light, sounds, the absence of sound as a new and recreational quality etc. We feel that there is huge potential for new applications and ideas, either through developing new functionalities or through the combination of existing technologies (real-time sound analysis app "singing bird detector" e.g.). These may include ambient displays in combination with data from crowd sensors in order to influence the guest's decision making within the hotel premises.

We also highlighted the special challenges for the hospitality industry: balancing safety and surveillance technologies with the high preference for non-intrusiveness seems of high importance. Also integrating technology in nature themed ambiances, which are quite common for most tropical high-end resorts, is a particular design setting, where the idea of the disappearing computer and ambient intelligence literally seems predestined to offer solutions.

For research in the field of aesthetic intelligence the hospitality industry seems a very fruitful domain to test and explore heuristics for the design of aesthetic systems, especially in relation to building brands. In combination with social media – before, during and after the stay may also open up new possibilities; we did not touch upon those here, but they could be explored in future research.

Overall we assume, that the high-end hospitality could become an innovation driving industry for the application of ambient intelligent systems. Similar to the role of luxury brands, from these premium services the mass-market suppliers may benefit and adopt strategies for the future. We could imagine, that the high-end hospitality industry could help to explore and establish highest standards for ambient and aesthetic intelligence. There seems an abundance of opportunities for the progress of luxury hospitality through new applications and research offering feasible, yet innovative and commercially viable perspectives.

References

1. Leonidis, A., Korozi, M., Margetis, G., Grammenos, D., Stephanidis, C.: An intelligent hotel room. In: Augusto, J.C., Wichert, R., Collier, R., Keyson, D., Salah, A.A., Tan, A.-H. (eds.) AmI 2013. LNCS, vol. 8309, pp. 241–246. Springer, Heidelberg (2013)
2. Manes, G.: The tetherless tourist: ambient Intelligence in travel & tourism. Inf. Technol. Tourism 5(4), 211–220 (2002)
3. Röcker, C., Kasugai, K., Plewe, D., Kiriyama, T., Rozendaal, M.: When design meets intelligence: incorporating aesthetic intelligence in smart spaces. In: Augusto, C. (ed.) AmI 2013. LNCS, vol. 8309, pp. 241–246. Springer, Switzerland (2013)

4. Röcker, C., Kasugai, K., Plewe, D., Kiriyama, T., Lugmayr, A.: Aesthetic intelligence: the role of design in ambient intelligence. In: Paternò, F., de Ruyter, B., Markopoulos, P., Santoro, C., van Loenen, E., Luyten, K. (eds.) AmI 2012. LNCS, vol. 7683, pp. 445–446. Springer, Heidelberg (2012)
5. Kasugai, K., Röcker, C., Plewe, D., Kiriyama, T., Oksman, V.: Aesthetic intelligence: concepts, technologies and applications. In: Wichert, R., van Laerhoven, K., Gelissen, J. (eds.) Constructing Ambient Intelligence, Communications in Computer and Information Science Series. Lecture Notes in Computer Science, vol. 277, pp. 1–4. Springer, Germany (2012)
6. Röcker, C., Kasugai, K., Plewe, D., Kiriyama, T., Lugmayr, A.: Aesthetic intelligence: the role of design in ambient intelligence. In: Paternò, F., de Ruyter, B., Markopoulos, P., Santoro, C., van Loenen, E., Luyten, K. (eds.) AmI 2012. LNCS, vol. 7683, pp. 445–446. Springer, Heidelberg (2012)
7. Bremner, C.: Travel and tourism: travel industry forecast review. In: Euromonitor International (2014)
8. Bremner, C.: Luxury goods: euromonitor from trade sources/national statistics. In: Euromonitor International (2013)
9. Bremner, C.: Game-changing technology key to capturing the new online travel consumer. In: Euromonitor International (2014)
10. Bremner, C.: Understanding the 21st century traveller. In: Euromonitor International (2013)
11. Röcker, C., Etter, R.: Social radio – a music-based approach to emotional awareness mediation. In: Proceedings of the International Conferences on Intelligent User Interfaces (IUI 2007), pp. 286–289. ACM Press, New York (2007)
12. Ziefle, M., Röcker, C., Holzinger A.: Medical technology in smart homes: exploring the user's perspective on privacy, intimacy and trust. In: Proceedings of the IEEE 35th Annual Computer Software and Applications Conference Workshops (COMPSACW 2011), pp. 410–415. IEEE Press (2011)
13. Ziefle, M., Röcker, C.: Acceptance of pervasive healthcare systems: a comparison of different implementation concepts. In: Proceedings of the 4th International ICST Conference on Pervasive Computing Technologies for Healthcare (PervasiveHealth 2010). Munich, Germany, March pp. 22–25. CD-ROM (2010)
14. Röcker, C., Janse, M., Portolan, N., Streitz, N.A.: User requirements for intelligent home environments: a scenario-driven approach and empirical cross-cultural study. In: Proceedings of the International Conference on Smart Objects & Ambient Intelligence (sOc-EUSAI 2005), October 12–14. Grenoble, France, ACM International Conference Proceeding Series, vol. 121, pp. 111–116 (2005)
15. Lahlou, S., Langheinrich, M., Röcker, C.: Privacy and trust issues with invisible computers. Commun. ACM 48(3), 59–60 (2005)
16. Sack, O., Röcker, C.: Privacy and security in technology-enhanced environments: exploring users' knowledge about technological processes of diverse user groups. Univ. J. Psychol. 1(2), 72–83 (2013)
17. Röcker, C., Feith, A.: Revisiting privacy in smart spaces: social and architectural aspects of privacy in technology-enhanced environments. In: Proceedings of the International Symposium on Computing, Communication and Control (ISCCC 2009), 9–11 October 2009. Singapore, pp. 201–205 (2009)
18. Röcker, C.: User-centered design of intelligent environments: requirements for designing successful ambient assisted living systems. In: Proceedings of the Central European Conference of Information and Intelligent Systems (CECIIS 2013), 18–20 September Varazdin, pp. 4–11 (2013)

19. Streitz, N.A., Prante, T., Röcker, C., van Alphen, D., Stenzel, R., Magerkurth, C., Lahlou, S., Nosulenko, V., Jegou, F., Sonder, F., Plewe, D.: Smart artefacts as affordances for awareness in distributed teams. In: Streitz, N., Kameas, A., Mavrommati, I. (eds.) DC 2007. LNCS, vol. 4500, pp. 3–29. Springer, Berlin (2007)
20. Kasugai, K., Röcker, C.: Computer-mediated human architecture interaction. In: O'Grady, M.J., Vahliai-Nejad, H., Wolf, K.-H., Dragone, M., Ye, J., Röcker, C., O'Hare, G. (eds.) AmI Workshops 2013. CCIS, vol. 413, pp. 213–216. Springer, Heidelberg (2013)
21. Röcker, C., Kasugai, K.: Interactive architecture in domestic spaces. In: Wichert, R., van Laerhoven, K., Gelissen, J. (eds.) Constructing Ambient Intelligence, Communications in Computer and Information Science Series. Lecture Notes in Computer Science, vol. 277, pp. 12–18. Springer, Germany (2012)
22. Heidrich, F., Ziefle, M., Röcker, C., Borchers, J.: Interacting with Smart Walls: A Multi-Dimensional Analysis of Input Technologies for Augmented Environments. In: Proceedings of the ACM Augmented Human Conference (AH 2011), March 12–14, Tokyo, Japan, CD-ROM (2011)
23. Youngblood, G.M., Cook, D.J., Holder, L.B.: Managing adaptive versatile environments. Pervasive Mob. Comput. 1(4), 373–403 (2005)
24. Doctor, F., Hagras, H., Callaghan, V.: A fuzzy embedded agent-based approach for realizing Ambient Intelligence in intelligent inhabited environments. IEEE Trans. Syst. Man Cybernet. Part A Syst. Hum. 35(1), 55–65 (2005)
25. Hagras, H., Callaghan, V., Colley, M., Clarke, G., Pounds-Cornish, A., Duman, H.: Creating an ambient-intelligence environment using embedded agents. IEEE Intell. Syst. 19(6), 12–20 (2004)
26. Abowd, G.D., Mynatt, E.D. Designing for the human experience in smart environments. Smart Environ. Technol. Protoc. Appl., 151–174 (2004)
27. Nest. The Learning Thermostat. Home: http://www.nest.com/
28. Yang, R., Newman, M.W.: Living with an intelligent thermostat: advanced control for heating and cooling systems. In: UbiComp, pp. 1102–1107, September 2012
29. Cook, D.J., Augusto, J.C., Jakkula, V.R.: Ambient intelligence: technologies, applications, and opportunities. Pervasive Mob. Comput. 5(4), 277–298 (2009)
30. ALADIN. http://www.ambient-lighting.eu
31. Kleinberger, T., Becker, M., Ras, E., Holzinger, A., Müller, P.: Ambient intelligence in assisted living: enable elderly people to handle future interfaces. In: Stephanidis, C. (ed.) Universal Access in Human-Computer Interaction. Ambient Interaction. Lecture Notes in Computer Science, vol. 4555, pp. 103–112. Springe, Springer (2007)
32. Friedewald, M., Costa, O.D., Punie, Y., Alahuhta, P., Heinonen, S.: Perspectives of ambient intelligence in the home environment. Telematics Inform. 22(3), 221–238 (2005)
33. Peterson, K.E.: If high-tech it is your idea of paradise, welcome to Valhalla (2002). http://www.10meters.com/homelab3.html
34. Plewe, D., Röcker, C., Autexier, S.: Aesthetic intelligence for ambient intelligence. In: Proceedings of 2014 European Conference on Ambient Intelligence (in press)
35. Lahlou, S., Jegou, F.: European disappearing computer privacy design guidelines V1.0. Ambient Agoras Report D15.4. Disappearing Computer Initiative (2003)
36. Prante, T., Röcker, C., Streitz, N.A., Stenzel, R., Magerkurth, C., van Alphen, D., Plewe, D.A.: Hello.Wall – beyond ambient displays. In: Ljungstrand, P., Brotherton, J. (eds.): Video Track and Adjunct Proceedings of the Fifth International Conference on Ubiquitous Computing (UBICOMP 2003). Seattle, pp. 277–278, October 12–15, (2003)

Vision 2020: The Future of Software Quality Management and Impacts on Global User Acceptance

Robin Poston[1]([⊠]) and Ashley Calvert[2]

[1] University of Memphis, Memphis, USA
rposton@memphis.edu
[2] System Testing Excellence Program, Canada, USA

Abstract. This paper explores the future evolution of software quality management (SQM), testing, and global user acceptance approaches keeping in mind the evolution in software and technology quality management in general, including new technologies and the increasing adoption of new software development life cycle methodologies such as Agile and Scaled Agile. These evolutions are forcing quality organizations to change the way they approach software quality processes, including increased outsourcing of development, and the need to update traditional testing and user acceptance testing approaches which lag behind with manual and invasive techniques. User acceptance as we know it today must evolve.

This discussion about evolution should deemphasize the role of the end user in "testing" and emphasize the end user's role in acceptance, adoption, and ability to influence the quality and usability of software much further upstream in the development life cycle. User acceptance teams should increase their role in user experience, the development of usability standards, non-invasive automation techniques gathering usage data, etc. All of these mechanisms should increase the ability of the end user to influence product quality and enhance the user experience and acceptance. Perceptions of end user's participation in user acceptance events need to be transformed away from just another cycle of software testing. User acceptance should not be about testing, but about validating that the end user needs and expectations have been met. All testing and other quality processes should be completed and defects corrected before the end user is engaged in the process of "accepting" the deliverable.

Thus, this effort will explore the future of SQM and its impacts on global user acceptance. We will discuss how organizations involve users throughout the development life cycle to facilitate adoption, user experience, and usability of new technologies. This discussion will be embedded in the use of futuristic new technologies and development methodologies. To explore these notions, this study gathers input from technology visionaries about best practices approaches for facilitating SQM and user acceptance throughout the development life cycle.

Keywords: Global user acceptance · User acceptance testing · Software development life cycle · Software quality management

© Springer International Publishing Switzerland 2015
F.F.-H. Nah and C.-H. Tan (Eds.): HCIB 2015, LNCS 9191, pp. 748–760, 2015.
DOI: 10.1007/978-3-319-20895-4_70

1 Introduction

Software quality management (SQM) has been a key driver enabling teams to deliver software at the user-accepted quality levels. The focus of these management approaches is to adopt specific quality assurance activities throughout the development life cycle with input from developers, customers, and users (Poth and Sunyaev 2014), that ultimately improve customer's acceptance of software quality at release time. Prior research has examined various supporting mechanisms including the adoption of total quality management principles and process knowledge management (Shang and Lin 2009), among others. While software testing activities tend to remain relegated to the final stages of development work, SQM brings a more holistic approach to ensure user acceptance, keeping in mind today's global reach of enterprise user groups.

Development life cycles have evolved over time increasing in quality management focus. Starting with structured formalized methodologies in the 1960s and1970 s, early approaches required each stage of the life cycle from inception of the product to release of the final system performed under a rigid, sequential timeline. Still in use today, these plan-driven methods typically have hierarchical organization structures, formalized project manage processes (Agarwal and Sambamurthy 2002), and tend to be characterized by predefined process phases, pre-approved designs, and agreed-to requirements documentation. More recently, industry has moved toward agile methodologies in the 1990s and 2000s, characterized by flexibility and openness to embrace and learn from changing work routines, requirements, and designs being responsive to shifting customer demands (Conboy 2009, Ramesh et al. 2006). Today, methodologies, such as Scaled Agile Framework (SAFe), offer guidelines for adopting agile in large enterprises, by addressing challenges with architecture designs, integration activities, funding mechanics, governance oversight, and role assignments. However, quality management and development life cycles will continue to evolve as innovative, cutting-edge technologies are introduced, e.g., artificial intelligence, visualization tools, and augmented reality.

With the focus on quality management and more rapid flexible software development capabilities, user acceptance testing will inherently need to adapt. The purpose of user acceptance testing is to gather software product feedback from actual system users, those who have experience with the business processes and will be using the system to complete related tasks (Klein 2003, Larson 1995). Actual users bring knowledge of processes and work activities and are able to assess how the system meets what is required of it. UAT typically occurs after development is complete but before the product is released. As business systems become more complex and decentralized, UAT on a global scale becomes more complicated to perform (Poston et al. 2014). The execution of UAT events needs effective participation of geographically distributed actual system users. The evolution toward increasing global dynamics, quality focus, and more rapid development life cycles is forcing UAT organizations to change the way they approach software quality processes. Organizations are beginning to see the need to update traditional UAT approaches which lag behind with manual, invasive, and time-consuming techniques (Poston et al. 2014). Thus, how will UAT evolve?

This study examines the future evolution of UAT through an assessment of the future of SQM and impacts on global user acceptance. The evolution should deemphasize the role of the end user in "testing" and emphasize the end user's role in acceptance, adoption, and ability to influence the quality and usability of software much further up-stream in the software development life cycle. User acceptance teams should increase their role in user experience (UX), the development of usability standards, non-invasive automation techniques gathering usage data, etc. All of these mechanisms serve to increase the ability of the end user to influence product quality and enhance the user experience and acceptance. Perceptions of end user's participation in UAT events needs to be transformed away from just another phase of software testing to become about validating that the end users' needs and expectations have been met. All testing and other quality processes should be completed and defects corrected before the end user is engaged in the process of "accepting" the deliverable. The idea is to move toward an 'operational readiness' mindset.

This study set out to describe the future of SQM and its impacts on global user acceptance. We will discuss how organizations involve users throughout the software development life cycle to facilitate adoption, user experience, and usability of new technologies. This discussion will be embedded in the use of futuristic new technologies and development methodologies. To explore these notions, this study gathers input from technology visionaries about best practices forward-thinking approaches for facilitating SQM and user acceptance throughout the development life cycle.

2 Literature Background

The goal of SQM is to place the focus on how software is progressing in quality as it is being developed. A quality software product will meet its requirements as set by the users or how much it satisfies user needs. The idea is to create a culture of quality within the organizational environment holding everyone responsible for evolving a product's quality throughout the development life cycle. Keeping this in mind, testing and global user acceptance approaches are well aligned to help support SQM. While regulated to the end of the waterfall life cycle, testing and user acceptance activities have been migrating toward the earlier stages of software development. With the introduction of agile methodologies, testing and user acceptance team members become equally important on software development teams. With the move to greater quality management, the infusion of new technologies, such as artificial intelligence and virtualized automated autonomous testing, becomes even more promising. See Table 1 in the Appendix A for advances in these technologies and their potential implications for quality management. As the Table illustrates, research has advanced our understanding of how smarter tools can be created to support SQM goals. This paper explores the use of such technologies in advancing how user acceptance techniques might evolve in the 21st century based on interviews with top visionary of the field.

3 Exploratory Study Methodology

The research methodology follows an exploratory approach in gathering case study data on automated testing and artificial intelligence practices in order to provide descriptive and explanatory insights into the management activities in software development work. This approach has been used successfully in prior research (Pettigrew 1990, Sutton 1997) and allows us to induce a theoretical account of the activities found in empirical observations and analysis of team member's viewpoints. This approach is also known to lead to accurate and useful results by including an understanding of the contextual complexities of the environment in the research analysis and outcomes. This approach encourages an understanding of the holistic systematic view of the issues and circumstances of the situation being addressed, in this case the issues of managing development projects from team member perspectives about their testing practices (Checkland et al. 2007, Yin 1984). To identify the future of user acceptance practices and tools, we interviewed experts in artificial intelligent systems, software testing, user experience, and automated systems.

4 Data Collection

The results reported in the present study are based on interviews with identified experts in the fields predicted to influence the software development life cycle, e.g., artificial intelligence, visualization tools, and augmented reality. Our data gathering began with the creation of semi-structured interview protocols which comprised both closed and open-ended questions. To inform our interview question development, we reviewed documentation about the technology, and the relevant scholarly literature. The data collection methods focused on interviewees' perspectives on visualized automated testing and artificial intelligence issues, roles played by various stakeholders involved, and the challenges of UAT. Face-to-face and phone interviews of approximately 1 to 1.5 h were conducted. In total, we held 33 interviews, conducted between November 2014 and January 2015, with additional follow-up clarification Q&A sessions conducted over e-mail. The expertise of those interviewed is available upon request. Each expert provided input on their field of expertise and extrapolated ideas to proposed future scenarios of SQM.

By collecting and triangulating data across a variety of methods, we were able to develop robust results because of the perspectives we gained about testing and user experience technologies and issues. This approach provides in-depth information on emerging concepts, and allows cross-checking the information to substantiate the proposed future of SQM (Eisenhardt 1989, Glaser and Strauss , 1967, Pettigrew 1990).

5 Findings

In this research, we gathered and analyzed interview data from a panel of experts. Our findings offer insights into the future of SQM and the impacts on global user acceptance. The future will entail better tools and techniques for user centric design and development of software systems. Future process will infuse end user perspectives in the design and validation of new software at the front end of the development life cycle. Similar to the Boeing's 777 design where significant user input was used (Birtles and Boeing 1998, Weiner 1990), enterprise systems development will incorporate input from more and more end users or employees via the use of automation. Boeing was able to coordinate over 200 design teams with about 40 members each by automating the process by using three-dimensional CAD software systems enabling team members to assemble and simulate a virtual aircraft to verify that the thousands of components would work together properly (Norris and Wagner 1999). Boeing also successfully used visualization systems for design reviews and production illustrations (Abarbanel and McNeely 1996). The Boeing 777 is successfully being used by dozens of airlines today. Figure 1 illustrates the vision of the future of SQM best practices.

5.1 Scaled Agile Frameworks

Agile software development is increasing in prevalence and should be considered in any vision of the future. Agile is being found across settings to deliver faster time to market, improved productivity, better quality, and greater morale. Agile methods are increasingly being used in high assurance and regulated environments where the cost of errors is high. For large scale software development, Scaling Software Agility (Leffingwell 2007) and Agile Software Requirements (Leffingwell 2011) have been shown to apply at enterprise scales. Agile methods, when properly implemented, enable teams to focus on better understanding the end user needs, and building high-quality software, including highly reliable and safe systems. While there will always be the need to address defects, Agile methods are being usefully applied across industries and project

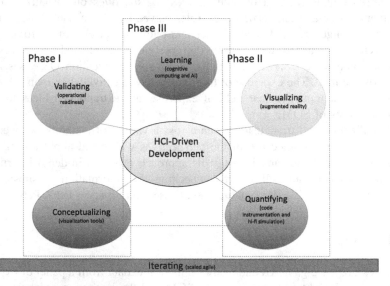

Fig. 1. Conceptual model of HCI-driven software development

sizes. User acceptance validation becomes an integral part of agile frameworks given the method calls for active, continuous user, i.e., user proxy, participation or operational readiness input.

5.2 Operational Readiness

Utilizing all or some of the concepts and tools above, user acceptance testing teams can implement quality assurance plans covering the entire development life cycle. By measuring technical debt along the life cycle, acceptance teams can measure a technical debt ratio as exit criteria for input to go/no go decisions. This is essentially a risk profile of weighted features that becomes an operational readiness score, customized for that release for that system, and acceptance teams become readiness evaluators. This process can be built into scaled agile frameworks and application life cycle management systems.

Creating a quality management plan at the beginning of a project, quality teams can expand acceptance criteria beyond simply defect counts and classifications, to develop a new "Risk Profile" model. Using a "Technical Debt" ratio (e.g., configuration control or software versioning) becomes a rated criteria), test environment availability becomes a rated criteria. Continuous integration, automated testing and other forms of testing also become rated criteria. In this way, "user acceptance testing" becomes "operational readiness evaluation"; test cases become "operational readiness scenarios"; and exit criteria become "operational readiness score".

5.3 Visualization Tools

The next generation of automating testing activities will involve requirements visualization tools, e.g., iRise (see: www.irise.com/). These tools enable user input into requirements through visual formats, enabling more descriptive communications and knowledge transfer of software product development. Enabling all of the software development stakeholders, including users, to virtually 'see' product designs, these tools create visualizations that look and act almost identical to the real end product. End users may not be necessary if proxy combinations of experts are involved, e.g., those trained in user experience, architectures, development, operations, and quality analysis. Visualization helps users and those who create new software to illustrate what the product will do before a single line of code is written, helping people understand what the product is going to be like.

Visualization tools with high-fidelity representations have been known to reduce costs and decrease development time. They create and communicate innovative, revenue-enhancing ideas without coding, helping global teams to deliver apps that delight the first time, virtually eliminating the re-work that many companies have been forced to expect. Through simulations, software designs will be refined with the end users' needs and interests in mind.

5.4   Augmented Reality, Code Instrumentation, and High-Fidelity Simulation

Along with instrumentation, future generations of automating testing activities will involve augmented reality, which will be used to support user-system interactions offering additional informative overlays of explanation of system features. Instrumented code provides the ability to monitor the software's performance, diagnose errors, and track information values and usage. Special code instructions monitor specific parts of the system. Operational scenarios then can be provided via augmented reality while enterprise users are performing daily activities, while instrumented code tracks how users respond to the overlays. Video snippets, sensory awareness, and other tools can offer users more informative direction for testing actions. This approach can be modelled by companies such as User Testing (see: www.usertesting.com/) or Applause (see: www.applause.com/) supporting distributed testing based on concepts of cloud-sourced testing. Building on systems such as LARIAT, the Lincoln Adaptable Real-time Information Assurance Testbed, which uses automated high-fidelity real-time evaluations of system usage (Rossey, et al. 2002), artificial intelligence techniques can be used to learn then mirror and simulate the real-time user experience as input to continuous automated testing systems. With applications embedded into production systems, intelligence systems can monitor user interactions with technology and model users and their behaviors. Artificially intelligent testing systems then mimic real users and be used to realistically evaluate new software development designs and coded products.

5.5   Cognitive Computing and Artificial Intelligence

Cognitive computing systems learn and interact naturally with people to extend what either humans or machine could do on their own. Future generations of automating testing activity will involve cognitive chips, e.g., the latest SyNAPSE chip by IBM (see: www.research.ibm.com/cognitive-computing/neurosynaptic-chips.shtml#fbid= h9hs1Q-C8Ra). This chip is expected to initiate a new type of software applications that can respond to sensory information. The IBM chip is built based on a brain-inspired computer architecture with 1 million neurons and 256 million synapses. This technology has the potential to utilize a cognitive hardware and software ecosystem within a business enterprise that learns user work habits and software usage anomalies. Utilizing technology that can gain an automated profound understanding of the actual facets of how employees use enterprise software will enable real-time virtualized testing and quality management to be performed throughout the SDLC. The technology will be able to mimic a greater breadth and depth of user experiences as it monitors everyday use to understand how, when, and where users get work done across the enterprise network.

5.6   Vision 2020: Future of Completely Automated User Testing

Combining cognitive chips, augmented reality, visualization tools, agile frameworks, and operational readiness measures, tomorrow's end user acceptance activities will take on a new look. In the future, virtual end users based on artificially intelligent autonomous systems will interact with simulated versions of new software to utilize reality-driven operational scenarios to perform user acceptance validation before code is written. More efficient and faster than humans, these systems will deploy more scenarios continuously augmented with every day usage behaviors. Neural networks will continuously collect the activities of real-time global users to update scenarios. An event that occurred yesterday will be replicated in simulation and testing scenarios today. Problems will be addressed in real-time. This approach eliminates the need to incur the expense of flying globally located users to a central location to review and provide input on software requirements and manually test software products. Figure 2 delineates the environmental components needed to make HCI-driven software development a reality.

Autonomous testing systems with automated learning will not be constrained by one person's understanding of system use, but will incorporate the mission of many user types, understand a more holistic environmental scope, and potentially outthink the devices under test. These test vehicles will be fed in real-time the artificial intelligence gathered about users around the globe to continuously build and update test scenarios. This approach eliminates the issue of test team members joining user acceptance teams as user proxies with operational knowledge which becomes obsolete with time. The goal is to shift user validation left as a virtual activity before software is coded, through the combined use of augmented reality, cognitive computing, and artificial intelligence. To further support this approach, code and simulations can be modified with instrumentation to measure usage patterns.

UAT events will change based on advances being made in code instrumentation and simulation. The focus is to design requirements visually within simulation to allow real end users to 'test drive' the software before it is created. Using operational

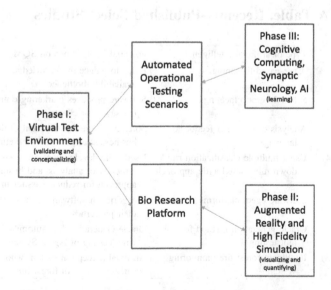

Fig. 2. Vision 2020: HCI-driven development environment

scenarios in the simulations based on known usage patterns, autonomous artificial intelligence systems can use neural networks to scan actual live production systems for real user activities. The operational scenarios can be continuously updated based on how users change how they use the software and anomalies in usage. These systems can provide real world operational scenarios to the simulations. Thus, the scenarios are updated in real-time to correctly map to actual system user usage activities and patterns. Eventually the simulations become autonomous testing devices that represent end user actions. Consistent with the concepts behind the Internet of Things, autonomous devices can be programmed and updated to think like end users and change as users change their usage activities. Using autonomous devices updated in real-time eliminates reduces the need for human involvement, removing issues of a non-representative sample of end users or outdated knowledge regarding current business processes. Autonomous UAT devices will perform mission-based scenarios with real environmental parameters, representing the current user experience, and be able to outthink humans as UAT participants, e.g., a faster supercomputer processes 8.2 billion megaflops (million operations per second) and the human brain only 2.2 billion megaflops (Fischetti 2011).

Software development processes will focus more on design and prototypes, with great user involvement. The next generation high-fidelity simulations, e.g., iRise, will offer developers the means to involve greater user input. With instrumentation, augmented reality, and artificial intelligence, user proxies will eventually replace actual users. In addition augmented reality can be added to production systems to introduce future system modifications to users prior to their development in order to collect feedback. As these systems autonomously gather usage information, operational scenarios can be augmented by the feedback and used in test lab environments.

Appendix A Table. Recently-Published Select Studies

Citation	Type of artificial intelligence	Potential implications on SQM
Khan(2014)	Case-based reasoning	Helps to reduce the knowledge availability bottleneck
Mims(2014)	Schedule group meetings	Software produces marketing e-mail messages for clients
Rusli(2014)	Analysis of customer feedback language	Software in the development of their business strategies and marketing
Han et al. (2014)	Using multiple classification ripple down rules based agile approach	Used agile development for overcoming difficulty of analysis, and business rules approach for reducing issues in maintenance
Zapf (2013)	Software agent platforms	Categories of software agent systems and their properties
Padgham et al. (2013)	Oracle generation method for unit testing	Oracle Generation for Automated Unit Testing of Agent Systems
Šerić et al.(2013)	Intelligent forest fire monitoring system	Artificial perception system whose aim is early detection of forest fires

(*Continued*)

(*Continued*)

Citation	Type of artificial intelligence	Potential implications on SQM
Simonite (2012)	Artificial chat partner	Development of chat software for instant messaging
Powell (2011)	people are the only solution to software problems	Requirements gathering and software modeling through artificial intelligence
Oprea (2011)	University knowledge management system	Software tools that assist the decision making process
Henderson-Sellers (2011)	Meta-models and ontologies	Contribution of meta-models and ontologies for software engineering
Omoteso et al. (2010)	Information and communications technology (ICT) tools	Software development to help auditors match the complexity of their clients' information systems
Chang 2010	Artificial slow intelligence systems	Applications of slow intelligence Systems in software engineering
Cohen et al. 2010	Herbal toolset	Development of intelligent agents using established software-engineering principles
Singh et al., 2010	Predicting software development effort using artificial neural network	Software effort estimation of cost, time and manpower using feed forward network trained using back-propagation algorithm using training and validation data of 650 projects
Schneidewind (2010)	Applying neural networks to software reliability assessment	Neural networks to assess the reliability of software, employing cumulative failures, etc., method proved superior for reliability.
Farah(2009)	Techniques developed in artificial intelligence (AI)	Artificial intelligence techniques in software engineering
Kapur et al. (2008)	Software reliability assessment using artificial neural network	Apply neural networks to build software reliability growth models. Logistic function provides improved goodness-of-fit.
Sagarna and Lozano 2008	Dynamic search space transformations for software test data generation	Propose test data generation with definition of the initial search space using static information extracted from source code. Grid search method is promising option for test data generation
Citation	Type of Autonomous Systems	Potential Implications on SQM
Warwick (2014)	Automatic control systems	Use of autonomous and nondeterministic control systems in aeronautics
Safiullah (2014)	Methodology techniques	Strategy for testing the autonomous system integrations domain
Garcia et al. (2011)	Multiagent systems	Evaluation and comparison of MAS software engineering techniques
Jiao (2011)	Autonomous software entities	Autonomous component to model independent software entity
Jiao et al. (2010)	Automated assembly of internet-scale software systems with autonomous agents	Systems are modeled by dynamic trial-and-evaluation strategy to select high quality agents to facilitate the interoperations among autonomous agents

(*Continued*)

(Continued)

Citation	Type of artificial intelligence	Potential implications on SQM
Trivino et al. (2009)	Semiautonomous robot tele-control systems	Role of operator and autonomous behavior of the robot
Citation	Type of Augmented Reality	Potential Implications on SQM
Sangani (2013)	Developing applications	Benefits & obstacles associated with the augmented reality GPS
Ferran and Salim (2012)	Distributed cognition supported by technology for knowledge sharing	Minimize knowledge bottlenecks with virtual reality and internet-based distributed cognition.

References

Abarbanel, R., McNeely, W.: Fly Thru the Boeing 777. ACM Siggraph, New york (1996)

Agarwal, R., Sambamurthy, V.: Principles and models for organizing the information technology function. Manag. Inf. Syst. Q. Executive 1(1), 1–16 (2002)

Birtles, P.: Boeing 777, Jetliner for a New Century. Motorbooks International, St. Paul, Minnesota (1998)

Chang, S.: A general framework for slow intelligence systems. Int. J. Softw. Eng. Knowl. Eng. 20(1), 1–15 (2010)

Checkland, K., McDonald, R., Harrison, S.: Ticking boxes and changing the social world: data collection and the new UK general practice contract. Soc. Policy Adm. 41(7), 693–710 (2007)

Cohen, M., Ritter, A., Haynes, F.E., Steven, R.: Applying software engineering to agent development. AI Mag. 31(2), 25–44 (2010)

Conboy, K.: Agility from first principles: reconstructing the concept of agility in information systems development. Inf. Syst. Res. 20(3), 329–354 (2009)

Eisenhardt, K.M.: Making fast strategic decisions in high-velocity environment. Acad. Manag. J. 32(3), 543–576 (1989)

Engr.Farah Naaz Raza.: Artificial intelligence techniques in software engineering (AITSE), In: International MultiConference of Engineers and Computer Scientists (1). (2009)

Ferran, C., Salim, R.: Distributed cognition supported by information technology can help solve the knowledge management bottleneck. Acad. Bus. Res. J. 4, 432–454 (2012)

Fischetti, M.: Computers Versus Brains, Scientific American, 12 October 2011

Garcia, E., Giret, A., Botti, V.: Evaluating software engineering techniques for developing complex systems with multiagent approaches. Inf. Softw. Technol. 53(5), 494–506 (2011)

Glaser, B., Strauss, A.:The discovery grounded theory: strategies for qualitative inquiry (1967)

Han, S., Yoon, H., Kang, B., Park, S.: Using MCRDR based agile approach for expert system development. Computing 96(9), 897–908 (2014)

Henderson-Sellers, B.: Bridging metamodels and ontologies in software engineering. J. Syst. Softw. 84(2), 301–313 (2011)

Jiao, W.: Using autonomous components to improve runtime qualities of software. IET Softw. 5 (1), 1–20 (2011)

Jiao, W., Sun, Y., Mei, H.: Automated assembly of Internet-scale software systems involving autonomous agents. J. Syst. Softw. 83(10), 1838–1850 (2010)

Kapur, P.K., Khatri, S.K., Basirzadeh, M.: Software reliability assessment using artificial neural network based flexible model incorporating faults of different complexity. Int. J. Reliab. Qual. Saf. Eng. **15**(2), 113–127 (2008)

Khan, M.J.: Applications of case-based reasoning in software engineering: a systematic mapping study. IET Softw. **8**(6), 258–268 (2014)

Klein, G.S.: Time user acceptance testing. Qual. Assur. **10**(2), 91–106 (2003)

Larson, G.B.: The user acceptance testing process. J. Syst. Manag. **46**(5), 56–62 (1995)

Leffingwell, D.: Scaling Software Agility: Best Practices for Large Enterprises. Addison-Wesley Professional, Boston (2007)

Leffingwell, D.: Agile Software Requirements: Lean Requirements Practices for Teams, Programs, and the Enterprise. Addison-Wesley Professional, Boston (2011)

Mims, C.: Artificial intelligence comes to your inbox. Wall Street J. – East. Ed. **264**(47), B1–B2 (2014)

Norris, G., Wagner, M.: Modern Boeing Jetliners. Minnesota: Zenith Imprint, Minneapolis (1999)

Omoteso, K., Patel, A., Scott, P.: Information and communications technology and auditing: current implications and future directions. Int. J. Auditing **14**(2), 147–162 (2010)

Oprea, M.: A university knowledge management tool for academic research activity evaluation. Informatica Economica **15**(3), 58–71 (2011)

Padgham, L., Zhang, Z., Thangarajah, J., Miller, T.: Model-based test oracle generation for automated unit testing of agent systems. IEEE Trans. Softw. Eng. **39**(9), 1230–1244 (2013)

Pettigrew, A.M.: Longitudinal field research on change: theory and practice. Organ. Sci. **1**(3), 267–292 (1990)

Poston, R., Sajja, K., Calvert, A.: Managing user acceptance testing of business applications In: Proceedings of 16th International Conference on Human-Computer Interaction, Creta Maris, Heraklion, Crete, Greece, 22–27 June 2014

Poth, A., Sunyaev, A.: Efficient Quality Management: Risk- and Value-based Software Quality Management, IEEE Software (2014)

Powell, J.: Leadership by walking around: 21st century people solutions for software problems. Contract Manage. **51**(5), 56–65 (2011)

Ramesh, B., Cao, L., Mohan, K., Xu, P.: Can distributed software development be agile? Commun. ACM **49**, 41–46 (2006)

Rossey, L.M., Cunningham, R.K., Fried, D.J., Rabek, J.C., Lippmann, R.P., Haines, J.W., Zissman, M.A.: LARIAT: Lincoln Adaptable Real-time Information Assurance Testbed. IEEE (2002)

Rusli, E.M.: Deep dives into buyer minds. Wall Street J. – East. Ed. **263**(87), B5 (2014)

Safiullah, F.:Some Practical Considerations and a Methodology for Testing Autonomous System Integrations, Int. J. Softw. Eng. Appl. (IJSEA), 5 (2014)

Sagarna, R., Lozano, J.A.: Dynamics search space transformations for software test data generation. Comput. Intell. **24**(1), 23–61 (2008)

Sangani, K.: Developing AR apps. Eng. Technol. (17509637) **8**(4), 52–54 (2013)

Schneidewind, N.: Applying neural networks to software reliability assessment. Int. J. Reliab. Qual. Saf. Eng. **17**(4), 313–329 (2010)

Šerić, L., Štula, M., Stipaničev, D.: Engineering of holonic multi agent intelligent forest fire monitoring system. AI Commun. **26**(3), 303–316 (2013)

Shang, S., Lin, S., Wu, Y.: Service innovation through dynamic knowledge management. Ind. Manage. Data Syst. **109**(3), 322–337 (2009)

Simonite, T.: Artificial intelligence, powered by many humans. Technol. Rev. **115**(6), 14–16 (2012)

Singh, Y., Kaur, A., Bhatia, P.K., Sangwan, O.: Predicting software development effort using artificial neural network. Int. J. Softw. Eng. Knowl. Eng. **20**(3), 367–375 (2010)

Sutton, R.I.: Crossroads-the virtues of closet qualitative research. Organ. Sci. **8**(1), 97–106 (1997)

Trivino, G., Mengual, L., van der Heide, A.: Towards an architecture for semiautonomous robot tele control systems. Inf. Sci. **179**(23), 3973–3984 (2009)

Warwick, G.: Enabling autonomy. Aviat. Week Space Technol. **176**(20), 28–29 (2014)

Weiner, E.: New Boeing Airliner Shaped by the Airlines, The New York Times, 19 Dec 1990

Yin, R.K.: Case Study Research: Design and Methods. Sage Publications, Beverly Hills (1984)

Zapf, M.: Two decades of software agent platform engineering. PIK - Praxis der Informationsverarbeitung und Kommunikation **36**(4), 235–242 (2013)

Early-Stage Software Start-up Survival: the Effects of Managerial Actions on Firm Performance

Yunfei Shi[(✉)], Dongming Xu, and Iris Vessey

UQ Business School, The University of Queensland, Brisbane, Australia
{y.shi,d.xu,i.vessey}@business.uq.edu.au

Abstract. The emergence of software start-ups contributes to society by driving innovation as well as by creating jobs. Research, to date, mainly concentrates on either start-ups in general or established software firms. Little research has been conducted directly into software start-ups. The objective of this research is to understand how early-stage software start-ups survive. We develop a conceptual model for explaining early-stage software start-up survival. The conceptual model illustrates important resources, capabilities, and managerial actions that facilitate high levels of software start-up performance. Our research contributes theoretically to IS literature in general by developing a theory of how software start-ups survive in the early stages and to resource-based research specifically by explaining the actions management takes in deploying resources and capabilities to achieve high levels of performance.

Keywords: Software start-up performance · Resources · Capabilities · Managerial actions · Company life-cycle early-stage

1 Introduction

Software start-ups are high-tech start-up firms that develop cutting edge software products and/or provide services based on the software they create. The majority of software start-ups are product-based [1]. Software start-ups are a very active component of the start-up market. In 2013, for example, U.S. software start-ups accounted for the largest proportion of new investment (23 %), followed by media companies (16 %), and health-care services/medical devices and equipment (14 %) [2]. The demand for the products or services of software start-ups is evidenced also by job creation rates almost twice that of the private sector as a whole [3]. The impact of the software industry on economic growth, in general, is reflected in the phrase "software is eating the world" [4].

Despite obvious successes, the failure rate for software firms also is high compared with that of other high-tech industries. Although numerous software start-ups appeared in the marketplace during the Internet bubble of the 1990s, attracting large amounts of venture capital, few of those start-ups survived in the longer term [5]. For example, nearly 80 % of start-up firms failed within their first three years [6].

The objective of this paper is to understand how early-stage software start-ups survive. Early-stage software start-ups refer to software start-ups that are engaged in conceptualizing and developing software products. Understanding early-stage software

© Springer International Publishing Switzerland 2015
F.F.-H. Nah and C.-H. Tan (Eds.): HCIB 2015, LNCS 9191, pp. 761–771, 2015.
DOI: 10.1007/978-3-319-20895-4_71

start-ups is important for two reasons. First, little research has been conducted directly into software start-up survival. An extensive literature on entrepreneurship focuses on explaining the survival of start-ups, in general, where the major emphasis is on manufacturing and therefore on engineering [7, 8]. In contrast, the core elements of the production process in software start-ups are IT skills and IT innovation. To date, IS studies most often examine performance in established firms [9]. The reasons for firm failure are different in new firms and established firms however. For example, established firms often do not succeed because they fail to adapt to changing environment, while the failures of new firms are often attributed to managerial deficiencies of using resources and capabilities [10].

Second, little research has examined the role of management in helping firms survive during the start-up stage of a new software firm. Scholars typically base their investigation of such issues on the resource-based view of the firm, primarily by documenting the resources that lead to effective performance or competitive advantage [11]. The availability of resources is not, however, sufficient to explain why some start-ups survive while others do not. The way in which firms use their resources may explain the variance in firm performance when resources are similar [12]. In other words, management needs to understand how to deploy resources effectively. That is, they need to focus on the actions managers take to manage a firm's resources thereby creating value for customers and owners [13]. Henceforth, we refer to this phenomenon as "managerial actions."

Extant resource-based research provides little information regarding the actions managers might best take to facilitate start-up survival and/or competitive advantage [13, 14]. This aspect of RBV is an emerging research stream in management and promises to extend the understanding of the resource-based approach by examining how resources are managed to create business value [13, 15, 16].

We investigate managerial actions that facilitate early-stage software start-up survival. Our paper seeks to address the overall research question: how do resources, capabilities, and managerial actions influence early-stage software start-up performance. Specifically, we view resources and capabilities as the fundamentals that managers draw on to perform managerial actions.

The remainder of the paper proceeds as follows. The next section, Sect. 2, introduces the theoretical background, while Sect. 3 presents the development of the theory of early-stage software start-up survival. We present our conclusions in Sect. 4.

2   Theoretical Background

Because literature on managerial actions grounded in resource based theory, we first review resource based theory (RBT) followed by the research associated with managerial actions.

2.1   Resource Based Theory

RBT focuses on "describing, explaining, and predicting organizational relationships" [11]. Scholars increasingly use the term RBT rather than resource-based view (RBV) due to the fact that "resource-based research has reached a level of precision and sophistication such that it more closely resembles a theory than a view" [11, p. 1303]. Here, we consider first RBV followed by the notion of dynamic capabilities.

From the perspective of RBV, firms invest in valuable, rare, inimitable, and nonsubstitutable (VRIN) resources to gain a competitive advantage [17, 10]. Resources are important in a stable environment. However, in a changing environment, it is not sufficient to consider resources alone. That is, RBV is not applicable in a dynamic environment [19, 20]. Firms therefore need to develop the ability to configure resources to respond to rapidly changing environments [19, 21]; that is, they need to develop dynamic capabilities.

Dynamic capabilities reflect a firm's ability to modify its resource base, thereby transforming RBV from a static view to one suitable for a changing environment. The core idea of dynamic capabilities is that a firm responds to a changing environment by developing capabilities to extend or modify resources [15]. Such capabilities help a firm to cope with rapid [19], as well as minor changes [15, 19, 21–23]. Although the notion of dynamic capabilities advances the usefulness of RBV in a dynamic environment, it does not explain how resources are deployed or configured to create business value [24].

Within RBT-based research, two important but underdeveloped areas need to be addressed further. First, most of existing literature on RBT does not address the process of resource deployment [11]. Deploying resources and capabilities is as important as possessing those resources and capabilities [25]. The value of resources and capabilities can be realized only when they are deployed effectively [13]. Second, extant literature does not acknowledge the role of management in deploying resources [13, 14]. Apart from performing operational activities such as control or supervision, managers play a prominent role in strategic functions such as integrating complementary resources to develop firm-specific capabilities [15].

2.2   Resource Orchestration

Resource orchestration is a recent stream of research that seeks to understand resource deployment, a vital but under-researched aspect of RBT [11]. Resource orchestration describes "the actions leaders take to facilitate efforts to effectively manage the firm's resources" [26, p.64]. Managerial actions in resource orchestration take three forms: structuring, bundling, and leveraging. Each category is made up of specific actions. Structuring refers to managing a firm's resource portfolio that includes both tangible and intangible assets. Structuring includes acquiring, accumulating, and divesting resources. Bundling refers to developing new capabilities and modifying current capabilities. Bundling includes stabilizing, enriching, and pioneering resources. Leveraging refers to using capabilities to compete within the target market or to satisfy customers. Leveraging includes mobilizing, coordinating, and deploying [16].

Effects of managerial actions are contingent on a firm's external environment. Except for divesting and stabilizing, managers perform such actions when a firm faces high environmental uncertainty. Divesting creates business value only when it sheds a firm's resources without sacrificing the firm's current or future competitive advantage [16]. In a highly-uncertain environment, managers are unable to evaluate accurately a resource's potential for competitive advantage. Therefore, divesting resources may reduce a firm's potential to create value for customers [16]. Further, stabilizing does not enhance a firm's competence to maintain its competitive advantage in a highly-uncertain environment. It is easy for competitors to outperform a firm that relies on stabilizing because stabilizing involves making only minor changes to a firm's current competence [16].

3   Theory Development

In this section, we first introduce the foundations on which our conceptual model is based, followed by the model itself. We then introduce the boundaries of our conceptual model.

3.1   Theoretical Foundations

We first define early-stage software start-up life cycle followed by early-stage software start-up performance. We then present fundamental premises of our conceptual model.

Early-stage Software Start-up. The early stage of a software start-up refers to the period during which a software start-up converts a business idea into a viable solution designed to realize the core functions of the software innovation [27]. First, a start-up faces technical problems associated with software development. Second, there is no structure or formality in such a firm. Rather than a formal organization, a software start-up is likely to be a task group. Entrepreneurs are central to the organization as a whole and they carry out most of tasks.

Early-stage Software Start-up Performance. In this stage, the major focus of a software start-up is software development. Good performance in this stage indicates the potential for first mover advantage. Early-stage software start-up performance can be viewed from both product and process perspectives [28]. From a product perspective, software development performance is reflected in product effectiveness. Product effectiveness refers to the extent to which the prototype fulfils the functional goals of the innovative software product [29]. From a process perspective, software development performance is reflected in process efficiency. Process efficiency refers to the extent to which the software development adheres to an established budget detailing the time and cost of converting an idea to a software prototype [30].

Fundamental Premises. Three premises underlie the development of our conceptual model.

Resources and Capabilities Create Business Value Through Managerial Actions. This premise reflects our belief that (a) resources or capabilities are essential for firms to create business value, and that (b) their effects are realized through managerial actions. Specifically, resources are factors that a firm owns, controls, or has access to, while capabilities relate to deploying resources [31, 32]. Compared with resources, capabilities are unique because they are developed internal to a firm by integrating technical and physical resources [15, 33]. A firm that possesses effective resources and capabilities has the potential to achieve high levels of performance. Such potential is realized when managers take actions to use resources and capabilities effectively [13, 15, 16].

A Software Startup Operates in a Highly Uncertain Environment. A software startup introduces an innovative software product and subsequent innovations to the market-place. It operates, therefore, in a highly uncertain environment. The high environmental uncertainty of a product-based software startup involves both technical uncertainty and market uncertainty. From a technical perspective, uncertainty relates to incomplete information regarding the possibility of achieving technical success and the cost associated with it [34]. From a market perspective, uncertainty arises mainly from the competition among rival firms. A software startup normally competes with firms all over the world and enjoys less home-advantage than startups in other industries, such as manufacturing and retailing [35]. Note that, divesting and stabilizing are not appropriate to a firm in a highly-uncertain environment, and therefore do not apply to the product-based software startup that we examine in our research [16].

A Software Startup Operates as an Independent Organization. We view a software startup as an independent organization in the process of becoming an established firm. In a high-tech industry such as the software industry, an established firm often acquires new technology by taking over small innovative firms [36]. In this case the software startup will be incorporated into a larger firm and will therefore cease to exist as such.

3.2 Conceptual Model of Early-Stage Software Start-up Survival

We draw on the theory of resource orchestration [13] to develop a conceptual model of early-stage software start-up survival (see Fig. 1). We now present our independent constructs, the associations between them, and propositions for the associations.

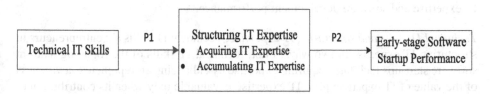

Fig. 1. Conceptual model of software start-up survival

Constructs. We first examine the constructs of technical IT skills and structuring IT expertise, followed by the associations between the constructs.

Technical IT skills. The realization of an innovative idea relies largely on the technical competence that entrepreneurs bring to a start-up [37]. Therefore, structuring IT expertise is a very important aspect of a software start-up. To structure IT expertise, entrepreneurs need to use technical skills that either exist within a start-up or to which a start-up has access.

Technical IT skills refer to the generic and explicit skills needed for developing IT applications [38, 39]. Generic IT skills include, for example, knowledge of programming, system integration, database management. Explicit IT skills include, for example, the knowledge that is codified in equations, blueprints. Internal technical skills are possessed largely by its founding team in the early stages of development because most of software start-ups consist only of the co-founders. Technical IT skills are not, however, restricted to those within the software start-up itself. The required skills may be provided by IT professionals external to the start-up firm.

Structuring IT expertise. Structuring IT expertise refers to managing the specialized IT knowledge of a start-up [16]. Because software development is knowledge work, its success mainly relies on IT expertise [40]. A team's expertise derives from the aggregation of individual skills [41]. A start-up operates at a resource disadvantage in its early stages of development [26]. Therefore, entrepreneurs need to acquire necessary knowledge from the external environment. Further, individual knowledge may not be readily transferrable and is, therefore, resistant to elaboration across an organization [42]. Hence, entrepreneurs need to promote internal learning and training to accumulate and structure knowledge within their software start-ups.

Specifically, structuring IT expertise includes two types of actions: acquiring and accumulating expertise. Acquiring refers to obtaining IT expertise from the marketplace [43]. For example, entrepreneurs obtain advice from external IT experts or hire new IT staff to enrich their firm's IT expertise. Accumulating expertise refers to developing IT expertise internal to a firm. Highly firm-specific resources cannot be bought as commodities from the marketplace; rather, they require internal accumulation [44]. For example, the understanding of the software innovation is the knowledge that needs to be accumulated through learning-by-doing and learning-by-trying [45].

Associations between Constructs. We first examine the association between technical IT skills and structuring IT expertise, followed by the association between structuring IT expertise and software development performance.

Technical IT skills and structuring IT expertise. Technical IT skills aid entrepreneurs in structuring IT expertise in two ways. First, technical IT skills of the founding team in software start-ups facilitate acquiring expertise by enhancing entrepreneurs' awareness of the value of IT expertise [46]. IT expertise is valuable only when its contribution to a firm exceeds the cost of acquiring it [43]. Appropriate technical IT skills enable entrepreneurs to evaluate more precisely the potential business value provided by IT personnel. Such evaluation is critical for entrepreneurs to prioritize their marketplace acquisitions. That is, entrepreneurs focus efforts on acquiring IT expertise that is most needed in their start-ups.

Second, to accumulate IT expertise, internal technical IT skills must already be in place. Accumulating IT expertise requires training programs [16, 44]. Technical IT skills provide a rich environment in which entrepreneurs design internal training programs. For example, entrepreneurs assign less-experienced IT personnel to work on a software development project along with IT experts that has adequate IT technical skills, which helps nascent employees develop their skills thereby enriching the specialized knowledge of the software start-up. Hence, we propose the following proposition:

P1. Technical IT skills of the founding team are positively associated with structuring IT expertise.

Structuring IT expertise and software development performance. Structuring IT expertise contributes to software development performance because entrepreneurs acquire and accumulate specialized knowledge for prototype development. When IT expertise is present, the likelihood of developing a successful software prototype is high [40]. First structuring IT expertise is critical for ensuring the effectiveness of a software prototype. If entrepreneurs structure a set of specialized knowledge regarding prototype development, they will help their start-ups develop an accurate understanding of the software functionality and conceptualize a software solution to realize the required functionality [47]. The more effectively entrepreneurs structure IT expertise, the better the possibility of realizing the software innovation.

Second, structuring IT expertise is beneficial for enhancing the efficiency of software development. If entrepreneurs structure their IT expertise appropriately, they are better placed to obtain the knowledge necessary to overcome the technical barriers encountered, thereby accelerating the pace of software development. Further, if entrepreneurs structure IT expertise, a software start-up will be likely to develop a reasonable software development plan based on cost, risk assessment, and schedule [48]. Therefore, we propose the following proposition:

P2. Structuring IT expertise is positively associated with software development performance.

3.3 Boundaries of the Conceptual Model

Three premises underlie our model of early-stage software startup survival. The model will not hold when any of the fundamental premises is violated.

First, the model is only suitable for explaining firm failure due to inefficient managerial actions. For example, failing to structure IT expertise may lead to a software startup's failure in software development. Expect from inefficient managerial actions, various factors may cause a firm to fail in the marketplace. For example, although the actions entrepreneurs take may be effective for managing a software startup's resources, a software startup may exit from the industry because of the negative impacts of financial crisis. Such kinds of circumstances are not accounted for in our model.

Second, our theory is only applicable for a software startup that introduces the initial software product and subsequent innovations to the marketplace. Two types of software startups are not accounted for in our model. One refers to software startups that focus on providing outsourcing services for other firms. Such firms repeatedly engage in the process of software development but are not responsible for introducing the software innovation into the marketplace. The other one refers to software startups that outsource completely development tasks to other firms, and therefore they do not engage in product development activities. Technical uncertainty and market uncertainty for such firms are low, so managers may maintain current competitive advantage by stabilizing existing business processes. Managers may also divest resources when they have a full understanding of business environment [16].

Third, a software startup is taken over by another firm is not addressed in our model. Some startups are designed to be sold because their entrepreneurs are more likely to have entrepreneurial preferences [49]. Entrepreneurs, who enjoy starting a new business from scratch, may sell their business after their firms demonstrates viable prototypes and then engage with a new business.

4 Conclusion

We first present the potential contributions of our research, followed by its practical implications. We then present research directions

4.1 Expected Contributions

Our research seeks to contribute theoretically to existing literature in two areas: IS research in general and resource-based theory.

First, our research contributes to IS research by developing a theory of how an early stage software start-up survives. It is important for IS researchers to understand what management in software firms needs to do to facilitate survival. To the best of our knowledge, IS research to date provides few insights into the development of a software start-up.

Second, our research contributes to resource-based theory by explaining how resources and capabilities are deployed to achieve high levels of performance at early stage of a software start-up. Prior research primarily focuses on documenting that a set of resources and capabilities lead to firm performance. Such research is silent on how resources and capabilities are deployed [11, 50]. In our research, we examine the role of managerial actions in using resources and capabilities to achieve firm performance.

4.2 Practical Implications

Our research has major implications for practice. We identify the actions entrepreneurs need to take to manage a software start-up's resources in the early stages of a software start-up. Resources themselves cannot create value for customers and owners. It is the use of resources that directly leads to business value. Entrepreneurs may facilitate the delivery of innovative software applications and thus compete successfully in the marketplace by effective resource management and resource utilization.

4.3 Research Directions

We present the possibilities of furthering our research. First, researchers can develop measures for the concepts in our conceptual model and collect empirical data to test our conceptual model. Second, researchers can examine the development of software start-ups that are in the late-stage of startup life cycle. Firms in different life-cycle stages require different resources and actions into managing resources [13]. It is meaningful to examine the effects of resources and managerial actions on performance across start-up life cycle stages.

References

1. Hilmola, O.P., Helo, P., Ojala, L.: The value of product development lead time in software start-up. Syst. Dyn. Rev. **19**(1), 75–82 (2003)
2. Jeffrey, O: The Angel Investor Market in 2013: A Moderating Recovery Continues, Center for Venture Research (2014)
3. Hathaway, I.: Tech starts: high-technology business formation and job creation in the United States. Kauffman Foundation Research Series (2013)
4. Andreessen, M: Why software is eating the world. Wall Street Journal, 20 (2011)
5. Perkins, A.B., Perkins, M.C.: The Internet Bubble: the Inside Story on Why It Burst-and What You Can Do To Profit Now. HarperBusiness, New York (2001)
6. Feinleib, D.: Why Start-ups Fail: And How Yours Can Succeed. Apress, NY (2011)
7. Chrisman, J.J., McMullan, W.: Outsider assistance as a knowledge resource for new venture survival. J. Small Bus. Manage. **42**(3), 229–244 (2004)
8. Li, S., Shang, J., Slaughter, S.A.: Why do software firms fail? capabilities, competitive actions, and firm survival in the software industry from 1995 to 2007. Inf. Syst. Res. **21**(3), 631–654 (2010)
9. West, G.P., Noel, T.W.: The impact of knowledge resources on new venture performance. J. Small Bus. Manage. **47**(1), 1–22 (2009)
10. Thornhill, S., Amit, R.: Learning about failure: bankruptcy, firm age, and the resource-based view. Organ. Sci. **14**(5), 497–509 (2003)
11. Barney, J.B., Ketchen, D.J., Wright, M.: The future of resource-based theory revitalization or decline? J. Manage. **37**(5), 1299–1315 (2011)
12. Barney, J.B., Arikan, A.M.: The resource-based view: origins and implications. In: Hitt, M.A., Freeman, R.E., Harrison, J.S. (eds.) The Blackwell Handbook of Strategic Management, pp. 124–188. Blackwell Publishers Inc., Malden (2001)
13. Sirmon, D.G., Hitt, M.A., Ireland, R.D., Gilbert, B.A.: Resource orchestration to create competitive advantage breadth, depth, and life cycle effects. J. Manage. **37**(5), 1390–1412 (2011)
14. Augier, M., Teece, D.J.: Dynamic capabilities and the role of managers in business strategy and economic performance. Organ. Sci. **20**(2), 410–421 (2009)
15. Helfat, C.E., Finkelstein, S., Mitchell, W., Peteraf, M., Singh, H., Teece, D., Winter, S.G.: Dynamic Capabilities: Understanding Strategic Change in Organizations. Blackwell, Malden (2007)
16. Sirmon, D.G., Hitt, M.A., Ireland, R.D.: Managing firm resources in dynamic environments to create value: looking inside the black box. Acad. Manage. Rev. **32**(1), 273–292 (2007)
17. Wernerfelt, B.: A resource-based view of the firm. Strateg. Manage. J. **5**(2), 171–180 (1984)
18. Barney, J.: Firm resources and sustained competitive advantage. J. Manage. **17**(1), 99–120 (1991)
19. Teece, D.J., Pisano, G., Shuen, A.: Dynamic capabilities and strategic management. Strateg. Manage. J. **18**(7), 509–533 (1997)
20. Helfat, C.E., Peteraf, M.A.: The dynamic resource-based view: capability lifecycles. Strateg. Manage. J. **24**(10), 997–1010 (2003)
21. Eisenhardt, K.M., Martin, J.A.: Dynamic capabilities: what are they? Strateg. Manage. J. **21**(10–11), 1105–1121 (2000)
22. Helfat, C.E., Winter, S.G.: Untangling dynamic and operational capabilities: strategy for the (N) ever-changing world. Strateg. Manage. J. **32**(11), 1243–1250 (2011)
23. Winter, S.G.: Understanding dynamic capabilities. Strateg. Manage. J. **24**(10), 991–995 (2003)

24. Barreto, I.: Dynamic capabilities: a review of past research and an agenda for the future. J. Manage. **36**(1), 256–280 (2010)

25. Hansen, M.H., Perry, L.T., Reese, C.S.: A bayesian operationalization of the resource-based view. Strateg. Manage. J. **25**(13), 1279–1295 (2004)

26. Hitt, M.A., Ireland, R.D., Sirmon, D.G., Trahms, C.A.: Strategic entrepreneurship: creating value for individuals, organizations, and society. Acad. Manage. Perspect. **25**(2), 57–75 (2011)

27. Kazanjian, R.K., Drazin, R.: An empirical test of a stage of growth progression model. Manage. Sci. **35**(12), 1489–1503 (1989)

28. Ravichandran, T., Lertwongsatien, C., LERTWONGSATIEN, C.: Effect of information systems resources and capabilities on firm performance: a resource-based perspective. J. Manage. Inf. Syst. **21**(4), 237–276 (2005)

29. Cooprider, J.G., Henderson, J.C.: Technology-process fit: perspectives on achieving prototyping effectiveness. Proc. Twenty-Third Annual Hawaii Int. Conf. **3**, 623–630 (1990)

30. Pavlou, P.A., El Sawy, O.A.: From IT leveraging competence to competitive advantage in turbulent environments: the case of new product development. Inf. Syst. Res. **17**(3), 198–227 (2006)

31. Amit, R., Schoemaker, P.J.: Strategic assets and organizational rent. Strateg. Manage. J. **14**(1), 33–46 (1993)

32. Grant, R.M.: The resource-based theory of competitive advantage: implications for strategy formulation. In: Zack, M. (ed.) Knowledge and Strategy, pp. 3–23. Butterworth Heinemann, Boston (1991)

33. Grant, R.M.: Toward a knowledge-based theory of the firm. Strateg. Manage. J. **17**(S2), 109–122 (1996)

34. Beckman, C.M., Haunschild, P.R., Phillips, D.J.: Friends or strangers? firm-specific uncertainty, market uncertainty, and network partner selection. Organ. Sci. **15**(3), 259–275 (2004)

35. Buxmann, P., Diefenbach, H., Hess, T.: The Software Industry: Economic Principles, Strategies, Perspectives. Springer, Heidelburg (2013)

36. Granstrand, O., Sjölander, S.: The acquisition of technology and small firms by large firms. J. Econ. Behav. Organ. **13**(3), 367–386 (1990)

37. Van de Ven, A.H., Hudson, R., Schroeder, D.M.: Designing new business start-ups: entrepreneurial, organizational, and ecological considerations. J. Manage. **10**(1), 87–108 (1984)

38. Mata, F.J., Fuerst, W.L., Barney, J.B.: Information technology and sustained competitive advantage: a resource-based analysis. MIS Q. **19**(4), 487–505 (1995)

39. Ray, G., Muhanna, W.A., Barney, J.B.: Information technology and the performance of the customer service process: a resource-based analysis. MIS Q. **29**(4), 625–652 (2005)

40. Faraj, S., Sproull, L.: Coordinating expertise in software development teams. Manage. Sci. **46**(12), 1554–1568 (2000)

41. Brown, J.S., Duguid, P.: Knowledge and organization: a social-practice perspective. Organ. Sci. **12**(2), 198–213 (2001)

42. Von Hippel, E.: Sticky information and the locus of problem solving: implications for innovation. Manage. Sci. **40**(4), 429–439 (1994)

43. Barney, J.B.: Strategic factor markets: expectations, luck, and business strategy. Manage. Sci. **32**(10), 1231–1241 (1986)

44. Dierickx, I., Cool, K.: Asset stock accumulation and sustainability of competitive advantage. Manage. Sci. **35**(12), 1504–1511 (1989)

45. Tsang, E.W.: Acquiring knowledge by foreign partners from international joint ventures in a transition economy: learning-by-doing and learning myopia. Strateg. Manage. J. **23**(9), 835–854 (2002)
46. Morris, M.H., Kuratko, D.F., Allen, J.W., Ireland, R.D., Schindehutte, M.: Resource acceleration: extending resource-based theory in entrepreneurial ventures. J. Appl. Manage. Entrepreneurship **15**(2), 4 (2010)
47. Tiwana, A., Bharadwaj, A., Sambamurthy, V.: The antecedents of information systems development capability in firms: a knowledge integration perspective. In: Proceedings of International Conference on Information Systems, Seattle, pp. 246–258 (2003)
48. Ravichandran, T., Rai, A.: Quality management in systems development: an organizational system perspective. MIS Q. **24**(3), 381–415 (2000)
49. Stam, E., Thurik, R., Van der Zwan, P.: Entrepreneurial exit in real and imagined markets. Ind. Corp. Change **19**(4), 1109–1139 (2010)
50. Kraaijenbrink, J., Spender, J.C., Groen, A.J.: The resource-based view: a review and assessment of its critiques. J. Manage. **36**(1), 349–372 (2010)

An Architecture-Oriented Design Method
for Human-Computer Interaction Systems

Yu-Chen Yang[1(✉)], Yi-Ling Lin[1], and William S. Chao[2]

[1] Department of Information Management, National Sun Yat-sen Univ.,
Kaohsiung, Taiwan
{ycyang,yllin}@mis.nsysu.edu.tw
[2] Association of Chinese Enterprise Architects, Taipei, Taiwan
architectchao@gmail.com

Abstract. In this paper, we propose an architecture-oriented design method for human-computer interaction systems. This design method adopts the structure-behavior coalescence (SBC) architecture as a systems model. SBC architecture design method starts from the preparation phase and then goes through the creative thinking, concept, preliminary design, and detailed design phases of SBC architecture construction. SBC architecture design method uses six fundamental diagrams to formally design the essence of a human-computer interaction system and its details at the same time. In the concept phase, architecture hierarchy diagram and framework diagram are used. In the preliminary design phase, component operation diagram and component connection diagram are used. In the detailed design phase, structure-behavior coalescence diagram and interaction flow diagram are used. With the above six diagrams, we then can effectively design the structure, behavior, and information of human-computer interaction systems; resolve uncertainties and risks caused by those non-architecture-oriented design methods.

Keywords: Architecture-Oriented design method · SBC architecture · Human-Computer interaction system

1 Introduction

In general, a human-computer interaction system is exceptionally complex that it includes multiple views such as structure, behavior, and information views [8, 10]. The systems model designs the human-computer interaction system multiple views possibly using two different methods. The first one is the non-architecture-oriented method and the second one is the architecture-oriented method [1, 6]. Non-architecture-oriented systems model respectively picks a model for each view [7, 9]. The architecture-oriented system model, instead of picking many heterogeneous and unrelated models, will use only one single coalescence model [2, 11].

An architecture-oriented design method for human-computer interaction systems adopts the SBC architecture [3–5] as a systems model. With SBC architecture, we then can effectively design the structure, behavior, and information of human-computer interaction systems; resolve uncertainties and risks caused by those non-architecture-oriented design

© Springer International Publishing Switzerland 2015
F.F.-H. Nah and C.-H. Tan (Eds.): HCIB 2015, LNCS 9191, pp. 772–780, 2015.
DOI: 10.1007/978-3-319-20895-4_72

methods. Overall, SBC architecture design method helps integrate different stakeholders' works on the same track and unfold the backbone of human-computer interaction systems. The human-computer interaction system design result of SBC architecture can be used as human-computer interaction system blueprints to improve the acceptance and effectiveness of the development of human-computer interaction system.

The remaining of this paper is organized as follows. We first give a brief review of the differences between non-architecture-oriented and architecture-oriented models. Section 3 outlines the SBC architecture design method for human-computer interaction systems. Section 4 concludes the paper by summarizing the contributions of the SBC architecture design method.

2 Non-Architecture-Oriented and Architecture-Oriented Systems Models

A systems model is a virtual system, distinguished from a physical system, used to design either the physical or virtual systems. A physical system, e.g., house, tree, river, airplane, etc., exists in the physical world. A virtual system, e.g., symbol, language, diagram, software, virtual reality, thought, etc., exists in the virtual world.

A human-computer interaction system is exceptionally complex that it includes multiple views such as structure, behavior, and information views. The systems model designs the human-computer interaction system multiple views possibly using two different methods. The first one is the non-architecture-oriented method and the second one is the architecture-oriented method.

The non-architecture-oriented method respectively picks a model for each view as shown in Fig. 1, the structure view has the structure model; the behavior view has the behavior model; the information view has the information model. These multiple models are heterogeneous and unrelated of each other, thus there is no way to put them into a conformity model [7, 9].

The architecture-oriented method, instead of picking many heterogeneous and unrelated models, will use only one single coalescence model as shown in Fig. 2. The structure, behavior, and information views are all integrated in this multiple view coalescence (MVC) systems model [1–6, 11].

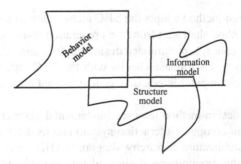

Fig. 1. The non-architecture-oriented approach

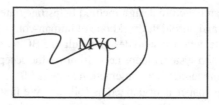

Fig. 2. The architecture-oriented approach

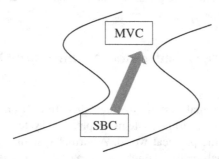

Fig. 3. SBC facilitates MVC

Figure 1 has many models. Figure 2 has only one model. Comparing Fig. 1 with Fig. 2, we unquestionably conclude that an integrated, holistic, united, coordinated, coherent, and coalescence model is more favorable than a collection of many heterogeneous and unrelated models.

Since structure and behavior views are the two most prominent ones among multiple views, integrating the structure and behavior views apparently is the best approach of integrating multiple views of a system. In other words, structure-behavior coalescence (SBC) facilitates multiple view coalescence (MVC) as shown in Fig. 3. Therefore, we claim that SBC architecture is an architecture-oriented systems model.

3   SBC Architecture Design Method for Human-Computer Interaction Systems

SBC architecture design method adopts the SBC architecture as a systems model. SBC architecture design method shall start from the preparation phase and then goes through the creative thinking, concept, preliminary design, and detailed design phases of SBC architecture construction. Each phase checks with the SBC architecture to make sure the constructed human-computer interaction system is what the users want as shown in Fig. 4.

SBC architecture design method uses six fundamental diagrams to formally design the essence of a human-computer interaction system and its details at the same time. In the concept phase, architecture hierarchy diagram (AHD) and framework diagram (FD) are used. In the preliminary design phase, component operation diagram

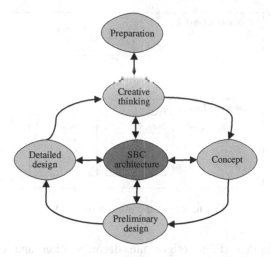

Fig. 4. SBC architecture design method

(COD) and component connection diagram (CCD) are used. In the detailed design phase, structure-behavior coalescence diagram (SBCD) and interaction flow diagram (IFD) are used.

3.1 Concept Phase

Through architecture hierarchy diagram (AHD), designers shall clearly observe the multi-level decomposition and composition of a human-computer interaction system. As an example, Fig. 5 shows that Multimedia KTV is composed of Song_Selection and Songs; Songs is composed of Song_1 and Song_2. Among them, Multimedia KTV and Songs are aggregated systems while Song_Selection, Song_1 and Song_2 are non-aggregated systems.

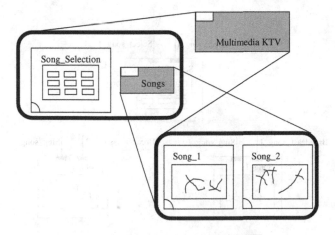

Fig. 5. AHD of the multimedia KTV

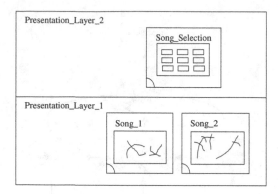

Fig. 6. FD of the multimedia KTV

Framework diagram (FD) designs the decomposition and composition of a human-computer interaction system in a multi-layer manner. Only non-aggregated systems will appear in the FD.

As an example, Fig. 6 shows a FD of the Multimedia KTV. In the figure, Presentation_Layer_2 contains the Song_Selection component; Presentation_Layer_1 contains the Song_1 and Song_2 components.

3.2 Preliminary Design Phase

For a human-computer interaction system, we use a component operation diagram (COD) to design all components' operations. Figure 7 shows a COD of the Multimedia KTV. In the figure, component Song_Selection has two operations: Select_Song_1 and Select_Song_2; component Song_1 has two operations: Broadcast_Song_1 and Sing_Song_1; component Song_Selection has two operations: Broadcast_Song_2 and Sing_Song_2.

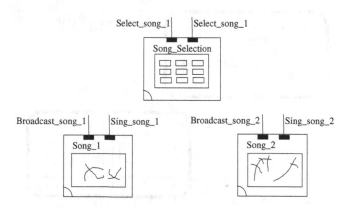

Fig. 7. COD of the multimedia KTV

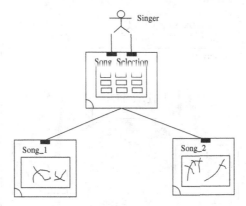

Fig. 8. CCD of the multimedia KTV

We use a component connection diagram (CCD) to design how the components and actors (in the external environment) are connected within a human-computer interaction system. Figure 8 exhibits a CCD of the Multimedia KTV.

3.3 Detailed Design Phase

In a human-computer interaction system, if the components, and among them and the external environment's actors to interact, these interactions will lead to the systems behavior. That is, "interaction" plays an important factor in coalescing structures with behaviors for a human-computer interaction system.

We use a structure-behavior coalescence diagram (SBCD) to design how the structure and behavior are integrated within a human-computer interaction system. Figure 9 exhibits a SBCD of the Multimedia KTV. In this example, an actor interacting with three components shall represent the overall systems behavior. Interactions among the Singer actor and the Song_Selection and Song_1 components generate the KalaOK_Song_1 behavior. Interactions among the Singer actor and the Song_Selection and Song_2 components generate the KalaOK_Song_2 behavior.

The overall behavior of a human-computer interaction system is the collection of all of its individual behaviors. All individual behaviors are mutually independent of each other. They tend to be executed concurrently. For example, the overall Multimedia KTV's behavior includes the KalaOK_Song_1 and KalaOK_Song_2 behaviors. In other words, the KalaOK_Song_1 and KalaOK_Song_2 behaviors are combined to produce the overall behavior of the Multimedia KTV.

The major purpose of adopting the SBC architecture design method, instead of separating the structure model from the behavior model, is to achieve one single coalesced model. In Fig. 9, designers are able to see that the systems structure and behavior coexist in a SBCD That is, in the SBCD of the Multimedia KTV, designers not only see its systems structure but also see (at the same time) its systems behavior.

The overall behavior of a human-computer interaction system consists of many individual behaviors. Each individual behavior represents an execution path. We use an

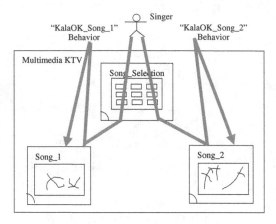

Fig. 9. SBCD of the multimedia KTV

interaction flow diagram (IFD) to design this individual behavior. The overall Multimedia KTV's behavior includes two behaviors: KalaOK_Song_1 and KalaOK_Song_2.

Figure 10 shows the IFD of the KalaOK_Song_1 behavior. First, actor Singer interacts with the Song_Selection component through the Select_Song_1 operation call interaction. Next, component Song_Selection interacts with the Song_1 component through the Broadcast_Song_1 operation call interaction. Finally, actor Singer interacts with the Song_1 component through the Sing_Song_1 operation call interaction.

Figure 11 shows the IFD of the KalaOK_Song_2 behavior. First, actor Singer interacts with the Song_Selection component through the Select_Song_2 operation call interaction. Next, component Song_Selection interacts with the Song_2 component through the Broadcast_Song_2 operation call interaction. Finally, actor Singer interacts with the Song_2 component through the Sing_Song_2 operation call interaction.

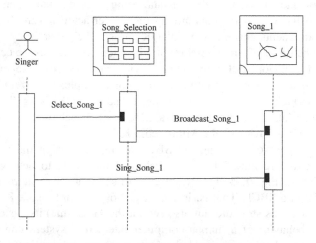

Fig. 10. IFD of the "KalaOK_Song_1" behavior

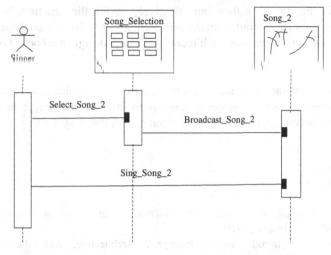

Fig. 11. IFD of the "KalaOK_Song_2" behavior

4 Conclusions

A human-computer interaction system is very complex that it includes multiple views such as structure, behavior, and information views. The systems model designs the human-computer interaction system multiple views possibly using two different methods. The first one is the non-architecture-oriented method and the second one is the architecture-oriented method.

Non-architecture-oriented systems model respectively picks a model for each view. These multiple models are heterogeneous and unrelated of each other, thus there is no way to put them into a conformity model. Architecture-oriented systems model, instead of picking many heterogeneous and unrelated models, will use only one single coalescence model. The structure, behavior, and information views are all integrated in this multiple view coalescence (MVC) systems model.

Since structure and behavior views are the two most prominent ones among multiple views, integrating the structure and behavior views apparently is the best approach of integrating those multiple views of a system. In other words, structure-behavior coalescence (SBC) facilitates multiple view coalescence (MVC). Therefore, we claim that SBC architecture is an architecture-oriented systems model.

SBC architecture design method adopts the SBC architecture as a systems model. SBC architecture design method starts from the preparation phase and then goes through the creative thinking, concept, preliminary design, and detailed design phases of SBC architecture construction. SBC architecture design method uses six fundamental diagrams to formally design the essence of a human-computer interaction system and its details at the same time. In the concept phase, architecture hierarchy diagram and framework diagram are used. In the preliminary design phase, component operation diagram and component connection diagram are used. In the detailed design phase, structure-behavior coalescence diagram and interaction flow diagram are used.

With these six diagrams, we then can effectively design the structure, behavior, and information of human-computer interaction systems; resolve uncertainties and risks caused by those traditional non-architecture-oriented design methods. Overall, SBC architecture design method helps integrate different stakeholders' works on the same track and unfold the backbone of human-computer interaction systems. The human-computer interaction system design result of SBC architecture can be used as human-computer interaction system blueprints to improve the acceptance and effectiveness of the development of human-computer interaction system.

References

1. Bass, L., Clements, P., Kazman, R.: Software Architecture in Practice, 2nd edn. Addison-Wesley, Boston (2003)
2. Bernard, S.: An Introduction to Enterprise Architecture, 2nd edn. AuthorHouse, Bloomington (2005)
3. Chao, W.S.: General Systems Theory 2.0: General Architectural Theory Using the SBC Architecture. CreateSpace Independent Publishing (2014)
4. Chao, W.S.: Systems Thinking 2.0: Architectural Thinking Using the SBC Architecture Description Language. CreateSpace Independent Publishing (2014)
5. Chao W.S.: Systems Modeling and Architecting: Structure-Behavior Coalescence for Systems Architecture. CreateSpace Independent Publishing 2014
6. Clements, P., Bachmann, F., Bass, L., Garlan, D., Ivers, J., Little, R., Merson, P., Nord, R., Stafford, J.: Documenting Software Architectures: Views and Beyond, 2nd edn. Addison Wesley, Boston (2010)
7. Dennis, A., Wixom, B.H., Roth, R.M.: Systems Analysis and Design, 4th edn. John Wiley & Sons, Hoboken (2008)
8. Jacko, J.A.: Human Computer Interaction Handbook: Fundamentals, Evolving Technologies, and Emerging Applications. CRC Press, Boca Raton (2012)
9. Kendall, K.E., Kendall, J.E.: Systems Analysis and Design, 8th edn. Prentice Hall, Upper Saddle River (2010)
10. MacKenzie, I.S.: Human-Computer Interaction: An Empirical Research Perspective. Morgan Kaufmann Publishers, Burlington (2013)
11. Maier, M.W.: The Art of Systems Architecting, 3rd edn. CRC Press, Boca Raton (2009)

Author Index

Printed in the United States
By Bookmasters